HOME OF THE FIRST GOVERNOR OF CALIFORNIA.

A MEMORIAL AND BIOGRAPHICAL HISTORY

OF THE COUNTIES OF

Santa Barbara, San Luis Obispo and Ventura, California.

ILLUSTRATED.

Containing a History of this Important Section of the Pacific Coast from the Earliest
Period of its Occupancy to the Present Time, together with Glimpses of its
Prospective Future; with Profuse Illustrations of its Beautiful Scenery,
Full-Page Steel Portraits of its most Eminent Men, and
Biographical Mention of many of its Pioneers and
also of Prominent Citizens of to-day.

BY MRS. YDA ADDIS STORKE.

"A people that take no pride in the noble achievements of remote ancestors will never achieve anything worthy
to be remembered with pride by remote descendants."—*Macaulay.*

CHICAGO:
THE LEWIS PUBLISHING COMPANY.
1891.

Notice

In many older books, foxing (or discoloration) occurs and, in some instances, print lightens with wear and age. Reprinted books, such as this, often duplicate these flaws, notwithstanding efforts to reduce or eliminate them. The pages of this reprint have been digitally enhanced and, where possible, the flaws eliminated in order to provide clarity of content and a pleasant reading experience.

*A Memorial and Biographical History of the Counties of
Santa Barbara, San Luis Obispo and Ventura, California.*

Originally published:
Chicago
1891

Reprinted by:

Janaway Publishing, Inc.
732 Kelsey Ct..
Santa Maria, California 93454
(805) 925-1038
www.JanawayGenealogy.com

2007, 2012

ISBN: 978-1-59641-153-1

Made in the United States of America

SANTA BARBARA REGION.

IN GENERAL—
First Visit of Whites	9
First Exploration and Founding of the Missions	10
An Invasion	17
Miscellaneous	18
War with Mexico	24
Dress and Manners	26
Dana on Santa Barbara	29
Pioneers and their Descendants	31

SANTA BARBARA COUNTY.

IN GENERAL—
Boundary	38
Exports	39
Items of Interest, 1850–'90	39
Description	52
Land Grants	54
The Channel Islands	56
Climate	58

CITY OF SANTA BARBARA ... 62
Haley Survey	63
Miscellaneous Items	66
Public Library	67
Natural History Society	68
Fraternal Organizations	69
Churches	70
Banks	71
Court-House	72
Jail	72
County Hospital	73
Railroads	73
Water Supply	74
Electric Light	74
Minor Items	74
The Mission	75
Schools	76
Medical Profession	79
Bench and Bar	79
Crimes	86
The Press	89

EASTERN PORTION OF THE COUNTY ... 90
Montecito	91
Hot Springs	93
Summerland	93
Carpenteria	94
La Patera	96
Goleta	96
The Hollister Place	98

THE WESTERN PORTION OF THE COUNTY ... 99
Lompoc	100
Ranchos	103
Los Alamos Valley	105
Santa Ynes Valley	108
Ballards	110
Ranchos	110
Santa Maria Valley	112
Ranchos	114
The Lost Woman	116

RESOURCES ... 121
Hogs	121
Bee Farming	121
Fishery	122
Minerals	123

SAN LUIS OBISPO COUNTY.

IN GENERAL—
Origin and Description	126
Organization	129
Annals, 1851–'90	130
Land Grants	134
Topography	137
Soil	138
Climate	140
The Coast Region	143
Coast Towns	143
Cambria	144
Morro	145

TOWN OF SAN LUIS OBISPO ... 146
ARROYO GRANDE ... 150
OTHER POINTS—
Newsom's Hot Sulphur Springs	153
Pizmo Beach	154
Los Berros	154
Nipomo	154

EASTERN PORTION OF THE COUNTY ... 154
San Miguel	155
Paso Robles Hot Springs	156
Templeton	157
Rancho Santa Margarita	158
The Southern Border	160
Salinas Valley	160
The Painted Rock	161
Monte Diablo Mountains	161
Creeks	161
Ranchos	162

CONTENTS.

RESOURCES—
   Agriculture........................... 163
   Horticulture and Viticulture............. 164
   Mineral Resources...................... 166
   Bituminous Rock....................... 170
   Dairying.............................. 171
   Exports............................... 173
BENCH AND BAR............................ 174
MISCELLANEOUS—
   County Officers........................ 177
   Postoffices............................ 177
   Schools............................... 178
   Light-House........................... 179
   Railroads............................. 179
   The Breakwater Question................ 179
   Fraternal Organizations................. 180
   The Press............................. 181

VENTURA COUNTY.

   Early settlement....................... 183
   Government and Business................ 184
   Division from Santa Barbara............. 186
   Organization and Annals................ 188
GENERAL DESCRIPTION—
   Water Supply......................... 195
   Timber Supply........................ 196
   San Nicolas Island..................... 197
   Geology............................... 198
   Climate............................... 199
   Churches of Ventura................... 201
   Public Schools......................... 201
EASTERN PORTION OF VENTURA—
   Santa Clara Valley..................... 203
   Rancho La Colonia..................... 203
   Hueneme.............................. 203
   Guadalasca Rancho..................... 206
   Las Posas Rancho...................... 206
   Simí Rancho........................... 207
   Rancho Tapo.......................... 208
   Springville............................ 208
   Calleguas Rancho...................... 208
   Rancho El Conejo...................... 209
   Newbury Park......................... 209
   Timberville............................ 210
CENTRAL PORTION OF VENTURA............. 210
   Rancho San Miguel.................... 211
   Rancho Santa Paula y Saticoy........... 211
   Town of Santa Paula................... 212
   Saticoy............................... 216
   New Jerusalem........................ 218

   Montalvo.............................. 218
   The More Murder...................... 219
   Rancho Sespe......................... 223
   Fillmore............................... 223
   Bardsdale............................. 224
   An Earthly Paradise, Piru City........... 224
   Rancho Camulos....................... 225
   Rancho San Francisco.................. 225
WESTERN PORTION OF VENTURA............. 226
   Rancho Cañada San Miguelito........... 226
   Rancho Cañada Larga o'Verdo.......... 226
   Ojai Rancho........................... 226
   The Ojai Valley....................... 227
   Santa Ana Valley...................... 228
   Rancho Santa Ana..................... 228
SAN BUENAVENTURA....................... 229
   Its Institutions........................ 230
   Floriculture........................... 232
   County Hospital....................... 233
   Court-House........................... 233
   Jail................................... 233
   Banks................................ 234
   Churches.............................. 234
   The Press............................. 240
   Bench and Bar........................ 241
RESOURCES—
   Agriculture........................... 241
   Horticulture.......................... 245
   The Year's Exports.................... 249
   Stock-Raising......................... 249
   Bee-Keeping.......................... 252
   Mining................................ 252
   Mineral Oils........................... 256

ILLUSTRATIONS.

Residence of the first Governor of California.
   ....Frontispiece
Mission Santa Barbara....................... 12
Mission San Miguel.......................... 16
View of Santa Barbara....................... 62
View of Ventura............................ 229
San Buenaventura Mission................... 229
Residence of A. S. Pietra................... 261
Drying Prunes in the Upper Ojai Valley..... 345
Orange Orchard in the Ojai Valley.......... 345
Myron Angel............................... 441
P. J. Barber............................... 553
J. B. Shaw................................ 633
W. W. Hollister............................ 649

BIOGRAPHICAL SKETCHES.

Abernethy Bros..........366	Arnold, H. H............332	Ball, John..............609
Allen, B. G.............302	Arnold, Leroy...........578	Ballard, E. B...........264
Alvord, J. B............344	Arnold, M. H............545	Ballou, S. D............648
Anderson, A. L..........522	Atmore, Mathew..........329	Barber, P. J............553
Anderson, S. D..........333	Atwood, E. A............353	Bard, C. L..............487
Angel, Myron............441	Austin, W. H............607	Bard, T. R..............471
Anthony, C. J...........602	Avila, J. V.............628	Barker, J. A............677
Anthony, G. T...........603	Axtell, J. D............560	Barker, J. L............307
Arata Bros..............356		Barkla, J. S............412
Argabrite, J. L.........668	Bailard, John...........282	Barker, Wm..............387
Armstrong, W. M.........508	Baker, F. W.............369	Barnard, A. D...........498
Arnold, C. R............332	Baker, H. W.............536	Barrows, F. P...........585
Arnold, E. F............454	Ball, Elbridge..........416	Barrows, Thomas.........519

CONTENTS.

Barry, E. S.	298
Bartlett, C. G.	378
Battles, R. E.	393
Bean, E. P.	669
Beattie, James	382
Beckett, J. F.	408
Beckwith, F. J.	313
Beebee, W. L.	358
Benn, Wm	528
Bennett, E. M.	642
Bennett, Fayette	461
Bennett, J. R.	505
Bennett, W. C.	354
Bennison, H. G.	576
Benton, A. F.	483
Bish, Harrison	462
Bither, Tyler	623
Blackburn, D. D.	580
Blanchard, Nathan W.	459
Blochman, L. E.	409
Blood, J. A.	477
Blumberg, A. W.	292
Boeseke, A. J.	521
Boll, Michael	518
Bonestel, C. D.	449
Booth, A. R.	347
Borchard, John	560
Borland, W. E.	626
Boronda, E.	482
Boyd, A. M.	356
Bradley, Charles	609
Bradley, John	322
Bradley, Paul	419
Branch, F. Z.	421
Branch, J. F.	605
Brewster, J. C.	455
Bridge, J. H. & R. E.	269
Broughton, R. J.	491
Broughton, W. W.	371
Browne, A. W.	384
Buell, A. W.	332
Bunce, I. H.	353
Burdick, H. J.	606
Burgess, F. P.	606
Byers, P. L.	342
Call, S. B.	654
Call, S. J.	645
Camarillo, A.	584
Canet, A.	404
Canon, W. S.	515
Carle, O. C.	557
Carnes, H. S.	481
Carr, Robert	425
Carter, C. E.	431
Cass, James	316
Casteel, Jesse	610
Castro, J. C.	658
Cavanaugh, T.	669
Cawelti, John	594
Chaffee, W. S.	484
Charlebois, P.	647
Cheal, James	523
Chediston House	523
Chiesa, F.	496
Clark, C. H	474
Clark, H. F.	467
Clark, I. M.	438
Clark, Thomas	296
Cleveland, E. M.	548
Cody, N. T.	547
Coffin, G. W.	512
Cohn, Simon	589
Coll, Jose	520
Collins, J. S.	492
Conaway, J. A.	316
Connelly, A.	573
Cook, F. E.	605
Cook, R. D.	514
Cook, W. C.	300
Cotton, A. R.	656
Cox, A. W.	407
Crabb, Alonzo	593
Crane Bros.	282
Crane, G. G.	304
Crane, H. G.	562
Crane, J. L.	542
Cravens, T. A.	294
Crawford, J. M.	287
Cummings, J. F.	566
Cunnane, W. B.	272
Currier, C. J.	289
Dalidet, Jr., P. H	666
Dally, H. J.	583
Dana, D. A.	419
Dana, H. C.	424
Dana, W. G.	569
Davidson, B.	403
Davis, Charles	570
Davis, F. C.	639
Day, J. A.	622
Decker, C. H.	323
De la Guerra, Emanuel	654
De la Guerra, E. B.	654
De la Rosa, José	568
Dennis, A. C.	522
De Rome Bros.	392
Dimmick, L. N.	532
Dimock, Joseph	417
Dimock, H. C.	446
Donlon Bros.	580
Donlon, John	588
Dormer, & Challenor	603
Douglas, Cyrus	409
Draper, J. B	614
Dubbers, Henry	371
Dunham, F. H.	318
Duval, C. S.	284
Duval, E. A.	541
Dyer, A. H	420
Dyer, Wallace	417
Ealy, R. J.	318
Earll, F. A.	352
Earls, J. F	436
Eastin, L. F	646
Eddy, W. M.	594
Elliott, Nathan	363
Emerson & Co.	342
Estrada, Joaquin	672
Estrada, Nicolazo	437
Evans, James	509
Evans, W. A.	307
Exline, Levi	376
Faeh, Ambrose	378
Fagan, Michael	335
Fandrey, Joseph	486
Farrelly, P. F.	357
Faulkner, C. P.	582
Faulkner, G. W	559
Fernald, Charles	674
Fernandez, E.	673
Field, F. F.	619
Fisher, I. K.	534
Fisk, Rufus	575
Fluegler, Emil	666
Flynn, Michael	410
Ford, H. C.	485
Forrester, L. L.	436
Forrester, P. A.	653
Foxen, W. D.	667
Frankl, Leopold	277
Franklin, B. H.	280
Freire, M. P.	478
Frink, C. H.	301
Frost, F. D.	642
Gagliardo, G. B.	354
Gally, B. W.	586
Garcia, Mrs. Julian	608
Garcia, Philemon	514
Gardner, C. O.	601
Garrett, Russell	661
Garrison, A. M.	336
Gates, L. D.	531
Gerry, Waite	552
Gilger, C. T.	587
Gisler, S. L.	304
Glass, J. H	355
Goodyear, J. D.	544
Gordon, A. L.	594
Gosnell, T. B.	411
Gragg, G. T.	671
Graham, J. W.	601
Graham, Z.	568
Grant, K. P.	549
Graves, Ernest	672
Graves, J. M	425
Graves, Murphy	540
Graves, William	655
Gregg, V. A.	303
Gregory, D. S.	607
Green, J. E.	546
Greenlee, D. M.	600
Greenwell, W. E	595
Greer, Mrs. E. A.	602
Gries, J. K.	465
Grimes, Brice	319
Gruenhagen Bros.	270
Guiberson, S. A.	315
Gutierrez, A. G.	526
Gutierrez, B.	510
Haines, Abner	632
Hall, C. L.	527
Hall, E. B.	590
Hall, E. P.	507
Hall, E. S.	445
Hardison, Harvey	434
Hardison, L. A	321
Hardison, W. L.	620
Harkey, J. S.	511
Harloe, Marcus	394
Harris, Joseph	510
Harris, R. R.	383
Harrold, E. W	307
Harrold, Michael	583

CONTENTS.

Hart, Reuben	614
Hartman, F.	365
Harwood, Thomas	308
Hathaway, F. C.	370
Hawley, O. F.	561
Haydock, R. B.	447
Hayne, W. A.	524
Hazard, R. J.	627
Hendricks, J. W.	411
Henning, J. S.	385
Hepburn & Terry	648
Herbst, J. H.	448
Herrera, Dolores	386
Higgins, P. C.	281
Higuera, T. B.	479
Hillard, Fred	538
Hill, Jesse	435
Hill, J. G	463
Hill, R. W	448
Hill, Samuel	349
Hobart, Joseph	290
Hobson, P. J	637
Hodges, T. E.	346
Hogg, S. T.	641
Hoit, E. M.	499
Hollister, John H	326
Hollister, Joseph H	326
Hollister, W. W.	649
Holt, Herman	622
Horstman, A. F.	265
Hosmer, Thomas	276
Houk, John	394
Hudiburgh, I. N.	345
Hudson, A. J.	640
Irwin, John	314
Jack, R. E.	303
Jackson, Wm	413
James, D W	350
Jameson, T. C.	364
Jamison, W. C.	264
Jatta, J. N.	403
Jeffreys, W. M.	657
Jenkins & McGuire	517
Jesse, J. V.	615
Jewett, Henry	438
Johnson, C. H	563
Johnson, G. W. F.	638
Johnson, H. H	658
Johnston, W. F.	497
Jones, E. M.	461
Jones, W. S.	619
Kaiser, Joseph	424
Kaltmeyer, G. E.	577
Kamp, H. L	566
Kays, J. C.	626
Keene, Josiah	328
Keller, J	506
Kellogg, F. E.	500
Kellogg, P. E.	458
Kelsey, J. B.	624
Kennedy, J L	414
Kilson, G. E.	274
Kimball, C. N	550
Kirkpatrick, R. R.	277
Krill, F. A	520
Kuhlman, J. H.	470

Lamy, Louis	666
Larsen, S.	599
Larzelere, C. W.	407
Law, S. L & Co.	591
Lazcano, Alonzo	390
Lazcano, Bernardo	391
Lazcano, Mariano	389
Le Blanc, J. B	644
Lee & Rice	323
Lee, R. E	655
Leedham, E.	612
Levy, Achille	469
Levy, Leon	488
Lewis, Henry	343
Lewis, W. S.	363
Lewty, David	616
Liddle, James	643
Lillingston & Perry	293
Lima, J. P.	668
Linbarger, L.	432
Lindner, J. D.	375
Lloyd, L. M.	380
Logan, Anna M	325
Long, G. H.	405
Long, John	613
Loose, August	660
Low, C. P.	267
Lucas, W. T.	501
Lugo, Bernardino	476
Maddox, B. F	285
Maggi, G. R	540
Mallagh, W.	667
Mallagh, S. P.	665
Mancilla, V.	611
Maris, W. S.	496
Marks, Joshua	567
Martin, Andrew	277
Manderscheid, G.	616
Maulhardt, Jacob	559
Maulsby, O. W.	398
McCabe, G. W.	502
McClure, J. F.	398
McCoy, J. E.	408
McDonnell, John	669
McFerson, J. C.	275
McGee, W. J.	384
McGlashan, J.	418
McGrath, D.	565
McGuire, I. N	517
McGuire, Wm	295
McHenry, Patrick	467
McKee, James	453
McKeeby, L. C.	400
McKevett, C. H	535
McMillan, Peter	336
McNulta, Thomas	535
McPhail, A. F.	598
Mears, John	338
Mehlman, H.	506
Merritt, C. W.	617
Meyer, J. F.	593
Middagh, Gilbert	288
Miller, D. S.	496
Moody, J. P.	662
Moore, E. E.	310
Moore, F. A.	592
Moore, S. T.	513
More, T. R	546
Moreno, F. P.	618

Murphy, P. W	625
Muscio, Abram	331
Myers, J. R.	402
Nance, T. C.	433
Nelson, Andrew	372
Newby, J. F.	368
Newsom, D. F	488
Nichols, A. J.	600
Nichols, G. B.	529
Nichols, M. S.	379
Nicholson, E. H.	422
Nicoles, E. R.	422
Norcross, D. C.	426
Norton, Thomas	506
Nott, Samuel	297
Nuttall, R. W.	506
O'Hara, William	340
Old, Henry W.	482
Oliver, L. G.	268
Ortega, J. C.	542
Orton, R.	623
Palin, J. B.	576
Patter, L. L.	520
Percy, James	629
Petersen, H.	263
Pezzoni, Antonio	415
Phillips, C. H.	532
Pico, B.	537
Pico, Z. A.	536
Pierce, B. B.	346
Pietra Bros.	261
Pippin, W. T.	391
Poland, Henson	373
Polley, H.	579
Pomeroy, F.	610
Porter, Arza	399
Prefumo, P. B.	665
Prell, J. G.	430
Price, J. M.	476
Proctor, G. W.	283
Pyster, John	286
Quarnstrom, John	263
Quintana, J.	658
Quintana, Pedro	658
Ransom, John	521
Ready, P. F.	670
Ready, W. E.	562
Redrup, C. G.	416
Reed, A. S.	530
Reed, John	370
Reed, N. H	540
Reilly, W. H.	495
Remick, A. C.	551
Rice, J. C.	324
Rice, J. H.	404
Rice, T. A.	334
Richardson, Frederick	306
Richardson, G. M.	305
Richards, G. W.	423
Richards, J. T.	549
Richards, W. D. F	548
Riley, C. C.	312
Riley, W. S.	406
Roach, W. H	431
Robbins, G. W.	663
Roberts, George	454

Robinson, Richard...583	Smith, Frank...321	Utter, M. S...567
Robinson, S...644	Smith, G. C...617	
Robinson, Thomas...420	Smith, H. B...265	Vance, J. R...471
Robison, T. J...509	Smith, N. B...397	Van Gorden, Geo...658
Rochin, J. M...364	Smith, N. D...339	Van Gorden, Ira...571
Rogers, A. C...564	Smith, R. D...266	Veneble, McD. R...524
Rogers, J. W...286	Smith, Solon...531	Von Schroeder, Baron...479
Root, Orville...616	Snow, H. K. Jr...352	
Ross, W. L...418	Snyder, J. D...518	Walbridge, O. C...452
Rotsler, G. F...311	Soule, C. E...444	Walden, G. R...464
Rucker, G. F...425	Sparks, I. J...392	Walker, Alfred...618
Rucker, Z. T...426	Spanne, John...385	Walker, James...462
Ruffner, Joseph...395	Spence, John...428	Ward, A...611
Ruiz, Gabriel...269	Sperry, H. A...673	Ward, F. P...440
Rundell, Eli...490	Sprout, W. P...598	Warden, L. M...625
Ryan, W. H...474	Squier, O. P...299	Wason, Milton...528
Rynerson, A. C...585	St. Clair, C. L...655	Webb, H. P...630
	Steele, E. W...525	Webster, Gaius...261
Salzman, H. W...415	Steele, Sebern...377	Webster, L. T...287
Sanborn, E. P...341	Stevens, R. K...278	Weill, Isidore...382
Sauer, G. F...668	Steward, Marvin...498	Welch, G. C...337
Saulsbury, Thomas...437	Stiles, H. M...468	Wells, M. T...628
Saunders, C. L...430	Stock, Frederick...327	Wells, S. T...572
Saunders, W. A...390	Stoddard, Henry...599	Wells, Timothy...348
Saunders, Z. W...604	Stone, George...627	Whitaker, W. S...278
Scarlett, John...588	Stone, W. R...439	White, F. M...630
Schiefferly, J. J...664	Storke, C. A...537	Whitney, B. P...601
Scott, John...645	Stowell, E. A...646	Whitney, S. E...626
Seaton, J. H...512	Stowell, George...412	Wigmore, J. & A. A...508
Sedgwick, Charles...490	Streeter, W. A...494	Wiley, B. T...396
Sessions, O. V...466	Summers, Henry...406	Wilkinson, J. M...396
Sewell, G. G...543	Surdam, R. G...632	Willett, Jacklin...401
Sexton, Joseph...591	Sutton, R. S...293	Williams, B. T...451
Shackelford, Otto...354	Sweet, J. W...610	Williams, E. B...309
Shackelford, R. M...374	Swift Brothers...272	Williams, H. L...273
Sharon, Thomas...573		Williams, Julia F...298
Sharp, J. M...520	Taggart, Edwin...541	Williams, J. F...503
Shaw, J. B...633	Tallant, E. C...592	Williams, T. J...423
Sheldon, C. H...539	Taylor, G. O...618	Williamson, A...379
Shepherd, W. E...427	Taylor, James...659	Willoughby, J. R...502
Sheppard, S. A...504	Taylor, W. H...345	Wilson, A. C. J...327
Sheppard, T. A...587	Tebbetts, G. P...492	Wilson, I. L...670
Sherman, C...613	Thompson, C. A...301	Wilson, J. C...344
Shick, J. W...432	Thompson, John...656	Woodberry, W...662
Short, J. M...324	Thornburgh, M...440	Woolever, A...631
Short, W. N...410	Thornazzini, A...273	Wolff, M. L...460
Show, W. C...491	Tognazzini, A...273	
Simmler, J. J...516	Townsend, J. B...604	Young, C. J...429
Simpson, John...387	Toy, Daniel...401	Young, J. V. N...612
Simpson, V. A...458	Truitt, D. T...388	
Sittenfeld, A...294	Tucker, B. F...381	Zeller, W. M...467
Skellenger, L...310	Tutt, E. R...388	
Smith, D. A...457	Twitchell, F. C...574	

THE SANTA BARBARA REGION.

A HISTORICAL SKETCH OF THE COAST COUNTIES OF SANTA BARBARA, VENTURA, AND SAN LUIS OBISPO, FROM THEIR DISCOVERY TO THE PERIOD OF AMERICAN OCCUPATION.

THE FIRST VISIT OF WHITES known to have been made to the waters washing the shores of the three present counties composing our group, was that of Juan Rodriguez Cabrillo and his sturdy men, in his two vessels, the San Salvador and La Victoria. Having enjoyed the shelter of the "land-locked and very good harbor" at San Miguel (San Diego), touched at Santa Catalina and San Pedro, and sailed past Santa Monica, they discovered, on Tuesday, October 10, 1542, a great valley, opposite which they anchored, seeing on shore some villages of peaceable Indians, with whom they traded and whom they called "los pueblos de las canoas," because these people had a great many canoes. These towns were in 35° 20′, being near the present San Buenaventura, the valley that is now called Santa Clara.

Here the Spaniards remained four days, taking formal possession, and communicating as best they could with the natives, who came off in fine large canoes, each carrying a dozen or so of men, who averred that other whites, like unto these visitors, were in the interior, and who told of maize growing in their own valley. Fishermen were these Indians, dressed in skins, and living largely on raw fish and agaves. Leaving this anchorage on Friday, October 13, the Spaniards passed, at some seven leagues distance, two large islands about four leagues long each, and about four leagues from the mainland. There were many cabins and trees along the coast, and continually the ships were boarded by natives from their canoes, who pointed out to the navigators and named the villages, whose names were certainly strange enough to the ears that then heard them—Xucu, Bis, Sofono, Alloc, Xabaägua, Xotococ, Potoltuc, Nacbuc, Misinagua, Misesopano, Elquis, Coloc, Quelqueme, Mugu, Xagua, Anacbuc, Partocac, Susuquey, Quanmu, Gua, Asimu, Aguin, Casalic, Tucumu, and Incpupu.

On the 15th they passed an island fifteen leagues long, very populous, with six villages, which they named San Lucas (now Santa Cruz). Two days later they were in latitude 34° 28′, abreast of the present Gaviota Pass, where the natives ate no maize, went clothed in skins, and wore their very long hair tied up with cords placed within the hair, from which dangled many small daggers of wood, bone and flint. Still northward, passing many points and capes, now and then the mouth of a river emptying into the sea, and everywhere evidences of a numerous population. Past San Simeon Bay and Las Piedras Blancas (between which now stands San Luis Obispo), and on up the coast to a little northward of 40°, whence they returned southward, until, on November 23, they were once more at their old harbor on San Miguel Island. And here they remained for nearly two months, and re-named the island Juan Rodriguez, for their stanch captain, who found a grave there; for on January 3, 1543, Cabrillo died from the results of a broken arm, aggravated by the exposure of the voyage. At his instance, urged while dying, the expedition once more sailed northward, under Bartolomè Ferrelo, and reached about 44°, then returned, reaching their home port, Navidad, on April 14.

And it was sixty years before the whites again visited these shores.

Then, in 1603, came Sebastian Vizcaino, commanding an exploring fleet of three Spanish vessels. It would seem that he knew naught of the discoveries of Cabrillo; for to all the points of interest he gave new names, mostly from the saint claiming the day of their discovery. And it must be said that many of the names applied by Vizcaino are those in use to-day. After exploring, recuperating, and re-naming San Diego, and also San Clemente and Santa Catalina Islands, they came to "a regular row of islands from four to six leagues distant from each other." Vizcaino was the first to note the parallelism of this chain of islands with the coast of the mainland, and he it was who gave to the intervening broad passage the name El Canal de Santa Barbara. Being anxious to reach northern latitudes whilst the favorable winds should last, Vizcaino did not anchor here. He had, however, a visit from an Indian who appeared to be the king of the coast, who came off in a boat with four paddles, and urged the visitors to land. Noting the absence of women in the vessels, he offered ten for each man! But on to the northward went Vizcaino, as far as Cape Mendocino, and the rest of his voyage has no local connection with the scene of the present writing.

FIRST EXPLORATION, AND FOUNDING OF THE MISSIONS.

It will be remembered that the Mission of San Diego was not yet formally founded, when the commandant, Gaspar de Portolá, zealous for the extension of the territories to be dominated by the missions, set forth northward, to reach Monterey Bay by a coast route. His party comprised sixty-four persons, who left San Diego July 14, 1769.*

Just one month later they "crossed from a point near the mouth of the Santa Clara to the shore farther north, where they found the largest Indian village yet seen in California. The houses were of spherical form, thatched with straw, and the natives used boats twenty-four feet long, made of pine boards tied together with cords and covered with asphaltum, capable of carrying each ten fishermen. A few old blades of knives and swords were seen. Some inhabitants of the Channel Islands came across to gaze at the strangers. Previously the inhabitants had bartered seeds, grass baskets and shells for the coveted glass beads, but now fish and carved bits of wood were added to the limited list of commercial products. Thus more food was offered than could be eaten. This fine pueblo, the first of a long line of similar ones along the channel coast, was called

* Bancroft.

Asuncion, and was identical in site with the modern San Buenaventura."

Proceeding on northward toward Monterey Bay in 1769, the route of Portolá and his command, from the middle of August through the first week of September, followed the coast of the Santa Bárbara channel westward, through a dense population of the natives, gathered into many large villages or rancherias. These Indians showed unfailing hospitality. All along this way the Spaniards remained in sight of the Channel Islands. On August 18 they came to a settlement which they called Laguna de la Concepcion, which was near the present Santa Bárbara, it being supposed that this city indeed occupies the exact site of that aboriginal village. The Spaniards stayed not here, but marched on northward, and here, as in San Buenaventura, the project of settlement was left in abeyance for some years.

Before returning to San Diego this expedition pushed northward to San Francisco Bay. Of their passage through the district at present under consideration, traces still survive, in the way of names applied by them then, as La Gaviota, Los Osos and El Buchon.

Although of the present group the most northern county was then the territory most remote from San Diego, the first base of operations, it was nevertheless to receive the attention of the Spaniards earlier than either Ventura or Santa Barbara.

The mission and presidio of San Carlos Borromeo de Monterey having been founded in June, 1770, the colonists there found themselves, in May, 1772, almost destitute of provisions, owing to the delay in arrival of the supply vessels. Late in this month Captain Lages took thirteen men to the Cañada de los Osos (Gulch of the Bears), where they staid for three months hunting bears, whose meat supplied the presidio and the mission until the arrival of the ships.

When this succor at last came, the president, going southward, resolved that on the way he would establish one of the new missions at this famous cañada, where there was abundance of game and good land. Accordingly, on September 1, 1772, Padre Junipero raised the cross and said mass, thus founding the Mission of San Luis Obispo de Tolosa, which he left in charge of Padre Cavaller, with five soldiers and some Indians. The natives, no doubt gratefully bearing in mind Fages' exploits among their ursine neighbors, were well disposed toward the newcomers, whom they assisted by their labors, and by contributions of seeds to the commissary. Perhaps the father, too, derived some solace and encouragement from their readiness to accept the rite of baptism for their children.

In Palou's report on the missions, forwarded to Mexico at the close of 1773, San Luis Obispo is stated to have but twelve converts. "It is," so says the report, "hard to attract the people here to the mission. The population is very numerous, and of friendly disposition toward the missionaries; but as the Indians, having plenty of deer, rabbits, fish and seeds, are better supplied with food than are the Spaniards, they cannot be controlled by self-interest. Moreover, as there is no rancheria close by, they do not stay in the vicinity of the mission. The buildings here are somewhat less extensive than at some of the other establishments, but there is plenty of fertile land, well wooded and well watered, and there has been a small crop of beans and corn even this first year." By 1780 San Luis had some 2,000 bushels surplus of maize.

It was not until April, 1782, after the founding of the missions of San Carlos, San

Antonio, San Gabriel, San Francisco and San Juan Capistrano, and the beginning of pueblos and presidios, that further measures were taken toward the settlement of these districts.

Then, indeed, there came up thither the largest expedition as yet seen in California, comprising, besides the officers, seventy soldiers and their families. Coming from San Gabriel, they reached March 29, the first rancheria on the Santa Barbara channel, that village which had been called Asuncion in 1769 by Portolá's party, and which had been selected long since as a suitable site for a mission. Here, near the beach, and in close vicinity to the native huts of straw and tule, shaped in conical fashion, the cross was duly raised beneath its arbor-like shelter, and, on the 31st, the mission was formally founded and dedicated to the "seraphic doctor," Giovanni di Fidanza. Padre Junipero Serra himself it was who preached the dedicatory sermon. There were present many natives, who expressed much pleasure in the establishment of the mission, to the building of whose edifices they cheerfully lent their labors.

The facilities here were good for irrigation, also for procuring good building material. By April 12 of that year, there had been completed an enclosure of 40 x 50 varas (a vara is $33\frac{1}{3}$ inches) of palisades four varas high, having two ravelins, a gate and a small warehouse.

Padre Cambon remained until May in charge of the new mission; then Padre Francisco Dumetz and Padre Vicente de Santa Maria arrived there as regular ministers. Notwithstanding the cordiality of the natives, only two adults received the rite of baptism during 1782.

The first marriage ceremony performed at the mission church was that of Maria Concepcion Martiel, of Alamos, Sonora, Mexico, and Alejandro Sotomayor of Fuerte, Mexico, Padre Dumetz officiating, on August 8, 1782. The first baptism was that of José Cresencio Valdez, son of Eugenio Valdez Español, on April 27, 1782.

About the middle of April, leaving a sergeant and fourteen men as a guard at the newly founded mission, the governor and the president with the rest of the party journeyed on up the coast to establish the presidio of Santa Barbara.

The site chosen was probably that which Portolá's expedition of 1769 had called Laguna de la Concepcion. Here work was begun at once, and on April 21, Padre Serra formally established the fort, with the saying of mass and the chanting of an *alabado* (a hymn of praise; a *Te Deum*). The fort was constructed on an eminence, near some springs and a lagoon. The palisades were of oak from the neighboring timber, and the first enclosure was sixty varas square. This stockade was replaced later by a solid wall, around an area eighty yards square. The natives were friendly, and their labors here were repaid with food and clothing. The chieftain of the native town here had authority over no less than thirteen rancherias, and his support was of great value to the settlers. So favorably did matters progress here, that soon irrigation works were constructed, and farming was begun on a small scale.

The founding of a mission here was long postponed, owing to the enmity of the secular authorities toward the friars; but at last, 1786, more than two years after the death of the devoted Padre Junipero, the president with two friars of recent arrival went to the presidio and made preparations for the formal founding of the mission, the tenth to be established in Alta California. Thus, on December 4, 1786, the cross was raised and blessed, and the mission dedicated to Saint

MISSION SANTA BARBARA.

Barbara, Virgin and Martyr, the patroness of artillerymen in the Spanish army. The ceremonies were not completed at this time, as Fages, the governor, was absent, and he had ordered operations to be suspended until his arrival. If he had meant to impede the proceedings of the clergy here, he appeared to think better of it upon reflection, and, after his arrival, the first mass was said by Padre Paterna, a sermon was preached by Lasuen, and thus was completed the founding of *la Mision de Santa Barbara, Virjen y Martir.* The first baptism was on December 31, and the rite was administered at the presidio, as the rains prevented the erection of buildings at the mission itself for the time. However, a church 18 x 90 feet was completed in 1789, and by the end of 1790 there were numerous mission buildings, well built of adobes, and roofed with tiles. By this time, the number of baptisms here had reached 520, and the 102 deaths left 438 neophytes at that date. At this time, Santa Barbara mission owned 296 head of large, and 503 head of small, stock, and the agricultural products amounted to about 1,500 bushels.

Yet the mission had poor resources, and owing to this lack of means to support the Indians, only voluntary converts were admitted at first.

The formal founding of the third of the channel missions took place on December 8, 1787, this day being selected as being that dedicated to "Our Lady of the Immaculate Conception." This because it had been determined to consecrate this new mission to that service, and it was accordingly called "de la Purisima Concepcion." The mere act of founding accomplished, this mission was left alone until March, 1788, when a detachment returned thither to prepare buildings. By August, 1788, there had been enrolled seventy-nine neophytes. The site of this mission was changed somewhat later, as will be shown.

There were in the Purisima district over fifty rancherias, or Indian villages.

At this time, the white population of Santa Barbara presidial district was about 220, or 360, including Los Angeles. The natives were employed as hired laborers, and they did their work well. The neophytes of this entire district, including San Gabriel and San Fernando, numbered at this period nearly 4,000.

The presidio had eight guns, all but one of brass, from one to six pounds of caliber. Half of these were distributed among the missions, but they were not in use, as there was no hostility among the Indians, and the foreign disturber as yet appeared not.

At San Buenaventura, Padres Dumetz and Santa Maria had continued as ministers throughout this decade; and so zealous were they that the lukewarmness of the Indians was overcome, so that the neophytes increased from twenty-two to 388 within this period, besides 115 who died as converts. The large stock had now increased from 103 to 961, the small stock from forty-four to 1,503; and the crops for 1790 were over 3,000 bushels. The natives hereabouts continued friendly; but, in view of the great number of them, it was deemed prudent to maintain here a larger guard than at the other missions. However, this "large guard" would seem to have been absurdly inadequate to hold in check the hordes of Indians, had they chosen to be hostile, for the force numbered now fifteen, and now only ten men.

On November 10, 1793, Vancouver anchored at Santa Barbara, where he was courteously received by the commandant, Goycoechea, and hospitably entertained by the padres, who saw the importance of a favorable impression to be made upon visiting foreigners.

The Englishman pronounced the appearance of the place "far more civilized than any other of the Spanish establishments, * * * the buildings regular and well constructed, the walls clean and white, and the roofs of the houses covered with a bright red tile." "The presidio," he wrote, "excels all the others in neatness, cleanliness, and other smaller though essential comforts; it is placed on an elevated part of the plain, and is raised some feet from the ground by a basement story which adds much to its pleasantness." When Vancouver sailed on the 18th for San Buenaventura, he carried a passenger—Padre Santa Maria, who took that opportunity of making a visit to the neighboring mission, at the same time that he combated, by the force of his own experience, the prejudice and fears of the Indians, as against foreigners. The padres were very hospitable and courteous toward this traveler.

Padre Antonio Paterna, the founder, and a pioneer of 1771, died in 1793, at Santa Barbara mission.

On January 10, 1794, took place the first public execution, when Ygnacio Rochin paid the penalty for murder. Death was inflicted upon him by shooting, there being no hangman in the province.

The English merchant ship Phœnix touched here in August, 1795. Communication with the outside world had now begun to increase with each succeeding year.

In February, 1798, died Captain José Ortega, former commandant of Santa Barbara.

During this decade the number of neophytes increased from 438 to 864. Horses and cattle had multiplied from 296 to 2,492, and sheep from 503 to 5,615. The crops in 1800 were 3,000 bushels, although the crop three years earlier was 5,400 bushels. During this period many improvements in building had been made at the mission. In 1791 were added three tool houses and a guard-house; in 1792, two large stone corrals. In 1793–'94 was erected a new church, built of adobes and plastered, with tiled roof; its ground space was 28x135 feet, and it had a brick portico, and a sacristy 15 x 28 feet. In 1794 were built a granary and a spinning room, set on stone foundations; also an enclosure 48 x 135 feet, for a cemetery; also a sheepfold. In 1797 a corridor with brick pillars and tile roof was added, on the side of the quadrangle nearest to the presidio, and another alongside the spinning room; four new rooms were completed for the friars; and beams of pine were placed wherever alder and poplar had been used for that purpose. In 1797 were completed several rooms for granaries, store-rooms, and offices. In 1799 were built for the neophytes nineteen adobe houses, each 12 x 19 feet, plastered, whitewashed, and tile-roofed; also an adobe wall nine feet high was carried 1,200 yards around the garden and vineyard, and a warehouse was built. In 1800 were built thirty-one more adobe houses in a row, the three remaining sides of the square were completed, and measures were taken for the construction, from brick and mortar and stone, of a reservoir for drinking water. In 1800 sixty neophytes were engaged in weaving and its attendant processes. Others were taught carpentry, and others tanning.

The same priests remained in charge of San Buenaventura until 1797, when Padre Dumetz was succeeded by Padre José Francisco de Paula Senan. The only notable event of this decade would seem to have been a fracas between the Christian Indians and the unconverted, in which the former, while they had several men wounded, were victorious, killing two chiefs of the pagans, and taking six or seven captives. The authorities punished impartially the leaders on both sides, one of the neophytes being put to labor in irons.

By this time, although there had been 412 burials among the converts, the number of neophytes had increased to 715; and, although the population here was less than at any other of the older missions, San Buenaventura in 1800 had more cattle and raised more grain than any other place in California. There were 10,013 head of cattle and horses, and 4,622 sheep; and the crop of 1800 was 9,400 bushels, the smallest crop being 1,500 bushels in 1797, while the average yield was 4,800 bushels. Wheat was little grown until 1798, when this became the chief crop, reaching over 8,000 bushels per year.

The buildings here were superior in construction, having been rebuilt after the old ones had been swept away by fire. The church alone, of the mission quadrangle, was not complete. It was begun about 1793, and completed during the decade, being built of stone. Vancouver, who landed here November 20, 1793, pronounced this mission of "a very superior style to any of the new establishments yet seen." "The garden of Buena Ventura far exceeded," he wrote, "anything I had before met with in these regions, both in respect of the quality, quantity, and variety of its excellent productions, not only indigenous to the country, but appertaining to the temperate as well as the torrid zone; not one species having yet been planted or sown that had not flourished. These have principally consisted of apples, pears, plums [sic], figs, oranges, grapes, peaches and pomegranates, together with the plantain, banana, cocoa-nut, sugar-cane, indigo, and a great variety of the necessary and useful kitchen herbs, plants and roots. All these were flourishing in the greatest health and perfection, though separated from the seaside only by two or three fields of corn, that were cultivated within a few yards of the surf."

San Luis Obispo reached its maximum of population, 946, in 1794, but it had, in 1800, the considerable number of 726, from 605 in 1790. At this date, the cattle and horses had increased to 6,500 head, and sheep to 6,150. There were raised this year 2,700 bushels of grain, the average number being 3,200, while in 1798 the harvest was 4,100 bushels. This mission raised no barley.

During this decade had been completed an adobe church, with portico and tile roof, a house for the ministers, a guard-house, workroom, and barrack, and a mill run by water-power. The huts of the natives there were well built.

This mission was fortunate in receiving a miller, blacksmith, and carpenter, sent hither to impart instruction.

In 1794 there was at San Luis a certain excitement, resulting from the efforts of several gentile chiefs to incite a revolt among the Indians hereabouts. Those at Purisima were approached by agents of the malcontents, but the neophytes scorned the presents offered for the purpose and were so loyal to the Spaniards that five of the unruly Indians were delivered over for punishment.

For a long time there had been entertained by the authorities of the church a project to found a series of new missions to lie between the old ones, and as nearly as might be equidistant from each two of them, all of these to be situated somewhat farther inland than those of the original chain. Practically, the sites had been chosen by the friars; but for form's sake, the priests made, in 1794–'95, an exploration, in conjunction with the military. After this, and some preliminary correspondence, the five new missions were organized.

On June 11, 1797, was founded San Jose;

on June 24 San Juan Bautista, and on July 25, San Miguel, being the third of the new missions, and the only one with which we have to deal in the present chapters on this section.

San Miguel was founded by Padre Lasuen and Friar Buenaventura Sitjar, on a site which the natives called Vahiá or Vaticá, and the Spaniards Las Posas. It was between San Luis Obispo and San Antonio, Padres Sitjar and Horra, generally called Padre Concepcion, were appointed ministers. The founding was attended by a great number of Indians, fifteen of whose children were presented for baptism on that day; and this good disposition seemed to continue, for by the end of 1800 there had been baptized 385. The other missions had contributed a few head of stock, which by the end of the decade had increased to 372 large and 1,582 small animals. The total product of crops for these three years was 3,700 bushels. The church was built of wood, with a mud roof, and it continued in use for some years.

In 1801 the safety of the whites of Santa Barbara was jeopardized, from a singular cause. An epidemic of lung disease had been causing great mortality among the Indians, when a neophyte claimed to have seen in a dream or trance, Chupu, the deity of the channel natives, who announced that all the baptized Indians would fall victims to the evil unless they would renounce Christianity and perform certain rites to Chupu. The natives of most of the channel rancherias hastened to comply, while the padres remained in ignorance of the movement; and it is not quite clear what withheld the fanatics from proceeding to attack the Spaniards.

On September 17, 1804, was founded the nineteenth of the Alta California Missions, dedicated to Santa Ynes (Saint Agnes), Virgin and Martyr. As far back as 1795 the Spaniards had made explorations for a mission site here. The spot chosen was called by the Indians Alajulapu (*rincon*, a corner or nook). Mission work here was begun with the baptism of twenty-seven children, and the enrolling of many catechumens, among them three captains or chiefs. By the end of the year Santa Ynes had 225 neophytes, but at least half of them came from other missions. The church here was a very poor one in this decade. The crops here averaged 2,700 bushels yearly, and by 1810 the live stock numbered 3,200 cattle, 420 horses, 61 mules, 11 asses, and 2,300 sheep.

At this time was agitated the question of founding a mission on one of the Channel Islands, but an epidemic of measles carried off over 200 of the natives, and the president had to admit, moreover, that the facilities of lands and the water supply were unfavorable to the project.

At Santa Barbara, during each year from 1801 to 1805, from thirty to fifty adobe dwellings for the neophytes were built, and their numbers reached 234, they being enclosed on three sides by an adobe wall, constructed in 1802. Other erections of this period were three large warehouses, a major-domo's house, a tannery, and several other buildings, one of which was 120 feet long. Meanwhile, at the Indian rancheria of Mescaltitlan, by the Spaniards called San Miguel, six miles from Santa Barbara, there had been built an adobe chapel, 66 x 27 feet, a stone prison building, a reservoir of masonry, a fountain, arranged with washing places for the laundresses, a pottery, and more than a score of adobe-built dwelling houses.

In 1805–'6, the presidial company at Santa Barbara was increased from fifty-nine to sixty men by the process of recruiting, and there were thirty-five invalided soldiers, mostly living at the presidio. The total white

MISSION SAN MIGUEL.—SAN LUIS OBISPO COUNTY.

population, including Santa Bárbara, San Buenaventura, Purisima, Santa Ynes, San Fernando, San Gabriel, Los Angeles and the ranchos (all these points were under the military jurisdiction of Santa Barbara presidio) was 825, having gained 150 during the decade. Without Los Angeles and the ranchos, there had been an increase to 460 from 390.

The greatest number of neophytes at San Luis Obispo, 854, was reached in 1803, but by the end of the decade it had declined to 713. Although the smallest of the old missions, excepting San Carlos, this was far above the average in the production of livestock. Its agricultural results were less satisfactory. The friars there were somewhat noted for their discouraging treatment of foreign vessels.

At San Miguel, this period was characterized by the death of Padre Pujol, and the violent illness of two other priests, all supsupposed to have been poisoned by the neophytes. There was also some trouble over the defiant attitude of Cuchapa, one of the Indian captains, who was, however, subdued by judicious treatment.

A great loss was sustained at San Miguel in 1806, in a fire which destroyed that portion of the mission buildings used for manufacturing purposes, with the implements and a large quantity of raw material, including wool, hides, cloths, and 6,000 bushels of wheat.

In population San Miguel grew from 362 to 973, the greatest gain of the decade, except at San Luis Rey and San Fernando. Its death rate was only forty-nine per cent. of the baptisms. This had more sheep than any other mission save San Juan Capistrano.

The chapel at Santa Barbara presidio had its walls badly injured by an earthquake in March, 1806, and just two months later, the edifice was almost totally destroyed by a great storm.

At intervals through this decade, no little local excitement was wrought up over three criminal cases of a repulsive nature, and by a case of alleged blasphemy.

The channel was visited during this period by the Hazard, the Lelia Byrd, the O'Cain, and the Albatross. There were in this presidial jurisdiction, which included San Gabriel, 6,500 neophytes (round numbers), the gain over the previous decade being 2,500.

By 1810 the numerical decline of the neophyte population had begun; although there was an actual increase from 864 to 1,355, this was a considerable drop from 1,792, the figure which had been reached in 1803. Santa Barbara by this time led all the other missions in the whole number of baptisms for the decade, and in the highest number for one year. The large stock of this mission had increased from 2,492 to 5,670; there were 1,390 horses and mules in 1810. The small stock increased from 5,615 to 8,190. The average crop for the decade was of 6,216 bushels per year; at one time there were produced 10,150 bushels.

AN INVASION.

On October 6, 1818, the American brig Clarion brought to Santa Barbara the news that there were being fitted out at the Sandwich Islands two privateers, carrying collectively fifty-four guns and 250 men whose purpose was to make a cruise on this coast. Commandant Guerra at once despatched messengers at all speed to Governor Sola at Monterey, and to the friars of the southern missions. Sola at once issued orders that all church vessels, ornaments, and other articles of intrinsic value, should be packed up and sent to points of safety inland; the women and children made ready to retire thither also;

provisions and ammunition prepared for attack; live-stock driven inland; soldiers and settlers summoned for defense at their respective presidios, as well as the native archers; sentinels and couriers stationed at convenient points; and, in fact, every preparation made for resistance, at the same time that all precautions must be taken to prevent the expected vessels from effecting a landing upon any pretense. The missionaries, too, were officially notified of the expected attack, and earnestly recommended to co-operate with the commandants.

Taken all these prudent measures nearly two months elapsed without sign of hostile approach, and Sola ordered the civilians dismissed to the attention of their own affairs. Guerra and some others considered this relaxation premature, in which the events sustained them; for on November 20, the dreaded vessels were descried approaching Monterey. The account of the ravages there committed by their crews is not strictly germane to the subject of these pages. Suffice it to say that, after destroying all they could in that quarter, and losing three of their men—one an American—as prisoners, the two ships came southward, the news being brought by a returning corporal and six men whom the prudent Guerra had sent up to re-enforce Monterey. The marauders landed at the Rancho Refugio of the Ortegas on December 2, the family having abandoned the place on their approach. Here they killed cattle, and plundered and fired the buildings, while they were watched by Spaniards assembled at Santa Ynes, who captured, from an ambush three of the " pirates." Sailing hence the two ships anchored at Santa Barbara on December 6, and Bouchard, the commander, sent ashore with a flag of truce a letter to the commandant, promising to leave the coast without further hostilities after an exchange of prisoners. Guerra replied, avowing his positive yearning to fight, but consenting to consider the other's proposition, "from feelings of humanity," and to forward the letter to the governor. Further urgency from Bouchard impelled Guerra to consent to an immediate exchange, but, on coming to the point, he found that but one prisoner was offered for three. To Guerra's indignation on this score, Bouchard averred that he had but one captive, and this one, when delivered over for Bouchard's three useful men, proved to be a drunken vagabond named Molina, who had stumbled into the arms of the invaders while they were at Monterey, and who was a nuisance to the community! Besides his chagrin at this victimizing of the wily Bouchard, poor, plucky, sincere Guerra had to bear the blunt of Sola's reproaches for consenting to terms with the cheating rascals. Perhaps the worst of the matter, however, after all, touched Molina, for he was sentenced to six years in the chain gang, after 100 blows on his bare back. Bouchard, after some lingering, finally disappeared on December 12 from Santa Barbara, and the troops at this point were then hurried southward, to assist in the defense of San Diego and the other southernmost missions, and Guerra himself followed.

This invasion was the principal event of the decade. In April, 1820, there were rumors of the arrival of four insurgent vessels from Chili, and orders for protectionary measures were again issued, but these fears proved unfounded.

MISCELLANEOUS.

During this decade, the total white population of all this district had increased from 460 to 740. This included forty-five men of the company brought to Alta California by Portilla. The presidio contained sixty-six men, besides its officers, and twenty-seven to thirty-one invalids. With the Los Angeles contingent, there was a total of 1,355. The neophytes had diminished 100, being now 6,400. The padres had granted the land of the San Julian Rancho as a loan, and it was stocked with some 650 tithe cattle, for a source of meat supply for the soldiers. This proved very successful.

In 1812 occurred the severe series of earthquakes that so seriously damaged many of the missions. At Santa Barbara the shocks began about December 21 and lasted several months, during which time the people, who had abandoned their dwellings, lived in the open. Several buildings were ruined and others damaged, both at the presidio and the mission; springs of asphaltum were opened; the mountains cracked, and the general signs thoroughly justified the alarm of the people. The other events were not numerous; a few Indian expeditions were made, and a certain element of excitement was introduced by the foreign vessels and the other hunters, now arriving with more frequency. Times were very dull throughout the province, and here as elsewhere.

In 1813 a chapel was built at the presidio, of wood, with a tiled roof, and it was even proposed to remove the whole presidio to another site, in consequence of the damage from the earthquake. A primary school for girls, taught by a woman, was opened here in 1817, and a lady at the mission administered medicines to the sick at the presidio, whose cemetery was not used for interments after 1818. About this time, too, there was a controversy regarding a piece of land between the mission and the presidio.

At the mission extensive repairs were made on the old church to remedy the earthquake's damage, and also a new church was begun in 1815, for which Captain Wilcox in the Traveler went to bring the timber from Santa Cruz Island. On September 10, 1820, this edifice was consecrated, the ministers having the assistance of three visiting priests, with Governor Sola acting as sponsor in the presence of the commandant, soldiers, and citizens. This ceremony was celebrated by a banquet and general festivities. The church was described as "of hewn stone and mortar, with walls very strongly built with good buttresses, a tower of two stories holding six bells, a plaster ceiling frescoed, marbled columns, and altar tables in Roman style, one of them having a pulpit. In the front an image of Santa Barbara in a niche, supported by six columns, and at the extremity of the triangle the three virtues, all four of the figures being of cut stone, painted over in oil. The floor of bitumen, polished; sundry decorations in the church and the sacristy. All being attractive, strong and neat."

With the downfall of the Spanish rule in Mexico, California became a province of the Mexican empire, to which the oath of allegiance was taken on April 13, 1822, at Santa Barbara, four days after the news was formally announced in *junta* (council) at Monterey. Shortly thereafter, Francisco Ortega was chosen *elector de partido* from Santa Barbara and five missions, to elect a deputy to the court at Mexico. The election sent Sola to that office.

On September 13 of this year, the American schooner Eagle was seized at Santa Barbara. For several years she had been on this coast engaged in smuggling. While at this port her crew attempted to seize the San Francisco de Paula, formerly the Cossack, there lying at anchor, on the plea of an irregularity of sale. In towing this prize out of the harbor, the Eagle ran herself aground, and was captured with the aid of the garrison men and cannon. For some time the vessel could not be floated, but she later sailed as the Santa Apolonio, having been bought, it seems, by the Santa Barbara padres, when both vessels and their cargo were sold at auction after confiscation. They brought about $3,000, which, pending instructions from Mexico, was directed to be used for the good of the province. It would seem, however, that in those days existed the same affinity as at present between dollars and fingers, as seven years after, investigations were still making to ascertain what had been done with this money.

Duhant-Cilly, who wrote of the place in 1827, said: "The presidio of Santa Barbara is, like that of Monterey, a closed square, surrounded with houses of a single story. Near the northwest corner rises an edifice a little more prominent than any other, and ornamented with a balcony. It is the residence of the commandante. At the opposite corner, protecting the way to the shore, it was evidently the intention of the Californian engineers to build a bastion; but to believe that they had succeeded would be great good nature."

By this time the port was often visited by foreign vessels, trading for hides and tallow. Some grain and vegetables were raised by the inhabitants. Most of the commerce was carried on by foreigners, with whose methods the Californians were unable to compete. The only manufactures were coarse woolen cloth and hats produced at the mission. Native wine and brandy might have been produced with profit but for the free importation of foreign liquors.

In 1826, Father Luis Martinez built on the beach and launched, at Avila Landing, now in San Luis Obispo County, a two-masted vessel of about seventy-five tons' burthen, in which he used to ship to Monterey grain and other products, which he sold so profitably that in a few years he had become wealthy, and he then went to Lima on Captain Wilson's vessel, carrying his golden doubloons quilted into a queer leathern tunic, which he wore, for the greater safety of his fortune and his person. But this golden coat of mail was so heavy and uncomfortable that he had to confide its contents to Captain Wilson, who cared for it safely throughout the voyage.

About 1828 there was built at Santa Barbara a schooner of thirty-three tons, built for Carlos Carrillo and Wm. G. Dana for the coasting trade and otter hunting

Santa Barbara participated to a considerable extent in the dissensions of local magnates, as Alvarado and Carrillo, from 1836 to 1838; and from this cause proceeded the battle of San Buenaventura, on March 27, 1838, in which the church walls were somewhat injured. Santa Barbara favored Alvarado.

During the decade 1830-'40, the white population of this district grew from 630 to 900, while the Indian population fell from 4,400 to 1,550. These figures were exclusive of San Fernando, although that point was legally within this jurisdiction. The presidial organization was still kept up here, José de la Guerra y Noriega being its captain, and after 1837 its regular commandant. The force was something like eighty.

From 1821 to 1829, the presidial force of Santa Barbara stood at about sixty-six men and twenty-six invalids; in 1830 there were about eighty souls, all told. The white population at the presidio had gained little in the decade, being now about 500; the whole presidial district, including the missions, with Los Angeles and its ranchos, had, 1,790, a gain of 435 during the decade. Meanwhile, the neophyte population had declined; having lost 2,000, there were now 4,400 Indians. During this decade, Southern California, including the two districts, San Diego and Santa Barbara, had increased from 1,800 white population to 2,310, while the neophyte population, from 11,600 fell off to 9,600.

There were at this time resident in the district at least ten foreigners,—*i. e.*, whites not Mexican or Spanish.

The Barbareños were quite conservative, and shunned the various "plans" of opposition. They took no part in the revolt against Victoria in 1831, and their partisanship of Alvarado, as against Carlos Carrillo, one of the most popular of their own men, once secured through the influence of de la Guerra and Duran, they were always loyal in their adherence to his cause.

There is considerable vagueness of definition between the municipal and the military jurisdiction at this period, as the records were not preserved.

It is notable that, of some twenty ranchos granted to private owners in this decade, none of the titles were lost in subsequent litigation. The neophytes of this mission decreased from 711 in 1830 to 556 in 1834, the year of secularization, and by 1840 they were only 250. Stock continued to gain during the earlier half of this period, and until the last the crops were good. The mission buildings here were in better repair than at the other establishments. Writing in 1846, Sir James Douglass placed Santa Barbara as a larger town than Monterey, and estimated the annual output of hides and tallow at $25,000.

At San Buenaventura there was a perceptible check in the falling off of neophyte population. In 1834 there were 626 in this section. Live-stock continued to increase, and crops continued good. Even after secularization there was a loss of only about fifty per cent. in herds and flocks, while there was an increase still in horses, then as now a special product of Ventura. By this time there were some 500 Indians left in the district.

At Santa Ynes there were frequent changes of ministers. Down to 1834 the decrease in neophytes was about fifteen per cent, thereafter about twelve per cent. until 1840, when there were 180 Indians in the community. This mission held its own in live-stock down to secularization, and then showed a decided gain. The church property was valued at $11,000, other property at about $45,000, and the debt was reduced two-thirds, so that this was the most prosperous of the Southern missions. It was not secularized until 1836.

At Purisima the neophyte population diminished little until 1834, when there were 407 Indians; but by 1840 they had run down to 120. In possessions there was a decrease throughout the decade. The value of the Purisima estate about 1835 was approximately $60,000. Secularization was done here early in 1835.

At San Luis Obispo there was little loss of neophytes down to 1834, when there were 264, which after secularization in 1835 ran down to 170 by the end of the decade. Agricultural matters were not flourishing, and the live-stock diminished about one-half in the last lustrum. The possessions were valued at $70,000 in 1836, and at $60,000 three years later, after which the decline was rapid.

At San Miguel the neophyte list fell off from 684 to 599, in 1834, and to about 350 by 1840. Crops ran down but little until after secularization in 1836, and there was an actual gain in cattle. The inventory at the transfer showed a valuation, exclusive of church property, of $82,000, which by 1839 had dwindled to $75,000. None of the lands here passed to private ownership during this decade, and the establishment had several ranchos, with the corresponding buildings, and two large vineyards. At these ranchos, as well as at the mission, dwelt the Indians. Owing to their contiguity and intimacy with the Tulares, they were sometimes refractory; yet the real decline here hardly began before 1840.

Santa Barbara shared in the notoriety of the Graham affair in 1840, in that ten foreigners resident here were arrested under Governor Alvarado's order, on the pretext of intended revolt against the authorities.

January 11, 1842, was marked by the arrival of Bishop Garcia Diego, who came to take up his residence at this, the best preserved of the missions. He was received with enthusiastic demonstrations.

A report on the southern missions, dated February, 1844, states that "Santa Barbara has left 287 neophytes, whom she supports with the greatest difficulty; that Purisima remains with some 200, unprovided with lands to sow, or other property provision than a moderate-sized vineyard; that Santa Ynes has 264 neophytes, and the wherewithal to support them; while San Buenaventura is in very fair condition, with sufficient resources;" these two last named being the only ones of the eleven secularized missions not utterly ruined.

Bishop Garcia Diego cherished a utopian project of establishing at Santa Ynes an ecclesiastical seminary, and he applied for and on March 16, 1844, obtained a grant of six leagues of land, subsequently augmented. On May 4, he formally founded the college of Maria Santisima de Guadalupe de Santa Ynes.

In May Governor Micheltorena declared the roadstead of Santa Barbara open to the coasting trade. It is probable that the difference was one of formality merely.

In the strifes and struggles between local personages, Micheltorena and Alvarado, the Picos, the Carrillos, and all the rest of their associates, Santa Barbara figured inevitably to some extent, by virtue of her importance as a town, and the strong individuality and influence of some of her citizens. But here as elsewhere the characteristic conservatism of the Barbareños was conspicuous; moreover, these matters, besides being far too cumbrous to be treated in detail in a work of restricted magnitude as the present, were of little real importance in the development or building up of the section.

By 1845, Santa Barbara had about 1,000 white population, and about the same number of ex-neophyte Indians. At the presidio were enrolled between thirty and forty men, with ten to fifteen on actual duty. Captain José Antonio de la Guerra y Noriega, that conspicuous character of early days, retired from the commandancy in 1842. Municipal affairs were managed by judges of the peace or by alcaldes, and the records are meager and unimportant. Visits from trading vessels now were frequent, and the hospitable and amusement-loving character of the Barbareños made this a favorite stopping-place. Travelers were sure to comment upon the features of social superiority here over other coast points. Sir George Simpson wrote in 1842: " Santa Barbara is somewhat larger than Monterey, containing about 900 inhabitants, while the one is just as much a maze without a plan as the other. Here, however, anything of the nature of resemblance ends, Santa Barbara in most respects being to Monterey what the parlor is to the kitchen. Among all the settlements as distinguished from the rascally pueblos, Santa Barbara possesses the double advantage of being both the oldest and the most aristocratic. The houses are not only well finished at first, but are throughout kept in good order; and the whitewashed adobes, and the painted balconies and verandas form a pleasing contrast with the overshadowing roofs blackened by means of bitumen, the produce of a neighboring spring."

At the mission there were 260 Indians at the end of this half decade, the community being broken up in 1845. At Santa Ynes the estate was restored to the management of the padres in 1843. The ex-neophyte population in 1845 was 270. From 12,000 in 1841, the live-stock decreased to 2,000 in 1845; and the whole value of property declined to $20,000 from $49,000, or even more. This estate was rented in 1848 to José M. Covarrubias and Joaquin Carrillo for $580 per year.

At Purisima the remnants of the property were turned over to the padres in 1843, having been in charge of the manager of Santa Ynes during the preceding year. From this time on, there was no resident priest. In 1844 most of the 200 remaining Indians died of small-pox, so that there were not over fifty left in 1845, when the Purisima Mission, barring the church property, was sold for $1,110, the purchaser being Temple, though the title was made out to J. R. Malo. During the same year, Santa Barbara was rented to N. A. Den and Daniel Hill for $1,200, San Buenaventura to Arnaz and Botello for $1,630, and Santa Ynes to Covarrubias and Carrillo for $580. There is no further record concerning this mission, which appears thenceforward to have been entirely abandoned.

The end of San Luis Obispo as a missionary establishment came with an order of the Governor in July, 1844, for the complete emancipation of the Indians and secularization of the mission. Accordingly a regular pueblo was formed, the town lands comprising all the vacant mission lands near, and distribution being made to the ex-neophytes. However, no claim for pueblo lands was ever entered by the town. In December the ex-mission buildings, having the curate's house and some reserved for public uses, were sold for $510 to Scott, Wilson and McKinley.

After 1842, San Luis had spiritual charge of San Miguel. The *administrador* found himself unable to control the Indians, and Governor Alvarado instructed him to abandon the effort. By 1845 all the property had disappeared, save the buildings, and these, valued at $5,800, were ordered sold at auction.

On July 16, 1844, San Luis Obispo was formally secularized and converted into a pueblo; its buildings were devoted to public uses, barring the missionary house, to continue as a parsonage; the ditches remained free for the use of all; and to the pueblo were given two adjacent orchards and a league of land at La Laguna. At the same time, San Miguel received the vineyard called La Vina Mayor (the Greater Vineyard). The United States Courts confirmed this grant in later years.

The lessees of Santa Barbara Mission probably kept possession during 1846, 1848, and, although Den's title was confirmed by the Land Commission, it appears to have been practically annulled by later litigation.

On June 8, 1846, San Buenaventura was sold to José Arnaz for $12,000. The title of Arnaz as purchaser was not recognized during the transition period of 1846-'48, and in 1848 he was supplanted even as lessee, Isaac Callaghan obtaining a lease from Colonel Stevenson. There was a long litigation over Arnaz's title, which was finally confirmed.

On June 10, Santa Barbara was sold to Richard S. Den for $7,500.

On June 15, 1846, Santa Ynes was sold for $7,000 to Joaquin Carrillo and José Maria Covarrubias, who kept possession until after 1848,—this under their lease, however; their title by purchase was afterwards declared invalid.

In 1845 San Luis Obispo Mission was sold to Scott, Wilson and McKinley for $510.

They were not disturbed in their possession, and their title subsequently was declared valid.

San Miguel was subject, spiritually and temporally, to the powers that were, in San Luis. It is known that this mission was sold, July 4, 1846, to Petronilos Rios and William Reed. The latter had lived here since 1745 or earlier, and in September, 1847, the Government gave orders that he be left in possession, the title to be left for later settlement. In December, 1848, Reed's home was visited by a party of five American tramps, formerly soldiers, whom he entertained for some days with a hospitality characteristic of the man. He was, however, unwise enough to let them know that he had in his possession a considerable sum of gold, he having recently returned from the mines where he had sold a flock of sheep. The dastards set out apparently to continue their journey, but, going only to Santa Margarita, they returned at night to the ex-mission, and basely murdered all its inhabitants, heaping the corpses all in one room, and plundering the place of the gold and its other valuables. The victims were William Reed, his wife Maria Antonio Vallejo with her unborn child, Josefa Olivera, a midwife who had gone thither to attend Mrs. Reed, José Ramon Vallejo, brother to Mrs. Reed, a daughter of the Reeds aged fifteen, a son of two or three years, a nephew of four, a negro cook, an Indian servant over sixty years old, and his five-year-old nephew. When the news of this awful crime reached Santa Barbara a force of men set out in pursuit of the murderers, whom they overtook on the present site of Summerland (see "Bench and Bar.") One of the members, after being fatally wounded, shot and killed Ramon Rodriguez, who had rushed single-handed toward the marauders; one jumped into the sea, swam out beyond the kelp, and was drowned; and the other three, named Joseph Lynch, Peter Quin and Peter Raymond or Renner, were captured and taken to Santa Barbara, where they were executed on December 28.

THE WAR WITH MEXICO—CHANGE OF RULE.

A very small part indeed, comparatively speaking, was that taken by Santa Barbara in the important occurrences of 1846-'47, which resulted in the conquest of California by the Americans.

On May 13, 1846, was issued a call for a *consejo general de los pueblos unidos* (gengueral council of the united towns) to meet at Santa Barbara on June 15, to discuss the actual and the impeuding situation, and to deliberate on the future. This council was to consist of the governor and eighteen delegates from the respective towns, together with certain representatives from the ecclesiastical and the military element. It was freely rumored that the object of this convention would be to invoke English interference between Mexico and the United States; but on June 3 the Assembly suspended the action of the *bando* or call.

Equally futile was the proclamation, summoning to a patriotic resistance the Mexican Californians, which Pio Pico issued from Santa Barbara on June 23, on learning of the taking of Sonoma. The Barbareños would seem to have been practical, progressive and cautious.

On August 4 or 5, Stockton, on his way down the coast, touched here and raised the American flag, leaving also a garrison of ten men under a midshipman, thus formally putting Santa Barbara under the rule of the United States. These men were taken away on the Congress on September 7, being replaced somewhat later from Fremont's battalion.

When Gillespie's tactless and overbearing rule in Los Angeles brought about there an uprising, which resulted in his abandoning the field and marching to San Pedro, the Californians, having disposed of the Los Angeles garrison, set about dispossessing those of San Diego and Santa Barbara. Accordingly, about the first of October, a small force under Manuel Garfias demanded the surrender or parole of Lieutenant Talbot and his nine men. These were youthful but experienced mountaineers, and to avoid parole, they took to the open; for a week they kept in sight of the town, which they hoped might be retaken by a man-of-war. Then, being hard pressed by the Californians, who fired the brush to drive them out, they crossed the mountains and reached Monterey. After the flight of this garrison, the Americans living at Santa Barbara were arrested, and some were sent to Los Angeles as prisoners, but most were paroled. In December, 1846, and January, 1847, John C. Fremont with his battalion rested here for a week, on the way to Los Angeles and Cahuenga.

On April 8, 1847, companies A, B and F, of Stevenson's regiment, under Lieutenant-Colonel Burton, arrived at Santa Barbara, where Company F remained during its term of service. The other two left on July 4 for La Paz. Captain Lippitt remained in charge of this post.

Toward the close of 1847, there were apprehensions of attack upon the Americans at Santa Barbara under Captain Lippitt, and the Governor, Colonel Richard B. Mason, went thither, where he was satisfied that the strain of feeling, if any, was caused by the improper conduct of some of the Americans composing the garrison.

In April, 1848, during the organization of forces to fight Indians, it transpired that a plot was on foot to direct these bodies toward wresting from the Americans the towns of Santa Barbara and Los Angeles.

At this time, while popular excitement and official fears were both wrought up, the affair of "the lost cannon" happened, materially increasing the feeling of insecurity. This was a brass gun—some say a six-pounder, some say of twice that caliber—which had belonged to the Elizabeth. It was left on the beach, while awaiting trans-shipment to Monterey, to be placed on the fortifications there. It disappeared on the night of April 5, and all efforts to find it were unsuccessful. Some said it had been carried on a cart toward Los Angeles; others averred it had been put aboard a vessel; the authorities inclined to connect its disappearance with flying rumors of revolt, and to believe that it had been sequestrated by the Barbareños, with a view towards turning it against its former owners. Local officials and prominent citizens were very indignant at this distrust, but the gun was not forthcoming. Therefore Governor Mason imposed a military fine of $500 upon the town, to be paid *pro rata* by all its inhabitants; the whole sum to be repaid to the town on discovery of the guilty individuals, or proof that they were not residents of Santa Barbara. A list of property-holders was made out, and each was assessed his portion of the $500. This caused great excitement and indignation, and not least among the American residents; the alcaldes offered their resignations, which were, however, not accepted; a company of dragoons was sent for from Los Angeles to enforce the payment of the fine. Still, while some paid, others would not do so, and so much of their property as was necessary to satisfy their assessments was seized and sold at public auction. It afterward transpired that five men had dragged away the gun with the aid of a yoke of oxen, and buried it in the sand, at a spot that they could not relocate. Their idea may have been one of pecuniary profit, or they may have designed to use the piece in a possible uprising against American rule. Be that as it may, no less than three streets of Santa Barbara still bear the names of men in commemoration of this event:—Mason, Quinientos [Five Hundred], and Cañon Perdido [Lost Cañon] streets.

Not only in the nomenclatures of streets did the Barbareños indicate the impression left by this affair: the first seal of the city had emblazoned in its center the picture of a cannon encircled by the words " Vale quinientos pesos "— it is worth $500. This seal was used from 1851 to 1860, when a new one was devised, leaving out this emblem.

The military governor of California in 1850 returned to the prefect of this district the $500, with instructions to employ it in the construction of a jail. The city authorities endeavored to obtain the money from its depository, and place it in the city treasury; but the prefect stated that, as he held the money in trust for a specific purpose, and was ready to pay it over when, but not before, the city was ready to build the jail. The city attorney was instructed to begin a suit against the prefect to recover the money, and he accordingly did so. As the District Judge was a family connection of the defendant in the action, the case could not be tried here, and so was transferred to San Francisco. The papers relating to the matter were unaccountably lost, the trustee of the fund died, and as no new suit was instituted against his estate the fund was never recovered for the city.

In the year 1858, a heavy rain caused the pent-up waters of the Estero to cut through the sand-bank separating it from the ocean, and the mystery of the lost cannon's whereabouts was solved as it was now discovered protruding from one of the banks of this new channel. Some of the native Californians completed its disinterment, and hauled it in triumph up State street to de la Guerra. It was uninjured, clean, and bright. It was sold for $80 to a Jew, who sent it to San Francisco and sold it at a large profit for old brass. Thus Santa Barbara displayed no little inconsistency, in failing to retain and preserve here a relic of such memorable importance in local history.

DRESS AND MANNERS.

For fifteen or twenty years before American occupation, the general conditions were much the same, save in a political sense, as they were for fifteen or twenty years after that period; as the reader and the traveler of the present day find those conditions full of picturesqueness and romance, it is desirable to give herein some account of the manners, customs, and usages of those times.

At this period, Santa Barbara was, next to Monterey, the most important town in the territory. Here, as a general thing, paused *en route* for Monterey the governors sent up hither from Mexico, to rest and to learn something of the duties of their office. These and other visiting magnates usually were guests of the de la Guerras, the Carrillos, or the Ortegas, these being the principal families.

Here was the center of trade for a hundred miles around, and hither tended all roads and all riders.

The houses were generally built in the shape of a parallelogram, sometimes of adobe walls only, sometimes a framework of timbers, filled in with adobe. The simplest form was a habitation of one room, with bare walls and clay floors. Houses of the better class had a species of piazza on one or more sides. Thatch roof were sometimes used, although tiling was the preferred material; not seldom the rafters were crossed by rods or tules, covered with a layer of mud or of asphaltum. Generally the door, window-frames and rafters constituted the only wood about the structure. The walls often were whitewashed. The best of the houses were built after the Spanish fashion around a *patio* or court, containing plants and sometimes a fountain. The floors were sometimes boarded, but more frequently were of earth. Some of the wealthier inhabitants had glass to their windows, but a grating was the more general rule. The kitchen was apart, in a separate shed or hut. The houses had no fire-places.

In the poorer houses, the only furniture would be a handmill or a *metall* for grinding corn, and a few pieces of pottery or ironware for cooking purposes, the beds being composed of rawhides spread on the ground, and perhaps a hammock. Sometimes there was a table, and stools or benches. Joints of a whale's vertebræ were often used for chairs. Some had beds of poplar, lined with leather, and fitted with pillows, sheets, and blankets. Where there was linen, the slips were frequently used over silk, and enriched with drawn-work. After 1824, some of the richer families had rather handsome furniture— mirrors, bureaus, and tables inlaid with shell, etc., brought from Peru or China.

Up to 1834 the chief features of men's costumes were: Short and wide breeches, fastened at the knee above deerskin boots, made like gaiters or leggings, and held up by gaily-embroidered garters or by bunches of ribbons; a wide and loose waist-coat, usually blue, open at the lower part to show the silken sash, generally crimson, or indeed, the two or three sashes with which the men often swathed themselves; over this a blue jacket, trimmed with big metal buttons. A silk handkerchief was knotted about the throat, another on the head; and the hat was wide-brimmed, low-crowned, and fastened by a string or loop passing under the chin. The hair was in a queue.

Women of the middle class wore chemises with short sleeves, richly embroidered and trimmed with lace, a muslin petticoat flounced and belted with scarlet, shoes of velvet or satin, a cotton *rebozo* or headscarf, pearl necklace and earrings, and the hair hanging down the back in one or two braids. Others, of the higher class, dressed in the English style, wearing, instead of the *rebozos*, rich and costly shawls of silk, satin, or Chinese crape. The skirts were so narrow as to impede freedom of step in walking.

When the Hijar-Padres colony arrived, they brought new fashions. The breeches were replaced by *calzoneras*, a kind of trousers, whose outside seams were left unjoined, to be closed by means of buttons and button-holes. The hair was cut short in the back, but left quite long in the front.

The women now exchanged their narrow skirts for more ample draperies, and coiled their braids on the crown of the head, around a comb. All women of means and position wore hose, as it was deemed immodest to let more than the face and hands remain uncovered. The poorer women, and old women in general, wore no gown over the petticoat, and on the waist a chemise with sleeves falling below the elbow. The neck and breast were covered by a black kerchief, of silk or cotton, doubled cornerwise, the corner being fastened at the back, the two points passing over the shoulders, and crossing, being fastened at the waist by pins. The more humble women retained and wore continually the *rebozo*. Shoes had points turned up at both toe and heel.

The dress of the Barbareños is described as having consisted of "a broad-brimmed hat, usually black, with a gilt or figured band around the crown, and lined with silk; a short jacket of silk or figured calico, the European skirted body-coat never being worn; a shirt usually open at the neck; a waistcoat, when worn, always of rich quality; the trousers wide, straight, and long, usually of velvet, velveteen, or broadcloth; occasionally knee-breeches are worn with white stockings; shoes of deerskin are used; they are of a dark brown color, and being made by the Indians, are commonly much ornamented; braces are never worn, the indispensable sash twisted around the waist serving all their purposes; the sash is usually red, and varies in quality according to the means of the wearer; if to this is added the never-failing cloak, the dress of the Californian is complete. The latter article of dress, however, is a never-failing criterion of the rank or wealth of its owner. The caballero, or gentleman aristocrat, wears a cloak of black or dark blue broadcloth, with as much velvet and trimming on it as it is possible to put there; from this, the cloaks gradually descend through all grades until the primitive blanket of the Indian is reached. The middle class wear a species of cloak very much resembling a table-cloth, with a large hole in the center for the head to go through; this is often as coarse as a blanket, but it is generally beautifully woven with various colors, and has a showy appearance at a distance. There is no working class amongst the Spaniards, the Indians doing all the hard work; thus a rich man looks and dresses like a grandee, whilst even a miserably poor individual has the appearance of a broken-down gentleman; it is not, therefore, by any means uncommon to see a man with a fine figure and courteous manner, dressed in broadcloth or velvet, and mounted on a noble horse, completely covered with trappings, who perhaps has not a real in his pocket, and may even be suffering from absolute hunger."

There was one feature peculiar to the women of Santa Barbara, all of whom wore a *camorra*—a black silk kerchief, folded into a band about two inches wide, tied around the forehead and into a knot under the nape of the neck.

Wealthy women wore diamond rings, pearl or golden necklaces, and ear-hoops or rings and other jewelry.

At this time, almost the only means of communication between ranchos or settlements was by horse; and no race in the world, perhaps the Bedouins not excepted, were better riders than the Californians. Horses were constantly kept standing saddled at the doors of stores and dwellings, and walking was a means of progression in great disfavor, even for the shortest distances. Tailing the bull, lasso-throwing, and many other feats of strength and skill were practiced by the young Californians. They were great lovers of sport and amusements, and races, dances, etc., were improvised upon the slightest inducement. The guitar was almost the only musical instrument, although a few harps were introduced during the last few years before American occupation.

The arrivals of the trading ships were events among these people. The vessels had a cabin fitted up as a shop or salesroom, and thither flocked the housewives, to buy domestic utensils, trinkets, and fabrics, often of the very finest, to be paid for by the head of the house in hides and tallow. As payment on a cash basis hardly even entered into the transaction, the rancheros keeping a running account with the traders, these latter practically had the simple-hearted provincials at their mercy, all the more that the price of wares was rarely asked before or at the time of purchase.

Perhaps the most graphic description of the country and its people is that given by Richard Henry Dana, in his "Two Years Before the Mast," which is an account of his voyage to, and sojourn on, the coast of California, in a trading vessel, 1836-'38. Accordingly some extracts are given.

DANA ON SANTA BARBARA.

The bay, as it was commonly called, the *canal* [channel] of Santa Barbara, is very large, being formed by the main land on one side [between Point Concepcion on the north and Point San Buenaventura on the south], which here bends like a crescent, and by three large islands opposite to it and at a distance of some twenty miles.

These points are just sufficient to give it the name of a *bay*, while at the same time it is so large and so much exposed to the southeast and northwest winds that it is little better than an open roadstead; and the whole swell of the Pacific Ocean rolls in here before a southeaster, and breaks with so heavy a surf in the shallow waters that it is highly dangerous to lie in near to the shore during the southeaster season, that is, between the months of November and April.

Two points run out as the horns of the cresent, one of which, that to the westward, is low and sandy, and that to which vessels are obliged to give a wide berth when running out for a southeaster; the other is high, bold, and well-wooded.

In the middle of this crescent, directly opposite the anchoring ground, lies the Mission and town of Santa Barbara, on a low plain, but little above the level of the sea, covered with grass, though entirely without trees, and surrounded on three sides by an amphitheater of mountains, which start off to a distance of fifteen to twenty miles. The Mission stands a little back of the town, and is a large building, or rather collection of buildings, in the center of which is a high tower with a belfry of five bells. The town lies a little nearer to the beach—about half a mile from it—and is composed of one-story houses, built of sun-baked clay or adobe, some of them whitewashed, with red tiles on the roofs. I should judge that there were about a hundred of them; and in the midst of them stands the presidio, or fort, built of the same material and apparently but little stronger. The town is finely situated, with a bay in front and amphitheater of hills behind. The only thing that diminishes its beauty is that the hills have no large trees upon them, they having been all burnt by a great fire which swept them off about a dozen years ago, and they have not grown again. The fire was described to me by an inhabitant as having been a very terrible and magnificent sight. The air of the valley was so heated that the people were obliged to leave town and take up their quarters for several days upon the beach. * * * We lay at a distance of three miles from the beach, and the town was nearly a mile farther, so that we saw little or nothing of it. * * * We were pulled ashore in the boat, and took our way for the town. There everything wore the appearance of a holiday. The people were dressed in their best, the men riding about among the houses, and the women sitting on carpets before the doors. Under the piazza of a pulperia two men were seated, decked out with knots of ribbons and bouquets, and playing the violin and the Spanish guitar. These are the only instruments, with the exception of the drums and trumpets at Monterey, that I ever heard in California, and I suspect they play upon no others, for at a great *fandango*, at which I was afterward present, and where they mustered all the music they could find, there were three violins and two guitars and no other instruments.

Inquiring for an American who, we had been told, had married in the place, and kept a shop, we were directed to a long, low building, at the end of which was a door with a sign over it, in Spanish. Entering the shop we found no one in it, and the whole had an empty, deserted air. In a few minutes the man made his appearance and apologized for having nothing to entertain us with, saying that he had had a fandango at his house the night before, and the people had eaten and drank up everything. "O, yes!" said I, " Easter holidays!" "No," said he, with a singular expression on his face, "I had a little daughter die the other day, and that's the custom of the country." At this I felt somewhat awkwardly, not knowing what to say, and whether to offer consolation or not, and was beginning to retire, when he opened a side door, and told us to walk in. Here I was no less astonished for I found a large room, filled with young girls, from three or four years old up to fifteen or sixteen, dressed all in white, with wreaths of flowers on their heads, and bouquets in their hands. Following our conductor among these girls, who were playing about in high spirits, we came to a table at the end of the room, covered with a white cloth, on which lay a coffin about three feet long, with the body of his child. The coffin was covered with white cloth and lined with white satin, and was strewn with flowers.

Through an open door we saw in another room a few elderly people in common dress, while the benches and tables, thrown up in a corner, and the stained walls, gave evidences of the last night's "high go." Feeling like Garrick, between tragedy and comedy, an uncertainty of purpose, I asked the man when the funeral would take place; and, being told that it would move toward the Mission in about an hour, took my leave. To pass away the time, we took horses and rode to the beach. * * * From the beach we returned to the town, and finding that the funeral procession had moved, rode on and overtook it, about half way up to the Mission. Here was as peculiar a sight as we had seen before in the house, the one looking as much like a funeral procession as the other did like a house of mourning. The little coffin was borne by eight girls who were continually relieved by others running forward from the procession and taking their places. Behind it came a straggling company of girls, dressed, as before, in white and flowers, and including, I should judge by their numbers, all the girls between five and fifteen in the place. They played along the way, frequently stopping and running altogether to talk to some one, or to pick up a flower, and then running on again to overtake the coffin. There were a few elderly women in common colors, and a herd of young men and boys, some on foot and others mounted, following them, or rode or walked by their side, frequently interrupting them by jokes and questions. But the most singular thing of all was that two men walked, one on each side of the coffin, carrying muskets in their hands, which they continually loaded and fired into the air. Whether this was to keep off the evil spirits or no I do not know. It was the only interpretation that I could put upon it. As we drew near the Mission, we saw the great gate thrown open, and the padre standing on the steps with a crucifix in his hand. The Mission is a large and deserted-looking place, the out-buildings going to ruin, and everything giving one the impression of decayed grandeur. A large stone fountain threw out pure water from four mouths into a basin before the church door; and we were on the point of riding up to let our horses drink when it occurred to us that it might be consecrated, and we forbore. Just at this moment the bells set up their harsh, discordant clangor, and the procession moved into the court. I wished to follow and see the ceremony, but the horse of one of my companions had become frightened and was tearing off toward the town, * * * and I was obliged to leave the ceremony and ride after him.

A very apposite phase is illustrated by the following description:

Great preparations were now being made on shore for the marriage of our agent, who was to marry Doña Anita de la Guerra y Noriega y Carrillo, youngest daughter of Don Antonio Noriega, the grandee of the place, and the head of the first family in California. Our steward was ashore three days making pastry and cake, and some of the best of our stores were sent off with him. On the day appointed for the wedding we took the Captain ashore in a gig, and had orders to come for him at night, with leave to go up to the house and see the fandango.

At 10 o'clock the bride went up with her sister to the confessional, dressed in black. Nearly an hour intervened when the great doors of the Mission church opened, the bells rang out a loud discordant peal, and the bride, dressed in complete white, came out of the church with the bridegroom, followed by a long procession. Just as she stepped from the church door, a small white cloud issued from the bows of our ship, which was full in sight, the loud report echoed among the hills and over the bay, and instantly the ship was dressed in flags and pennants from stem to stern. Twenty-three guns followed in regular succession, with intervals of fifteen seconds between, when the cloud blew off and our ship lay dressed in colors all day. At sundown another salute of the same number of guns was fired, and all the flags run down.

The bride's father's house was the principal one in the place, with a large court in front upon which a tent was built, capable of containing several hundred people. Going in, we found nearly all the people of the town—men, women and children—collected and crowded together, leaving barely room for the dancers; for on these occasions no invitations are given, but everyone is expected to come, though there is always a private entertainment within the house for particular friends. The old women sat down in rows, clapping their hands to the music, and applauding the young ones.

The music was lively, and among the tunes we recognized several of our popular airs, which we, no doubt, have taken from the Spanish. In the dancing I was much disappointed. The women stood upright with their hands down by their sides, their eyes fixed upon the ground before them, and slid about without any perceptible means of motion; for their feet were invisible, the hem of their dresses forming a circle about them, reaching to the ground. They looked as grave as if going through some religious ceremony, their faces as little excited as their limbs, and, on the whole, instead of the spirited, fascinating Spanish dances which I had expected, I found the California fandango, on the part of the women at least, a lifeless affair. The men did better. They danced with grace and spirit, moving in circles around their nearly stationary partners, and showing their figures to advantage. A great deal was said about our friend Don Juan Bandini, and when he did appear, which was toward the close of the evening, he certainly gave us the most graceful dancing that I had ever seen. He was dressed in white pantaloons, neatly made, a short jacket of dark silk, gaily figured, white stockings and thin morocco slippers upon his very small feet. His slight and graceful figure was well adapted to dancing, and he moved about with the grace and daintiness of a young fawn. He was loudly applauded, and danced frequently toward the close of the evening. After the supper the waltzing began, which was confined to a very few of the "gente de razon," and was considered a high accomplishment and a mark of aristocracy. Here, too, Don Juan figured greatly, waltzing with the sister of the bride (Doña Angustias, a handsome woman and a general favorite) in a variety of beautiful figures, which lasted as much as half an hour, no one else taking the floor. They were repeatedly and loudly applauded, the old men and women jumping off their seats in admiration, and the young people waving their hats and handkerchiefs.

The great amusement of the evening—owing to its being the carnival—was the breaking of eggs filled with cologne or other essences upon the heads of the company. The women bring a great number of these secretly about them, and the amusement is to break one secretly upon the head of a gentleman when his back is turned. He is bound in gallantry to find out the lady and return the compliment, though it must not be done if the person sees you. A tall, stately Don, with immense gray whiskers, and a look of great importance, was standing before me, when I felt a hand upon my shoulder, and, turning round, saw Doña Angustias (whom we all knew, as she had been up to Monterey and down again in the Alert), with her finger upon her lip, motioning me gently aside. I stepped back a little, when she went up behind the Don and with one hand knocked off his huge sombrero and at the same instant with the other broke the egg upon his head, and, springing behind me, was out of sight in a moment. The Don turned slowly around, the cologne running down his face and over his clothes and a loud laugh breaking out from every quarter. A great many such tricks were played, and many a war of sharp manœuvering was carried on between couples of the younger people, and at every successful exploit a general laugh was raised.

Another of their games I was for some time at a loss about. A pretty young girl was dancing, named—after what would appear to us an almost sacrilegious custom of the country—Espiritu Santo, when a young man went behind her and placed his hat directly upon her head, letting it fall down over her eyes, and sprang back among the crowd. She danced for some time with the hat on, when she threw it off, which called forth a general shout, and the young man was obliged to go out upon the floor and pick it up. I soon began to suspect the meaning of the thing, and was afterward told that it was a compliment, and an offer to become the lady's gallant for the rest of the evening, and to wait upon her home * * *

These fandangos generally lasted three days. The next day two of us were sent up town and took care to come back by way of Señor Noriega's and take a look into the booth. The musicians were again there upon their platform, scraping and twanging away, and a few people, apparently of the lower classes, were dancing. The dancing is kept up at intervals throughout the day, but the crowd, the spirit, and the elite, come at night. The next night, which was the last, we went ashore in the same manner, until we got almost tired of the monotonous twang of the instruments, the drawling sounds which the women kept up as an accompaniment, and the slapping of the hands in time with the music in place of castanets.

We heard some talk about "caballos" and "carrera," and seeing the people streaming off in one direction, we followed, and came upon a level piece of ground just outside of the town, which was used as a race-course. Here the crowd soon became thick again, the ground was marked off, the judges stationed, and the horses led up to one end. Two fine-looking old gentlemen—Don Carlos and Don Domingo, so-called—held the stakes, and all was now ready. We waited some time, during which we could just see the horses, twisting aound and turning, until at length there was a shout along the lines and on they came, heads stretched out and eyes starting, working all over, both man and beast. The steeds came by us like a couple of chain-shot, neck and neck, and now we could see nothing but their backs and their hind hoofs flying through the air. As fast as the horses passed, the crowd broke up behind them and ran to the goal. When we got there we found the horses returning on a slow walk, having run far beyond the mark, and heard that the long bony one had come in head and shoulders before the other. The riders were light-built men, had handkerchiefs tied around their heads, and were bare-armed and bare-legged. The horses were noble-looking beasts, not so sleek and combed as our Boston stable horses, but with fine limbs and spirited eyes.

THE PIONEERS AND THEIR DESCENDANTS.

At each of the California missions a company of soldiers was stationed. In Santa Barbara the soldiers occupied a square called the presidio. This was about 250 yards square, surrounded by a high adobe wall, inside of which were a church and buildings, constructed of adobe, roofed with tiles, and used for shelter by the soldiers. This church was standing until 1853, when a portion of the roof fell; the adobe walls, being thus exposed to rain, soon crumbled away. A part of one of the buttresses still stands near Santa Barbara Street, west of Cañon Perdido Street.

A portion of the Californian population of Santa Barbara are descendants of the soldiers of this garrison, who married natives; others are descendants from immigrants from old Spain and other parts of Europe, from Mexico, South America, and the United States.

It is generally conceded that the leading Spanish family in Santa Barbara has been that of de la Guerra, often wrongly called Noriega, from a misapprehension of the Spanish custom by which the children of a family add their mother's patronymic with the prefix "y" ("and") after their father's; this, however, is a matter of compliment to the mother, and the father's remains the lawful family name. Thus the founder of this family, from its mother being a Noriega, was called de la Guerra y Noriega, while his children, whose mother was a Carrillo, wrote their name de la Guerra y Carrillo.

Don José de la Guerra y Noriega was born in 1776, at Novales, province of Santander, Spain, of an honorable amily, whose coat of arms carries their record back to the time of the Moors. The house where he was born still stands, an imposing edifice of Novales, over a century old, with the family arms cut in stone over the two great gateways; it covers a block of land in the principal town of the province.

Young de la Guerra was sent out to a kinsman, a wealthy merchant in Mexico, but he soon sought and obtained a cadetship in the royal army, and in 1800 was appointed ensign in a company stationed at Monterey, California, where he joined it in 1801. In 1804 he married Doña Maria Antonio, daughter of Don Raymundo Carrillo, then commandante of the presidio of Santa Barbara; and in 1806 he was sent hither as the company's lieutenant. In 1810 he was appointed Habilitado General from both Californias to the Vice-Royal Government in Mexico, and, proceeding toward the capital with his family, he was captured at San Blas by the Mexican patriots, then in revolt against the government of Spain, he escaping with his life, while the other men captured with him were assassinated. The revolution had deprived him of his office; therefore he started back to California; and, performing on the way military service which gave him a better footing with the government, he was appointed in 1811 to the command of troops stationed at San Diego, where for several years he dwelt with his family. In 1817 he was appointed captain and commandante of the troops and Santa Barbara, and here was his home thereafter, with a brief interregnum, when he went to Mexico again as Habilitado General. He was continued in office as captain and commandante until 1828, when he was sent as deputy to the Mexican Congress; but, on reaching the capital, he found his seat contested, and his opponent triumphed. Don José now renounced politics and engaged in farming and stock-raising on a large scale, favored by the secularization of the missions. Within a few years he was owner of eight of the principal ranchos of the district, including Las Posas, Simí, Conejo, San Julian, and others. The ability, integrity, and kindness of this man made him a power among his neighbors, his advice and influence being almost without limit. He was always an arbiter in misunderstandings among his own people, as well as between these and the foreigners who soon came into the country.

His wife, Maria Antonia Carrillo, was regarded as one of the most charitable and benevolent women of the age.

This worthy pair had seven sons and four daughters, and a brief *resumé* of their marriages and descendants will show the important part that this family has continued to play in local history, as well as the fertility of the race.

The eldest son, José Antonio de la Guerra y Carrillo, married Concepcion Ortega. Their children were: José Antonio, José Ramon (graduated at Georgetown, District of Columbia), Guillermo and Alejandro, sons; Dolores, Catarina, Lola, Cristina, and Juana, daughters.

Second son, Juan, was considered the ablest in the family, but died early; was educated in England, being graduated from three colleges.

Third son, Francisco, married Ascencion Sepúlveda, and by her had a son, Francisco, and a daughter, Maria Antonia. His second wife was Concepcion Sepúlveda, sister of the former wife; by her he had Juan, Osboldo, José Hercules, Pablo, and Hanibal, sons; and Anita (Mrs. F. W. Thompson), Herlinda, Rosa, and Diana, daughters.

Fourth son, Pablo, married Josefa Moreno, and had Francisca (Mrs. T. B. Dibblee), Delfina (one of twins), Herminia, and Paulina, all daughters.

Fifth son, Miguel, married Trinidad Ortega; their children were: Gaspar, Ulpiano, and Leon, sons, and Maria (Mrs. Taylor), Josefa, Olympia, Joaquina, and Paulina, daughters.

Sixth son, Joaquin, was for a time sheriff of Santa Barbara County. He never married.

Of the daughters of José de la Guerra y Noriega, Teresa, the eldest, married William E. P. Hartnell, of England, and by him had twenty-two children, as follows: Guillermo, Juan, Alvano, Nataniel, George, Franco, Benjamin, Teresa, Matilde, Anita, Magdalena, Amelia, and others whose names cannot be had.

The second daughter, Maria de las Augustias, was married to Manuel Jimeno of Mexico, who was subsequently secretary to several of the governors of California, and intimately connected with land matters after secularization of the missions. Maria had Manuela, Maria Antonia, Augustias, Carolina, daughters; and José Antonio, Porfirio, Santiago, Enrique, Belisario, Juan and Alfredo, children by this marriage; and by her second marriage to Dr. Ord, of the United States navy, one daughter, Rebecca Ord.

The third daughter, Ana Maria Antonia, married to Alfred Robinson, of Boston, Massachusetts, had James, Alfredo, Miguel, and another James, sons; Elena, Maria, Antonia, and Paulina, daughters.

This lady was the bride referred to in Dana's account of Santa Barbara. Alfred Robinson came from Boston in 1829, on the ship Brooklyn, owned by Bryant, Sturgis, and others. He was for many years engaged in mercantile business, and was the first agent of the Pacific Steamboat Company in 1849. The first son, James, for whom the youngest was named, died at West Point when seventeen years old.

The fourth and youngest daughter of Don José de la Guerra y Noriega, named Antonia Maria, married first Cesario Lataillade of Spain, by whom she had Cesario, Jr., and Maria Antonia; contracting a second marriage with Gaspar Oreña of Spain, she had Anita, Serena, Rosa, Acacia, and Teresa, daughters; and Leopoldo, Dario, Orestes, and Arturo, sons. This lady, Mrs. Oreña, was considered the greatest beauty of the de la Guerra family, or even of the coast.

One of the sons of Don José was Don Pablo de la Guerra, a member of the first constitutional convention of California, who, in his life-time, was severally Senator, District Judge of the Fourth Judicial District, and Lieutenant Governor of the State. He was a courteous, intelligent, upright man. He died February 5, 1874.

His predecessor as District Judge was Don Joaquin Carrillo. Judge Carrillo was the first County Judge of this county, and was elected to the district bench in 1852, and served in this capacity eleven years. He neither spoke nor understood the English language; all proceedings in his court were conducted in Spanish. His mind was broad and easily grasped and mastered the most subtle and complicated cases. He based his decisions upon the principles of equity, rather than law. Don Joaquin Carrillo was a warm friend of the Americans. He died February 19, 1868, beloved and lamented.

Another of the prominent families, whose members are now counted by the hundred, was founded by Don Raymundo Carrillo, one of the first commanders of the posts of San Diego and Santa Barbara. He married Tomasa Lugo, daughter of one of the oldest soldiers stationed at Santa Barbara. They had four sons and one daughter, Maria Antonia, already mentioned as the wife of José de la Guerra y Noriega, and mother of the de la Guerra y Carrillo family.

The first son of Raymundo Carrillo, Carlos Antonio, married Maria, sister of Governor Castro, and by her had sons: José, who married Catarina Ortega; Pedro, who married Josefa Bandini; José Jesus, wedded to Tomasa Gutierrez; and daughters, Maria Josefa, who married William G. Dana; Encarnacion, wife of Thomas Robbins; Francisca, wedded to Alpheus Thompson; Manuela, married to John C. Jones; Maria Antonia, spouse of Lewis C. Burton; and two other daughters, who died young—in all ten children.

Anastacio, Carrillo's second son, married Concepcion Garcia. Their children were: Raymundo, who married Dolores Ortega; Francisco, dead; Luis, married to Refugio Ortega; Guillermo, whose wife was Manuela Ortega; and daughters, Micaela, dead; Manuela, married to Joaquin Carrillo; and Soledad, dead.

Domingo Carrillo, the third son, married Concepcion Pico. They had sons: Joaquin, married to his cousin, Manuela Carrillo; José Antonio, who married Felicitas Gutierrez; Francisco, whose wife was Dorotea Lugo; Alejandro, dead; Felipe, dead; and daughters, Maria, wife of J. M. Covarrubias; Angela, married to Ygnacio del Valle; and Maria Antonia, dead.

José Antonio Carrillo, the fourth son, married Estefana Pico. His daughter was Luis (or Lewis) Burton's second wife, mother of Ben Burton.

The Ortega family was of the *sangre azul*, or blue blood of Castile, Spain. Some of this family emigrated to Guadalaxara, Mexico, and the founder of the California branch was for a time commandante of a cavalry company at Loreto, in La Baja, or Lower California, where were born to him, Captain José Maria Ortega, and his wife, Antonia Carrillo, seven children: Ygnacio, José Maria, José Vicente, Francisco and Juan; and Maria Luisa and Maria Antonia, daughters.

Ygnacio Ortega married Francisca Lopez, and had sons: Martin, married to Ynocencia Moraga; José Vicente, who married Maria Estefana Olivera; and Antonio Maria José Dolores, José de Jesus and Joaquin, who did not marry; also daughters, Pilar, spouse of the doughty Santiago Arguello; Soledad, wife of Luis Arguello; Maria de Jesus, married to José Ramirez; Concepcion, who married José Antonio de la Guerra; and Catarina, wife of José Carrillo.

José Vicente, second son of Captain Ortega, was the founder of the Refugio Rancho, which is still possessed by the family.

Juan Ortega, the fourth son, married Rafaela Arrellanez. Their children were: Emidio, married to Concepcion Dominguez; and daughters, Maria, wife of Guadalupe Hernandez; Buenaventura, wife of Joaquin Cota; Maria Antonia, wife of Pedro Dejeme; and Maria de Jesus, who married Fernando Tico.

José Vicente, son of Ygnacio, and grandson of Captain Ortega, married Maria Estefana Olivera, daughter of Ygnacio Olivera, of Los Angeles. The Oliveras were of old Castilian stock, with chivalric ideas of courtesy and honor. Diego Olivera, who died a few years since, wore the old-time garb, with silk stockings, shoes with jeweled buckles, and the sword to bear which he had hereditary right. It bore engraved the time-honored Spanish motto—"*No me saques sin razon, no me envaines sin honor* ("Draw me not in unjust cause, sheath me not with honor dimmed"). This Diego Olivera was brother to Maria Estefana, who gave her husband children as follows: Two sons named Luis, who both died young; Manuel, who died somewhat later; Pedro, and one daughter, Rafaela Luisa, wife of Daniel Hill.

Daniel Hill and his wife, Rafaela Luisa, had children as follows: Rosa, wife of Nicholas A. Den; Josefa, wife of Alexander S. Taylor; Susana, wife of T. Wallace More; Maria Antonia, wife of H. O'Neill; Lucrecia, died young; Adelaida, Helena, daughters; and Vicente, Jose Maria, Juan, Tomas, Ramon, Enrique and Daniel, sons.

The Cotas were another important family, allied by intermarriage with various names which appear on the page of history. At least two women of this family are deserving of mention here, they being also granddaughters of that Corporal Antonio Maria Lugo who came up from Los Angeles to assist in repulsing the "pirate" Bouchard, in 1818. Maria Los Angeles Cota de la Torre, daughter of Don Pablo Cota, ensign of the Santa Barbara company, and of Doña Rosa Lugo, was born at Santa Barbara in 1790. At thirteen years of age she was married to Don José Joaquin de la Torre, cadet and commissary at Monterey, and afterwards secretary to Governor Sola. She died at Monterey in 1877, aged eighty-seven years, after seventy-four years of married life. She left three sons, three daughters, forty-three grandchildren, thirty-four great-grandchildren, and several great-great-grandchildren.

Maria Ysabel Cota de Pico was born at Santa Barbara, May, 1783. At nineteen years old she married José Dolores Pico, one of three brothers who came to California with the first Mexican colony as officers in the military service of the Spanish Viceroyalty in Mexico. Her husband died in 1827, after fifty years of military service. Of this marriage were born thirteen children, who, with their cousins, the Castros, children of their father's brothers, and allies by marriage, were all powerful in the affairs of government in California at the time of the American invasion. This lady was over eighty-six years old when she died. Her descendants numbered over 300, including one of the sixth generation; nearly all live in this State, and they bear the names of the most prominent native families, as well as of many leading American citizens intermarried with them.

Raymundo Olivas, born in Los Angeles in 1801, came northward in 1821. He was the original grantee of the San Miguelito or Casitas Rancho, granted in 1840. He and his wife had twenty-one children. In 1883 he had under his roof in Ventura County, he then being nearly eighty and his wife sixty years old, forty-three descendants, of whom eighteen were their sons and daughters. Moreover, a daughter living at Santa Cruz had already done somewhat toward sustaining the family record, in presenting the country with ten children.

There were other eminent families, bearing the names of Del Valle, Arnaz, Camarillo, etc., although the Del Valles, a notable family, now belong properly to Ventura County.

Among the pioneers not of Spanish or Mexican blood were the following:

Joseph Chapman, of Massachusetts, captured from Bouchard's privateer in 1818; settled for a time in Los Angeles County with the Lugos; married Guadalupe Ortega, of Santa Barbara; he built and lived in the adobe house still standing in the rear of the Episcopal church; died in 1848, leaving many descendants.

Captain James W. Burke, a native of Ireland, arrived here from Lima in 1820, and settled permanently in 1828.

William E. P. Hartnell, an Englishman, came here in 1822. He was a notable linguist; was Government translator at Monterey, and translated the statutes into Spanish. He married Teresa de la Guerra, daughter of Don José, and they had twenty-two children, of whom a number are still living in this county and San Luis. He died in 1854.

Captain Thomas Robbins, a native of Nantucket, came here in 1827. He owned the Rancho Las Positas y Calera, adjoining Santa Barbara. Died in 1857.

Captain William G. Dana came from Boston in 1827. He lived mostly at his rancho, Nipomo, in San Luis County, where he died in 1857, and where are still living a number of the twenty-two children borne him by his wife, Maria Josefa Carrillo.

Alfred Robinson came hither from Boston in 1829, on the ship Brooklyn. He married Ana Maria Antonia de la Guerra; was the first agent of the Pacific Steamship Company in 1849, and was for many years a leading merchant. He is a gentleman of intelligence and refinement, and generally esteemed. He still lives in San Francisco. He is the author of a work, "Life in California," published in 1846, and now quite rare.

Robert Elwell, of Boston, arrived in 1825. He was favorably known by all the old citizens. He had a pithy way of expression. One of his sayings was the following: "In politics, I am a Whig; in religion, a Unitarian. I am also a Freemason, and if these won't take a man to Heaven, I don't know what will." He died in 1853.

Daniel A. Hill, of Billerica, Massachusetts, came from the Sandwich Islands to Monterey in 1823, and settled in Santa Barbara the following year. He was the original grantee of La Goleta Rancho, where he died in 1865. He left a large family, who, with their descendants, still reside in Santa Barbara County.

James Buck, of Boston, Massachusetts, arrived from the Sandwich Islands in 1829. His descendants still have a home here.

Captain Alpheus B. Thompson, of Brunswick, Maine, arrived here from Honolulu in 1834. As merchant and ship-master he did business here many years. Three of his children, C. A. Thompson, A. B. Thompson and Mrs. E. Van Valkenburg are now residents of this vicinity. A. B. Thompson was for twelve years the County Clerk of Santa Barbara County. Captain Thompson died at Los Angeles in the year 1870.

Augustin Jansen, of Belgium, arrived here from Mexico in August, 1834. He has been County Assessor of this county, and a member of the common council of Santa Barbara city.

Julian Foxen arrived in 1828 from England. He was a man of notable character. He died on his rancho, the Tinaquaic, in February, 1874, leaving many descendants.

Lewis F. Burton, of Henry County, Tennessee, came here in 1831, and engaged in otter-hunting, and later he conducted a mercantile business in Santa Barbara for more than thirty years. He was nearly killed by robbers, in the early days, near the site of the present Port Harford, but was nursed back to health by the ladies of the Carrillo family, one of whom he married later on. He died in 1880.

Captain John Wilson, of Scotland, who came hither via Peru in 1830, was long a merchant here. He died in 1860 at San Luis Obispo.

Francis Ziba Branch, of New York, came here from New Mexico in 1833. He engaged in mercantile pursuits; died in 1874 at San Luis Obispo.

Isaac J. Sparks, of Maine, came overland in 1832. He was a merchant, and the first postmaster appointed; he built the first brick house in Santa Barbara, erected in 1854, which now forms a part of the old Park Hotel.

James Scott, of Scotland, came here in 1830 with Captain Wilson, and was his partner in business. He died in 1851.

George Nidever, of Arkansas, came overland in 1834, reaching Santa Barbara in 1835. He was a mighty hunter. He it was who rescued "the lost woman" from San Nicolas.

Captain John F. Smith, native of France, came in 1833 via the Sandwich Islands, built the first wooden dwelling in Santa Barbara, still standing near the gas-house. He died in 1866.

Nicholas A. Den, of Waterford, Ireland, arrived in 1839. He was the grantee of the Rancho Dos Pueblos. He married a daughter of Daniel A. Hill. He died in 1862, leaving ten children.

John C. Jones, of Boston, came hither in 1835 from Honolulu, where he had been United States Consul. He married Mannela Carrillo, whose wedding portion was one-half of Santa Rosa Island, which he, with A. B. Thompson, a brother-in-law, stocked with horses, sheep and cattle. He removed with his family to Boston, and died about 1850.

Albert Packard, a New Englander, arrived via Mazatlan about 1845, and lived here for many years, being well-known as a prominent lawyer and a wealthy orchardist. He still lives.

Henry J. Dally, of New York, reached Monterey in 1843, and removed to San Luis Obispo in 1848, and to Santa Barbara in 1853. He was an otter-hunter.

Wm. A. Streeter, a New Yorker, came here via Peru in 1843. A wheelwright by trade, he officiated as a dentist and a physician, and was and is skillful at almost every kind of practical mechanics. He still lives, engaged in various and versatile sorts of handicraft.

SANTA BARBARA COUNTY.

IN GENERAL.

BOUNDARY.

After the signing of the treaty of peace between the United States and Mexico, February 2, 1848, the establishment of the new government was pushed forward as speedily as practicable. One month after the adoption of the Constitution, the first Legislature met at San José, which was made the capital.

The act subdividing the State into counties, and appointing the county-seats therein, approved February 18, 1850, contained passages as follows:

"Section 1. The following shall be the boundaries and seats of justice of the several counties of the State of California until otherwise determined by law.

"Section 2 created San Diego County.

"Section 3 created Los Angeles County.

"Section 4. COUNTY OF SANTA BARBARA. Beginning on the sea coast, at the mouth of the creek called Santa Maria, and running up the middle of said creek to its source; thence due northeast to the summit of the Coast Range, the farm of Santa Maria falling within Santa Barbara County; thence following the summit of the Coast Range to the northwest corner of Los Angeles County; then along the northwest boundary of said county to the ocean and three English miles therein; and thence in a northwesterly direction, parallel with the coast, to a point due west of the mouth of Santa Maria Creek; thence due east to the mouth of said creek, which was the place of beginning, including the islands of Santa Barbara, San Nicolas, San Miguel, Santa Rosa, Santa Cruz, and all others in the same vicinity. The seat of justice shall be at Santa Barbara.

"Section 5. COUNTY OF SAN LUIS OBISPO. Beginning three English miles west of the coast, at a point due west of the source of the Nacimiento River, and running due east to the source of said river; thence down the middle of said river to its confluence with Monterey River; thence up or down, as the case may be, the middle of Monterey River to the parallel of thirty-six degrees north latitude; thence due east following said parallel to the summit of the Coast Range; thence following the summit of said range in a southeasterly direction to the northeast corner of Santa Barbara County; thence following the northern boundary of Santa Barbara County to the ocean, and three English miles therein; and thence in a northwesterly direction parallel with the coast, to the place of beginning. The seat of justice shall be at San Luis Obispo."

A subsequent act, defining the boundaries between Santa Barbara and San Luis Obispo Counties was passed May 13, 1854. The northern line of Santa Barbara County was declared to be from where the eastern line intersected the southern line of Township 10 north, San Bernardino base; thence west, on said township line to the Santa Maria River, thence down said river and down the creek which divides that part of Guadalupe Rancho known as La Larga from that known as Oso Flaco, to a point in the Pacific ocean opposite the mouth of said creek.

The act passed March 2, 1850, providing for the holding of the first county election, and that passed March 23, 1850, providing for general elections, applied to these as to the rest of the newly designated counties.

THE EXPORTS

from Santa Barbara from March to September, 1847, amounted to $27,780.

In the summer of 1848 the United States steamship Edith went ashore on the coast between Point Sal and Point Arguello. There were assertions that she was purposely wrecked, as some of the crew were eager to leave service and go to the newly discovered gold mines. The wreck was sold to Captain William G. Dana, owner of the great Nipomo rancho, who entertained at his house the officers and the crew until arrangement could be made for their transportation to Monterey, then the State capital and headquarters on this coast for the army and navy.

ITEMS OF INTEREST, 1850–'90.

The first supply of public money for Santa Barbara County was obtained for licenses for selling liquor and merchandise. The treasurer's account began August 23, 1850. An accounting was made January 4, 1851, when he was charged with State taxes, $5,507.18; county taxes, $2,753.59; total, $8,260.77. The total of credits was $5,667.53, leaving for salaries, etc., $2,593.24.

Apropos to the subject of licenses, there would seem to have been some thirst-inspiring property in the climate of Santa Barbara at this period, for, of the fifty licenses issued from August, 1850, to February, 1851, thirty-two were for the sale of liquors. It should be said, however, that the sales were mostly to foreign customers, for the native Californians of that day were not excessive drinkers, but it is surprising to see how many of the aristocratic old families took out licenses to sell liquor.

It is said that the three lustrums from 1850 to 1865 were a period of great peace and order in Santa Barbara. No place in California, nor even in all the United States, it is declared, with an equal population, was more free from crime than was this city at that period. The county jail served as the place of incarceration of all the town prisoners, as well as those of the county; yet, as we are told, more than half the time during those fifteen years the jail door stood wide open, the edifice being without an occupant. Many of the new-comers had intermarried with the natives, and these relations served to bind the diverse elements together in harmony. There were occasional strifes over the possession of land outside of the city, such as always occur in a new country, but these were not frequent in the earlier times, for land was not considered worth enough to warrant dispute.

It was, however, inevitable that owing to a not unnatural friction, should be occasional passages which caused strained relations between the Californians and the Americans. For instance, two men coming up the coast to buy cattle were murdered near the San Gabriel River by one Zavaleta and another native, who came to Santa Barbara to spend the money taken from their victims. The murderers were recognized by description, and were arrested by the sheriff, Valentine Hearne, aided by a number of citizens. Some of the native families, including that of Captain de la Guerra, protested against the treatment of the men, as based on insufficient evidence, and inspired by race prejudice. Hence considerable ill-feeling was engendered. An escort of twenty-five men was made up to accompany the accused back to Los Angeles, and a semi-official demand, accompanied by a menace, was made for a supply of horses to be furnished for the purpose, by the citizens of Santa Barbara. The men were tried, and confessed the murder in detail, pointing out the burial place of their victims, so that they were hung by the people of Los Angeles. Notwithstanding this justification, Dr. Den and the de la Guerras were so much displeased with Hearne for having arrested the men, that they withdrew from his bond, and so forced him to resign his office of sheriff. It is said that W. W. Twist, his successor, was not even an American citizen.

Again, trouble arose from the dissatisfaction of American newcomers with the system of large holdings of land by the natives, and from such a cause arose one of the celebrated cases of the county. John Vidal, a member of Carnes' Company in Stevenson's Regiment, had rented for a time a tract of land on the Arroyo Burro, a small creek emptying into the sea near Santa Barbara, and when his lease expired, he claimed the land under the pre-emption laws as Government land. Suit being brought in the respective courts, the land was adjudged the property of Dr. Den, of whom Vidal had rented, and the sheriff (Twist) was ordered by the court to evict Vidal and put Den in possession. Vidal was known to have many friends among the gamblers, and the attempt to disturb him was considered very dangerous. When the sheriff called out a posse to execute the writ of ejectment, the people began to take sides, and Vidal's friends gathered upon the disputed territory, some say merely in friendly union, others declare to fortify and hold the place at all hazards. The sheriff enlisted some 200 men, engaged a surgeon, and secured a small cannon to be used, if necessary, in demolishing the fortifications. At this juncture, Vidal and a few of his companions rode up to the assembled force, whether with hostile intent or in the hope that the issue might be determined by amiable parley. Two of his companions lassoed the cannon, and made as if to drag it away, upon which pretext Twist fired upon them, and at once the fight became general. One of Vidal's companions rushed at Twist, and attempted to plunge into him a long knife, which was deflected by a rib, so that the wound was not dangerous. Vidal was shot, and fell from his horse, but, although terribly wounded, he lingered under Dr. Brinkerhoff's care for fourteen days, unable to speak, even regarding a ring he wore, which he evidently wished to leave to some one. Twist soon recovered. These were the only serious casualties which occurred, although a running fight lasted for some minutes. By advice of their leading men, the Californian citizens remained within doors that day, and Pablo de la Guerra proceeded to the spot with a flag of truce, and persuaded the Vidal adherents to submit to the legal authorities. The next morning, a ship-of-war anchored here, having been despatched from Monterey to enforce order if necessary.

The land in dispute was afterward pronounced public ground, although Vidal had practically acknowledged Den's ownership by possession, by his payment of rental for it. Vidal appears to have been largely a scapegoat in the matter, as he was a man of some worth. He was justice of the peace when killed, and had been associate justice with Joaquin Carrillo.

The feverish excitement, the disorganized conditions of society, and general lawlessness, naturally led to a vast deal of gambling, drinking and other vices, as well as systems of outlawry,—practically highway robbers.

One gang, which flourished in the early '50s, had its headquarters at the Los Alamos and Purisima Ranchos. It was headed by Salomon Pico, a connection of Don Pio and General Andres Pico; and this prestige of blood no doubt greatly facilitated the gang's operations, by procuring shelter, protection, aid, and warnings of danger, from the powerful rancheros. The ostensible occupation of this set was driving and trading in stock, and the consequent irregularities of movement greatly facilitated the suppression of strangers who came thither, well supplied with money, to purchase cattle. Many were the disappearances noted of such individuals, and after years brought to light many skeletons, on which were signs of violence telling of robbery and murder.

Jack Powers was another bandit, and one of the most remarkable and most successful of the epoch. He had been a member of Captain Lippett's Company F, Stevenson's Regiment, and is said to have enjoyed at one time a good reputation and standing. After being mustered out, he took up the career of a gambler, in which he was very successful, and when Salomon Pico's band was dispersed, Powers brought its remnants together under his own leadership, and for a time they terrorized the section for a period of about four years. He was deemed the best rider in the State,—no slight compliment, as the Californian boys were very like unto centaurs. Powers once at San José rode for a wager 150 miles in fourteen hours, changing steeds at will. This skill as a rider, and his command of good horses, made him appear fairly ubiquitous, as was reputed to be Joaquin Murieta. Powers had a gray mule, which, it was said, would carry him 100 miles in twelve hours. He was once in Santa Barbara within ten hours after he had committed a robbery near San Luis Obispo. Many anecdotes are told of Powers' exploits.

Another of the fraternity of "holy terrors" was Patrick Dunn, who had the name of belonging to Powers' gang. Dunn, while intoxicated, shot a stranger, a passenger from a steamer; the murder, done in the square before the de la Guerra House, was witnessed by several ladies of that family. But such was the terror of incurring the enmity of the gang, that only the court's solemn assurance of protection could induce them to testify. Whilst the trial was in progress, the judge, the district attorney and the sheriff, each received a warning that they would be killed if they prosecuted the case, and no doubt murder would have been done in open court, had not six deputies been sworn in, with instructions to shoot instantly Powers and Dunn, at any attempt to interfere with the proceedings. Dunn pleaded justifiable homicide in self-defence, and after a trial of twenty-one days, the jury disagreed. A similar result followed a second trial, held at Los Angeles.

Dunn was again tried for an attempt at murder, he having loaded a double barreled shot-gun to kill one Martin, who had offended him. Both barrels snapped without effect, but Dunn was sentenced to State's prison for a term of years. It became known that Powers had determined to rescue Dunn on his passage from the jail to the boat, and twenty-five men were sworn in as deputies, with instructions as before, to shoot both Dunn and Powers upon any attempt at a rescue. Powers, so Russell Heath, the sheriff, assured him, would be the first to fall.

The deputies followed the van containing the prisoner from the jail to the shore, where he was transferred to the lighter without interruption, although Powers and his friends, about thirty in number, had assembled at the beach on horseback. Powers left California about 1850, and went to Mexico, where he was shot. Dunn died in Arizona in 1866.

Up to 1856, the mail facilities for Santa Barbara were very sketchy; Lewis T. Burton was the first postmaster. When the Panama steamers began to touch here, they carried letters between this point and San Francisco, but the mail-bag was treated with so little consideration that it was often wetted in transit between the steamer and the landing, and on one occasion several gallons of water were turned out of the bag, along with the letters and papers. The dispatching of the mail was treated as a matter of little moment, and the letters received for distribution were kept in a candle-box, where each could help himself to his own—or his neighbor's—missives. In March, 1856, William Carey Jones, in a letter addressed to the Postmaster-General, set forth the disadvantage and detriment suffered from this lack of postal service, cited the superior means of intercommunication enjoyed under the Spanish rule eighty years previous, and advocated the establishment of a regular weekly mail, to be carried by couriers, between Monterey and San Diego. Within a year or two, the overland stage, carrying mail and passengers, was established by the United States Government, at a cost of about $500,000 per annum. It was designed to open a line of settlements from Texas to California, in the interest of the Southern States. Few passengers took this route, and as the schedule time was but little less than by steamer, the large Eastern mail continued to be transferred by the main lines of passenger travel. The stage route lay through the coast counties, and afforded their people the long-needed facilities. The war of the Rebellion scattered the stock, and put an end to this line.

At a little after 8 A. M., on January 9, 1857, was felt the premonitory shock of one of the severest earthquakes ever felt in California. The morning was clear, sunny and cool, with no forecast of the *temblor* whose shocks continued at intervals until the next day, their force extending from Point Concepcion to Los Angeles. The most violent alarm was felt by the people at Santa Barbara; but, fortunately, there was no loss of life, and but little damage to property beyond cracking the walls of some of the houses. The reservoir at the mission rocked so violently that the water slopped over at each of its sides so plentifully as to set quite a stream running; and near the hot springs great boulders were detached from the cliffs and rolled into the valley. At San Buenaventura, the mission church was badly injured, the roof partly falling in, and the belfry suffering considerable injury. The tower of the Point Concepcion light-house also was much damaged.

The *Gazette* died this year, the plant being sold to parties who removed it to San Francisco. It is believed that no file of this paper was preserved.

The whole tax rate for this year was 1.62\frac{1}{2}$ on the $100. In September there was in the county treasury $8,724.77$\frac{1}{4}$, the largest sum yet known, and the supervisors took the subject in hand, fixing the treasurer's bonds at $20,000. The system of accounts in this department was very obscure and imperfect, and it is said that the amounts on the stubs of the warrants gave the only clue to the condition of the funds. There seems to have been a pretty continual agitation on this subject during this period, and inspections were ordered made of the books of the auditor also. The same trouble ran into the succeeding year.

The whole number of votes cast at the county election in 1858 was 319. The total of tax rates for this year was $1.52½ on each $100. A road tax of $2.00 was levied on every man between twenty and forty years old. It was now ordered that one-sixth part of all taxes raised be set apart as a hospital fund.

On June 17, 1859, Santa Barbara was visited by a hot, sirocco-like wind from the northwest, which began about 12 M., and blew furiously until about 3:30 P. M., killing birds, rabbits, lambs, etc., blasting fruit, scorching the leaves on the wind ward side of trees, and sending the mercury up to 136° F.

In 1860 Santa Barbara shared in the split in the Democratic party on the slavery question, and the electoral ticket was divided. It was this year that San Buenaventura became ambitious of planning the town plat after regular, and laying out a street in front of the mission, between it and the orchard. After some controversy, this was carried into effect, and the fine main street of the town, which serves as its base line, dates from this beginning.

In 1861 there was a general resolve to discharge the heavy debt incurred by previous mismanagement and extravagance, and a law looking to that purpose was enacted by the Legislature, by the expressed wish of the people. The tax rate for this year was $1.90 on the $100. An appropriation was made by the Legislature of $15,000 for the construction of a county road, bids were made, and the contract was awarded to T. Wallace More; but he, after some little time, declared his inability to complete the undertaking, and suit was brought against him for the performance of the contract. The question was ultimately compromised.

The elections passed off very quietly this year, perhaps because of the absence of a newspaper to incite violence of political feeling.

Santa Barbara shared in the excessive rains that fell all over California in the winter of 1861-'62, and many changes were wrought in the way of changing the beds of rivers, filling up estuaries, etc. Until this season, the estuary of the Goleta was a sort of harbor, accessible to small crafts, which might have been made into a safe harbor of refuge from storms, but this season's freshets filled it with sand and gravel from the mountains, beyond the hope of clearing. In other places, the swollen streams swept out channels through the *bolsas*, or miry lagoons, in which they had terminated. The appearance of the country was also much changed by slides in the mountains. At San Buenaventura there was a slide along almost the whole face of the hill where ran the aqueduct, and the canal was so nearly destroyed as to require rebuilding. Many cattle perished this winter, but they were hardly missed, as stock was even over-abundant.

The taxes for 1863 footed up to $2.52 on the $100. The election of this year showed a notable increase in the population, as indexed by the number of voters. The salaries of the county judges, the sheriff, and the county clerk were fixed this year, respectively, as follows:—$1,000, $1,000, and $500 per annum. It was about this season that the enormous increase of the herds had brought down beef to a price that hardly repaid the killing. The loss in the hard winter of 1861-'62 was speedily recouped, and the droves had now attained proportions that demanded diminution. Particularly in the southern counties was this result made necessary, for here the distance from the markets, the long drives thereto over closely-grazed country, the inevitable shrinkage contingent upon the journey, and the inferior quality of the beef after the drive, all tended to depress greatly the value of this product. This led to the institution of a *matanza*, or species of wholesale slaughter, which reached, it is asserted, far toward 100,000 head. The slaughter-works were situated on the seashore between Santa Barbara and Carpenteria, that the refuse might be swept away by the tide. The carcasses were put into steam baths, and subjected to such heat that the flesh fell from the bones and became a mass of jelly and fat. This was put into a mighty press, and every particle of the tallow extracted; the jelly went to the manufacture of glue, the horns were sent East to be made into combs and other such matters. The cake or pressed meat was fed to hogs, so that every portion of the beef was utilized. Yet, notwithstanding this economy and the low price paid—$5 per head—the enterprise was unprofitable to its projectors.

In 1864 began the development of misfortunes arising from various causes. The excess of cattle and low prices of beef; the number of mortgages incurred as lands were changing owners; the purchase of goods, often superfluities, on the credit system, to be paid for with heavy interest—all these factors entered into the conditions. Mortgages on ranchos were given as security for comparatively small debts, and they were seldom redeemed. As land was held at about 25 cents per acre, an indebtedness of a few thousand dollars not infrequently laid a mortgage on a rancho of eleven leagues, or 44,000 acres. In this manner the Santa Clara del Norte, the Las Posas, the Simí, and other fine ranchos were alienated from their original owners. The sum of $20,000 or less would have saved to the mortgageor the ranchos Simí Las Posas, Conejo, San Julian and Espada, aggregating 200,000 or more acres. Nearly all the principal rancho-owners this year asked and obtained considerable reductions on their assessments.

The whole number of votes cast in this year's election was 429.

To add to the general drawbacks of this year, the great drouth created terrible havoc, compared to which that caused by the floods had been trifling.

This drouth, though severe throughout the State, was much more disastrous in the southern counties than elsewhere. The country was overstocked with cattle, and the dried grass was eaten close to the ground before the time came for the usual rainfall. Then a little rain fell, early in December, but barely enough to lay the dust in Santa Barbara. December and January passed with no more rain. The grazing grounds were absolutely bare, and there was no grass nearer than the snow-watered valleys over the Sierra, across the rainless desert. The cattle were unfit for a day's drive, far less 400 miles. There was no remembrance of a season without rain, but this season felt not those of either winter or spring. The cattle died daily by hundreds, and the whole country was strewn with their heat-dried carcasses. The assessment-roll of 1863 had showed over 200,000 cattle in Santa Barbara alone, and this probably was not more than two-thirds of the real number; yet when the grass sprung up under the welcome rains of the winter of 1864–'65, there were less than 5,000 cattle left to graze upon it. The great herds were gone, and the reign of the cattle kings was over. Their possessions were for the most part hopelessly mortgaged, and within the next five years had passed from their hands. It was sensationally reported during the drouth that the people of the southern counties were reduced to subsisting upon the flesh of cattle that had died of starvation, and that famine was imminent. The people of San Francisco promptly raised $3,000 and forwarded food and delicacies by steamer. This generosity was greatly appreciated, although it was not needed, as there was no destitution which could not be relieved in the district.

As regarded county politics, Santa Barbara was democratic; but owing to the influence exerted by a few of the leading families, 343 of the votes cast were in favor of the Republican presidential electors. A representative of one of these families, Antonio Maria de la Guerra, raised a company of native cavalry, about 100 strong, which, although they did not reach the field of most active fighting, did excellent service on escort and scout duty on the frontier, their expert horsemanship eminently fitting them for work in the rough country where they served.

In this year the oil interests attracted much interest and immigration, of which account will be given elsewhere, under the respective captions.

The assessment roll of 1865 showed many changes, old names disappearing, and being replaced by new. The total assessments on real estate were $520,591; on personal property, $227,594; total, $748,185, this being nearly $300,000 more than in 1860.

In 1866, the supervisors deliberated upon the practicability of building a new jail, as recommended by a report of the grand jury, which condemned that in use; the decision was that the state of the exchequer did not admit of the requisite expenditure. It is a noticeable feature that the record of this deliberation was spread upon the minutes in the Spanish language. The tax rate established this year was $2.43 on the $100.

Up to this time, the irregularities practiced at elections were the source of much dissatisfaction and inconvenience, admitting as they did, of great fraud in voting. In one instance, a whole tribe of Indians was voted; in another, a Panama steamer list was copied entire, and a precinct known to contain but twenty voters was made to give returns of 160. The new law, which went into operation this year, provided for the inscription upon the great register of the name of every voter, together with particulars of his birth, or naturalization, age, residence, and business, such as to identify him fully; and it was further provided that each should be restricted to voting in his own precinct. Most of the smaller precincts were abolished, this measure also tending to obviate many sources of fraud and error.

The supervisors here at this time were seldom in touch with the other county officials, now one and now another of whom fell under the supervisorial displeasure. This year it was the district attorney who fell under the ban of their displeasure, and his office was by them declared vacant, after some previous differences of opinion had been followed by the demand that he file new bonds for an additional $10,000 for the collection of the delinquent taxes, and his refusal to comply. The contest was somewhat long as well as acrimonious, ending in the district attorney's continuance in office. Yet the board of supervisors, which, by the way, contained a majority of native Californians, would appear, reviewing the events, to have had right and reason on their side.

The total tax rate for 1867 was $3.08 on the $100; the proportion of school tax, 35 cents, shows that provision was being made for the public schools. The whole county vote at this year's election was 624, being a considerable increase on the last vote. At this time Thomas R. Bard was elected to the board of supervisors, a circumstance notable in that it marks the entrance into public official position of men trained to business habits, who would give personal attention to official matters instead of referring them to a commission.

It may be said that the ensuing year of 1868 marked a new era in the history of Santa Barbara, a revolution in all its conditions. The drouth of 1863-'64, and its consequent financial disasters, caused the breaking up of many of the great ranchos, whose land was now put on the market, at prices sometimes as low as 25 cents per acre; this attracted a large immigration, whose members instituted many industries hitherto unknown here. It was found that much of the land was highly appropriate to the cultivation of wheat, under proper care and attention; and this staple, which had been produced in but small quantities, for the manufacture of a little flour of inferior grade for home consumption, was now raised in great quantities, sufficient for heavy exportation. Here arose the need for a new development; to ship it, there was need to lighter the wheat to the vessels, at risk of great loss in the surf. Hence, wharves were projected and constructed to facilitate commerce in this product.

Up to this time, all ships touching at Santa Barbara anchored a mile or two from the shore, whence their freight was transferred by surfboats. Thus the goods, as well as the mails, were liable to injury or loss. The passengers, too, were carried ashore from the boats on the backs of sailors. This method of landing was considerably modified when, in the summer of 1868, the Santa Barbara wharf was constructed by a company of citizens. This structure extended beyond the surf only under the ordinary conditions of winds and tides, and only lighters could approach it with safety, no vessel of more than 100 tons making fast to it. The stairs were unrailed, and the surf sometimes broke upon them, and this cause and seasickness often occasioned considerable difficulty and even danger to the passengers landing, one lady falling into the water, whence she was rescued with much exertion. As the towns along the southern coast were already competing for immigration, a Los Angeles newspaper took occasion to remark of this that passengers for Santa Barbara were dumped into the sea, to swim ashore or drown! The Santa Barbara *Post*, just established in this year, took the statement *au serieux*, and denied it with much acrimony!

With the utterances of the newspaper, politics, whose fire for some time had lain dormant, kindled anew, and a Republican meeting, held in September of this year, was called the largest assemblage which had as yet met in Santa Barbara.

The total vote of this year was 729, having almost doubled since the breaking up of the cattle ranchos.

The grand jury of June, 1868, reported $2,490 in the city treasury, and a total county debt of $37,006.24; this body had gone somewhat deeply into official matters, and they reported finding systematic fraud practiced in the city government; that the records were kept in Spanish; that but one of the five trustees spoke English; that within the past two years 7,000 acres of the public lands had been granted away for less than $6,000; that these lands had not been granted for settlement or improvement, but for speculation; and that some of the members of the council were implicated. The recorder's books showed conveyance to one man of 900 acres for $888, when lands of a similar class were selling for $6 per acre. At least one-third of the members of this honest and energetic jury were native Californians.

The road fund now amounted to a respectable sum, and its disbursement was generally judicious and proper. Road districts were formed, and competent road-masters appointed. Private road enterprises also were undertaken. Among these were the Santa Ynes turnpike road, organized August 6, 1868, and the Tulare Turnpike Road Company, organized December 15, 1868.

A number of Protestant churches were organized this year, as will be set forth under the respective headings.

The Ranchos Zaca and Corral de Cuati, containing 17,760 acres, were sold for $26,700, and 900 acres of the Santa Paula tract were sold for $13,000.

Eighty new buildings were erected this year; $70,000 worth of lumber was used, and 600,000 brick. The estimated increase of property in the county was $1,000,000. The acres assessed were 1,154,106¾; real estate and improvements, $695,565.48; personal property, $478,229.72; total value, $1,137,795.10.

In 1869 the assessed value of real estate was $755,864; personal property, $626,267; total, $1,482,131. Of live-stock, there were 5,057 horses, mules and asses; 11,094 cattle; and a great quantity of small stock. The estimated population was 8,600, of which 700 was subject to road tax. In September of this year, William H. Seward visited Santa Barbara and addressed the people. This year was stigmatized by an unseemly newspaper war between local editors, calculated to convey but a poor impression of the refinement and discretion of the citizens. The whole vote of this year numbered 1,172. The rates of assessment, provided by law to be based on a cash value, this year gave rise to a vast deal of complaint, land being assessed so low that the great rancheros paid but nominal taxes, while the levies on land improvements and stock, being the largest items on the roll, carried rates that bore heavily on their owners, thus virtually laying a penalty on the industry which created these improvements. Land was sold in hundreds of instances for five, ten, or twenty times its assessed value, and in at least one case, a tract which had paid taxes on a valuation of $275 per acre sold for $100 per acre. Such was the resistance offered to this abuse, and such the stir created through the press, that in 1870 assessments on large tracts were nearly double what they had been.

During these years, from 1868 on, there was an almost continual agitation over the question of securing a railroad for Santa Barbara; and editorials, railroad meetings, and applications for charters were rife. As a concession to symmetry, the facts and details necessary to a proper exposition of this subject will be given in another chapter.

In 1870, the census report gave as 7,987 the population of Santa Barbara, which then included Ventura.

On September 25, 1871, was held a special election for State Senator from the Second District, to fill the vacancy caused when Pacheco resigned, he having been elected Lieutenant Governor.

The total tax rate for 1871 was $2.08½; road poll tax, $2.

The First National Gold Bank was organized in March, 1872; prior to this, Mortimer Cook, the president of this new bank, had been conducting a private banking house, the pioneer estbalishment in the county, of that character.

The election of November, 1872, was the last held previous to the division of the county, Ventura being set off, January 1, 1873. The town of Santa Barbara now registered more votes than had existed in the whole county twenty years earlier. At that time there had been but one school district, with some sixty pupils, as against some twenty at this period; while against the one little store kept by Lewis T. Burton in those earlier days, there were now many flourishing commercial houses.

The law creating Ventura County went into effect January 1, 1873; thus from this date on the history of the two counties requires separate treatment. Some little confusion in the board of supervisors arose from this division, but the matter was adjusted. From the same cause arose the need to redistrict Santa Barbara County, and three townships were accordingly determined.

The elections this year were the occasion of a good deal of enthusiam, " smashing the machine" being the active principle to a large degree.

The tax rate was $1.47; the assessment roll bore: real estate and improvements, $3,637,364; personal property, $1,415,200; money, $33,000. This total of $5,085,564, the board of equalization augmented by a sum which raised the figures to $5,223,094. The increase in valuations from the preceding year was $626,014.

In the days of the discovery of gold, and the consequent mining fever, not only had the newcomers passed by the southern portion of the State to the rich mining districts beyond, but also many dwellers here were drawn there, to settle and remain in the larger centers of wealth and population to the northward; and this section was left comparatively deserted. Thus Santa Barbara had lain slumbering peacefully in her balmy golden sunshine, remote, unheralded, difficult of access, until a whisper began to float beyond, of the delights and virtues of her climate. Then came now and again a weary seeker after health, that greatest of boons and blessings, and each one spread the fame of the land to others. And with some of these wayfarers in 1872 came that prince and pioneer of boomers, "California" Nordhoff, whose rapturous articles on the charms of this country awoke to interest myriads of readers all over the United States, and even Europe. Then, with the great influx of newcomers, the prices of property were run up to fabulous prices, and the climate and other attributes of the country, were " puffed " beyond all truth and reason, *ad nauseam*. Once the tide of immigration set in, the hotel accommodations were entirely inadequate for the visitors who came pouring in by scores from every steamer, and, although the citizens endeavored to prevent extortion, overcharges and abuses were very common. From this cause arose various rival schemes for hotel buildings. " The Seaside Hotel Company," formed in 1874, proposed to purchase the Burton Mound property, comprising about eighteen acres, and there erect a hotel which should eclipse all others on the coast. During the agitation of this project the citizens in the rival, upper portion of the town, also started a hotel project, which they pushed with so much vigor that the Arlington is the present visible result, while the " Seaside Hotel " is still on paper only.

Nearly all the wharves were erected within a few years after the first great immigration. The Santa Barbara wharf was the first built. The franchise for the San Buenaventura wharf was granted to J. Wolfson, January 1, 1871; the Hueneme wharf to Thomas R. Bard, C. L. Bard and R. G. Surdam, August 4, 1871; the Gaviota to W.W. Hollister, Albert Dibblee and Thomas B. Dibblee, November 6, 1871; and Point Sal to G. W. Foster, August 4, 1872.

The summer of 1874 witnessed a novel kind of political canvass. The Legislature had passed a law authorizing each municipality to determine for itself whether saloons should be licensed in the towns. By an apparently concerted movement, the ladies of the State undertook to secure the prohibition of license, and they organized entertainments, dinners, etc., and carried on a spirited canvass, inducing thousands of drinking men, even, to vote against license. The ladies of Santa Barbara displayed quite as much energy as those of other sections, and giant meetings were held in the county-seat and elsewhere. The city election resulted in a majority of 119 in favor of no license. At Montecito the meeting was characterized by great feeling on both sides; the liquor dealers sent thither a great quantity of liquors, which were given away freely and openly, notwithstanding the law prohibiting the sale or other disposal of liquors on election day. The "no license" party carried the day by a majority of one. At the Patera, 97 out of 128 voters were in favor of no license. The business of liquor selling went on much as before; various persons were tried for illegally selling liquors, but they were dismissed. At last a case from another county was appealed to a higher court, and the law was declared unconstitutional, on the ground that the Legislature had no right to delegate its powers to another body or municipality. When the news of the decision reached Santa Barbara the saloon-keepers held a joilification with bonfires, speeches, and other demonstrations.

Santa Barbara was full of enterprising and brilliant plans at this period. The movement to form a new county from the third township, the wise and wholesome effort to secure the construction of a sewer system, and attempts to build a woolen factory, and foster various manufacturing institutions, were among the chief plans.

The year 1874 witnessed the building of the Arlington Hotel, at a cost of about $80,000; the three-story Odd-Fellows' Hall, cost $20,000; City Hall, cost $8,000; Presbyterian Church, cost $15,000; new St. Vincent's School on the ruins of the old building, cost $15,000; Tebbetts' three-story building, cost $13,000; John Edwards' dwelling, cost $8,000; Charles Pierce's two-story store, $8,000; Russel Heath's stores, $8,000; and T. Henry Stevens' two-story brick dwelling, which cost $4,000.

The assessment roll for this year showed values of $6,010,309, with sixteen taxpayers on $16,000 and upwards.

In the winter of 1874–'75 there were severe storms, one of which flooded a part of the city—2.75 inches of water fell within seven hours—while Stearns' wharf was somewhat injured.

In August, 1875, Santa Barbara had six wholesale and retail grocery stores; nine retail; four dry goods stores, one clothier; three wholesale and retail boot and shoe stores; two manufacturing boot and shoe stores; ten fruit, candy and vegetable stores; three of hardware; thirteen saloons; one tenpin alley; five billiard rooms; two banks; two auction and commission merchants; five real estate and house agencies; two warehouses; seven hotels; three restaurants, various private boarding and lodging houses; four barber shops; three bathing houses; sixteen laundries; two paint shops; four furniture stores; eight meat-markets; four drug stores; four tobacco and cigar stores; five livery stables; four wholesale sugar stores; one ice cream and oyster saloon; three saddle and harness shops; four jewelry shops; three grocery and liquor stores; three book stores; two crockery and glass stores; six millinery and dressmaking establishments; three tailor shops; two sewing-machine agencies; two clothing, boot and hat stores; two brick yards; three lumber yards; three sash and door factories; three planing mills; one flouring mill; one candy factory; one cigar factory; three carriage and wagon shops; four blacksmith shops; two architects and builders; one marble-worker; three daily and four weekly newspapers.

The Santa Barbara County Bank was opened in November of this year.

In 1875, all Santa Barbara mourned over the death of Father José Maria Gonzales, the superior of the Franciscans on this coast, whose missionary career had lasted two generations. He was a saintly man, beloved by all denominations.

In 1876, the county jail was built. The Centennial celebration drew forth much enthusiasm. The political campaign of this year was a very closely contested one.

In 1876 the city of Santa Barbara alone cast a total of 789 votes, whereas in 1850 the whole vote of the county, which then included Ventura, had been only about 300. During this year, a remarkable enthusiasm over Spiritualistic doctrines existed among many citizens.

During 1876 the western portion of the county began to agitate the project of forming a new county, to be called Santa Maria, the scheme coming to naught, however.

The season of 1876-'77 was termed a dry season, although the drouth was far less disastrous than that of 1863-'64. Grain hardly sprouted, and most of the fields thus sown remained brown all winter. Many sheep died, and more were driven away and never brought back; it is estimated that the flocks diminished one-half at this time.

Because of the dry season, for want of railways, or by reason of the general hard times, real estate here depreciated vastly—some good judges say as much as $2,000,000, and lands of every description were placed on the market at one-half the figures of two years earlier. The improvements of 1877 were estimated at $192,000.

On January 1, 1877, a violent storm of wind and rain prevailed for about an hour, during which a house was blown down, and a portion of the debris fell upon and killed a son of W. F. M. Goss, an estimable youth of eighteen or twenty years.

The total tax rate for 1877 was $1.85 on the $100. The assessment roll for this year held $4,187,175.

On January 19, 1878, occurred a very severe storm, which destroyed nearly all the light shipping in the harbor, driving some of it through the wharf. This storm injured nearly all the wharves on the coast. The old wharf at Santa Barbara was demolished, and some 155 feet of Stearns' wharf destroyed. The debris from these wharves destroyed all but about 100 feet of Smith's wharf at Carpenteria. The Bennett Bath Houses, built some six years before, were carried away, causing a loss of some $1,300. Much damage was done in the district by freshets, cloudbursts, etc. The steamers could not land during the storm, and for some time thereafter, whilst the wharves were under repairs, passengers and freight were landed by recourse to the old system of lighters.

About this period there was some little agitation over the tax keeping of the county records, and investigations were ordered, and made, showing great disorder and confusion in the keeping of the accounts.

The total tax rate for 1878 was $1.65 on the $100.

This year was marked by J. C. Benton's offer to exterminate the squirrel pest by means of a wholesale an inexpensive poisoning; in this Mr. Benton succeeded far beyond the general expectation, and the board of supervisors carried on the work.

At this time, communication north and

south from Santa Barbara was had only by way of the Rincon and along the shore, where the water, at high tide dashing against the cliffs, often cut off connection. It had been found difficult to secure the opening of other roads in the county. The Sycamore Cañon road had been located for some time, but some parties whose lands were crossed by it, positively refused to have the road opened.

In September, 1878, a public demonstration was held in honor of the opening of the Casitas Pass road, which, while it was in Ventura County, and built by the sale of Ventura bonds, was greatly to the benefit of Santa Barbara County. Indeed, complaint was made later that Santa Barbara profited more than Ventura.

In 1879, there were inscribed in the great register of this county 2,384 voters.

In the tax list of 1880 appeared 128 names of citizens paying taxes on $5,000 or upwards. It was remarkable that among these there were hardly a dozen of the old families who, twenty-five years before, had practically owned the county.

The summaries for this year showed valuations as follows: value of city and town lots, $489,350; improvements on same, $515,580; real estate other than city and town lots, $2,785,554; improvements on same, $339,920; money, $38,634; personal property, $1,306,834; total, $5,507,727; deductions on account of mortgages, $769,668. The total tax rate for this year was $2 on the $100. About 50,000 acres were cultivated, yielding 214,937 bushels of barley; 198,293 bushels of wheat; 60,000 bushels of corn; 20,000 of potatoes; 80,931 of beans; 714,700 pounds of wool; 125,000 pounds of butter; 256,000 of honey; besides a multitude of other products. The population, by the census of this year, was 9,522.

There were three parties in the field at this year's election, Republicans, Democrats, and Workingmen; the last never gained much foothold in Santa Barbara. The road fund this year amounted to $10,000. Official mileage was now established.

In March, 1881, was held an art loan exhibition to raise money for public purposes, and many rare and valuable treasures were presented for exhibition. This enterprise was not only pleasing, but profitable, netting $500. A floral and citrus fruit fair was also held this spring. About this time was opened a cannery, to furnish a market for fruits which otherwise would decay and waste.

The bean crop of Santa Barbara County, which in 1880 had been 85,273 bushels, in 1881 amounted to 87,000 bushels, and the following year to 146,700 bushels.

The tax rate for 1883 was 1.69\frac{1}{4}$ on the $100 for State and county; the city tax eighty-five cents. The board of equalization this year raised Santa Barbara's assessment roll twenty per cent., the increase aggregating $1,134,300.

In 1884 the county had outstanding bonds amounting to $46,500; cash in the treasury, $34,318.75; county property, about $85,000. The county clerk's estimate gave the county this year at least 2,600 voters, this, by the usual process of rating, giving a county population of about 13,000 people. By 1886 it was estimated at 16,529, a gain in six years of 7,007, or seventy-three per cent. It must be remembered, too, that this increase was prior to the presence of the railroad, which subsequently brought a vast immigration with the opening up of the extensive tracts of farming country. Of the population perhaps one-fifth is of Spanish descent, the rest Americans, largely from the middle western States.

The school census of June, 1885, reported 8,777 children of school age, and 1,294 under five years old; total, 5,071. There were forty-four school districts.

The State and county taxes collected in Santa Barbara in 1885 were $140,967.96—a decrease of some $800 from the preceding year. The total valuation of Santa Barbara, after the addition of the fifteen per cent., was $9,635,803.

Santa Barbara carried off the first premium for county exhibits at the State fair at Sacramento, in 1885.

DESCRIPTION.

In describing the topography of California, the following comparisons have been frequently and very appositely instituted to give an idea of the general characteristics: The coast of the State is some 750 miles long, in the latitude corresponding to that on the Atlantic coast of a strip extending from northern New Jersey to the seaboard of Georgia. This distance may be divided into three fairly equal parts, the first point from the northward down marking the situation of San Francisco, and the next toward the south falling at the spot where the coast makes a sharp eastward turn and thence has a general direction almost due east and west for a distance of about seventy miles. This knee-like bend contains the county of Santa Barbara, the aforesaid east and west line forming the county's southern coast line and boundary. This trend it is, too, in a great measure, that insures to Santa Barbara her delightful peculiarities of climate. This county has the shape of an irregular parallelogram, extending from this corner or knee of land bending in the Pacific to where the coast line resumes its general southeasterly direction below Ventura. The county is about seventy miles long by forty-five wide, and it comprises about 2,000,000 acres, of which about one-third is arable land. Most of its fertile valleys contain prosperous towns, and are rapidly settling up. This development has been greatly assisted by the branch line of the Southern Pacific Railway, which, connecting with the main line at Newhall, continues up the coast and affords facilities for travel and shipments.

The arable land of Santa Barbara is for the most part composed of either alluvial soil or adobe. The alluvial, which is found mostly in the lower levels, is very deep and fertile. When underlaid with clay, it possesses great powers of resisting or enduring drouth, the clay acting as a hard pan to retain the moisture instead of allowing percolation, as is the case with a gravel substratum. This soil produces in rich abundance all the year around all manner of garden vegetables and deciduous and citrus fruits. Patches of this soil are found on the mesa and hillside lands which are especially adapted to the growth of the olive and grape.

The adobe soil is generally black, and of considerable fertility, albeit hard to work, on account of its clay-like consistency. To produce the best results this soil needs intelligent cultivation and irrigation. It is best adapted to wheat, barley or flax.

This county contains no arid, sandy or desert tracts. The valleys are threaded with streams from the cañons; several of these water-courses, such as the Santa Maria, the Santa Ynes, and the San Antonio, being of sufficient importance to take the name of rivers.

The timber supply of this section is somewhat deficient. The live oak grows rather abundantly, furnishing pleasant parks on the high lands, and in the thicker growth in the low lands and cañons valuable supplies of wood for fuel. The mountain sides are clothed with a dense growth of *chapparal* (low brush) consisting of buckeye, sumach and a number of bushes peculiar to this country. Redwood also is found, and some say mezquite, although the present writer believes that this mimosa is not found on the hither side of the Colorado River.

The summits of the San Rafael Range, in the eastern part of the county, and the northern part of Ventura, is clothed in patches, sometimes covering 100 or 200 acres, with a fairly thick growth of fir, pine and cedar, the latter species, which grows lower down than the pine, being a scrub cedar, particularly valuable for posts and ties.

The Santa Maria and Santa Ynes are the principal rivers, the former being the longer and carrying the greater volume of water. It rises in the Sierra Madre del Sur, and the San Rafael mountains, draining by its branch the Cuyama, the southern slope of the former, and by the Sisquoc the northern slope of the latter, and it flows into the Pacific about seven miles north of Point Sal. The Tepusque, Los Encitos, Cañoncito, Agua Sacado, and Potrero are small tributaries.

The railroad bridge across the Santa Maria River is 1,982 feet in length.

The Santa Ynes rises in the Santa Ynes mountains, in Ventura County, and flows westerly, draining the south slope of the San Rafael and the north slope of the Santa Ynes range, and reaching the ocean five miles south of Purisima. Its feeders are the Sal Si Puedes, Zaca, Alisal, Alamo Pintado, Santa Cruz, Caballada, Los Laureles, Indio, Mono, Agua Caliente, and a few others.

The southern slope of the coast mountains waters the valley below through the Rincon, Carpenteria, Santa Monica, Paderon, Toro, Ficay, Hot Springs, Cold Stream, Mission Creek, Maria Ygnacia, San José, San Pedro, Carneros, Tecolote, Armitas, Tecolotito, Dos Pueblos, Las Varas, El Capitan, Refugio, Hondo, Costa, Molinos, Las Cruces, Agua Caliente, Santa Anita, San Augustin, Rodeo, Cañada Honda and the San Antonio and Cosmalia creeks. Of these mountain streams the Rincon, Carpenteria, Mission, El Capitan and Dos Pueblos are the most important, flowing into the sea in ordinary years, while most of the others shortly after leaving the foot-hills partially or wholly disappear during the dry season. There are in the county several small lakes and lagoons, the Guadalupe and the Zaca being the largest.

Over the Santa Ynez mountains run several horseback trails and two good wagon roads, through the Santa Ynes and Gaviota passes. The greatest elevation of the San Marcos Pass is 2,240 feet. It is reached by following up the San José, descending the mountains on the north side, along the Los Laureles by what is known as the Frémont trail. The Gaviota Pass lies along the Las Cruces, crossing the mountain on the old Spanish grant of that name at an altitude of 1,500 feet. One horseback trail starts from the foot of Montecito Valley, follows up the Ficay to its head, and then bears a little northeast to the Najalayegua Cañon. Another crosses the mountain by Cold Stream Cañon, near the head of this valley. A good trail also ascends the Pedregosa, the east branch of Mission Creek, to near its source, where it divides into two forks.

Much of Santa Barbará County is hilly or mountainous; the Santa Ynes, a low range of mountains, follows the trend of the coast across the southern part of the county, and the Sierra de San Rafael, a higher range, strikes through the center of the county, and extends almost to its northern limits. These mountains, with the foothills and spurs, impart to the whole country a rugged and diversified aspect.

Separated by these ranges are the four large valleys of the county, from which branch out a number of smaller and tributary valleys. These four main valleys, beginning at the south, are: Santa Barbara, Santa Ynes, Los Alamos and Santa Maria.

Between the Santa Ynes and the sea lies the unparalleled valley of Santa Barbara proper, forty-five miles in length, with an average width of perhaps three miles, and an area of 86,400 acres. Although this is the smallest in acreage of the four chief valleys into which the county is divided by the configuration of its surface, yet it is the most important, by reason of its natural characteristics, which have attracted the largest population.

For its rare advantages of climate and its wonderful fertility, it has become famous all over the world. This valley extends from the Rincon to Point Concepcion, and it comprises the Carpenteria Valley, from the Rincon to a small spur of the Santa Ynes, called Ortega Hill, a distance of nine miles; the Montecito, from Ortega Hill to the city limits; the city of Santa Barbara, spreading beyond its two miles square; and eight miles beyond, on the Patera, the village of Goleta. Still following the same broad avenue, are found the great ranchos of Dos Pueblos, Nuestra Señora del Refugio, and those owned by Hollister and Cooper; then comes the Gaviota Pass, and a few miles past it, Point Concepcion, where the Santa Ynes range runs boldly into the Pacific, forming the terminal wall of this valley.

Beyond the Santa Ynes range, and between it and the San Rafael, opens the lonely Santa Ynes Valley. The Santa Ynes River here runs almost due west from its mountain source, watering a vast extent of farming lands and passing through the broad Lompoc Valley before it empties into the sea, between Point Concepcion and Point Purisima. This valley contains the towns of Santa Ynes and Lompoc.

LAND GRANTS.

After secularization, land in abundance could be had for the asking, and large tracts were given to the heads of families. The policy of the Mexican government had been to limit each holding to eleven leagues, which would contain something above 48,000 acres. The wide territories required for stock-raising caused this to be considered a small tract, and many families acquired several times that much, whether by exchange, purchase, or government favor. For instance, the Noriegas at one time owned no less than 200,000 acres. The following list from Hoffman's report on land cases shows the ownership of many of the old grants, some dating back to 1790, though mostly made subsequent to secularization. In the case of lands lying in other counties, they are included here because they were assigned to members of families living in Santa Barbara.

Rancho Nipomo, granted to William Dana (member of Carrillo family), April 6, 1837. Acreage, 32,728.62.

The Lompoc, granted to José Antonio Carrillo, April 15, 1837. Acreage, 35,335.78.

San Julian, granted to George Rock, April 7, 1837. Acreage, 48,221.68. The claim was purchased and the title perfected by José de la Guerra y Noriega.

Guadalasca, granted to Ysabel Yorba, May 6, 1846. Acreage, 30,593.85.

Simí, or San José de Gracia, to Patricio Xavier and Miguel Pico, in 1795, by Governor Diego de Borica; claim revived by Alvarado to de la Guerra, April 25, 1842. Acreage, 92,341.35.

Sespe to Carlos Antonio Carrillo, November, 1833; six leagues. In the trial this number was pronounced fraudulent, and *dos* (two) was substituted.

San Buenaventura to Fernando Pico, March 24, 1845; 29.90 acres.

Guadalupe to Diego Olivera and Teodoro Arellanez, March 21, 1840. Acreage, 30,408.03.

Cuyama to José Maria Rojo, April 24, 1843. Confirmed to Maria Antonio de la Guerra and Cesario Lataillade; 22,198.74 acres.

Huerfano (San Luis Obispo), granted to Mariano Bonilla; confirmed to Francis Branch (member of the Carrillo family).

Tequepis to Joaquin Villa; confirmed to Antonio Maria Villa; 8,919 acres.

Sisquoc to Maria Antonio Caballero, June 3, 1833; confirmed to James B. Huie; 35,485.90 acres.

Santa Rosa Island to José Antonio and Carlos Carrillo, October 4, 1843. Acreage, about 60,000. This island was given to Jones and Thompson, who married into the Carrillo family.

Cañada Larga de Verde to Joaquin Alvarado, about 2,220 acres.

Punta de la Laguna to Luis Arellanes and E. M. Ortega, December 24, 1844. Acreage, 26,648.42.

Conejo to José de la Guerra y Noriega, by Governor Sola, October 12, 1822. Acreage, 48,674.56.

Arroyo Grande or San Ramon (in San Luis Obispo) to Zeferino Corlon, April 25, 1841; confirmed to Francisco Branch, who married one of the Carrillos.

Ojai to Fernando Pico, April 6, 1837. Acreage, 17,792.70.

Rancho (name unknown) to Teodoro Arellanes, January 22, 1846. Small.

Mision de San Diego to Santiago Arguello, June 8, 1846. Small extent.

Island of Santa Cruz to Andres Castillero, May 22, 1839. About 60,000 acres.

Mision Vieja de la Purisima to Joaquin and José Antonio Carrillo, November 20, 1845; 4,440 acres.

Corral de Cuati to Agustin Davila; confirmed to Maria Antonia de la Guerra Lataillade; 13,300.24 acres.

Tequepis to Tomas Olivera, April 7, 1837; confirmed to Antonia Maria de Cota; 8,900.75 acres.

La Laguna to Miguel Avila, November 3, 1845; confirmed to Octaviano Gutierrez; 18,212.48 acres.

Tinaquiac to Victor Linares, May 6, 1837; confirmed to Wm. D. Foxen; 8,874.60 acres.

La Calera or Las Positas to Narciso Fabregat, May 16, 1843; confirmed to Thomas M. Robbins and Manuela Carrillo de Jones; 3,281.70 acres.

Todos Santos to Salvador Osio, November 3, 1844. This tract contained 22,200 acres; another tract on the Cosumnes, granted at the same time, to the same party, contained 26,640 acres. These tracts were confirmed to William E. P. Hartnell.

Cañada de San Miguelito to Ramon Rodriguez, March 1, 1846. Acreage, 8,880.

Alisal to William E. P. Hartnell, January 26, 1843; Acreage, 2,971.26.

La Zaca to Maria Antonia de la Guerra Lataillade, 1838. Acreage, 4,480.

Lomas de la Purificacion to Agustin Janssens, December 27, 1844; contained 13,320 acres.

Las Posas to José Carrillo, May 15, 1834; confirmed to José de la Guerra y Noriega; 26,623.26 acres.

San Marcos to Nicolas A. Den, June 8, 1846. Acres, 35,573.

One square league to —— Marcelina, August 16, 1843; confirmed to Maria de la Guerra Lataillade.

San Francisco (partly in Santa Barbara County) to Antonio del Valle, January 22, 1839; confirmed to Jacob Feliz.

Las Huertas confirmed to Maria Antonia de la Guerra Lataillade; granted July 26, 1844; 13,000 varas square.

Los Alamos to José Antonio Carrillo, March 9, 1839. Acres, 48,803.38.

Santa Clara del Norte to Juan Sanchez, May 6, 1837; 13,988.91 acres.

Callegnas to José Pedro Ruiz, May 10, 1847; 9,998.29 acres.

San Miguel to Raimundo Olivas, July 6, 1841; 4,693.91 acres.

La Liebre to José Maria Flores, April 21, 1841; eleven square leagues.

———— ———— three square leagues to José Ramon Malo, April 12, 1845.

Santa Rosa to Francisco Cota, three and a half leagues, granted July 30, 1839; and a subsequent addition November 19, 1845.

Purisima to Ramon Malo, December 6, 1845; 14.927.62 acres.

Ex-Mision San Buenaventura to José Arnaz, June 8, 1846; confirmed to Poli.

Camulos to Pedro C. Carrillo, October 2, 1843; 17,760 acres.

Nojogui to Raimundo Carrillo, April 27, 1843; 13,522.04 acres.

Santa Ana to Crisogono Ayala and others, April 14, 1837; 21,522.04 acres.

———— ———— to José Chapman, 4,440 acres. 1838; confirmed to Guadalupe Ortega de Chapman.

Dos Pueblos to Nicolas A. Den, April 18, 1842; 15,535.33 acres.

Cañada del Corral to José Dolores Ortega, November 5, 1841; 8,875.76 acres.

La Goleta to Daniel Hill, June 10, 1846; 4,440 acres.

Temescal to Francisco Lopez, March 17, 1843; 13,320 acres.

Nuestra Señora del Refugio to Antonio Maria Ortega, August 1, 1834; 26,529 acres.

Jesus Maria to Lucas Olivera, April 8, 1837; 42,184.93 acres; two-thirds confirmed to Lewis Burton.

San Carlos de Jonata to Joaquin Carrillo, September 24, 1845; 26,631.31 acres.

Mision Santa Ynes to José Maria Covarrubias and others, June 15, 1846. This claim was rejected by the commissioners.

Pueblo de Santa Barbara to the Common Council; granted in 1782; claim filed February 1, 1853; rejected by commissioners August 1, 1854; confirmed by District Court March 1, 1861.

Island of Catalina to Thomas Robbins, July 4, 1846.

Santa Paula y Saticoy to Manuel Jimeno Casarin, April 1, 1843; 17,733.33 acres.

Casmali to Antonio Olivera, September 12, 1840; 8,841.21 acres.

College Rancho or Cañada del Pino; 35,499.37 acres.

Santa Barbara Mission to Richard S. Den, June 10, 1846.

Mission lands allotted after secularization: San Buenaventura, 36.27 acres; Santa Barbara, 37.83 acres; Santa Ynes, 17.35 acres.

By the methods already cited, some of the influential families obtained territory enough for a small kingdom. Thus the Carrillo family had twelve grants, the Castros twenty, the de la Guerras twelve, Fosters eight, Limantour eight, Murphy thirteen, Ortega nine, Pacheco eight, Rodriguez seven, Sanchez twelve, and Vallejo fourteen.

THE CHANNEL ISLANDS.

"An enterprising party named Cabrillo headed the first special excursion party to Santa Barbara and its islands, that was only 345 years previous to our present boom, but there is a record to the fact that the old sea-rover and his crew of buccaneers were as well pleased with the country as are the tourist parties of to-day. Sailing under direction of no special hotel syndicate or real estate monopoly, Cabrillo and his companions made free to choose their own winter quarters in the fairest spot on all the coast, an island opposite to where our city now stands." Such is the humorous beginning of a paper on the Channel Islands, written in 1887 by a Barbareño, referring to the two-months sojourn of the pioneer explorer, Juan Rodriguez Cabrillo, and his men, on San Miguel, in the winter of 1542–'43. We have already read how Cabrillo there died, and was buried; also how Sebastian Vizcaino sailed up hither, sixty years later, and named the channel, and renamed the other points of interest. And from that time down to the present, these islands have been conspicuous features in the landscape, objectively and subjectively.

Until their examination by the Coast Survey, nothing accurate was known of the numbers, position, extent, or peculiarities of the islands off the coast, from San Diego to Point Concepcion, but the chart published by this body shows clearly the beautiful parallelism, to which Vizcaino first called attention, between these islands and the adjacent mainland. The four islands Anacapa, Santa Cruz, Santa Rosa and San Miguel, with the rocks extending from the last named, have their longer axis parallel to the trend of the shoreline, which is the general direction of the Sierra Santa Ynes, immediately behind it. Cortez Shoal, Santa Catalina, San Clemente, and John Biggs' Rock, have their longer axes northwest by west and parallel to each other, while Santa Barbara Island is the prolongation of the longer axis of San Clemente.

Navigators, in making the Santa Barbara channel from the northwest, readily note the neighborhood of these islands through thick, foggy weather, by the peculiar odor of the bitumen which issues from the bottom or the shore some eight miles west, and floats upon the water, working against the winds far beyond Point Concepcion. Vancouver was the first to call attention to the presence of this bitumen. Sir Edward Belcher, in October, 1839, also remarked the phenomenon.

The current among these islands runs southward as far as San Nicolas. On the Cortez Shoal it frequently runs against the northwest wind at the rate of nearly two miles per hour; while again it has been found to run nearly as strong in an opposite direction.

Santa Cruz, lying almost in front of the city of Santa Barbara, at twenty-five miles distance, contains 52,760.33 acres, and its mountains rise to 1.700 feet in height. It is owned by a French company, who devote it to sheep-raising. There is no settlement on this island, beyond the rancho-houses. Santa Rosa contains 52,696.49 acres, and rises to a height of 1,172 feet. It belongs to A. P. More, and is used for sheep-raising. San Miguel, the most western of the group, is seven and a half miles long, two and a half wide, and contains 15,000 acres. It belongs to the United States Government, and is held in reserve, being unsurveyed. Waters and Schilling occupy it by possessory right, for sheep-raising.

Santa Cruz is irregularly shaped, having a rough surface, with a few tracts of level lands. The owners have a fine wharf, with a harbor safe in all but northeast winds. The climate is much the same as on the main land, though the ocean winds are stronger. Citrus and deciduous fruits will do well here. This was formerly the resort of great numbers of seal, but continued slaughter has almost extinguished them. Santa Cruz was used by the Mexican Government only as a penal colony—a sort of Botany Bay, whose few tenants were yet a constant menace to their mainland neighbors.

Santa Cruz was afterward given by Mexico to Castillero, in reward for his discovery of quicksilver at New Almaden. He sold it to the sheep companies. Occasional matanzas, or systematic slaughters of stock, are held here.

More than half of Santa Rosa is adapted to tillage. It is nearly quadrilateral in shape. In 1834 it became the joint property of Carlos and José Antonio Carrillo, and was given as a dowry to the two daughters of Carlos, who, on the same day married J. C. Jones and A. B. Thompson.

The grooms raised sheep on the island, with great success. After some family litigation, Santa Rosa became the property of A. P. and P. H. More, and is now owned by the former. The natural grasses are of very fine quality, and the humid atmosphere keeps them green throughout the year, so that the sheep business is here conducted under particular advantages.

One of the most notable events in the history of these islands was the wreck here, in the early days of the Pacific Mail Steamship Company, of their steamer Winfield Scott. It is said that her wreck was visible beneath the water for twenty years thereafter.

These islands, with their cave dwellings, their kitchen-middens, their battle-grounds, and their obscure history, are full of interest to the ethnologist, the archæologist, and the antiquarian. Cabrillo described the inhabitants of the Channel Islands as fairly white, with florid complexions.

Accounts vary as to the extinction of these people. Some authors opine that they were extirpated by the inhabitants of Russian-America, who used to come to these islands to hunt the sea-otter, and who are known to have slain, even during the present century, all the male inhabitants of San Nicolas, whose effects and women they appropriated. Again it is suggested that a famine reduced the natives to the necessity of preying upon each other, to their extermination; or else that they were fallen upon by the cannibalistic inhabitants of the islands of the western Pacific. Some appearance of probability is given to this theory by the state of the human bones found on the island, many of which have been cracked, as if for the purpose of extracting the marrow. On the other hand, the idea of a famine is counteracted by the existence on the rocks of shell-fish enough to sustain a population of thousands. There are, however, many indications of a terrible drouth experienced here at some time, and the inhabitants may have perished for lack of fresh water.

CLIMATE.

Of Santa Barbara, as of other portions of Southern California, it must be said that the terms "rainy season" and "dry season" are in some measure a misnomer, as conveying too extreme an impression. Dr. J. P. Widney's suggestion of "rain season" is more apt, as signifying the period during which rain does fall, as distinguished from the time of the year when it does not fall. It is practically true that from April to November no rain falls, yet even during these months there have been known occasional showers. From November to April the rainfall occurs, in Santa Barbara averaging seventeen inches per season. The rains are not continuous, but distributed, coming in heavy storms, with days or often weeks of intervening delightful weather. While there is no regularity about the rains, no two seasons being alike, there is usually a heavy rain about the first of December, followed by another heavy storm about the beginning of

January, then others scattered through January, February and March, with the final or "clearing up" storm about the first of April. February and March are the real spring months of Santa Barbara. Then the results of the rains are fully apparent, the flowers of the plains and cañons are in season, the foot-hills are brilliantly grass-clad, the streams are full, and nature appears in her brightest, gayest aspect.

The rainfall for 1867–'68 was 25.19 inches; for 1868–'69, 15.77 inches; for 1869–'70, 10.27 inches; for 1870–'71, 8.91; for 1871–'72, 14.94; for 1872–'73, 10.45; for 1873–'74, 14.44; for 1874–'75, 18.71 inches.

In 1872 there were only thirteen days when the mercury rose above 83°. The highest temperature was 86°, and the lowest 40°. In 1875 the mercury rose above 83° only seven times; the highest was 88°, and the lowest 38°, this last being the register for seven o'clock A. M. on January 24.

Observations made from June to December show the mean temperature of the sea water to be 64°, the thermometer being sunk four feet below the surface of the water, where it is twenty feet deep, at the point one-third of a mile from land, and at 11 A. M. Observations made at the same time show the mean temperature of air in the shade to have been 71°.

In 1885 there were thirty-one days in which the mercury rose above 80°. These were distributed through seven months, of which two were December and February. There were only thirteen days when it did not fall at night below 60°, and these were scattered through three months, including December. There was but one night in the year when the mercury fell below 40°. In 1885 there were thirty-one days in which rain fell, but only nine of them could be called rainy days, since, in the remaining twenty-two it rained only in the night, or in brief showers during the day.

In 1886 there were twenty-three days, distributed through seven months, in which the mercury rose above 80°, and thirteen nights when it did not fall below 60°. The greatest height of the mercury during this year was 85°, and the lowest point reached was 35°. The mean temperature for January was 55°; for July, 66.3°; for October, 58.3°. The mean temperature for the three winter months was 56.81°; for the three summer months, 65.51°; for the three autumn months, 59.46°. Thus it will be seen that the difference between the mean of January and that of July was 11.30°, and between the mean winter and mean summer temperature 8.7°.

In 1886 the mean temperature of the warmest day in the year was 73.5°, this falling in January; of the warmest day in August, 72°; the mean of the coldest day, being in February, was 45°; the highest temperature reached was 85°, in January, February, and August; the lowest was 35°, in January. The annual average temperature was 59.6°. The total rainfall was 13.86 inches.

In 1887 the mean temperature of the whole year was 59.7°; while that of the three summer months was 64.4°, a difference of less than 5°. The means of the three warmest days were 79°, 71°, and 74°, in June, July and October, respectively. There were during this year twenty-six days in which the mercury registered more than 80°, and of these only six were in the summer. On the warmest night of the year the temperature fell to 65°, and there were but fourteen nights in the whole year when it did not fall to or below 60°, and of these, four were in the summer. The mean temperature of the coldest day was 47.5°, in November. The three hottest days being in May, June, and

October, reached respectively, 86°, 95°, and 91.8°. The three lowest fell in January, February, and December, reaching 37°, 37°, and 38°.

There was a total rainfall of 17.09 inches, being .72 above the average for the last twenty years. Rain fell on twenty-four days. Of 289 days observed this year, 214 were recorded as clear, forty as fair, and thirty-five as cloudy.

Such statistics as these refer more particularly to that portion of the country south of the mountains; that is to say, Santa Barbara Valley. In the northern valleys there is more wind, and the mercury falls lower and rises higher. During seven months, beginning with March of the year 1888, the lowest mean in the Santa Maria Valley was 57°, in April; the highest, 63.5°, in July—a difference of only 6.5°. In the Santa Ynes Valley the mercury has fallen to 18° and has risen to 100°. Even these valleys, however, are generally equable, and the more marked changes they do undergo prove an attraction to many persons liking variety,

There is a table of comparisons often submitted, as illustrative, to those knowing the Eastern resorts, of Santa Barbara climate. This says:—January at Santa Barbara is equivalent to May at Nantucket; February to May at Atlantic City; March to May at Norfolk; April to May at Portland; May to May at New Haven; June to May at New York; July to May at Philadelphia; August to May at Washington; September to May at Brooklyn; October to May at New London; November and December to May at Portland.

These climatic conditions naturally and inevitably make Santa Barbara one of the most healthful sections in the world. The experience of the years has fully attested this, and the fame of this climate has gone throughout the world. Even from the earliest period of Spanish settlement here, these phases have been noted.

During the mission period, the deaths in proportion to baptisms were less at Santa Barbara and Purisima than at any other of the missions, thus attesting the healthfulness of this region.

In the spring of 1798 the ship Concepcion brought hither several cases of small-pox, and the passengers were prematurely released from quarantine, against the orders of the Governor, who, it may be said *en passant*, was raging in consequence. He threatened to hang the commandant should the disease spread; but, happily for that functionary as for the community at large, the excellently healthful climate protected the people from this scourge, and infection did not spread.

The census returns for 1870 show that in Santa Barbara County, which then included what is now Ventura, the total of deaths from consumption that year was *five* out of 7,984 population, or one in every 1,567. The deaths from all causes were but sixty-three, of which but one-twelfth were from consumption. The deaths from this disease in Massachusetts are one in every 283, in New York, one in every 379; in Florida, one in 1,433. The ratio of deaths in Massachusetts is 17.7 in each 1,000; in New York it is 15.8 in the 1,000; in Florida 12.1 in 1,000; in Santa Barbara 8 in 1,000.

The following extracts relative to the healthfulness of Santa Barbara are taken from a paper written by the late Dr. S. B. Brinkerhoff, who practiced medicine here from 1852 to 1880:

Santa Barbara is protected from northern blasts by the Coast Range of mountains, which average from 3,000 to 4,000 feet in height. The heat of summer is tempered by gentle breezes from the sea, the average summer temperature being less than 70°. The average winter temperature is 55°. The changes in the seasons are scarcely perceptible in temperature. Frosts are of rare occurrence, and disagreeable fogs seldom prevail. There are but comparatively few days in the entire year when one cannot be out of doors during the day without discomfort. The nights are always cool and sleep-inviting. * * * The softness and general uniformity of the climate, its freedom from dampness and sudden changes, the opportunities for diversion and recreation, render Santa Barbara pre-eminently a desirable place of resort for persons suffering from bronchial and pulmonary affections. Although many persons suffering from these complaints have come here too late to receive any permanent relief from the restorative effects of climate, yet the greater portion of cases which have come under my observation have been permanently relieved, and many, in a surprisingly short space of time, have been restored to health. The climate of Santa Barbara possesses elements of general healthfulness in an eminent degree, and perhaps, also, some latent peculiarities in its favor too subtle for ordinary observation. I may instance the following facts in this connection: During the eighteen years of my active practice here I have never known a single case of scarlet fever or diphtheria. I have known of only three cases of dysentery, neither of which proved fatal, and of only three cases of membranous croup. The epidemics and diseases incident to childhood, which in other parts of the country sweep away thousands of children annually, are here comparatively unknown. Cases of fever and ague I have never known to originate here, and persons coming here afflicted with it rarely have more than two or three attacks, even without the use of anti-periodics. I have known instances of small-pox at three different times; in each of the first two instances occurring several years apart, the disease was confined to a single case, and was contracted elsewhere. Neither of these cases proved fatal. In the year 1864, when this disease prevailed so extensively and proved so fatal throughout the State, there were two cases of the disease, contracted elsewhere and developed here, which proved fatal. Three other persons residing here contracted the disease at this time, all of whom recovered. Although no unusual precaution was taken to prevent the spread of the disease, it was confined to the cases mentioned. Yet hundreds of the native population, either from ignorance or prejudice, had never been and would not suffer themselves to be vaccinated. In the years 1869–'70, when this disease in its most virulent form prevailed so generally throughout the State, not a single case occurred at Santa Barbara, although in daily communication with other parts of the State by stage and steamer.

Some ten miles from Santa Barbara, in a westerly direction, about one and a half miles from the shore, is an immense spring of petroleum, the product of which continually rises to the surface of the water, and floats upon it over an area of many miles. * * Having read statements that, during the past few years, the authorities of Damascus and other plague-ridden cities of the East have resorted to the practice of introducing crude petroleum into the gutters of the streets to disinfect the air, and as a preventive of disease, which practice has been attended with the most favorable results, I throw out the suggestion, but without advancing any theory of my own, whether the prevailing westerly sea breezes, passing over this wide expanse of petroleum-laden sea, may not take up from it and bear along with them to the places whither they go, some subtle power which acts as a disinfecting agent, and which may account for the infrequency of some of the diseases referred to, and possibly for the superior healthfulness of the climate of Santa Barbara.

Dr. M. H. Biggs, for many years resident in Santa Barbara, in his report to the State Medical Society on the "Vital Statistics and Medical Topography of Santa Barbara," corroborated the testimony of Dr. Brinkerhoff, saying: "There are no malarious fevers. Persons who come here afflicted with fever and ague rarely have more than two or three attacks. They soon become well, often without the use of anti-periodics. The climate seems sufficient to cure the malady. During a residence of over eighteen years I have seen only one case of membranous croup, and heard of two others. There is no disease endemic in Santa Barbara— nothing but what can usually be referred either directly or indirectly to some indiscretion in eating or drinking or unreasonable exposure."

Dr. Thomas M. Logan, ex-president of the American Medical Association, and secretary of the State Board of Health, made a statement in favor of Santa Barbara as a suitable place for a State sanitarium. In his first official report, published in 1871, is expressed this opinion:

"The secretary informed the board that he had been occupied of late in visiting several localities in the southern part of the State, noted for salubrity, as San Rafael, Santa Cruz, Montery, San Luis Obispo, Santa Barbara and other places. * * * While most of the localities named are possessed of climatic elements adapted to different stages and characters of pulmonary diseases, that of Santa Barbara appeared to present that happy combination of the tonic and the sedative climate which would seem to render it suitable to a greater variety of phthisical affections, and at the same time better adapted to the different stages of cachexia than any other place visited."

Elsewhere Dr. Logan wrote as follows:— "In vain, heretofore, since my appointment to the responsible position of Health Officer of the State, have I sought for such a combination of sanitary qualities as are now presented. * * * As to the climate of Santa Barbara it will be seen that, although lying in about the same latitude as Charleston, South Carolina, yet it is totally different, and that the isothermal line would be deflected toward St. Augustine, Florida."

In short, the testimony alike of physicians, tourists and invalids attests the delightful and healthful qualities of the climate here. Even the present winter, afflicted with a cough of several years' standing, pronounced by physicians sure to result fatally, has found it almost quite disappear in a residence of two months here, with practically no medicaments, and even without the exercise of precautions against cold, etc.

THE CITY OF SANTA BARBARA.

From Point Concepcion the Santa Ynes mountains follow eastward the line of the coast, at a little distance from the shore. The mountains rise rocky and rugged, 3,000 to 7,000 feet high, and the strip of land between these and the sea, two to five miles wide, slopes gently toward the south, is thoroughly protected on the north, and is composed of very rich soil, which has received the wash of the hills for ages. Seven or eight miles to the westward runs a range of hills, which behind the town reach their greatest height, of 500 to 600 feet. Their level tops form the *mesa*—table or plateau land. From the surf-bound beach, the land rises gradually toward the northwest until it is 350 feet above the sea at two miles inland. Thus the town lies on a southeastern slope shut in and protected on the north and northwest by a range as high as the Green Mountains, and on the south and southwest by the *mesa*. Thus the trade winds cannot reach this place; the close vicinity of the sea prevents the heats of summer from reaching the degree attained at inland points in this latitude and the neighboring mountains absorb dampness and give tone to the atmosphere.

The topography of Santa Barbara is not a little baffling to the stranger, who, accustomed to regarding the Pacific Ocean as the western boundary of this continent, distrusts his own senses when he sees the sun rising out of that body of water. While the general trend of the coast from Ventura to Santa Barbara is straight westward, just at this city it curves outward, and for a short distance runs southwestward, the city being laid out on this southwest curve, with its streets at right angles to that part of the beach west of the wharf. State street runs almost directly northwest from the ocean, while the cross-streets extend almost due northeast and southwest. This arrangement of the streets was determined by the Spanish settlers who preceded American surveying, and the "bias" arrangement, confusing as it at first is, has some manifest advantages over the arrangement of most cities, planned with the points

VIEW OF THE CITY OF SANTA BARBARA.

of the compass. As the city lies on a slope, the streets should properly take the direction that most facilitates drainage. Then, a house whose corners, rather than its sides, are toward the cardinal points of the compass, receives the sunlight in each room some time during the day, as would not happen in houses set "square on."

The few buildings here previous to 1850 were placed without regard to regularity or to the location of their neighbors, and there were no streets. The first grant of which the archives, such as they are, contain a record, was made February 14, 1835. Previous to this, the commandante gave verbal permits to occupy small lots, the right continuing as long as the occupancy; and these rights were generally respected as valid prior to 1851. Most of the lots of land in the central portion of the city were granted during the period from 1846 to 1850, while the old ayuntamiento system of town government was continued, with the offices of prefect, alcalde, regidores, and sindico. In 1851 the town council passed a resolution that no title to a town lot should be deemed valid unless it should be recorded in a book kept for that purpose. This book contains the record of 196 lots, varying in size from a few varas to 150 varas square. (A vara is thirty-three and one-half inches.) The descriptions of the land were for the most part given with so much vagueness and uncertainty as to give rise to many lawsuits.

Four leagues of land were confirmed to the mayor and common council of the city of Santa Barbara, by the United States District Court, and, the appeal having been dismissed, the decree of the Federal Court became final. The final survey was approved April 8, 1870. A patent for these four leagues was issued by the United States on May 31, 1872.

It is difficult to speak with any degree of certainty as to special proceedings prior to 1850, since the archives of that period are missing.

THE HALEY SURVEY.

The city of Santa Barbara was laid out into streets and blocks in 1851, when the town council directed Captain Salisbury Haley to make a survey and a map of the town. The intention was to have each block 150 yards square, and each street sixty feet wide, except State and Carrillo streets, which were to be eighty feet wide. At that time the value of land was not great, and the surveyor gave good measure, and that not always exact. The streets were straight, and cut each other at right angles, but the blocks were not all alike. In the year 1871 most of the old Haley stakes, set to make the survey, had disappeared, and the council instructed the town surveyor, James L. Barker, to retrace the Haley survey, and this retracing was adopted by ordinance, and this confirmed or ratified by the Legislature. There was, however, some contention for the exact measuring of the blocks, which had the effect of changing the location of most of the streets. Near State and Carrillo streets, this difference is but a foot or two, but near the outskirts of the city, it amounts to as much as ten or twelve feet in one direction, and is about forty feet in the other.

Subsequent to the Barker survey, W. H. Norway was authorized to make another survey, beginning at the initial point, and making the blocks all similar, of the size before stated. The resulting discrepancies are the cause of litigations still pending and unadjusted. There are numbered on the map 369 whole blocks, ten more fractionally numbered, and still more fractional blocks not numbered. The blocks being 450 feet square, ten of them are reckoned as making a mile. The nomenclature of the streets is highly suggestive of the city's picturesque early history, many of whose events are thus commemorated.

As elsewhere seen, no less than three of the streets take their names from the episode of "The Lost Cannon." The first street at the northeast of the city is called San Buenaventura, from the then village of that name, thirty miles away, which was the nearest to this town when the street was christened; Pitos street was thus named because there grew the reeds from which were made *pitos* (flutes or whistles); Punta Gorda, from its running into a cape-like bluff; Yudio Muerto, from some Indian found dead thereabouts; Cacique, from the title of the tribal chiefs of the Indians; Yanonali, from the name of a famous old Indian chief who lived there; Montecito, from its leading to the beautiful valley bearing that name. Carpenteria street, too, was named from its running the route to the present settlement of Carpenteria, twelve miles east of this city; and this spot in its turn took the name (Carpenter Shop) from the presence near its creek of a shop of that sort. Gutierrez street was so called after Don Octaviano Gutierrez, a noted member of the town council. Haley street was named after Salisbury Haley, who made the famous "Haley Survey" in 1850; and Cota, Ortega, and de la Guerra streets after the respective families of these names. Carrillo took its name from Don Joaquin Carrillo, the District Judge, whose house fronted upon it; Figueroa was named after José Figueroa, Governor of California during the Mexican rule; his bones lie in the vault of the Mission church here. Micheltorena for Manuel Micheltorena, Governor in 1842; Arellaga from José Joaquin Arellaga, Governor in 1792–'94; Victoria for Manuel Victoria, Governor of this department in 1831; Sola from Vicente Sola, Governor from 1815 to 1823. Anapanau was named for an Indian chieftain who held sway from Santa Ynes to San Fernando; Valerio for a renowned Indian robber who dwelt in a cave in the Santa Ynes mountains; Yslay comes from the fruit of a tree used as food by the Indians. Pedregoso means stony, and the street is thus called because cut through by the creek named Arroyo Pedregoso (Stony Gulch). Mission street takes its name from its proximity to the mission of Santa Barbara.

Of the streets which run southeast and northwest, Salinas was so called because it runs into a salt sink or pond; Cañada, from its running into a ravine; Soledad (a solitude), because that part of the town was uninhabited and solitary when the name was applied to it. Voluntario (volunteer), because it runs into the hill whereon was encamped Fremont's volunteer battalion; Alisos (sycamores), from the trees of that variety there growing; Milpas (sowed fields), from the sowing patches of the Indians in that locality; Nopal, from the prickly-pear cactus there growing in abundance; Quarentena, because at its foot some vessels were put into quarantine; Salsipuedes ("Get out if you can"), from the gulches and ravines crossed by it, which rendered travel on this street a serious business. To Canal street was given the name from its being the first on that side extended to the channel; Laguna, because it traverses a system of lagoons; Jardines, or Garden, street is so named for that it cuts through the gardens of Captain de la Guerra and others. Santa Barbara street has a name of obvious origin. Anacapa street points toward the island of that name. State, the principal street, takes its name from the commonwealth of California. Chapala was so named in honor of a town and a lake near Guadalaxara, Mexico, from which came some of the early emigrants to Santa Barbara. De la Vina, or Vineyard street, was laid out through a vineyard planted in 1802 by Governor Goycoschea. Baños (Baths) street was so called from its leading to that part of the beach most used for bathing. Castillo or Castle street led to the hill on which stood an old Spanish fort, mounted with cannon. Rancheria comes from a cluster of Indian tents that formed a native village at that point. San Pascual street commemorates the field of a battle fought between the American forces and the Californians in 1846. San Andres (Saint Andrew) is claimed to honor Andres Pico, who figured conspicuously in that battle. Chino street is said also to derive its name from the Chino Rancho, in that same district. Gillespie street was named from Lieutenant—afterwards Captain—Gillespie, who figured in the American occupation; and Robbins street took its name from Captain Robbins, who owned the Rancho Los Positas, to which this street extends.

The situation of Santa Barbara is particularly favorable for effective sewage, the slope of State street being at no point less than nineteen feet in the mile. This street is sewered throughout, starting with eight-inch pipe and terminating with twelve-inch. This line, which is two miles long, is terra-cotta to the wharf, whence it is iron pipe, extending 1,000 feet into the sea. Chapala street is sewered from Gutierrez to Yslay, a distance of fifteen blocks; and de la Viña has three blocks of sewer, and Pedregosa also is sewered from Santa Barbara to State street. All this is after the Waring system.

From State street run two storm conduits, extending in two directions, to the creek and to the Estero; their cost was $20,000.

The city has a Fire Department, partly paid and partly volunteer, comprising one steam and one hand engine, two hose-carts with 2,000 feet of hose, and one hook and ladder company. The quarters are in the City Hall building. The number of members is about thirty. The fire alarms are given according to wards.

The watering of streets is provided for with four water-carts, and also a patent street-sweeping machine operates on State street.

Santa Barbara contains, besides the institutions and practitioners elsewhere mentioned, six large hotels, three surveyors, about twenty private boarding-houses, three restaurants, eight dry-goods houses, twenty grocery and general merchandise stores, three feed stores, two nurseries, one florist, one tea and coffee store, two feed, lumber and planing mills, three fruit stores, three confectionery stores, five bakeries, two fish dealers, seven meat markets, three wholesale liquor houses, twenty-one saloons, four hardware stores, five drug stores, one foundry, four furniture and upholstery shops, three second-hand stores, four tailor shops, two men's clothing stores, four shoe stores, three stationers, two curiosity and shell stores, two Chinese fancy goods stores, eight or ten Chinese general merchandise shops, one crockery store, four milliners, five jewelry stores, seventeen feed and livery stables, four house decorators, six painters, eight carpenters, nine blacksmith and carriage shops, eight barbers, four photographers, seventeen insurance and real-estate offices, one skating rink, one theater building, one gas company, one ice company (stock imported from Truckee), four saddle, harness and leather goods shops, one luggage transfer company, four tobacconists, and numerous gurneys, hacks, omnibuses, etc.

The Santa Barbara Cottage Hospital Association, mainly composed of ladies, have contracted for a cottage hospital building, to cost when completed $12,000 to $15,000. The contract was made in November, 1889, and the work as thus far completed comprises a two-story building with attic, ninety-one feet front, in which twenty-five or thirty patients could be accommodated, besides the offices, etc. The outlay thus far, for grading, bridge (across irrigating ditch), building, etc., has been $7,735.29. The funds have been raised partly by donations, partly by a local Trades' Carnival.

MISCELLANEOUS ITEMS.

From the United States census returns for the year ending June 1, 1870, are taken the following statistics:

Population of the town, 2,970; number of births, 131; deaths of children under one year of age, 9; ratio of births to deaths, $14\frac{1}{2}$ to 1. Total number of deaths, including adults, for the same period, 23; percentage of deaths for the whole population, 1 in 136, or $\frac{77}{100}$ of 1 per cent. Population of the county, 7,987; number of births for above period, 235; total number of deaths of children under 1 year of age, 15; ratio of births to deaths, $15\frac{3}{4}$ to 1, or nearly 16 to 1. Total number of deaths in the county, 64, two being accidental; percentage of deaths in total population, 1 in 125, or $\frac{80}{100}$ of 1 per cent.

In 1871, the letters of Charles Nordoff, in *Harpers' Monthly Magazine* and other Eastern periodicals, directed the attention of Eastern pleasure and health seekers to Santa Barbara and its vicinity. Then followed from 1871 to 1875 a great influx of immigration to this county. Blocks in the city of Santa Barbara, which in 1870 found a slow sale at $100, rapidly appreciated in value, until they readily brought $5,000 and $6,000. The city was transformed from a Mexican village of 1,500 population to a charming town, with all the characteristics of New England villages except as to climate. Lands in the county which theretofore had been used exclusively for grazing, now became farming and fruit lands. From this period dates the beginning of the olive and the walnut culture; almond trees were extensively planted; corn and barley were produced in large quantities. The cultivation of the bean was begun in Carpenteria and La Patira. The failure of the Bank of California, in 1875, brought all this advancement to an end, and the county slumbered until the boom of 1887.

In June, 1886, the Southern Pacific Railway Company formed an auxiliary corporation entitled the Southern Pacific Branch Railroad Company, and began the construction of a railroad from Soledad in Monterey County, then the terminus of the Northern Division of said company, to Saugus, a station near Newhall, on the Southern Pacific main line. For several years a steady advance in the values of real property had been going on in Los Angeles and adjoining counties. The construction of this branch line extended this impulse in prices to the counties of Ventura, Santa Barbara and San Luis Obispo. A general advance sometimes trebling and quadrupling the original price was had along the line of the Newport road. A period of building activity sprang up; the population of these counties was rapidly increased. New hotels and business houses were constructed in all the principal places—the Rose and the Anacapa at Ventura, the Arlington at Santa Barbara and the Ramon in San Luis Obispo. Ventura town laid many miles of concrete sidewalk, and generally graded and improved its streets. State street in Santa Barbara was paved with bituminous rock for a distance of two miles, at a cost of $180,000. In August, 1887, the railroad ceased construction, and immediately, presto, change! a sudden cessation of activity took place. Property, which had rapidly changed hands, now became slow of sale, and a considerable drop in prices occurred. Building operations largely ceased and further improvements were not attempted.

Recently, under promises of a speedy resumption of work upon the railroad, financial affairs have assumed a better aspect, and a more healthful feeling has been given to business.

During the boom of 1887 there were recorded twenty-eight sales ranging from $10,000 to $250,000, which alone aggregated $1,679,000. There were, further, about $500,000 worth of property covered by bonds; and at the lowest estimate $3,000,000 in sales of smaller figures than those just given; thus during seven months of that year over $5,000,000 changed hands.

During the same period of seven months, at least $500,000 were expended in improvements, buildings, etc.

The Santa Barbara postoffice is of the second class; its staff comprises a postmaster (salary $2,300) and three assistants. The total receipts of the postal account average $8,000 per annum. The registry business comprises about 3,000 pieces yearly. The money order business, domestic and international, and postal notes, paid, for 1890, are estimated at $35,000; postal money orders and postal notes issued approximate $25,000 per annum. There are in this office 675 boxes, of which perhaps eighty per cent. are rented at 75 cents per quarter.

Santa Barbara has had free postal delivery since July 15, 1890, there being three carriers, at $600 per year.

The city officials of Santa Barbara, September, 1890, are as follows: Mayor, P. J. Barber; Councilmen, Jos. B. Wentling, Frank P. Moore, M. F. Burke, C. E. Sherman, H. B. Brastow; Police Judge, W. H. Wheaton; Assessor, A. Davis; Treasurer, Ulpiano Yndart; City Attorney, Thomas McNulta; Tax Collector, W. S. Maris; Clerk, F. N. Gutierrez; Surveyor, Engineer and Street Superintendent, John K. Harrington; Janitor and Fire Engineer, J. T. Stewart; Marshal, D. W. Martin; Night Watchmen, G. J. Fullington, Thomas Knightly; School Trustees, C. A. Storke, George F. Trenwith, and J. T. Johnston.

The old graveyard adjoining the Santa Barbara Mission must have received 6,000 to 10,000 dead into its narrow limits.

Soon after the coming of the Americans, a site for a new cemetery was chosen on the hillside, immediately north of the town. The town plat, when surveyed, was found to include portions of this ground; and as the city was built up about it, much complaint was made of the interment of bodies there, and further use was prohibited by a city ordinance. This was, however, disregarded by the then president of the Mission, and so the grand jury took up the question, in September, 1873, and burials here were then discontinued. Thomas Hope donated a tract of ——- acres in a district lying about five miles from Santa Barbara, toward the Patera, and this is the present Roman Catholic burying ground.

THE PUBLIC LIBRARY.

The first movement toward the establishment of a public library originated with the order of Odd Fellows, which organization had procured a collection of books, and maintained for a time a library under their own auspices. Circumstances arose which caused the discontinuance of this library, and the books were removed from circulation and stored away for a considerable time.

Under the regulations of "An Act to Establish Free Public Libraries and Reading Rooms, approved by the Legislature of California, April 26, 1880, the city council, in session of February 16, 1882, adopted a resolution to establish such an institution, and five trustees were accordingly voted for at the next election of city officers, T. B. Dibblee,

James M. Short, O. N. Dimmick, W. E. Noble, and S. B. P. Knox being elected.

After a number of preliminary meetings a permanent organization was effected, Dr. S. B. P. Knox being elected permanent president, and James M. Short permanent secretary.

The custodians of the former Odd Fellows' Library donated all the books, etc., which had belonged to that institution, and which were formally accepted by the trustees of the Santa Barbara Free Public Library.

The books so delivered comprised 2,921 volumes; to these, during the first year, were added by purchase 300, and by donation 252 volumes.

A set of very liberal rules and regulations were adopted, and Mrs. Mary Page was elected librarian.

The library at present contains 5,740 well-selected volumes, and it issues 3,974 cards, each representing a drawer of books. Fiction represents the greatest demand from readers, and next come travels, history, and miscellaneous works. The rooms are comfortably fitted, and every care is taken to provide for their profitable use by readers and students. Mrs. M. C. Rust, the present librarian, has been the incumbent for the past few years, and Mrs. F. C. Lord her assistant. Both ladies are attentive, courteous and capable in the discharge of their duties.

THE SANTA BARBARA NATURAL HISTORY SOCIETY.

In December, 1876, this society was organized with a list of twenty-one members and the following officers: President, Rev. Stephen Bowers; Vice Presidents, Mrs. Ellwood Cooper, H. C. Ford, L. N. Dimmick; Treasurer, Dr. Mason; Corresponding Secretary, Mrs. H. G. Otis; Recording Secretary, Miss Abbie I. Hails; Curator, Prof. Alphonse Bel.

The objects of the society, as set forth in its constitution, are, "The increase and diffusion of knowledge of the natural sciences, by the establishment of a museum, the reading and publication of original papers," etc.

For the first two years of its existence, the society met in the Santa Barbara College building. Its property at this time consisted of a few specimens, contained in one case, and a few books and pamphlets. Removing hence, the society occupied until 1883 a place in the public library, owned by the I. O. O. F. During this period, little progress was made. In 1883 a new impetus was given by the transfer of about 1,200 volumes of Government publications, which had been in charge of the Santa Barbara College. Funds were now donated by the citizens for the purchase of necessary furniture and book-cases.

In 1884 the society removed from rented rooms to two fine rooms adjoining the Free Public Library, liberally offered by the proprietors of the Clock Building. During this year, from the proceeds of an entertainment given by the citizens, there was purchased a collection of archæological specimens, valued at $300.

For many years, large numbers of fine ethnological and archæological specimens, impossible to replace, had been unearthed and carried from this section by Government expeditions, agents of foreign museums, collectors for institutions in other States, and innumerable individuals collecting for speculation. The Natural History Society has done energetic and most desirable service in checking this movement, and in collecting and preserving for the use of this section relics thereunto appertaining. The museum and library have been steadily increasing, by donations and by purchase. This society's library is a depository—and the only one south of San Francisco—of all the publications issued by the United States Government, exceedingly useful as works of reference. These rooms are accessible to all during the public library hours, but books may be taken out only by members of the society.

The museum contains: In entomology, 299 species; ornithology, 85 mounted birds, 6 nests, 132 eggs; mammals, 5 species, mounted; conchology, about 900 species marine and fresh-water shells; crustacea, 12 marine specimens, numerous corals; reptiles, 33 species, in alcohol; botanical, marine algæ, 330 species; flowering plants, about 2,000 mounted specimens, 80 miscellaneous varieties; geological, 69 fossils, corals, crinoids, fish, shells, and insects; minerals, over 500 specimens; Indian relics, over 700 varieties, very interesting; bound volumes, 2,053; pamphlets and parts of volumes, 3,534; a large painting, by Henry C. Ford of "the Grizzly Giant," Sequoia gigantea; a stone chair used by the Incas of South America, found near Guayaquil; numerous photographs and curios.

The present officers of the society are: President, H. C. Ford; Vice Presidents, L. G. Yates, James W. Calkins, Mrs. A. A. Boyce; Treasurer, Mrs. Mary A. Ashley; Corresponding and Recording Secretary, L. G. Yates; Curator and Librarian, Mrs. C. F. Lord; Publication Committee, H. C. Ford, L. G. Yates.

The society has a membership of over forty-five, of whom, however, not very many are active members. It is proper to note that Henry Chapman Ford, president of the society, is a painter of some distinction, and that to his devotion and enthusiasm are due his charming etchings and studies in oil of the old missions, being the only pictures in existence of the entire chain of those historic structures, now mostly fallen to ruin.

Dr. Lorenzo Gordin Yates, corresponding and recording secretary, has been honored by election as a Fellow of the Linnean Society of London, a distinction enjoyed by only six citizens of the United States. Dr. Yates, assisted by John Gilbert Baker, F. R. S., of the Royal Herbarium at Kew, is about to publish a list of "All Known Ferns," which will be a valuable contribution to fern knowledge.

The librarian and curator, Mrs. C. F. Lord, is most energetic, assiduous, and efficient in her duties, and courteous in her treatment of persons visiting the rooms.

FRATERNAL ORGANIZATIONS.

The fraternal organizations of Santa Barbara are as follows:

Santa Barbara Lodge, No. 192, F. & A. M.: E. G. Dodge, W. M.; W. B. Squier, Secretary.

Magnolia Lodge, No. 242, F. & A. M.: B. F. Thomas, W. M.; R. D. Smith, Secretary.

Corinthian Chapter, No. 51, Royal Arch Masons: J. W. Hiller, High Priest; A. B. Williams, Secretary.

St. Omar Commandery, No. 30, Knights Templar; Sir F. M. Casal, E. C.; Sir J. H. Austin, Recorder.

Santa Barbara Lodge, No. 156, I. O. O. F.: D. O. Kelly, N. G.; T. R. Dawe, Secretary.

Channel City Lodge, No. 232, I. O. O. F.: C. S. Sawyer, N. G.; W. H. Stafford, R. S.

Santa Barbara Encampment, No. 52, I. O. O. F., organized December, 1875: J. M. Holloway, C. P.; Fred Forbush, Scribe.

Santa Barbara Lodge, K. of P., No. 25, organized in 1876: S. W. Ireland, C. C.; A. Davis, K. of R. and S.

Castle Rock Lodge, K. of P., No. 151, organized in 1886: L. Brooks, C. C.; J. L. Hurlbut, K. of R. and S.

A. O. U. W., Lodge No. 172, organized in 1881: J. T. Johnson, W. M.; W. H. Myers, Recorder.

Santa Barbara Parlor, No. 116, Native Sons of the Golden West: W. H. Maris, President; C. J. Murphy, Secretary.

Branch No. 39, Young Men's Institute: L. F. Ruiz, President; Rudolph Wakurka, Secretary.

Young Men's Christian Association and Free Reading Room, organized April, 1888.

Starr King Post, No. 52, Department of California, G. A. R.: H. M. Van Winkle, Post Commander; F. A. Rowan, Adjutant; A. Davis, Quartermaster.

Starr King Woman's Relief Corps: Florence Salada, Mrs. E. J. Thompson, Secretary.

Marguerite Chapter, No. 78, O. E. S.: Mrs. N. M. Axtell, W. M.; Eli Rundell, Secretary.

Woman's Christian Temperance Union: Mrs. H. D. Vail, President; Mrs. M. F. Clapp, Secretary.

CHURCHES.

With the advent of Americans, other than Catholic churches were speedily organized in the county. As early as 1854, Rev. Adam Bland, Presiding Elder of the Los Angeles Circuit of the Methodist Episcopal Church, held services here, and thus this denomination may be called really the pioneer of Protestantism in this county, although not the first to organize.

The circumstances were adverse to organization up to 1868, when the Rev. R. R. Dunlap was appointed to the charge of the community embracing Santa Barbara, La Patera, Montecito, Carpenteria and San Buenaventura, although there was no organized society in any of these places. In 1868, Rev. P. Y. Cool was appointed to the service, and succeeded in organizing a church with eighteen members, and building a parsonage and chapel. The first worship was conducted in the court-house, then called the Egerea House. The native population were much opposed to having Protestant service in the town, but offered no violence, although resorting to annoying disturbances, such as causing the squealing of hogs and the howling of dogs to interrupt the service. The public schoolhouse also was at one time used for holding service.

On July 17, 1869, the contract was let for a new brick church which cost $5,824.75, which was dedicated December 5, 1869. At the end of Mr. Cool's three-year pastorate, there were sixty-one members and parishioners. When the present incumbent, E. W. Caswell, was appointed, September, 1888, the charge numbered 210 members and parishioners, with an average attendance of 128 Sunday-school scholars.

The Parochial Church (Catholic) of Santa Barbara was built in 1853 by the Franciscans. In 1855 Bishop J. Amat arrived and took possession. In 1865 the church was burned, and rebuilding was begun in 1866. The first pastor was V. R. B. Rajo, who remained in charge only ten months, being succeeded by Rev. F. Torrentian, who was in 1887, in his turn, succeeded by V. R. F. James Vila, the present incumbent, who has the entire charge, wholly independent of the mission, the friars having nothing to do with the administration of the parish. Father Vila is assisted by Father M. G. G. B. F. Cesari.

Trinity Church.—In March, 1867, Rev. T. G. Williams having been sent to Santa Barbara by the bishop, a meeting of Episcopalians was held, a board of trustees elected, and a church incorporated under the name of "Trinity." Services were held regularly in the old brick school-house until Christmas-day, 1869, when, a brick church having been built, the first Protestant place of worship in the county was opened. The interior of the church at that time was unfinished. This church was used continuously up to

1887. Late in 1886, in anticipation of the speedy arrival of the railroad, and the consequent probable great increase of the congregation, movements were taken to secure larger quarters. Wm. R. Broome donated a valuable lot, and a handsome building was thereupon erected. Although the edifice was not yet complete, on Easter Sunday, 1888, Rev. Dr. John Bakewell held the first service therein, to a congregation of over 500 persons; and on July 29, Rt. Rev. Bishop Kip, assisted by the Dean of the diocese, formally opened the new church, under the old name of "Trinity." This church has now (October, 1890) been without a pastor since August.

St. Mark's Episcopal Church was organized in the spring of 1876, with Rev. Robert Scott as pastor. A suitable edifice was built, but it was sold to the Baptist congregation when St. Mark's re-united with Trinity Church, from which it was an offshoot.

The *Congregational Church* had services here as early as 1866, when Rev. J. A. Johnson preached his first sermon in the courthouse. At the close of the service, a resolution was adopted, asking him to remain in the town and organize a church society, which he did. In 1867 a permanent society was organized. Mr. Johnson's ministry closed in 1869. In 1870 a new brick church was dedicated, built at a cost of $9,000 on a lot donated for the purpose. The present pastor, Rev. C. T. Weitzel, was installed in 1887.

The *Presbyterian Church* was organized in June, 1869, under Rev. Thomas Frazer, with an enrollment of nineteen members, many being ex-members of the congregation organized by Mr. Johnson. Rev. H. H. Dubbins was the first pastor, and the next, Dr. Phelps, who increased the congregation to nearly 100. In 1874 was built a church costing $15,000. The present pastor is A. H. Carrier.

The *Baptist Church* was organized in 1874. The first pastor was H. I. Parker. In 1875 this congregation purchased the old Presbyterian chapel, and in 1882 St. Mark's (an offshoot from Trinity), which is still their place of worship. Rev. Alex. Grant is the present pastor.

The *Unitarian Church* was organized about 1880. The present place of worship is a chapel on State street, near which is building a handsome new stone chapel for this denomination at a cost of $28,000. Rev. Philip S. Thacher is pastor.

The *Christian Church* was organized here in 1888. Rev. T. D. Garvin is pastor. Service is held in the old Trinity chapel.

The *Holiness Church* was organized in 1884. The pastor is J. A. Foster.

The *Faith Mission* was established in 1884. Mrs. E. J. Scudder is pastor.

In 1889 a very handsome church was built, a ta cost of $16,000. In 1887, the East Santa Barbara Methodist Church was organized, a lot was purchased, and a new church erected, at a cost of $2,100.

The Methodist Church, South, was organized in 1889, and a church building is being erected.

BANKS.

The First National Bank is the pioneer financial institution of this county. It was organized in 1873; its president being Mortimer Cook, and the other officers the present ones. In 1876 was completed the present bank block at the corner of State street and Cañon Perdido, an imposing three-story brick structure.

This bank at present controls a system of safe deposit vaults also.

The officers are: J. W. Calkins, president; Hugh D. Vail, vice-president; A. L. Lincoln, ashier; H. P. Lincoln, assistant cashier.

The Santa Barbara County National Bank was organized in July, 1875, as a State institution, being then known as the Santa Barbara County Bank, with a paid up capital of $50,000. In February, 1880, it was reorganized under the National Banking Laws, taking its present title. About the end of 1886 its capital was increased to $100,000. Its statement for August, 1887, showed an increase in business of nearly $200,000 over that shown in December, 1886. The officials of the bank are as follows: William M. Eddy, president; John Edwards, vice-president; Eugene S. Sheffield, cashier; Charles A. Edwards, assistant cashier. These officers are the same in charge since the beginning, save the assistant cashier, lately added.

The Santa Barbara Savings Bank was incorporated September, 1886, opening its doors for business in December, 1886, with a capital of $50,000. In October, 1887, it was merged in the Commercial Bank, incorporated August, 1887, which commenced business October 1, 1887. Its officers at organization were: John H. Redington, president; E. B. Hall, vice-president; W. B. Metcalf, cashier. The present officers are: George S. Edwards, president; E. B. Hall, vice-president; W. B. Metcalf, cashier. This bank expects to occupy, by January 1, 1891, its own new edifice, now building on State street.

THE COURT-HOUSE

was built in 1872. For years past, constant complaints had come in from successive grand juries of the total inefficiency of the court-house and jail, from which prisoners could escape almost at will. The murderer of Abadie had thus escaped, after some $1,700 had been spent for guarding him. After many delays on the score of deficiency of funds, the board of supervisors requested the legislature to pass a bill authorizing the issue of bonds, not to exceed $50,000, bearing interest at seven per cent. per annum, payable in thirty years from date. The bill was passed, and plans called for, that of P. J. Barber being selected from among the many offered. From the many bids received, that of Edward R. Fogarty, for $16,825 for carpenter work, was accepted, and two bids of Stevens and Joyner, for $16,595 and $1,922, for regular and for supplementary mason-work, respectively. The corner-stone was laid on October 5, 1872. The architecture is pure Corinthian in order. The edifice has a cupola, and a surmounted dome, with lantern finish. The general plan has the form of a Greek cross. The material is brick and iron, upon a stone foundation. Originally, and for many years, the jail was situated in the basement of the main building. Besides the court-rooms and judges' chambers, the court-house contains the offices of all the county officials except the recorder. The building cost some $60,000. Within the last few years there has been placed in it a fine steel lined vault for the safe-keeping of the county's treasure and court records.

THE COUNTY JAIL

was built in 1876, at a cost of about $9,000. It is 28 x 36 feet, and contains an office, sitting-room, dining-room, kitchen, pantry, closet, and hall. In the second story are three large cells for female prisoners, the main entrance to which is through a wrought-iron skeleton door. The prison part of the jail is 28 x 31 feet over the ground, and one story high. The floor is of stone, save in the prisons, where it is of three-eighth inch steam-boiler iron, overlaid with wood. Entering through the iron door, one reaches the hall, which is six feet wide, and runs the full length of the building. This hall is made of iron bars, three fourths of an inch square, set on end, three inches apart, between the floor and the ceiling, with iron doors at the left and right, opening into the cells, eight in number. The doors are opened by levers from the main hall. The cells are seven feet long, six wide, and eight high. During the day, the prisoners have the freedom of the hall, being locked up at night. The ceiling, floor, partitions, and doors of the cell, are all made of the boiler iron aforesaid.

THE SANTA BARBARA COUNTY HOSPITAL, POOR FARM, AND ALMS-HOUSE,

(for these establishments are combined in one), is situated just outside the city limits on the east. The grounds cover an area of about ten acres, sufficing for the raising of fruits and vegetables in a garden and orchard attached to the premises. The board of supervisors each year appoints a county physician and a hospital superintendent, and nurses are employed as needed. There are at present one female and about twenty male inmates. The percentage of females seeking assistance here is small, owing to the same reason which accounts for the fact that the character of the inmates is rapidly changing; formerly they were mostly acute cases, but now they are mainly chronic. This is because very many of those received here are either tramps, or sick persons who reach Santa Barbara with means of support for a few days only, after which they become objects of charity. Dr. S. B. P. Knox, who is the present incumbent, has been county physician for some eight years in all, at one time filling the office for six years in succession.

Besides the inmates of the poor farm, the county has some forty pensioners, mostly of Spanish-American blood, who live at their own dwellings, or with relatives, and receive a monthly allowance of $4, $6, or $8.

RAILROADS.

From time to time movements have been made in Santa Barbara to secure the running of railways, of various lines, through this section. Meetings had been held, resolutions adopted, and memorials drawn up, but all to very little, in fact to no, purpose.

Only when it was clear that self-interest was thoroughly warranted, when further delay would positively divert an important and desirable revenue into other channels, when the rich products of this section guaranteed freight shipments to warrant extortions, the railroad at last condescended.

On the afternoon of Friday, August 19, 1887, the first regular passenger train pulled into Santa Barbara, with a large number of visitors from Los Angeles, Ventura, and other neighboring cities. At the same time arrived a special excursion train from San Francisco, with a load of railway officials and other parties interested in Santa Barbara. Altogether, it is estimated that about 5,000 people visited the city during this railway jubilee celebration. The hotel accommodations proving inadequate, the houses of the citizens were thrown open in generous hospitality to the visiting strangers, who were met at the station, with bands and conveyances, and driven about the city. In the evening was given at the Arlington a grand banquet, at which sat down fifty of the guests, with fifty of the leading citizens. Also there were read many letters and telegrams of regrets from prominent State officials and railway magnates. Speeches and toasts were offered, and congratulations on this event for Santa Barbara. The next day, Saturday, August 20, there was a grand parade at 10 A. M., in which participated the public organizations of Santa Barbara and other points in the county, as well as many features of individual representation. The procession was headed by the Presidio Band, of San Francisco, and the local bands followed at intervals. One of the most interesting features was the illustration of the successive stages of progress in land transportation— the pack-mule, the stage coach of 1860, and the Pullman car of 1887. Many of the designs displayed upon floats in the procession were developed in the flowers for which this section is justly famous. At noon, the procession moved to Burton Mound, where the Santa Barbara ladies served a complimentary luncheon to the citizens and the visitors, after which this large and enthusiastic throng listened, before adjourning, to other speeches.

At different periods efforts have been made to secure from Congress appropriations for a breakwater at Santa Barbara, but all such movements have been tentative or initiatory only, and leading to no practical result.

THE WATER SUPPLY

of Santa Barbara is purveyed by the Mission Water Company, incorporated in 1872, which in the following year made through its pipes and mains a regular service. For this purpose the living springs of Mission Cañon have been tapped, and the waters of Mission Creek utilized. There are two reservoirs, whose total capacity is some 4,000,000, that of the storage reservoir being 3,000,000 and of the distributing reservoir 750,000 gallons. The distributing reservoir is about 200 feet above the highest, and 325 feet above the lowest, portion of the city, thus giving sufficient pressure to throw a stream over the highest building in the city. There are in use several miles of distributing pipes, four to six inches in diameter.

ELECTRIC LIGHT.

Since November 1, 1887, Santa Barbara has been municipally lighted by the electric system. There are two towers 150 feet high, each having four 2,000-candle power lamps, and twenty-eight masts sixty and eighty feet high, each with one 2,000-candle-power lamp. State street is thus lighted throughout its entire length, and the rest of the lamps are distributed about the city. This system costs the city about $500 monthly. Besides the city lights, there are in use over sixty arc -lights of 1,200candle-power, and a large number of incandescent lights of various powers, used for the lighting of mercantile houses, hotels, and other private establishments.

MINOR ITEMS.

The telephone office at this city was opened July 10, 1886, with a list of thirty-five subscribers, now increased to 149, all within the city limits.

There are in Santa Barbara County post-offices as follows: Santa Barbara, Santa Maria, Lompoc, Los Alamos, Guadalupe, Summerland, Stuart, Sisquoc, Serena, Santa Maria, Santa Ynez, Nojoqui, Montecito, Los Olivos, Goleta, Carey, Carpenteria and Ballard's. Of these, the first five are money order offices, that at Santa Barbara having international exchange.

The Santa Barbara county officials at present date, September, 1890, are as follows:

District Court Commissioner, Charles Fernald; State Senator, E. H. Heacock; Assemblyman, C. A. Storke; Superior Judge, R. M. Dillard; County Court Commissioner, S. W. Bouton; Clerk, F. L. Kellogg; Official Court Reporter, C. F. Reynolds; Recorder, C. A. Stuart; Sheriff, R J. Broughton; Under Sheriff, R. D. Smith; Auditor, J. T. Johnson; Tax-Collector, M. F. Burke; Treasurer, E. S. Sheffield; Surveyor, A. S. Cooper; District Attorney, W. B. Cope; Assessor, Frank Smith; Deputy

Assessors, J. L. Barker, Santa Barbara; C. J. Young, Lompoc; B. M. Smith, Carpenteria; George Smith, Los Alamos; School Superintendent, G. E. Thurmond; Public Administrator, W. B. Hosmer; Coroner, A. M. Ruiz; Supervisors—Thomas Hosmer, H. G. Crane, A. M. Boyd, D. T. Truitt, A. W. Cox.

THE MISSION.

As the Mission (now a college of Franciscans) is one of the most notable features of the place, from its historic associations, and for its present picturesqueness, a brief recapitulation of its history here will hardly be superfluous. On the feast of Santa Barbara, Virgin and Martyr (December 4), 1786, on the site occupied by the present edifice, Very Reverend Father Fermin Francisco de Lasuen, President of the Missions, and successor to Padre Junipero Serra, raised the cross and founded the Mission, being assisted by Padres Antonio Paterna and Cristobal Oramas. On December 15, Padre Lasuen celebrated mass and preached in a hut or booth, built for the occasion from boughs or branches of trees. At this service was present the Governor, Pedro Fages, accompanied by a few soldiers. In the year 1787 were built a house for the priests, 36 x 15, and a church or chapel, 30 x 15, having adobe walls three feet thick, and temporary roofs made of heavy rafters, across which were tied long poles or canes, over which was spread a layer of mud or clay, the whole then thatched with straw. In the following year, the Fathers, with the 200 Indians then living at the Mission, began the manufacture of tiles, with which they then roofed the buildings.

By the year 1789 the first church was razed, as too small, and a new one, 85 x 15, was erected, as also many new houses for dwellings for the Indians of the Mission, by this time numbering nearly 500.

In 1793 was begun, and in 1794 was finished, the third church of this Mission, a large adobe structure, $127\frac{1}{2}$ x $25\frac{1}{2}$, containing six chapels and a large sacristy. It had a brick portico, walls well plastered with mortar, and tile roof. In this year died Rev. Father Antonio Paterna, the first minister of this Mission.

As the Indians here now numbered 782, and were increasing rapidly, it became necessary to form a village and give a separate house to each family; and so, in 1798, there were erected nineteen houses for as many Indian families; and during the years following an average of thirty-five new houses per year, so that by 1807 the Indian village contained 252 houses and as many families. In 1806 was built a reservoir of mason-work, 116 feet square by seven feet deep, to collect water for the gardens, orchard, etc., and this tank is still in existence, used for water storage by the water company. In 1808 was built in the space before the Mission an ornamental stone fountain and lavatory, still existing and regarded as a "show" feature.

During the latter part of December, 1812, the severe earthquake shocks which then occurred so damaged all the Mission buildings, and particularly the church, that it was deemed expedient to take this down and build another. From this period, then, dates the fourth and present Mission church, which was begun in 1815, and finished and consecrated in September, 1820. Its dimensions are 170 feet long, forty feet wide, and thirty feet from floor to ceiling. The walls, nearly six feet thick, are of large cubes of cut sandstone, plastered over, and they are strengthened by heavy and massive stone buttresses along the sides and at the angles, thus making it the strongest of the Mission edifices.

Hitherto Upper and Lower California had been under the spiritual jurisdiction of the

Bishop of Sonora, Mexico. But in 1835 the Mexican Congress which revoked the decree of 1833 and gave back to the Missions the property of which they had then been despoiled, decreed also that the California provinces should have a special or local bishop, whose interest would be devoted exclusively to the welfare and advancement of this section. Such a prelate was not assigned, however, until 1840, when Pope Gregory XVI. elected Right Rev. Francisco Garcia Diego y Moreno, a Franciscan father, who was solemnly consecrated to the bishopric October 4, 1840. On January 11, 1842, he arrived at Santa Barbara, and amidst great rejoicings took possession of the diocese, selecting the Mission as his residence, and thus making Santa Barbara the Episcopal city. The bishop died at the Mission, April 30, 1846, and Very Rev. José M. Gonzalez Rubio, O. S. F., became administrator of the diocese, surrendering his charge in 1850 to the Right Rev. J. S. Alemany, who had that year been consecrated Bishop of Monterey, and who in 1835 became Archbishop of San Francisco.

The Mission under its present aspect is still very picturesque, although at close range something of its charm is lost through the results of "restoration," which has destroyed the creamy, time-mellowed tints of the surfaces, and imparted a certain obtrusive and common-place setness to its appearance. Nevertheless, in its architectural fitness, in its dimensions, and in its situation, lying as it does on a commanding site, where it is sure to catch promptly the attention of the traveler, whether by land or by sea, the Mission bears strong witness to the taste and judicial discrimination of the Padres. The building has a very oriental aspect, what with its long arcade and two twin towers. Within, the organ loft is at one end, and the high altar at the other. In the vault beneath reposes the mortal part of the first Bishop of the two Californias, Francisco Garcia Diego, above whose tomb hangs his antique hat. This vault was recently reopened to receive the body of the venerable Father Sanchez, who had ministered here since.

At the left of the church is a wing 130 feet long, with the pillars and arches of its corridor well preserved. On one side is the old olive orchard, and scattered near are the remains of many now ruined buildings of industrial use in the days of the Indian converts.

This probably went to decay less than any of the other missions, and it was, furthermore, put in repair for the celebration of the centennial of its founding. On this occasion, December 4, 1886, visitors from all parts of the State came hither.

Masses and services are held regularly at the mission, which is in charge of Rev. Joseph O'Keefe, who is accompanied by some three or four fathers, and about a dozen lay brothers.

Visitors to the mission are courteously received. Ladies are prohibited from entering a certain one of the gardens.

THE SCHOOLS.

It would appear that the first beginnings of public instruction of Santa Barbara were such rudiments as were imparted by one José Manuel Toca, a *grumete*, or ship-boy, from one of the transports. This required a remuneration of $125, of which each soldier paid $1. By the governor's orders, the first feature of these presidio schools was the teaching of Christian doctrine, then reading and writing. Toca taught from the close of 1795 to 1797, when he was called on board ship, being replaced in school by another ship-boy.

A primary school for girls was opened by a woman in 1817, but it would seem to have closed rather speedily.

During the last years of the decade 1810–'20, a school was maintained, with Diego Fernandez as teacher, on a monthly salary of $15; but in 1828 not one pupil was in attendance, and the alcalde was directed to enforce compulsory education.

Up to 1856, the English language was not taught in the common schools, owing to the opposition offered thereto by the Spanish element of the population. But in that year, the county superintendent, George D. Fisher, and the school commissioners, Hill, de la Palma y Mesa and Huse, held an examination of teachers, at which applied Pablo Caracela, Mr. Baillis, Victor Mondrau and Owen Connolly, the two latter of whom were there authorized to teach school for one year, at a monthly salary of $75. Through the failure of the county superintendent to report, it is said for lack of mail facilities, one appropriation of the State school fund was lost; and an attempt was made in the Legislature to so remedy the matter that Santa Barbara might receive her quota. In objection it was urged that Santa Barbara had no school-house, and that the English language was not taught there at all. Accordingly, the teaching of English was this season begun, and after some difficulty the quota due Santa Barbara was paid over. In 1854 there had been levied a school tax of five cents on each $100, and this fund provided for increased facilities and accommodations. In a letter to the school board from Owen Connolly, teacher of the first and then only school taught in English, he asks for an increase of salary, based on the flourishing condition of the school. It numbers, he says, seventy-eight pupils between the ages of four and fifteen years, half of whom were young ladies (age not stated!) one-third were Americans, the rest of Spanish or Mexican blood. The studies were orthography, penmanship, reading, arithmetic, geography, grammar and analysis, of both English and Spanish.

In 1879 there were thirty school districts and 2,976 children of school age.

For the year ending June 30, 1884, the children of school age were 3,445; school districts, forty.

With the increased proportion of Anglo-Saxon population, they here as elsewhere arranged for the maintenance of that great necessity, good public schools, and the system has steadily advanced in the county to its present proportions.

The School Department of Santa Barbara County is now composed as follows, as prescribed by the new State constitution of 1879–'80: The County Board of Education consists of the county school superintendent, *ex officio* its secretary, and four others, two of whom must be teachers holding the highest grade of certificate. This board prescribes the course of study, the list of text-books, and list of books for school libraries; and it holds semi-annual examinations, in June and December, of teachers for the county schools. Every autumn is held a county institute, which every teacher is required to attend, unless excused by the superintendent for sufficient reasons.

There are three grades of schools, namely, primary, grammar grade and grammar school course, that receive State appropriations; and a high school, located in the city of Santa Barbara, and supported by county tax. The city in the autumn of 1887 contained five public-school buildings, accommodating twelve primary, five grammar and one high school. There was then an enrollment of 1,031 pupils, taught by twenty teachers.

The school census of Santa Barbara for the year closing June 30, 1886, shows as follows: Total number school census children, 3,844, divided as follows: white boys, 1,937; white girls, 1,888; negro boys, four; negro girls, six; Indian boys, four; Indian girl, one. Under five years old there were 1,495 white and three negro children. The county then contained four Chinese children under seventeen years of age, four deaf and dumb and seven blind children.

The births during the year were 129 boys and 115 girls; total 244.

The number of children who attended public school during the year were 2,650 white, seven negro and two Indian.

There were 136 attending private schools.

In November, 1887, there were in the county forty-six school districts, supplied by about seventy teachers. The number of children enrolled, between five and seventeen years of age, was 3,948, as against 2,696 in 1886. The total of appropriations during that year for school purposes was $46,990.20, and the amount paid for teachers' salaries was $37,947.95.

There are at present in Santa Barbara County fifty-three school districts, with eighty-six incumbent teachers, of whom sixty-one are women and twenty-five men. The ladies receive an average salary of $61, the gentlemen of $75. There are 4,429 children of school age in the county, of whom are enrolled 3,648, comprising 1,800 girls and 1,848 boys. The average daily attendance is 2,254.

For the school year closing June 30, 1890, the State apportionment for this county was $42,840, and the county apportionment, $27,791.45. From this total of $70,631.45 the amount paid for teachers' salaries was $50,247.50; for school buildings, $15,395.06; for school libraries, $994.96; for apparatus, $1,045.45; for rent, repairs and contingent expenses, $12,440.16. Total of expenditures, $80,123.13. The school bonded indebtedness in the county is $81,450.

The county owns school-houses and furniture to the value of $143,300; the school libraries contain an aggregate of 8,936 volumes, valued at $10,080, and the apparatus supplied to the schools is worth $5,730, thus placing the valuation of school property at $159,110.

The County Board of Education at present is composed of School Superintendent G. E. Thurmond, T. N. Snow, Miss Josephine Rockwood, Mrs. Ida M. Blochman and Holton Webb.

There are in the city of Santa Barbara 1,630 census children, of whom 1,228 are enrolled in the schools, the average attendance being 840. The number of teachers is twenty-four. There are five school buildings of plain but substantial style, the valuation of buildings and furniture being $50,000. The corps of teachers numbers a city superintendent and twenty three assistants.

St. Vincent's College was established 1858, by the Sisters of Charity, noble, unselfish and energetic women, who have conducted it very successfully up to the present. Early in its career St. Vincent's possessed an excellent four-story brick building, which was destroyed by fire March 15, 1874, the loss being about $20,000. This calamity, as it veritably was to Santa Barbara, was soon repaired by the erection of the present building on the site of the burned structure. The institute is now a fine three-story brick edifice of composite architecture, where the Sisters teach all common branches of instruction. Only girls are received here.

The Santa Barbara College was instituted in 1869, by a joint-stock company of the citizens, and an edifice (at present the San Marcos Hotel) was built at a cost of about $35,000. It had an efficient corps of teachers, qualified to fit pupils for a business life or for the university. It had an average of perhaps eighty pupils. It suspended operation about 1878.

There are now in Santa Barbara three private schools besides St. Vincent's, viz.: the Collegiate School, Miss Thayer's School for Girls, and the School for Girls kept by Professor Alfred Colin and Madame Colin.

THE MEDICAL PROFESSION.

In the early days the care of the sick was of lay origin; that is, by domestic remedies, mainly herbal, and in not a few instances borrowed from the superstitious rites of the aborigines. Surgical operations, too, were performed mostly after a rough and amateurish fashion. As late as June, 1846, Francisco de la Guerra wrote to the Governor that for the want of good medical men in the country he had been under the necessity of employing the surgeon of a British man-of-war.

William A. Streeter, as stated elsewhere, practiced here as a physician, albeit not regularly qualified, from 1845 forward.

Dr. Nicholas A. Den had arrived here as early as 1836, but it would appear from Don Francisco's expressed want that Dr. Den did not at once begin to practice, nor is the date of his embarking in this profession obtainable by the present writer.

Dr. Samuel Bevier Brinkerhoff, who arrived here in 1852, soon became a general favorite practitioner, and when he died he probably knew as many family histories and family secrets of the section as a father confessor, besides having opened or closed the gates of life to a vast number of the community. Up to the time of his death he was a successful practitioner.

Among the earlier physicians who came to Santa Barbara were: Drs. Alexander Perry; Wallace, who came in 1850; Shaw, who practiced with Dr. Burris, who came hither from Mexico; English, Freeman, Ord (a direct descendant of George IV. of England and Mrs. Fitzherbert), Biggs and Bates (in partnership about 1873), Winchester (came about 1873), S. B. P. Knox, Logando (came about 1875), etc.

There are at present about twelve regular practicing physicians in the city of Santa Barbara, and five practitioners of the homeopathic school. In the outside towns there are ten practicing physicians, as follows: At Carpenteria, three; at Santa Maria, two; at Santa Ynes, one; at Los Alamos, one; at Lompoc, two; at Los Olivos, one; all these being of the allopathic school, save one homeopath at Carpenteria. Most of the physicians in the city belong to the State Medical Association, but there is no county association, although various efforts have been made to establish one.

BENCH AND BAR.

The following account of the bench and bar of Santa Barbara County and the Second Judicial District in the early days was kindly prepared for the present work by Judge Charles Fernald:

"The bench and bar in newly organized communities must always be an interesting subject to all readers, professional and lay as well. The well-being of the community in general depends largely upon the character of the bench and the bar, at all times, under our system of government. The rights of person and property find their surest guaranty in the character of both. Accordingly we have striven to ascertain, as best we may at this late date, just how the courts were organized, and the character of the judges, magistrates, attorneys and counsellors practicing here from the adoption of the constitution and the organization of the courts from 1850 to the election and inauguration of Abraham Lincoln in 1861.

"The judicial system of the State under the judicial act of 1850 and 1851 was radically different from that adopted by the new constitution of California in 1879 under the influence of the "sand lot," as it has been called. The former was much more simple in structure, and we can but think a careful comparison of the two will show the old system very much more effective in its scope and practical operation. We have not space here to analyze and compare the two systems, and it is not our purpose to do so.

"The act of April 11, 1851, provided for the organization of a Supreme Court, consisting of a chief justice and two associate justices, to be elected by the people. The State was divided into eleven judicial districts, and provision was made for the term of six years for the election of a district judge for each district, embracing one or more counties according to population. The first district embraced the counties of San Diego and Los Angeles, and the second the counties of Santa Barbara and San Luis Obispo, Santa Barbara County at that time including in its territory the present county of Ventura, cut off from Santa Barbara in 1872, by an act of the Legislature. The act of 1851 also provided for the organization of a superior court of the city of San Francisco, and for a county court for each of the counties of the State, with original and appellate jurisdiction, and for the election of appointment of county judges to preside over said courts. Also for a court of sessions for each of the counties, over which should preside the county judge and two associate justices, to be appointed by the judge, or to be chosen by the justices of the peace of the county when elected.

"The term of district judges was for six years and of county judges four years. The district court, the county court and the court of sessions exercised substantially the same jurisdiction as the superior courts now do under our present judicial system. The county judge also acted as surrogate or probate judge, and the court of sessions was charged with all of the duties of the present boards of supervisors for each county.

"As we have had occasion to say elsewhere in speaking of the character of the immigration to this State in 1849–50, we now repeat here what is undeniably true, that there came to the State in those early days the excellence and culture of the older States east of the Mississippi River. It would be difficult to point to a more able body of men, taken altogether than those assembled at Monterey in 1850 to frame a constitution for the State of California. Such men as William M. Gwin, Winfield S. Sherwood, Henry W. Halleck, L. W. Hastings, Jacob R. Snyder, Charles T. Botts, Henry A. Tefft, Thomas O. Larkin, Rodman M. Price, J. McHollingsworth, Myron Norton, Edward Gilbert, Benjamin S. Lippincott, Thomas M. Vermeule, Louis Dent, Abel Stearns and the late Pablo de la Guerra. There were other able, experienced men—merchants, lawyers and farmers. The average age of these men was about thirty-three years; many of them were less than twenty-seven years of age.

"And it has been a matter of frequent assertion that the first Legislature of the State of California contained more able men than any succeeding one.

"The first judge of the district court of the second judicial district, embracing, as we have stated, the counties of Santa Barbara and San Luis Obispo, was Henry A. Tefft, a native of Washington County, New York. At the date of his appointment he was twenty-six years of age and resided at Nipomo, San Luis Obispo County. He served but one year as district judge, having perished at the steamboat landing at San Luis Obispo in the winter of 1851-'52, in endeavoring to land from the steamer in an open boat during a heavy storm.

"Henry Storrow Carnes, still living in Santa Barbara, was appointed by the governor of the State to fill the vacancy caused by the death of Judge Tefft. Carnes held the office until the general election in November, 1852, at which election the late Joaquin Carrillo was elected by the people for the balance of the term. Carrillo continued to hold the office until the year 1863-'64, when the late Don Pablo de la Guerra was elected for the term of six years. De la Guerra held the office until his death in 1873. Walter Murray of San Luis Obispo County, was appointed by the governor to finish the unexpired term. Judge Murray died in June, 1875, and Eugene Fawcett was then appointed by the governor until the next succeeding general election. Judge Fawcett was afterward elected to the office and held the same until the adoption of the new constitution in 1879.

"The first county judge of Santa Barbara County was Joaquin Carrillo. He held the office from the date of the organization of the court in 1851 until his election as District judge in November, 1852, at which time he resigned the office of county judge, and the Hon. Charles Fernald was then appointed by Governor Bigler as his successor."

"Judge Charles Fernald arrived in California in 1849, and in Santa Barbara in 1852. A native of Maine, Judge Fernald had acquired much of his legal training at Dorchester, Massachusetts, where his favorite recreation had been to attend the court of Chief Justice Lemuel Shaw. In attendance upon noted cases, he had had the great privilege of listening to such lights of the bar as Webster, Choate, Benjamin R. Curtis, E. R. Hoar, W. R. P. Washburne, etc., etc. Judge Fernald was elected without opposition, by the people, at every judicial election thereafter until 1861, and held the office until the beginning of 1862, at which time he resigned to enter upon the active practice of his profession. At the time of his appointment to the position of county judge, Judge Fernald was scarcely twenty-two years of age, but he possessed the rare advantage of a thorough and proper training for the discharge of the duties of the office, which few young men then competing here possessed.

"At the resignation of Judge Fernald, Governor Downey appointed as his successor the late J. M. Covarrubias, who held the office until the ensuing general election, when the late Hon. F. J. Maguire was elected; and he continued to hold the office by election up to the time of the adoption of the new constitution.

"From every point of view, the character, integrity and ability, the Bench was an able one, and the records of the Supreme Court show that the decisions of the judges of these courts were rarely, if ever, reversed. And when it is considered that during that period some of the most important principles of law of real property, the construction of the new constitution, the statutes relative thereto, and the rules of the civil law and of the civil law as adopted in Spain and Mexico, were often involved and at issue, it will be admitted that this is high praise.

"At the date of the organization of the above named courts there were here and at the bar from the beginning men of descent and training; among them was Edward Sherman Hoar, a son of the Hon. Samuel Hoar of Concord, Massachusetts; he was a graduate of Harvard and one of the brightest intellects of all that gifted family. He was the confessed leader of the bar of Southern California. Next must be mentioned Augustus F. Hinchman of New Jersey, also a graduate of Harvard and a classmate of Mr. Hoar, a man of varied learning, culture and acquirements. Judge Fernald having been thus early appointed to the Bench, practiced at that time only in the Federal courts, up to the time of his resignation in 1862. Next came James Lancaster Brent, a native of Maryland and brother of the attorney-general of that State, an accomplished orator and advocate, as well as a learned lawyer. Brent resided at Los Angeles and was associated with Jonathan R. Scott, a giant physically and mentally, who came from St. Louis, Missouri. Although resident at Los Angeles, they often appeared before the courts of Santa Barbara and San Luis Obispo counties. Benjamin Hayes, a resident of Los Angeles, and afterward judge of the first judicial district for many years, often appeared in the courts of this county prior to his election as judge. Myron Norton, one of the leaders of the bar of Los Angeles, was often called here in important cases.

"Then came L. C. Granger, who recently died in Chico, Butte County, a man of recognized ability and learning. William J. Graves, who came from St. Louis, Missouri, to San Luis Obispo, became well known throughout the State as a man of marked ability at the bar, and deeply learned in the law; he was a worthy competitor of the able men before mentioned. Well worthy of mention comes Russell Heath, now living at the Carpenteria, who came to this State and settled in this county about the beginning of 1851. Mr. Heath was a native of Little Falls, Herkimer County, New York, being a lineal descendant of General Heath, of Revolutionary fame. He made the journey to California overland on horseback through Northern Mexico. From the time of his arrival here, early in 1851, at about twenty-three years of age, he took a prominent position at the bar. He was appointed by Judge Fernald, then presiding judge of the court of sessions, to the important position of district attorney in January, 1853. He discharged the duties of the office judiciously and with great intelligence. In 1856 a strong man was needed for sheriff of this county, and Judge Fernald selected Mr. Heath for that position, which he held until 1854, and his administration was strong and gave great satisfaction to the people. Since that time Mr. Heath has creditably represented this county in the State Legislature two terms.

"Early in 1852, Eugene Liés appeared here as one amongst the most versatile at this bar. He was born in the city of New Orleans, of French parentage. Early in life he was taken to Paris, where he was educated and trained to the bar. Returning to this country, his parents settled in New York, and young Liés was admitted to the bar in that State, whence he came directly to Santa Barbara County, and here commenced his professional career, achieving pronounced success. In 1859–'60, he was elected to the Legislature of this State, and at the close of the session of that year he took up his abode in the city of San Francisco, attaining immediate recognition as among the ablest of the bar of that city. He was an accomplished linguist, an able lawyer, and a successful advocate. With him was associated in practice here and at San Francisco Albert Packard, of Rhode Island. Mr. Packard had early come to this State and settled in Los Angeles. He was recognized as a man of unusually strong intellect. Then last, but not least, must be mentioned Charles E. Huse, from Newburyport, Massachusetts. He was a graduate of Harvard, where he took a course of study for the ministry, afterwards adopting the profession of law, becoming a painstaking, laborious and zealous practitioner. There were many others who occasionally appeared in our courts, such as Parker H. French, the late D. S. Gregory, and until his death recently Superior Judge of San Luis Obispo County; Hon. Francis J. Maguire, afterwards County Judge; E. O. Crosby, who had been a member of the Constitutional Convention, and Walter Murray, of San Luis Obispo, a laborious, reliable and successful practitioner up to the time of his appointment to the bench, as before stated.

"All of these men were lawyers of marked ability and learning, and compared favorably with the members of the bar in any part of the State. And, while later on in the '70s men like Fawcett and other able young men came to the bar here, we feel warranted in expressing the opinion that the men we have named were altogether exceptional in point of ability and learning. They had to deal with new questions and principles in settling the law in many of its branches, and well their work was done, as the reports of their cases in the Supreme Court will abundantly show."

The machinery of government of Santa Barbara County went into working in August, 1850: Joaquin Carrillo was county and probate judge. The first case brought before him regarded the estate of James Scott, deceased, who had been a partner in trade of Captain Wilson. The will was approved, and N. A. Den and Pablo de la Guerra were appointed appraisers.

When Henry A. Tefft took his seat as judge of the Second Judicial District August 5, 1850, John M. Huddars acting as Clerk, Eugene Liés, of New York, was admitted to practice, and he was sworn in as interpreter and translator. José Antonio de la Guerra y Carrillo having been judge of the Court of the First Instance, the records of that court were demanded from, and refused by, the Alcalde Joaquin de la Guerra, perhaps to show contempt for this new court which superseded the old authorities.

The court ordered made a county seal, described as follows:

"Around the margin the words, *County Court of Santa Barbara County*, with the following device in the center: A female figure holding in her right hand a balance, and in her left a rod of justice; above the figure a rising sun, and below, the letters CAL.

The first district attorney was Edward S. Hoar. He returned in 1857 to his old home at Concord, Massachusetts. It is said that the clerk of this court was a mighty hunter and fisherman, and that he was wont to carry about in his coat-pocket the memorandum book which contained the only court records kept for some months. Judge Fernald pronounces this story apocryphal, however.

The first sheriff was José Antonio Rodriguez; he was killed early in 1850, on the present site of the gas wells at Summerland. He was leading a party of some fifty men in pursuit of those who murdered the Reed family at San Miguel, in San Luis Obispo County, and, disapproving of the reluctance of his followers to close with the murderers, Rodriguez dashed forward and tore from the saddle one burly fellow, who thereupon raised himself upon his knees and killed the sheriff with a shot-gun. One of the miscreants plunged into the sea and swam out beyond the kelp, where he was drowned; the others were captured, tried, and shot at Santa Barbara.

The next sheriff was named Heavy. He was waylaid and shot on the Santa Ynes mountains.

J. W. Burroughs was the first county clerk, auditor, coroner, and justice of the peace. His deputy was A. F. Hinchman, now of San Francisco. Nicholas A. Den was made foreman of the first grand jury, but the names of the other jurymen were not recorded. A better record was kept of the next session, held April 7, 1851; the following persons were empaneled: Antonio Arellanes, John Kays, Rafael Gonzalez, Octaviano Gutierrez, Manuel Cota, Raimundo Olivera, Estevan Ortega, George Nidever, Augustus F. Hinchman, José Lorenzano, Juan Rodriguez, Ygnacio Ortega, Antonio Maria Ortega, Guillermo Carrillo, Edward S. Hoar, A. F. Hinchman, José Carrillo, Lewis T. Burton, Augustin Janssens, Joaquin Carrillo, Vicente Hill. Eight individuals were fined $25 each for not answering to their names on this panel. The grand jury found indictments for murder against Guadalupe Sanchez and Francisco Figueroa, and offered a complaint against the jail as unfit for use. In the case of the People vs. Francisco Romero et al., the witnesses were discharged, and the sureties relieved, as the defendants had escaped from custody, because of the jail's insecurity.

The roll of attorneys of Santa Barbara County shows the following names:

J. L. Barker, A. T. Bates, I. R. Baxley, S. W. Bouton, J. J. Boyce, R. B. Canfield, J. G. Deadrick, Charles Fernald, William Gallaher, G. H. Gould, E. B. Hall, F. Leslie Kellogg, Thomas McNulta, Walter H. Nixon, A. A. Oglesby, Joseph J. Perkins, S. S. Price, A. E. Putnam, J. T. Richards, C. A. Storke, W. C. Stratton, J. W. Taggart, B. F. Thomas, C. A. Thompson, J. B. Wentling, H. G. Crane, W. N. Haverly, C. F. Carrier, J. F. Conroy, W. P. Butcher, W. C. Gammill, Grant Jackson, W. S. Day, E. R. McGrath, Eugene W. Squier, Walter B. Cope and Paul R. Wright, all of Santa Barbara; B. F. Bayley and W. W. Broughton, of Lompoc; S. E. Crow and Caleb Sherman, of Santa Maria.

Many of these are not now engaged in active practice.

Among those now actively engaged in the practice in the center of the county, prominently stands Hon. Charles Fernald, whose biography is given at length elsewhere.

J. J. Boyce is a native of Utica, New York, where he was born April 28, 1852. He entered the law office of Seymour & Weaver, upon arriving at majority, and pursued for a time the study of law. He came to Santa Barbara in 1876, and resumed his law studies under the instruction of Judge Fernald. He was admitted to the practice of law by the Supreme Court, in 1878, and has since been actively engaged in the practice of his profession at Santa Barbara.

R. B. Canfield graduated from Columbia, in 1862, and studied law in the law school attached to his alma mater. He came to the Pacific Coast in 1865, and spent three years in the mines in Nevada. In 1868, returning to New York and resuming his legal studies, he was admitted to the New York State bar, in 1869. In 1876 he came to Santa Barbara, where he has since resided. Mr. Canfield was married in 1873 to Mrs. Davidson. Mr. Canfield is a keen lawyer, with a judicial brain. He is quiet and unobtrusive in his habits, and does not seek notoriety. By appointment he has for a year or more presided over the Superior Court of this county, and has won golden opinions from his constituency.

Ephraim B. Hall is a native of Virginia, born in 1823. He has occupied in his native State many offices of great trust and responsibility. At one time he was Attorney General of the State, and at another judge of the *nisi prius* courts of the county in which he resided. He was also a loyal member of the convention that passed the ordinance of secession, by which Virginia attempted to sever its relations with the sister States. He is now declining the active business of the county.

Thomas McNulta was born in New York in 1845. He possesses to a large degree the confidence of the community. He was admitted to the Illinois bar about 1871, and for several years parcticed law with his brother, Hon. John McNulta, at Bloomington, Illinois. Coming to Santa Barbara in 1874 he soon became a prominent member of the local bar. He has, at various times, held the office of city attorney and district attorney, and has had charge of many important cases. He is an eloquent speaker, somewhat inclined to be impetuous.

B. F. Thomas was born in Missouri, February 22, 1846. He studied law with ex-Congressman Tully, of San José, and was admitted to the bar January 13, 1874. His first labor in a legal way was at Guadalupe in this county. In 1875, Mr. Thomas became district attorney and filled the office with credit. He is a slow thinker, but of great industry and perseverance, by the aid of which he has become a prominent member of the local bar, and has secured a lucrative practice.

Jarrett T. Richards was born in Chambersburg, Pennsylvania, in 1842. After spending three years in Europe in classical study, he returned to his native land, and entered Columbia College Law School, where he graduated in 1866, receiving a special prize of $150 for a thesis on municipal law. After graduation he went to Erie, Pennsylvania, where he alternated the practice of law with editorial work. In 1868 he came to Santa Barbara, and formed a law partnership with Hon. Charles Fernald. He has been mayor of Santa Barbara and city attorney. In 1879 he was nominated for Associate Justice of the Supreme Court, but with his ticket was defeated. Mr. Richards is a strong and classical writer. His mind is eminently judicial, and he is probably better fitted to act as a judge than as a pleader. His advice is much solicited.

W. C. Stratton was born in New York December 14, 1826. He was a resident of New Jersey from 1849 to 1856, coming to California in the latter year. In 1858 he was elected to the Legislature by the Democrats of Placer County, and then became Speaker of the House. From 1860 to 1870, he was librarian of the State Library. In January, 1873, he came to Santa Barbara, and was for several years attorney for the city. Mr. Stratton has a lucrative practice, which he has obtained by thorough study of his cases. He is a good jury pleader, and coming into court with his cases thoroughly understood and properly prepared, he generally is successful.

W. S. Day was born in Smith County, Tennessee, on the 14th day of March, 1848; was educated in the common schools of Illinois. Began the study of law in 1872, at Jonesboro, Illinois, under Judge Monroe C. Crawford, and was admitted to practice before the Supreme Court of Illinois in June, 1874. He then practiced law in the city of Jonesboro from 1874 to 1888, holding during that time the positions of State's Attorney and member of the Legislature. He removed to Santa Barbara in June, 1888, and at once formed a partnership with Paul R. Wright, an old and respected attorney of the city of Santa Barbara, under the name of Wright & Day. Mr. Day is a clear, methodical thinker, and has in his short residence at Santa Barbara added to his previous excellent reputation.

S. S. Price was born in Morristown, New Jersey, on the 27th day of January, 1840; was educated at Lombard College, at Galesburg, Illinois, and was studying law at Jerseyville, Illinois, at the outbreak of the war. He enlisted in Company F, Fourteenth Illinois Infantry in 1861, and followed the fortunes of that regiment until the battle of Shiloh, in which he was badly wounded, necessitating his discharged. Having partially recovered from his wounds, he renewed his legal studies at the Law School of Michigan University, where he graduated in the spring of 1865. Opening a law office in Salem, Missouri, he practiced for three years and more in Dent County, and then moved to Falls City, Nebraska. From 1869 until 1883 he was actively engaged in legal pursuits at Falls City, and moved to Santa Barbara in 1883. His old wounds having disabled him from active practice, his work in Santa Barbara has been that of an adviser and counsellor rather than advocate. In 1886 he was elected District Attorney.

Walter B. Cope is a son of Hon. W. W. Cope, of the Supreme Court Commission. Walter B. Cope came to Santa Barbara a few years since, and at the last election but one he was chosen for District Attorney. The election of November, 1890, has placed him upon the bench of the Superior Court of this county.

CRIMES.

Since the dispersion of the bands of outlaws gathered during the disorder of the transition period Santa Barbara has been, all things considered, reasonably free from crime. There have been notable cases, but these were of individual, rather than public, bearing. The most conspicuous crimes committed hereabouts were the following: In January, 1864, Mr. and Mrs. Wilson Corliss were murdered, and their bodies consumed in their dwelling; the criminals were not discovered. Later in that year, Samuel Barthman was robbed and murdered, and his body concealed in the woods between Lompoc and La Purisima. His murderers were discovered and brought to justice. In June, 1868, one Bonilla, a young man of twenty years, shot to death Mr. Domingo Abadie, a respected and prominent citizen, in a quarrel. Bonilla was sentenced to thirty-five years' imprisonment. In January, 1874, William Shedd, a cruel and intemperate husband, stabbed his wife to death, and then blew his own brains out. Perhaps the most flagrant case was the murder of John C. Norton, a rancher on Rincon Point; Norton's wife had an intrigue with one Jack Cotton, a farm-hand of her husband, and the two killed Norton and buried him in the sand-hills. Then, giving out that he had died in Los Angeles, they disposed of his property and left the country together. The crime was discovered, and the guilty pair captured in Nevada, and returned to Santa Barbara for trial, being sentenced to imprisonment for life.

There have been a few murders of minor notoriety, the perpetrators in some cases remaining undiscovered. There was, too, early in the '80's, a good deal of excitement over the stage robberies committed in the western portion of the county by Dick Fellows. He was a man of education, who from confinement wrote very good articles for publication. His characteristics and the desperate efforts he made for liberty aroused much sympathy for him, notwithstanding which he was sent to prison.

The crime, the case *par excellence* of Santa Barbara, was

THE GRAY-GLANCEY MURDER.

This was one of those criminal cases which become *causes célébrés* throughout the State. Theodore M. Glancey, a native of Illinois, came to California in 1873, and was for a time editor and general manager of the Los Angeles *Herald*. Resigning this position, he had removed to Placer County, and here and in Sutter County he was engaged in the journalistic profession. After a few years he was tendered the editorship of the *Press* at Santa Barbara, and, accepting, he removed here, conducting the *Press* with the same devotion to truth and duty that had marked his career hitherto. He was a veteran of the civil war, a man of nerve, and true to his convictions. He was, further, a man of liberal education, with legal training, and just views of matters in general. He was polite and urbane in manner, notwithstanding the positive character of his mentality.

Clarence Gray came to this county in 1870, and was immediately recognized as its natural leader by the lawless element composed of the roughs, the gamblers and disorderly parties in general. While there were not more than 200 of these characters, they were formidable, holding in many instances the balance of power. Gray had a bad record, so far as it was known. It was asserted that his real name was Patrick McGinnis, and it was understood that he had been closely connected with the Molly Maguire assassins in Pennsylvania, which State he had been obliged to leave. He was reckless, unscrupulous, audacious, brilliant, enterprising, witty and obtrusive, being ready always to thrust himself into notice. Ostensibly a lawyer, his knowledge of the law consisted mainly of an understanding of its defects and weaknesses, whereby he became the natural defender of violators of the law. Like all men of that class, he relied upon personal prowess for security in his personal rights, and he had committed personal assaults on many occasions. It is said that he had been arrested more than twenty times for breaking the peace. While nominally a Catholic, he beat a Catholic priest to insensibility for a reproof justly administered, and was fined therefor. When a fire occurred in the *Press* office, he was so strongly suspected of having caused it that he left the State for a year or two, but returned and resumed his former career.

On one occasion the Republican party nominated him for District Attorney, and, in consequence of his bad repute, a public meeting was held to consider the means of defeating his election, which, it was deemed, would endanger the safety of the community. Nevertheless, so strong was the lawless party that he came within seven votes of election. When the new constitution was adopted in 1880, the country was in doubt whether the officials elected the previous year should complete the usual terms, or whether a new set would be elected. Pending the decision the Republicans held a convention and nominated candidates for the supposed vacancies, among them Clarence Gray for District Attorney. When the Supreme Court decided that no election was necessary that season, the *Press*, of which Mr. Glancey was editor, commenting upon the reasons for satisfaction therefor, said: "Not the least of these in this county is the fact that the Republicans here will be relieved of the necessity of defeating the candidate for District Attorney. The nomination was disgraceful in every respect, and while it is extremely disagreeable for earnest Republicans to take such a course in a presidential year, there is no difference of opinion among those who have the good of the party at heart. They are convinced that all such candidates should be beaten, and Republican conventions taught, if they do not realize it already, that the decent people of Santa Barbara County will not submit to having the officer for the administration of justice chosen from among the hoodlums and law-breakers." While this language was moderate, compared to what had been printed many times before, Gray's friends urged that it was a gratuitous insult, as no election was to take place, and Gray set about finding the party responsible for the article. Meeting John P. Stearns in Judge Hatch's office, he inquired if Stearns was responsible, and was met with a prompt "I am, sir!" Nevertheless, something, possibly the number present, induced him to defer shooting until a more convenient season. Later, he met Stearns at home, but again postponed his proposed punishment. On the evening following the issue of the article, Gray met Glancey, and inquired if he was responsible for the article in question. Glancey replied in the affirmative, whereupon Gray drew a revolver and attempted to shoot, when Glancey caught his wrists, saying, "You shall not draw a revolver on me; I am unarmed." A bystander separated them, but Gray again leveled his revolver and fired at Glancey whilst retreating through the door of the Occidental Hotel; the ball took fatal effect, striking Glancey in the wrist, and thence passing into the abdomen, and out near the hip. Glancey's vitality enabled him to walk to a hotel in the same block, where he fell. Gray meanwhile followed him, endeavoring to obtain another shot. Glancey was attended by three physicians, but was past help, and died the next day.

While the lawless element justified Gray's deed, the better portion of the community emphatically denounced it. The press of the State, too, condemned the dastardly act unequivocally, as did the pulpit unitedly.

Yet hardly were the funeral ceremonies over before Gray's friends were planning an active defense, $4,000 were raised to employ counsel, and all the technicalities of the law were invoked to delay or thwart justice. Although he had uttered numerous threats that Stearns or Glancey must die before night, Gray pleaded self-defense and sought to prove by witnesses that Glancey made the first attack. The jury failed to agree, and the case was transferred to San Mateo County, where Gray was found guilty and sentenced to twenty years' imprisonment. Eminent legal talent was employed in this trial. One most censurable feature of the case was that Gray was permitted many privileges seldom granted to persons on trial for high crimes, in that he was allowed, during his term of incarceration, to visit processions, shows, etc., and to visit and dine at the houses of his friends. His partisans made application for a new trial, which was granted on such singular grounds as to become historical. This feature is explained in the appended statement of Justice Thornton:

"The trial commenced on the first of June, 1881, and terminated on the morning of the 12th of the same month, about 9 o'clock, when the jury rendered the verdict, and were discharged. As soon as the jury was complete, they were, by the order of the court, placed in charge of the sheriff, and instructed as to their duties. They remained in charge of the sheriff, not being allowed to separate until they were discharged on the morning of the 12th. After the jury was complete, and before the cause was submitted to them, on the afternoon of the 11th of June, about 5 o'clock, a period of about eight days, four five-gallon kegs of beer were brought into the room at the Tremont House, where the jury was kept by the sheriff, of which about seventeen and a half gallons (of the beer) were drank by them; that during the same period a two-gallon demijohn of wine was brought in and drank by them; that during the same period some of the jurors drank claret wine, amounting to three bottles, at their meals; while some of them drank whiskey at their meals; that all this drinking was done before the case was submitted to them on the afternoon of the 11th of June; that on the 11th of June, during the noon recess, two of the jurors procured each a flask of whiskey; that one of the jurors (Price, the foreman) drank nothing; that all the drinking by the jurors was without the permission of the court, or the consent of the defendant, or of the counsel engaged in the cause, and, in fact, without the knowledge of either of them; that all the beer, wine, and whiskey drank were procured by such of the jurors as desired it of their own notion and at their own expense; that the verdict was agreed on about 8:30 o'clock on the morning of the 12th. Further, the evidence affords strong reason to suspect that one of the jurors drank so much while deliberating on the verdict as to unfit him for the proper discharge of his duty. * * * For the reason above indicated, the judgment and order are reversed, and the cause remanded for a new trial."

This conclusion was concurred in by Justices Myrick, McKinstry, Ross and Sharpstein. The third trial of Gray occurred in the same county, in December, 1882, and it resulted in his acquittal.

The summer of 1890 has been stigmatized by two very flagrant murders—that of "Billy" Kays, by Eduardo Espinosa, in a street brawl, and the unprovoked slaying of Mary Dezirello, an innocent and worthy girl, brutally shot by a worthless fellow named Ramon Lopez, in revenge for her refusal to accept his addresses. The wanton and dastardly character of this crime so aroused the citizens that Lopez was taken to Los Angeles to avert a lynching. These two murderers are now on trial.

THE PRESS.

The first newspaper in this county was the Santa Barbara *Gazette* issued weekly by Wm. B. Keep and R. B. Hubbard, practical printers. Its first publication was on May 24, 1855. During the first six months one page was printed in Spanish for the benefit of citizens of Spanish descent. Old residents declare that it was edited as ably as any provincial paper in the State, and that it did great credit to the intelligence and the enterprise of its publishers. Its circulation was limited, as was the population, and it maintained only while it had the publication of legal notices. A law was passed by the Legislature which substituted for advertising the posting of public notices, in writing, in three public places, thus rendering unnecessary publication of such notices. Therefore the proprietors of the *Gazette* sold out to Torres & Fossas, who printed in Spanish one side of the sheet, Democratic in politics, and in English the other, of Whig proclivities, thus aiming to suit all tastes and all parties. After one year the publishers removed with their plant to San Francisco; but they continued to issue the Santa Barbara *Gazette*, as well as the San Luis Obispo *Gazette* and the Monterey *Gazette*, all alike, except in the headings. These papers were sent for distribution by every mail, which arrived by steamer, and only twice a month. The mail was carried from Santa Barbara to San Luis Obispo on horseback, as no stage roads then existed, and vehicles could not go up the coast. Thus the news was usually somewhat stale before reaching the subscribers. The *Gazette* continued, printed in San Francisco and brought here for distribution for about a year, when it ceased publication.

The next newspaper was the Santa Barbara

Post, first issued in May, 1868, printed and published by E. B. Boust. After about a year, one-half of this paper was sold to Joseph A. Johnson, who became one of its editors. He afterwards purchased the other half, and changed the name to the Santa Barbara *Press*, July 1, 1869. It is said that the efforts of Mr. Johnson did more to build up this county and draw population to it than the labors of all the other men combined; and that he added millions to the value of property in this county. The *Daily Press* was first issued July 1, 1871. The *Press* passed into the hands of H. G. Otis, and soon declined sadly. After many vicissitudes this paper has finally been established on a satisfactory basis, and it is now issued as both daily and weekly, by the *Press* Publishing Company, Walter H. Nixon managing editor. This is the third oldest newspaper in Southern California. It is not a party organ, but is Republican in politics.

The Santa Barbara *Times* was established in the interest of settlers, its first number being issued January 30, 1870. After various changes, it was absorbed by the *Press* in 1874.

The Santa Barbara *Index*, established by Wood & Sefton, was first issued August 31, 1872. It was subsequently sold to William F. Russell.

The Santa Barbara *News*, established by Al. Pettigrove and Miss Nettie La Grange, was issued as a daily, May 3, 1875. Mr. Pettygrove subsequently became the sole owner, and continued the publication until it was merged in the *Press*, May 15, 1876.

A small sheet styled the Santa Barbara *Tribune* was issued weekly for over two years, by a lad of twelve years, named Walcott. Its publication was suspended at last, owing to the ill-health of its youthful conductor, whose enterprise and ability attracted considerable attention.

In January, 1878, Fred. A. Moore started the *Democrat*, a weekly, which discontinued issue after some six months, when Mr. Moore started the *Independent*, as a weekly, with Warren Chase as editor. In 1879 Mr. Moore bought out and consolidated with his paper the daily and weekly *Advertiser*. He sold the *Independent* to G. P. Tebbitts, who still continues its publication. The *Independent* was first issued as a daily in 1884. In politics it is nominally independent, albeit with Democratic proclivities.

The *Weekly Herald* was established in April, 1885, by Messrs. Felix Lane and S. W. Candy. In 1886, Mr. Lane became the sole proprietor of this paper, which he conducts at present. The *Herald* is the only avowed organ of the Democratic party in this county.

Outside of Santa Barbara, there are issued in the county the following journals, all weeklies: The *Reconstructor*, at Summerland; *Argus*, Santa Ynes; *Progress*, Los Alamos; *Times*, and also *Graphic*, Santa Maria; *Record*, and also *People's Journal*, Lompoc.

THE EASTERN PORTION OF SANTA BARBARA.

The Ortega hill is a lateral spur from the mountains, perhaps 600 feet high, projecting into the sea so boldly as to make difficult the building of a road around it. The beach below the hill is passable at low water, but at high tide the surf dashes against the rocks, cutting off the passage. This was a point of dread to the earlier boards of supervisors, for they were continually called upon to repair the road, this then being the only avenue of communication with what is now Ventura County. The road was built along the edge of the bluff, and every rain would so damage it by landslides, etc., as to necessitate costly repairs. Many thousands of dollars were expended before the completion of the fine grade around and over the hill. This was also a serious stumbling-block to the railway companies.

MONTECITO.

To the eastward of Santa Barbara lies a tract of land extending easterly to the Ventura County line, a distance of some fifteen miles, with a breadth of seven or eight miles, from the channel on the south of the summit of the Santa Barbara Range on the north. The face of this section is diversified by hills, plains and valleys, and it comprehends some of the most valuable agricultural lands in California.

Beginning some four miles east of Santa Barbara is the district of Montecito, one of the most favored sections imaginable. All that productive soil, benignant climate, pure water and the most striking scenery to be produced by the juxtaposition of sea, and vale, and mountain—all that such elements can contribute to the charm of a section has been bestowed upon Montecito.

This valley of the "Little Wood" is not large; its length, parallel with the coast, is about seven miles; and its width, between shore and mountain, three-quarters of a mile to two miles wide. Northward are the Santa Ynes mountains, of panoramic beauty; eastward the hills between this and the Carpenteria Valley, and westward the hills running down to the shore between the Montecito and Santa Barbara. Southward, beyond the sweep of water, the Channel Islands lie, with glimpses of the open sea glinting between them.

This, as has often been said, is a valley of homes, nestling among the groups of live-oaks that give its name to the district.

The first American settler in this valley was Newton M. Coats, who arrived in 1858. A full flood of tillers of the soil and men of leisure have followed after. Messrs. Dinsmore, Hayne, S Bond and Robert W. Smith, who became residents here in 1867-'68, are among the oldest and most prominent settlers. This has come to be one of the show spots of Southern California. The bulk of the improvements have been made by men of leisure and means, who have brought their families hither to form attractive homes amidst the rare charms afforded here by the attractions of balmy climate, fertile soil and picturesque and romantic scenery and surroundings. In the eastern part of this section is the San Ysidro Rancho, belonging to Johnston & Goodrich, from which an annual yield of about 300,000 oranges and 100,000 lemons finds a ready market. Down the valley, towards the ocean, is the old Coats Rancho, fertile and heavily timbered, now the property of Messrs. Sperry and Crocker, who are making upon it extensive improvements, planting orchards, etc. The "Hunter Place" contains one of the finest general orchards in the section. At "Inglenook," a pretty red cottage shows through the branches of a fine olive grove, in profitable bearing. Along the Hot Springs avenue is a succession of tasteful dwellings with carefully-tended grounds. Among these are:—the Gould mansion, with its hedged grounds, its leafy oaks and rippling streams; the Hall cottage, with clustering vines and its smooth lawns, commanding a broad outlook down the coast; the Magee homestead, where stands Montecito's famous grape-vine; the high, many-gabled Anderson villa, and above it a residence of true Southern aspect, as well it may be, since here lives Colonel Hayne, of the celebrated Southern family of that name; across from Colonel Hayne's is the fine collection of palms and other handsome plants of the Sawyer—formerly the Bond—place, where thrive in great luxuriance many rare shrubs and trees. West of the avenue, on a broad ridge which divides the valley into two parts, often distinguished as "Upper" and "Lower" Montecito, stands prominently in an orange grove the comfortable home at "Riven Rock," the Stafford place. On a knoll toward the sea is the dwelling of N. K. Wade, commanding a superb view on all sides. In the "Upper" Montecito, west of Mr. Stafford's place, are the dwellings of Messrs. Stoddard and Stevens, and above them, toward the mountains, the picturesque home of Mr. Eaton, full of artistic treasures collected at home and abroad.

The situation and climate of this valley in many respects resemble those of the celebrated Riviera of Italy, except that the *mistral*, the chilly afternoon wind, does not blow here. Frost is a very rare visitor in this valley, and tender exotics thrive well here. There are many fine collections of choice plants in this valley, embracing vines, shrubs and trees of the Eastern States, as well as rarer specimens from the old world, South America, and the Pacific Islands. The banana here ripens fully, the oranges raised here are particularly juicy and delicate of flavor, while figs, nectarines, lemons and apricots are exceptionally fine. Strawberry plants bear abundantly throughout the year, and have been known to bear fruit in thirty days from planting. The odors of fragrant flowers develop exceptionally, and the manufacture of perfumery is a potential future industry. Twenty or more varieties of palm are grown here, including the "Toddy Palm," the Coquito, various dracoenas, the "Umbrella Palm," "Thatch Palm," "Royal Palm," wild date and others. Pomegranates, yuccas, guavas, alligator pears, chirimoyas, etc., all grow here as if in their native habitat. This valley has, even in the dry season of summer, a notably fresh and green appearance, due to the large number of non-deciduous trees and shrubs. Although irrigation is seldom used here, except for citrus fruits, yet the water supply is ample. A local company brings down water in pipes from the Hot Springs stream, and the subterranean flow is large, wholesome and easily obtained by sinking wells.

The famous "Big Grape-vine" of Montecito grew on the domain of Doña Maria Marcelina Feliz de Dominguez, who died in 1865 at the advanced age of 107 years. Doña Maria Marcelina disclaimed all knowledge of those romantic but apocryphal stories which assign as the origin of this monster plant a shoot given by a lover to his sweetheart for a riding switch, and planted by the girl. The great vine was nearly four feet six inches in circumference, and six feet to the lowest branches. It spread over an area of about an acre, and bore several tons of grapes yearly—it is said sometimes as much as six tons. It was about sixty years old. From the deprivation of its accustomed share of water it died, and in 1876 it was taken up and conveyed to the Centennial Exhibition at Philadelphia, where it was left on show as one of the products of California. On the same estate as the former "big vine," is another, somewhat inferior in size, but still of very large growth, which attracts many visitors. It is said to have been a cutting of the former vine.

Lying as it does contiguous to the sea, Montecito possesses the attractions lent by bathing, boating and fishing; on the other hand, the close vicinity of the mountains give delightful excursions along winding cañon roads and up picturesque trails. The San Ysidro, the Cold Spring and the Hot Springs, all are cañons of many attractions.

This section has a station, Montecito, on

the railway, four miles south of Santa Barbara.

THE HOT SPRINGS.

The Montecito Hot Springs are about six miles from Santa Barbara, beyond Montecito, up quite a steep ascent of the mountains, at about 1,450 feet above the sea.

It is said that while California still appertained to Mexico, and this, as a province, to the crown of Spain, a commission sent out by the government to examine and report upon all the mineral waters then known to exist in Mexico and the Californias, reported most favorably upon the properties of the Montecito springs for the curing of cutaneous diseases. As to their later discovery, the story goes that in 1855, Mr. Wilbur Curtis was wandering in search of some spot which should restore his health, broken in the rough life of the mines, when he chanced upon a party of Indians encamped at the mouth of this cañon. Telling them of his condition, they took him to these springs, and one veteran of over 100 years old told how he had bathed here and drunk since childhood from the waters, to whose virtues he ascribed his longevity. Mr. Curtis drank, bathed, and was healed; and with the genuine American practicality, he took up a claim, foreseeing that this property would be of great value in the future. From a blanket camp, through the progressive stages of a tent, a hut, a cottage, the evolution has progressed to the present conditions, provisions and building materials being carried for years over a rough trail, which has now been widened into a good stage road. Gushing from crevices in the solid rock, on the premises are some thirty mineral springs. Some of these are sulphurous, others saline and chalybeate, ranging in temperature from 99° to 120° Fahrenheit. Seven of the principal springs are used for drinking and bathing purposes.

These waters are of great value in the treatment of rheumatism, gout, joint affections, Bright's disease, liver trouble and bladder irritation; being antacid, considerable benefit may be derived from the waters in dyspepsia, and acid conditions of the blood and urine. Perhaps the greatest benefit accrues from bathing in the sulphurous and saline waters, especially in syphilitic and scrofulous contaminations, grandular enlargements, and chronic skin diseases. The waters much resemble the famous Hot Springs of Arkansas. Of late, the arsenical spring has been developed, with excellent results.

There is now at this resort a good hotel, well managed, with the modern comforts and conveniences, and particular attention is paid to the opening up of trails, etc., to the end of affording diversion and exercise for the guests and patients.

Dr. Brinkerhoff wrote, regarding these springs: "I do not regard the use of these waters by any means as a panacea for 'all the ills which flesh is heir to,' but for the cure of certain diseases they are unmistakably efficacious. I have known some cases which seemed to defy all powers of medication, cured in a surprisingly short space of time by the waters of these springs, advisedly used as a beverage and for bathing purposes. The indiscriminate use of them may be disadvantageous, and even positively injurious, and before resorting to them patients should always consult some experienced physician as to their proper use."

Some two miles beyond El Montecito is

SUMMERLAND.

Summerland is situated six miles from Santa Barbara, on a portion of the old Ortega Rancho. It lies between the sea and the Santa Ynes mountains. Some 1,050 acres of this rancho became the property of H. L.

Williams, who, after the subsidence of the boom of 1886–'88, laid out 160 acres in town lots, and, by means of judicious advertising, collected here a colony of citizens of Spiritualistic belief, who have organized quite a thriving community. Most of the 160 acres has been sold, mainly to mechanics, carpenters, etc., who have found ample employment in the little hamlet, as building has been lively. Some sixty houses have been built, and the population is now about 300; at the recent election some forty-one votes were cast. There are now three stores of general merchandise, shoes and groceries, one blacksmith, one restaurant and bakery, one public school with some thirty pupils, a public library, a postoffice with two daily mails, express office and railway ticket office. The water supply here is lifted by a hydraulic ram to a reservoir on a hill, giving some 200 feet pressure; the water being piped free to every house in the colony.

A very strong impulse has been given to the interest felt in Summerland through the discovery here in June, 1890, of natural gas, in wells tapped near the beach and just above the railway. There are now some nine wells burning, the gas from which is used in Summerland for domestic purposes, illuminating, fuel, etc.; and the Summerland Gas Company, recently organized, expects to bring the gas into Santa Barbara within two months.

Summerland has also fine industrial resources in the shape of the presence on the tract of large beds of superfine brick clay, sewer-pipe clay, limestone, gypsum, and sandstone.

These elements, taken in conjunction with the possibilities for manufacturing afforded by the natural gas product, offer for Summerland a bright commercial future.

Farther down the coast from Summerland lies the fruitful district of

CARPENTERIA.

The central and more thickly settled portion of Carpenteria Valley is twelve miles east of Santa Barbara. This valley was a part of the pueblo lands of Santa Barbara, apportioned out by the prefect to the people, who used these lands as *temporales*, or fields for the cultivation of summer crops. No titles to the soil were given until after the coming of the Americans.

From the point dividing the Montecito and Carpenteria, the beach curves gently to the bold, rocky point at Rincon, giving to the whole valley a southern exposure, it being practically enclosed, moreover, from point to point, by a deep semicircle of mountains, up which open picturesque cañons. Sea and mountains bound a sheltered corner containing about ten square miles of deep and fertile soil, mostly alluvial.

There are also mesa or upland and adobe soils, though in small quantities. The adobe soil is found in inconsiderable tracts, being in patches all through the bottom lands. It is difficult to work, but, when properly treated, very strong and productive.

Thus this valley does not border a stream, but fronts the ocean, extending for eight or nine miles along the beach, giving an area of 8,000 to 10,000 acres. These peculiarities of situation give the climate here characteristics quite different from other sections.

The annual rainfall is about the same as at Santa Barbara. The usual winter temperature is about 60°, and the summer temperature about 65°. The climate is agreeable and healthful. There is some fog in summer, but it originates from the sea, and is of that character called "high fog." It is not insalubrious, and it is considered beneficial to vegetation.

The name of the valley, Carpenteria (Spanish for carpenter-shop), is derived from the existence, in early days, on the bank of one of the streams here, of a workshop of that nature.

In the early history of this valley it was deemed an unsuitable locality for horticultural pursuits, as the existing streams could not be made available for irrigating purposes. Experience showed that the soil, deep and loamy, by proper cultivation could be made to retain so much moisture as to render artificial irrigation unnecessary.

More recently it has been discovered that the water supply is enriched by the existence of artesian water. A weak flow was obtained at seventy feet deep, and an abundant flow at ninety feet. A number of these wells have been sunk, and the new town of Carpenteria is in this manner supplied with pure and cheap water. To the colony grounds on the foot-hill slope between Carpenteria and Fenlon, a supply of mountain water will be piped.

Carpenteria is divided for the most part into small farms; and so wonderfully rich is the soil that a few acres will support a family. The low foot-hills at the base of the mountains are sometimes cultivated to their very summits. All the best of the cañons, being mostly Government land, have been taken up. The chief product of these cañon farms is honey, the bees thriving on the wild flower-food of these sections. On mesas and rolling lands are produced great crops of hay, and wheat and barley produce heavily.

The Lima bean is one of the staple and most profitable products. This crop alone has averaged for some years past 800 tons annually, this being worth $60 per ton, delivered at the wharf, has brought in a revenue of $48,000 per annum.

Almonds and walnuts are extensively raised also, the walnut grove of Mr. Russell Heath, comprising nearly 180 acres, being the largest in California, and producing as high as 3,000 bushels in a season. The same gentleman is a large grower of red peppers, which yield as high as $1,000 in a year. Among the other crops are common and castor beans, corn, potatoes, squashes, flax and barley.

As in most parts of Santa Barbara County, there is produced here a great variety of fruits, as apples, apricots, blackberries, figs, nectarines, olives, pears, peaches, peanuts, plums, strawberries and walnuts.

The products of this section are shipped partly by rail, and partly over the Carpenteria wharf, the property of the Smith Brothers, built in 18—, since which time it has experienced many mishaps, having been rebuilt after at least one severe storm. The wharf proper is 800 feet long, reaching water deep enough for any vessels navigating on this coast. Large and commodious warehouses, with a railway connection to the sea end, render shipping over it safe and easy. Until the advent of the railway, great quantities of lumber were imported, mostly for building and fencing.

A postoffice was established at Carpenteria in 1868, or about ten years after the original settlement here by Americans. The First Baptist Church was dedicated June 1, 1873. The town of Carpenteria is well laid out, the lots for residence purposes being of 50 feet frontage by 140 deep, and business lots 30 x 140 deep. The railway traverses the settlement. The town itself is somewhat scattered, the buildings being rather widely interspersed among the fruitful orchards. Contiguous to the railway station there is a tract of twenty acres, subdivided into town lots, and one block from the line is an elegant hotel, combining the Eastlake and Queen Anne styles, which cost $10,000. There are in the valley congregations of the Baptist, Methodist and Presbyterian churches, and a branch of the Holiness Band, lodges of Knights of Pythias, and Good Templars. There is a capacious hall for public meetings or general assemblages, and there are three school-houses, two general merchandise stores, two saloons, a butcher shop, two blacksmith shops, etc., besides two railway stations. Several new small towns have been projected in this valley.

LA PATERA.

This term is the general designation of the district lying to the west of Santa Barbara, and comprising all that portion of the valley between the city and the Rancho Cañada del Corral. Westward from Santa Barbara, the first grant is the Calera, or Las Positas, of 3,281 acres, made to Narciso Fabregat in 1843, and confirmed to Thomas M. Robbins and Manuela de Tines. Westward of this lies the Rancho Goleta, of 4,440 acres, and beyond that the great Dos Pueblos grant of 15,535 acres, while still farther westward is the Rancho Cañada del Corral.

Since the influx of Americans these grants have been broken into smaller tracts, farmed in a progressive manner, and there is not in California a more productive region than the Patera. This name, by the way, means "the place of ducks," and was applied from the number of that species found upon the *esteros* or lagoons of this section. The greater portion of this region is mesa, that is to say, bench or table-land, of the greatest productiveness. These *mesas* begin at the western extremity of La Patera in a series of low plains or plateaus, some fifty or sixty feet above sea level, and rise to a height of 600 to 800 feet as they approach Santa Barbara. To the westward, a line of low hills starts from the Santa Ynez mountains, and trends toward the coast, west and southwest, completing the inclosure of the valley.

GOLETA.

Goleta (a schooner) was the name given to a rancho of 4,440 acres, granted to Daniel Hill in 1846, by Governor Pio Pico. The soil of large portions of this and other ranchos is of the richest adobe, carrying an uncommon amount of subsoil moisture, probably from the existence of a subsoil pervious to water which allows the upward passage of the moisture from lower depths, whence it is constantly drawn by capillary attraction. This peculiarity insures this section against the failure of crops in dry years.

The little town or village of Goleta was laid off in 1875. As recently as 1877 it contained only a church, a school-house, post-office, store, lumber-yard and blacksmith shop. At the last general election 116 votes were cast at Goleta, which is the polling place for the precinct, whose whole population probably is about 750. There are now two churches, Methodist and Baptist, and a number of shops, business places and dwellings. The school now requires two teachers, has a fine reputation, and about eighty pupils in daily attendance. The community is strongly temperance in principles, and for many years tolerated no saloon. There is one now running, but nearly a mile distant from the village. Goleta is seven and three-fourths miles west of the Santa Barbara postoffice. The town site consists of 250 acres, situated in the southwestern part of the old grant. The shipping is chiefly done over the Goleta wharf, about one mile south of the village, a commodious structure, fully equal to the requirements. This valley originally contained dense forests of live-oak, of which a good many still dot the region, as also do sycamores. There still remain large supplies of wood in the little cañons and along the foot-hills. The varied Goleta soil presents a corresponding degree of eclecticism in its products. The main valley soil, with its peculiarity of moisture already noted, its remarkable depth and richness, produces, without irrigation, a surprising variety of farm and orchard products. Apples, peaches, pears, prunes, lemons, figs, loquats and English walnuts rarely fail to yield abundant crops.

Almost every variety of garden vegetables grows luxuriantly. This district is especially famous for its enormous squashes, which are continually awarded the premiums at the county fairs. One prize squash weighed over 270 pounds. Another was so large that, when it was bisected, the eighteen-year-old daughter of the farmer who grew the mammoth was placed in the cavity, and the halves were closed about her! This incident having given rise to a fable to the effect that eighteen-year-old maidens are sometimes found in Goleta squashes, it is said that a lively demand grew up among bachelor farmers for seeds of this remarkable and desirable variety of "garden truck!" The best lands hereabouts will produce ten or fifteen tons of squashes to the acre, twenty or thirty tons of beets, or one ton of beans. Until quite of late, farmers considered beans the most profitable of the crops, but now they find that other products yield better returns. A few have tried pampas grass culture with very satisfactory results, one crop amounting to 250,000 plumes, selling at $40 per 1,000, which realizes as high as $1,600 per acre. Dairying, too, appears to pay better than ordinary farming. But the most promising industry seems to be the culture of the English walnut, of which the natural home seems to be this valley. One six-year-old orchard brought its owner $30 per acre, while from orchards of fifteen to seventeen years old as much as $200 per acre is realized.

At one time several years' experiments proved that tobacco could readily be produced in the Goleta region, one farm yielding 60,000 pounds per annum, or 5,000 pounds to the acre. The San José vineyard is one of Goleta's notable places, containing 2,400 vines planted by the Mission Fathers nearly a century ago, and at least an equal number planted by Mr. James McCaffrey, the present owner, of late years. This vineyard has produced an average product of 8,000 gallons of excellent wine yearly. The Santa Barbara nursery, owned by Mr. Joseph Sexton, is perhaps the chief show-place of Goleta, from the character of its stock, which includes forty acres of useful and ornamental trees, hundreds of rose-bushes, some 200 species of pinks and carnations, and many beautiful floricultural specialties. The San Antonio Dairy Farm also is a conspicuous feature of Goleta, and a source of good revenue.

Goleta is on the former site of an Indian village, the residence of the aboriginal princess Ciacut. The antiquarian has found here grounds for delightful revels, and about ten tons of Indian relics found in this locality have been shipped to the Smithsonian at Washington.

In the cliff rocks adjoining the wharf is found asphaltum in vast quantities, and of the purest quality. The deposit is in fissures and pockets. During the past twenty years probably 30,000 tons of asphaltum from this place have been shipped, going mainly to San Francisco, and bringing from $12 to $20 per ton.

The Dos Pueblos Rancho was granted to Nicholas A. Den, but he dying the property passed to his widow, who was a daughter of Daniel Hill, and to her family. Through recent subdivisions this rancho is now in the ownership of the Den heirs, the estate of John Edwards, G. C. Welch, S. Rutherford, L. G. Dreyfus, the Tecolote Land and Water

Company, the Hollister estate, Elwood Cooper, C. A. Storke, J. W. Swett, Mrs. S. Tyler, W. W. Stow, and W. N. Roberts, the last two under title through Daniel Hill, of the Goleta, to whom N. A. Den sold during his lifetime. About two-thirds of the original rancho is arable land. Mr. G. C. Welch sold to Mr. J. H. Williams some 700 acres of the old Den place, including the home rancho-house, where he has founded the seaside town of Naples.

Six miles beyond Goleta is the famous Rancho Elwood, owned by Elwood Cooper. Ground was broken here in 1870, and by 1878 Mr. Cooper had planted 200 vines, 400 assorted fruit trees, including apple, peach, plum, cherry, etc., 200 fig, 3,500 olive, 4,000 English walnut, 12,500 almond, and 25,000 eucalyptus. This tree, it may be said, was introduced into Southern California by Mr. Cooper, whose rancho is bordered by splendid rows thereof, comprising about fifty varieties, whose growth is almost marvelous. It is estimated that they aggregate 1,000,000 trees. Mr. Cooper's acreage was formerly 2,000, now reduced to about 1,700. This place is a veritable botanical garden, containing over 1,000 species of trees and plants from all over the world, from the various climates of the temperate and the tropical zones. For, although slight frosts fall here in winter, they are not sufficient to injure the most delicate plants. While this soil is excellently adapted for citrus-fruit growing, only enough for family use is raised of these varieties. An interest which has been promoted lately is the raising of Japanese persimmons, a fruit which grows finely here, and which, as it contains more sugar than most fruits, is when properly cured a very palatable and wholesome article. The principal market for this product is Chicago, as also for nuts. Of the 12,500 almond trees already mentioned, only about one-half now remain, covering 200 or 300 acres; and while the yield per tree is not great, the aggregate is a good many tons of almonds per year, and as these nuts bring a high price, even a small crop pays better than grain-growing.

Of walnut trees, which must be planted on the best soil, there are about 3,000, which are very prolific. Of walnuts and almonds together, some twelve or fourteen car-loads are raised annually. Of olive trees there are about 8,000 in various stages of bearing, which will yield, when all come into bearing fully, 50,000 bottles of oil. The yield from the crop now on the trees is estimated at 25,000 bottles. This is a crop which produces in alternate years, requiring rest for the trees between crops. Mr. Cooper's oil is considered among the best made in this State or in Europe, and it is sold all over the United States. To the perfecting of this branch Mr. Cooper has given most careful study of foreign methods, and the results of much exercise of inventive genius on his own part, many of his appliances being of his own devising. Mr. Cooper's profits are greater because the location of his orchards and his careful methods of cultivation do away with the need for irrigation. The soil here is a sandy loam, adobe, clayey, and deep cañon soil or alluvial detritus. It may be said further that here is perhaps the largest and most varied collection of flowers and ornamental shrubs and plants to be found anywhere on the Pacific coast, outside of public parks or ornamental grounds. As indicating the fecundity of yield, it may be said that from one Sicily lemon tree here no less than 5,000 lemons were picked in one season.

THE FAMOUS HOLLISTER PLACE

includes about 3,200 acres of the old Dos Pueblos grant, lying about twelve miles west of Santa Barbara, about five-sixths of it being rich, arable land, adapted for most agricultural pursuits. The tract extends one and one-half miles along the highway, and has a depth of over three miles back to the mountains. Through it run three streams of living water, ample for irrigation. The soil is mostly made up of detritus from the mountain range, and it is of exceeding fertility. This property is approached by a broad highway from Santa Barbara. Colonel William Wells Hollister bought this property in 1869-'70 from the executors of the Den estate, and forthwith instituted notable improvements, upon which was expended a great sum of money, although probably very much less than the rumored sum of $400,000. The business center of the property was located at " the Lower House," where the laborers were lodged and boarded, and the dairy was situated. Two miles distant from this, through an avenue lined with lemon trees, was situated "Glen Annie," the family residence, so named in honor of Mrs. Hollister, being situated at the head of a beautiful little cañon, traversed by the Tecolotito (Little Owl) Creek. The native timber on this estate is principally live-oak, with smaller quantities of sycamore and willows, and the beautiful California laurel. The forage is burr-clover, red and white clover, and alfileria. The planted trees are eucalyptus, pepper, many varieties of acacia, palms, walnuts, etc. Fruit culture on this estate was carried to an advanced degree. Irrigation was practiced only with the citrus fruit trees, the water being piped some eight miles through the adjacent mountain streams. Under Colonel Hollister's wise administration, this estate was maintained in model condition, but since his death, his heirs have permitted it to run down, owing to continued litigation, which menaced its possession; and in effect, after fourteen years or more of litigation, a recent decision has adjudged the ownership of this property to the Den heirs, owing to an informality in the probate sale.

THE WESTERN PORTION OF SANTA BARBARA.

For convenience and for geographical and social reasons, this district will be regarded as comprising the following ranchos, wholly or in part: Lompoc and Mission Vieja de la Purisima, Punta de la Concepcion, the west half of Nuestra Señora del Refugio, San Julian, Cañada de Salsipuedes, Santa Rosa, Santa Rita, Mission de la Purisima, and the southern half of Jesus Maria. It has a coast of thirty-seven miles, extending from La Gaviota Pass or Landing westward to Point Concepcion, and thence southward to Point Purisima. At Point Concepcion, the Santa Barbara Mountains, which protect the Santa Barbara Valley against the cold winds from the north, terminate abruptly in the Pacific; and the west coast valleys to the northward of this point are exposed to the full force of the trade winds, which, particularly at night, supply much moisture for the crops of summer. The climate here is accordingly cool and bracing, stimulating the system to labor, and promoting healthful sleep. The interior valleys are less subject to winds and fog, and they are warmer in the day, and cooler at night.

Until within the last twelve or fourteen years, the only use made of all this section was for the raising of live-stock, and the only population consisted of the few herders and vaqueros necessary to look after the stock. The number of acres of arable land in this district is estimated at 35,000, in a total of 223,487.45. The chief products are wheat, barley, beans, corn, potatoes, mustard, flax, honey, butter, cheese, wool, hogs, cattle, horses, and sheep. In 1881, this district supported 817 horses, 3,253 cattle, and 95,703 sheep. The annual production of wool is about 650,000 pounds. The soil is rich and productive, but requires early seeding and deep and thorough cultivation. Fruit culture is successful in the valleys which are sheltered from the strong and continual trade-winds of the Pacific.

LOMPOC.

The Lompoc Colony Lands embrace all the territory of the Lompoc and Mission Vieja de la Purisima ranchos; the title is by United States patent. These lands border for seven miles on the Pacific Ocean, and extend back from the coast about twelve miles. The original Lompoc rancho, containing 38,335.78 acres of land, was granted by the Mexican Government to José Antonio Carrillo, April 15, 1837, and the Mission Vieja to Joaquin and José Antonio Carrillo, November 26, 1845, this containing 4,440 acres. Carrillo sold the Lompoc to the More Brothers, they to Hollisters, Dibblees and Cooper, who sold to a joint stock company 46,499.04 acres, of which about 24,000 acres are plain land. The main valley contains 16,000 acres. The Santa Ynez River runs westerly through these ranchos, and for some twelve miles forms their northern boundary.

The name Lompoc is from the Indian for lagoon or little lake, probably at first two words—Lum Poc. This was modified by the Spanish to Lompoco, whence the present name. The history of Lompoc colony proper begins only as far back as 1874, when a company of California farmers and business men organized a joint-stock company, under the auspices of the California Immigrant Union of San Francisco, and bought from Hollister & Dibblee the Lompoc and Mission Vieja ranchos, giving $500,000, payable in ten annual installments. The capital stock was divided into 100 shares of $5,000 each. In the deed was placed a clause of an iron-clad nature, providing against the manufacture or sale, upon the lands to be acquired in the colony, of any intoxicating beverages. The lands were now surveyed, and divided into tracts of five, ten, twenty, forty and eighty acres. For a town-site was reserved a tract one mile square, nine miles from the coast, and near the center of the valley. The water supply was sufficient for a population of 25,000.

On November 9 were held the sales of lots, amounting to more than $700,000 for city and farm tracts, leaving unsold about 35,000 acres, for which the company were offered $370,000 by the former owners. Building and farm operations were immediately begun, and within two months eighty families were occupying their new homes. A new county road was now built, connecting Lompoc with La Graciosa. Lompoc put forward a claim to be made the county-seat of a proposed new county, to be formed from a portion each of San Luis Obispo and Santa Barbara.

By 1875 the town was flourishing. It supported a newspaper—the *Record*, started April 10—a physician, a justice of the peace, and a notary public. There was a Sunday school of 100 members. Communication with the outside world was had by means of a tri-weekly stage. About this time it transpired that one Green, a druggist, was retailing liquor contrary to the terms of the land sales, and some 200 of the most reputable men and women assembled, and, first searching but vainly, for liquor in the other business houses, they proceeded to Green's drug store, and prepared to destroy his stock of liquors. Green resisted, and threatened violence, but submitted when it was intimated that the besieging party might proceed to a lynching settlement. The matrons then broke up the barrels, casks, etc., spilling the liquor, and then withdrew to their homes. This affair caused a great sensation, of more than local discussion.

The first marriage in Lompoc was that of Jesse I. Hobson and Miss Lyndia Spencer, July 25, 1875.

During this year Father McNally agitated the question of building a Roman Catholic Church at Lompoc; and so successful were his efforts that Protestants and Catholics alike gave liberally, especially the old ranchos. Thus the church was soon built; it was christened "La Purisima," and in its tower was placed one of the bells from the old neighboring mission of La Purisima.

The first school in Lompoc was opened on May 3 by Rev. J. W. Webb, who was Grand Secretary of the order of Good Templars in Southern California. The census of this year found 225 children in Lompoc school district. On October 16 the town voted an appropriation of $3,000 to the school-house fund. On the first anniversary of its founding, the colony contained 200 families, and good church and school facilities, although the school-house, whose fund was raised by the sale of bonds, was not built until 1876.

In June, 1876, Lompoc was visited by the severest storm ever known in that section. The Lompoc *Record* stated that the waves ran twenty feet above the wharf. At Point Sal a $20,000 vessel was driven ashore and totally wrecked. The Lompoc wharf at Point Purisima, thirteen miles up the coast from Lompoc, was completed this year. (In the summer of 1884 this wharf was extended sixty feet, the rest of it was repaired, and a new warehouse, 50 x 100 feet, was built.)

Not one name of a property owner in this district was in the delinquent tax list this year.

The events of 1878 were: the building of a $600 bridge across the Santa Ynez at Lompoc, completed February 4; and a revival of the question of county division. Although nothing came of it, there was much discussion over this subject, as the section found it very detrimental to do business with so distant a center as Santa Barbara. By this time certain unfavorable conditions had produced a state of depression in the affairs of this section. To assist in tiding over the juncture, the original owners volunteered to remit certain portions of the moneys still due them from the purchasers; Colonel Hollister, holding five-twelfths, and Albert Dibblee and Thomas Dibblee each holding two-twelfths of the company's indebtedness, remitted all of the accrued interest for three years and two and one-half months, from the time of purchase, October 15, 1874, to date, January 1, 1878; also Mrs. Sherman, P. Stow, and Mr. and Mrs. Jack, each holding one-half of the indebtedness, remitted one year's interest, the whole rebate amounting to $130,000, lifting a heavy burden from the colonists.

In 1880 Lompoc contained 200 inhabitants. There were Methodist, Roman Catholic, Christian, Cumberland Presbyterian, and South Methodist church organizations, the three first named owning church structures. There was a good school-house, a public hall 30 x 60 feet, a public library, three hotels, a Good Templars' library, a fifty-horse-power steam flouring-mill, and about thirty business establishments. There were societies of Odd Fellows, Good Templars, Knights of Pythias, and Patrons of Husbandry, also a literary and musical society and a uniformed brass band; two justices of the peace, two constables, two doctors, one lawyer and one notary public, a daily mail, and express and telegraph offices.

The population of the colony lands was now 1,400. The territory was divided into six school districts, each having an ample school building. Moreover, a public park of five acres had been set apart for the general use.

Regarding the entire acreage this year planted as 100, the percentage of the various principal crops was as follows: wheat, .36; barley, .36; mustard, .10; beans, .7; corn, .6; hay, 4.; flax, .$\frac{1}{4}$; potatoes, .$\frac{1}{4}$.

In 1881 the liquor question once more came to the surface, producing the usual effect of strong waters—uneasiness and disorder. In April there was an explosion in the Lompoc Hotel, caused by the loading with gun-powder of wood to be consumed in the store. This had once before happened while the hotel was under the management of a man who sold liquors, but who, after the explosion, closed out his business and left the town. Against the traffic the local paper inveighed most bitterly, like all the citizens, and public meetings were held, numerously attended and full of enthusiasm. At last, toward midnight on May 20, a large bomb was thrown into George Walker's saloon, it being known that no one was in the building at the time. So large was the bomb, and so violent the concussion, that Mr. Walker discontinud the business in Lompoc; the sides were thrown out, the second floor and the roof crushed in, and in fact the building was quite demolished.

Lompoc was very proud of two celebrations held this year. The first, on May 9, was the eighteenth anniversary of the Knights of Pythias of San Luis Obispo, Santa Barbara and Lompoc, on which occasion there were processions, literary exercises, picnics, a barbecue and a grand ball. The Fourth of July was also celebrated in an attractive manner.

Lompoc now has a daily mail, a bank, express and telegraph offices, six organized churches with fine congregations, and the usual number of business houses warranted by a population of 2,000. The schools of this colony are considered among the best in the State. They employ twelve teachers. The town school is especially well conducted, and will soon be raised to a high-school grade.

The town is laid out in rectangular blocks 300 x 500 feet, the streets being eighty and 100 feet wide. The blocks are bisected by an alley twenty feet wide, and the lots are 25 x 125 and 25 x 140 feet. The business houses are substantial, and the dwelling houses are mostly of the latest design. Plans have been submitted and bids advertised for a new public hall, 50 x 130 feet, which will cost some $6,000, and will be the finest hall in the county. An election has been called to vote bonds for a $10,000 school-house. The present year will witness building in the town and valley to the amount of $150,000.

The town is incorporated, and it owns its own water supply.

There is a project, too, of putting in an electric light plant.

Lompoc now contains five general merchandise establishments, aggregating about $50,000; two hardware, of $10,000 and $20,000; one shoe store, $1,000; one furniture, $5,000; two drug stores, $4,000 each; one jeweler, $7,000; two lumber-yards and planing mills of $25,000 and $20,000; two hotels; two tailor shops; two fruit stores; two saloons; two large livery stables; two harness-shops; two barber shops; four large blacksmith shops; two butcher-shops; two physicians; one dentist; two lawyers; and four real-estate dealers.

The grazing lands are excellent, and there is a large business done in live-stock. At present this valley has no railroad facilities. To the shipment of the section's products, there have been built three wharves—one at

Lompoc Landing, Point Purisima, thirteen miles away, and at Point Arguello, fourteen miles distant, and one at Gaviota, twenty-four miles distant. Passenger travel is by stage via Gaviota or Los Alamos.

The census for 1885 showed Lompoc to have 195 boys, and 232 girls, or 427 children, of school age.

The wheat crop of Lompoc and Santa Maria Valley for 1885 was about 100,000 centals. The average yield was the best in the county—about five sacks per acre. Santa Maria Valley yielded about three sacks per acre.

In 1886 Lompoc reported a grand aggregate of domestic exports from that region to the value of $337,000. This was produced by 400 families, thus giving each $815, besides the products consumed at home. Of the crops raised, English mustard yielded 1,250 tons, of $75,000 gross value; beans 40,000 sacks, worth $50,000; wheat, $40,000; barley, $78,000; cheese and butter, $25,000; eggs and poultry, $15,000; beef cattle, $20,000; hogs, $15,000; horses sold, $12,000; 100 tons honey, $7,000.

An unusually industrious and intelligent class of people has been attracted to Lompoc by the fame of the colony's high moral character. This causes this district to be regarded with particular favor for family settlement.

Adjacent to this colony are many large ranchos which will be subdivided and placed on the market in homestead tracts at an early future date.

Lands of the greatest fertility in this valley can be bought for $125 per acre. Grazing lands sell for $10 to $40 per acre.

The land of Lompoc Valley is a rich alluvial soil, and it is very productive. Artesian wells supply water for irrigation where necessary. Thus the country tributary to the town is adapted to agricultural and grazing purposes. Here 3,700 pounds of beans have been raised upon a single acre, and barley has been known to yield 100 bushels to the acre, eighty bushels being not uncommon. The English yellow mustard is an important product. It is sowed in May, and harvested in July, yielding 1,800 to 2,200 pounds to the acre, worth $2\frac{1}{2}$ to $3\frac{1}{2}$ cents per pound. The wild mustard grows so large and in such profusion that men have earned $2.50 per day cutting it for market. Wheat, corn, rye, potatoes, flax, and fruits are also grown, and the output is simply enormous. Bee-keeping also yields a considerable revenue to augment the sum total.

The apples from Lompoc were awarded at the New Orleans Exposition the first silver medal over all the other sections of the Pacific States and Territories.

RANCHOS.

The Santa Rita Rancho, granted to Ramon Malo by Governor Pio Pico, April 12, 1845, contained "three square leagues, a little more or less," the patent issued June 25, 1875, calling for 13,316.05 acres. The Santa Rita Valley, which opens northeasterly from the Santa Ynez, is in part a *sobrante* (remainder) from the Rancho de la Purisima. In early years it was used exclusively for grazing, and at that time supported a small settlement, which was the scene of many a bloody encounter. It is owned at present mainly by Jesse Hill, and is used mainly for grazing, although it is farmed somewhat, and has several smaller owners.

East of Santa Rita lies the Rancho Santa Rosa, a magnificent estate, well watered by the Santa Ynez River, amply supplied with live-oak for fuel, and with a deep, rich soil, which, even to the hill-tops, affords the richest pasturage. In 1881, there were grazing here

17,000 sheep, seventy-eight cattle, and twenty horses, with feed for several thousands more. Upward of 5,000 acres of valley and foothill lands are arable. From twenty acres of wheat have been harvested 1,100 bushels of grain, even with great loss in harvesting. About 100 acres are farmed to hay. The wool clip in 1880 amounted to 120,000 lbs., sold at 22½ cents per pound, from twelve to thirty-five men being employed in this interest, at different seasons of the year. This rancho is now owned by J. W. Cooper.

The Rancho Cañon de Sal si Puedes is so named from a cañon winding through it, so tortuous as to deserve the Spanish name, "Get-out-if-you-can." Prior to 1874 it passed into the possession of Hollister & Dibblee, who used it for sheep grazing. It is accredited by the United States patent with 6,656.21 acres. It is now the exclusive property of the Hollister estate.

The Rancho San Julian, of 48,221.68 acreage, was granted to George Rock, April 7, 1837, and the claim was purchased and its title perfected by José de la Guerra y Noriega. It is singularly diversified and attractive in its topography, being made up of rolling hills and dipping valleys, watered by running brooks and numerous living springs of pure water. Its largest and loveliest valley is the Cañada San Julian, a branch of the old Purisima Mission, where the padres used to make wine. The soil is deep, rich, strong, and productive to the tops of the hills, the grass being thick, deep and dense. The leading trees are the live-oak, willow, sycamore, manzanita, and madroño. In 1881, there were estimated to be 70 horses, 575 cattle, and 64,703 sheep, upon the San Julian and the Sal si Puedes ranchos. The natural increase of flocks in this favored section is little short of marvelous. The San Julian Rancho now belongs to T. B. & A. Dibblee.

About three miles east of Point Concepcion begins the coast line of the Rancho Punta de la Concepcion, comprising the ranchos La Espada and El Cojo, and including an area of 24,992.04 acres, belonging to P. W. Murphy. The coast line extends northwesterly about twenty miles, the interior boundary of the rancho lying nearly parallel to, and about three and a half miles distant from its coast line. In the northern part, this rancho partakes of the general character of the Lompoc lands, being chiefly mesa and low valley hill lands; in the southern portion, near Point Concepcion, it is composed of very ragged and picturesque outlines. The body of the land adjacent to the point is, in a fair year, good pasture, being a part of the Rancho el Cojo, famous for its rich grazing and fine beef. Some cereals are raised in the northern part of the rancho, but cattle-raising is the principal business. This rancho is characterized by that bold promontory, some 220 feet high, situated where the coast trends suddenly from east and west below to a line almost at right angles north and south. This point, whose position is given by the Coast Survey as latitude 34° north, longitude 120° west, has been termed the "Cape Horn" and the "Cape Hatteras" of the Pacific, on account of the heavy northwesters here met on emerging from the channel, the climatic and meteorological conditions also changing with remarkably sudden and sharp definition, so that vessels coming from the eastward with all sails set, are at once reduced to short canvas on approaching the cape. This point was discovered by Cabrillo in 1542, and called Cape Galera, which name was afterward changed to the present. The view from the headland is extended and magnificent. It bears a lighthouse, whose lantern, 250 feet above the water, can plainly be seen in clear weather from the Santa Barbara hills, forty miles away. The light shown is a white revolving half-minute flash, of the first order of the Fresnel system. This light was built on land supposed to belong to the Government, but which proved to be a part of the grant purchased by the Murphys. After much delay as to repairs, etc., because of the insecurity of title, the United States in 1881 purchased from the owners for $10 000 a title to the lighthouse buildings, etc., and thirty acres of land adjoining. At Point Arguello, about twelve miles north of Point Concepcion, the Sudden Wharf was built in 1881. About three miles from Point Arguello, on the Espada Rancho, there are hot sulphur springs.

The Rancho Nuestra Señora del Refugio, containing 26,529 acres, was granted to Antonio Maria Ortega, August 1, 1834. It has a coast-line of about twenty miles, and from the coast an average depth of three miles. The rancho is divided into two nearly equal parts by the Gaviota Pass, about sixty feet wide, the only natural gateway into the Santa Barbara mountains between the San Buenaventura River and Point Concepcion. This pass is an important outlet for a wide scope of country behind the mountains, including most of the western portion of the country. Its landing at Gaviota is good and safe, having the substantial wharf, 1,000 feet long (built by Hollister & Dibblee in 1875) to accommodate a large shipping business. And, in effect, a large business is done here, principally in live-stock, wool, general merchandise, sacked grain, miscellaneous farm and ranch produce, and lumber. This wharf is about thirty-eight miles from Santa Barbara, and twenty-eight miles from the Lompoc wharf. A peculiarity of this locality is a strong off-shore wind, which somewhat interferes with the landing of sailing vessels, while, in consequence of the strong blast

always coming down the pass, no vessel is ever thrown against the shore. The scenery hereabouts is very picturesque.

The topography of the Rancho de Nuestra Señora del Refugio is very similar to that of the San Julian. It is mainly utilized as a sheep rancho.

LOS ALAMOS VALLEY.

The next valley is Los Alamos. It is watered by an arroyo of the same name, which rises in the San Rafael Mountains, and, sometimes sinking out of sight, empties into the sea between Point Purisima and Point Sal. This is a long valley, being in its broadest part scarcely more than two miles wide. It contains but one town, Los Alamos.

Lying between the Santa Ynes and the Santa Maria Valley, stretches this valley, some twenty-five miles long by two miles wide. It is drained by an arroyo of the same name, which flows almost due west, sometimes with sinks below the surface. This district comprises the ranchos of La Laguna, Los Alamos, Todos Santos, north half of Jesus Maria, Casmali, the hill lands of Point Sal, and adjoining Government lands. The total area of these ranchos, as shown by the United States patents, is 149,305.60 acres. Until a comparatively recent date, cattle and sheep raising were the principal industries, but now immense quantities of wheat, barley, beans, hay, hogs, bricks and lime, as well as horses, cattle and wool, are shipped annually. The grazing interests on May 1, 1881, were represented about as follows: horses, 495; cattle, 1,400; sheep, 50,000. There are in this district about 40,000 acres adapted to tillage. The soil is mixed, the greater portion being heavy loam, particularly in the valley proper. There is also adobe and sandy loam, with bits inclining to a shaly character. The rainfall is somewhat less than at Santa Barbara, varying from seven to fifteen inches. The temperature is very equable, averaging 65° the year around. The hottest weather comes here in September, when the record occasionally reaches 95° to 115°, though these extremes are very rare, and of brief duration. The sea-breeze tempers the climate notably. Save for trees in their first year, there is no necessity for irrigation, but an inexhaustible supply of surface water is obtained by digging ten to twenty feet. These wells afford the domestic supply. The perfection of the crops here is attributed to the great depth of soil, the nearness of water to the surface, and the protection from drying winds afforded by the hills. The hillsides afford good feed in all seasons. Wheat, barley, corn, beans, flax and hemp are the staple products of the soil; flax and hemp grow so luxuriantly as to promise an important revenue, not only from the fiber but also the seed. The yield of wheat in 1880 was 115,000 centals, and the acreage is constantly increasing, the yield being twenty to forty bushels to the acre; barley averages twenty-five to sixty bushels to the acre; hay reaches three and a half tons to the acre in an ordinary year. Butter and cheese also are produced.

The prosperity of this section is evinced by the excellent condition of all improvements, public and private. Roads kept in good order, fences, dwellings, barns, and outbuildings all of the best kind, are an index to the status of the community.

Within this district are three sea-shipping points, distant as follows from the town of Los Alamos: Point Sal, twenty-five miles; Chute Landing, twenty-two miles; Lompoc Wharf at Point Purisima, twenty-five miles.

La Laguna Rancho lies at the head of this valley. It was granted to Miguel Avila, November 3, 1845, and confirmed to Octaviano Gutierrez, the United States patent calling for 48,703.91 acres. This rancho has suffered many decimations. It is traversed by the county road.

The Rancho Los Alamos was granted to José Antonio Carrillo, March 9, 1839, consisting of 48,803.38 acres. The United States patent was issued September 12, 1872. It embraced about one-third of the entire valley. A heavy lawsuit has made this rancho conspicuous. On the original tract were pastured on March 1, 1881, 300 horses, 500 cattle, and 25,000 sheep.

Todos Santos Rancho originally contained 22,200. It was granted to Salvador Osio, November 3, 1844, and confirmed to William E. P. Hartwell; the patent calls for 10,722.17 acres. The live-stock here on March 1, 1881, was 50 horses, 200 cattle, and 3,000 sheep.

The Rancho Jesus Maria was granted to Lucas Olivera, April 8, 1837, containing 42,184.93 acres, and the southern two-thirds portion was confirmed to Lewis T. Burton. Some 10,000 acres of this land is adapted to cereals. Its stock on March 1, 1881, consisted of 40 horses, 500 cattle, and 10,000 sheep.

The Casmali Rancho was granted to Antonio Olivera, September 12, 1840, it containing 8,841.21 acres. It has a two-mile coast line, and extends some six miles into the interior. It produces some cereals, but stock-raising is the main interest. On March 1, 1881, there were here 25 horses, 150 cattle, and 6,000 sheep. The black sand of the shore is mined for gold, in a small way. In 1875 was made an unsuccessful attempt to colonize this rancho.

Point Sal is at the extremity of a prominent cape that projects into the Pacific from the Government lands lying between the Casmali and the Gaudalupe. It is about twenty-four miles from Los Alamos, and twenty-one miles from Lompoc. For some years freight was discharged here by lighter through the surf. Then, after the rejection of several petitions, a wharf was built in 1874; it was carried away by a storm in 1876; was rebuilt the next spring, and washed away again the following winter; then, being rebuilt, it still remains.

The coast here is bold and rugged, rising twenty to 100 feet above the water. At the point is a laguna, some three miles long, covering about 3,000 acres, which is a great resort for water-fowl, many of which are shot for their feathers.

Owing to dissatisfaction with the administration of the Point Sal wharf, a stock company was formed, and a chute landing constructed near by, where there was a sheltered and safe anchorage. The first grain was received for shipment in 1880, and 13,000 tons of grain were handled here the first two years. In this time, it is said, the chute landing saved to the farmers its full first cost, in freight and wharfage. After some years this wharf was bought out by a steamship company, for the purpose of forcing the traffic over another landing, already established by the company.

Adjacent to the mouth of Los Alamos Arroyo is Lompoc Wharf, built in 1876.

The name Los Alamos means "The Cottonwoods," which trees were conspicuous by their absence, upon this rancho. In 1867 John S. Bell bought from José Antonio de la Guerra y Carrillo that portion of the rancho whereon the town now is situated, which, for some ten years thereafter, he devoted to the raising of sheep and cattle. In 1873 the stage route which hitherto had passed through the Tiniquiac rancho was so changed as to run through Los Alamos, and then buildings were erected for a barn and eating-house for passengers.

In 1876 John Purkiss built at Los Alamos the pioneer mill of Santa Barbara County, and during the same year, C. D. "Patterson" tested the farming capabilities of the region with such success that the future of the valley was assured from the agricultural standpoint. A store and a hotel were built, and in 1887 Mr. Bell, together with Dr. J. B. Shaw, who had now acquired a portion of the rancho, laid out the town of Los Alamos, and built a steam flouring-mill. In 1882 Mr. Peter Conyer built a public assembly hall. Dr. Shaw donated a lot, and a fine school-house was built upon it. In October, 1882, the Pacific Coast Railway reached the place, and built a fine depot and water tanks, and established a telegraph line. On January 24, 1884, was issued the first number of a newspaper, the Los Alamos *Herald*. By this time the town had eight business houses, shops and stores, and 100 dwelling houses, all occupied.

There are now in Los Alamos two large general merchandise houses, two good hotels, one drug store, two livery stables, two blacksmith shops, one barber shop, several carpenters, one paint shop, one hardware store, one meat market, two laundries, one steam roller flouring-mill, one brewery, one stationer's shop, one lumber yard, one harness shop, one millinery shop, several saloons, a money-order postoffice, an express office, and one practicing physician.

The public shool-house is a fine $5,000 building, containing two departments. The Methodist congregation has a fine brick church, which is used also by the Presbyterians. Each of these denominations has a resident clergyman.

Los Alamos has the usual number of justices, constables, notaries, insurance agents, etc. There is also a live weekly newspaper, the *Progress*. The population is about 500.

Los Alamos is on the line of the Pacific Coast Railway, between San Luis Obispo and Los Olivos.

There is here an abundant rainfall, insuring good crops every year, the quantity of water falling here exceeding that in most other localities. No irrigation is required for crops. This section abounds in living springs, and good water can be obtained almost anywhere at a depth of ten or fifteen feet.

Not least among the advantages is the fact that good live-oak wood can be obtained here in any quantity for but little more than the price of cutting. There is also plenty of game in this vicinity.

On July 28, 1886, the schooner Columbia, with a cargo of 100,000 feet of lumber and 3,000 posts for the Lompoc Lumber Company, went ashore in a fog, at the mouth of Los Alamos Creek, and was a total loss. Most of the cargo, being strewn along the beach, was saved.

SANTA YNES VALLEY.

The Santa Ynes is the largest of the five valleys, including an area of 120,000 acres of farming land and 280,000 of pasturage.

The Santa Ynes Valley is in the form of a horseshoe. The San Rafael Mountains on the north and the Santa Ynes range on the south meet at the eastern extremity of the valley, which they divide from the narrow strip of land in the vicinity of Santa Barbara. These mountains meeting form the toe of the horseshoe, where rises the Santa Ynes River, which runs westward through the whole valley, emptying into the Pacific a few miles north of Lompoc. The western end of this valley is open to the Pacific, which largely accounts for the delightful climate of this section, the western trade winds being felt all the length of the valley. This valley may be divided into two parts, the upper or Santa Ynes Valley proper, and the lower or Lompoc Valley. The former comprises the following large ranchos: San Carlos de Jonata or Buell, Corral de Quati, De Zaca, Cañada de los Pinos or College Ranch, San Marcos, Tequepis, Nojogui (often misspelled Nojoqui), Los Prietos y Najalayegua, Las Lomas de la Purificacion, and part of Las Cruces; in all about 223,185 acres, of which at least 50,000 acres are adapted to agriculture and horticulture. There are also Government lands obtained from Mision Santa Ynes, and comprising the Alamo Pintado, some 6,000 acres in extent. Most of the soil is a rich, gravelly loam, which is very easy to cultivate, and which, when kept loose by cultivation, retains sufficient moisture to keep fruit trees of all kinds, and vines, to grow entirely well without irrigation through the dryest season. Some of the rich bottom lands of this district will raise the finest of summer crops, of corn, beans, etc., without irrigation.

The whole valley is magnificently watered by the river and by tributary creeks from the mountains on both sides. Good well water is had almost everywhere at ten to 100 feet below the surface, and there is no doubt that on a great portion of the land artesian water can be had at little depth. The entire valley is beautifully wooded with scattered oaks and sycamores. White, red, and green chestnut oaks (Quercus lobata, rubra, and demiflora) are found, the white oak supplying the farmers with fence posts at very small cost. Along the creeks are found the alder, the bay or sweet laurel, and the willow. A species of pine is found in the San Rafael mountains.

The valley is reached from Santa Barbara by the San Marcos Pass over the mountains, this route being forty-five miles; or else through the Gaviota, a natural pass or defile through the Santa Ynez mountains, it being sixty miles by this way.

This valley hitherto has been so difficult of access, and the removal of crops to market has been so expensive, that the farmers' profits have been small, and land has been held very low.

Until recently, this valley was used exclusively for grain, great quantities, of a very fine quality, being raised annually. There is no rust or blight found here, and wheat has yielded thirty to fifty bushels to the acre. Barley also yields exceedingly well.

Some years ago, Mr. A. Hayne, Jr., of Montecito, became satisfied that the Santa Ynes, particularly the Alamo Pintado, otherwise Ballard's Valley, was thoroughly adapted to the culture of the olive. This idea was based on the gravelly nature of the soil, and the extreme dryness of the climate, the absence of the fogs felt on the coast obviating the ravages of the olive's worst foe, the black scale. Accordingly, in 1884 he set out 5,000 young trees just below the old Mission. Two years later they bore fruit. Mr. Hayne, with the Messrs. Gould, of New York, has since planted another orchard of 5,000 trees; Mr. Ben. Hayne planted 2,500, and now olive culture has become the leading industry of the valley. Next in importance comes vine-planting, the vineyard of Mr. Louis Janin having demonstrated that the raisin grape will do splendidly anywhere in the valley and on the foot-hills.

Apricots, nectarines, apples, pears, peaches, quinces, and the small fruits thrive well, and are remarkable for the fineness of their flavor. Prunes do excellently well in the valley, and no doubt their curing will shortly be added to the local industries.

The sugar beet promises to do well, and a sugar factory is within the probabilities for the near future.

There are four settlements in the valley; the town of Santa Ynes, lying in the middle of the College Rancho; Ballard's Station, and Childs' Station, on the San Carlos Jonata Rancho, and Los Olivos.

The road on the southern slope of the Santa Ynez mountains was built by the late J. A. Brown at a cost of $18,000, or $3,000 for each of the six miles of the road.

The Atlantic & Pacific Railway is surveying the San Marcos Cañon, through which this road passes, where it is designed to make a tunnel two miles long.

Santa Ynez is the town founded in 1882, distant from San Luis Obispo eighty miles, of which seventy-five are traversed by the Pacific Coast Railway running to Los Olivos, whence the remaining five miles are by stage.

The town supports two hotels, two or three stores, two livery stables, six or seven saloons, and a blacksmith shop, and it has a number of sightly cottages and other dwellings.

The Santa Ynez Land and Improvement Company has a fine office here.

There is a band consisting of fifteen members, which discourses good music.

Santa Ynez has one of the finest schoolhouses in the county. It is a two-story wooden structure, just completed at a cost of $6,000. It is eligibly situated on a commanding site.

Santa Ynez is the Spanish for "Saint Agnes."

The Rancho Las Cruces is of divided ownership. It is a tract of about two leagues (8,888 acres), lying north of the summit, and on the main county road to Gaviota Landing. Stock-raising is its chief industry. The so-called town of Las Cruces is three and one-half miles from Gaviota Wharf, north of the pass, forty-two miles from Santa Barbara. It consists only of a postoffice, a store, and half a dozen surrounding dwellings. Less than a mile distant are the Las Cruces Hot Sulphur Springs, the principal one of which flows a volume of about ten inches, at a temperature of 90°. The Tulare Indians used to fight hereabouts with the coast tribes, their warfare ranging down as late as American occupation. On one occasion they raided the adobe rancho house of Las Cruces, shooting the walls full of arrows, and carrying off the horses of sixteen Californians, besieged within the dwelling. They were pursued, the horses retaken, and all but one of the Indians slain.

Within two miles of Ballard's, and five of Santa Ynes, stands the young town of Los Olivos, started in 1886–'87. It is supported by the surrounding farming country with its rich yield of wheat and barley, and the numerous young fruit and olive orchards. The population of this little town is about 150. There is one hotel (another was burned recently), two general merchandise houses, one drug store, two bars, two blacksmith shops, one livery stable, one lumber yard, a railroad station-house (of the Pacific Coast Railway, south from San Luis Obispo), post-office with daily mail, express office, one church, one school-house with one teacher, and accommodations for four departments.

About five miles from Los Olivos, and adjoining Santa Ynes, is the Indian reservation called Zanja de Cota, where live nine Indian families, or thirty to forty souls, remnants of the Santa Ynes Mission Indians, who live by farm labor, fishing, etc.

BALLARDS.

This little town was laid out in 1881, by George W. Lewis. It is in the Santa Ynes Valley, three miles from the old mission of Santa Ynes, and four from the Santa Ynes College. A fine wheat-growing region surrounds the town, having yielded an average of twenty centals to the acre of as good wheat as is found on the coast. A large irrigating canal runs through the place, and its many advantages promise a flourishing future.

RANCHOS.

The Rancho San Carlos de Jonata, otherwise known as "the Buell Ranch," is a tract of land of almost square shape, comprising 26,634.31 acres, lying on the north bank of the Santa Ynes. It is estimated to contain 10,000 acres of fine, rich, sandy loam soil, well watered by the Shasta Ynes and numerous creeks. This rancho is owned by H. I. Willey and others. This is used for grazing, although the lowlands are good grain lands, suitable for corn, wheat, barley and beans. The northwest portion, known as Red Rock, contains large bodies of asphaltum as yet undeveloped.

The Rancho Corral de Cuati was granted to Augustine Davila, and confirmed to Maria Antonio de la Guerra y Lataillade, 13,300.24 acres—United States patent 13,322.29 acres. The main county road runs from north to south through its eastern portion, the distance to Gaviota being twenty miles, and to Los Alamos eight miles. The surface is rolling hills, mostly tillable, but used chiefly for grazing. This rancho, together with La Zaca, carried in 1881 the following stock: horses, 20; cattle, 1,114; sheep, 3,400.

The Rancho La Zaca was a grant of 4,480 acres, made to Maria Antonio de la Guerra y Lataillade in 1838—United States patent 4,458.10 acres. Its chief industry is stock-raising. At the head of La Zaca Creek is Zaca Lake, a beautiful sheet of water of about 100 acres area, 2,000 to 3,000 feet above the sea.

The College Rancho, otherwise Rancho Cañada de Los Pinos, is owned by the Roman Catholic Church, being under the control of the bishops. It was a grant of

35,499 acres. The rancho is a nearly square tract of land, on the north bank of the Santa Ynes. Two living streams, the Santa Agata and the Cañada de Los Piños, flow through it. The elevation above the sea is about 596 feet. Its shipping points are Gaviota Pass and Los Alamos, each about sixteen miles distant. Some 15,000 acres are rich, arable lands, especially adapted for wheat-growing. This land has produced about 1,600 pounds of wheat to the acre. This rancho is the site of the old Santa Ynes Mission, now fallen into disuse. One mile from the mission is the College of Our Lady of Guadalupe, organized to educate missionaries for the conversion of the Indians. On this rancho is the town of Santa Ynes, already described.

The Rancho San Marcos is a tract of nearly circular form, comprising 35,573.10 acres, granted to Nicholas A. Den, June 8, 1846. By the San Marcos toll-road the nearest point to Santa Barbara is twelve miles distant. Its surface is very rugged, therefore stock-raising is about the only industry practicable. Quail, pigeon, deer, bear, California lion, trout and other game is very abundant in its wild fastnesses. This rancho is owned by the Pierce Brothers.

The San Marcos Sulphur Springs are found seven miles northwest of Santa Barbara. They have a temperature of 120° F., and are used locally for skin diseases, etc.

The Rancho Jequepis was granted to Joaquin Villa and confirmed to Antonio Maria Villa. It is a tract of 8,919 acres, divided into two nearly equal portions by the Santa Ynes River. The surface of this rancho is much broken, and is used almost entirely for grazing.

The Rancho Los Prietos y Najalayegua was originally granted to Francisco Dominguez by the Mexican government, with very indefinite boundaries. Owing to the rugged and mountainous character of the land embraced within its confines, the rancho was considered of very little value and was not presented to the land commissioners for confirmation. Finally falling under the control of Thomas Scott, he secured the passage of an act of Congress securing the title to said grant in 1866. Then followed several years of litigation, during which the grant owners tried to secure a location of the grant on the south side of the Santa Ynes mountains and adjacent to the pueblo lands of the city of Santa Barbara. Many settlers who had located on these lands, attempting the securing of title to them as pre-emptors and homesteaders, contended that the grant should be located north of the Santa Ynes. In the midst of this contest the development of the quicksilver interests north of the mountains gave promise of great results; and, influenced by this consideration, the grant owners consented to a location of the grant to the northward of the mountains. This was consequently done, and patents were issued accordingly.

The Rancho Las Lomas de la Purificacion, lying south of and across the river from the College Rancho, was granted to Agustin Janssens, December 27, 1844, and contains 13,320 acres under United States patent. It is owned by the heirs of the T. W. Moore estate. This is chiefly grazing land. By San Marcos toll-road, which traverses the rancho, it is twenty-two miles from Santa Barbara.

The Rancho Nojogui (in general wrongly written Nojoqui) adjoins the Rancho de Jonata, from which it is separated by the Santa Ynes River. It was granted to Raymundo Carrillo, April 27, 1843, containing 13,522.04 acres — United States patent, 13,284 acres. This rancho is finely situated in and about a well-watered cañon, and along the county road leading through the mountain to the Gaviota Pass and Las Cruces. It is well watered by the Santa Ynes and its tributaries. It is owned by the Pierce Brothers, and the heirs of Dr. de la Cuesta. It contains excellent farming and grazing lands. The principal crops are wheat, flax and barley. Najogui is about eleven miles from Gaviota, twelve from Los Alamos, and forty-six from Santa Barbara. On the Cañada Najogui, about five miles northeast of Las Cruces, and about 1,009 feet above the sea, are the beautiful falls of Najogui, leaping down 700 feet, which have been compared to the storied falls of Minnehaha.

SANTA MARIA VALLEY.

The Santa Maria Valley occupies the northern part of Santa Barbara County, extending from the Pacific ocean to the Sisquoc range of hills, thirty-five miles eastward; and from the San Luis Obispo county-line on the north to the low range of hills separating this valley from that of Los Alamos. From Guadalupe, the main valley extends easterly twenty miles, and its continuation, the Sisquoc Valley, stretches still farther southeastward, the extreme eastern end forking into the Sisquoc hills on one side and the Foxen cañon lands on the other. The valley here is bordered on the north by the Santa Maria hills, and on the south by the clay mesas. The county near the coast is skirted by a range of low, fertile hills, mostly included in the Casmalia, Laguna and Guadalupe land grants. All the drainage of the Santa Maria and Sisquoc rivers falls into the Santa Maria Valley. These streams drain an enormous country—a region that has twice the average rainfall of the same character of hilly land from Los Angeles to San Diego. Large and swift streams as they are in winter, they sink in summer. Besides this water-supply, and the possibilities of artesian irrigation, the abundant crops of this valley, particularly near the coast, are nurtured by the heavy mists and fogs prevalent during the summer months.

This valley was named from an Indian called Santa Maria, and the title at first related to but a small part of it, but it was later extended to the whole valley and stream. The greatest dimensions of the valley proper are about twenty-five miles long by twelve wide at the upper, and narrowing until it averages about four miles. It includes the Guadalupe, Punta de la Laguna, Tepusquet, Sisquoc, and Tinaquiac ranchos, their total acreage, as per the United States patents, being 123,590.77, at least 65,000 acres being tillable land. Ten years since, these ranchos carried some 13,950 head of sheep, 3,860 cattle and 879 horses, grazing then being the chief interest.

The town of Santa Maria is about twelve miles from the coast, twenty-nine from San Luis Obispo, and eighty-four from Santa Barbara. It was first settled in 1867, by Mr. B. Wiley, who, after investigation of the title, located a quarter-section each for himself and three other gentlemen, who were followed during the next two years by some half-dozen others. The first well was dug by Mr. Wiley; it was twenty-four feet deep and curbless, but it lasted for some four years. The first house in the valley was built by Mr. Prell. The first birth was that of Thomas Miller, May 17, 1869. The first funeral was that of Mr. Rosenburg, who accidentally shot himself in the summer of 1869.

The first settlers put in large fields of grain. There was much trouble and threatened violence over the actions of the speculators with school-land warrants, who located over the claims of actual settlers that had made valuable improvements.

Tha winters of 1869-'70 and 1870-'71 were very unprosperous, owing to drouths, to damage done by occasional heavy storms, and by grasshoppers. The year 1871 marked the beginning of fruit-raising here.

The settlement, notwithstanding all opposing elements, waxed so strong and populous that the town of Central City (now Santa Maria) was laid out in 1875. The first hotel was built this year, and several shops, etc., opened.

In 1877 was organized a Union Sunday-school, and in 1878 the Methodist Episcopal church was built. The first public school was opened in 1881, the church building being used for a time. In September the town issued bonds for a two-story school-house, worth $1,000, and within one year there were eighty pupils enrolled. In 1882 was started the Santa Maria *Times*, independent in politics and devoted to local matters.

The present population of the town is about 1,000, while the surrounding country is thickly settled. The voting precinct contains some 1,500. The town is neatly laid out in squares, the principal streets, 100 feet wide, running east and west, crossed at right angles by subordinate ones, eighty and sixty feet wide.

Some of these streets are planted with shade trees, and the approaches to the town are all beautiful drives. The streets are crowned and graveled, some having concrete, and some plank walks, and they are kept sprinkled. The chief business thoroughfare is Main street, 120 feet wide, in which are many substantial business buildings. The town covers an area three-quarters of a mile square. The water is partly supplied from wells, and in part by two water companies, the water being forced by steam-power pumps to large reservoirs, at about fifty feet altitude, whence it is piped for distribution. There are in the town three good assembly halls, a Presbyterian, a Christian and a Methodist Church, a free public library and a fine $12,000 brick school-house, with four teachers in as many departments. Fraternal societies are represented by organizations of Masons, Odd Fellows, Good Templars, Knights of Pythias, Chosen Friends, Native Sons, Grand Army and Woman's Christian Temperance Union. There is a fine band, "The Fairlawn," of twelve pieces.

In September, 1883, Santa Maria suffered from a severe fire, consuming several business houses, at a loss of $5,000, of which $2,000 was covered by insurance. Again, in June, 1884, another fire here destroyed $29,650 worth of property.

There are in Santa Maria two practicing physicians, two attorneys, one dentist, two drug stores, three general merchandise houses, one grocery, one hardware store, one jeweler one stationer, one saddle and harness shop, one shoe store, two bakeries, three confectionery and fruit stores, five real-estate offices, one butcher shop, four blacksmith shops, two barbers, four painters, one fine patent-roller flour-mill, with a daily capacity of about fifty barrels, one lumber yard, two furniture stores, one bank, one newspaper,—the Santa Maria *Times*,—four millinery stores, two tinshops one photograph gallery, one merchant tailor, one toy and notion store, one steam barley-crushing mill, three large hotels, four restaurants, one large lodging-house, five saloons and three livery stables. There are two large nurseries, that of T. A. Garey having some 300,000 trees, while another nursery has sold 40,000 to 50,000 trees this year. Still another has 50,000 trees. Within half a mile of the center of the settlement, there is a half-mile race track, and a prettily planned park of ten acres.

This town is the distributing point for an area reaching fifty miles to the eastward, twenty toward the south, ten to the north, and westward to the coast line; also for the mines, seventy-five miles distant.

A through line of railway is greatly needed, and the people are anxiously looking forward to the completion of the Southern Pacific Coast Line.

The main industries of this valley are: dairying and stock-raising in the hills and lands toward the coast and about the Gauda lupe region; wheat, barley, oats and corn in the central and upper parts of the valley and the mesas; beans and potatoes from the line of the railroad westward; eastward from the railway fruit-raising is rapidly becoming an important industry, apricots, prunes, and Bartlett pears being the varieties mostly cultivated. At the western end of the valley, the potato, bean, and summer crops are steadily encroaching on the dairy tracts. The upper valley and surrounding hills will be largely planted to fruit. Citrus fruits will grow well in the more sheltered valleys and cañons. In 1880 the *average* yield of wheat on valley lands was twenty centals ($33\frac{1}{3}$ bushels) per acre; on mesa land, 17 centals or $28\frac{1}{3}$ bushels; the average yield of barley was, on valley land, 25 centals, or $41\frac{2}{3}$ bushels; mesa land, 20 centals, or $33\frac{1}{3}$ bushels. The whole wheat and barley crops amounted to about 625,000 centals in this valley in 1880, this being rather above the average yearly yield.

As special illustrations of the products, it may be mentioned that Mr. Isaac Miller has twenty-five acres of apricots, five years old, and fifteen acres of French prunes, four years old, with 108 trees to the acre. In 1889 he sold thirteen tons of dried apricots, at $200 per ton. This year the trees were loaded almost to breaking, and the crop of prunes brought $3,000, while the apricots. sold at 16 cents per pound, produced $7,000.

The prunes yield very largely, and, dried with their pits in, bring 5 cents per pound.

The district of La Graciosa, otherwise known as Fruit Vale, eight miles south of Santa Maria, being composed of rolling hills and small valleys, has mostly been converted into orchards. Here are planted hundreds upon hundreds of acres of peach, plum, nectarine, walnut, and orange trees,—in short, almost all known fruits. Here may be seen walnut trees ten feet high, two years old.

The Guadalupe Rancho of 30,408.03 acres, was granted by the Mexican government to Diego Olivera and Teodoro Arellanes, March 21, 1840. The claim was confirmed in 1857, and in 1870 a patent was issued for 43,680.85 acres. It has a coast line of ten miles, and extends eight miles back from the coast. The first farming here was done in a small way in 1867, by John B. Ward, who married a daughter of Estudillo, then owner of the rancho. He built a road from Point Sal to the rancho, nine miles distant, in consideration of a tract of land at the former place, voted him by Congress, for the construction of a road from Point Sal to Fort Tejon. As there was already a natural route between Fort Tejon and Guadalupe, Ward claimed the land and secured a patent for it, at the time when the Point Sal landing was first built. In 1872 was founded the town of Guadalupe, situated in the extreme northwestern corner of this county, about seven miles from the coast, ninety-five miles from Santa Barbara, and twelve miles from Los Alamos. The climate here is cool, bracing and healthy. This little town made considerable growth up to 1882, when the building of the Pacific Coast Railway stimulated the development of Santa Maria, at the expense of Guadalupe, which thereafter lost ground markedly. The present population is about 300.

The soil around Guadalupe is mostly a deep black adobe, which yields large returns. Wheat succeeds only on the extreme upper end of the tract. Barley has produced 100 bushels to the acre, and beans yield a more prolific crop even. Corn is an unreliable factor. Vegetables, including pumpkins and potatoes, score a marked success, but melons are a failure. The air here is too bleak for fruit-raising, and orchards fail unless protected by wind breaks, usually of cypress or eucalyptus. Stock-raising is a great industry, owing to the excellent watering and the freedom from noxious weeds or plants, enjoyed by the pasturage of this rancho. Therefore it is regarded as one of the best dairy ranges in California, and occupied largely by Swiss dairyman, who milk a vast number of cows, their products selling at an advance of one or two cents a pound on the prices of butter from the upper coast; several tons are shipped thence weekly. Good water is found here within two to sixteen feet of the surface, and artesian wells 110 feet deep yield as much as ten gallons per minute.

The Rancho Punta de la Laguna lies immediately eastward of the Guadalupe, further up the Santa Maria Valley, being an irregular strip of territory, ten miles by seven miles in extent. It was granted to Luis Arellanes and E. M. Ortega, December 24, 1844, when it contained 26,648.42 acres, extending a little way into San Luis Obispo County. Like the rest of the valley it was once a great grazing region. The soil is mostly a sandy loam, on which the cereals and all kinds of vegetables grow to perfection. The best of water is procured from wells twenty to sixty feet deep.

The Rancho Tepusquet was carved out of Government land surrounding it on all sides but the southeast, where it joins the Sisquoc. It contains 8,900 acres under United States patent, lying in the upper part of the Santa Maria Valley. It consists of low, rolling hills, the approaches to the lofty Sierra de San Rafael lying to the eastward. While the cereals are cultivated to some extent, stock-raising is the principal industry. The surface is rugged, and there is a stream affording ample water-power for manufacturing enterprises. Once the property of the Foxen Brothers this rancho now belongs to the Ontiveras family.

The Rancho Sisquoc lies at the very head of the Santa Maria Valley, extending back into the hills eight or ten miles. It comprises 35,485.90 acres of land, mostly rolling country. The cereals are produced, but stock-raising is the chief interest. This property belongs to the Stone estate.

The Rancho Tinaquaic is nearly rectangular in shape, measuring three by five miles, lying at the head of the Santa Maria Valley, it contains appropriately two leagues of land. It is traversed by the main county road. This rancho, which is now the property of the Foxen heirs, was originally granted to Victor Linares, May 6, 1837, and confirmed to William D. Foxen, the title calling for 8,874.60 acres. Its surface is hilly, but large tracts are sown to grain yearly, although stock-raising is by no means superseded.

The Rancho Cuyama, now belonging to Haggin & Perkins, and to Gaspar Oreña, was granted to José Maria Rojo, April 24, 1843, and confirmed to Maria Antonio de la Guerra and Cesario Lataillade, whose heir is Mr. Oreña. Its acreage, as by the United States patent, was 71,620.75 acres. In the spring of 1881 it was estimated to support 3,000 cattle. The Cuyama River, the northern boundary of the county, cuts this rancho into two nearly equal portions. Thus, lying in the extreme northern portion of the county, and separated from the rest thereof by the high Sierra de San Rafael, this isolation is so complete that even the returns of the elections are received from this district more tardily than from any other in the county. The only industry here is stock-raising.

THE LOST WOMAN.

The purpose of a historical sketch like the present would fall short without an account of "the Lost Woman of San Nicolas," appertaining as it does to the history of both Santa Barbara and Ventura counties.

This story has often been told, too frequently with embellishments and exaggerations which only serve to diminish the force of the simple facts, which certainly are sufficiently romantic, dramatic, and even tragic. The Alaskan Indians were in the habit of making to the channel islands periodical visits, to secure otter and other pelts, making fierce war upon other hunters who should seek to follow the same field. Supplied as they were with fire-arms, they were savage and powerful, dangerous even to the whites, and far more so to the natives, armed only with stone weapons.

Of the island of San Nicolas a party of these Indians took possession, and slew every male of the thick population upon it, keeping possession of the women. When the otter-hunting season was over, the Alaskans departed, leaving these women to what fate might befall them. About the middle of the year 1835 the padres made arrangements for the succor and removal of the surviving women, by Isaac J. Sparks and Lewis T. Burton, American otter hunters, settled at Santa Barbara, who had chartered the schooner Peor es Nada ("Worse is Nothing") for the purposes of their calling. With a crew composed mainly of Kanakas, they sailed to San Nicolas, and assembled the Indians upon the beach, ready for embarking. One of the women then signified by signs that her child had been left behind, and she was allowed to go to fetch it. She delayed some time, and meanwhile a strong wind sprang up. The water about the island is quite shoal, and becomes very rough in a storm, and there is no sheltering harbor, so that the schooner dared not tarry, but ran before the wind, leaving the woman behind. The vessel arrived safely at San Pedro, where the Indians were landed, some being taken to Los Angeles and some to the Mission of San Gabriel. The captain of the vessel designed to return to the island as soon as possible to fetch away the woman. But, being ordered to San Francisco, she capsized there, and, there being now no craft large enough to attempt the passage of the channel, no attempt was made to rescue the woman, and after some years it was generally believed that she must have perished.

In 1851 John Nidever, with a man named Tom Jeffries and a crew of Indians, had occasion to visit San Nicolas. Landing on the lower end of the island they shortly found on the bank near the beach the footprints of a human being, probably made during the preceding rainy season, as they were deeply impressed in the ground, now very hard and dry. The size of the tracks indicated they were made by a woman. After walking some distance, the men discovered on rising ground about 200 yards back from the beach three structures of human creation. Standing about a mile apart, these enclosures were circular in shape, six or seven feet in diameter, with brush-built walls, five or six feet from the ground, on stakes of driftwood stuck into the earth, pieces of dried blubber, apparently placed there a month or two before, and in good condition. Other than the meat there was no sign of recent occupation of the enclosures. A wind came on, which increased to a gale shortly after the men had regained their vessel, and as soon as practicable, which was not for eight days, they left the vicinity of the island.

In the winter of 1852, Nidever, accompanied by Charles Brown and a crew of Indians, made a second visit to the island, in quest of otter, of which he had seen great numbers on his former visit. Landing at the old place, they walked toward the head of the island, where the woman, if still alive, was likely to be found, as fish and seal are more plentiful, and water better and more abundant in that quarter. The huts were seen as before, the old blubber seeming to have been replaced by fresher. About half a mile from the head of the island and extending across it, was a flat, low and sandy; and here, thought the men, the woman must be living, as the ground to the north and eastward was high and windswept. After searching for some time, without finding a trace of the woman, the men decided that she must have been devoured by wild dogs' of which they had seen a number, resembling the coyotes, but black and white in color. When just about to return, Nidever noticed in the crotch of a small tree a basket, covered over with sealskin, which, on being examined, proved to contain a carefully-folded dress made of the skins of shags, cut in square pieces and sewn together; a rope made of sinews, and divers small articles such as needles made of bone, abelone, fish-hooks, etc. Brown compassionately proposed to replace the basket where they had found it, but Nidever shrewdly preferred to scatter the articles about the spot, as their replacement on a future visit would prove the woman's existence and presence there. Accordingly this was done, and the men returned to their schooner. For some days they were busy hunting, and then a gale forced them to make off without renewing the search.

In July, 1853, Nidever once more returned to San Nicolas with Brown and four Mission Indians, this time with the intention of making a thorough search for the missing woman. After selecting a camp, they followed the shore to the head of the island, which Brown rounded; and some distance down the other side he found fresh tracks of the woman, which he followed up from the beach and over the bank, losing them on the ridge where the ground was covered with moss. The following day, going to the sandy flat before mentioned, they organized a regular search, for some time without results. Brown followed the track he had found the previous evening, until he found a piece of driftwood, apparently dropped by the woman; and farther along the ridge he discovered three huts, made of brush, disposed over the ribs of a whale, set in the earth. These tenements were, however, open on all sides, and tall grass grew within them, proving the long time that had elapsed since their occupation. Ascending to one of the highest parts of the ridge he gazed about on all sides. Most of the searchers were in sight, and far away he could see moving a small black object which he at first took to be a crow. On walking toward it, he discovered that this was the Indian woman, whose head and shoulders just appeared above the rim of an enclosure like those already described. Close to her were two or three dogs like those the men had seen already. They growled at Brown's approach, whereupon the woman uttered a sort of yell, and they slunk out of sight. The woman was sitting cross-legged on some grass within the enclosure, which doubtless served her for a bed. She wore a sort of gown, made of shag-skins cut in squares and sewed together, with the feathers pointing downward. The garment left her neck and shoulders bare, reaching to her ankles. Her hair was thickly matted upon her head, being yellowish-brown in color, probably from exposure to the weather The ends seemed to have rotted off. She was engaged in stripping the blubber from a piece of sealskin held across her knee, using a knife rudely fashioned from a piece of iron hoop. A fire was smouldering within the enclosure, and close by was a large heap of bones, which would denote that for a long time this had been her domicile.

The woman appeared much interested in the movements of the men who were scouring the flat below; every now and then she would shade her eyes with her hand and direct a long and steady gaze upon them. And all the while, from the time Brown first came within hearing distance, she kept up a continual talking to herself.

As the men drew near, Brown motioned to them to spread out in such shape as to surround her and intercept her, should she attempt to escape; then, just before the others reached her little camp, Brown, whom she had not yet seen, stepped around in front and in sight of her. To his great surprise, instead of exhibiting signs of fear or distrust, she received him with an air of welcome, bowing and smiling with mingled cordial politeness and dignity. Her self-possession and ease was considered by her discoverers remarkable. As each man came up he was greeted in the same manner, and she continued to talk unceasingly. But although the Indians of the schooner's crew could muster several native dialects, not a word of her speech understood they.

When the men were all seated upon the ground around her, she took from a grass-woven bag some of the bulbous roots called by the Californians *cacomites*, and another species of root, and having first roasted them upon the fire, she offered them to the men, who found them very palatable.

Wishing to convey her on board the schooner, the men tried to inform her by signs of their intentions; but while she seemed pleased with their company, and gave no reason to apprehend that she would try to escape, she seemed to not comprehend their intentions until they signified that she must gather up all her food stores. Then, indeed, she obeyed with the greatest alacrity, and seemed anxious to preserve everything capable of sustaining life, thus pathetically demonstrating the sharp experiences she had undoubtedly undergone during her eighteen years of solitude. Carefully she collected and placed in a large *cora*, or basket, such as was generally used by the Indians of this coast, the considerable quantity she possessed of the dried blubber of the seal and sea elephant. She even insisted upon carrying away a seal's head so decayed that the brains were oozing from it; and when all else was ready she took a burning stick from the camp-fire. The men distributed her effects for carriage, and all set forth toward the vessel. She trotted along at a good pace, and presently led them to a spring of good water which issued from beneath a shelving rock near the beach. Here were more pieces of dried blubber, hung on stakes beyond reach of the dogs and foxes; and here, too, further pathetic evidence of the privations she had suffered, in the shape of bones stored away in the crevices of the rocks. It was clear that when food was scarce, her resource was to come hither and suck the scanty nutriment remaining in these bones! All these matters were respected and preserved by the men, who thus gained the poor, deserted creature's confidence. Near the landing was another spring which the woman would seem to have used for bathing, as she stopped to wash her face and hands in it.

She readily obeyed the signaled instruction to step into the boat, in whose bow she kneeled, holding to the sides; and on reaching the vessel she hovered in the vicinity of the stove, another indication of the hardships she had suffered on the island. From the first she preferred to her own the food given her by her rescuers.

Brown immediately contrived for her a petticoat of bed-ticking, which, with a man's shirt and necktie, composed a new wardrobe, of which she was very proud, continually calling to it the attention of her companions. While Brown was engaged upon her skirt, she made signs that she wished to sew also; and being given a needle and thread, she could not understand, until she was taught, how the needle was threaded; but she used the needle deftly, mending with infinite patience the many rents in an old cape, very torn and tattered, which one of the men bestowed upon her, and which she repaired into a garment quite serviceable in cold, rough weather. In sewing, she thrust the needle into the cloth with her right hand, pulling it through, and drawing the thread tight with her left hand.

The men on the next day moved ashore, where they remained for about a month, otter-hunting. They constructed for the woman, at a short distance from their camp, a shelter similar to their own; and here she remained very well contented, evincing no disposition to leave them, but assisting in the work of the camp, bringing wood and water at need, and wandering about the island, talking and singing.

When the woman was found, she had in construction several vessels for carrying water, they being really unique. They were woven of grass, in shape somewhat like a demijohn, although wider in the mouth, and lined with a thin coating of asphaltum, which she applied with some ingenuity. Putting into the basket several pieces of the asphaltum, which was found along the beach in great quantities, she threw upon them some heated pebbles, and when these had melted the asphaltum, she would distribute it evenly over the inside by giving the basket a rotary motion, throwing out the surplus and the pebbles. These baskets were water-tight, and very enduring. She worked upon them fitfully, a few minutes at a time, putting one aside to take up another.

One rather touching trait of her character is illustrated by the following occurrence. The men one day killed a large female otter which was with young, and when they were about to throw it into the sea, as they usually did the bodies after skinning, the woman, in her mute way, protested. She took out the young otter, which was nearly to be born and covered with fur, and when it had been stuffed it looked quite natural. Of this little creature the woman made a sort of doll, suspending it from the roof of her shelter, where for hours she would swing it, all the while talking to it in a kind of sing-song.

After about a month's successful hunt, Nidever's party embarked for Santa Barbara. Not long after they sailed there arose a furious gale, which threatened to engulf the little vessel. Then the woman made signs that she could calm the wind, and, kneeling down with her face toward the quarter whence it blew, she commenced to make prayers or incantations, which continued a long time, and were renewed at intervals during the storm. When the wind abated and patches of clear sky appeared, she pointed in triumph to these tokens of good weather, as who should say, "See what I accomplished!"

The shore was neared early one morning, and it was evident that the woman had never seen this nor any of the ordinary appearances and sights of a settlement. It was hard to tell whether pleasure or wonder predominated in her when there passed on the sands a Spanish cart, drawn by an ox team. Every feature of it was delightful to her, and she imitated with curious gestures the rotary motion of the clumsy wheels, talking, laughing and gesticulating, all at the same time. When landing had been made, she was much taken up with a horseman who came to the beach, and her courage was shown by her readiness to touch this great unknown, and to her doubtless fearful, creature. After touching both horse and man, she turned to her captors, and proved that she grasped the situation by straddling over her left thumb the first two fingers of her right hand, while she moved her hand to imitate the galloping of a horse, shouting the while with delight.

The woman was taken to Nidever's house, where his wife cared for her; and soon the news spread that the lost woman of San Nicolas Island was found. Her case had excited great interest among the warm-hearted people of the region, who had discussed in the safety of their homes for many a year the possibilities of her still surviving on that desert sea-girt isle, with wild beasts for her only companions. And as the years went by, it was generally believed that she must surely be dead, devoured, in all likelihood, by the wild dogs. The padres of the mission had interested themselves for her, and had offered a reward of $200 for information that should lead to her recovery.

And now the lost was found, and was here within the limits of civilization. Hundreds flocked to Nidever's house to see her. Among others came the Fathers, Sanchez, Jimeno and Gonzalez, the latter of whom in particular had earnestly insisted upon the probabilities of her survival. But none could communicate with her, save by the imperfect sign language, although the padres knew all the dialects of the coast. From Santa Ynes, from Los Angeles, and from other places Indians were brought to see her, but they too found not one word in common with her. Every one showed her the greatest kindness. Nearly every one would give her a present of money, of clothing, or of trinkets, all of which she would at once give to her friends, or to the children who visited her. The Panama steamers were touching at Santa Barbara in those days, and the passengers were always eager to see this poor savage heroine. She would often put on her best dress of feathers, and for their gratification perform movements which might be called dancing. She soon became very expert in conversing by signs, and thus related the history of her adventures, relating that when she went back after the child, she wandered a long time without finding it; that when she concluded that the dogs had eaten the child, she lay down and cried for so long a time that she sickened, could not eat, and became too weak to walk; then, recovering somewhat, she began to walk about and to eat. Often she had seen vessels upon the sea, but none ever came near to take her away, so that in time she became reconciled to her fate, and her monotonous life of hunger, cold and the fear of wild animals. She was supposed to have been about fifty years old at the time of her rescue. Her face was smooth, although the skin on her body and limbs was badly wrinkled. It was gathered from her signs that at the time when she was left on the island she had two children, one a nursing babe, the other some years older.

The woman was much attached to the family of Mr. Nidever, who in turn were fond of her. Mr. Nidever repeatedly refused large sums which were offered him as an inducement to her public exhibition in San Francisco. It was only a short time before her death that her protectors succeeded in making her understand their wish to learn some words of her language, and the following comprise about all the terms they gathered from her: a hide, "tocah;" man, "nache;" the sky, "toy gwah;" the body, "puoo-chay."

With regard to practical matters, she was like a child, and childish was her want of control over her appetite. Being excessively fond of fruit, she would eat it at all hazards, and this self-indulgence produced a dysentery which terminated fatally, in spite of careful attendance and nursing. During her illness, it was thought that she might be relieved by a diet of seal's flesh, to which she had been so long accustomed; and accordingly some was procured and roasted for her. But she laughed and shook her head over it, passing her finger over her worn-out teeth, to indicate that they were too old and spent for such use. It was about four months after her rescue that she died. She was buried by the padres. Most of her trinkets, including the finer of her feather dresses, were sent to Rome.

It may be wondered that the woman should have been left so long for want of a boat to fetch her from the island; but it must be remembered that when the Boston ship Monsoon visited Santa Barbara in 1839, the captain of the port had no boat in which to make his official visit. Chagrined by the situation, he petitioned for a boat, which the government accordingly provided for him.

RESOURCES.

The resources of Santa Barbara county have been pretty thoroughly indicated in connection with the respective sections, save in the directions set forth hereafter, as follows:

HOGS.

With reference to hog-raising in this county, an estimate of the possibilities may be formed from the following extract from a paper by Mr. L. Babcock: "Hogs can be raised here with little trouble after you are prepared, as we do not have any or but few storms during each year, and no fatal diseases such as cholera. Neither have we any trichinæ in the bacons on this coast. On May 19, 1881, I purchased 120 acres of land in the Lompoc Valley, all fenced and improved ready to go into the business of raising and preparing hogs for the market. I also bought 600 head of hogs, big and little, and the growing crop, at a cost of $13,066. I raised grain on 100 acres of the ranch. On the last of August, 1881, sold to Sherman & Ealand, of Santa Barbara, 302 head of hogs. They received them on the ranch and paid me $1,962.50. In September, 1882, I shipped to San Francisco 323 head of hogs off the same ranch, and sold them for $3,801.26, and after deducting all expenses of driving, shipping, commission, etc., I got a net return of $3,282.63. And I have 100 or more still on the ranch."

BEE-FARMING.

In 1860 or '61, a party named Miner—he who built the first frame house in Santa Barbara—imported eight or ten swarms of bees, which sold readily for $50 per swarm. In December, 1873, Mr. Jefferson Archer brought hither some forty-five stands of bees, and went into apiculture exclusively. The industry increased to such an extent that at the close of the season of 1880 there were in the county about 3,300 stands of bees, yielding a product of over 128 tons or 256,000 pounds of extracted honey.

While that portion of this county adapted to profitable honey-raising is small, compared with the territory devoted to this industry in some other counties, the quality of honey produced is unexcelled. The honey-producing plants are abundant; the mountain redwood, sumac, grease-wood, coffee berry and the various sages, all in their respective seasons, supply the raw material to the humming, busy workers. This is an enterprise yielding large returns from limited capital; it is by no means uncommon to derive a profit of over 400 per cent. from single swarms, and almost as high a figure has been realized from an entire apiary. With a fair season, a good swarm will yield 150 to 250 pounds of extracted honey in a season, besides its increase of one or two swarms in a season, the increase not seldom reaching to five and even ten swarms in one season. One apiary of 400 stands in the county produced during the season of 1884 no less than 730,000 pounds of pure strained honey and 2,000 pounds of beeswax. Apiculture suffers occasional drawbacks; an insufficient rainfall lessens or cuts off altogether the honey yield, and a general drouth affects bees as it does cattle and other stock.

FISHERY.

Santa Barbara Channel and its adjacent waters are especially rich in good fishes. The ocean temperature here is particularly mild and equable, never falling below 60° nor rising above 66° F., thus resembling the Mediterranean, which produces many of the finest market fish in the world.

This temperature, the calmness of the waters, and the quantity of marine vegetation nourished therein, make these parts the natural home of the finest tribes.

In 1881 David S. Jordan and Charles H. Gilbert were sent by the United States Government to the Pacific coast to investigate the fish interests of this section. They found Santa Barbara Channel one of the richest points on the coast, and the results of their investigation surprised even those best acquainted with the wealth of these waters. In their report the following fishes are mentioned as abundant in this locality:

Herring: Clupea mirablis. Runs during the winter. Is like the Atlantic herring in size and general character. Is marketed, dried and salted.

Sardine: Clupea sagax. Two species—the larger " American " sardine, sometimes reaching a length of nine inches, and a smaller species, exactly the same as that of the Mediterranean.

Barracuda: Sphyræna argentæ. The favorite fish of this part of the coast. Runs four or five months during the summer. Averages under ten pounds' weight. When dried, is an excellent substitute for codfish.

Albacore: Orcynus alalonga. Average weight, twelve to fifteen pounds. Very good food fish.

Spanish mackerel: Sarda chilensis. Average weight eight to ten pounds. Used for the most part dried and salted.

Pompano: Stromaticus simillimus. Averages one-half pound weight; length eight inches. Scarce in winter.

Yellow-tail or white salmon: Seriola lalandi. Weight forty to fifty pounds. Length four to five feet.

Smelt: Atherinops affinis. About one foot in length.

Flying fish: Exocœtus californicus. Length about fifteen inches; weight about one and one-half pounds. Excellent food. Appear toward the middle of summer.

Mullet: Mugil albula. Fifteen inches long. Flesh coarse, but good food when taken in clear water.

Rock cod: Serranus maculofasciatus. Fifteen inches long; weighs two to three pounds.

Kelp salmon: Serranus clathratus. Eighteen inches long; weight five pounds.

White sea bass: Alroctoscium nobile. Length about four feet; weight under fifty pounds.

White-fish: Dekaya princeps. Length two feet; weight ten to fourteen pounds. When salted is excellent.

Conger eel: Muræna mordax. Length about five feet; weight fifteen to twenty pounds. Flesh very fat. Excellent food.

The local market for fish is not large, and a very few fishermen supply the local needs and such small exportations as have been made. But the fish interest could be made a source of important revenue by the development of some practical plan for exportation, for which purpose a number of the species named above are eminently suitable. The white-fish, the barracuda, and the herring are particularly adapted for preparation and shipment, and it must be noted, too, that the herring is here brought into natural contact with his regular post-mortem element, olive oil. Thus a sardine cannery hereabouts would seem to be an inevitable outgrowth of these natural provisions.

MINERALS.

(From the State Mineralogical Report.)

On the San Marcos Rancho there is said to be a lode that assays well in both gold and silver. Gold-bearing rock has also been found on the Buel Rancho, near Los Alamos. Placer claims have been worked at Pine Mountain, also at the headwaters of Zaca Creek, and at several places in the San Rafael Mountains. A very few colors of gold are occasionally found in the creeks running from the Santa Ynes Range. Gold-washing has also been carried on upon the seashore; the most successful operations were at Point Sal, in the northwestern corner of the county. Point Sal is situated upon the southern bank of the Santa Maria River. Gold-washing has been intermittently carried on here by the Point Sal Mining Company. The gold is found in streaks of black sand from three to four feet below the surface of the beach. They run from one inch to two feet in thickness, usually being about one foot, and from thirty to forty feet in length. The bank of the beach runs north and south, the streaks of sand east and west toward the ocean. Beneath the black sand is blue clay in some places, and sandstone in others. The richest deposits are found on the sandstone where it is worn into ridges, being favorable to the concentration of the gold. The sand is run into a hopper, where a stream of water carries it over amalgamated plates. About twenty-five tons of this sand yielded $137.

On the Jonita Rancho, near Los Alamos, rock containing gold and silver has been found. This at last induced William Buel to explore the formation of his rancho by running a tunnel over 400 feet. This tunnel, which is situated a little over 1,000 feet above the level of the sea, is run in a southwesterly direction through a sedimentary formation, which dips to the sea at an angle of about 45° * * * Here and there throughout the tunnel are a few seams and pockets of clayey matter, which are said to show a few colors of gold. * * * The tunnel does not appear to be following any vein.

Copper is said to exist in paying quantities on the southern bank of the Santa Cruz River, where it was worked by the old padres; also at several places in the San Rafael Mountains.

Quicksilver is said to exist at Los Prietos, nine miles north of Santa Barbara, on the upper waters of the Santa Ynes River, in considerable quantities. It is claimed that a great deal of the ore will average from two to three per cent. The Eagle Quicksilver mine was also worked in 1867, by Captain Samuel Stanton, on the Cuchama River, in the San Rafael Mountains.

Float rock containing galena is said to be found at the mouth of Dry Creek Cañon, on the Buel Rancho, near Los Alamos; also on the Spinnocia Rancho, about twelve miles east of Santa Ynes, in the San Rafael Mountains.

Manganese occurs in the San Rafael Mountains, about seven miles north of the town of Santa Ynes.

Coal has been found at several places in Santa Barbara County, notably in the Loma Paloma, head of Santa Ynes Creek, Montecito Hot Springs and at the Mission.

Limestone is widely distributed in the county, but as yet has been burned only for local use. It is found upon Moore's Rancho, a few miles west of Santa Barbara. Immediately north of Mr. Moore's house, distant about two miles from the seashore, are the foothills of the Santa Ynes Range, spurs of which run down nearly to the water's edge; these are composed of sandstone, varying from coarse to fine. At one point they are traversed by a vein of calcite about four feet wide, running nearly east and west.

The gypsum deposits of Santa Barbara occur upon the southern side of Point Sal, and can be reached by road either from Guadalupe or Santa Maria. Point Sal gypsum mines lie back in the mountains about one and one-half miles from Point Sal Landing. They occur as a vein having a head-wall and foot-wall of clay slate. There are six openings on this property from which gypsum are taken. * * * The finest quality of the material is said to be obtained in the upper workings. The other openings are of less importance, and no gypsum at present is taken from them. The lower vein can be traced for about two miles. This mineral can be mined and placed on board the vessels at Point Sal for about $2 per ton.

There are several mineral springs in this county, but few of them have as yet become places of resort. At Montecito the water from the springs reaches 117° Fahrenheit. On the Santa Ynes Mountains, near Santa Barbara, there is another hot spring; also in the Santa Marcos Cañon, where the water is said to reach a temperature of 120° Fahrenheit. In the cañon and the Cuyama Valley are also springs.

There are, so far as known at the present time, no oil wells producing anything in Santa Barbara County, though several have been sunk there. But there are great deposits of asphaltum and other bituminous matters at several localities in the county. "El Rincon" Creek, some three or four miles east of Carpenteria, is, for some little distance near the coast, the boundary line between Ventura and Santa Barbara counties. At Rincon Point, on the shore just west of El Rincon Creek, the railway company has recently done some heavy grading in the construction of their road. Amongst other unaltered rocks here, which dip toward the north, they have cut through a heavy body of bituminous shales, which contain a sufficient quantity of bituminous matter, so that, when once ignited they continue to burn for a long time like the waste heaps from a coal mine.

The Rancho of Mr. P. Clark Higgins, mentioned as the "Carpenteria bed," is only about one mile east of the new Carpenteria railway station. The bluffs here fronting the sea-beach are fifty to seventy-five feet high. The lower portion of them consists of tertiary rocks, out of which the petroleum oozes. * * * Anywhere within one quarter of a mile or more back from the edge of the bluffs it is no uncommon occurrence for the plow to turn up bituminous matter. * * *

The outcrop of asphaltum and other bituminous matters in the bluffs extends for a distance of three-quarters of a mile along the shore and to within half a mile or less of the new railway station at Carpenteria. * * * This bitumen is very dirty, but might possibly be used for street pavements.

On Ortega Hill, about six miles east of Santa Barbara, and near half way between there and Carpenteria, Mr. H. L. Williams has drilled a well. The locality is within 500 or 600 feet of the seashore, and 250 feet above high tide. Mr. Williams here went down 455 feet. * * * The shale is very close, and contains neither water nor oil. The sand above was free from water. But the oil which it contains makes it act like a quicksand, and it rose 100 feet in the pipe. * * * In attempting to draw the casing, in order to substitute drive pipe for it, the casing parted in the upper sand and they could not get the lower part of it out, and were therefore obliged to abandon the hole. Then they swung the derrick around about ten feet, and started another one.

Just northwest of Ortega Hill, in the Montecito Valley, two little creeks join, and just below their junction there is a small outcrop of asphaltum in the bank. * * *

At the foot of the hills, on the shore, a quarter of a mile east of the well, the rocks are exposed at low water, and it looks as if there were an anticlinal fold here. There is also some seepage of oil from these rocks, and Mr. Williams states that after a slight earthquake shock one night, in 1883, a jet of oil "as large as a man's arm" spurted out here for a little while, but did not last long. Considerable gas also escapes from these rocks. Their strike is about east and west. Mr. Williams' wells are just about on the line of the anticlinal axis in these rocks, while the old well at the foot of the hill is on the north side of it.

A little over one mile east of here a low bluff makes out a short distance into the sea, and there is also some seepage of oil. There are also said to be extensive seepages in "Oil Cañon" and one other cañon in the Santa Ynes range of mountains, some three miles in an airline northeast from Ortega Hill.

In 1885 the "Santa Barbara Oil Company" sunk two wells some 500 or 600 feet deep in "Oil Cañon," at a point 1,400 or 1,500 feet above tide. There was much gas here. But at last, either by accident or malice, the tools were lost in one of the wells, and the work was abandoned. * * *

Moore's Landing is near the village of Goleta, about seven miles west of the city of Santa Barbara. Easterly from the landing, for a distance of a mile of so along the shore, the bluffs are forty to seventy-five feet high, of light gray sandstone, * * in which there are enormous quantities of asphaltum, which occur in all imaginable forms. There are occasional well-defined veins of it, from the thickness of a sheet of paper up to two or three feet thick, which extend for short distances through the heavy-bedded sandstone, and then run out completely. Again it occurs in heavy masses twenty or thirty feet and more in diameter. In some places very heavy beds of it run nearly parallel with the stratification of the sandstone, while on the other hand many of the small *veins* of it cut straight through and across the bedding at all angles. Most of it is largely mixed with sand and pebbles; but there are large quantities of it which look very pure. No liquid oil is visible here, nor any soft pitch either, except what is washed up in small flakes by the surf on the beach from beneath the waters of the sea.

Something like a mile to the west of the landing there is a place in a creek in the salt marsh where a good deal of gas bubbles up; and two or three miles farther southwest is Salinas Point, which projects some distance into the sea, and about half a mile outside of which is one of the large and famous petroleum springs beneath the ocean. The depth of the water where this spring issues was asserted by one man to be only about fifty feet, but by another to be fifty fathoms. The latter is more probable. About eighteen miles off shore here in the channel, and some two miles north of the island of Santa Cruz there is also said to be another very large oil spring under the water.

Mr. H. C. Hobson, of San Luis Obispo, states that there are very large quantities of asphaltum on the Sisquoc Rancho, in the northern part of Santa Barbara County, on one of the upper branches of the Santa Maria River. Sisquoc Creek joins the Santa Maria River at Fugler's Point, some fifty miles south of San Luis Obispo.

SAN LUIS OBISPO COUNTY.

IN GENERAL.
ORIGINAL AND DESCRIPTIVE.

San Luis Obispo was one of the original twenty-seven counties created by act of Legislature, approved February 18, 1850. The boundaries of this county, as described by section 5 of this act, were as follows: " Beginning three English miles west of the coast at a point due west of the source of the Nacimiento River, and running due east to the source of said river; thence down the middle of said river to its confluence with Monterey River; thence up or down, as the case may be, the middle of Monterey River to the parallel of thirty-six degrees north latitude; thence due east following said parallel to the summit of the Coast Range; thence following the summit of said range in a southeasterly direction to the northeast corner of Santa Barbara County; thence following the northern boundary of Santa Barbara County to the ocean, and three English miles therein; and thence in a northwesterly direction, parallel with the coast, to the place of beginning. The seat of justice shall be at San Luis Obispo."

The area of the county, as originally defined, contained about 3,250 square miles. This territory was but sparsely populated; the census for 1850 gave a total population of 336. The only occupied sections were the large ranchos, where were found but the dwellings of the proprietors and their employés. The only focus of population was at the Mission of San Luis Obispo; this was the central point of the district, before the creation of the county; here was the seat of justice for the surrounding region, and here were held elections. But even here there was no assemblage of houses beyond the mission buildings and a few neighboring adobe structures.

This county has about ninety miles of coast, extending along the Pacific Ocean, northerly and northwesterly, from opposite the mouth of the Santa Maria River to where the Sixth Standard South, Monte Diablo Base, enters the ocean, or to a point about ten miles northwest of the Piedras Blancas.

Soon after California became a possession of the United States, this coast was surveyed under the suprevision of Prof. A. L. Bache, of the United States Coast Survey, the first report on the survey being published in 1852. The surveys have been continued under the charge of Prof. George Davidson, whose volume, published in 1869, entitled " Coast Pilot of California, Oregon, and Washington,' is the authority for many of the present statements.

The coast of this county has a natural division into two distinct sections, one of which extends from Point Sal, in Santa Barbara County on the south, to Point San Luis on the north. This division is an indentation called San Luis Obispo Bay; north of Point Sal the mountains fall back, and the shore is formed of sand-hills. The general trend is north, until the coast commences sweeping westward to form the bay of San Luis Obispo, and the shores become high and abrupt. From Point Sal to Point San Luis the distance is about seventeen miles in a northwesterly direction, the beach running somewhat east of north for about fifteen miles, when it curves to the northwest, west, south, and southeast, in a line of ten miles, forming San Luis Obispo Bay.

A few miles north of Point Sal the Santa Maria River, emptying into the ocean, forms the division line between this and Santa Barbara County. A few miles north of this is the Oso Flaco, and midway of the beach the Arroyo Grande empties, having received near its mouth the Pizmo and Arroyo Verde creeks. The San Luis Creek enters the northern side of the bay.

The first or lower division of this coast is called Pizmo Beach. Landing was formerly effected here in fair weather by means of small boats, and lines through the surf. As increasing agricultural interests demanded better facilities, the Pizmo wharf was here constructed in 1881, extending through the surf to deep water, opposite the Pizmo Rancho.

On San Luis Obispo Bay the Coast Survey made the following report, published in 1852, and republished in 1867: "This bay is an open roadstead, exposed to the southward, and even during heavy northwest weather a bad lateral swell rolls in, rendering it an uncomfortable anchorage. The landing is frequently very bad, and often impracticable, but the best place is the mouth of the creek, keeping the rocks at its mouth on the starboard hand. Fresh water may be obtained at a small stream opening on the beach half a mile west of the creek. In the coarse sandstone bluff between these two places are found gigantic fossil remains.

"Off Point San Luis, which forms the southwest part of the bay, are some rocks, and in making the anchorage vessels should give this point a berth of half a mile. * * * The distance from this rock to the mouth of the creek is a mile and a half. * * * Four fathoms can be got about a fourth of a mile from the beach. In winter, anchor far enough out to clear Point San Luis if a southeaster should come up. During southerly weather landing is frequently effected at the watering place when impracticable at the creek."

In the ante-wharf days, landing was effected here as elsewhere by means of boats and lighters, and the disembarking was often, when the swell was heavy, very dangerous, as only those places were selected which were accessible to teams or pack trains on the shore. In 1860, a small wharf was built at a spot called Cave Landing, and here passengers and goods were landed. In 1869 a larger structure, called the People's Wharf, was built at the Avila Beach. Here vessels and steamers could make fast to discharge and receive cargo. This wharf was exposed to the violence of the ocean during southwest storms, preventing landing, and more than once breaking away the structure.

It was observed that vessels remained more securely farther to the westward, where the waves broke less heavily; but here the beach was very difficult of access, high, rocky bluffs coming to the edge of the water. Here Mr.

John Harford and others resolved to construct a landing, and accordingly in 1872 work was begun, to quarry a way for a railroad, and build a wharf to deep water. By 1873 the enterprise was so far advanced that shipping was received and goods transported over the railway, then operated by animal traction, to a point accessible to teams, a distance of some two miles. Such was the origin of Port Harford, which now has a wharf 1,800 feet long, with warehouse and offices upon it, and a large hotel at the land end. Vessels of up to 3,000 tons' burthen touch at this wharf regularly, and it is constantly crowded with business. Passengers and freight are conveyed to San Luis Obispo and other towns by the Pacific Coast Railway, whose trains run out upon the wharf twice a day.

The second division of this county's coast is an irregular shore line, extending northward from Point San Luis to where the Santa Lucia Range abuts upon the coast, at the northern extreme of the county. Concerning this section, the Coast Survey's report says:—

"To the northwest of the bay of San Luis Obispo rises to a great height the Monte de Buchon, which is readily distinguished in coming from the northward or the southward. * * * From Point San Luis the coast trends in a straight line west-northwest for eight miles, and close along the shore of this stretch are several large rocks. Thence the coast trends abruptly to the north, to the high, conical rock called El Morro, distant eight miles—these two shores forming the seaward base of Mount Buchon. From El Morro the shore line gradually trends to the westward, thus forming a deep indentation or bay, designated as Estero Bay on the Coast Survey chart. Behind El Morro are several lagoons or streams, where a harbor for light-draft vessels could be made at comparatively small expense, and the high land etreats for some distance, leaving the shore low and sandy, while the north shore is rugged and guarded by rocks. The northwest point of the bay is called Punta de los Esteros, on the old Spanish charts, distant thirteen miles. A line joining these points shows that the bay is about five miles deep.

"In this bay is the landing of Cayucos where Captain James Cass, in 1873, built a substantial wharf, with tramway, warehouses, etc.

"From Point Los Esteros to the western point of anchorage of San Simeon, the coast runs nearly straight northwest by west for a distance of fifteen miles. The shores are not so bold as to the southward or northward, and the mountains fall back, leaving a fine, rolling country of no great elevation, and well suited to agriculture. We have seen wild oats growing here over six feet in height—not one or two stalks, but in acres.

SAN SIMEON BAY.—"This is a small, exposed roadstead, but affords tolerably good anchorage during northwest winds. * * * The indentation of the shore line forming the bay trends between northwest and north for half a mile, and then sweeps away to the westward about a mile and a half, gradually taking a southeast direction. The land behind the bay is comparatively low and gently rolling, the high hills retiring well inland. The high hills behind this shore are marked by redwood trees along their crest line, and upon some of their flanks. * * * It was in this bay that the steamship Pioneer, in 18—, put in leaking badly, was driven or dragged upon the beach, and after being abandoned by the underwriters was got off and carried to San Francisco.

"In making this harbor from the northward vessels must sight the Piedras Blancas

(White Rocks) four miles west, three-quarters north of the southwest point of San Simeon. They are two large, white, sharp-topped rocks, and nothing else like them is found on this part of the coast. When the outer rock bears north-northwest about two miles distant, it bears a very striking resemblance to a lion *couchant*. The geographical position of the outer and larger rock is, approximately, latitude 35° 39' north; longitude, 121° 15' west. * * * From Piedras Blancas the coast trends northwest half west for a distance of fifty-seven miles, in an almost perfectly straight line."

ORGANIZATION.

In the division of the State into Assembly and Senatorial districts, San Luis Obispo was allowed to elect one Assemblyman, and San Luis Obispo and Santa Barbara counties were united in a Senatorial district to elect one Senator. Don Pablo de la Guerra of Santa Barbara was sent out as Senator, although it was claimed that more votes were cast for Captain William G. Dana, of San Luis Obispo. Henry A. Tefft was the first Assemblyman from this county. Santa Barbara and San Luis Obispo composed the Second Judicial district, in which court was ordered to be held in the more northern county-seat, beginning on the first Monday of March, of July, and of October, in each year. At the election held April 14, 1850, J. Mariano Bonilla was elected County Judge; Henry J. Dally, Sheriff; Charles James Freeman, County Clerk; Joaquin Estrada, County Recorder; John Wilson, County Treasurer and Collector; Joseph Warren and Jesus Luna, Justices of the Peace. The statute creating the courts authorized the Court of Sessions to order elections to fill vacancies, and also to fill vacancies *pro tem.* Here as elsewhere the court consisted of the County Judge and two Justices of the Peace. The first session, held in July, 1850, appointed Francis Z. Branch, Assessor; William Hutton, County Surveyor, and William Stenner, Harbor Master; also Stephen Purdie to fill the office of County Recorder, resigned by Joaquin Estrada; and in August, when Purdie in his turn resigned, his successor, S. A. Pollard, was appointed. There were in this county several incumbents of the office of *Juez de Campo* (Judge of the Fields or Country), a feature adapted from the old Spanish règime. This officer had supervision over the ownership, branding, driving, and killing of cattle, and other questions relating to this subject, and in those counties containing the great stock ranges his functions were very important.

The first mention of any other township than that of San Luis Obispo is in the records of the Court of Sessions which appointed these judges of the fields and prescribed their duties. Here reference is made to the township of Nipomo, and to that of the Third Precinct.

At the election held in 1853 there were cast 137 votes in San Luis.

After a meeting of the board of supervisors, August 3, 1859, which added three more precincts to those already existing, the county contained election precincts as follows:—San Luis Obispo, Paso Robles, Arroyo Grande, San Miguel, Costa, and Estrella.

For a number of years all the proceedings of the Court of Sessions of San Louis Obispo were conducted in Spanish, and all the accounts, and such records as were kept, were entered in that language, which alone was spoken by the great majority of the people, and by those who composed the official corps and the juries.

ANNALS OF THE COUNTY—1851–1890.

In the early days an act of the Legislature provided for public advertising in this county, requiring that all public notices should be posted at the houses of three specified citizens of the county.

The total vote here at the first election under American rule was twenty-nine. The first after the constitution was adopted was forty-five. At the election of 1851 for governor, San Luis Obispo gave eight votes for the Democratic, and fifty-eight for the Whig, candidate, this being the lowest vote polled in any county in the State, whose whole vote was 46,009. This county continued Whig for some years.

During the '60s the inequitable assessments on lands caused great dissatisfaction in San Luis Obispo as elsewhere, and, a test case having been carried through various courts, it was declared that the action of the Board of Equalization, in increasing the assessments, was unjustifiable in law. The taxes were therefore paid according to the original asesssment. The assessed valuations this year were: real estate, $177,711.60; personal property, $311,121.25; total, $488,832.85. The tax rate was $3.85; total tax, $18,598.90. There was in the county treasury a total of $4,881.50.

During the decade of 1850–'60 San Luis Obispo County was indeed "a dark and bloody ground," where the peaceable and law-abiding citizen was far enough from finding security and protection. In 1853 a gang of eight or ten men committed murders and robberies hereabouts, and then left for Los Angeles, where they were captured, five paying the supreme penalty for their crimes, and the rest escaping. For the next five years, hardly a month passed without the disappearance of some traveler, or the finding of one or more bodies of men slain for plunder.

The murder of George Fearless in 1856, presumably by Jesus Luna, unpunished; the murder of the two Frenchmen, Obiesa and Graciano, on the Nacimiento, in December, 1857, by Jack Powers, Pio Linares, and the Huero Rafael, who all escaped justice; the cold-blooded murder at San Juan Capistrano of the French rancheros, Baratie and Borel, and the abduction of Mme. Baratie by eight men who had enjoyed their hospitality, are among the most flagrant cases of those days. Of these criminals six paid the forfeit of their lives, either by hanging at the hands of the law, or by shooting by their pursuers.

These crimes were of unspeakable detriment to San Luis Obispo County. A deputy United States surveyor was at the time engaged in surveying the public lands, and dividing them from those comprised in the Spanish grants, many choice locations thus being found available for settlement. Further, many of the old ranchos were changing hands. The San Simeon rancho had been sold to a Spanish gentleman named Pujol, a part of the San Geronimo to one Señor Castro, the Blackburns of Santa Cruz had gathered about them on the Paso Robles quite a colony of Americans, and the Frenchmen Borel and Baratie were cultivating the San Juan Capistrano rancho when they met their untimely end. Naturally enough, the evil fame of these atrocities spread far and wide, and deterred from immigration many worthy people whose advent would have contributed greatly to the development of the section.

Opposite the priests' house, in Monterey street, the padres had erected a whipping-post, whereon to punish refractory Indians. After the coming of the Americans, they still used it as a means of punishment, up to 1854 or 1855. It was made of stone, with a base two and one-half feet square, and four feet high, from which arose a cylindrical column, some eighteen inches in diameter, and six feet high, all well cemented and smooth. On the top was a stone sun-dial, which marked the time for the padres, who were very scantily supplied with clocks and watches.

It is stated that one sheriff here whipped a Mexican, for a heinous crime, so severely that the creature died in consequence.

As late as 1862 there was in San Luis no watchmaker, and all time-pieces to be repaired had to be taken to San Francisco.

In 1864 the Steele Brothers made a cheese eighteen inches thick, and over twenty feet in circumference, with a weight of 3,580 pounds. They presented it to the Sanitary Commission, who placed it on exhibition at the Mechanics' Institute Fair in San Francisco, and then sold it for the benefit of sick and wounded soldiers, it bringing over $3,000.

In September, 1883, a fire at Corral de Piedra destroyed 260 tons of hay, and buildings, harness, etc., to the amount of about $5,000, uninsured.

In October, 1883, was organized a local Society for the Prevention of Cruelty to Animals.

A fire at San Luis during this month burned portions of several buildings, including part of the Cosmopolitan Hotel, causing losses to the amount of $8,000.

In December, 1883, the town had a population of over 3,500.

The unusually rainy season of 1883–'84 caused great damage here as elsewhere in Southern California; landslides, destruction of roads and bridges, and some loss of life ensued from the excess of waters, with delayed mails and traffic incidental.

In January, 1884, the community was much exercised over the murder of Francisco Correa, shot in a lonely spot. It was generally supposed, and all the circumstantial evidence tended to prove, that he was killed by his step-son, José Correa; but, although the young man was taken into custody several times, it was found impossible to convict him.

In March, 1884, the sheriff, with a *posse*, captured a gang of counterfeiters and their mint, on San Bernardo Creek, they having been on the books of the authorities for some time.

In the closing days of March, 1884, a severe hail-storm caused such deposits of frozen drops that a regular siege of snow-balling followed—a thing unprecedented in the experience of many native born here.

In the spring of 1884 work was begun on the "Andrews" Hotel, the contract being for $62,497. The site was valued at $20,000, and other costs brought the value of the completed building up to $100,000. The Andrews was in its day the largest California hotel outside of San Francisco, excepting the Del Monte. This large, fine, elegantly furnished structure stood near the court-house. It was the property of an incorporated company, being named for Mr. J. P. Andrews, one of the syndicate, who was at that time president of the San Luis Obispo Bank. It contained 112 rooms. It was open to guests in June, 1885.

In July, 1884, was organized the Gentlemen's Social Club of San Luis Obispo, with forty members. The officers were: C. H. Phillips, president; Wm. L. Beebe, vice-president; J. A. Goodrich, secretary; J. P. Andrews, treasurer; J. M. Fillmore and R. E. Jack, directors.

In August, 1884, died on board the steamer Los Angeles, Judge W. J. Graves, of congestion of the brain, superinduced by over exertion in reaching the steamer. Judge Graves, the recognized head of the bar of San Luis Obispo, was a pioneer, having arrived in California in 1849, and in 1852 in San Luis, where he had, with an interval of a few years, resided ever since. He was an ex-Assemblyman and ex-State Senator. Appropriate resolutions of respect and regret were adopted by the local bar.

On September 27, 1884, Jeff Drake, who kept a saloon about four miles from the town, shot and mortally wounded in his bar-room one man, and wounded another so as to cause loss of one arm.

The flouring-mill was converted into a roller mill in September, 1884.

During 1884 about $8,000 worth (or from 30,000 to 40,000) of fruit trees were planted in the Estrella region.

Early in November, 1884, the Mission District school-house was burned, a loss of $6,000, with $3,000 insurance. This was the second attempt by incendiaries within a few weeks to destroy the building, in which burned many valuable books, records, etc.

Of the Southern California counties of San Diego, San Bernardino, Los Angeles, Ventura, Santa Barbara, and San Luis Obispo, this county in 1884 stood first in the yield of wheat and oats, the average yield there being twenty-four and sixty bushels respectively to the acre; and in the yield of barley second, with an average product of thirty-six bushels to the acre.

In 1884 San Luis County contained twelve road districts, six judicial townships, and five supervisional districts.

In the spring of 1885 the fine new steamer Santa Rosa was put on the service of the Pacific Coast Steamship Company.

On the night of Tuesday, January 13, 1885, a fire destroyed the costly and elegantly furnished residence of Mr. Ed. Smith, in the Los Tablas Valley, the net loss being about $15,000.

In the early part of July, 1885, two men were killed and four wounded on the Estrella plains, in a shooting affray growing out of an old feud.

On August 16, 1885, Dr. J. P. Mooklar shot and killed Robert C. Lowrie at San Miguel, in a quarrel while under the influence of liquor. This was one of the *causes célèbres* of the county.

In November, 1885, occurred the phenomenal storm wherein eleven inches of rain fell, of which nine inches came within twelve hours. Through the washing away of roads and bridges, the railroad, breaking of telegraph lines, and stoppage of travel, traffic and the mails, damages were done amounting, in the city alone, to some $20,000. About 200 feet of Pizmo wharf was washed away by the breakers.

In December, 1885, the population of San Luis County was estimated at 17,500; of the city, 3,000; and of the school district of San Luis, 3,500. The rate of taxation for State and county was $1.50. and for city purposes $0.50.

During 1885 260 passengers came from Los Angeles to Port Harford by steamer.

San Luis County in 1885 stood twenty-second in school rank among the fifty-two counties of the State, and received from the State School Fund $4,807.84.

In 1885 there were collected and paid to the county treasurer of San Luis Obispo, $147,536.50.

In 1885 an ice factory was constructed at San Luis Obispo.

In 1885 the Methodist congregation made various additions and improvements to their church edifice, at a cost of about $1,000.

The Young Men's Home Association was organized in 1885.

The postmaster's annual report for 1885 showed a total of 2,959 registered pieces handled, the gross receipts of the office being $2,746.61.

In January, 1886, the new mission school-house was completed, to replace the structure burned in October, 1883.

On March 19, 1886, died Charlotte L., wife of Myron Angel, the well-known journalist and author of San Luis Obispo. Her funeral was most largely attended.

On March 31, 1886, Peter Hemnie, a resident of the county since 1851, and his eighteen-year-old son, shot and killed, in their garden at Arroyo Grande, Eugene Walker and his wife. The cause was a sense of injury over the deprivation of a small piece of land which Hemnie had fenced in as part of his pre-emption claims, but which had been patented by Walker. The citizens of the outraged community that night formed a party, took the murderers from custody and hanged them from the timbers of the railroad bridge.

On Sunday, April 18, 1886, the Andrews Hotel caught fire from a defective joint in a terra cotta chimney, and in less than three hours it was but a mass of embers. The loss in the hotel alone was $75,000, and in its furniture $20,000; no insurance. The flames were communicated to neighboring buildings, with the result of losses as follows: San Luis Obispo Bank building, value $35,000, insured for $10,000; brick building adjoining, belonging to the bank, $10,000, insured for $5,000; postoffice, belonging to the bank, $1,000; Payne & McLeod's livery stable, $1,200. Other losses to individuals, guests, employés, etc., brought the aggregate up to at least $1,600,00, with $19,000 insurance. The court-house, over 100 yards distant, caught fire, and was saved only by prompt and great exertions, as was also the case with the flouring-mill of Steele & Wheelan. The buoyant citizens, within twenty-four hours of the burning, had raised $31,050 toward the building of a $200,000 successor.

On July 5, 1886, another large fire, caused by the celebration pyrotechnics, consumed $10,550 worth of property, which breakages, thefts, etc., increased to a grand total of $15,150; insurance, $3,700.

In August, 1886, a Kindergarten was opened in San Luis Obispo.

In 1886 there were collected and paid to San Luis Obispo's county treasurer $150,125.28 of taxes.

A board of trade, organized in February, 1887, expired after about two years' duration.

In February, 1887, an insane man named Dougherty, who had been at large some time, being well known in the county, set out running amuck with the avowed intention to kill his wife and other persons, and he was shot down by armed citizens as a protective measure.

In 1887 "the boom" struck San Luis Obispo, and in the week from March 11 to 17 the prices of real estate advanced fifty per cent., in many cases 100 per cent. Building received an impetus.

In the spring of 1888 the steamer Queen of the Pacific sunk at Port Harford, owing to the entrance of water through an open deadlight in a side compartment of the hold. She was raised within a few days, and restored to service.

The year 1888 witnessed the construction of a handsome hall of records, built in an elegant, modern style of architecture, at a cost of $14,000.

It was also during this "boom" period that arrangements were made with the noted engineer, Colonel George Waring, to make plans for a system of sewage. To this purpose he visited the town and made the plans, at a cost of $800 to the municipality. The city was surveyed, but no further movement was taken in the matter. The fulfillment of the plans would have required an expenditure of $150,000, for which it was purposed to vote bonds of the city. The question has not yet been submitted to the people.

The report of the county school superintendent, rendered in June, 1888, showed the county to contain 4,149 census children; total number enrolled in public schools, 3,249; average daily attendance, 1,797; average number belonging, 1,958. There were eighty-six school districts, and 100 teachers, who received an average salary of $73 for the men, and $62.50 for the women. There were received from all sources for school purposes $94,476.74.

Owing to the lowered rates on imported ice, the iceworks was sold, and the plant removed, December, 1889.

The school census report of June 30, 1889, showed a total of 4,402 census children in the county; a total enrollment of 3,510; an average of 2,284 belonging; and an average daily attendance of 2,097. There were now 105 teachers, supplying eighty-nine districts. The average salary for men was $75, and for women $62.50. The total receipts for school purposes was $79,869.84.

The assessment roll for 1889 was made up as follows: Real estate, $9,068,636; improvements on same, $725,564; city lots, $1,316,108; improvements on same, $677,566; improvements on land of others, $84,891; mining claims and improvements, $1,825; money and credits, $97,215; telegraph and phone lines, $9,922; personal property, $2,358,429; total, $14,340,256.

This increase of about $600,000 over the roll of the preceding year was not due to the increase of values, but to the addition to the roll of about 60,000 of pre-empted lands, etc.

The acreage of wheat this year was 96,385; oats, 4,246; barley, 48,360; corn, 765; hay, 25,780; acres table grapes, 432; wine grapes, 426; number vines, 514,835; number fruit trees, 38,325.

The tax levy for 1889–'90 for State and county purposes is $1.42 on the $100.

In January, 1890, natural gas was discovered on the Tar Spring Rancho. As yet, it has not been developed.

The total rainfall from October 8, 1889, to May 11, 1890, was 38.71 inches, a very unusual quantity.

The auditor's report, at the close of the last fiscal year, June 30, 1890, showed the county's money to stand as follows:

Gold	$28,274.00
Silver	3,594.84
Currency	5,658.37
County Warrants paid during the month	108.75
Certificates of Deposit	25,000.00
Total	$62,635.96

LAND GRANTS.

The land grants in San Luis Obispo County, according to geographical position, ranging from north to south, are as follows:

Piedra Blanca, eleven leagues; grantee and confirmee, José de Jesus Pico; surveyed and finally confirmed by natural boundaries; patented October 9, 1876, for 48,805.59 acres. Subsequent owners, Juan Castro, heirs of Mariano Pacheco, Peter Gillis, George Hearst, and others.

San Simeon. One league. Grantee, José Ramon Estrada; confirmee, José Miguel Gomez. Patented April 1, 1865. Contains 4,468.81 acres.

Santa Rosa. Three leagues. Grantee and confirmee, Julian Estrada. Survey includes 13,183.62 acres. Patented March 18, 1865.

San Geronimo. Two leagues. Grantee and confirmee, Rafael Villavicencio. Patented July 10, 1876, and then surveyed; 8,893.35 acres.

Morro y Cayucos. Grantees, Martin Olivera and Vicente Feliz. Confirmee, James McKinley. Patented January 19, 1878, and surveyed; 8,845.49 acres. Subdivided and sold in farms and dairy ranchos.

San Bernardo. One league. Grantee and confirmee, Vicente Canet. Surveyed and patented April 1, 1865; 4,379.42 acres.

San Luisito. One league. Grantee and confirmee, Guadalupe Cantua. Patented March 18, 1860, and surveyed; 4,389.13 acres.

Canada del Chorro. One league. Grantees, James Scott and John Wilson. Confirmed to John Wilson. Surveyed and patented March 29, 1861; 3,166.99 acres.

Huerta de Romualdo or El Chorro. Grantee, Romualdo, an Indian; confirmee, John Wilson. Confirmed by District Court of the United States, February 9, 1857; one-tenth of one square league, or 117.13 acres. Patented April 13, 1871.

Canada de los Osos, y Pecho, é Yslay. Grantees, Victor Linares, Francisco Badillo, James Scott, and John Wilson. Finally confirmed, surveyed, and patented to John Wilson, September 23, 1869; 32,430.70 acres.

Potrero de San Luis Obispo. Grantee and confirmee, Maria Concepcion Boronda. Finally confirmed, surveyed and patented, July 1, 1870; 3,506.33 acres.

Santa Fé. Grantee, Victor Linares. Confirmed and surveyed. Patented August 19, 1866; 1,000 varas square; 156.76 acres.

La Laguna. One league Mission land. Confirmed to Archbishop Joseph Sador Alemany and patented; 4,157.02 acres.

San Miguelito. Three leagues. Grantee and confirmee, Miguel Avila. Patented August 8, 1867, and surveyed; 22,135.89 acres.

Corral de Piedra. Seven leagues. Grantee and confirmee, José Maria Villavicencio. Surveyed and patented October 29, 1867; 30,911.20 acres.

Pismo. Two leagues. Grantee and confirmee, Isaac J. Sparks. Surveyed and patented, November 16, 1866; 8,838.89 acres.

Arroyo Grande or San Ramon. One league. Grantee Zeferino Carlon; Confirmee, Francis Z. Branch. Patented and surveyed April 10, 1867; 4,437.58 acres.

Santa Manuela. Grantee and confirmee, Francis Z. Branch. Patented August 22, 1868, and surveyed; 16,954.83 acres.

Bolsa de Chemisal. Grantee, Francisco Quijada; confirmee, Lewis T. Burton. Surveyed and patented August 27, 1867; 14,335.22 acres.

Nipomo.—Eleven leagues. Grantee and confirmee, William G. Dana. Patented December 14, 1868, and surveyed. 37,887.91 acres.

Suey. Five leagues. Grantee and confirmee, Ramona Carrillo de Wilson. Patented August 10, 1865, and surveyed; 24,497 acres of this rancho are in San Luis Obispo County, and it also contains 23,737.77 acres in Santa Barbara County.

Huasna. Five leagues. Grantee and confirmee, Isaac T. Sparks. Patented January 23, 1879, and surveyed; 22,152,99 acres.

Santa Maria, or Tepusquet. Two leagues, partly in Santa Barbara County. Grantee, Tomas Olivera. Confirmed to Antonio Maria de Cota and others. Patented February 23, 1871, and surveyed. 8,900.75 acres, of which 2,950 are in San Luis Obispo.

The land grants lying on the east side of the Santa Lucia Range are as follows:

Santa Margarita. Four leagues. Grantee and confirmee, Joaquin Estrada. Surveyed and patented April 9, 1861; 17,734 acres.

Atascadero. One league. Grantee, Trifon Garcia; confirmee, Henry Haight. Surveyed and patented June 18, 1860; 4,348.23 acres. Lies west of Salinas River, between the ranchos Santa Margarita and Asuncion.

Asuncion. Ten leagues. Grantee and confirmee, Pedro Estrada. Patented March 22, 1866, and surveyed; 39,224.81 acres.

Paso de Robles. Six leagues. Grantee, Pedro Narvaez; confirmee, Petronilo Rios. Patented July 12, 1866, and surveyed; 25,993.18 acres. North of the Asuncion, and west of the Salinas River. This rancho has the Paso de Robles Hot Springs in its northern part.

Santa Ysabel. Four leagues, 17,774.12 acres. Grantee and confirmee, Francisco Arce. Surveyed and patented May 21, 1866. Lies east of Paso de Robles and the Salinas River.

Cholamie. Six leagues, lying partly in San Luis Obispo, and partly in Monterey County. Grantee, Mauricio Gonzalez; confirmee, Ellen E. White. Patented April 1, 1865, and surveyed; 26,627.10 acres.

Huer-Huero. Three leagues; 15,684.95 acres, to which Flint, Bixby & Co. added 31,150 acres of Government land. Grantee, José Mariano Bonilla; confirmee, Francis Z. Branch. Patented August 9, 1866, and surveyed. Lies between the Salinas and Estrella rivers.

Mission San Luis Obispo; 52.72 acres, comprising the present church buildings, and land covered by the city of San Luis Obispo. Property of the Roman Catholic Church, confirmed to Archbishop Joseph Sadoi Alemany. Patented September 2, 1859.

Lot in Mission San Luis Obispo, containing one acre, confirmed to John Wilson.

1 Cuyama. Grantee, José Maria Rojo; confirmee, Maria Antonio de la Guerra and Pesario Lataillade. Patented July 20, 1877, for 22,193.21 acres.

2 Cuyama. Grantee, José Maria Rojo; confirmed to the heirs of Cesario Lataillade. Patented January 10, 1879.

Guadalupe. Grantees and confirmees, Diego Olivera and Teodoro Orrellanes. Patented June 30, 1866; 30,408.03 acres.

Punta de la Laguna, containing 26,648.42 acres. Grantees and confirmees, Luis Arrellanes and E. M. Ortega. Patented October 2, 1873.

The Cuyamas, two-thirds of the Guadalupe, and the Punta de la Laguna, excepting about 700 acres of the last mentioned, lie within Santa Barbara County, but the United States maps place them in San Luis Obispo County, with which they are often reckoned.

Besides the large granted tracts, individual purchases have been made of Government land, whose extent in the aggregate exceeds the grants made under the Mexican system. Among these are the following:

Las Chimeneas, containing 20,000 acres, situated near the head of the San Juan River, in the southern part of the county.

La Panza, extending twenty-two miles along the San Juan River valley; 31,000 acres.

El Saucito, in the western part of the Carriso Plains; contains 2,560 acres.

La Cometa, lying northwest of La Panza, containing 36,139 acres.

San Juan, comprising 39,780 acres, on the San Juan River, north of La Panza.

California, comprising 18,155 acres, lying west of the San Juan.

Estrella, containing 25,140 acres, on the Estrella River, near the junction with the San Juan.

Sacramento, of 15,900 acres.

Whim Rancho, in the southwestern part of Carriso Plain; 30,000 acres.

McDonald Tract, comprising 57,386 acres, lying in Carriso Plain and Carriso Valley.

Schultz and Von Bergen Tract, 21,000 acres, in the Carriso Plain.

Morrow Tract, 33,000 acres, in the upper portion of the San Juan Valley.

St. Remy, consisting of the Arroyo Grande Rancho of 4,437.29 acres, and 1,500 acres lying at the head of the Arroyo Grande.

Among the great land-owners before the beginning of American rule, were William G. Dana, John Wilson, John M. Price, Francis Z. Branch and Isaac J. Sparks, of the foreign element, besides many native Californians.

TOPOGRAPHY.

San Luis Obispo, classed as one of the southern coast counties of California, has as its western boundary the Pacific Ocean, and for its eastern the Monte Diablo Range, which separates the county from the Tulare Valley, this boundary following the summit of the mountains in a trend northwest and southeast; the northern boundary is a direct east and west line; the southern follows the Santa Maria or Cuyama River. Thus the general shape of the county is a parallelogram, averaging sixty-five miles long by fifty wide, with a total area of 3,250 square miles. The county lies between the thirty-fifth and thirty-sixth degrees of latitude, and the longitude runs from about 119° 20′ to 121° 20′ west from Greenwich. The territory is rolling, and traversed by several ranges. The chief physical feature is the Santa Lucia Range, running almost parallel with the coast, and dividing the county into unequal parts, of distinctive characteristics. West of the Santa Lucia lies about one-fourth of the county, the mountains toward the south trending eastward, continuing to a junction with the Monte Diablo Range, and dividing the Cuyama from the headwaters of the Salinas and San Juan rivers. From Estero Bay the Mount Buchon Range extends about twenty miles southeastward, 1,200 to 2,000 feet high; it is cut through by the San Luis and Arroyo Verde creeks. Between these ranges is a succession of detached buttes, as the Mission and Bishop's Peaks, having an elevation of 1,500 and 1,800 feet. This butte range on the southeast gradually runs into low, scattered hills, while on the northeast it terminates in Morro Rock, in Estero Bay. Westward to the ocean from the Santa Lucia flow very many small streams, such as the San Corcopero, Santa Rosa, Toro, Old Creek, San Luis, Arroyo Verde, Arroyo Grande, and others, beside the numerous branches. These streams are marked by many cañons, with valleys of considerable extent, which, as well as much of the hill lands, are very fertile. The Salinas River flows from south to north through nearly the whole extent of that portion of the county east of the Santa Lucia. Its tributaries are: from the west, the Santa Margarita, Atascadero, Paso Robles and San Marcos creeks; from the east, the Estrella and its branches, the Huer-Huero, San Juan, and others; the San Juan in its turn receiving the Carriso, La Panza, Montezuma, French, and other small streams. These smaller streams generally are so nearly dry as to fail to reach the main water courses. This region generally has very fertile soil; it is mostly hilly, and in the southern portion mountainous, and is well wooded in oaks and pines. The extremes of heat and cold here are greater than in the district west of the Santa Lucia. East of the San Juan Creek is a high, treeless basin, called the Carriso Plain. It is forty-five miles long by eight to ten wide. It ranges from 1,000 feet elevation in the center to 1,300 at the extremes. The drainage goes to the central depression, which during the dry season is a great bed of salt, one to two miles wide and five miles long. This becomes a lake in "wet" years. The stock-raisers for miles around have long resorted hither to salt their flocks and herds. Very densely salt water is obtained by sinking some four feet. For a few miles north of this lake the soil contains some little alkali, but most of the plain is of fine agricultural possibilities.

This land was mostly bought up some years ago by capitalists of San Francisco, with a view to speculation, J. M. and R. H. McDonald, 1. Glasier, Schultz & Von Bergen owning about 50,000 acres, 47,000 acres, and 21,800 acres respectively, while large tracts were held also by Haggin & Carr and others.

The following description of the geographical divisions of the county is from a report of the State mineralogist: "The Santa Lucia Mountains, which are the westerly-lying ridge of the coast range, strike northwest and southeast across the entire length of this county, the other branch of the coast range, though more broken, occupying its easterly portion. Between these mountain ranges, and flanking them on the east and west, occur many valleys and much low hill land, constituting the principal agricultural districts of the county. Wild oats and the native grasses grow abundantly all over this county, making it one of the best grazing regions in the State. As a consequence, large numbers of cattle and sheep, the most of them improved breeds, are pastured here.

"The cereal crops and fruits of most kinds are also largely produced, both the soil and the climate being highly favorable to their growth.

"The county is watered by the upper tributaries of the Salinas River, flowing north; San Simí Creek, running southwest and emptying into San Luis Bay; and by the Cuyama River, flowing across its southern border, and forming in part the dividing line between this and Santa Barbara County. The timber here consists chiefly of oak, madroño and manzanita, with a little scrubby pine on the mountains.

"The trend of this range is north 46° west The general altitude is 2,500 to 3,000 feet, but in the south there are peaks rising as high as 7,000 feet. The strip of land between the western base of the foot-hills and the sea is five to fifteen miles wide.

"The aspect of this range, as seen from the west, is of precipitous and forbidding mountains; in reality, the mountain-wall is broken by many inlets, which follow little streams, such as the Arroyo Grande, Lopez Creek, Corral de Piedra, San Luis Chorro, Morro, Van Ness, Santa Rosa, Old Creek and others, opening into delightfully fertile valleys. Those valleys on the northeastern side of the range are much higher than that of San Luis Obispo, which is 190 feet above sea level, while Santa Margarita Valley is nearly 800 feet higher, and the Cuesta is 1,350 feet above the sea.

"These mountains viewed from the east appear more accessible, being made up of many detached buttes and lateral spurs, interspersed with deep, romantic cañons, broad valleys and verdant pastures. This region is well covered with noble white oaks of wide spread, together with a smaller variety scattered among nut pines on the ridges; laurel, balm of Gilead, cottonwood and sycamore in the cañons, and live oak and chemisal on the mountain sides.

"On this slope the Salinas River and its branches take their rise, the principal tributaries being the Santa Margarita, Atascadero, Paso Robles and Nacimiento."

THE SOIL.

The county, owing to the direction and character of the Santa Lucia Range of mountains, is naturally divided into two sections, the western and eastern—the coast and interior. Conforming to this division are the two distinctions of soil, elsewhere noted, which make the general character of the eastern and western portions of the county divergent. Lying open to the sea, that portion between the Santa Lucia Range and the Pacific enjoys the refreshing coolness of the ocean, has a greater rainfall, and enjoys many advantages peculiar to itself as compared with the eastern portion of the county, while on the other hand the latter enjoys a climate and warmth that must give it some pre-eminent advantages over its western counterpart. Another more obvious and practical distinction is that of the rancho and public lands. San Luis Obispo County has a total area of 2,290,000 acres. Of this 561,073 acres are included in the Spanish grants, leaving 1,728,926 acres of public lands. The grants lie along the coast or on the Salinas River, with the greater number on the coast, thus leaving the interior portion of the county mostly public lands. The grants include much of the rich bottom along the streams, but by no means all of the good land of the county. The thousands of acres of Government land are among the most fertile of the State. There are in all thirty-five grants in the county, thirteen of the largest of which, aggregating 200,000 acres, have been subdivided and sold off in smaller lots or are now on the market. So rapid have been the sales of these lands, that of the three or four great ranches placed upon the market in the year 1887, but a comparatively small portion remained unsold. As the market calls for it, as the increase of taxes and of value render it advantageous, the owners of others of the very best and largest grants will be forced to place them on the market, thus affording opportunity for others to secure homes under San Luis Obispo's genial skies. The Government land, as already stated, embraces by far the greater portion of the county. Of late, settlers have been flocking in, and the land is being rapidly settled up; still there are thousands of acres of the finest kind of rolling land, adapted to mixed farming, stock raising, and more especially fruit-raising; the latter kind of land being the most valuable when lying along the hills or at the foot of the mountains. All of the public land that is open to settlement can be acquired under the pre-emption laws of the United States at $1.25 per acre, and San Luis Obispo County can heartily say to the intending settler, "Come, settle in our midst and enjoy the luxuries, pleasures and beauties of our California home." To the man of means who does not care to undergo the hardships incident to taking up land fresh from the hand of nature, and by his own sturdy labor surround himself with all the comforts and luxuries of a home, there are thousands of opportunities to purchase improved farms at almost any price to suit his fancy or funds. If he desires to follow simple farming, as already noted, there are numberless opportunities to secure the fertile ranch lands that are on the market, at from $10 to $50 per acre. For grazing purposes the hills offer ample room for all, at a cost but little in advance of Government prices. Along the coast some of the finest dairying land in the world may yet be had, at from $10 to $14 per acre. Elsewhere, along the hills or in the valleys, can be obtained for fruit-raising, the finest farms in the State, at prices which of course are high, but considering the return on the investment made far exceed the profits of grain or stock raising. Along the creeks or on the alluvial bottoms, is to be found a great deal of improved gardening lands, varying in price from $100 to $500, and the famous bean lands of the county, which, cleared and ready for cultivation, sell so readily for $300 per acre, but the returns from which make it one of the best investments in the county. The lands now offered for sale are in every particular as good as many of the famous orchards and vineyards of Los Angeles, San José and other famous portions of the State, where land sells at from $300 to $1,000 per acre. But this county, heretofore shut off from outside communication, except by a tedious stage journey of 200 miles or an equally disagreeable sea trip, now offers opportunities at one-tenth of the cost of these sections. Here, as there, may be found every variation of quality and adaptability.

CLIMATE.

The climate varies slightly with the locality, as the sea breeze blows direct from the ocean or deflected by the hills. The meteorological record that has given us the rainfall, shows the mean temperature of the four warmest months of summer to be 64 degrees, and of the four coldest months of winter 51 degrees, taken at 7 A. M., 12 M. and 9 P. M., constituting a climate as equable and salubrious as man can desire. The thermometer seldom measures over 90 degrees, and frosts are rarely seen, even in the low, damp valleys. The prevailing wind is from the west, often causing foggy or hazy mornings.

There are no extremes of wind, or heat, or cold. The desiccating northers experienced at intervals in almost every section of California are never known in this coast region. The heaviest winds are those that bring the winter rain; and the highest wind known, forty-four miles an hour, is regarded as a gale of extreme and rare occurrence. The heaviest summer wind rarely reaches twenty miles an hour, usually ranging from one to eight miles. These are from records kept through a series of years.

The physical features of this county resemble the State in miniature, with its seacoast, the bordering mountains and valleys, the Sierra (Santa Lucia) and the interior large valleys and river and mountain ranges, giving a variety of climatic conditions. The coast climate is modified by the neighborhood of the sea and the winds therefrom. The usual temperature of the water of the ocean is about 53 degrees, varying but one or two degrees summer or winter. There is little change during the year in the temperature of the coast sections, the summers of which are cooler, and the winters warmer, than in the region east of the Santa Lucia range. While the summer winds are sometimes unpleasantly strong, as they come from across the wide expanse of the Pacific waters, they blow pure, fresh and healthful, instead of bearing malaria from decaying vegetation, or germs of disease taken up from agglomerations of human abodes. Snow sometimes falls on the mountains, and on the high Carriso plain.

The meteorological record for 1874 and 1875 shows that there was a difference of only 2.08 degrees in the mean annual temperature during those two years. Taking the record of the four coldest months, it shows a difference of only 2.31 degrees in mean temperature between the two winters; and a similar comparison gives but .84 of a degree in difference between the mean heat of the two summers. The same records note the greatest difference for the two years to be but 13.78 degrees. As between the extreme hottest and coldest months of this period, the difference was 19.37 degrees.

COMPARATIVE MEAN TEMPERATURE OF SIX COLDEST MONTHS.

Temperature of six coldest months at San Luis Obispo, as compared with the most noted places in the world, regarding climate:

PLACE.	STATE.	DEG. FAH.
San Luis Obispo	California	56.15
Santa Barbara	California	56.55
City of Mexico	Mexico	56.03
City of Lisbon	Portugal	54.70
City of San Remo	Italy	53.89
City of Mentone	France	53.21
City of Nice	Italy	48.45

SAN LUIS OBISPO COUNTY.

WEATHER REPORT.

The United States Signal Service established a station at San Luis Obispo, in July, 1885, and a fire occasioned its removal after March, 1886. The following table gives the observations for the eight months of its existence. The remaining four months are always uniformly fair and pleasant:

1885 AND 1886.

	Aug.	Sept.	Oct.	Dec.	Nov.	Jan.	Feb.	Mar.	Total.
*Days upon which rain fell	0	0	0	17	5	13	3	9	47
" " " snow "	0	0	0	0	0	0	0	0	0
" " " frost app'd	0	0	0	0	3	0	0	0	3
" " " fog	9	0	0	0	0	0	1	0	
" " were cloudy	0	0	0	11	7	12	10	11	34
" " clear	31	31	31	6	5	8	17	15	
" " fair	0	0	0	13	19	11	1	5	
Mean temperature	62.0°	63.2°	63.0°	56.7°	55.7°	52.7°	58.4°	50.4°	57.8°
Highest velocity of wind, Miles per hour	5	.28	.32	.44	.36	.34	.28	.15	.167
Total number of days	31	30	31	30	31	31	28	31	243

* Rain usually falls during hours from sunset to sunrise.
† Fog and light frosts appear only, late in the evening and early in the morning.

The reports of the temperature, wind, and rain, published in the *Daily Republic*, which kept the only complete record in the county, showed the rainfall for the wet season of 1886–'87 to be as follows: October, .25; November, 1.25; December, 1.06; January, 1.10; February, 9.62; March, .75; April, 1.69; May, .40; thus making for the season a total of 16.12 inches, and the average for the eighteen years past 20.79½ inches, as against 21.07 at which, the preceding year, stood the average for seventeen years previous. As compared with other agricultural counties of the State, this was a very favorable showing. The reports for the same year showed the following record of rainfall from the respective localities: San Francisco, 18.97 inches; Templeton, 9.51; Paso Robles, 8.02; San Miguel, 7.05; San Ardo, 6.85; Kings City, 6.45; Soledad, 5.88; Salinas, 8.27; Monterey, 7.95; Hollister, 6.09; Gilroy, 9.06; San Luis Obispo, 13.96; Creston, 12.74; San José, 9.98; Menlo Park, 8.26; Fresno, 4.95; San Diego, 5.60; Stockton, 5.61; Sacramento, 11.40; Woodland, 8.52; Pajaro, 11.12.

COMPARATIVE ANNUAL RAINFALL.

Rainfall at San Luis Obispo as compared with other points in California and the United States:

PLACE.	STATE.	IN.
San Francisco,	California,	21.46
*San Luis Obispo	"	21.07
Sacramento	"	17.25
Santa Barbara	"	15.31
Los Angeles	"	14.92
Monterey	"	13.01
Salinas	"	12.03
Stockton	"	11.37
San José	"	10.62
Chualar	"	10.18
San Diego	"	9.44
Soledad	"	7.75
Riverside	"	7.66
Bismarck	Dakota	21.27
Dodge City	Kansas	20.09
North Platte	Nebraska	19.97
St. Vincent	Minnesota	18.62
Lewiston	Idaho	17.14
Salt Lake City	Utah	16.91
Helena	Montana	15.13
Denver	Colorado	14.98
Prescott	Arizona	14.51
Boise City	Idaho	13.30
El Paso	Texas	12.11
Cheyenne,	Wyoming	10.85
Phœnix	Arizona	7.53

*Average as taken at San Luis Obispo City for the last seventeen years.

SAN LUIS OBISPO COUNTY.

in the thermal belt surrounding the Sacramento Valley, and these are the favorite fruit sections of the north. But in those localities frosts are quite heavy in winter, which is favorable for deciduous fruits, but not quite sufficiently severe to be damaging to citrus fruits. In such comparison we might say that all the coast region of San Luis Obispo was in the thermal belt, but it is not so estimated. The thermal belt is that region where frosts are unknown, where the winds do not sweep too severely, where the air is unburdened by fogs, and the genial sun of summer fructifies and enriches the fruits of the earth. Along the coast, throughout this county, frost is rarely seen, in many places never; and still near the ocean grapes do not ripen, nor do citrus fruits grow successfully. There is here a distinctive thermal belt, such as we have mentioned, lying between the altitudes of 100 and 600 feet of elevation, where not a damp and level valley. All the little ridges of this region lift themselves above the frosts of night, and everywhere all delicate plants grow without danger. The distinctive belt is that lying east and north of San Luis Obispo city, skirting the base of the hills and extending along the mountain side. There, frosts are unknown, and tomatoes and other delicate plants furnish their flowers and fruits, regardless of the months or the seasons. There are the oldest orange trees of the country, growing from the seed planted as an experiment, and coming into bearing when eight years old, producing an excellent fruit. With this proof of success, others made the trial, and the most delicious oranges known now grow in the belt. Wherever it may be followed, north or south, to the elevation of 600 feet, this band of genial temperature will be found, the most certain in its products of any portion of our favored region.

RAINFALL AT SAN LUIS OBISPO DURING THE PAST SEVENTEEN YEARS.

	August	Sept.	Oct.	Nov.	Dec.	Jan.	Feb.	Mar.	April	May.	June.	July	Total
1869-70			.84	.66	.76	.71	4.85	.74	2.40	.85			11.83
1870-71			.68	.38	2.90	1.51	4.43		2.79	.28			12.97
1871-72				2.40	18.93	3.45		.71	1.37				27.02
1872-73					6.00	5.16	3.45						12.79
1873-74					7.96	5.00	1.79	3.23	1.00				20.53
1874-75			4.28	2.05	4.29	4.04		.50	1.2				19.69
1875-76				6.20	2.20	12.10	.28	5.29	1.74				30.12
1876-77					.48	9.87	5.29	.42					8.15
1877-78			1.16		4.83	7.88	11.91	2.74	2.75				30.60
1878-79				1.42	3.90	1.78	2.15	1.60	1.80	.25			11.66
1879-80				1.50	2.58	1.75	7.23	2.36	8.78	.52			25.82
1880-81			.75	1.40	3.03	4.71	1.90	1.40	1.85				23.69
1881-82				.48	13.85	.85	3.40	6.75	1.73				17.03
1882-83	.46	1.65	.25	2.00	1.50	1.60	4.88	1.10	8.85				17.01
1883-84		.69	2.95	.44	10.57	10.21	12.41	3.39		2.26			42.40
1884-85		2.17	.13	8.56	2.25		.94	3.15	.10				17.59
1885-86		.04	12.90	8.85	3.67	5.78	.73	2.37	3.75				29.30

Average for seventeen years, 21.07 inches.

THE THERMAL BELT.

This is a pleasant term for that ill defined region which is supposed to border every valley, and to extend at a certain elevation along the coast of Southern California. Almost every section of California has its "thermal belt," each differing from the other according to locality and the latitude, for it is certain there are climatic changes with the latitude, though slight. Thus the foot-hills of the Sierra Nevada, and the slightly elevated regions of Vacaville, and Madison, and winters in the Coast Range are

THE COAST REGION.

The coast slope of the range is usually regarded as comprising one-third of the county, but this is reckoning from the summit to the ocean.

Between the foot of the range and the ocean are a succession of valleys of various areas, aggregating about 300,000 acres. This is the oldest settled portion of the county, was nearly all included in the old Mexican grants—now mostly subdivided and sold in farms—and until recently was regarded as comprising all that was valuable.

Of these fair valleys are the San Simeon, Santa Rosa, the coast borders of Cayucos and Morro, the larger mountain valleys of Las Tablas, Nacimiento, Old Creek and of other streams, the Chorro and Los Osos, Laguna and San Luis, Corral de Piedra, Verdi, Arroyo Grande, Ranchita, Los Berros, Nipomo and Oso Flaco, winding in and winding out among the hills, of greater or less dimensions and all lovely and fertile. The scenery is varied and picturesque; a few level plains extending one or two miles in width, exist, but the country is undulating and broken, with precipitous peaks and rocky projections. This unique formation adds attractiveness and character to the scenery, and appears to govern the climate, so influencing the winds as to modify the effects of the cool sea breeze of summer, and to cause a greater precipitation in winter, the rainfall being greater than in other southern coast counties, or in the agricultural counties of the interior, the average for the past nineteen years being $20.79\frac{1}{2}$ inches.

COAST TOWNS.

The most northern of the coast towns is San Simeon. The bay of San Simeon has, in past years, attracted much attention as a probable commercial port for the productions of the neighboring country. Mr. George Hearst, proprietor of the Piedras Blancas Rancho, which surrounds the landing, in 1878 invested a considerable sum in the improvement of the port. This year also a new wharf was built, to replace the old, which for some time previous had been inadequate to the needs of commerce. The new wharf began on the northeastern side of the bay, terminating at a distance of 1,000 feet, where at low tide there is twenty feet of water—a depth sufficient for the largest merchant steamer. The wharf is excellently built, with commodious warehouses for the reception of goods. It cost $20,000. The building of this structure gave a new impetus to business at San Simeon. This name is applied also to the township, which embraces the northwestern part of the county, extending to the Monterey County line. The township embraces the whole of the Rancho Piedras Blancas, consisting of eleven Spanish leagues (48,000 acres), of which a very large proportion is cultivable land. While the climate is somewhat raw and damp, with fogs and winds, it is excellent for dairying purposes, the grass being always green, wherefore the milk production is of the the highest. Thus far, the chief products of this rancho are butter and cheese, although the lands are excellently adapted for the cultivation of corn, oats, barley, peas, and beans.

To the north of this rancho lies the old property of Juan Castro, a large tract of grazing lands, besides 900 acres of arable land of very high order. On this land stands the Piedras Blancas Light-house, which is 100 feet high, built of brick and iron, and cost $100,000. It contains a Fresnel light of great power, and is one of the marked features of the coast.

On this coast there are a number of whaling stations—at Monterey, San Simeon, Point San Luis, and Point Concepcion. The whaling business was begun here as early as 1864, and it has proved quite profitable. The least catch during the season was three whale, the greatest twenty-three. The whale hunts, conducted in open boats off these rugged coasts, is exciting but dangerous sport.

CAMBRIA.

The town of Cambria had its beginning about 1866. Its site was claimed as a portion of one of the large grazing ranchos, part of whose territory later became known as Government land. The greater part of the tract whereon Cambria is situated is composed of undulating ground, rising into low, smooth hills, or sinking into valleys fertile though small, through which flow numerous streamlets. In 1867 the land now occupied by the town was covered by a virgin forest of pines; and the lumber from these woods has created an industry which has done much to support and build up the section. As long ago as 1869, two saw-mills worked here steadily, and the houses of the vicinity have been built from lumber of home production. Early in the '60's, a copper mining excitement broke out in this section, leading to the establishment, a year or two later, of the town of Cambria. In 1867, there was no means of communication between the village and the county-seat, save by private conveyance. In 1868 a weekly mail service, by means of a spring-wagon, was instituted. Travel was slight, and passengers few. Within a year, a tri-weekly service, with a covered stage, replaced this, and now the patronage greatly increased, as the comforts of this line exceeded those of travel by mustang.

Although born of the mining interests, Cambria survived these, basing its growth and prosperity upon agricultural industries. School-houses were built, mills were erected, stores were opened, and evidences of substantial prosperity multiplied. The first building in Cambria proper was a store built by George E. Long and S. A. Pollard.

The name of the new town was a subject of dispute for some time. Some of the settlers favored the name of Rosaville; others inclined to the Spanish term of Santa Rosa; and others insisted upon San Simeon, notwithstanding there was already a port of that name in the county. At last a compromise was effected upon the present name. A steady growth now ensued in this section, and the port of San Simeon became frequented by vessels which conveyed to market the products of the region. In 1871 was built near Cambria a cheese factory, which consumed daily 9,000 pounds of milk, manufacturing therefrom 1,200 pounds of cheese. One feature of the early history of Cambria was the co-operative movements of the agriculturists for mutual benefits, social and commercial. One of the phases of this development was the establishment in 1872, of the "Farmers' and Stock-Raisers' Co-operative Store," for the purpose of lessening the retail price of articles formerly purchased through middlemen. This enterprise had a stock of $40,000, divided into 2,000 shares at $20 each. In April, 1881, the weekly output of butter in the vicinity of Cambria was 21,900 pounds.

The present population of Cambria is about 300. The town contains three general merchandise stores, all carrying heavy stocks, "everything from a needle to an anchor," two drug stores, one variety store, one stove and tin shop, one blacksmith shop, five saloons, one shoe shop, two carpenter and undertaker shops, one butcher shop, one saw-mill, one hotel, and one boarding-house. There is a public school with two departments, a Presbyterian and a Catholic church, telegraph, express and postoffice with daily mail. The only brick building in the town is the Odd Fellows' Hall, a handsome two-story structure. The town is picturesquely situated amidst pine-covered hills, and surrounded by a wide expanse of very fertile country. The principal industry continues to be dairying, and the section is exceedingly prosperous.

Santa Rosa Valley is six miles long, by half a mile to one mile wide, and through it flows the Santa Rosa Creek, a living stream of pure water. This valley is quite thickly settled, and few farming localities show greater signs of prosperity. The rich alluvial soil appears adapted to the growth of almost every kind of grain, fruit or vegetable. At the head of this valley stands Mammoth Rock, a rocky promonotory 200 feet high, with perpendicular sides, separated from the hills on the north by a narrow pass through which the Santa Rosa Creek runs into the valley below. It seems as if some tremendous force has riven the rocky wall, to give passage to the little stream skirting the mountain's rocky base.

Passing down the coast from San Simeon Bay, about six miles south, was formerly found Leffingwell's Wharf, a good landing place for small vessels, which supplied the neighborhood with lumber and sent out a portion of the native products. This wharf was washed away in 1881–'82.

The next landing place is Cayucos, thirteen miles south of Cambria, an entrepot of considerable commercial importance, with certain advantages as a harbor. In the early days, when boats made of skins were used in plying between the shore and visiting vessels, those light canoes were called *cayucos*, whence the name of the rancho and the town. Captain James Cass, who came to this point in 1867, and engaged in the business of lightering, saw the necessity of a wharf, and accordingly built one; this proving inadequate, it was extended, making a structure 940 feet long, extending to twenty-one feet of water, with a warehouse, store, steamship and telegraph companies' offices. Cayucos is now quite a thriving trade center, being surrounded by a rich dairy and farming country. The population is 600 to 700, of whom many are Swiss. The town was laid out in 1875, with streets 100, and eighty feet wide. The beautiful belt of land between the beach and the hills, reaching to Morro, was surveyed into lots of five to ten acres each, to be occupied as homesteads, and made accessible by a beautiful beach road. The region about here, known as the Rancho Morro y Cayucos, is very fertile and productive. Greatly in its favor are its ease of access and its natural advantages of climate and water. There are hereabouts over 8,000 acres of the best dairies on the coast.

The Rancho Morro y Cayucos was acquired in clear title by Don Domingo Pijol, by a decision of the Supreme Court of California. It was subdivided into small farms about 1877. Eight miles south of Cayucos is

MORRO.

This is a small village on the southern part of Estero Bay, where a lagoon extends some five miles inland from the sea, having a narrow entrance, and forming an excellent harbor for light-draught vessels. At the entrance of the lagoon is a wharf, receiving lumber from the north and produce from the interior. From the ocean in front of the village rises the Morro Rock, belonging to the National Government, a grand feature of natural scenery. It is a great cone, rising precipitously from the water to a height of 580 feet, upon a base of about forty acres. It is composed of trachyte, a valuable building material, which may be quarried here in large quantities, and loaded upon vessels with great convenience. The ambition of Morro is to have its promising harbor for light vessels perfected, and to become a traveling center by means of a road leading directly east to the Salinas Valley.

The Rancho San Miguelito, of 22,136 acres, borders on San Luis Obispo Bay, and includes the most feasible landing place. It was granted by the Mexican Government to Don Miguel Avila. In 1867, when Mr. John Harford built "The People's Wharf," the town of Avila was laid out by the Avila Brothers, and the prospect was fair for the growth of a lively village. Busy times prevailed here for a time, when two lines of steamers were contesting for the trade, but the construction of the railroad wharf in 1873, and the transfer to it in 1875 of the railroad terminus deprived Avila of its business and its hopes of commercial importance.

Port Harford is treated elsewhere, and the town of San Luis Obispo also is described separately.

THE TOWN OF SAN LUIS OBISPO.

When the county was organized, San Luis Obispo, the only town within its limits, consisted of a few adobe houses irregularly gathered about the Mission buildings. There was one main road, running southwest and northeast, crossing the San Luis Creek about half a mile below the Mission, and following up the right bank thereof. Except the cultivated grounds surrounding the Mission, all was open country. That main road became Monterey street, and the trail north of the Mission became Chorro street. The first frame building in the county was one built by Captain Dana in 1850, of material brought from Chili. It fronted on Monterey street, and stood near an ancient, large palm tree.

Shortly after this, Captain John Wilson erected another frame house, a little southwest of the Mission, the material for it having been brought around Cape Horn.

The rest of the buildings, in 1850, consisted of a two-story adobe, quite a pretentious building, at the corner of Monterey and Chorro streets, used for a restaurant and dance hall; an adobe store built by Beebe & Pollard; another adobe store where afterwards was the *Tribune* office; and another where the French Hotel stood.

In 1851, on the site afterwards occupied by the Bank of San Luis Obispo, Captain Dana erected a large building. Its walls were of adobe, its roof of sheet iron; its timbers were hauled by oxen from the Santa Rosa Creek, and the flooring and doors were brought from the Atlantic coast. So grand an edifice was this then considered, that it was called "Casa Grande." This was the first hotel in San Luis Obispo, and it was the scene of festivities on all gala days, whether of church or state, while on the grounds adjoining were held the bull-fights, bear-baiting, and other characteristic sports of the times and place. The Casa Grande was subsequently used as a court-house, serving in that capacity up to 1870.

In August, 1850, William R. Hutton was authorized by the court of sessions to survey and lay out the town of San Luis Obispo. He was directed to make the main street twenty yards wide, and all the other streets fifteen yards wide, while the town should extend to the limit of the lots.

The question of the existence of a pueblo and the right to pueblo lands was a very important one in the early history of the town. In 1853 the pueblo claim was presented to the Land Commission, and in September, 1854, it was rejected; San Luis Obispo had been a recognized pueblo, and as such was entitled to the four leagues of land assigned to such entities. But the Land Commission rejected the claim, because they alleged there was not adduced sufficient proof in behalf of it. In consequence of this decision, and the failure to take possession, the lands reverted to the public domain, and were surveyed by the United States government in 1867. The town acquired a title to only 640 acres, in conformity with the act of Congress of August, 1867. The remainder of the pueblo lands were acquired by individuals under the United States and State land laws.

In 1862, William C. Parker, civil engineer, made a map of the town after Hutton's survey, which included the land northwest of the creek, and the streets, nearly as at present; southeast of the creek, there was some cultivated land, and the territory was variously marked as "Priests' Garden," "Marsh Land," "Corral," etc.

The streets were not named, and it was not until some years later that any except the main ones were opened.

In February, 1871, the town authorities received from the United States Land Office a certificate of purchase for the town site of the town of San Luis Obispo, covering the following tracts of the United States land survey: being parts of sections 26, 27, 34 and 35 in township 30 south; range 12 east of Mount Diablo, base and meridian containing 552.65 acres. This afforded a sense of great relief to the people of the town, who had felt much uneasiness on account of the uncertainty of title, whereas the United States patent would thenceforward give a basis of title, either to those in possession, receiving title from the town authorities, or to future purchasers.

The town of San Luis Obispo was organized under the laws of California in May, 1859. Charles H. Johnson was president of the board of trustees, and Thomas H. Bouton was clerk. Ordinances were passed to provide for naming streets, keeping them in repair and clean, licensing business, maintaining order, etc. But little attention was paid to the incorporation, which very nearly expired; but when, in 1867, the public lands were surveyed, the town authorities found it necessary to display greater energy.

In 1874, under the provisions of an act of the Legislature, passed the preceding session, town bonds were issued to the amount of $10,000, bearing interest at eight per cent. per annum, and payable in fifteen years. These bonds were sold for ninety per cent. of their par value, and the proceeds were applied to the construction of bridges, street-grading, and other improvements of valuable and permanent importance to the town.

By an act of the Legislature passed March 20, 1876, the city of San Luis Obispo was incorporated, succeeding to all the rights, interests, possessions and liabilities of the former town. The limits of the city were extended; and provision was made for the election of city officers, legislative power being vested in a common council, consisting of five members, the mayor acting as president of the body.

MODERN INSTITUTIONS.

The city blocks are not regular in size or shape, and the streets, as has been seen already, follow in various instances the desultory lines of old-time roads and trails. Monterey street, so called from being a part of the old road from Santa Barbara to Monterey, winds past the old mission into the valley of the creek, and onward northeastward by well graded roads over the summit of the Santa Lucia mountains. This street, for the most part sixty feet wide, has recently been widened to seventy-five feet in some quarters. Various other streets are of uneven width, ranging from fifty-five to sixty feet in different portions of their length, as the widening was left to the option of property owners. An ordinance passed in 1888 ordering sidewalks of cement, bituminous rock in some streets, and of gravel in others, has been largely but not fully carried out.

The central addition is a very eligible portion of the town, lying on a gentle rise at the side of San Luis. It consists of some fifty acres, divided into nineteen blocks, 450 x 170 feet, one of which is occupied by the hotel, the rest being divided into building lots. Edwin Goodall of San Francisco was the promoter of this enterprise, and the projector of the Ramona, but the property was purchased in April, 1890, by the West Coast Land Company, who are not putting it upon the market, but rather holding it back until there shall ensue a season of greater growth and prosperity. This is the only portion of San Luis having a satisfactory sewer system. The Ramona Hotel, owned by the California Southern Hotel Company, was opened September, 1888; it cost, exclusive of the grounds (that is, for the building and furniture), some $150,000, and it is a well-equipped and well-conducted hostelry.

There are in San Luis Obispo two school-houses, containing twelve school-rooms, administered by eleven teachers. There are primary and grammar school courses. The city schools have an attendance of about 500.

The Court school-house, in the northern part of the town, is an eight room frame building, erected at an expense of about $14,000.

The Mission school, in the southern part of the town, is a four-roomed brick structure, which cost $10,000, to which may be added $3,000 for furnishings, etc.

The San Luis Obispo Thomson-Houston Electric Light Company was incorporated July 29, 1889, and the circuit was opened in October of the same year.

The city system comprises seven 1,200-candle-power masts of about fifty feet height; the county pays for one similar mast, and the Hotel Ramona for another. There are, moreover, between forty and fifty arc-lights and some 300 incandescent lights supplied to stores, hotels, etc.

The city system costs the municipality $70 per month.

The value of the plant is estimated at $1,500. The arc-dynamo is of 1,000-volt current, and the incandescent of 1,200 volts, alternating currents.

The company has four employés in San Luis.

San Luis Obispo has a street railway, running between the railway station and the Ramona Hotel, with two and one-half miles of track, and a plant worth $20,500, employing ten animals and four people. The company is not incorporated; it opened operations October 18, 1887.

The San Luis fire department was organized under new ordinances in 1889, and it is now in good working order, comprising about 100 members, divided as follows: San Luis Hook and Ladder Company, No. 1; Goodwill Hose Company, No. 2; Vigilance Hose Company, No. 3; and San Luis Fire Engine Company, No. 4. The last named company owns a steam engine of the Silsby rotary patent, purchased in 1889 at a cost of $5,000.

The sewerage of the town is performed by San Luis Creek, which runs through the corporation and washes away the sewage, the water being stored by means of dams for purposes of flushing. There are sewage conduits from that portion of the town about the Ramona Hotel, and from a few other blocks, leading to the creek.

In 1886 an arrangement which cost the city $800, was made with George Waring, the celebrated engineer, to furnish plans for a sewage system, and he visited San

Luis accordingly. The city was surveyed, but no further measures were taken. The execution of the plans would require an expenditure of $150,000, for which it was purposed to vote bonds of the city. The matter has not yet been submitted to a vote of the people.

The hospital system here was organized by Dr. W. W. Hays, and by him so conducted for some years in an admirable manner. The present hospital was built in 1878. The site is some thirteen acres upon a foot-hill bench about a mile southeast of the town, in what is locally known as "the thermal belt," a region free from frost, where the most delicate semi-tropical plants can be grown successfully. Water from the adjacent hills is brought down to a reservoir, 20 x 20 x 6 feet, from which the house and irrigation needs are supplied. The main building is two stories high and fifty feet square. The lower story contains the reception room, physician's office and dispensary, the steward's room, dining room, kitchen, and commissary store-rooms. Above these are rooms designed for use by non-indigent patients.

There is in the rear a ward with eight beds, which can be augmented if needful, and in an adjoining building is a one-story ward 47 x 25 x 16 feet, with the necessary closets sitting room, etc.

There has been constructed lately a new ward of seven rooms, 75 x 26 x 16 feet, with porch and ten-foot lean-to, which cost $2,900.

With this addition, the institution can accommodate thirty-five to forty patients. The present number is fourteen, all male. The percentage of female patients is never large.

The establishment is well sewered, and supplied with hot and cold water.

Driveways curve around the building in such fashion as to render the approach a pleasant feature. A system of drainage has been constructed whereby all the surface water running from the earth and the water pipes is conveyed away to irrigate the trees of the small orange grove.

The gardens are well kept, being cared for by the stronger of the patients; the whole place is exquisitely neat and orderly, and the inmates show conscientious treatment. The system of purchasing supplies, etc., by wholesale, is very economical; and, while the patients are furnished abundant, wholesome and satisfactory food, their cost to the county is said to be cheaper than at any similar establishment in the State, amounting to but seventeen cents per patient per diem.

The hospital is under the management of Dr. W. W. Hays, county physician, and Mr. J. M. Lewis, steward, both most efficient officials.

San Luis Obispo has two large well arranged and ornamented cemeteries, namely, the Catholic and the Odd Fellows', the last being the Protestant burial-place, under control of the Odd Fellows, but having plats devoted to the Masons, the Jewish people, and the Chinese. A cemetery formerly existed near what is now the central part of the city; but as the town grew, the two present pantheons were laid out, and the bodies from old ground removed thither, about 1870. The Catholic cemetery occupies about six acres, and the Protestant twelve. Each contains many fine monuments, and the inscriptions constitute quite a history of the prominent pioneers, of both the Spanish and the American races.

The banks of San Luis Obispo are: The First National Bank, founded in 1884, with $75,000 capital, as a private enterprise of Jack, Goldtree & Co. On March 1, 1888, it was changed to the National system, with a capital of $100,000, increased March, 1889, to $150,000. Its statement for July, 1890, showed a surplus of $35,000. The officers are J. P. Andrews, president; Wm. L. Beebe, vice-president; R. E. Jack, cashier; R. W. Martinoff, assistant cashier. This house does a general banking business.

The Commercial Bank was opened May 14, 1888. Its paid up capital is $100,000. Its statement December 31, 1889, is as follows: Assets—cash on hand, $12,104.12; cash on call in other banks, $17,457.42; loans and discounts, $273,427.26; real estate, vault and fixtures, $8,852.21; total assets, $321,841.01; surplus, October, 1890, $7,500.

Liabilities—Capital paid up, $100,000; surplus and profits undivided, $4,877.76; due banks and bankers, $5,330.21; due depositors, $210,883.04; interest on certificates, $750. Total liabilities, $321,841.01.

The officers are: McD. R. Venable, president; L. M. Kaiser, vice-president; H. Brunner, cashier.

In connection with this house was instituted in October, 1890, the California Mortgage and Savings Bank, capital $250,000. McD. Venable, president; L. M. Kaiser, cashier; H. Brunner, manager.

The Bank of San Luis Obispo has a capital stock of $100,000; surplus, $246,392.49. Its president is James L. Crittenden, its cashier, W. E. Stewart.

ARROYO GRANDE.

The township of Arroyo Grande was established in 1862 by the board of supervisors of San Luis Obispo County. It consists of a strip entirely across the southern end of the county, comprehending an area of about 300 square miles, embracing all of that territory situated between the Corral de Piedra Creek on the north, Santa Barbara County on the south, the Santa Lucia Range on the east, and the Pacific Ocean on the west. This includes the valleys of the Arroyo Grande, Santa Maria, Cuyama, Huasna, Alamo, Dry Creek, Verde, Villa, and other streams. In this area are the old Spanish grants of Corral de Piedra, Pizmo, Bolsa de Chemisal, Santa Manuela, Arroyo Grande, Huasna, Nipomo, Punte de la Laguna, Guadalupe, Suey, and Cuyama (or parts of the four last), aggregating 189,668 acres, being the chief area and nearly all the agricultural land of the township. On the upper waters of the Arroyo Grande and east of the Huasna grant, and in various nooks and corners, were considerable tracts of public lands, most of which are now occupied by prosperous farmers.

The first settlement here was when the priests of San Luis Obispo Mission established, about 1780, on that portion of the Arroyo Grande bottom, afterward farmed by W. S. Jones, a garden and plantation, where were raised large quantities of corn, beans, potatoes, etc., etc., to supply the mission.

The next settlement was the Rancho Bolsa de Chemisal, containing 14,335 acres, granted to Francisco Quijada, May 11, 1837. Quijada and his heirs transferred the grant to Lewis T. Burton, he to F. Z. Branch, and Branch to Steele Brothers, who subdivided it in September, 1873.

The Nipomo Rancho was granted to Captain William G. Dana, about 1838. It contained over 33,000 acres; it is now owned and occupied by his heirs at law.

The Santa Manuela Rancho was granted to Francis Z. Branch, April 6, 1837, and August 22, 1842. It contained 16,954 acres, and passed to the hands of Branch's heirs, and others.

The Pizmo Rancho, containing 8,838 acres, was granted to José Ortega, November 18, 1840. Ortega sold to Isaac J. Sparks, he to John M. Price and David P. Mallagh, each one-half. Mallagh sold his portion to F. Z. Branch, and he to Steele Brothers and others.

The Corral de Piedra Rancho was granted May 14, 1841, to José Maria Villavicencia, as containing 8,876 acres, which on May 28, 1846, was extended by Governor Pio Pico to include "all lands included in map," which brought it up to about 34,000 acres. This sweeping grant thus absorbed the Mission farm on the Arroyo Grande, and the lime-works, which were some four miles southeast of the Mission church. This grant passed into the hands of Ramon J. Branch, W. S. Jones, John Corbit, Steele Brothers, and others.

The Arroyo Grande Rancho, containing 4,438 acres, granted April 25, 1842, to Zeferino Carlon, was by him transferred to F. Z. Branch, afterwards passing into the hands of Steele Brothers and Wittenberg Brothers, who used it for dairying purposes.

The Huasna Rancho, containing 22,190 acres, was granted to Isaac J. Sparks, December 8, 1843, reverting upon his death to his daughters, Mrs. Mark Harloe, Mrs. Amy Porter, and Mrs. Harkness.

Of the Suey Rancho, of eleven leagues, granted to Don Mariano Pacheco, father of ex-Governor Pacheco, about one-third is in this township, and the rest in Santa Barbara County.

These vast tracts of land covered almost every desirable homestead in the township.

The dry season of 1864, the trespass act, the United States surveys, and the proceedings of the State Board of Equalization, have all proved instrumental in subdividing these wide domains and opening them up to immigration, so that, instead of the original eight patriarchal holdings, hundreds of smaller fertile farms, carefully cultivated, now smile and bloom for the maintenance of a numerous, thrifty population.

The Arroyo Grande Valley was first opened for settlement in 1867–'68, when a blacksmith shop and a school-house were built on the north bank of the creek, on the stage road between San Luis and Santa Barbara.

The growth of the settlement was necessarily slow, as the valley was then a tangled mass of woods and brush, almost impenetrable, save by the bear trails running through it,—a sort of semi-wilderness called by the Spanish term "monte."

But the fertility of the soil soon demonstrated its merits, and what had been a dense and useless thicket became a famous garden-spot. The lands were rather high-priced for that time, for, while they sold at $15 to $60 per acre, the cost of clearing averaged $100 per acre.

In 1876 Arroyo Grande had a school-house, two hotels, two well supplied stores, a post-office, a livery and feed stable, a wheelwright and blacksmith shop, butcher shop, laundry, two saloons and many dwellings. Manufactures were well represented in the district. Ramon J. Branch managed for the Branch heirs the Arroyo Grande flour-mills, with a capacity of thirty barrels per diem; and the water-power of this mill was used at times to run a small circular saw for sawing shingles and small timbers; a steam grist-mill was in operation, as also Newsom's tannery, the Nipomo lime works, McDougall's asphaltum works, and Marsh's smithy and carriage shop.

A decided impulse was given to the prosperity of this section by the building of the Pacific Coast Railway and the People's Wharf at Pizmo, in 1881, these media of transportation giving the producers of the valley competitive advantages in conveying their wares to market.

In 1882 the Arroyo Grande Irrigating Company was organized, and the two ditches thereupon constructed are capable of irrigating 5,000 acres of land.

The climate here is excellent, but diversified. The larger valleys are subject to late frosts in the spring, but in the fall they are exempt to a remarkable degree. The smaller valleys are almost free from frost, and from extreme heat in summer.

The soil also has great variety, and therefore is quite eclectic in its products. Wheat, barley, oats, corn, beans, peas, peanuts, tobacco, garden vegetables of all kinds, apples, peaches, plums, apricots, almonds, figs, olives, grapes, etc., are grown to perfection. In fruits, apricots are a never-failing staple, yielding 200 to 250 pounds to the tree at five years old; apples, 300 to 400 pounds to the four-year-old tree; strawberries, 16,000 quarts per acre; peaches, plums, prunes, cherries, grapes, raspberries, blackberries, olives, walnuts, oranges, lemons and limes, all do well here. Garden vegetables do exceedingly well; on one acre of monte land any one of the following items may safely be counted upon as a fair yield; 4,000 pounds beans; 25,000 pounds potatoes; 80 tons beets; 65 tons carrots; 45 to 50 tons cabbages; 500 hundred-weight onions; 50 tons squashes; 12 to 14 tons alfalfa. Squashes weighing from 200 to 250 pounds, cabbages weighing 60 to 95, carrots of 75 pounds' weight, are not uncommon productions.

On September 21, 1886, the people of this section met and organized a Fair Association, the first in the county. It held its first annual fair in October, 1886, and the second on October 6, 7 and 8, 1887. Among the exhibits were:—a pear weighing 1 pound 14 ounces; a cabbage of 94 pounds, and several others from 50 to 80 pounds weight; potatoes of 3 to 9 pounds each; carrots three feet long; a squash of 217 pounds weight; five others aggregating $822\frac{1}{2}$ pounds; a muskmelon weighing $20\frac{1}{4}$ pounds; an onion of 5 pounds $2\frac{1}{2}$ ounces; corn 15 feet high, ears 2 inches in diameter, 13 inches long, solidly filled; five quinces weighing 6 pounds 15 ounces; 5 pears weighing 9 pounds 3 ounces; 5 fall pippins weighing 5 pounds 10 ounces, and many other remarkable products.

Arroyo Grande furnished all the exhibit from this county at the Mechanics' Institute Industrial Exhibition of 1887, receiving special silver medal for display, diploma for best potatoes, and silver medal for best apples; and also the first premium at the Sixteenth District Agricultural Exhibition for best general display of fruits and vegetables.

As a general rule, no irrigation is required here, but occasionally the application of water saves a crop or economizes time in working the land. The water supply is derived from the Santa Maria River, Alamo, Huasna, Berros, Arroyo Grande, Pizmo, and Carrol de Piedra creeks, and numberless springs and brooks. Several of these streams are well stocked with trout, and salmon are caught often. There is never fear of a "dry year" here, and one of the most favorable features of this valley is its facility of irrigation.

The village of Arroyo Grande is pleasantly situated on the bank of the creek under a range of hills. It is but three miles from the famous Pizmo Beach, and almost every house in town commands a view of the valley and the ocean. The present population is about 600 in the village, 1,000 in the district, and 1,500 in the voting precinct. There are three churches, Catholic, Methodist and Cumberland Presbyterian, each supplied with a minister, and the Methodist Episcopal Church South holds monthly service in a hall.

The school is the second largest in the county, having a fine large school-house with three teachers.

There are lodges of Masons, I. O. O. F.,

G. A. R., W. R. C., and a Good Samaritan Temperance order.

There are general merchandise stores, mechanics' shops and professional offices to the usual number to be found in settlements of this rank. A Woman's Relief Corps was organized here in October, 1886.

Arroyo Grande has a postoffice, telegraph office, express office, trains and mails daily (excepting Sunday), a newspaper, the *Weekly Herald*, a practicing physician, a pavilion and hall, a jeweler and photographer, a millinery store, a produce and commission merchant, two hotels, several general merchandise stores, and two butcher shops.

On September 2, 1890, the Catholic church and parsonage here were burned, the loss being about $6,000. The fire at one time appeared to threaten the town, and the engine was called out from San Luis, but it was not sent out, as the call was countermanded.

NEWSOM'S HOT SULPHUR SPRINGS.

Newsom's Springs are situated in a pretty little natural park, at the base of a large, singularly formed hill of silici-calcareous rock, through whose summit runs a strong ledge of pure limestone, which it has been demonstrated is very valuable for making lime. The body of the hill is believed to be valuable for making cement. The hot sulphur spring shows a temperature of 100 degrees, and analysis of the water shows silica, sodium chloride, sodium sulphate, potassium sulphate, calcium carbonate, magnesium carbonate, ferrous carbonate, alumina and sulphate of magnesia, the combination showing the medicinal properties. Considerable gas arises from the water, and arrangements have been made to utilize it for cooking and heating purposes.

The owner of these springs has surveyed a plat of six acres near by, bordering the Arroyo Grande, which he designs to donate to the State, with water privileges, on condition of the establishment there of a technical school.

They are reached by rail to Arroyo Grande, thence by easy stage or drive from Nipomo. The altitude is about 400 feet. The grounds and springs are well kept. The ocean beach road affords a superb drive. There is always bathing, fishing and clamming. Hotel and cottages for guests.

The climate is almost perpetual sunshine. On the place are three principal springs, whose waters range in temperature from 40° F. to 100° F., flowing some 49,000 gallons per hour. The waters are salino sulphureted, and have considerable reputation in the treatment of old, chronic rheumatism, and gout, catarrhal affections of the bladder and bowels, skin diseases, etc. For uterine troubles the hot sulphur douche has been of great benefit. There are warm and hot plunge and tub bathing facilities. The following is the statement of an analysis made by Dr. Winslow Anderson, 1888:

Temperature, 100.5° F.
U. S. gallon contains—

	Grains.
Sodium chloride	4.10
" carbonate	1.75
" sulphate	3.92
Potassium carbonate	15.00
" sulphate	2.90
Magnesium carbonate	6.41
" sulphate	2.47
Calcium carbonate	8.25
" sulphate	.76
Ferrous carbonate	3.98
Alumina	.33
Silica	2.03
Organic matter	.27
Total solids	37.32

Gases—

	Cubic inches.
Free carbonic anhydride	14.90
" sulphureted hydrogen	3.56

Four miles westward is the

PIZMO BEACH,

a stretch of twenty miles of sand along the ocean shore, popular as a drive and resort for bathing and pleasure. Near this is the surveyed route of the Southern Pacific Railroad, and along the beach have been laid out the towns of Pizmo and Grover, expecting to grow into prominence as coast watering places upon the completion of the railroad.

LOS BERROS

is a village of recent growth, being in a pretty and fertile valley of that name, on the Pacific Coast Railway, three miles from Arroyo Grande, and the same from Nipomo. The land was formerly the property of Mr. William G. Dana, and purchased of him by Messrs. C. R. Callender and J. W. Smith, who also purchased several thousand acres of the Nipomo rancho, laying out the town site and subdividing the ranch into farming lots of various areas, which are offered for sale. These surveys have been made during the present year, and a village with several handsome residences, a store of general merchandise, a postoffice and hotel are there, and recently an election was held which voted to expend $1,500 for building a school-house. A block of the village lands has been devoted for the purpose of the school. All the neighboring land is very fertile, and when occupied will afford ample support for a pleasant and thriving village.

NIPOMO

is a village of recent growth, on the line of the Pacific Coast Railway, nine miles south of Arroyo Grande. This is upon the Nipomo grant, made by the Mexican government to William G. Dana in 1838, and recently subdivided and in part sold by the grantee's heirs. The grant was one of the first made in this county, and as may be presumed the first selection was an exceedingly choice tract. The village is but two years of age, and so rapidly is it growing that an estimate of its population is hardly likely to approach accuracy, although it is estimated at 700. There are two hotels, two large stores, a newspaper, the Nipomo *News*, and many handsome residences. The village is well supplied with water by a system of water-works, with reticulation pipes through all the houses.

THE EASTERN PORTION OF SAN LUIS OBISPO COUNTY.

East of the Santa Lucia Mountains is a large area comprising about three-fifths of the county, being included in the Salinas Township, which by the census of 1880 had a population of 1,209, and San José Township, which had 872; thus this district had 2,081, or about one person to the square mile, in a total county population of 9,142. Between the Carriso Plain, already described, and the Tulare Valley, extends the southern end of the Monte Diablo Range, a line of low sandstone mountains, generally treeless, trending northwest and southeast, which constitute the division line between this and Kern County. Westward a low ridge separates the plain from the San Juan Valley, and one of its branches, Carriso Valley; and on the northwest a like barrier lies between the plain and the main Estrella River. The streams are 200 or 300 feet below the general level of Carriso Plain.

The San Juan is the southern branch of the Estrella River, albeit the summer season finds only occasional pools in its broad, sandy channel. The rains convert this into a veritable river, fifty to 100 yards wide, running through small valleys and hills softly rounded, clothed in a luxuriant growth of alfilaria, wild oats, bunch-grass and flowering shrubs.

This section is a paradise to the stockman, being devoted almost entirely to pasturage. Nevertheless, its resources would suffice for varied industries. There is here much oak timber, the soil is very fertile, there are mineral springs, ore-bearing rocks, and diverse elements to support a large population.

This valley may be considered as including the following tracts: That section between the San José Range and the Carriso Plain; the ranchos Las Chimeneas and Avenales in the southern part; La Panza and the mining district in the central part; and La Cometa or Comate, California, and San Juan Capistrano in the north.

Among the old settlers were: John Gilkey, on the Comate, murdered in 1858; Baratie and Borel, on the San Juan Capistrano, murdered in 1858; Philip Biddle, Robert G. Flint, James Mitchell, Joseph Zumwalt, D. W. James and John D. Thompson, all of whom located there twenty to thirty-five years since.

In the northern portion of this section is

SAN MIGUEL.

The Mission of San Miguel Arcangel was established July 25, 1797, being the sixteenth in order of date in Alta California. Its site was in the midst of wide reaches of grazing land, on the west bank of the Salinas, just below where this river receives the Estrella. The two streams here run through broad valleys, where flourish willows, cottonwoods, sycamores, oaks and other trees.

This Mission is thirty-four miles north of the city of San Luis Obispo, and some four miles south of the county line between this and Monterey.

San Miguel, like most of the twenty-one mission establishments, is the site of a flourishing settlement of later times. This place was never quite abandoned, and even during the unsettled times of the American occupation a few Mexican settlers kept their abode in the decaying habitations of the mission buildings. Its position on the main—if not the only—road, between the northern and the southern settlements, gave San Miguel a certain importance as a station, where an eating-house, etc., were established. The population was of course small for many years. On the vote upon the new constitution, in 1879, San Miguel precinct cast thirty-four votes. About 1876 a certain degree of activity began here; the old mission buildings were fitted up for a hotel, and various shops and other enterprises were opened. In 1877 the population was reckoned at thirty, and there were fifteen buildings, including a school-house, postoffice, express office, store, blacksmith shop, carriage shop, and two saloons. This year was a "dry season," and two-thirds of the sheep and cattle from this grazing country either died or were driven away to more favorable pastures, and a brief revival of prosperity the following year was followed by drouths again in 1879.

An excitement arose here in 1881, over the expectation of the immediate building of a portion of the Atlantic & Pacific Railway through the district.

Since the actual advent of a railroad, San Miguel, which is the most northerly town on the line in this county, has taken an important rank hereabouts, standing as the second point in the county, before it fell behind Arroyo Grande. The population is now between 400 and 500; there is a money-order postoffice, a $10,000 school-house, a newspaper—the *Weekly Messenger*—and a very full complement of business houses, stores, shops, professional men, etc.

The Bank of San Miguel, on October 26,

1889, reported its assets and its liabilities each as $87,966.51.

The Episcopal church at San Miguel, completed in 1884, cost $1,200, and is a handsome Gothic structure, with a seating capacity of 100. It is said to be the handsomest church building in the county.

The Mission church still stands,—an immense structure, 230 feet long, forty-four wide, with a height to the eaves of forty-five feet, and walls seven feet thick of concrete. There remains a portion of the wing, once 400 feet long, and until about a year since there still existed the ruins of the former dwelling-houses of the neophytes, which covered an area of more than forty acres. The quaint old church on its adjacent ruins constitutes a very picturesque feature of the village, a vivid contrast of the medieval period with the present. The floor of the church is of brick, or tile, as is a broad front porch. The inner walls are plastered and frescoed, to represent a gallery with pillars, the colors now appearing as fresh as when newly painted. The sacred ornaments of this church have survived all the vicissitudes and spoliations which the venerable pile has suffered. Over the altar in the western end stands the patron saint, Michael the Archangel, life size and handsomely depicted, gorgeously arrayed in gold and crimson, holding aloft his sword of light, beneath a broad banner on which is emblazoned the all-seeing eye from which radiate rays of light. To the right of the altar stands the brightly-painted statue of St. Joseph, holding the infant Jesus in one arm and bearing on the other the shepherd's staff. Opposite stands the statue of St. Francis de Assisi, the founder of the order of Franciscan monks, under whose charge were established the missions of California. Beside the altar is a painting of St. John the Evangelist, with one foot resting upon a skull. There are also other paintings of various sacred subjects, generally in bright colors, and these, with the bright altar ornaments, form a vivid contrast with the neglect, decay and ruin seen elsewhere about the old mission. The many small pictures hung on the walls are dimly seen in the faint light, and the thickness of the walls keeps the atmosphere generally in a chilly, cellar-like condition; the windows are few, small and high out of reach. Services are held fortnightly in this church.

THE PASO ROBLES HOT SPRINGS

take their name from the rancho on which they are found, El Paso de Robles (the Pass of Oaks). They are about thirty miles north of San Luis Obispo and sixteen miles from the Pacific ocean, in the beautiful valley of the Salinas River, which the Santa Lucia range protects from the cold sea winds and fogs. For miles around the springs stretch level plains, now and then broken by low hills, and shaded by graceful groups of white and live oaks—a charmingly picturesque setting for the springs whose curative waters have become famous.

The missionaries and early Spanish pioneers, and the Indians before them, knew the health-giving qualities of these waters and benefited by them. Prior to American occupation the principal spring had been rudely walled in with logs, the better to fit it for bathing purposes, this being done before the founding of San Miguel Mission. It is declared that even the wild beasts of the forest came to profit by these waters, and stories are told of an immense grizzly that was in the habit of plunging into the pool nightly, adding to the joys of his bath by swinging himself up and down by the low-growing branch of a great cottonwood that grew near by, extending its limbs over the water.

The Paso de Robles Rancho, including the springs, was purchased in 1857 by D. D. Blackburn, James H. Blackburn and Lazare Godchaux. The springs at that time were in the condition in which the missionaries had left them, with no sign of improvements by the decaying logs of the old abutment placed there many years before, while the thickly-strewn bear-tracks added to the general air of desolation. From such a condition as this has grown the present settlement of 820 population, supplied with an excellent hotel and annex cottages, with postoffice, express and telegraph offices, billiard halls, etc.,—in short all the modern improvements for the convenience of visitors.

The chemical analysis of the principal Hot Spring, as made by Professors Price and Hewston, of San Francisco, is as follows:— Temperature, 110° Fahrenheit. One imperial gallon, of 7,000 grains, contains—

	GRAINS.
Sulphureted Hydrogen Gas	4.45
Free Carbonic Acid Gas	10.50
Sulphate of Lime	3.21
Sulphate of Potassa	.88
Peroxide of Iron	.36
Alumina	.22
Silica	.44
Sulphate of Soda (Glauber's Salts)	7.85
Bi-Carbonate of Magnesia	.92
Bi-Carbonate of Soda	50.74
Iodides and Bromides	Traces.
Organic Matter	1.64
	93.44

The great and distinctive feature of Paso de Robles is the Mud Bath, whose analysis is as follows: Temperature, 140° Fahrenheit. One gallon, of 7,000 grains, contains—

	GRAINS.
Sulphureted Hydrogen Gas	3.28
Carbonic Acid Gas	47.84
Sulphate of Lime	17.90
Sulphate of Potassa	Traces
Sulphate of Soda	41.11
Silica	1.11
Carbonate of Magnesia	3.10
Carbonate of Soda	5.21
Chloride of Sodium	96.48
Organic Matter	3.47
	168.30

There are several other springs, such as the Sand Spring, the Soda, the White Sulphur and the Iron or Chalybeate Spring.

Paso de Robles, the town, dates from 1886. The present population is rated at 820.

The Paso de Robles Rancho has been subdivided, and its lots are now offered for sale by the West Coast Land Company.

Lots eighteen and nineteen of the subdivision were reserved and laid out for the town of

TEMPLETON.

These lots embrace 160 acres, of which 100 are on a level plateau, twenty or twenty-five feet against the Salinas River. This site is covered with oak timber, and is one of the most picturesque spots in the county. Previous to the completion of the railroad to this point this region of country was but a vast cattle range. In March, 1886, the West Coast Land Company was formed with a capital of $500,000, and purchased the Santa Ysabel and the Eureka ranchos, and portions of the Paso de Robles and the Huer-Huero ranchos, comprising a compact and contiguous body of 63,000 acres of land, equal to any in the State for cereals, fruits, vines, grasses or almost any product of California. This immense body of 500 square miles of territory was at once surveyed and subdivided into small tracts and the town laid off. It was at first called Crocker, which name was shortly changed to Templeton. Within ninety days after its foundation Templeton contained one extensive and two smaller but quite respectable hotels, three general merchandise stores and two more in immediate prospect, a handsome and well-stocked drug store, a very neat structure for the office of the West Coast Land Company, a well-supplied meat market, a shoeshop, two blacksmith shops, five saloons, a billiard saloon, a large lumber yard, a sash and blind shop, several building and painting establishments, two barber-shops, a public hall, a postoffice with daily mail service and probably twenty-five to thirty dwelling houses. The intellectual and educational wants of the community are provided for by a weekly newspaper with a good circulation and advertising patronage, and the Templeton Institute, with a good pupilage in its primary department, and prepared to receive students in the higher and collegiate departments. The railroad buildings consist of a handsome depot and freight warehouse, a turn-table and round-house and other appointments of a first-class station, provided with telegraphic and express facilities. The religious want is attended to by an excellent Presbyterian clergyman who, with his family, resides in the town, and a Sunday-school with a good attendance of scholars and teachers is held every Sunday in the building of the primary department of the Templeton Institute.

The establishment of a brickyard gives an added impetus to building, as clay of a very superior quality is abundant almost within the town limits, and wood is very cheap.

THE RANCHO SANTA MARGARITA

has been noted for its fertility since the days of its tillage by the Mission fathers. It consists of a tract perhaps eight or nine miles long by two wide, in the form of a valley—the bottom lands along the Salinas River. It was granted to Joaquin Estrada, and to him afterwards confirmed and patented. During the Mexican regime it was given up to grazing. The surroundings were very wild, and bears were frequent visitors to the rancho houses.

The San José Valley, once called the Rancho San José, lies about twenty miles east from San Luis Obispo, and southeast of the Santa Margarita Rancho. It was supposed that Don Ynocente Garcia had a grant for the whole of the land in this valley, to the extent of five or six leagues. Later on, he decided to treat the place as Government land, and recorded possessory claims upon the best of the tract, finding that he had only applied for the grant, no action having been taken upon his petition. The land here is fertile, and the climate warmer than nearer the coast. Corn, beans, etc., are raised unirrigated. The cultivated land is of greater than a township area; the postoffice is Pozo (a hole or well), from the form of the valley.

On the headwaters of the Atascadero is the Eagle Rancho, purchased in 1876 by Mr. A. F. Benton, a settler in this county since '69. He raised here a great number of hogs, this industry being favored by the existence of marshy places and oak groves. The many grizzly bears, however, were a great obstacle to the entire success of this industry. The existence of this "big game" gave the rancho a great reputation amongst hunters. Among others, Baron Von Schroder was attracted thither, and, after a long sojourn amidst the game-infested mountains, he purchased the rancho, upon which he has since expended a good deal of money, to make of it a country resort for himself and his friends. The rancho comprises some 500 acres, extending through several small valleys, and commanding an extensive range of pasturage, over adjoining public and railroad lands not desirable for cultivation. Upon a small knoll in the first valley is built a handsome dwelling, surrounded by drives and avenues leading to the neighboring falls and grottoes.

The water supply, difficult to secure at this altitude of 1,500 feet, was obtained through tunnels, tapping large springs from which an abundant supply is had. Perhaps the largest prune orchard in the world is that upon this rancho, which contains something over 200 acres, growing in a fine rich slate loam. Ten tons of dried fruit, grown on these young trees three years after planting, took the first premium at the Mechanics' Institute Fair for 1889, in San Francisco, as the best French prunes raised in California. It is estimated that the yield of this orchard for 1890 will reach five tons to the acre, worth seven cents per pound, or $700 per acre, four years after planting. A short distance from this place are the Falls of the Atascadero, where the scenery is exceedingly wild and picturesque. The cañon is spanned by a massive dyke of serpentine and trachyte, over which leaps the stream to a fall of about forty feet, in several cascades, of which the highest is twenty feet. The stream in very low water is about four feet wide, and three or four inches in depth. From below the falls the rocky banks rise perpendicularly to over 100 feet, clad in beautiful ferns and shrubbery.

As the valley of the Salinas stretches northward toward its junction with the Estrella, the mountains sink into rolling hills, bearing groves and clumps of oaks, while the streams are fringed with willow, sycamore and cottonwood. On the left bank of the Salinas are the ranchos Asuncion, Atascadero, Paso de Robles, and ex-Mission of San Miguel, and on the right bank are the Eureka, Santa Ysabel and Huer-Huero; the settlement of the Estrella is on the banks of that stream, and the Cholame Rancho is in the northeastern part of the county. On the western slope, opposite Von Schroder's, in Van Ness Cañon, Hon. Frank McCoppin, ex-mayor of San Francisco, has a vineyard of over 30,000 choice vines, four or five years old, bearing heavily.

Farther south, on the western slope, on the headwaters of the Arroyo Grande, A. B. Hasbrouck has a vineyard of over 30,000 vines, which produce an abundance of the most luscious grapes from which most excellent wine is made. There are many other small vineyards and orchards throughout the range, but the above are mentioned as examples. In the many valleys and slopes of this grand range these vineyards and orchards may be multiplied indefinitely, and with a success challenging the most favored or noted region of the State, or of the world.

Hasbrouck's Rancho is located twenty-two miles from San Luis, on the main southern road to Steele's. The Santa Mannela grant of 16,955 acres crosses and occupies a wide extent of this valley. Between it and the Arroyo grant was a strip of a mile or more of Government land, now owned and occupied by well-to-do settlers. The Arroyo Grande grant, of about 4,500 acres of the Ranchita, embraces different branches of he stream for about four miles, about 1,500 acres being arable. This was leased by the Steele Brothers to Mr. Hasbrouck, who occupied it for a number of years, brought a large area under cultivation, and finally, in 1883, purchased the land at the stated price of $27,000. In 1880, Mr. Hasbrouck had bought of A. C. McCleod, the Musick heirs and others, a large tract of excellent pasturage similar to the Ranchita, where he has made his home. Here is the postoffice named Musick. The dairy here is a model institution, the building appointments being admirably adapted to their purpose. The dairy is mainly devoted to cheese-making, and several hundred cows are kept, each yielding an estimated product of $55.00 per annum. The grounds of Mr. Hasbrouck's rancho are splendidly kept, and are a noted show-place in this district. Two miles south of Musick rises Mt. Hasbrouck, a cone-like bald mountain which is one of the highest peaks of the Santa Lucia range.

THE SOUTHERN BORDER.

The Santa Maria River, which in its upper part bears the name of Cuyama, forms the southern boundary of the county, separating it from Santa Barbara. The Cuyama Valley is an extensive region, stretching like a division between two systems of geological formations from the Mojave Desert on the east to the Pacific Ocean on the west. The greater portion of the region is unoccupied or devoted to grazing, and its resources unknown and undeveloped. It opens a feasible railroad route from the high interior to the coast, and when such a road is constructed an undoubtedly valuable section will be opened. A few streams run from the Santa Lucia to the Cuyama, as the Alamo, Huasna, Suey and others, and on these are valuable ranches, the Huasna grant of five leagues and the Suey of the same, being of these, and with the Santa Margarita and the speculative purchases the principal ones of the county not subdivided. North and east of these grants the land was all public, there being much yet remaining unsurveyed and unoccupied, yet very suitable for culture and grazing. Upon the Suey, the property of Messrs. Newhall, of San Francisco, large quantities of wheat are produced, and oranges, lemons and grapes are grown successfully.

THE SALINAS VALLEY.

Opposite the head of the Alamo, in the Santa Lucia range, is the source of the Salinas, which runs northwesterly through San Luis Obispo and Monterey counties to the Bay of Monterey. This collects the waters of the greater portion of the eastern section of the county. A large number of streams empty into the Salinas, making it a mighty torrent in seasons of heavy rains.

The region of the Salinas, or that east of the Santa Lucia range, comprises about 1,100,000 acres, of which fully two-thirds is vacant, held for speculation or occupied for nothing more than grazing purposes. It appears almost incredible that such a vast area should, at this date, lie an unoccupied waste if it is susceptible of profitable cultivation. But such things have been in other parts of California, and the condition still exists in the southeastern part of San Luis Obispo County. Until within the last two or three years the same condition obtained in the northeastern part of the county, but this has been partly changed by the incoming of a large number of settlers on public lands, and the subdivision and sale of the great ranchos of Huer-Huero, Eureka, Santa Ysabel and Paso Robles, influenced by the construction of the Southern Pacific Railroad in that quarter.

The writer has traversed a greater portion of this region, and noticed the uniform good character of the soil, the abundant herbage, the many large trees and density of chapparal, or the broad plains ready for the plow, and wondered at its lack of occupancy.

The chief reason, however, why it is not thickly settled is, undoubtedly, because of its distance from railroad communication. This lack will probably be supplied in the near future.

The principal valleys of this region are the San José, Santa Margarita and Salinas along the latter river; the Carriso, La Panza and San Juan along the last named stream, the Estrella on the Estrella River, the Huer-Huero, Cholame, Pala Prieta and other smaller valleys in the north, and the great plains of the Estrella and Elkhorn in the southeast.

Across the Santa Lucia to the eastward is the Carriso Plain, already described, in whose southeastern part is one of the most interesting objects in California. This is the antiquarian monument known as

THE PAINTED ROCK.

Conical in shape, it rises abruptly from the plain to a height of about 140 feet, on one of whose sides is an opening twenty feet wide; extending to 120 feet on the inner side, where it expands to 'a length of 225 feet, forming a grand natural room or hall, open to the sky,—a veritable majestic temple of the wilderness.

It is evident that this great chamber was used by some pre-historic people for purposes of worship or of council, as is evinced by the strange paintings upon the inner face of the walls. These paintings are done in pigments of three colors, red, white and black, still distinct after exposure to the weather through untold ages. The strange characters and figures there depicted with evident careful design somewhat remotely resemble the hieroglyphics of Egypt or the picture writings of Yucatan and other portions of Mexico, being homogeneous with the other aboriginal paintings found in various portions of Southern California. In other parts of this county, as in that of Santa Barbara, are found other "painted rocks," of similar origin, but none so grand or so interesting as this great natural temple of the Carriso Plain.

This plain is separated from the Tulare Valley by the Monte Diablo range of mountains, and from the San Juan Valley by a low ridge. The small valleys and rounded hills here are clothed in wild oats, alfilaria, and bunch-grass. This valley has been much settled up of late years.

THE MONTE DIABLO

range of mountains runs along the eastern boundary of the county, separating it from Kern County and the Tulare Valley. A range of uplifted sandstone divides the San Juan Valley from the Carriso Plain, and between the San Juan and the Salinas is the La Panza range, quite prominent mountains, with gold placers in many of its gulches, which are mined with fair remuneration. The greater portion of the country is of rolling hills, with scattering oaks, giving it a very pleasant and park-like appearance. The beauty and resources of this section cannot be fully described in the limits of this article.

Throughout the region, wherever tried, fruit in many varieties and of the finest quality is grown. At the recent county fair held in the city of San Luis Obispo, peaches, apples, pears and grapes of superb appearance and quality, were on exhibition from the vicinity of Poza on the upper Salinas. This is an elevated region, and the production is an evidence that the very best of the most delicate and valuable fruits can be grown through every limit and extreme of the county.

CREEKS.

Southeastward from the old Mission of San Miguel, the valley of the Estrella Creek stretches toward the mountains dividing San Luis from Kern County. This large tract until very recently was unoccupied and useless, save as grazing ground for a few cattle and sheep. Up to the '70's it was regarded as a portion of some Mexican grant; then the discovery was made that this was Government land, open to settlement, and, while bare in appearance, of great fertility of soil, and well adapted to agriculture. Thus a rapid immigration set in, settlements were made, schoolhouses built, and a vast change effected. Good crops were had in 1876 and 1878, and by 1880 at least forty families had settled upon this wide and fertile tract. In 1887 the total acreage in wheat and barley, from Santa Margarita on the south to San Miguel on the north, and from Paso de Robles to Sheid's, was 8,625 acres, of which thirteen-sixteenths was wheat. The land here is a rich, sandy loam, sparsely covered with nutritious grasses, and with live-oak and white-oak trees scattered at intervals. Water is had at an average depth of thirty feet.

Las Tablas Creek rises in the hills near the Hot Springs and flows northwesterly into the Nacimiento. The fertile tract along its valley supports a quite considerable population, chiefly engaged in grazing and farming. This region is somewhat elevated, its soil mostly a black adobe, very fruitful, and its grazing facilities excellent. Mining, too, has helped the various settlements in this district, as several important quicksilver mines have been located and worked hereabouts. Adelaide is the postoffice for this region, and the postal facilities are well maintained. In schools and churches, also, Las Tablas has taken an advanced position.

RANCHOS.

Between the Salinas and the Estrella are the ranchos Santa Ysabel, Huer-Huero, and Eureka, aggregating about 70,000 acres.

The Santa Ysabel consists of 20,200 acres, adjoining the Rancho Paso de Robles at the northeast. For ten miles the Southern Pacific Railway runs along and within one-fourth mile of its boundary. It is covered with white and live-oak timber, although less thickly than the Paso de Robles. There are, substantially, 16,000 acres of plow land, the rest fruit and grazing land. The soil is rich and deep, and will produce wheat of the finest, barley, oats, corn, all fruits and vines, and olives. Wine and raisin-making will, no doubt, be important industries of this section. On this rancho are twenty miles of running water, besides numerous living springs. Well water is had at ten to forty feet deep.

The Huer-Huero adjoins the Santa Ysabel and the Eureka on the east. It comprises 8,000 acres of valley, 23,000 acres of level and rolling farming lands, and 15,000 acres of hill grazing lands. In two years, 34,000 acres were sold to settlers, mostly of wealth and position, and the region is thickly settled. Wheat, olives, fruit and vines have been planted. About 12,000 acres of this rancho are still unsold.

The Eureka Rancho adjoins Santa Ysabel on the south, and Paso de Robles on the east, comprising about 11,000 acres, of which some 9,500 acres are plow land, and 1,500 grazing. This rancho has a rich, deep soil, and is well watered, and wooded with white and live oak.

These three ranchos last-named were purchased two or three years since by the West Coast Land Company, and have been subdivided and put upon the market by this company, which already has founded the promising town of Templeton, and settled up a great deal of country hitherto unoccupied.

In the extreme northeastern part of the county is the great Cholame Rancho, comprising 26,622 acres, long the property of Messrs. R. E. Jack and Frederick Adams, who have used it mainly as a sheep range. It is similar in its features to the region just described, and is a valuable property. It extends over the boundary line into Monterey County.

As an evidence of progress, the development of the Huer-Huero may be cited. This tract of land, comprising about 48,000 acres, was regarded as an exhausted sheep range, and less than four years ago was sold at $3 an acre. Mr. J. V. Webster, an experienced horticulturist of Alameda County, purchased a large area and soon commenced its cultivation. At the county fair, in the middle of October, 1888, he exhibited from the land grapes of the most choice varieties in large bunches. Also fig and peach trees of six feet growth in the last six months; samples of amber sugar cane, yielding at the rate of 144,000 pounds per acre, and sorghum at the rate of 175,000 pounds per acre. He also exhibited hops of exceedingly thrifty and rich growth, flax of good quality, melons, squashes and a great variety of products grown without irrigation, but with good cultivation.

This detail could be carried on to a tedious extent, and is only introduced to illustrate what can be done on lands called a desert, simply because it was the stupid custom to follow the expression of some very stupid man.

In this region is the little village of Creston with two stores, hotel, school, postoffice, shops, saloons, and residences, with many thrifty farms in the vicinity, all where four years since existed only a wilderness.

RESOURCES.

AGRICULTURE.

San Luis Obispo County with over 2,000,000 acres of land, offers to the farmer unequaled inducements to pursue his calling within its domains, as at least three-fourths of that number of acres is adapted to general farming, and is particularly suited for the raising of grain; as in other places there are certain portions of the county especially desirable for grain; in the northern portion, and east of the Santa Lucia range, fully 200,000 to 300,000 acres of land will bring to the cultivator thereof a rich return, the soil being rich and deep, and though in parts mountainous, is mainly composed of good rolling and valley lands, embraced within the districts known as the San José Valley, the Cholame, and the Ranchos Eureka and Santa Ysabel, Paso Robles, Huer-Huero and Santa Margarita and Salinas Townships.

The country surrounding the city of San Luis Obispo, north and south, in the Osos Valley, is also a rich, grain-producing region, comprising many thousand acres. The average yield of wheat is forty-five bushels to the acre and of oats 150 bushels to the acre.

Around Arroyo Grande and Nipomo, is found, probably, as rich land as lies in any other portion of the county, and possibly the best soil is in these portions. That at Arroyo Grande is particularly fine for beans, a very remunerative and easily handled product, and an industry constantly increasing, the yield being in 1886 nearly 105,000 bushels, and in 1887 in advance of any yield heretofore had; the average yield of beans being forty bushels to the acre.

The county possesses one advantage over other southern counties which an eastern man will appreciate; we refer to the immense water facilities, and moreover the fact that irrigation is never needed; from north to south on an average of every six or seven miles, perennial streams flow to the ocean. With the advent of the railroad easy and accessible shipping points are had; the towns of San Miguel, Paso Robles and Templeton on the Southern Pacific Railroad are the centers for large agricultural districts, and their shipping points for San Francisco.

San Luis Obispo receives from the surrounding country, shipments by the Pacific Coast Railway, which also brings the products of Nipomo and Arroyo Grande and the southern portion of the county to Port Harford, where the Pacific Coast Steamship Company receives for both north and south. A growing industry is the raising of alfalfa, which requires a moist, rich soil. Alfalfa is being raised all over the county; it requires to be cut five times during the year, averaging two tons to the acre at each cutting. All grasses for feed and general use are raised in abundance; timothy, clover, etc., are found in many portions of the county and grow as luxuriantly as in any portion of the East.

Potatoes yield abundantly, averaging over 200 bushels to the acre, equal to the finest grown in Utah, varying in price from 80 cents to $2 per 100 pounds, according to the season. They are of large size, white, mealy and delicious.

All kinds of garden vegetables, such as beets, peas, beans, tomatoes, cucumbers, turnips, onions, etc., are successfully and profitably cultivated, the crop is enormous, the quality good, and the market for all that is not needed at home is sure and at paying prices.

Nearly every farmer has his garden well stocked with all kinds of vegetables.

Cabbages are raised weighing ninety pounds per head; and sweet corn, sorghum, lettuce, melons, radishes, egg plant, etc., are noticeably thrifty and superior. The market is a consideration not to be overlooked by intending settlers, since abundant crops would be of little value if no market at remunerative rates was to be had close at home, or within easy reach by rail.

HORTICULTURE AND VITICULTURE.

While San Luis Obispo County has a wide reputation for its dairying interests, its large cattle interests, and capabilities as a grain county, it stands second to none in adaptability for fruit-raising. A fruit-raiser is not confined to any one particular kind of fruit, but if that is his ambition, may raise nearly every known species, peculiar to either northern or southern California, the soil, climate and topography of the county combining advantages which few counties or other countries possess. The finest qualities of apples, pears, peaches, plums, cherries, apricots, prunes, olives, figs and oranges, and all kinds of nuts,—in fact all fruits, as well as berries of all varieties, grow in abundance with but ordinary care.

East of the Santa Lucia Range, a large section of the country is specially suited to fruit culture; notably around Creston, Templeton, Paso Robles and in fact all of the Salinas basin and the San José Valley.

In the valley around the city of San Luis Obispo, the fruit-raiser reaps a rich reward for his labors, especially with nuts, oranges, lemons, figs and olives, the latter being a very remunerative fruit and growing luxuriantly. The southern portion of the county is well adapted to all fruits; especially must the valley of the Arroyo Grande be named, and it would be hard to say that one portion of the county is better than another for general fruit-raising.

There is a large market for the fruit-grower, both at home and abroad, and now that the railroad traverses the county the Eastern market opens its doors for the reception of our fruits.

With a full-grown, bearing orchard, the profits are sure and large, fruit always being in demand, and the finer the quality, the greater the return.

Within three years after setting out the orchard, the grower will commence to reap his reward, increasing of course as the years roll around. With olives, walnuts and oranges, it takes somewhat longer, it being about seven years before the walnut is in full bearing, about six for the orange, and from five to seven years for the olive.

There is one never failing, ever increasing market for the raiser of fruit; namely, the canning industries growing continually on this coast, which are making the raising of fruit a very profitable industry.

At no far distant day this county will assuredly take a high rank as a grape and wine producing section of the State; a large area of the hill land of the county is peculiarly adapted for the grape, favored with soil and climate for every species of this luscious fruit. Heretofore the mission grape has been more largely cultivated than any other and the success attained with that variety has induced local viticulturists to try the other, favorite species and with marked success; Black Prince, Flame Tokay, Muscat, Black Hamburg, Black Morocco, Zinfandel, Riesling and Frontignan flourishing wherever planted. The raisin and wine industries are rapidly increasing, and, the profits being large, they are bound to increase still more, as there is much room for settlers who wish to engage in this pleasant and profitable business. The principal home market for wines is of course San Francisco, where there is a heavy demand by the large houses which supply the East with California wines, so rapidly growing in favor.

To show what success San Luis Obispo County vineyards have attained we quote the following from an article on the subject prepared by Mr. P. H. Dallidet, Jr., entitled "Specific Instances:"

"From the information acquired through that and other sources in the last twenty years in the county, I am of the opinion that the wealth of San Luis Obispo County can and will be greatly increased by the planting of vineyards, because of the certainty and abundance of their returns. I will endeavor to give facts in a few cases of people living at considerable distances from each other in the county, and any one desiring the full particulars can write to them for further information, and I have no doubt that they will be pleased to give it. Mr. W. N. Short, in the neighborhood of Temblor Ranch on the eastern border of the county, has a young vineyard which surprised him by the numbers of bunches each vine yielded on the fourth year, the bunches filling well and berries growing to perfection. On the Temblor and Cuyama ranches, fifty miles apart on the same belt, there may be found trees and vines growing without attention that do wonders in the way of yield. Mr. Gillis, near Adelaide, told me three years ago, that his two-year-old vines, Muscats, and wine grapes, bore from ten to thirty pounds each, berries very large and sweet, with a beautiful bloom on them. His place is thirty miles from San Luis Obispo in a northerly direction. On W. S. Hinkle's farm some three miles from this city are some ten vines in arbor form, that were literally purple with grapes of the Mission variety every year from the year 1860 to 1882, yielding three to five tons of grapes annually. Mr. Dolores Herrera, near Pozo, planted some vines near his house that have borne very well, but said Mr. Herrera, 'I had a few cuttings left over after planting my vineyard; so I thought I would experiment, and I therefore set them out on a dry-looking hill about half a mile away from the house, and left them there to live or die as they chose. After some months I saw they grew nicely: so I pulled up some of them and left the others till the next year. When my grapes were ripening, I thought of the hill vines and went to see if they were yet alive, when imagine my surprise on finding from three to five bunches on each little vine, each bunch weighing from a half to three-quarters of a pound of the finest white grapes I ever tasted.' Pozo is thirty miles east of us and forty miles from the ocean. Mr. E. W. Howe, near Morro, has a very nice little vineyard which yields good crops of thirty pounds and upwards to the vine.

"F. Guillemin, just over the mountain to the east of us, has a small vineyard set out after the manner of his country, that is, the vines from two to four feet apart, which bear from five to fifteen pounds each, and of part of his crop he makes a light wine which connoisseurs pronounce to be equal to the famous petit vin du Jurat of France.

"Mr. Hasbrouck has some twenty acres or more of vines at the Ranchita which are growing very nicely. Mr. Henry Ditmas, of Musick, has some boxes of raisins made by him on his place that were equal in point of size, color and taste to the best San Bernardino raisins.

"Mr. P. H. Dallidet, Sr., has a vineyard from four to twenty years of age, and he has taken from his oldest vines, which at seven years of age had had good care, as high as twenty pounds to the vine, and out of eight acres of grapes made one season 6,300 gallons of wine.

"Hon. Frank McCoppin, Dr. W. W. Hays, E. W. and Hon. George Steele, J. P. Andrews, Goldtree Bros., W. H. Taylor and E. A. Atwood, all have fine young vineyards and orchards. Besides these gentlemen who are largely interested, there are a great number of persons who have from one acre and upwards in full bearing who all say that vines are a success with only moderate attention. Out of perhaps 150 persons who have vineyards, I know of but two that irrigate, and that because they have an abundance of water which would otherwise be entirely wasted. As it is, they get a good growth of wood, whether at the expense of quantity in fruit is a question, but certainly, at the expense of quality. Of the persons named above only Mr. Guillemin irrigates.

"Having observed closely the yield of grapes for a number of years past, I can say without fear of exaggeration that vines of full bearing age will yield an average one year with another of thirty pounds to the vine."

MINERAL RESOURCES.

The following account is partly extracted from the report of the State Mineralogist:

Gold, silver, lead, copper, quicksilver, chromite, gypsum, onyx, silica, salt, lime, coal, and petroleum have been found in the mountains of this county. Some of these have been found in sufficient quantities to pay for working, and it is quite likely that a careful investigation of the remote mountain regions would result in additions to the mineral resources. * * * It is a matter of history that gold was shipped from San Luis Obispo and neighboring counties prior to its discovery by Marshall in 1848. The explorers of the Pacific Railroad reported gold west of Salinas in 1854, though its existence in the San José Mountains had long been known. Gold has been and is still washed from sands in the bed of the San Marcos Creek, about four miles northwest of Paso Robles, during the wet months of the year, yielding, it is said, as high as from $3 to $4 per man per day. Placer claims have also been worked thirty miles southeast of Templeton since 1870–'71, ground sluicing and panning when water has been plentiful, having yielded from $2 to $4 per day.

The placer mines of the La Panza District are the best known, and are probably of the most importance. They are situated at the southeastern part of the San José range, which rises as a formidable mountain joining the Santa Lucia, and over $100,000 in gold have been taken out. During 1878 there was quite a rush to these parts, and prospecting was carried on in nearly all the gulches leading from the San José range to the San

Juan River. The chief interest was centered in the de la Guerra Gulch, where the most mining was done,—even as late as 1882; also upon the Navajo Creek, which is a stream of constantly flowing water. Some of these placers have yielded as high as $4 per day. The gold was coarse, pieces worth 50 cents or 80 cents being of frequent occurrence. Haystack Cañon also has running water, and gold. Near the head of this cañon are falls of twenty feet, where the water descends into a basin nearly twenty feet across, and ten or twelve feet deep.

These streams reach the channel of the San Juan during very wet weather. Of late years these mines have not been actively worked, chiefly on account of the scarcity of water. In the southern portion of the county gold has also been found in sands on the seashore in considerable quantity. They are reported as yielding from $1.50 to $2 per day to the miner, and, as the gold dust appears to be renewed by the washing of the sea, the deposits are practically inexhaustible. San Luis Obispo is credited with the production of $6,200 in gold during the year 1889, as reported by the director of the United States mint.

San Luis Obispo, in common with all of the California missions, holds to the customary legends of rich silver mines having been formerly worked within its borders by the Indians and old Spanish padres.

In 1862, during the great copper excitement, several copper mines were opened in the northwestern part of the county. Green Elephant and North Mexican were among the most promising. In 1863 copper was obtained and smelted in the neighborhood of these mines, and shipped to San Francisco. Sulphurites, carbonates, and silicate ores are widely distributed throughout the county, the float rock being often very rich. Cubanite, a sulphide of copper and iron, is said to exist abundantly upon Santa Rosa Creek.

Quicksilver was discovered in 1872, by a Mexican, in the mountains west of San Simeon, although it was long known to exist in the county by the Indians, who used it as a paint, and were in the habit of visiting the Santa Lucia range of mountains to procure it for that purpose. Over 150 quicksilver claims are recorded in the San Simeon district. In 1871 discoveries of cinnabar were made at Cambria; also about eight miles north of the first discovery, near the northeast corner of Piedras Blancas Rancho, which led to the discovery of the Pine Mountain lode, on the summit of the Santa Lucia. On this lode eight claims were located, from which a large quantity of ore, stated to average $2\frac{1}{2}$ per cent., has been extracted. The Gibson and Phillips claims, the Santa Maria, Buckeye, and Jeff Davis, are all located on the same lode. The San José mines were located in 1872 upon the eastern slope of the Santa Lucia range. The principal mine that has been developed is the Oceanic. The original claims, three in number, were located in 1874, and are situated on the north side and three-quarters of a mile from Santa Rosa Creek, and five miles from Cambria. The ledge runs east and west, dipping to the north at an angle of about seventeen degrees; the vein is said to vary from eight feet to thirty-two feet in width. At times over 300 men were employed in these works. Three furnaces were erected, at a cost of $90,000. Good returns were made on the capital while the price of quicksilver was high, but when it fell to 40 cents per pound it was found impossible to produce it at a profit, and work was suspended.

Large deposits of chromite exist in various parts of the county, but mining has been principally carried on in the Santa Lucia and Buchon ranges. Rackliff's mine is situated five miles northwest of the county-seat; is leased to William Copeland & Co. Developments have been carried on here to a limited extent during the past year, and between 100 and 200 tons of the chromite were shipped to San Francisco; price paid at San Luis Obispo, $9.00. The San Juan, Castro, Primera, El Salto, and El Devisadero, which are situated northeast of San Luis Obispo, are the property of Goldtree Brothers. These mines have not been worked during the current year, there being sufficient chromite already on the dump to satisfy the demand. The price obtained is $8.50 per ton at San Luis Obispo. The principal shipments have been to Germany. William Goldtree states that it would not pay to work these mines unless $12 per ton could be obtained for the average product. The mines are patented. G. Jasper is working a mine seven or eight miles distant from San Luis Obispo, and he ships about 150 tons per year to Baltimore. The price obtained is $8 per ton. It is the opinion of those conversant with chromic mining in the county that a miner could only make wages by working his own mines at such a figure.

Several deposits of electro-silicon occur in the county, particularly in the vicinity of the bay of San Luis Obispo and San Carpojoro. The deposits at the latter place have so far proved of the greatest value, great quantities having been shipped for polishing purposes. The name of Salinas (saline) was given to the principal river of San Luis Obispo and Monterey counties because of the saline springs along its banks and tributaries. In the mountains, about the rivers' headwaters, are many salt springs of the strongest brine, and large deposits of salt rock. Black Lake is a small sheet of water, half a mile in diameter and of irregular contour, situated near the summit of the San José mountains, and is so intensely salt as to form a brine suitable for the preservation of meat without further concentration. The salt deposits of the Carriso Plain appear like a dry lake, being five miles in length and from half a mile to two miles in breadth. The salt covers the bed to a depth of from six inches to two feet, and is sufficiently pure to be used for many purposes. It is much used for stock, being hauled away in wagons to the ranchos, twenty or more miles distant. Water intensely salt is found at a depth of two or three feet beneath the surface in the vicinity of this deposit.

Limestone is found in many localities in this county. In the vicinity of Nipomo Rancho is a large body of soft, marly limestone, that produces a fair article of lime. A good supply of limestone suitable for lime is now being obtained in Lopez Cañon, about eight miles east of the town of Arroyo Grande, and lime burning has been commenced there with a good prospect of success. The immense bed of fossil clams and oysters, near the Oceanic mine, and on the Santa Margarita Rancho, and the huge *Ostrea titans* occurring in several places, when burnt, yielded a fair article of lime, which has been used extensively in retorting at the quicksilver mines in this county.

Gypsum is found at the headwaters of Arroyo Grande and on Navajo Creek.

Coal was discovered in this county as early as 1863 on the beach at San Simeon, by William Leffingwell, who used it for blacksmithing. The San Simeon Coal Mining Company was subsequently started by C. B. Rutherford, of Oakland. This is said to have been the first mining company started in the county. The outcrop of the vein was two feet in width, and usually covered with water at high tide. A shaft was sunk to a depth of about 100 feet, at which point the coal dwindles to a mere seam, and mining was abandoned. Coal has also been found in the mountains east of the town of San Luis Obispo, but not in sufficient quantities to pay for working.

There are several varieties of building stone in the county. The range of peaks which extends from San Luis Peak to Moro Rock are composed of trachytic porphyry, which is used locally, and of late there has been some talk of establishing a quarry either at Moro Rock or some of the neighboring peaks. A sandstone crops out also a half mile southeast of Arroyo Grande, and extends to Los Varos Creek. At the latter place a quarry has been opened by Hugill Brothers. About fifty feet of rock are here exposed, which is a light buff-colored sandstone, soft when quarried, and can be sawed into cubes, but becomes hard upon exposure to the atmosphere. This stone has been much used for chimneys and foundations in this vicinity. A quarry of similar rock is said to have been opened by J. S. Rice five miles from Pismo wharf.

There is a notable onyx mine five miles from Musick, in the heart of the Santa Lucia mountains, amidst rugged, precipitous spurs and ridges, which make the scenery exceedingly wild and grand. Here, ten years ago, David Musick, while hunting for deer, discovered the character of the rock, and claims were made as for a gold or silver bearing vein, as the locality was Government land. A company was formed and prospecting was done, but the locators, not seeing their way clear to develop the mine, presently sold it for $250 to J. and F. Kessler, marble-workers of San Francisco, who have jealously guarded and extended their claim, and, having perfected the title, are now ready to open the property. A road is in course of construction from Musick along arroyos and over ridges to the ledge, being built for the comparatively small sum of $1,300. The summit of this ridge is 1,900 feet above sea level, the Santa Lucia range here reaching an elevation of 2,000 to 3,500 feet, and forming the watershed of the Arroyo Grande flowing southwest, the Huasna flowing south, and the Salinas north by west. The surrounding country affords good grazing and an abundance of live oak and chapparal.

The onyx ledge runs athwart the ridge bearing slightly west of north and east of south. Faces of from twenty to forty-five feet in height have been opened on the ledge on each side of the ridge, the northern one showing a brilliant white mass of rock in seams of two to sixteen inches in thickness, standing nearly perpendicular. The southern opening is about half a mile from the first, of similar formation, but showing rock of various colors, of yellow, green, blue, golden, white and other shades, giving it the highest value for ornamental work. This, Mr. Kessler claims is the most beautiful and valuable deposit of onyx known in the world. The ledge is sixteen feet in thickness and the opening exposes to view more than a thousand tons of the rock. The outward appearance is of a rusty, rugged stone, not attractive until broken and the lines and waves of the blending colors seen. A few tons have been dragged down the mountain in sleds and taken to San Francisco, where it was sawed into slabs or cut into such shapes as required and polished. A piece eight inches square and half inch thick, was sold to Gov. Stanford for $25. In a rough state it sells readily for $100 a ton. The proprietor showed a fragment of eight feet in length, by sixteen to eighteen inches in breadth and thickness, which he said would be worth $300 in San Francisco. This would be cut into thirty slabs half an inch thick, and polished, and be worth $10 a square foot at least, or bring a return of $3,600. Others become valuable according to their colors and the forms they are worked into. The labor this will employ and the value resulting is inconceivable. There is now a rage for colored onyx in a vast variety of forms,—of mantels, tables, counters, pillars, panels, frames, ornaments, etc. But the customers are among the rich of the East and Europe. It cannot be utilized but to a slight extent in California. The railroad forbids, and the high rates of labor give, an advantage elsewhere. The raw material will go by sailing vessel to Atlantic and European ports for $9 a ton. In New York it can be worked by labor at $1.50 a day; in France and Italy at 50 cents a day, and in Belgium at 25 cents a day, while in San Francisco such labor demands from $3 to $4 a day. Thus it will be worked abroad, and, what Californians want, will pay the railroad $45 a ton and vast profits to the employers of cheap labor. But San Luis Obispo will have the honor of supplying the beautiful material in its crude state and profit on the glory.

Near the summit on the divide and on the line of the onyx ledge is a spring of very singular water. It tastes like the water from oysters, and a common glass full is a strong purgative. Bruises, cuts, poison oak and other sores are quickly cured by bathing in it. For medicinal purposes this water appears very valuable, and what it is, is a mystery.

"At and in the immediate vicinity of Port Harford there are extensive bodies of serpentine.

BITUMINOUS ROCK.

"On the 'Rancho El Pismo,' about seven miles southeast of San Luis Obispo, * * * great quantities of all the rocks are saturated with bitumen. There are, it is true, places where the rock is free from bitumen and other places where the percentage which it contains is small. But the greater portion of it, where the quarry has been opened, is about as full of bitumen as it can hold, and the quantity easily available here is practically inexhaustible. A short sidetrack from the Pacific Coast Railway runs directly to the quarry. [Blasting is required, and the quarrying is often perilous, from the clinging for a while of a portion of the very tough rock, which will afterwards fall suddenly, in pieces of many tons' weight, which drop without warning.—Y. H. A.] They are now shipping this rock both to Los Angeles and San Francisco for pavements, for which it seems to be admirably adapted.

"At a point about three-quarters of a mile from this quarry, there is another large deposit of bituminous sandstone very heavy-bedded, on the 'Corral de Piedra' Rancho. It is called 'Oak Park.' But very little work has been done yet at this locality, and the exposures are not so good as could be desired.

"Mr. J. J. Schifferly also has a rancho of 1,344 acres, about one mile westerly from Adams & Nicholls' quarry (these gentlemen own the two first mentioned), where most of the hills are full of bituminous rock. There is probably enough of this material within a few square miles in this vicinity to pave all the cities in the United States.

"Mr. A. B. Hasbrouck, who owns a rancho called 'Ranchito,' in the Santa Lucia range of mountains, about twenty-two miles southeast of the city of San Luis Obispo, and on the headwaters of the Arroyo Grande, states that on his place there are large quantities of asphaltum, with some petroleum springs and much sulphur water."

The large deposits of asphaltum and the presence of rock saturated with bitumen suggested the presence of petroleum, and in May,

1886, Messrs. Nicholls, Adams & Walker undertook the boring for oil in the valley of the San Luis Creek, about two miles from the ocean. At a depth of 600 feet a body of hot sulphur water, accompanied by gas was struck. The boring was continued to a depth of 900 feet, when an accident occurred that caused the further prosecution of the work to cease.

At this depth the flow of water is about 3,000 barrels a day, with a jet of gas burning with a flame three feet high from an aperture two inches in diameter. The water has a temperature of 100 degrees, and the "oil well" has become the Hot Sulphur Well, and the locality improved as a bathing and health resort. A hotel and bathing-houses have been erected, and, the site possessing many attractions, it bids fair to become one of the many popular resorts of the coast.

The boring for oil led the same parties to investigating the formation of the rocks in the neighborhood, and over a large area it was found that certain sandstones were saturated with bitumen, forming a rock very valuable for paving purposes.

Through a region of twenty miles in length by four in width, were found many high, rocky projections almost rising into mountains, largely composed of this bituminous rock. These barren ridges, previously regarded as of little value, immediately became objects of great demand. A paving material of such value, in such unlimited abundance and of so easy access appears a discovery of inestimable value to the world.

This material is used in paving in San Francisco, Los Angeles, San Diego and other cities, causing a demand at this early day of its development of some 3,000 tons a month. The consumption of this rock will largely increase, creating a very important business and become a great source of wealth to the county.

The main bituminous rock mines are situated in a belt one mile wide and ten miles long, extending from San Luis Creek to Arroyo Grande, and from five to fifteen miles south and southeast from San Luis Obispo. About 30,000 tons were mined and exported last year. The quantity in the hills is infinite. The chemical analysis of this substance is as follows: finely divided sand, 65.917; bitumen, 16.255; iron and alumina, 8.405; calcium carbonate, 8.212; magnesium carbonate, 1.003; undetermined, .208; total, 100. Some seven or eight companies are engaged in mining this rock. The S. L. O. Bituminous Rock Company, it is said, will build a wharf about a half a mile south of Cave Landing. The company is developing the rich mine within 1,500 feet of the proposed wharf.

DAIRYING.

We believe that California has advantages second to no State in the Union for dairying and cattle raising; the only drawback being the high price of labor; but the soil, climate and native grasses are all exceedingly favorable, making San Luis Obispo County one of the best, if not the banner county for this industry.

Although one of the youngest counties in the business, and for many years comparatively inaccessible, it has long occupied the second place for productiveness, and now claims the first place.

The rainy and consequently grass season is expected in November or December and lasts till June—that is, the season for green and growing native grasses produced spontaneously, wild oats and volunteer grain often being five inches high during the first of December. The climate is peculiarly fitted for dairying, on account of the feed grasses, and general vegetation being constantly kept in good condition by the moisture from the ocean, besides the regular rainy seasons, and there being no necessity for irrigation; the trade winds make the climate warmer in winter, keeping off frosts and freezing weather.

As a result of such a climate and soil we have a luxurious growth of the most nutritious grasses known on this coast; all kinds of small grain, corn, roots, alfalfa, Australian rye and orchard and other foreign grasses are grown successfully.

At the commencement of the rainy season the native grasses, to-wit, wild oats, alfilaria, various kinds of clover and bunch grass spring up as if by magic. Later comes the alfalfa, which continues green all the year except during the very few frosty nights when it is cut down; but the first crop in winter, being rank and sour, is cut and used for hay. The dairy cows are also fed green corn, and later, roots, squashes and hay; the squashes will keep nearly all winter if well matured, and the carrots and beets may remain in the ground till needed, and will keep growing, and are often carried over until the next season. In that case they will come in for feed when the native grasses begin to mature and dry, and consequently need something to go with them.

Thus it will be seen that there is no need of resorting to silos in order to have the proper milk-producing feed the year round. The native grasses, when they mature dry and remain upon the ground, make a very good quality of hay in this climate, and the seeds of the burr clover, particularly, are like grain, on which the stock cattle and dry cows subsist during the whole dry season. The number of squashes and roots that can be grown to the acre is wonderful—from twenty to forty tons of green corn, alfalfa and squash; from fifty to 100 tons of roots; the writer has weiged single mangel-wurtzels that averaged over 100 pounds, and squashes 270 pounds. He also made a three-days test of the milk from 150 cows while grazing on the native grasses, to ascertain the value of the milk for butter and cheese. The cream was separated from the milk by a Lavel Separator, and 17.76 pounds of milk made a pound of butter, eight and three-eighths pounds of milk made one pound of cheese from the press, good solid cheese; thus demonstrating the native grasses to be the very best cheese and butter producing food. In most localities it takes about ten pounds of milk to make one pound of cheese, and twenty-five pounds of milk to make a pound of butter on the average. The above test was made from all the milk of 150 cows for three consecutive days, furnishing a test of the most conclusive character.

For thirty years there has not been a day in which there has not been made cheese or butter in some of the dairies there. When put to extra expense, by raising feed, prices of produce are higher. By milking the year round they keep their best help, distribute the calf-raising, keep their business organized and their stock in good condition. Thus they can dairy profitably the year round.

A Holstein cow that was fed bran and shorts in addition to grass, and milked twice a day, made by actual weight 17,270 pounds of milk in one year. It was her first year in the county, and she was carrying a calf during eight months of the time. Several of two-year-old Holstein heifers, under precisely the same treatment, made about 10,250 pounds of milk in one year. It can safely be said from the above showing that San Luis Obisbo is the banner dairy county, and that her cows and grasses can not be excelled in this or any other State.

EXPORTS.

Perhaps, on the whole, no better judgment may be found of the resources of the county than that founded upon a resume of the exports of material produced over and above those needed for home consumption. To this end is hereinafter given a statement of the exports from Port Harford for the last four years.

FOR THE YEAR ENDING NOVEMBER 30, 1886.

	Tons.
Beans	3,369.8
Wheat	13,847.5
Barley	9,024.8
Oats	657.1
Rye	83.0
Flax seed	306.9
Other grains	203.9
Wool	334.6
Lumber	9,903.0
Wood	1,192.0
Coal	465.3
Asphaltum	415.2
Bituminous Rock	
Chrome ore	912.6
Butter	892.0
Cheese	181.7
Hides and pelts	81.2
Cattle	1,416.0
Hogs	1,213.8
Sheep	649.8
Other live-stock	78.9
Agricultural implements	134.4
Merchandise	9,189.9
Total	54,552.4

FOR THE YEAR ENDING NOVEMBER 30, 1887.

	Tons.
Beans	3,062.9
Wheat	7,271.3
Barley	9,423.6
Oats	237.5
Rye	74.2
Flax seed	47.4
Other grains	896.3
Wool	271.1
Lumber	17,677.4
Wood	1,473.4
Coal	174.9
Asphaltum	383.4
Bituminous rock	2,470.1
Chrome ore	1,115.4
Butter	853.1
Cheese	167.2
Hides and pelts	93.8
Cattle	451.3
Hogs	1,635.3
Sheep	200.9
Other live-stock	134.8
Agricultural implements	52.2
Merchandise	12,262.9
Total	60,430.4

FOR THE YEAR ENDING NOVEMBER 30, 1888.

	Tons.
Beans	1,338.5
Wheat	8,383.9
Barley	16,724.8
Oats	1,173.1
Rye	25.8
Flax seed	86.7
Other grains	197.7
Wool	145.1
Lumber	21,770.3
Wood	1,524.0
Coal	8,310.9
Asphaltum	190.2
Bituminous rock	19,063.0
Chrome ore	635.0
Butter	978.7
Cheese	117.9
Hides and pelts	100.2
Cattle	585.9
Hogs	1,027.3
Sheep	120.0
Other live-stock	204.6
Agricultural implements	196.6
Merchandise	18,652.5
Total	91,502.7

San Luis Obispo County shipped last year (1889) via Port Harford, by steamers of the Pacific Coast Steamship Company—not to mention shipments by other conveyances and from other landings—the following:

	Pounds.
Asphaltum and bituminous rock	27,773,200
Butter	2,014,800
Cheese	192,800
Wheat	15,699,200
Barley	26,762,800
Beans	2,998,400
Ore	1,368,000
Hogs	769,800
Sundries	7,835,200
Total	85,414,200

Six hundred and seven steamers arrived and departed during the year, besides a large number of sailing vessels.

The reports of shipments for 1890 are not yet rendered, but the officials estimate that the export of bituminous rock will be one-third greater than last year. On the other hand the excessive rains of last season having caused a light grain crop, the aggregate of exports probably will not exceed that of last year.

BENCH AND BAR.

After the adoption of the constitution of the State of California, the office of county judge of San Luis Obispo was first held by Don José Mariano Bonilla, a native of the city of Mexico, who had been judge of the first instance under the Mexican rule, and sub-prefect and alcalde under the military government, after annexation and prior to the adoption of the constitution. It is related of Señor Bonilla that his keen sense of justice was once severely outraged in the trial of a case between two Mexicans, involving the ownership of a horse. Judge Bonilla and W. J. Graves were the only lawyers in the county, and, Graves having been retained by the plaintiff and Bonilla occupying the bench, the defendant was left without an attorney. This seemed to the judge such a hardship that he summoned the sheriff to preside over the court, while he himself descended from the bench and devoted to the cause of the defendant all his ability and energy. That he was thoroughly impartial and unbigoted appears from the fact that, after due deliberation, he rendered judgment for the plaintiff, against his own arguments!

To Judge Bonilla succeeded (elected in 1850) John M. Price, who also had been alcalde. He served less than one year, when he was followed by William J. Graves, who had been a member of the State Assembly and of the State Senate.

O. M. Brown was next elected to this office, taking his seat in March, 1853. He held the position for two years, and was succeeded by Romualdo Pacheco, a member of one of the old Spanish-American families, prominent in California both before and after annexation. Mr. Pacheco held various important offices in the State, including that of Governor.

In 1857 José Maria Muñoz was elected county judge to succeed Pacheco. Judge Muñoz was a native Californian, well educated in Spanish, but unable to speak English. His opposing candidate was ex-Judge José M. Bonilla. Judge Muñoz held the office until 1861, when he was succeeded by Dr. Joseph M. Havens, one of the pioneers of California.

In 1863 Dr. Havens was succeeded by Wiliam L. Beebee, one of the oldest and most respected citizens of San Luis Obispo. Again Mr. Beebee was elected in 1867, and was confirmed in his seat after a protracted and expensive litigation, the election having been contested by Charles Lindley.

In 1871 the choice for county judge was McDowell R. Venable, who since 1869 had held a high position at the bar here. In 1875 he was the only candidate for county judge, and received almost the entire vote of the county. He continued in this office until it was abolished by the adoption of the new constitution.

The constitution provided for the division of the State into judicial districts, and that at its first session the Legislature should elect for each district one district judge, who should hold office for two years from the 1st of January succeeding his election, after which the judges should be elected at the general election, to hold office for six years. This court was given original jurisdiction in law and equity; in all civil cases where the amount in dispute should not exceed $200, exclusive of interest; in all criminal cases not otherwise provided for, and in all issues of fact joined in probate court.

Henry Amos Tefft was the first gentleman elected by the Legislature judge of the district comprising San Luis and Santa Barbara counties. He held the office until February 6, 1852, when, returning from holding court at Santa Barbara, he was drowned in San Luis Obispo harbor while attempting to disembark from the steamer Senator.

The sad death of Judge Tefft left vacant the chair of this district court, and to it was appointed, in February, 1852, Joaquin Carrillo, then county judge of Santa Barbara. This gentleman was a grandson of Raymundo Carrillo, the first commandante of Santa Barbara presidio. Judge Carrillo was not familiar with the English language, and when cases were tried in that language it was necessary to interpret to him the court proceedings. Yet the Carrillo family having high rank and influence, he was elected without opposition district judge at the ensuing general election, and he continued to hold the office until 1863. He was in character at once imperious and convivial, as appears in an incident related by Mr. D. F. Newsom, who was appointed county clerk in 1853. Judge Carrillo one day asked Mr. Newsom to join him in a social glass, and Mr. Newsom declined, as he never took wine or liquor. Thereupon the judge took umbrage, declaring that a man who would not drink was not fit to be clerk of his court, and that for the discourtesy he would remove him from office; accordingly the sheriff was called upon to furnish a deputy to act as clerk. Now there was here no one qualified for this position save Mr. Newsom, whose knowledge was of the greatest usefulness and importance in the public functions, badly organized as generally were the offices. Therefore the sheriff promptly appointed Mr. Newsom deputy sheriff, and detailed him to act as clerk, which office he continued to fill without opposition or comment from Judge Carrillo.

After the census of 1860 the State was re-apportioned into judicial districts, and San Luis Obispo, Santa Barbara, Los Angeles, San Bernardino, and San Diego counties were grouped into the first district. An amendment to the constitution hereafter segregated the judicial from the political election, ordering them to be held at different times. At the election in 1863 the candidates for judge of the first district were Pablo de la Guerra and Joaquin Carrillo, of Santa Barbara, and Benjamin Hayes of Los Angeles, the first mentioned being elected. Judge de la Guerra was one of the most notable of the Spanish-American citizens of California. He was born in Santa Barbara, his father at the time commanding the presidio of Santa Barbara. Don Pablo de la Guerra filled a conspicuous *role* in public affairs in California, both before and after annexation. He held at different periods the offices of supervisor of customs, judge of the first instance, member of the constitutional convention, State Senator, president of the Senate, and, by succession, Lieutenant-governor. He was re-elected to the office of district judge until 1869, and remained the incumbent until failing health compelled his resignation in December, 1873, he dying some two months later.

On the resignation of Judge de la Guerra, Governor Booth appointed to the vacant position Hon. Walter Murray, who in 1869 had been a candidate for the position, carrying San Luis Obispo County, but being defeated by the large vote cast in Santa Barbara County in favor of Don Pablo de la Guerra. He was a man of firm convictions, immovable principles, and great independence of character. Unfortunately, he survived his predecessor but two years, dying at San Luis Obispo, October 5, 1875.

In the campaign of 1875 Walter Murray was the promising candidate to succeed himself; but, he dying just before the election, the next preferred was Eugene Fawcett, of Santa Barbara, who continued in this office until it was abolished by the new constitution. He was then, in September, 1879, elected in Santa Barbara County to the new office of superior judge, created by the new constitution; and, taking his seat January 6, 1880, he died within three days.

The new constitution, adopted in 1879, entirely reconstructed the judiciary system in California, abolishing the district courts, and replacing them by superior courts, one to each county. In San Luis Obispo, Louis McMurtry was elected superior judge on a union ticket, defeating the nominee of the workingmen and new constitution parties. Mr. McMurtry at this time had been district attorney since 1877. He fulfilled the duties of this new office with great credit, but was shortly stricken with disease, and died February 11, 1883.

The vacancy left by the decease of Judge McMurtry was filled by appointment, Governor Stoneman attending the prayers of a preponderance of constituents in selecting Durrell S. Gregory, to whom had been paid the compliment of admitting him to practice by special act of the Legislature. Judge Gregory had a brilliant reputation in his profession, and had served two terms as State senator. He had been district attorney in Monterey County, and in 1860 he had been sent as a delegate to the memorable Charleston convention. Judge Gregory discharged the duties of this office for some years, and until his death, which befell on June 5, 1889.

During the last few months of his incumbency San Luis County had had a second judge in the person of Hon. V. A. Gregg, who had been appointed February 8, 1889, by virtue of a special act of the Legislature. Judge Gregory's office ceased with the expiration of his incumbency,

Though the election records of 1850 do not mention the office of district attorney, O. M. Brown, afterward county judge, was appointed by the court of sessions to fulfill the duties of such office.

After him, in 1851, was appointed Parker H. French, of unsavory record in connection with Walker's filibustering expedition to Nicaragua, and other questionable proceedings.

Hubbard C. M. Ely was elected to this office in 1853; and W. J. Graves was elected in 1855; and he, being elected the following year to the Assembly, was followed by James White, appointed by the board of supervisors.

Walter Murray was elected in 1859, and P. A. Forrester in 1861; James White followed him in 1863; and Walter Murray once more became district attorney in 1867. He was succeeded by Newton Dennis Witt, who filled the term. Then, in September, 1871, was elected A. A. Oglesby, who was re-elected in 1875. After Mr. Oglesby came Louis McMurtry, afterward superior judge. He was district attorney from 1877 to 1879, when Ernest Graves, son of the pioneer, Hon. W. T. Graves, was elected by the workingmen and new constitution parties. Graves was re-elected in 1882.

Mr. F. A. Dorn is the present district attorney (October, 1890), the former incumbent, Mr. Arthur R. Earll, having died in June, 1889.

In the early days there were few lawyers

in San Luis Obispo, yet since the organization of the county the bar here has comprehended eloquent and able lawyers. Among these may be mentioned Frederick Adams, Judge Robt. C. Bouldin (died December 16, 1879), R. M. Preston (died in Sonoma County, 1882), W. H. Spencer, J. M. Wilcoxen, Jasper N. Turner, C. H. Clement, J. R. Patton, and R. B. Treat, who, with those already mentioned, and others now practicing, present a fine array of talent.

There is no regular bar association in San Luis County, although there is a good mutual understanding among the attorneys. There are seventeen lawyers resident at the county-seat, and various others in the interior towns. The oldest and best known of these gentlemen are:— Judge McDowell R. Venable, Cyrus Wren Goodchild, Ernest and William Graves, William Spencer and J. M. Wilcoxen.

San Luis Obispo County contains thirty-seven election precincts, as follows:—Arroyo Grande, No. 1, Arroyo Grande, No. 2, Avenales, Beach, Cambria, Carriso, Cayucos, Cholame, Chorro, Corral de Piedra, Creston, Cuesta, Estrella, Huasna, Josephine, La Panza, Las Tablas, Los Osos, Lynch, Morro, Nipomo, Orcutt, Oso Flaco, Painted Rock, Paso Robles, No. 1, Paso Robles, No. 2, Piletas, San José, San Juan, San Luis Obispo, No. 1, San Luis Obispo, No. 2, San Luis Obispo, No. 3, San Luis Obispo, No. 4, San Miguel, San Simeon, Santa Margarita, Templeton.

MISCELLANEOUS.

COUNTY OFFICERS.

Virgil A. Gregg	Superior Judge
A. C McLeod	Sheriff
Chas. W. Dana	Clerk
F. A. Dorn	District Attorney
B. F. Petitt	Treasurer
C. A. Farnum	Auditor
J. T. Walker	Collector
J. Feidler	Recorder
J. M. Felts	Assessor
W. M. Armstrong	School Superintendent
G. B. Nichols	Coroner
T. A. Greenleaf	Public Administrator
Geo. Story	Surveyor

SUPERVISORS.

J. C. Baker	1st District
F. F. White	2d District
P. F. Ready	3d District
G. T. Gregg	4th District
J. V. Webster	5th District

BOARD OF EDUCATION.

A. F. Parsons	Arroyo Grande
D. M. Meredith	San Luis Obispo
Miss C. B. Churchill	Paso Robles
B. H. Franklin	Cambria
Wm. Armstrong, ex officio	San Luis Obispo

THE POSTOFFICES

in the county are twenty-nine, as follows:— Adelaida, Arroyo Grande, Avenal, Cambria, Cayucos, Cholame, Creston, Dove, Edna, Estrella, Goodwin, La Panza, Linne, Los Berros, Morro, Musick, Nipomo, Painted Rock, Paso Robles, Port Harford, Pozo, Root, San Luis Obispo, San Miguel, San Simeon, Santa Margarita, Simmler, Starkey and Templeton.

Of these, seven are money-order offices, and the San Luis Obispo issues also international money orders. This is a third-class office. The postmaster is W. S. Cannon. He has two assistants,—young ladies. The semi-annual statement of this office, from October 1, 1889, to April 1, 1890, shows that the total number of letters and parcels handled during that period was 3,613; second-class matter sent was 5,934 pounds; money orders issued amounted to $12,547.03; money orders and postal notes paid, to $12,319.86; total receipts for fees, stamps, etc., $3,972.06; net income from the office, $1,447.86.

From May 5 to May 12, 1890, this office handled 417 pounds, eight ounces, or 6,477 pieces of mail, the income amounting to $94.41.

The office now contains 352 boxes and twelve drawers, and the newly-leased quarters could accommodate just twice that number should increased population require it.

SCHOOLS.

The first school in San Luis Obispo, under the new *régime*, was opened in 1850, in a room of the mission building, the Spanish language being the medium of instruction. The teacher was Don Guillermo Searles, born in Chili, of English parents. This was a gentleman of education, and his administration gave satisfaction. The population being then very sparse, the one school district covered the whole county. Searles' successor was Michael Merchant, an Irishman, who came thither via Mexico. He taught in Spanish. It appears that during his administration the county fund failed, and the pupils were required to pay $5 per month tuition. Mr. Merchant was succeeded by Mr. Parker, who, instead of teaching in Spanish, and simply repeating the lessons, required his pupils to translate from one language to the other, they attaining to considerable progress by the drill. In 1854 Mr. D. F. Newsom was the teacher, and he gave his instruction in English, and required his pupils to translate the lessons into both languages. At that time there were in the county but forty children able to speak English. To Mr. Newsom is due the honor of having organized the schools of San Luis Obispo upon the basis followed until now. At this time the assessor was ex-officio superintendent of schools, but little or no attention was paid to the department until Mr. Newsom's incumbency.

The progress of the schools was slow during the first decade, and there was but one district until 1861, when San Simeon district was formed where several American families had settled on a small area of Government land along Santa Rosa Creek. The two districts comprised the county, the dividing line being entirely indefinite. There were now 735 children of school age, and 230 under the limit, that is, a total of 965 children under eighteen years old, in the county. Of these, sixty-two attended the mission district school, and thirteen the San Simeon school in 1861. The records are much broken up to 1866, since when they are complete.

In 1870 there were 1,275 children of school age in San Luis Obispo County, of whom 566 attended the public, and 109 attended private, schools. In 1880 the total number of school census children was 2,752, of whom 1,805 were in the public, and seventy-eight were in private, schools. In twenty years the number of public schools here increased from two to fifty-three, the corps of two was enlarged to one of fifty-nine teachers. In 1863 the appropriation from the county for the school fund was $613; the county tax rate for this purpose in 1882–'83 was fixed at twenty and one-half cents on each $100.

The school reports for June 30, 1890, show there are 4,733 census children in San Luis; the total enrollment to 3,845; the average number belonging, 2,515; average daily attendance, 2,307. The number of districts has increased to ninety-two, with 112 teachers, of whom the men receive an average salary of $75, and the women $63. The total amount received from all sources, for school purposes, for this year, was $93,822.10.

The districts are all well supplied with good school-houses, barring such as come under the law of one year's probation. The buildings are neat in style, and some care is had with regard to the condition of the grounds. The best edifices are those of San

Luis, San Miguel (where the main building cost $10,000), Paso de Robles, which town has lately expended $8,000 upon two buildings, and Nipomo, where the school-house cost $5,000.

LIGHT-HOUSE.

During the month of July, 1890, the light was shown at the new light-house on Point San Luis Obispo. This is a light of the fourth order, showing alternate red and white flashes, with thirty seconds interval, illuminating 240 degrees of the horizon; the focal plane is 133 feet above mean low water, and in clear weather the light can be seen at a distance of seventeen and one-half miles, from the deck of a vessel, fifteen feet above the sea.

The approximate geographical position of this light-house is as follows: Latitude north 35°, 9', 32"; longitude west 120°, 45', 42".

This edifice was constructed from an appropriation of $50,000, made during the Cleveland administration. Its estimated cost as per the Government architect should be $38,000, but the contractor built it for $17,000, at a severe loss to himself.

The light is shown from a black lantern surmounting a square frame tower attached to the southwest corner of a frame dwelling one and a half stories high, painted white, with brown roof, green blinds and lead colored trimmings. Some fifty yards eastward stands another similar dwelling; between the two, some fifty yards southward, is the steam fog-signal house, painted like the dwellings, and having two black smokestacks. The fog signal was put in place some weeks later than the light. Stephen D. Ballou is light-keeper.

RAILWAYS.

The Pacific Coast Railway, at that time known as the San Luis Obispo & Santa Maria Valley Railway, was opened from Avila to Castro, some seven miles distant, February 1, 1876. Thence it was extended from Castro to San Luis Obispo, operations being begun August 16, 1876. The next section opened was from Avila to Port Harford, December 1, 1876; and the next, from San Luis to Arroyo Grande, the extension being completed and operations begun October 16, 1881. Then followed the section from Arroyo Grande to Santa Maria, June 1, 1882; thence Santa Maria to Los Alamos, October 4, 1882; and from Los Alamos to Los Olivos, the present terminus, November 17, 1887. The total length of the road is now 76.1 miles in this county.

THE BREAKWATER QUESTION.

Since the days of the wreck of the iron bark Harlech Castle, off Piedras Blancas, in August, 1869, the need of a breakwater at Port Harford has been apparent.

In January, 1850, the citizens of San Luis Obispo held a meeting and passed resolutions to petition Congress for an appropriation for the construction of a breakwater at the harbor. In accordance with the spirit and instructions of these resolutions, Hon. H. Y. Stanley, member of the Assembly from San Luis Obispo in the legislative session of 1880 introduced the following resolution:

"*Resolved*, By the Assembly, the Senate concurring, that our senators and representatives in Congress be and are hereby respectfully and earnestly requested to procure an appropriation from the general Government, to be expended in the construction of a breakwater for the harbor of San Luis Obispo, and to make said harbor a port of entry. The Governor of this State is hereby requested to transmit a certified copy of the foregoing resolution to each of our senators and representatives in Congress."

The resolution was adopted, but while Congress voted many millions for improvements of rivers and harbors, the breakwater of San Luis Obispo was ignored. The port, including Port Harford, Avila, Pismo Wharf and all points in the bay, was made a port of delivery, where ships may discharge foreign cargo.

From this period forward the Luiseños have kept up a pretty persistent clamor for a breakwater at Port Harford. Myron Angel in particular kept the matter constantly before Congressman Markham, a member of the River and Harbor committee, as well as the representative from the Sixth District. Thus it came about that in the session of 1885–'86, Mr. Markham obtained an appropriation of $25,000 for the aforesaid purpose. This became ineffective because President Cleveland "pocketed" the bill. However, the matter had now been presented to Congress in such a fashion as to facilitate its revival at a future date.

In the following Congress, Representative Vandever was petitioned to secure an appropriation, and further, the citizens of San Luis raised a fund and sent to Washington a special emissary, Rev. R. L. Breck, whose efforts conduced largely toward the desired end. In this manner was definitely obtained an appropriation of $25,000. The contract was now let and the breakwater begun, $23,000 being expended on the contract, and $2,000 on superintendence.

During the Fifty-first Congress was made another appropriation, this time of $40,000, for continuing work on this breakwater, whose completion will certainly secure to San Luis Obispo one of the finest harbors on the coast of California. It is designed to connect this harbor with the Tulare Valley, this being the tide-water point nearest to that section.

FRATERNAL ORGANIZATIONS.

The pioneer secret society in San Luis was San Luis Obispo Lodge, No. 148, F. & A. M., which was organized May 16, 1861, by charter from the Grand Lodge of California. The members were Dr. Joseph M. Havens (who was county judge, also Past Master in Masonry), Michael Henderson (who was a '49er, and one of the oldest Masons in the State, his initiation dating from Tuolumne County, in 1850); Thompson D. Sackett, Abraham Blockman, Walter Murray, James McElrath, David F. Newsom, Joseph Riley, Joseph See, and James White. During the year, Governor Romualdo Pacheco and seven or eight others joined this lodge. The famine years, 1863–'64, caused such changes in the population that but few of the old members remained here, and this lodge surrendered its charter. Some of the members joined other lodges, but San Luis Obispo County was without a Masonic organization until early in 1869, when San Simeon Lodge, No. 196, was founded under dispensation, and in October under charter, at Cambria.

The need for the Cambria Lodge to visit the town of San Luis to bury a prominent Mason led to the organization of King David's Lodge, No. 209, June 21, 1870, under dispensation, and November 1, under charter. This lodge in 1875 constructed a fine Masonic hall in San Luis Obispo.

San Luis Obispo Chapter, No. 62, R. A. M., was constituted on April 28, 1883.

In March, 1870, the Odd Fellows of San Luis Obispo organized Chorro Lodge, No. 168, and the order has instituted a number of imposing anniversary celebrations.

On September 28, 1870, Hesperian Lodge, No. 181, I. O. O. F., was organized at Cambria, with seven charter members.

The first Rebekah Degree Lodge was Morse Rebekah Degree Lodge, No. 25, instituted at Cambria, June 10, 1877. Immediately following was Friendship Rebekah Degree Lodge, No. 36, organized at San Luis Obispo, July 12, 1877, with twenty-eight charter members.

Park Lodge, No. 40, Knights of Pythias, the first of the order in the county, was organized December 20, 1876, at San Luis Obispo, with seven charter members, by district officers from Santa Barbara.

On April 18, 1878, was instituted Section No. 147, Endowment Rank, K. of P.

In June, 1873, was founded at Cambria the Cambria Grange, No. 25, of California Patrons of Husbandry; in September, 1873, the grange at Arroyo Grande, and in 1874, five granges in this county reported to the State Grange.

San Luis Obispo Lodge, No. 122, I. O. G. T., was organized in February, 1878; Corral de Piedra Lodge, I. O. G. T., in February, 1883; Obispo Council, A. L. of H., on May 9, 1881; San Luis Obispo Division Independent Order of Missourians, on March 8, 1879; Society of Pioneers, on June 14, 1879; the Temperance and Life Insurance Society, on May 9, 1870; the San Luis Obispo Agricultural Society, on March 25, 1875; the Order of Chosen Friends, on March 30, 1883, and the Irish Land League, May 13, 1883.

THE PRESS.

San Luis Obispo had been an American town for more than twenty years, and a county-seat for nearly eighteen years before she had a newspaper. This because the ways of life there were not such as tended to create excitement or foster greed for news. The chief interest of the country was in cattle-raising, and the section took life and variety from the consequent movements of the herds and drovers.

On January 4, 1868, was issued the first number of the San Luis Obispo *Pioneer*, the first newspaper published in this county. Its publisher and proprietor was Rome G. Vickers, and it was by its own showing "an independent weekly journal, devoted mainly to the interests and advancement of San Luis Obispo County." It was a four-page paper, and it appears to have had good patronage for a time although it proved a financial failure at last.

The *Pioneer* inclined to the Democratic doctrines, and the Republican element combined to establish for themselves a party organ. Thus was issued on August 7, 1869, the first number of the San Luis Obispo *Tribune*, also a four-page paper, one or two of whose columns were printed in Spanish, as the language spoken by a majority of the people in the county. The paper was first under the proprietorship of H. S. Rembaugh & Co. In 1871 an interest in it was owned by Mr. James J. Ayers, one of the founders of the San Francisco *Morning Call*, now of the Los Angeles *Herald*. He remained but a few months with the *Tribune*.

The *Pioneer* lived but about two years, and it was succeeded on February 12, 1870, by the *Democratic Standard*, between which and the *Tribune* was waged a warfare of words more forcible than elegant.

On March 20, 1878, appeared the first number of *The South Coast*, a four page paper dedicated to the interests of the section. It was established by Mr. Charles L. Wood, a gentleman of considerable attainments. *The South Coast* was issued until August, 1879, when its plant was sold to the *Southern California Advocate*.

Undeterred by the non-success of their predecessors, Messrs. C. H. Phillips and George W. Mank issued, on August 2, 1879, the *Southern California Advocate*, a folio of seven columns to the page. This paper underwent various changes of proprietorship, continuing its issue until its fifty-second number, when its subscription list was sold to the *Tribune*, and the material turned over to its creditors.

The *Mirror* was established by Messrs. Doyle & Crenshaw in October, 1880, as an organ of the Democratic party. It was a large, well-managed folio sheet, issued weekly.

On January 15, 1883, was issued the first number of the *Republic*, which was the first daily published in the county. The weekly edition followed promptly. The founders were Messrs. E. F. O'Neil, A. Pennington and G. W. Jenkins.

The county-seat now has two good journals, the *Tribune*, daily and weekly, edited by Benjamin Brooks, being Republican in politics; and the *Republic*, an independent sheet, with Democratic proclivities, owned and edited by Messrs. Angel & Hughston. Both papers are well conducted and contain much information concerning the surrounding section.

Outside of the county-seat there are no daily newspapers; and the following is a list of the county weeklies: the *Advance*, of Templeton; the *Moon* and the *Leader*, Paso de Robles; the *Courier* and the *Messenger*, San Miguel; the *Herald*, of Arroyo Grande.

The Templeton *Times*. the Nipomo *News*, and the Cambria *Critic* were issued for a time, but they have now suspended publication.

VENTURA COUNTY.

EARLY SETTLEMENT.

Although quite a number of Americans, being traders, sailors, or adventurers, had settled in various parts of the territory now known as Santa Barbara County, none of them had located permanently at San Buenaventura up to the time of American military occupation, since Santa Barbara, the more important town, had superior attractions for them. When Stevenson's regiment arrived in Southern California, Isaac Callahan and W. A. Streeter were put in charge of the mission at San Buenaventura. A few years later Russel Heath, in connection with Don José Arnaz and one Morris, established the first store within the present county limits. In 1850 came C. C. Rynerson and wife from the Mississippi Valley, camping at first at the mouth of the river San Buenaventura; they afterward moved northward. The first American farmer was A. Colombo, and Mr. Ware was the first blacksmith. Even as late as 1857 there were in the whole district but two houses of entertainment. One of these was a tent on the Sespe Rancho, and the other a little hostelry established in rooms in the east wing of the ex-mission buildings. It is worth while to note here a tribute to the climate of Ventura County, paid by John Carr and wife, who kept this little inn or tavern. They had lived together for twelve years in childlessness, but within two years of their arrival in San Buenaventura they had presented their country with no less than five children, products, so they declared, of the matchless climate!

The first lumber-yard was kept by Thomas Dennis, but the date of his arrival is not given. Very early in the '50's T. Wallace More obtained a title to an immense tract of the richest land in the region; he claimed over *thirty miles* along the Santa Clara and in other districts, possessions about as enormous, over which grazed 10,000 head of cattle. These lands were valued at ten to fifty cents the acre. During this period the whole Colonia Rancho was sold for $5,000, and this price the purchaser finally concluded was exorbitant. About 1854 W. D. Hobson removed to the Sespe, where he built a house and there lived in 1859. In 1858, the Americans resident in San Buenaventura were: A. M. Cameron, Griffin Robbins, W. T. Nash, W. Williams, James Beebe, —— Park, W. D. Hobson, —— McLaughlin and one other, name unknown. As late as 1860 there were but nine American voters in the precinct. Chaffee & Robbins, and afterward Chaffee & Gilbert, kept the only store in the town for many years. In 1860 the Fourth of July was celebrated here with a regular program of exercises, and much enthusiasm was displayed. About this time the American population was agmented by the arrival of John Hill, V. A. Simpson, Albert Martin, G. S. Briggs, G. S. Gilbert, W. S. Chaffee, W. A. Norway, H. P. Flint, the Barnetts and Messrs. Burbank, Hankerson, Crane and Harrington.

In 1861 a postoffice was established at San Buenaventura, and V. A. Simpson became postmaster. The mail matter received, apparently, was not extensive, for it is related that on its arrival the postmaster was in the habit of depositing it in his hat, and then walking around among the citizens to deliver the letters. "This," says a previous historian, "may be regarded as the first introduction of the system of letter-carriers in California." This year the first brick house in town was built by W. D. Hobson, who moved hither from the Sespe.

During the winter of 1861-'62, there was an excessive amount of wet weather; rain fell for sixty consecutive days; all the land to a great depth was saturated and reeking; live stock was reduced almost to starvation, the animals dying in great numbers. Landslides were very frequent, half of the soil in certain localities being moved to a greater or less distance. The soil would often be displaced in patches of an acre or more. In the town various houses were submerged, or carried away bodily. The only life lost was that of Mr. Hewitt, a resident of Santa Barbara, who was drowned while on a prospecting tour up the Piru Creek. Travel was rendered almost impossible for twenty days. In 1862 Messrs. Waterman, Vassault & Co., owning the lands of the ex-mission, laid out a town there. This enterprise had been projected as early as 1848, when Don José Arnaz laid out here a town site, and advertised the advantages of the spot in Eastern journals, offering lots to those who would make improvements upon them. This offer had not elicited response, and the subject had not been revived until the project above mentioned. The survey made in this instance was rejected by the board of trustees after the town was incorporated, and another was substituted. The first attempt to incorporate was in 1863, when a number of citizens met and drew up a petition addressed to the Legislature, asking for incorporation. Ramon J. Hill, at that time a member from Santa Barbara County, opposed the proposition, and the subject was dropped for the time.

The following is given as an accurate list of the foreign (*i. e.*, not Spanish or Mexican) citizens resident in San Buenaventura in 1862: Baptiste Ysoardy, who came in 1858; Agustin Solari, in 1857; Victor Ususaustegui, in 1852; Ysidro Obiols, in 1853; Antonio Sciappapietra in 1862; John Thompson, in 1862; Oscar Wells, George V. Whitman, Albert and Frank Martin, in 1859; Myron Warner, in 1863; William Pratt, 1866; William Whitney, 1864; Thomas R. Bard, in 1865; Henry Cohn, in 1866; Joseph Wolfson, 1867; —— Clements, 1868; Thomas Williams, 1866; A. T. Herring, 1863; Henry Spears, 1865; Walter S. Chaffee, Volney A. Simpson, John T. Stow, Griffin Robbins, William S. Riley, William T. Nash, Jefferson Crane, John Hill, Henry Clifton, Marshall Routh, George S. Gilbert, James Beebe, William H. Leighton, Samuel Barnett, Sr., Samuel Barnett, Jr., William Barnett, W. D. Hobson, Alex. Cameron, Melvin Beardsley, George Dodge, George S. Briggs, Albert de Chateauneuf and Henry Dubbers.

GOVERNMENT AND BUSINESS.

In 1864 the question of incorporation was renewed and accomplished, but it was not until thirteen years later that the patents to the town site were received from the Government. This was the year of the disastrous "dry season;" the rains of the preceding season had not wet the ground deeper than three inches, and the feed was therefore a failure. From this cause two-thirds of all the stock in Ventura famished.

The beginning of growth and development in Ventura is agreed to date back to the subdivision into small tracts of the large ranchos, thus inducing immigration and settlement by small farmers and fruit-raisers. In 1866, the Briggs tract was cut up and put on the market, and two years later began a general influx of Americans, from which directly resulted an epoch of prosperity which became assured with the breaking up and selling to actual settlers of the great ranchos of Santa Paula y Saticoy and Colonia or Santa Clara.

The first cultivation of grain in Ventura County was by Christian Borchard and his son, J. A. Borchard, on the Colonia Rancho in 1867. Thirty acres each of wheat and barley were sown. The rust destroyed the wheat crop, but the barley yielded eighteen centals or hundreds per acre.

The first Protestant church (Congregational) was organized in San Buenaventura in 1867.

Again in 1867 was San Buenaventura visited by devastating waters. On Christmas Day of that year the Ventura River overflowed, and the water rose to a depth of three feet in Main Street. The lower part of the town was submerged, and the safety of the inhabitants was endangered. The land from the Santa Clara House to the river was flooded, and forty-seven women, gathered from the imperiled houses, were assembled in one small adobe shanty. Some of these had been brought from their flooded homes on horseback, and others had been carried on the shoulders of men. This episode gave rise to various feats of real gallantry, courage, and daring. The immediate cause of the freshet was supposed to be the melting of heavy deposits of snows about the river's source, through the agency of warm rains falling upon them.

In 1868 came hither Dr. Cephas L. Bard, the first American physician in San Buenaventura.

In September, 1870, San Buenaventura and Santa Barbara were placed in telegraphic communication.

Anticipating the needs and opportunities to result from the creation of the new county, in immediate prospective, John H. Bradley in April, 1871, started the Ventura *Signal* at the proposed new county-seat. Mr. Bradley was a good and practical business man, and an editor of some experience; and so, avoiding the political issues not properly within the province of a country newspaper, he devoted his attention to the production and publication of matter relative to the recommendations and resources of the section; such as would contribute to the advancement and advertisement of the region and its merits.

Contemporaneously with the formation of the county, work was begun to provide canals to supply water for domestic and irrigating purposes. The old Mission water-works, which brought a supply from six miles up the Ventura River, was overhauled and repaired, portions of the aqueduct having been destroyed by the excessive rains of 1861-'62.

Owing to the difficulties attending the disembarkation of freight and passengers by means of lighters to transport them between the vessels and the shore; it became evident that a wharf was an absolute necessity to the public. Accordingly, in January, 1871, a franchise was procured, and work was begun upon the structure, by Joseph Wolfson. The beginning of operations was signalized by formal ceremonies. In August of this year the right to construct a wharf at Hueneme was granted to Thos. R. Bard, C. L. Bard and R. G. Surdam.

By February, 1872, the Ventura wharf was so far completed as to obviate further necessity for lightening steamers now discharging directly upon it. Rates of toll were instituted, and an instrument of great public utility was firmly established.

In May, 1871, was formed the Santa Clara Irrigating Company, designed to water the fertile lands of the Colonia Rancho from the Santa Clara River. The canal therefor was twelve miles long, twelve feet wide, and two feet deep, with branches of smaller dimensions.

In 1871 also surveys were made for "The Farmers' Canal and Water Ditch," taking water from the Santa Paula Creek, and conveying it some eight and a half miles down the valley.

In December, 1871, Ysabel Yorba sold to Dickenson & Funk the Guadalasca Rancho, comprising 22,000 acres, for $28,500.

In 1872 many property owners refused to pay taxes, owing to the abeyance of financial settlement between Ventura and Santa Barbara counties.

In July, 1872, the first gold was taken to Santa Barbara from the Sespe mines.

On September 16, 1872, the corner-stone of the high school building at San Buenaventura was laid. This building was the first public building erected in the county. The total number of school children in the county at that time was 800.

SEGREGATION OR DIVISION FROM SANTA BARBARA COUNTY.

The inception of the plan for setting off Ventura from Santa Barbara County dates as far back as 1868. In that year began a new era of growth, increase in population, and prosperity in business. This was mainly owing to the subdivision into small tracks of several important ranchos in the district. The sale of these tracts to small farmers and fruit-growers brought immigration, the establishment of industries, production, and the circulation of money. As the country became populous, the citizens desired local, independent government, and so began to agitate the project of creating a new county. This question was made an issue of the election of 1869, and Mr. A. G. Escandon was elected to the Assembly for the purpose of furthering the plan, but the measure miscarried in the Legislature, thanks to the opposition offered by the northern part of the county. The Venturans were not vanquished by this defeat, but continued to carry on a vigorous fight for division. The Ventura *Signal*, established largely with a view to that end, was a powerful weapon in this struggle, devoting itself to demonstrating the advantages of such division. It is not uninteresting to note some of the statistics presented in this discussion. Santa Barbara County then had a total area of 5,450 square miles, or 3,491,000 acres, of which 1,570,419 acres were covered by Spanish grants, 1,920,581 acres being public lands, the most of which were of an inferior character. The proposed new county comprised 20,600 acres of improved land and 2,000 acres of wooded land, probably of individual ownership, and 390,000 acres of unimproved land, of private holding. It was estimated that the real estate was worth $3,018,200; personal property, $911,000; the total valuation for the projected new county being $3,929,200. There were 2,800 head of horses and mules, 6,000 horned cattle, and 7,400 sheep,—worth in the aggregate, $442,000; the wool clip was 350,000 pounds; there were produced 35,000 pounds of butter and 20,000 pounds of cheese annually, the revenue from farm products being $307,000. The new county would contain, as per the *Signal* of February 17, 1872, an area of 2,000 square miles, and a population of 3,500, with an assessment roll of $1,200,000, leaving Santa Barbara with 3,000 square miles, 7,000 inhabitants, and an assessment roll of $2,000,000.

By the opening of the session of the Legislature of 1871-'72, there had been engendered so strong a public sentiment as to result in organized action, and W. D. Hobson, a prominent citizen, was chosen and sent to Sacramento to work for the desired end. So successful were the measures now taken that the bill, when presented to the Assembly, passed with but one dissentient vote; and in the Senate it was approved also, March 22, 1872, and it was ordained to be in force on and after January 1, 1873. The boundaries prescribed for the new county were as follows: Commencing on the coast of the Pacific Ocean, at the mouth of the Rincon Creek, thence following up the center of said creek to its source; thence due north to the boundary line of Santa Barbara County; thence in an easterly direction along the boundary line of Santa Barbara County to the northeast corner of the same; thence southerly along the line between the said Santa Barbara County to the Pacific Ocean and three miles therein; thence in a northwesterly direction to a point due south of and three miles distant from the center of the mouth of Rincon Creek; thence north to the point of beginning and including the islands Anacapa and San Nicolas.

Contemporaneously with the passage of the bill for county division, great activity sprang up in Ventura. During the summer, the immigration was so extensive that the accommodations were insufficient to hold the new arrivals. Municipal improvements were instituted, new buildings were erected, including a hotel and a $10,000 school-house, water companies were established to supply the needs for irrigation and domestic purposes, and the county-government was organized, with the usual complement of officers, the county to contain three townships, three supervisorial districts, and eight election precincts. The townships were: Ventura, Saticoy, Hueneme; the supervisorial districts coincided with the respective townships; the election precincts were: San Buenaventura, La Cañada, Mountain View, Sespe, Saticoy, Pleasant Valley, San Pedro, and Hueneme.

The Legislature appointed a board of commissioners, consisting of S. Bristol, President; Thomas R. Bard, Secretary; W. D. F. Richards, A. G. Escandon, and C. W. Thacker, to put into action the government of Ventura County. Meeting on January 15, 1873, this board issued a proclamation calling for an election to be held on the 25th day of February following, to elect district attorney, county clerk, school superintendent, sheriff, assessor, county treasurer, county surveyor, coroner, and supervisors.

The county was divided into three townships, Ventura, Saticoy, and Hueneme, the islands of San Nicolas and Anacapa being attached to and forming a part of Hueneme Township. The voting places were established for the various election precincts, numbering eight.

As soon as the county government was established, certain changes were made in the road districts.

All the territory in the first supervisorial district was made into the San Buenaventura road district; the third supervisorial district was designated as constituting the Saticoy road district, and Mountain View and Sespe road districts were united into one under the name of Sespe road district.

The first election was held on February 25, 1873. The Republicans had desired a fusion of parties and nominations irrespective of politics; but, the Democrats opposing this proposition, the usual course was followed, the result being a Democratic victory. The total vote polled was 630. The officers elected were as follows: District judge, Pablo de la Guerra; county judge, Milton Wason; district attorney, J. Marion Brooks; county clerk, Frank Molleda (dying very shortly, S. M. W. Easley was appointed); sheriff, Frank Peterson; treasurer, E. A. Edwards; assessor, J. Z. Barnett; superintendent of schools, F. S. S. Buckman; surveyor, C. J. De Merritte; coroner, Dr. Cephas L. Bard; county physician, Dr. S. P. Guiberson; supervisors, James Daley, J. A. Conaway, C. W. Thacker; justices of the peace, J. W. Guiberson, W. D. Hobson, F. A. Sprague, J. G. Ricker, John Saviers, R. J. Colyear.

On April 13, 1873, a final settlement with Santa Barbara was effected under the terms of the act of Legislature of March 22, 1872. The commissioners from Ventura were Thomas R. Bard and Charles Lindley, and from Santa Barbara, Ulpiano Yndart and C. E. Huse. Their report was as follows:

Assets to March 20, 1873	$10,693.87
Old court-house and lot	3,000.00
Present unfinished court-house with proceeds of bonds	50,000.00
Interest paid and unpaid on same	1,652.76
Cost of advertising	400.00
Delinquent taxes collected to date	3,810.78
Funds for interest on hand	2,698.92
Total assets	$72,256.33
Bonds of 1856 and subsequent indebtedness	$19,796.42
Court-house and jail bonds	50,000.00
Interest due on same	777.76
Total indebtedness	$70,574.18
Excess of assets	1,682.15

of which the proportion belonging to Ventura County was fixed at $581.52.

ORGANIZATION AND ANNALS.

The supervisors in May, 1873, ordered the issue of $20,000 in interest-bearing bonds, to meet current expenses, and advertised for bids for the same; they also authorized the transcription of such portion of the records of Santa Barbara as related to Ventura County, paying F. A. Thompson $4,000 for that service. The county-seat was appointed by the creating act to be at San Buenaventura, and the question of county buildings at once assumed importance, as the rental paid by the county for the use of private buildings amounted to $1,044 per annum, besides $3 per diem paid for guarding the prisoners, in the absence of a jail building. Hence the supervisors appropriated $6,000 of the funds resulting from the sale of the bonds, to the erection of a court-house, on condition that private parties should donate $4,000 and also a suitable site for the purpose.

Bishop Amat, head of the Roman Catholic diocese of Southern California, now renewed his previous offer of three blocks of the old mission garden, on condition of the erection within two years of a $10,000 building. These terms were accepted, the $4,000 subscribed by the citizens, and the court-house was promptly built.

In the autumn of 1873 took place the regular State and county election, resulting in the seating of the entire Republican ticket except the school superintendent.

By the following enumeration of holdings may be seen what radical changes by this time had come about in land ownership since 1868, when the whole territory of the present county had been owned by a handful of men in great ranchos, largely uncultivated. In 1873 there were: ninety-five ranchos of 100 to 200 acres; nine ranchos of 200 to 400 acres; seven of 500 acres; two of 600 acres; six of 800 acres; two of 900 acres; seven of 1,000 acres; one of 1,100 acres; three of 2,000 acres; one of 2,500 acres; one of 4,000 acres; two of 4,500 acres; two of 6,500, and one each of 8,000, 9,000, 10,500, 12,500, 13,500, 17,090, 23,000, 24,000, 42,000 and 131,083 acres. Total number of acres assessed, 338,761; value assessed $1,554,951.

A very sensational tragedy had place in the record of this year. At the Colonia Rancho, George Hargan, after disputing George Martin's land boundaries, shot and instantly killed Martin, and he was immediately captured and lynched by the neighbors of the murdered man.

In April, 1873, extensive bodies of gypsum were found on the Ojai Rancho.

On June 23, 1873, the Ventura Reading Club was organized.

In 1873 Mr. Bradley, on account of ill-health, retired from the *Signal*, Messrs. W. E. Shepherd and John T. Sheridan succeeding him.

In January, 1874, was published the first report of the county treasurer, which showed that the preceding year's receipts were $20,522, and the disbursements $5,018, leaving a balance of $15,504.

In 1874 were made extensive additions and improvements to the wharf constructed at San Buenaventura in 1871.

On November 23, 1874, the Ventura Library Association was incorporated.

During 1874 there was a notable advance in population and in wealth throughout Ventura County, and many new and important institutions were organized. The Fourth of July was here celebrated with a vim and an originality perhaps not equaled elsewhere in the State. In August, the question of local option in regard to the traffic in liquor came up in Ventura, but on putting it to a vote of the people, the temperance faction was put badly in the minority. On September 19, the bank of Ventura was founded; on September 20, the trotting park was opened to racing. At the election this year, some attention was paid to the nativity of the voters, and the population was found to be very cosmopolitan, numbering members from almost every country. The tax list showed thirty-five citizens owning from $10,000 to $187,000 each worth of property. A notable feature of this year's record was the remarkable lowering of rates and fares. The jealous competition between the South Pacific Coast Steamship Company and the California Steam Navigation Company, brought the fare from Ventura down to $3 to San Francisco, and $4 to San Diego, while merchandise was transported for $1.50 per ton. The shipments of produce from San Buenaventura for the six months ending May 1, 1874, were: wheat, 5,600 sacks; barley, 23,000 sacks; corn, 6,000 sacks; beans, 2,100 sacks; wool, 1,000 sacks; hogs, 300; sheep, 700; petroleum, 1,876 barrels.

The winter of 1874-'75 was an exceptionally wet one. In one week of January, 1875, $9\frac{32}{100}$ inches fell at San Buenaventura, while the fall in the Ojai Valley was tremendous, it being estimated that ten inches of water fell within twenty-four hours, whereas, even in those sections where the fall sometimes amounts to sixty inches in the season, a fall of three inches in twenty-four hours is considered excessive. Peculiarly enough, too, the excessive fall here was not general throughout the State that season. The phenomenal quantity here was attributable to cloudbursts. The rivers, San Buenaventura and Clara, were for days at a time impassable.

The year 1875 witnessed the establishment

of various institutions of the highest importance to the comfort and advancement of the section. The "Monumentals," a fire company, was organized, comprising in its officers and members many of the most respected citizens of San Buenaventura. The Ventura Gas Company was also instituted, the city appreciating the need of efficient street illumination; and an impulse was given to manufacturing industry, in the opening of a large steam planing-mill.

The *Free Press* was first issued November 30 of this year, running for a very few months as a daily, and continuing as a weekly.

The diversity in the California field of politics at this time bore its natural fruits here as elsewhere. There were three State tickets before the people, and Ventura entered into the canvass with great energy and enthusiasm; the Republicans, fearing injury to their cause by the disaffection of the temperance people, prepared a ticket to unite these two factions. Nevertheless, the Democrats elected most of their candidates. This election took also the sense of Ventura for the new Constitutional Convention, at this time offered for suffrage.

It was on April 13 of this year that a final settlement of finances was effected between this and the mother county of Santa Barbara, under the terms of the act of March 22, 1872. The commissioners from Ventura, Thomas R. Bard and Charles Lindley, met with C. E. Huse and Ulpiano Yndart, of Santa Barbara, and, making the estimates and balancing accounts, they found Ventura entitled to $581.52.

Early in 1876 came a disaster for Ventura, in the loss of the Kalorama, which was an iron schooner-rigged steamer of 491 tons' burden, belonging to the Coast Steamship Company; she had accommodations for sixty-three cabin, fourteen steerage and thirty-nine deck passengers. Built in England, and purchased for the coast trade, she had been since the beginning of 1873 plying between San Francisco and San Diego, and way ports, alternating with the Constantine. On Friday, February 25, 1876, she lay at Wolfson's wharf, when, being chafed by the roll of the surf, she was ordered to move out to the floating buoy. On the way thither, the screw fouled with the mooring line, and left the vessel at the mercy of the wind, which drove her ashore at once. No lives were lost, but as she lay on the beach the heavy machinery broke loose in her hull and beat her to pieces; the loss was $77,500.

Ventura, always fond of civic displays, celebrated the Fourth of July in this the Centennial year, with actual pomp. Besides the program of parade, orations, music, etc., a dinner was prepared on the grounds for no less than 3,000 individuals. At Sespe also, there was a spirited celebration.

There had now been added two more precincts (Santa Paula and Conejo) to the original eight in the county, and they polled at the presidential election in this year an aggregate of 1,097 votes. The Hayes electors received 608 votes, the Tilden electors 590; Pacheco, Republican nominee for Congress received 694, and Wigginton, Democratic candidate, 532. There were now 1,400 names on the Great Register, and an estimated population of 7,000, being just double that in the county at the date of organization. There were now twenty-seven citizens paying taxes on $10,000; twelve paying on more than $15,000; seventeen on $20,000 to $50,000, and one each paying respectively $75,000, $100,000, $150,000, and $200,000.

The year 1877 was made fairly calamitous by a drouth of excessive severity. Great numbers of sheep and cattle perished from the lack of feed caused by the dry weather, and multitudes were saved only by transportation to distant pastures where feed was plentiful. T. Wallace More, of Ventura, sent 10,000, and Metcalf & Co., 6,000 head of sheep through the Soledad Pass to Elizabeth Lake, in Los Angelos County, where good grazing was found and great herds of cattle were sent by various owners to Arizona.

On March 29, 1877, the brig Crimea, of 223 tons, loaded with lumber, while made fast to the wharf, parted her lines and was beached during a heavy westerly gale and sea; loss $9,200. It was reported also that a portion of the wharf was washed away.

On the evening of October 22, Charles Bartlett and Walter Perkins walked down the wharf to watch the heavy rollers, caused by a southeaster. Finally, alarmed by the tremendous height of three, the largest they had ever seen, the gentlemen decided to beat a hasty retreat, and they ran up the wharf at full speed. When they had covered some two-thirds of the distance to shore, the first of the rollers struck and breached the wharf, and at the progress of the wave the piles bent down before it like grass-stalks. The two fleeing men barely saved themselves from being overtaken by the waves, and the wharf reeled and rolled beneath their feet as they fairly flew along it.

On December 1, the brig Lucy Ann, of 199.61 tons, here parted her moorings in a northwesterly gale and a heavy sea, and was wrecked, with a loss of one life and $6,500.

These repeated disasters caused the people of Ventura to yearn for a Government appropriation for a breakwater, and they accordingly entered a petition therefor. In consequence of their representations, Lieutenant Seaforth, of the United States Engineers, examined the port or roadstead, and made an exhaustive report, adversely, however, to the construction of the breakwater.

Ventura County made substantial progress this year; business was in a prosperous condition, and manufacturing interests were beginning to awaken. A substantial brewery had been erected, with a capacity of 1,500 gallons per week. The Casitas Pass road was inaugurated this year, under an $8,990 contract, the expenses being met by the issue of bonds for $8,000, which were sold for $8,580 to Sutro & Co., of San Francisco, thus indexing the solvent condition of the county; the assessed value of all taxable property here had now risen to $3,270,161.

The election this year distributed the offices pretty evenly between Democrats and Republicans. One office was yielded to the Democrats with considerable bitterness of spirit by the Ventura constituency, who, with the Republicans of Santa Barbara and San Luis Obispo, had nominated T. R. Bard, the reputed wealthiest man in the county, as the Republican candidate for the State Senate, as against Murphy, a wealthy land-owner of San Luis Obispo. Mr. Bard was nominated without a dissenting voice, and received a handsome majority in his own section, but the Democratic vote in the other two counties elected his opponent.

The chief item recorded for 1878 is the arrival from San Francisco, in January, of the apparatus of a hook and ladder company, following the "Monumentals," long the only fire company in Ventura.

The record of public events for 1879 is mostly political. This was the year of the Workingmen's agitation, so that three tickets, partial or entire, were in the field. White and Perkins, two of the three gubernatorial candidates, addressed the people of Ventura, as did also Denis Kearney, the agitator-in-chief of the Workingmen; he, however, was not received here with enthusiasm. The result of the election was a pretty fair distribution of the offices among the three parties.

The progress of matters agricultural in this section may be judged from the following figures: With a total population of about 7,000, the assessed valuation of property was about $3,394,000, with a cultivated area of 75,000 acres. The crops comprised: barley, 36,000 acres; corn, 19,000; wheat, 13,000; beans, 1,800; flax, 1,250; alfalfa, 900; oats, 550; potatoes, 300; canary seed, 285; and 570 of vegetables, peanuts, tobacco, etc. In orchards and vineyards there were 37,000 acres, of which 1,500 acres were planted to English walnuts, 300 to oranges, 210 to grapes, 75 to lemons, and about 1,100 to other fruits.

Early in 1880, the people of Ventura were thrown into violent excitement by an affair whose mystery continued unraveled. Miss Jennie McLean, an accomplished young lady, a favorite in the community, while alone and engaged about household matters, was attacked and struck down by a terrible blow on the head, dealt by some unknown party, who beat her into insensibility. Her jewelry was not taken, and it was never known whether her assailant was man or woman, nor whether the object was plunder, jealousy or revenge, although Miss McLean was not known to have an enemy in the world. The deed had the seeming of a frenzy of insanity, rather than the act of an ordinary criminal, and it is not impossible that it was such, and that a connection might have been traced between this and an occurrence some three weeks later. On June 15, a young man named Mills, nephew of Governor A. A. Low, boarded the stage at Ventura, and after traveling a few miles it was noticed that he held a new hatchet, with which he threatened to kill the driver unless he kept out of the way of parties who, Mills fancied, were in pursuit of himself, in order to take his life. The driver was compelled to keep his horses lashed to a run for miles, to avoid having his head split open. The unsatisfactory passenger, on reaching Newhall's Rancho, sprang to the ground with his hatchet, and with deer-like speed ran to the hills. Some days later he was found, being reduced to a famishing condition.

On the 26th of December, the ill-fated wharf met with another misfortune, the waves carrying away 200 feet of its outer end, together with some freight piled thereon.

The traffic from this port had now attained such proportions that the facilities for transportation were entirely inadequate.

In round numbers, San Buenaventura exported in 1880, 4,000,000 pounds of corn, 800,000 of barley, 1,400,000 of wheat, 1,100,000 of beans, and 60,000 of potatoes. From Hueneme were shipped during this period about 2,100,000 pounds of corn, 240,000 of barley, 2,200,000 of wheat, and 64,000 pounds of wool. From the three counties of San Luis Obispo, Santa Barbara, and Ventura, were shipped 1,800,000 pounds of wool during this year.

The events of 1881 were neither exciting nor of a nature to make a permanent impress upon the community. There were two murder cases, of a commonplace character, upon the docket; there was some animation in local musical circles, and there was a temperance agitation, which led to the establishment of four lodges of Good Templars, with an aggregate membership of over 300. Also, eighty feet of extension were added to the wharf, Beyond these, and the Garfield funeral exercises, which were of a character truly impressive, there were chronicled no points of especial interest. Assessed valuations, $3,347,787.

Ventura's bean crop for 1880–'81 amounted to 35,000 bushels.

The season of 1882 appeared less prosperous than many preceding years, to judge by the assessment roll, which showed a diminution from that of the preceding year, being at present $3,171,127. This loss was due mainly to the decrease in sheep, of which large numbers died in the winter and early spring.

The State election, held November 7, 1882, gave the Democratic candidates slight majorities, ranging from six to forty-five votes. There were cast here thirty-five votes for the Prohibition candidate for Governor.

The assessment roll for this year showed a depreciation, enumerating property worth $3,171,127 only, while the previous year had shown $3,347,787. This was mainly due to the loss in sheep, of which large numbers died in the early spring. This county produced 30,000 bushels of beans in the season of 1881–'82.

The delinquent tax list of Ventura for 1883 was so short, being only one and a half columns, that the *Signal* printed it gratis as a matter of news, and the *Free Press* officially at a nominal price.

Ventura County was awarded the first premium for county exhibits at the Mechanics' Institute Fair of 1885 in San Francisco.

The next succeeding feature of general interest, was the construction, in the fall of 1886, of the Coast Line branch of the Southern Pacific Railroad, whose advent brought new life and development to the section.

The following figures, taken from the official returns for 1887 of the county clerk, county auditor, and county assessor, will serve as a basis of comparison of the developments of the past few years:

1885, Total value assessed property,	$4,574,208
1886, " " " "	4,693,698
1886, " county indebtedness,	22,000
Number acres assessed	449,937

Real estate, other than town property,	$4,050,467
Real estate improvements thereon,	322,865
Real estate, city and town property,	618,107
Improvements on same,	245,939
Total value real estate,	4,668,574
Total value real estate improvements,	568,804
Total value personal property,	1,178,694
Total assessed valuations,	$6,415,572
Total county indebtedness, bonds outstanding,	$22,000.00
Cash in county treasury, November 5, 1887,	14,292.14
Amount thereof applicable to indebtedness,	6,684.79
Bonds paid January 1, 1888,	8,000.00
Total county indebtedness, July 1, 1888,	14,000.00

The rate of taxation for 1887 was $2 on the $100.

For 1887 there were shipped from the ports of San Buenaventura and Hueneme the following, all of which were produced in Ventura County:

Beans,	sacks	114,989
Corn,	"	58,486
Wheat,	"	93,558
Barley,	"	424,485
Potatoes,	"	4,686
Flax Seed,	"	7,150
Eng. Walnuts,	"	1,171
Mustard,	"	1,004
Bird Seed,	"	1,638
Eggs,	cases	1,040
Honey,	"	9,630
Oil,	bbls.	31,170
Oil,	tanks	2,362
Wool,	bales	1,755
Lemons,	boxes	2,007
Hogs,	No.	11,978
Sheep,	"	7,445
Hides,	"	916

The estimated population being 7,500, this would allow to each of 1,500 families of five persons in Ventura County an income of $1,328.

For 1888–'89 the San Buenaventura Wharf Company's statement showed export shipments of 174,158 packages, and import shipments of 113,227 packages of merchandise and 5,715,140 feet of lumber.

Over the Hueneme wharf were exported during this period 534,757 packages, of which 436,539 were sacks of beans, 18,143 sacks of wheat, 30,302 sacks of corn, and 32,864 barrels of oil, thus showing the chief staples for the year.

In addition to the above shipments out of the county over the Southern Pacific were as follows, in pounds: beans, 1,766,700; grain 1,110,900; potatoes, 147,500; cattle, 160,000; sheep, 100,000; hogs, 2,360,000; flour and mill stuff, 384,000; bees and honey, 214,300; dried fruit, 218,400; green fruit, 1,090,000; nuts, 40,800; wool, 402,300; hay, 1,871,000; brick and tile, 357,200; stone, 3,176,340; oil, 41,268,000; asphaltum, 261,500; miscellaneous, 2,861,000.

Late in 1889 the statistics gathered from the Southern Mill and Warehouse Company showed shipments as follows: Barley, 2,676,123 pounds; Lima beans, 2,109,090; common beans, 756,243; corn, 308,750; walnuts, 10,000; honey, 74,463; apricots, 145,726; miscellaneous, 300,000. Total shipments, actual weight, 6,380,395 pounds.

At the same time there was in the warehouse: of barley 2,089,090 pounds; wheat, 453,010; honey, 54,853; common beans, 136,839; making a grand total of 9,114,187 pounds of farm products, from which, making a low estimate, the farmers of this vicinity must have derived an aggregate revenue of $200,000.

The statement of the San Buenaventura Wharf Company for the year ending May, 1890, shows transactions over that structure as follows: 44,748 bags corn, 54,692 bags beans, 25,370 of barley, 1,393 of potatoes, 2,737 of wheat, 1,199 of dried fruit, 2,323 of walnuts, 86 of popcorn, 83 of almonds, 221 of peanuts, 35 of mustard seed, 9 of garlic, 1,220 packages of merchandise, 234 of household goods, 3,167 cases honey, 90 cases lubricator, 215 of coal oil, 262 of eggs, 1,207 empty beer kegs, 1,362 boxes oranges, 1,047 boxes lemons, 294 boxes raisins, 4 of butter, 393 green apricots, 607 of apples, 18 of persimmons, 15 of peaches, 38 of nectarines, 104 of pears, 74 of limes, 20 of prunes, 1,333 barrels asphaltum, 1,091 of distillate, 6,045 of crude oil, 322 barrels of empty bottles, 209 of tallow, 624 tons asphaltum, 89 tons of old iron, 527 bales wool, 1,350 bales hides, 153 bales pelts, 27 bales seaweed, 31 coops live fowls, 1 steam engine, 4 horses.

The imports were 93,563 packages merchandise, and 261,059 feet of lumber.

The value of the wharf warehouses and fixtures is placed at $79,000 at this time.

Some idea of the relative charges on freight may be formed from the statement that the income of this wharf from all sources was $11,754.43 during the year.

The Hueneme Wharf Company for 1889-'90 shows exports as follows:—279,613 sacks barley, 17,018 of wheat, 34,638 of corn, 396 cases honey, 13,462 sacks beans, 1,447 bales wool, 295 sacks mustard seed, 223 of walnuts, 4,824 of potatoes, 519 cases eggs, 1,202 hogs, 2,117 sheep, 249 boxes butter, 46 coops fowls, 489 bundles hides, 122 bundles pelts, 86 barrels tallow, 29 sacks apricots, 30 of onions, 2 of beeswax, 3 of peas; miscellaneous packages, 963.

Ventura County at present, October, 1890, contains twenty-one election precincts, as follows:—San Buenaventura precincts, Nos. 1, 2 and 3; La Cañada, Rincon, Santa Ana, Ojai, Cuyama, Piru, Camulos, Sespe, Santa Paula, Nos. 1 and 2, Saticoy, Mound, Pleasant Valley, San Pedro, Simí, Conejo, Springville and Hueneme.

The postoffices in Ventura County are Ventura, Hueneme, Santa Paula, Saticoy, Nordhoff, Bardsdale, Camulos, Fillmore, Matilija, Montalvo, Newbury Park, New Jerusalem,

Piru City, Punta Gorda, Simí, Springville, and Timberville. The first five are money order offices, and Ventura has international exchange.

There are four banks in Ventura County, aggregating paid up capital amounting to nearly $400,000.

The present officers of Ventura County are are as follows:—

E. H. Heacock	State Senator
G. W. Wear (with Kern County)	Assemblyman
B. T. Williams	Supreme Judge
W. H. Reilly	Sheriff
L. F. Eastin	County Clerk
W. H. Jewett	Auditor and Recorder
Orestes Orr	District Attorney
Paul Charlebois	Treasurer
James Donlon	Assessor
C. L. Bard	County Physician
F. M. Patton	Coroner
C. T. Meredith	Supt. Public Schools
J. T. Stow	County Surveyor
A. W. Browne, B. W. Dudley, F. A. Foster, C. N. Baker, E. H. Owens	County Supervisors.

OFFICERS OF THE U. S. CIRCUIT AND DISTRICT COURTS
SOUTHERN DISTRICT OF CALIFORNIA.

Stephen J. Field	Circuit Judge
Lorenzo Sawyer	Circuit Judge
Erskine M. Ross	District Judge
George Denie	U. S. Attorney
David R. Risley	U. S. Marshal
William M. VanDyke	Clerk of Circuit Court
E. H. Owen	Clerk of District Court
Charles L Batcheller	Standing Master and Examiner in Chan.

COMMISSIONERS.

William M. VanDyke	Los Angeles
E. H. Owen	Los Angeles
Charles Fernald	Santa Barbara
L. C. McKeeby	Ventura
Charles G. Hubbard	San Diego

GENERAL DESCRIPTION.

Ventura County lies 300 miles southeast of San Francisco, and twenty-five miles northwest of Los Angeles. It is bounded on the west by Santa Barbara County, on the north and east by Kern and Los Angeles counties, and on tha south by the Pacific Ocean. It also includes the islands of San Nicolas and Anacapa, lying respectively about eighty and eighteen miles from the mainland. These islands are resorts for seals, sea lions, otter, and aquatic birds. They are included in the total area of 1,296,000 acres, divisible into arable land, pasture land and mountain land. There are about 200,000 acres of very rich country, of which as yet little over 70,000 acres have been brought under cultivation.

This county contains various fertile valleys, the most important being the Santa Clara, Ojai, Simí, Conejo, and Sespe, besides some small mesa and mountain valleys. The soil is mainly a rich, dark brown, sandy loam, 10 to 150 feet deep. The surface is nearly level, or but enough diversified to add to the beauty of the situation.

WATER SUPPLY.

Ventura County perhaps is the best watered county in Southern California. The Santa Clara River, which rises in the Soledad Mountains near the Mojave Desert, enters the county at the southeast corner, traverses its entire length, furnishes an abundant supply for a large portion of the Santa Clara Valley, and is a never failing stream. It flows in an easterly direction about sixty miles through the southeastern portion of the county, and empties into the ocean about six miles southeast of San Buenaventura.

The Santa Clara River takes its rise seventy miles inland, in the rugged cañons of the Soledad Pass. Hence it flows west by south, swelled by several large tributaries, mostly coming from the northward. It passes through the Santa Barbara range at Santa Paula, some fifteen miles from the coast, and ends at the seaside in an estero or lagoon, which shows no communication with the sea, save when the winter floods tear away the intervening bar of sand. At Santa Paula this river receives the waters of the Santa Paula Creek, formerly called the Mupu; east of this, the Sespe empties, and near the boundary line, the Piru.

Tributary to the Santa Clara are the Santa Paula, Piru, Big and Little Sespe, which are fine, clear, living streams, furnishing an unfailing supply of water for all that portion of the county comprised within the original grants of Sespe, Santa Paula, Saticoy, and San Francisco ranchos. The Lockwood, Alamo, Hot Springs, and Pine are feeders of the Piru and the Sespe.

The Ventura River rises in the Santa Ynez Mountains, in the northern portion of the county, and flows in a southerly direction, and through the beautiful Ojai Valley to the sea at San Buenaventura, which city it supplies with pure water and excellent water-power. Its tributaries are the Arroyo San Antonio, Cañada Leon, Santa Ana, Cañada Larga, and Los Coyotes, which water large portions of the Ojai, Cañada Larga, and Santa Ana ranchos.

These rivers are fed by numerous springs and mountain streams which run into them from almost all the cañons. The Ventura River alone furnishes water enough to irrigate, were it necessary, every acre of land in the valley through which it flows. This river furnishes the water-power to run the large flouring-mill at Ventura, which at need could be kept running day and night throughout the year.

In that section of country lying southeast of the Santa Clara River in the neighborhood of Hueneme, artesian water is obtained at from 50 to 100 feet, which is a constant flow of good, pure water. Besides these there are a great many small mountain streams in various portions of the county that never go dry. It is estimated that the water supply is sufficient to bring it on every part of farm land if it were necessary to do so, but from a comparison of the per cent. of farmers, whose experience is given elsewhere in this paper, it will be seen that irrigation is not necessary except in case of a dry season, and excepting also for citrus fruits, which some think ought to be irrigated.

It is a peculiarity of this section that no irrigation is needed to raise the most abundant crops, of whatever nature. This may be due to the humidity derived from the sea. At all events, the fact accounts for the rarity of attempts to divert the abundant water into ditches, as is done in most other parts of Southern California.

THE TIMBER SUPPLY.

Ventura County is well supplied with forest timber of live-oak, cottonwood and other deciduous and evergreen trees, much of it being easily accessible to the various railway stations in the county. But the greatest and most valuable timber consists of the great pineries in the remote and almost unknown mountain regions in the northern part of the county. These extensive pine forests contain an immense quantity of valuable timber which some day will be reached by roadways and brought to market. When that day comes, as it surely will, a rich harvest awaits the lumberman's ax. It is now a wild and inaccessible forest, inhabited only by the mountain goat and the fleet-footed deer, with a smart sprinkling of the more ferocious lion and grizzly bear. It is here that nature, in its wildest and most chaotic state, holds undisputed sway, but with an increased population in this county will be made to yield to the demands of civilization—the demand for lumber and other building material.

The following details are extracted from a paper by Dr. Stephen Bowers, in the State Mineralogical Report.

"The county includes the islands of San Nicolas and Anacapa. The former is about eighty miles south of Ventura, and the latter eighteen miles. The area of the entire county is 1,869 square miles, or 1,196,000 acres.

"The valley of the Santa Clara extends along the seashore from San Buenaventura to Point Magu, a distance of over twenty miles, and extends in an easterly direction across the county, narrowing to two or three miles on the eastern border. A chain of mountains extends from Newhall in Los Angeles County westwardly to within about ten miles of the ocean, separating the upper portion of the Santa Clara from the Simí and Las Posas valleys. The chain is narrow and comes to a sharp ridge or comb at the top, averaging about 2,000 feet in altitude.

"Thirteen miles north of San Buenaventura is the Ojai Valley, about ten by five miles in extent. It is divided into two valleys, upper and lower. The latter is 800 feet above the sea level, and the former about 1,700 feet. These valleys are surrounded by mountains, opening along the Ventura River to the south. On the eastern portion of the county is the Cornejo Plateau, which is several miles in extent and elevated 900 feet above the ocean. It is really a succession of hills and valleys. The rock exposures here are principally trappean and metamorphic. The remaining portions of the county are mainly mountainous, giving a diversity of soil and climate.

"It is by far the best watered of all the southern counties. The Santa Clara River runs through the county in a westerly direction, reaching the ocean a few miles west of San Buenaventura. The Matilaja, San Antonio, and Coyote creeks unite and form he Ventura River, coming in from the north, and supplying the town of San Buenaventura with an abundance of water. The Santa Paula, Sespe, and Piru flow into the Santa Clara from the north and west, the Sespe having its rise in Santa Barbara County. The Lockwood flows into the Piru at the western base of the Almo mountain. The Cuyamo rises near Mount Almo, and runs westwardly to the county line, some fifteen miles distant. The Las Posas Creek waters the Las Posas and Simí valleys on the eastern side of the county. In addition to these rivers and streams, are numerous small creeks and springs scattered here and there throughout the county."

SAN NICOLAS ISLAND.
BY DR. BOWERS.

"San Nicolas Island belongs to Ventura County. It is nearly eighty miles south of Ventura, the southesatern end being in latitude 33° 14' north, and longitude 119° 25' west from Greenwich.

"The area is about nine miles long and four miles wide, containing 32.2 square miles, or 20,608 acres. Its longer axis is northwest by west. What is known as Begg Rock is situated on the prolongation of the longer axis of the island, bearing northwest, and is seven miles distant. Soundings show that there is a submarine ridge connecting this rock with San Nicolas, and that it was probably once above the surface. Breakers extend for several miles to the westward, and also for nearly two miles on the eastern shore line of the island, indicating shallow water. Begg Rock is bold and precipitous, rising to the height of forty or more feet, and plainly visible from San Nicolas.

"There is an abundance of water on the

island, but it is slightly brackish; it is entirely destitute of timber, but evidently has not always been so. At the present time there is not even a bush growing on it except a stunted kind of thorn, scarcely two feet high, and a few species of the tree cactus.

"The surface is comparatively level, sufficiently so to till with little trouble. The cultivable land embraces about two-thirds of the island's area, and much of it is apparently rich and fertile. * * * Coral Harbor, located about three miles from the extreme western point, is reached by an opening in the rocks, some twenty feet wide. The water in this opening is sufficiently deep to admit a schooner of twenty tons' burden.

"The only animals found on San Nicolas are, a small fox, a kangaroo mouse, and a diminutive sand lizard. The fox is little more than half as large as the gray or silver fox of the mainland. As far as I have been able to learn, the species is confined to the Channel Islands. Several species of land birds are found. Amongst them may be mentioned the bald eagle, ground owl, raven, crow, and plover. Water fowl are abundant, and among them gulls, pelicans, cormorants, sea-pigeons, and others. Beetles, crickets, spiders, butterflies, house and other flies are met with, but no poisonous or noxious animals or insects. * * * San Nicolas Island must have once supported a large population. In whatever direction one turns, he comes in contact with human skeletons, broken mortars, pestles, ollas, bone implements, etc., and shell heaps. * * * I judge that the natives of this island were physically and intellectually superior to those inhabiting the other islands and the mainland, where, in previous explorations, I have exhumed several thousands of skeletons. Many of the skulls on San Nicolas closely resemble those of the Caucasian type."

GEOLOGY.

The following account of the geological formations of Ventura is by a writer whose name the present editor has been unable to learn:

Ventura County exhibits many interesting geological features. On the eastern side is a volcanic uplift extending westwardly under the ocean forming the island of Anacapa, Santa Cruz, Santa Rosa and San Miguel. This uplift may be traced eastwardly through Los Angeles, San Bernardino and San Diego counties, with an outcrop near Yuma, and probably extending far into Mexico. In Ventura County it is composed largely of rhyolite, trachyte and vesicular basalt. The mountains here have been lifted to a height of nearly or quite 4,000 feet, their serrated summits presenting a rugged outline against the sky.

Another trappean uplift occurs in the northwestern corner of the county running parallel with the first described, leaving a space of over fifty miles between them. It is most likely the two are synchronous. One of the characteristic rocks of the latter is amygdaloid filled with zeolites of quartz, chalcedony, agate, opal, calcite, natrolite, etc., and inspissated bitumen.

The mountains on the northern portion of the county are composed principally of granite rocks, while the characteristic rocks on the southern side, as we approach toward the ocean, are largely sandstone.

There are no large areas of horizontal rock strata in the county. Formerly tilted, folded and plicated rocks of this section bear evidence of sudden upheaval. But it is evident that the lateral pressure that has raised the mountains of Ventura County from 2,000 to over 9,000 feet above the sea level has probably done its work so gradually as not to "disturb the flight of an insect," apart from the volcanic disturbances above mentioned. The uplift is still going on, but so gradually and silently as to be imperceptible to the casual observer. Along the seashore, and indeed all over the county where the older rocks are exposed they are found tilted, shoved and heaved at every conceivable angle of inclination, with alternating anticlinal and synclinal folds.

The Santa Clara River enters the county on the eastern side and traverses it in a westerly direction to the sea. Three or four streams flow into it from the north which will be described in due time. One of these, the Sespe, heads not far from the Santa Barbara line and runs in an eastwardly direction for some distance, gradually bending southward through the center of the county. This stream seems to mark the division between the Cretaceous and the Tertiary periods. At least some of the fossils which the writer found north of the stream he must refer to the Cretaceous, while all south of it belong to the Miocene and Pliocene epochs. It is probable that all the northern portion of the county was lifted from a Cretaceous sea, and what now forms the northern boundary of the Sespe was for ages the shore line against whose rocky ribs the waves of the Pacific Ocean expended their fury. The strata south of this are at an entirely different angle and to some extent different in composition, and seem to have been raised independently, leaving a fissure between the two formations and along which the stream has cut its gorge.

The Piru Creek, running in a parallel direction, but several miles north of the Sespe, has cut its way through mountains of granite, slate and diorite. In some places the walls are nearly or quite a half mile high and perpendicular, the tortuous bed of the stream appearing as a ribbon far below.

In the southern portion of the county are vast beds of Pliocene fossils. They are found in the foot-hills skirting the sea shore from the extreme southern corner of the county to the county-seat, and on the north side of the Santa Clara to the Sespe, on the south side of the Santa Paula mountains, in the Las Posas and Simí valleys, and elsewhere. Joining the town of Ventura the remains of the fossil elephant, llama and other animals are found. Near Santa Paula the remains of an extinct horse (*Equus occidentalis*) have been found.

Miocene fossils are found in the Ojai Valley, Conejo plateau, along the south side of the Sespe from its source to its mouth, in the mountains east of Santa Paula and other places. Among these may be mentioned the remains of whales, seals, sharks, etc. Indeed the entire county, apart from the volcanic uplifts referred to and the granitic formations on the northern portion, abounds in most interesting remains, including hundreds of species of invertebrate and vertebrate animals, many of which are extinct, while others are still found in the ocean. This county is a paradise for the geologist and paleontologist, much of which has never been subjected to a thorough scientific investigation.

In this connection we may add that the botanist, zoologist, ichthyologist and entomologist will find an ample field for investigation and study in their respective departments in this county.

CLIMATE.

The climate of Ventura County is difficult to overestimate. Near the coast the mercury seldom falls below 43° or rises above 83°; but in some places back from the ocean, in the mountains and valleys, it is somewhat warmer in summer and cooler in winter.

Taking it altogether, the evenness of the climate is unexcelled. Thermometrical observations, extending over a series of years, indicate an average temperature of about 58°. By careful study of the various places in Southern California the reader will perceive that Ventura County is not excelled in point of climate. Near the coast frost is seldom or never seen; but several miles back from the ocean a little frost occurs in winter, yet not sufficiently severe to injure orange trees or the most tender vegetation, except in rare instances. Large banana trees may be seen growing a dozen or fifteen miles from the coast. The same kind of clothing is worn winter and summer. While nearly all kinds of northern and semi-tropical fruits flourish here, roses, fuchsias, geraniums and many other flowers bloom constantly, and strawberries may be procured nearly any day in the year. The days are warm but not sultry; hence sunstroke is unknown in this county. The nights are cool and induce refreshing sleep. For invalids, and especially for persons disposed to pulmonary troubles, this county offers superior inducements. It is seldom that lightning is seen or thunder heard, and no tornadoes, cyclones or other disturbances of the forces of nature exist here. The islands south of Ventura County deflect the warm ocean currents from the equator, turning them to the very shore line and giving a higher temperature than is realized some hundreds of miles south, and thus securing good bathing the entire year.

For Santa Paula the average temperature for winter is about 45° and for summer is about 85°. The highest given is 100° and the lowest 30°. For Saticoy the average for winter 55° and for summer 85°; the lowest given is 40° and the highest 100°. The variations at Camulos are from 25° to 100° and and at Nordhoff is 30° to 100°. The average at Hueneme is, for winter, about 50° and for summer 75°; the highest given is 85° and the lowest 38° and for New Jerusalem it is about the same.

THE TEMPERATURE.

RECORD OF TEMPERATURE AT SAN BUENAVENTURA.

Table showing average temperature per month at San Buenaventura for the three consecutive years 1880, 1881, 1882, as kept by I. T. Saxby, Voluntary Observer for United States Army Signal Service.

The following is a table showing the average rainfall at San Buenaventura, California, for the past eighteen years. And it should be remembered that what is called the "rainy season" generally includes the following months: October, November, December, January, February, March and April. During the remainder of the year there is usually no rain at all.

SEASON	INCHES	SEASON	INCHES
1870–1871	9	1879–1880	22.06
1871–1872	5.12	1880–1881	13.81
1872–1873	17.25	1881–1882	11.98
1873–1874	15	1882–1883	11.68
1874–1875	15.25	1883–1884	35.74
1875–1876	21	1884–1885	9.46
1876–1877	4.62	1885–1886	20.92
1877–1878	20.22	1886–1887	12.95
1878–1879	11.79	1887–1888	20.24

THE CHURCHES OF VENTURA.

The county is well supplied with churches. The Catholics have, besides the old Mission at San Buenaventura, which was founded more than a century ago, a good church house at New Jerusalem. Each of these churches have regular pastors.

The Baptists have organizations in Santa Paula, Hueneme and Springville. At the latter place there is a house of worship owned by an independent Baptist organization.

The Methodists have houses of worship at San Buenaventura, Hueneme, Santa Paula, Sespe and Piru. They also have organizations at Cienega, Saticoy, Springville, Conejo, Fillmore and other places.

The Presbyterians have houses of worship at Ventura, Nordhoff, Saticoy, Santa Paula and Fillmore.

The Universalists have a parish at Santa Paula and services at Ventura.

The Congregationalists have a house of worship in San Buenaventura and Nordhoff; an academy at Santa Paula.

The Episcopalians have a church organization and edifice at Ventura.

The Swedenborgians have a church organization and edifice at Bardsdale.

In addition to the above there are two or three union or independent churches in the county. All of the churches named above are supplied with regular pastors.

THE PUBLIC SCHOOLS.

The school system of Ventura County is much like that of other counties of the State, but quite unlike that of most of the other and old States east of the Rocky Mountains.

The public schools of Ventura County are of three kinds or grades: primary, grammar and high school; the first being found in the sparsely settled portions of the county; the second in the more thickly settled, and the third or high school only in San Buenaventura. In the primary school instruction is given in reading, orthography, practical and mental arithmetic, geography, United States history, physiology, penmanship, elements of book-keeping, industrial drawing, vocal music, practical entomology and the rudiments of technical English grammar. Grammar schools are established in those parts of the county, in the country towns, where there are a number of children who desire to pursue, in addition to the studies of the primary grade, such branches as algebra, natural philosophy, natural history, and when, owing to the increased number of children attending school, there are funds enough to admit of paying a higher salary to the teacher in return for a greater and more advanced work. It is proper to remark here, however, that in every one of the primary schools of the county the teacher is competent to teach algebra and such other grammar-grade studies, so that no pupil is debarred from pursuing each study if desirable.

The high school in California or the grammar school course—which is a course in advance of the grammar school as given above—is intended to prepare the pupils who graduate from the public schools, having finished the work of the grammar grade for entrance into the State University. This adds to the grammar school such branches as rhetoric, advanced English and American literature, chemistry and mineralogy. But this course can be pursued only in such localities as have a representation of pupils sufficient to supply a number of teachers, since no one person could do the work required in a school with all grades from primary to and including the grammar school course; and in general the grade of a school depends upon the number of children in it.

By a provision of the State law, all pupils who finish the course of study laid out for the grammar grade and pass a satisfactory examination therein upon questions prepared by the County Board of Education, are entitled to a diploma of graduation from the grammar school. This admits them to the lowest class in the State Normal School, or to the high school or grammar course. Completion of the studies in the course, upon satisfactory examination, admits the graduate to the University of California at Berkeley.

As another prominent feature of the schools it may be observed that each district in Ventura County draws from the public funds annually from $30 to $50, to be expended only for school apparatus or library books.

Accordingly we have in this county schools which possess valuable libraries, having in the course of the past few years accumulated a set of cyclopædias, all requisite books of reference, besides complete sets of the poets and standard novelists, and comprising many works on history, biography and travel.

As an index of the growth and development of the county, as represented by the growth of the schools, there follows a comparative statement of the condition of the public schools in each alternative year since 1884.

In 1884 Ventura had twenty-four school districts, and school property worth $33,417, as follows: buildings, $30,113; libraries, $1,932; apparatus, $1,366. There were 1,667 census children, of whom 1,270 were enrolled, with an average attendance of 743.

The total receipts for school purposes were $34,429; total expenditures, $30,677.

In 1886 there were in Ventura County 1,889 census children; enrolled were 1,439; the average attendance was 911. The value of school buildings was $50,800; of school libraries, $1,610; of apparatus, $1,500; total value of school property, $53,910. The total expenditures for schools were $23,399, and the total of revenues for school purposes $28,328.

In 1888 there were 2,284 census children in Ventura County, which had gained ten school districts in two years; 1,889 were enrolled in the public schools, and the average daily attendance was 1,069. There were now school buildings to the value of $64,900; libraries, $1,825, and apparatus, $1,410; total, $69,035.

There are now in Ventura County forty-three school districts, employing fifty-seven teachers. The number of census children is 2,703; number enrolled, 2,244; the average attendance is 1,339. The amount received from county school tax for 1889 was $11,366; from all sources for 1889-'90, $65,791.42. The total expenditures were $51,457.31. Of the teachers in the county, twenty are graduates of the State Normal School, and three are from Eastern high schools. The average monthly salary of men teachers is $75; of women, $63. The total value of school buildings in the county is $102,050; of school libraries, $2,850; of apparatus, $2,955; total, $105,855. During the eight years that C. T. Meredith has been county superintendent of schools, there have been built new school-houses in thirty-two districts. San Buenaventura has school-houses worth perhaps $35,000; the Avenue building another worth $6,000; those at Santa Paula cost $10,000; at Hueneme, $9,000; the Montalvo building cost $5,000, to which must be added another $1,000 for grounds, improvements, etc., and the Saticoy school-house cost $1,500.

It is rather a remarkable feature that there is a small attendance of the Spanish element in the schools of this county.

THE EASTERN PORTION OF VENTURA.

THE SANTA CLARA VALLEY.

The lower Santa Clara Valley, bordering on the ocean, comprises the ranchos San Miguel, Santa Paula y Saticoy, Santa Clara del Norte, La Colonia, and part of Guadalasca, besides Government lands. Through the hills skirting the eastern flank of the main expanse break two fine valleys, with wooded hills and cultivated dales. The more northerly of these contains the ranchos Las Posas and Simí; the southern, being El Conejo Valley, embraces the ranchos Callejos, El Conejo, and the upper end of the Guadalasca. Close down to the channel of the Santa Clara on the north come the Santa Barbara Mountains, jagged and distorted, while to the south, above Santa Paula, they are much lower and more rounded, although still mostly untillable. The northern slopes are set with groves of pine and live-oak; the southern are covered with grass, flowers and the honey-bearing sage. The principal trees along the water courses are sycamore, walnut, cottonwood, and some inferior varieties of pine.

RANCHO LA COLONIA.

The Rancho La Colonia, or Rio de Santa Clara, as finally confirmed, comprises a tract of about 48,883 acres, lying south of Rancho Santa Clara del Norte, and north and west of the Pacific Ocean, the Guadalasca Rancho, and a small piece of Government land. This tract was granted in 1837 to eight old soldiers, by Governor Alvarado, the record of possession bearing date September 28, 1840. The commissioners rejected this claim in 1854, but the grant was declared valid, reversing the former decision, in 1857, thus confirming the land to Valentine Cota, although it was also claimed by the widow of Joseph Chapman, of the Ortega Rancho affair.

During the '60's many squatters settled upon this tract, and its boundaries were modified by various surveys. It was first cultivated in 1867, when Christian Borchard and his son settled on the rancho, in an old adobe house formerly occupied by the Gonzales family, of the original grantees, and planted crops of wheat and barley, the first grain sown in Ventura County, thirty acres of each being sown in the spring of 1868. The barley yielded eighteen centals to the acre; the wheat rusted and was left standing. This rancho was so thickly covered with wild mustard that two men, in two and one-half months, gathered with an old-fashioned header, twenty-five tons of mustard seed, which sold for 2 cents per pound. This section has been steadily settled, and that with an industrious and excellent class of citizens. "Tom" Scott, the railroad king, who purchased this rancho from the Spanish owners, in 1869 sold it for $150,000 to Thomas R. Bard, under whose auspices it has been improved greatly. The Colonia includes most of the Santa Clara Valley, oceanward.

HUENEME.

Hueneme is situated upon a projection of the Colonia Rancho, a point running into the sea, some twelve miles south of San Buenaventura, and the same distance north of Point Magu.

The town was started in June, 1870, by W. E. Barnard, G. S. Gilbert and H. P.

Flint. It was declared that the town would be overflowed at high tide, and cut off from the surrounding country by the neighboring swamps and morasses. Moreover, the proprietors of the Colonia Rancho claimed the land, and tried to dispossess the founders of the new town.

The Hueneme Lighter Company began to make shipments of lumber in June, 1870, in connection with the steamer Kalorama, and, against all predictions to the contrary, this enterprise proved eminently successful. During the first year 60,000 sacks of grain were shipped by means of the lighters. Still there were some losses, notably that of some costly machinery destined for the oil works, and therefore, with a view to the possibilities of future traffic, T. R. Bard and R. G. Surdam obtained the right to construct a wharf at this point, and the work was begun and finished within the month, that of August, 1871. The wharf was 900 feet long, reaching to water eighteen feet deep. It was connected by tramway with the shore, where was built a warehouse, also corrals for stock. At once this wharf was made the medium of a very heavy business. The board of supervisors fixed the maximum rates of wharfage, which was moderate.

Already in July, 1871, much attention had been attracted to the artesian wells about Hueneme. One owned by T. R. Bard, although but 147 feet deep, threw up such an immense volume of water it flooded several acres, and flumes had to be constructed to carry away the surplus water.

The first two houses in this town were built in 1871, by Messrs. Thompson and Judson. The town was laid out by T. R. Bard. The Pioneer Hotel was built in 1871 by D. D. McCoy, who then removed hither from San Buenaventura.

Shortly after the settlement at Hueneme,

T. R. Bard, who had purchased the Colonia Rancho in 1869, denied that the site of the town was public land, as claimed by its founders, and to enforce his claim he set a party to fence in the proposed wharf site. Enraged by this measure, the settlers assumed a threatening attitude with regard to the fence-builders, and it is probable that bloodshed was prevented only by the fact that Mr. Bard's party possessed fire-arms, while the settlers were without them. They finally dispersed, and later both claimants gave bonds for a title to the land when the ownership should be established by issue of the case then pending before the United States authorities.

After this difficulty was adjusted, the new town received numerous additions, and within a year after its founding it had seventeen families and forty-eight school census children. Several stores and a second hotel were opened this year.

In September, 1872, Hueneme contained one grocery, one fruit and confectionery store, two of general merchandise, one restaurant, two lumber yards, one livery stable, one carpenter shop, two blacksmith shops, two barber shops, one hotel, and one private school. Many vessels were loading or discharging at the wharf. There were shipped this year 86,900 centals of grain.

On May 5, 1873, was established the Hueneme public school district; also road districts for the vicinity, and many artesian wells were sunk hereabouts during this summer. During this year 145,000 centals of grain were shipped hence.

In 1874 Hueneme had become a lively town, with several large stores, and most of the trades represented.

The shipments of grain this year were 198,500 centals.

In 1877 was established a matanza, or

slaughter-yard, to kill and utilize cattle and sheep which otherwise would probably perish during the disastrous season already begun.

In 1878 were received 264,336 sacks of grain, of which 140,217 sacks were shipped during the year. Other shipments were: 4,070 hogs, 32 calves, 53 boxes eggs, 862 barrels petroleum, 1,228 bales hay, 1,231 bales wool, 37,735 pounds rock soap, 2,224 sacks mustard, 1,002 sacks beans, 6,680 sacks corn, 50 sacks wheat, 3,893 sacks barley, 190 tons miscellaneous freight. There were received about 1,000 tons of freight, besides 800,000 feet of lumber.

In April, 1879, was organized the Hueneme Lodge of Good Templars, No. 236.

During the year ending March 31, 1880, there were shipped from Hueneme 16,888 sacks of corn, 232,995 sacks barley, 2,012 sacks flaxseed, 352 sacks rye, 21,479 sacks wheat, 3,156 sacks beans, 406 sacks mustard, 140 sacks oats, 149 boxes eggs, 418 sheep, 10,035 hogs, 64,000 pounds of wool.

In view of the growing business, the wharf was now extended to a total length of about 1,500 feet.

The receipts of the business for that year $20,100.92; expenditures, $10,461.96; earnings, $9,638.96, or about 1 1-6 per month on the cost.

In 1883 Hueneme contained a hotel, several business houses, a telegraph office, postoffice, wharf and steamship offices, good school-house and some twenty-five dwellings. There were four large warehouses, with an aggregate capacity of about 300,000 sacks, or 684,120 cubic feet.

In the earlier months of 1884, a waterspout appeared on the ocean before Hueneme, whence it passed to the land, tearing up trees, and wrecking to total demolishment the house of H. F. Coffman, the occupants escaping injury as by a miracle.

For the year ending March, 1886, the shipments over the Hueneme wharf were as follows: Sacks barley, 121,336; wheat, 53,628; corn, 8,291; beans, 2,035; walnuts, 111; mustard seed 153; cases honey, 481; bales wool, 722½; bales hay, 172; hogs, 5,300; sheep, 3,147; lambs, 599; boxes butter, 50; cases eggs, 479; coops live fowls, 72; hides, 213; bundles pelts, 70; barrels tallow, 23; sacks castor beans, 13; miscellaneous packages, 641.

Over the Hueneme wharf were exported during the year ending March, 1887, products as follows: Sacks barley, 394,024; sacks wheat, 80,174; sacks corn, 23,426; sacks oats, 12; sacks beans, 1,286; sacks walnuts, 81; sacks mustard seed, 1,004; clover seed, 201; potatoes, 2,880; onions, 167; bales wool, 1,352; bales hay, 139; cases honey, 2,803; cases eggs, 427; head hogs, 7,005; head sheep, 7,443; lambs, 207; boxes butter, 40; coops live fowls, 49; hides, 216; bundles pelts, 60; barrels tallow, 44; miscellaneous packages, 105.

During the year ending March 31, 1888, there was shipped from the port of Hueneme, of corn, 12,534 sacks; wheat, 16,073 sacks; barley 508,118 sacks; mustard seed, 3,934 sacks; beans, 1,556 sacks; eggs, 387 cases; pelts, 304 bundles; hides, 116 bundles; wool, 1,023 bales; hogs, 2,249 head; honey, 2,803 cases; potatoes, 2,597 sacks; sheep and lambs, 8,339 head; butter, 146 cases; tallow, 26 barrels; hay, 102 bales; fowls, 158 coops; castor beans, 12 sacks; onions, 167 sacks; petroleum, 1,785 barrels. During this year, 169 steamers, 23 schooners and 44 steam schooners, making a total of 236 vessels, touched at this port.

The town site is almost level, with only a sandy beach between it and the sea. The climate is mild and the air very pure and free from malaria. This is the "embarcadero" or sea shipping point for a large back country.

The rich agricultural and grazing lands of the Simí, Conejo and Santa Clara ranchos, the Colonia Rancho, and Pleasant Valley, lie behind it.

The Hueneme light-house is situated one mile west of the wharf. It is a two-story brick structure, combining the Swiss with the Elizabethan style. It contains ten large rooms, with closets, offices, etc., being designed to accommodate two families. The revolving light is of the fourth order, red flash, with fine French prisms and concentrators. It is fifty feet above the sea level and is perceptible from forty miles away. It consumes about three gallons of oil per week. A record is kept of all details, time of lighting and of extinguishing the lamp, etc. The light was first shown December 15, 1874. The successive keepers have been: Samuel Ensign, J. A. McFarland and E. H. Pinney.

Hueneme has post, express and telegraph offices and daily mail by stage from Ventura. There are two hotels, one school—a $9,000 building—one church, one weekly newspaper, the *Herald*, three stores of general merchandise, one for furniture, one drug store, one tobacconist, one blacksmith, one carpenter-shop, one barber, one bakery, one agricultural implement depot, one saddlery and harness-shop, one grain, wool, and produce depot, one insurance agent, one livery stable, one lumber yard, one meat market, one painter, one plumber, one stove and tinware house, two notaries public, two attorneys at law, one physician and one dentist. Here is situated the mammoth tank, of 36,000 barrels capacity, into which a line of four-inch pipes conveys the oil from the wells in the mountains, and whence it is piped into vessels built expressly for transporting it to San Francisco, San Pedro, etc.

THE GUADALASCA RANCHO.

This rancho lies in the extreme southern part of Ventura, southeast of the Colonia. It borders on Los Angeles County about two miles, on the coast about eight miles, and extends about ten miles into the interior. The place is historical, being the site of Xucu or "The Town of the Canoes," described in the voyage of Cabrillo, 300 years since, this having been the most densely-populated portion of the coast. In one of the valleys, La Jolla, seems to have been a favorite ground of the Indians, it being rich in kitchen-middens, bones, etc., and having a trail, worn deep, from the landing over the hill. The Guadalasca was a grant of 30,593.85 acres, made May 6, 1846, to Ysabel Yorba, whose title was confirmed by the United States Land Commissioners. Of this estate, 23,000 acres were purchased some years since by William Richard Broome, an English gentleman of leisure, living in Santa Barbara. Several thousands of these acres are on the fertile Colonia plain, where flowing wells of artesian water can be had at 100 to 150 feet deep. "The Estero" is the termination of the Guadalasca Creek, being a basin some four miles long, in some parts 1,000 feet wide, and deep enough to float large vessels. Near Point Magu is a landing for vessels, safe in any weather, and considered one of the best harbors on the coast. The mountains here abound in game, such as bear, deer, California lions, wild cats, coyotes, rabbits, hare, and quail, while the sea is here swarming with fine fish and shell-fish, as in the days when sea products here supported the dense aboriginal population.

THE LAS POSAS RANCHO.

This rancho occupies the lower end of the Las Posas and Simí Valley, debouching upon the great Santa Clara plain. Las Posas, embracing 26,623 acres of land, was granted to José Carrillo May 15, 1824, and confirmed to José de la Guerra y Noriega, being held by him and his heirs until 1876, when it was sold to a company, who have kept it undivided until the present day, raising wheat, barley, corn and stock.

At the date of sale, the Las Posas and the Simí, containing an aggregate of about 125,000 acres, were sold for $550,000, being assessed at the same time at but $172,000.

The rancho is located about twelve miles east of Hueneme, within sight of the ocean, in the southern part of Ventura County. The property is crossed by the proposed Los Angeles and Hueneme Railroad, and will be, when that road is completed, about fifty miles by rail from the metropolis of Southern California. The great Simí ranch borders it on the east, the Calleguas on the south, the Santa Clara del Norte on the west, and a range of mountains on the north.

Las Posas could take in every resident of Ventura County, give each voter of the county ten acres of land, and leave nearly 1,000 acres on which to build the towns. Considering the fact that this county is as thickly populated outside the villages as perhaps any in the State, the foregoing statement gives the reader some idea of the extent of this great ranch.

Probably 12,000 acres of the Las Posas are arable, 13,000 suitable for grazing, and the mountain land availing only for bee-keeping. It has no timber. The wide fields are mostly unfenced. Most of the farming is carried on by renters, who raise wheat, barley, corn, and beans, grown without irrigation. All the grains and semi-tropical fruits succeed here, and there are several thousand acres perfectly adapted to the growth of the orange, lemon, fig, almond, and apricot. Artesian water is easily obtainable.

On a part of this Rancho, Peter Rice, the owner of a farm of 280 acres, has an orchard, bearing all kinds of fruit, including oranges and lemons, walnuts, figs, grapes, apricots, prunes and peaches.

The sale of the Scott estate lands on the adjoining rancho, La Colonia, in July and August, 1888, aggregated over $525,000, in five days.

THE SIMI RANCHO.

The Simí Rancho is a vast tract of 96,000 acres, completely walled in by continuous ranges of hills and mountains, on all sides save the west, where lies the narrow valley of the Las Posas Rancho. To the north lies the upper Santa Clara Valley, and to the south the Conejo Valley, on the south and east being also the Santa Susana range, separating the Simí from Los Angeles County. The Simí was formerly called San José de Gracia. It was granted to Patricio Javier and Miguel Pico, in 1795, by Governor Borica. In April, 1842, when Alvarado revived, or renewed, the claim to Noriega, it contained 92,341.35 acres. It contained 114,000 acres between sixty and seventy years since. Since that time, to settle a dispute as to title $\frac{15}{113}$ of the whole, comprising about 14,000 acres, were conveyed to Eugene Sullivan. This portion, comprehending the homestead of the de la Guerra family, now known as the Tapo Rancho, lies in the northeast corner of the Simí Valley. To Mr. Chaffee were sold other 2,000 acres of the Simí, leaving the rest in the ownership of Andrew Gray. Of this tract, only about 11,000 acres are suitable for farming; 67,000 acres are grazing land; and 20,000 acres are available for bee-raising only. The altitude of the valley is about 700 feet above sea-level.

Having passed into the hands of "Tom" Scott, this rancho, on his death, remained in use only for grain farming and sheep and cattle raising, as the executors of the estate could not dispose of it in small parcels, and the heirs seemed not inclined to put it on the market. Of late it has passed into the hands of the Simí Land and Water Company, of Los Angeles, who have divided it into stock ranges, containing from 1,000 to 10,000 acres each, at from $5 to $15 per acre, each division being supplied with abundant water from the living springs which are found in almost every part of the Simí.

It is understood that there is abundant water on Simí for the irrigation of all fruit land *which will need* irrigation. No crop ever raised there has ever been irrigated. Some of the best fruit land on the rancho has flowing water tributary to it which can be piped at small expense. This water will be supplied as the needs of settlers may require. On the ordinary farming lands in the valleys water is easily reached by boring a short distance, and in many places artesian wells can be found.

The climate of Simí is most desirable, and it is destined to become an important health resort for persons afflicted with weak lungs or throat trouble. The elevation of the valleys average over 1,000 feet above the sea level, and the air is pure and dry, at the same time the temperature is even and pleasant. The ocean breeze begins to blow gently in the morning and continues through the day, making their air pleasant in the warmest days of summer. At the eastern end of the rancho is a beautiful oak grove of about 2,000 acres, which affords a charming place for camping and picnic parties, an attraction not often found in this part of the State.

Land on the Simí can now be bought in tracts to suit at $5 to $15 for stock ranges, and from $20 to $75 for farms and colony tracts. At present the nearest railroad point is San Fernando, a station on the Southern Pacific Railroad, twenty miles north of Los Angeles.

The Simí Hotel is twelve miles west of this point. Visitors can go to San Fernando by rail from Ventura or Los Angeles, and thence to Simí by four-horse stage.

RANCHO TAPO.

The Tapo Rancho, before mentioned as having been set off from the Simí, belongs to the estate of Francisco de la Guerra. It has been established for more than sixty years. Lying at the northeastern part of the Simí Rancho, only some 1,500 of its 14,000 acres are arable, the rest being grazing land. This rancho, being protected by a mountain wall, is peculiarly adapted to fruit-growing. Superior wines and brandies have been made from a vineyard here, planted nearly fifty years ago.

SPRINGVILLE.

This is a little village located near where the ranchos Santa Clara del Norte, Las Posas and La Colonia come together at the west end of what is known as Pleasant Valley. Past this hamlet goes a great deal of local travel. The village has a postoffice, one church, one store, one smithy, and a small number of dwellings. Adjoining Pleasant Valley is the magnificent Calleguas Rancho of 22,000 acres, and close to Springville is the large stock rancho of Gries & Bell.

CALLEGUAS RANCHO.

This lies over the hills, south of the Las Posas, and east of La Colonia (from which it is separated by Government lands), north of the Guadalasca, and west of El Conejo. The extension of Pleasant Valley forms a portion of it. This was granted to José Pedro Ruiz in May, 1847, the area called for being 9,998.29 acres, of which about half is fit for stock-raising only. The rest is arable, producing excellent flax and cereals, corn being considered the best crop. Much of this rancho contains living springs, which appear in many places, but which have not been utilized, although irrigating a large surface, which they render peculiarly suitable to fruit-raising. A small vineyard here produces wine of excellent quality.

RANCHO EL CONEJO.

The Conejo (Rabbit) Rancho was granted by Governor Sola to José de la Guerra y Noriega, October 12, 1822. It contained 48,674.56 acres. It lies east of the Calleguas and Guadalasca ranchos, and south of the Simí, which also borders it on the east. Los Angeles bounds it on the east and south.

It is cradled between the Guadalasca or Conejo range south and westward, the Susana hills extension on the north, and the Susana and Santa Monica mountains on the east. The altitude is about 700 feet. The soil is a deep and rich black loam. The grazing lands are unsurpassed, and the cañons and mountains afford fine bee-pasturage. In 1872–'73 H. W. Mills purchased one-half of the Conejo grant from the heirs of Captain José de la Guerra. In 1882 were sold at $5 per acre 2,200 acres of the Newbury tract, and in the same year 6,000 acres above Newbury Park were sold to Russell Brothers for $15,000. Of this rancho 1,800 acres are fertile and even-surfaced. The water here is good. The distance of this section from Hueneme is twenty-five miles.

NEWBURY PARK.

In the southern end of Ventura County, and in the lower part of the Conejo Rancho, is located the town of Newbury Park—or rather there is in this beautiful little valley a post-office known by that name, at which a score or more of prosperous families get their daily mail. The postoffice is located in an old building belonging to the Russell Brothers, on the old stage route from Los Angeles to Ventura, about fifty miles from the former and thirty from the latter. The inhabitants of this locality are farmers living for six or eight miles up and down the old stage road, and in the " Portrero," a narrow cañon leading out of the larger valley, hemmed in by rugged hills and covered by some of the finest forest trees to be found in Southern California. The territory covered by the ranches in this vicinity embraces about 30,000 acres, mostly devoted to stock-raising. The country is diversified, as is the greater part of California. Along the roads, which are extra good, are here and there pretty farm houses, and large barns filled to overflowing with farm products. On the hills are fat cattle and fine horses. Good fences, good roads and good buildings, all speak of thrift and industry.

The valleys being well covered with large oak trees, the drive through them is delightful. Upon the rancho of A. D. and H. M. Russell, embracing 6,000 acres, are kept 500 head of cattle, 100 horses and 500 hogs.

W. H. Crolley has a rancho of 2,260 acres, which in two years, under his care, has been brought—from a property that did not make enough to pay taxes—into the most thrifty condition, showing what a little care and good judgment can do in a short time on California soil. He keeps about forty fine horses, 200 Durham cattle and fifty hogs, besides a good quantity of poultry, all of which does very well.

O. A. Wadleigh, from Canada, rents the Edwards rancho of 6,400 acres, and is carrying on the dairy business. He keeps 125 cows, 150 hogs and a large lot of poultry.

R. O. Hunt has a splendid little rancho of about 1,000 acres, on which he raises all kinds of crops and keeps all kinds of stock. He raises a great deal of poultry—chickens, ducks and turkeys. He says he never saw a place where poultry did as well or could be raised as easily, or where it would pay as well.

H. Hadsell, from Chicago, and his brother, N. D. Hadsell, from Ohio, have a nice little farm of 200 acres, on which they raise wheat and various other crops with success. They are planting fruit trees of all kinds, which are making most remarkable growth.

H. T. Stebbins, from Ohio, who has lived on the Conejo for fourteen years, has a charming little place of eighty acres, divided into tillage and pasture, where he keeps twenty horses, twenty-five cattle and 120 hogs, besides a liberal supply of fine poultry. Mr. Stebbins says he has killed 350 deer on this ranch since he has lived here. From his porch he looks out upon the rugged mountains of the Coast Range; the "Triunfo," where it is said the Mexicans fought a successful battle with the Indians years ago, and up the lovely Potrero Valley.

Three miles further up is the 8,000-acre rancho of "the Banning boys," where 500 to 1,000 cattle are kept and fattened for market.

The only means of public transportation into this valley are the mail-carts.

TIMBERVILLE.

This is the name of an old settlement on the Conejo Rancho, some eight or nine miles from Newbury Park. It is situated in a quiet valley of great fertility, abundantly watered, and surrounded by hills whose slope furnish fine grazing. There are here a post-office, hotel, store, blacksmith shop, tannery, Chinese laundry, a good school-house, and one or two church organizations. Here lives Mr. Borchard, the pioneer grower of wheat in Ventura County. He now is engaged in general farming, and also makes butter by the ton. Game is very plentiful in this section.

THE CENTRAL PORTION OF VENTURA.

The Santa Clara Valley, above Santa Paula, is narrow and tortuous, with but a meager amount of arable land; below, it spreads out nearly level, in the approximate shape of an isosceles triangle, whose longest side extends from San Buenaventura to Point Magu, the southernmost point of the county, about twenty-four miles; the apex of this figure is Santa Paula, distant about thirteen miles in a direct line from each of the other points. The upper Santa Clara Valley contains the Rancho Sespe, occupying its lower and central portions, parts of the San Francisco and Camulos ranchos, next to the eastern county boundary line and Government lands.

The soil south of the Santa Clara, and also the whole valley above Santa Paula, is a dark loam of the strongest kind, adapted to the cultivation of almost every vegetable, grain, fruit and flower. Extending along the channel of the Santa Clara, above Santa Paula, is a tract of sand about one mile wide and twelve miles long. The soil of the lower main valley, south of the river, varies from sandy to adobe. Grain generally succeeds in this valley without irrigation; but the climatic conditions are such that the land, with proper irrigation, regularly produces two crops each year.

Extensive asphaltum and sulphur deposits are found in this valley, and oil indications throughout it. In the upper part are numerous irrigating ditches, while there is in the Santa Clara River, four miles above Santa Paula, abundant water to irrigate all the land between the river and the ex-Mission hills, Santa Paula and the sea. In the southwestern part artesian wells furnish an ample supply of water. Good water for drinking purposes is found only in favored localities, although it is affirmed that the best of water can be found in wells of more than 100 feet deep. The Santa Clara River and its tributaries furnish abundant first-class water-power.

The range of temperature in the lower valley is small, reaching neither hot nor cold. In the upper valley the range is greater; at Santa Paula snow has been known to fall, and the thermometer has registered 108°, although such freaks are of great rarity. This part of the county has, perhaps, more than its share of windy days. Most of the towns of the county lie within this district; the county-seat is but two miles beyond its northwestern point; Santa Paula guards the entrance of the upper valley; Hueneme is the landing-place, and various other towns are found here.

THE RANCHO SAN MIGUEL

lies in the extreme western part of the Santa Clara Valley. It was a grant of 4,693.91 acres, made to Raymundo Olivas, July 6, 1841. Of this, 2,400 acres are now owned by Dixie W. Thompson, who has 1,700 acres under cultivation. The surface of the land, for the most part, has a gentle slope back from the sea, which it borders for about four miles.

THE RANCHO SANTA PAULA Y SATICOY

was originally granted to Manuel Jimeno, April 28, 1840, he taking possession that year. In 1847 Jimeno petitioned the alcalde, Pablo de la Guerra, for judicial possession, and the neighboring land-owners were summoned to witness his installation, and to attest the boundaries, which originally were described as follows:—" From the Arroyo Mupu (now Santa Paula Creek) on the east, to the small mountain on the west, and from the small mountain (supposed to be Sulphur Mountain) on the north to Las Positas on the south." Jimeno was given possession of about 30,000 acres. The name of the rancho is partly derived from the Saticoy tribe of Indians, who made their headquarters at the springs of that name. (Saticoy is said to be the Indian term for "Eureka!") The tract is about twelve miles long, extending from the San Miguel Rancho to the Sespe Rancho, with an average width of two miles between the Santa Clara River on the southeast and the lofty ex-Mission hills on the northwest. Its upper portion overlaps the river channel, including a narrow strip of the southern slope. Being one of the choicest pieces of land in the county, it was one of the earliest settled ranchos, as it is now the most thickly populated sections of the county.

One of the most important events in the history of this rancho was the enterprise of Mr. George G. Briggs, of Marysville, Yuba County, who conceived the idea that in the Santa Clara Valley existed such combinations of soil and climatic conditions as would constitute an ideal fruit-growing district, whence he could place his fruits on the San Francisco market some weeks in advance of all competitors. To this end he purchased of the More Brothers four leagues of land for $40,000, and in March, 1862, he planted 100 acres to fruit trees of various kinds to the number of several thousands, the site of this great orchard being two miles up the river from the Indian town of Saticoy. Carefully nurtured for five years, the orchard succeeded in all other respects; but, failing to mature early, the project was abandoned. In 1865 the grass was as high as a man's head, over the valley, and of 25,000 trees, but a few poor stragglers remained in a few years. In 1867 Mr. Briggs subdivided the rancho and sold it for small farms. In this year there were upon this rancho the following settlers:—J. L. Crane, who had come to the site of Saticoy in 1861; Dr. Millhouse, in the Wheeler Cañon; Colonel Wade Hampton, in the Cañada Aliso; Messrs. Montgomery, Horatio Stone, Charles Millard, Edward Wright, Wm. Garden, Andrew J. Nutt, A. Gray, E. S. Woolley, Wm. McCormick and George M. Richardson.

During the winter of 1871-'72, which was a very severe one, much of the stock perished, and the prosperity of the settlement received a severe check. At this time the present site of

SANTA PAULA

was a wilderness, the only signs of human habitation being one or two old adobe houses, an ancient barn, and the traces of an irrigating ditch—relics of a mission once established there. In 1872 Messrs. Blanchard and Bradley laid out some town lots, and built a flouring-mill on the Santa Paula Creek, one-half mile above the town, whose site is on the creek, about one mile above the Santa Clara River, in the upper part of the rancho. Some half-dozen lots were sold, but a small saloon was the only building erected up to the summer of 1875. In June, of that year, the valley was more extensively laid out. In December there was a snow-storm almost unprecedented in that section.

The drouth of 1877-'78 gave a severe check to the growth of this place. In the fall of 1878 there was sufficient prosperity to support a Baptist Church, having a church building and a membership of thirteen, October of that year witnessing the second anniversary of the congregation's existence. By 1879 there was a membership of 250.

In 1880-'81 many of the farmers turned their attention to the raising of pork, which staple was then dear, while the wheat and barley crops brought very low rates. In 1880 no less than $40,000 were realized from the sale of hogs raised in the vicinity of Santa Paula, and twice that sum in 1881. The hottest weather ever felt in the town was during September of that year, when the mercury rose to 100° in the shade for several days in succession, once rising to 108°.

Naturally the growth of Santa Paula was slow, as long as the only means of travel was by staging. But since the extension of the line of the Southern Pacific to Santa Barbara, the increase has been steady.

The following account of Santa Paula, her resources and surroundings, was written by Mr. C. J. McDivitt, editor of the Santa Paula *Chronicle:*

Santa Paula is situated on the Southern Pacific Railroad, between Santa Barbara on the west and Los Angeles on the east, and on what will be the main through line of that road up the coast from Los Angeles, and the east from San Francisco. It is in the Santa Clara Valley, sixteen miles east from Ventura and the ocean, and nineteen miles from Camilos, the last station eastward in Ventura County, on the road to Los Angeles, and distant from that city sixty-five miles. It is located at the mouth of the Santa Paula Cañon, near where Santa Paula Creek forms a junction with the Santa Clara River, and near the center of the county.

There are four passenger trains daily, two each way; giving the people of the valley four daily mails and easy communication either north or south. The town is located in the midst of a fine agricultural region. The land on every side is capable of the highest production of all the cereals and almost all the fruits and nuts peculiar to this coast; and all this, with the single exception of oranges and lemons, without irrigation. The town contains more than 1,000 inhabitants, with a voting population of 400. (The last census showed 1,200.)

Santa Paula is not incorporated, but her public-spirited citizens have secured many advantages to be imitated profitably by towns which boast of incorporation. Private enterprise has placed on a large portion of the main street cement sidewalks twelve feet wide, and on many of the other streets good walks, now of asphaltum and now of boarding. "The Avenue" is a drive of at least a mile long, smooth and well-kept, with its trees on either side all its length forming an arch-like perspective, and this is kept sprinkled through its full length. The other streets of the town also are well sprinkled.

Santa Paula is the headquarters of the petroleum oil industry of Southern California. Here are located the Hardison & Stewart Oil Company, the Mission Transfer Company, the Sespe Oil Company, the Torrey Cañon Oil Company and several parties who are operating in a private way and disposing of their product to these companies. Here the Mission Transfer Company has erected a refinery with a capacity of 10,000 barrels of crude oil per month, which they manufacture into lubricating oils of fine quality for use on all sorts of machinery, from the locomotive to the spindle. The different brands are known to the trade under the names of engine oil, extra engine oil, car-box oil, journal and gear oil, heavy machine oil, light machine oil, valve oil, wool oil, and black lubricating oil. They also manufacture several grades of naphtha; several grades of asphaltum; distillates for enriching illuminating gas, and several other products. The refinery works cover about four acres of ground, and give employment to a number of skilled workmen. Inside the inclosure there is a tankage capacity of 40,000 barrels, and a perfect network of pipes running in every direction connecting the tanks and works. The erection of the refinery was begun in the fall of 1887, and the first manufactured product was turned out in March, 1888.

The Mission Transfer Company handles the entire product of oil from all the companies, and owns and uses more than 100 miles of pipe line in Ventura County, having a pipe line connecting every well with the storage tanks at Santa Paula. This company also has a pipe line from Santa Paula to Hueneme, and another to Ventura, on the ocean, and so loads vessels at either port direct from their own tanks. There is tankage capacity of 100,000 barrels, of forty-two gallons each, all in this county, except one large tank at San Francisco. In addition, this company owns fifty four tank cars with a capacity of 5,500 gallons each.

The companies are now (September, 1889) pumping about fifty wells. The daily product is near 700 barrels, with a gradual increase, and excellent prospects for the future, as they are all the time developing new territory, have recently struck some good wells, and are now at work on several that give promise of being good ones. The oil interests give employment to 125 men, and pay out in wages not far from $10,000 monthly.

The Mission Transfer Company owned the steamer W. L. Hardison, built by themselves expressly to carry the product of the wells up and down the coast to a market, but it was recently burned at the wharf while loading at Ventura. The company is now considering plans to replace it with a vessel of steel.

The Hardison & Stewart Oil Company has also erected at Santa Paula large boiler works and machine shops where all work connected with the oil business is done. New boilers are built and repairs made to engines, boilers and all kinds of machinery used in this or neighboring counties. The plant is a valuable one, the company having recently put in a new ten-horse-power Charter gas-engine, which uses no boiler, makes the gas to feed it while running, and requires little or no attention. Work is turned out here which is not obtainable elsewhere in Southern California.

One of the largest fruit-driers in the State is located here. This was built in 1888 by an organized company, composed of farmers and fruit-growers, at a cost of $14,000. The same year the company handled more than 500 tons of apricots. When running at its full capacity of twenty-five tons per day, the drier requires 150 hands to operate it. Both hot air and steam are used for drying. In 1889 over ninety per cent. of the fruit dried was of the first quality, bringing the highest price in the market.

The "Santa Paula Water Works" supplies the town with good, pure mountain water, taken from the Santa Paula Creek several miles up the cañon. The reservoir, with a capacity of about 5,000,000,000 gallons, is located 200 feet above Main street, giving a pressure of ninety-five pounds to the square inch. There is a magnificent system of mains and pipes running all over the town, and a water supply fully adequate to the needs of a city of 50,000 inhabitants. This system is owned by W. H. Bradley.

In the Sespe Cañon, a few miles east of Santa Paula, are the quarries of the Sespe Brown Stone Company. This stone is used in some of the finest buildings in the State, among others the elegant new building of the San Francisco *Chronicle*. The quarries are extensive, there being practically no limit to the supply. It is of a rich brown color, and in color and texture closely resembles the noted brown stone of Nova Scotia. It has been tried by all tests known to science, and is pronounced the finest quality found. When subjected to a white heat and dropped into water, it turns to granite instead of crumbling as other stones have done in large fires.

While the material interests of the town are being developed and business projects rapidly pushed forward, the intellectual, moral and religious advantages have not been neglected. There are four church organizations and two buildings, Presbyterian and and Methodist. The Presbyterian is the finest in the county, having been erected in 1888 at a cost of $14,000. The pastor is Mr. Logan. The Methodist Church, dating from 1882, is worth some $5,000. Its pastor is Mr. Ashley. The Baptist Congregation worships in the Methodist Church and the Universalists in Cleveland hall. Mr. Andrews ministers to the Universalists. There is no Baptist pastor at present. The Roman Catholics are about to build a church; the officiating priest lives at New Jerusalem. There are four well attended Sunday-schools at Santa Paula.

The town has a graded school of four departments, each with a large attendance—about 200. The public school building is a fine structure standing in the center of a large enclosed square of ground. This school contains a well-selected library. Here also is located Santa Paula Academy, opened September 16, 1889, for the second term of school. This is an elegant and commodious building, costing, with the five acres of ground upon which it stands, $17,000, all of which was contributed by the people in and around Santa Paula. While its articles of incorporation provide that a majority of its directors shall be of the Congregationalist persuasion, this school is non-sectarian in character.

The land around Santa Paula is well adapted to the growth of all kinds of deciduous fruits, there being no less than 800 acres of bearing walnuts, almonds, pears, peaches, prunes, figs, grapes and many varieties of other fruits, together with all the small fruits in abundance. These trees make wonderful growth in the rich soil and warm temperature of this valley. There are in the grounds of W. L. Hardison mulberry trees of five years' growth, which measure thirty-two inches in circumference, and thirty feet in height, with a twenty-five-foot spread to the limbs, and from which 300 pounds of choice fruit were gathered in one year. Apricot trees on the same place, of the same age, are twenty-nine inches in circumference, twenty-five feet high, and with a twenty-foot spread of limbs. The apricots have been cut back each year, the mulberries but once, and neither have had any irrigation. Both varieties have been bearing fruit for three years. These are by no means exceptional cases. The orchard of Mr. Nathan W. Blanchard, one of the best and most profitable in the State, is located here. In 1889 he sold over $15,000 worth of fruits. He has 100 acres of seedling oranges and Lisbon and Eureka lemons, which always yield the highest market prices. The lemons are picked during every month of the year. Mr. Blanchard has planted many more oranges lately. This is one of the largest orchards in the State, though it is not yet all in bearing.

On Mr. F. J. Beckwith's place, he has 100 acres sown to Lima beans, which last season yielded 2,275 pounds to the acre. Another 100 acres, planted to corn, yielded ninety bushels to the acre. These staples are not the exclusive products; all these farms have a comprehensive variety of growth, including hay, grain, fruits and walnuts. Almost within the city limits, Mr. Warhan Easley has a tract of forty acres, from which, last season, he realized a net income of $3,000, as follows:—1,200 boxes pears, at fifty cents per box, $600; twenty-five tons apricots, at $20 per ton, $500; oranges, $100; walnuts, $200; peaches, $100; prunes, $100; apples, $200; pumpkins, $100; hay, thirty tons, at $10 per ton, $300; potatoes, 500 sacks, at $1.50 per sack, $750; garden truck, $150; total, $3,100. From this was paid $100 for harvesting, all the rest of the work being done by the owner. Besides all this, there were raised several tons of grapes, which were made into wine.

From the famous orange grove of N. W. Blanchard, which began to pay running expenses only three years since, the shipments from the 100 acres last season amounted to twenty-eight car-loads, the sales footing up to nearly $15,000. More profitable than his oranges is Mr. Blanchard's fifteen-acre tract set to lemons, from which he harvested last season about 3,000 boxes, at an average price of $4 per box.

Mr. G. G. Sewell, Mr. C. H. McKevett, Mr. H. Crumrine, and Mr. J. R. D. Say are all equally successful growers of oranges, although not so extensively. This whole section is, thus far, entirely free from scale, or other insect pests. In the grounds of Mr. Hardison are to be found Washington Navel orange trees which have yielded two boxes of fruit to the tree five years from planting, and in the grounds of Mr. McKevett and Mr. G. G. Sewell are trees which bore some fruit the second year from planting.

Mr. Crumrine has six acres of seedling oranges from which he received $2,600 last season. This, it should be remembered, on ground that was, as late as 1886, considered poor for citrus fruits.

Prunes are becoming an important feature of orchards here, and walnuts also are quite extensively planted. There are two nurseries in Santa Paula, one of which has a large general stock.

In the growth, breeding, and improvement of horses and the raising of fine cattle, this neighborhood shows commendable enterprise. There are a number of fine herds of cattle and some choice short-horns in this vicinity, the foot-hills being particularly adapted for pasture lands. There is one choice herd of Holstein cattle here hard to beat anywhere. The gentleman imported twenty-one head of cows four years ago, and has sold $11,000 worth from their increase, besides keeping good the original number.

The owners and breeders of fine stock in and around Santa Paula have the laudable ambition to make Ventura County and the Santa Clara Valley still more famous for good horses; and to this end Messrs. F. E. Davis, J. K. Gries, W. L. Hardison, and C. H. McKevett have organized into an association, procured a track—the Santa Paula Driving Park—and put up training stables, at their own expense, with no other object in view than the improvement of the horses of the county. They own and keep at the track some very fine stallions, among them Black Pilot, half-brother of Stamboul, Richwood, a Richmond stallion, Eli, and others.

In the way of business enterprises Santa Paula has:—the First National Bank (successor to the Bank of Santa Paula), with a capital stock of $75,000.

The president is C. H. McKevett; vice-president, G. H. Bonebrake; cashier, J. R. Haugh; the Petrolia Hotel, which cost $15,000, opened about January 1, 1889; six general merchandise stores; one grocery; two cigar and news-stands; two hardware stores, of which one has a full line of oil supplies not to be found elsewhere in the State; the Ventura Lumber Company, which has seven yards in the county, unloading at Ventura the lumber received from the north, and carrying on a very heavy business; one planing-mill, conducted by the same company; one fruit-drier of twenty tons' daily capacity; two drug stores; one weekly newspaper, the *Chronicle;* two hotels; three restaurants; one shoe store and one cobbler shop; one men's furnishing shop; two milliners; two real estate offices; two practicing physicians; one dentist; one furniture store; two livery stables; one bakery; two butcher shops; three barbers; one harness shop, and two blacksmiths.

In common with other portions of Ventura County, Santa Paula enjoys a very even temperature from one season to another, with more, bright, clear, sunshiny days than is usual so near the coast. For the greater part of the year the breeze is landward, coming up the valley without interruption, cooling the air in summer and warming it in winter; and with no extremes of heat or cold, the town is a delightful place of residence, both for the health-seeker and the man of business.

SATICOY.

Saticoy is situated at the lower end of the old Santa Paula y Saticoy Rancho, on the Santa Clara River, about eight miles east of San Buenaventura, nine miles north of Hueneme Wharf, and eight miles southwest of Santa Paula. Here are the famous Saticoy Springs, with their many bloody traditions of the Indian tribes, by whom the springs were discovered; the word Saticoy is said to mean in the dialect of the Indians who settled here the same as the word "Eureka." Until the last twenty years, the chieftainess Pomposa, and a number of the tribe, were still living at these springs, and the early settlers tell how, even after their advent, here were wont to gather annually the remnants of the various tribes of Southern California.

It is declared that at each of these gatherings a human sacrifice was made, one of those assembled being put to death by poisoning. To this effect, there were made as many cakes as there were guests at the feast, one of the cakes containing the fatal potion. None knew which cake held the poison, so that the sacrifice was entirely at hazard.

In November, 1861, J. L. Crane settled upon the site of the village, and others came in at about the same time. These early settlers were men of sterling qualities, who made the most of their surroundings. A school was opened as early as 1868. In this year came hither Mr. W. de F. Richards, another of the pioneer settlers.

While quite a thick settlement was in existence, and a postoffice had been for some years established, the building up of the town proper dates mainly from the advent of the railway. The town with its adjacent farms covers about eight miles square of territory, within which extent are some of the most prolific farms and fruit orchards of Southern California. Being well watered, and having soil of exceptional strength and fertility, this famous valley produces crops of extreme richness and value. Corn, beans, flax-seed, canary seed, hops, castor beans, sugar beets, hay, etc., are among the fruits of the soil, and the product is not infrequently 2,000 to 3,000 pounds of beans, or 2,000 to 6,000 pounds of corn, per acre. From the farm of M. E. Isham, who has 80 acres in fruit—consisting of 500 walnut, 600 apple, 3,000 apricot, 100 lemon, 300 lime, 500 peach, and 100 pear trees—were produced last season, 10,000 cans of fruit, and about 3,000 glasses of jelly, which respectively brought $2.25 and $1.50 per dozen in Ventura, without casing. This, besides a great deal of green fruit sold, and about 100 barrels of cider vinegar. On the 180-acre farm of James Evans, another old settler, were raised in 1878 as much as 4,400 pounds of shelled corn to the acre, this average being reached again in 1884.

In 1882 Mr. Evans raised 2,200 pounds of flaxseed to the acre. His barley hay in 1889 gave three tons to the acre. These are by no means exceptional holdings. As indexing the products of this district, a few statistics gathered from the shipping clerk at the Southern Mill and Warehouse Company will be interesting: barley, 2,676,123 pounds; Lima beans, 2,109,090; small beans, 756,243; corn, 308,750; walnuts, 10,000; honey, 74,463; apricots, 145,726; miscellaneous, 300,000. Total shipments, actual weight, 6,380,395 pounds.

In addition to above there were in October, 1889, in warehouse, of barley, 2,089,090 pounds; wheat, 453,010; honey, 54,853; small beans, 136,839; making a grand total of 9,114,187 pounds of farm products, which at a low estimate must have distributed not far from $200,000 among the farmers of this prosperous community during the past year.

Saticoy contains over fifty houses, a beautiful new church building, a $15,000 schoolhouse, three hotels, one of which cost $10,000, two dry-goods stores, three grocery stores, one drug store, a town hall, a warehouse 50 x 300 feet, etc. Good water is obtainable here in wells ten to seventy feet deep.

Eastward, and across the river from the lower portion of the Santa Paula y Saticoy, is the Rancho Santa Clara del Norte, which comprises 13,988,91 acres, granted to Juan Sanchez, May 6, 1837, and to him confirmed. This rancho lies six miles east of the county seat, and borders three miles of the Santa Clara River. It is watered by the Santa Clara ditch, and by good artesian wells. Three-fourths of this land is tillable, the grazing land supports 8,000 head of sheep.

One vineyard on this rancho, about twenty years old, produces 10,000 gallons of excellent wine annually, selling at 50 cents per gallon. In one orchard of 500 trees, there are representatives of every variety of fruit grown in this county. Large quantities of flax are grown here.

NEW JERUSALEM,

situated near the northern boundary of La Colonia Rancho, is some two miles from Montalvo, and half way between Ventura and Hueneme. Its chief attraction is the magnificent surrounding country. The location of the town is favorable, and it will doubtless become a good town with transportation facilities and the dividing-up of the Colonia and Santa Clara del Norte ranchos, with the attendant settling of more people. In the vicinity of this town are some very fine farms, which yield prolifically. This town has two large, well-filled general merchandise stores, a church and various other business institutions.

MONTALVO.

Montalvo is a station five miles east of Ventura, on the Southern Pacific Railroad. It is the nearest railroad station for New Jerusalem and for Hueneme, being about two miles from the former and seven from the latter. At this place is one of the Southern Mill and Warehouse Company's large warehouses. Montalvo, although not having the appearance of much of a place, is, nevertheless, quite an important little one, being situated, as it is, on the railroad, at a point where all the travel from the Simí, Las Posas and the southern portion of the county crosses to Ventura. The town was laid out about two years ago. Water was piped to all parts of the tract, being first pumped from a well to a large reservoir on a hill back of the town. Two store buildings have been erected, something like a dozen houses, and one of the finest school-houses in the county, costing $6,000.

The development of Montalvo has been somewhat retarded by the ownership by one man, a Santa Barbara capitalist, of 2,300 acres of land, lying upon the road to Montalvo and the ocean. This tract, if subdivided, would make beautiful home lots, and so induce immigration. This is a great region for beans and fruit.

Mr. Barnett has a place of only thirty acres, from which he reaps a large harvest of fruits, mostly apricots. When the trees were nine years old the twenty-five acres of apricots produced fifty tons of fruit. The owner of this valuable property has recently erected a fruit dryer with one of Thomas Pilkington's furnaces.

The celebrated Alhambra Grove of sixty-six acres is owned by Judge S. R. Thorpe from Louisana. This is one of the first apricot orchards in the county and produces as rich fruit as any seen. In 1889 the crop amounted to two tons of green fruit to the acre; in 1888 it was four tons. This place is equipped with all necessary appliances for carrying on an extensive business. It is an interesting sight to see the fruit as it is prepared and cured in the improved evaporator.

A field of 250 acres of beans is worked by W. S. Sewell, a native of Iowa. He says his beans average 1,400 pounds to the acre and his corn seventy-five bushels.

In this same neighborhood Charles G. Finney, Esq., a retired lawyer from New York, has an interesting place of 150 acres covered with fruit of all kinds. He has 500 bearing pear trees. The fruit he sells dry in cans and green; he has also thirty acres in walnuts in profitable bearing, also 1,000 White Symrna figs, which, not proving what he expected, he feeds to hogs, and finds them exceedingly profitable for this purpose. He says that the same amount of ground in corn will not make one-fifth the pork these figs will. Why not raise figs to feed hogs on? He has 5,000 apricots, 120 prunes and other fruits, which do well. When Mr. Finney came here, fifteen years ago, there was but little, if any, orchards between his place and Santa Paula. Briggs of Marysville had been here before him and tried to raise fruit and failed, and when Mr. Finney started in, everybody said he would fail, but he kept steadily on and succeeded, as his place most emphatically proves.

THE MORE MURDER.

The murder of Thomas Wallace More was a *cause celebré*, not only in Ventura County, but also throughout the State, and it was undoubtedly the most notable criminal case in the annals of the county. The victim was one of four brothers, who had made extensive purchases of the old landed estates of the Spanish-American families, acquiring in this manner the Santa Rosa Island, the Patera, a portion of the Hill estate, the Santa Paula y Saticoy, the Lompoc and Purisima Vieja, and the Sespe. They at one time owned a tract thirty-two miles long on the Santa Clara River. The murder in question was the result of land difficulties over the Sespe possessions.

In November, 1829, Don Carlos Carrillo received from the Mexican government a grant of the Sespe tract, the extent of which is not known, some arguments indicating that it comprised only 8,880 acres, or two leagues, while other accounts are to the effect that there were six leagues granted, this last being the territory upon which Carrillo was installed by the local government. In 1884 T. Wallace More purchased Carrillo's grant, supposing that he was buying six leagues, as he paid full value for that quantity, and he prosecuted the title to the land, using the name of Carrillo as one of the parties in interest. The Land Commissioners, too, on April 18, 1853, had confirmed the grant title to "six leagues and no more."

The United States, as the adverse party, appealed the case to the United States District Court for the Southern District of California. When the plat (diseño) was brought into court, it for the first time was remarked that the numbers of the grant had been manipulated, and it was therefore asserted that, by the erasure of the figures, six had been substitued for two, thus fraudulently increasing the grant. The impression of the old settlers in the section was that the original grant had been made for six leagues. The smaller quantity, however, was that confirmed to More by the court, a patent being issued March 14, 1872. In 1875 More endeavored to purchase the other four leagues, under sections 7 and 8, codes of 1866. The settlers on the land alleged that the claim had been settled in full; that they had for years been settled upon the land, and had pre-emption claims antedating this law; and they appealed to the law of March 3, 1861, section 13, which declares that all lands, the claims to which have been finally rejected by the Commissioners in manner herein provided, or which shall finally be declared invalid by the District or Supreme Court, and of all lands, the claims to which have not been presented by said Commissioners within two years after the date of this act, shall be deemed, held and considered as part of the domain of the United States. Mr. More's attorney had made application for permission to purchase, to the Register of the Land Office; and, on that officer refusing the permission, the petition was lodged with the Commissioners at Washton, where it was pending at the time of the murder.

During several years preceding the murder, More often had difficulties with the settlers who, to the number of sixty, had established themselves upon the land he claimed. Among them was one Joseph Bartlett, and him More had dispossessed by the sheriff, while the matter was in dispute, his squatter's cabin being torn down and then burned. The place was afterward reoccupied, and the tenant then was poisoned, accidentally or otherwise. Of this affair an account was published in the San Francisco *Bulletin*, couched in such terms that More sued the *Bulletin* Company for $100,000 damage for libel. The case was tried in Santa Barbara, where the popular animus was very strong against More at that time, so that, although the jury found a verdict for him, they gave him only nominal damages, fixed at $150, thus practically sustaining the *Bulletin*, although the evidence showed charge of poisoning to be unfounded, and the casualty owing to the universal free use in the district of poison for coyotes, squirrels and other vermin.

During the years which followed, More was endeavoring to perfect his title to the land, whilst the settlers, remaining in possession, had formed themselves into a league for mutual defense and assistance. It is commonly asserted, although it has been disputed, that the death of More had been decreed by this league, as a protectionary measure. The fact remains that he was commanded to abandon his proceedings to secure the land, in letters of incendiary and menacing character.

During the unusually dry winter of 1876–'77, More, while in company with his son-in-law, C. A. Storke, engaged in inspecting the cutting of a ditch to convey water upon his land, was attacked by F. A. Sprague, armed first with a shot-gun and then with a pistol, with which he twice attempted to shoot More, being prevented by Storke and More, who turned the shots into the air. For this assault Sprague was arrested, but was discharged by the magistrate. The attack was not made upon Sprague's land, the ditch in question tapped the Sespe River below Sprague's land, and the tract he held by More fourteen years before Sprague settled upon and claimed it.

Such was the condition of affairs on the night of March 23–24, 1877, when More slept at one of his rancho houses, where there were, besides himself, a hired hand named Ferguson, a Mexican named Olivas, and Jim Tot, a Chinese cook. At about 12:30 the barn, distant from the house 200 feet, was fired, and More, Ferguson and Olivas, being aroused by the Chinese cook, rushed forth, to endeavor to save the contents of the barn, consisting of twelve work horses, their harness, about 2,000 sacks of wheat, some barley, and several tons of hay. These men were joined by one Ramirez, an employé who had slept outside that night, and all were engaged in trying to save the property, when More, carrying out a load of harness, was fired upon by two masked men, guarding the gate of the corral, or barnyard, who shot him in the thigh near the groin; at this, the employés of More scattered toward shelter, and More also ran toward cover, but fell, and was overtaken by three masked men, who then riddled his body and head with bullets, of which three entered his head, and several his body. A number of these shots, after he had fallen, and after he had entreated his assailant not to kill him, were fired at such short range that his features were almost obliterated by powder and smoke. After this dastardly deed, the murderers turned at the cry of their leader, "Come on, boys!" and deliberately left the scene.

This murder excited the greatest horror throughout the State. While the sympathies of the people were with the settlers, the cowardly and brutal nature of the murder inspired great abhorrence.

The coroner's jury found that "deceased came to his death on the morning of March 24, 1877, by gunshot wounds inflicted by divers persons upon the head and body of said deceased, by parties unknown to the jury; and that the jury further find and declare the said crime to be a case of wilful murder."

Shortly after the murder, a meeting of the settlers upon the Sespe was held at the house of F. A. Sprague, being convened on the evening of March 28, to give expression to public sentiment in regard to the lately committed crime of murder and arson. At this meeting, N. H. Hickerson being chairman and F. A. Sprague secretary, resolutions were passed condemning the action in question, and tendering sympathy and offers of assistance and co-operation in detecting and bringing to justice the offenders.

Early in 1878, one Austin Brown, one of the Sespe settlers, had some dispute with J. T. Curlee, in consequence of which Brown sought an interview with the administrator of More's estate, and made a statement that F. A. Sprague and J. S. Churchill had conspired to kill More, giving details as to parties involved, time set, etc., this statement being given in confidence, as not to be divulged to the public until Brown could remove from the settlement to a safe place, as he feared for his life, having been threatened by More's murderers, in event of his disclosing the secret. In consequence of this movement, Brown sold his place, and removed to the county-seat, where he was considered safe. These and other newly-developed circumstances led to the arrest of F. A. Sprague, J. S. Churchill, J. T. Curlee, Jesse M. Jones, Ivory D. Lord, Charles McCart, H. Cook and J. A. Swanson, on a warrant dated March 28, 1878. These parties were brought before R. C. Carlton, examining magistrate, April 1.

About this time, it was learned that new evidence had been obtained. N. H. Hickerson, being ill and in expectation of death, and being informed of Brown's statement and the arrest of the assassins, came forward to make a statement of a secret weighing upon his soul, to the effect that he had been the recipient of Sprague's confession of his planning and execution of the murder of T. Wallace More.

As yet the stories of Hickerson and Brown had not been made public. The detectives and prosecutors who had the matter in hand brought about an interview with Jesse M. Jones, one of the parties implicated. This was a young man, only twenty-three years old, and it was considered that he was a tool rather than an active agent in the affair, and that, under assurance of protection and ultimate pardon, he might be induced to turn State's evidence. Although Jones had no knowledge of the revelations of Hickerson and Brown, with whom he therefore could not have been in collusion, he told a story of the murder, substantially the same as that related by Hickerson, save that Jones declared that W. Hunt was present at the murder, but not Jule Swanson.

On the preliminary examination, H. Cook and J. A. Swanson were discharged, and during the hearing, Charles McCart and W. H. Hunt were arrested as accomplices in the murder. In the following June, the grand jury was organized, and it returned a true bill against F. A. Sprague, John Curlee, Jesse M. Jones, J. S. Churchill, Charles McCart, W. H. Hunt, and I. D. Lord. The lawyers for the prosecution were: J. G. Howard and Frank Ganahl, of Los Angeles, L. C. Granger (acting district attorney), W. T.

Williams, B. F. Williams, and N. Blackstock of Ventura. The counsel for the defense were: J. D. Fay, Creed Haymond, and W. Allen, from abroad; and J. D. Hines, J. M. Brooks and N. C. Bledsoe, local lawyers. Eugene Fawcett presided over the court. The prisoners demanded separate trials, thus entailing heavy unnecessary expense upon the county. Hickerson died prior to the trial, but his affidavit was introduced as evidence. The testimony was complete, not a link being wanting, and it appeared that even the discrepancies of testimony as to the different parties engaged, arose from the fact that the disguises were donned before they came together, so that only two or three knew all the persons present. In the case of Sprague, the jury rendered a verdict of murder in the first degree. Curlee was next tried, and found guilty, with punishment fixed at imprisonment for life. The jury in Lord's case disagreed. These three trials had exhausted the material for a jury. On August 5, 1878, the death sentence upon Sprague was pronounced by Judge Fawcett. The court now adjourned for the term, as the three trials had extended the July session into near the middle of August. Jesse M. Jones, the State's witness, had been discharged from the indictment for more than a month, being maintained by the county as an indigent witness in a criminal case. He was under pressure of poverty, and denied access to his wife, by her father, on account of his betrayal of his confederates. At this juncture, full of discomfort for the present, and of dread of a forbidding future, he was approached by emissaries of counsel for the defense, conducted to the presence of those attorneys, and there seduced and suborned into retracting his former statements, and made affidavit that his former testimony was given under compulsion and fears for his own safety. Upon this recantation the other accused were dismissed, it being impossible to convict them without Jones' testimony, and even great efforts were made to have the sentence against Sprague quashed. This not being done, the death sentence was commuted to imprisonment for life. Jones, having scoffed at and defied the power of the law, was absolutely beyond its vengeance, owing to the provisions of the penal code making absolute and unconditional the discharge of an accomplice, that he may become a witness for the people; and the improved and comfortable financial conditions with which he was thereafter surrounded, proved what inducements had secured his perjury. Sprague spent ten years in the penitentiary, was then pardoned out by Governor Stoneman, and now lives in Ventura County. Curlee, having been granted by the Supreme Court a new trial, was dismissed like the others, after Jones' defection, and now lives in San Diego County, as does Hunt. Churchill, after acquittal, went to Oregon, where he probably died, being consumptive. Jones lives in San Bernardino County, and scattered are the rest whose dastardly deed has left a black blot upon the fair fame of Ventura County. While the settlers believed that they were on Government land, and resolved to defend their rights thereto, inspired by the God-given love of home, there is no doubt that More also believed that he was right, being firm in the conviction that he had bought six leagues in his Sespe purchase. As to the rights of possession, the present writer does not assume to judge, but only to condemn, as ever, the cowardice and unfairness of the means employed against one man by many. The commission gave the disputed land to More's heirs, the Secretary of the Interior, Carl Schurz, reversed this decision; and although two succeeding commissions have pronounced in favor of the heirs the land is held by the settlers.

RANCHO SESPE.

The Sespe Rancho adjoins the Santa Paula y Saticoy on the northeast, extending eight miles up the Santa Clara, and embracing most of the arable land in the valley on both sides of the river within those limits— an extent of two leagues, or some 8,880.81 acres. This land encloses but does not include a tract of Government land. The title to the rancho is by United States patent.

The story of this rancho is remarkable, involving, in the struggles made for its possession, episodes of trespass, misdemeanor, fraud, arson, attempted homicide and murder.

The rancho was used many years mainly for pasturage for stock, although it possessed such remarkable advantages of soil, water and climate as to render it an uncommonly desirable territory for the production of vegetables, cereals, grapes, citrus and most varieties of deciduous fruits. The upper portion of this rancho contains the noted oil wells. The elevation of this tract is some 2,000 feet above sea level.

Among the earliest settlers here were living, in 1861, the More brothers, W. H. Norway and Captain William Morris. Their nearest American neighbors, for at least a part of the year, were at San Buenaventura. The first crop of grain was sowed in the winter of 1860-61, the More brothers putting in about 200 acres of wheat. It was harvested by W. S. Chaffee and W. H. Norway, Alexander Cameron being the contractor. The grain was cut with a reaper and threshed out by horses.

In 1876 this rancho, then owned by T. Wallace More, was assessed at $9 per acre, whereupon he entered suit to have a portion of the taxes refunded. It was maintained that the land could be sold for twice that sum within twenty-four hours.

In March, 1877, took place the murder of T. Wallace More, the owner of the rancho, a full account of this crime being given elsewhere.

This rancho is becoming settled rapidly, many people being attracted thither by the rare advantages of soil and climate. While there are no large towns on this territory, not a few villages and centers of population are found here.

La Cienega (Spanish for a marsh) is the name of a postoffice which was established in 1875, up the valley some fourteen miles from Santa Paula, and twenty-one miles from Newhall. Near La Cienega is the "Buckhorn Ranch," Mr. B. F. Warring's famous place, whose owner settled here in 1869, upon 160 acres, to which, after ten years' litigation, he obtained a United States patent. Lying on the old stage road, and midway between Los Angeles and Santa Barbara, this in time came to be a regular eating-place and relay stage station, widely and favorably known to the pilgrim guild. It took its name from the great antlers hung over the gate, trophies from many a proud buck brought down by the gun of the ranchero. This is a sheltered spot, free from frosts, well-watered and blessed with a rich soil. In the neighborhood are many farms where grow plentifully grain, vegetables and fruits.

FILLMORE.

This is a small town, started by the Sespe Land and Water Company, just after the advent of the railway. It lies in a charming situation, and in the midst of a fruitful country, full of profitable farms. About 200 people take their mail from this office. The settlement nucleus has a Presbyterian church, a school-house, two hotels, several stores, a lumber-yard, a blacksmith-shop, etc. Near this was started at about the same time another little town called Sespe, but a church is about the only claim to importance to be seen here.

BARDSDALE.

In January, 1887, R. G. Surdam, one of the founders of Nordhoff, bought of Thos. R. Bard, of Hueneme, 1,500 acres of the old Sespe grant, and soon thereafter founded the now thriving little town of Bardsdale. It is in a beautiful valley, appropriately termed a "dale," the ground lying between mountains, and sloping gently from the range to the river. Bardsdale is a little south of Fillmore, on the Southern Pacific Railway, fifty-six miles from Los Angeles. It is the only town in the Santa Clara Valley south of the Santa Clara river. The land here is of a superior quality of soil, and its sheltered position insures a delightful climate. There is an abundant supply of water for domestic and irrigation purposes, brought from the Santa Clara River, through strong wooden flumes, constructed at a cost of some $8,000. Thus irrigation can be applied to hundreds of acres, planted to barley, potatoes, etc., there being at least ten miles of these flumes. As an exponent of the productiveness of the soil, it may be said that potatoes yield easily 75 to 150 sacks per acre, which rarely sell for less than 75 cents to $1.25 per sack. On one farm of about 100 acres, the owners, beginning with a crop of sixty bushels of corn per acre, have every year increased the yield until it has reached an average yield of ninety bushels per acre; in other words, there have harvested from this field during the last twelve years not far from 90,000 bushels of corn, grown without irrigation or fertilizer.

AN EARTHLY PARADISE.

Three or four years ago Mr. David C. Cook, the Chicago publisher of Sunday-school literature, came into Ventura County and purchased that portion of the Temescal or Old Camulos Rancho which extends up the Piru Cañon. Since then he has added considerable to it, bringing it up to nearly 14,000 acres and calling it the Piru. This ranch is located on the Piru Creek, including the mouth of the stream and a small portion of the Santa Clara Valley. As most of the ranch was mountainous it was formerly thought to be only suitable for grazing purposes, but Mr. Cook has already demonstrated that it is valuable for something else. He has planted out and has growing 400 acres of oranges, 300 acres of apricots, 180 acres of figs, 200 acres English walnuts, 130 acres of olives, 80 acres of grapes, 30 acres of chestnuts, 20 acres of almonds, 10 acres of pomegranates and 10 acres of Japanese persimmons. He has in his nursery 150,000 citrus trees ready for planting this fall, and 3,500 fig trees.

He has laid out eight miles of avenues and has ten acres devoted to ornamental shrubs and trees. The latter embraces trees, shrubs and plants from about every northern and semi-tropical clime, and in great variety. All this has been done so noiselessly that not half the people of Ventura County are aware of its having been accomplished. A fine stream of water traverses the entire length of the rancho, and is entirely utilized for irrigating purposes, which is useful in starting citrus and other trees, and also is helpful when some kinds are fruiting. Mr. Cook's experiments only indicate the possibilities of this wonderful soil and climate.

As an illustration of what has already been said of this county's productive soil, and adaptability to fruit raising, one has only to make a trip to the little town of Piru City, which was laid out and dedicated in March, 1888. It is located on the Ventura division of the Southern Pacific Railroad, thirty miles southeast of San Buena Ventura at the junction of the Piru and Santa Clara rivers; contains about twenty buildings including Methodist Episcopal Church with a membership of fifteen; one general merchsandie store, meat market, paint-shop and depot. They also have telegraph, express and post offices, and their population is now about 100.

RANCHO CAMULOS.

On the line of the railway, forty-seven miles northwest of Los Angeles, and in the extreme eastern portion of Ventura County is that fertile 2,000-acre tract known as the Camulos. This was once a part of the great San Francisco Rancho, belonging to Los Angeles County. This portion of the original grant was established as placed in Ventura when the boundary lines were settled between this county and Santa Barbara. The San Francisco Rancho was granted in 1841 to Antonio del Valle, and upon his death passed to his son, Ygnacio del Valle, who held it intact until 1866, when he sold all but 1,500 acres to a Philadelphia company. When he acquired the property, in 1861, Ygnacio del Valle removed his family to reside on the Camulos, somewhat improved already. From that time improvements here have been constantly in progress, but the picturesque and romantic features of the rancho have been preserved. Don Ygnacio died in March, 1880, leaving a widow and five children. The present owners have added 500 acres to the original reservation, and the whole has been improved until it is now one of the most productive and profitable properties in Ventura County. This rancho is divided about equally into farming and grazing land. The pastures raise horses, horned cattle, sheep and hogs. All farming on the Camulos is carried on with irrigation, and the whole Santa Clara River could be diverted into the great ditches running across the rancho. Here are grown excellent crops of wheat, in quality very superior, also bountiful crops of barley, rye, oats, corn, potatoes, sweet potatoes, pumpkins, melons, and all kinds of vegetables, harvested from the same land year after year with no indication of exhausting the soil.

The vineyard here is of 50,000 vines, which for many years have yielded 10,000 to 20,000 gallons of wine per year. From an orange grove of 2,000 trees, 1,200 boxes of fruit were shipped last season. The returns are handsome from 500 walnut trees, as also from the oil and pickled olives from a fine grove of 1,000 olive trees. Almost every kind of fruit grown in the United States is raised here.

This rancho was the scene of Mrs. Helen Hunt Jackson's novel of "Ramona," and the del Valle family have suffered not a little from the inconvenient notoriety thus given their property, and the consequent invasion of inquisitive and often intrusive and unmannerly visitors to the site. In the immediate vicinity of this rancho there is a large settlement of Spanish-Californian farmers, who employ the most improved implements and methods, and raise good crops of corn, beans and barley. The next great estate is the

RANCHO SAN FRANCISCO,

containing about 11,500 acres of grazing, and 3,000 acres of tillable land, which is divided into nearly equal portions by the Santa Clara River, and of which about 13,000 acres belong in Ventura, and the rest in Los Angeles county. This rancho was granted January 22, 1839, to Antonio del Valle, and confirmed to Jacoba Feliz and others, then containing only some 10,000 acres. It now belongs mostly to the estate of H. M. Newhall, the well-known auctioneer of San Francisco.

Save at Newhall, in Los Angeles County, few houses appear on this rancho, whose rough mountains and coarse, wild sage-brush and weeds appear like worthless waste land. Yet these very brush-lands are admirable bee pastures. Here, too, are oil interests not yet developed.

THE WESTERN PORTION OF VENTURA.

The country drained by the San Buenaventura River is mostly comprised within the limits of the following ranchos:—The Cañada San Miguelito and a part of the ex-Mission, both bordering on the ocean; the Cañada Larga or Cañada Verde, and the Ojai on the left bank, and the Santa Ana on the right bank.

The vast domain of the ex-Mission Rancho was granted as six leagues to José Arnaz, by Governor Pio Pico, June 8, 1846. Arnaz sold it to M. A. R. Poli in 1850. The claim was confirmed May 15, 1855, by the Land Commissioner, and finally, on April 1, 1861, by the United States District Court. In August, 1874, a patent was issued to the grantees for 48,822.91 acres. Poli sold the property to the San Buenaventura Manufacturing and Mining Company. He afterward died insolvent. This rancho derives its name from the fact that a division was made of the lands held in the name of the old Mission, the church retaining the old orchard and $36\frac{27}{100}$ acres contiguous; all lands outside these are called ex-Mission lands. At the sale of lands for delinquent taxes, February 16, 1874, the ex-Mission lands were offered for sale without a buyer, the taxes amounting to $3,163, drawing interest at two per cent. per month. This region is one of almost continuous settlements, with easy outlets. The soil is exceedingly rich to the very crests of the hills, and the climate is unsurpassed. The lands are agricultural and grazing. This territory is luxuriantly covered with wild oats, wild burr-clover, and alfilaria. A short distance back from the sea are forests of oaks, not readily seen save from close at hand. The bee pasturage is rich and extensive. The oil belt underlies a portion of this rancho.

THE RANCHO CANADA SAN MIGEUELITO.

This is next northwest of the ex-Mission Rancho. It has about three miles of coast line. This grant of 8,877.04 acres was confirmed to J. F. Rodriguez and others. This rancho consists almost wholly of rich pasture lands, raising great numbers of sheep. Very little timber is found here. The ocean road from San Buenaventura to Santa Barbara passes along the beach here. On Government land close by this rancho is a mine of so-called rock soap, being an infusorial earth resembling marl. It has been exported for polishing silverware, and for use by jewelers for burnishing purposes.

THE RANCHO CANADA LARGA Ó VERDE

was granted to J. Alvarado, who pushed the claim to confirmation. It contains about 2,220 acres, of which all is grazing land but about 1,000 acres, which are well cultivated, and upon which are found fine orchards and handsome homes.

THE OJAI RANCHO.

This is a wedge-shaped tract, which was granted to Fernando Tico, April 6, 1837, and afterward confirmed to him; acreage 17,792.70. In 1864 this rancho was bought by the California Petroleum Company. It was then a very wild place; a dozen or more grizzly bears were killed in Ojai Valley in one winter, and hundreds were thereabouts, as well as California lions, wild cats, etc.

Lion Cañon was so named from the great number of these panthers that it harbored. Dr. Chauncey Isbell lived here as early as 1866, and in October, 1868, Robert Ayers removed thither his family, the first American household in the valley, where a few Spanish-Californian families were living. In 1870 but two houses, one frame, one adobe, were in the Upper Ojai. In 1872 this rancho produced about 16,200 bushels of wheat, averaging thirty to forty bushels to the acre. A grange was organized here in 1874, and, in 1875 there were two school districts, the Ojai and the Nordhoff. The settlement of this section has been most rapid; within four years from the time when the inhabitants were less than half a dozen it had nearly 100, forming an enterprising and intelligent community. The fertility of this soil is hardly surpassed in California; here the wheat crop reaches its maximum as to quality and quantity. No irrigation is used for the small grain crops. Artesian water is obtained at Nordhoff, but it rises little above the surface. On the hills all the usual northern farm crops thrive remarkably well, as also many fruits, etc., considered semi-tropical in character.

THE OJAI VALLEY.

Almost in a straight line due north from San Buenaventura, from which town it is fourteen miles distant, lies the valley of the Ojai, shut in by high mountains, that determine the amphitheater-like shape whence it takes its name (a nest).

The mountains on the north side take a snowy covering in winter, in sharp contrast with the slopes of sulphur mountain, covered with live-oaks on the south side. Overlooking the others rises Mount Topotopa, between 5,000 and 6,000 feet high, also snow-mantled in the winter.

The drive to the lower Ojai follows an easy grade along a beautiful clear stream where trout sport and twinkle. The Upper Ojai, to the eastward of the main valley, is reached by a steep grade up an oak-covered ridge leading out of the lower valley. The soil here is rich and fertile, and plentifully watered, and its crops never fail.

Attention was first called to this valley by Charles Nordhoff, who visited it in 1872, and soon after, in his book on California, gave an enthusiastic description of it.

The lower valley is five miles long, and 800 feet above sea-level; the upper is smaller, with an elevation of about 1,200 feet. This basin is well-timbered, and its soil is very productive, giving the largest yield in the county of wheat per acre. It is also well adapted for raising the finest varieties of citrus fruits. Mr. Elwood Cooper, the famous olive-grower, says that the Ojai is also the best olive-growing district in California.

The scenery here is truly wonderful; the softy and balmy air, the park-like groves of oaks, their mistletoe, the vines and mosses, the bird voices within their leafage, the grandeur of the surrounding mountains, the cloud effects—all combine to give an indescribable charm to the Ojai Valley.

But there is another advantage; the delightful climate is of great benefit to sufferers from affections of the throat and lungs, and the famous Ojai Hot Springs in the Matilija Cañon are possessed of strong curative properties.

The Ojai Hot Sulphur Springs are beautifully situated in Waterfall Cañon, about five miles from Nordhoff and fifteen from Ventura. The altitude at the springs is about 1,000 feet. The flow is about 50,000 gallons per hour, and the temperature ranges from 60° F. to 74° and 104° F. Several of the springs are carbonated and others are sulphureted. The Ojai waters contain: sodium, potassium and magnesium carbonates and sulphates, calcium and ferrous carbonates, silicates, carbonic anhydride and sulphureted hydrogen. The waters have a reputation for whitening and softening the skin, and improving the complexion. These springs are the resort of many people afflicted with stiff joints, rheumatism, gout and skin diseases.

Almost in the center of this lovely valley, and nearly 900 feet above the sea, is the village of Nordhoff, so named in recognition of Charles Nordhoff's offices in heralding to the outside world the merits of this quarter.

Mr. R. G. Surdam, if not the first, was one of the prime movers in starting this flourishing little town, he having bought sixty acres, which he laid off in blocks and lots in 1874. He gave a one-third interest to A. M. Blumberg, on condition that he build a hotel. That structure, which at first was made of light scantling covered with cloth, has developed and grown into quite a sightly hostelry, the nucleus of a thrifty little village. Nordhoff contains some 300 inhabitants, many of whom are recuperated invalids from nearly every State in the Union. There are here two hotels, nestled under the splendid oaks, two churches, two schoolhouses, two general merchandise stores, two blacksmiths, a builder, contractor and lumber-dealer, and a butcher-shop. There is a weekly newspaper and a postoffice with daily mail.

SANTA ANA VALLEY.

Westward from the Ojai are a number of broad mesas and thickly-populated uplands, which constitute the Santa Ana Valley, on whose well-cultivated farms and orchards are raised as fine fruits as any Ventura County produces. This is all a fine grain country, where wheat reaches its maximum as to height, quantity and quality. This valley is a twin sister to the Ojai in its climate, soil and resources, and also probably with quite as much water and timber, but this valley contains less arable land than the Ojai.

Here is a region of forests; timber of majestic size, and an undergrowth of wild oats, wild grasses, wild gooseberries, rhododendron and honeysuckle, while wild grapes clamber over the trees along the creeks and the river.

A portion of this territory has as great an altitude as the Ojai, but it is much lower where it approaches the San Buenaventura Valley. Above this section the Ventura River descends rapidly, passing by cascades over highlands, but it flows more tranquilly when it reaches the table-like lands of the Ojai and Santa Ana ranchos. Here it gathers volume from the water of the San Antonio and Coyote creeks, the former flowing from the east, the other from the west; and hence forward to the sea it flows with gentle current. All three of these are fine trout streams.

THE RANCHO SANTA ANA.

This tract of 21,522.04 acres was, in April, 1837, granted to Crisogono Ayala and others, and to them confirmed. This lies but two miles from the Santa Barbara line, and it is the most northerly rancho in Ventura County. The Coyote Creek crosses this forest-hooded rancho, of which nearly 10,000 acres would be good arable land, if cleared of its timber. In May, 1875, this rancho was surveyed in lots, which were to be sold on terms similar to those of the Lompoc colony lands. The capital stock of the company was fixed at $60,000, in shares of $100 each. Among the estimated resources were 6,000 acres of arable land, other 6,000 tillable with side-hill plows, and 75,000 cords of wood. The temperance principle was to be a leading feature of this settlement. The project was never carried to fulfillment.

MISSION SAN BUENAVENTURA IN 1875.

BIRDS-EYE VIEW OF THE CITY OF VENTURA.

THE TOWN OF SAN BUENAVENTURA.

The capital, or county-seat, of Ventura is situated a few miles east of Point Rincon, near where the Ventura River empties into the ocean. The "Small City," or "Palm City," as it loves to call itself, spreads over an area extending to about twenty blocks long by six wide. The sea washes the southern boundary, the Ventura River skirts the western, a high hill looms on the northern side, whilst the fertile Santa Clara Valley stretches out eastward.

The old town was grouped about the adobe buildings and the semi-tropical gardens of the mission, and it was long isolated for lack of railway communication, being accessible only by means of the steamers of the coast line, at that time generally small and uncomfortable for purposes of travel.

This has, however, always been an important shipping point. In the mission days, when the hides and tallow produced from the broad lands ruled by the fathers were carried hence by Indians and wading sailors, as related by Robinson and Dana, and in later days when a substantial wharf, large warehouses and frequent service of steamers facilitated the export of products from the rich tributary country.

Since the coming of the railway, in 1887, San Buenaventura has veritably entered upon a new epoch of existence, with a new lease of life, and the outside world has begun to learn somewhat of her resources.

The town is eighty miles distant from Los Angeles, thirty from Santa Barbara and 300 by sea from San Francisco.

Lying upon a narrow plain between the foot-hills and the sea, the town, like many others of the older Spanish settlements, naturally enough grew along one main business street. When the Americans came they spread out across that narrow plain, and began also to climb the hills in search of places whereon to build homes. Thus San Buenaventura to-day has five long streets, Front, Meta, Santa Clara, Main and Poli, in the order named from the water front back which run east and west, parallel to the shore, and crossed at right angles by nineteen other streets, running north and south. These all have either wooden or concrete walks eight and ten feet in width. Probably no other town in the State of the same population has the same quantity of sidewalks. In the last two years Ventura has built 11,310 feet of cement sidewalks, at a cost of $25,188, and 39,104 feet of wooden sidewalks, costing $32,100, making in all nine and one-half miles of walks, at a cost of $57,288. Aside from this there are eight and one-half miles of graded streets, prepared at a cost of $38,145. The system of sewerage is good, there being three miles of sewer pipe that cost $20,000.

Here, as in Paris, France, there are city ordinances forbidding the casting down of paper, etc., upon the streets, or the throwing into them of any sort of litter, and these precautions, together with the services of men employed to do weeding, etc., keep the streets and sidewalks of this town in fine condition. Provision is made, too, against the bane of Southern California during the dry season—dust. By an ordinance approved in November, 1888, constantly three, and occasionally four, sprinkling carts are kept at work on the city streets, at a cost of about $2,500 per year.

There is also a good system of sewerage, based on the Waring plan, comprising 17,914 feet of pipe, of diameters ranging from six to fourteen inches, constructed of the best vitrified ironstone piping, at a cost of $25,000. The sewering is greatly facilitated by the natural slope of the town site.

Running for several miles northward along the border of the Ventura River is a beautiful valley, or narrow strip of land, called "The Avenue." It is laid off into small farms and villa lots, skirted by hills on either hand, and here live many of Ventura's people, amidst a wealth of fruit and flowers. The street which runs through this valley is broad, level and very nearly straight, extending six or eight miles. It is set with shade trees nearly the whole distance, and the enterprise of the residents here provides for its sprinkling from end to end. This is the boulevard of Ventura, and its beautiful bordering of tasteful houses, and its well-kept orchards and gardens, make it indeed an attractive drive.

On the avenue grows a monster grapevine, about seventy-five years old, whose main vine is over three feet in circumference. It is trained over framework, and produces annually several thousand tons of grapes.

San Buenaventura is a town of the sixth class. Its population is 2,350, of which about sixteen per cent. consist of the Spanish-American element.

The assessed valuation of city property for the fiscal year ending June 30, 1890, shows as follows: town lots, $814,385; improvements, $375,370; personal property, $391,529; money, $18,871; mortgages, $171,103.

San Buenaventura was incorporated as a town March 10, 1866, and re-incorporated March 29. 1876.

The municipal officers are: A board of town trustees, consisting of J. S. Collins, President; and Peter Bennett, C. D. Bonestel, E. M. Jones and J. R. Willoughby; Marshal, Frank S. Cook; Clerk, J. F. Newby; Attorney, Lloyd Selby; Treasurer, Chas. McDonald; Engineer, G. C. Power.

There is a volunteer fire department, equipped with two hose carts and hook-and-ladder paraphernalia. There are about forty members.

The town hall and library building, in one, built in 1883, is owned by the city. It is a one-story brick of fifty feet frontage on the main street, with a depth of seventy feet The construction is such as provides for the ready and economic addition of another story.

The town hall contains a fine cement and brick fire-proof vault of the latest improved order, whose capacity is sufficient to make it the receptacle of the municipal records and documents for at least twenty-five years to come. This building is valued at about $7,000.

The cemeteries, Protestant, Roman Catholic and Jewish, are situated on a beautiful location in the eastern addition. With the exception of the Roman Catholic one, they are owned and managed by the municipal jurisdiction, the town clerk giving deeds for lots, while the sexton reports to the town trustees.

The Ventura postoffice is of the third class. The postmaster is Nathan H. Shaw, and he has one assistant. The postmaster refuses to give any information regarding the business of the office, such as is customarily given to the public press once or twice a year; therefore no comparison can be made of the relative importance of this with other county-seat postoffices. The Postoffice Department at Washington, at the request of citizens here, recently changed the name of this postoffice from San Buenaventura to Ventura. Much mail and express matter designed for this office found its way to San Bernardino, and vice versa. Then the name was too long to write and too difficult for strangers to pronounce.

For a number of years the town was lighted by gas, there being twenty-five street lamps, paid for by the city; but since September 1, 1890, the municipality has adopted the electric light system, of which there are two circuits. The gas company still lights many stores, offices, etc.

Ventura has no street railways, but a franchise to build one has recently been granted.

In February, 1888, the telephone service was introduced, under the management of an experienced electrician. Beginning with thirty connections, the patronage has steadily increased to sixty, and connection will soon be made with neighboring towns. The service is in great favor here.

Ventura has in force various ordinances highly favorable to public morals, among others, one prohibiting boys under sixteen years old from being in the streets after 8 P. M.

The high-license law has been in operation for one year. The license is $600 per month, of which one-half goes to the town and one-half to the county.

Located in San Buenaventura, as the county-seat, are various county institutions, hereinafter described, as the hospital, the court-house, etc.

Within the city limits there is a half-mile race-track, of private ownership.

There are several excellent hotels, among them the Rose, a handsome three-story brick, cost $120,000; artistic in furnishing, and excellently managed, it is safe to say this is the best hotel in Southern California.

The following report was prepared by Mr. J. F. Newby, who was for ten years librarian of the Ventura Library Association:

"This association was incorporated November 23, 1874, with Milton Wason, James Daly, C. G. Finney, L. F. Eastin, G. S. Gilbert, Jr., C. H. Bailey, J. J. Sheridan, T. B. Steepleton and L. C. Granger as incorporators. The association arranged for a fair and festival, the proceeds of which went to purchase books and furniture. All members were required to pay $5 per annum toward supporting the library, and those who did not pay the $5 for membership paid twenty-five cents a month for the privilege of drawing books. A room was secured and some 600 volumes purchased, Mr. J. W. Maxwell being the first librarian, succeeded by Miss Cecelia Perkins. The library was kept up until the spring of 1878, when it became involved in debt and was closed.

"In August, 1878, the library trustees, Messrs. James Daly, M. H. Gay, C. H. Bailey, L. F. Eastin and J. J. Sheridan, made a proposition to the board of town trustees to transfer the assets of the association to the town, provided the town would pay the library indebtedness, and agree to levy a library tax under a State law allowing incorporated towns to levy a library tax. The town board accepted the proposition and took charge of the library August 21, 1878, with J. F. Newby as librarian, he continuing to fill the position until February 1, 1888.

"The library was a success from the time the town took charge of it and levied an annual tax to support it. New books were added two or three times each year, until the library now contains 4,000 carefully selected volumes. A reading room is attached to the library, in which one finds the standard periodicals of the day. There were over 10,000 books drawn from the library last year by citizens. The town has lately added an addition to the library room, and the library now has two large, well-lighted rooms.

"Miss Florence Vandever, daughter of General Vandever, is the present librarian, and under her management the place is made attractive, as shown by the increased attendance.

"The library is one of the best small libraries in the State, and is the pride of the citizens of Ventura. The success of the library is mainly due to the intelligent and constant supervision of Messrs. James Daly, W. E. Shepherd and Judge S. A. Sheppard, and especially to James Daly, who was one of the original founders, and since then almost continuously one of the trustees, he having been untiring in his efforts to build up the library and make it a success.

"The library is open every afternoon and evening, and it is largely patronized, the Venturans taking great pride in the institution."

A feature æsthetic as well as practical of the town is

FLORICULTURE.

A few years ago Mrs. T. B. Shepherd of San Buenaventura, possessing a love for flowers and rare plants, sought, through a system of mutual exchange, to add to her collection and at the same time furnish persons in other parts of the country with such seeds and bulbs as she grew at home. In her zeal and anxiety to secure for herself some varieties grown by Eastern florists, she occasionally applied to them, proposing to furnish from her stock such as they might wish to propagate. These applications were often entirely unnoticed. Peter Henderson, however, the noted seedsman and florist, wrote her encouragingly and advised her to raise seeds and bulbs for the Eastern market. This was four years ago; but, having no capital and only a limited experience, her progress was necessarily slow. But with a courage born of love for the business, she went to work upon about two acres of ground adjoining her residence. As fast as the income from her sales would permit she would order seeds and bulbs from prominent florists in Europe and America. Her ground had to be prepared and necessary buildings put up, and all from the income of the garden. Thus has she worked along, experimenting sometimes though rarely failing, until she has demonstrated that this country, and right here in Ventura, is one of the best places for cultivating flowering plants for profit in the world. Of all the European plants and bulbs she has cultivated, those raised here are superior to those raised in their own country. Her business has increased until it requires the constant attention of two men under her supervision, and her sales to Eastern seedsmen and florists alone will amount to $2,000 this year. This amount does not include her sales to individuals and those who purchased for their own use, which sales are very considerable. She values her stock at $5,000, and fully expects to realize that amount upon her next year's sales. Eastern florists who would not deign to answer her letters when, as an amateur, she applied to them for favors, now send her orders for seeds and bulbs. She shipped, in one year, on orders from the Eastern States, 10,000 calla lilies, 20,000 Freesia refracta alba and 1,750 Canna Ehemani. She has already received orders for thirty-three pounds of smilax seed, and has sent to one order $45 worth of fuchsia seed. Mrs. Shepherd states that her business is increasing rapidly, and that, as Southern California becomes better known for the excellence of its seeds and bulbs, she cannot supply the demand, notwithstanding the fact that she is now improving and planting out five acres in addition to the above floral park.

It having become noised abroad that Mrs. Shepherd was willing to impart to others the results of her experience, she has been besieged with letters, often from people who write from curiosity only. This is obviously unfair to the lady; for, while she is always ready to give information to persons interested in pursuing this new field of labor she has shown to be open to and practicable for women, she has not the time nor the strength to attend to the merely curious.

THE COUNTY HOSPITAL.

This institution is situated in a central portion of San Buenaventura, on the same tract as the court-house and other county edifices, where the county owns one half-block.

The building has recently been renovated; its walls calcimined and cheerful pictures hung upon them; the wood-work is clean with fresh paint, and carpets are laid on most of the passage-ways. In the lower hall is a case containing a number of books and periodicals.

The office contains a supply of medicines; the wards are well lighted, well ventilated, commodious, and comfortably fitted. There are four wards upstairs and two down, - in all about eighteen beds. At present thirteen beds are occupied—eleven by men, and two by old ladies of neat and tidy appearance, disabled by rheumatism from work.

The kitchen is well kept, and it and the pantry seem to be supplied with viands of a better quality than is usual in such institutions.

The outhouses are ample and orderly, the grounds cheerful with flowers, and the kitchen-garden filled with vegetables.

This hospital seems less formal and more homelike than most refuges of the sort.

It is under the management of Dr. Cephas R. Bard, the county physician, and of Dr. Joshua Marks, hospital superintendent. The cost of the hospital was $10,000.

Until within the past few years the poor were "farmed out;" then the atention of Mr.

W. H. Jewett, county auditor and recorder, having been called to an act of the Legislature of 1882 to provide aid for the indigent sick, he looked up the records, and claims were made out for $1,800. This being allowed, the matter was pressed, and Ventura County was found to be entitled to $10,700 from this source, and the amount was duly collected from the respective fund or appropriation.

THE COURT HOUSE,

built in 1872, originally consisted of the main square building, to which was added, some six years later, a wing containing an enlargement of several offices in two stories, and a vault for the storage of records. In 1884 four rooms were added to the west end. It now contains the quarters of the sheriff, assessor, district attorney, clerk and auditor and recorder, on the ground floor; and the court-room and chambers, jury-room, and the offices of the county surveyor and school superintendent. The treasurer is quartered elsewhere. The building is of brick, stuccoed, with fittings rather comfortable, although somewhat out of repair and antiquated. At the time of the present writing, an addition is in progress, to contain the papers of the clerk's office and and the supervisors. The cost was $20,000.

THE COUNTY JAIL,

erected in 1888, is a substantial brick building of two stories and a basement, its woodwork being of Oregon pine, sugar pine, redwood, and white fir, all the materials being of the best quality. The cells, locks, etc., are of the most modern and complete designs, and the jail is a model of this sort of institution. It cost $20,000.

The valuation of Ventura's county property as per the rates of the present year, 1890, is as follows: court-house, $20,000; hospital, $10,000; jail, $20,000; records, books, improvements, furnishings, etc., $35,000; total, $85,000.

BANKS.

The pioneer banking establishment of this county is the Bank of Ventura, which was founded in September, 1874, with a capital of $250,000. Its officers were: L. Snodgrass, President; M. Cannon, Vice-President; H. M. Gay, Cashier and Secretary. This bank now has a paid up capital of $100,000; surplus, $50,000. Its present officers are: E. P. Foster, President; L. C. McKeeby, Vice-President; J. A. Walker, Cashier; A. Bernheim, Secretary.

The bank of William Collins & Sons was opened in September, 1887. The following is its comparative statement:

RESOURCES.

	Sept. 1, 1889.	Sept. 1, 1890.
Loans and discounts	$172,727.11	$203,076.05
Bonds	35,500.00	30,000.00
Warrants	3,192.96	678.50
Cash	15,762.60	24,815.68
Due from Banks	9,929.96	73,341.28
Real Estate, furniture, fixtures	21,000.00	21,000.00
	$257,212.63	$352,911.51

LIABILITIES.

Capital stock	$100,000.00	$100,000.00
Surplus and profits	26,719.70	38,116.38
Deposits	130,140.07	212,708.06
Due other Banks	352.86	2,087.07
	$257,212.63	$352,911.51

Reserve fund.........................$38,116.38

In the city of San Buenaventura there are 679 census children, of whom 464 are enrolled in the public schools, the average attendance being ninety-seven per cent. of the enrollment. There are some 125 or 130 children of Spanish blood in attendance. There are three departments—primary, grammar and high schools. The corps comprises Professor Black, principal of the city schools, and nine other teachers. The school buildings are: the High School-house, which cost $30,000; the Poli street building, worth $2,500, and the Meta street building, worth $2,000. The High School was established in 1889, by the people voting a special tax for the purpose, the vote being unanimous but for two votes. This department has three courses, scientific, literary and classical, and it prepares pupils for the colleges and for the State University. There are thirty-three pupils in the High School, of whom eight are seniors, who will be graduated in 1891.

CHURCHES.

It will readily be seen from the following list of the different denominations and their churches that Ventura County will rank among the first as a church-going people; and while the compiler has not been able to get the whole number in the county, the following brief sketches of the principal churches of San Buenaventura will be found nearly correct:

Catholic.—There are 1,500 Roman Catholic parishioners in the district of La Mision, and 850 in Ventura, where Father Cipriano Rubio is pastor, officiating in the old Mission church. This sanctuary has been extensively repaired, but with consistency preserving as far as might be the ancient characteristics. The earthquake of 1857 caused the roof to fall in, lodging in the garret, where it was held by the vigas (beams). Thereupon the present roof of shingles was put in place. Twenty years ago new altars and flooring were supplied, and about the same time the pews were placed. Within the last three years, many modifications have been made, but with discretion. The sanctuary, being of insufficient space, was raised, and extended to the body of the church; and a new chancel railing was put in. The main altar was built in 1886—

'88, and two side-altars in 1889. Since 1885 there has been a resident priest at New Jerusalem, eight miles from Ventura. Previous to that, Father John Pujot had officiated there at intervals since 1875 or 1876.

Congregational Church.—The Congregational Church was the first Protestant church in the county, having been organized in 1867, at the time the land known as the Briggs tract was thrown upon the market and opened to settlement, the founding of said church being the result of the settlement of the above mentioned tract of land by American citizens.

There being no Protestant church at that time nearer than Santa Barbara, the services of Rev. M. B. Starr were secured to act as missionary for $1,000, donated by the Society of Missions.

The first members consisted of Revs. Bristol and Harrison, Eliza A. Shaw, Francis L. Saxby, Isabella L. Hobson, Hannah E. McCarty, Mary A. Herbert, Matilda P. Barnard, George Beers, Sarah Beers, Edward B. Williams, Elizabeth A. Williams, Amanda Baker, Maria A. Wason, Nancy L. Banning, Celia A. Simpson, Fanny Williams, W. E. Barnard and G. S. Gilbert, the two latter persons being deacons, and the latter of these clerk.

A simple and inexpensive church, 28 x 40 feet, costing but a few hundred dollars, was soon erected. The Ventura Land Company donated the lot on which the church was built, and the Rev. Mr. Warren, of San Francisco, preached the first sermon in the new edifice, the Rev. Mr. Harrison occupying the pulpit from October, 1869, until March, 1870. Rev. W. E. Merritt officiated from July 30th of that year until the following October. Rev. S. Bristol preached at intervals until 1875, when Rev. T. C. Jerome, of Illinois, was engaged and remained until June, 1876; Rev. R. B. Snell from August 1, 1876, to January 1, 1878; Rev. Charles B. Shelden from January, 1878, to ——. Rev. T. D. Murphy began his services here October 26, 1884.

The church building now occupied was finished, furnished and dedicated free from debt, without missionary help, May 3, 1885. It has a seating capacity for 350 persons. An annex, 24 x 30 feet, has recently been added.

Methodist Episcopal Church.—In 1867 Rev. R. R. Dunlap was appointed to the pastorate of Santa Barbara, his charge embracing the whole county, which at that time included the county of Ventura. In 1867 Rev. P. Y. Coole took charge of the western district and Mr. Dunlap was sent to San Buenaventura and Saticoy, and he organized the church in San Buenaventura. In 1870 Rev. George O. Ashe was sent to this circuit and became popular at once. He held services in the room which afterward became the public reading room. Mr. Ashe's family responsibilities crowded upon him. He worked during all his spare time at the printer's case, thus obtaining but a small pittance, upon which the average Methodist minister in all new countries is supposed to keep the wolf from the door. In 1871 the Rev. B. Holland was sent to the circuit, and, like his predecessors, received a very small allowance, but conversions followed his labor, part of the converts joining the Methodist Church and part joining other churches. In 1872 Rev. G. O. Ashe was returned to the circuit for a second time and much good was done during his year. Rev. Adam Bland officiated in 1873, and was instrumental in building the Methodist Church, at a cost of $1,700, the lot upon which the same was built costing $400, and when the church was completed the society found itself in debt $1,000.

Mr. Bland seems to have been the first pastor who received a fair salary, he receiving $200 from the Missionary Society and $500 from the people.

In 1874 Rev. W. A. Knighten became pastor, Ventura being set apart as a station with a missionary appropriation of $500. After arriving at the place, he and others concluded that the house rent was so high that it would be better to build a parsonage; consequently the lumber was bought, and the house was completed in about six days, most of the work being donated. During this year the Sunday-school was organized and an organ purchased for the church. A ladies' "Aid Society" was organized and rendered efficient financial aid, paying a large portion of the church debt, and furnishing the parsonage. Mr. Knighten was returned for the third time. This year was marked with financial prosperity. During the three years that Mr. Knighten was pastor, he had the pleasure of seeing the membership increase from seventeen to seventy-five.

Rev. F. S. Woodcock was appointed pastor by the conference of 1877 and remained one year. Owing to the severe financial depression of that year, the church was considerably crippled, but maintained its spiritual power. In September, 1878, the Southern California Conference held its session in San Buenaventura. The sittings were attended by the people generally and greatly enjoyed. At this session Rev. E. F. Walker was appointed pastor, but he became discouraged and remained only ten months. At the next session of the conference the Rev. J. A. Van-Anda was appointed, and the work of the church proceeded. The Rev. J. H. Peters served the church during 1880–'81, and during his pastorate the church enjoyed a good degree of prosperity, and reduced its indebtedness. During 1882 Rev. A. N. Fields was pastor and had a fair share of success, and did good work. Rev. James A. White was sent to the charge by the conference of 1883. Improvements on the church property were immediately commenced. The parsonage was removed from behind the church to the corner of the lot and enlarged. The church edifice was dedicated during the year. Mr. White remained three years. Rev. J. A. McMillan followed in the fall of 1886 and had a successful year. During this year the church debt was entirely paid off. He was returned for another year, but owing to ill-health was compelled to abandon his work at the end of three months, the pulpit being supplied until the end of the conference year by various ministers.

In April, 1888, Rev. W. L. Douglass was transferred from the New York East Conference and placed in charge of the church.

Presbyterian Church.—Rev. T. E. Taylor, a missionary to the Sandwich Islands in 1847, and founder, in 1852, of the first church for foreigners, having returned and settled in Virginia City, Nevada, was petitioned by a number of Ventura citizens to organize a Presbyterian Church in this place. He answered at once, and on Sunday, January 31, 1869, in the school-house just north of town, he met the friends of the enterprise. At the close of his sermon ten members were enrolled by certificate, who at once elected as elders, M. J. Ashmore, E. B. Conklin and B. Lehman. The following gentlemen were elected trustees: M. J. Ashmore, A. D. Barnard, E. B. Conklin, George A. Gilbert and S. W. Chaffee. Mr. Taylor was invited to remain as their pastor. T. R. Bard gave the ground on the northeast corner of Oak and Meta streets, 80 x 200 feet, for the church building, and by March 27, 1870, the present house of worship was finished, paid for and dedicated, all in fourteen months from the organization of the society. The total cost was $2,511.60. Mr. Taylor found it necessary to resign shortly after the completion of the church. He was followed for short terms by Revs. William Campbell and H. H. Dobyns, and November 1, 1873, Rev. Mr. Taylor was recalled, continuing his pastorate to the close of the year 1876. The parsonage on Meta street had been built in the meantime, entailing a heavy debt upon the young and struggling church.

The year 1877 was wholly given to the experiment of a "union" with the Congregationalists, the points of which were, that for that term both organizations worship together in the Presbyterian church, under the pastorate, first, of Rev. Mr. Snell, now of the Snell Academy, Oakland; second, that of Rev. Charles B. Sheldon, of the Anoka Congregational Union, Minnesota; but the ecclesiastical, like the domestic step-fathership, was not satisfactory to all the parties concerned. The debt had increased, while death and removals had weakened the already feeble church. As a result, Sunday, January 6, 1878, the "union" was, on motion of Mr. N. Blackstock, dissolved. No permanent supply for the pulpit was secured till July 1, when Rev. S. T. Wells, of Oakland, amid great discouragements, began his pastorate, which continued for three years and resulted in greatly strengthening the church and freeing the property from encumbrance.

Mr. Wells resigned the pastorate in July, 1881, but as "honorably retired" continues, with his excellent wife, foremost in every good work. His successor, Rev. F. D. Seward, of New York, carried forward the work with rare energy and faithfulness from October, 1881, until September 1, 1887, when he took the field of Synodical Missionary for Southern California; and Rev. James M. Crawford, the present pastor, was called to the church from Greenville, Ohio. Under its various leaders the church has steadily increased in membership, while the Sunday-school and prayer-meetings have shared in the prosperity of the congregation.

The church building, now eighteen years old, and by no means attractive in its exterior, is, inside, not surpassed in the county for the cheerfulness and good taste of its furnishings; and though quite ample for all the uses of the church, is being so fully occupied as to make it evident that more churchly and commodious quarter, is only a question of the near future. From a dependent of the Presbyterian Board of Home Missions and church erection, it has become self-sustaining, and at the same time a generous contributor through the nine great agencies of that church to the world's evangelization. It has steadily fostered the work at Saticoy, and been largely instrumental in securing to that community a beautiful church building, a church organization and Sabbath-school.

Besides the officers already alluded to, Messrs. T. R. Bard, D. S. Blackburn, George W. Chrisman, J. L. Kenney, James R. Boal, J. P. Cutter, Frank Dennis, E. A. Edwards, A. J. Collins and Rev. S. T. Wells have served as trustees. Messrs. E. A. Duvall, J. P. Cutter, J. C. Brewster, N. Blackstock, George P. Waldon, Hon. William Vandever, A. D. Seward, L. W. Hare and Luther Skellenger have been elders.

Rev. James Monroe Crawford, pastor of the First Presbyterian Church of Ventura, was born in Trimble County, Kentucky, August 12, 1836. His father, John Crawford, of Westmoreland County, Pennsylvania, was of Scotch descent, and brought up in the Presbyterian Church; his mother was Clarissa Bell, a native of Culpeper Court-house, Virginia, who, from childhood, was a devoted member of the Methodist Episcopal Church.

At the time of their marriage they were residents of Madison, Indiana, which city continued to be the family home, with the brief exception of two years spent in Kentucky, until 1876. The subject of this sketch was the oldest son of twelve children; the foundation of his education was laid in the private and public schools of that city. At the age of sixteen he was apprenticed to learn the pattern-maker's trade, that being his father's business. During the three years' term of service he had taken a preliminary course in theology, aided only by the text books and such comments on them as he was able to read in the people about him. Admitted into the Southeast Indiana Conference as an itinerant minister of the Methodist Episcopal Church, in October, 1856, he entered fully upon the double work of student and pastor.

On September 14, 1858, he was united in marriage to Miss Clarissa L. Golay, the daughter of Constant and Louisa Golay, of Switzerland County, Indiana, both of whom were descendents of prominent Swiss families.

August, 1862, during the gloomiest period of the war, he enlisted a full company of volunteers from his congregation in Dearborn County, Indiana. On their "muster in" as Company H, Eighty-third Indiana Volunteers, he was unanimously elected, and Governor Morton commissioned him, Captain; two months later he was appointed Chaplain; and during the siege of Vicksburg was compelled to resign on account of wretched health. After five months' rest he resumed his work. While closing his term as pastor of Trinity Methodist Episcopal Church, Indianapolis, Indiana, having fallen a victim to insomnia, he gave up active service, spending the next six years in a fight for life and health. It was at the close of that period, with returning health, that he severed his ecclesiastical connection with the Methodist Episcopal Church, and united with the Presbytery of Indianapolis. The cause of the change was no grievance, neither a want of appreciation of Methodism, nor disappointment as to his private ambitions; but rather a conviction that had sprung up early in his ministry and strengthened each year that both the teachings and methods of the Presbyterian Church would be more helpful to his Christian experience and add largely to his ability to make full proof of his ministry.

Mr. Crawford was called immediately to the pastorate of the Sixth Church, Indianapolis, Indiana, and thence to Greenville, Ohio, and from the latter church to this, September 1, 1887, of which he continues pastor at this writing. Of their family of eight children, three died in early childhood; three are yet with them; two, Edward S. and Louisa, are in the East, the former as foreman of the pattern department of the Malleable Iron Works, Indianapolis, Indiana, and the latter, as wife of Rev. Berthold Seeholzer, a minister of the North Ohio Conference of the Methodist Episcopal Church.

Episcopalian.—During the summer of 1887, an informal meeting of four or five persons interested in the Episcopal Church was held at the residence of Judge L. C. McKeeby, to consider the propriety of organizing such a church in San Buenaventura. As a final result of the preliminary conference, the Rev. A. G. L. Trew, Dean of the Diocese, visited Ventura on the 7th of December, 1887.

Services of the Episcopal Church were held in the house of worship of the Congregationalists, who kindly placed their edifice at the service of the Episcopalians for the purpose.

A mission was organized under the name of St. Paul's, and the announcement made that the bishop had appointed Rev. F. R.

Sanford, of Connecticut, as missionary rector thereto. January 15, 1888, the first regular service was held in Odd Fellows Hall.

At this time there were but five communicants of the church. On Easter Sunday of 1888, solemn confirmation service was administered to a class of fifteen adults, and the church thus strengthened began preparations for a church building.

A most eligible lot on the corner of Oak and Santa Clara streets was purchased, and the present church edifice was erected, being opened for services in December, 1889.

The church property is valued at not less than $8,000, the lot having cost $3,000.

Rev. W. A. M. Breck, the present incumbent, began his rectorship in May, 1890.

The membership comprises thirty communciants, besides the uncomfirmed.

Since his arrival, Mr. Breck has instituted services at the mission stations, Nordhoff, Santa Paula and Hueneme, there being fifteen communicants at the last mentioned place, eight at Santa Paula, and six at Nordhoff.

The Methodist Episcopal Church, South, was organized in Ventura, July 29, 1888, under the ministry of Rev. J. W. Allen, presiding elder of the San Luis Obispo District, Los Angeles Conference, and Rev. D. C. Browne, pastor of the Trinity Methodist Episcopal Church, South, Los Angeles. There were thirteen charter members, and five more were added by the end of the conference year October 2.

Rev. D. C. Browne succeeded Rev. J. W. Allen as presiding elder of the district, and was also appointed pastor of the church at Ventura. During this year, from October, 1888, to October, 1889, twenty-five were added to the membership, and the church, led by Hon. L. M. Lloyd, secured the building of a house of worship, on the corner of Main and Kalorama streets. The church services this year were held in the Young Men's Christian Association Hall.

On September 30, Bishop R. K. Hargrave, with appropriate services, laid the corner stone of the new church building. Rev. J. M. Neems was appointed to the pastorate by Bishop Hargrave, October 6, 1889, and entered at once upon his work. The services were held in the Hare school building on Main street, from October, 1889, to May, 1890. May 4, 1890, the church held their first service in their new building, in the Sunday-school room, with much rejoicing. And on July 27, following, they entered their beautiful auditorium with grateful hearts to Him who had so wondrously led them in this work. During the year, from October 6, 1889, to September 11, 1890, fifteen were added to the membership, and the church building was finished and furnished at a cost of $7,000.

The Methodist Episcopal Church, South, in Ventura, while not strong in either numbers or wealth, yet has thus far met all claims against it, and looks to the future with hopeful hearts, believing that He whose hand hath led them thus far will lead them on.

Christian Church.—Charles Bradshaw began to preach in July, 1870, at Pleasant Valley. There were a few members who continued to meet occasionally until December 25, of the same year, when the church was organized with fourteen members at Pleasant Valley. The following were the charter members: Charles Bradshaw and wife, J. S. Harkey and wife, Martha White, Fanny and Laurence White, William Cagle, D. W. Gilbert, Mrs. Gilbert, S. Wallbridge, and Amy and Ollie Wallbridge and Mrs. Bear. The church continued to meet for three years, when a land decision occurred adverse to the settlers, at the end of which time there were about fifty members.

As most of them were deprived of their homes, they began to scatter until there were only a few left, but they continued to meet until the summer of 1876, when all had left but three.

In October, 1876, Elder G. R. Hand came to Ventura and engaged to preach for one year. The church then reorganized with thirty members. Rev. Hand preached until May, when he left and went East. The members continued to meet and worship until the spring of 1879, at the school-house. From 1875 to 1883 there were no meetings of the church. About July, 1883, Rev. J. S. Harkey, who has been elder of the church ever since the first organization in the county, called the membership together, and they covenanted to meet and worship together, and they have been doing so from that time until the present. They are now meeting at Good Templars' Hall on Main street. There has been added since the organization up to the present time by letter, confession and obedience, forty-eight members. There are, as near as can be ascertained, between fifty and sixty members in the county. Elder F. W. Pattee, formerly from Pasadena, is now preaching on the first Lord's day in each month. The church meets every alternate Sunday for social worship in the above named hall, and a Sunday-school meets every Sunday in the same place, at two o'clock. It has about fifty scholars and teachers enrolled, with Miss Annie Linn as superintendent.

A lot has been donated to the church at the western end of the town, and the congregation hope soon to erect a suitable house of worship upon it.

Y. M. C. A.—The Young Men's Christian Association of San Buenaventura was organized in September, 1887, with sixteen charter members. It has now a membership of sixty-four. The president is J. S. Collins; vice-president, Dr. C. F. Miller; treasurer, J. C. Brewster; and general secretary, Moore Hesketh. The rooms are in Collins' Block, Main Street, and are comfortably furnished, being open daily, Sunday excepted, from 8:30 A. M. to 10 P. M. The association is liberally supported by the Christian and business people of the town. It has already a building fund, and is now endeavoring to secure a suitable lot on which to erect a permanent home. During the nine months of its existence it has helped a number of young men to better and purer lives, and is now exerting a silent influence for good in the community.

THE PRESS.

As has been seen, the *Signal* was established in 1871, by John H. Bradley, who in 1873 retired from its management, on account of ill-health, being succeeded by Messrs. W. E. Shepherd and John J. Sheridan.

In November, 1875, was first issued the *Free Press*. Its editor was O. P. Hardy, and its politics nominally independent. The two papers fell into a hot controversy, in which was displayed much personal acrimony.

In November, 1883, the *Democrat* was founded by the Democrat Publishing Company, and subsequently purchased by John McGonigle, its editor from the beginning.

The *Vidette* was founded in May, 1888, by F. E. Smith, and an interest in it was subsequently purchased by Dr. Stephen Bowers.

The newspapers at present in the city of Ventura are: The *Free Press*, daily and weekly (publishers, Leonard & Sykes); the *Democrat*, weekly; the *Republican*, weekly.

In other towns of the county are published the following: The *Chronicle*, Santa Paula; the *Herald*, Hueneme; the *Recurrent*, Nordhoff.

Of
FRATERNAL ORGANIZATIONS

Ventura has the usual number. The Masons own a handsome hall.

THE BENCH AND BAR.

As the judiciary of Santa Barbara for many years included that of Ventura, the names of the earlier Bar members in the older county comprehend those of the younger. As to those of later date, a report on this subject has been promised the editor by B. T. Williams, Esq., Superior Judge of Ventura County, but, as it has not yet been received, the present writing must go to press without treating of this subject.

RESOURCES.

Chief among the resources of Ventura County is

AGRICULTURE.

From the time of its first settlement by the Mission fathers, over 100 years ago, Ventura County has been more or less given over to agriculture; but her grand capabilities in this line are only beginning to be understood.

When he came to Ventura County the man whose ideas of farming were formed amid the summer rains and the corn-fields of the Mississippi had to learn over again how to farm, and, now that he has learned the lesson, is growing rich on the land which at one time was deemed comparatively worthless.

A mistaken idea has prevailed to some extent among people in the East that farming is only carried on in Southern California by means of irrigation, and that without it crops would be a failure. Irrigation is not used at all in Ventura County, except for alfalfa, and for all small grains and winter crops it is not used in other countries. They are cultivated just as they are in the Mississippi Valley or the Atlantic States, and need only the regular rains of the winter and spring, or wet season, to mature them. Corn, a summer crop, is irrigated in some counties, but never here, as the natural moisture of the soil is sufficient to mature the crop. In some sections, after a winter-sown crop, raised without irrigation, has been harvested, another crop is raised when the rains are over by means of irrigation, and thus the land does double duty. In Ventura County, however, as our farmers do not desire to get rich in a day, corn is planted after the winter rains are over, and but one crop a year is raised and that without irrigation.

In many places land will be seen which is never free from a growing crop from year to year, except during the few days when plowing for the new planting. In counties where irrigation is used, where water from the river is used, the sediment held in suspension constantly renews the fertility of the soil over which it is spread.

Southern California throughout is a wonderfully rich farming section, and Ventura County is richer than any. She raises enough for her own consumption and exports more than any other county in the south. Her markets are at her very door. Lying between Los Angeles and Santa Barbara, neither of which raises enough for home consumption, the question of disposing of her products is a simple one. Many things, especially beans and fruit, are shipped to the East, although the bulk of exports' goes by steamer to San Francisco. But the supply is never half equal to the demand, which makes Ventura a splendid field for the industrious farmer. It is a better field than any other in Southern California, if for no other reason than that it is the only county where irrigation is not needed and not used. The number of acres under cultivation in this county is estimated at 100,000 this year.

Anything that grows in Ventura county—and anything will grow—yields a good profit to the tiller. But of course there are some things much more profitable than others. Heretofore barley has chiefly occupied the attention of the farmer, with satisfactory results; but year by year the tendency is to forsake barley and go over to

THE BEAN.

Before all others Ventura is pre-eminently a bean county. This is conceded on all sides, and one of the facts that has not been denied in other counties. The cultivation of the bean dates back to the earliest settlement of the county; and bean culture has always been successful. The season of 1864–'65 was the dryest and most unpropitious ever known here, and even then a large quantity of beans were exported. About the year 1875, Mr. Crane began cultivation of the Lima bean in the valley, and it is now thought to be the most valuable bean produced in the county. The Lima bean is a very prolific product. More than a ton is often raised on an acre of ground, while twenty-three hundred pounds of the White Navy beans are frequently raised on one acre. Lima beans have often brought as high as 5 and 6 cents a pound, returning to the producer the handsome figure of $100 per acre, but $50 is probably a fair average.

This year Limas will bring $2\frac{1}{2}$ cents a pound. Estimating 1,800 pounds to the acre, at $2\frac{1}{2}$ cents, the yield in money per acre will be $44 and the profit about $32 or $33. Bean raising costs about $7.50 per acre. This estimate includes everything—cost of seed, planting, cultivating, cutting and harvesting. And it is a liberal estimate.

Beans are planted with a bean planter, a simple machine. Two, three, and sometimes four rows are planted at a time. Cultivation after they are planted consists simply in keeping the field clear of weeds. They are planted in May, after the winter rains are surely over, never irrigated, cultivated once or twice after planting, and then nothing more is done until they are ready to cut, which is generally in August or September. At first beans were pulled by hand, but by degrees improvements on this slow method were invented, until now the harvesting of the bean is a very inexpensive, rapid and simple process; and herein lies much of the profit. They are cut with a bean cutter, also a very simple machine. It is a V-shaped knife, the blades of which are five or six feet long and are attached on either side of a wooden sled about eight feet long, one foot wide and one deep. Three horses are attached to the cutter, which is guided between the rows by one man. This way beans can be cut at an expense of about 50 cents an acre, and one man and three horses will cut fifteen acres a day. Lima beans are planted in rows three feet apart and drilled. Small white beans are planted thirty inches apart and drilled. The latter are cut earlier than the Limas. After the beans—of any variety—are cut, they remain in piles in the field for about four weeks to dry, when they are taken to the machine and threshed at an expense of about 15 cents per 100 pounds. Seven dollars and a half will easily cover the cost of seed, planting, cultivating, cutting and harvesting an acre of beans. The demand for beans is always good. Limas bring from $2\frac{1}{2}$ to 3 cents a pound, the small whites from 2 to $2\frac{1}{2}$ cents. Farmers in Ventura have often cleared $50 an acre on a crop of Lima beans, and never less than $30. So it will be seen that bean land is not shockingly dear at even $200 an acre. Land that will pay fifteen per cent. on money invested is not exorbitantly high: it is reasonably cheap. But there is plenty of land suitable for bean culture that can be had for $150, some at $100, $75, $60, $50—according to location and facilities for shipping. The highest priced lands in the poorest season will pay fifteen per cent. on money invested. The Santa Clara Valley has heretofore been considered the home of the bean. Before this season farmers who were not fortunate enough to own land in this favored section were afraid to embark in anything but grain, but this year some tillers of Las Posas soil were bold enough to pioneer bean planting, and crops resulting from their experiments demonstrate the fact that beans can be successfully grown in other sections besides the Santa Clara Valley. Rice & Bell on the Las Posas have as fine a crop of beans as can be found in the county —a crop that will certainly average a ton to the acre. Beans have also been raised this year on the Ojai, the Conejo, and a few in the Simí. Unquestionably the soil and climate of the Santa Clara valley is more suited to the cultivation of the bean than any one of these latter valleys, which are mostly given over to grain-growing. In the Santa Clara Valley farmers often raise 2,000 to 3,000 sacks of beans a year. A sack of Lima beans contains about sixty pounds, and about seventy pounds of small whites.

In the Las Posas Valley, good bean land—land that will raise as good beans and as heavy crops as grow anywhere in the county—can be had at $60 an acre.

First-class bean land can be bought and paid for with two years' crops. No bean land can be bought in the Santa Clara Valley—the alleged home of the bean—for less than $100 an acre, and most of it runs from $150 to $200. The latter price would seem enormously high to the Eastern farmer unacquainted with the profits of bean raising.

A California bean field often embraces hundreds of acres, all in sight from a given point. The vines run along the ground and not on poles as in the Eastern States.

Next to fruit growing, bean raising is undoubtedly the most profitable industry in the farming line in Ventura county; and it is more profitable than some kinds of fruit growing.

OTHER PRODUCTS.

No spot in California can excel the Santa Clara Valley in the production of corn. It grows without irrigation and has reached as high as 72 centals or 120 bushels to the acre. It is planted in April or May after the rains are over, and frequently nothing more is required till it is ready for gathering in autumn. Should it rain after the ground is planted the farmer frequently finds it advantageous to plow it up and plant it a second time; otherwise cultivation will be necessary to overcome the weeds. After the corn is gathered and husked it may be thrown into open pens and left uncovered for a year or more, if not sooner shelled or fed to stock. Everything in connection with corn-raising except the gathering is performed by machinery. Until lately corn was raised extensively here and fed to hogs, but now, notwithstanding the heavy yield per acre, the ground is generally considered more profitable for some other kinds of crops. Ventura is the only county in Southern California where corn is raised without irrigation.

Barley is the chief cereal crop of Ventura County. Its yield is large in the Santa Clara and other valleys. On the west side of the river it has reached 52 centals, or 104 bushels, to the acre. There is always a demand for barley, and there is so much land in the county exactly suited for its production that it is likely to continue one of its staple products. It may be sown after the autumn rains or early in the spring. Cut green it is used for hay, and is highly relished by stock. Year in and year out the profits from barley-raising will average from $15 to $20 per acre. The Simí Valley yields larger crops than any other portion of the county.

Wheat is an important crop in Southern California, but is not as extensively grown in Ventura County as barley. The Ojai Valley, Simí and Conejo plateaus are better adapted to wheat than the land immediately on the coast, as they are less subject to fogs which occur in some seasons of the year. Wheat-raising in California is another and different thing from what it is in the East. After it ripens it may be left standing for weeks with impunity, the husk closing around the grain and holding it intact. When the farmer is ready he enters the field with headers and a thresher and cuts, threshes and sacks the grain the same day. The sacks are put in large piles and left in the field uncovered for weeks, or even for months, until he is ready to haul them to market. The wheat of California has a world-wide reputation. The State ships on an average some 15,000,000 bushels annually.

Alfalfa, or lucerne, which is being extensively grown in Ventura County, is known botanically as *Medicago sativa*. It has been grown in Greece for about 3,000 years as a forage plant and for hay. The Romans esteemed it very highly, and Columella wrote that it yielded four to six crops a year. In France it is known as lucerne and in Spain as alfalfa. It came from Spain to South America, and thence by way of Mexico to California. It is grown extensively in Southern Europe. It is a most successful crop in this county, but in most places needs irrigation. From six to eight cuttings are harvested in a year. It yields from two to three tons to the cutting, and readily nets from $60 to $75 to the acre. It is fed to cows, horses, hogs and poultry, all of which thrive upon it.

While oats are not extensively raised here, yet they grow to perfection and make excellent feed. In some portions of the county oats grow wild, covering foot-hills and sides of mountains, and they are prized by stockmen for all kinds of stock, including sheep.

In this connection should be mentioned bur clover, which covers the mountains, foot-hills and valleys in winter with a carpet of green. It bears a bur which contains small seeds, which are highly relished by cattle, horses, sheep, goats, hogs, and upon which they thrive. About the first of June it dies and drops the burs containing the seed, sometimes covering the ground to the depth of an inch or more, and remains good until the November rains. When the country was new no provision was made to feed stock any season of the year. They were sustained during the winter and spring months by the abundance of grass which grows luxuriantly in the valleys and on the mountains, and during the summer and autumn lived on bur clover.

Vegetable-raising has been largely relegated to the Chinese, who pay as high as $25 an acre rent for land. Of late, however, white men are turning their attention to this important industry in Southern California. Of late, white men have begun to see that there are possibilities for profit in the humble cabbage, cauliflower, tomato and potato, not exceeded even by the noble orange. Train-loads of vegetables are now sent East from Southern California every winter, although not by any means so many as should be sent. These vegetables arrive East when everything is frozen, and fetch very high prices. The industry is growing rapidly, and offers excellent opportunities to men of moderate means, as it is not necessary to wait several years for a return. A thrifty man can support a family n this manner from the product of five acres, or even less.

Potatoes yield two crops a year and bring as much as $200 an acre. At present there is not enough raised in the county, and, with the demand East, ought to develop into a great industry in the rich valleys of Ventura County. Sweet potatoes yield immense crops and always command a good price.

Tomatoes ripen nearly all the year round, the same vines bearing for years in the more sheltered spots. Asparagus, onions, beans of all kinds, peas, cabbage and cauliflower, squashes, melons, pumpkins, and in short, nearly or quite every vegetable known to the northern or semi-tropic climes grow here to perfection.

Fruit culture in Ventura County is yet in its infancy, but it is growing rapidly. There are a few spots on earth so favored by nature, and none where the horticulturist receives larger profits for his labor. The possibilities of horticulture in this county seem almost without limit. Year by year the area devoted to it is being enlarged, and as the county is settled up orchards and vineyards increase and multiply. The profits are much greater than from grain-growing, while the labor is much lighter and pleasanter. It requires no extraordinary stretch of the imagination to see the county in a few years transformed into one vast orchard and vineyard; to see the large farms now in grain subdivided into small tracts, with a happy home in each surrounded by fruits and flowers. The great Simí, the Las Posas, all the great ranchos now supposed to be good for little but grain, will one day be an unbroken line of orchards. The growth of some of the most populous and wealthy countries of the old world has been based upon horticulture and viticulture. The chief income of the Mediterranean countries, occupying a similar latitude to Southern California—Asia Minor, Greece, the Ionian Islands, Italy, Southern France, Spain and Portugal—is derived from their export of oranges, lemons, figs, olives, olive oil, dates, raisins, dried prunes, chestnuts, preserved fruits, wines and brandies. The United States imports annually $15,000,000 to $20,000,000 of fruits and nuts, all of which, in quantity to supply the United States, may be grown within the limits of Ventura County, and, in addition thereto, all the wine and brandy which is consumed in this country, with a large surplus for export. Horticulture, therefor, furnishes a pretty solid basis for a large population in this county, apart from its other numerous resources.

Fruits are at home in Southern California, and particularly in Ventura County. They seem at once to take kindly to its soil and climate, no matter whence they are brought. In the early days—during the '50s—there were only a few inferior varieties of grapes and oranges grown in Southern California. The Mission grape was about the only variety grown in California at that time. There were a few old orange trees in Los Angeles County, around the missions, introduced by the Catholic fathers a century ago. The success of these led to others being planted in other sections, and so the orange industry has increased until the present day. There are seedling pear trees at the missions a hundred years old. The first grafted fruit trees were brought to California in 1851, 1852 and 1853. Fruit trees at that time were a dollar apiece, and the fruits were sold at enormously high prices—from $1 to $2 per pound. As time passed, more fruit trees were planted, nurseries established, and the price of fruit and trees diminished, and before railroads reached our coast the price of fruit was not remunerative, orchardists lost their interest in fruit-raising, and it was some years before fruit was shipped East with profit.

The olive is said to be the most valuable tree known to man. This is undoubtedly true in Ventura County as elsewhere. It will grow in almost any kind of soil, although it is a mistake to imagine that it prefers soil nearly destitute of life-giving qualities. The olive will grow on the hill side, among rocks, and flourish where other trees would die. But that is no reason the olive prefers that kind of soil. It will do better in rich soil, which is natural. But the cheap lands of Ventura County—the hillsides now covered with chapparal—will undoubtedly be most used in the cultivation of the olive, for these lands would not be suitable for other trees. Such land can be procured at from $10 to $30 an acre.

The profits from olive-growing are enormous. Olive trees are planted twenty feet apart, or 108 to the acre. The olive grows from cuttings, which can be had at from five to ten cents each. At present the cost of setting out an olive orchard in Ventura County, including cost of land, trees and planting, would scarcely exceed $35 an acre. This is a reasonable estimate and may be too high. The olive bears at six or seven years from the cutting.

At seven years an olive tree will bear about 120 pounds to the tree. About twelve pounds will make one large bottle of oil, which will sell readily at from $1.50 to $2 a bottle. Mr. Cooper originally sold his at $1 per bottle, but the demand was so great that he was compelled to raise the price to $2. Twelve pounds to the bottle would be ten bottles to the tree, or in round numbers 1,000 to the acre. At $1.50 per bottle this would be $1,500 income from an acre of seven-year-old trees. Say that in curing the olive and making the oil and keeping the trees clean, two-thirds—an over estimate—of this sum is expended, we have left as profit the enormous sum of $500 an acre. These are astonishing figures, but when one reflects on the demand for and price of olive oil they will not seem without the bounds of reason. As the olive has off years in bearing, divide this estimated profit of $500 by two, and you still have a yearly profit per acre of $250 from an olive orchard. Ten acres would be enough, it has been often said, and such is the fact. Truly the olive is the most valuable tree known to man. The above estimates are based on the average yield of the orchard of the pioneer olive-grower of the State.

At present there are but two varieties of the olive most largely grown, that is, the Mission and Picholine. Both have advantages. The Mission will perhaps grow on a drier and poorer soil than the Picholine. The planting of the Mission is much advocated by many, because the fruit is a large berry and the tree a rapid grower.

The walnut prefers a moist rich soil, and is at home in Ventura County. The older variety of the trees are very slow in coming into bearing, requiring about ten years or more, and this fact has discouraged many an orchardist from setting out this valuable fruit; but there is a variety of soft shell walnut that requires but six years in which to bear, and once bearing it keeps on increasing (as is the case with all kinds of walnuts) its crop for fifty years or more. Sometimes these soft-shell walnut trees bear in five years—four years from the nursery—and this year there are some five-year-old trees in the county—notably at the Rice & Bell place on the Las Posas—that are loaded with nuts. This is an exception, however, the tree not usually bearing short of six years.

The walnut groves of Ventura County will and do net their owners an average of $100 per acre year in and year out, and there are some groves of old trees that net yearly twice that sum. No crop is more easily gathered than the walnut, and it is ready to be gathered after all other crops are in. The best thing about the walnut is that it is not perishable, and the owner of a grove is never forced to sell his crop at a loss or small profit to keep it from spoiling on his hands. Then another thing is that the area in which the walnut will thrive is so small that there can never be any danger of an overstocked market.

Walnut lands in Ventura County sell for from $100 to $400 an acre, according to location, and any of it, after an orchard has been in bearing a couple or three years, will pay ten per cent. interest on $1,000 an acre.

There is abundant acreage in Ventura County adapted to culture of the almond, but as yet little has been done in this direction. Mr. Joseph Hobart some fifteen years ago put out 300 almond trees in the Upper Ojai Valley, and he is almost the only grower of this article. So satisfactory does he find the enterprise that he is planting out a large number of these trees, which he regards, each for each, as more profitable than apricots, prunes, or peaches. Some of the pleasant features of this business are as follows: its successful treatment requires neither great haste nor a large crew of workers; the gathering of the crop comes in cold weather, and wet days can be utilized for hulling; the care of the orchard is less than with other fruit trees, and the cost of handling a crop of almonds is only about twenty-five per cent. of what it costs to handle apricots, peaches, etc.

Probably all kinds of apples that can be grown in any country are grown here. They are of very superior quality and there is no place in the United States where they keep better than in this climate. The dried apples sent from this county have commanded double the price of ordinary dried fruit. Pears of superior quality are raised here and are found profitable both for drying and canning purposes.

The soil of this section seems to be exactly suited to the apricot. Here it finds its special adaptation, yielding immense quantities of fruit of large size and excellent flavor. This is a very profitable industry and is becoming a source of immense revenue to the county. As the district of country in which they can grow to such perfection is limited, it is not likely the business will be overdone, but there will be an increasing demand for this fine fruit year after year. So far the apricot has had no natural enemy. Neither insect nor disease of any kind has ever attacked it in this region. As instances of the profit derived from this fruit we may cite the following: A farmer sold the fruit of a nine-acre orchard of four-year-old trees for $1,000, the purchaser gathering the fruit, from which he also derived a handsome profit, having obtained it for about one cent per pound. The fruit in another orchard of five-year-old trees sold for $200 per acre, the purchaser in this instance also realizing a handsome profit by drying the fruit. In another orchard three years old, the owner gathered fifty pounds to a tree, which more than paid for the trees and their cultivation up to that time. A gentleman planted seventy-five acres of apricot trees on land which cost $25 per acre; he raised two crops of beans between the trees, which more than paid the cost of cultivation of his orchard, and the third year sold it for $150 per acre. This is not a solitary instance, for there are scores of individuals in this county who are quadrupling the value of their land in a similar manner.

One of the largest orange and lemon orchards in the county is near Santa Paula

The orange trees of this orchard of nearly 100 acres are bearing and doing well. The lemons have been more thoroughly tested and are superior to most others grown in the State. The soil is very deep, a rich, well drained alluvial or sedimentary deposit, and is pronounced by Prof. E. W. Hilgard superior to any of his acquaintance for "easy cultivation and power to raise moisture jointly." The lemons grown thus near the coast are not superior to those further inland. At the citrus fair held at Riverside in 1883, a committee was appointed to make thorough scientific tests for the purpose of comparison of lemons grown in California with imported lemons. The analysis embraced, first, appearance, including size and quality of rind; second, bitterness; third, percentage of acidity. The committee compared the California lemon with those freshly imported from Messina, Malaga and Palermo, and reported as follows: "From a careful analysis of the foregoing it will seem that the California budded lemon properly grown and handled is the equal in every respect of the imported lemon." The committee further says: "It is noticed in the examination that the lemon of Santa Barbara, Ventura, Los Angeles, Anaheim and San Diego are nearly globular in form, and all having a smooth, morocco-like texture of the rind, while those of the same varieties found in San Gabriel and Pasadena are now elongated in form and not as smooth, and those of Riverside and vicinity are still more elongated and rougher in rind. It is noticeable that the smoothness and thinness of rind indicates greater quantity of juice." This testimony from a Riverside committee carries great weight as to Ventura's ability to successfully grow lemons, which branch of the citrus culture it is believed will be most profitable in the future.

The growing of oranges and lemons has been successfully tested at the Camulos, Sespe, Ojai, Matilija and other portions of the county. There are also thousands of acres on the Simí, Las Posas and other portions of the county that will doubtless produce oranges, lemons and limes of good quality. This industry is yet in its infancy in Ventura County, while its possibilities are beyond computation.

Farmers and fruit growers have not turned their attention largely to grape culture, but as far as tried they do remarkably well. Raisin grapes are grown successfully and produce the finest raisins in the land. This is especially true at Sespe and Ojai valleys. At the Camulos, in the northern part of the county, a fine quality of wine has been successfully manufactured for years. The county contains thousands of acres of land not yet brought under cultivation, where every variety of grape known on the coast can be successfully and profitably grown. For size and flavor the grapes grown in this county will compare favorably with the best. A few miles from Ventura is one of the largest grape-vines in the world.

Prunes do well and yield profitable crops. The French prune grows to great perfection, yielding largely, and promises to become one of the paying industries of the future. Peaches of all varieties do exceedingly well in this county. They seldom or never fail; and this may be said of nearly all kinds of fruits grown here. Some years the yield is not as great as others, but is never a total failure.

In addition to the fruits mentioned above, the following also do very well in Ventura's soil: Limes, guavas, loquats, currants, pears (which bear enormously), cherries, plums, figs of all kinds at all seasons, pomegranates, quinces, nectarines, persimmons (Japan), strawberries (ripe the year round), raspberries and blackberries.

THIS YEAR'S EXPORTS.

The barley product of Ventura County for this year is about 120,000 sacks, the arveage yield being about 350,000 sacks; the low product this year is due to last year's unusually wet winter. Of wheat there were about 20,000 sacks, which is a fair average, comparatively little land being sown to wheat. Of hay are raised about 2,500 tons annually. This year hay is more abundant than usual in this county. Of corn about 150,000 will be this year's harvest, the average yield increasing from year to year, as barley-raising is abandoned for the culture of corn and beans. Of beans—that great Ventura staple—18,200 acres were this year sown to Lima beans, yielding about 1,000 pounds to the acre, this being somewhat below the average of 1,500 pounds to the acre. About 2,500 acres were put to other varieties of beans, yielding about 1,500 pounds to the acre. The apricot and walnut yield was very large also, about 300 car loads of green apricots having been shipped to Newhall alone, for the purpose of sun-drying.

The shipment from this county of fresh apricots, delivered at the railway stations at $20 per ton, amounted to about $100,000 last season.

So abundant was the crop that one grower, Mr. A. D. Barnard, of the Cañada Larga Rancho, invited through the newspapers all parties who would, to take away from his orchard all of this fruit that they would haul, without money or price. Of walnuts twelve to fifteen car-loads, or 240,000 pounds, will have been shipped this year. There are about 200 acres of walnut trees bearing, and 350 acres not yet bearing, in this county.

Of oranges and lemons, the total value will probably approach $40,000. Olives will not reach a large figure, outside of the Camulos Rancho. Peanuts enter into the exports, as many as 500 sacks, or 25,000 pounds, having gone out; potatoes amount to about 200 carloads; a variety of promiscuous products also are exported, including hogs, of which a large number are raised, sometimes as many as 10,000 a year. The yield for this year is not determinable.

STOCK RAISING.

This industry has been carried on in Ventura somewhat extensively for many years. When under Mexican rule it consisted solely of cattle and horses, but when the Americans took possession they made sheep-raising a specialty. Under their supervision the county has supported as many as 250,000 head at one time. At the present time there is somewhat over 75,000 head in the county. Recently imported draft and other horses have been introduced, the assessment roll indicating several thousand American horses, some 3,000 of which are graded. Percheron, Hambletonian, Belgian, Morgan and other breeds have been imported. Among cattle there have been imported Durham, Shorthorn, Jersey and Holstein breeds, making the grade of cattle the very best. The county is far in advance of many others in the best breed of horses and cattle, farmers having reached the conclusion that good stock can be as easily raised as the poorer varieties and to much greater profit. The raising of hogs is also engaged in extensively and profitably. Diseases among stock are unknown here, except scab in sheep, which has not proved destructive.

A gentleman of Santa Paula imported twenty-one head of Holstein cows four years ago and has already sold $11,000 worth from their increase, while keeping up the original number. This is a fair sample of what is being done in this and other portions of the county in improved stock of nearly every kind.

The resources and capabilities of Ventura County in this regard may be best judged by the following *resumé* of the fine stock ranchos in this county: Three miles from Hueneme on the road to Ventura, and about half way between the former place and Montalvo, the first station on the Southern Pacific Railroad east of Ventura, is the splendid stock ranch of Mr. J. G. Hill, one of the representative and wealthy men of Ventura County.

The property embraces 630 acres of the La Colonia ranch, and is as desirably located and composed as as good soil as any part of the 45,000 acres of this magnificent property. The whole ranch is very nearly a mile square, and is fenced and cross-fenced into suitable fields for tillage, grain or grazing.

The owner of this valuable place is doing much toward the improvement of horses in this section. Several years ago J. C. Simpson, of Oakland, brought to California from Chicago the beautiful dapple-gray stallion, A. W. Richmond, which he sold to a Mr. Patrick, the latter to H. Johnson, he to Hill & Greis, and finally Mr. Greis sold his interest to Mr. Hill, the horse dying on the latter's hands last November, at the age of twenty-seven years. This horse was said to be one of the finest, if not the best, carriage or driving horses on the continent. He was the sire of Joe Romaro, record 2:19$\frac{1}{2}$; Arrow, record 2:13$\frac{1}{4}$; Columbine—the dam of Anteo and Anterolo, the only mare in the world that has produced two sons to beat 2:20; Rosewall, who has just made himself a record, taking six straight races, against stock imported to beat him; and a host of the finest driving stock on this coast. Being owned by Mr. Hill and Hill & Greis for some five or six years, his colts have become numerous, and are considered the best stock in the county. Most of the colts strongly resemble he sire, being showy and of a gentle disposition. Some of his progeny develop great speed, but more of them become intelligent, attractive family carriage horses, and are owned and prized by many of the best families in this part of the State.

Chief among the valuable horses Mr. Hill has at the present time is Ulster Wilkes, a two-year-old stallion by Guy Wilkes, record 2:15$\frac{1}{4}$, dam by Ulster Chief by Hambletonian No. 10, second dam by May Queen, record 2:24. This is considered one of the finest-bred colts in America. He is very handsome and will, without doubt, make an extra fine horse. Fayette King, a dark brown stallion, three years old, by The King, son of George Wilkes, first dam by Beecher, second dam by imported Consternation, full thoroughbred. This is a fine horse. Sterlingwood, another chestnut stallion, three years old, by Sterling, first dam by Nutwood, second dam by John Nelson. This is also a valuable animal.

Another beautiful black two-year-old stallion, Steve White, by A. W. Richmond, first dam by Ben Wade (thoroughbred), second dam by Traveler, third dam by Son of John Morgan, fourth dam by Tiger Whip, is one of the prettiest colts in the county.

Aside from the above list Mr. Hill has other fine stallions and some splendid mares by Joe Daniels, Ben Wade, Wild Idler, Corbitt and other horses of high record, in all about 120, the majority of which are unusually fine animals. He has a three-quarters of a mile track on the ranch, and keeps a man who thoroughly understands the business to train his stock. Aside from one or two running horses, one of which is Dottie Dimple, record 48$\frac{3}{4}$, half mile, this breeder gives his attention almost exclusively to carriage and trotting horses, and has certainly done Ventura County much good in introducing a class that would do credit to the blue-grass region of Kentucky or any other section of America or the world.

This rancho is supplied with every necessary appliance, commodious buildings, well watered and fenced, and is one of the best for stock-raising on the Pacific coast. Aside from his stock of horses, Mr. Hill keeps some 400 hogs, and raises large quantities of corn, hay and barley.

About a mile from the above rancho is that of J. D. Patterson, of Geneva, New York, covering 6,000 acres. This was also a part of the La Colonia property, and is probably the largest horse rancho on the south side of the Santa Clara River. The whole of this, however, is not devoted to stock, 1,000 acres or more being planted to barley, the product of which was 27,000 sacks last year. This farm keeps 500 head of horses, mostly of the French draft species. Of this number 150 are brood mares.

Mr. Patterson is the owner of the celebrated Montebello, a pure Boulornais stallion a beautiful mahogany bay, foaled at Jabeka, Belgium, in 1875, and imported into this country in August, 1876. His weight is 1,800 pounds. He has taken first premiums wherever exhibited, as well he might, for a finer horse of its kind would be hard to find.

Another noble stallion of this ranch is Black Lewis, a California-raised black fellow, nearly as heavy as his sire. This horse is five years old. Leopold, another son of Montebello, a beautiful dapper-bay stallion, weighing 1,850 pounds, a pure blood, three years old. Cæsar, another three-year-old, and Philipi, another of the same age, Victor, Bonita and Patera, the last three yearlings, are all fine stallions by same sire out of the imported six-year-old mares Marie and Lady Henrietta, and the pure blood, four-year-old, California-raised mare Florence, and are all splendid specimens of this species of horses.

The owner of this property began raising this breed of horses in 1880, and has been very successful. He sells them all over this coast and farther east.

To Mr. Patterson is due the credit of introducing an excellent strain of draft horses.

This ranch, besides raising barley and horses, also produces large quantities of hay and corn; also keeps some 2,000 hogs. The location, soil and equipments are all superb. The fences are good and everything bears the unmistakable evidence of thrift and prosperity.

On the same old La Colonia, about four miles from these, is located another horse ranch owned by J. K. Greis, of Nordhoff, and Thomas Bell, of New Jerusalem, known as the Greis & Bell Ranch. This is a smaller one than the others, containing only about 425 acres, but on it are kept some very fine horses, mostly of the Richmond breed. This rancho keeps several fine stallions; and, like the two above mentioned, keeps a large number of fine brood mares, and makes a business of raising colts that develop into the best carriage and family horses. They pay special attention to the breeding of fine carriage stock and train them for this purpose, not, of course, discouraging speed in trotting or racing. Their place, which is located near Springville, is a valuable one, and is kept in "apple-pie order," being like the other two a credit to the owners and to the county.

Such marked success has attended the development of this industry here that it seems hardly extravagant to predict that the day will come when California shall lead the world in fine horses. The desirable mountain ranges of Ventura County, with the rich alfalfa fields of the valleys, are just the thing to develop the fine form and strong limb of this noble animal; and it would be no unnatural thing for this little seaside county to wave the banner of victory over the world, having achieved the honor of producing, if not the fastest running, the fastest trotting and the finest driving stock on the continent.

BEE KEEPING.

There are about 18,000 hives of bees in this county. In a good year the county produces about 3,000,000 pounds of honey, sufficient to fill 150 cars. In many cases 400 pounds of honey to the hive have been produced. One apiary of 700 hives, and surrounded by bees amounting in all to 1,800 hives within the radius of two miles, averaged 130 pounds each. Another apiary, containing 445 hives in the spring, increased to about 1,200 and yielded eighty tons of honey. These are presented as fair examples of the products of the honey bee in this section.

The bee-keepers of this county use honey extractors, replacing the comb. They have learned to handle it economically in a wholesale way, and receive their full share of the profits. The Langstroth hive in its simplest form is almost the only one in use. The principal part of the honey is put up for shipment in sixty-pound tins, two tins in a case. Some is put up in twelve pound tins, and considerable in one and two pound tins for the English market. But the larger portion is sold by commission merchants in San Francisco, orders being received by them from all parts of the world. Some send their honey by the car-load to the interior States, at a cost of about two and one-half cents a pound; others send it by sailing vessels around Cape Horn to the Eastern States, at a cost of less than one cent a pound.

This industry can be greatly extended in this county. The best locations are at the mouths of cañons where water is plentiful. Some apiarists cultivate a little land while taking care of their bees, and others indulge in stock-raising.

MINING.

Mining in Ventura is as yet comparatively undelvoped.

The mountains of this county are as yet but partly explored, and the most scientific explorers who have visited this section are unacquainted with much they contain. They will yet doubtless yield valuable returns to the faithful investigator in precious metals, valuable minerals and not unlikely gems.

Piru Mining District. This district is several miles in extent, and, in scenery, abundance of timber, excellency of water, salubrity of climate in summer and healthfulness, is hard to excel. The mountains are covered with pine and oak timber; and in the Lockwood and Piru creeks, which traverse the entire district, and are never failing streams fed by springs, abundance of water can be procured for running stamp mills and other mining purposes. Most of the ore is easily accessible and can be worked with comparatively small cost. Considerable placer mining has been done in this district, in which dry and wet washers have been used. Men have made from $1.50 to $5 a day, but the principal wealth lies in the quartz ledges, which require stamp mills to reduce the ore.

Some of the mineral-bearing peaks rise 8,000 feet, and one, Mount Pinos, over 9,000 feet above sea level. Gold was discovered here long before the excitement of 1849. The territory of this district on the northern line of the county has the honor of furnishing the first gold mines discovered and worked in the State.

Professor Whitney says it was somewhere in this vicinity that gold was first obtained in California in considerable quantity, and that was as early as 1841. M. Duflot de

Mofras says that the locality was in the mountains six leagues from San Fernando and fifteen leagues from Los Angeles, where gold was first discovered. Bancroft makes mention of the fact of this locality having been worked more or less during the first half of the present century. It is evident that the yield of gold and silver of this locality has amounted to a large sum in the aggregate.

The director of the mint, in one of his annual reports to the Government, claims that Frazer mountain alone had yielded $1,000,000 in gold.

To preserve the chronological symmetry of the present work, is introduced an extract from the report of the director of the mint for the year 1882. Dr. Bowers gives this at the end of his own paper on these mines, to which recurrence will be made hereafter.

"The Piru District takes its name from the Piru Creek, which runs through it in a southerly direction, carrying, according to season, from 100 to 1,000 inches of water, and has placer diggings along its banks that have been profitably worked. It is about fifty miles in length by twenty-five in width, and is a strongly-marked mineral belt, carrying mineral veins of almost every kind, such as gold, silver, copper, lead, tin, iron, bismuth and antimony. It is abundantly supplied with timber of all kinds and grass. It seems never to have attracted the attention of that class of men who get up booms in mining camps. Those who frequent it are poor men, who go there to make a raise, working the rich gold quartz they find, in arrastras. The district is in Ventura County, and the part around which the principal interest centers and the work is mainly done is distant fifty-five miles from Bakersfield.

"The principal lode is called the Fraser mine. During the time it was worked, a period of eight years, until operations ceased, October 31, 1879, because of litigation arising from disputed ownership, it is believed to have yielded about $1,000,000 in gold. The difficulty is now said to be on the eve of settlement, and it will be worked by improved methods and on a larger scale than heretofore. The vein varies from two to sixteen feet in width, and will average eight feet. The ore contains a small percentage of silver, which seems to increase with depth. At the depth of 250 feet it amounts to $6 per ton, while there was only a trace at the surface. The ore contains iron and other sulphurets that assay from $3.00 to $3.50 per ton. They are all saved, but there is no means of treating them at the mine. The yield in free gold is from $15 to $25 per ton. There are many other claims in the vicinity that are successfully worked, yielding from $500 to $3,500 yearly by the arrastra process. One of these, the Castac, has yielded about $1,500.

"Some of the most valuable lodes cannot be worked by the free-milling process, because they contain lead, and therefore lie idle for the present. One of these, the Mountain Chief, a large, well-defined vein, gives an average of $31 in gold and $40 in silver per ton. The ore is also charged with rich sulphates. Probably one of the most valuable lodes in the district, if it were in some other place, is a vein of magnetic iron fifty feet in width, containing fifty-two per cent. of this useful metal.

"In this district are Frazer, Fitzgerald, Alamo, Brown and other mountains, all within the boundary line of Ventura County. In these are found true fissure quartz veins with granite walls, yielding gold and silver in paying quantities. Unfortunately for the development of these ledges they have generally fallen into the hands of persons who have had little or no capital to work them.

They are holding their claims by doing the necessary assessment work from year to year, awaiting the advent of men who can command the means to purchase and develop them.

"Gold has also been found in the Guadalasca range on the eastern side of the county, not far from the sea shore. The mountains rise from 3,000 to 4,000 feet above the sea level a few miles back from the ocean, and contain numerous quartz deposits in which free gold is found. It has never been successfully mined in this locality, but prospectors have recently brought in some fine-looking ore carrying a considerable quantity of free gold. This section still lacks thorough scientific investigation.

"The San Emidio Antimony Mine was located by its present owners in 1872. It is claimed that this ledge was known to the Jesuit Fathers at an early day and was worked under their direction. I learn that there is a record to this effect in some of the old missions, and that implements have been found here and elsewhere in this portion of the country, indicating their use in these mines many years ago.

"Professor William R. Blake, who visited this locality in 1853 as geologist and mineralogist of the expedition surveying a route for the Pacific Railroad, refers to this deposit of antimony and says that in one place he found the remains of some old smelting works. Mr. Blake revisited this locality some years afterward, being much impressed with the character of its mineral deposits. In his reports he believed the antimony of sufficient importance to pay for its transportation to San Pedro on mules, a distance of over 100 miles, to what was then the nearest seaport. The ore is principally sulphuret of antimony. The vein crops out on the summit of the San Emidio Range, and is from thirty to 100 feet in width. The hanging and foot walls are composed of granite. The ore is carried on donkeys over a trail two and one-half miles to smelting works in San Emidio Cañon, which is 2,500 feet below the vein at the place where it is being mined. Here is a pulverizer and three concentrators, with other machinery, run by steam power.

"Messrs. Bouchey & Co., the owners of this mine, are preparing to erect a tramway or slide from the mine to the works, which will be about one and one-half mile in length. There is an abundance of pine timber growing near by that may be utilized for the purpose, while in the cañon where the smelting works are located is a never-failing stream of water. The ore averages from thirty to thirty-five per cent. of antimony. It is also stated that it contains from $4 to $16 per ton in gold, and from $10 to $14 in silver. * * * The mountain west of this ledge is capped with metamorphic sandstones, which Mr. Bouchey has tested for lining the furnaces of his smelting works, and pronounces it equal to the best imported fire-bricks."

A large bed of gypsum occurs in the Ojai Valley, crossing the hill below the grade road that ascends to the upper valley. There is an exposure in the cañon on the south side of the road, some fifteen or twenty feet wide, dipping slightly to the east. It disappears under the mountain, but crops out nearly a mile distant on the opposite side. It is situated so that it can be easily worked, requiring the construction of a wagon road but about 2,000 feet along the side of the cañon. A large deposit of gypsum is reported to have been found recently in the western portion of the county. It is also found in small quantities in other portions of the county.

A ledge of bituminous rock was discovered a few months since in Diablo Cañon, about five miles from Ventura, and is worked by Messrs. Cyrus Bellah & Son. It is on the side of the cañon, and has been prospected a distance of forty feet and forty feet deep. The deposit gradually increases in thickness, and gives promise of being practically inexhaustible. It has been tested by the Southern Pacific Company and others, who pronounce it of most excellent quality. The town authorities of San Buenaventura have ordered sidewalks to be constructed of this material on one of its principal streets, which will test its durability and value for paving purposes. Small deposits of this mineral are found in the upper Ojai Valley and other places in the county.

The county abounds in hot and cold mineral springs. The most noted of these are situated in the Matilaja Cañon, fifteen or eighteen miles from San Buenaventura. They have been in use several years by persons suffering from rheumatism, indigestion, and cutaneous and other diseases. They are found somewhat abundantly for two or three miles along the cañon, varying in temperature from cold to hot. Several medicinal springs are found on the Piru and at other portions of the county, but they have not been brought to the notice of the public.

Already all the following named minerals have been found in Ventura County, and doubtless others will be discovered in other portions of the section that as yet have not been critically examined:

Agate, analcite, actinolite, aragonite, antimony, amygdaloid, azurite, alabaster, auriferous quartz, argillaceous ironstone.

Bitumen, basalt, bromide of silver, bituminous rock, breccia, banded agate, brown coal, bituminous shale.

Copper, calcite, cinnabar, chalcedony, chert, chrysolite, conglomerate, calcareous tufa, carbonaceous shale, chrysocolla, compact gypsum, coal, chimney rock.

Dolomite, dendrite, dogtooth spar, diorite, diatomaceous earth.

Epsomite.

Feldspar, fortification agate.

Gold, garnets, granite, graphite, galenite, gypsum, granular gypsum, fibrous gypsum, graphic granite, gneiss, grit rock, granular quartz, gray kip ore.

Hornblende, hornblendic gneiss, hyalite.

Iron, ironstone, iron pyrites, infusorial earth, jasper, jelsonite.

Kaolinite, lava, limestone lignite.

Mercury, marble, moss-agate, manganese, magnetic iron, marl, mica, mica schist, mottled jasper, massive calcite, micaceous granite, massive gypsum.

Natrolite, native sulphur, nickel (?), naphtha.

Opal, obsidian, oxide of iron, orthoclase.

Porphyry, petroleum, pumice-stone, pudding-stone, pitch-stone, potters' clay, petrified wood, pyrites, picrolite (?).

Quartz, quartzose granite.

Rose agate, ruby silver.

Silver, satin spar, salt, sulphur, shale, silica, silt, stalactite, stalagmite, slate, syenite, steatite, serpentine, selenite, semi-opal, shell marble.

Tin (?), trachyte, talc, talcose slate, tufa, trap, travertine, vesicular basalt, wood opal, zeolite.

Potters' clay, pipe clay, brick clay and several other kinds that may be utilized and their manufacture grow into important industries, are found in this county. Also mineral soap is found in large quantity. This soap is composed of nearly pure silica, being the remains of infusoria, a microscopical organism that existed in vast numbers in past time. These deposits have detergent qualities, and are a valuable substitute for manufactured soap in many respects. It is also valuable for the manufacture of dynamite, in which it soaks up and retains the liquid nitro-glycerine, and is valuable for some other purposes.

Ventura County contains enough good building stone to supply the State of California for centuries to come. A ledge of brown sandstone begins at the Sespe and continues in a westerly direction (probably curving northwardly) for over twenty-five miles to the ocean. It is several miles wide and of unknown depth. It crops out in various accessible places and varies in texture and hardness. But in every instance, so far as known, it is an excellent building stone. In some places this vast ledge has been lifted to a vertical position and in others it is horizontal. It can be quarried in any size required by builders.

This stone is being used extensively for the finest buildings in San Francisco and Los Angeles, and this promises to be one of the permanent and profitable industries of the county, whose development will furnish employment for thousands of workmen, skilled and unskilled.

Other building stone is found in various portions of the county, as greenish and gray sandstone. In some places these are found in extensive ledges, but they are not equal in texture and beauty to the red sandstone above described. In the northern portion of the county may be found millions of tons of granite, syenite and mica slate. The former contains large rose-colored crystals of orthoclase, giving it a most beautiful appearance, which is heightened by polishing. The mica, feldspar and quartz are distributed in such a manner as to make the granite durable and valuable for building and monumental purposes. The syenite is exceedingly tough and durable. In other portions of the county vast quantities of compact slate rock may be obtained, and also diorite. Compact basaltic rocks in almost unlimited quantity may be found at the southeastern and northwestern portions of the county.

Altogether the building stone of Ventura County is inexhaustible. In quality it is probably unexcelled in the State. Henceforward the "Ventura brownstone" will go into the finest buildings in every city in California.

The asphaltum or bituminous rock mines form one of the coming great interests of Ventura County. Up to this time a vast quantity has been shipped to various cities for street paving, etc., and large contracts are being filled for contractors working in Colorado and Utah. The output over the Ventura wharf will average perhaps ten tons daily. New deposits have been discovered lately, and preparations are making to ship in large quantities as far east as New York. It is hoped that this county will soon be able to supply the demand for this article, formerly supplied from the Trinidad Islands. These beds of asphalt, along the San Antonio Creek, were first examined before the war, and before the oil discoveries in Pennsylvania, by Professor Silliman of the Smithsonian Institute. His report called attention to this territory, and led to the organization of the California & Philadelphia Petroleum Company.

MINERAL OILS.

(From the State Mineralogical Report.)

Owing to the vast mineral oil deposits in this section, Ventura is known as the "oil county" of California. The oil belt lies in the mountains to the north of the Santa Clara River; it starts from near the eastern boundary of the county, and runs in a southeasterly direction to the San Buenaventura River. It is also found near the Conejo Rancho and in other places in the county.

The wells are mostly situated from three to six miles north of the edge of the Santa Clara Valley, in and about a series of cañons which run southerly to the Santa Clara River. The names of these cañons in order, from east to west, are as follows: Piru, Hopper,

Sespe, Santa Paula, Adams, Saltmarsh (a branch of Adams), Wheeler, West Wheeler (a branch of Wheeler), Sulphur and Coche (these two being branches of the Cañada Larga). There are also a few wells in the Ojai Valley.

Westerly from Santa Paula Creek, between the Ojai Valley on the north and the Santa Clara Valley on the south, there extends an unbroken mountain ridge, whose highest crest is about 2,000 feet above the sea, as far west as the San Buenaventura River This ridge is called "Sulphur Mountain," and all the cañons above named to the west of Santa Paula Cañon lie on the southern flank of Sulphur Mountain.

Piru Canon.—From Camulos station it is about six miles to the well of Messrs. Rhodes & Baker, head of Brea Cañon. * * *

The well is about 250 feet north of the anticlinal axis, and is now (July 12, 1887) 715 feet deep. * * They have stopped drilling this well for a while, because their water supply for the engine gave out. There is a moderate quantity of gas in the water from this well. The oil from the well is dark brown in color. This is said to be the only well in or about Piru Cañon. And certain it is that in the Piru Cañon itself the visible surface indications of bituminous matter are very slight. From 200 to 300 feet south of the well there is an extensive deposit of asphaltum mixed with surface sand, and numerous little springs of black maltha scattered over perhaps an acre of ground. Next west of Piru Cañon comes

Hopper Canon,—at whose mouth * * * a well was drilled in 1877, by M. W. Beardsley, to a depth of 800 feet, * * * when the work was stopped for lack of funds. * * * Even at that depth * * * it would probably have yielded three or four barrels per day of light green oil. From this well, in an air line * * about one and one-half miles, * * * are two wells about 200 feet apart. The lower one is ninety feet deep, and was abandoned because the hole became irretrievably crooked. There was here a good deal of heavy black oil. The other well is a new one just started, * * * yet they have a little heavy black oil on the tools even now.

All the way from here down to the mouth of the cañon there is liquid oil floating on top of the water in the creek. Some of it is green and some of it is black. The aggregate quantity of oil which thus oozes out and floats away on the water is, of course, not large; nevertheless it is greater in this cañon than in any other cañon yet seen in Southern California.

About opposite Waring's house, in the hills on the south side of the Santa Clara Valley, on the Simi Rancho, and on the northern slopes of the San Fernando range of mountains, there is a large deposit of asphaltum, together with extensive outflows of liquid petroleum, where, some years ago, a man gathered for a while about ten barrels of oil per day. Oil men believe that with the expenditure of a moderate amount of labor a surface flow of forty barrels per day could be obtained there. Mr. Hugh Waring states that this is the most westerly point where asphaltum is found in the San Fernando Range. He also says that east of there, in the hills somewhere to the south of Camulos, he has seen cattle mired and dead in pools of viscid and muddy maltha.

Sespe Canon.—Sespe Creek, occupying the cañon next west of Hopper Cañon, is the largest and longest northern branch of the Santa Clara River in Ventura County. It heads far back in the mountains to the north of the Ojai Valley, and at first flows nearly east for a number of miles, passing entirely around the head branches of Santa Paula Cañon, and then curves around so that its general direction for the last ten or twelve miles of its course in the mountains is nearly south. The mouth of the cañon is something like ten miles east of the town of Santa Paula. "Tar Creek" and the "Little Sespe" are two different branches of the main Sespe Cañon, both of them coming in from the east, the mouth of Tar Creek being several miles above that of the Little Sespe. The latter is a short cañon not more than four or five miles in length, but Tar Creek is a longer stream. * * * Near the mouth of the main Sespe Cañon one small oil spring occurs in the bed of the cañon. In the Little Sespe there is a nice little spring of water, and occasional small oil springs and seepages. * * * In the Little Sespe are the so-called "Los Angeles" wells, of which there are two. One of these is about 1,500 feet deep, and is said to have yielded at first, for some time, about 150 barrels per day. But about the year 1882, in the course of a "freeze out" game amongst the owners, while still yielding some forty barrels per day, it was maliciously plugged by somebody, and thus ruined. The other one went down about 200 feet, when it became crooked.

The present wells of the "Sespe Oil Company" are scattered about the upper branches of Tar Creek. * * * Well No. 1 is on the right bank of the main Tar Creek. It was begun January 26, 1887, and finished February 12, 1887; is 196 feet deep, and pumps about forty barrels per day of a very dark-colored greenish-brown oil. This well first started off at about 100 barrels per day.

No. 2 is about 300 feet southeasterly from No. 1. It was drilled in April, 1887, and is 206 feet deep. It first started off at about 150 barrels per day, but afterward fell off, and now flows about seventy-five barrels per day of a dark green oil. It also produces considerable gas.

No. 4 is probably 1,200 feet northwesterly from No.

1, and is a new well, not yet drilled. Nos. 1, 2 and 4 are nearly in a straight line. No. 5 is on Oil Creek. Here they have not begun drilling.

No. 3 is down about 500 feet, and they are still drilling.

No. 6 is located some 500 feet easterly from No. 1. Here the grading has been done, but the derrick is not yet erected.

The foregoing statements refer to the condition of the wells July 25, 1887. Some months later No. 2 was reported pumping instead of flowing; beginning with 225 barrels per day, it continued with about 140 per day. No. 4, now about 400 feet deep, was pumping twenty-five barrels per day. Nos. 3 and 4, having gone down about 700 feet, proved dry holes.

The report of the State Mineralogist for 1888 contains the following:

In addition to the report relating to these deposits, published by the Mining Bureau, last year, I have to say that work has steadily progressed, and the output of oil for the last fiscal year has increased from 62,500 barrels to 226,050 barrels.

The following is a statement of the work which has been done in this district during the year ending September 18:

Hopper Cañon.—Considerable work has been done here, but the returns have been meager. The formation is so broken up that it is not unlikely the oil exudes at the surface as rapidly as it is elaborated below. In order to thoroughly test this locality two wells have been drilled during the past year, one 400, and the other about 800, feet deep. In the deeper well a small amount of oil was struck, and a large flow of water. In the 400-foot well a flow of soda water was obtained, which is said to be of excellent quality, and may be profitably utilized.

Piru Cañon.—Like Hopper Cañon, this seems to be outside of the paying oil belt. Two new wells have been drilled here during the past year. One was sunk to a depth of 1,000 feet, but no oil was obtained, and it was abandoned. Another well was sunk one-fourth of a mile away, but it was abandoned for the same reason.

Sespe Cañon.—The efforts of the oil company have been much more successful here. Eight new wells have been dug here during the year, which, in the aggregate, yield a large quantity of oil.

No. 7 is located about thirty rods southwest of No. 5. The depth reached was 300 feet. When first completed the well produced twenty barrels a day, but now yields ten barrels daily.

No. 8, located about eighty rods north of No. 4, was drilled to a depth of 650 feet, and yielded seventy-five barrels a day; now reduced to forty-five barrels daily.

No. 9, located about 600 feet from No. 4, is down to a depth of 400 feet, and is producing about eight barrels a day.

No. 10 is about 500 feet south of No. 7. It is 350 feet deep and pumps seventy-five barrels a day.

No. 11 is southwest of No. 8, and is down to a depth of 400 feet. It produced thirty or forty barrels a day, but quickly ran down to its present product of about nine barrels.

No. 12 is north of No. 8, and is about 650 feet deep. This well produces seventy-five barrels daily.

No. 13 is one-half mile north of No. 12, on Irelan Creek. It is 600 feet deep, and pumps ten barrels a day.

No. 14 is west of No. 13, and was drilled as a test well, going down 1,400 feet. About 500 feet below the surface a small deposit of oil was struck, but the well is practically dry.

No. 15 is south of No. 13, and is still drilling at a depth of 700 feet. Considerable water has been struck, and a small quantity of oil.

No. 16 is down about 100 feet, and still drilling.

These wells are located twenty-five miles from the ocean, at an altitude of 2,800 feet.

Adams Cañon.—Well No. 16, which was completed in January, at a depth of 730 feet, is the largest flowing well ever struck in California. The oil, when reached, shot up to the height of nearly 100 feet, and flowed at the rate of 800 or 900 barrels daily. Before it could be controlled it sent a stream down the cañon for a distance of seven miles. After the lapse of nine months it continues to flow at the rate of 500 barrels daily.

No. 17 is drilled to a depth of 1,400 feet, but is a small producer, barely paying for pumping.

No. 18 is located about 400 feet south of No. 9, and is about 900 feet deep and still in process of drilling.

The Adams Cañon wells are about the head of the cañon, and most of them strung along a very narrow belt about three-quarters of a mile long. These wells are quite productive. No. 13, when one year old, had produced 74,000 barrels, and is still producing 220 barrels daily. There is considerable asphaltum on the surface of the ground in Adams Cañon. The largest patch covers probably one or two acres of ground and contains numerous little springs of black maltha. Adams Cañon well, No. 16, is probably also the largest gas well on the Pacific Coast. At the present time it is producing sufficient gas to run all the works and machinery in the cañon.

Saltmarsh Cañon,—named after John Saltmarsh, promises well.

Well No. 1 was completed in January, 1888. It is 290 feet deep, and produces seventy-five barrels daily.

No. 2 was abandoned on account of "crooked hole" and caving, at 350 feet deep.

No. 3 is finished to a depth of 400 feet. It is producing forty barrels per day.

Santa Paula Cañon,—formerly called "Mupu Cañon," contains the group called the "Scott" wells, situated about five miles from the town of Santa Paula. They are from three to ten years old. There were eleven or twelve in all, some five or six only of which are now producing an aggregate of about eleven barrels per day. They range from 200 to 1,000 feet deep The oil is black.

Wheeler Cañon—contains three wells, drilled in 1887-'88, which yield only about ten barrels per day in the aggregate.

Aliso Cañon—promises to produce oil in paying quantities.

During 1887-'88 the Hardison & Stewart Oil Company erected at Santa Paula refining works which are claimed to be the most complete of the kind in the country. The machinery and equipment in general include the latest improvements for oil refining. This company manufactures benzine, illuminating oil, gas and domestic fuel; distillates, wool oil, neutral oil, lubricating oils, and maltha. The crude oil yields from fifteen to twenty per cent. of illuminating oil, and from thenty to twenty-five per cent. of maltha or asphaltum. The illuminating oil is of excellent quality, and claimed to be superior to any that has been made on the Pacific Coast. It burns with a clear and steady flame, and is free from smoke or disagreeable odor. The asphaltum is used for pipe dipping, for the manufacture of paints and varnishes, and for coating roofs, bridges, etc. It is a beautiful glossy black, absolutely impervious to water, and particularly adapted to coating iron. The lubricating oil is said to have a lower cold test than any other ever discovered in the United States. It does not harden until it reaches a much lower degree of cold than any other oil known, hence is adapted to locomotives and other machinery subject to cold weather.

The oil regions of California have headquarters at Santa Paula, where there are six companies, viz.: the Hardison & Stewart Oil Company, Sespe Oil Company, Torrey Cañon Oil Company, Mission Transfer Oil Company, Ventura Oil Company, and O'Hara Brothers. The most extensive petroleum oil operations are on the Rancho ex-Mission, situated along the south side of Sulphur Mountain, beginning about four miles northwest of the town, and extending westerly eight miles. These works are owned and operated by the Hardison & Stewart Company, incorporated with a capital stock of $1,000,000. Lyman Stewart is president and general manager; W. L. Hardison, vice-president and treasurer; Alex. Waldie, secretary. This company has been most successful in its development, having a large production from their many wells and tunnels. There is connected with the company's offices at Santa Paula a complete telephone system. The region is a network of pipe lines conveying the oil to Santa Paula, Ventura and Hueneme. The next most extensive oil developments in this region are located at Sespe, and are owned and operated by the Sespe Oil Company, with its office at Santa Paula. The company has a capital stock of $250,000. Thomas R. Bard is president; D. McFarland, vice-president; W. L. Hardison, treasurer and general manager; Alex. Waldie, secretary. The Torrey Cañon Oil Company is opearating three miles south of Piru Station. Its officers are: Thos. R. Bard, president; W. S. Chaffe, vice-president; I. H. Warring, secretary; W. L. Hardison, superintendent. The production of the region is also very large, and is piped to Santa Paula. The wells have telephone connection with the main office. These four companies keep a large force of men constantly engaged in the drilling of new oil wells; and thus the production is being constantly augmented. The Mission Transfer Company has a capital stock of $500,000; T. R. Bard is president; Lyman Stewart, vice-president; W. L. Hardison, treasurer and general manager; I. H. Warring, secretary. This company has about 100 miles of pipe lines and forty tanks, the largest one holding 30,000 barrels. They have fifty-two oil-tank cars, and have a refinery, where they make all the various products usually manufactured from petroleum, notably lubricating oil, gas oil and naphtha. Asphaltum (maltha) is also refined in large quantities, and is used extensively both on this coast and in the East for coating pipe and other iron goods, for roofing, and for paving purposes. No industry in the Golden State promises better results than its oil developments; and nothing is more beneficial to Ventura County, and to Santa Paula in particular, than the business of these four oil companies. With an abundance of cheap petroleum for fuel no section offers better advantages for manufacturing purposes than Santa Paula.

The prospects of this industry are now brighter than ever before. The Sespe Oil Company has now drilled thirty-one wells, varying in depth from 450 to over 1,800 feet, yielding at this time an average product of 7,000 barrels monthly. The last well, No. 29, promises to give 150 to 300 barrels per diem. Developments have just begun on the "Kentucky Oil Claim," where, in well No. 2, was struck near the surface sand-rock so full of oil that it could not be drilled over 200 feet; after exhausting this well by pumping, work will be continued. The Sespe Oil Company has a lease of about 7,000 acres of the best oil lands on the Simí Rancho, and are beginning to drill thereon, the territory being deemed rich in oil. The production of the Hardison & Stewart Company is increasing very rapidly, being 8,000 to 9,000 barrels per month. Adams Cañon well, No. 13, opened August, 1887, has to date produced 125,000 barrels, which, at the average price of fuel oil—$1.75 per barrel—has been a fortune in itself. They have in all drilled thirty-four wells, the last of which, in Adams Cañon, averages over 125 barrels per day. They have at present three sets of tools, each employing four experienced drillers, pushing developments more rapidly than ever before, and the expectation is that 20,000 barrels per month will be reached before the close of the year. No part of the development has paid better than the oil tunnels. Adams' Tunnel, No. 3, where three men were killed in April, 1890, by a gas explosion, was at that time 950 feet long; work has just been resumed, and it is expected to reach 1,000 to 2,000 feet further into the mountain, which it will drain of oil.

In 1889 work was began in the Upper Ojai Valley, and two wells are yielding average production, with a third well now in process of drilling.

RESIDENCE OF A. SCHIAPPA PIETRA.—SAN BUENAVENTURA, VENTURA COUNTY, CALIFORNIA.

BIOGRAPHICAL SKETCHES.

SCHIAPPA PIETRA BROS., upright and capable business men of San Buenaventura, came here as pioneers in 1857, when there were scarcely any Americans in the whole county. They are natives of Italy. Sr. A. Schiappa Pietra was born February 2, 1832, and in 1853 came to California, and after spending six months in San Francisco he came to San Luis Obispo and opened a general merchandise store, which was conducted successfully for fourteen months. He then sold out and went to San Fransisco in search of a locality for business, but, failing, he visited San Diego, San Bernardino and other places in Southern California and located in Santa Barbara, engaged in general merchandise; and while there, in 1857, he started a store in San Buenaventura, and in 1878 sold out his business there. In 1864 he bought the Santa Clara del Norte ranch of 13,900 acres and stocked it with sheep; 30,000 or 40,000 are now kept upon it. Also there are planted on the ranch trees of various kinds, including olives and oranges, and they are doing well. Formerly about 4,000 acres were devoted to barley, but this year it is the intention to plant 5,000 acres to beans.

The younger brother, Sr. Leopold Schiappa Pietra, was born February 3, 1842, and came to California in 1866, since which time his business was united with that of his brother. He married Miss Amparo Arenas, a native of California, and they have a son and a daughter, both of whom are deceased.

In 1877 the brothers built their present fine residence, and have made it a place of unusual beauty. The grounds are planted and decorated with artistic skill, and are extremely well cared for. They are also the owners of the St. Charles Hotel at Santa Barbara and the Palace Hotel in San Buenaventura. They are zealous members of the Holy Catholic Church, and are exemplary citizens.

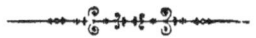

GAIUS WEBSTER, of San Miguel, was born in Delaware County, New York, November 22, 1842, his father, John Webster, being a respectable farmer and justice of the peace. Was educated mainly in the public schools; qualified himself for teaching, and taught school in the winter of 1861–'62.

In August, 1862, enlisted in Company A, One Hundred and Forty-fourth Regiment, New York Volunteer Infantry, and served until July, 1865, being discharged by reason of the close of the war.

Returning to his native county, he spent a month or two visiting relatives and friends, and packing his gripsack started for Oregon alone. There was not a soul on the Pacific coast that he had ever seen, but he was determined to carve a way for himself among strangers in a new and rising country. Stopping in Douglas County, Oregon, he worked for a time in a logging camp, afterward attending an academy at Roseburg, reviewing the studies of former years and pursuing such sciences as the curriculum of the institution included.

In 1866 he entered as a law student the office of Hon. S. F. Chadwick, who afterward became Secretary of State and Governor. Having read the usual course, he was examined in the Supreme Court and admitted to the bar September, 1867. In the spring of 1868 he purchased the Roseburg *Ensign*, which he carried on as editor and publisher until the spring of 1870, and also attending to such law business as presented. In the political campaign of that year he became the candidate of the Republican party for the office of County Judge, but was defeated with the whole ticket. It was during this period that he became acquainted with Miss Anna West, an estimable lady teacher, to whom he was married in 1870. Near the close of that year, having disposed of the newspaper, he moved to the adjoining county of Coos, settling at Marshfield, on Coos Bay, and engaged in the practice of his profession. In 1872 he was nominated and elected State Senator for the district including Douglas, Coos and Curry counties. He occupied a seat in the State Senate during the sessions of 1872 and 1874, being the youngest member of that body. From 1875 to 1877 he was associated with D. L. Watson, Esq., in the publishing of the *Coos County Record*, a Republican paper, the editorial management of which devolved upon Mr. Webster. On the opening of the year 1878, with I. Hacker, he established the newspaper known as the *Coast Mail*, which he edited for two years, at the same time attending to a considerable law practice.

In 1880 he sold the paper, and for two years devoted his entire attention to the law. In the meantime pulmonary and bronchial disease developed in his family, and in the winter of 1882 he moved to Santa Cruz, California, where in the following year he resumed the practice of the law. The coast air of that beautiful place proving unfavorable to his family he moved to Los Gatos, where he purchased an interest in the Los Gatos *News*, but devoted his time to the profession of the law.

In February, 1886, being impressed with the central location and favorable surroundings of San Miguel, he established at that place the *Inland Messenger*, afterward changed to the San Miguel *Messenger*, which he carried on with his law business for two years, when he sold the property to F. J. Burns, its present proprietor.

Mr. Webster's family consists of his wife and two sons, and two daughters, all nearly grown. His time is now fully and profitably occupied in his profession; he is also improving a fruit farm near town, where he has about thirty acres planted in choice varieties. He is Commander of John Buford Post, No. 136, G. A. R.; Overseer of San Miguel Grange and Notary Public. Mr. Webster is looked upon by his fellow citizens as one of the most enterprising and public-spirited men of San Miguel, and takes an active part in promoting the interests of the place. He stands high in his profession and enjoys a good practice, and looks exceeding young for one who was for the three worst years of the war engaged in the great and saving struggle for National life, and appears as if he was good for another half century of usefulness.

HON. H. PETERSEN is one of the leading business men of Templeton, San Luis Obispo County, California. He is a native of Hamburg, Germany, born July 5, 1840. His parents, Adolph and Augusta Peterson, were Germans who emigrated to the United States, in 1855, bringing their family of six children with them, the subject of this sketch being the second child of the family. They settled near Davenport, Iowa, on a farm of 150 acres, which they bought. They built a home on the property, and made other improvements.

Mr. Petersen had received his education in Germany and was fifteen years of age when they came to America. When he began life for himself, he had twelve dollars. He engaged in farming on shares, and continued it until 1868, when he moved west to Grundy County, and purchased 160 acres of prairie land, at five dollars per acre. Here he built a house and improved the property, and lived for fifteen years. At this time the railroad was built to Reinbeck, and Mr. Petersen moved into town, and opened a hardware and agricultural implement business. He built one store and purchased another, and did a prosperous business until 1886, when he sold out. He was elected a member of the Twenty-first General Assembly by the Democratic party, while there, and served the term of office with credit to himself and his constituents. In the spring of 1886 he visited California, and traveled the State over, looking for a place to settle. In 1887 he came to San Luis Obispo County, and invested in 200 acres of land near Templeton and bought two village lots. In October, 1888, he brought his family to their new home. He bought the hardware business of Mr. E. Griffith, the principal business of the place. It had been started in the spring of 1887. Mr. Petersen has since continued the business, and has made a success of it. He deals in both hardware and agricultural implements, and his trade extends out for twenty-six miles. His lands are rented and he is getting a share of the crops. He has engaged, to some extent, in the culture of fruit on his lands, principally French prunes.

Mr. Petersen was married in Iowa, in 1863, to Miss M. Klein, a native of Saxony, and of German parentage. They have had ten children, seven of whom are living, viz: Teresa, Ida, Antonette, Henryetta, Carl, Rudolph, and Hubert, all born in Iowa. Teresa and Antonetta are married, one in Kansas, and the other in San Bernardino, California. Mr. and Mrs. Petersen are Lutherans, and he is an Odd Fellow. He is still a member of the Democratic party; is a man having well defined business and political ideas; has a general information on all topics; gives his business close personal attention; and is withal a worthy citizen and desirable acquisition to the new town in which he has cast his lot.

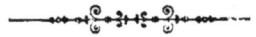

JOHN QUARNSTROM is one of the business men of San Luis Obispo County. He was born in Sweden, of Swedish parents, January 26, 1851; and came to the United States March 28, 1884. Previous to his arrival in America, he was a merchant and contractor in his native country. His first business enterprise in the United States was in Minneapolis, Minnesota, where he carried on cabinet-making, and also did a real-estate business. In 1887 he came to Templeton, California, bought out a store, conducted it two years, and then joined the corporation comprising the Bank of Templeton, and the general merchandise firm of J. Quarnstrom & Co., and also the general merchandise firm at Paso Robles of the Nelson Quarnstrom Company. He has also become interested in lands and is engaging in fruit culture. He has build a block in Templeton, and erected one of the finest residences in the town, where he resides with his family.

Mr. Quarnstrom was married to Miss S. C. Erksen, a native of Sweden, and their union has been blessed with two children, Annie C. and Ernest L. Both he and his wife are members of the Lutheran Church. Mr. Quarnstrom is a member of the I. O. O. F., and in his political views he is independent. He and his family are worthy people, a credit and an important acquisition to the community in which they reside.

B. BALLARD is one of the prominent ranchers of Huer-Huero, two and a half miles southwest of Creston, San Luis Obispo County, California. He is the owner of a beautiful estate of 640 acres. The house and farm buildings, which he planned and erected, stand on an eminence somewhat back from the highway, and present a home-like and picturesque appearance. The undulating hills, dotted over with majestic white oaks, form a fine back and fore ground to the picture.

Mr. Ballard is a native of England, born September 23, 1860. He received a liberal education in England, and in March, 1880, came to America in search of health and fortune. He went first to Iowa, and from there to Minnesota, where he purchased 640 acres of land which he still owns. In 1883 he came to San Luis Obispo County, California. Cressey, Adams & Ambrose purchased the property and placed it in the hands of C. H. Phillips for subdivision and sale. As soon as it was subdivided Mr. Ballard was one of the first buyers. He is now engaged in diversified farming, raising hay, grain, horses and mules.

Mr. Ballard had the asthma very bad, and has found the climate on his ranch very salutary and is now quite free from the disease.

In January, 1889, Mr. Ballard was united in marriage with Miss G. Hayes, a native of Maryland, and daughter of Dr. W. W. Hayes who is the pioneer physician of San Luis Obispo.

Mr. Ballard's ancestors for five generations have been in the English navy, and up to his father, Captain J. B. Ballard, they have all risen to the position of Admiral. His younger brother, Casper, has now entered the navy with the intention of keeping up the family line in that department. His grandfather, Admiral V. V. Ballard, had the honor of being the captor of the Island of Guadaloupe and Cape Town, South Africa. Mr. Ballard's mother, Charlotte (Hale) Ballard, was the daughter of a land-holder in Hampshire, England.

Mr. and Mrs. Ballard are members of the Episcopal Church. They are highly entertaining and courteous people.

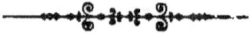

C. JAMISON, a rancher of Santa Ynez, was born in Redwood, Santa Clara County, December 25, 1860. His father, T. B. Jamison, is a native of Maryland, and came across the plains to California in 1854, and again in 1859, with his family, settling in Santa Clara County. In

1865 he was a pioneer to Salinas City, Monterey County, and built the first house. In 1872 he moved to Guadalupe, being among the first to enter that valley. W. C. Jamison lived at home during the several changes of the family, and in 1882 they again broke up; at the opening of the Santa Ynez Valley, went there and established themselves. He rents about 680 acres of land from the Santa Ynez Improvement Company, which he cultivates to wheat and barley, principally grain. This year (1890), the hay crop being short, he is cutting everything for hay; will cut about 275 tons and 150 acres for grain. He uses all heavy machinery, and presses hay in the field.

Mr. Jamison was married at Santa Ynez, December 18, 1889, to Miss Alice B. Mills, a native of California.

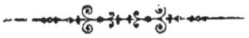

ADOLPH F. HORSTMAN, one of the prominent business men of Templeton, is a stockholder and the cashier of the Templeton Bank, and a member of two general merchandise firms at Templeton and Paso Robles, namely, Quarnstrom & Co. and the Nelson Quarnstrom Company, both doing an extensive mercantile business. He is also interested in ranch property and horticulture. Mr. Horstman is a native of Davenport, Iowa, born in July, 1865. His parents, William and Amelia Horstman, were both natives of Germany, and came to the United States in 1861, settling in Iowa on a farm. They were poor people and honest and industrious, and worked by the day and month. After a time they purchased eighty acres of land, which increased in acres and value, until in the course of years they had several thousand acres of valuable land. His father and family came to California in September, 1887, and is now retired from active business, and resides in a pleasant home in Templeton, where he expects to spend the evening of life, amusing himself in the cultivation of fruit and the ornamentation of his grounds.

Mr. Adolph F. Horstman, our subject, was educated at Vinton, Iowa, in the Tillford Academy. He engaged in the grain business, as book-keeper for his father for four years. When he was nineteen years of age his father started him in the merchandise business, in Sutherland, O'Brien County, Iowa. He continued the business successfully until 1887, when he sold out and came to Templeton, where he established the bank, and engaged in banking business, to which he now gives his personal attention.

Mr. Horstman was married in 1887, to Miss Hatty Sibert, of Reinbeck, Iowa, daughter of Dr. J. G. Sibert, of that State. Mr. Horstman is a member of the Masonic fraternity, and also of the Independent Order of Odd Fellows. He has taken an active part in politics, when he resided in Sutherland, Iowa, and was elected Recorder of that town by the Democratic party, of which he is a member.

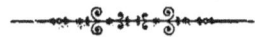

H. B. SMITH, a prominent citizen and Justice of the Peace of Creston, is a native of Southern Ohio, born near Sandusky, July 9, 1841. His father, William Smith, was a native of Connecticut, and a soldier in the war of 1812. He was in the Ninth United States Infantry, and at the battle of Sackett's Harbor. Mr. Smith has the pocket-book his father carried in that war, and many other interesting relics. His father married Lucy Turner, a native of New York, and daughter of Mr. Samuel Turner, who was a soldier of the Revolution. Mr. Smith's grandfather, Eri Smith, was also a soldier of the Revolution; so that, as far as patriotism is concerned, he can claim as good ancestry as the best. His parents had eleven children, four of whom are now living. He was the youngest except one. He lived in Ohio until thirteen years of age, when, in 1854, the family removed to Illinois. His youth was spent working on the farm in summer and attending the district school in winter, finishing his education at the Lombard University, Galesburg, Illinois. He then carried on farming and also taught school in the winter for eleven years. In Illinois he bought forty acres of land, which he improved by building, etc., and which he sold before removing to Southern Nebraska. In that State he purchased a farm of 320 acres, which he also improved, building a house on each quarter section, and on this property he resided ten years. At this time, 1885, a throat trouble caused him to sell out, leave his Nebraska home, and come to California with a hope of obtaining relief from his disease; and he has been greatly benefited. He owns 306 acres of land, located 260 rods northeast of the village of Creston. Mr. Smith has built on the crest of the hill and will soon have a very attractive home. He has planted a large variety of fruit trees, comprising the following: prunes, apricots, pears, peaches, plums, figs, apples, almonds, nectarines and also grape vines. Wheat is his principal crop, and in 1889 he raised 1,665 bushels on 105 acres.

Mr. Smith was united in marriage, in 1863, with Miss Emma Stone, a native of West Virginia, and daughter of Mr. Anson Stone, a native of Virginia, and a soldier of the war of 1812. This union was blessed with nine children, five of whom are living, all natives of Illinois, viz.: Bertha D., Clark S., Fred H., Paul L., and Lillie M. After eighteen years of wedded life, Mrs. Smith died. Her loss was greatly felt by her many friends and her bereaved family. A beautiful character was hers; a devoted wife, a loving and indulgent mother, and a true Christian. She had long been a consistent member of the Methodist church. In 1882 Mr. Smith was again married to Miss Lizy Nesmith, a native of Pittsburg, Pennsylvania, daughter of Mr. Thomas Nesmith. She is a member of the Methodist church. While in Illinois, Mr. Smith was elected by the Republican party, Justice of the Peace, for the years 1870 to 1874. He was also elected on the Board of Supervisors in that State. While in Nebraska, he was selected by his party to fill the office of Justice, in 1875. He cast his first vote for Abraham Lincoln, and has since adhered to the Republican party. In 1889 his fellow-citizens elected him Justice of the Peace, which office he now holds. Mr. Smith is a careful, painstaking, conscientious officer, and as such is respected by all. He is a member of the Grange, and is strictly a temperance man.

RUFUS DANA SMITH was born at Newark, Caledonia County, Vermont, May 2, 1846. His parents were natives of that State. His father in early life followed the trade of joiner, but after forty years of age devoted himself to tilling the soil. In the gold excitement of 1849 he visited California, spending one year in the mines very successfully, then returning to his home in Vermont, in 1868, he moved to Minnesota where he died at the age of eighty years. The subject of this sketch, being filled with youthful patriotism, enlisted at the age of fifteen years, in Company K, of the Eighth Vermont Infantry, Colonel Thomas in command. The regiment was mustered in February 10, 1862, and was immediately ordered South, going to Ship Island, where they joined the troops under General Butler and from there to New Orleans, then to Algiers. He was taken prisoner at Bayou des Allemands in September, 1862; a detachment of 150 were sent then to guard a bridge, and they were surrounded by about 1,500 men and all captured. They were then sent to New Iberia on Bayou Teche, where they passed ten weeks in a prison camp and suffered terribly from short allowances of food and water, and the little food received was worm-eaten and the water stale and muddy. Many died from the effects. From New Iberia they were taken to the Vicksburg jail, and in November, 1862, were paroled, and our subject joined his regiment. In 1863 they were under General Banks, marching through the same swampy, malarious district, and in April, 1864, Mr. Smith was discharged, owing to disability caused by imprisonment and exposure. He then returned home to recuperate, and February 10, 1865, re-enlisted in Company D, Ninth Regiment Veteran Reserve Corps, composed of veterans more or less disabled. They were first stationed in Northern Vermont to guard the banks and private property from the depredations of Rebel sympathizers, then living in Canada. Later they were sent to Washington and served as guard about the White House, and were mustered out at that place, November 18, 1865.

The subject of this sketch then returned to Vermont and followed farming until 1867, when he was married at Barton, Orleans County, Vermont, January 9, to Miss Lucy M. Lebourveau, and in May of the same year they went to Spring Valley, Minnesota. He then farmed for five years, and, on account of failing health, went into a store and clerked four years. He never recovered from the exposure of the war, and for a milder climate went to Santa Barbara in 1876, and there had his leg amputated. After recovering, in 1877, he was elected Justice of the Peace, and re-elected in 1879, but resigned in March, 1880. He was then appointed Under Sheriff by C. E. Sherman, and later by R. J. Broughton, thus holding the office continuously to the present date.

Mr. and Mrs. Smith have five children living, and have lost one son. He is a member of Magnolia Lodge, No. 242, F. and A. M., and Starr King Post, No. 52, Department of California, G. A. R.

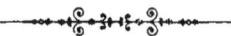

CAPTAIN CHARLES P. LOW, of Santa Barbara, was born in Salem, Massachusetts, in 1824, and when he was four years of age his parents moved to Brooklyn, where his father became a member of the firm of Seth Low & Co., merchants of New York. Of his parents' twelve children he has four brothers and one sister still living, and they are all in Brooklyn; the brothers are all merchants, doing business mainly with China. His nephew, Seth Low, has been mayor of Brooklyn, and is now president of Columbia College. At the age of eighteen years the subject of this sketch began a seafaring life, having studied seamanship ever since he was twelve years old. He began before the mast on the Horatio and the crack East Indiaman, commanded by Captain Howland. This vessel made a ten-months trip to China. Then Mr. Low went to London on the packet ship, Toronto, Captain Griswold, of the London Packet Company. Then he shipped for Rio Janeiro, then on the Houqua, Captain N. B. Palmer, the first clipper ship out of New York to China. He was a seaman for eight years, being third mate, second and first mate, and finally Captain at the age of twenty-three years. While Captain, in 1848, he experienced a most terrible typhoon in the Indian Ocean, a regular cyclone which lasted twelve hours and swept off the deck all the railing, masts and boats. The Captain was washed overboard, and, after being twice engulfed, he caught a rope, and as soon as he got his head above water he gave orders to cut away the masts, and so saved the ship from foundering. As a testimonial of their approbation, the Atlantic, Sun, Mercantile and Union Insurance Companies of New York, presented Captain Low with a beautiful chronometer, with this inscription: "Captain Charles P. Low, late Captain of the ship Houqua, as a testimonial of their approbation of his good conduct in saving said ship and cargo after having been thrown on her beam ends in the Indian Ocean, on the 5th of January, 1848, in a violent typhoon and nearly filled with water; but by the extraordinary exertions of the master and crew, was righted and subsequently taken by them to her port of destination, which was 3,500 miles distant."

After having arrived at Hong Kong, the Captain re-rigged her with his own crew, and after three voyages up and down the coast he returned to New York. There he took charge of the Samuel Russell, January 16, 1850, from New York to San Francisco, making the passage in 108 days—ten days quicker than any vessel before had made the trip. He carried 1,000 tons of freight, on which he received $60 a ton, which was more than the original cost of the ship. Then, by way of China, he completed his trip around the world, within the year. He next took charge of the N. B. Palmer to San Francisco, to China and to New York, by way of the Cape of Good Hope. In 1859 he took command of the Jacob Bell and made a voyage to China. Next he took command of the N. B. Palmer, being on board of that vessel twenty-one years, with the exception of the last trip to China referred to. He has been around the world seven times, making twenty-six voyages to China, and being thirty-one years at sea. In 1873 he left the sea and came to Santa Barbara and purchased eighty acres of land on the mesa. In 1875 he was the originator of the Agricultural Association, of which he has been president; and he has also been president of the Cemetery Association, and also the first president of the Young Men's Christian Association.

He was married at Peabody, Massachusetts, in 1852, to Miss Sarah Maria Tucker, a native of Salem, whose father was a merchant. She has also made trips to China and been around the world four times. They have five sons and two daughters. Three sons are in business in San Francisco. One is connected with the American Oil Company, one is agent for a firm in Japan, and one is in the hardware business; one son is a physician and one is at the State University.

L. G. OLIVER, who owns and cultivates a beautiful farm on the mesa, overlooking the sea, was born in Clermont County, Ohio, in 1826. His father was a farmer, and in 1841 moved to Des Moines County, Iowa, and there continued farming. The subject of this sketch worked at home until twenty-one years of age; then, in 1850, he bought the farm of 160 acres of his father, and continued in general farming until 1854, when he sold out and erected a steam saw and grist mill at Kossuth, Iowa, which he operated for two years; then sold out and returned to farm life, purchasing eighty acres on Round Prairie. In the Pike's Peak excitement he fitted out an expedition for the mines, driving five yoke of oxen and taking four persons. After traveling 130 miles west of the Missouri River, they were discouraged by the tide of emigration returning, so abandoned the project and spent the summer near Brownsville, Nebraska, in breaking prairie, and in the fall he returned to his home at Kossuth. In 1861 he sold his farm and came to California, across the plains, driving a team composed of four yoke of oxen and one yoke of cows. He started April 10, 1861, with his family, and joined other emigrants at the Missouri River. They were five months and a half en route. He sold his team at Little Lake Valley and at Marysville took steamer for San Francisco. He then went to Humboldt Bay and engaged in farming near the town of Arcata; but, owing to frequent depredations by hostile Indians, he sold out in 1864 and went into the Napa Valley, where he engaged in farming, and later, in Solano County, until the fall of 1868, when he came to Santa Barbara. He then purchased 104 acres on the mesa, at $20 per acre, and engaged in general farming, being one of the pioneer farmers on the mesa. He continued farming about twelve years, then went into the hog business, breeding the Essex, Poland China and Berkshire breeds, fattening about 100 hogs each year, which he manufactured into lard and bacon. For the past two years he has sold his increase to the butchers, as, with the increasing years, the responsibility was greater than he cared to assume. He now devotes more time to farming, and grows extensively the Chevalier barley, with soft beard, which is more suitable for hay.

Mr. Oliver was married in Kossuth, Iowa, in the spring of 1851, to Miss Catharine J. Blair. This union has been blessed with three children, two of whom survive: C. A. Oliver, a doctor in Chico, California, and J. B. Oliver, who is foreman of a stock ranch in Sonora, Mexico.

J. H. AND R. E. BRIDGE are two of the prominent ranchers of San Luis Obipo County. They formerly had a large ranch in Mexico, and farmed there one year. Then they sold out and came to San Luis Obispo County, California, and purchased two ranches, one of 2,200 and the other of 320 acres. The last named property is located one mile south of Creston. They are engaged in raising grain, horses and cattle, and have also commenced the cultivation of fruit. They have fifty acres in olives, twenty-five acres in figs, fifteen acres in French prunes, and ten acres devoted to a variety of fruit. They are farming for profit and are making a grand success of it. Both gentlemen are valuable accessions to the county. They expect soon to build a fine residence on their ranch.

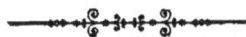

GABRIEL RUIZ is one of the native sons of California, born in Santa Barbara County in 1817. His father, José Ruiz, was born in Mexico and came to California many years ago. At one time he owned some land where Ventura is now located, having had a grant of 1,000 acres of land from the Mexican Government for services rendered the government in California. The ancestors of the family were officers in the Mexican army. Mr. Ruiz has a pleasant home and a fine ranch of 151 acres, called the Santa Anita Rancho, and he also owns some lots in Santa Barbara; also in Ventura. He has always lived the life of a farmer and stock-raiser. They came to this locality in

1879. Here Mr. Ruiz raises Norman and Richmond horses and some fine grade cattle.

The subject of this sketch was married in 1859 to Miss Rafaela Cota, daughter of Balentin Cota, a native of Mexico. They have fourteen children, all born in Southern California, and thirteen of them, at the present writing, make their home with their parents. Their names are as follows: Arthur, Doraliza, Lazaro, Ulpiano, Thomas, Albertina, Anzelmo, Petra, Josepha, Lucy, Balentin, Gabriel and Acacia. They have all been sent to the English schools and can speak both the English and Spanish languages. All are members of the Catholic Church. Three of the sons are engaged in business. Thomas assists his father in the management of the ranch and is agent for the Spanish people in the vicinity of Santa Ana, acting as their interpreter and obtaining employment for them. He is also a fine musician, playing both violin and guitar. He and his brothers form a band and furnish good music for social parties. Arthur has a saloon and the best billiard rooms in the county of Ventura. Ulpiano is a freighter and teamster, having a large, strong wagon, to which he drives four, and sometimes six, fine horses. They are a family of intelligent and refined people, and are well worthy the success which is attending them.

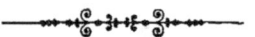

GRUENHAGEN BROS., the pioneer merchants of Creston. Robert W., the senior brother, was born in Oshkosh, Wisconsin, in 1855, and Edward H. was born in the same place in 1859. Their parents, William F. and M. Gruenhagen, were natives of Germany, and came to the United States when they were respectively eight and ten years of age. They settled first in Milwaukee, and afterward in Oshkosh, Wisconsin, where they and lived raised their family. They came to California, October 2, 1884, and now reside at Creston, San Luis Obispo County. The brothers opened a store, seventy-two feet long, and have it stocked with merchandise of all kinds, drugs, jewelry and farm implements; their business extends about fifty miles. They own a ranch of 740 acres thirty miles northeast of Creston, where they are raising horses and cattle.

Robert W., in 1880, was married to Miss Bertha Zick, a native of his own town. They have three children, viz.: Ed. H., Elsie and Robert W. Edward H. Gruenhagen was married in 1889 to Miss Feda Ploetz, a native of Wisconsin. He enjoyed the distinction of being postmaster of the town during the administration of President Cleveland; in politics he is a Democrat. His brother, Robert W., is a Republican.

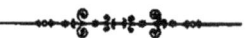

R. R. KIRKPATRICK, of San Miguel, is one of the prominent citizens of San Luis Obispo County, a man of large experience in various directions, and a veteran of both the Mexican and the great civil wars. His grandfather, John Kirkpatrick, was a Scotch-Irish man, who came to America before the Revolution, and did the colonists valuable service as a soldier; later he was in the war of 1812. He settled in Pennsylvania, and there his son, John L. Kirkpatrick, the father of the subject of this sketch, was born. He married Miss Nancy Larimore, also a native of Pennsylvania, and they have four sons and three daughters, of whom R. R. was the fourth child. He was born in Armstrong County, Pennsylvania, December 9, 1826, and as he grew he learned the use of carpenter's tools from his father, who was a boat-builder. Immediately after the declaration of war with Mexico he enlisted at Louisville in the Fourth Kentucky Infantry, and under the command of General Winfield Scott his regiment held the city of Mexico from January until July 4. Returning then to Louisville, he was there discharged. He was afterward at several places, and in two or three businesses until in July, 1862, when he enlisted in Company A, Twenty-ninth Iowa Infantry, of which company he was elected Second Lieutenant. In October, 1862, the company was mustered in and marched 100 miles to St. Joseph, and thence to St. Louis, where for a time they were on provost duty. From there they were ordered to Columbus to intercept General Forrest; next they were sent to the White River expedition, returning to Helena. Soon afterward they were engaged in a fight at Fort Pemberton, and again at Helena. Mr. Kirkpatrick was then detailed with a company of sharpshooters, and had several engagements with guerrillas. When in Helena with about 3,000 men, they were attacked by General Price with 25,000 men. This rebel General thought he had a "sure thing," and had been boasting that he would "eat breakfast in Helena or in hell." The attack was made at daylight, and the Union forces killed and took more prisoners than they had men; Price was defeated and failed to get the bounteous breakfast prepared for him by the citizens of Helena; their houses were filled instead with wounded men. A shell in that engagement tore Mr. Kirkpatrick's clothes, but did not draw blood. The soldiers were sent to Little Rock and participated in taking that place.

The next campaign in which Mr. Kirkpatrick was engaged was that of General Banks at Shreveport. A piece of shell struck him in the groin, and for a long time he was paralyzed. His hip was also injured at the same time, from which wound he never fully recovered. He has a pension of $12.50 per month from the Government. As this wound incapacitated him from marching, he was sent on detached duty as a recruiting officer in Iowa; and he was also engaged in conducting recruits and drafted men to the front. He also served as Quartermaster, having charge of Camp Distribution from Fort Gaines. Next he was sent to the Rio Grande, and finally to New Orleans to be discharged. In the summer of 1865 he was mustered out at Davenport, Iowa.

Then he was engaged in express business between Omaha and Council Bluffs, making money; next he was in a grocery at Council Bluffs, and then in the ice business. In 1877 he came with I. E. Blake to San Francisco, in order to establish the Continental Oil and Transportation Company, and Mr. Kirkpatrick took charge of the Oakland office five years. Then in 1882 he came to San Luis Obispo County, and filed a claim to his present ranch of 320 acres of choice land, three miles due east of San Miguel. On a sightly and picturesque spot on a hill, in the midst of trees, vines and flowers, he has built a pleasant and commodious residence; and he has a large variety of fruit trees growing luxuriantly, and many of them loaded with fruit. The prevailing sorts are peaches, pears, apricots, prunes, figs, almonds and filberts. The locality is 1,250 feet above the sea, and he does not irrigate. He is also raising hay and grain, besides horses, cattle and poultry. He is a Freemason and an Odd Fellow, and Chaplain of the G. A. R. Post at San Miguel. For a time he held the office of Justice of the Peace. Mr. Kirkpatrick is a well-informed gentleman, of pleasant manner, and remarkably successful in his comparatively new vocation of farming and fruit-raising on his "Pleasant Dale" ranch.

In 1849, in Allegheny City, he was united in matrimony with Miss Libby Lloyd, a native of that city; five of their six children are now living. The first four were born in Allegheny City, viz.: Inez, Alice, Ida and Albert; Ellen was born in Nebraska, and Libby in Sioux City. Inez married J. W. Perregoy, a wholesale tobacconist of Council Bluffs; Alice lives with her father, and has 160 acres of land near him; Ida is married to Mr. Frank E. Shepard, and they reside at Council Bluffs; Elliot is also married and lives on the San Marcos in this county; and Libby, with her husband, Charles E. Fowler, occupy land near their father's. After fifteen years of wedded life, Mrs. Kirkpatrick died, and in 1874 Mr. Kirkpatrick married his present wife, who was Mrs. Annie Walker, the widow of Frank Walker, and a native of Ohio. Mr. and Mrs. Kirkpatrick are Presbyterians.

SWIFT BROTHERS.—W. D. and Charles Swift, who own adjoining ranches in the eastern part of the Montecito Valley, were both born at Lyons, Wayne County, New York. Their father had passed many years as a prominent hotel-keeper in New York, Illinois, and later at Virginia City, Nevada; and in June, 1868, he came to Santa Barbara and purchased a ranch of 333 acres in the Montecito Valley. This part of the country was then sparsely settled, and scarcely a fence was to be seen in the valley. But by industry and perseverance the ranch now stands out prominently as one of the best in the valley for agricultural purposes. Since the father's death in 1880, the ranch has been divided, and the sons now own about 100 acres. They carry on general farming and devote a considerable acreage to beans. They are jointly interested in the oil wells which are now being developed near their ranch, in the Santa Ynez Mountains, a stock company carrying on the developments. They also have mining interests at Fort Tejon, in the Santa Anita Mountains.

W. D. Swift, being unmarried, supplies a home for his mother, who is now seventy-six years of age. Charles Swift was married in Montecito in 1875, to Miss Laura Pettit, and they have two children.

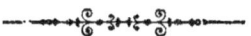

DR. W. B. CUNNANE, the only resident physician of the Santa Ynez Valley, was born at Edinburgh, Johnson County, Indiana, in 1854. His father was a farmer and distiller. The subject of this sketch was educated at the Sturgeon High School of Boone County, Missouri, but was taken from school in 1870 to accept a position with P. Corrigan, who was then general roadmaster of the Wabash Railroad, with headquarters at Moberly, Missouri, remaining two years and learning telegraphy. He was then employed by the Western Union Telegraph Company, for five years, at stations throughout the southwest. Having a desire for a medical education, he employed every odd moment in medical studies, and in 1877 he resigned his position to enter the Medical University of Louisiana, at New Orleans, taking the three years' course and also the special course of toxicology and chemistry, graduating with honor in 1881. He then went to Queen City, Cass County, Texas, where he practiced for two years, and in 1883 he came direct to Santa Ynez, to grow up with the new town, which was then being established. He now has an extensive practice throughout the valley. In 1885 he built his present residence, and in September of the same year was married, at Santa Ynez, to Miss Mabel Johnston, a daughter of W. F. Johnston, an extensive rancher of Santa Maria and also a descendant of that celebrated family of Johnstons of Virginia. Doctor and Mrs. Cunnane have one child.

HENRY L. WILLIAMS, the owner of the Ortega ranch and the founder of Summerland, was born in Massillon, Ohio, in 1841. His father, G. W. Williams, was a financier and was connected with the Union Bank of Massillon. In the spring of 1861, at the age of twenty, Henry L. enlisted in Company A, of the Nineteenth Ohio Infantry, under command of Colonel Samuel Beatty and Captain C. F. Manderson; the latter is now United States Senator from Nebraska. The regiment, which was stationed with the Army of the Cumberland, joined General Grant's forces on the second day of the battle of Shiloh. They were in the three-days' fight at Stone River, where one-half of the regiment was lost, and were also in many small skirmishes. Mr. Williams, however, did not receive a scratch, although his clothing was many times pierced with bullets. In April, 1863, he was appointed State pay agent for Ohio, and on June 30, 1864, he received the appointment of paymaster in the United States army, and was stationed with the army of the Cumberland, with headquarters at Louisville, Kentucky. He was mustered out of the service on November 15, 1865. He then became engaged in the coal business in Ohio, as manager and part owner of the mines, and remained there until the spring of 1776. In that year he was appointed by the United States Treasury Department to examine the books of the Collectors of Customs through Pennsylvania, New Jersey and Delaware, with headquarters at Philadelphia. In June, 1881, he was stationed at Tucson, Arizona, to look after the frontier offices from El Paso to San Diego and Santa Barbara; but, finding the weather very warm at Tucson, he resigned October 15, 1882, and came to Santa Barbara, where his family were already settled. In April, 1883, he purchased the Ortega ranch, of 1,000 acres, located at the east end of the Montecito Valley, and has since made that his home. He has a small walnut grove and fruit only sufficient for family use.

Mr. Williams brought the location of Summerfield before the public in November, 1888, by laying out the town and piping water to every lot, and advertising it extensively through the country. The town is established on the faith of Spiritualism. Already 1,450 lots have been sold to parties from all over the United States, some of the purchasers being in Australia. Many fine cottages have been built, and a library of 500 volumes, with a building costing $4,500, has already been erected. A weekly newspaper named the *Reconstructor* has also been started.

Mr. Williams has been twice married, the last time at Summerland, to Mrs. Agnes S. Morgan, in September, 1889.

A. TOGNAZZINI, one of the most successful business men and dairy men of Cayucos, is the son of Swiss parents, and was born in the city of Ticino, Switzerland, in 1847. May 26, 1864, he came to San Francisco after a journey from his native land of seventy-five days. He was the only son and youngest child of a family of five children. He was raised on a farm and attended the common schools, and finished his education in the high school. His father was a dairy man, and his son also learned the business. He was seventeen years of age when he came to California, and engaged in the stock and dairy business, having learned that California was a fine State for that business. He began work in Marin County, at $15 per month, but afterward his wages were raised to $30 a month; he worked here about a year. In the fall of 1866 he started in business on his own account, having learned the Spanish language of Mr. Marshall, for whom he had been working, and of whom he rented 100 cows and land, most of which were milch cows, and paid a rent of $20. That season butter was thirty cents per pound, and he cleared $1,100, and he thought himself rich. In 1868, in Marin County, he bought 150 cows, and rented 1,400 acres of land, and conducted it for six years, from which he made some money.

Mr. Tognazzini then came to San Luis Obispo County, and bought 700 acres of land, and has since added to it until he owns over 1,000 acres. He bought 150 head of stock and put it upon the ranch, which his nephew conducted, while he continued the business in Marin County. He finally moved here and rented 2,000 acres at seventy-five cents an acre for five years. When he rented this land people thought it would prove a failure; but it has since proved a success. In 1881 he bought a ranch in Santa Barbara, consisting of 3,200 acres, which is one of the best dairy ranches in the county. He has 250 cows and made 505 boxes of butter in the year 1889. In 1884, with a partner, he purchased 7,000 acres in Santa Barbara County, which was divided into dairies.

Mr. Tognazzini was one of the incorporators of the Commercial Bank of San Luis Obispo and is one of the directors. He has built a very pleasant home on his ranch, one and a half miles northeast of Cayucos, which is surrounded with trees and shrubs. He is now the owner of 1,800 acres of land in Cayucos, on which he raises a few horses that have frequently taken the premium at the fairs. He also raises cattle and hogs.

Mr. Tognazzini was united in marriage, in 1867, at San Francisco, to Miss Madaline Reghetti, a native of Switzerland. They have had five children, four of whom are living, viz.: Virgilio Valerio, now at college, studying engineering; Americo and Celia. Mr. and Mrs. Tognazzini are members of the Catholic Church. Mr. Tognazzini is a member of the Odd Fellows Lodge, and is also a Mason. In his political relations he is a Republican, and is an illustration of what an honest man can become in the county of San Luis Obispo.

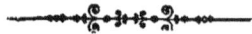

C. E. KILSON was born in Iowa, January 29, 1857. His parents, Lewis and Caroline Kilson, were natives of Bergen, Norway. They emigrated to America in September, 1838, and went to Cincinnati, the journey at that time being a most arduous one. They soon afterward settled in Adams County, Illinois, on a farm they bought and improved. Later, they sold it and moved to Wisconsin, and, after a year spent in that State, removed, in 1855, to Butler County, Iowa. They entered 240 acres of land for a homestead, and this they developed into a fine farm. They built a nice home, and there resided until their deaths, which occurred, the mother's on November 10, 1881, and the father's November 28, 1889.

The subject of this sketch was the fifth of a family of seven children. He was reared in Bristow, Butler County, Iowa, and received his education in the public schools of that town. He assisted his father on the farm until the age of twenty one years. At that time he came to California to carve his own destiny in the land that offers so many inducements to the worthy citizen, arriving in the Golden State February 7, 1882. He had already obtained some knowledge of telegraphy, and his first move was to finish learning that business, at Pino, Placer County. He was afterward sent to Arizona and at different times had charge of several stations: was three months at Yuma, one year at Dragoon Summit, the highest point on the Southern Pacific Railroad, and was two years at Nelson.

Mr. Kilson was married to Miss Laura F. Williams, December 17, 1886. She is a native of California. From Nelson Mr. Kilson moved to Saticoy on the 20th of November, 1887. Here he has the position of ticket and station agent. He is an active and capable business man, and at once became identified with the best interests of Saticoy; has bought property and built a neat and pleasant home, where he resides with his family. Mr. and Mrs. Kilson have two children: Lewis, born at Nelson, and Elmer, at Saticoy.

In his political views, Mr. Kilson is a Republican. He is a member of the K. of P., Eden Lodge, No. 101, at Nelson, Butte County, California.

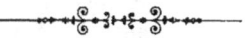

C. McFERSON, one of Cambria's old-time citizens, and one of its most reliable and influential ranchers, is public-spirited and alive to the interests of the community. He is also a California pioneer, having come to this State with the last train that crossed the plains in 1849. There were sixty people in the company, and it was conducted by Turner, Allen & Co. Every passenger paid $200 for passage and everything was furnished. They rode in three seated covered carriages, each drawn by four mules, and six passengers to a carriage. They arrived in Weaverville, one and a half miles south of Placerville, October 15, 1849. There is but one man living that Mr. McFerson knows of that came in that company, who is Lloyd Tevis, now a man of wealth in San Francisco.

Mr. McFerson is a native of Ohio, born in Brown County, August 5, 1824. His father, Samuel McFerson, was a native of Ohio, born in 1789, and died in 1833. The ancestors of the family were from Scotland: his mother, Martha (Culter) McFerson, was a native of Ohio, and of English ancestry. His parents had seven children, of whom he is the youngest of the three now living. He was reared on a farm in Ohio, where he worked in summer and attended the county schools in the winter. He moved to Washington County, Indiana, and attended the Seminary there for two years. He commenced the study of medicine, and after a year's study the great California gold excitement broke out and he, like others, was taken with the fever. He went into the gold diggings in El Dorado County, and remained there until 1857, meeting with good success. For one day's work he received $115, the most he ever received; a single pan contained $25; he frequently made $100 per day. He was taken with typhoid fever, and was sick at the camp four months; in addition to his other troubles he had scurvy. The first onion he bought cost him $1, and potatoes were $1 a pound. There, after his recovery, he continued mining. He afterward purchased a hotel, which he operated for two years at Indian Diggings, El Dorado County.

August 6, 1855, Mr. McFerson was mar

ried to Mrs. Guegnor, a native of Virginia, but resided in Ohio. They continued the hotel business for two years, when they sold out, in 1857, and removed to Mariposa County. He engaged in cutting cord-wood at $5 per cord for General John C. Fremont. There he made $10 per day, and followed the business for eighteen months. He then removed to Tulare County, and purchased eighty acres of land and engaged in farming. He built a house and fenced the property, and remained there until 1865, when he sold it and came to San Luis Obispo County, and settled on his present ranch, then unsurveyed Government land. Mrs. McFerson came in a spring wagon, driven by her son, Joseph Barrickman, and Mr. McFerson, with two others, drove the stock. She arrived first, and stopped at the house of George E. Long; Mr. McFerson was ten days on the road. They first lived in a little 10 x 12 log cabin. Mr. Long showed them the land, and they took 370 acres, which he still retains, and is conducting a stock-raising and dairy business. He built a nice house in 1868, and has planted an orchard for home use, with a large variety of fruit. The train with which Mrs. McFerson came to California was commanded by Senator Hearst, who was a warm friend of the family, and with whom Mr. McFerson had been on many trips, when they had to sleep on the ground many nights together. Mr. and Mrs. McFerson have helped to organize the Presbyterial Church at Cambria, in 1871, of which they have been faithful members since. He held Sunday-school in the little log school-house before the church was organized, and has been Sunday-school superintendent ever since. He is a trustee and elder of the Church. He is a member of the Odd Fellows Lodge, of which he has passed through all the chairs, and in 1889 was district deputy grand master of the order. In his political views he has always been a Democrat.

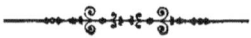

THOMAS HOSMER, a resident of Montecito, was born in Freedom, Maine, in 1833. His father was a mechanic and a manufacturer of edged tools, and after leaving Freedom moved to Springfield, Massachusetts, where he carried on a large establishment. Thomas learned his trade of machinist at Belfast, Maine, in the shop of Messrs. White & Kimball, who did general country machine work, but especially work for shingle and saw mills. He remained with them four years, and in the spring of 1858 came to California, first settling at Sacramento, where he followed his trade for five years. In 1863 he became interested in a silver mine at Sonora, Mexico, went there and put up a quartz mill, and after a year of hard labor and much expense he gave it up as an unprofitable investment, and returned to San Francisco to follow his trade, working about three years for the Government at Mare Island, and the rest of the time in San Francisco until the fall of 1871. In January, 1872, he came to the Montecito Valley and purchased nineteen acres of land where he now resides. He began with the almond culture, but after two years of heavy bearing the crop failed. He then grafted the trees with plums and prunes, but, not meeting with success, the trees were taken out and oranges were put in their places, which are now doing well. He has about 700 orange and lemon trees.

Mr. Hosmer was elected Supervisor in 1884 and re-elected in 1888, proving an able and efficient officer. He was married in San Francisco in 1863, to Miss Frances Dinsinore, a native of Anson, Maine, who came to California with her parents in 1861, making the journey by steamer. Her father came to Montecito in 1868, bought what is now known as San Ysidro ranch, and planted the first orange grove in the valley, containing 1,500 trees. The ranch has since been sold to J. Harleigh Johnston, who has brought the fruit to a high state of perfection. Mr. and Mrs. Hosmer have four children, three daughters at home, and one son, who is a member of the firm of Hunt, Hosmer & Co., of Santa Barbara.

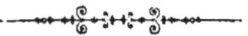

LEOPOLD FRANKL, the founder of San Simeon, is a '49er, and a prominent business man of San Luis Obispo County; he was born in Vienna, Austria, April 7, 1818, the son of Adolph Frankl, a native of Austria, and a merchant all through his life. His grandfather, on the maternal side, was Alios Leathern, a mail-carrier in Austria for years, and lived to the great age of 110 years. Mr. Frankl's mother, Catherine (Leathern) Frankl, was a native of Austria. They had six children, of whom three are living, the eldest, the middle one and the second. The eldest is now eighty-five years of age, the youngest, the subject of this sketch, is seventy-two years. He was educated in Austria, and learned engineering, and worked in the mines in California as a mining engineer. From 1856 to 1860 he was with General John C. Fremont in his mining enterprises in Mariposa. He built the railroad and 100-stamp mill at the Benton Mines, named by Fremont after Jessie Benton, his wife's name before marriage. He afterward worked in the mines, and had 250 men at work. When Fremont went to Europe, in 1860, Mr. Frankl rented the mill, and sent the gold to Krahaugen & Cruse, and to Davison, agent of Rothschild's Bank, in San Francisco, General Fremont went to England to raise money, and the arrangements were about consummated when the civil war broke out, and the unsettled condition of the country prevented the closing of the business. In 1865 Mr. Frankl sold the mines to T. W. Parks, by order of General Fremont. He then was engaged in the mines at Mexico, for Tilliughast, agent of a London mining company, for fifteen months. He became sick and came to San Simeon, and for years was wharfinger and agent for the Pacific Steamship Company. In 1875 Mr. Frankl opened a general merchandise store in San Simeon, and has conducted it until the present time, enjoying a great portion of the business for miles around. He received the appointment of Postmaster in 1874, and has held the position ever since. He sold seven leagues of land to Senator Hearst for $85,000, and has done most of the building in San Simeon. He also owns very valuable property, and for the past few years has been reducing his real estate; he has made lately two sales of $10,000 each. He has a large mercantile business, conducted by his nephews in Lake View, Oregon. He was raised to the Hebrew religion, and in his political views is a Republican.

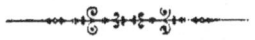

ANDREW MARTIN, one of California's early pioneers, was born in LaFayette County, Missouri, in 1824; his father was a pioneer to that State. In 1837 they moved to Platte Purchase, and took up 160 acres of heavily timbered land. Andrew prepared to leave home at the age of twenty-one years, but owing to his father's illness he remained at home and looked after his interests. June 15, 1856, he entered the Government service at Fort Leavenworth, under Colonel Price, as teamster during the Mexican war, driving the ammunition wagon. At Taos, in January, 1847, he volunteered under Lieutenant Dyer, of the artillery, and fought all day through that engagement. A few fights subdued the Mexicans, and he then returned to Santa Fé, and later to Fort Leavenworth, where he was mustered out in June 22, 1847. The following year he worked at home, except four months, engaged in driving freight teams to Santa Fé. In July, 1848, he was married in Clay County, Missouri, to Miss Mary L. Bradbury. After spending the winter in Kansas, in May, 1850, they started across the plains for California, driving an ox team of five yoke, and one horse for his wife to ride. They joined a train commanded by John Morris, and after many hardships with the Indians, sickness among the company, cholera and short supplies, they arrived in California by the Carson route, having been four months on the road. Mr. Martin first mined in Amador County one winter, then in 1851 he went to Cold Springs, where his camp was burned and all his effects were lost. In October, 1852, they came to Santa Clara County, and in 1853 went to Half Moon Bay, San Mateo County, and there remained eight years. They took up what was supposed to be Government land, but which proved part of a grant, and they were finally put off, thus losing eight years of labor during the best part of his life. In the spring of 1866 he took up land at Pescadero, San Mateo County, and remained there until 1873, raising hay and teaming in the Redwoods, and also making pickets and shingles. Mr. Martin then passed one year in Oregon, and in 1874 came to Carpenteria Valley, purchasing fifty-five acres of valley land, which was covered with live-oak timber, with the exception of five acres. He then began clearing and planting, and now has a beautiful ranch, under a high state of cultivation. He has set out about seventy walnut trees, and has about 2,000 trees in nursery. He also plants about forty acres in beans.

Mr. and Mrs. Martin have five children, four sons and one daughter. Their present spacious residence was built in 1888, under the assistance and direction of the sons, who are all at home. Mr. Martin located a homestead on Mount Hor in 1887, consisting of 120 acres, eighty acres of which is tillable land, and fifty acres are now under cultivation.

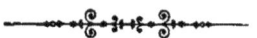

R. K. STEVENS, proprietor of the Palm and Citrus Nursery, in the west end of Montecito, makes a specialty of palms (of which he has forty different varieties), and tropical fruit trees, many very delicate and sensitive, but his locality is rarely visited by frost. Banana fruit ripens on the plants; orange, lemon, lime, and the olive also do well. The ranch is well supplied by water, and of the 260 acres the greater part is under cultivation.

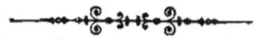

W. S. WHITAKER came to California in 1853, and ranks among the pioneers of the State. He was born in Indiana, February 18, 1832, and is the son of John M. Whitaker. His father, who was born in 1802, and who is still living, was a member of the Legislature of Iowa for twenty years off and on, and had the honor of selecting the State University lands. He married Mrs. Jane Phillips, a native of Ohio, and daughter of William Phillips. They had six children, five sons and one daughter, all of whom are now living.

The subject of this sketch was reared and educated in Van Buren County, Iowa, and lived on a farm until twenty-one years of age, when he came to California. He first engaged in mining at Dry Town, Calaveras County, and prospected without any success there; he then went to Grizzly Flats, El Dorado County, where he worked two years and saved $2,000. He was one of four men who took out twenty-six ounces of gold, worth $468, in one day. It was nothing unusual to take out from six to twelve ounces per day. This luck came to him the last winter spent in the mines. The first winter he spent in the mountains, six miles above Grizzly Flats, he prospected without any success, and during that time he suffered a great deal, the snow being three feet deep. He became afflicted with the scurvy, and walked out through the snow three feet deep to Grizzly Flats, where he could get a vegetable diet. In the summer of 1856 he and his partner thought they had about exhausted their claim, and, receiving a good offer for it, sold out. Mr. Whitaker received $600 for his interest. The parties who bought it afterward took out large quantities of gold.

Mr. Whitaker returned to Iowa with his money, arriving June 17, 1856; he engaged in the mercantile business until 1863, in which year he went back to California. He settled in Marin County, remained there during the winter, went to Nevada, mined and prospected six months, and October 7, 1863, came to San Luis Obispo County. He purchased a ranch, on which he lived during the winter, and in the spring helped organize the firm of Grant, Lull & Co. Mr. Lull went to San Francisco after goods, and while he was away Mr. Whitaker moved the logs of a log house down the San Simeon Creek and rebuilt it near the Coast road for a store. It was ready when the goods arrived, the stock —not a large one—costing $1,800. Mr. Whitaker relates many interesting incidents which happened during his business experience at that place. Among the goods was a crate of crockery, and at first they had little hope of disposing of it, but there was no crockery in the country and it proved to be just the thing wanted. Mr. Whitaker kept the cash account. One day they received nothing until nearly night, when a Spaniard came in and bought a drink of whisky and saved the day! One of the partners, Mr. Lull, has kept that coin as a memento of the day's business and their little pioneer store at the mouth of the San Simeon Creek. One night, while they were at supper, an Indian broke into the store through the window. When they found the store had been entered, they first went to the money drawer, nothing had been taken from it. A drunken Indian fast asleep on the beach was enough to tell the story of the robbery, and, as the tide was coming in, had they not found him when they did, he would doubtless have been drowned. After doing business for six months in this locality, they removed to Cambria. They built the first store at that place and put in $8,000 worth of goods. From that time Cambria began to build up. The first hotel was built by Mr. Rice. Mr. Proctor built his blacksmith shop; and the work of settlement and development has gone on. Mr. Whitaker's firm continued the business until 1867. He then sold his interest, removed to San Simeon and took charge of the wharf for the Steamship Company and acted as their agent. He bought the hotel and ran it for some time, then prospected and mined, and now has charge of the San Simeon wharf and is agent for the Pacific Coast Steamship Company. During the quicksilver excitement of 1875–'76, he had an interest in the mine with Mr. George Van Gordon and others. They a made a contract for a new process of saving the quicksilver; but, after much expense, it proved a failure. The machine did not separate as represented. They lost money, but still retain the mine, expecting ultimately to make it pay.

Mr. Whitaker and his son do a dairy business on their ranch at the mouth of the San Simeon Creek—the first land he took up. They own 420 acres of land which joins the San Simeon grant—three leagues of land that could, at one time, have been purchased for $5.000. It is now worth a vast sum of money. The dry season of 1864 caused immense loss to the cattle men, and nearly all the early settlers were engaged in that business. The people were greatly discouraged, and it seemed to them that California was worthless, but it has since proved a wonderfully productive country, and large sums of money have been made in the dairy and cattle business.

Mr. Whitaker has three children, Ira R., Alice and Lotty. The first and second were born in Winchester, Iowa, and the youngest in San Luis Obispo County. Politically Mr. Whitaker is a Democrat.

B. H. FRANKLIN, one of Cambria's most active business men, being a merchant, Postmaster and Justice of the Peace, and President of the Board of Education of the county. He is a son of Colonel Willliam H. Franklin, now of San José, but a native of New Jersey. He served under General Scott, and was also a veteran of the great civil war, and for a time held the position of Provost Marshal of the city of Washington. He was advanced to the rank of Colonel in his regiment, and was several times wounded while in command of his men on the battle-field. His grandfather was Benjamin Franklin, a native of New Jersey, and his great-grandfather was the world-renowned Benjamin Franklin, the first Postmaster General of the United States. His mother was Morgiana R. (Hurber) Franklin.

Benjamin H. Franklin, our subject, was born in Philadelphia, September 1, 1856, and was the eldest in a family of nine children, only four of whom survive. He was reared and educated at San José, and is a graduate of the business college, high school and normal school. In 1876 he came direct from school to Cambria, where he taught school for two years. For a time he was engaged in real-estate and money lending, and purchased county warrants. He was appointed Postmaster in 1882, but was removed by the administration of President Cleveland and re-installed when Harrison was elected President. He has been a member of the Board of Education of the county nearly ever since coming to the county. For five years he clerked for the firm of Grant & Tull, and at the same time was telegraph operator and Postmaster. In 1885 he opened a variety store, which has consequently grown until he now has a large general stock, the largest in town. When the fire broke out he owned 100 feet on Main street, the theatre building, and a building rented for a saloon and his store. The rate of insurance had been raised to nine and a half per cent., and while trying to get the price down the fire caught him without a dollar of insurance. The fire originated in a hotel, a block from him, and he succeeded in saving $2,000 worth of goods, the rest was a total loss, amounting to about $10,000. The next morning after the fire he opened his store in the parlor of a dwelling house, and in five days had a building, 26 x 40 feet, into which he moved and conducted the only mercantile business in town. He has since added to the building thirty feet, and is carrying a very large line of goods. As a justice of the peace he makes it a point to have all the cases that come to him settled, and this does the litigants a service, saving both them and the county costs. He is a member of the Odd Fellows lodge, and has passed through all the chairs; he is now secretary of the order. Mr. Franklin has a ranch of 500 acres on the Santa Rosa Creek, run for him on shares, seven miles from Cambria; it is nicely improved and has on it about 100 head of cattle; they milk about seventy cows. He has a nice residence in Cambria, and a business block in San Luis Obispo, on which he has three stores, rented.

Mr. Franklin was married in 1876, to Miss Mabel Runyon, a native of Colfax, on the Sacramento River, near where Courtland now stands. She is the daughter of Alexander Runyon, a rancher horticulturist. They have four children, three sons and a daughter, all born in Cambria, viz.: Benjamin H., Raymond, Alexander and a baby unnamed. Mr. Franklin is a man of business sagacity and integrity. In addition to the other offices which he has held is trustee of the school board. He speaks English, Spanish and German. He furnishes a little music for the people in the Presbyterian church. It is questionable whether the renowned Benjamin Franklin had as much business on his hands as his great-grandson. The following story is told of Benjamin Franklin the first, not narrated in his history. It is said that when his father took him to church, he was annoyed to see his son gazing about and not apparently paying much attention to the sermon. He said to him when they came out, "Benjamin, you pained me by the poor attention you seemed to be giving to the sermon; I don't think you know what it was about." "Oh, yes, father," replied Benjamin; "I can tell you the text, and a good deal that the minister said." And he began and gave a nice little outline of the sermon, and when he stopped he said, "And now, father, I can tell you how many rafters, posts and collar braces there are in the church." And so it can be said of the subject of this sketch,— that there is not much going on where he is that he does not take in.

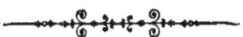

P. C. HIGGINS, a rancher of Carpenteria Valley, was born in Galesburg, Illinois, in 1842. His father had large farm interests in the locality of Galesburg and much city property. His father and mother are still living, each at the age of seventy five years, and they are looking forward to their golden wedding in April, 1891. P. C. Higgins was married at Galesburg in 1864, to Miss Mary Jenks, and they then moved to Altona, Knox County, Illinois, to take charge of one of his father's farms. In 1867 they moved to Forest, Livingston County, where Mr. Higgins bought 160 acres of land, and carried on general farming for thirteen years, dealing largely in hogs, which he fattened for market. In 1880 they sold out and moved to Prairie City, Iowa, where he engaged in the hardware business, and remained three years. Through an unsatisfactory partner they made no progress, and in 1883 Mr. Higgins sold out and came to Carpenteria Valley, where he bought 108 acres of cleared land, all under cultivation. His main crop is Lima beans, the leading industry of the valley, of which he plants about ninety acres, with an average yield of from 1,500 to 2,000 pounds per acre. Mr. Higgins has a bituminous rock bed on his place, bordering on the sea, which, after careful examination is found to cover several acres in area, at an average depth of sixteen feet. They have taken out about 5,000 tons, which was used in the paving of State street in Santa Barbara. In boring for artesian water he struck natural gas, at a depth of 500 feet, although not in paying quantities: still by storing it was found to burn very rapidly. He raises, lemons and other fruits, but only for home use. Mr. and Mrs. Higgins have six children, all living.

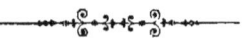

CRANE BROTHERS are the leading merchants of Saticoy. The business was established by E. C. Crane in 1886. he conducting it until 1889, when his brother, L. P. Crane, became a partner, taking a half interest in the business. The store was first located on the Telegraph road, and in 1887 it was removed to a point one-half mile northwest of where the depot now is. After the depot was built, as they are buyers and shippers of produce, and as the new hotel is at the station, they saw it would be to their interest to again move their store, and accordingly located near the station. They are now building a large store-room at the rear of the main building, making the whole depth of the building 110 feet. Over the store is a large hall which is used for public meetings. Both of these gentlemen are enterprising and are active in all measures tending to build up the town. Both are native sons of the Golden West, having been born in Ventura County, within a few miles of Saticoy, their father, J. L. Crane, being one of the earliest pioneers of this part of the country. (A sketch of his life appears elsewhere in this work.)

E. C. Crane, the senior member of the firm, dates his birth in 1863. He was reared on a farm and educated at Carpenteria. In 1884 he was united in marriage with Miss Mary E. Cross, a native of Wisconsin. They have three children, Cora L., Ella and Clarence. Mr. Crane's political views are Democratic. He was Postmaster under the Cleveland administration. Mr. Crane resides in a neat cottage which he built not far from their place of business.

L. P. Crane, the junior member of the firm, received his education in the public schools of the county. He is a successful farmer, owning a fine ranch in the Santa Clara Valley, one mile from their store, and is conducting this in addition to his other business. He has built a nice residence and barn and resides on the ranch. He was married in 1888, to Miss Abby Briggs, a native of Yuba County, California, and a daughter of John G. Briggs. They have one son, Bertie, born in Saticoy. L. P. Crane shares his brother's political views.

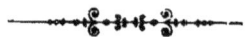

JOHN BAILARD.—One of the largest ranches in the Carpenteria Valley is that owned by the estate of Andrew Bailard, which is under the direct management of his widow and John Bailard, his eldest son. Andrew Bailard was born in Germany, and came to this country in his boyhood, with his parents, who settled on a farm in Missouri. In 1853 Andrew came to California, across the plains, first settling in San Mateo County, where he purchased a ranch of 400 acres, and carried on general farming, making grain, barley, hay and potatoes the principal crops. In 1857 he was married to Miss Martha C. Schultz, a native of Missouri, who came across the plains in the same train with Mr. Bailard. In 1868 Mr. Bailard sold his ranch and in August of the same year he moved his family to the Carpenteria Valley. He here purchased 400 acres of wild land from Dr. Beggs, who owned a large Spanish grant. He at once began clearing and as soon as practicable planted corn and beans. At that time the small bean was cultivated, the Lima bean being a later production. Mr. Bailard died in December, 1876, leaving his widow and nine children. His eldest son, John Bailard, was born in San Mateo County, in 1859; received his education there and at the Santa Barbara College. He has taken an active part in the management of the ranch, which has since been enlarged by 100 acres that Mrs. Bailard inherited. The valley land has mostly been cleared of the live oaks since his father's death; and of the 500 acres, 400 are under cultivation, the uplands during the alternate years and valleys every year. The machinery used is of the most improved kind, throwing all labor possible upon the team rather than the driver. Two hundred acres of this ranch is planted to Lima beans, which has become the principal crop of the valley. Mr. Bailard has recently purchased forty acres more, which is largely under cultivation.

In June, 1887, Mr. Bailard was married in Carpenteria, to Miss Kitty Cravens.

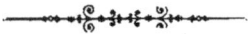

GEORGE WILLIAM PROCTOR was born in East Providence, Rhode Island, May 5, 1823. His father and grandfather, William Proctor, Sr. and Jr., were both natives of New Hampshire, and were the descendants of English settlers in this country. His mother, Betsey (Thompson) Proctor, was born in Andover, New Hampshire, and was a daughter of Peter Thompson, a Revolutionary soldier. Mr. Proctor's father was twice married, and he was the youngest of a family of four children by the first marriage. He was reared at Andover, attended the district school, worked on the farm and learned the blacksmith's trade. He then went to Ashburnham and worked with his brother, after which he took a contract to make 100 tons of railroad spikes, at Nashua. That completed he entered the railroad shops, and worked for the company three years. November 29, 1848, he went to work for the Passumpsic Railroad Company at Wells River, Vermont, having charge of a shop. May 20, 1850, he commenced work for the Eagle Screw Company of Providence, Rhode Island. Next he went to Maidstone, Vermont, and helped to build a saw-mill, and from there he went to Guildhall, Vermont, where he set up a blacksmith shop, and continued the business there until 1858.

In that year Mr. Proctor came to California. He engaged in work on a quartz mill at West Point, Calaveras County, and also became interested in mining. They had rich rock, but, owing to the dishonesty of some of the parties, it did not pay. From there he went to Pine Grove. No survey had been made at that place. Mr. Proctor fenced in 100 acres of land, and also built a shop. In 1859 he planted an orchard of apples, pears, and peaches. This property he sold, and removed to a place twenty-two miles from Sacramento, which he named Elliott. He located a quarter section of land, and built a shop, and was there about five years. During that time he did a good business and also cultivated an orchard, which proved a great success, this being the first orchard planted on the red land. He sold the property for $2,000, and removed to Cambria, San Luis Obispo County. Here he got land to the amount of 400 acres. He was a pioneer builder of the town, and in every way did all he could for the development and growth of the place; built a large shop, aided in building the Masons' Hall, built a three-story hotel, and several other houses. The hotel was destroyed by fire in 1889, and was a total loss.

In 1880 Mr. Proctor moved from Cambria to near San Miguel. He took up Government land, and, as at other places where he had located, he built a shop. He for a time ran the shop in San Miguel, with George Washington Proctor, besides his shop across the river from San Miguel. This shop he ran for five years, in company with G. E Proctor. Now, he owns 800 acres of land, six miles east of San Miguel. Other members of his family have 560 acres adjoining his, making 1,360 acres in all. A fine spring is located on his place. He is engaged in raising wheat, cattle and horses. In 1888 Mr. Proctor built the Occidental Hotel, which was opened in February of that year. It is being conducted by his son-in-law, George S. Davis, who is an experienced hotel man, and who keeps a good house.

Mr. Proctor married in 1844 Miss Elvira Cooper, a native of New York, daughter of Rev. David Cooper, a Universalist minister of Saratoga, New York. They had two children: Elvira E., born in Ashburnham, Massachusetts, now the wife of George S. Davis; and George E., born in Nashua, New Hampshire, who resides on his ranch, two miles east of San Miguel. After four years of wedded life, Mrs. Proctor died. Several years later Mr. Proctor married Miss Lucinda T. Norris, a native of Corinth, Vermont, a daughter of Rev. John Norris, and they have had seven children.

Mr. Proctor has been a leader; where he has gone others have followed. He has both thought and labored for the interest of the society in which he has lived. Has aided in organizing four granges in the county. In politics he is in favor of reform. He was reared a Methodist, but his religious views have been modified. He is a believer in one God, and in the principle that " If we do right in this world we will be all right in the next if there is one, and we will be all right in this world whether there is another or not." This mode of expressing his doctrine was used by a Unitarian minister on the occasion of the funeral of his beloved uncle, Hon. John Proctor, at Andover, New Hampshire. Mr. Proctor has been an Odd Fellow, a Son of Temperance, a Good Templar, and has helped to start a number of lodges and reform movements.

C. S. DUVAL, the builder and proprietor of the Charles Hotel, Saticoy, was born in Maine, August 4, 1858. He is a son E. A. Duval, mention of whom will be found in another part of this book, where the history of the family is given as far as known. Mr Duval came with his father to Saticoy in 1868, and was engaged in the general merchandise business, under the name of Crane & Duval, for two years. He sold his interest and purchased lots of the Pacific Improvement Company, with the understanding that he would build a hotel for the accommodation of their trains. He accordingly erected the Charles Hotel, 56 x 100 feet, two stories high, having a balustrade on three sides, and containing twenty-five rooms. It was built at a cost of $12,000, and was opened to the public June 2, 1889, being the first hotel in this part of the valley. After being successfully conducted for eight months, it was destroyed by fire. The cook upset a pot of lard on the range, and, there being a strong wind blowing, the whole house was soon in flames. Their best efforts to save the building was ineffectual, only a portion of the foundation being left. The property was insured for $8,000, which the company paid in full; and Mr. Duval commenced the erection of a new building on the 3d of March, 1890, which was opened for business April 4. It contains eighteen rooms and is suitably finished and furnished throughout. It is the eating-house for the traveling public between Santa Barbara and Los Angeles, trains stopping for both dinner and supper. This house is being conducted in a first-class way, and Mr. Duval, by his genial and accommodating manner, has secured a good patronage.

Mr. Duval was married in 1879 to Miss Mary E. Knox, a native of Iowa, and daughter of John Knox of that State. This union has been blessed with three children, Elmer H., Lawrence and Melvin, all born at Saticoy.

Mr. Duval belongs to the Regulators of Santa Clara Valley. In politics he is Republican.

B. F. MADDOX, one of the business men of Nordhoff, is a native of Kentucky, born in Pendleton County, January 12, 1844. He is a son of William Maddox, a native of Ohio, who for many years resided in Kentucky, was married to Miss Brandenburgh, and lived on a plantation. Mrs. Maddox died of cholera in 1857. His father was afterward married to a second wife, and was the father of eighteen children, ten by his first wife and eight by the second, all except two living to adult age.

When the subject of this sketch was ten years of age the family moved to Illinois. In December, 1861, he enlisted in Company E, Fifty-seventh Illinois Volunteer Infantry, as a private soldier, and participated in all the engagements of the West from Fort Henry to Fort Donelson, the battle of Shiloh, the advance on Corinth and the battle of Corinth in 1862. He was with General Sherman on his memorable march from Atlanta to the sea, and was at Washington during the grand review, when the magnificent victorious army made its triumphant march through the great capital of the country their deeds of valor had saved. Mr. Maddox received no wound, but suffered much from diarrhœa, from the effects of which he has never fully recovered. Four of his brothers were also in the Union army, one of whom lost his life and another came near dying in prison.

At the close of the war Mr. Maddox was mustered out, and went to Kansas, where he took a Government claim which he improved and on which he lived until 1874. In that year he came to Ventura County, California. Mr. Maddox was a carpenter, and worked at his trade five years in Ventura, where he met with a very slight accident which resulted in the loss of the use of his right hand. He received a wound from a scratch-awl, and went to a physician to have something applied to remove the soreness. The doctor injected carbolic acid, full strength, and blood poisoning did the rest, causing Mr. Maddox to be a cripple for life. He then took up a small piece of land in the Matilija Cañon on Ventura-River, and kept an apiary. He was there elected road commissioner, and held the office eight years. In 1886 he came to Nordhoff, purchased a lot, and erected a very pleasant home. He also bought another lot and built a livery stable, and dealt some in real estate, being very successful in his transactions. His livery stable is now the only one in the town. It is well equipped throughout, Mr. Maddox keeping sixteen horses and ten conveyances. He has one team composed of fine grays, Richmond stock, that being considered the best stock in the country.

In 1872 Mr. Maddox was married to Miss Jennie R. Whaley, who was born in Canada, and is a daughter of William Whaley, a native of Ireland. Their union has been blessed with two sons and two daughters—Lela, Eugenia, Harry E. and Foster F. In political matters Mr. Maddox is a Democrat. His wife is a member of the Presbyterian church.

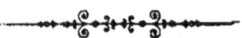

JOHN PYSTER.—On the county road, about two miles east of Carpenteria, lies the fine ranch of John Pyster, who was born in Bavaria, Germany, in 1840. He worked on the farm of his father until eighteen years of age, when he came to America, and went to Northern Wisconsin, where he worked at farming two years. He then went to Jefferson County, New York, and worked for one farmer three years. In 1863 he came to California, and was occupied as circumstances offered during the first year. He then went to Half Moon Bay and rented a farm of 200 acres of Mr. Andrew Bailard, doing general farming and remaining until 1869, when he came to the Carpenteria Valley, working one year for Mr. Bailard, who came down in 1868. In 1870 Mr. Pyster purchased adjoining land to the amount of 191 acres, of Dr. Biggs, who owned the Spanish grant. The land was all wild and largely covered with brush and live-oak which abounded all through the valley. He immediately began clearing and cultivating and putting in the standard crops of the valley—beans and barley. Mr. Pyster inherited the thrift and industry of his country, and now possesses one of the finest large farms of the valley. He is a breeder of a fine class of farm and draft horses, and his stallion "Montebello, Jr.," a Belgium horse, is one of great beauty, is four years old and weighs 1,750 pounds.

Mr. Pyster was married in Santa Barbara, November 15, 1870, to Miss Christiena Lieb, a native of Würtemburg, Germany. They have five children, four sons and one daughter, all at home. Mr. Pyster is quite up with the times in his agricultural work, and is now (May, 1890) putting in thirty-five acres of beans of choice varieties, for seed purposes, to supply the seed-store of George Haskell & Co., of Rockford, Illinois, they finding the seed grown in California to be of better quality than that grown in the East.

J. W. ROGERS, a resident of the Carpenteria Valley, was born in Peru, Clinton County, New York, in 1825. He was the youngest son of a family of seven children, all of whom are now living excepting the eldest son, who went south in early life and was stricken with yellow fever. At the age of two years, with his parents he moved to Boston, Massachusetts. His father was then connected with a manufacturing house, and introduced the first cast-iron plow into the State of Maine. As agent for a Boston firm he was also interested in the lumber business. In 1841 he moved his family to Augusta, Maine, on account of his lumber interests; was very successful, owned a ranch of 1,000 acres, and also owned a line of coast schooners which operated between Augusta, Boston and New York; but owing to a terrible freshet his lumber interests suffered to such an extent as to wipe out all of his accumulations.

J. W. Rogers was educated at the public schools of Boston, after which he took charge of his father's farm, which adjoined the city of Augusta, carrying on dairying, general farming and raising stock, etc. In 1852 he was married in Augusta, to Miss Charlotte C. Kenney, and together they passed the following winter in Virginia. In the spring they went to Wisconsin, where Mr. Rogers took up 160 acres of Government land, and for seven years was engaged in general farming. While living in Illinois he deeded to the Home for the Friendless, of New York city, one farm of 120 acres, and Mrs. Rogers became a life member of the society, and also a member of the Chicago Home for the Friendless, for the support of which institution she has contributed and also raised moneys from friends. In 1860 Mr. Rogers sold out and returned to the East, and in 1862 he brought his parents to Fairbury, Livingston County, Illinois, where Mr. Rogers purchased a small farm near the town, and also town property, and there remained until 1880, interested in gardening and the dairy business. The next year he passed in Montana, and his health failing there he came in 1881 to California. He purchased thirteen and a fourth acres of land in the Carpenteria Valley, which was at that time covered with dense underbrush and live-oaks. Mr. Rogers built a small house in the brush and then worked himself out. He now has one of the finest and most productive small ranches in the valley. He has since added to his residence, and in place of the brush it is surrounded with flowers and fruit. Mr. Rogers keeps four horses and three cows; and his strong growth of barley, beans, vegetables, alfalfa and corn bears evidence of the quality of his soil.

Mr. and Mrs. Rogers have an adopted son which they took in infancy. They are also bringing up a colored girl who was left an orphan. In conclusion we state that Mr. Rogers has just deeded a handsome lot, 50 x 150 feet, to the Methodist Episcopal society for church purposes, upon which is now erected a beautiful little chapel, where services are held every Sunday.

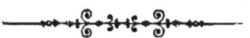

L. T. WEBSTER.—At the east end of the Carpenteria Valley lies the beautiful ranch of L. T. Webster, who was born on the shore of Lake Erie, in Lorain County, Ohio, in 1845. His father was a farmer, making the production of fruit his chief business. At the age of nine years his parents moved to Wisconsin, and his father purchased a small farm near Madison. At the age of fifteen years young Webster started out in life for himself. He first went to Iowa and began work on a farm, but with the firing on Fort Sumter his loyalty was aroused, and, though a mere boy, he enlisted in Company E, of the Second Iowa Infantry, for three years, under command of Colonel Curtis, Captain McCullough being in charge of the company. The regiment was engaged with the Western army and was at the battle of Fort Donelson, where 209 men were killed and wounded from their regiment, this being their first heavy battle. They were at the battle of Corinth; and at Shiloh the regiment sustained a severe loss, Company E going in with thirty men, nineteen of whom were killed and wounded. At the end of three years Mr. Webster was mustered out at Louisville, Kentucky, and returned home for the summer, but in the fall he again enlisted, in the Second Ohio Cavalry, under Colonel Nettleton. They were stationed in Virginia, Maryland and around Washington, but were in no engagements, and were mustered out at St. Louis in September, 1865. Mr. Webster then returned to his home in Ohio, and resumed farming.

In the fall of 1871 he was married to Miss S. E. Hammond, a native of Ohio. In the spring of 1881 they came to California, settling, in the fall of that year, in the Carpenteria Valley, where they purchased sixty acres of valley land as level as a floor. The farm was somewhat improved, a house and barn having been built on the place. Mr. Webster had done much to increase its productiveness, and it is now in a high state of cultivation. He has a fine walnut grove of thirty-one acres, six acres in a variety of fruits for family use, and two acres in alfalfa, which, at each cutting, produces about two tons to the acre. He plants six acres to corn and thirty-four acres to beans. The beautiful condition of this ranch is a significant history of the success which has attended its owner. Mr. and Mrs. Webster have two children, both living at home.

GILBERT MIDDAGH is one of the old-time Californians. He came to the State in 1854, and to his present ranch in 1869. While driving the corner stake in the homestead claim Mr. Middagh had taken, the Government surveyor stopped and said: "That's right. You're all right. Stick to it." And he has strictly followed the advice given him, and has not only stuck to it, but has added to the ranch until he now owns three-quarters of a section of land. They gathered a little drift wood and erected a temporary structure which they covered with the wagon cover. This crude affair served for a house until their nice little adobe home was finished. It stands near the stream, beside a huge white oak, which now measures fifteen feet and eight inches around the trunk and its branches extend eighty-one feet in width. Here they planted the fig and the vine until the house is embowered with fruit tree, vine, shrub and flower, and it forms a quiet, snug little home to which Mr. Middagh returns from his broad acres when his day's work is done.

He has engaged in fruit culture and has a fine orchard now in bearing, principally grown from the seed planted and budded by his own hands, and in this work he takes just pride, pleasure and profit. Few realize the hardships and self-denials that the pioneer had to undergo. The nearest place from which they could obtain supplies was Port Harford, and that was forty-five miles distant. One of the first improvements made on this ranch was a well, from which the wife lifted the dirt in an iron kettle. The well was completed and has since done good service. Mr. Middagh has trees that he planted ten years ago which now measure three feet and ten inches in circumference. Fruit trees seven years old, grown from the seed, measure two feet and four inches around, and are loaded with fruit.

Mr. Middagh's ancestors came from Holland and Germany. His grandfather, Martin Middagh, was a Revolutionary soldier, and a lieutenant at the battle of Bunker Hill. During that conflict he was struck in the face by a ball which carried away some of his teeth. His father, George Middagh, participated in the war of 1812. His mother was Mary (Goble) Middagh, and both his parents were natives of Pennsylvania. His own birth occurred in Canada, October 29, 1826, and he is one of a family of nine children, only three of whom are now living. On account of his American sentiments his father had to leave Canada in 1837, and, with his family, located in Illinois. From there he went to Iowa, was a pioneer of both States, and, of course, school opportunities for his family were limited.

In 1854 the subject of this sketch went to Shasta County, California, and engaged in mining two years. He then removed to Oregon, and both mined and farmed there for thirteen years. When he went to Oregon he had two old horses and twenty-five cents in money, and when he left, in 1869, he had saved $1,000. In that year, as already stated at the beginning of this sketch, he located in San Luis Obispo County, California.

In 1852 Mr. Middagh married Miss Mary Huston, a native of Burlington County, Hanover Township, New Jersey. Her father was Robert Huston, a native of Ireland, and his father was a Scotchman who settled in Ireland and was killed there in the time of the Rebellion, and his head was placed on a pole. His family escaped to America. Mrs. Middagh's grandfather Sherry, on the maternal side, was a Highland Scotch drummer-boy in the English army in the Revolutionary war, and deserted to join Washington and the cause of the Colonies. With his clothes tied on his back, he swam across a river to reach the American lines. He was with Washington at Valley Forge. His feet were protected with some old rags tied around them, and he was wounded in the ankle. After peace was declared he settled in New Jersey.

Mr. and Mrs. Middagh have had five children. All are now deceased except one daughter, Mary Abigail, who resides with them. She has 160 acres of land adjoining her father's property, on which she is raising stock. Mr. Middagh is raising horses and cattle. His farm products are grain and hay. He has a sample of Egyptian oats, grown on his place, that measures seven feet in length. One stool of wheat contained twenty-six heads, with 100 grains to the head.

Mr. Middagh is a political reformer. He is a Granger, and is treasurer of the Farmers' Alliance, a new society recently organized at Estrella.

CAPTAIN C. J. CURRIER, a veteran of the late war, is a prominent citizen of San Miguel, having a large ranch in that vicinity and being United States Pension Agent at San Francisco. He is a native of Derry, New Hampshire, born September 19, 1844. His father, David Currier, is also a native of that State and a banker of the city of Derry for thirty years, where he raised his family. The Captain, the seventh of nine children, was educated at Pinkerton Academy in his native town, and was but little past sixteen years of age when the country was plunged into a great war. He endeavored to enlist, but was rejected on account of his youth and the strenuous opposition of his parents. As the great struggle progressed his interest increased and his zeal fired up at the news of each battle, and in the spring of 1862, when not yet seventeen years of age, he broke over all restraints and enlisted as a private soldier in Company I, Eleventh New Hampshire Infantry, and was assigned to the Ninth Army Corps, under command of General Burnside. In three months he was promoted to be Second Lieutenant of his company. His regiment had been in several skirmishes, but in no decisive battle until December 12 and 13 at Fredericksburg, when they were put to the test and their gallantry and bravery were displayed. Of the survivors none fought more gallantly than our Lieutenant, and his services were fittingly recognized at the time by his superior officers. In the spring of 1863 his regiment was sent to the West and was under the command of General Grant as long as Captain Currier was able to remain in it. The regiment took part both in the siege and the capture of Vicksburg and pursued General Joseph E. Johnston. In November Mr. Currier was at the siege of Knoxville, and in the campaign in Virginia in 1864. On the second day of the battle of the Wilderness, in May, 1864, Captain Currier, commanding his company in advance of their line, was cheering on his men. In the assault the Captain fell with a bullet in his face, and after temporary treatment on the field he was sent to the hospital at Washington. As soon as he recovered he joined his regiment and for his bravery was promoted First Lieutenant and soon afterward Captain. He was at the siege and battle of Petersburg; at the battle of Poplar Grove Church. September 30 he was twice wounded, one ball striking him in the hip and one in the jaw. The latter passed through his head, taking out part of his jaw and most of his teeth, and cutting his tongue nearly in two. He lay on the battle-field four hours, crawling slowly and painfully to the rear, as the balls of the contending forces were passing over him. At night he was picked up nearly dead, cared for, and the second time sent to the hospital at Washington. Lying on the field, wet and cold induced rheumatism, with which he has ever since suffered to some extent. The war closed before he was able to leave the hospital. He was twice brevetted for bravery— once at the battle of the Wilderness and once at the battle of Poplar Grove Church. As soon as he was able, he accepted a position, after being mustered out, as clerk in the War Department at Washington, where he remained a year. He was then commissioned Second Lieutenant of the Twenty-first Infantry. In 1869 his regiment, commanded by General Stoneman, came to California.

He remained with it until 1870, when he resigned his commission and retired to private life.

In 1874 he came to San Luis Obispo County, purchased a ranch of 1,000 acres and engaged in stock-raising. His home is a quiet retreat on the Salinas River, about a mile northeast of San Miguel, but since his appointment as pension agent he has to spend much of his time in San Francisco. He is a member of the G. A. R. at San Miguel, Independent Order of the Loyal Legion and also of the Odd Fellows Encampment and Masonic Chapter. He still carries in his cheek a dimple made by that rebel ball, which, however, in no way detracts from his fine, gentlemanly personal appearance. It is indeed as graceful as a physical defect can be. In his political principles he is an ardent Republican, but he has declined office. He and his wife are members of the Episcopal Church.

In 1869, at Manchester, New Hampshire, he was united in matrimony with Miss Nataline Smith, a native of Providence, Rhode Island, and daughter of Waterman Smith, president of the First National Bank of Manchester. They have a son and daughter, both born in San Francisco, namely: Charles Waterman, who graduated with honor in the class of 1889 at the California Military Academy at Oakland; and Harriet Nataline, at present a pupil of Snell's Seminary in Oakland.

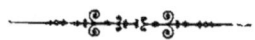

JOSEPH HOBART is a pioneer of the State of California and one of the most prominent horticulturists of the Upper Ojai Valley. His life history would make a book of most interesting reading, but in the short space allowed in a work of this character only a brief outline can be given. He comes of hardy New England ancestry; and in the early pioneer days of California, only the men of strong will power braved the dangers of the long journey to the far West and, once there, stayed and helped to make the country what it is to-day; and it is to their indomitable qualities that California owes the proud position she now occupies among the sisterhood of States.

Mr. Hobart is a native of Abington, Plymouth County, Massachusetts. His father, Benjamin Hobart, was a native of the same town, was a graduate of Brown University, Providence, Rhode Island, later became a manufacturer and made the first tacks ever made in the United States. He was a member of the Congregational Church. His death occurred in 1875. Mr. Hobart's grandfather, Colonel Aaron Hobart, was born in the same town, and was a foundryman. He cast cannon to be used in the Revolutionary war. The original ancestor of the family in America landed at Hingham, Massachusetts. in 1632, and was one of the first pastors of the Hingham Church. Mr. Hobart's mother, *nee* Deborah Lazell, was a descendant of the Huguenots, and was the mother of twelve children, five daughters and two sons still living. Mr. Hobart received his education at the Phillips (Exeter, New Hampshire,) Academy and at the Leicester Academy, Massachusetts. Being feeble in health and afflicted with asthma, he was advised to go to sea, and his second voyage brought him to San Francisco, in 1849. He returned to that city in 1856, and, in company with his brother, engaged in the wholesale boot and shoe business, which proved a success and which they conducted until 1864. He then sold his interest and went to New York and Boston, and in 1871, health again failing, returned to San Francisco. Being troubled with asthma, he then came to Southern California, first to Santa Barbara and then to Upper Ojai Valley. Being delighted with the country, and finding it conducive to health, he purchased 441 acres of land on which he built and planted and on which he has since resided. The altitude of this land is 1,100 feet above sea level, and it is located four miles east of the village of Nordhoff. With him everything was experimental, and those who have not experienced the disappointments and failures know nothing of the difficulties under which the early settlers labored; but intelligent industry has gained the victory, and Mr. Hobart now has one of the finest fruit ranches in this beautiful valley. During his eighteen years' residence in the Ojai Valley he has never had an attack of asthma. He has 1,500 large bearing apricot trees, loaded with fruit; 1,000 French prunes in the same fine condition; 1,000 almond trees also bearing abundantly, and a large orchard devoted to a general variety of delicious fruits. He keeps his ranch in a most excellent condition, has his own fruit-dryer, and has a nut-huller of his own invention that makes hulling of the nuts quite easy. To give an idea of the productiveness of the land we state that, in 1888, from 285 almond trees, Mr. Hobart sold $784 worth of nuts, and the prospect is still better this year. Mr. Hobart has also given some attention to the raising of fine horses and cattle, principally for his own use.

The subject of this sketch was married in 1860, to Miss Elizabeth Hutchinson, a native of Philadelphia, a Quaker, and a lady of Scotch-English descent. This union has been blessed with two daughters, Margaret and Gertrude. Their cozy California home, embowered with trees and vines, at once denotes the intelligence and refinement of its inmates.

Mr. Hobart is a gentleman pleasant in his manner and pronounced in his ideas on all subjects. He takes an active interest in educational matters, and is School Trustee of his district. He is a decided Republican, and a man of influence in the county.

W. BLUMBERG is the proprietor and manager of the Ojai Hot Springs, in the Matilija Cañon, located fifteen miles from Ventura and five miles from Nordhoff. Here Mr. Blumberg has what might be called a village for the sick, the halt and the invalid of every description, and here are located three springs. The Hot Sulphur Spring is 104° and is impregnated with sulphate of soda, magnesia and other healing properties, and is the safest and most healing to be found. Every one who has tried its efficiency speaks in the most emphatic manner of the benefits derived. Another fine spring is called the Fountain of Life, which is tonic in its effect. The third spring Mr. Blumberg calls the Mother Eve spring. It is alterative and cathartic in its effect. It is one of the unexplained mysteries of nature how these delightful health-giving fountains should flow from our beneficent mother earth in the same locality. The cañon in which the little health town is located has a beautiful, clear mountain stream, the San Buenaventura River, running through it, filled with a great many shy little trout, that all can fish for but only the expert can catch. This romantic spot is hemmed in by mountains 1,000 feet high on either side, and those who enjoy wild and rugged scenery can here find a place of delight. It is about nine hundred feet above the sea, and is completely shut in from the breezes of the great Pacific, fifteen miles away. Mr. Blumberg has eighty acres of land, in the center of which he has built the Matilija House, which is designed with kitchen, dining-room, parlor and office, near which are five or six cottages in which guests may have the quiet of home. There are also some tents, the bath-house, a store and postoffice, all built and conducted by Mr. Blumberg, who is also the Postmaster. He is an enterprising business man, well informed, pleasing in his manner, and takes great pains to look after the comfort of his guests. Consequently, his resort is fast becoming a popular one.

The subject of this sketch was born in Roxbury, Delaware County, New York, July 9, 1836, the son of Christopher Blumberg. His grandfather, George Blumberg, came from Germany, was detained in the British army, and afterward became a settler of Delaware County, New York. Mr. Blumberg's mother, nee Jane Mackey, was a native of New York. Her father, Thomas Mackey, was also born in the same State. They were of Scotch ancestry. Mr. Blumberg received his education in New York, and afterward went to Iowa, where he was admitted to the bar. In 1872 he came to California, and after residing in Los Angeles one or two years came to Ventura County, where he has since remained. He built the first hotel in Nordhoff, for which he received the twenty acres of land on which it stands. He arrived in Nordhoff January 12, 1874, and at that time the town was in the embryo state. Mr. Blumberg named the hotel which he built The Nordhoff, but it has since been called the Ojai House. For three years he was its proprietor and conducted it successfully. The land for the town site was bought for $4.25 per acre, and sixteen years later Mr. Blumberg sold one-fourth of an acre for $5,000. He still has considerable real-estate interests in the town. He started the Hot Springs enterprise January 20, 1887.

Mr. Blumberg was married in 1859, to Miss Catherine E. Vancuren, a native of New York, daughter of Calvin Van Curen, also a native of New York. Their union has been blest with five children, four of whom are living, viz.: Inez O., Wheeler C., Birdsel W. and Irene M. The last named was the first child born in Nordhoff. Mr. Blumberg is a Republican and was elected Justice of the Peace by his party. He is a Master Mason.

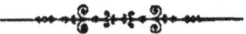

LILLINGSTON & PERRY.— Among the progressive developers of Santa Barbara County the firm of Lillingston & Perry holds a prominent place. All who visit the beautiful valley of Carpenteria should take that lovely drive up through the Lillingston Cañon, which is suggestive of the primeval forests, with its dense underbrush and its gnarled and twisted live-oaks which have stood the storms of centuries. Far back in the cañon lies the "Glen Rosa" Ranch and ostrich farm, which was started by Mr. Lillingston in 1885, at which time he made the purchase. The ranch is composed of 160 acres, largely mesa and upland. He carried on general farming until September, 1888, when he sold a half interest to Mr. Perry, his fellow countryman, and together they conceived the idea of starting an ostrich farm. They purchased four fine birds from Mr. E. Cawston, of the Norwalk Ranch, near Los Angeles. Two of the birds were imported from Africa and are now eleven years old. The other two are eighteen months old, and were raised in California. The birds were placed on the ranch in October, 1889, and are now (May, 1890,) laying and doing well.

During the year 1890 Mr. Perry bought another ostrich ranch, at Santa Monica, Los Angeles County, where there are about thirty birds, in fine condition.

Mr. Lillingston was born in London, England, in 1861, and before twelve years of age had circled the world in his travels with his parents. His father, Rev. F. A. C. Lillingston, is a prominent clergyman of the West End of London. Mr. Lillingston was educated in the Haileybury College of England, and afterward studied in Germany. In 1878 he entered the National Provincial Bank of England, going in as clerk and rising to assistant cashier, remaining seven years. In 1885 he came to California.

Mr. Harold Burder Perry was born in London, England, in 1869. His father was editor and proprietor of *Perry's Gazette*, a bankruptcy journal of great prominence. Mr. Perry was educated at the Repton School, and came to America in 1887. The next year, as already stated, he purchased an interest in the "Glen Rosa" Ranch.

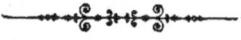

B. S. SUTTON was born at Romulus, Seneca County, New York, in 1828. He was educated at the Ovid Academy, at Ovid. His father was a farmer, and to this calling the subject of this sketch was reared, and has followed through life. After remaining at home until twenty-three years of age, he started out for himself, first going to McLean County, Illinois, where he purchased 242 acres of prairie and timber land, and engaged in general farming, raising corn, cattle, hogs, etc. In 1863 he sold out and went to Livingston County, same State, near the town of Forest. He there bought 200 acres and carried on the same class of farming, until 1873, when he again sold out and came to California. He first stopped at Ventura, but in November, 1873, he came to Carpenteria and bought forty acres of land. This he immediately improved by building a house and barns. During the boom of 1877 he sold thirty acres, continuing to hold ten acres, which is largely devoted to alfalfa and orchard.

Mr. Sutton was married in Bloomington, Illinois, in 1854, to Miss Mary Barnard, a native of Ohio, who moved with her parents to Illinois in 1840, being among the first pioneers. They have five children, all of whom are living.

A. CRAVENS.—Among the California pioneers of 1849 was T. A. Cravens, who was born in Marion, Alabama, in 1828. His father, Jesse P. Cravens, was a physician and surgeon of Marion, and enjoyed a large practice. T. A. Cravens was educated in Marion, and at the age of twenty-one, during the California gold excitement, started on that long, tedious journey across the plains, taking the southern route, through New Mexico and Arizona. Upon his arrival in California he went to the mines on the American River, and there, and at other points, he was engaged in placer mining for about two years, with reasonable success. He then went to Eureka and engaged in lumbering, owning his own saw-mills and remaining about three years. In January, 1856, Mr. Cravens was married in Marysville, Yuba County, to Miss Elizabeth Humes, a native of Missouri. They then went to Plumas County, and Mr. Cravens again engaged in placer mining, about three years. In 1859 they removed to Sonoma County and purchased a farm of 160 acres, and carried on general farming until 1865, and in Monterey County, until 1868, when they came south, spending the winter in Los Angeles, and in the spring of 1869 locating in the Carpenteria Valley, where they purchased a ranch of sixty acres, on which was a small adobe house. Land was mainly unimproved, being covered with brush and a heavy growth of live-oaks. Then the work of clearing and improving began, and the broad, beautiful fields in a high state cultivation now surround their more modern house and more complete out-buildings. They have added seventy acres to their ranch, all valley land, of which 100 acres are yearly planted to Lima beans, with an average yield of 2,000 pounds to the acre. They keep eight or ten horses and mules and several cows, but only for ranch purposes.

Mr. Cravens was a man popular among his associates and much respected by all. He served his county one term as Supervisor. At the age of sixty years, after an active life of much labor and hardships, he passed away. His widow has since managed and carried on the ranch. Mr. and Mrs. Cravens have been blessed with eleven children, eight of whom survive, one daughter being married to John Bailard and living in the valley, and seven children living at home.

SITTENFELD, the pioneer merchant of San Miguel, and one of its most prominent citizens, is a native of Prussia, Germany, born in 1855, of German parents. He received his early education there, and served an apprenticeship to the mercantile business, which proved of great value to him in after years. He came to the United States in 1870, and accepted a position as clerk in San Luis Obispo County, with the firm of Goldtree Bros. After being in their employ four years they started a store at San Miguel, in 1874, and Mr. Sittenfeld became a partner in the business, and was assigned the management of it; it was located near the old Mission building. There had been another man in business at that place, but he soon sold out to them, and for a number of years he had the only store in the town. The trade continued to grow under Mr. Sittenfeld's management until 1886, when the railroad was built. He then sold out to his partners, the Goldtree Bros., and organized the present firm of A. Sittenfeld & Co., general merchandise dealers, Mr. Mandersheid being the other member of the firm. They have established their store in the business center of the town and carry a large stock, which is kept up in excellent style, neatness and order prevailing throughout the store. Mr. Sittenfeld, as a business man, is a "success," collecting about him a large circle of friends and still keeping his old customers with him. They have a branch store at Cholame, employing six men in both stores, including themselves, both taking an active part in the business. Mr. Sittenfeld has purchased a 160-acre ranch, a mile and a quarter from town, on which he takes great pleasure in making improvements. He has planted a large variety of trees and vines; and there are a large number of oak trees on the ranch, which naturally add to the beauty and picturesqueness of the place. The farm is devoted to wheat. For many years Mr. Sittenfeld was the Postmaster of San Miguel, and for twelve years was Wells, Fargo & Co.'s agent, and has also held the office of Justice of the Peace at Parkfield, Monterey County.

Notwithstanding the amount of business he is doing, and the length of time in business, he is still a young and single gentleman, but the fixing of this nice place so near the town would seem to indicate that Mr. Sittenfeld does not always intend to board at the hotel, and that there are to be still other chapters of interest in his history!

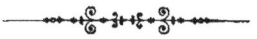

WILLIAM McGUIRE was born in Coshocton County, Ohio, April 29, 1846. His father, Thomas McGuire, was also a native of Ohio, and his grandfather, Francis McGuire, was born in Virginia. His great-grandfather, William McGuire, was a native of the north of Ireland, came to America before the Revolution, participated in that struggle, and lost his life for independence. Mr. McGuire's mother, nee Sarah Johnson, was born in Orange County, New York, daughter of Henry Johnson, a native of the same county. They were of German ancestry, and are in the line of heirs of the New York Trinity Church property. Mr. McGuire's parents had three children, of whom the subject of this sketch and his sister, a resident of Ventura County, are living. Mr. McGuire was reared in Ohio. He began life as a photographer. On account of ill health he was obliged to abandon it and engage in out-door employment. In 1875 he came to Ventura County, California, and bought a small place on the Avenue near San Buenaventura city. He built upon and improved the property, and when his health recovered he engaged in milling with Thomas Clark, in the Ventura mill. After this, Mr. McGuire purchased 262 acres of land in the beautiful Upper Ojai Valley, and has here erected a comfortable house and barns, and is engaged in stock-raising, and also producing large quantities of hay, which he feeds to his horses and cattle.

Mr. McGuire was united in marriage, in 1875, with Miss Nancy Darrah, a native of Ohio, and daughter of William and Elizabeth Darrah. This union has been blessed with eight children, all but one living, and all born in Ventura County, viz.: Corena, William, Myrta A., Thomas, Sarah, Claus and Katie B.

Mr. McGuire is an enterprising, intelligent business man, one whose influence for good is felt in the community. He is now serving his district as School Trustee. Politically he is a Democrat; and socially affiliated with the Masonic fraternity.

THOMAS CLARK, a pioneer citizen of the Ojai Valley, was born in Ireland, November 14, 1842. His parents, Bernard and Annie (McCarron) Clark, were also natives of Ireland. The subject of this sketch was educated in his native country, and, in 1855, came with his parents to the United States and settled in Wisconsin, where his father purchased a farm. Mr. Clark, Sr., was a faithful member of the Catholic Church all his life, and died in 1865. Mr. Clark is one of a family of three children, all now in California, and his sister, Mrs. Thomas Thompson, lives on an adjoining farm. After working for some time on a steamboat, Mr. Clark next engaged in the saw-mill business, and sawed lumber to aid in keeping the rebels out of New Orleans. In 1861 he returned to Wisconsin and there met the lady who afterwards became his wife and has been a faithful helpmate to him thus far on life's journey. She is also a native of Ireland, and of the same town in which Mr. Clark was born, her maiden name having been Annie Murphy. She was a daughter of Hugh Murphy, who was a native of Ireland, a devout Catholic all his life, and who lived to the advanced age of ninety-nine years. After his marriage, Mr. Clark worked a year in Chicago and then, in 1864, came to Sonoma County, California, where he rented a farm. In 1868 he bought 150 acres of land in the upper Ojai Valley, lived on it for a year, and then moved upon his present ranch of 180 acres. Here he has expended much labor in improving the land, clearing off the brush and stones and "making the wilderness to bloom like the rose." He has erected a comfortable home and has one of the finest ranches in the valley, and his success is due to his own industry and enterprise. On this ranch is plenty of fruit, which was planted for home use, but they now have more than is needed for that purpose. Mr. Clark has a splendid vineyard and makes his own wine, a superb article, and has it in his cellar for years, growing better as it gets age. In addition to cultivating his own land, he rents other lands and raises large quantities of choice wheat. Mr. Clark is giving some attention to the raising of Morgan horses, Poland-China and Berkshire hogs and Jersey cattle. They also raise a great many fine chickens. Mrs. Clark is a lady of refinement and takes much pleasure in the cultivation of flowers, which are found in profusion around her home, and in bloom all the year. The beautiful pictures and many ornaments which are found in her cosy parlor also go to show her good taste.

One day a minister called to see Mr. Clark while he was at work in his vineyard, and, after following him around a while, he said: "Mr. Clark, I must congratulate you. The Lord has placed you in a fine vineyard." "Yes," said Mr. Clark, "but the Lord had nothing but brush and stones here when I came here." When they first settled in the valley, there were only three families in it—the families of Messrs. Ayers, Lucos and Proctor. The grizzly bears were plenty and quite familiar. Mrs. Clark says they would lift a panel of fence and set it to one side and pass through easier than a man could. They were thinned out and gotten rid of by poisoning. During eight years of his residence here, Mr. Clark owned and ran the Ventura grist mill, in company with Mr. McGuire.

The subject of this sketch belongs to the Democratic party and is often a delegate in their county conventions. Both he and his wife are members of the Catholic Church.

SAMUEL NOTT is one of the worthy business men of San Miguel. His father, John Nott, was a native of England, a hardware man there, and afterward continued the business in New York city; so that Mr. Nott, the subject of this sketch, inherits the business, or, as he says himself, was born a hardware man and a tinner. He made his arrival in this mundane sphere September 17, 1840, in England. In 1852, at the age of twelve years, he came to New York. His mother, Elison (Wardrope) Nott, was a native of Scotland, and her ancestry can be traced back to the Scottish chiefs. His grandfather was killed in the battle of Bothwell Bridge. However, Mr. Nott takes little stock in ancestry except as a matter of history. He is one of those plain, common-sense men who hold that it is not who a man's father was, but what he is himself that tells the story. There were nine brothers and sisters in his father's family, all born in England, and all living. This gentleman does not dispute that who a man's parents are has much to do with his longevity. Their mother is the only one of this large family who is now deceased. Her death occurred in New York city, in 1873.

Mr. Nott went to Honolulu in 1866, and opened a hardware business, and continued there until 1885. He then sold out and came to California. At Los Gatos, Santa Clara County, he bought a fruit orchard and a nice home. As there was no opening for his business he came to San Miguel, and opened his present hardware store, and he here enjoys a good trade which extends over an area of seventy miles in width. Mr. Nott still retains his valuable property in Los Gatos. He bought the lot and built his store, and also a home in San Miguel.

At Honolulu, he met and married the lady of his choice, Mary E. Andrews, who was born in Honolulu, daughter of Rev. Lorrin Andrews, one of the first missionaries sent there by the American Board of Missions, in 1828. Mr. and Mrs. Nott have eight children, all except one born on the Islands, viz.: Annie W., Samuel W., Robert H., William W., Mary A., Sarah T., Elizabeth W. and Lorrin A. They are members of the Congregational church. Mr. Nott is an Odd Fellow, and a member of the G. A. R. His war record is as follows: he enlisted in the Union army in October, 1862, at Canandaigua, New York, Company G, One Hundred and Forty-eighth New York, at a time when the great civil war had reached vast proportions, when the two great armies had become in dead earnest and were struggling for supremacy and many thousands of precious lives were being sacrificed. He enlisted as a private soldier and went to the front to do his share in putting down the great rebellion and saving the Union. He participated in eighteen battles, among them were Cold Harbor, the siege of Petersburg and Fort Harrison; and was with General Grant during 1864 and 1865, up to the surrender of General Lee.

He was present at the surrender, and his corps, the Twenty-fourth, was left in charge of the captured city of Richmond. He passed through the deadly struggle without receiving a scratch, but his health was impaired by exposure and fatigue, from which he has never recovered. He was discharged at Richmond, and returned to his home and took up his old trade, the hardware and tinning business, as already referred to. He is a quiet, painstaking, and industrious business man, and deservedly enjoys the confidence and respect of his fellow citizens.

MRS. JULIA F. WILLIAMS, who for twenty-five years has faithfully served the light-house department in discharging her duty at the light-house on Santa Barbara Point, like the wise virgins with lamps always filled and trimmed ready to light at the appointed time, was born on Campo Bello Island, New Brunswick, July 12, 1826. She passed her childhood at Eastport, Maine, was married there to Albert J. Williams, and she and her husband resided at Waterville, Maine. Her husband came to California in 1849, and she followed him in 1852, coming by the Isthmus of Panama, and arriving in San Francisco, February 22, 1853. The trip up from Panama was fraught with much discomfort, as ship-fever was among the passengers and there were seventy-five deaths and burials at sea. Mr. and Mrs. Williams lived in San Francisco until 1856, when they came to Santa Barbara. The light-house was then being built, and as soon as it was finished Mr. Williams received the appointment of keeper, from President Franklin Pierce, and the lamp was first lighted December 19, 1856. In 1857 there was a severe earthquake which shook the stone light-house, rattled the blinds, threw the chimney, from the lamps, and even the earth could be seen to quake. On December 25, 1857, Mrs. Williams gave a Christmas dinner at the light-house to all the American families in town. About thirty persons were present. After dinner they played base-ball, and at midnight sang "Home, Sweet Home," and withdrew. In 1860 Mr. Williams was superseded, and in February, 1865, Mrs. Williams received the appointment from Commodore Watson, light-house inspector at San Francisco, which was confirmed at Washington. Mrs. Williams was the first woman appointed light-house keeper in California and is now the oldest incumbent in the light-house service of the State. For twenty-five years she has rendered most faithful service, filling and trimming her own lamps. With the exception of three weeks, when ill, she has lighted the lamp at sunset, changed it at midnight, never retiring until that duty was performed, and extinguishing the lamp at sunrise. She keeps her own books, recording each day the amount of oil used, hours the lamp burned and the condition of the weather, making monthly, quarterly and annual reports. Now, in her sixty-fourth year, she is still regular in the discharge of her duty.

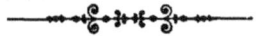

S. BARRY is one of the public-spirited citizens and prominent business men of San Miguel. He came to the coast in 1869. Mr. Barry is a native of Galena, Illinois, born February 22, 1845. His father, Richard F. Barry, was born in Washington, District of Columbia, and his grandfather, Commodore Barry, was first commodore of the United States navy. The ancestors of the family were originally from Ireland, having settled in America before the Revolution. His mother's maiden name was Emily Weber. She was a native of France. There were only two sons in the family, J. D., now living in San Francisco, and E. S., the subject of this sketch. He was educated in St. Louis, Missouri, and started in business in that city as entry clerk in a large wholesale dry-goods house. During the war he was chief clerk in the disbursing office at Little Rock, Arkansas. At the close of the war he continued in the occupation of entry clerk in the wholesale business. After coming to this coast he was paymaster for Wells, Fargo & Co., on their route between Salt Lake and Fort Benton, on the head waters of the Missouri River; was in that business three years, and made payments along the route for 1,100 miles, while the country was infested with stage robbers and Indians. After that Mr. Barry spent some time in the White Pine country, Nevada.

In 1869 he came to California and was in the employ of the Northern Pacific Transportation Company, Holladay & Brenham agents, San Francisco. Afterward with the Southern Pacific Railroad Company, and after that engaged in mining. In 1879 he went to Soledad and engaged in stationery and express business, and has been with the company ever since. Mr. Barry is a prominent Odd Fellow, has passed through all the chairs, and is now District Deputy.

He was married in 1874, to Miss Ella M. Little, of Hollister. Their union has been blessed with three children, viz.: William B., born in San Francisco, in 1877; Edward L., in Soledad, in 1885, and Gail W., in San Miguel, in 1888. Mrs. Barry is a Presbyterian. In his political views, Mr. Barry is a Democrat.

In speaking of his ancestors, it should be further stated that his grandfather, on the maternal side, Captain John H. Weber, a noted sea captain, had the honor of having Weber River and Weber Cañon named for him.

P. SQUIER was a descendant of one of the early pioneers of Ohio, who emigrated to that country when it was wild and unsettled. He was born in Sandusky County in 1838, and is one of a family of eight children, only four of whom are living. His father was a merchant at Taylorville, Illinois, where he moved in 1844, and where the subject of this sketch received his education. As soon as he heard of the firing on Fort Sumter in 1861, he was thrilled with patriotism and enlisted April 19th in the Illinois State Militia, and, under the next call of the President for more troops, was transferred to Company H, Fourteenth Illinois Infantry, Colonel John M. Palmer in command, and Andrew Simpson as Captain of the company. Mr. Squier went out as Second Lieutentant, and for gallant and meritorious service at Shiloh was promoted to Captain of Company H, Captain Simpson having been wounded. In 1861 the regiment was in the campaign of the Missouri, under General Fremont, and in 1862 joined the forces under General Grant, and were at Forts Donelson and Henry, Shiloh, Corinth, Metamora, the siege of Vicksburg and many skirmishes. He was wounded at Jackson, Mississippi, by a cannon ball, July 6, 1863, and was mustered out at Springfield, Illinois, in August, 1864. He returned home and served as enrolling officer, not being able to attend to more active duty.

Mr. Squier learned the trade of carpenter and builder at Taylorville, Illinois, where he served two terms in the city government, and worked at his trade until 1875. In that year he came to California, coming direct to Santa Barbara. He began work at once and superintended the construction of many of the best residences in the upper part of the city. He bought block 234 on the west side of the city, in 1884, and erected his present residence in 1886. In 1888 he was elected city Councilman from the second ward.

Mr. Squier was married at Taylorville, Illinois, January 17, 1865, to Miss Priscilla Keller, a native of Pennsylvania. They have four children, all living in Santa Barbara. Mr. Squier is a member of the Masonic order, and at Taylorville held the responsible position of Master and High Priest for a number of years; and was Master of the Santa Barbara Lodge, No. 192, F. & A. M., for two years. He is also a Knight Templar.

WILLIAM C. COOK, one of the prominent business men of New Jerusalem, Ventura County, California, was born in Toronto, Canada, October 28, 1856. His birth occurred in Canada while his mother was there on a visit, so that he is the son of a United States citizen. His father, William Cook, was born in England, came to America in 1837, and settled at Buffalo, New York. His mother, Hannah (Chappel) Cook, was also a native of England Of the five children born to them, William is the only surviving one. His early life was spent in Rochester, New York, at Buffalo and at London, Canada. He graduated at a high school and also spent one year at the Huron College. For nearly a year he sailed on the steamship Oceanic, White Star Line, between New York and Liverpool, after which he traveled in England, Ireland and France. His father sent him a ticket to return to America on the Atlantic. He missed that ship, however, and sailed in the Oceanic. On that voyage the Atlantic went down near Halifax, Nova Scotia, with 950 souls on board! His parents thought he was on the lost ship, and it was a glad surprise, indeed, when he reached them in safety. His father thinking it best for him to learn a trade, he chose carriage-making, and worked at it three years, receiving $25 per year and his board. After his term of apprenticeship had expired he worked in the same shop for a while, and later in Detroit and Chicago. He then accepted the position of brakeman on the New York Central Railroad. After being thus employed for two months he went home on a visit, and in May, 1876, came to California. He worked in Saticoy two years, then went to the Conejo Valley, and next came to New Jerusalem. A year and a half he worked here for wages, and then was employed for four years in Hueneme. He returned to New Jerusalem and formed a partnership with Mr. Wilkes and opened his present carriage and blacksmith business. The firm now, 1890, is Cook & Joy, Mr. Joy having bought out Mr. Wilkes. Mr. Cook owns a five-acre lot, on which he built his residence. He also owns another house and lot.

The subject of this sketch was married November 26, 1876, to Miss Annie Groves, a native of Canada. They have a family of two sons and two daughters, all born in Ventura County, viz.: Hannah, Emma, Charles and Willie, Mr. Cook is a Republican and takes an active part in political matters. He holds the office of Justice of the Peace, and is clerk of the board of trustees of the school district. He has recently been appointed Postmaster of New Jerusalem. He is Deputy Grand Master of the A. O. U. W., and a charter member of the order at Hueneme, where he aided in establishing a lodge. Mr. Cook has recently united with the F. & A. M.

It should be further stated, in connection with the history of Mr. Cook's family, that his father, brother and an uncle were Union soldiers in the late war. His brother and uncle both died at the Andersonville prison.

CHARLES A. THOMPSON was born at Santa Barbara in May, 1845. His father, A. B. Thompson, was a native of Portland, Maine, and came to Santa Barbara at an early age. He was a seafaring man, and was largely engaged in trading with the Sandwich Islands, taking out hides and tallow and exchanging for silks, dry goods and other merchandise, which he sold through his stores in Santa Barbara. He owned three vessels, which he ran between the California coast and the Sandwich Islands. He was also owner at one time of the Santa Rosa Islands, where he kept a large number of sheep. The family was composed of six children, namely: Frank A. Thompson, now residing at Ventura; Mary Isabelle, who married E. Van Valkenburg, and resides at Santa Barbara; Ellen Ann, who married George Tyng, a descendant of the eminent divine, Doctor Tyng, and lives in the city of Mexico; Frances Caroline, who married John F. Dana, and resides on the Nipomo Ranch in San Luis Obispo County; Albert F. Thompson, the youngest, who died in New Mexico, February 16, 1885, where he was assisting to compile new laws for the Territory; and Charles A., the subject of this sketch, who was educated at the Santa Clara College. After leaving the college in 1858 he went into the County Clerk's office, under Charles S. Cook for one year. Then, on the election of his brother, F. A. Thompson, to the office of county clerk, which he held for twenty one years, Charles A. continued deputy throughout the several terms. He then studied law, and was admitted to the bar in November, 1875. Mr. Thompson has served as deputy County Assessor, as City Assessor and as a member of the city council. His practice has been largely in searching records and proving titles.

He was married in Santa Barbara, in 1876, to Miss Maria E. Andonaegui, whose parents were natives of San Sebastian, Spain. They have two children, Charles Lawrence and Francis.

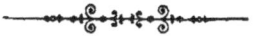

C. H. FRINK, the proprietor of "The Great Wardrobe" clothing store, Santa Barbara, was born at Philadelphia, Jefferson County, New York, in 1849, a descendant of the Frinks of Stonington, Connecticut, his grandparents immigrating to Jefferson County among the earliest pioneers. At the age of sixteen years Mr. Frink began his mercantile life at Bedford, Michigan, where he clerked in a dry-goods store three years. He then returned to Philadelphia, and in 1869 bought an interest in a general merchandise store, carrying on the business for three years under the firm name of Rouse & Frink. He next passed three years at Albion, New York, returning to Philadelphia again, in 1876, and remaining until 1879. In that year he sold out and came to California, first settling at Antioch, Contra Costa County, where he was again connected with his former partner, Mr. Rouse, in general merchandise business. In 1883 Mr. Frink bought out his partner and continued alone until 1886, at which time he came to Santa Barbara and opened the clothing store known as "The Great Wardrobe." It is now

(1890) the leading store in clothing and gents' furnishing goods in the city. Mr. Frink keeps on hand a large line of the finest quality of ready-made clothing, manufactured by the leading houses in Syracuse, Rochester, Chicago and New York city; also deals in the Stetson & Dunlap hats.

Mr. Frink is a courteous and pleasant gentleman who commands the respect and confidence of all who meet him. He was married at Antioch, California, in 1880, to Mary Elizabeth Ross, a native of St. Lawrence County, New York. The union has been blessed with one child, Clarence Harlow.

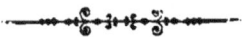

B. G. ALLEN is one of San Miguel's prominent citzens and business men. He came to California in 1856, and is a native of the city of Utica, Oneida County, New York, born April 21, 1849. His father, Elihu Allen, was a native of Oneida County, New York; came to California in 1849; and was a member of the fire department of San José in 1854. Mr. Allen has a framed certificate of his membership. The Allens were originally from Schenectady, New York, and belong to the posterity of Ethan Allen, of Revolutionary fame. His mother was Mary Ann (Graves) Allen, a native of New York, and daughter of Benjamin Graves, from Connecticut, a prominent citizen, who removed to Oneida County, New York, and reared a large family there. Mr. Allen's mother was a descendant of Mollie Stark, of Revolutionary fame.

The subject of this sketch is the only survivor of a family of four children. He received his education in the public schools of San José, and also took a year's study in the East, at the Business College of Utica, New York. In 1867 he engaged in farming in San José, and was very successful, farming 400 acres for several years; and afterward, by the failure of crops and other causes, he lost what he had made. Then he obtained the position of clerk in a store, and afterward he became manager of the Los Gatos store, which position he held for four years. He then opened a general merchandise business for himself in that town, and remained there two years. In 1887 he moved to San Miguel, and opened a general merchandise store, and has conducted a successful business, enjoying the patronage and confidence of the people. The trade extends in the surrounding country for fifty miles. Mr. Allen also owns a ranch of 160 acres, which he farms, raising wheat and hay. It is improved with good house, barns, fences, etc. He has also invested in lots in the town. He built his store in the business center of the city, on Mission street, between Twelfth and Thirteenth streets.

Mr. Allen was married in 1871 to Miss Hattie Ables, a native of Big Valley, Sonoma County. She was the first white child born there. Her father, William C. Ables, was a native of Ohio, and came to California in 1852. He was a leading Methodist and prominent rancher in California from 1852 to 1885, when his death occurred. Mr. and Mrs. Allen have two sons, Edgar E., born in Castorville, and William B., born at San José. The family are attendants of the Episcopal Church. Mr. Allen is a prominent Odd Fellow, being a member of San José Encampment, No. 34, and Nacimiento Lodge, No. 370, I. O. O. F. He is also a member of the A. O. U. W. In politics he is a stanch Republican, and takes a lively interest in any public enterprise that tends to improve the community where he resides. He has unbounded faith in the upper Salinas Valley, and thinks the planting of fruit will soon make it compare favorably with any county in the State. Mr. Allen speaks both the English and Spanish languages.

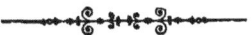

R. E. JACK, of San Luis Obispo, was born in the State of Maine, in September, 1841, and very early in life evinced a high order of talent for business. Accordingly he went to New York, where he was connected with a commercial house on Wall street. In 1864 he came to California and at once engaged in wool-growing. He is now the owner of Cholame Ranch of 40,000 acres, but he devotes his time to banking, in his city, being cashier of the First National Bank of San Luis Obispo; is also the principal of the Bank of Paso Robles, in that town, the Bank of Santa Maria and the Bank of Lompoc in the county of Santa Barbara. Mr. Jack represents the progressive element in business, and is prominent in all matters connected with the welfare and prosperity of San Luis Obispo. In politics he is a leader, and at the present time is President of the city council.

He was married in 1872, to a daughter of Colonel Joseph Hubbard Hollister, and has a family of four children.

VIRGIL A. GREGG, Superior Judge of San Luis Obispo County, was appointed to the office he now holds by Governor Waterman, February 8, 1889. Mr. Gregg was born in Des Moines County, Iowa, in 1844. His father was born in Virginia, in 1810, and his mother in Tennessee, in 1819. Both parents were pioneers of Iowa, when it was a part of Michigan Territory. The subject of this sketch at the age of thirteen years, entered the Iowa Wesleyan University at Mount Pleasant, Iowa, where he continued until he entered his senior year in 1862. He then left college and entered the volunteer service in the war of the Rebellion, in the Twenty-fifth Iowa Volunteer Infantry, and continued in the army with Sherman until the close of the war. Then he entered the law department of the University of Michigan, in September, 1865, and graduated with the class of 1866, and located first for the practice of law in December, that year, in Memphis, Tennessee. Being in poor health, he left Memphis and traveled for nearly a year, and then settled in Council Bluffs, Iowa, and there practiced law and took an active part in politics, as a Republican, always participating in every canvass as a speaker. In 1873 he came to California, at the instance of his friend Josiah Earl. Mr. Earl having succeeded by a visit to Washington City in having a United States land office located at Independence, Inyo County, California, and being appointed Register, he got Mr. Gregg to come to California to put the new office in working condition. Mr. Gregg left Inyo and located at Bakersfield, Kern County, California, in 1876, and was there elected on the Republican ticket a member of the California Constitutional Convention that met at Sacramento in December, 1878, and that formulated the present Constitution of California, and Mr. Gregg had the honor of serving on the Judiciary and Corporation Committees of that body. Mr. Gregg has been a resident of San Luis Obispo for seven years, and of the State for seven years. He has always been a Republican in politics, and has for his party canvassed the State at one time, and several counties at different times. He is a Grand Army man, a member of George H. Thomas Post, No. 2, San Francisco, and is in receipt of a pension of $16 per month from the Government for wounds received during the war. He has a wife and five children, having married at Mount Pleasant, Iowa, in 1879.

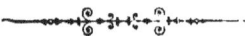

GEORGE G. CRANE, one of the prominent citizens of Saticoy, was born in Sharon Township, Medina County, Ohio, July 7, 1835. His father, George W. Crane, was a native of Massachusetts, born in 1809, and removed to Ohio in 1834, bought a farm in that new country, cleared it and made it his home until his death, which occurred in 1884. Mr. Crane's grandfather, Barnabas Crane, was born in Dighton, Massachusetts, in 1774. Their ancestors were English and Scotch, and were among the first settlers of the new world. Mr. Crane's mother, Louisa (Briggs) Crane, was a native of New York, born in 1815. She is now (1890) a resident of California. Her brother, George G. Briggs, was the pioneer in and promoter of the raisin-grape industry in California, devoting as many as 1,000 acres to their production. She is the daughter of Thomas Briggs, who was a native of Massachusetts. Mr. Crane is one of a family of seven children, all now living except one, and was reared and educated in his native place. When a young man he came to California, worked in the mines and by the month, after which he returned to his native State and purchased 125 acres of land. After residing on that farm twelve years, he sold out and removed to Cass County, Missouri, where he bought a farm and lived six years. He then disposed of his property there and went to Denver, Colorado, engaged in the wholesale fruit business, and later in quartz mining, continuing the latter business six years. In 1884 he bought his present home place of 140 acres, situated in one of the very best valleys in Southern California, and improved the property by building, tree-planting, etc. He has fifty acres in English walnuts, four years old, and one-half acre in eucalyptus trees, planted in rows six feet apart and four feet apart in the row, now over fifty feet high, which will furnish all the wood needed on the farm. Mr. Crane raises from sixty to 110 tons of beans each year.

He was married in 1859 to Miss Adaline Huntly, a native of Ohio, born in Granger Township, Medina County, in 1836. They have two children, both born at his home in Sharon, Ohio,—Amie and Abbie. Amie is the wife of E. E. Huntly, and resides at Saticoy. Mr. and Mrs. Crane are members of the Universalist church, and are liberal in their religious views. In politics he is a Democrat, and has held the office of Supervisor both in Ohio and in Missouri. He has always taken an active interest in schools, and has frequently held the office of school trustee. He is an intelligent and agreeable gentleman, and is highly respected by his fellow-citizens.

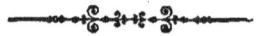

S. L. GISLER is a well-to-do citizen and an early settler of New Jerusalem. His father, Max Gisler, a native of Switzerland, was a poor but worthy and industrious man, with a wife and thirteen children. With the intention of trying to improve his financial condition and to better provide for his family, he borrowed the money to pay his passage to California, and came to Ventura County in 1876. The second eldest son came with him, and together they worked as sheep herders for two years, and during that time they saved money enough to pay the borrowed money and also to bring the eldest daughter and son to this country. S. L. Gisler and two brothers were the next sent for. By the united efforts of all, the mother and other members of the family were brought to California, and here prosperity has been the reward of their labor. When persistent effort is coupled with a determination to succeed in any undertaking, it is seldom that failure is the result. Mr. Gisler purchased sixty-five acres of land adjoining the town of New Jerulsalem, on which he built a fine residence, where he and a part of the family now reside. Five of the children are married and settled in this county.

S. L. Gisler dates his birth June 6, 1861. He arrived in California May 6, 1878, and his first work here was as a farm hand and teamster, for Edward Borchard, remaining with him six years and three months. He next worked two seasons on a thresher, at $55 per month and board. In 1886 he opened his Swiss saloon in New Jerusalem, which he is still conducting. Mr. Gisler was married December 1, 1888, to Miss Theresa Puentener. Both are members of the Catholic church. His political views are Democratic.

GEORGE M. RICHARDSON is one of the oldest settlers of Santa Paula. He was born in Kennebec County, Maine, on the last day of the last week of the year, and on the last day of the last month of the year 1821. He was the son of George and Lovicy (Robins) Richardson, the former a native of Attleborough, Massachusetts, of English extraction, and the latter was born in Orange, Massachusetts. They had a family of twelve children, of whom five sons and one daughter are now living. The subject of this sketch left his native State in 1836, and settled in the town of Moscow, Hillsdale County, Michigan, just about the time Michigan was admitted into the Union as a State, thus becoming a pioneer of that new country. He bought a farm, built a house and improved the land, and lived there for ten years. He then sold out and removed to Jackson County, same State, where he purchased eighty acres of land and again built and made improvements; and, while there, split more rails than Abraham Lincoln did. In 1852 he disposed of his property in Michigan and came to the Pacific Coast, reaching San Francisco December 31. Upon his arrival here he was short of money, and he and his brother went to Petaluma, having only seventy-five cents left when they got there. They at once went to work in a saw-mill; but, soon afterward Mr. Richardson, observing the high price paid for potatoes, decided to engage in their production, which he did, paying eight cents per pound for seed; at digging time potatoes were so plenty there was no sale for them. He then went to the redwoods and there worked two years at $60 per month; got out timber for himself and others, which was split with a froe, making good siding. After this he rented a place and made enough to buy out a squatter, in the neighborhood of Vacaville. He lived on this place ten years, built a house and made many improvements; and then discovered that the title was not good. After having paid for it twice, he loaded his things in wagons and started for Southern California with his family. Seven of them rode in the covered wagon, which took the place of both wagon and house for weeks while they were traveling; and after they reached their destination they lived out of doors through the day and slept in it at night, until they got the house built. At that time, 1867, there were no houses on the road between Santa Paula and San Buenaventura, and his wife remarked to him, "You have brought us to the jumping-off place now." Mr. Richardson's first house built there is still standing and speaks plainly of pioneer days. It is 16 x 24 feet, one story high, and the lumber, of which it was built was hauled from Ventura. The property is located three-quarters of a mile southeast of the now beautiful town of Santa Paula. When Mr. Richardson located there his neighbor, Mr. Montgomery, lived a mile and a half away; and the Ventura school district was the only one in the county. The first year Mr. Richardson sowed wheat and barley, and the wheat rusted; the second year he sowed again, with the same result; and the third year he did not sow. There was not a mill in the county, and his son Fred went with a wagon to Los Angeles, with wheat and corn to mill, sleeping in his wagon at night, the trip requiring a week's time. The younger boys would go up the Sespe River fishing, and be gone two or three days, returning with plenty of fish and other game. They would take their blankets and go on the top of the mountains at night, in order to be ready for game in the morning. A great share of their provisions at that time was venison. Mr. Richardson has been principally engaged in raising hogs and cattle; but at present he is extensively engaged in the production of Lima beans, for which this part of the country is so well adapted.

Mr. Richardson was married July 4, 1848, to Miss Nancy Mull, a native of Ohio. They had one child, Fred, whose history appears in this book. After four years of wedded life, Mrs. Richardson died. And for his second wife Mr. Richardson married Miss Jenette Sims, a native of Indiana. To them were born five children: Emma, who died at the age of twenty-one years; George, born September 21, 1860; Louis, born December 22, 1862; Frank, born April 8, 1864; and Harry S., October 1, 1873. Mrs. Richardson died June 22, 1877.

George Richardson has a ranch of 160 acres adjoining his father's. He married Miss Ida Kellog, a native of Illinois, born December 2, 1860, and daughter of Norman A. M. Kellog, who was born in New York. George and his wife live with father Richardson. They have a family of five children, all born in Santa Paula: George Lawrence, born December 16, 1882; Olinda, June 7, 1884; Charles K., July 27, 1885; Yale, March 6, 1887; and Mark, January 24, 1889.

The subject of this sketch was reared a Democrat, but has been a Republican since the organization of that party. He has been a member of the Methodist Church for thirty-five years. Well has he earned the name of pioneer, having been an early settler of both Michigan and California. By his industry and economy he has acquired a competency, and is now enjoying the fruits of a well-spent life.

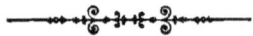

FREDERICK RICHARDSON is one of the reliable and prosperous ranchers of Santa Paula, and a pioneer of this part of the county, having come to California in 1855 with his uncle. The subject of this sketch was born in Jackson County, Michigan, near the Hillsdale County line, June 18, 1849, and was in his sixth year when he removed to the Golden State. He received his education in Solano County, and was reared to farm life. In 1867 he came to Santa Paula, and to his present home in 1876. He at once began the work of planting and improving, and he now has a comfortable home surrounded by bearing fruit-trees. He has ten acres of alfalfa for cows, ten acres planted to English walnuts (Lima beans are grown between trees till in bearing), one acre of blackberries, one acre of raisin grapes, four acres of fruit-trees common to the country, including orange, lemon, and Japanese fruits. Two acres are devoted to eucalyptus for fire-wood, and the rest of the grounds are planted to corn, hay and Lima beans.

In 1876 Mr. Richardson married Miss Edith Ireland, a native of Atchison, Kansas, born in 1856, and daughter of Newcomb J. Ireland, who was born in New York. From this union two children have been born: George S., born in Santa Paula, April 17, 1877, and Paul F., born at Nordhoff, December 16, 1881. Mrs. Richardson was a victim of consumption, and in 1881 died of that relentless disease. October 31, 1883, Mr. Richardson wedded Miss Lottie Sewell, a native of New York, born in 1847, daughter of Rensselaer Sewell, of that State. This union has been blessed with two children, twins, Frank R. and Faith H. Mr. and Mrs. Richardson are both worthy members of the Methodist church. His political views are Republican.

C. W. HARROLD is one of the many prominent citizens who live in the beautiful valley of Saticoy. He was born in Wayne County, Indiana, November 8, 1839, and is the son of Jonathan Harrold, a planter, born in Virginia, of English ancestry. When the subject of this sketch was two years old his parents removed to Illinois, where he was reared and educated. For a number of years he was engaged in stock-raising for beef, conducting the business on a large scale. He moved from that State to Texas, where he spent ten years in the same business. In 1886 he came to San Francisco, and from there to his present ranch, five miles and a half nearly due west of Santa Paula, where he owns 2,500 acres of choice land. He has erected a new house on an eminence overlooking the whole valley, the view from which is exceedingly beautiful. The entire valley, with its fine ranches and comfortable homes, and the mountains opposite, is a picture that the visitor beholds with delight and does not soon forget. Mr. Harrold's residence can be seen for many miles in every direction. A large portion of the ranch is planted to olives. They are devoting 375 acres to walnuts, and fifty acres to corn. Some thoroughbred Jersey cattle are kept on the ranch for home use.

Mr. Harrold was married in 1886, in San Francisco, to Miss Clarise Harris, a native of Maryland, an accomplished lady, the daughter of J. B. Harris, who was born in New York in 1830. He has for some time been prominent in railroad building; was assistant superintendent of the construction of the Central Pacific Railroad, superintendent of the South Pacific to Fort Yuma, of the western part of the Northern Pacific; is now engaged in the construction of the Nicaragua Canal. Mr. and Mrs. Harrold have two interesting children: John H., born in Texas, June 24, 1887, and E. B. Harrold, Jr., born October 28, 1888. Mrs. Harrold is a member of the Episcopal church. Mr. Harrold's political views are Republican, but he is liberal and independent in politics as well as other topics.

J. L. BARKER, one of the most intelligent and enterprising young men of Santa Barbara, is a native of Methuen, from which town the manufacturing city of

Lawrence, Massachusetts, was founded by the celebrated Lawrence family of Boston. His father, James K. Barker, was a civil engineer and was engaged in building the dam and canal at that place and took an active interest in the early history of the town, being elected Mayor in 1861.

After graduating at the Lawrence High School, Mr. Barker entered Amherst College, graduating in the class of 1865 with high honors, although the youngest member in his class. He then returned to Lawrence and entered the office of Daniel Saunders, a prominent lawyer, with whom he read law for three years and was admitted to practice. He also devoted much time to the study of engineering with his father. When his father died, in 1868, Mr. Barker succeeded to his business, which he continued about eighteen months. Consumption being hereditary in the Barker family, as a preventive, J. L. decided to come to California, which he did in 1869. After locating in Santa Barbara, his mother followed him the next year. He engaged in surveying, and in April, 1871, was appointed to the position of City Surveyor. He made the well-known and much-talked-of Barker retracing. The town was laid off in 1851 by Salisbury Haley, in blocks 450 feet square; but, owing to imperfect measurement and loss of many stakes, it became difficult to identify blocks, and the question arose whether a survey should be adopted which would correspond to exact measurements or whether old Haley's stakes should define boundaries; and Mr. Barker made the retracing, following the Haley survey as near as practicable without regard to exact measurements, which retracing has been gradually adopted. This question is still a prominent feature in local politics, and enters into the election of city officers.

Mr. Barker resigned his office in July, 1873, to visit the East, but on his return was re-appointed in January, 1874, serving to the end of the term. He was appointed Deputy County Assessor in 1880, under J. M. Garrison, and was re-appointed by Frank Smith, Mr. Garrison's successor, who was elected in the fall of 1882. Mr. Barker continues to hold that position.

The subject of this sketch owns 340 acres of foot-hill lands and much city property. He is a large stockholder in the Stearns Wharf Company. Mrs. Barker is now seventy years of age; resides with her son in East Santa Barbara. They own and occupy the old adobe house formerly occupied by that historic character, George Nidever, the trapper, who discovered and rescued the woman from San Nicolas Island. Mr. Barker is a Royal Arch Mason, and a royal representative of the citizens of Santa Barbara.

THOMAS HARWOOD, of Saticoy, is a California pioneer, who came into the State in 1850. He was born in Gibson County, Indiana, November 24, 1841. He was the son of Thomas Harwood, Sr., a native of New York, and the grandson of Ruthland Harwood, who came from England. His mother, Sarah Harwood, was a native of England. They had six children, only three of whom survive. Thomas Harwood obtained most of his education in California, as he was only nine years of age when he came to this State. For fifteen years he was engaged in the freighting business from Marysville to Virginia City, with a ten-mule team and a large wagon. The distance was 120 miles, over mountain roads; the round trip was performed in twenty days. They hauled five tons and cleared nearly $500 each trip. Some of the mountain sides were steep, and the road formed many loops to make the grade possible, and then the hind wheels were dragged down on shoes to keep them from revolving. From there Mr. Harwood went to Butte County, and engaged in ranching; he had 2,400 acres of land, on which he kept about 2,000 sheep. The net income while he was on this ranch was about $3,000. He continued in this business about twelve years when he sold out and came to Ventura, and bought a fine ranch where he now resides. The ranch contains 152 acres, for which he paid $18,000. There are twenty-five acres of bearing apricot trees, the fruit of which they market both green and dry, and a large orange and lemon grove and other citrus fruits; and he is now raising large quantities of beans and corn, both being a paying crop. In two years, at the present prices, the property will have paid all expenses and will have returned the purchase money. He raised 2,100 pounds of Lima beans to the acre, on forty acres of land, which are now worth five cents per pound; the land only cost him $70 per acre. He has raised ninety bushels of shelled corn to the acre, and it is now worth $1 per hundred pounds; he is also raising some Belmont horses.

Mr. Harwood was married in 1876, to Miss E. A. Mastin, born November 14, 1859, in Quincy, Plumas County, California; her parents were natives of Georgia and South Carolina. They have four children, three born in Butte County, California, as follows: Thomas F., born September 26, 1879; Oliver, December 4, 1881; Henry Irvin, October 9, 1883; and Frederick W., born in Ventura County, August 21, 1887. Mr. and Mrs. Harwood are members of the Congregational Church. In his political views Mr. Harwood is a Republican, and has frequently held the office of School Trustee. He is an intelligent Californian, and is alive to the interests of his State, and highly esteemed by his neighbors.

C. B. WILLIAMS is a native of New York city and dates his birth March 7, 1828. He is a son of Clark Williams, who was born in Rensselaer County, New York, in 1801. The family were of Welsh origin and were pioneers of the eastern part of this country. His mother, Lucinda (Brewer) Williams, was born on the Hudson River. His parents had thirteen children, ten sons and three daughters, nine of whom are now living. His father was largely engaged in business, was a merchant in New York, had canal boats and was also a lumber dealer. Mr. Williams was educated in New York and, being the oldest son, aided his father in both the store and in the charge of the boats, from Buffalo to New York city. He afterward became a boat owner and did a freighting business for thirteen years.

In 1858 he came to California and settled in San Francisco, where he took charge of the spice factory of Hudson Company. He conducted that business for nine and a half years, sending their spices to all parts of the State. Mr. Williams came to Santa Paula in 1867 and started the first grist-mill in the county, at Saticoy, which was run by horse power. The machinery was afterward moved to Santa Paula, where Mr. Williams used the water power. He bought property here and devoted a part of his time to agricultural pursuits. In 1868 Mr. Williams went to Ventura with a colony to organize the Congregational church, and was one of the charter members, the pastor being Rev. M. B. Star.

Mr. Williams was married, in 1850, to Miss Elizabeth Rogers, daughter of Peter and Hester Rogers, of Oneida County, New York. Her father was a native of Massachusetts. Their union has been blessed with five children: Edward D., Eldret M., Fanny, B. H., Llewellyn A. and Charles A.

In 1884 Edward B. and Eldret purchased a valuable ranch, a mile square, one mile west of Santa Paula. This is principally a stock farm, and they are raising draft and blooded horses, grade Durham cattle and Berkshire hogs These young men were educated in San Francisco and are practical stock men. Eldret M. has special charge of the horses. Their property is beautifully located in one of the richest valleys in Southern California.

Edward B. Williams dates his birth December 21, 1851. He was married in 1881 to Miss Lizy Butcher. She was born December 29, 1860, in Canada, and removed with her father to Michigan when she was quite young. They have two children: Aneta, born in Ventura, April 6, 1886; and Howard, born in Santa Paula, October 10, 1888. He and his wife are members of the Presbyterian Church.

Eldret M. was born December 3, 1854, and is still a single man; one of excellent habits and character.

C. E. MOORE, of Santa Paula, is a pioneer of the State of California. He was born in New York, of which State his father, John Moore, was also a native, and his mother, whose maiden name was Lydia Todd, a daughter of Jared Todd. The ancestors of the family on both sides have been Americans, tracing as far back as the early settlement of this country. In John Moore's family were ten children, five of whom are still living. The subject of this notice was born September 5, 1837, and was three years old when the family removed to Hillsdale County, Michigan, where he was brought up on a farm. In 1859 he came to California and engaged in mining in Placer County, and afterward eight or nine years in the State of Nevada, with varied success. In 1869 he came to what was then Santa Barbara County, now Ventura, and bought a squatter's claim a mile and a quarter east of Santa Paula, built a house and improved the place (160 acres), which he still owns and to which he has added other ten acres by purchase. He carries on general farming. He has recently built a nice town residence on Eighth street, Santa Paula, where he now resides with his family, in a quiet and unassuming way, surrounded with the comforts of life, the well earned results of strict economy and industry. Mr. Moore has ever been a Republican; is a generous neighbor and kind husband and father. In 1872 he married Miss Annie Warren, a native of Wisconsin, born August 19, 1855, and they have one son, Enos Leroy, born in Santa Paula, August 26, 1877.

LUTHER SKELLENGER, of Santa Paula, is a native of New Jersey, born in the town of Decker, Sussex County, March 20, 1825. He followed the contractor and builders' trade until in April, 1861, when President Lincoln made his first call for volunteers to put down the Rebellion, he enlisted as a private in Company C, First New Jersey Volunteer Infantry. At the expiration of six months he re-enlisted in Company

C, Seventh New Jersey Volunteer Infantry, and was detailed on recruiting service. He raised a company, of which he was elected First Lieutenant.

When he returned for the service he bought a small flour-mill and was engaged in the milling business several years. Mr. Skellenger came to California in 1887, on account of his wife's health, and in San Buenaventura started a large furniture store. Mrs. Skellenger did not recover her health, and died soon after coming here. He sold his furniture store in 1889, and bought a ranch in Wheeler Cañon consisting of 800 acres, on which his son, Fred, is in charge. They removed to Santa Paula, where he bought property and built a home and furniture store. The business is under the firm name of Skellenger Brothers. They are doing the principal business in their line of goods in the city. Mr. Skellenger has retired from active life, and his sons are conducting the ranch and store; the store is in charge of Walter H. Skellenger. They are enterprising men of high character.

The ancestors of the family came from Amsterdam, Holland, and settled on Long Island. At one time most of the island was owned by the family, and some of it is still in the family, which was obtained in 1842. W. H. Skellenger's son, Frank Herbert, is the last of an unbroken line of eight generations, as follows: Jacob Skellenger was born in Amsterdam, Holland, in 1625, and came to America in 1653. His son was Jacob (second); his son was Daniel, born on Long Island; his son was Daniel (second), and was also born on Long Island; his son, Elisha P., was born in Morris County, New Jersey, and was a shoemaker; he died in 1839, at seventy-two years of age; his son, Elisha, was born in Sussex County, New Jersey, November 24, 1800. He was the father of Luther, the subject of this sketch, who was the father of Walter H., the father of Herbert Frank.

Mr. Skellenger, our subject, is a member of the G. A. R., and of the I. O. O. F. In the East the family were Congregationalists; but in Santa Paula, as there is no church of that denomination, they have united with the Presbyterian Church. Walter H. is a member of the choir, and also superintendent of the Sunday-school. He is a member of the K. of P., the K. of H., the S. of V. and the I. O. F. Since the death of his wife Mr. Skellenger makes his home with his son in Santa Paula.

Mr. Skellenger was married in 1847, to Miss Maria Vaness. They have had three children, all of whom are deceased. After six years of wedded life Mrs. Skellenger died, of consumption. In 1855 he was again married, to Miss Ada C. Kelsey, a native of New Jersey, born June 30, 1837, and daughter of J. B. Kelsey, also a native of New Jersey. They have four children, two boys and two girls, viz.: Walter H., born in Newark, New Jersey, May 31, 1856, and was married in 1879 to Miss Maggie A. Nichols, a native of New Jersey, born in 1860. They have three children: Frank H., born in Paterson, New Jersey, in 1882, Luther J., born in Newark, in 1886, and Marion Ethel, born June 6, 1890, at Santa Paula, California. Fred, born October 17, 1859; Mary Ida, April 15, 1862; and Clara K., March 6, 1864.

G. F. ROTSLER is one of the prominent ranchers of Santa Paula, Ventura County, California. He came from Missouri to his present locality in 1874. Mr. Rotsler was born in Baden, Germany, January

4, 1831. His parents were natives of Germany and his father was a machinist. Young Rotsler obtained his education in Germany and in 1849, at the age of nineteen years, came to the United States. He located in New York and worked in a machine shop in Green County, putting up machinery in woolen factories. He next engaged in the manufacture of straw paper, in Columbia County, and after running the paper-mill two years, he built a flouring-mill in Green County, which he ran two years. He sold out, conducted a mercantile business four years, sold it in 1866 and in 1867 went to Missouri. He purchased 130 acres of improved land in Audrain County, and a new house and eight acres of land in Martinsburg. Here for four years he was engaged in agricultural pursuits, after which he again sold out, went into a merchant mill at Mexico, Missouri, ran it three years, then disposed of it, and, in 1874, came to California. He purchased seventy-five acres of land near Saticoy, built a house and improved the property; sold out ten years later; lived in Ventura one year; went to Los Angeles, bought and sold property there; and then came to his present locality. Here he purchased twenty acres of choice land, built a very attractive house and fine barn and has made this property a valuable one. He is engaged in raising Lima beans. Ten acres of this land are devoted to walnuts, and Mr. Rotsler also has a large variety of fruit trees for family use.

He was married in Green County, New York, in 1854, to Miss Sarah E. Golden, a native of that State. They had three children: Georgiana G., born in Green County, New York, married Scott Gibson, and is a resident of Saticoy; Charles D., also born in Green County, died at the age of twenty-three years; and Willie S., born in the same place, married Sarah Middleton, and lives in Los Angeles. After seventeen years of wedded life, Mrs. Rotsler died. In 1872 Mr. Rotsler married Miss Hannah E. Lewis, a native of New York, daughter of Abel Lewis of that State. Their union has been blessed with two sons, both born in Saticoy, L. F. and S. L.

Politically Mr. Rotsler is a Democrat.

C. C. RILEY was born in Tennessee, February 9, 1818. He is a son of Stephen Riley, who was a native of South Carolina, and was of Irish ancestry. His mother, Nancy (Walker) Riley, was the daughter of Rev. West Walker, a Baptist minister of Tennessee. C. C. Riley was the fourth of a family of ten children, five of whom are living. He was reared and educated in Tennessee and Missouri, and when he became a man he purchased a farm of 161 acres in the latter State, and was engaged in agricultural pursuits there for seven or eight years. In 1853 he sold out and went to Oregon. He there improved 160 acres of land, on which he lived until 1869, when he again sold out and located in San Luis Obispo County, California. In 1872 he came to Ventura County, bought a Government claim, built a good home and planted trees. The location of this ranch is a fine one. Looking at it from the highway, it presents an inviting and home-like appearance, and plainly indicates the industry and thrift of the owner. Mr. Riley's son, West, is conducting the farming operations, and is a most industrious and worthy man.

Mr. Riley was married in 1843, to Miss Sarah Loveall, a native of Kentucky, and daughter of Abraham Loveall, a Baptist minister. Mr. and Mrs. Riley have had a family of nine children, six of whom are living, viz.: West, Stephen A. Douglas,

George B. McClellan, Lucinda, Rachal and Nancy Jane.

At the age of thirty years Mr. Riley was ordained as a Baptist minister, and has been an efficient laborer in the vineyard of the Lord. Recently, on account of advanced age and ill health, he only preaches occasionally. He was the organizer of the first Baptist Church in San Luis Obispo, and has been a leader in many revival meetings. Through his instrumentality many souls have been lead to accept the offers of salvation and obey the Lord's command. Mr. Riley's political views are Democratic.

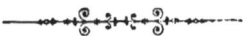

FRANCIS J. BECKWITH is one of the reliable ranchers of the section of the county where he resides. He was born in Ontario County, New York, August 14, 1834, of Scotch ancestry. His father, Nathan Beckwith, Jr., was born about the year 1798, resided in the State of New York for many years, and removed to Iowa, and from there back to Ontario County, New York, where he died at the age of sixty-five years. His grandfather, Nathan Beckwith, Sr., was a resident of Oswego County, New York, for many years, and an early settler there. Three of the Beckwiths were in the war of 1812. Mr. Beckwith's mother, Phebe (Granger) Beckwith, was born in Ontario County, New York, in 1808. She was the daughter of Elihu Granger, who came from New Jersey and settled in New York, where he resided for many years. Their ancestors had for a long time been residents of America. Mr. Beckwith was the youngest of a family of seven children, three of whom are now living. The family moved to Indiana when he was quite young, and he was reared on a farm and educated in the public schools of that State. Early in life he lost his father, and he remained on the farm with his mother until he was twenty-seven years old, and has made farming his life occupation. When Mr. Beckwith left home he removed to Michigan and purchased a farm near Vermontville, Eaton County, where he resided for two years in a log house of his own building—the only kind in which the early settlers lived. He sold out and worked in a mill for three years. In 1874 he came to California, and September 21 he came to his present ranch. He remained with his brother, Appleton Beckwith, who owned the ranch, for two years. Then he returned to Indiana, and two years later came back to California and worked for his brother nearly a year. February 3, 1881, Appleton Beckwith died, bequeathing his ranch to the subject of this sketch and another brother. This brother Mr. Beckwith has since bought out, and now owns the whole ranch, about 700 acres. Three hundred acres are farming lands, and the rest is pasture and waste land. The location of this property is in a beautiful farming country. Hogs and cattle were formerly the chief products of this district, but now the principal crop is corn and beans, twenty-five centals of corn to the acre and 2,000 pounds of Lima beans per acre being an average crop. Mr. Beckwith has made most of the improvements on the place. The grounds, with trees and flowers, everything about the house, the large barns and well-filled corn-cribs, all denote plenty and comfort. Twelve acres are in bearing English walnut trees, sixteen years old, and there is also a fine orchard containing a variety of fruit. The walnut grove yields at present $100 per acre.

In 1859 Mr. Beckwith married Miss Sarah Greenmayer, who was born in Ohio, July 5, 1841. Her father, Jesse Greenmayer, was a native of Pennsylvania, born in 1818, of Pennsylvania-Dutch ancestors. They have had a family of four children, all living. The two oldest were born in Indiana: Caroline M., September 20, 1860, now the wife of George A. Jones, and resides near Ventura; Charles F., January 12, 1862. Delbert T. was born in Michigan, January 31, 1869, and Emma G. was born in California, October 22, 1878. Charles and Delbert are settled near their father, and Emma is at home with her parents. Mr. Beckwith's political views are Republican.

JOHN IRWIN is one of the business men of Santa Paula. A brief sketch of his life is as follows: Mr. Irwin was born in Cherry Tree, Venango County, Pennsylvania, May 4, 1841. His father, William Irwin, was a native of the same place, and his grandfather was one of the early settlers of that county, and lived to be eighty-seven years old. His great-grandfather, Richard Irwin, was born in County Armagh Ireland, in 1740, and immigrated to Pennsylvania in 1761, at the age of twenty-one years. In 1809 John Irwin built the first grist-mill in Cherry Tree, and the first saw-mill in the township was built by Ninian Irwin in 1823. Both John and Ninian Irwin were appointed justice of the peace and held the office for years. Most of this early history was obtained from Judge John Irwin, a judge and prominent citizen of Cherry Tree for many years in the early history of the county of Venango. Mr. Irwin's mother's maiden name was Eliza Stewart. She was a native of the same State, and was a daughter of Elijah Stewart, who was also born in Pennsylvania. When the subject of this sketch was nineteen years old his father died, and upon him devolved the care of the farm and his mother and six children. His early educational advantages were limited, and he is evidently a self-made man. He remained with the family until twenty-eight years of age. When John was quite a small boy his father kept a dairy, and the boys early learned to take charge of the stock. Mr. Irwin says that when he was only eleven years old he both bought and sold cows. He was thus inured to hard work in early life and also learned something of the management of the farm and stock; although he was a slight lad, at twenty-one weighing only 100 pounds. His birth-place was only four miles from the first producing oil well in the oil regions of that State, the Drake, which was opened in 1859. When his farm work was done, Mr. Irwin often worked at the oil wells for wages, and after a time purchased an outfit and took contracts to sink wells. The owner of the well furnished the boiler and engine and wood rig; the other material was furnished by the driller. After working in this way for twelve years, he took an interest in wells and became an oil-well owner. In speaking of productive wells, Mr. Irwin says the most productive well he had anything to do with was the "Old Sherman." It flowed 1,200 barrels per day, and it was estimated that it flowed 1,900,000 barrels, and it was then pumped for twenty years. This well was 600 feet deep.

Mr. Irwin had always taken an interest in stock-raising, and in 1883 came to California, prospecting. Mr. Lyman Stewart came at the same time and together they looked the oil region over. After looking the country over they decided that there was a good opening for development. Mr. Stewart telegraphed Mr. W. L. Hardison, and at once they began to make roads to the localities of this work, of which Mr. Irwin was superintendent. Mr. Hardison came out and arrangements were made, and in May, 1883, he went back for machinery and men. Mr. Irwin made the preliminary preparations for the wells at Newhall and then came to Santa Paula Cañon and engaged in preparations to drill and develop. When a man goes into new fields in this way, such work is called by oil men wild-cating. Mr. Irwin has done much of this work. He continued at Santa Paula until 1887, when he went to Sespe Cañon, eighteen miles east of Santa Paula, where they now have wells, with a pipe line to the refinery. Mr. Irwin is superintendent of field work, having a complete supervision of the whole business of sinking the wells, of their production and of making the roads to them. This is the Sespe Oil Company. Thomas R. Bard is president and W. L. Hardison is general manager.

Mr. Irwin was married in 1868, to Miss Caroline B. Canfield, of Niagara County, New York. They have one son, Ralph, who was born in Cherry Tree, Venango County, Pennsylvania, September 9, 1874.

Mr. Irwin cast his first presidential vote for Abraham Lincoln, and has been a Republican ever since. He is the owner of property in Santa Paula and a nice cottage near the center of the town. Mr. Irwin is a well informed man, and has had a long experience in the oil business. His efforts in that direction in Ventura County have been crowned with success, and are resulting in the growth and upbuilding of Santa Paula.

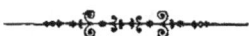

A. GUIBERSON, one of the early settlers and prominent ranchers of Ventura County, was born in Holmes County, Ohio, January 1, 1838. He was the son of Rev. J. W. Guiberson, a native of Pennsylvania, and a minister of the Methodist church for many years. He removed to Ohio and from there to California, where death his occurred at the age of seventy years, caused by the bite of a rattlesnake in the hand; he only lived seven hours after receiving the wound. Mr. Guiberson's grandfather, Samuel Guiberson, was born in New Jersey, and removed to Ohio when it was a wilderness. When he reached majority there was some member of the Whig party who objected to his voting, although he had been raised a Whig; he was so enraged at them that he voted the Democratic ticket, and for several generations, to the present time, the Guibersons have voted that ticket. Mr. Guiberson's mother was Catherine (Knight) Guiberson, a native of Ohio, born in 1805. She was the daughter of Mr. George Knight, a native of England. They have six children, three boys and three girls, four of whom survive.

Mr. Guiberson, our subject, was educated in Ohio, and raised on his father's farm. In 1860, when twenty-two years of age, he came to California, and settled at Placerville, engaging in contracting. He then went to Napa Valley, and leased land, and in 1869, came to what was then Santa Barbara County, now Ventura County, and settled upon what he supposed to be Government land, where he remained three years, and on discovering his mistake he left it and went to his present place, twelve miles east of Santa Paula and three miles from Fillmore Station. Here he has a fine ranch of 1,300 acres, and in 1888 built a fine residence upon it. He is engaged in raising grain and stock, but his specialty is stock; he is raising Berkshire hogs, Durham cattle and draft horses.

Mr. Guiberson was married in 1860, to Miss Ellen Green, a great-granddaughter of General Nathaniel Green, of Revolutionary fame. She was born in Missouri, in 1840, and is a daughter of Mr. Joseph N. Green, a native of Virginia. They have eight children, five boys and three girls. The first two were born in Napa County, and the others on the ranch in Ventura County, viz.: Lorane, J, W., N. G., S A., W. R., Zuleki, Carrie, Blanch. J. W. is a merchant in Santa Paula; Nathanial S. is clerking for his brother in the store; he is nineteen years of age, being six feet seven inches high, and weighing 225 pounds. Lorane is in business in Arkansas. Mr. Guiberson and his two eldest sons are members of the Masonic fraternity. Mrs. Guiberson is a member of the Methodist church at Fillmore. He has been too much occupied on his ranch to give much attention to politics, but has been appointed deputy sheriff, and also deputy assessor of the county of Ventura. Notwithstanding the hardships of pioneer life for thirty years, he still is a young-looking man, and has a long life before him in which to enjoy the fruits of high cultivation that has now come to the beautiful valley, and which he has helped to bring about.

J. A. CONAWAY, residing near Fillmore, is one of California's pioneers. He was born in West Virginia, April 4, 1830. His father, Eli Conaway, was a native of Virginia, and his great-grandfather was born in Ireland, and came to America before the Revolution. His mother, Mary (Baker) Conaway, was a native of Virginia, of Welsh ancestry. They had a family of nine children, of whom Mr. Conaway was the sixth. He was educated in Virginia, and finished his education in Iowa. He left home in 1849, and remained in Wisconsin two years; he then went to Missouri, and he worked in Ashley, Pike County, that State, part of the time as an overseer on a plantation; the rest of the time he was in a shop running an engine and sawing lumber. In 1853 he crossed the plains to California, with an ox team, having a prosperous and safe journey. He settled on a ranch in Amador County, and engaged in raising stock. He then removed to San Joaquin County, and settled upon a Government ranch, where he perfected the title and made it his home for twelve years; he improved the place by building upon it and planting a vineyard and orchard. For his present place he bought a Government claim, and also paid the railroad for it. The railroad soon after wanted the right of way, and he received his money back. Mr. Conaway took the place when it was wild and uncultivated, and has since built a fine house, and planted fruit of all descriptions, and the whole place shows the work of a first-class farmer; every tree and shrub has been planted by his own hands. He is engaged in general farming, and his orchard contains fruit of nearly every variety.

Mr. Conaway has held public office in the county for years; he was one of the first Supervisors of the county, and Assessor seven years. He and his wife are members of the Methodist Church at San Buenaventura. Mr. Conaway is a Democrat and a temperance man.

He was married in 1859, to Miss Lizzie Jane Blamey, a native of England. They have had thirteen children; only ten are now living, five boys and five girls, all born in California, viz.: May, Kate, Austin E., Alice P., Jennie B., Charles W., Lulu V. and Lelia V., twins, Ethan W. and Albion N. (twins), and T. Benton.

JAMES CASS, one of the pioneers of California, who came to the State July 8, 1849, by sea, on the ship Orpheus, was a sailor before the mast. Mr. Cass was born in Somerset, England, November 24, 1824, the only child of James and Harriet Cass, of English descent. He went to sea at the age of ten years, and came to the United States in 1836. He made New York his headquarters, but sailed on the coast of the United States until 1841. He then returned to England and attended school for one year, and then resumed his occupation as a sailor. He was promoted mate of the brig Trio of New York. In 1849 when the gold fever was raging, he came to California, and was employed on the schooner, Olevia, to run on the Sacramento River, at $150 per month. He sailed for three months, carrying supplies up the river for the miners. In September, 1849, he went to the mines at Coloma, and from there he went to Dry Town, where he mined in the winter and sailed on the river in the summer. When at the mines he did well until he was attacked with the chills and fever. He became a pilot on the river, and was paid $250 a month. In the fall he again tried mining, and took out about $2,500 in two weeks. He then formed a company with Joseph Cracborn, Charles Salmon and Levi Shepherd, and started the Boston Store on Dry Creek, two and a half miles north of the Q Ranch. It was opened November 1, 1850, and the following June he sold his interest and purchased 160 acres of land and engaged in farming. He was inexperienced in the business and met with unlooked for difficulties, the floods being the most serious difficulty. His farming venture proved a failure, and he again engaged in store-keeping at Mule Town, on his own account, but afterward Mr. Walden Lords became a partner in the business. They continued for six months, when they sold out and took up Government land, each taking a quarter section and engaged in the raising of hogs. They paid high prices for their stock, and when they were ready to sell them the prices had gone down and they met with heavy losses. From 1858 to 1859 he remained on his ranch with various experiences. In November, 1867, he sold out and came to Cayucos (an Indian name for canoe) and took up 320 acres of Government land, one and a half miles out of the town. He engaged in raising stock and farming until 1869, when he sold the property and engaged with Captain Ingals in building the wharf. There have been some changes in proprietorship, and Mr. Cass is now the sole manager of the business, owning a half interest.

Mr. Cass is a member of King David's Lodge, F. & A. M. of San Luis Obispo. He has passed through all the chairs of the Odd Fellows Lodge; he is also a Knight Templar. In his political views he is a Republican. As Mr. Cass has been connected with the construction of his own wharf, and has had much experience in the expense connected with the destruction of piles by the teredo, he has set his mind to work to provide a remedy, and has the credit of having invested and patented a pile preserver, which, at a small expense, preserves them for many years, and his system has been adopted by wharf owners all along the coast. Thus by his genius he has not only saved his own company large expense, but has given a valuable invention to the world. He is a pioneer of the State, but is still a strong and hearty man. Within a few rods of his store and wharf he has built a beautiful residence, where he and his wife and daughter reside, surrounded by trees, flowers and shrubs, a fitting place for a pioneer of California to spend the evening of life.

In 1854 Mr. Cass was united in marriage to Miss Mary Stone, a daughter of William Stone, a native of Holdham, England. They have four children, all of whom are living, viz.: Sarah, Charles A., Emily and Henry K. Mrs. Cass died in 1858, and in 1860 he was again married to Miss Mary McMurry, a native of New York. They have one daughter, Rosa M.

R. J. EALY, a rancher near Fillmore, was born in Johnson County, Iowa, February 12, 1853. His father, William C. Ealy, is a native of Pennsylvania, born November 3, 1815; was an architect and builder, and is now a resident of Kansas. His grandfather, John Ealy, was German, as was also his ancestry. He emigrated with his brother to this country during the Revolutionary war, in which they both took part, on the side of American liberty. One of the brothers settled in New York, the other (John) in Pennsylvania, and from these sprang two distinct lines, one called the Yankee and the other the Dutch. Mr. Ealy's mother, *nee* Margaret Ellen Williamson, was born in Kentucky, March 19, 1824. Her father, about thirty years before the civil war, was the owner of a number of slaves in Kentucky, and, becoming convinced that slavery was wrong he voluntarily freed them. William C. Ealy's eldest child is now Mrs. Lizzie Jepson, of Ventura County. His second son, John William, is a publisher in New York city. The third child, Henry B., is a dealer in agricultural implements in Keokuk, Iowa.

The subject of this sketch, the youngest son, was reared and educated in Iowa City, and there learned the tinner's trade, which he followed for nineteen years. He had a hardware store in Dysart, Tama County, Iowa; but, being in poor health, he disposed of his business interests there and came to his present location in Southern California. He purchased from the railroad company and Government a ranch of 200 acres, and secured satisfactory title to the same. This property is located two miles and a half east of Fillmore, in one of the most productive sections of the country, and is each year becoming more valuable. Mr. Ealy at once set about its improvement. built a home and planted a large variety of fruit trees and also walnut trees. A fine spring and two wells furnish an ample supply of water for the place. Mr. Ealy also started a general merchandise store, and for four years was Postmaster. Since coming to this sunny land he has fully recovered his health, and is now in a fair way to enjoy life.

He was married in 1872, at Iowa City, Iowa, on Christmas eve, to Miss Ella Whisler, daughter of John Whisler, a native of Pennsylvania. She was born and reared in Cedar County, Iowa. Their union has been blessed with two children, Willie C., born in Dysart, Iowa, January 7, 1876, and Ray J., born in Ventura County, California, October 20, 1884. Mr. and Mrs. Ealy are members of the Christian Church. Mr. Ealy is a life-long Republican.

B. H. DUNHAM is one of the most prominent business men of Santa Paula, is a stockholder in and a director of the Hardison & Stewart Oil Company, and Superintendent of the Mission Transfer Company's oil refinery. There are four companies here interested in the oil development: the Hardison-Stewart Company, the Sespe Oil Company, Torrey Cañon Oil Company, and also the Mission Transfer Company, which latter are refiners and marketers of the oil and transfer it from the wells to their refinery and see to its shipment.

Mr. Dunham was born in Fairhaven, Massachusetts, October 26, 1855. He is a son of Rufus A. Dunham, a native of Massachusetts, born in September, 1819. His grandfather, George Dunham, was also born in Massachusetts. They are of English ancestry. Robert Dunham, who is the progenitor of the American branch of the family, was born in England about the year 1760. When sixteen years of age he was drafted into the English army to fight the American Colonies. When he reached America he took the first opportunity offered to join the American forces, and at the close of the war he made his home in Massachusetts. He was a descendant of Sir R. Dunham, a Knight of the west of England. They had a family coat-of-arms, which is yet in existence, and it is stated that at the close of the war he expected to found an estate in America, but was not successful as it was contrary to the ideas of the founders of a republic. Mr. Dunham's mother's maiden name was Hannah Morton Westgate. She was born in Rochester, Massachusetts, in 1821. In speaking of Mr. Dunham's paternal ancestors, it should be further stated that his great-grandmother, *nee* Mary Albertson, was a direct descendant of Peregrine White, one of the original Pilgrims of the Plymouth Colony. The subject of this sketch was the seventh of a family of twelve children, ten of whom are now living. He was reared and educated in his native town, graduating at the high school at the age of sixteen. When he was eighteen years old he engaged in the steam laundry business, in which he continued six years. He then removed to Olean, New York, and went into the employ of the Acme Oil Company, remaining with them seven years and in that time learning the business thoroughly. From there he came to Santa Paula, California, to superintend the construction of the oil refinery and to operate the works, in which business he is still engaged. The capital stock of the Mission Transfer Company is $250,000, and their refinery is the most complete of all on the Coast. The quality of their refined petroleum is unsurpassed by any in the world. Mr. Dunham is a most competent man in his line of business. He is a man of few words, but has a fine business head and is a gentleman of first-class business integrity.

Mrs. Dunham is a native of Massachusetts, born in April, 1863. Her maiden name was Alice M. Green, and she is the daughter of Captain Paul Green, of that State. She and Mr. Dunham were married in 1882. They are both Methodists and he is a steward and trustee of that church. Mr. Dunham is affiliated with the Independant Order of Odd Fellows. Mr. and Mrs. Dunham reside in a beautiful and substantial new house of their own planning and building. The grounds are being ornamented with trees and flowers, and the place is fast becoming one of those delightful homes, of which there are so many in Southern California.

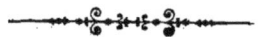

BRICE GRIMES is one of the prominent pioneers of Ventura County, having arrived in what was then Santa Barbara County in 1866, and was intimately connected with the formation of the county of Ventura. He was born in Missouri, December 12, 1829. His father, Thomas H. Grimes, was a native of Kentucky, and his grandfather Grimes was born in Virginia, of Scotch-Irish ancestry, the original American ancestors of the family having settled in the "Old Dominion" as early as 1748. Mr. Grimes' mother, *nee* Sarah Gibson, was born in St. Charles County, Missouri, daughter of

Joseph Gibson, a native of South Carolina, of English ancestry. The subject of this sketch is the oldest of a family of ten children, five of whom are living. His father owned a large farm in Missouri, and there he was reared and received limited school advantages. In 1852 he came to California, and engaged in mining with the usual success and reverses of the miner. While he was mining in Shasta County he lost $1,600 by the failure of the Adams Express Company, besides suffering other heavy losses about the same time. After three years spent in the mines, he went to Napa County to regain his health. Upon his recovery he went to work again with that indomitable will which is always sure to overcome reverses. He engaged in draying for a time, then built a warehouse, was in the forwarding and commission business, and afterward turned his attention to general merchandise. He remained there until 1860, when he located in San Luis Obispo County. While there was under sheriff for two years, and had some of the roughest characters to arrest and imprison, having as many as fifteen in jail at one time. Murders and robberies were frequent at that time, and the utmost care and shrewdness was required in the detection and arrest of the perpetrators of crimes. Mr. Grimes removed to Los Angeles County and farmed there three years, after which he came to San Buenaventura and, in partnership with Mr. Edwards, opened the pioneer hardware store of the city, and also did a produce business. Two or three years later he sold out to his partner, who afterward sold to Mr. F. W. Baker. Mr. Grimes came to his present locality and purchased 160 acres of land in the picturesque cañon which bears his name. He has here planted several thousand trees, French prunes, apricots, peaches, nectarines, apples, pears, and other varieties, including oranges and lemons. Mr. Grimes is now a dealer in lumber and builders' hardware at Fillmore.

In 1858 Mr. Grimes wedded Miss Elenora Hogle, a native of Jefferson City, Missouri, whose father, John Francis Hogle, was born in Canada; her mother, Jane (Jacoby) Hogle, was a native of Kentucky. Mr. and Mrs. Grimes have four children, George H., Frank, Lillie and Robert. Those of the children not at home are married and settled near by. Mrs. Grimes is a worthy member of the Christian Church, and her husband's preferences are for that denomination.

At the time of the formation of Ventura County, Mr. Grimes was an active worker in that movement and one of the committee to help draft the bill for the division of the county, as he also was in the construction of the fine brick school-house in San Buenaventura, which was built at a cost of $10,000, and was considered a grand achievement for the place. He has long been a school trustee, and at that time was clerk of the school board, and much of the management of the building devolved on him. When he removed to the Willow Grove district he helped to build the school-house there; was afterward cut off into the Bardsdale district, and was also instrumental in the erection of a fine school-building there. Mr. Grimes has been a prominent Democrat, has been a delegate to many of the State and county conventions. In 1884 he made many speeches, advocating Grover Cleveland's election for President, and in 1886 he made a strong speech in favor of ex-Congressman Berry for Governor. Was one of the candidates for the election to the State Constitutional Convention, and ran ahead of his ticket more than 2,000 votes; and in 1890 he was much talked of by the papers and his friends as an available candidate for Congress in the Sixth District of California

In speaking of his experience as a miner, Mr. Grimes says that a man who was at work for him on the Yreka flats, in 1853, picked up a nugget of solid gold that was sold for $1,028, a little over four pounds in weight of very pure gold. Notwithstanding his long pioneer and business career, Mr. Grimes is still an active business man, and bids fair to spend many years in the enjoyment of his home in Grimes Cañon.

FRANK SMITH.—One of the hustling business men of Santa Barbara is Frank Smith, who was born on the frontier, in Kendall County, Illinois, December 30, 1845, his father having immigrated to that country from New Hampshire in 1844 with a family of nine children, Frank making the tenth and being the youngest of the family, of whom two sisters and five brothers are still living. Frank received a limited education at the high school in Joliet, Illinois. At the age of eighteen years he was employed by H. C. Carpenter, a prominent grain buyer of Joliet, as book-keeper, remaining five years. He was then employed by Carpenter, Truby & Company, grain buyers, who operated on the line of the Illinois and Michigan Canal, until 1870, when in company with two brothers, N. D. and J. M. Smith and a nephew, J. T. Johnson, they came to California. The firm of N. D. & Frank Smith established themselves at Carpenteria as pioneers in the lumber and shipping business, using surf boats as communication between land and vessels. In 1874 they built a wharf, when deliveries to and from the vessels were made much easier. In 1876 Frank bought out N. D. Smith and took in his brother, J. M. Smith, as partner, which continued until January, 1889, when Frank bought out J. M., and now carries on the business alone. Mr. Smith is also Postmaster of Carpenteria.

In connection with above interests Mr. Smith moved his famly to Santa Barbara in 1872, and entered the employ of J. P. Steams as wharfinger. In January, 1888, Mr. Steams organized a stock company of his wharf interest, called the Steam Wharf Company, in which our subject bought stock and was appointed a director and secretary of the company. In the fall of 1882 Mr. Smith was elected County Assessor, and was re-elected in 1886 in opposition to Mr. Garrotson, the former popular assessor who was the nominee of the Democratic party, winning by the handsome majority of 700 votes. Mr. Smith employs five deputies through the country.

Mr. Smith was married in Kendall County, Illinois, in 1868, to Miss Annie Corey, and they have four sons, all living. Mr. Smith is a member of Santa Barbara Lodge, No. 156, I. O. O. F., and of the A. O. U. W.

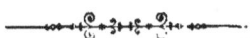

LEWIS A. HARDISON is a native of Maine, born August 9, 1853. His father, Oliver A. Hardison, was born in the same State, May 18, 1830. Their ancestry is the same as that of W. L. Hardison whose history appears in this book, and who is an uncle of the subject of this sketch. Lewis A. Hardison's mother, *nee* Mary O'Leary, was born at Frasier Mills, New Brunswick, in the year 1824. He was the oldest son in a family of seven children, four sons and three daughters, five of whom are now living. Mr. Hardison received his education in the public schools of his native State, and remained on the farm until he was nineteen years of age. At that time he went to the oil regions of Pennsylvania, and in 1872 became a driller of wells, working seven years for wages. In 1879 he got an outfit and began to drill wells under contract. During the eleven years that he worked there he was engaged on as many as fifty-three wells, their average depth being about 1,400 feet, and average cost of drilling $1,000 each. Four men are employed on each well, and termed a drilling crew, two drillers and two tool-dressers, one of each for each tour, changing at 12 M. and at midnight. When the Hardison-Stewart Oil Company commenced operations in California, in 1883, he came to Santa Paula and for four years did the company's blacksmith work at Pico and Santa Paula. Mr. Hardison is the inventor and has patented a well drilling machine of great simplicity and merit, which he used with great advantage in putting down water wells in New York during the fall and winter of 1882-'83. For some time he has been the master mechanic of the Hardison-Stewart Oil Company, built their tanks and rigs, and superintended the putting up of their telephone lines and the laying of their pipe lines. He is now superintendent of the Mission Transfer Company, and looks after the gauging of the oil, sees where it goes and keeps an account of the barrels of oil that go through their pipes. They have seventy miles of telephone and ninety miles of four and two-inch pipe lines.

December 25, 1877, Mr. Hardison was united in marriage to Miss Margaret A. Brooking, a native of St. Johns, New Foundland, born July 22, 1851. They have had seven children, five of whom are living, viz.: Oliver J., Clara E., Arthur J., Bert and Lewis. He and his wife are members of the Universalist Church of Santa Paula. His political views are Democratic, and independent when he pleases. He was made a Master Mason July 14, 1875. Mr. Hardison has a pleasant home situated on Eighth street, between Santa Paula street and Railroad avenue.

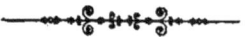

JOHN BRADLEY was born in Northumberland County, Upper Canada, in 1833, his father being interested in the lumber business in that county then. They emigrated to Michigan in 1843, where his father engaged in farming. Mr. Bradley's uncle, George Bradley, was an Indian agent, one well-known and much respected. John Bradley started for California, across the plains in 1852, traveling with strangers. On Bear River Mountain he was seriously ill with mountain fever. After recovering, he strayed from his train while hunting, and got lost at the head of the Humboldt River. He then traveled alone and met with many hardships. On his arrival in the Golden State he visited the mines, and the following ten years were passed in the several mining districts, prospecting, placer mining and butchering. In 1862 Mr. Bradley made a rich strike. He shortly afterward started for the East, and at Battle Creek, Michigan, in the same year, was married to Miss Velona M. Van Buren. He then returned to California, bringing his wife, and after two more years in the mines, he began farming in Yolo County. The land was held by the land league and they tried to drive off all settlers, but Mr. Bradley persisted, amid many dangers, and really opened up the country. In 1870 he came to Santa Barbara, bought 100 acres of land at the head of the Montecito Valley, cleared it, and engaged in farming. In 1873 he sold his ranch and purchased seventy-five acres of tide land, where he now resides. Mr. Bradley has taken great interest in training horses, and has a short method of training them without cruelty. He built a race track, which he found very profitable for about four years.

Mr. and Mrs. Bradley have been blessed with five children, all living and at home. Mr. Bradley is a worthy and respected citizen. At present he is School Trustee of Montecito district.

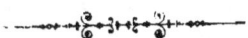

C. H. DECKER is a pioneer of California, having come to the State in 1855, to Santa Paula in 1867, and to his present ranch in 1870. He was born in Kennebec County, Maine, August 20, 1832. His father, Stephen Decker, was a native of Maine, and was a merchant and farmer there; and Joshua Decker, his grandfather, was also born in that State. Great-grandfather Decker was an Englishman by birth. Mr. Decker's mother, nee Phelinda Pratt, was also a native of Kennebec County, Maine, and her father, David Pratt, was born in that State, and was at one time a hotel-keeper. Her ancestors were English people.

The subject of this sketch was the youngest, except two, of a family of fifteen children, six of whom are now living, three sons and three daughters. He was reared on his father's farm and received his education in his native State. When he came to California he engaged in mining, in Yuba County, three years, and was partially successful. For two years he furnished blocks for flumes, and from that turned his attention to the lumber business in the redwoods, being engaged in the latter business eight years. Since then he has resided in Ventura County. He is the owner of 146⅜ acres of well-improved land, and is engaged in raising fruit and walnuts. The walnut trees were planted in 1878 and began to bear at five years old. They now average from fifty to sixty pounds to the tree. He has a few orange trees that are doing well. At the time he settled here, Mr. Decker supposed his ranch to be Government land, and has had not a little trouble in securing proper title to the land. At last, after an expensive suit, he now has both Government title and a deed from the railroad.

Mr. Decker was married, in September, 1853, to Miss Mary Lewis, a native of Maine. To them was born a daughter, Frances, June 14, 1854, who is now the wife of George P. Willer, and resides at Newton. He was again married, August 12, 1873, to Miss Emily M. Rowell, a native of Maine. They had three children, all born at their present home in Ventura County: Burtis L., May 17, 1874; George V., October 12, 1876, and Bertha N., October 16, 1878. Mrs. Decker's death occurred October 22, 1885. June 2, 1888, Mr. Decker wedded Miss Gertrude Hill, at Santa Paula. She is a native of Missouri, born in Richmond, November 18, 1865. They have one daughter, Ruth, born October 22, 1889.

Mr. Decker is a member and a trustee of the Sespe Methodist church. Politically he is a Prohibitionist. He is a man who has been identified with the best interests of the county ever since he took up his residence here: has served the public as School Trustee, and also as Postmaster of Fillmore, having been the first postmaster, when the office was established in 1870.

MESSRS. LEE & RICE.—As one approaches the town of Santa Paula in any direction he will see a star on the stones and boulders, and when he arrives in the city he will find several stars in front of a neat and tasteful clothing store. This is the Star Clothing House of Santa Paula, the firm being Lee & Rice.

F. E. Lee, of this firm, was born in Detroit, Michigan, March 23, 1859. He is the son of John L. Lee, who was born in England and came to the United States in 1850. Mr. Lee was educated in the city of Lansing, taking a thorough course in a commercial college. He commenced business as a pressman, in the State printing office at Lansing, and was engaged in press work there for five years. Then for a time he was in a store with his brother, in Lincoln, Nebraska, after which he spent five years in Chicago, on press work. From there he came to Los Angeles, California, and held the position of foreman in the press-room of the *Times* office, five years, until he came to Santa Paula. Mr. Lee is married to Miss Balcom, one of the fairest young ladies of Santa Paula, daughter of W. E. Balcom, a wealthy and influential citizen of Santa Paula.

J. C. Rice, who is manager of the store with Mr. Lee, was born in Cleveland, Ohio, in 1854, and completed his education at the Michigan State Normal School, at Ypsilanti. He has had experience in the clothing business with the best wholesale houses in the East, and in Los Angeles, both as a salesman and traveling man. He has thus gained a knowledge of the cost of goods which is of much value to him in their present business. Mr. Rice was married, September 22, 1889, to Miss Fanny M. Baker, daughter of C. N. Baker, a prominent resident of Santa Paula and a member of the Board of County Supervisors.

These gentlemen are both talented business men. They established their business in Santa Paula September 22, 1889. They purchased the building in which their store is located, in the business center of the town, have a fine stock of goods, and quite an extensive trade. Both Mr. Lee and Mr. Rice are Republicans and both are worthy members of the K. of P.

JAMES M. SHORT, of English-Welsh descent, was born at North Swansea, Massachusetts, in 1835. His ancestors came to Massachusetts in 1840, and shared the hardships of the early Indian wars, the war of the Revolution, and also the war of 1812. His father, Henry S. Short, was a machinist by trade. James M., after leaving the public schools, finished his education at the Warren Institute at Rhode Island and at the Maine Wesleyan Seminary at Kent's Hill. He started for California in January, 1858, on the steamer Star of the West, via the Isthmus, and arrived in San Francisco on the steamer John L. Stephens, making the voyage safely in twenty-four days. After spending a few days in San Francisco, he went to Eureka, Humboldt County, and afterward to Arcata, where he engaged in teaching in the public schools, remaining about five years. It is quite interesting to hear him relate his experience in the Indian troubles that prevailed there for several years. In the fall of 1864 Mr. Short gave up teaching to accept the office of County Clerk, to which he was elected, and was re-elected in 1866. In November, 1868, he came to Santa Barbara and purchased property at East Santa Barbara. In 1870 he bought an interest in the Las Cruces Ranch, and engaged in sheep-raising for about twelve years, and disposed of this interest in 1862. From 1879 to 1882 Mr. Short was a member of the Board of Supervisors of Santa Barbara. For six years he has served as School Trustee, and has been trustee of the city library since its organization. He engaged in the culture of pampas in 1882, and has since been interested in its production.

Mr. Short was married at Eureka, California, in 1865, to Miss Margaret Singley. They have one son, Henry S., and a daughter, Lillian L. Mr. Short is a veteran Odd Fellow of nearly thirty years' standing, and is a member of Channel City Lodge, No. 232.

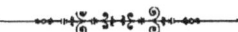

ANNA M. LOGAN.—On one of the nicest residence streets in the heart of Santa Paula, and in one of the most artistic houses in the place, lives Mrs. Anna M. Logan, widow of Dr. Marshall L. Logan, who was a prominent citizen and dentist of Tyrone, Pennsylvania. The Doctor was born at Saulsburg, Huntingdon County, Pennsylvania, August 21, 1844. When quite young he was bereft of his parents by death, and left to his own resources, but succeeded in gaining a liberal education in the public schools and in the Philadelphia University. When the great civil war broke out, with the patriotism of a hero and the ardor of youth, he enlisted in the service of his country in the Twenty-second Pennsylvania Volunteer Cavalry, and fought through that great struggle with distinction and honor, until he beheld the banner of victory floating over a preserved and undivided country. He returned to his home and took up the study of dentistry, and in 1871 went to Tyrone, where with signal success he practiced his profession for fifteen years. He rapidly rose to a position of distinction in his profession, and conducted it in a strictly upright and honorable manner, and enjoyed the respect of his fellow-citizens and a lucrative practice. He was the inventor of the Logan Tooth Crown, which is now in use by dentists throughout the world. Dr. Logan was married November 23, 1869, to Miss Anna Raney, a native of Pennsylvania, born October 27, 1846. Her father, Alexander Raney, was a native of Pennsylvania, a well-to-do farmer, who like many others lost his eldest son in the great Rebellion. The Doctor and Mrs. Logan had a family of three children, two daughters and a son, all born at Tyrone, Pennsylvania: Gertrude E., Mary A. and George Burkett. Dr. Logan had received two wounds while fighting in the defense of his country, one by a spent ball in the left lung, and one in the back of his head, and it is believed that the wound in the lung induced consumption, which terminated in his death. It first manifested itself in 1883, and December 9, 1885, he died. At the time of his death he was a member of the school board, a member of the Masonic fraternity, and of the independent order of Odd Fellows. He was also an honorable member of the Pennsylvania State Dental Society. Dr. Logan had been for years a consistent member of the Methodist church, and a regular attendant at church and Sabbath-school. He was a man of pleasing manner and fine ability, and took an active part in the organizations to which he belonged, as well as in the schools and public welfare. His loss was felt not only by his bereaved wife and children, but by the whole county in which he lived. Resolutions of high esteem and condolence were tendered to Mrs. Logan by his societies and the school board of which he was a member. His funeral was one of the largest ever known in that county.

In 1887, after settling up her business in Tyrone, Mrs. Logan, with her children, came to Santa Paula and invested $4,000 in the property where she now resides. Besides the beautiful residence which, with her children, she occupies, she owns three other houses which she rents, all being valued at

$12,000, and she lives upon her rents and interest. She is a lady of refinement and intelligence, and has been very successful in business.

JOSEPH HUBBARD HOLLISTER, deceased, a son of John and Philena (Hubbard) Hollister, was born in Licking County, Ohio, March 9, 1820. His parents were from Connecticut. His father in early life moved to Ohio, where he established himself on a farm. Joseph here grew to manhood. In 1853 he came to California, with his brother, Colonel W. N. Hollister, crossing the plains with a large flock of sheep,—said to be the first lot ever brought to California from the East; the brothers sold their stock at an excellent profit, and our subject returned East for more in 1856. Coming West this time with his flock in partnership with J. W. Cooper of Santa Barbara, he met with a detention in Utah, the Mormon troubles there causing them some embarassment to travelers. Mr. Hollister deviated from his route to the South, entering into Mexico, and, owing to the lateness of the season, he was obliged to spend the winter there. The next year he reached California. In 1860 he returned to Ohio for his family, and came to California with them in 1865. In that year he purchased the Chorro and San Luisito ranches in San Luis Obispo County, and he also owned a portion of the Lompoc Rancho in Santa Barbara County. He was said at one time to be also the largest sheep owner in California. He made his home on the Chorro ranch, five miles distant from San Luis Obispo, north, and lived there until his death, January 5, 1873.

June 8, 1843, he married Miss Ellen, a daughter of Joseph Mossman, of Ohio, and had four children, all of whom are now living, viz.: Mrs. Phineas Banning, a widow of Los Angeles; Mrs. R. E. Jack, of San Luis Obispo; Mrs. Sherman P. Stow and John H. Hollister, also of San Luis Obispo, whose sketch is given at length.

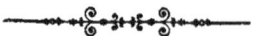

HON. JOHN H. HOLLISTER, one of the most prominent citizens of San Luis Obispo County, is the only son of Joseph Hubbard Hollister, deceased, whose sketch is also given. He was born in Newark, Ohio, November 27, 1856. When he was seven years of age the Hollister family removed to California, where the father had acquired large property interests; and since that time the subject of this sketch has made California his home, his name being conspicuous among those who have aided the development of the agricultural interests of the State and more especially of San Luis Obispo County. He received an excellent education, finally graduating with honors at the State University at Berkeley. Since 1866 he has made the county of San Luis Obispo his home, his present residence being in the city. His country home, on the beautiful Chorro Rancho, containing 2,000 acres, is located five miles northwest of San Luis Obispo. He is a large property holder, and extensively engaged in the cattle business, both in this State and Arizona. In partnership with Judge Frederick Adams of San Luis Obispo, he has two ranches in the latter Territory, namely, the Santa Rosa in Pima County, fifty miles southeast from Tucson, and the Las Cienegas in Graham County, on the Gila River; and on these are 5,000 head of cattle. Mr. Hollister is also one of the owners of Chimnicos Rancho of 20,000 acres, in San Luis Obispo, which is used for stock purposes.

In matters political Mr. Hollister is a conspicuous figure. When but twenty-three years of age he was a Supervisor of the county,—the youngest who was ever a member of the board, as well as one of the most active, competent and intelligent. In 1882 he was the Republican candidate for the Assembly, when the Democrats were well organized and in the majority, and he made a spendid canvass, gaining the election. His record in the Assembly was distinguished by able and conscientious work. He introduced measures, which were passed, becoming the anti-oleomargarine law, the law to extirpate fruit-tree pests and to prevent diseases in fruit trees, etc., laws of importance to the agriculturists. He is a member of the orders of Patrons of Husbandry, Knights of Pythias and Free Masons, is in the State Militia, from which he has passed through the different grades from private up to the rank of Major. He is interested in all matters connected with the progress of this State.

April 22, 1880, is the date of his marriage to Miss Flora May Stocking, a native of Sonoma County, this State, and they have had five children, four of whom are now living: John Hubbard, William M., Mary Banning and Flora Hollister.

C. J. WILSON was born near Wheeling, West Virginia, in 1822. His grandfather emigrated to Virginia in early days when the State was so thinly settled that for months he would not see a white face. The subject of this sketch is the only living member of a family of seven children. He was reared on his father's farm and remained there until the age of twenty-eight years, when he came to California, and was among the first to cross by the Nicaragua route. He arrived at San Francisco, August 17, 1850, and went to the mines in Tuolumne County, near Sonora, where he remained seventeen years, working at placer and quartz mining. He was once buried twenty-four hours in a caving mine, and fully realized the sensation of being buried alive!

Mr. Wilson was married at Sonora in 1857, to Margaret Ann Calder. They came to Santa Barbara in 1867. Here Mr. Wilson purchased three blocks, or about fifteen acres, at East Santa Barbrra, and has since continued to make this place his home. Building was difficult and expensive in those days, and for a month he lived in his first house without a door. During his residence here Mr. Wilson has been engaged in stock-raising and speculation. Mr. and Mrs. Wilson have had three children, but only one daughter survives. She is now the wife of Harmon Bell, of Kansas City.

FREDERICK STOCK.—The able and efficient manager of the works of the Los Angeles Granite and Brown Stone Company, at Sespe Cañon, Ventura County, California, is the gentleman whose name heads this sketch. He is a thoroughly competent superintendent, having been reared to the business in his father's quarry in England. The quarry which this company is operating is located eight miles east of Santa Paula, on the banks of the Sespe River. The brown stone here obtained is exceedingly durable and of a splendid texture. For uniformity and permanency of color it is unsurpassed by any brown stone on the continent. The works, under Mr. Stock's management, are being run to their greatest capacity, filling orders for many public buildings of the country. They are now at work on orders for the Academy of Science and the Concordia Club building, San Francisco, also the Keating Block, San Diego. They also furnish the stone for the Reform School building. The stone for the Whittier building was supplied by them, the corner-stone of which weighed ten tons. They are now getting out six stones, fifty-two feet cube, each weighing seven tons.

Mr. Stock was born in England, October 9, 1859, the son of John and Ann (Thomas) Stock, natives of England. John Stock was the owner of a quarry, and both his sons learned that business with him. The quarry is still in the possession of the family, and is now being conducted by his son Charles. Mr. Stock was married in 1878 to Miss Alice Emily Player, a native of Bristol, England. They have three children, born in England: Walter, Victor and Greta. Mr. Stock is a member of the Congregational church of Los Angeles city.

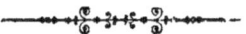

JOSIAH KEENE was born in the State of Maine, December 19, 1828. His father, Jeremiah Keene, was also born in the "Pine Tree State," and his grandfather, Isaac Keene, was a native of Massachusetts, and served in both the Revolution and the war of 1812. The Keenes were of Scotch-English descent. Josiah Keene's mother, *nee* Rebecca Kendall, was born in Maine, a daughter of Colonel David Kendall, who was also a native of Maine and a soldier in the war of 1812. They were of Welsh ancestry, who came to America in the early Colonial times. Mr. Keene's grandmother, on the maternal side, was a Cobourne, a cousin of Governor Cobourne of Maine, and a member of one of the oldest families of the State. The subject of this sketch was the fifth of a family of fourteen children. All but two are still living. There were three pairs of twins in the family. In 1888 a reunion of the family was held in Minnesota, and members of the family from all parts of the country assembled there, ten grey-haired men and women being present.

Mr. Keene was reared and received a good education in the public schools of his native State. At the commencement of the great civil war, he enlisted, in April, 1861, as a private soldier, He served nearly three years, or until the time of losing his left arm at the battle of Chattanooga. He participated in twenty-two hard-fought battles, first at Mills Springs, then at Pittsburg Landing, Corinth, Stone River, Perryville, Franklin, and all the engagements of his regiment. After he was wounded he was taken prisoner, and his arm was treated in the Rebel lines. Twelve days later he was exchanged Mr. Keene considers it one of Mr. Lincoln's best acts when he exchanged 10,000 able Confederate prisoners for 10,000 maimed men, of whom he was one. It was a year before he was able to work, and then he obtained a clerkship in the Treasury Department at Washington and served ten years in that capacity. The close confinement was injurious to his health, and, in September, 1874, he came to California, and spent months in looking over the coast before he finally settled. He purchased three acres of land at San Buenaventura, on which he built a small house. After the boom he erected a very fine residence on that beautiful street, Ventura Avenue, where the family now reside. In the fall of 1875 he took a Government claim of 160 acres of land and also a timber culture of 160 more. This is located six miles due east of Santa Paula. He has planted seventy-five acres to trees and vines. Twenty-five acres are in olives, forty acres in raising grapes, two acres in a variety of fruit and the rest in Eucalyptus trees.

Mr. Keene was married, January 1, 1874, to Miss Lucy E. Monroe, a native of Massachusetts, and a daughter of Rev. Calvin H. Monroe, of that State, a minister of the Baptist church. Their union has been blessed with five children. Kendall C. was born in the city of Washington. The following were born in Ventura, California; Allen H., Herman B., Robo-Vesta and Helen L. Mr. and Mrs. Keene are members of the Methodist Church. He is a Republican and an active member of the Grand Army of the Republic.

MATHEW ATMORE, of Santa Paula, is another one of the many brave and worthy pioneers of the great State of California, and is justly entitled to honorable mention in a work of this character. A sketch of his life is as follows:

Mathew Atmore was born in England in 1837. His parents, Mathew and Maria (Pond) Atmore, were English people, and his father was a Methodist minister. The family came to America in 1846, when the subject of this sketch was nine years of age, and settled at Battle Creek, Michigan. There young Atmore was sent to school. When seventeen years old he ran away from home with an older brother, Charles (now of Denver), came across the plains to California, and went into the mines in El Dorado County, where he mined for a year, making $600 clear. They then returned to Michigan and remained at home during the winter. The following spring their father furnished them with money to come back to California, and when they reached the mines they were $600 in debt, which they paid after mining three months. The second year they engaged in freighting from Sacramento to Virginia. Some idea of the difficulties and expenses of freighting in those days may be obtained from the following facts: seven yoke of oxen and a large wagon cost $1,400; the cost per yoke to shoe the oxen was $7. Seven yoke of oxen were required to each wagon; their freight was heavy castings for stamp-mills, each wagon being capable of hauling six tons, and the price per pound for freighting being thirteen cents; in addition to the castings they also carried a ton of hay and a ton of ground feed; the roads down the mountain sides were very bad, and the grade so steep in some places that the rear wheels were run down with wooden shoes; the toll on these mountain roads was $40 for a single trip, and twenty-two days were required to make the journey. On two trips they brought back silver ore, in sacks of $250 each. On the last trip one of the sacks was stolen, and they afterward refused to take the risk of freighting silver. They followed this business two years, always receiving their pay in checks, the only kind they dare take, for the country was infested with thieves.

At this time the great war of the Rebellion burst upon the country, and when the news of the firing on Fort Sumter, and, later, the battle of Bull Run, reached the far West, the patriotic enthusiasm of every loyal man was fired, and each stood ready to serve his country. Mr. Atmore enlisted in 1861, in Company K, Second Cavalry, California Volunteers, and was in garrison in San Francisco until the following July. At that time the Utah expedition was organized and placed under command of Colonel P. Edwin Conner of the Third Infantry. Six companies of cavalry and ten of infantry started for Salt Lake City July 10, 1862. In Nevada the expedition was reorganized, and in September the march was continued. They established Fort Ruby, and two companies were left to garrison the fort. At the Jordan River, forty miles south of Salt Lake City, they were met with orders from Brigham Young to proceed no farther. The answer sent to Mr. Young was that they would cross the Jordan River if hell were at the bottom. At sundown, October 10, the bugle sounded for dress parade. They formed in line when the answer was read, and the order given to march at 3 o'clock the next morning and take eighty rounds of cartridges; the artillery were to take all the ammunition they could carry. At 3 o'clock in the afternoon of the next day, they were in Salt Lake City. Mr. Atmore's company was in the advance, and as they entered the city there was not a Mormon in sight. They were hailed with delight by the American residents, and the Governor of the Territory made them a speech of welcome on the public square. On an eminence overlooking the city, two and a fourth miles away, with the mountains in the rear, with a splendid view of the country for forty miles in front, and with a bountiful supply of water, they went into temporary quarters. They dug holes, ten feet square and four feet deep, and placed logs around the top, on which they built their tents. In these they passed the winter, and here they permanently established Fort Douglas, which still stands there, although efforts have been made for its removal. The object of this expedition was to protect the Americans at Salt Lake City from any rebellious movement on the part of the Mormons, and also to prevent the renegade Indians from their frequent deeds of murder and plunder. At this time their deeds had been formidable, and many American citizens had been surprised, murdered and robbed by them. There was a band of some 600 red men overrunning that part of the country, and the soldiers under Colonel Conner had had several skirmishes with them. Many of the soldiers had crossed the plains and had sustained not a little suffering from the hands of the Indians, one man having been scorched to the knees by them; and the determination of the commander was to punish the Indians for these outrages.

Colonel Conner waited until the snow was two feet deep, and the Indians had established their winter quarters, when he decided to make an attack. The Indian camp was 140 miles away, fourteen miles from the town of Logan, with only an Indian trail from Logan to the camp. The expedition consisted of 256 cavalry, and twenty-five infantry to escort the wagon train. They took one 12-pound howitzer, with six men, all under the command of Lieutenant Honeyman Hough. The distance was made in four days and nights, and the advance guard captured four Indians at the town of Logan, to prevent news of their arrival being carried to the camp. They left Logan in the evening and the next morning at sunrise drew up on the south bank of the Bear River, a quarter of a mile below the Indian camp. The river at the ford was three feet deep, with ice on either bank, and great difficulty was experienced in getting the broncos across. The Indians were ready to receive them, there being 1,100 in camp, men, women and children, with 600 braves, some of the latter being mounted and riding around in circles, as if to intimidate the whites. The order was given to dismount and charge, when within a short distance of the enemy. Mr. Atmore and his comrade took aim at the chief nearest them, and, without orders, fired, and the chief Bear Hunter, dropped from his horse. When within ten feet of the Indians, the order was given to fire. The fight lasted until about half-past nine o'clock. The Indians had had a black flag out all morning, indicating no quarter. About 10 o'clock a white shirt was hoisted in its place. The interpreter was ordered to tell the women and children to come out, and a call was made for ten volunteers to go down to the head of the ravine and keep them from escaping to the hills. Twelve went, Mr. Atmore being one of the number. They were met by forty Indians and a fierce conflict ensued. Inside of twenty minutes two of the whites were killed and four wounded. (Adolphus Roe, Company K, of Berrien County, Michigan, and J. Adams, same company, Third Infantry, from Roxbury, Massachusetts, were the killed.) At this time the troops were ordered to close in, and in less than fifteen minutes the fight was over. Orders were given to kill the wounded Indians, and the men who had suffered by them in crossing the plains were not slow to obey the command. The Union loss was twenty-two killed and fifty-four wounded, out of a total of less than 300 men. Not more than 100 fighting Indians got away, the women and children were not molested, and the command returned with about 600 ponies; twenty-five of the best horses they could not catch, and they were shot. The camp was full of plunder and the soldiers were six days in returning to the fort. In the spring they started after Pocatello, the chief of the renegade Snakes, who, however, made good his escape. That summer they were engaged in fighting the Indians on the overland route. In October they made peace, and thus ended the Indian troubles. Mr. Atmore returned to Salt Lake City, was mustered out of service, and went East. Twenty-six of them each paid a man $100 to take them to the Missouri River, and most of the way they found it necessary to walk to keep from freezing.

Mr. Atmore then settled in Van Buren County, Michigan, and remained there twelve years; then spent a winter in Nebraska, after which he came to Santa Paula, California, in 1876. He worked for two years by the day, and then bought a Government claim of sixty-two acres, located six miles east of Santa Paula. He also purchased a water-right and afterward sold a part of it for $3,000, reserving four inches of water. He then bought twenty-five acres of land at $100 per acre. He has here erected a comfortable home, surrounded by trees of his own planting.

Mr. Atmore was married in 1865 to Miss Mary E. Gorham, a native of England. They have four children: Haidee, Grace D., Runsen D. and Frank. Mrs Atmore was in delicate health before coming to this State, and the invigorating climate of Southern California has greatly benefited her, and her life has been prolonged. Mr. Atmore is a Republican and a worthy member of the Grand Army of the Republic.

BRAM MUSCIO, a prominent rancher of San Luis Obispo County, was born March, 1849, in Someo, Canton Ticino, Switzerland, the youngest of nine children, whose parents are still living, at the old Switzerland home. Abram left home in November, 1866, and arrived at New York, the principal port of the New World, during the next month; but he came at once to California, by way of Panama, arriving at San Francisco January 12, 1867. He first settled in Marin County, and was engaged there ten years principally in the dairy business, with Batista Tomasini. In 1876 he came to San Luis Obispo County, locating on the coast four and a half miles north of Cayucos, renting a ranch of 1,300 acres. In 1884 he was able to purchase this property, on which he now resides, engaged chiefly in dairying, with good success. The dwelling and dairy buildings are models, and there is no prettier front yard in the county. The highest esthetic taste is exhibited in the architecture of the residence and the plan of the grounds. Mr. Mu cio also owns a rancho of 1,450 acres in Green Valley, which he has rented; but the stock thereon, 170 cows, he owns. He is also a prominent man in many business enterprises; is a stockholder in the Commercial Bank of San Luis Obispo, etc.

He was married in June, 1871, to Miss Assonta Righetti, and has six children, whom he is educating with care. The two oldest sons are now pursuing their studies at San Francisco.

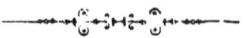

A. W. BUELL, whose handsome residence stands out very prominently among those of East Santa Barbara, was born at Essex, Vermont, March 18, 1836. His grandfather, Samuel Buell, was a resident of Connecticut, but, being drill-master during the Revolutionary war and located in Vermont, he became familiar with that country and later went there with his family and located. He moved in the winter on an ox sled, and it is said of his wife that when not too cold as she journeyed, she passed the time in knitting. Mr. Buell's father, Linas Buell, was born in Vermont, and lived to the ripe old age of seventy-one years. The old homestead, which was built 105 years ago, is still in the Buell family. A. W. Buell lived at home until twenty-one years of age, when he started for California, March 17, 1857. First went to St. Louis by rail and boat, and there joined a party of sixteen men, one woman and child, all from Vermont, which composed what was known as the Yankee train. With three wagons, each drawn by three yoke of oxen, about eighty head of loose stock and 3,500 sheep, they started on their long march across the plains, taking the northern route. After ten months of travel and a hard, tiresome passage, they arrived at San Francisco, the "Mecca of their pilgrimage," December 25, 1857. He then joined a brother who came to California in 1853, and together they engaged in farming, planting potatoes and sowing barley, with good results. Then for several years Mr. Buell engaged in the dairy business, keeping 160 cows, and in one year making 60,000 pounds of cheese and three tons of butter, and selling $1 500 worth of hogs. In 1867 he came to Santa Barbara and bought a one-fourth interest in the Juanita ranch, of about 26,664 acres. Later he traded his interest for the Cañada Corral Rancho, at El Capitan, and there resided until May 1, 1889, engaged in stock-raising and dairy business. Mr. Buell brought the first American dairy cows to the county. He sold his ranch and stock interests May 1, 1889, and moved to his present spacious residence, which he had built in 1888, and there he has since resided in quiet contentment.

Mr. Buell was married on the Buena Vista ranch, Monterey County, December 25, 1868, to Miss Marter Carter, a lady whom he had known in childhood. This union has been blessed by seven children.

HENRY H. ARNOLD, the oldest of the Arnold brothers, who came to California in 1852, and settled in Ventura County, two miles east of Hueneme, in 1871, was born in De Kalb County, Illinois, November 10, 1837. (For the father's history, see the sketch of Mathew H. Arnold, in this book.)

Henry H. left his native State when fourteen years of age, and came across the Isthmus of Nicaragua to California, with the family, and settled in Marysville, in 1857. He located 160 acres of land in Lassen County, built a house and made it his home for fourteen years, being engaged in raising grain and stock. He sold out and came to Ventura County in 1871, as already stated, his father having come to this county two years previous to that time, thinking he had found the finest tract of Government land. They were more then a month coming from Lassen County, and their outfit consisted of four wagons drawn by horses, the party numbering Henry H. and Leroy Arnold, B. J. Robertson (father-in-law of the subject of this sketch), his son Frank, and their wives and children—eleven in all. They camped out every night, and as there was plenty of deer, antelope, and quails, they had all the meat they wanted. In their journey across the plains and in their pioneer life in the far West they had become accustomed to that kind of life, and enjoyed it. When they arrived at their destination they found a squatter's board shanty on nearly every quarter-section of land. Mr. Arnold went up the Sespe River to look for a place, but returned and settled in his present locality. This land proved to belong to Thomas Scott, and Mr. Arnold bought 160 acres, on which they camped for three monnths, or until he got a house built. In 1881 he built a better house, and in 1889 he added to it and remodeled it, until he now has a commodious home. Mr. Arnold's principal crop has been barley, and he has farmed from 300 to 1,200 acres of land. He is also engaged in raising horses, Belgium stock, and is the owner of Dandy Dick, a fine thoroughbred, seventeen and a half hands high, weight 1,720 pounds.

Mr. Arnold was married in 1866 to Miss Permilia Robertson, a native of Illinois. They have five children, Charles R. and Annie G., born in Lassen County, and the three younger, Lizzie, Nellie and Eliza, born in Ventura County. Charles R. married Miss Helen Hodge, a native of California. They have a little daughter, Hazel. This son also has a nice house on the ranch.

The subject of this sketch belongs to the A. O. U. W., and has been a life-long Republican. His first vote was cast for that great, good man, Abraham Lincoln. The Arnold brothers own large tracts of land adjoining each other, and are all prominent ranchers of the county.

SAMUEL D. ANDERSON was born in the State of Pennsylvania, May 4, 1830, the son of John and Elizabeth C. (Roe) Anderson, both natives of Ohio. They had a family of nine children, eight of whom are living, Samuel D. being the oldest. When he was a boy the family removed to Iowa. He attended the public schools of that place and finished his education at a college at Princeton, Kentucky. After reaching the years of maturity, his first work was in the milling business. He soon afterward turned his attention to theology, and became a minister in the Cumberland Presbyterian Church, and was pastor of a charge. The church prospered under his ministry for a number of years, and he has ever been a worthy Christian man. The greater part of his life, however, has been spent on a farm.

Mr. Anderson was married in 1854, to Miss Nancy J. McClaran, a native of Ohio, who removed to Iowa when quite young. Mr. and Mrs. Anderson had one child, Mary Elizabeth, born September 24, 1855, and died October 15, 1858. Having no family of their own left, they adopted a little girl, Elizabeth Jane Hill, taking their own name, and a boy, Thomas Thurman. The former, at the age of twelve and a half years, sickened and died. The latter, Thomas Anderson, is still with them, and is now twenty-five years of age.

Mr. Anderson is the owner of a beautiful home in the prosperous town of Santa Paula; and here his cozy home, like its possessor, has an unassuming appearance; but its neatness and thrift and the flowers in the well-kept yard, all indicate peace and contentment —a fitting place in which to pass the closing days of a well-spent life. Mr. Anderson and his son are farming ninety acres of land, seventy acres of which they devote to beans, a crop for which the soil of this country is so well adapted. Mr. Anderson has been a Republican since the formation of that party. He was made a Mason in 1860, and was one of the charter members of Santa Paula Lodge, No. 291.

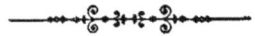

THOMAS A. RICE, a prominent and influential citizen of Ventura County, came to California in 1859. He comes of a good old Southern stock, which originated in England, his great-grandfather Rice having come from England to this country and settled in North Carolina. To him was born a son, Archibald, who wedded Miss Richmond, whose ancestors were the founders of Richmond, Virginia. To them was born a son, William. He married Miss Louisa Ish, a native of Tennessee, and daughter of William Ish, also a Tennesseean. This worthy couple were the parents of seven children, of whom the subject of this sketch, Thomas A. Rice, was one. He was born in Jackson County, Missouri, January 24, 1849. His ancestors, on both sides, participated in the Revolutionary war. One branch of his maternal ancestry is among the oldest Virginia families.

When Thomas A. was ten years of age, the family removed to California, coming across the plains and bringing with them 1,000 head of cattle. Here the father was largely engaged in stock-raising, both in Merced and Contra Costa counties. They had 2,000 acres of land in Contra Costa County, where the family resided, and where the father's death occurred in 1885. He had been a Democrat all his life, was a strict member of the Baptist Church, and was a leading and prominent man. He was possessed of those generous and courteous manners so characteristic of the Southern gentleman. It was said of William Rice that he lived an exemplary life.

Thomas A. Rice received his education in a private school at his home, and began life as a farmer on his own fine ranch, in 1876. His father had given him 470 acres, and to this he has added until he now has 900 acres in one body, located seven miles northeast of Hueneme and ten miles southeast of Ventura. He has converted it into a magnificent ranch; has a whole village of ranch buildings on it and his own school-house. He has recently built the finest residence in the county. It is artistic in design and is planned with every modern comfort, including electric bells, gas and hot and cold water. Mr. Rice is carrying on general farming, and is much interested in the breeding of fine horses, both driving and draft. In addition to the property already described, he also owns 320 acres of land about two miles from his home ranch, which is leased and which is being cultivated to beans and corn.

In 1877 Mr. Rice was united in marriage with Miss Lilian Flournoy, a native of Santa Clara County, California, daughter of Thomas Flournoy, now a resident of Danville, Contra

Costa County. Their union has been blessed with four children: N. Blanche, Madge, P. Alvin, and Merrill. They are being educated at home by their governess. Mr. Rice does not give much attention to politics, but is a Democrat, and has held the office of Supervisor. He inherits those generous traits of character for which his ancestors were distinguished; is affable alike to both stranger and friend, and is much respected and highly spoken of by his fellow-citizens. November 4, 1890, he was elected to the State Assembly, on the Democratic ticket by a majority of 175. He ran 300 ahead of his ticket in his county, Ventura, the highest compliment ever paid to a candidate in that county.

MICHAEL FAGAN is a pioneer of California and of Ventura County. He was born in Pennsylvania, August 26, 1840, the son of John and Annie (Dinnell) Fagan. The father was born in Dublin, Ireland, and emigrated to Canada when a boy. Michael Fagan is one of a family of nine children, five of whom are now living. After living in Illinois nine years he came across the plains with ox teams to California, arriving August 13, 1852, and he was reared and received his education in Calaveras County, California. His mother died in 1851, and his father in November, 1852. He spent the years 1852–'53–'54 in mining, and when he was eighteen years of age he had about $11,000. Then for a time he was engaged in stock-raising. In 1862 he went to Arora, where he was interested in quartz-mining. About that time he met with reverses and lost nearly all that he had made. In 1863 he engaged in farming in San Joaquin County, in partnership with his brother. They sowed 1,000 acres in wheat, and, the season being dry, the crop was a failure. In March, 1864, Mr. Fagan sailed for Mexico, where he engaged in cotton-raising, and the last six months of his stay there he was in a store. He sold out, prospected a year in Arizona, with but little success, returned to California and settled in Stanislaus County, where he purchased 640 acres of land at Dry Creek. Two years later he again sold out, went to San Joaquin, engaged in the meat business with his brother, and after remaining there a year, disposed of his interest in the meat market, in 1869, and came to Ventura. Here, for four years, he was engaged in sheep-raising, having as high as 3,500 head of sheep at one time, and a part of the time being in partnership with Mr. Snodgrass. He traded the last of his sheep for property in Ventura, and during the boom sold it and bought 100 acres of land in the vicinity of Saticoy. He planted the first orchard there, improved his property, and, in 1884, sold it for $75 per acre. He then bought his present ranch, 740 acres, and erected his pleasant home in a most picturesque spot. The property is principally a stock-farm, is fenced in two fields, and an abundance of water is supplied for stock from a sulphur spring on the place, the water being brought in pipes. Mr. Fagan has some fine Durham cattle. His property being located so near Santa Paula, he pastures a great many horses for other people. In addition to other improvements made, Mr. Fagan has planted a large variety of fruit trees, principally for home use

He was married, April 9, 1879, to Miss Hattie Tillotson, a native of New York. They have five children, all born in Ventura County, namely: Frank D., Cora May, Ettie Bell, Walter Miller and Marion Morris. The children are all at home with their parents, and attend school at Santa Paula.

Mr. Fagan is a member of the Masonic fraternity, and votes the Democratic ticket.

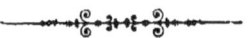

N. GARRISON is a veteran of the great war of the Rebellion. He was born in Tompkins County, New York, March 26, 1845, the son of John and Sarah (Cooper) Garrison, both natives of New York, the former born in 1820. His grandfather, Abram Garrison, was also born in that State, in Putnam County, his ancestors being among the early settlers of the State. The subject of this sketch was the third of a family of five children. He was reared and educated in that State, and spent some time clerking in a store.

The war broke out, the old flag was fired on at Fort Sumter, and the fires of patriotism burned in the hearts of the loyal people of the North. President Lincoln called for volunteers. War meetings were held. Every little town had its company of volunteers, and the larger places more. The fife and the drum could be heard every day. When the strife began Mr. Garrison was only sixteen years old, and, although eager to enter the service, could not on account of his youth. The following August, 1862, when seventeen years of age, he enlisted in Company H, One Hundred and Seventh New York Volunteer Infantry. It was in answer to Mr. Lincoln's 300,000 call; and they went forth into the deadly strife singing, "We are coming, Father Abraham, 300,000 more." In a little over a month they were in the battle of Antietam; and the peaceable farmer boy and clerk and student from school had, as by a miracle, been transformed into a hero. Then they were at Chancellorsville, Gettysburg, and at the battle of Lookout Mountain, and in the great and notable march with General Sherman from Atlanta to the sea. He participated in all the battles that his regiment was in during the last three years of the war, and never received a scratch, nor was sick a day— a noble record for a youth of seventeen. He came in at the grand review at Washington, when the war veterans, crowned with victory and glory, made their triumphant march through the beautiful capital of the great country that their heroism had saved. What a glorious chapter in a man's life was that!

On being mustered out of the service, Mr. Garrison returned to his home and was in the oil regions for a time; and not long after engaged in business in Saginaw, Michigan, four years as a merchant and four years as a dealer in stock and produce. In 1876 he came to the Golden State, and was engaged in farming and stock-raising in Yuba County. While there he was burned out and met with several financial reverses. He is now, 1890, located in Ventura County, four miles east of Hueneme, on an 800-acre ranch, raising barley, hogs, horses and cattle, and is very successful. Last year he sold $3,000 worth of stock from the ranch. Everything about the place indicates industry and thrift.

August 11, 1877, Mr. Garrison wedded Miss Mary Bayley. She is a native of Vermont, daughter of George B. Bayley, also of the Green Mountain State. In his political views Mr. Garrison is a Republican.

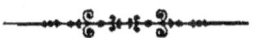

PETER McMILLAN, one of the pioneers of Santa Paula, Ventura County, was born in Canada, March 31, 1834. His parents, Donald and Mary McMillan, were natives of Canada, and both of Scotch descent. Mrs. McMillan's maiden name was the same as her husband's, while they were not relatives. In 1870 Mr. McMillan came to Santa Paula. For eighteen months he was employed on a ranch, working for wages, after which he rented lands and, for two years, raised barley and corn. He was not successful in that enterprise, and again worked by the month for a year. In 1874 he built a livery stable—the third building in Santa Paula—which served as a station on the stage route between Santa Barbara and Los Angeles. Mr. McMillan had the charge of eight stage horses all the time, turning out that many at 4 o'clock every morning, and the same number at 9 o'clock in the evening. His livery stock consisted of two horses, a wagon and a spring buggy. One of the horses with which he began business, Salem, is now twenty-six years old, is a good horse yet and is some times let for light work. Mr. McMillan bought the ground for his stable and also the lumber to build on time. For eight years he worked along without getting much ahead. He then purchased three acres on Main street for $350, and from this he sold the lots on which Cleveland Hall and the Petrolia Hotel are built, for $45 per foot front. He also owns two acres a little further out on the same street, his home property and some other lots. His livery business has increased until he now has nine rigs and fourteen good horses, and is raising some valuable colts. Mr. McMillan has been fairly successful in his business enterprises, and is one of the reliable old settlers of Santa Paula.

December 24, 1884, Mr. McMillan, like his father, wedded a lady of his own name, Mrs. McMillan. She was born in New Brunswick; is the daughter of John Murray and widow of William McMillan. She has two children by her first husband, William and Nellie. Mrs. McMillan is a member of the Presbyterian Church. Mr. McMillan is affiliated with the I. O. O. F. fraternity, and in his political views is a Republican.

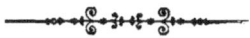

C. WELCH, who occupies a spacious home in East Santa Barbara, has suffered all the experiences and privations incident to pioneer life. Coming to the far West at an early day, he has seen the wonderful growth and development of this country. Mr. Welch was born in Linden, Vermont, August 26, 1826. His father, Jacob Welch, was a farmer and miller, owning both flour and lumber mills. He was a descendant of Jacob Welch, of England, who emigrated to America in early days. Mr. Welch's mother was a daughter of Captain De Merritt, who was a soldier in the Revolutionary war, and assisted at the retaking of Briggs Hill.

The subject of this sketch learned the trade of scale-maker, in the factory of Fairbanks & Company, at St. Johnsbury, Vermont, now called Fairbanks village. He served an apprenticeship of three years, and also received an academical education in the same town. He came to California in 1849, via the Isthmus route, landing at San Francisco on December 12, 1849. For one year he mined near Sonora, and, although very successful, did not like the life of a miner; so he purchased a ranch of 320 acres, near Stockton, and engaged in general farming, his principal crop being hay, which sold from $25 to $50 per ton. Here he contracted fever and ague, and in 1854 he came south, first settling at Ventura and later at Santa Barbara. In the latter place he started a blacksmith shop, and also planted a vineyard of 6,000 vines on the border of the Santa Clara River. In those days wine was made in raw-hide sacks, the grapes being treaded out by the Indians in bare feet. In 1862 Mr. Welch took a trip on horseback to Prescott, prospecting, and going by way of La Paz. With Daniel Lount and brothers he built a cabin near the present city of Prescott, they being the first white settlers of that place. In 1865 he rented the orchard and vineyard of the Los Dos Pueblos ranch, which was owned by the Den estate, and in February, 1866, Mr. Welch married the widow of Nicholas Den. He then engaged in stock-raising, keeping about 3,000 sheep and 800 head of cattle. He bought his present place in Santa Barbara in 1878, built a house and moved his family here on account of the illness of his wife. Mr. Welch lived mainly at the ranch, making frequent visits to town. Mrs. Welch died in 1883. Two years later the subject of this sketch sold his stock and his interest in the ranch, and did not again engage in business. He was married again, at Santa Barbara, in June, 1884, to the widow of Ramon J. Hill. By this marriage he has one son.

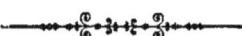

JOHN MEARS is one of the pioneers of California who came to the State in 1859, and to Ventura in 1869, before the county was formed. Mr. Mears was born in Ireland, in 1844, and at the age of eleven years came to the United States and lived with his aunt, his education being principally obtained in this country. When only a large boy he started for Illinois and went from there to Pike's Peak. After he had made enough money to purchase an outfit, he decided to cross the plains for California. He found some difficulty in getting any one to go with him, but at last a young German agreed to accompany him. They secured a one-horse wagon and covered it with canvas, having a pole in it in place of thills. They attached four yoke of oxen to the wagon and, with provisions enough to last, set out on their perilous journey June 20, 1859, from that part of Colorado where Denver is now located. They were not many days on the way until they encountered swollen streams. The first they crossed without sustaining any serious loss, but the second proved more difficult, as their wagon was wrecked and the most of the provisions lost. The German could not swim, so clung to a part of the wagon. Mr. Mears, while trying to get out of the wagon, got his foot fastened and hung with his head in the water, and would shortly have been drowned had not some plunge of the oxen set him free. He then succeeded in reaching some logs and was carried down the stream nearly a quarter of a mile, when some other emigrants who had come up rescued him. He found the German on the bank, minus his hat. One of the wheels of the wagon was broken, and their clothes, money and provisions lost in the stream. Their first conclusion was to return, and Mr. Mears let an emigrant who had helped them have one yoke of the oxen to add to his team, on the condition that if he did well he would send back the pay for it. They found a sack of their flour, and the German proposed that they rig up the rear wheels of the wagon, start forward and overtake the emigrants, and in company with them work their way through. With willow bark they fastened the end-board of the wagon on the hind axletree and secured the sack of flour to that; and, cold and wet and hungry, they started on and in time fell in with the emigrants. By shooting game they managed to subsist until they reached California, six months later.

While at Pike's Peak Mr. Mears had become acquainted with a number of young Indians, and run races and jumped with them, and an Indian chief had taken a great fancy to a navy-blue coat he had, which Mr. Mears gave him. The Indian in return presented Mr. Mears with a buffalo robe. While out on the plains Mr. Mears was some distance from the train hunting, and on his return saw about fifty Indians about the emigrants, the emigrant train, which consisted of about fifteen wagons, having been stopped by the Indians. Mr. Mears was somewhat alarmed, but knew it was useless to attempt an escape, so walked up. The chief recognized him as the gentleman who had given him the coat, shook hands and gave him to understand that they wanted water for a sick man. The emigrants fearing they would not have a sufficient supply for themselves, had refused to give them the water. Mr. Mears gave them water and also a little whisky for the sick man, for which the Indians gave signs of great satisfaction, and the train was permitted to proceed.

When Mr. Mears came to Ventura County he first settled on the Santa Ana. At that time there were no settlers there except Mr. Arness and another gentleman. Between where he now lives and San Buenaventura there were only about five houses, which were occupied by Mr. Montgomery, Mr. McKenna, Mr. Peter Boyle and others. In 1870 Mr. Mears moved upon the quarter-section of land three miles north of Santa Paula, which he had purchased from the Government, and there kept bachelor's hall for four years, being engaged in sheep-raising, having as many as 8,000 head of sheep and employing ten men, Americans and Spaniards, to assist him in their care. His wool was sent by schooner to San Francisco, and they drove the fat sheep to that city for market. It required two months to make the journey, taking 2,000 sheep at a time. Mr. Mears has added to his first purchase until he now has 1,700 acres, and is engaged in general farming, raising sheep, horses and cattle, and beans, barley, corn and hay. His pasture land is valued at $10 per acre, and the farming land at $150 per acre.

In 1874 Mr. Mears married Miss Ellen Lavelle, at Ventura. She is a native of the "Emerald Isle," born in 1856. They have built a comfortable home, surrounded with trees, on the banks of the Santa Paula River. They have a family of six children: John W., Frances E., George H., Florence, Ellen C. and Lawrence M. L. Their first born, a beautiful little girl, they lost when two years and nine months of age. A bean got fast in her windpipe, and before medical aid could be obtained it went to her lungs and caused her death. A fine picture of this little daughter hangs in their parlor.

Mr. and Mrs. Mears are members of the Catholic Church. For the past fifteen years Mr. Mears has served as a School Trustee in his district. His political views are Democratic. Notwithstanding all that he has seen and experienced of pioneer life and adventures, Mr. Mears is still a young man. He is a worthy and respected citizen, and holds a prominent place in the community in which he resides.

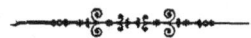

D. SMITH began his pioneer life at the age of eleven years by moving with his parents from Hanover, New Hampshire, where he was born in October, 1833, to Kendall County, Illinois, where his father followed farming. Our subject worked at farming until 1870, when he came to California in compay with his two brothers, J. M. and Frank Smith. They settled at Carpenteria, and N. D. and Frank were pioneers in the shipping and lumber business, taking all merchandise through the surf to vessels, shipping wood and grain. In 1874 they built a wharf and deliveries were made much easier. In 1876 he sold his interest to Frank and J. M. Smith and the subject of this sketch came to Santa Barbara and started merchandise business at 618 State street. under the firm name of Smith & Johnson. In 1886 Mr. Smith bought Mr. Johnson's interest and has since continued alone; he carried a full line of groceries, crackers and provisions.

He was first married in Kendall County, Illinois, in 1859, to Miss Louise Frise, who died in 1877. He then married Miss Carroll Edwards in Santa Barbara in 1879. They have one child: Bernice Dee Smith. who was born March 28, 1880.

WILLIAM O'HARA, a rancher near Santa Paula, is a native of Bangor, Maine, born May 4, 1841. His father, Henry O'Hara, was born in Ireland, in 1804, and his mother, Nancy (Galaher) O'Hara, was born in the same country, in 1806. His parents were married in 1824, and emigrated to the State of Maine, where they lived on a farm, excepting two years spent in Illinois. In 1849 Mr. O'Hara's father came to California, and engaged in mining for two years in Tuolumne County, and returned to his home in Maine. Soon after his return the family removed to the State of Illinois, where they remained until in 1867 they came to Contra Costa County, California, where they engaged in farming until his father's death. The subject of this sketch was a miner in Virginia City, Nevada, two years. He was then sent on a mining and exploring expedition into the wilds of Arizona in search of gold, in company with C. L. Strong, and backed by the Bank of California; the expedition consisted of 100 men. They were harassed by the Indians, and a good many of their company were murdered. They fed the Indians in the day-time, but in return they made treacherous attacks upon them in the night. The expedition was finally abandoned, with a heavy loss.

In 1865 Mr. O'Hara came to Santa Paula and bought 150 acres of land, known as the Briggs tract. He afterward sold it and bought his present ranch of 160 acres, two and a fourth miles west of Santa Paula. He bought of a party who took it for Government land, and it was supposed to have been grant land, but after lawing over it for nine years to perfect his title he was obliged to buy of the ex-mission. At that time the valley was a vast mustard field, containing only a few settlers. Among them was John Montgomery, E. B. Higgins, Peter Boyle and William McCormack. Mr. O'Hara built a small house and engaged in stock-raising. He remained here for twelve years, cooking his own food,—a second Robinson Crusoe. The little house has since been destroyed, and a stately mansion is now occupied and filled with the comforts and luxuries of life. Beautiful grounds surround the house, planted with beautiful trees and shrubs, and the whole property is transformed into a most delightful home, with its large barns and beautiful fields. The whole valley is now dotted with fine houses, beautiful trees, and wide, well cultivated fields.

Mr. William O'Hara was married in 1877, to Miss Mary E. Kelley, who was born in Napa County, California, February 17, 1858, the daughter of Michael Kelley, a native of County Kilkenny, Ireland. Her mother, Maggie (Whalen) Kelley, was also born in

Ireland. Mr. and Mrs. O'Hara have two children, a boy and a girl, both born in their present home, viz.: Henry, born January 21, 1880; and Georgia, born December 12, 1886.

Mr. O'Hara's first efforts on the ranch was stock-raising, principally cattle, but afterward in raising barley, corn and hogs. At one time he had as many as 3,000 head of stock, which never had any disease among them; the wild-cat and coyote had to be watched to keep them from stealing the young pigs. The price received for live weight was from two and a half to seven cents per pound. He is now engaged in bean raising; in 1889 he harvested fifty-seven tons, and the price is now five cents per pound; the general price is from two and a half cents to five cents, according to the market. He has added to his original purchase forty acres of hill land, and has planted 27,000 gum trees, which are doing nicely. He is also interested with his brothers, George and Hugh, and his nephew, John McClosky, in 320 acres of oil land, and their producing wells give thirty barrels per day. They have all the machinery and tools connected with the business. Mr. O'Hara built his present residence in 1887, and it is an ornament to the country. He is a member of the I. O. O. F., and cast his first vote for Abraham Lincoln, and has continued to vote for the Republican party.

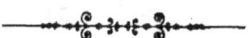

P. SANBORN was born in Kennebec County, Maine, November 1, 1844. His father, Captain John Sanborn, sailed in the West India trade. In a storm his ship was wrecked and all on board lost except the captain and one other man, who were rescued, but died two years after from the effects of exposure and hunger. Young Sanborn was reared on a farm and attended school in his native State. When the war of the Rebellion burst upon the country he was only seventeen years old, but the patriotic fire burned in his young heart, and he enlisted September 7, 1861, in Company C, Eighth Maine Volunteer Infantry. When his term expired he re-enlisted and served gallantly all through that great struggle, being mustered out January 18, 1866. Their regiment started in April, 1864, with 900 men, and after the battle of Cold Harbor, June 3, 1864, they numbered only 160 efficient soldiers. At that battle Mr. Sanborn, while making a charge, received a gun-shot wound in his shoulder, which disabled him from duty for four months. He participated in many important engagements, and through all acted well the part of a brave soldier. Entering the army as a private, he was promoted to Orderly Sergeant and carried the colors for six or seven months. He knows what it is to bear the old flag aloft in the midst of shell and shot, and lived to see it wave over a united country.

In 1867 Mr. Sanborn came to California and settled in Solano County, where he worked six months on a farm, and afterward farmed on the shares and accumulated a little money. He then went to Sacramento County and bought 200 acres of land, which he improved, and on which he engaged in farming. This land flooded and the property became worthless. Mr. Sanborn was then foreman on a large stock ranch for ten years. He bought thirty acres of fruit land at $1.40 per acre, in Vaca Valley, which he improved and afterward sold for $300 per acre. He then went to San Mateo County and purchased 3,000 acres of stock ranch, and afterward sold it at a profit, and went to King City, Monterey County. He there took the position of foreman on a 25,000-acre stock and grain ranch. Some time after this he went to San Diego and operated in lands and invested in city property, and also shipped 157 head of horses from the North, meeting with success in all of these enterprises. He came to his present property in March, 1888, bought forty acres of the finest land in the valley, and built a house and large barn. In 1889 he realized $2,100 from the products of the farm.

Mr. Sanborn married Miss Emily Palmer, a native of Maine, daughter of Reuel Palmer of that State. They have one daughter, Elteen, born in 1877, in Sacramento County, California.

Mr. Sanborn is a Republican, a member of the G. A. R., and a most worthy citizen.

EMERSON & COMPANY.—The proprietors of the handsome and commodious shoe store at 716 State street, Santa Barbara, are both natives of Wakefield, Massachusetts, and are descendants of shoe manufacturers, even to their remote ancestry.

Daniel W. Emerson, the senior partner, was born at Wakefield, and was a manufacturer of shoes in Wakefield and Haverhill. He came to California in the interest of gold mining in 1867, having purchased interests in the East, but the mines proving a failure he bought the co-operative boot and shoe business of San Francisco, manufacturing shoes in the city wholesale and retail trade, and also running retail stores in the country, One being established in Santa Barbara in 1873. Mr. Emerson continued manufacturing until 1886, when, after doing a prosperous business he sold out his interest and came to Santa Barbara to live a more retired and quiet life.

He was married in Wakefield, in 1865, to Miss Ellen Wiley, and they have two children: Percey W. and Fred W.

F. M. Emerson, the junior partner of the firm was born in 1856, and was educated at Haverhill, Massachusetts, where his parents removed in his early life. He learned the trade of shoe manufacturing in the establishment of his father. He came to California in 1875, and settled at San Luis Obispo, where he opened a shoe store, continuing four years. He then sold out and came to Santa Barbara in 1879 to take charge of the present store for his uncle, D. W. Emerson, and in 1883 was taken in as a partner under the firm name of Emerson & Co. It is the oldest shoe store in the city, and they carry a fine and well assorted stock.

Mr. Emerson was married at Santa Barbara, in September, 1884, to Miss Agnes Calder, a native of Massachusetts. They have two children: Helen Calder and Barbara. Mr. Emerson is a member of the I. O. O. F.

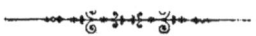

P. L. BYERS was born in Armstrong County, Pennsylvania, December 15, 1845. His grandfather, David Byers, came from Germany about the year 1768, and settled in Pennsylvania where Peter Byers was born in 1812. He was a well-to-do farmer and wedded Miss Susanna Sourwine. They were the parents of thirteen children, the ninth one being P. L. Byers, the subject of this sketch. He was reared and educated in his native State, and when eighteen years of age entered the war, enlisting in Company K, Eighth Ohio Cavalry. He was in the Army of the Potomac and participated in all the battles of the campaign. At the battle of Winchester, September 19, 1864, he was wounded in the right arm and laid up for three months in the Little York hospital, Pennsylvania. Upon his recovery he returned to his regiment at Beverly, West Virginia, and served until the close of the war, being mustered out August 5, 1865. On account of the wound received, he gets a pension of $2 per month.

After leaving the service, Mr. Byers returned to the quiet life of the farm, and has been engaged in agricultural pursuits ever since. He came to Santa Paula, June 25, 1875, and after seven years gardening, he purchased his present home property of five acres. He has built a nice house, planted a hedge and all kinds of fruit trees and small fruit, and has one of the neatest little places in all the county. Mr. Byers was married, in 1870, to Miss A. Davidson, of Illinois. She was born in 1850, daughter of John Davidson of that State. Her ancestors were natives of Kentucky, but her father was born in Pennsylvania. They have had eight children, six of whom are living. The first two were born in Missouri and the others in California. Their names are Norman O., Ona M., John L., Creed H., Marge E. and Earl. Mrs. Byers is a member of the Presbyterian church. Mr. Byers has never joined any society, is a strictly temperate man, Democratic in his political views, is an industrious man, and one highly respected by his fellow citizens.

HENRY LEWIS, one of the early pioneers in the Carpenteria Valley, was born near Manassas Junction, Virginia, in 1830. His father was a farmer, and Henry followed a like occupation, although a part of his boyhood was passed in a store in Washington, District of Columbia. Mr. Lewis was married at the age of twenty years to Miss Chattin, of Virginia, and he then bought a farm and began what has proven his life work. He sold out all interests and came to California in 1857. The next year he went into the mines in Tuolumne County, and after six months' experience he came out "with rheumatism and little else," which has remained with him through life. In December, 1858, he moved to Half Moon Bay, and there farmed for three years. In the spring of 1862 he come to Carpenteria Valley, purchased eighty-eight acres of land and pitched his tent near where his house now stands. He bought this property from the city of Santa Barbara at $1.25 per acre, the land being wild and uncultivated and covered with brush and live-oak trees. He drove down from Half Moon Bay, looking along for a desirable situation, and the Carpenteria Valley was the first location which seemed practicable. He immediately began cutting and clearing, and now has one of the most complete ranch properties in the place. The only white people then in the valley were Colonel Russell Heath and Mr. Lowrie. As rapidly as land was cleared he began the cultivation of Lima beans, corn and barley. In 1864 they had a very dry year, no crops maturing and horses and cattle dying for want of sustenance. Mr. Lewis has since added twenty acres to his ranch, which now numbers 110 acres, ninety acres of which he plants to Lima beans, with an average crop of 2,000 pounds to the acre. The thirty-five-acre field in front of his residence has produced an annual crop of beans since 1865, and yearly becomes more productive.

Mr. Lewis lost his first wife in February, 1863, and in 1879 he was married to Mrs. Bebecca Mullin, of Carpenteria. He has seven children by his first wife and three by his second, all living. His handsome two-story residence, fine barns and suitable outbuildings all go to show the thrifty and successful farmer, and his well kept ranch is significant of the prosperity which has attended Mr. Lewis.

J. B. ALVORD, a prominent rancher and educator of Ventura County, was born in New York, November 10, 1849. He is the son of Alvin W. Alvord, a native of Vermont, and the grandson of Julius Alvord, who was born in Massachusetts. Their ancestors were English. His great-grandfather was Seth Alvord, whose grandparents came to America in the year 1700. Mr. Alvord's mother, Electa R. (Todd) Alvord, came from Scotch ancestors. She was born in Herkimer County, New York, daughter of Mr. Bela Todd. The subject of this sketch is the only son in a family of three children. He received his early education in the public schools of New York and Ohio, and was also a student at the Northwest Normal School of Pennsylvania. He began teaching at the age of nineteen years, and has been a teacher almost continuously for fifteen years.

On coming to Ventura County, Mr. Alvord bought a small farm, but afterward sold it. In 1884 he purchased his present fine ranch of 160 acres, seventy acres of which he sold for more than the whole cost him. He remodeled the house and made many improvements, and the land is now under a high state of cultivation, his principal crops being beans and potatoes. The beans averaged a ton to the acre, and a portion of the land produced as high as 3,500 pounds per acre.

Mr. Alvord was married, in 1879, to Miss Ida Ricker, a native of Iowa, and daughter of John G. Ricker, who was born in Maine. They have four sons, all born in Ventura County, the three eldest named respectively Hartwell, Vernon M. and David E. Mr. and Mrs. Alvord are refined and intelligent people. They are members of the Universalist church of Santa Paula. In his political views, Mr. Alvord is a Republican. For eight years he has been a member of the Board of Education of the county. As a teacher he has been very successful, but is at present devoting his attention to agricultural pursuits.

JEROME C. WILSON, proprietor of the Black Hawk stables, Santa Barbara, has been successful in his line. He was born at Sutton, Vermont, in 1849. He is of Scotch-English descent, and his grandfather was one of the early settlers of Vermont; his mother was a native of Vermont, but of Scotch descent. Jerome C. was educated at the high school of Sutton. In 1868 he went to Boston and remained until 1885, engaged in a mercantile and speculative business. He came to San Francisco in March, 1885, where he was engaged in business until September, 1886, when he came to Santa Barbara. He rented the corner of Cota and Chapella streets, and started a small livery business of five horses and one bus, which was the nucleus of his present complete establishment. In 1887 he bought out the Black Hawk stable on the present sight, and he built his commodious building of 75 x 152 feet, and keeps ninety horses, twenty-five of which are especially trained to the saddle. He has a fine stock of carriages and the popular three-seated wagon, which, with four horses makes the favorite rig of the tourist. It was said of Mr. Wilson when he came to town that "he would not stay a week," but he attended to his own business and is now proprietor of one of the finest livery stables in California. Investing only $3,000 at first, he is now worth fully $70,000.

DRYING PRUNES IN THE OJAI VALLEY.

AN ORANGE ORCHARD IN THE OJAI VALLEY.

Mr. Wilson is a Royal Arch Mason, Corinthian Chapter, No. 52, of the Blue Lodge, No. 282, of the Knights and Ladies of Honor. He is also a member of the Knights of Pythias, Independent Order of Foresters, an Odd Fellow and a Good Templar. May 6, 1890, he married Miss Lettie Renwick, and they made their wedding trip to the principal Eastern cities.

W. H. TAYLOR, a stock-farmer of San Luis Obispo County, is one of a family of four sons. Born in Virginia, in 1829, his early life was spent at home. At the age of eighteen he engaged in the business in which for a period of forty years he was a prominent figure, namely, the livery and stage business. It is difficult to conceive of more varied, exciting or interesting experiences than Mr. Taylor relates of his stage life on the plains and over the mountains and various part of California. Coming to California in 1861, he was connected with the Pioneer Stage Company of this State, their line extending from California to Virginia City, Nevada. He was employed by this company for four years, being superintendent the latter part of the time. This Pioneer Stage Company was a famous one, and operated their line in the best manner ever known. He was also superintendent for the Overland Mail Company, between Salt Lake City, Utah, and Virginia City, Nevada, previous to the building of the Central Pacific Railroad, and was Wells, Fargo & Co.'s superintendent and paymaster several years on their stage and express lines in Utah, Idaho and Montana. He next ran a stage line from Soledad to Los Angeles for a period of thirteen years; and it was related that during that time, either winter or summer, there was never a delay of over two days in the arrival of the mails which were carried by these coaches. With well organized railroad and steamship companies at the present time, we need only to refer to the season of 1889–'90 to find delays of a week or more in the delivery of these same mails. The Coast Line Stage Company, which had been controlled by Flint, Bixby & Co., passed in 1878 into the hands of William Buckley and Mr. Taylor, the latter being superintendent. This arrangement lasted until 1886, when he retired. A remnant of this well managed stage line is now found between San Luis Obispo City and Santa Margarita Station.

Mr. Taylor first settled in Monterey County in 1873, and engaged in the hotel business for a time. He then settled down on the Buena Vista Stock farm, San Luis Obispo County, in 1884, where he now resides. It comprises 267 acres, and is located on the Pacific Coast Railroad three and a half miles from San Luis Obispo on the way to Port Harford. On this place are raised some of the finest horses in the State, and there are few better judges of the points of a horse that Mr. Taylor. He has been an invalid for some time, and is now confined to his house with a nervous affection.

I. N. HUDIBURGH was born in Morgan County, Indiana, January 4, 1848, son of Samuel and Nancy Hudiburgh, both natives of Indiana, and the former of German descent. He was the sixth of a family of eight children, was reared on a farm and received his education in the public schools, going to school in the winter and working on the farm in the summer. At the age of seventeen he tendered his services to his country, enlisting, in 1865, in Company H,

Eighty-third Illinois Infantry. He was transferred to Company I, Sixty-first Illinois Infantry, and was ordered to Clarksville, Tennessee, and from there to Nashville. While his regiment was in the latter place, General Lee surrendered, and on the 8th of September, 1865, he was mustered out by reason of the close of the war. He then returned to his home, where he remained a year; next removed to Missouri and worked in Bates County eight years; then went to Linn County, Kansas, where he resided eight years. In 1882 Mr. Hudiburgh came to California, and since that time has resided at Santa Paula. Is engaged in the remunerative business of cultivating Lima beans, devoting forty acres to their production.

He was married, in 1869, to Miss Margaret J. Cleek, a native of Virginia, and reared in Missouri. Their union has been blessed with five children, namely: Charles M., born in Bates County, Missouri, July 19, 1870; Alfred, in Kansas, February 20, 1877; Walter, also born in Kansas, August 3, 1878; Samuel, in Santa Paula, California, July 17, 1884, and Ethel May, in Santa Paula, November 6, 1887. Mrs. Hudiburgh is a member of the Baptist church. Mr. Hudiburgh is a strict temperance man, a good citizen, and in politics is a Democrat.

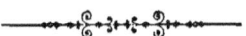

T. E. HODGES, a resident of the lower portion of the Arroyo Grande, was born in Missouri, in August, 1846. At the age of eighteen years he enlisted in the Union army, and was in the ranks until the close of the war. In 1865 the family removed to Kansas, where young Hodges lived for eleven years, except the time he was in school, at the age of twenty-three. In 1876 he came to California, and was for two years employed upon his farm in See Cañon; was one year on John McGlashan's place, and then came to his present property in the lower part of the Arroyo Grande Valley. It comprises fifty-three acres, twenty-five of which are in orchard, an object of pride to its owner. It contains apricots, peaches, apples, pears and prunes. Many of the branches on the trees at the time this sketch was written were bolstered up by strong ropes, in order to help sustain the enormous quantity of fruit. Mr. Hodges has had great success also with his English walnut trees; and this year he will plant many more of these trees in his twenty-acre bean-field. His drying house is a considerable invention, and is the largest and most complete in the valley.

Mr. Hodges was married in the fall of 1872, to Miss Sarah E. Weininger, of Kentucky, and they have six children.

B. B. PIERCE, another of the early settlers of California, came to the State in 1869. He is a native of Howard County, Missouri, born March 31, 1851. His father, John M. Pierce, a native of Virginia, came to California in 1869, and lived to be eighty-one years of age, dying September 21, 1878. His grandfather, John Pierce, was also a Virginian, and a soldier in the war of 1812. They were of Scotch-Welsh ancestry. John M. Pierce was twice married, and had four children by the first marriage and two by the second. The subject of this sketch was the younger child born of the last wife. His mother, *nee* Nancy L. Johnson, was a native of Kentucky, and a daughter of Benjamin Johnson, who was born in Virginia. Mr. Pierce comes from good old Virginia and Kentucky stock, an ancestry noted for chivalry and hospitality.

Mr. Pierce was reared in the State of Missouri, and came with the family to California, when eighteen years of age. They first settled in Hollister, San Benito County, and for seven years lived on a farm, which they supposed was Government land, but which the railroad company claimed and took from them. They then came to San Luis Obispo County, in 1876, and purchased 640 acres of land on the Los Osos. This property they improved by building, etc., engaged in raising cattle and horses, kept a dairy, and farmed for ten years, when he sold it for $24,000. Then he took up 160 acres, and afterward bought 480 acres adjoining it, on which he built a good residence, planted an orchard and vineyard, and is now engaged in raising stock on this property. He keeps about 150 head of cattle, the stock being graded up to a high standard of Durham cattle, the blooded stock being from the herd of Senator Hearst. They farm about 130 acres of the property. Mr. Pierce has bought property in Paso Robles, and has built a comfortable home and a good barn. He resides at this place, and has a meat market in the town. They raise and kill their own beef.

Mr. Pierce was married, November 11, 1879, to Miss Mary E. Knaus, a native of Missouri. They have two daughters, born in Los Osos, Maud Adeline and Mable J., and one son, John F., born in Paso Robles. Mrs. Pierce is a member of the Christian Church.

For five years Mr. Pierce served as a member of the Los Osos School Board, and he has been much interested in educational matters. He was elected Road Supervisor in 1884 and in 1888, and since then has been elected in District No. 12, by the largest majority ever obtained in the city. He is an Odd Fellow, and is a member of the board of trustees, and in politics he is a Democrat. Mr. Pierce is a driving, pratical business man, full of fun and ever ready to both give and take a joke.

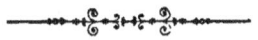

A. R. BOOTH, a prominent business man of San Luis Obispo County, has been on the Pacific Coast thirty-two years. With other old-timers he has had his share of pioneer life and also great influence in shaping the destiny of the great State of his choice. His long business career in this country makes him good authority on its varied resources, and he is one of the enthusiasts who believe that it is difficult to overdraw the grand resources and capabilities of California. He was born in Mount Clements, Michigan, July 28, 1835. His father, John Booth, a native of England, was brought by his parents to America when a child. His mother, *nee* Jane A. Wisdom, was born in Philadelphia. He was next to the youngest of their ten children. Received his education in Kalamazoo, Michigan, and opened his first drug-store in Fenton, same State. He removed to Eastern Oregon in 1858 and was located at the Dalles. He then spent ten years in Washington Territory and British America, speculating in mines and engaged in general business. He was also in Idaho and Nevada in the same business, and also in the drug trade; and he finally came to San Luis Obispo and later to El Paso de Robles, from choice, after deliberate investigation, and even before the town was established. He accordingly has taken hold and done his share toward the upbuilding of the place, which bids fair to be the largest town in the county. He is senior partner in the proprietorship of two drug stores,—one at San Luis Obispo and the other at El Paso de Robles. Booth & Latner have a fine drug store at the former place, while Booth &

Jannie have a similar one in one of the best localities in the latter place. He is also a member of the firm of Stowell & Booth, real estate and sole agents for the El Paso de Robles town site.

Mr. Booth is a Republican in politics, is a Master of the Masonic Lodge, and a Knight Templar.

He was married in 1878 to Miss Susan Reynor, a native of Missouri, and they have had three sons born in San Luis Obispo and a daughter in Paso Robles, viz.: Fred, Frank, Eugene and Clara J.

Following is an interesting anecdote from Mr. Booth's experience illustrating the condition of society in frontier life. He was taken for a minister, and it came near proving a serious inconvenience to him. One day, while riding one horse and leading another in a thinly inhabited portion of the frontier, and wearing a "boiled shirt," which was rare and almost unheard of in that country, he asked a settler on the approach of evening whether he could stay all night with him. "No; don't keep hotel," was the answer. Mr. Booth added, "I don't care for a hotel; all I want is a little hay for my horses; I can lie down anywhere." "Well, can't keep you," was peremptorily repeated by the resident. Mr. Booth asked, "Will you sell me a little hay for my horses; I can feed them out here." "No; I've got no hay to sell," replied the frontiersman. Mr. Booth, getting mad, said "G—— d—— you! Can you tell me where there is an Indian camp; an untutored savage would not turn me away like that."

Then the settler came out, grasped his hand and said, "Who be you, anyhow?" "G—— d—— me if I didn't think you was one of these preacher fellers. Git down; I'll keep you." And Mr. Booth says he was well entertained!

Mr. Booth has seen the early rough times of Western society transformed into those of refinement; the church and the school-house to ornament the land; and all the institutions of refined civilization of America to be established throughout the Pacific Coast. Physically he is still fresh and hale, and bids fair to live to see the whole coast thickly populated with the most intelligent and civilized people on the face of the earth.

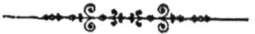

TIMOTHY WELLS, one of the prominent citizens of El Paso de Robles, is a native of Ohio, while his father, Timothy Wells, Sr., was a native of New York, and his grandfather of Rhode Island. The last mentioned took an active part as Captain of a force of scouts during the Revolutionary war, their principal errand being the search for Indians and Tories, in which they rendered the Continental cause good service. The Wells family had its origin in England. The mother of Mr. Wells, *nee* Elizabeth Hatch, was a native of Connecticut and also of English ancestry; so that Mr. Wells, although an American, is of pure English blood, equalled by that very few who have descended from those of American birth from the period before the declaration of independence.

The subject of this sketch, the youngest but one of a family of seven children, was brought up on the Western Reserve in Ohio, removed to Sycamore, Illinois, and embarked in the general merchandise business until 1857, when he sold out and remained out of active business life until the great civil war came on. In 1862 Governor Yates, of Illinois, appointed him Quartermaster, which position he filled until the close of the war, and he had the pleasure of seeing the grand review of the victorious soldiers of the Union army at Washington. After the war he engaged in stock-raising and buying and shipping cattle from the northeast corner of Kansas to St. Louis and Chicago, until 1874. In 1875 he came to the Pacific coast and was engaged in mercantile business at Redwood City for three years. Selling out, he returned to Missouri and remained there four years; then he came again to California and spent the first two years in San Bernardino County, at the Hot Springs of Governor Waterman, his brother-in-law, in order to recover his health. He then came to El Paso de Robles and bought 560 acres of land four miles from town, which he is now improving and developing. The railroad runs through the property, there is a warehouse there, and a portion of the ground is platted for a town site, a portion planted to prunes, and still another part is devoted to the production of milk. Mr. Wells is also doing a real-estate business in the city, where he has bought a lot and built a nice cottage, and he and his sister, Lucy A. (these two being the only survivors of the family), are spending the evening of their days. He has long been a leading Congregationalist, and is at present a deacon of his church at San Miguel. His political views are Democratic, and he is a pleasant, entertaining and public-spirited gentleman.

At Sycamore, Illinois, in 1844, Mr. Wells was united in matrimony with Miss Mary Howard Waterman, a daughter of John Waterman of that State, and a sister of Governor Waterman of this State. Of his five children, four are living; three were born in Sycamore, and the youngest in Wayne County, Ohio. They are: Helen L., who married William R. Thomas, and resides in Oakland, California; Mary E., who is now the wife of C. N. Chase, and resides in Vermont; Abby J. is the wife of Andrew J. Kinney, and their home is at East Orange, New Jersey; and John P. is married and resides in Warrensburg, Missouri. After forty years of wedded life, Mrs. Wells, the loving wife and the kind mother, died, September 26, 1881.

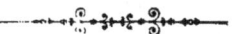

SAMUEL HILL is a pioneer of California and one of the prominent ranchers of Ventura County. He was born in England, March 21, 1816. His parents, Samuel and Mary Hill, were both natives of that country. Mr. Hill remained in England until nineteen years of age, and in 1835 went to Quebec, Canada. He soon afterward located in Toronto, where he was engaged in the milling business for a year and a half. From that place he went to Dubuque, Iowa, and worked in the mills for seven years. He then went back to England, but soon, however, returned to Iowa, and in 1850 came to California. He first worked in the mines at Placerville. At Fort John he had a small store of miners' supplies, was there two years, and then went to Amador County, where he engaged in quartz mining. At the latter place he lost all he had previously made. Next he went to Buckeye Valley, same county, pre-empted a farm of 160 acres and purchased 840 acres more. He also bought a large house that had been built for a hotel and located on the same land. One hundred and sixty acres of land he devoted to grain and sheep-raising, remaining on the farm twenty-five years. He then rented it, removed to Ventura County, and bought 5,368 acres of land in the Conejo grant, and moved upon it with his family in 1877. Has been engaged in raising sheep, horses and cattle, and has kept as many as 12,000 sheep at a time. His horses are principally roadsters, twenty-five head being used on the ranch.

Mr. Hill was married in 1865 to Mrs. Sarah Middleton, a native of England, and the widow of Thomas Middleton. By her former husband she had five children, all born in America. By Mr. Hill she has had one son, Samuel Hill, Jr., who lived to be twenty-four years of age, and his death was occasioned by an accident. His mules ran him against a fence, injuring him internally and causing his death soon afterward. He left a wife and son, Samuel H., Jr. They reside in Sacramento. Mr. and Mrs. Hill were reared in the faith of the Episcopal Church. Mr. Hill affiliates with the Democratic party. He has just built a comfortable residence, and here in the sunny climate of Southern California he expects to spend the evening of his life.

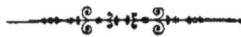

HON. D. W. JAMES, one of the founders of the beautiful young city of Paso Robles, came to this State across the plains in 1849, and has ever since been intimately connected with the growth and development of this State, and had he not the sturdy elements of a courageous frontiersman, and of a persevering and successful business man, he would not have encountered the obstacles and survived the great disasters which come so thick and fast around the pioneer.

Drury J. James was born in Russellville, on the Whip-poor-will River, in Logan County, Kentucky, November 14, 1824, the son of Jackson James, who was born near Richmond, Virginia. His grandfather was Martin James, who came from England before the Revolution, and settled in Virginia, and aided in the Patriot war as an aide to one of the generals. Mr. James' mother was a native of Virginia, and the daughter of a soldier who fought on the Patriot side during the same struggle. The subject of this sketch, the youngest of eight children, was but three months old when his mother died, and but a little over a year old when his father died. His eldest sister, Mary, took charge of the family. She afterward married John Mimms. He lived with them until he was eighteen years of age, employed upon their tobacco plantation and attending school. After that he was engaged with his brother William in mercantile business in Oldham County, Kentucky, on the Ohio River; but soon afterward he enlisted in the war with Mexico, in one of the companies of the Louisville Legion. Going to the front as a private, he participated under General Taylor in the battle of Monterey. On the evening of the second day they entered the city and marched to the plaza. The Mexicans raised a flag of truce, and the city was surrendered, and the Legion was left to garrison the place while the rest of the victorious command, numbering about 4,000 men, marched forward, to meet the forces commanded by Santa Ana, numbering about 22,000 men. The Legion was then ordered forward to join Taylor's force, which they reached in time by excessive marching. In the effort Mr. James crippled himself by bursting one of the veins in his leg, from which injury he has never fully recovered. The Americans were victorious in the battle of Buena Vista, fought against fearful odds, and the Legion was ordered back to Monterey. His time of enlistment having expired, Mr. James was honorably discharged, and resumed business at his home, in company with his brother.

Directly after the news of the gold discovery in California reached him, he joined a company of thirty men, left Fort Kearney the last of May, 1849, and crossed plain and mountain, safely landing at Weaverville, August 6. He engaged in mining at this place and at Hangtown for nine months, with reasonable success. In the spring of 1850 he engaged in buying cattle to supply the mines with beef, buying first at Santa Clara, at $20 per head, and selling them at the mines at sixty cents per pound on foot, and dressed meat at $1 per pound. In 1851 he went to Los Angeles and bought cattle at $15 to $20 per head and realized about $40 per head at the mines. Starting his drove of cattle from Los Angeles, he would make a trip and return to San Luis Obispo, Monterey and Santa Clara counties, sometimes taking three droves a year, of 500 to 700 head each time. At one time he drove from Los Angeles 1,500 head. This business he continued successfully until 1860, when, in company with John B. Thompson, he bought 10,000 acres of Government land at La Panza, at $1.25 per acre. They stocked it with 2,500 head of cattle, which he drove to Tulare and Buena Vista lakes, and thus saved them all, while others lost nearly all they had. In 1868, when he sold out, there were 9,000 or 10,000 head of cattle on the ranch, he could not tell how many. In 1859 he bought a half interest in the El Paso de Robles Hot Springs, and the one league of land embracing it, of his brother-in-law, D. B. Blackburn. They built the hotel and surrounding cottages as fast as they required them, and also, from time to time as their business grew, they increased the facilities of the place for bathing; and now the place as a health resort has grown in great favor throughout the State, and is known to many in the East. They have the largest bath-house in the State, and the hotel and cottages around have grown to be quite a village.

Mr. James and his partner are the founders of the now incorporated city of El Paso de Robles (the pass of oaks), generally called by the shorter phrase, Paso Robles. It began its rapid growth in 1887, and already has a nice park, fine brick business blocks, palatial residences, school-houses, churches, etc. His firm have now in process of construction one of the finest brick hotels in the county. It is 185 x 300 feet in dimensions, three stories and basement in height, and will be furnished with all modern improvements. The brick used in this building will number 500,000. The old hotel and cottages are directly in front, but they are to be removed when the space is devoted to hotel grounds. The establishment also fronts the park and will be a delightful place when completed.

Since coming here Mr. James has continued to be interested in stock-raising and farming. He has also been a stock-holder and director of the Bank of San Luis Obispo, in the steam flouring-mill of the same place, and other business enterprises. A sketch of his partner, already mentioned, also appears in this volume. They married sisters, at the same time and place, he choosing Miss Louisa Dunn, who was born in Sacramento, this State, the daughter of Patrick Dunn, of Irish ancestry, who came from Australia to California. Mr. and Mrs. James have seven children, all born in Paso Robles, viz.:— Mamie, William, Nellie, Lena, Charles, Carrie and Edward. Carrie and Charles are twins; Nellie is the wife of Edward Bennett, now Postmaster at that place; and the other children are still with their parents. They have a nice residence on a block reserved for that purpose. Mr. James was fittingly elected President of the first Board of Trustees, and continues to hold that position. He has also held the office of Supervisor for about ten years, and was elected a Representative to the State Legislature from his district in 1888, and this position he also holds. Although he has experienced an unusual number of hardships, during pioneer days, and has had so many heavy business cares for many years, he is still an active business man, taking great pride in the improvement and adornment of his pet little city. He is a member of the I. O. O. F. and of the Masonic order.

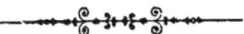

H. K. SNOW, Jr., a native son of the Golden West, was born in Vallejo, Solano County, September 5, 1865 His father, H. K. Snow, was born in Whitefield, New Hampshire, in 1833, and his grandfather, James Snow, was an Englishman who settled at Whitefield, New Hampshire, in an early day. They were prominent people there. Mr. Snow's mother, Cynthia O. (Downs) Snow, was born in Wisconsin. They had eight children, the subject of this sketch being the fourth. He was reared and educated at his native place, Vallejo, until he was twelve years of age, at which time the family moved to Santa Ana, now Orange County, where his father bought a ranch and engaged in the culture of oranges and grapes, and where he still resides. In 1887 they purchased 171 acres of land, one-half mile from New Jerusalem, Ventura County, where Mr. Snow is engaged in the culture of walnuts, having 100 acres of English walnut trees, all doing well. Between the trees they raise large crops of Lima beans and peanuts, one of the future industries of California. The rest of this ranch is devoted to nurseries, there being more than 50,000 trees of different kinds. They intend to do a large business in fruit and ornamental trees. They also grow some alfalfa and barley. A sightly residence, surrounded with flowers and shrubbery, is an attractive feature of this place.

Politically, Mr. Snow is affiliated with the Republican party. He is a member of the Tustin Lodge, I. O. O. F., and is a young man of fine business qualities.

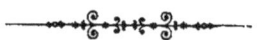

FRED A. EARLL was born in Shasta, Shasta County, California, May 13, 1857. His parents, Warner and Comelia (Scoville) Earll, were both natives of Onondaga County, New York. Warner Earll followed Fremont's trail to California in 1848, and was City Judge of Tehama for a number of years; he was also an Associate Justice on the Supreme Bench of Nevada. He was a prominent lawyer of California, residing at Shasta and Red Bluff for years. He also held the position of attorney for the Central Pacific Railroad, in Arizona. His three children were Arthur R., Fred A., and a daughter, A. H., who is now Mrs. Webb, and resides in Oakland, California. Arthur R. was a graduate of the Law School of California; was elected District Attorney of San Luis Obispo, and died three months after. Their father's death occurred in 1888.

The subject of this sketch attended St. Augustus College, and at the age of fifteen years, having obtained a good English education, he started out to work for himself, and since that time his education has been more of a practical character—obtained behind the desk. He worked for E. M. Derby & Co., lumber dealers, of Alameda, four years. He then engaged in business for himself, dealt in wood and coal, and did a thriving business; but, being anxious to make a fortune by quicker methods, he speculated in mining stocks, and lost his coal business. After that he went to

Arizona, and opened a stationery and cigar business, which he conducted three years; then removed to Ventura County, bought twenty acres of land, and, after planting an orchard, sold the property and returned to the lumber business. Saxby & Collins offered him the management of the lumber yards in San Buenaventura, which he accepted and conducted for two years. He then went to San Francisco and from there came to Paso Robles, to take charge of the warehouse, lumber yard, storage and shipping business at this point. At the time he came, November, 1886, there was nothing in the town. The railroad had just been built, and the station was in a box-car beside the track. Since then the shipping interests of the town have taken a great start. Shipments of wheat for the past year were about 9,000 tons. Mr. Earll has made real estate investments in the town.

He was married in October, 1879, to Miss Ida Barnes, a native of Dixon, Illinois, daughter of A. M. Barnes, of Ventura. Their union is blessed with two daughters, Bertha May, born in Arizona, and Helen, in Paso Robles.

Mr. Earll, being a native of California, took an active part in the organization of the Paso Robles Parlor, No. 122, Native Sons of the Golden West. They started with twenty-four members, composed largely of the best young business men of the town. Mr. Earll was elected its first president, and still holds that position of honor.

A. ATWOOD, a horticulturist of San San Luis Obispo County, was born in Androscoggin County, Maine, in 1828, of New England parents. After receiving a good common-school education at home he engaged in mechanical pursuits; later he entered the grocery business; in 1862 he came to California. For a number of years he was engaged in the manufacture of pumping machinery at San Francisco, and had a profitable trade. A serious catarrhal trouble compelled him to move from that city, and in 1876, after prospecting around for a year or so, he came to San Luis Obispo County, and settled on the property where he now resides, consisting of sixty-five acres, and located on the railroad between San Luis Obispo and Port Harford. He is eminently successful in fruit culture. At the county fairs he always captures some premiums. At one competition he took the first premium on several varieties of fruits. From a wild, unsettled country, when he first came to the ranch, the place has been changed to a finely developed piece of property. Mr. Atwood has a wife and one daughter, both natives of Maine.

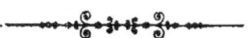

ISAAC H. BUNCE, a rancher of San Luis Obispo County, was born in Auburn, New York, December 24, 1831. On his father's farm he received his early training, and at the age of twenty-two he came to the golden center of the world's excitement, by the Panama route; but he had no luck whatever in his search for the shining nuggets, and he went to San Francisco and worked at his trade, carpentering, and a year afterward he began work on a saw-mill in Monterey County, the first mill of that kind in the county. He lived in Santa Cruz County for four years; and then, in the spring of 1858, he came to San Luis Obispo County, and worked at his trade at the county-seat for many years, being engaged in some of the most important structures of the city. He was for a time a member of the firm of Boland & Bunce. In 1870 he settled upon his present ranch near the oil wells. It is known as a part of the Avila place, and consists of twenty acres. In 1868 he met with a severe accident, falling from a building at Chorro, and he has not yet fully recovered from the effect.

August 22, 1862, he married Miss Juanita Avila, a daughter of Don Miguel Avila, and has nine children: Eliza, Lydia (now Mrs. B. L. Smythe), Charles, Henry J., Alfred Lyman, Martha, John, Minnie and Isaac William.

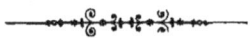

G. B. GAGLIARDO, the hotel-keeper at Port Harford, was born in Italy, January 18, 1853, came to California in the fall of 1869, and located in Columbia, Tuolumne County. For many years he engaged in mining. In 1881 Mr. Gagliardo, married Victoria Marré, of Jackson, Amador County, and has three children. In 1883 he came to San Luis Obispo County, since which time he has been conducting the hotel at Port Harford, owned by Luis Marré, and named Hotel Marré. It is a popular resort.

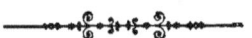

W. C. BENNETT, one of the prominent young business men of El Paso de Robles, was born in Van Buren County, Michigan, July 7, 1864, the son of G. H. and Mary (Brain) Bennett, natives of England, who came to Michigan in 1855, the father engaging in contracting and building until 1887, when he retired from business, and the family came to California; they now reside in El Paso de Robles. Of their seven children six are living. The subject of this sketch was educated in Michigan and learned the foundry business, following it for five years; then he was two years in the drug business in the East; and in 1885 came to Tulare County, California, and managed a drug store there for three years; and in 1888 he finally came to El Paso de Robles, where he has since been engaged in the same trade. He started here in the brick store on the corner of Twelfth and Pine streets; he afterward bought a lot on the corner of Twelfth and Park streets and erected a nice drug store building, where he is enjoying a fine patronage. He has doctors' offices well arranged and furnished in the rear portion of the building, and they are now occupied by Dr. Glass. Mr. Bennett's brother, R. W., is his assistant in the business and is an accomplished druggist.

Mr. Bennett was married in 1889, to Miss Dove McCubbin, a native of Illinois and a daughter of T. C. McCubbin, a capitalist. Mrs. Bennett is a member of the Christian Church and of the Rebekah-degree Lodge of the I. O. O. F., and also of the O. E. S.; while Mr. Bennett is a Congregationalist, a Republican, a Master Mason and also a member of the O. E. S. Both Mr. Bennett and his father have built delightful residences near each other in a sightly portion of the town, and they are highly esteemed members of the community. They have recently bought one of the finest fruit ranches in San Luis Obispo County, and also own real estate in Tulare County.

OTTO SHACKELFORD is a native son of the Golden West, and is one of the prominent young business men of El Paso de Robles. He was born in San Francisco October 7, 1869, and is a son of R. M. Shackelford, a native of Kentucky and a prominent California business man. Their ancestors for generations were residents of Kentucky. Mr. Shackelford's mother, *nee* Mary M. L. Questen, is a native of Wisconsin, he being the only child. He was reared and educated in San Mateo and in the city of Hollister; and for some time was book-keeper for his father. In 1886 he came to El Paso de Robles, and was engaged in the warehouse, grain and lumber business until September, 1889, when, with others, he organized the hardware and agricultural implement firm of Bennett, Shackelford & Le Blanc, the principal store of the kind in the town.

Mr. Shackelford's religious opinions are in accordance with the Methodist doctrines. He is a young man of fine business ability, and is held in the highest esteem by his fellow citizens. His prospects for a successful business career are most promising.

DR. J. H. GLASS, El Paso de Robles. In the early part of the seventeenth century Scotland furnished her full quota of hardy sons to settle and reclaim a portion of America, by laying the foundation of a free and independent people. They were self-reliant, persevering and possessed of a high degree of common sense. The progenitor of the Glass family came from Scotland and settled in one of the colonies of the mother country. His son, Hiram Glass, was born in Tennessee, and his son, Dr. Wilson H. Glass, was born in Wytheville, Virginia, where for years he followed the practice of medicine. There he married Miss Martha J. Minter, also a Virginian, the daughter of Charles Minter, and a descendant of one of the old Virginia families. They removed to Kentucky, where their children were brought up. Notwithstanding the Southern birth and education of his parents and ancestors, Dr. Wilson H. Glass was an avowed Abolitionist; and when the great civil war was sprung upon the country, compelling all men to take sides, he tendered his services to the United States Government and served as Surgeon in the Union Army with distinction until the close of the war. Mrs. Glass' youngest brother, L. C. Minter, was a Captain of the Eighth Kentucky Volunteer Infantry, and while commanding his company at the battle of Stone River he received a wound which resulted fatally. He was buried by the roadside, and six years afterward his grave was identified, the remains were brought home and interred in the family burying ground.

Dr. Glass, our subject, was the second of his parents' four children. He was born in Kentucky, July 28, 1857, and was brought up in his native State, studied medicine under his father's instructions, attended a medical college course at Keokuk, Iowa, and practiced his profession six years in his native town, in connection with his father. He then attended the College of Physicians and Surgeons at Baltimore, graduated in 1884, practiced two years longer at his Kentucky home, in 1886 went to Florida and thence came to Santa Clara County, this State, and in a short time, in 1887, to El Paso de Robles. He had been through the county of San Luis Obispo in 1886, and became favorably impressed with the character of the country. The building of the railroad satisfied him that Paso Robles was destined to be a good town, and he accordingly located here; and from that start he has enjoyed a good patronage in his practice as a physician, which he deserves, on account of his moral integrity and reliability. He has bought city property and built upon it a pleasant residence, and is identified with all the interests of the town.

He was married March 29, 1885, to Miss Mettie Hogg, a native of his own town in

Kentucky and daughter of Stephen P. Hogg, a lawyer. They have one child, Carl, born in Santa Clara County, April 23, 1886. Mrs. Glass is a member of the Christian Church, and is the present Worthy Matron of the Eastern Star Chapter. The Doctor is a Freemason, an Odd Fellow and a Republican.

ALDEN MARCH BOYD, a rancher in Santa Ynez Valley, is one of the promoters of the olive industry of the Alamo Pintado Valley, whose beautiful "Rancho de los Olivos" lies gently elevated, south of the town of Los Olivos. He was born in Albany, New York, in 1863. Much of Mr. Boyd's life previous to coming to California was passed abroad. He spent two winters at Nassau, in the Bahama Islands, and made two trips to Europe, where a large part of his education was received; on his return he attended the Phillips Academy, of Andover, preparatory to entering college. Owing to failing health, he gave up college and went to Europe, and on his return in 1883, he came direct to California, spending one winter at San Francisco, and in travel about the State. The summer of 1884 he passed with his family in the Montecito Valley, remaining until August, 1885, when he purchased his present ranch in the Santa Ynez Valley. On the place was a small house, and about four acres in a variety of fruits. Mr. Boyd immediately began improving his ranch with a view of establishing an olive grove. In 1876 he planted 2,500 trees, adding 2,500 more in 1877, all of the Mission varieties, coming from the nursery of Mr. Hayne, of the Montecito Valley. The trees began bearing from two years of planting, and the present year promises a very satisfactory crop. He has about seventy-five acres in olive trees.

In November, 1888, Mr. Boyd was elected Supervisor for the Third District, which covers the Santa Ynez Valley.

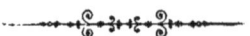

ARATA BROTHERS.—The brothers, F. L. and R. J. Arata, composing the firm of Arata Brothers, were born in Santa Barbara. Their father, Juan Arata, was formerly an extensive stock-raiser, keeping as many as 3,000 head of cattle. He was also a prominent merchant about 1857, continuing for several years. The brothers were educated in the public schools, and F. L., the senior member of the firm, obtained his education at the Franciscan College, then located at the old mission building in Santa Barbara city. In 1877 he began his mercantile life as clerk with L. M. Kaiser & Co., of Guadaloupe, remaining with them until 1882, when he came to Los Alamos, with a member of the same firm; the firm name being A. Weill & Co. Mr. Arata also bought an interest in the drug store, in 1882, continuing under the name of Walker & Arata. Mr. Walker conducted the business until February, 1886, when Mr. Arata bought his interest and has since conducted the business, aided by a druggist's assistant. Mr. Arata clerked for Weill & Co. until January, 1887, and in September, 1887, the firm of Arata Bros. & Co. was established, F. L. being associated with his brother R. J. Arata and W. F. Wickenden. In October, 1888, the brothers bought the interest of Mr. Wickenden, and have since continued alone.

R. J. Arata began his clerkship with O. I. Weil of Lompoc, in 1880, continuing until 1884, when he came to Los Alamos. He carried on a grocery, cigar and fruit business until the establishing of the above firm. They carry a general merchandise stock, keeping all supplies necessary to the family or ranch, in hardware and other requirements. They also own ranch property aggregating 500 acres, four miles from town, where they do general farming, and breed horses, cattle and hogs; they also own town property.

REV. P. F. FARRELLY, the resident pastor at Santa Ynez Mission, was born near the town of Virginia, County Cavan, Ireland, March 10, 1859. He was educated in the College of All Hallows, Dublin, and was ordained at the college by Bishop Crane, of Australia, on June 24, 1883, and in September, of same year, left for the United States. He then came to California, being first stationed with Father Marron, at Watsonville, Santa Cruz County, where he remained until 1886. He was next assistant to Father Ubach, of San Diego, for six months, afterward at Santa Cruz with Father MacNamee. During Bishop Moran's visit to Europe, Father Farrelly was nine months pastor at Watsonville, and on October 15, 1887, he was appointed as rector of Santa Ynez, Lompoc and surrounding towns.

His parish extends from Point Concepcion to Santa Barbara, and from Santa Maria to the sea; his residence is at the old Santa Ynez Mission, which was established by Father Estevan Tapiz on the 17th of September, 1804. He then translated the Spanish catechism into the Indian vernacular. Father Tapiz was a Catalonian by birth, and a man of great learning. The Mission was built at the expense of the Catholic Monarch, Charles IV, King of Spain and the Indies. The Mission was founded by the College Missionaries of San Fernando, Mexico, and was endowed by King Charles IV, who gave full administration of the possessions to the missionaries. It stands on an elevation, overlooking the beautiful valley of the same name, and was called by the Indians "Alajulapu, which means "higher," as the mission points to a higher life. In the day of founding at the feast of the Stigma (wound) of St. Francis, September 17, 1804, Father Tapiz, President of the Missions, associated with the missionaries from San Fernando College, first blessed the water according to the right of the Catholic Church. He then proceeded to the ceremony of blessing the Mission and the buildings, dedicating to God our Lord, and then erected the big cross on the land, singing the Litany of the Saints. After that he celebrated the mass in a brush tent that had been prepared with all possible decency, in which he preached to several white persons, among whom was President Raymundo Carrillo, Commandant of the Presidio at Santa Barbara, and a great multitude of natives from the missions of Purisima and Santa Barbara. Afterward, they sang the Te Deum, and other hymns and psalms to the greatest honor of God and His Holy Name, and the good of their souls. The first missionaries were Father Antonio Calzada and Father José Romaldo Guttierez, and that day were baptized twenty-seven Indians and children. Father Carrillo was sponsor for the twelve boys who were first baptized, and Doña Francisca, wife of José Maria Ortega, for the fifteen little girls. The mission was established, because of the large number of Indians in the valley, and the great distance between the two missions, Purissima and Santa Barbara; the college grant was given to the bishops in 1844 to aid them in establishing an ecclesiastical seminary for the education of students aspiring to the priesthood, and children. The college was first established at the mission, in September,

1845, by Father Sanchez, Father Romano and others. After college buildings were constructed it was moved to them in 1863, and continued until 1864, when the diocese was divided.

WILLIAM L. BEEBEE.—Of the pioneers who came to California before the advent of the gold-seekers, but few remain to tell the tale of that interesting period when the western coast of the American continent was to most people an unknown land, yet one is occasionally met with here and there throughout the State, and, indeed, rarely one may yet be found in business and mercantile pursuits. An example in point is the gentleman whose name heads this sketch, who has been, since the pioneer days, one of the most prominent figures of commercial circles in this entire region. A brief *resumé* of some of the salient features in his life therefore becomes valuable and indeed essential in a volume of this nature.

He is a native of Oswego, New York, born November 21, 1829, his parents being William L. and Mary (Douglas) Beebee, both of whom were natives of New York, the mother born in Onondaga County and the father probably in New York city. The latter was a merchant by vocation, who, in 1834, removed with his family to Cleveland, Ohio, where he contracted malaria, with results which proved fatal about a year after his arrival there. His widow, with her family, consisting of our subject, a younger brother and a sister, then went back to New York to live with her father. They resided at Auburn and at Skaneateles, but most of the time at the former town, and in these places William L. Beebee was reared to his fourteenth year. The Beebees of New York and Philadelphia, bullion and stock brokers—one of whom, Samuel J., was the founder of the New York Merchants' Exchange—were half-brothers of his father, and the lad of fourteen went to the Quaker City to commence a business career in their office in that city.

He remained with them about two years in this office in the two cities, and then an event occurred that changed the whole trend of his life. Among the appointments made by James K. Polk after his accession to the Presidential chair, was that of William G. Morehouse as consul to Valparaiso; and, having an opportunity to accompany that gentleman to the scene of his labors, our subject, who was by no means averse to a little adventure, readily availed himself of the chance, his uncle providing for his comfort and convenience on the trip as far as possible. In November, 1846, he sailed on the bark Hortensia, from Baltimore, her expected route being to the South American city by way of Cape Horn, and his fellow passenger, besides Consul Morehouse and his wife and child, being Henry D. Cook, who afterwards became Governor of Washington under President Grant, and two young Californians. The bark proceeded on her journey without an especially noteworthy incident until about the latitude of the Bermudas, when she encountered a terrific storm, and was tossed about at its mercy for six days—days of ceaseless agony to those on board. When at last the war of the elements abated, the vessel was found to be off the northeast of the Bermudas. The storm had played sad havoc with the bark, which was left without masts, her deck swept away of everything and with a hole in her bow, a condition of things which called for prompt action to insure her reaching a port in safety. They rigged up a jury mast, and the nearest land they could reach in their condition with the prevailing winds was the Island of St. Thomas, in the West Indies. The vessel's head was turned in that direction, and the island reached in safety. There the passengers learned for the first time that the British had a regular line of steamers plying between Southampton and Chagres, while on the Pacific side a connecting line furnished steam transportation between Panama and Valparaiso. Singularly enough, the fact did not seem to be known at that time either to the United States Government or the merchants of New York engaged in the foreign trade, a condition of ignorance as surprising as it seems to have been complete.

At the island of St. Thomas a little Boston pilot boat was chartered, and the party proceeded to Chagres, availing themselves of the information thus fortunately gained. The trip from Chagres to Panama occupied about a week, the distance from Chagres to Gorgona being accomplished by poling up the Chagres River, where they hired mules and rode to Panama. After waiting about ten days at that place they took passage on the regular steamer for Valparaiso, which was reached without special incident. Young Beebee found the city full of life and business, but after looking around a good deal saw that there was nothing there in the way of employment or business opportunities to suit him, though he could easily have obtained situations at office work had he so desired. However, he spent some five or six months in Chili, principally in Valparaiso, though visiting occasionally Santiago and other places.

While in South America the war of the United States with Mexico was probably the principal event engrossing the attention of the world, and our subject was not lacking in appreciation of the opportunities which in the future would be afforded by that portion of the old possessions of Mexico known as California. One day there appeared in the port Valparaiso the United States storeship Southampton, whose officers included among their number Lieutenant Commander Thornton and Executive Officer Worden, afterward the world-renowned commander of the Monitor. Young Beebee, who made his headquarters about the American Consulate, there met and formed the acquaintance of the officers of the Southampton, who, when they learned that he was not exactly satisfied with his stay in the Chilean City, asked him to accompany them on their cruise to California as a passenger. Of this opportunity he was not slow to avail himself, a visit to that comparatively unknown land having just the tinge of adventure that suited his disposition. On the way he became sufficiently acquainted with Executive Officer Worden to learn that that gentleman was very much disgusted with seafaring life, indeed, so much so that it did not then seem he would be in the service when the time came for him to achieve never-dying fame by his prominent connection with the naval duel between the Monitor and the Merrimac, which revolutionized the naval warfare and the service of naval architecture.

On the Southampton there was besides Mr. Beebee but another passenger, G. D. Brewerton, a lieutenant in Stevenson's New York Regiment, which, by the way, was en route just ahead of them. August 25, 1847, the vessel put into the harbor of Monterey and joined there the squadron under command of Commodore Shubrick, operating in connection with the land forces under Colonel Mason.

Mr. Beebee landed from the ship, and looking about Monterey found the place to be the scene of considerable sickness, and the funeral of a lieutenant in progress. He went hunting in the vicinity of the site now occupied by the Hotel del Monterey, and from the exposure of the hunt was taken down, after he returned to the ship, with what was known as the Monterey fever, and after that the physician on board could not allow him to go ashore again. Wishing to go to San José, where his friend Cook had preceded him, he obtained the sought-for opportunity aboard a little vessel called the Malacadel, which had been recently purchased at auction by an old shipper. Having a nephew about our subject's age, the vessel's owner invited him to go along as company, and the offer was gladly accepted. He packed his duds, bade good-bye to his friends on the Southampton and boarded the Malacadel, which set sail for Sausalito. The vessel was almost constantly disabled, and it was well in September before she reached her destination. Then all vessels entering the bay went first to Sausalito for water, Yerba Buena being practically without a fresh water supply. Arriving at Yerba Buena eventually, our subject went ashore. There he met one or two young men whom he had fallen in with in Panama, and who by their conversation there had first turned his attention to California. Their names were respectively Ruckle and Farnham, the latter of whom was subsequently a well-known figure and the author of a widely circulated work on California. Meeting Joseph S. Ruckle in Yerba Buena, Mr. Beebee learned that he and his former fellow-passenger, Henry D. Cook, were in partnership in business at San José, and he accepted an offer to accompany Mr. Ruckle to San José, where he entered their employ as clerk. The incumbency of their position did not prevent him from taking a trip anywhere throughout the State at any time his inclination led him to desire a change and recreation.

California, inhabited as it was by the generous ranch owners and their help, was a land of ideal hospitality, and one could travel for a year throughout its length and breadth without the opportunity to expend anything for entertainment. If it were to remain such forever there was no necessity for a care for the future. It was almost a pity to break up such a condition, even to make way for the march of modern improvement, with its ruthless disregard for sentiment.

On one of these trips of vacation from the store he accompanied a party of Mexicans on an elk hunt as far away as the San Joaquin River, they seeking the animals for their hide and tallow. He also often rode to Monterey and to Yerba Buena, and he saw in its primal state the future great commercial city of San Francisco, its few streets as yet untrodden by the feet of the gold-hunters, who were to make for California a new history. While with others he foresaw that a great commercial center was to spring up on the bay of San Francisco, yet it was at that time an almost unreasonable stretch of imagination to locate it on the sand hills by the bleak mountain side, where fate had mapped out its streets and blocks, while much more desirable appearing sites seemed ready made at other points along the bay, and while many of the shrewdest men of the day had selected Benicia as the site of the future metropolis of the Pacific. Mr. Beebee recalls, as incidental to the horseback rides he was accustomed to take at that day from San José to the bay, that the only disagreeable portion of the trip was the last three or four miles, where the tall, narrow mounds of sand impeded the view and obstructed the way so that it was necessary to pursue an extremely tortuous course in the latter part of the journey to Yerba Buena. Yet, where these very sand hills made life miserable for the traveler of that day, now lies the most valuable portion of San Francisco; where property is valued at thousands of dollars to the foot, and the sand of early times is to-day but a memory, cannot the wise men of to-day now understand why the bright young man of '48 did not lay the foundation for fortunes of millions by buying up all the fifty-vara lots they could get at the regular price of $16.75. Mr. Beebee did become the owner of one of these lots, and when in 1849 he sold it for $1,600, he was looked upon as a very shrewd and fortunate man of business.

At last the discovery of gold by Marshall occurred, and the news reached San José through a messenger who passed through on his way to Monterey to exhibit results of the find to the Governor. Our subject was among the early ones to go to the mines, prompted in this course as much by love of adventure as a desire for personal aggrandizement. At the mines he had what would be looked upon as excellent success, though not caring particularly to accumulate the sudden riches that one might suppose there was a chance for. As an illustration of this lack of greed for gold then existing among some of the young men, an incident not devoid of an amusing side may be related. One day, on which the sun shone with unusual intensity, our subject was reclining, in company with a young blacksmith, under the grateful shade of a tree. About three o'clock in the afternoon, the temperature having begun to moderate, the blacksmith proposed to Mr. Beebee that they resume prospecting. The proposition being satisfactory, work with the pick began in a shaded place, and before sundown our subject had washed out nearly $400 worth of gold! As a sequel to a typical tale of the time, it may be stated that a couple of days later the pair were seeking new and better diggings!

In the fall Mr. Beebee left the mines and went back as far as Yerba Buena, where he was taken sick with the Sacramento fever. The winter passed without incident other than the excitement of the new life, caused by the fever, and in May, 1849, Mr. Beebee left the scene of his early experience in the northern counties for San Luis Obispo, in company with Samuel A. Pollard, the present city clerk of this place, who had been down in this country before. Messrs. Beebee and Pollard opened a store for the sale of general merchandise, putting up the first store building, an adobe, which still stands on the corner of Monterey and Chorro streets, adjoining Sinsheimer's store. The conditions of trade at that early day were vastly different from those existing at present. Custom came to this store from the ranches all round, some as remote as forty miles away. After two or three years in merchandising, which was somewhat unprofitable, Mr. Beebee withdrew from the firm and engaged in ranching at a place eight miles south of San Luis Obispo, where he continued in the cattle business until the dry year of 1864–'65. During that drouth his 1,500 head of cattle lay down and died, and he experienced a great financial set-back. It was not long afterward that he sold his ranch of 1,200 acres to Steele Bros., whose property it yet remains.

Meantime, however, Mr. Beebee had entered the realm of politics. He was one of the few Republicans who resided hereabouts at the outbreak of the Rebellion, and he was one of the principals in the movement to build up and crystalize Union sentiment, organizing a strong Republican constituency with the aid of the Spanish recruits. He was appointed by Governor Stanford as Judge of San Luis Obispo County, and having served a year by virtue of the commission he was elected to succeed himself, and re-elected at the expiration of that term. His part in building up the Republican party in this county was an active one, but he has since excluded politics, and gives it only the attention necessary in the exercise of his privileges as a citizen.

Having sold his ranch, he moved into town, and in 1869, in company with John Harford, who owned the landing facilities, and L. Schwartz, of Santa Cruz, who resided in the timber district, he embarked in the lumber business, Mr. Schwartz doing the buying, Mr. Harford the shipping, while Mr. Beebee did the selling and managed the business. Mr. Harford afterward retired from the firm and went to Washington Territory, where he now resides, and Messrs. Beebee and Schwartz have since carried on the trade, the former having exclusive management of the business for some ten or fifteen years, when, having placed it on a permanent footing, he gradually began to retire from the aggressive part he had so long taken in its conduct. Some idea of the magnitude of the operations of this house may be gathered when it is stated that their trade has in the past reached all the way from 5,000,000 to 10,000,000 feet of lumber per year, they supplying the trade to the remote interior. All these years they have practically controlled the lumber trade of this part, and have had extensive interests in the shipping which touched at Port Harford. They now own yards at Cayucos, where they are interested in the wharf as members of the firm of James Cass & Co. of Santa Maria and at San Luis Obispo.

Mr. Beebee has independently large shipping connections, being extensively interested in fine vessels engaged in the coast and foreign trade, one of which, a fine schooner, bears his name. These, however, are but a portion of his investments, among the others of which may be mentioned banking, he being vice-president of the First National Bank of San Luis Obispo, and a stockholder in the Bank of San Luis Obispo, of which he was one of the organizers. He has some agricultural interests as a partner, and some entirely on his own account, among the latter a dairy ranch of 500 acres, between San Luis and Cayucos, and fifteen miles from the former.

Having gotten his various business properties under control, Mr. Beebee has allowed his former taste for travel to revive to some extent, and in 1886 visited Alaska, following this in the succeeding year with a tour of Europe, occupying six months of constant travel and sight-seeing. In 1888 he made a trip to Yellowstone Park, and drank in the beauties of that favored center of nature's fairest phases.

He has been twice married. His first wife, whom he married here, was Miss Alida St. Clair, who died in 1878. By this marriage there were two children, of whom one is living. viz.: William D., aged fourteen, in 1890; the other, Addie B., having died at the age of seven years. Mr. Beebee's present wife was formerly Miss Arletta S. Beswick, and to her he was united in marriage in November, 1879.

Mr. Beebee is a good type of the successful, spirited pioneer of California. Coming here long before the tide of immigration set in this direction, he has, ever since reaching manhood's estate, held his place well in the front rank of business men, through all the various changes of condition and circumstances which have taken place since the early days. He has seen California in all her various phases from the days when he rode horseback over her great ranches until a new civilization has grown up and she occupies a place among the most favored and most advanced of the States of the Union. As a business man, he couples with aggressiveness and shrewdness a spirit of toleration and moderation which goes far to explain his popularity socially. His only affiliation with social or fraternal bodies, however, is that of his connection with the San Francisco Society of California Pioneers, of which he has long been a member.

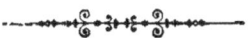

W. S. LEWIS, dealer in hardware and agricultural implements at El Paso Robles, was born in Santa Rosa, Sonoma County, this State, August 12, 1865. His father, I. M. Lewis, is a native of Missouri, and his mother, whose maiden name was Elizabeth Horn, was a native of North Carolina. He is the third in a family of seven children; was educated in the public schools, and was brought up on a farm in San Benito County, California. When the town of Paso Robles was begun, he started in business there, in 1887, in cigars, tobacco and fruit. A year and a half afterward he sold out and embarked in the hardware business, as a member of the firm of Holiday & Lewis; six months after that he sold his interest to a Mr. Fletcher and opened a store for the sale of agricultural implements and hardware, which business he still continues, and it is growing. His trade extends forty miles to the east. Mr. Lewis is also agent for four large insurance companies,—the Hartford, North American, Commercial of California, and Liberty of New York. He is not a member of any of the fraternal organizations, and in political matters he is a Democrat. At the last city election he was chosen Treasurer of Paso Robles, against the cashier of the Bank of Paso Robles, by a majority of three. Commencing without capital, Mr. Lewis has succeeded finely in business, having accumulated his present handsome property by industry, honesty and economy.

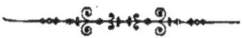

NATHAN ELLIOTT, a prominent business man of El Paso de Robles, came to California with his family in 1864, and has been a continuous resident of the State for the last quarter of a century. He was born near Greensboro, Henry County, Indiana, January 21, 1835, of English and Scotch ancestry. His father, Obadiah Elliott, a native of North Carolina, removed to Indiana in 1833, a pioneer there, entering land and bringing up a family, and remaining there until his death. He was a Quaker and a zealous Abolitionist. His wife, whose maiden name was Armella Hinshaw, a very pious lady of the Society of Friends, was also a native of North Carolina, and daughter of Seth Hinshaw, a prosperous and prominent free-labor merchant of Southern slavery times. The subject of this sketch, the fifth in the family of eight children, was brought up on a farm and learned the trade of brickmaking and bricklaying, but soon embarked in mercantile pursuits, which he conducted with success in Indiana and Iowa until 1864, when he sought the Pacific coast. The first seven years here he resided in Woodland, Yolo County, engaged in the manufacture of brick and in contracting. In 1873 he removed to San Francisco, where for fourteen years he drove a prosperous fruit and merchandise commission business; and finally, in 1886, he came to El Paso de Robles, as the town was just starting. He attended the first sale of town lots, and made purchases, subsequently of several blocks, and started the first brick-yard in the place, and has manufactured the brick for nearly all the brick buildings in town, including the brick hotel, which required 1,500,000 brick. He erected some buildings himself and has just broken ground for a large business block. Only three and a half years ago, when he first came here, it was only a cattle ranch; he has been an important factor in building up this pretty place. The city is now incorporated, and has one of the most palatial hotels, and a bath house on the coast; a large flouring-mill with roller process and a capacity of 150 to 200 barrels of flour per day, two school-houses and four churches, a good system of water works, electric lights, etc. Mr. Elliott is a Freemason, and both himself and wife are members of the O. E. S.

He was married in 1855, to Miss Emily I. Haskit, a native of Indiana, and daughter of Thomas and Sarah Haskit. Of their four children three are living and are married: Charles F., is a merchant of El Paso de Robles; Mary S. is the wife of Charles H. Arnold, and resides in San Francisco; Laura is now Mrs. S. P. Stephens, and resides in El Paso de Robles; the one now deceased, Sarah Armella, was a star in the family, and much loved and esteemed by all. The grandchildren are five in number and are: Pearl H. and Meta Jane, Elliott and Susa V, and Elliott Stephens and Armella E. Arnold.

C. JAMESON, one of the prominent young business men of El Paso de Robles, was born July 6, 1860, in Providence, Rhode Island. Thomas Jameson, his father, came from Scotland to America when a boy and now resides in Monterey County, this State. He married Miss Ellen Curran, a native of Scotland and a descendant of the Irish Currans who left Ireland soon after the Irish rebellion. His parents' family were three children, of whom he is the youngest. He was but seven years of age when he came with the family to California. In completing his education he took a thorough business course at the business college of San Francisco. He learned the tinners' trade and opened a shop at Castroville, and carried it on four years; selling out, he came to El Paso de Robles and in 1888 bought out a firm dealing in stoves, hardware and tinware, and he has since continued the business, enjoying a good patronage. He has orders from a distance of thirty miles. He is a Republican in his political views, a Master Mason and is highly esteemed by his fellow townsmen.

He was married in 1884, to Miss Emma Trafton, a native of Watsonville, California, and a daughter of George A. Trafton, a grain dealer of that place. Mr. and Mrs. Jameson have two children: Mabel, born in Castroville, and Alma, born in El Paso de Robles.

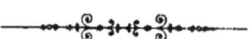

M. ROCHIN, of Los Alamos, was born March 19, 1822, in the State of Sonora, Mexico, and at the age of fifteen years moved to Guadalupe y Calvo, State of Chihuahua, Mexico, which is a nice, new, rich mining town, and there he followed the trade of goldsmith, separating gold from silver and silver from lead,—a trade he learned from one of his uncles, who was one of the best mechanics in the country. He also engaged in buying gold and silver for a merchant there, for a large commission, as he had no opposition, making sometimes as much as $200 to $250 a week; but he was young and inexperienced, and the money went out some way about as fast as it came in. In time, of course, opposition in his business sprang up, and he could not make more than any one else.

In December, 1849, when the California gold fever was at the highest and business in his place dull, he came to California, landing at San Fransisco. He left home December 2, went to Mazatlan on muleback, arriving there on the 9th, and then found that all the berths on steamers were taken for two to three months ahead. He had therefore to wait for the first sailing vessel. Soon a little German schooner came along, and he and fifty other Mexicans and fourteen Americans embarked upon it, being all that it could carry; but it was a fleet vessel. He and an American gentleman and his family and six other persons took all the berths that the vessel had. They arrived at San Francisco January 1, 1850, making a quicker trip than had ever before been made from that point by a sailing vessel. He went direct to the mines, and for three years was engaged all through the mining section, in every occupation which the district afforded, having his "ups and downs," as has been the experience of all miners. In 1853 he went to Los Angeles, where he passed one year. In 1854 he came to Santa Barbara, where he began what has since proven a very extensive stock experience. He began by renting land and keeping native stock of cattle, and in 1875 started the breeding of fine horses. He commenced his herd by purchasing forty picked mares from the stock of Dr. Richard Den and thirty from Mr. Ruiz, of Santa Barbara County; in 1873 was said to have owned more horses than any other man in the county. In 1873 he sold 200 choice mares to Sepulveda, of Los Angeles. In 1875 he traded 200 mares far the stallion "Newry," who was a full brother to Norfolk, and fleet runner, and bred by Mr. Alexander, of Kentucky. Mr. Rochin lost "Newry" in 1883, through the burning of one of his stables. He now keeps three stallions,—Antioch, Don Ramon and Captain Martinez, - and breeds for both running and trotting, having forty choice mares. Since 1876 Mr. Rochin has given special attention to the breeding of fine cattle, and his herd averages about 1,500 head.

Mr. Rochin was married at Los Angeles, in 1853, to Miss Lorenza Ordaz, a native of California. She died January 1, 1889, leaving one daughter. Mr. Rochin bought a ranch of 1,250 acres near Lompoc, in April, 1877, where he kept his horses, but sold again in 1880, feeling that it was cheaper to rent than to purchase. He has since been a large renter, also owning considerable city property in Santa Barbara and Los Alamos. He has always had the reputation of dealing conscientiously, and of breeding the best that could be obtained.

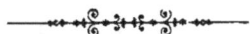

FRIDOLIN HARTMAN.—Among the early residents, prominent citizens and business men at San Buenaventura, we find the subject of this sketch. As his name indicates, Mr. Fridolin Hartman was born in Bavaria, Germany, and he dates his birth February 2, 1844, his parents being Bavarians. He was reared and educated in his native country. At the age of twenty-one he traveled in Austria and France, and was in Paris when war was declared with Germany. He came to the United States, landing in New York August 26, 1870. He first went to Philadelphia, then to Pittsburg, and on to St. Louis, Missouri, where he accepted a situation as foreman in a malt house. He next went to Kansas City, then to Denver, Colorado, and from there to Sacramento, spending a year and a half in the city brewery at Sacramento. Then he went to San Francisco, and, after spending two or three months there, he came to Ventura, in 1873, where he accepted a position in Mr. Greenwood's brewery. It was then a little wooden shanty, and, after working a year, he bought the property. He was so successful in his business that, two years later, he built the present two-story brick brewery.

Mr. Hartman saw the desirability of owning real estate in a growing county like Ventura and in the city of Ventura, so he has made a number of investments. He bought lands, which he subdivided and sold, and in this way his property has accumulated. He became the owner of eighty feet on Main Street, extending the whole length of the block on Palm Street. On this he built a commodious residence. Seeing the need of a larger hotel in Ventura than the town possessed, he took stock for the purpose of building one. His lot on Main street being a central position, he put it in as stock, and Anacapa Hotel was erected upon it. This building is a very good one and would do credit to any city. It is 80 x 130 feet, is three stories high, and contains 100 well planned, spacious rooms, lighted by electricity and furnished in good style. The building has a mansard roof, and under veranda on Main and Palm streets, the whole length and width of the buiding. When it was opened in 1888, it was crowded with guests, and has since been a popular hotel. Mr. Hartman has since invested in the stock of the company until he owns the controlling interest in the whole property, and is now proprietor of the hotel. He also owns, and is conducting a ranch of 300 acres, about three miles north of the town. This property he has improved by planting twenty-five acres in walnuts, also a large number of all kinds of trees, both deciduous and citrus. A portion of the farm is devoted to corn, wheat, barley and beans, and the rest is in pasture. Another piece of town property he owns is 100 feet front on the south side of Main Street, between Palm and Figueroa streets.

Mr. Hartman was united in marriage, in 1874, to Miss Katherine Kaufman, a native of Minnesota. Her father, Michael Kaufman, came to the United States in 1820, and in 1849, with an ox team, crossed the plains to California. In crossing the plains, their company had a convoy of soldiers, which escorted them until it was thought they were out of danger. After the soldiers left them they were attacked by the Indians. Two men were killed and one of the women captured. They made every effort to regain the woman, but failed. Mr. and Mrs. Hartman have had eleven children, all born in Ventura, in their present home, and all are living except one. Those living are Ludwig, Theresia, Fridoline, Karl, Katie, Anna, Lena, George, Fanny and Willy. The whole family are members of the Catholic Church. Mr. Hartman is a Democrat, and has three times been elected to the office of City Trustee. He resigned his trusteeship when he was elected a Supervisor of the town. He has served in this office four years, and was chairman of the Board of Supervisors. During his term of service he was strongly in favor of improvements. The addition to the court-house was made, and the substantial brick jail and the hospital were erected. Mr. Hartman's success in life would indicate that he is a good financier

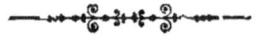

ABERNETHY BROS. are the leading livery and feed stable men of El Paso de Robles, and they are also prominent in the rearing of horses and cattle. The three brothers were born in the north part of the

County Tipperary, Ireland,—John in 1848, Edward in 1849 and Joseph in 1851. Edward came to America in 1868, Joseph in 1869 and John in 1873. They took up Government land, 480 acres, in Monterey County, built upon it a residence, etc., and raised stock and grain for seven years, when they sold out and came to their present place of residence. Here they bought lots and erected the buildings they occupy, their establishment being known as the Fashion Stables. They have ten carriages and thirty-five head of horses. They also have a ranch, where they are raising cattle and horses, of which John is in charge, while Joseph and Edward conducts the business in town. They own a fine French-Canadian Messenger horse and several valuable brood mares, and they are raising some good horses. In their political views these gentlemen are Democratic, and in religious matters they were brought up in the doctrines of the Established Church of England. Edward Abernethy is married and has five children.

STANLEY UTTER is a native of the Empire State, and dates his birth November 11, 18—. His father, T. L. Utter, is also a native of New York, his ancestors being English, but for two generations having resided in New York. His mother, Frances A. (Wilson) Utter, was a native of New York, as also was her father, Jeremiah Wilson, her ancestors, too, being English. Mr. Utter's father was a Union soldier in the late war. The subject of this sketch is the second child of a family of three sons and two daughters. His education was obtained chiefly in the public schools, later taking a course in the Curtis Business College, in Minneapolis. He began a fruit, confectionery and tobacco business in that place and continued the business very successfully for four years. His health failing at this time and being desirous of a change of location, he was influenced in deciding on California as his future home by reading, in the San Francisco *Chronicle*, a description of San Luis Obispo County. The fine springs, the new railroad, the central location of El Paso de Robles, and the delightful climate, were the attractions which brought him to this sunny land; and his expectations have been fully realized, both in the growth of the place and also in the improvement of his health. When he arrived the railroad had just been completed. The whole business of the town was done in the old "trap" where the hose cart is now kept. It contained a general stock of provisions, groceries, hardware and drugs, and also the postoffice. The change that has come over the town, in this respect, is marvelous; its many nice brick blocks, with fine stocks of merchandise, show a wonderful change in three years. Mr. Utter bought a block, corner of Twelfth and Olive streets, and at once commenced the erection of three cottages. They were completed in two months, and he moved his family into one and rented the others. He also bought a barley mill and engine, and has been doing the crushing for this section of the country, and in this way has become acquainted with most of the people in the county. He purchased 172 acres of land, and has since sold twenty-five acres at double what it cost him. The rest of the land he is devoting to the production of grain and also to the cultivation of some fruit. Mr. Utter still owns a fine home in Minneapolis, and other property there.

He was married in November, 1880, to Miss Mary C. Hewins, a native of Indiana, and daughter of Donavin and Emaline Hew ins. Her father is a farmer near Petersburg, Indiana, on lands he bought in an early day, and for many years has been postmaster of that town. Mr. and Mrs. Utter have two children, Irene, born in Indiana, and Darwin, born in Paso Robles, California.

Mr. Utter is a Republican, and a worthy citizen of the town of his adoption.

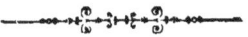

J. F. NEWBY, an influential citizen of Ventura, was born in Wayne County, Indiana, January 3, 1841. His father, Gabriel Newby, a native of North Carolina, was an enthusiastic supporter of Henry Harrison. He served as County Commissioner of Wayne County for eight years, and was highly commended for services rendered. Thomas Newby, of the firm of Morrison & Newby, of Cambridge City, Indiana, an uncle of the subject of this sketch, was one of the highest Masons of the United States. The Newby Lodge there was named for him. Mr. Newby's grandfather, Gabriel Newby, of North Carolina, was one of the first settlers of that State. The family have been noted for their patriotism, love of liberty and hatred of oppression. His great-grandfather liberated all his slaves, numbering more than 100 persons—an act very unusual at that early day. Mr. Newby's ancestors were Quakers, the original progenitors of the family having come to America from England and Scotland. His mother was Rebecca (Harvey) Newby. It is his impression that she was a native of North Carolina. She died when he was only four years of age, and the family afterward moved to Lee County, Iowa. His father was long a leading business man of Cambridge City. Mr. Newby was next to the youngest of a family of eight children. In 1857 he went to Leavenworth, Kansas, and while there was an enthusiastic supporter of James Lane, being there during the time of the Kansas troubles. From there he went to St. Louis, and then to St. Joseph, Missouri, where, for a time, he clerked in the postoffice. In 1859 he removed to New York city, was there four years, a portion of that time being clerk in the St. Nicholas Hotel; and from there he returned to Leavenworth, and was in partnership, dealing in dry goods and notions with Mr. Bloomingdale, now a wholesale merchant of New York city. In 1864, during Price's raid, word was sent to Leavenworth that Price was going to burn the town. A meeting was called to devise means for protection, of which meeting Mr. Newby was elected chairman. They decided to raise and equip a company from the business men of the town. Mr. Newby was Orderly Sergeant of this company. General Curtis met and defeated Price, and the town was saved. Owing to the excessive rents, they moved to St. Joseph and continued business there about two years. Fire caught in an adjoining building and his store was burned out. Mr. Newby was a severe loser. He was not out of business long, however, for he soon engaged in ornamental tree planting, and was very successful.

In 1874 he came to California. After he had been two years in San Buenaventura the town was reorganized, and in December, 1877, he was elected Town Clerk and Assessor, and has held the office ever since with the exception of two years, his last majority being the largest of any town officer. He has thus far performed the duties of this office with credit to himself and satisfaction to his fellow-citizens. Mr. Newby was one of the men who was helpful in organizing the Town Library, of which the residents are now so justly proud. Some objection was made to it on the ground of expense to the town; he was instrumental in overcoming these objections, and was elected its secretary and librarian, holding the office for ten years. During his city clerk and assessorship he has collected large amounts of money to pay the school district bonds for the construction of the splendid school building, and paid off the bonds.

Mr. Newby was united in marriage, April 27, 1864, to Miss Permelia E. Sheridan, a native of Summerville, Kentucky. Her father, S. N. Sheridan, was Sheriff of Buchanan County, Missouri. Their union has been blessed with three sons and two daughters, viz.: Thomas S., John W., Edward M. and Nellie, born in St. Joseph, Missouri, and Minnie, born in Ventura.

Since his residence here Mr. Newby has been very successful in the investments he made, and he now owns a good home and several other places from which he receives rents. He is the agent of the Gas Company of Ventura. His political views have ever been in harmony with the Republican party. Mr. Newby is a gentleman who is held in high esteem by a large circle of friends and acquaintances.

W. BAKER is one of the representative business men of the city of Ventura. He was born in Boston, Massachusetts, May 7, 1853, the son of F. W. and Mary L. (Eaton) Baker, the former a native of Vermont, of Scotch descent, and the latter of Cambridge, Massachusetts, of English ancestry. Mr. Baker was the oldest of four children. He attended the Winchester High School and also the Massachusetts Agricultural College. His first work for himself was in the dry-goods business with Jordan, Marsh & Co., of Boston. Not being suited with that position, he obtained a place in the wholesale hardware store of Hogan, Clark & Sleeper, and remained with them two years, when the great Boston fire occurred and they were burned out. He then accepted an offer to travel for Baker & Hamilton, a San Francisco hardware house, remaining in their employ four years. At the expiration of that time he engaged in business for himself in Napa, under the firm name of Stone & Baker, doing a tin and hardware business. Two years later he sold out to his partner, returned to San Francisco, and again entered the employ of Baker & Hamilton, working for them two years longer.

Mr. Baker then came to Ventura and purchased the store of E. A. Edward, who had been the pioneer hardware man of the place. This purchase was made in April, 1879, and, with the exception of one year, Mr. Baker has conducted the business and has been very successful. From time to time, as necessity demanded, he has increased his facilities for doing business. The little building that once served for a store room has given place to a fine two-story brick, 30 x 75 feet, and the first building, moved to the rear, is used for a warehouse. The store occupies both the lower and upper story of the new building. Mr. Baker has the only elevator in the city. He owns a factory, 30 x 50 feet, in which he manufactures tinware, honey and fruit cans in large quantities. He employs five men all the time and in the busy season seven or eight. His business extends all over the county, and some of his manufactures are shipped all over the State. In one season he made 12,000 sixty-pound honey cans, and many thousand smaller ones. They adopted a plan that every person who purchased $1 worth of goods should have a guess on how many cans they were making. The one who guessed the nearest was paid $50, the next

$25, and the third $10. This store is No. 216 Main street, between Oak and Palm.

Mr. Baker was united in marriage to Miss Annie M. Sheriden in 1880. She was born in St. Joseph, Missouri, the daughter of S. N. Sheriden, of Ventura. They have three interesting children, two sons and a daughter, all born in Ventura, viz.: George L. Frederick N. and Annie M.

Mr. Baker is Senior Warden of the Masonic Lodge, F. & A. M.; is also a K. of P., and was District Deputy of the order to the Grand Lodge. Politically he is a Republican. Mr. Baker is a stockholder in the Ventura Gas Company, and does his full share in all public enterprises. He is the owner of a good home, where he resides with his family, and also owns other valuable real estate.

Mrs. Baker is a member of the Congregational Church.

JOHN REED, one of the founders of the Lompoc Colony, and the surveyor of the town, was born in Milton, Norfolk County, Massachusetts, in 1826. His father was a farmer and carpenter. The subject of this sketch received his preliminary education at Milton, and graduated at Williams College, in 1848. He then acted as tutor in Virginia and South Carolina for about two years. He was married in Boston, in 1853, to Miss Amanda S. Baker, and together they went to San Antonio, Texas, where for two years they were engaged in teaching. In 1854 they came to California, by the Nicaragua route, landing at San Francisco, where his family resided for four years, while he was engaged in surveying Government land. In 1858 he moved to Santa Clara County, bought a farm of 120 acres, and for sixteen years thereafter was engaged in farming. In 1874, at the founding of Lompoc Colony, he came to the valley with other interested co-operators; Mr. Reed is one of the few surviving resident members of that early period. He surveyed the town and part of the surrounding country, and was one of the original purchasers of the grant. He also bought 160 acres near the center of the valley, which he has since sold, and now owns 160 acres at Santa Rita, and one block within the corporate limits.

Mr. Reed was County Surveyor of Santa Clara County in 1862–'63, and of Santa Barbara County from 1878 to 1887. In 1886 he was elected Justice of the Peace of Lompoc, and in April, 1890, was elected Town Clerk.

His first wife died at Santa Clara, in 1874, and in 1882 he was again married, to Mrs. Ella Miller, of Lompoc, which union has been blessed with one child.

C. HATHAWAY, the present manager of the Los Alamos Rancho, owned by John S. Bell, was born in Sanilac County, Michigan, in 1863. His father was a seafaring man, and during his later life was captain on the Lakes. The subject of this sketch left home at the age of eighteen years, and for many years followed the milling business, learning the trade of millwright at Montrose, Colorado. He worked there three years in the lumber mill, then, in 1884, went to Denver, where he engaged in the coal and wood business. In 1885 he came to California, settling at Santa Cruz, where for two and a half years he managed a sawmill. He came to the Los Alamos Rancho in the spring of 1887, in the employ of Grover & Rosener, who had contracted to purchase the ranch; but failing to meet their obligations in March, 1889, the ranch reverted to Mr. Bell, and Mr. Hathaway continued its efficient manager. He received a diploma in 1888 from the Mechanics' Institute of San Francisco, for the products of the ranch, in fruits and vegetables. The ranch consists of 14,000 acres; 2,000 is rented and under cultivation. They keep about 100 cattle and 175 head of horses, with stallions " Othello," " Robbery Boy," and " Arab," all running horses. They also have about twelve acres in deciduous fruits. In 1888 Mr. Hathaway bought thirty acres of valley land in the east end of the valley, where he is building a house and outbuildings, with a view of making that his permanent residence. He has a small vineyard and intends setting ten acres to mixed fruits.

Mr. Hathaway was married at Los Alamos, in 1889, to Miss Jennie E. Wait.

W. BROUGHTON came to California in the summer of 1859, and has resided in the State ever since. He is a New Yorker by birth, born July 29, 1836, at Tonawanda, Erie County. New York. He read law in the office of W. W. Thayer, since Governor of Oregon, and now an able Judge on the Supreme Bench of that State. Was admitted to practice in California, in 1863, and since that time has favored the profession with a strong tendency to newspaper life. Several papers have been founded, edited and published by him in various parts of the Pacific coast. In 1874 he owned and edited the Santa Cruz *Enterprise*, which has since been merged into the *Local Item*. In 1865 the *New Age*, the first Odd Fellows weekly paper in the United States, was founded by him in San Francisco and is now in its twenty-fifth year. In 1875 he established the Lompoc *Record*, at the founding of the Lompoc Colony, in Santa Barbara County, California, which he is now editing. In 1880 he founded the *Arizona Bulletin*, in that Territory, but discontinued the publication. Mr. Broughton was the original projector of the Lompoc Colony, and performed herculean work in its organization and in locating colonists. The success of the colony is mainly attributed to his enterprise in publishing the local paper and diffusing throughout the land the facts concerning the most desirable region of the Pacific coast for homes.

In 1862 Mr. Broughton was married to the only daughter of Mr. George T. Anthony, a highly respected citizen of Santa Cruz. A family of seven sons and five daughters is the result of this happy union. In politics, Mr. Broughton of late years has been a Democrat, and in 1886 was the nominee for the State Senate of that party for the district embracing San Luis Obispo, Ventura and Santa Barbara counties. At present Mr. Broughton is at Lompoc, practicing his profession and publishing his paper, the Lompoc *Record*, a paper recognized to be one of the ablest in the county.

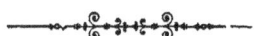

HENRY DUBBERS, a rancher residing in Ventura, came to Ventura in 1862, and as he is one of its most worthy pioneers, this history would not be complete without recording his life. He was born in Holstein, in the year 1819, and came to America in 1851, coming direct from Germany to California. His parents were both natives of Germany, and his father was a merchant. When Mr. Dubbers came to San Francisco he was sick, and his intentions were to go to South America; but becoming acquainted with other Germans, who were engaged in farming, he was induced by them to stay in California. They had rented land in San Mateo County at $4 per acre, and induced him to put capital in the business; he soon discovered that there would a be loss in the venture, and took it under his own management. He soon after bought the property—500 acres—and made good to the other parties all that they had put in and more. The property advanced on his hands, and he sold it at a liberal advance. He then came to Ventura, but the title to the lands was so unsettled that he did not buy at that time. A few years afterward oil was discovered, and it was pronounced very rich; New York and Philadelphia capitalists came in, and as he could talk Spanish he was taken in with them. They bought a large tract of land, and Mr. Dubbers took charge of the receiving of the machinery and supplies for the oil wells, and forwarding it to the wells. When Mr. Dubbers came to Ventura only two or three schooners stopped here during the year, to bring supplies and provisions, and for a good while the country was very much isolated from the outside world.

He bought an interest in the Santa Ana ranch, and owns about 930 acres; he is raising wheat and barley on it. He had fifteen acres in city tracts, which he subdivided, and has sold about half of it at remunerative prices.

In 1859 Mr. Dubbers was united in marriage to Miss Wilhelmina Osterman, a native of Germany. They had four children:—Henry, born in San Mateo; Hattie, born in Ventura, and is married to Mr. J. B. Ward, a civil engineer from Cleveland, Ohio; Alfred, born in Ventura, and is now at the Berkeley University; Emma, born in Ventura, and is now with her sister in Pittsburg. Henry is married, and lives at Point Reyes.

Mr. Dubber's ancestors are all deceased, in Germany, but he thinks of making a visit to that place; he has lived in Brazil and Buenos Ayres, and can speak English, Spanish, French and German. When he came to Ventura there were only a few Americans in the place, and no mail conveniences. When the postoffice was established, Mr. V. A. Simpson was the first postmaster, and a stage route was established twice a week from Santa Barbara to Los Angeles. Mr. Dubbers is leading a quiet and retired life, in his old-style, adobe house, surrounded with life's comforts. He is spending the remainder of his life under the shade of some large trees planted by his own hands.

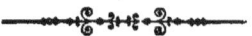

ANDREW NELSON, a prominent business man and rancher of El Paso de Robles, was born in Sweden, in 1846, both his parents being natives of that country. At the age of nineteen years Mr. Nelson entered upon a seafaring life, continuing thus engaged for twelve years and during that time seeing a large portion of the world. In 1870 he came to New York and was there variously employed, first as night-watchman in a large warehouse. Next he was at Pittston, Maine, two years, employed in sawmills. Then, going to Chicago after the great fire there, he engaged as a carpenter. Returning in 1874 to Maine, he worked at Portland, building the Grand Trunk elevator. Later he went to San Francisco and worked as a laborer on the Baldwin Hotel. The next year, 1877, he was married in San Francisco to Miss Annie S. Akblom, a native of Sweden. They moved to Seattle and there bought seven acres of land located five miles out in the woods near Talmonkay, which he cleared and devoted to the culture of small fruit, remaining in that place until 1888. Mr. Nelson was successful in Seattle in the fruit business and also in his investment in real estate. He still owns property in that place, and also fifty shares in the Puget Sound Creosote Company. He sold out and came to El Paso de Robles, purchased 160 acres of land near the town, on the northwest, built a good residence, and is making notable improvements in the way of clearing away brush and planting trees and vines. He has also purchased 160 acres farther from the town, in the same direction, and owns property on which he has built a good residence. On his ranches, Mr. Nelson is raising some fine horses.

In addition to his other interests in this place, Mr. Nelson is senior member of the firm of Nelson-Quarnstrom Company. The paid-in cash capital of the company is $9,000. They have a general merchandise store on Twelfth street, and do the principal business in their line in town, their trade extending from forty to fifty miles east.

Mr. and Mrs. Nelson have five children, four sons and one daughter, all born in Washington Territory, viz.: Robert, Fredrick, Earnest, Albert and Mable. Mr. Nelson and his wife are members of the Methodist Church. He is a Master Mason, and in his political views is a Republican.

HENSON POLAND, one of the original founders of the town of Lompoc, was born in Randolph County, Virginia, now West Virginia, December 13, 1838. His father was a farmer, who in 1844 emigrated to Chariton County, Missouri, and bought 292 acres of land and carried on general farming; he also raised tobacco, which was then a staple product. Henson was educated in the subscription schools of that period, then attended the Brunswick Academy, and finished at the Bluff High School, which was founded by Thomas M. Crowder, a graduate of the University of Virginia. Mr. Poland then taught school in Prairie Township, now called Salisbury, Missouri, but owing to the breaking out of the war and the exciting political feeling of Missouri, his school was dismissed before the term expired. Being a strong advocate of Unionism, contrary to the expressed sentiments of his family, and yet not caring to take up arms against a people in which was represented his own kin, Missouri became too hot for him and he went to New York. In 1863 he took the steamer, *en route* for California, by the Isthmus of Panama, arriving in San Francisco on April 28, 1863. He farmed in San Joaquin County during the summer, and in the fall started for the Arizona mines, but at Los Angeles was diverted to the Soledad mines, where he passed four months, returning to Santa Cruz County in March, 1864, where for six years he worked in timber, furnishing lime kilns and the California Powder Company with fuel and stove wood. In 1870 he was employed by the California Powder Company as manager of outside hands, and at his departure received highly commendatory certificates. In the fall of 1874 he came to Lompoc, at the founding of the colony, and was one of the syndicate which purchased a part of the Lompoc ranch, namely 46,500 acres, and has since bought five town blocks, twenty-five acres, four and a half of which he still owns. He improved his city property, and leased 200 acres, which he cultivated in grain, until 1888. He set out twelve acres in deciduous fruits, 1,000 trees, apples, pears, plums, all of which are now in bearing and doing well.

In 1888 he was elected Town Clerk and

served one term, and in April, 1890, was appointed Postmaster by President Harrison, assuming his office July 1, 1889. He has fitted up his office at his own expense, making it comfortable and convenient, and is a very acceptable postmaster.

Mr. Poland was married at Santa Cruz, August 4, 1868, to Mrs. D. W. Scoville, a native of New York State, who crossed the plains to California in 1863. Mr. Poland has served as presiding officer of Lompoc Lodge, No. 262, F. & A. M., and was also a charter member of the San Luis Obispo Lodge, No. 62, Royal Arch Masons. He was a charter member of the Odd Fellows Lodge, No. 248, which was instituted July 10, 1876, and has been continuously an officer until June 1, 1889, having passed through every chair. He was present to represent the Santa Cruz Lodge, No. 38, F. & A. M., at the laying of the corner-stone of the Mercantile Library at San Francisco, in March, 1867, which ceremony was performed by the Grand Lodge of California, F. & A. M. Mr. Poland is a man of progress and public spirit, charitable in all his dealings, and a conscientious and honored citizen.

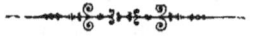

HON. R. M. SHACKELFORD, an eminent business man of El Paso de Robles, is a native of the Blue Grass State, where his ancestors for generations, both on the maternal and paternal sides, have lived. The Shackelfords of Kentucky claim both Scotch and English progenitors, while Mr. Shackelford's mother's family, the Dickersons, claim English forefathers only. Mr. Shackelford was born in Kentucky, and came to California in 1853, when a lad of seventeen years. Having been identified with California during the whole of its history as a State, and having received his education here, he claims the right and distinction of being a Californian in the fullest sense. While Mr. Shackelford has made a remarkable business success in life, yet like most pioneers he has seen hard times and many reverses, notwithstanding the misfortunes and trials have been to him, as he expresses it, "golden experiences." To appreciate health we must know what it is to be sick; and to enjoy sunshine we must have been in the deepest shades.

Mr. Shackelford's business career has been a remarkable one. A portion of his boyhood was spent in Missouri; and he was but fourteen years of age when the gold excitement occurred in California. As soon as he was old enough he came to this coast, a poorly educated boy, seventeen years of age. In Tuolumne County, he worked hard all day, and at night studied until ten and eleven o'clock, in the winter time, and in this way he received his education. For five years he dug in the mines in Tuolumne and El Dorado Counties, both placer and quartz, with but fair success. In 1858 he engaged in draying and handling freight with ox teams over the mountains. He received eighty cents per hundred for a single trip, the price of a pair of oxen. They took their provisions and camped out at night; he followed this business successfully for eighteen months. At Marysville he engaged in a flour-mill, forwarding and commission business until 1863. By this time he had made a little money and had it invested in this business: his warehouse was full of flour and grain, but the floods of 1862 and 1863 filled the warehouse with water, and the accumulation of years of industry was destroyed. He was compelled to start out again with ox teams, hauling freight from Marysville to Virginia City. He then went into the lumber business, which he manufactured until 1865. In this year he was elected a member of the first Legislature of the State of Nevada, by the Republican party, and served one term. In the fall of 1866 he returned to Los Gatos, California, where he opened a general merchandise store and lumber business connected with it. In 1868 he sold out, and in connection with two other gentlemen bought 22,000 acres of land, on which the town of King City now stands. In 1873 he sold out his interest and settled at Hollister, California, and engaged in a mill and warehouse. In this business he is still interested, the property having been transferred to the Central Milling Company. In November, 1886, he removed to El Paso de Robles, and engaged in the construction of warehouses, and started lumber yards along the line of the railroad between Soledad and San Margarita. He organized the Southern Pacific Milling Company, etc., and they have nine warehouses fifty feet wide and aggregating nearly a mile in length, and as many lumber yards.

Mr. Shackelford has purchased 1,700 acres of land adjoining Paso Robles, and has organized a company known as the Stock and Fruit Company's Association. On this land they have established a breeding farm, are raising fine horses, and have also a very large orchard. Mr. Shackelford is one of the directors and a stockholder of the water works of the town, and is a stockholder and director in the Central Milling Company. Mr. Shackelford, with Messrs. Steele & Wheelan, organized the Southern Mill and Warehouse Company; they have six warehouses and lumber yards, and the planing-mill at Ventura City.

Mr. Shackelford's father and grandfather were both born in Kentucky, and both bore the same name, James Shackelford. The grandfather was a soldier in the Revolution, and in the war of 1812 died fighting the Indians, at the battle of Hall's Gap. James Shackelford, Jr., married Sarah A. Dickerson. Her father, Beverly Dickerson, was a stock-raiser and tobacco planter. Mr. Shackelford's parents had twelve children, of whom ten are living. He was the fourth child in this numerous family, and was born in Kentucky, January 17, 1835. He was married in 1861 to Miss Mary Louise McQueston, a native of Wisconsin. They have one son, Otto Shackelford, a promising young merchant of El Paso de Robles. Mrs. Shackelford's father, John McQueston, is a native of Michigan, of Scotch descent. Mr. and Mrs. Shackelford are members of the Methodist Church, and were important factors in the building of the neat church and parsonage in their town. Mr. Shackelford was a trustee, and gave the ground and $1,200 to aid in the building.

In March, 1887, Mr. Shackelford built on a block of good ground, purchased for that purpose, a beautiful cottage, in which he resides with his family. He is a Knight Templar, a member of the Independent Order of Odd Fellows, and a member of the Ancient Order of United Workmen. He has been a Republican since the organization of that party.

J. D. LINDNER is the son of J. D. Lindner, Sr., and was born in Stark County, Ohio, February 20, 1839. His father came from Germany in 1830, stopped for a time in the State of New York, then became a pioneer of Ohio, and afterward of Iowa. He had been a Democrat, but, upon the organization of the Republican party, joined its ranks. In his religious views he was a Lutheran. He wedded Rosa Mary Sargent, a native of Saxony. They were parents of nine children, only four of whom are now living. Mr. Lindner was the fifth child of this family. He came to California in 1859, at the age of nineteen years, and engaged in farming in Sonoma and Marin counties, and also worked some at the carpenter's trade. He afterward removed to San José, where he was engaged in contracting and building until 1870. In that year he came to Monterey County, settled on a Government ranch, ten miles east of San Miguel, remaining on it six months, the want of water inducing him to abandon it. Mr. Lindner went to the coast, seven miles above Cayucos, San Luis Obispo County, and entered a homestead. For fifteen years he lived there, engaged in raising stock and grain, and improved the place by building, etc. He sold out and returned to San José, where he bought eight acres of land adjoining the city. On this property he built a house and planted the land to fruit trees, and a year later sold out and returned to the southern part of the State. At Creston he farmed a large tract of land on shares for three years, after which he came to his present location. He has eighty acres of choice land, two miles from Paso Robles, and ninety acres near Creston.

Mr. Lindner married Mrs. Maule, a widow with four children. They have had three sons, Virgil, Warren and Milton. Virgil was born in San José, Monterey County, and Milton in San Luis Obispo County. Of the three sons only two are living, Milton dying in the second year of his age. Mr. and Mrs. Lindner are members of the Grange, and Mr. Lindner is Master of the lodge at Paso Robles, and is much interested in its workings. He has voted with the Greenback and Prohibition parties, but takes no interest in the older political organizations. He is radical on all the topics of interest in the county and is well informed. He is by nature endowed with the ability to make an interesting speech, and had he followed the profession of either a lawyer or minister he would have been a success.

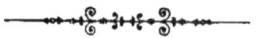

LEVI EXLINE is the pioneer horticulturist of Paso Robles. He is a native of Ohio, born January 15, 1844. His father, Adam Exline, was a native of Pennsylvania, of German ancestry. His mother, *nee* Christine J. Saucerman, was born in Ohio. They had a family of nine children, of whom Levi is the youngest except one. In 1843 his father moved to Indiana, and was a prominent pioneer of that State. He took up a Government homestead, reared his family on it, and there lived until 1862, when his death occurred. On a corner of his farm stood a log school-house, with benches made from split logs; and here Mr. Exline received his education, and learned the lessons of fortitude and self-denial which served him so well in after life. From this old home of his childhood, in 1868, he came to California, to make a home in a more salubrious climate. For a time he worked a place of his brothers, in San Luis Obispo County. He then removed to El Dorado County, and in the mines, twenty-five miles east of Placerville, he met with good success. He then came to his present locality, three miles northwest of Paso Robles, and took up 160 acres of land. By purchase he afterwards acquired 160 acres adjoining this land. When Mr. Exline came into the county it was principally occupied by sheep ranchers, who had no love for the settlers who wished to till the soil. First, they told him nothing could be raised and, second, they claimed to own the land; and it was by no means a friendly and warm reception he received. He knew that they had no legal claims to the land, for he had himself been to the land-office and made investigations. So, in spite of all objections, he sat down to stay. He built a very comfortable adobe house, and by his own industry and the help of his ever faithful companion, it was soon surrounded with flowers and fruits, and covered with thrifty grape-vines; and thus by their united efforts has the barren sheep pasture been transformed into one of the most delightful shady nooks for a home imaginable. A little cooling brook gurgles its way through their grounds, and lends a charm to the beautiful scene. Mr. Exline has thirty acres devoted to fruit of nearly every deciduous variety, and has fourteen acres planted to watermelons. He also raises blackberries and raspberries; and finds a ready market for all his fruit.

Mr. Exline's wife was *nee* Miss Emma Stone, a native of Wisconsin, a daughter of Samuel Stone, now a farmer of Fresno, California. They were married in August, 1879. Three children have come to brighten their home: Vernon, Clytie and Hazel. Mr. and Mrs. Exline are consistent members of the Methodist Church. They also belong to the Grange. Mr. Exline has been Overseer of the Grange since its organization here. He is also President of the Farmers' Alliance, and he has often been elected School Trustee of his district. For years he was an active Republican, and is now looking eagerly for other advance measures that will ameliorate and advance the condition of the American citizens, namely: lower rates of interest, cheaper and safer railroad facilities, better methods of dealing with intemperance, cheaper methods of obtaining the implements of husbandry, and other measures that will benefit the humblest citizens. Mr. Exline is a gentleman of intelligence and integrity, and his plans and ideas are in harmony with those of his companion.

In speaking of the undeveloped condition of the county when he came here, Mr. Exline says that the settlers were few and far between, and that there was but one store in San Luis Obispo. Three bullsdogs were tied to the back door of it, as if to keep people from coming in the back way. Now San Luis Obispo has many magnificent residences and places of business, and three other towns have started up between his home and that city; the county is being swiftly settled up with happy, refined and industrious people, and still there is room for more.

SEBERN STEELE, a rancher of Lompoc, was born in Randolph County, Illinois, June 2, 1844. His father was a farmer of that county, and in 1851 moved to Mount Vernon, Missouri. In 1853 he came to California, driving an ox team across the plains and being exactly five months on the road, arriving at Stockton, September 17, where he settled and for the following nine years passed much of his time at the mines. Sebern graduated at Benicia College, in 1864, and began the business of building in 1865. He was in the employ of S. E. Hoisington, who was a very superior mechanic, and with whom he remained about eighteen months. He then started out independently, and has since been alone in business. He worked at building and contracting in Stockton and Santa Barbara until the spring of 1875, when he came to Lompoc, and followed his trade about fifteen months. He bought 2,110 acres, on August 12, 1876, which was a part of the Lompoc grant, then a wild howling wilderness, covered with brush and timber, which by persistent energy has been transformed into beautiful farming and grazing land, with about 1,400 acres cleared. He sows a large acreage to barley, and raises horses, cattle and hogs. His land fronts upon the ocean, about two miles in extent, and is near the memorable spot upon which was wrecked the steamship Yankee Blade, in 1853. His residence overlooks the sea, and he has three other dwelling houses on his ranch, with the necessary out-buildings. Mr. Steele engaged in building until 1882, but since then his contracting has been in the nature of road-building or clearing timber land. He now has a contract for clearing 300 acres of brush and timber, upon which he uses the Hawkeye stump puller, pulling out large trees by the roots, saving time and labor of cutting them down or digging about.

Mr. Steele was married at Stockton, December 23, 1868, to Miss Laura J. Parnell, whose parents were natives of Cornwall, England. Her father was a pioneer of 1849 to California, and a member of the Society of California Pioneers of Stockton. She died December 25, 1889, leaving six children,—four sons and two daughters.

CHARLES G. BARTLETT, one of the prominent business men of San Buenaventura, was born in the southern part of England, February 23, 1852. His parents, Samuel and Elizabeth (Griffin) Bartlett, were both natives of England. His paternal grandfather, Richard Bartlett, kept a hotel, in earlier times called an inn, at Axworth, and his maternal grandfather was a flax merchant. Charles G. Bartlett came to the United States when five years of age with his parents, and settled at Adrian, Michigan. In that State he was raised, educated and learned his trade of jeweler. In the year 1872 he came to San Francisco, and worked in a large establishment on Montgomery street, for three years, where they were doing a large jewelry business. In 1875 he came to Ventura, and with his brother, Albert G. Bartlett, opened a jewelry, stationery and music store, which has grown from a little room 10 x 15 feet into their present large business. Bartlett Bros. have now a second store in Los Angeles, of which Albert G. is manager; Charles G. is manager of the business in San Buenaventura. They enjoy the leading jewelry trade of the city; they have also had the Pacific coast steamship passenger agency for ten years. They employ three men in their San Buenaventura store. It is remarked about Mr. Bartlett that he devotes more time to his business than any other man in the city. Mr. Bartlett has built a very artistic and beautiful home on Santa Clara street, in the best portion of the city, where he enjoys the comforts of home with his industrious family.

He was united in marriage to Miss Alice Day, a native of Oshkosh, Wisconsin, and daughter of James Day, of Ventura. Mrs. Bartlett had one son by a former marriage, Charles, born in Ventura. They now have two daughters: Effie and Mabel, both born in Ventura. Mr. Bartlett joined the Independent Order of Odd Fellows in 1872; he is a fine musician, and has been one of the foremost in organizing the fine orchestra and band in Ventura. In politics he is a Republican, but is too much engrossed in business to give much attention to political matters.

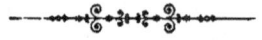

AMBROSE FAEH was born in Illinois, June 9, 1862. When he was thirteen years of age, the entire family came to California, one of whom, a married sister, was in very delicate health, and it was for her benefit that the change of residence was made.

She subsequently died of consumption. The family settled on Monterey street in the city of San Luis Obispo. Here young Faeh received the advantages of a good schooling, as the opportunities for study were excellent. In 1882 he purchased a ranch on the Salinas River and made that his home for one year, at the end of which time he sold out. At present he is residing on a ranch near San Luis Obispo, engaged in farming, cattle-raising, etc.

A period of Mr. Faeh's life, which probably he regrets very much and which forms a part of his early history, he relates for publication. It occurred between the years 1876 and 1879. Without the knowledge of his mother or family, he left them at their home in San Luis Obispo and engaged in ranching in some remote part of the county. He was gone two years and a half and no one of the family knew of his whereabouts. Being only fourteen years of age, of course his continued absence caused no little anxiety. All the time, however, he was rapidly gaining a thorough knowledge of ranch life, whether or not he was sowing his "wild oats," and that experience has been of great value to him since, if it was not so to his family.

Mr. Faeh was married in 1887, and has one child.

M. S. NICHOLS, a retired rancher of Lompoc, was born in Lewis County, New York, in 1840, where he was also educated. At the breaking out of the war he enlisted at Boonville, in October, 1861, in Company B, of the Ninety-seventh New York State Volunteers, under Colonel Charles Wheelock. The regiment was in the First Corps, and brigaded under General Duryea, and began active service at the battle of Cedar Mountain, in August, 1862, which was followed by Rappahannock, Second Bull Run, Antietam, Fredericksburg, Chancellorsville, and Gettysburg. Under General Grant they were at the battle of the Wilderness, Cold Harbor, Malvern Hill, siege of Petersburg, and many smaller engagements and skirmishes. Mr. Nichols was wounded several times, from which he has never recovered. They were mustered out in October, 1864.

Mr. Nichols then returned home, where he passed one year. In the fall of 1865 he came to California by water, and the Isthmus of Panama. After arrival at San Francisco he went to Santa Cruz, where he had brothers living, and in partnership with them he entered the lumbering business, which he followed for four years. He was engaged in butchering until 1874, when he came to Lompoc, with the original incorporators of the colony. He attended the first sale and bought some inside property; he also rented 150 acres, which he farmed. In 1878 he took up 160 acres of Government land, north of town, and also rented 500 acres additional. He improved his ranch and carried on general farming up to January, 1890, when, owing to lameness caused by his army disabilities, he rented his ranch, and moved his family in town, where he owned improved property.

Mr. Nichols was married in California, in 1872, to Miss Pastora Dakan, and the union has been blessed with three children.

A. WILLIAMSON was born in Scotland in 1835, and received instruction in his school-days from the celebrated Scottish historian, Dr. McIntosh. He served an apprenticeship in the tin and hardware business, after which he went to sea and visited the different ports in Europe, and finally doubled Cape Horn and came to California. On the day of landing at San Francisco, he was engaged by a mercantile house in that city, his various duties consisting of those of steward, waterman and copying clerk, which duties occupied his time from 4 A. M. to 10 P. M. After three years' service in this business, he gave the placer mines a trial, soon returning, however, to San Francisco, where he made the acquaintance of the senior member of a large English mercantile house and was given the position of trading agent. During his engagement with that firm he saw the important cities of the world.

It was in 1868 that Mr. Williamson came to San Luis Obispo, where he has ever since been actively engaged in business. He is the pioneer merchant in the tin and hardware business, and relates some very interesting stories of the experience of merchants in those early days of San Luis Obispo. Every thing, he says, was in an embryo and unsettled state of affairs, but money was plentiful, the soil new, and new people were coming into the town and county every day, bringing their families with them, their efforts all seeming to tend to establish an endless prosperity and a rapid growth of both town and county. But the dry years came and the county suffered many serious drawbacks. Mr. Williamson is a firm believer in a splendid future for this country and is of the opinion that it is not far distant.

He was married in 1866, at Santa Cruz, and has seven children, five sons and two daughters.

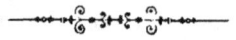

L. M. LLOYD, a prominent business man of San Buenaventura, and a large property holder, was born in Lee County, Virginia, November 23, 1835. His father, Absalom Lloyd, was also a Virginian; but his great-grandfather, J. Lloyd, came from Wales. His mother, Elizabeth (Willis) Lloyd, was born in Johnson County, Tennessee, the daughter of Rev. Louis Willis, a clergyman of the Methodist Church; they were of German descent. Mr. Lloyd's father was married twice, and he was the first child of the second family. He studied law under the direction of General Tutt, of St. Joseph, Missouri, three years, and then was admitted to the bar. In August following he enlisted in Company C, Third Missouri Cavalry; was at first elected a First Lieutenant, and was afterward promoted to Captain. His term of service expiring at the end of three years, he went to Colorado and engaged in freighting from Nebraska to Denver. He was the first returned Confederate soldier that was admitted to the bar in Nebraska, awaiting the decision concerning the test oath, by Chief Justice Mason until sometime in 1866; he continued in his profession in Nebraska City until 1871, when he returned to his old home in Missouri and lived there many years engaged in his calling. In 1874 he was elected States Attorney for two years, on the Democratic ticket, and in 1876 was re-elected. In 1878 he was elected to the State Senate from the Sixteenth Senatorial District, and also for the revision session of the State Constitutional Convention, serving three sessions. In 1884 he was appointed assignee of the Newton County Bank, under a bond of $190,000; and in 1888 he closed the estate, having settled every claim against the bank. In 1886 he visited California and Ventura County, and made investments which proved very successful. He bought 4,000 acres joining the town of San Buenaventura and partly in the corporation. A part of this property he sold at greatly advanced prices. He also owns three-fourths of the stock of the Ventura Land and Water Company, which firm owns 5,200 acres of land, subdivided, one of the finest stock and fruit ranches in the county. They have settled upon it a colony with a school-house. On his property here in the city he has built a beautiful residence, laid out large grounds and planted flowers, shrubs and ornamental trees; it will soon be the most delightful suburban resort and property in the whole country. This ranch is stocked with cattle and horses. He has also a three-fourths interest in a fine large furniture store in Ventura, stocked heavily with choice cabinet-ware, over which Warren E. Lloyd, his son, presides. While it is his good fortune to have quite a good share of this world's goods, it does not render him in the least vain; and he may be seen at work with shovel and spade with his men, planting his trees and ornamenting his grounds,—as hard at work as if for wages to support his wife and children. He is a sagacious, well-informed business man and enjoys the good-will of his fellow citizens. He is a member of the Masonic fraternity and of the A. O. U. W. Also one of the promoters and trustees of the Scorrit College at Neosho, Missouri.

In 1864 he married Miss Sarah E. Bramel, born in 1839, in Missouri. Her father, John H., was a native of Virginia. They have six children: Lee W., now in the University at Berkeley, will graduate in 1892; Lora V., married to Mr. M. L. Montgomery; Warren E., at home with his father; Roberta T., also now in the University; Ralph B. and Eleanor P. Mr. Lloyd and his wife and family are members of the Methodist Church, South. They have been largely instrumental in the erection of a fine church edifice in Ventura, having donated about one-third of the cost of the property. They believe that Christianity should be the paramount principle in life, and that Christian institutions should be liberally supported.

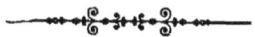

BENJAMIN FRANKLIN TUCKER, the first Postmaster of the town of Lompoc, and the present efficient agent of Wells, Fargo & Co.'s Express, was born in Washington County, Maine, in 1829. At an early age he began working at lumbering and saw-mills, until 1850, when, in February, he went to Boston to visit an uncle. In 1850 he sailed for California, around Cape Horn. They made but one landing, at Valparaiso, on July 4, and arrived at San Francisco September 22. Mr. Tucker shipped before the mast, which has proved to be his first and last voyage. The vessel was loaded with lumber, and they carried but one passenger. He passed the winter in San Francisco, and in June, 1851, went to the mines in Tuolumne County, remaining about one year, when he went to Santa Cruz. After one year at farming he began the carpenter's trade, which he continued for twenty years, the last ten of which were passed in the employ of the California Powder Company, in putting up their buildings and then acting as repair hand. He became interested and purchased stock in the Lompoc Colony, and to attend the first sale of lands he came to Lompoc, in the fall of 1874, but only bought town lots. In March, 1875, by Postmaster General Jewell, he was appointed first Postmaster at Lompoc, and held the office continuously for ten years and nine months, up to President Cleveland's Democratic administration. At the establishment of Wells, Fargo & Co.'s express agency in Lompoc Mr. Tucker was appointed agent, which office he has held up to the present time. He served one term as Justice of the Peace, having been elected in the fall of 1884, and has worked more or less at carpentering ever since he settled in the valley.

Mr. Tucker was married at Santa Cruz, in October, 1853, to Miss Emily R. Hecox, and they have four children. Mr. Tucker was a charter member of Lompoc Lodge, No. 248, I. O. O. F., which was established July 10, 1876, and also a charter member of Lompoc Lodge, No. 57, Knights of Pythias.

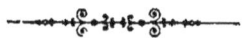

AMES BEATTIE, the prominent merchant tailor of Santa Maria, was born in the city of Cork, Ireland, in 1852. His father soon after moved to London, where he carried on his trade of tailoring, and by whom our subject was taught to follow in the same industry. In 1872 he came to the United States, first settling in Boston, then in New York, Philadelphia, Washington, District of Columbia, and Chicago, in each city finding ready occupation with the leading tailoring establishments. On account of poor health he left Chicago in 1880 for the warmer Pacific coast. He first settled in San Francisco, engaging with Bullock & Jones, the leading merchant tailors of that city. After one year he came to Chico, and in 1884 to Santa Maria, where he established a first-class shop, and with a fine line of imported and American cloths he finds a very satisfactory market, both at home and from the adjoining towns. He likes the town and climate, and has fully recovered his health. In the spring of 1888 Mr. Beattie built his present store building, 24 x 40 feet on Main street, and is prepared to meet the requirements of the people.

He was married in Washington, District of Columbia, February 15, 1877, to Miss Sarah Reddy, who died in 1879, leaving a little daughter, Elizabeth, who was born November 20, 1877. Mr. Beattie is a member of Santa Maria Lodge, No. 302, I. O. O. F.

ISIDORE WEILL, one of the leading merchants of Lompoc, and the vice-president of the Lompoc Bank, was born in Möwenheim, Alsace, in 1845. His father was an extensive dealer in stock and grain. Isidore came to America in 1862, and immediately offered his services and life, if need be, in the defense of the land of his adoption. Soon after his arrival he enlisted in Company B, Seventh Massachusetts Infantry, under Colonel Masey. The regiment was in the Second Corps, under General Hancock, and they were in the battle of Wilton Station, Spottsylvania, siege of Petersburg and all the engagements through Virginia. The regiment attended the Grand Review at Washington, in 1865, and was then sent to Boston, Massachusetts, where they were mustered out and discharged. Mr. Weill then went to Memphis, Tennessee, where a brother was living, and he there began his mercantile life, which has proved so successful. In 1867 he made a visit to his native country, but returning the same year came direct to California, where he arrived in September, 1867. He then went to Solano County and was employed by Blum Bros. in general merchandise, with whom he remained until 1875, when he opened business for himself, with a Mr. Davidson. After three years he sold out and came to Ventura County and opened a store at Hueneme, continuing until 1880, when he again sold out and came to Lompoc. He opened a general merchandise store on H street, in May, 1880, with fresh goods and a fine assortment, carrying on a very satisfactory business. In February, 1889, he moved to his present spacious rooms on Ocean avenue. He keeps everything in the line of farm implements or family requirements. He owns considerable city property and much ranch property, in San Luis Obispo County. The Bank of Lompoc was organized May 20, 1890, and Mr. Weill was elected vice-president and manager. He has been acting as agent for the Commercial Bank of San Luis Obispo for several months; he originated the idea of starting a local bank.

Mr. Weill was married in San Francisco, in 1875, to Miss Hannah Kaiser, a native of Alabama. They have two children, Maier and Reine.

R. HARRIS was born in Missouri in 1832. He received his education in his native place, and at the age of eighteen years, like many an ambitious youth, he decided to go West. It was in 1850 that he set out for California, across the plains and alone. This journey, which he describes as a very tedious one, was made with a wagon and pack, but Mr. Harris walked the greater part of the time. Upon his arrival in the Golden State, he settled in Nevada City, October 5, 1850, where he remained one year, after which he went to Sacramento, where he spent a short time in the mines, without any very great success, however. He next found employment in the Water Ditch Company, remaining in their service for two years. The winter of 1854–'55 Mr. Harris spent in San Francisco, at that time a very small, sparsely settled and unattractive place; and in the spring he joined a Government surveying party, as an assistant surveyor, and for three years filled that position in all the important Government surveys.

In 1857 the subject of this sketch took up his residence in the northern part of San Luis Obispo County, where he engaged in stock-raising. For the next eight years he was engaged at this calling, with considerable success. At the end of that time he went back to his profession of surveying, which he has since continued to follow. His long and varied experience in this capacity in different parts of the State has been of inestimable value to those who have been so fortunate as to secure his services. Indeed, it would be hard to find any one who could take his place.

Prominent in politics and a stanch Democrat, Mr. Harris has held for many years a conspicuous position among his fellow citizens in the management of the city and county affairs. To mention the public offices which Mr. Harris has held, or for which he has been the nominee of his party, would be to mention every important office in the gift of the county. He was Supervisor in 1865–'66–'67, County Surveyor for twelve years, City Councilman for four years, and was also a member of the Board of Trustees for San Luis Obispo. When it is explained that Mr. Harris was elected to the offices mentioned above as the nominee of the Democratic party —a party greatly in the minority in this section of the State—his personal popularity is shown at a glance. He was twice a nominee for Sheriff and once for Assemblyman, but was defeated by his opponents.

Mr. Harris is the owner of a very valuable ranch, which consists of 300 acres and which he purchased in 1880. This property is located four miles from San Luis Obispo, on the road to Santa Margarita. Mr. Harris was married in 1870, and has ten children. Their home is distinguished for its hospitality. After a beautiful drive from the city, the visitor is welcomed by Mr. Harris and his family with that cordiality and polite attention always so characteristic of the Cali fornian. During the past six months (1890) Mr. Harris has been stricken down with disease, and, though recovering slowly, is not able, at the present writing, to engage actively in business affairs.

M. W. BROWNE came to Ventura County in the fall of 1873, from his native city, Philadelphia, where he was born February 9, 1852. His father, N. B. Browne, was born in Philadelphia, in 1818; was a lawyer and a Representative in the Legislature from his district; held the office of Postmaster of Philadelphia under the administration of President Lincoln; was Sub-Treasurer and had charge of the Mint and Custom House; helped to organize the Trust and Safe Deposit Company of that city; was president of the company, and it might be said that he was the originator of that enterprise. The ancestors of his family were originally English. Mr. Browne's mother, *nee* Mary Jane Kendall, was a native of Reading, Pennsylvania, and also of English descent. The subject of this sketch was the third of a family of two sons and two daughters, and his mother's death occurred when he was only four years old. Mr. Browne received his education at Sanders' Institute, Philadelphia, and at Williston Seminary, East Hampton, Massachusetts. For five years he was employed in the Trust and Safe Deposit Company, Philadelphia, beginning as errand boy and rising to the position of receiving teller.

He came to California and engaged in sheep-raising, in Ventura County, ten years, being in partnership with Levi Taylor. They had as many as 12,000 sheep at a time, divided in flocks of 2,000 each. He disposed of his sheep, and afterward purchased 5,000 acres of land and engaged in the cattle business on the ex-Mission ranch, ten miles east of Ventura. He sold out in 1887, and for a year was one of the managers of the Anacapa Hotel. In 1882 he had served as Supervisor, and resigned the office to go away with his sheep. He was again elected, in 1888, to represent the town of San Buenaventura on the County Board, which position he now holds. He is the secretary of the Republican Central Committee, of Ventura County, and is a tried and true Republican of intelligence and ability, and a leader in his party.

Mr. Browne was married, in 1878, to Miss Neotia Rice, a native of California, born in 1860. She is the daughter of Peter Rice, who traces his ancestry back to the Germans. They have four children, all born in Ventura County, viz.: Albert O., Valeria O., Nathaniel B. and Samuel H. Mr. Browne takes a just pride in being a member of the California National Guard, of Ventura; is Second Lieutenant of the Company.

W. J. McGEE, proprietor of the Pioneer Shoe Store of Lompoc, was born at Kingston, Canada West, in 1846. As his parents died when he was very young he was early apprenticed, and in 1862 began the trade of shoemaker, serving three years. In 1865 he went to the vicinity of Rochester, New York, where he worked until 1866, when he returned to Kingston. In February, 1868, he started for California, by water and the Isthmus of Panama. There were 1,300 passengers on board, and except being a little crowded they had a comfortable and rapid passage, arriving at San Francisco, March, 1868. He then went to Santa Cruz, and in the fall to Watsonville, where he began business, and remained until the spring of 1875, when he came to Lompoc, having many friends among the colonists. He very soon opened a shoe store and shop and has since continued the business. The first store was an old adobe at the Mission, and the first church services were held in a grove east of town. Mr. McGee keeps a full line of goods.

He was married at Kingston, in the spring of 1867, to Miss Jessie Legassick, a native of England. She had given much attention to music, and was the pioneer music teacher of Lompoc, at which she is still engaged. They have three children, two sons and one daughter.

Mr. McGee was a member of the first Board of Directors of the town, and served two years, and was again elected in April, 1890, for four years. He is a stanch Republican, and for about ten years has been delegate of the party to the county conventions. He owns a nice property on L street, where is located his present residence.

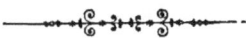

JOHN SPANNE, the City Marshal of Lompoc, and a leading dealer in agricultural implements, was born in Denmark, in December, 1857. His father was a blacksmith, and John learned the same trade at Schleswig, after an apprenticeship of three years. He then worked two years as a journeyman, and in 1880 came to the United States. He first settled in Ionia, Michigan, and worked one year in the carriage factory of M. J. Shields. He then came West to Leadville, Colorado, and was employed as blacksmith by the Leadville Lumber Company, remaining until January, 1883, when he came to Wilmington, Los Angeles County, in the employ of the Southern Pacific Railroad. After about fifteen months he took a trip to San Francisco; returning south he was engaged a few months at Los Alamos and Ballard's. He came to Lompoc in the fall of 1884, where he opened his present shop, corner of Ocean avenue and I street, purchasing the lot 50x150 feet, which he has since vastly improved. He carried on all kinds of blacksmith and repair work, and for two years has had the exclusive agency of Frank Bros., of San Francisco, who are extensive dealers in agricultural implements, and light and heavy wagons. Mr. Spanne is an active, energetic man, and is now doing the leading agricultural implement business of the valley. He has also erected a feed mill, and keeps barley and feed for sale. He was elected City Marshal in the spring of 1890.

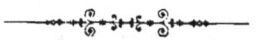

JOHN S. HENNING, a prominent contractor and builder of Lompoc, was born at Paris, Stark county, Ohio, in 1829. The father was a farmer, owning 112 acres. He died at the age of eighty-two years, and the mother is still living, at the age of eighty-two years; the land is still in the family. The subject of this sketch was educated in the common schools of Stark County, and at the age of nineteen years began to learn his trade, serving an apprenticeship with a Mr. Bowman at Canton, who later carried on business at South Bend, Indiana. After two years of training Mr. Henning took his first contract for a store building, which he carried through successfully; thereafter he did contract work about the county. In 1851 he started for Oregon, across the plains, wintering on the Missouri River, and arriving in Oregon September 9, 1852. Mr. Henning came with the Hardman family, which made up a company of twenty-two wagons. They had a very pleasant journey, with no deaths but three births. At Oregon City and Portland our subject worked at his trade until the fall of 1853, when he went to Olympia, Washington Territory, with the Government officials, who were sent there to take charge of the Territory. He followed his trade up to February, 1854, when he went to Seattle, and remained until 1857, building and contracting. He bought a place and built a house near Seattle, but was burned out by the Indian outbreak in 1855. Under Governor Stephens' call for volunteers Mr. Henning enlisted for three months, in Company H, Second Regiment, and was in a three-months engagement, mainly on scout duty. On January 13, 1856, he re-enlisted in Company A, First Regiment, and was in the fight at Seattle, Salmon Bay and Duwanish River, being in service about one year. He then returned to Seattle, and followed his trade until 1857, when he was again burned out by Indians. He then went into the logging business, furnishing Seattle mills.

In the fall of 1857 he came to California, and settled in Santa Clara County, where he bought 220 acres of land and built a house. He farmed a little, and worked at his trade. Mr. Henning remained in that county until February, 1877, when he sold out and came to Lompoc. He bought 120 acres of land, north of town, built his residence, and began working at his trade, which he has since continued. Prior to 1885 he erected nearly all the buildings of Lompoc. In 1885 he went to San Diego, and worked ten months, during the boom, and twenty months at Santa Barbara, building the Hawley Block, and some of the finest residences of that city. He returned to Lompoc, which has since been the field of his labors.

Mr. Henning was married in Santa Clara, in 1860, to Miss Mary Conner, a native of Massachusetts, who died in April, 1865, leaving three children. In 1868 he married Miss Mary Millikin, a native of Iowa, and they have had eight children; ten of all survive. The sons carry on the ranch, which consists of eight acres in prunes and other fruits, a fine tank house, and Mr. Henning will soon erect a more spacious residence.

DOLORES HERRERA is, in very plain English, an "old timer." He was born in New Mexico, in 1831, and came with his family to California in 1840. They went first to the San Gabriel mission, Los Angeles, where they lived one year. San Luis Obispo was their next home, and for twelve years they resided there. Mr. Herrera, Sr., kept a saloon in the place, which, as can well be imagined, was very primitive. Dolores assisted his father, and at various times was employed in ranch work near the mission. In 1853 he came to the San José Valley and settled where he is to-day, on a valuable property 400 acres in extent, through which the Salinas River winds, and also the Torro Creek. Here Mr. Herrera is engaged in farming and fruit-raising. An interesting feature of the place to a visitor is an enormous rock that rises out of the ground near the house. Thirty feet is a moderate estimate of its height on one side, and it is so conveniently situated that it forms the rear of one of the barns. A novel sight, indeed!

Mr. Herrera has been married three times, and has four children now living, all of whom are prominently identified with the interests of the San José Valley.

The subject of this sketch has an excellent memory, and, coming into this county as he did, early in its history, he relates some very interesting observations. When he first came to San Luis Obispo there were just two white people in the mission and about thirty Indians. The place was very desolate, and for a time there was little, if any, progress made in the development of the town. In San José Valley wild animals were plenty. Bears, wolves and lions were around stealing his pigs every day. Native Americans were few. Mr. Herrera relates that the creek which now is of great value to his property, was absolutely not to be seen when he first settled on his place, a fact to be accounted for only by the discovery and development of the mountain spring in 1862.

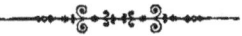

JOHN SIMPSON was born in Concord, New Hampshire, September 17, 1843, son of James and Eliza (Grant) Simpson. His father was born in Philadelphia, in 1808, his ancestors being natives of Massachusetts; and his mother was born in New Hampshire, in 1812. Her parents were also natives of the Granite State, and her father was a soldier in the Revolutionary war. John Simpson was the second of a family of four children. He was educated in Lowell, Massachusetts, after which he served an apprenticeship in his uncle John Simpson's machine shop.

When the call for volunteers resounded through the land, in 1861, he enlisted in Company K, Fifty-seventh Regiment, Illinois Infantry, and was in the service two years and a half. He participated in all the battles of the Army of the Tennessee, under General Grant and General Sherman, until the battle of Shiloh, where his regiment suffered heavily. Of the 520 who went into that engagement, 285 were lost. Mr. Simpson was wounded in the knee with a musket ball, and was crippled for six weeks. After he was wounded the army was driven back, he was captured on the field and was a prisoner four months in the South, at Mobile and Cahaba, Alabama, and at Macon, Georgia. While engaged with his regiment, supporting a battery, both the drums of his ears were so injured that he is quite deaf. After his exchange he served nearly a year on detailed duty, on account of his deafness. He was finally discharged for disability, and has since been in the railroad business. He learned telegraphy, and was in the employ of the Chicago, Burlington & Quincy, Central Pacific and Chicago, Milwaukee & St. Paul.

In 1877 he came to California and served as agent at Davisville, Yolo County, until 1884. In 1887 he came to Ventura and accepted the position of railroad agent, which he now fills.

Mr. Simpson was married in 1878, to Miss Lillie Pierce, a native of St. Louis, and daughter of Dr. T. B. Pierce, a dentist, of San Francisco. They have three children living: Arthur B. and George, born in Davisville; and Florence D., in Ventura.

Mr. Simpson is a worthy member of the G. A. R., of Ventura, and also of the Masonic fraternity.

WILLIAM BARKER, of Lompoc, was born in Santa Clara County, California, in 1857. His father was a farmer, having 160 acres of land, and carrying on general farming. William was educated at San José and Salinas, Monterey County, when, in 1868, his father moved and bought 849 acres of land and carried on farming more extensively. In 1873 William learned the photographic business, but in 1874 returned to the ranch, and remained until the fall of 1879, when he went to Chico to engage in mining. In July, 1881, he returned to San José, remaining until October, 1882, when he came to Lompoc; he bought forty acres of land and engaged in the nursery business. Selling out in 1885, he rented land until the spring of 1890, when he gave up the business, and on June 1, 1890, opened his present business, on H Street, consisting of fruits, cigars, nuts and candies.

He was married at San José, in 1876, to Miss Margarette E. McIlvain, a native of California. They have four children. Mr. Barker is a member of Lompoc Lodge, No. 248, I. O. O. F., and of Najoqui Parlor, No. 129, Native Sons of the Golden West.

D. T. TRUITT, the present Supervisor for Santa Barbara County, from the Lompoc District, was born in Salisbury, Worcester County, Maryland, in 1835. His father was a farmer, and in 1851 emigrated to Van Buren County, Iowa, where he bought a small farm. The subject of this sketch was educated at Mount Pleasant, Henry County, at the Iowa Wesleyan University, at which he graduated in 1861. He came to California across the plains in 1862, driving an ox team. They came by Sublette's Cut-off and down the Humboldt River, and arrived at Sacramento in the fall, after a six months' journey. He taught school in Yolo and Solano counties about one year, and in 1863–'64–'65 was employed by the United States Sanitary Commission, in collecting funds and supplies for the sick and disabled soldiers, working under O. C. Wheeler, of San Francisco. He was then employed by Bancroft & Co. in selling books until 1886, when he went East, by Panama, and returned to his home. He taught school in Schuyler County, Missouri, and in 1870 was elected County Clerk for a term of four years. He was then elected Superintendent of Schools for Schuyler County for two years. He was then cashier for the C. H. Howell Bank at Glenwood, Missouri, until the summer of 1877, when he came to Lompoc, arriving in August; he had land purchased for him before his arrival. He has since added to his first purchase 350 acres, about seventy-five of which is tillable, the balance being grazing land. He then built his present residence, known as the Mountain Home, doing most of the work himself; it was set in the midst of brush and timber, which has since been cleared away and improved, making a sheltered and comfortable home. He has about fifteen acres in deciduous fruits, apples being the main crop, which is doing especially well; also raises beans and English mustard. Mr. Truitt was elected Supervisor from the Fourth District, in the fall of 1883, and was re-elected in 1887, which proves him to be an efficient and acceptable officer. He was married in Schuyler County, Missouri, in 1868, to Miss Mary A. Saunders, a native of Iowa; they have four children, three daughters and one son. Mr. Truitt is a member of Lompoc Lodge, No. 262, F. & A. M., and of the Methodist Church of Lompoc.

C. R. TUTT, proprietor of the handsome and spacious hardware store of Lompoc, was born in South Bend, Indiana, in 1864. He was educated at the Notre Dame College, at South Bend, but left college in 1879 and went to Chicago to learn the tinning and plumbing trade with Craigon Bros. & Co. He was employed by this firm for eighteen months, but worked in the city until 1884, when he came to California, first to San Francisco, where he worked at his trade, and then to Ukiah, Mendocino County, where he worked for a while. At the end of this time he started in business, continuing until 1886, when he was burned out, and having no insurance, lost everything. Mr. Tutt then came to San Luis Obispo, and after a short time again started a shop, which he continued until 1888, when he sold out and went to Tulare City and bought property, but the climate being too hot he did not settle there, and he came to Lompoc in the fall of 1888. He at once located by buying city property and erecting his spacious store building, 25 x 140, which serves as a ware-room and shop, where he carries a full line of hardware, paints, oils and agricultural implements. Mr. Tutt is also connected with A. L. Hanck and Wm. Cantley in the lumber firm of E. R. Tutt & Co., which was established in 1889. They have a steam saw-mill, and also suitable machinery for jointing and moulding.

Mr. Tutt was married in San Luis Obispo, in 1887, to Miss Emma Adams, a native of Oregon, and daughter of Judge Adams, of San Luis. Mr. Tutt is now erecting a handsome residence on H street. He is a member of Park Lodge, No. 40, K. of P., at San Luis Obispo.

MARIANO LAZCANO, a brother of Bernardo Lazcano, was born in Mexico in 1825. Receiving a good education when a boy, he was placed in a store at the age of eleven years, and remained behind the counter thirteen years. In 1849, at the age of twenty-four, Mr. Lazcano came to California, and after spending six months in the mines came to San Luis Obispo, which place he reached in September of that year. Mariano preceded his brother by a few months, and, upon his arrival, they jointly engaged in business, conducting for nine years a general merchandise store. Their place of business was opposite the Mission building, in the French Hotel which they built. Theirs was the second store in the place: in fact there were only two altogether then, Pollard & Beebee having the other. Mr. Lazcano came to San José Valley in 1858. He first engaged in cattle-raising, building a home across the creek which runs through the valley. In 1864 was the disastrous dry year, and he lost so many cattle that he became greatly discouraged, and turned his attention to the raising of sheep. All went well until 1877, which proved to be a terrible year for them. However, Mr. Lazcano has been very energetic and industrious, and has prospered. It was in 1864 that the brothers came into possession of the fine property (1,440 acres), which they owned up to a recent date, when they sold a small tract.

Mr. Lazcano was married in 1855 to Serbula Ybarra. They are the parents of two sons and one daughter. Their splendid adobe residence was built in 1858. It was partially destroyed by fire in 1862, but the walls, two to three feet in thickness, were left unharmed, and the entire structure has been restored. Beautifully situated, the house and grounds are an attractive feature of the valley. In front of the house and extending above the entire front yard, is a fine grape-vine, affording excellent shade from the sun during the hot summer months, and in season bearing good fruit. This vine is exactly twenty-one years old, the age of Miss Mariana Lazcano, their only daughter. On entering this home the visitor is quickly impressed by the courtesy, cordiality and genuine hospitality for which Mr. Lazcano and his family are distinguished. The home is comfortably and substantially furnished. A piece of furniture rarely seen in the country in California, and of which there are none of finer quality in the city of San Luis Obispo, is the upright piano which occupies a conspicuous place in their parlor. Miss Lazcano is both an accomplished singer and pianist.

The subject of this sketch is busily engaged in the management of his ranch and expects to spend the residue of his life in this charming valley, of which he has now been a resident for over thirty years. A man closely identified with the early history of San Luis Obispo, prominent and alert in all matters affecting the locality where he now lives, this brief sketch forms a very important chapter in the history of San Luis Obispo County.

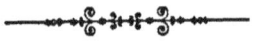

ALONZO LAZCANO, son of Mariano Lazcano, was born in San Luis Obispo, May 28, 1860. At the age of twelve years he came with his father to Pozo in the San José Valley. For four years he was employed as a clerk in the general merchandise store of Peter Agnellini, an Italian. During that period he gained a thorough knowledge of business life and habits. In 1884 Mr. Agnellini died, and Lazcano & Mancilla succeeded to the business. Mention of Mr. Mancilla's life appears elsewhere in this work. In 1888 the firm dissolved, Mr. Lazcano continuing alone at the old stand. He does a general merchandise business and keeps a fine assortment of everything needed in an ordinary life-time. He has also been Postmaster there since November 15, 1888.

Mr. Lazcano was married April 30, 1886, to Helen Herrera, daughter of Dolores Herrera, one of the pioneers of the valley. A sketch of his life will be found on another page of this work.

A fact worthy of publication and of very wide circulation is, that in an experience of ten years in the retailing of liquor at the bar and tobacco business (an important department of every general store), Mr. Lazcano has never smoked nor drank any intoxicating liquor, neither has he gambled. This is a record of which any one in these times may well be proud.

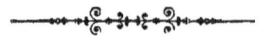

W. A. SAUNDERS, proprietor of a livery stable in Lompoc, was born in Birmingham, Van Buren County, Iowa, in 1850. His father was a cabinet-maker, and moved to Scotland County, Missouri, in 1858. W. A. Saunders began work in early life with his father and remained at home until twenty-one years of age, when he began farming on his own account, and in 1874 came to California. He passed two years in the redwoods of Santa Cruz County, and returned home in March, 1876, with the intention of remaining, not enjoying the climate of Missouri. He passed two months at home, and then returned to California, bringing his father with him. His father soon returned to Missouri and brought out his family to Lompoc, where he died in November, 1889, at the age of seventy-three years. The subject of this sketch came to Lompoc in the fall of 1876, and worked about one year. He then rented a stock ranch of 1,000 acres at La Honda, and began raising cattle, keeping about 300 head. He sold out in 1879 and returned to the Lompoc Valley, purchasing forty acres and renting 300 acres adjoining, where he farmed until 1885. He started the livery business at the

"Fashion Stables," under the firm name of Saunders & Calhoon. They bought 75 x 140 feet on Ocean avenue, and erected their large stable. In the fall of 1887 Calhoon sold his interest to James Rennie, and the firm of Saunders & Rennie has since continued. They keep twenty head of horses, and light and heavy wagons suitable for the trade.

Mr. Saunders was married at Lompoc, in 1885, to Miss Ellen Ruffner, a native of Santa Cruz County; two children have blessed this union. Mr. Saunders is a member of the Knights of Pythias.

BERNARDO LAZCANO was born in Mexico in 1820. At the age of twenty-six he came to California, and direct to the city of San Luis Obispo. With his brother Mariano, who had preceded him to this State, he built the small French Hotel opposite the mission building, the third house erected in the town, and conducted a store in it, under the firm name of Lazcano Brothers. For eight years they continued in business here, and there were no more familiar figures about town than the Lazcano brothers. In 1858 the subject of this sketch settled in the San José Valley, and was one of the first arrivals in this rich and fertile spot. He at once turned his attention to stock-raising. Every thing in this valley was then in a wild and uncultivated state. Bears, deer and wolves were plentiful and also very bold. Mr. Lazcano relates that many a time did these animals visit the kitchen of his house, if, indeed, on the way they were unable to capture any beeves. Bear were very plentiful and also exceedingly troublesome in those times to the cattle-raiser. Mr. Lazcano and one of his ranchmen found fourteen wolves in a gang one day. They had their dogs with them, but discreetly made up their minds not to provoke attack. Later on the dogs and wolves attacked each other, but were finally separated without serious loss. The dogs used to track many deer in this valley and on one occasion killed two within an hour's time. A magnificent hunting ground, that! To-day any one can go back in the hills and mountains and capture a deer without much trouble, and if still more ambitious he can find the California mountain lion. Mr. Lazcano's ranch in the San José Valley originally contained 1,440 acres. He has since disposed of all but 860 acres. His residence is an old adobe one, built in the year 1857.

Mr. Lazcano was County Treasurer in 1874. He is a man universally popular, as is shown in the result of this election. All the voting then in this part of the county was done at Santa Margarita, eighteen miles distant. All the voters from San José Valley and surrounding country had to be transported to this place, and Mr. Lazcano's friends all reached the polls through his efforts and expense. His political career is strictly Republican, and he never has received any funds to work and carry on campaigns. He has always worked at his own expense, from Lincoln's administration to date.

He has never married.

WILLIAM T. PIPPIN was born in Missouri, in 1855, and came to San Luis Obispo County, California, June 30, 1870. He first located in Morro, where he was engaged in ranching with his step-father for three years. At the end of that time he accompanied his parents to Arizona, the family making the trip by wagon. After remaining there for six months he returned to California, located at Chorro and engaged in dairying, renting a dairy of Mr. Lowry, of that place. After being thus engaged for one year, he was employed on a ranch, for wages. In 1876 he stocked a ranch, of which he was foreman, with 100 cows, and ran a dairy for six months, meeting with good success. At this time Mr. Pippin decided to make a prospecting trip in the north. December 17, 1879, he came to the San José Valley, rented a place of Captain Fletcher, and subsequently purchased the ranch, which contains 167 acres and which he now occupies. This property is located in the beautiful San José Valley, a mile and three-quarters from Pozo. Here Mr. Pippin is engaged in dairying, being very successful and receiving good prices for his product, which he markets with great care. He states that off of twelve cows (Devon) he has marketed one ton of butter, from September 1 to June 1, which is, indeed, a remarkable showing. Mr. Pippin also raises some fine fruit, the soil of the San José Valley being especially celebrated for this. As a health resort, Mr. Pippin speaks in the highest terms of the San José Valley. Since his residence here he has never had occasion to call a physician to his home.

The subject of this sketch was married, January 27, 1880, to Miss Lizzie L. Epperly. They have an adopted child.

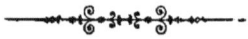

DE ROME BROTHERS, proprietors of a blacksmith shop and also agents for all kinds of agricultural implements in Lompoc. The firm is composed of A. P. and George E. DeRome. A. P. DeRome was born in Chicago, in 1856; his father was a cabinet-maker. In 1858 he moved his family to California, coming by water and the Isthmus of Panama. They settled in San Francisco, where A. P. was educated, and at the age of fifteen years began learning his trade of blacksmith at Kimball's manufactory, where he remained three years. He then passed two and a half years in Oakland, and in the fall of 1876 he went to Cayucos, San Luis Obispo County, and there opened a shop and remained twelve years in general blacksmith work. He sold out and in the spring of 1888 came to Lompoc.

George E. DeRome was born in San Francisco, in 1862, and also learned his trade at Kimball's manufactory, where he remained three years. He then joined his brother at Cayucos, working for wages until his brother sold out to go to Lompoc. In the spring of 1889 the present partnership was formed. They bought 50 x 140 feet of land on the corner of Ocean avenue and G street, and there erected their present spacious building, 50 x 60 feet. They carry on all the branches of blacksmithing, and are also agents for all kinds of agricultural implements. A. P. DeRome was married in 1884, to Miss Fanny Henning, a native of California. Four children have blessed this union, only three of whom survive.

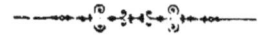

ISAAC J. SPARKS, deceased, was born in the town of Bowdoin, Maine, about year 1800, and was one of the great land-owners, and an early pioneer of this section of the State. His father fought in the war of 1812, and after its close moved his family to Ohio, and soon afterward to Saint Louis, Missouri, where he engaged in farming; he also died at this place. After his father's death our subject was obliged to take charge of the plantation. He had intended to become a doctor, but had to give up the idea on account of ill health. He was troubled with dyspepsia, and frequently went to the mountains for relief, and it was on one of these expeditions that Mr. Sparks met a party that was bound for the far West. Francis Z. Branch, elsewhere sketched in this work, and Oldman Yount, an old pioneer, were members of the party, he had no intentions of joining this party, but nevertheless was induced to do so, and he first settled at Los Angeles, California, in the early part of the year 1832, and a year later in Santa Barbara. Here Mr. Sparks followed Otter hunting, at which business he was very successful, being an excellent shot. He acquired large tacts of land, owning seven large ranches in Santa Barbara County, and the Huasna and Pismo ranches in San Luis Obispo County, at one time. The Huasna property, five leagues, now in possession of the daughters, was the smallest one. These large tracts were granted to Mr. Sparks by the Mexican government, chiefly as a protection against the Indians, the government freely giving the land if a settler could then be induced to occupy it, and thus in a measure keep off the hostile redskins. He was a resident of Santa Barbara when Fremont was there, and the General was very anxious that he should take up arms against the Mexicans, which he declined to do. He however aided Fremont in many ways, giving him provisions, clothing, horses, etc., to the value of $20,000 or more, for which he never received a cent in return. Mr. Sparks built and conducted the only store in Santa Barbara for some time, and also built the first brick house in the town, a relic of which now remains. He was a man tall and slim, but with a well formed frame, and had a fine commanding presence. His death occurred June 16, 1867.

He was married in Santa Barbara, to Miss Mary Ayers, a lady of Scotch descent, now living in that city, strong and hearty at the age of seventy-eight years. They had three children, —Flora, Rosa and Sallie, who are now Mrs. Captain Harloe, of San Luis Obispo; Mrs. Arza Porter, of the same place; and Mrs. Harkness of Santa Barbara.

R. E. BATTLES, whose fine ranch of 320 acres is attractively located on the mesa east of town, was born in Erie County, Pennsylvania, in 1848. His father was a farmer, and in early life our subject moved to Illinois, where he continued farming until 1855; then he moved to the town of Ipava, Fulton County, where he engaged in the blacksmithing business until 1860; then he engaged in a grocery until 1864, when he and his son again pushed West to California, crossing the plains with horse teams. They settled in Sacramento Valley, where they were engaged in farming until 1868, when they came to the Santa Maria Valley and took up 160 acres where Mr. Battles' father still resides, at the age of seventy-four years. The subject of this sketch lived at home until 1872, when he began farming on 160 acres, which he had preempted in 1868. About the year 1876 he sold out, and purchased his present fine ranch of 320 acres on the mesa, where he farms principally in grain. He has 160 acres of land near the town of Garey, which is devoted to stock for grazing. He also plants twenty acres in corn, and twenty-five acres in beans, and a small acreage to other summer crops. He averages about 300 hogs, which he fattens for market.

Mr. Battles was married in Santa Maria, in 1884, to Miss Mary E. Minor, and they have two children: Rollin Eugene and Myron H.

CAPTAIN MARCUS HARLOE is a native of Ireland, born March 17, 1833. His mother was a Scotch ship-master's daughter of Campbelltown, Argyleshire, and his father's ancestors were both Irish and English. Both are now deceased. Much of Captain Harloe's boyhood was spent in Ireland and Scotland, where he attended school. Early in life he evinced a strong desire for the sea, and in 1847 came to America. The next three years were spent on the sea, and in 1850 he came to California. With headquarters at San Francisco, for twenty years and more Captain Harloe has led a seafaring life on the Pacific, and more especially on the California coast. He has risen from the lowest and humblest position in the marine service to some of the most important in the gift of the Government. From 1862 to 1875 he was Captain of many of the steamers sailing between San Francisco and San Diego, and from San Francisco north to Portland. He was also engaged as commanding officer with the Pacific Mail Steamship Company for a time. Captain Harloe was Harbormaster at San Francisco for two years, 1865 to 1867, and in 1880 was appointed chief wharfinger, which includes the office of harbor-master, and served a term of four years, it being a political office and an appointment of some significance.

In 1866 the Captain married Miss Flora Sparks, the eldest daughter of Isaac J. Sparks, of Santa Barbara, by whom he has had seven children, two daughters and five sons.

Since 1875 the Captain and Mrs. Harloe have made their home in the Huasna Valley. Their ranch, consisting of two square leagues of land, is a part of the original Sparks grant. The Captain is engaged in farming, cattle-raising and dairying on this property, much of which is rented out. To the stranger, driving through this valley for the first time, the country appears like one huge park, so beautiful are the trees, hills and landscape. The Harloe home is built of adobe and is situated on a knoll, one mile from the Huasna postoffice. The house is an old one and was rebuilt and enlarged in 1868. Isolated as the house seems to be from the adjacent towns, one is quite impressed with the luxuries and comfortable appointments which greet the visitor as he enters. One noticeable feature of this attractive home is a splendidly equipped library, the property of Mrs. Sparks. Another is a fine Steinway piano. Since coming to the Huasna Valley, Captain Harloe has not entirely given up his sea life. He was for two years commander of the Santa Maria. During his residence in this place he has served as Supervisor for the Arroyo Grande District two years, 1876-1877. September 1, 1890, he was nominated for the Assembly by the Republican county convention.

An exceedingly popular man, Captain Harloe is held in the highest esteem by all who know him. As a ship-master, he won the respect, confidence and good will of all who traveled with him.

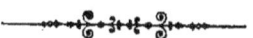

JOHN HOUK, one of the progressive ranchers of the Santa Maria Valley, was born in Germany, in 1852; his father was a nail-maker by trade. Labor being poorly paid, Mr. Houk emigrated to the United States with his family in 1855, going first to Cincinnati, Ohio, where he began farming. At the age of thirteen years our subject began his self-support. He went to Missouri and worked for two years on a ranch, then to Texas, where he followed the beef trade for two years, and then returned home, where he resided until 1874, when he came to California. After spending the winter at Sacramento he traveled north through Oregon and Washington Territory, but returned to Sacramento, where he worked at harvesting and in logging camps until the fall of 1876. He then came to Santa Maria and took up eighty acres in La Gracia country, remaining until the fall of 1880, when he sold out and bought 320 acres of the Suez school district. Mr. Houk has his ranch well fenced and improved. He raised principally grain until 1888, and now carries on general farming, with a small dairy of twenty cows. He is improving his stock by crossing with full-blood Holstein, owning some fine animals, and forty fine Berkshire hogs.

Mr. Houk was married at Sacramento, in 1875, to Miss Angelina Howerton, and they have eight children.

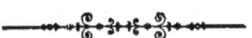

JOSEPH RUFFNER, one of the stanch and sterling citizens of Lompoc, was born at Luray, Page County, Virginia, in 1819. His father was an extensive farmer. Facilities for education were limited in those early days, but Joseph received the best that could be obtained from the old log school-house. In 1842 he went to West Virginia, part of the way by stage. Afterward he made a trip to Missouri, and returning to Virginia he followed farming until 1845, and in Kanawha County he was then superintendent of a salt furnace, in the manufacture of salt, until 1852. He then started for California by Major Amesby's covered wagon train, paying $200 for his passage from St. Louis to Sacramento, and being about four months on the journey. There were twenty passengers, but they were all amply fed, and, excepting one death from mountain fever, they came through without accident. At Sacramento Mr. Ruffner entered the stock business, buying for market, and at the close of the first week he had neither made or lost, and he gave up the business. In 1852 he bought a team of horses, drove to Santa Cruz, and there rented land and farmed for two years. He then bought 150 acres of land near the coast, where he made his home up to 1879, carrying on general farming. He was one of the original stockholders of the Lompoc Colony, and attended the first sale, purchasing eighty acres, which he sold later. In 1879 he closed his interest at Santa Cruz and came to Lompoc to reside. Mr. Ruffner rented the Thomas Wick's ranch of 250 acres, which was sold to Captain Sudden, in 1882, but Mr. Ruffner has continued on the ranch up to date (1890) and carries on general farming in barley, beans, mustard and potatoes, and also raises some horses. All of the ranch is under cultivation. In 1887 Mr. Ruffner made his first trip East, visiting his own home, going as far as Philadelphia. In 1887 he bought 123 acres of valley and grazing land, south of town, where his son now resides. He has seen some wonderful changes in the valley. When he arrived the question was, "What can we raise?" Nature herself has answered by giving abundant harvests, from any seed which are committed to her productive influences. Mr. Ruffner thinks California the best State in the Union.

He was married at Santa Cruz, in 1855, to Miss Elizabeth Williams, a native of New York State. Four children have blessed the union, two sons and two daughters, all of whom are married and living in the valley.

Mrs. Ruffner died in 1886, at the age of sixty-six years.

B. T. WILEY, one of the first locators of the Santa Maria Valley, was born in Autanga County, Alabama, in 1825. He was brought up on a farm, and at the age of fifteen years he went to Mississippi, where he was engaged in farming until 1847, when he enlisted for the Mexican war, in the Second Mississippi Regiment, under Colonel Reuben Davis. Their service was on Taylor's line, through Monterey and to Buena Vista, Mexico, but not being in time for the battle they were not in actual service, and were mustered out at Vicksburg, in July, 1848. Mr. Wiley returned to his home, and then to Greensborough, Mississippi, where he was engaged in farming until March, 1849, when he started for California. He drove five yoke of oxen across the plains, landing at Hangtown, now Placerville, in October, 1849, where he began mining, and continued for eight years. In 1857 he went to Amador County and began farming. He was married at Santa Cruz, in June, 1859, to Miss Minerva Clark, and they continued on the farm in Amador County until the fall of 1862, when they went to Santa Cruz County, and there located. A grant covered their ranch, and in 1864 they went to Mendocino County, and continued farming in different counties until 1868, when, having lost his wife, he took up land in the Santa Maria Valley, being the first man to locate. His land, of 160 acres, was a half-mile north of town; he built a little cabin and dug the first well, sixty-five feet deep without curbing, now considered a perilous proceeding. After two years he traded for other property, and in 1878 sold out and located his present ranch in Strawberry Cañon, southeast of town, and began improving by clearing off brush, fencing and building. He owns 320 acres, and carried on general farming. He has fifteen acres in fruit, and a fine garden with raspberries and strawberries every month in the year without irrigating. Corn is his principal crop, of which he plants about forty acres; he also keeps fifteen head of horses and cattle.

Mr. Wiley was again married at San Luis Obispo, in 1875, to Mrs. Abigail Bryant, and they have three sons. Mr. Wiley is particular that his children shall receive every benefit of an education.

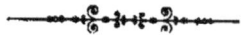

JOHN M. WILKINSON, a native of Missouri, was born March 2, 1837; was reared on a farm, attending school a part of the time, until seventeen years of age. In 1854 he came to California, crossing the plains with an ox team. He first settled in Butte County and spent some time in the mines. In the spring of 1855 he went to Napa County and for eight years was engaged in farming. Mr. Wilkinson relates that these days were the most prosperous ones of his life—he made money and made it fast.

Mr. Wilkinson was married in the fall of 1861 to Miss Wallace, of Napa County, by whom he had six children, only four of whom are living at present. In 1879 he was married a second time to Miss Hettie Stubblefield, of Santa Barbara, and by this marriage has had five children.

During 1863 and 1864 Mr. Wilkinson passed through a period of misfortunes, losing all the money he had ever made. This was in Washoe City, Nevada, where he was engaged in teaming and speculating in mining stock. Leaving this locality as soon as he could, he engaged in farming in Butte and Sonoma counties for six years, and in 1870 came to San Luis Obispo County. In 1875 he went to Santa Barbara County and settled on a ranch near Santa Maria, and for nine years lived there and did well. In 1884 he came to the Huasna Valley, where he has ever since resided. Mr. Wilkinson is engaged in fruit-raising and farming on his ranch of 160 acres. Like all the soil in this valley, it is rich and productive. Mr. Wilkinson has been particularly successful in raising grapes. He grows the Muscatel raisin grapes in large quantities and of excellent quality. The section of the Huasna Valley in which this property is located has been cultivated only in recent years. When Mr. Wilkinson came here in 1884 his ranch was one brush thicket, and now anything can be raised on it. Watermelons weighing from thirty to fifty pounds each are often picked from his vines, and one weighing sixty-five pounds was once grown, and is his best exhibit so far. To complete this illustration of the wonderful fertility of the soil in the Huasna Valley, Mr. Wilkinson has picked melons from his vines on Christmas Day, and has had them on his table for dinner. To people outside of the State of California, this story will appear quite impossible to believe, and perhaps to many in the State, but to the neighbors of Mr. Wilkinson it is an assured fact.

A. EVANS, a rancher of Lompoc, was born in Putnam County, Indiana, in 1834. In 1854 his father moved to Madison County, Iowa, being among the pioneers of that section. The subject of this sketch remained at home until 1857, when he came to California, by steamer from New York, crossing the Isthmus of Panama. From San Francisco he went to Oroville, Butte County, where he passed two years in a lumber camp. In 1859 he came to Gilroy, Santa Clara Valley, and worked in the redwoods, hauling and getting out lumber, remaining until 1862, when he went to the Powder River Mines, in Oregon, and worked one year. He then went to Boise City, Idaho, and was connected with mining interests until 1866, when he returned to San José and was connected with ranching at Gilroy and Castroville. In 1880 Mr. Evans came to Lompoc and bought eighty acres of land and has since devoted himself to the cultivation of beans, mustard and general farming. He has a small orchard sufficient for family use.

Mr. Evans was married at San José in 1869, to Miss Hannah Higginbotham, of Cheshire, England. They have one son, Oliver Samuel Evans, born in March, 1872.

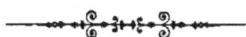

NATHAN BROOKS SMITH, is a native of the State of Massachusetts, born in Concord, January 17, 1850. He is the son of Joseph A. Smith, who was born in Concord in 1818, and still resides there, engaged in farming. He is a lineal descendant of Paul Revere, the hero of Revolutionary days. Mr. Smith's mother, Rebecca (Brooks) Smith, was born in Acton, a town adjoining Concord. She came of Puritan stock. Her father, Nathan Brooks, was a farmer, and her grandfather, Seth Brooks, was a Sergeant in the Acton "Minute Men," and was in the "Concord Fight" of 1775. There were six children in the family, the subject of this sketch being the oldest. He received his education in the institutions of learning in his native city; and afterward engaged in railroading in Kansas and Nebraska. Then he was book-keeper for Mr. Josiah Quincy, in Boston. Later, he went to Concord, bought a farm and engaged in general farming. That property he sold before coming to California. Upon his arrival on this coast, he located in Ventura County and engaged in sheep-raising, which proved a paying business. They had as many as 7,000 sheep at one time. This business he closed out, and, in 1882, with his partner, purchased his present fine fruit ranch of forty-five acres, on Ventura avenue. It is planted principally to walnuts, apricots, prunes and apples, but he also has a variety of other fruits. They are farming a large tract to wheat and barley, 4,000 acres being devoted to the cultivation of these crops, the yield being correspondingly large.

Mr. Smith, in 1875, married Miss Agnes E. Tolman, a native of Concord, daughter of Benjamin Tolman, also a native of that city, and the owner of a large printing house. They have one son, Allen Tolman Smith, born in Concord in 1880. Mr. Smith is a member of the Masonic fraternity. In politics he is independent.

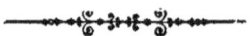

W. MAULSBY, of Santa Maria, was born in Wayne County, Indiana, in October, 1856, and moved to Dallas County, Iowa, in 1858, where his father engaged in farming. He was educated in the high schools, and at Tabor College in Fremont County, Iowa, after which he studied medicine two years. In 1878 he was married at Perry, Iowa, to Miss Linda E. Beeson, and in 1881 he went to Colorado and engaged in mining; he did the assessment work on the great Iron King Silver Mine without realizing a substantial benefit. In 1882 he came to Santa Maria, California, where he started a boot and shoe store; this he exchanged the following year for a farm, which he managed one year, then rented it and moved to Los Angeles, but returned to Santa Maria again in 1886 and engaged in the real-estate business. In 1887, associated with S. J. Jones, they bought sixty acres southeast of town, which they improved under the name of Olive Hill Orchard and Nursery.

Mr. Maulsby has bred some fine trotting stock which he is now having trained; he is a member of the County Board of Horticultural Commissioners for Santa Barbara County. Mr. and Mrs. Maulsby have two children, Luln A. and Flora B.

Mr. Maulsby is a member of Hesperian Lodge, No. 264, F. & A. M.

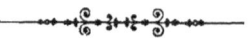

F. McCLURE, a rancher of Lompoc and one of the early settlers, was born in Caledonia County, Vermont, in 1844. Until 1866 he lived at home, and assisted his father on the farm. He was educated in Caledonia County and attended academies, and later taught the winter school. In 1866 he came to California, by the Isthmus of Panama, landing at San Francisco, and first bought a water route and sold water about the city. He then went to Nevada, and drove on a stage route, then conducted a dairy in Marin County, and later went back to San Francisco, where after three months he came to Santa Cruz and was in the dairy business for one year. In 1871 Mr. McClure returned for a visit to his old home in Vermont. On his return to San Francisco he engaged in the milk business, which he continued at Santa Cruz for one and a half years. In 1875 he came to Lompoc, and bought forty acres of land in the valley, to which he has since added another forty, and also eighty acres of hill and valley land. His main crops are beans, mustard, and barley for hay. He has a small orchard for family use, and about twenty-five horses for breeding and ranch purposes.

Mr. McClure was married at Santa Cruz, in 1874, to Miss F. L. Hall. They are blessed with three children, and a good, comfortable home in which to pass the decline of life.

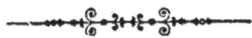

ARZA PORTER was born in Lima, Livingston County, New York, March 28, 1838, and was there reared and educated. Livingston County, besides being famous for its rich soil, magnificent farms, trout streams, trout ponds, etc., is also famous for its schools with well developed and well defined systems of study. The Geneseo Normal School, located at Geneseo in the beautiful Genesee Valley, is perhaps the largest of these institutions; but the Genesee Wesleyan Seminary, located at Lima, is the oldest and probably the best known throughout the country. It was the latter institution that Mr. Porter attended for a time, being engaged in his studies there up to the time the family decided to move West. On account of the delicate health of Mr. Porter's father, who was threatened with consumption, the family home was now moved to Morris, Grundy County, Illinois. Here Mr. Porter lived for four years on a farm owned by his father. He then made up his mind to go further west and seek new fields of labor. Hearing of the military excitement at Salt Lake City, in 1858, he crossed the plains with ox teams to that point. Finding nothing there to interest him, he planned to return home; but, owing to the heavy fall of snow, the trip across the plains was, of course, impracticable, and he decided to go to California, although he originally had no thought of going so far. The party of which he was a member then packed their blankets and walked from Salt Lake City to Los Angeles, California, the entire trip across the plains from Illinois consuming six months and a half of time.

Once in California, Mr. Porter has since resided here, only returning East once, in 1874, for a visit. Los Angeles was his home from 1858 to 1863. A part of that time he was in the employ of the Stage Company, as he was also subsequently, when he moved to Santa Barbara. Mr. Porter came to Santa Barbara in 1863, and with the best interests of this city and county he was very closely identified for many years. He was elected Sheriff of the county in 1865, and held the office for six years. For two terms he was also a member of the Common Council, commencing with the year 1873, or as near that as can be recalled.

It was in Santa Barbara that Mr. Porter was so fortunate as to meet Mr. Isaac J. Sparks and his family. Mr. Sparks, a sketch of whose life appears elsewhere in this publication, was then well advanced in years, but apparently strong and hearty. Mr. Porter was married in 1870 to Miss Rosa Sparks, and up to very recent years continued to make Santa Barbara his home. At present Mr. and Mrs. Porter reside with their family, which consists of six children, in the Huasna Valley, San Luis Obispo County. Their ranch consists of two square leagues of land (something over 10,000 acres), and is a part of the original grant of the Mexican Government to Mr. Sparks. This splendid property is situated in as healthy a spot as there probably is in the world. No damp winds and no fogs are to be found in this valley. The soil, as might be expected, is rich and productive, and for fruit purposes apparently cannot be excelled. Mr. Porter has recently set out an orchard of twelve acres, near his house, containing a grape vineyard, and peach, prune and apricot trees—a model in its way. The trees are only four to six years old and, without irrigation, the yield this year (1890) is something enormous, the peaches being especially large and of rare quality. As this was the owner's first experiment in fruit culture on the place it illustrates well the remarkable fertility of the soil and its special adaptability for fruit raising. Mr. and Mrs. Porter are universally popular; their home is distinguished for its hospitality, the visitor being welcomed with the kindness and attention so characteristic of the Californian.

Since making his home in San Luis Obispo County, Mr. Porter has held public office on one occasion. In 1884 he was elected Assemblyman, defeating Judge D. R. McVenable, his opponent, who was the following term elected to the same office over H. M Warden.

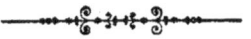

HON. LEMUEL C. McKEEBY came to Ventura in 1868 from Carson City, Nevada. He was born in New York city in 1825, and received his education there. His father, Edward McKeeby, was of Scotch descent and a native of New York. His mother, *nee* Catharine Miller, was born in New York and was a descendant of one of the old German families of that city. His great-grandfather was a soldier in the Revolutionary war. Mr. McKeeby served one year as private in the service of the United States during and until the close of the war with Mexico, when he was honorably discharged. He then made Milwaukee, Wisconsin, his home. In 1850 he came to California and engaged in mining, and was always a successful miner. He mined at French Corral and Sebastopol principally; was the first to introduce rubber hose for hydraulic mining, which was at Sebastopol, Nevada County. He there, with his associates, carried on a large mine, the weekly yield being from $2,000 to $4,000. His company also put a flume in the Yuba River twenty feet wide, at a cost of $20,000. During his mining operations his gold was sent by Wells, Fargo & Co's Express to Marysville and to San Francisco, where it yielded an average of $14 per ounce. From this mine he went to Carson City, and with others erected a factory and engaged in the manufacture of sulphuric acid. In this enterprise he was also successful. The expense at this time, 1863, of getting the material—some fifteen tons in all—to commence operations, to that place from San Francisco, was ten cents per pound. The demand for the acid diminished and he sold out. While there he was elected Justice of the Peace and Police Judge. He was also elected a member of the first Legislature from the city of Carson, State of Nevada, and had the honor, in joint convention, of placing in nomination Hon. J. W. Nye for United States Senator; Governor Nye and Wm. M. Stewart were the two first United States Senators elected from that State.

Mr. McKeeby came to Ventura and engaged in the mercantile business, but for the past ten years has been engaged in the active practice of his profession, and is considered a very careful and successful lawyer. He has always been identified with the business interests of the town and county, and was one of the organizers of the first bank in the city—the Bank of Ventura—and is now its attorney and vice-president. He also took a prominent part in the organization of the public library of the city. The first meetings for its organization were held in his house, and he has been President of its Board of Trustees for many years. He is a charter member of the Masonic order, helped in the organization of the lodge, and was its first W. M., and continued such for many years.

In 1857 he was united in marriage to Miss Caroline A. Sampson, a native of the State of Maine. She is a daughter of Mr. Sampson of that State, and a niece of Mr. Owen Lovejoy. Their union has been blessed with four children, three of whom are living, viz.: Charles B., born in Nevada County, California, now a farmer in Ventura; Mary A., also born in Nevada County, California, is the wife of A. G. Bartlett, of Los Angeles, a member of the firm of Bartlett Bros., of Ventura and Los Angeles; George L., born in Ventura, is now living with his parents.

Mr. McKeeby has been a Republican since the war. He and his family are leading members of the Episcopal Church. They are people of high standing in the city in which they have lived so long and are identified with all its best interests.

On June 1, 1890, he was appointed Deputy Collector of Internal Revenue for the First District of California, to reside at Los Angeles.

DANIEL TOY, a rancher of Santa Maria, was born in Wilmington, Delaware, in 1853. His father was a blacksmith, who followed his trade until fifty years of age; then, in 1865, he moved to Iowa and engaged in farming. Our subject lived at home until 1874, when he started in life for himself, continuing farming. In 1878 he bought a small farm; but, thinking he could do better in California, he sold out his interests in 1880 and came to Santa Barbara County. He first settled at Santa Ynez, where he was engaged in farming until 1885, and then bought his present ranch of 160 acres south of town, and there established himself for a permanent home, making improvements, with a view to future comfort and convenience. He raises the usual crops of hay, potatoes and beans, but makes corn the leading crop, of which he planted about twenty-five acres. He has planted a small orchard, and has trees in his nursery for fifteen acres more, all to be winter apples, the trees being imported from Illinois. He has set out 15,000 gum trees, for wind-break and fuel. Mr. Toy makes a specialty of small fruits, strawberries and raspberries doing remarkably well; he also keeps 200 fowls, and about fifteen head of horses and cattle, and his place bears evidence of his Eastern thrift coupled with intelligent farming.

Mr. Toy was married in 1877, at Storm Lake, Iowa, to Miss Laura Mudgett, a native of Maine, and they have four children:— Zalia, Susan, Rebecca and Hugh.

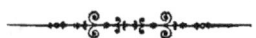

JACKLIN WILLETT was born in Columbiana County, Ohio, June 13, 1838, son of George and Elizabeth (Rhodes) Willett. His father was born in Virginia, May 10, 1809, of English ancestors, and his death occurred June 3, 1879, at the age of seventy years; and his mother was born in Loudoun County, Virginia, her father being of an old Virginia family, and her mother a Pennsylvanian. Mr. Willett was the third of a family of nine children. He received his education in Illinois, learned the blacksmith's trade and worked at it two years before coming to California, in 1859. He crossed the plains and went to the mines at Virginia City, and from there to Plumas County, where he continued to mine and where he met with financial losses. He then went to Santa Clara County and worked at his trade, and afterward engaged in farming. In 1863 he returned to Illinois and engaged in the general merchandise business at Jeffersonville, and also carried on a milling business at the same time, remaining there until 1873. At that time he returned to California and purchased fifty acres of land at Ventura, where he has since resided. It is a very sightly place, on Ventura avenue, and here Mr. Willett is engaged in raising fruit, grain and beans, the latter product being now more profitable than grain.

Mr. Willett was united in marriage, in 1864, to Miss Mary Holzhausen, a native of Ohio, born in 1843. She is a daughter of Henry Holzhausen, who came to this country from Germany when fifteen years of age. They have three children: Augusta, born in Illinois, now the wife of W. Reynolds, of Ventura County; George, born in Ventura; and Muktar, also born in Ventura. Mrs. Willett is a member of the Presbyterian Church. Mr. Willett is a Granger; was formerly a Republican, but is now an independent. In company with Mr. Chilson and others, Mr. Willett built the Ventura Flouring-mill. During the years 1879 to 1887 Mr. Willett was engaged in mining in Arizona, New Mexico and old Mexico.

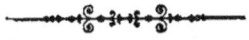

JOHN R. MYERS came to Ventura, in 1874, directly from his native State, Iowa. He was born in Clayton County, July 1, 1846. His father, Jacob K. Myers, is a native of Beverly, Randolph County, Virginia, born in 1824. His grandfather, John Myers, was also a Virginian. They were of German descent. His mother, Elizabeth (Wood) Myers, was born in North Island, Vermont, a daughter of Nathaniel Wood, of that State. Their ancestors, on the paternal side, were English, and on the maternal, Irish. Mr. Myers was the oldest of three children. He was reared on a farm and educated as other farmer boys, learning to work and getting his book education between times. This fitted him for the life of a farmer which he has since followed. When he was nineteen years old he bought a colt, which was the first property he ever owned. At that time he began to do for himself. When twenty-two years of age, he bought eighty acres of land in western Iowa. On this property he built and made improvements and, after farming it eight years, sold it to come to Ventura, California. His first purchase here was ten acres of land. He improved it and lived on it seven years, then sold, and in July, 1882, bought his present fine property of twenty-three acres, on Ventura avenue, the best street in the city. He has planted the property to English walnuts, apricots, apples and other varieties of fruit. Between the younger trees, as his groves were growing, he has raised large crops of Lima beans, which have proved very remunerative.

In 1869 he was united in marriage to Miss Elena Dodge, a native of Oswego, New York, daughter of Mr. Samuel Dodge, a farmer of that locality. Their ancestors were English. This union has been blessed with three children, a daughter and two sons: Verner D. and Mary E., born in Monona County, Iowa, and Frank S., born in Ventura. The eldest died in his fourth year. Mr. and Mrs. Myers are both members of the Methodist Church, and, in politics, he is a Republican. They are enjoying life in their beautiful California home, engaged in the general employments attending fruit culture.

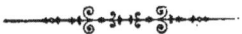

BYARD DAVIDSON, rancher west of Lompoc, was born in Nova Scotia in 1850, but in early life came to California with his parents, by water and the Isthmus of Panama. His father bought 1,700 acres in Marin County, and there carried on farming until 1870, when he cut up the ranch and divided it among his sons, Mr. Davidson receiving as his portion 330 acres. He then worked the farm until 1880, also conducting a dairy of forty cows. In 1880 he sold it, and in 1882 came to Lompoc. He bought 138 acres west of town close to the foot-hills, 300 acres being tillable land. He sows a large acreage in barley, and keeps a fine grade of stock. Mr. Davidson has fenced his ranch, and built a suitable house and outbuildings.

He was married in Marin County, in 1877, to Miss Malvina E. Farley, a native of California. Five children now grace their household.

JOSEPH NOAH JATTA, a rancher of Arroyo Grande Valley, was born August 6, 1842, on the St. John River, Canada, twenty-eight miles from Montreal. His parents, both French-Canadians, reared a family of eleven children. He was seven years of age when they removed to Monroe County, New York. Two years afterward they all returned to Canada except Joseph. He was placed in the family of a Mr. Lewis, who owned a farm three miles from the city of Rochester. Here he spent his boyhood, working on the farm and attending school, until twenty-one years of age. Mr. Lewis gradually entertained a higher esteem for young Jatta and took pains to make his place a pleasant home for him. In 1863 he came to California, by way of Panama, in company with William Hartley, an old schoolmate. For the first three years here he was employed in the dairy of G. D. W. Gorden, who at that time had leased some of the Steele Brothers' property in Marin County. He then followed agricultural pursuits on Governor Haight's property in Monterey for a year. Afterward he came to San Luis Obispo County, where he has since resided. For two years he was employed on the property of Corral de Piedra. Next he leased the fine Tar Spring ranch, then owned by Frank Branch, and for four years operated a dairy, with success. After the expiration of the lease he purchased his present ranch of 300 acres in the Arroyo Grande Valley, located in the forks of Lopez and Arroyo Grande creeks He also owns a place of twenty-four acres near the town of Arroyo Grande. His property adjoins the ranch of the Hamie estate.

Residents of the county will recall the horrible murder of Walker and his wife in 1886 by young Hamie, at the instigation of his father, and how both were quickly captured and subsequently hung from the railroad bridge at Arroyo Grande by a lynching party, the mob capturing the prisoners from the officers in charge. Mr. Jatta was returning from Nipomo at the time of the tragedy, and was not a witness to the preceedings, but being a neighbor of both the Hamie and Walker families he was naturally greatly interested in the shocking affair.

Mr. Jatta was married to Mary Hall (whose family reside in Ventura County), in the old adobe house on the road a short distance from the town of Arroyo Grande, where her people then lived. Mr. and Mrs. Jatta have ten children. He is a member of the Arroyo Grande Lodge, No. 160, K. of P.,—the only organization with which he is at present connected.

J. H. RICE, an early pioneer of California, and a prominent developer of the Santa Maria Valley, was born in Rhea County, Tennessee, June 20, 1832. His father was a farmer and a prominent trader of that period, who, ever in the advance line of civilization, pushed to the front in 1842 and emigrated to Arkansas, where he continued farming. The subject of this sketch was educated in the common schools, and remained at home until 1850. Then, "enthused" with the spirit of emigration and the gold excitement of California, he started across the plains with a mule team, and after a period of four months he arrived at Mud Springs, Placer County, August 10, 1850. He then began placer-mining, and for one year shook the pan or rocked the cradle on the banks of the Yuba and Auburn rivers; but, meeting with poor success, he resumed the industry of his youth, farming, and to that end settled in Sonoma County, in November, 1851, taking the "squatters'" claim and carrying on general farming for sixteen years. While there Mr. Rice was married, November 19, 1854, to Miss Mary A. Long, a native of Ohio, and they have six children, five sons and one daughter. In 1867 Mr. Rice removed to Monterey County, where he farmed for six years, and in 1873 they removed to Santa Maria Valley, settling near Guadalupe. Through litigation with grant-holders, he deemed it wise to change his present location, which he did in 1874, and purchased from Martin Murphy 1,831 acres of the Punta de Laguna Rancho, at $4.10 per acre, a barren tract, unfenced and no improvements upon it. Mr. Rice immediately began substantial improvements, and his well-fenced and well-stocked ranch is now satisfactory evidence of his progressive ideas with his energy and ability. The first ten years he farmed in wheat, barley and corn; but in 1884 changed to sheep, cattle and hogs, and in 1886 began his present successful and well-managed dairy, consisting of 160 cows. He makes the "R" brand of butter, shipping only in rolls, and averaging 2,000 pounds per month. His present farming is for feeding purposes, raising eighty acres in barley hay, which averages three tons to the acre; forty acres of pumpkins, of twenty tons to the acre, and ten acres in corn, averaging thirty bushels to the acre. His ranch is very rich and productive.

M. CANET came to Ventura in 1873. His native place was France, where he was born in 1833. He sailed for New York, and while there was engaged eight or nine years in the manufacture of bonnet frames. He returned to France, and then came again, to California, where he took up his present location of 137 acres of Government land. He afterward bought 270 acres, and has since added to his property until he now has between 1,300 and 1,400 acres of rich pasture and grazing land. The land was wild and uncultivated, but he is improving it, and as the country grows it will increase in value every year. He is raising cattle, horses and sheep, but most of his time is devoted to sheep-raising, keeping from 1,000 to 2,000. He employs from two to five shepherds, according to season, and hound-dogs to keep the wild-cats from his flocks. They shot fifteen during the last winter. When they are in pursuit of a wildcat they make the hills resound with their "music." In addition to his stock-farming Mr. Canet raises corn and barley, to which the land is well adapted; nor could it be surpassed for fruit.

Mr. Canet was married in 1864, to Miss Kate Brangan, who was born in Ireland. They have one son, Ed. C., born in New York, in 1865. In his political views Mr. Canet is mostly independent, but has lately voted with the Republicans. Mr. and Mrs. Canet are members of the Catholic Church.

GEORGE H. LONG, an early pioneer and prominent rancher of California, was born in Lancaster County, Pennsylvania, in 1815. His grandfather manufactured the first hand-sickles made in the United States, and his father was an extensive manufacturer of sickles and agricultural implements. George left home at the age of fourteen years, and went to Huntingdon County, Pennsylvania, where as hostler-boy he entered the service of Dr. Peter Schoenberger, an extensive manufacturer of iron, etc., from a fine quality of pipe iron ore, the doctor owning his own mines. By faithful service George H. was rapidly promoted, and before twenty years of age he became superintendent of the entire manufactory. After nineteen years of service, in partnership with his brother, he built a charcoal furnace, at Lewiston, Pennsylvania, but only continued until 1852, when he started for California in a sailing vessel, around Cape Horn. Sailing from Philadelphia, they were ninety days on the voyage to San Francisco. Mr. Long then went to the mines on the Yuba River, and, striking a rich claim, in ten months he had cleared $15,000, and then returned to the East by way of Panama. He was employed by the Pennsylvania Railroad Company for two years, but could never forget the genial climate and productiveness of California, and he returned to the State in 1856. He again sought the mines, but not with his previous success; still he followed mining through the mining districts of California and Nevada, with varied success. In 1860 he, with others, under guard of troops from Fort Mohave, located many rich claims about Prescott, Arizona; but at the breaking out of the war, in 1861, the troops were recalled, and all had to leave the country for fear of the Indians. Mr. Long then took a drove of cattle and sheep from Fort Tejon Rancho, in Los Angeles County, to Virginia City, and on his return was engaged by Thomas Dibble as superintendent of the Santa Anita Rancho, where he looked after stock interests. In 1864, when Hollister & Dibble bought the Lompoc Rancho, Mr. Long brought their sheep up to that ranch; when he came to the valley in 1865 there was not an American farmer nearer than Santa Barbara. The valley was covered with brush and timber, and filled with deer, grizzly bear and many other wild beasts, and people exclaimed at the idea of bringing sheep to the valley, thinking all would be devoured by the wild beasts. By careful herding, and poison for the wild beasts, few sheep were lost, and the wild beasts were exterminated. No farming was done in the valley until after 1874, when it was opened by the Lompoc Colony.

Hollister & Dibble had very large ranch interests, owning 136,000 acres, and as high as 70,000 sheep. Mr. Long acted as superintendent of this ranch for sixteen years, and in 1876 bought the Rancho la Honda, of 2,000 acres, where he raised cattle and horses. In 1888 he bought his present ranch of 250 acres, west of town, and in 1889 built his residence which, standing on an eminence, commands an extended view of ocean and valley. He sold Rancho la Honda in 1890, and now carries on general farming and raises hogs and a fine grade of horses.

Mr. Long was married at Santa Barbara, in 1870, to Miss Mary Davison, who died in 1886, leaving five children. Mr. Long was then remarried, in 1888, to Miss Mary Rios, and that union has been blessed with one child. Mr. Long has always been a stanch Republican; he voted for William Henry Harrison for President, in 1840, and in 1888 for his grandson, Benjamin Harrison, for the same honorable position.

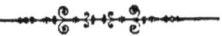

W. S. RILEY was born in Milford, Oakland County, Michigan, October 8, 1839. His father, Charles Riley, came from England, and was a hardware merchant in Milford. His mother, Sarah (Senior) Riley, was also born in England. They were the parents of eleven children, the subject of this sketch being the eighth child. He was reared and educated in his native town, and arrived in California September 5, 1861. After spending some months in Sacramento, he went to San Francisco. August 5, 1862, he left the latter place, and landed in Ventura August 6, at eight o'clock in the evening, and has been here ever since. Mr. Riley was first employed by the California Petroleum Company, J. P. Green, of Pennsylvania, being president. In 1873 he started a livery business in Ventura, beginning with a spring-wagon, carriage and four horses; and some time afterward, when he sold his business to Mr. Logue, his stock had increased to twenty horses and fifteen carriages. With Mr. E. S. Hall, he engaged in the real-estate business, making a great many sales and being very successful in this enterprise. He purchased twenty-two acres of land, four miles north of Ventura, where he built a good house and barn and planted variety of fruit trees.

Mr. Riley was married June 6, 1889, to Miss Janette Wakefield, who was born in Sonoma County, California, August 2, 1869. Her father, Wilson Wakefield, was born in Peoria, Illinois, March 17, 1836. Her mother, Mary (Hickman) Wakefield, was born in Indiana, October 23, 1834. They were both of Scotch-English descent.

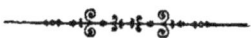

HENRY SUMMERS, a farmer and one of the first settlers of Lompoc, was born in Holstein, Germany, in 1830. He was raised on the farm of his father and remained until 1847, when he shipped on a whaling expedition to Greenland and returned in the fall, thus spending his winters at home. This he continued for five years, and in 1852, when Holstein rebelled against Denmark, Mr. Summers enlisted and joined the navy as third mate and served about eighteen months, passing through many engagements. He then shipped on a merchant vessel, and for two and a half years was engaged along the coast of South America. March 1, 1856, he took passage at Hamburg, on a sailing vessel for California, rounding Cape Horn, and arrived in San Francisco in September, 1856. He then went to the mines at Mountain Well, Nevada County, and there clerked in the store of his brother-in-law, remaining until 1860, when he bought out the business. He continued until 1869, when, on account of sickness, he sold out and came to Watsonville, and there farmed and teamed until 1874, when he came to Lompoc, having stock in the Development Company. He bought 160 acres, all wild and unimproved land, and turned the first furrow in the valley. He now has cleared and under cultivation 120 acres of rich and very productive soil. Mr. Summers carried on general farming, making mustard and beans his principal crop. He has also about fifteen brood mares, from which he raises some fast horses.

Mr. Summers was married in Nevada County, in 1861, to Miss Maggie Burner, a native of Holstein. They have eight children, six daughters and two sons.

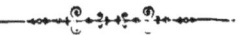

CHARLES W. LARZELERE, a prominent citizen and rancher of Lompoc, was born at Seneca Falls, Seneca County, New York, in 1834. His father owned a canal-boat which ran from Buffalo to Albany, and also traded, having a grocery at Seneca Falls. His uncle, Abraham Larzelere, built the first four-story building in Buffalo. His father emigrated to Lenawee County, Michigan, in 1836, when the country was very wild and unsettled; he took up land and also traded with the settlers. The subject of this sketch remained at home until 1853, when he came to Salt Lake with Colonel Steptoe, who had command of 600 soldiers and 100 work-hands. They passed the winter in camp at Salt Lake, and in the spring of 1854 the Government took up a reservation, eight miles square, at Rush Valley, and built barracks for the accommodation of officers and men. In 1854 Mr. Larzelere came to California and engaged in mining in Nevada County for two years, then to Humboldt Bay and to Jacksonville, Oregon, where the Government command was stationed during the Indian war of 1856. He remained at Jacksonville for five years, engaged in mining, farming and dairying. In 1859 he went to Coos Bay, Oregon, bought 160 acres of land and farmed and lumbered until 1866, when he was married to Miss Clarinda Rowley, a native of Illinois. They then came south and traveled through California and settled at Los Olivos, and with a friend took up 320 acres of land. After three years he traded his claim for a lumber-wagon, which is still in use. In 1870 he went to Santa Barbara and leased 175 acres, near the present town of Goleta. He there carried on farming until 1877, when he moved to his present ranch, which he had purchased in 1876 to the amount of 384 acres, 106 of which he has since sold. He started an apiary at Goleta in 1876, which he has since continued on his ranch at Lompoc and has about 350 stands, which average 100 pounds to the stand; but he has taken as high as 200 pounds from one stand. He has four children living, all at home.

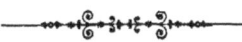

W. COX, an extensive and successful rancher of the Santa Maria Valley, was born in Hocking County, Ohio, in 1843. His father was a farmer, who in 1846 moved to Iowa, and in 1857 to Clark County, Missouri, where he continued his stock and farming interests. The subject of this sketch was educated at Iowa, and took a seminary course at Canton, Missouri. He then lived at home and followed farming until 1861, when his country called him, and he was prompt to answer, enlisting at Athens, Missouri, July 5, 1861, in Colonel Moore's Home Guards. After three months a general order came disbanding all independent companies, and he then enlisted at Warsaw, Illinois, in the Black Hawk Cavalry, under Colonel Bishop, which was later consolidated at

Macon City with the Seventh Missouri Cavalry, and Colonel Huston of the regular army was placed in command. They were then placed in the Department of Missouri, with headquarters at Macon City, their services being chiefly about Springfield and southwestern Missouri. They were at the battle of Prairie Grove in 1863, under Generals Herron and Blunt, a heavy engagement; then at Cape Girardeau, Missouri, and Little Rock, Arkansas, where there were 30,000 men under command of Colonel Fred Steele. The duty was chiefly skirmishing, as after four months the Confederates evacuated. They were then stationed at Little Rock until the close of the war, on detached duty, in raiding and guarding the frontier. Mr. Cox was then connected for nearly three years with the medical department on hospital duty, and was at the Post Hospital at Little Rock after the evacuation; he was mustered out with his regiment at St. Louis in November, 1865.

He then returned home and took up 160 acres of land in Jasper County, Missouri, which he improved. He was married in 1869 to Miss Mary Powers, and they continued to reside on the ranch until 1874, when he sold out and came to California, settling in the Santa Maria Valley, where he pre-empted thirty acres and rented 300 adjoining, which he farmed in grain. In 1879 he bought 320 acres southeast of town, and in 1882, 160 acres more, and here in 1888 he built his present comfortable residence where he now resides. He farms 500 acres in wheat and barley and keeps about twenty head of horses for ranch and breeding purposes, breeding only for general utility. Mr. Cox was elected Supervisor for the Fifth District in the fall of 1886, but is more particularly interested in the mangement of his extensive farming interests. Mr. and Mrs. Cox have three children, Ashbury Arthur and Chester. He is a member of Foote Post, No. 89, G. A. R.

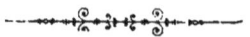

J. F. BECKETT, a real-estate dealer of Arroyo Grande, was born in Polk County, Iowa, in 1847. In 1852 the entire family removed to Oregon and in 1859 to California. Del Norte, Humboldt and Sonoma counties were their home in rapid succession, the Senior Beckett being engaged in agricultural pursuits at these various places. In 1869 the subject of this sketch came to San Luis Obispo city, striking out in the world for himself, and for fifteen years was engaged in teaching school, spending his winter vacations in planting and cultivating nursery stock. Thus he was in fact the pioneer nursery man of the county. Although he had taught school in Arroyo Grande as early as 1878, he did not make the place his home until 1880. He was School Superintendent of the county from 1880 to 1883; was also President of the Agricultural Association for one year, being the immediate successor of E. W. Steele, who was the first president of the Association. Since 1883 Mr. Beckett has been engaged in real-estate business in Arroyo Grande; and no man in that section has a better knowledge of the wealth and resources of that great valley. It is through his courtesy that the publishers of this work are enabled to give an accurate and full discription of the valley and its environs. He is the owner of one of the most important bituminous rock mines in the county near Steele's Station; also of another fine bituminous rock mine adjoining the town of Arroyo Grande. In company with others, Mr. Beckett bought 200 acres of this land some time ago, of E. W. Steele and others. Most of this property now belongs to Mr. Beckett. Among the important real-estate transactions which Mr Beckett has successfully negotiated are to be mentioned the Steele subdivision of the Corral de Piedra tract, and the Tallyho ranch of Mr. Vachell. He has a large and increasing business, owns steam water works in the town and is now preparing to pave the streets with bituminous rock.

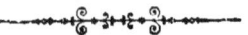

L. E. BLOCHMAN, an enthusiast on fruit and tree culture, was born in San Francisco in 1856. He was educated in the public and high schools of San Francisco, and studied for teaching, which he followed for three years. In 1879 he began his business career as book-keeper, to which he has devoted himself and become a scientific book-keeper and accountant. In 1881 he came to Santa Maria, and has since followed his profession, having been several years with the extensive general merchandise house of Weilheimer & Coblentz, as manager of their financial and accounting department. In 1885 Mr. Blochman became interested in land, and bought 160 acres southeast of town, where he experimented in various fruits, nuts and vines, and where he planted, and what has since been a very successful orchard of twenty acres. In 1887 he sold this ranch, that he might go farther up the valley. Thus, from the protection afforded by the outlying hills, he gets a warm summer temperature, and a large rainfall, free from the stormy coast winds, elements which he thought would conduce to a better fruit area. He bought 320 acres, some of which he is now improving. He has forty acres in peaches, apricots, Bartlett pears, apples and prunes, and ten acres in grapes, and contemplates setting out 500 almonds the coming season. In 1888 he organized a company of gum-tree growers, to raise trees to sell at cost, and thus induce an increased tree-planting, and which has been a success except from a financial standpoint.

Mr. Blochman was married in January, 1888, to Miss Ida M. Twitchell, a lady of high attainments, who graduated at the State Agricultural College of Iowa, and was valedictorian of her class, composed of men and women. For five years she taught, and was Principal of the Santa Maria School. She is now a member of the Board of Education, and a leading authority on school education. She is also connected with the scientific temperance work, and has notes prepared for a book on the subject.

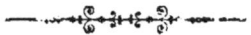

CYRUS DOUGLAS, a successful rancher of the Lompoc Valley, was born in Vermillion County, Illinois, in 1831. He lived at home assisting his father on the farm until the spring of 1852, when he started his ox team and prairie schooner for the Pacific slope. It was a large train, and through repeated delays they were seven months on the road. They came in through Oregon, and our subject located in Pierce County, Washington Territory, where for three years he worked at logging and in saw mills. In 1855 he came to Mendocino County, and worked ten years in logging in the red woods. In 1867 he went to Solano County, and bought 160 acres of land and raised wheat and barley, remaining until 1876, when he came to Hollister and put in one crop. In the spring of 1877 he came to Lompoc, and bought forty acres of land, and moved his family in the fall. His land was partly cleared, and he soon after built his house and out buildings. He also rents 200 acres across the river, where he raises wheat and barley. He has a small orchard for home use, and makes beans and mustard the principal crops. He keeps horses and cattle, but only for ranch purposes.

Mr. Douglas was married in Solano County, in 1867, to Miss Armilda F. Carter, a native of Missouri. They have seven children, all at home.

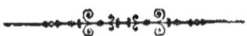

MICHAEL FLYNN, one of the prominent and progressive ranchers of Springville, Ventura County, was born in the west of Ireland, October 13, 1853, his parents, David and Ellen Flynn, also being natives of that country. In 1875 Mr. Flynn came to America and worked for one year in Boston, Massachusetts, and in 1876 came to San Francisco and engaged in teaming in the city two years. He then came to Ventura County and angaged in farming and sheep-raising, following that business five years, a part of the time in partnership with his brother-in-law. He bought out his partner's interest and continued the business alone for awhile. In 1885, the country becoming developed and much of the land being used for farming purposes, Mr. Flynn closed out this business and turned his attention to speculating in grain at San Francisco. A year later he removed to Los Angeles, and in October, 1886, came to his present location in Ventura County. He purchased 142 acres of land, on which he has since resided, and which he has improved by erecting a good dwelling-house and suitable out-buildings, surrounded by well-kept grounds. He has planted a quantity of walnut trees, and is going into that business quite largely. His present principal crop is beans and corn. Mr. Flynn is also engaged in raising horses, cattle, sheep and hogs, in partnership with Mr. Paulin, having some very fine specimens of horses. They are devoting about 800 acres of land to wheat and barley, and employ eight men and six teams.

Mr. Flynn was married in 1878 to Miss Lavelle, who was born near his own native place, her parents being Irish people. They have a family of six children, all born in Ventura County, viz.: David E., Robert E., Mary Grace, Albert E., Clarence E., and Sarah Clara. Mr. Flynn is a Democrat. He and his family are worthy members of the Catholic Church.

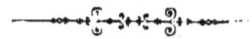

WILLIAM NEWTON SHORT, of Arroyo Grande Valley, was born in the town of Oquawka, Henderson County, Illinois, in March, 1838, one of eight children, all of whom are still living. When he was fourteen years of age the family came to California with ox teams, settling on a ranch near Watsonville. William, of course, was placed at farm work, but from time to time he went around prospecting in the mining regions, and visited Los Angeles and the northern part of the State. In the spring of 1876, in company with his brother, he bought twenty-two acres of land in the Arroyo Grande Valley, joining the present town of Arroyo Grande. They purchased of the Steele Brothers, and eleven acres of their first purchase is still the property of the subject of this sketch, on which he lives. When he first came here there was no town, and the only business establishments were Ryan's Hotel, one store and a blacksmith's shop. The valley was dense thicket, with here and there remotely a small cultivated spot. Stages were running from Soledad to Arroyo Grande, and, strange as it may seem, the mails came more promptly and earlier than they do to-day by rail.

Mr. Short was married April 4, 1869, to Miss English, a native of Missouri, whose parents moved to Texas when she was only a child, and in 1861 to California. Mr. Short has two daughters and one son.

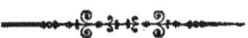

J. W. HENDRICKS, a farmer of Lompoc, was among the first settlers there. He was born in Dayton, Ohio, in 1823. His father, Aaron M. Hendricks, was by trade a carpenter, and a native of Tennessee. In 1812 he was at the battle of New Orleans as Sergeant, under General Jackson. In 1837 he emigrated to Indiana, where he followed his trade. The subject of this sketch lived at home until twenty-two years of age, and worked at farming. In 1846 he was married, at West Point, Tippecanoe County, to Miss Esther A. Wagner, a native of Ohio. Mr. Hendricks then rented a farm of about 150 acres and followed farming up to 1865, when he crossed the plains for California; P. W. Fondy was in command of the train, which was very large, and there was much sickness in the company. They were five months on the way, and came to California by Truckee. Mr. Hendricks then went to Marysville, where he bought 120 acres and farmed for four years, then going to Hollister, where he rented 600 acres, and carried on general farming up to the fall of 1874, when he came to Lompoc and bought sixty-eight acres where he now resides. Land was then covered with brush, and they could shoot wild-cats, deer and coyotes from the house. The land is now nicely cleared and under a high state of cultivation; mustard, beans and barley are now his chief crops, and he also raises a fine grade of horses. He has three children, all married. After many years of hardship Mr. Hendricks fully enjoys his present comfortable home.

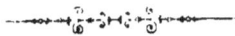

B. GOSNELL, a prominent rancher of Ventura County, was born in Newark, Ohio, November 2, 1848. His father, Nelson Gosnell, was also born at the same place, and his grandfather, Joshua Gosnell, was a native of New York, his ancestors having emigrated from England to that State. His mother, Samantha (Barrick) Gosnell, daughter of John Barrick, a native of Pennsylvania, traces her ancestry back to the Pennsylvania Dutch. Mr. and Mrs. Gosnell had thirteen children, seven of whom are now living. The family removed from Ohio to Illinois when the subject of this sketch was nine years old, residing there eight years. In 1865 they removed to Missouri and remained there ten years. Mr. Gosnell was reared a farmer, and also learned the carpenter's trade. He returned to Ohio, and, in 1885, came to his present locality. Here he purchased 102 acres of land on the Ventura avenue, and built on it two houses and a barn. He is now engaged in erecting a very fine family residence on one of the most sightly spots of the whole avenue, it being on a high point of land that overlooks the entire valley in every direction, with all the beautiful homes on Ventura avenue in full view. Mr. Gosnell has a family orchard with a variety of fruit of nearly all kinds, and also 300 walnut trees.

In 1879 the subject of this sketch was united in marriage with Miss Caroline McGuire, sister of William McGuire, a history of whom will be found on another page of this book. It was on account of Mrs. Gosnell's health that they came to California.

They are the parents of two children, Ira and Lena, both natives of Ohio. Mr. Gosnell is a Royal Arch Mason. Politically he is a Republican.

J. S. BARKLA came to California in 1853 and located in Ventura County in 1871. He was born in Cornwall, England, March 9, 1832. His father, John Barkla, was a mining contractor in England, and both his parents were natives of that country. Mr. Barkla was reared and educated there, and in 1849, at the age of seventeen years, came to the United States. His business, that of a copper miner and prospector in the employ of a copper mining company, took him into the States of Pennsylvania, Maryland and Virginia. The gold excitement of California brought him to this coast in 1853, where he engaged in mining for the precious metal. His operations began at Hangtown, now Placerville, where he spent six years, most of the time in tunnel mining, being very successful. In the summer of 1856 four men worked four days and cleared up fifty ounces of gold as the result of the labor, worth $925. After this he put $8,000 in one claim and worked hard for three years to get his money back again. After leaving the mines he came to Ventura County and bought forty acres of land on Main street, Santa Paula, and of this he retains five acres, on which his residence is situated, and on which is a variety of fruit trees, including oranges in bearing. Mr. Barkla also owns land in this and Los Angeles counties. During his residence in Santa Paula he has done his share toward the development of the town.

Mr. Barkla was united in marriage in Pennsylvania, April 17, 1860, to Miss Hannah Hinton, a native of England, born in 1840. When a child she came to America with her parents, and was reared in Massachusetts. They have three children living: Laura H., born in El Dorado County, March 23, 1861; Luna Jane, in the same place, August 31, 1863; Carl Benjamin, born on the Cosumnes River, El Dorado County, April 23, 1866. Mr. and Mrs. Barkla are Universalists in belief. In politics his views are in harmony with Democratic principles. From 1883 until 1887 he served as Supervisor of Ventura County. He united with the I. O. O. F. in 1855.

GEORGE STOWELL, a successful rancher of the Santa Maria Valley, was born in Ashtabula, Ohio, in 1830. His own home being broken up by the death of his parents, he lived with relatives until he was seventeen years of age. He then went to Lake County, where he learned the trade of carpentering, which he followed until 1853, when with his brother, Henry, they crossed the plains for California, landing in Hangtown, now Placerville, in August, 1853. The subject of this sketch then followed mining for two years, and in 1855, in company with two others, they began teaming across the Sierra Mountains; they were the first to freight across those mountains. They brought back the first load of quartz from the famous Comstock mines in Nevada, which they carried to Folsom, California, where it was shipped to England. Mr. Stowell followed freighting very successfully until 1867, when he came to San Luis Obispo County, and took up 363 acres of land in the Cayucos district, where he followed dairy farming, keeping seventy cows. In 1878 he sold his interest, and removed to Paso Robles Springs, where he put 500 acres in wheat. In 1882 he moved to Santa Maria Valley, where he bought 160 acres, his present elegant ranch, which he has since fenced and divided, and built substantial house and farm buildings. He farmed in barley and beans, giving particular attention to hogs, keeping about 150 head, and other stock only for ranch purposes.

Mr. Stowell was married in Hangtown, in 1855, to Miss Lydia Smith, a native of Michigan and they have three children: Susan A., Fanny E. and Guy J. Mr. Stowell is a member of Santa Maria Lodge, No. 302, I. O. O. F., and has been an Odd Fellow for thirty-two years; first joining at Hangtown.

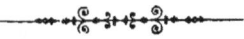

MAJOR WILLIAM JACKSON is one who has served both State and County, and was numbered among the earliest settlers of Lompoc; he was born at Newport, Cocke County, Tennessee, in 1822. His father, William Jackson, moved to Moniteau County, Missouri, in 1833, where he farmed and was also Public Administrator and Justice of the Peace. Our subject received a limited education in the log school-house of that day, and in 1854 was elected to the Legislature from Putnam County, Missouri, representing the county two sessions. During the exciting days of 1861, though a Southern man by birth, Mr. Jackson sympathized with the North, and early in 1861 he was elected from five counties as a delegate to the Constitutional Convention held at Jefferson City, Missouri, and at St. Louis, in four sessions. In June, 1861, he was one of fifty-six who deposed the Governor and all the staff officers, and elected a provisional Governor and full body of State officers, who carried on the State Government for two years, until loyal officers could be elected. In 1862 he enlisted from Chilicothe, Livingston County, Missouri, and helped raise the Third Missouri Regiment, and was appointed Major of the First Battalion. They went to Springfield, Missouri, which was chief headquarters, and was placed in the army of the frontier under General Halleck. The regiment was engaged in the battle of Springfield, January 8, 1863, against General Marmaduke, who it was said had 16,000 men, while the Union forces numbered 4,500, still fighting from within the fort; they were victorious and Marmaduke was repulsed. Major Jackson was in many skirmishes, and was discharged in the spring of 1863.

He then went home in the spring of 1864, with his wife and five little ones, and crossed the plains for California. After four months of travel they landed in Green Valley, Sonoma County, in September, 1864, where he rented land, and farmed and teamed until 1867, when he came to San Luis Obispo, and bought a claim of 320 acres, near the town, where he farmed and dairied, furnishing the town with butter and milk, and keeping about forty cows. In 1874 he came to Lompoc, where he attended the first sale and bought twenty-five acres of land, and built the first house of the colony, bringing with him a load of lumber for that purpose from San Luis Obispo. He also bought 320 acres west of the town, where he started a dairy, bringing his forty cows from San Luis Obispo; he rented 300 acres, which he farmed in wheat. In 1878 he sold his ranch and moved his house to the city lots. He then bought 1,100 acres at Arroyo Hondo, where he has since farmed and dairied, keeping about sixty cows. All his land is now rented, and he is improving his home property.

Major Jackson was one of the original directors of the colony for three years, and in

1888 was elected Justice of the Peace. He was Grange Master two years from San Luis Obispo, and two years from Lompoc. Major Jackson has been twice married, first to Miss Martha J. Bruce, of Missouri, whom he lost in 1862, leaving five children. He was again married in Kansas, in 1863, to Miss Mary C. Francis, and they have eight children. Mr. Jackson is a member of Lompoc Lodge, No. 262, F. & A. M., and is a worthy Master Mason, and was delegate to the Grand Lodge in 1889. He is also a member of Robert Anderson Post, No. 66, G. A. R.

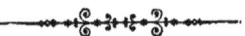

J. LOGAN KENNEDY, as his name indicates, is a descendant of the old Scottish chiefs. Kennedy, in Celtic, Ceannathighe, means the head of a clan or chieftain. Duncan de Carrick, living in 1153, was father of Nicholas de Carrick, whose son, Roland de Carrick, took the name of Kennedy, and from this origin the family springs. Their home was in Ayrshire.

This ancient family were prominent in political matters, were leaders in the Presbyterian Church, and were valiant soldiers in the cause of reform, liberty and religion. Albert Edward, Prince of Wales, is the present Earl of Carrick. They have been connected with the great house of Stewart and with the kings of Scotland and England. Colonel Gilbert Kennedy, who was with Cromwell at the battle of Marston Moor, had two sons, who were Presbyterian ministers. Rev. Thomas Kennedy, one of these sons, was Chaplain to General Munro, and went with the army to Ireland, in 1642. Mr. Kennedy afterward settled in Carland, and this accounts for the family being in Ireland. He died in 1714. Two of his sons were Presbyterian ministers. It is believed that William Kennedy, who emigrated from Ireland and settled in Bucks County, Pennsylvania, in 1830, was Colonel Gilbert Kennedy's descendant. This William Kennedy was born in Londonderry, Ireland, about 1695. He married Mary Henderson, and his death occurred in 1777. He was J. Logan Kennedy's great-great-grandfather. His son, James Kennedy, was born in Bucks County, Pennsylvania, in 1730, and married Jane Maxwell in 1761. They had twelve children. His death occurred October 7, 1799. His son, William Kennedy, born in 1766, married Sarah Stewart, and to them were born eight children. He served in the Continental army as aid to his uncle, General Maxwell. He afterward represented the counties of Sussex and Warren in the Legislature of New Jersey, several terms, and was chairman of the house, which position he filled with dignity and honor. He was also, for years, a judge of the courts. He was an elder in the Greenwich Presbyterian Church, and in politics was a Democrat. This was our subject's grandfather. His son, James J. Kennedy, was born in Warren County, New Jersey, July 14, 1793; and, January 28, 1819, he married Margaret Cowell. He removed to Chambersburg, Pennsylvania, in 1839; was a Presbyterian, a judge, a Democrat, and a prominent agriculturist.

His son, J. Logan Kennedy, was born and reared in Cumberland Valley, near the town of Chambersburg, Pennsylvania. He was the youngest of a family of nine children, six of whom are now living; and received his education at Chambersburg and Jonesville, New Jersey. For a time he read law in the office of his brother, T. B. Kennedy. He engaged somewhat in politics, and was elected treasurer of his county. In 1872 he came to California and settled in Ventura, where he engaged in the sheep business with

Thomas R. Bard, who had been his boyhood playmate and schoolmate. The firm was Kennedy & Bard until 1880. They engaged in this business on a large scale, having as many as 15,000 sheep at one time. Mr. Kennedy has also been engaged in buying and selling sheep and cattle, and he owns a livery in Ventura. He has been interested in lands, and now owns a ranch.

Mr. Kennedy was married in 1881, to Miss Netta E. Wright, a native of Wisconsin. She is the daughter of Philip V. Wright, who was born in New York. They are of Scotch-Irish descent, and their ancestors have been residents of America since the Revolution. They have one child, an interesting little girl: Carrie L., born in Ventura, April 25, 1882. Mrs. Kennedy is a member of the Presbyterian Church.

A descendant of a family of Democrats, Mr. Kennedy has ever been true to that party. He is a fine physical representative of his Scotch ancestry—blue eyes, fine complexion, tall and straight, and a fine well developed form. He retains his love for valuable horses and can be seen driving his fine horse on the beautiful avenues of Ventura, with his wife and little daughter, enjoying the delightful and balmy climate of Southern California. They have a nice home at the corner of Oak and Poli streets, surrounded with flowers and shrubs and everything that goes to make life a comfort.

ANTONIO PEZZONI, dairyman and farmer of San Luis Obispo County, near the south line of the county, was born in Switzerland in 1858, and at the age of fourteen years came on a prospecting tour to America. The first year in this country he was in Sonoma County, this State; then he came to San Luis Obispo County, attended school for fifteen months and returned to Sonoma County; there he remained four years engaged in farming and dairying, with good success. He then came to Guadalupe and was engaged with his brother two years on his place on the Oso Flaco, then settled on his present property just across the line, the Santa Maria River separating San Luis Obispo and Santa Barbara counties. There he has 850 acres of very rich land. His residence is a beautiful house, surrounded by a handsome lawn.

He was married in 1884, to Miss Bonetti, and has three children.

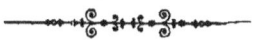

D. W. SALZMAN, of Lompoc, was born in Germany, in 1833. His father was a weaver by trade, and also owned a small farm. Mr. Salzman learned the trade of a mason and plasterer, at Hessen-Cassel, where he served a three-years apprenticeship. He then traveled three years and worked in Hanover, Hamburg and Bremen, which was considered necessary before one became a finished artisan. In 1856 he came to the United States, first working on Long Island, about Babylon, at his trade; then in the fall of 1858 he left for California, by the Isthmus of Panama. After arrival he went to Sacramento Valley, where he passed one year, and through an accidental injury he was admitted to the Marine Hospital at San Francisco. After recovering he worked on a milk ranch at the Presidio, until 1860, when he went to the mines in Tuolumne County, remaining ten years in that locality. In 1870 he went to Los Angeles, and resumed his trade, and in 1873 went to Santa Barbara, where he contracted, and did the plastering of the Arlington Hotel, Crane's Hall, and many of the residences. In 1876 he came to Lompoc Valley, and bought 460 acres in the San Pasqual Cañon and foothills, mainly grazing land, except about five acres in fruit. He keeps about sixty head of cattle, and several brood mares, and has a good apiary of 100 stands of bees.

Mr. Salzman was married at Lompoc, in 1880, to Miss Amelia Kriegel, a native of Germany, who came direct to California to perform the marriage vows. They have five children. Mr. Salzman still works at his trade about town, and also carries on the ranch.

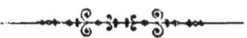

C. G. REDRUP was born in Cleveland, Ohio, February 29, 1844. His father, Joseph Redrup, was a native of England, born in 1813, came to America when a boy fifteen years of age, and lived in the United States sixty years. Mr. Redrup's mother, Evaline (Robinson) Redrup, was born in the State of New York, in 1814. They had a family of eight children, the subject of this sketch being the fifth. He received his education in the public schools of Mansfield, Ohio, and in 1872 became a book-keeper, holding that position five years. He then engaged in business for himself, dealing in machinery for nine years. In 1881 he married Mary E. C. Brown, a native of New Jersey. Mrs. Redrup, having poor health, preceded her husband to California, hoping to receive benefits. She purchased a valuable tract of land in Ventura, which, if it had not been for difficulty with the title, would have sold for a fortune during the past five years. Since Mr. Redrup's residence in Ventura he has been engaged in building, and has erected a number of houses. Since the title to their land has been settled, he is carrying on farming operations. Their property is in a fine location and will soon be very valuable.

Mr. Redrup is a member of the Baptist Church, in Ohio, and his wife is a Presbyterian. In politics he is a Republican.

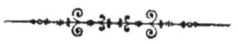

ELBRIDGE BALL, of Arroyo Grande, was born in Fleming County, Kentucky, in 1833. His father, who died in 1861, kept a tobacco plantation, on which Elbridge lived until he was sixteen years of age. From 1849 to 1853 he was a farmer in Kane County, Illinois; and then, "enticed by the wafture of a golden lure," he came to California and spent a year in the mines, however with but little success. He then went to Scott Valley to begin farming, but was limited in his operations by the scarcity and high price of agricultural implements. He made his own plow. The winter of 1852–'53 was a hard one for the farmers. Provisions were costly, salt being $16 a pound, and everybody was living on what he could get cheap. Mr. Ball lived in Scott Valley ten years, and then moved to Butte Creek, where he lived until 1884. At that place he still owns a ranch of 1,000 acres, in partnership with his brother, on which they raise cattle and horses and are conspicuously successful. In 1884 Mr. Ball came to San Luis Obispo County, since which time he has resided on a ranch of thirty-two acres in the Arroyo Grande Valley, engaged in farming and fruit-raising. He came here in the first place for the sake of his health. He is a bachelor. He was personally acquainted with the Modoc Indians, and lived for some time among them. During the Modoc war, he was often thrown in contact with Captain Jack and Scar-faced Charley—the celebrated warrior chiefs—and he knew them well. He was a witness of the celebrated three-days fight between these Indians and the United States troops, in which the redskins were victorious.

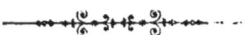

WALLACE DYER, of Lompoc, was born in Albany County, New Yorks in 1825. His father was a farmer, and a stanch Republican, dying in February, 1861, and casting his last presidential vote for Abraham Lincoln. His grandfather, Charles Dyer, was a Colonel in the Revolutionary war, and at the battle of Newport his horse was shot from under him, although not being wounded himself. Mr. Dyer's grandmother, a Miss Hazard, was an own cousin of Commodore Oliver Hazard Perry.

Wallace Dyer, our subject, was educated at the common schools, and then learned the trade of millwright, which he followed for twenty years. In 1852 he was married, at Greenville, New York, to Miss Mary Vincent, and they lived on the homestead of 100 acres, where Mr. Dyer carried on farming. In 1863 they moved to a fifty-acre farm, in the same county, where he farmed until 1875, when he sold both places and came to California, settling at Santa Cruz. He bought fifteen acres in the city limits, and 125 acres adjoining, in Scott's Valley. In 1881 he was elected Alderman, by the Republican party, serving two years. He resided at Santa Cruz until 1884, when he sold his property and came to Lompoc, and bought two blocks on Second street, and has since bought four blocks on H street. The Second street property he cleared of brush and timber, and is improved with two substantial residences. In 1888 he gave the Presbyterian society a church lot, 60 x 80 feet, and then drew the plans, and performed the most of the work on the church structure, the only expense to the society being the material. Mr. Dyer has been in no active business in Lompoc, except improving his property. In April, 1889, he was elected Justice of the Peace, and the same year was appointed Recorder, by the Board of Aldermen.

Mr. Dyer has two sons, Frank Marshall Dyer, who still farms in Green County, New York, and A. H. Dyer, who has a fine ranch across the river, north of town.

JOSEPH DIMOCK, one of the thrifty and successful ranchers northeast of Lompoc, was born in Newport, Hants County, Nova Scotia, in September, 1839. His father was a farmer and blacksmith, from whom Joseph learned the trade, and with whom he worked until 1861, when he came to California, by the Panama route. He arrived in San Francisco in May, and after a few months at Watsonville, he settled at San José, and carried on a blacksmith business until 1874, except one year, 1864, which he passed in Idaho. Mr. Lick, of observatory fame, was a patron of his shop at San José. In 1874 Mr. Dimock was among the first settlers in Lompoc, where he opened a shop and carried on business for three years. In 1876 he bought his present ranch of 160 acres, at the foot of the hills, northern part of the valley. During the past six years forty acres of his valley land has been washed away by the Santa Ynez River; he now has eighty acres of fine land, under a high state of cultivation, and about twelve acres in fruit, mainly of winter apples, though a full variety of deciduous fruits for family use. Apples are the main crop, which do very well, and about half of the orchard is now in bearing.

He plants fifty acres to beans, with an average yield of one ton to the acre. He raises a great many horses, both draft and trotting stock, and is one of the most successful ranchers of the valley.

Mr. Dimock was married at Gilroy, Santa Clara County, in 1868, to Miss Matilda A. Drake, a native of Iowa. They have two children, Shubael F. and Sadie A. The father and mother of Mr. Dimock are both living, at the ages of seventy-seven and seventy-two years respectively, and the winter of 1889 and 1890 they passed in California.

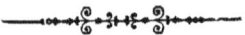

JOHN McGLASHAN, a citizen of the village of Arroyo Grande, was born in 1835, in Scotland. His parents emigrated with their family to Fulton County, New York, in 1843; and John was therefore raised in the Empire State, receiving his education in an old log school-house. Until twenty-three years of age he lived on his father's farm; and then, in the year 1858, he crossed the plains to Las Vegas, New Mexico, then a small settlement. Next he mined for a time in Colorado, and then came on to California, in the fall of 1858. At first he engaged in the mason's trade, which he learned in New York State. In 1875 he began farming in the Arroyo Grande, where he now lives. He has sixty-six acres on the Monte, principally in beans, and is doing well. He has been successful in almost everything that he has attempted to raise out of the soil on his place, fruit and vegetables being especially productive. He took a premium at the county fairs in 1889, on the white radish, the weight of which is recorded as being seventeen and a half pounds.

Mr. McGlashan was married in 1865, to Miss Rooker, and has four sons: John, who is now married and farming on the college grant at Santa Ynez; David, Joseph and Charles,—all at home.

W. L. ROSS was born in Virginia, December 2, 1845, being one of a family of eight children. His father, a farmer by occupation, is still living. Remaining at his home until the age of eighteen years, he then enlisted in the Confederate army, in 1863, joining the Fifty-first Virginia Regiment, Company D. Mr. Ross took part in several important engagements, among them was the retreat before Sheridan, during his famous run, which but a short time previous had almost been a great victory for the Confederate troops. After the war Mr. Ross spent a year at home, and finished his education in a town in North Carolina. He now returned to his home in Virginia, where he remained until 1869, in that year starting for the West. He spent a year in Kentucky and Tennessee, and in 1870 reached California. Taking up some land in Tulare County, he located there for four years, at the end of which time he disposed of his property. Since then this land has proved to be very valuable, and had Mr. Ross held on to it, it would have been a rich holding. Frequent attacks of chills and fever drove him to the coast and in 1875 he located in Cambria, where he was engaged in farming and dairying for three years. In connection with his brother, he owned some valuable stock. In 1882 he came to his present ranch, located on the Corral de Piedra Rancho. Mr. Ross has 1,240 acres, upon which he is engaged in dairying and stock-raising. This property is beautifully situated, has considerable oak timber, and is well adapted for stock-raising and diversified farming. The climate here is delightful. The frequent cool winds that are felt on the other side of the coast hills are not noticed in this valley. Mr. Ross is unmarried.

DAVID A. DANA, of Nipomo, was born at that place August 27, 1851. His share of the large property left by his father is a pretty ranch of 660 acres at the foot of the hills a mile from the village of Nipomo, and here he has a valuable dairy, to which he now devotes his entire time, having abandoned general farm work some time ago. Like all his brothers, he received a good education, attending for three years the college at Santa Ynez. He is a member of Nipomo Parlor, No. 123, N. S. G. W., and is now president of the same. He was married in 1885 to Miss C. Rojas, and has two children.

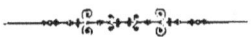

PAUL BRADLEY, an early pioneer of California, who surmounted the trials and disappointments of the early days, and whose broad acres in the Santa Maria Valley extend for miles, was born in Derbyshire, England, in 1822. At the early age of fifteen years he began working in the mines, on railroads and steam engines, and being mechanically inclined he soon became an expert engineer. In 1846 he emigrated to the United States, and was engaged about New York until January, 1850, when he shipped on the steamer Carolina for California, going around Cape Horn. The steamer was engaged to ply on the Pacific coast and took no passengers until arriving at Panama, and from there on was overcrowded, and arrived in San Francisco on May 6, 1850. The subject of this sketch then went to the mines at Stringtown on the Feather River, but soon became disgusted and returned to San Francisco. He then made several trips on steamships to Panama, and in the spring of 1851 began a market garden at San José, and also ran a ten-ton sloop to San Francisco, carrying passengers and freight. In the spring of 1852 he shipped on the Golden Gate, a new steamer, for Panama, and spent eight months there learning the Spanish language. He then took a cruise down the coast, in the employ of the Southern American Steamship Company, running between Callao and Valparaiso, trading with the natives, which was quite profitable. He then returned to San José, where he had left his oxen and effects, and went to Monterey County, where he found 150 acres of very desirable Government land, where he located, stuck his stakes and remained until 1868. Mr. Bradley then began improving and developing his ranch, where he first raised chickens and beans, but he said the coons destroyed his chickens, and he had to sleep with his beans to keep away the grazing cattle. The country was wild, unsettled and filled with outlaws, so that guns had to be taken into the field as a means of defense; but he still persisted and developed a very fine ranch. He also kept some cattle, but they became of no value except for hides and tallow, and he went into the sheep business, keeping about 2,000 head, and also a large number of hogs. His place became highly improved with good fences and buildings, and he sold it in the spring of 1868 for $5,250, which with his stock represented his accumulations. Mr. Bradley then came to Santa Maria in the fall of 1868, and bought 480 acres of school lands, and has since added to the amount of 4,000 acres. He still continued sheep raising, and in 1870 had a flock of 7,000 head, but they became very cheap and were only valued for their wool, and he reduced his stock, although he has always had a few, and he now has sixty very choice ones of South Down and Shropshire Down strains, which are a high grade and valuable for either mutton or fleece, as they do better than in their native Downs. He also keeps a number of cattle and about forty horses. He also rents land for both farm and pasture purposes, tilling only his home place of 160 acres, which is highly improved, with eighty acres set to fruit. In 1888 he built an elegant two-story residence.

In 1870 Mr. Bradley returned to England to visit his family and friends, and was there married to Mrs. Elizabeth Spencer, and they have one child, Ellen.

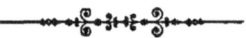

A. H. DYER, a farmer of Lompoc, was born in Albany County, New York, in 1856. His father, Wallace Dyer, whose biography elsewhere appears, was a farmer, owning 150 acres, and in 1863 moved to Greene County, where he continued at farming. A. H. Dyer lived at home until 1875, when, with his father, he came to California, and settled at Santa Cruz, where they bought town property and mountain land, covered with timber. In 1877 our subject came to Lompoc and rented land for general farming, and also ran a threshing machine with Charles Robbins. He bought his present ranch of 245 acres in 1883, and was married the same year at Lompoc to Miss Lulu Wilkins, a native of California. Mr. Dyer has about thirty acres in fruit, mainly winter apples, which are doing finely. Vines are also looking well, and his few orange trees show a rapid and healthy growth. He has also 300 walnut trees, which are doing well. He carries on general farming, but beans and mustard are the principal crops, with barley for hay and grain. He keeps twenty head of horses, and has bred some fine draft stock.

He has one daughter, Lulu May, born in August, 1884. Mr. Dyer is a member of Lompoc Lodge, No.. 262, F. & A. M., and Lompoc Lodge, No. 248, I. O. O. F.

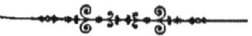

THOMAS ROBINSON, one of the prominent ranchers of the Lompoc Valley, was born in Yorkshire, England, July 1, 1822. He worked at home with his father, at farming, until 1847, when he came to the United States, first settling at Buffalo, New York, and there learned the trade of boat-builder and ship-carpenter, remaining about four years, when he returned to England. In 1851 he was married in Yorkshire, England, and the first year lived midway between Hull and Grimsby, an old and historic spot, as from that vicinity came the first Puritans to our then barren shores. Mr. Robinson was engaged in steam-threshing until 1862, running five engines and six threshers, as the business continued every month of the year. In 1862 he returned to the United States, and settled in Greenfield Township, Erie County, Pennsylvania, where he farmed one year, then went to Buffalo to work at his trade for a short time, then to Askhum, Illinois, where he bought eighty acres and remained until 1870. In the latter year he came to California, first settling in Sonoma County, taking up Government claims and farming for three years, then to Petaluma, and in the spring of 1874 came to Lompoc to attend the first land sale of the colony. He farmed with his son there for three years, and then gave up the land, and bought 370 acres farther out, of which he still owns 310 acres, 225 being tillable. He then engaged in the hog business, keeping about 250, and also in the raising of horses and cattle, which he still continues. His land was covered with brush and timber, and its present clean appearance speaks volumes for the energy of a master hand. Mr. and Mrs. Robinson have five children, four girls and one son.

FRANCIS ZIBA BRANCH.—The great land-owners in early times and pioneers, who were not native Californians, may be enumerated in this short list: Francis Z. Branch, Isaac J. Sparks, John Wilson, John M. Price and William G. Dana. Facts relative to the early history of the Branch family have been very difficult to obtain, as there are no notes in possession of the Branch family. Resource is therefore had to the admirable collection of sketches by Mr. F. H. Day, published in 1859. Mr. Branch was born in Scipio, Cayuga County, New York, in the year 1803. Both of his grandfathers served in the Revolutionary war. His father died before he was old enough to appreciate a father's care, and, his mother being poor, the children were scattered among relatives to be reared and educated. At the age of eighteen Ziba abruptly left his relatives and removed to Buffalo, with the view of making his own living. After remaining there some time he went on Lake Erie and followed the business of sailing for about five years. He then went to St. Louis, where he fell in with a trading party commanded by Captain Savory, and started with them for Santa Fé. This was the largest party that had ever come through, being composed of 150 men and eighty-two wagons. They made the journey in safety and reached Santa Fé in July, 1830, without having had a single skirmish with the Indians, which circumstance was accounted for by the fact that Colonel Riley and his party, who had been sent out by the Government and who had preceded them, had some field-pieces and also the first ox-team the Indians had ever seen. When the Indians attacked them Colonel Riley brought his field-piece to bear upon them, of course doing much damage in their ranks, and as Mr. Branch and his party had ox-teams along they were afraid to attack them, as they also had "shooting wagons." In the fall of 1830 Mr. Branch joined a trapping party in the Tulare Valley. They made the journey from New Mexico toward Big Salt Lake, across the head waters of Red River, and struck a stream supposed to be the Sevier River, which they followed until it emptied into Little Salt Lake, near the California mountains. It being the month of November, the country was covered with snow, and they found it impossible to cross the Sierra Nevada Mountains, and consequently struck off south for Red River. They were nine days crossing and had to break a path through the snow, which was two or three feet deep. They found but few beaver and no game, and soon their provisions gave out. When they started from New Mexico they had four oxen, and when near Little Salt Lake they killed their last ox and then had to subsist upon the flesh of their horses and mules, each man being put upon short allowances, which at best was very poor.

They traveled along Red River and reached the Mohave country, luckily escaping all attacks from the hostile tribes of Indians, and finally arrrived safely at San Bernardino, California, in February, 1831, and from there proceeded to Los Angeles, where the party disbanded. After leading a hunter's life for three years, Mr. Branch invested his bonds in a grocery store at Santa Barbara, which he subsequently sold to A. B. Thompson.

In 1835 he was married to Doña Manuela Corlona, and they settled in San Luis Obispo County, where in 1839 he obtained a Spanish grant of land of great value. This property consisted of 16,954.83 acres located on the Arroyo Grande. Mr. Branch afterward became the owner of much valuable property in addition to this, including the Huer-Huero, Pizmo and other large tracts, also vast herds of horses and cattle. The dry years of 1862–'63–'64 proved very disastrous to his enormous herds of cattle, numbering in 1863 over 70,000 head, and as a result he lost almost a fortune, when the value of cattle the year previous is taken into consideration. Mr. Branch profited by the favorable season which followed, though not for a long time did he make up for the disaster alluded to above. He has held public offices at various times, and was prominently identified with the affairs of the city and county. The public positions which he was called upon to fill were frequently important ones, but his work was always eminently satisfactory. He died at his home on Santa Manuela rancho, May 8, 1874, leaving a widow and four sons: Ramon, Frank and D. Fred, all of whom, with the exception of one, are still alive.

The splendid adobe house, the home of the Branch family, still remains, above and adjoining the home of D. Fred Branch. The house is not now occupied, but is in an excellent state of preservation, revealing clearly the fact that in its day it was a substantial as well as a beautiful home. Mr. Branch, like many of those early pioneers, reached California with nothing but his gun by which to make his living. This, however, proved in his skillful hand to be all the capital he needed, as with it he shot otter, the skins of which were very valuable, and always brought the ready cash in those times. His history bears with it a moral. He set out in life poor, and by his own energy and activity he became rich in the world's goods, and at one time was one of the wealthiest men in San Luis Obispo County.

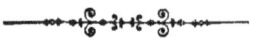

R. NICOLES, resident at Lompoc, Surveyor of Santa Barbara County.

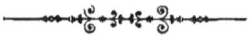

H. NICHOLSON, a careful and practical farmer of Santa Maria, was born in Winneshiek County, Iowa, in 1856. His father was an extensive farmer of that period, having 400 acres of land, which he farmed to general crops, and was also engaged in stock-raising. The subject of this sketch received a common-school education, and then attended the Cornell Methodist College at Mount Vernon, Iowa, where he finished in 1875. He then farmed on rented land, until 1878, when he bought a farm of 100 acres in the same county. He was married at Ossin, Iowa, in 1876, to Miss Agnes Hall, and they lived on this farm until 1881, when he sold out and came to California, arriving in Santa Maria, in May, 1881, and with his uncle, M. P. Nicholson, an early settler in the valley, they leased a farm of 3,000 acres, where they were engaged in raising grain; Mr. Nicholson took charge of the ranch. In 1883 he purchased the lease and stock and farmed the same tract until 1887, when he purchased his present beautiful ranch of 320 acres. In 1882 they raised from 3,000 acres, 3,300 sacks of grain, mainly wheat. In addition to his present ranch he rents 180 acres, and devotes the entire tract of 500 acres to grain, wheat being the main crop. He uses all heavy machinery of gang plows, headers and steam-threshers, and also does much threshing about the valley. He raises stock only for ranch purposes. He is making preparations for fruit culture, which he will enter quite extensively. Mr. and Mrs. Nicholson have two children, Harry Roland and Edith. Mr. Nicholson is a member of Santa Maria Lodge, Knights of Pythias, and also a member of the Farmers' Alliance.

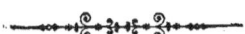

USTAVUS W. RICHARDS, who has had an extensive business as civil engineer, was born June 3, 1834, in New York city, the son of G. U. Richards, a prominent dry-goods merchant of New York. The subject of this sketch was educated at Portland, Maine, and there learned his profession, and up to 1875 was extensively engaged through the Eastern, Middle and Southern States. In 1865 he was married at Zanesville, Ohio, to Miss Eleanor MacLeod, a daughter of Robert MacLeod, who was born in Washington, District of Columbia, July 3, 1815. He was by profession a civil engineer, and did a large business throughout the East, until December, 1874, when he came to Lompoc. He bought 160 acres and farmed until 1878, when he sold out and moved to Santa Barbara, where he died January 23, 1880.

The subject of this sketch came to Lompoc in 1885, purchased sixty acres of land, and rented other land, and farmed for four years. He went to the mines in Arizona and for ten years was absent in mining and railroad engineering. His family meanwhile resided in Lompoc and Santa Barbara. All of the original purchase has been sold, excepting ten acres and their residence. Mr. and Mrs. Richards have seven children, six boys and one girl, all at home. Mr. Richards has had a varied experience.

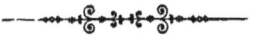

THOMAS JEFFREYS WILLIAMS, Superintendent of Arroyo Grande, Nipomo and Los Olivos Lumber Yards, generally known as Captain Williams, was born in Pennsylvania, of English parents. He received a good practical education at his boyhood home, leaving however, at the early age of sixteen years in company with a schoolmate for the gold fields of California; they reached San Francisco by way of Panama on October 5, 1853. After a few months' expierence in the then small but busy city at the bay, he joined his fortunes with others from the Keystone State, in a trip to the mines, arriving in Nevada City, Nevada County, in January 1854. It has been said by many, and the Captain says it is true, that this was the year of flush times in California. After two years of mining in the hills surrounding the city of Nevada, Captain Williams, in company with a Scotchman by the name of David Thorn, established the Nevada Foundry, under the firm name of Thorn & Williams; they were very successful, building many quartz and saw mills and hoisting works for deep mining. In 1861 Captain Williams sold out to Mr. Hugh, and engaged to go to Arizona, to superintend reduction works at the Patagonia mines, for Lieutenant Mowry, the pioneer of the Territory. He arrived there in April, 1862. After a few months successful working they were compelled to suspend on account of withdrawal of troops from the Territory. After indifferent success in mining in northern Sonora, Mexico, for the next two years, Captain Williams returned to California overland, by the way of Fort Yuma, in company with John Archibald, a merchant of Tucson. After a hard trip and many narrow escapes from the hostile Apaches, they reached Los Angeles in February 1865, where Captain Williams engaged to superintend mines for Colonel Rand, a gentleman from Boston, who purchased mines for a Boston syndicate at Havilah, Kern County. He remained here four years, taking out upward of half a million dollars in bullion. The company suspended work in 1869, when the Captain entered the field of politics, being elected Clerk of the County without an opponent, in 1870; resigning before his term expired, he purchased a ranch and engaged in stock-raising. After a few years he sold out and returned to the Mecca of all old Californians, San Francisco, where he received a State appointment. Seven years ago he was sent by the Pacific Coast Steamship Company to manage their lumber business on the line of their railroad, where he is still to be found. The Captain has three children, two sons and a daughter by a former marriage: his second wife who is still living was a Miss Hurlburt, of Middlebury, Vermont, a near relative of the Rockwells, and a direct descendant of the Mayflower Pilgrims. Captain Williams' future home will be at Santa Maria, Santa Barbara County, where he has an apricot orchard of sixty acres one mile from the town.

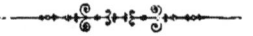

HENRY CAMILO DANA, engaged in raising cattle and sheep in the Nipomo, is a son of Captain W. G. Dana (whose sketch is given on a subsequent page) and nee Maria Josefa Carillo, and was born in Santa Barbara, July 14, 1839, one of twenty-one children, twelve of whom are now living. Mr. Dana has followed ranching all his life, on the old homestead. He now has 300 acres, beautifully situated in the Nipomo. He has never been away from Nipomo for any length of time, except in 1853, when he visited the Eastern States for a year and a half, especially New York and Massachusetts. He has been Deputy County Clerk of San Luis Obispo County, and frequently has been Clerk of Election.

He was married in 1884, to Josephine Blake, and has three children.

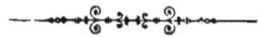

JOSEPH KAISER, a prominent real-estate dealer of Santa Maria, and President of Kaiser Land and Fruit Company, was born in the city of Mobile, Alabama, April 10, 1858. His father, Meyer Kaiser, was a wholesale and retail grocer of that city, who died in 1861. His mother and family came to San Luis Obispo in 1870, and established their residence. Our subject was educated at Mobile and San Luis Obispo, and finished at Heald's Business College at San Francisco. In 1874 he began business as book-keeper for his brother, at the general merchandise store of L. M. Kaiser & Co., at Guadalupe, continuing until 1880, when, associated with his brother, the general merchandise store of Kaiser Bros. was established at Santa Maria. They continued until 1882, when Blochman & Cerf were admitted, and the firm changed to Kaiser Bros. & Co., which dissolved in 1884, and the business was sold. There was then organized the Kaiser Land & Fruit Company, of which our subject was elected president. They have 300 acres west of town, known as Fair Lawn, which has been subdivided and platted into lots from two and a half to forty acres, offering special inducements to settlers. They also have 2,700 acres of ranch property, suitable for fruit or farming. In 1887 they began setting out trees, and have planted 130 acres to English walnuts and ninety acres to French prunes. The ranch property is leased, and under cultivation in general farm crops.

Mr. Kaiser has been treasurer of the Santa Maria Stock and Agricultural Association since its organization in 1886, his term of office having just expired. He is a member of Hesperian Lodge, No. 264, F. & A. M., and of Santa Maria Lodge, No. 90, K. of P.

JAMES MADISON GRAVES was born in San Luis Obispo, December 17, 1858, and is the son of William J. and Soledad (Pico) Graves. At an early age he attended school in his native city and later was a student at Berkeley. In 1881 was appointed Deputy Sheriff under Sheriff Oaks; afterward for a time was employed in the State Penitentiary. After the death of his father, in December, 1884, he resigned his position there and returned to his old home in San Luis Obispo. He then accepted a position in the sheriff's office, as deputy, and then Under Sheriff, acting in the latter capacity for three years. Mr. Graves is at present City Marshal, an office he has held three years, being twice elected.

He was married September 17, 1888, to Miss Martha de la Guerra, by whom he has two children.

GEORGE F. RUCKER, a rancher of Lompoc, was born in Saline County, Missouri, in 1851. His father was a farmer and a native of Virginia, and in 1852 emigrated across the plans to this undeveloped country, rich in minerals, called California. He settled near Santa Clara on a farm of 160 acres, and there engaged in general farming. The subject of this sketch was brought up on a farm, and in 1876 came to Lompoc, and very wisely selected fifty-six acres of rich loam soil, east of town, near the foot-hills, which he improved, and where he has since resided. He then devoted his time and energies to cultivating the land. He also rents eighty acres, and plants about sixty acres to beans and the balance to barley. He now has a finely developed ranch.

Mr. Rucker was married in Lompoc, in 1878, to Miss Susan Frances Barker; they have four children, who are now in school. Mr. Rucker is a member of Lompoc Lodge, No. 262, F. & A. M.

ROBERT CARR, a rancher, and one of the early settlers of Lompoc Valley, was born in Lancashire, England, January 1, 1833. His father was connected with railroad work, and was killed on the Liverpool Railroad, while in service. Robert entered the English army in 1855, when England, France and Turkey were allied against Russia, and they were in the first attack on Sebastopol, on June 18, 1855, and remained until after the first surrender, after a siege of eleven months. He then came with his regiment to Kingston, Canada West, where they were stationed one winter. In September, 1857, he was discharged, and he came to the United States, settling in Jefferson County, New York, where he remained two years, working on a farm. In the fall of 1859 he left for California, by water and the Isthmus of Panama, arriving in San Francisco January 9, 1860. He worked on a farm in Alameda County until 1864, and then rented one year. In 1864 he bought a ranch of 320 acres in the Livermore Valley, where he raised wheat and barley; he remained until 1875, when he sold out and came to Lompoc. Mr. Carr then bought eighty acres in the northwest part of the town, which was covered with brush and timber, but he has since cleared it and now plants thirty acres each to beans and mustard. He has built a house and farm buildings, and has five acres in a variety of fruits.

Mr. Carr was married in Jefferson County, New York, in May, 1859, to Miss Martha Rawley, a native of Long Island, Canada. Mr. Carr keeps six horses, and breeds for carriage purposes from a fine Bashaw mare.

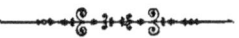

AVID COPELAND NORCROSS was born in Farmington, Maine, July 12, 1829. His boyhood was spent at home and he received his education at Abbott's School in Farmington. Coming to the State of California in 1851, he went at once into business at Sacramento, where he remained for a time. He afterward went to Arizona, being there interested in quicksilver mines. In 1865 he was in Monterey County, where he was engaged in the sheep business with Colonel Hollister. About 1867 he came to the county of San Luis Obispo, continuing sheep-raising at Mariano Springs. A stanch Republican and an active and enthusiastic worker, Mr. Norcross received in 1871 the nomination of his party for the office of Sheriff and was elected. In 1873 he was re-elected by a largely increased majority. At the conclusion of his term of office, he acquired the ranch known as Juerta de la Romualda, a few miles north of San Luis Obispo, where he resided until within a short time. This property was formerly held by Senator Stanford.

In 1872 Mr. Norcross was married to Miss Elida Woods, of San José, a sister of Mr. C. H. Phillips, of San Luis Obispo. Mrs. Norcross formerly lived in Wisconsin. By this marriage there have been four children born, all living at present.

Mr. Norcross died suddenly of heart disease, August 10, 1889. It was on returning to his home, then in the city, where, at the usual hour he had dined, that he complained of a pain in the region of his heart. His wife remained with him, and while they were conversing he gasped and settled back on his pillow unconscious, having died instantly. While the actual cause of his death will not, perhaps, be positively known, it is presumed by physicians to have been occasioned by a blood clot suspending the action of the heart. Few men in the county are more widely known or more popular than was David C. Norcross. Generous in disposition, genial in manner, devoted to his friends, a kind, faithful and loving father and husband, he is greatly mourned by his family and will be long remembered with sincere regret by his many friends.

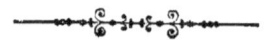

T. RUCKER, a prominent dealer in and trainer of trotting horses, was born in Saline County, Missouri, in 1846. In 1852 his father moved his family, across the plains to California, settling near Santa Clara, on a farm of 160 acres. Our subject lived at home until 1867, when he rented a farm of 200 acres and was engaged in raising wheat, which he carried on successfully. In 1875 he came to Lompoc and bought a one-half interest in the blacksmith shop of Joseph Dimmick, which they carried on for eighteen months. Then, in partnership, they bought a ranch of 128 acres, which, after working for two years they divided. Mr. Rucker has since added to his ranch to the amount of 122 acres, where he carries on general farming, making beans a leading crop, planting forty acres. All of the land is under cultivation. During late years Mr. Rucker has been giving his time and attention to the breeding of a high grade of horses, breeding from the old Percheron horse "Dexter," which he owned, and he has secured some very valuable colts, and now has about twenty-seven head of horses. He has charge of the race-track and stables and gives his entire attention to the training of trotting horses.

Mr. Rucker was married in Santa Clara County, in 1870, to Miss Emma Drake, a native of Iowa. They have five children, three of whom are now living.

W. E. SHEPHERD was born in Fairfield, Iowa, June 30, 1842. He is the son of Thomas Shepherd, a native of Ohio, who followed the business of tanning. His ancestors were Scotch-Irish. Mr. Shepherd's mother, Sarah S. (Edgar) Shepherd, was born in Ohio. Her parents were formerly residents of Pennsylvania, and her remote ancestors were English people. The subject of this sketch is one of a family of five children, and he was reared and educated in Iowa. His legal education was obtained at Oskaloosa. After his admission to the bar, he at once began the practice of his profession. When Mr. Lincoln was elected to the Presidency, Mr. Shepherd was appointed Postmaster of his town, and also held the office under Grant's administration. During the campaign in which Mr. Greeley was a candidate for President, Mr. Shepherd was on the Greeley ticket for Elector from his district, and he was defeated by General Weaver, who was then the candidate on the opposing ticket.

In 1873 Mr. Shepherd came to California, and, in Ventura, engaged in the newspaper business, and conducted the Ventura *Signal* for five years. Since then he has been engaged in the practice of law, and is one of the leading attorneys of the city, being associated with Mr. Blackstock. The firm stands high and enjoys a lucrative practice. Mr. Shepherd has a quick preception, a strong, resolute will, good reasoning faculties and fine argumentative ability, and is a fluent speaker. He is wide awake to the interests of his chosen city, and contributes his full share to its success. The side on which he arrays himself has in him a powerful advocate.

He was united in marriage to Miss Theodosia B. Hall, daughter of Augustus Hall, formerly a member of Congress from Iowa —a man of rare ability—and late Chief Justice of Nebraska. Mrs. Shepherd was born in Keosauqua, Iowa, October 14, 1845. Until 1873, except when in Batavia, New York, at school, she resided in Iowa and Nebraska. In that year, with her husband, W. E. Shepherd, and family, she came to Southern California, and soon found a home in Ventura. From those who know her well we learn she has been prominently connected with every movement for the good of the town and county; that it was greatly due to her and her lady co-workers that the town has a fine library of 3,000 volumes.

In addition to the care and education of her children, Mrs. Shepherd has, in the past five years, established a prosperous business, and formed in that business the nucleus of an important industry. When, five years ago, she told her friends that she intended to grow seeds and bulbs and to sell them in large quantities to Eastern dealers, she was met with good-natured but incredulous smiles. Knowing something of the magnitude of the demand, and having unbounded confidence in the soil and climate of the country, and being possessed with a passionate love of flowers, she went to work as the pioneer in this work—at first in a very small way. Her first green-house cost only the small sum of $2.50, and from year to year, without capital, she increased her facilities and trade. Now she keeps three men at work the year round; and has under her control, in addition to her beautiful two acre tract in town, five acres planted to calla lilies, similax and other rare plants and bulbs.

Mrs. Shepherd modestly attributes her success, which is really remarkable, to the glorious sunshine and soil of Southern California. Her friends insist, however, that her success is due to her pluck, perseverance, push and energy. They say not one in a thousand would have withstood the rebuffs of dealers, the discouragements, the disappointments, the lack of capital, the mishaps, the losses and the derisive smiles of friends. She was induced to go into the business through the advice and encouragement of the late Peter Henderson, of New York. He wrote to her a very kind letter, saying Southern California had the soil and climate for the production of bulbs and seeds and that he believed in fifty years it would grow seeds for the world. Mrs. Shepherd is a slight woman, weighing a little over 100 pounds. She has unusual executive ability. Her business correspondence now is very large, which she conducts herself, besides replying to letters from many women who write to her for advice as to how to go to work to do for themselves what she has done in her line. She takes a just pride in being known as the pioneer flower-seed and bulb grower of the Coast, and is entitled to all the praise she has received from the press of the State and from the many correspondents who have visited her grounds and written up her work.

When the writer went through her grounds and green and bath houses and packing house, heard her tell in her quiet, unassuming way, how she had worked, saw her directing her employés; considered what a vast amount of labor she must have personally performed, and what a tax on her memory it must be to hold at her tongue's end the names of her endless variety of plants and bulbs and shrubs; and then entered her parlors and saw her there with her husband, her daughters and son, the queen of the household, whom they all honored; saw there the evidence of culture and refinement,—when he saw all this, he gave a hearty assent to every word of praise so generously bestowed by her many friends in her home town.

Mr. and Mrs. Shepherd have an interesting family of four children: Augustus H. and Myrtle, born in Iowa; and Madge and Eda, in Ventura.

Mr. Shepherd enjoys the distinction of being a veteran of the late war. In his country's first call for volunteers, he enlisted in the Third Iowa Volunteer Infantry, for six months, and afterward in the three years' service. A part of the time he was in the postal service, by order of General Grant, under General A. H. Markland. He is a member of the G. A. R., and his political views are Democratic.

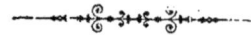

JOHN SPENCE, of Santa Barbara, is a native of England, born at Little Gransden, Cambridgeshire, January 14, 1848. He remained there until 1870, when he emigrated to America. He was, at fourteen years of age, apprenticed to learn the business of a landscape gardener, which he thoroughly mastered, and upon his arrival in America assumed charge of the gardens of one of the wealthiest men of Norwich, Connecticut. He there read of the natural beauties of California, and in 1875 came to Santa Barbara. He leased the ground, now comprising his present home, for five years, which he planted to fruit trees, small shrubery, flowers and palms. The sale of stock from this business brought him a handsome income, and he gradually added to it ornamental and fruit trees and shrubery. He also engaged quite extensively in the raising of Pampas plumes, and is a pioneer in this now important industry. At the New Orleans Exposition of 1885 he made an exhibit of 10,000 plumes, which attracted much attention, a portion of them being dyed in various beautiful hues, and most tastefully arranged. His design of the American flag, which spanned the California exhibit, a rainbow thirty-six feet in length and a pyramid thirty feet in height, were special features of the exposition. He had charge of the Santa Barbara County exhibit, and did himself great credit, as well as the county which he represented, in his management of affairs. He is one of the active members of the Santa Barbara Horticultural Society.

Mr. Spence was married in England, to Miss Helen F. Reeve. She is an enthusiastic admirer of flowers, and takes a lively interest in flower culture. They have four children, and one of the most beautiful homes in Southern California.

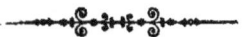

C. J. YOUNG, a rancher and Deputy Assessor for the city of Lompoc, was born in Shiawassee County, Michigan, in 1839. His father was a farmer and carpenter, and moved to Clinton County in 1849, where he continued his trade. Our subject learned the trade of carpenter with his father, and worked with him until the breaking out of the war, when he enlisted in August, 1861, at St. Johns, Clinton County, in Company D, First Michigan Cavalry, under Colonel Thornton F. Broadhead, for three years. He was discharged January 1, 1862, and then re-enlisted in August following in the Fifth Michigan Cavalry, under Colonel J. T. Copeland, the regiment being with the Army of the Potomac until June, 1863, when he joined General Custer's brigade. Their first heavy battle was at Gettysburg, and they were in every heavy battle fought by the Army of the Potomac. Mr. Young was taken prisoner near Richmond June 18, 1864, and was taken to Richmond. He was sent to Andersonville, where he remained three months, and suffered every possible deprivation in diet, being confined to poor food and water. He was then sent to the prison at Florence, South Carolina, where he was kept three months; there the water was fair but they had but little to eat. He was paroled in December, but remained as a prisoner until January 1, when he was sent home to Michigan, having lost seventy-five pounds during his six months' imprisonment. The exchange of prisoners was made in April, and then Mr. Young returned to his regiment, and they moved to Fort Leavenworth, Kansas, where they were discharged July 3, 1865.

After a visit to his home he went to Chicago, where he worked at his trade of carpenter and builder about seven years, when he came to California, arriving at San Francisco January 2, 1873. He then spent one year working at his trade in Monterey County, and in the spring of 1874 came to the Jonato Rancho, owned by R. T. Buell, to superintend building, and after completion he went to Lompoc and bought two blocks, built a house, and followed his trade of contractor. He then sold out, and in 1883 bought forty acres northeast of town, which he has since cleared and improved by building a house and planting a small orchard, and he now interests himself in the cultivation and improvement of his ranch, raising the general crops of the valley.

Mr. Young was married in St. Johns, Michigan, July 1, 1867, to Miss Naomi J. Everett, and they have nine children. Mr. Young was appointed Deputy Assessor in the spring of 1889, under Frank Smith, whose biography appears elsewhere.

CHARLES L. SAUNDERS, one of the prominent developers of Lompoc, was born in London, England, in 1827. His father was a carpenter and boat-builder, and moved with his family to Cleveland, Ohio, in 1841. In 1844 our subject was apprenticed to a carriage-maker at Brunswick, Ohio, where he remained four years. He then worked in an adjoining town until 1849, when he went to Independence, Missouri, and worked one year there. May 1, 1850, he started across the plains for California, with a mule team. They made a comfortable and rapid trip, and after three months arrived at Hangtown. He then went to the mines on American River, and in 1852 to the Yuba River, where he began trading, opened a store and boarding-house, which he continued until 1855. Mr. Saunders then went to Salmon River in Klamath County, where he kept a store and traded, and built two bridges across the Klamath River, remaining until 1864. He then came to Salinas, where he rented 2,100 acres of land and engaged in stock-raising, and also conducted a dairy of seventy-five cows. In 1876 he came to Lompoc, and bought thirty acres in the corporation, which he improved by building a house and setting out a small orchard. His family remained here while he managed the wharf down at the sea. In 1881 he sold out to Goodall & Perkins. In 1880 Mr. Saunders bought the lot on the corner of H street and Ocean avenue, and in 1881 he erected a two-story building for a hall and store, opening the store himself with a full stock of general merchandise. He continued this business until May, 1889, when he sold out. In 1885 he bought $387\frac{1}{2}$ acres in the San Miguelito Cañon, where he raises horses and cattle, and also carries on general farming. In 1887 he bought fifteen acres, his present residence property, where he built a house and barns. In 1889 he built the two-story hotel, 50 x 140 feet, on Ocean avenue, called the Saunders Hotel.

Mr. Saunders was married in Klamath County, in 1856, to Miss Jane A. Swan, a native of New York. They have five children.

JOHN G. PRELL is a native of the Old World, having been born near Leipsic, Germany, in 1837. At the age of fifteen years he was apprenticed, for a term of three years, to learn the trade of cooper. His father having previously died, in 1855, his mother with brothers and sisters emigrated to the United States and settled at South Bend, Indiana. The subject of this sketch worked at brick-molding until 1860, when he sought the mining regions of Pike's Peak, but after a brief experience of four months he pushed further West to California, and after a few months in the mines of El Dorado County he settled in San José for the winter. But still unsettled, in the spring he went to

Los Angeles, and there passed the summer, returning to San José in the fall, and finding a job of brick-molding he settled in that locality, and later engaged in farming, which he followed until 1866. He then returned to his old home in South Bend, but not liking the cold weather he went to southwestern Missouri, where he passed several months, and in 1867 returned to the more temperate climate of San José. He was engaged in farming until 1868, when he came to Santa Maria, and was among the first to locate land in the valley, and he claims the honor of having built the first house, November 7, 1868. In 1869 he moved his family here. He has since purchased 320 acres of land near by, where he follows grain farming, only raising sufficient stock for ranch purposes. He has four acres in orchard, and a large variety of fruit.

Mr. Prell was married at Rolla, Missouri, in 1867, to Miss Eliza Powers, a native of Ohio, and they have four children. He is a member of Santa Maria Lodge, No. 302, I. O. O. F., of Hesperian Lodge, No. 264, F. & A. M., and of the Chosen Friends.

C. E. CARTER, whose fine orchard and fruit ranch stands out prominently east of Lompoc, was born at Hopkinton, New Hampshire, in 1834. His father had extensive lumber interests, and owned and operated a saw-mill; he died when our subject was but ten years of age. After the death of his father Mr. Carter lived out, and worked at farming until 1856, when he came to California by water and the Isthmus of Panama, arriving in San Francisco, May 2, 1856. He then went to the mines in Sierra County, where he was engaged in mining and farming until the fall of 1869, when he moved to Watsonville, and bought fifteen acres of land and set out a small orchard in that locality. In 1876 he came to Lompoc, and bought 116 acres, ninety-six of which he still owns and which is highly developed. It was largely covered with brush and timber. In 1877 he began setting out his orchard, which now covers twenty-two acres, nearly all of which is now in bearing, mainly of winter apples, but he has also a large variety of fruit. He formerly planted beans, wheat, barley, mustard, etc., but now devotes his entire time to the orchard, and also raises hay for home use; he keeps several mares, and raises a high grade of draft and trotting stock. His attractive and substantial home is evidence of the years of labor which he has expended upon the improvement of his property. He was married in 1868, in Sierra County, this State, to Miss Lucy E. Glidden, a native of Maine.

W. H. ROACH was born in Sanel, Mendocino County, California, February 26, 1860, the son of Patrick and Catherine (Prucell) Roach, the former a native of Ireland and the latter of Detroit, Michigan, of Irish parents. They came to California in an early day and were pioneers of Mendocino County. They were the parents of twelve children, nine of whom are still living. The father has followed farming and stock-raising all his life, and reared his numerous family in the county where he still resides.

The subject of this sketch received his education in the public schools of his native county, and also took a course in Heald's Business College. For four years he was engaged in a meat market in his native town. He came to Ventura in 1888, and entered into partnership with Mr. George Saviers. They have two markets, one at Hueneme and the other at New Jerusalem. Being men well qualified for the business in which they are engaged, they have a thriving trade.

Mr. Roach has held the office of Justice of the Peace at Westport, Mendocino County, for two years, and also Notary Public two years. He is a member of the Masonic fraternity, Ventura Lodge, No. 214. Mr. Roach is a single gentleman and, no doubt, other chapters in his history will soon follow!

LEWIS LINBARGER, a California pioneer, came to the State in 1857. He was born in Illinois, January 6, 1836, son of Lewis and Jane (Henderson) Linbarger, the former of German ancestry, and the latter a native of Jackson County, Indiana. He was one of a family of eleven children, seven of whom are now living. The family removed to Missouri in 1841, and in 1843 emigrated to Oregon, where the subject of this sketch was reared and educated. When he came to California, he first located on a ranch of 160 acres in Contra Costa County, which afterward proved to be a grant. He then sold his improvements there and went to San Joaquin County, where he purchased property and engaged in farming; then sold out, went away and bought and sold again; returned to San Joaquin County, bought 160 acres of land, which he improved; then sold out, and this time came to Ventura County. He here engaged in stock-raising for five years; was then absent from the county for a period of time, after which he returned and continued the same business four years more. In 1882 he purchased his present ranch of 100 acres, located two miles west of Santa Paula. He improved the property by erecting buildings, etc., and engaged in raising barley and hogs, for four years. He then turned his attention to the production of Lima beans, of which he is now raising large crops, at remunerative prices. The work is all done by machinery, so that the labor is not severe.

Mr. Linbarger was married in February, 1858, to Miss Malinda F. Blevins, of Oregon, and daughter of Alexander Blevins, who emigrated there in 1843. They have three children: Mary J., born in Contra Costa County, is now the wife of Allen Baker, and resides in Santa Paula; Nancy Lucinda, born in San Joaquin County, married F. M. Edgar, and also resides in Santa Paula; and Charles L., born in Linn County, Oregon, is married and lives on his father's ranch. Mr. Linbarger is a Democrat.

J. W. SHICK was born in Georgetown, Brown County, Ohio, August 18, 1819. His father, Peter Shick, was born in Philadelphia in 1791, and his grandfather came to America from Germany. His mother was Elizabath (Woodruff) Shick, a native of Brown County, Ohio, born of English parents. Mrs. Shick was the third of a family of eleven children, five of whom are now living, and are scattered over the United States. He was educated in his native State. When he became of age he purchased the old homestead on which his father had lived six years, the youngest of the family were born, and on which his father died in 1835. It contained 100 acres. His father had settled on it in 1829, had reclaimed it from the bush, and, at his request, was buried on it. After living on this property five years, Mr. Shick sold out and went to Davis County, Iowa, where he bought eighty acres of improved land, farmed it for two years, then sold, and in the same neighborhood bought 100 acres. On this property he made his home for twenty years.

In 1861, when the war broke out, he enlisted in Company G, Second Iowa Volunteer Infantry, and served during the war. He made that remarkable march with General Sherman from Atlanta to the sea. On this march he was detailed to the ambulance corps, and drove the mail ambulance for General G. M. Dodge, of Iowa. On his way from Dallas, Georgia, to Kingston, after the mail, his team ran away and he was thrown from the wagon and run over, his left ankle being badly injured, also right shoulder and knee slightly. He has, to some extent, been a cripple ever since. At the time of General Lee's surrrender, he was in the hospital from the effect of this injury, where he was discharged on surgeon's certificate of disability July 10, 1865. He returned to his home and engaged in agricultural pursuits on his farm and, in winter, also taught school. In 1877 he sold his property and came to California. In Inyo County he bought 116 acres of land, and resided there ten years. He then sold and came to Santa Paula, where he bought the house in which he now resides with his family. He has received a small pension, dated from the date of discharge.

Mr. Shick was married in 1843, to Miss Eleanor A. P. Clark, a native of Kentucky, and a daughter of Mr. John Clark. They had one child, Elizabeth, born in Ohio, and is now the wife of Thomas Bates, of Missouri. Mrs. Shick died in 1845. For his second wife he wedded Catharine Srofe, a native of Ohio, and daughter of Elijah Srofe. Her father was born in Ohio, and was the son of a soldier of the war of 1812, who was wounded in the battle of Lundy's Lane. By this wife he had four children, two of whom are living: Mary A., born in Ohio, now married to A. J. Humphrey, and resides in Davis County, Iowa; David T., born in Davis County, Iowa, resides at his father's old home. This wife died in 1855. Mr. Shick's next wife was *nee* Martha J. Mohler, also a native of Ohio. She lived only a short time after marriage, her death occurring in 1858. He was afterward married to Annie M. Torrence. She, too, was a native of Ohio, and her death occurred a year after her marriage. Mr. Shick's present wife was formerly Mrs. Catharine Tull, widow of Mr. W. Tull, of Davis County, Iowa, and daughter of Mr. Thomas Clark. They have had four children, three of whom are living. Their eldest son, T. M., lived to be twenty-three years of age, and was murdered by one Henry Brown, who was convicted of the crime and sentenced to imprisonment for life. Ida May, and Rena C. and Francis M. were born in Davis County, Iowa, and now reside with their parents. Mr. Shick is a member of the Baptist Church, and her husband of the Christian Church He is a worthy member of the G. A. R. In Davis County, Iowa, Mr. Shick held every township office, and was Justice of the Peace for eight years. In Salt Creek, that county, he served as Postmaster. Notwithstanding his advanced age, seventy-one years, he is still hale and hearty, and bids fair to enjoy a long life in his happy California home.

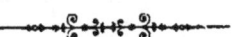

C. NANCE, a rancher of Santa Maria, was born in Randolph County, North Carolina, in 1839. His father was a farmer and stock-raiser by occupation. Our subject lived at home until sixteen years of age, engaged in farming and also learning the trade of carpenter. In 1855 he went to

Buchanan County, Missouri, to join his uncle, Rev. Isham Nance, who emigrated to Missouri in 1835, at the settling of the Platte purchase. Mr. Nance engaged with Colonel Fouts as overseer of his plantation and slaves near Rock House Prairie, remaining until 1858, when he started with a freight train of Guthrie & Mitchell for Salt Lake City. He engaged as cook, but was soon promoted second wagon boss. The train was composed of thirty-two wagons, six yoke of oxen to each wagon. In the spring of 1859 he started for Pike's Peak, with his own outfit, and returning again as assistant of John S. Woods. In 1860 he went to Nebraska, where he engaged in farming, and in 1862 moved westward to the mines in eastern Oregon, where he remained until 1866, meeting with good success. He then came south to San José and Castroville, where he worked at his trade, helping to build the first seven houses of that town. In 1867 he went to Salinas City, at the founding of that town, and engaged in the building of the first fifteen houses. He then returned to San José, and in partnership with W. T. Morris farmed the Parr ranch until 1870, when he took a trip East. On returning to California Mr. Nance continued his trade up to 1872, when he came to Santa Maria, and bought land, which he farmed and also worked at his trade as opportunity offered. In 1881 he bought 240 acres of grazing land in Cat Cañon, and he also rents 500 acres, which he farms to wheat and barley. He set out one of the first orchards in the valley, of 300 trees. He now devotes much time to stock interests, breeding a fine grade of horses for general utility purposes, keeping about twenty-five head. He owns two stallions, Frank Leslie, of Messenger stock, known as the trick horse, and the Rowdy Dutchman, of Hambleton stock.

Mr. Nance has been a director of the Santa Barbara Agricultural Society since its organization in 1884. He was Roadmaster for Santa Maria district two years, and in 1884 was appointed Deputy Sheriff, under R. J. Broughton, and is now serving his fourth term. He was married in Santa Maria, in 1881 to Miss Maggie Smith, and they have four children. Mr. Nance is a member of Hesperian Lodge, No. 264, F. & A. M.

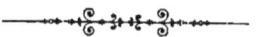

HARVEY HARDISON, deceased, late one of the prominent business men and oil-well operators of Santa Paula, was born in Aroostook County, Maine, February 9, 1844. Natives of the same State were also his father Ivory and his grandfather Joseph Hardison; and it is believed that the family originated in Sweden. Harvey's mother, Dorcas (Abott) Hardison, was born in China, Kennebec County, Maine, and her ancestors were English and Irish. In their family were eight sons and three daughters, all of whom excepting one are yet living.

Mr. Hardison, the subject of this memoir, was the eighth in this family, inheriting a fine physical organization and a good disposition, and was reared to strict temperance habits, using neither tobacco nor strong drink. At the age of twenty-one years he began work for himself in the oil regions of Pennsylvania, drilling for oil. About two years afterward he obtained an outfit, began to take contracts and for five years drilled wells for Lyman Stewart, now of Los Angeles. He then began drilling for himself, as well as for others, having an interest in Shangburg and in Venango County, Pennsylvania. He bored about 300 wells, ranging from 800 to 2,000 feet in depth. The time required for sinking the deepest well then required about three months; but now the same work can be done in about one month.

In 1883 Mr. Hardison came to Newhall, California, and superintended the putting down of the Hadison & Stewart wells at Pico. They sank four wells before "striking oil." The fifth well, called the Star, was a good producer, yielding fifty barrels per day. In Adams, Saltmarsh and Aliso cañons he superintended the drilling of oil wells. In tunnels from some of these electric lights are employed to work by, and all the latest improvements in the oil-well business are brought into use. One well in Adams Cañon gave a flow of 1,000 barrels per day. In the Saltmarsh Cañon the company has four producing wells, one of them having yielded 100,000 barrels of oil. In the Adams Cañon one well produced 125,000 barrels. These wells are from 250 to 1,750 feet deep. They have also producing wells in Santa Paula Cañon and three in the Aliso Cañon and five in the Ojai. At the time of his recent death, Mr. Hardison had a fourth interest in the Santa Paula Horse and Cattle Company, who have a ranch of 6,400 acres stocked with horses and cattle, some of which are thoroughbred stock. Mr. Hardison owned other property.

Mr. Hardison was appointed Postmaster of Santa Paula in April, 1889, and his daughter Ida was employed as assistant and his son Frank as deputy. Mr. Hardison was a member of the A. O. U. W., of the Universalist Church and of the Republican party. April 4, 1890, he met his death from explosion of gas in one of the oil tunnels in Adams Cañon, where he was superintendent. It was supposed that the explosion was so sudden and forceful that death was instantaneous. His bereaved wife and children bore the fearful calamity with great fortitude. Mr. Hardison was a noble, generous and large-hearted man, and a pleasant and kind husband and father, and was also esteemed highly by all who knew him.

His marriage took place in 1869, when he wedded Miss Delphina M. Wetherbee, a native of Crawford County, Pennsylvania, born September 14, 1848, a daughter of Franklin Wetherbee, who was born in New York. Mrs. Hardison is a member of the Presbyterian Church at Santa Paula, and has proved herself an excellent wife and mother. There are two sons and two daughters, all of whom are also members of the same church. Ida A. was born in Centerville, Crawford County, Pennsylvania, August 2, 1870; Franklin I., January 20, 1872, in Parker City, Pennsylvania; Seth J., November 14, 1874, in Turkey City, Pennsylvania, and Ruth M., in the same place, January 16, 1877.

JESSE HILL, one of California's pioneers, and an early settler of the Lompoc Valley, was born in Mason County, Virginia, in 1820. His ancestors were natives of the Old World, who came to this country at an early day, and both his grandfathers were soldiers in the war of the Revolution. Jesse lived at home, and engaged in farming until 1849, and then passed one year in Iowa, when, being thrilled with the California excitement, in the spring of 1850, he started for that undeveloped country, across the plains, by Salt Lake City and the Truckee route. He crossed on horseback. At Truckee he was shot by an Indian, but only laid up about fifteen days, and landed in California in October, 1850. He settled near the San Joaquin River, and bought out what has since been known as Hill Ferry, which he operated for ten years, and which became the popular crossing for the droves of cattle of Southern California, as they were moved toward the mines. In 1862 he sold his interest and then moved back to the foot-hills, where he embarked in the sheep business, keeping a herd of 5,000 sheep. In 1869 he drove his flock south to the Rancho la Purisima, 3,300 acres of which he still owns, also the Rancho Santa Rita of 2,500 acres. In 1877, the dry year, Mr. Hill lost about 15,000 sheep, and though still in the business has only continued in a small way, keeping about 1,600 head on Santa Rita. He also farms about 700 acres, 100 acres in beans, and the balance in barley, of which he rents a large portion. The Rancho la Purisima, Mr. Hill has given to his two sons, who carry on farming, but who are more particularly interested in the raising of horses and cattle, keeping about forty head, and breeding to running and trotting stock. In politics Mr. Hill is a Democrat, but takes no official distinction, and devotes his life to his family and farm.

He was married near San Juan, January 1, 1856, to Miss Harriet Rhea, a native of Illinois, but of French descent. They have four children, two sons and two daughters.

L. FORRESTER, a rancher of Santa Maria, was born in West Virginia, in 1850. He lived at home until eighteen years of age, and then worked in a saw-mill and in oil works in Parkersburg, and there learned the science of well-boring. He then went to Kansas, and for several years followed farming and stock-raising. In the spring of 1875 he came to California, and farmed one year in Butte County, then went to Tulare, where he ran a saw-mill and teamed until 1878, when he went to Oregon and helped build and run a saw-mill, until he returned to California and settled in Santa Maria, in 1880. He then opened a blacksmith shop in the Santa Maria district, which he continued until 1885, when he returned to Santa Maria and built his present spacious shop, 46 x 70 feet, corner of Chapel and Broadway streets. He also has a machine shop and barley crusher, all running by steam power, and he is prepared to do blacksmithing in all its branches, also carriage building and repairing, always keeping on hand two blacksmiths and one wood-workman. He also owns a ranch of 480 acres in Santa Maria district, 130 acres of which is tillable, and the remainder is good for grazing. He has twenty acres in fruit, mainly prunes and apricots, and also grows barley and beans. He breeds horses and cattle, keeping from forty to sixty head. In 1878 he started the water-works, pumping by steam from the well to an elevated tank, and is prepared to supply the town; this interest he sold to his brother in the fall of 1889. Mr. Forrester is a professional house-mover, and has moved some of the largest houses in the surrounding country.

He was married at Pottawattomie, Kansas, in 1872, to Miss Martha Clark, a native of Missouri, and they have five children. Mr. Forrester's father was born in Philadelphia.

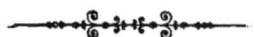

F. EARLS, one of the successful ranchers of the East side, was born in Boone County, Kentucky, in 1830. His father was a farmer, and in 1837 emigrated to Andrew County, Missouri, where he bought 320 acres, and engaged in general farming and stock-raising. The subject of this sketch lived at home until 1852, when he started for California, crossing the plains. He came out with Steele, McCord & Co., driving 800 head of cattle, and being 134 days in crossing, landing at Grand Island on the Sacramento River, where they sold their stock. Mr. Earls went to Santa Clara, where he rented and farmed until 1857, when he went to Monterey County, rented land and started a dairy, continuing until 1863. He then went to Virginia City, Nevada, and began teaming, which he continued until 1869, then to the White Pine country, where he teamed until 1874, and also engaged in farming, first purchasing 280 acres.

He was married in 1874, to Mrs. Martha Jane McMinn, and carried on his ranch until 1878, when he came to Lompoc, still retaining the ranch. At Lompoc he bought 120 acres, partly covered with brush and timber. He began clearing and improving it and now possesses a highly developed ranch, devoting himself to farming, making beans the main crop, of which he planted about seventy acres. They have two sons, both living under the parental roof.

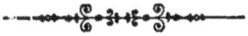

NICOLAZO ESTRADA, widow of Julian Estrada, was born in Monterey in the year 1820. She is the sister of J. Gaxiola, one of the oldest residents of the surrounding country, a brief account of whose life we append to this sketch. Mrs. Estrada is herself one of the earliest settlers of the place, having come to San Luis Obispo in 1846, as the wife of Julian Estrada. At that time there were but ten families living in the county, and where the city of San Luis Obispo now lies there was but one building and that was the old Mission. When Mr. and Mrs. Estrada moved to this county in 1846 they took up their abode on their Santa Rosa ranch, which was twelve miles square. Twenty-three years later they sold this ranch, excepting a small portion of it which they continued to occupy. During the past year this has been disposed of, and Mrs. Estrada is now occupying a residence within the city limits, where she is spending the closing years of her life with a portion of her family, Mr. Gaxiola and an unmarried daughter. Her husband died in the year 1869, leaving three sons and four daughters.

Mr. Gaxiola is one of the most prominent survivors of the Mexican war now living in this county. He fought under General Castro, and many are the stories told of his brave deeds during this period. He was a great favorite with his comrades and also with the officers. Of late years Mr. Gaxiola has led a quiet and retired life. He was married in 1835, but has no family.

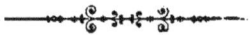

THOMAS SAULSBURY, a rancher of Santa Maria, was born in England, in 1830. He began work in the coal mines at Oleburg, at nine years of age, continuing six years. He then worked in the iron factory, and learned the trade of puddler. In 1848 he came to the United States, first settling in St. Louis, Missouri, where he worked at his trade, on the opening of the first iron factory in that city. He remained until 1852, when he came across the plains to California. He came with the freight train of Ben Holliday, as driver of a mule team, the train being loaded with whisky, dry goods and general merchandise. They landed at Sacramento, where Mr. Holliday established a store, and our subject remained with him for twelve years, much of the time being engaged in driving cattle from Salt Lake to California. At the time of the Mormon war, Mr. Holliday bought General Johnson's stock, consisting of 1,000 mules, all of them being driven to California, in Mr. Saulsbury's care. In 1864 Mr. Saulsbury began farming in Alameda County, where he bought land, and kept 100 head of cattle, remaining until 1873, when he came to Guadaloupe, and was one of the pioneers of that town. He bought 347 acres of land, and started the dairy business, keeping seventy-five cows, and making butter. He still owns the ranch, which he rents with part of his stock. He and his sons also own a stock-ranch of 2,000 acres in the Cuyamaca country, where he raises horses and cattle. He is now renting a ranch of 160 acres near town, thus affording his children the advantages of the school; he and his sons plant 120 acres in beans.

Mr. Saulsbury was married in Alameda County, in 1860, to Miss Isabelle Randall, and they have eleven children.

HENRY JEWETT, son of Samuel and Maria Rosaria (Herrera) Jewett, the former of Vermont and the latter of Mexico, was born in the city of Mexico in 1844. In 1850 the family moved to San Francisco, where two years later the father died from cholera. Alameda was next their home. Young Jewett was very fond of traveling and roamed around the country a great deal in search of new sights. He was for nine years engaged in ranching in New Mexico. In 1869 he came to San Luis Obispo, and there served as Constable, Deputy Sheriff and City Marshal. Mr. Jewett was married in 1869, in Los Angeles, to Elvira Andrada. They were the parents of ten children, six of whom are now living. After his marriage he went to San Francisco, believing he would prefer to settle there, but decided later that San Luis Obispo presented the best business opportunities for him. During the gold excitement Mr. Jewett went to the mines in San José and was moderately successful in his search. He was a member of the A. O. U. W., and also of the fire department. When he died, August 11, 1889, a worthy and respected citizen passed away.

J. M. CLARK, one of the intelligent ranchers of Lompoc, who farms with his head as well as his hands, was born in Monroe County, Michigan, in 1845. His father was a mechanic in early life, but devoted his later life to farming. He moved his family of eight children to California in 1856, and settled in Alameda County, where he died in 1876, at the age of seventy-one years. His widow is still living, hale and hearty, at the age of eighty-four years. The subject of this sketch passed his early life at home, and in March, 1865, enlisted at San José, having passed several years in the Home Guards, in Company E, First Cavalry, under Captain McElroy, and they were then sent to Arizona. Mr. Clark was mainly on escort duty with the paymaster, and during the year rode 3,000 miles. He was discharged at Drum Barracks, Los Angeles, in 1866. He then passed two years in roaming and riding over the country, and in 1868 settled in Pajaro Valley, near Watsonville, with his brother. They also had a stock-ranch in San Benito County, consisting of 900 acres, where they raised horses and hogs, and continued the partnership until 1878. Mr. Clark then became agent for Major J. L. Rathburn and the Athertons, who owned large ranches. He superintended the farming and attended to the sale of lands until 1885, when he came to Lompoc. He bought eighty acres of land, to which he has since added ten acres more, making his present attractive ranch. He makes beans his main crop, planting about forty acres; and during the wet season, when the potato crop is likely to be light on the wet lands, he pays careful attention to that crop. In 1889, from seven acres of land, he cleared $1,700, obtaining a yield of 275 bushels to the acre. Mr. Clark is a careful, systematic farmer, and now enjoys what in boyhood was his chief ambition, to have a nice farm, with every desirable tool, and sufficient horses to conduct his ranch.

On March 8, 1882, Mr. Clark received a certificate from Governor Perkins of California, in accordance with a passage of the Legislature, testifying the people's gratitude to the soldiers of the civil war. Though an ardent Republican, he aspires to no political distinction, but devotes himself to his family and the proper maintenance of his ranch. He is a member of Robert Anderson Post, G. A. R.

Mr. Clark has been twice married; first in Watsonville, in 1866, but his first wife survived but a short time. He was married the second time at San Jose, in 1869, to Miss Juliet Duncan, a native of Missouri, who came to California in infancy. No children have been born of this union.

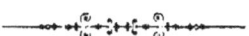

WILLIAM R. STONE, one of the leading business men of San Buenaventura, was born in Winchester, Middlesex County, Massachusetts, eight miles from Boston, August 17, 1854. His father, Hon. J. F. Stone, a native of New Hampshire, was a business man of that State for many years, and for the last eight years of his life represented his district in the Legislature of Massachusetts, as a Republican. His wife, *nee* Melvina Clark, is also a native of the Old Granite State. They have five children, of whom three are living. Mr. Stone, our subject, finished his education in a Bryant & Stratton business college, located at Boston, Massachusetts, and when of age he became a traveling salesman for John M. Davis & Co., in the line of gents' furnishing goods, and continued three years in their employ, with good success. Then, for four years, he had charge of the furnishing-goods department of C. C. Hastings & Co.; next he was salesman until 1885 in the hosiery department of Murphy, Grant & Co.; and then he embarked in business for himself in San Buenaventura, buying out John A. Walker's establishment of dry goods, fancy goods and gents' furnishing goods. He conducted the business with marked success until November 23, 1887, when he moved into his large, new store, the "White House," where he enjoys a large trade from the better class of customers, based on keeping fine fashionable goods. The store is kept well filled with stock; it has a nice, cosy office, and a gallery in the rear for a cloak department. Every feature is metropolitan, showing that the proprietor is a trained merchant of experience, although comparatively young. He is Master Workman of Ventura Lodge, No. 173, A. O. U. W., Chancellor Commander of the K. of P., a member of the K. of H., and is a prompt and efficient officer as First Lieutenant of Company D, Seventh Infantry, First Brigade, National Guard of California.

He was married in 1879 to Miss Minnie C. Clark, a native of San Francisco. By this marriage there was one daughter, named Maud C., born in San Francisco February 23, 1880. In 1882 Mrs. Stone met with a sad accident which caused her death; and in 1884 Mr. Stone was again married, this time to Miss Emma Ellinghouse, whose place of birth was San José; and by this marriage there is also one daughter, named Arlie B., and born in San Buenaventura, in 1886.

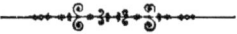 THORNBURGH, of Santa Maria, was born in Wayne County, Indiana, in 1835. His father, John Thornburgh, was a native of Tennessee, and emigrated to Indiana in 1819. He was a tanner and saddler by trade, and carried on that business in connection with farming. In 1864 he moved to Redfield, Iowa, and there engaged in wool manufacturing until 1870, when he came to California, spending one year in Ventura County. In 1871 he came to Santa Maria and purchased 160 acres of land on the corner of Main and Broadway, and was one of the founders of the town. He engaged in the merchandising business three and a half years, but his main interests have been in agriculture. He is still living, being hale and hearty at the age of eighty-one years. He married Elizabeth Hunt, a native of Guilford, North Carolina, of Quaker parentage, and Mr. Thornburgh, our present subject, was also brought up in Quaker principles.

Mr. Thornburgh, our subject, was educated in the common schools of Indiana, and then attended the Union College, in Randolph County, until 1855, when he returned home and engaged in farming. In 1858 he was married, in Wayne County, Indiana, to Miss Ellen McLucas. They then removed to Redfield, Iowa, where Mr. Thornburgh engaged in farming. In 1864 he assisted his father in building the Thornburgh Woolen Mills, and was engaged therein until 1870, when his father left for California. The subject of this sketch then became foreman for saw mills through Dallas and Boone counties until 1875, when he came to Santa Maria and took up a Government claim of 160 acres, and also clerked in the store of Thornburgh & Co. In 1876 he was appointed the first Justice of the Peace of the town by the Board of Supervisors, and thereafter continued by election until 1884, and one term since by appointment to fill a vacancy. In 1880 he was appointed the first Notary of the town. He organized the Central School district in 1882, and was Clerk of the Board of Trustees for six years.

Mr. Thornburgh is now living with his third wife, to whom he was married at Santa Maria, in January, 1887. Has two sons by his former wife. He was a charter member of the Hesperian Lodge, 264, F. & A. M.

P. WARD, one of the business men of San Buenaventura, alive to the interests of his town and ready to help it in every enterprise for the advancement of the city, was born in the State of New Jersey, April 30, 1853. His father, G. A. Ward, was born in the State of New York in 1832. As far as is known, the ancestors of the family were from New York. His mother, Margaret Graff, was born in New York city, and is of German descent. They had four sons and two daughters. Mr. Ward, the third child, was educated in New York and New Jersey, learned the carriage-making trade, working at it three and a half years, and, finding that it did not agree with him, removed to Chicago, where he was employed for years as carpenter and architect for Allen & Bartlett, prominent builders; he was in Chicago during the great fire of 1871. In 1876 he came to Yolo County, California, and began contracting and building, and had a large and successful business. In 1886 he came to Ventura, and has since built a fine

Myron Angel.

residence on the Floral tract, three-fourths of a mile from the business center of the city, and the structure exhibits the skill of the architect and builder. On arriving here he formed a partnership, which is known as the firm of Shaw & Ward. They were the builders of the Anacapa Hotel, the residence of Mr. Wells, and several other fine houses. They are also the architects of a new church which is now in process of erection for the Methodist Episcopal Church, South, of which Mr. Ward is a member of the building committee, and also district steward. He belongs to the order of F. & A. M. and the I. O. O. F., and his wife was also a member of the same church with him. He was married in 1886 to Miss Jennie Hill, a native of Yolo County, this State.

MYRON ANGEL is a native of the State of New York, born in Oneonta, Otsego County, December 1, 1827, a descendant of the first Puritan Pilgrims who landed on Plymouth Rock. His father, William Angel, desiring to advance the prosperity of Oneonta, established a newspaper in the village, and in this office the subject of this sketch often assisted in the mechanical and editorial departments, although then very young. In 1835 his mother died, and in 1842 his father, leaving him an orphan in his fifteenth year. The boy, inheriting a fair property, was enabled to acquire a fine education from district school to Hartwick Seminary, thence, in 1846, to the Military Academy at West Point, from which institution he resigned to join the excited throng bound for the gold mines in the newly acquired region of California.

At the date of the discovery of gold his elder brother, Eugene Angel, was practicing law in Peoria, Illinois, having recently been admitted to the bar, and was anxious to join the "Peoria Pioneers" in the journey overland. Urging the cadet to join him in Peoria, Mr. Angel, in January, 1849, started on his journey, crossing Pennsylvania to Pittsburg by stage—that being the only conveyance at the time, the New York & Erie Railroad only reaching to Port Jervis, on the Delaware River—and from Pittsburg to St. Louis by steamboat, thence a short distance up the Illinois River by boat, and a toilsome journey in mud-wagons to Peoria. In April the pioneers left that city, destined for St. Joe, on the Missouri, on the "utterly utter" verge of civilization. The treachery of the captain of the steamboat on which was that part of the company in which was Angel's party changed the fate of the young emigrants by landing at Weston and refusing to proceed to St. Joseph, this deciding the party to take the Arkansas and Gila route instead of the direct route to the gold mines via the South Pass. On the steamer was Captain William Kirker, an old mountaineer who had been guide to Colonel Doniphan in his march through New Mexico a few years previously. He told of gold mines in the Rocky Mountains, far richer than those in California, and a large sum was paid him by a collection of Illinois and Missouri people who then made up a company. Late in May the journey was undertaken, and in July prospecting parties entered the Rocky Mountains on the Rio Sangre de Christo and other localities which have since become famous for their mineral wealth; but, being entirely ignorant of the occurrence of gold, or how to obtain it, found nothing.

The mines of the Pike's Peak region were then condemned, and the route taken again for California, or somewhere, the travelers hardly knew where. Captain Kirker, the guide, said he knew of mines on the Gila River, and he would take them there. The captain was only playing his party, as he had a family at Albuquerque and he only wished to have an escort to take him safely there. The long journey was pursued many hundred miles south, along the Rio Grande, then westward into Sonora to the head of the Rio Santa Cruz, then northerly through Tucson to the Pima villages on the Gila River. From this point the two brothers Angel, becoming impatient to reach their destination, it being then October, went in advance of the train, each taking a small pack of clothing and food, and, after a journey of severe fatigue, reached San Diego about the middle of November, ragged and famished. The train, which had been left behind, dragged its weary way along, and in the spring of 1850 reached the mining region in Mariposa County.

At San Diego was a small hermaphrodite brig about to sail for San Francisco, and would take passengers at $100 each, the passenger to furnish his own subsistence. As a great favor, the owner of the brig accepted $150 as passage money for the two, that being the size of their pile after buying some provisions for the voyage. About half a dozen others who had reached San Diego with sufficient means also went as passengers, leaving near one hundred destitute emigrants bewailing their hard fate. A few days afterward the steamer Oregon called in on her way from Panama and took all remaining, free of charge.

On the 8th of December, 1849, the two brothers landed in San Francisco, in the rain and mud of a severe winter, in a condition that can better be imagined than described. A few days thereafter an incident occurred that helped much to relieve them of want when employment was unattainable. They had left in the wagon a trunk well filled with valuable books, some clothing, etc., to lighten the load. This was thrown out at the crossing of the Colorado. At that time Lieutenant Cave J. Coutts was in command of some soldiers stationed there (since called Fort Yuma), and seeing the trunk as jetsam on the sand he examined it, and, finding the books, papers and clothing of a cadet, quickly put it on an ambulance and hastened after the departed train. Finding that the object of his search had gone before, he pushed through to San Diego, but was still too late to overtake the owner of the things he had rescued at so much trouble. The kind officer then put the trunk in charge of a gentleman going to San Francisco with instructions to hunt up the owner and restore to him his property with the warm regard of a brother soldier. The trunk thus reached its destination, and the valuable books it contained sold for such prices as aided to pass the hardships of a winter which proved the last to many young and homesick pioneers.

The summer of 1850 was spent in mining at Bidwell's Bar, on Feather River, with rather poor success; and in 1851 the two brothers settled on a ranch at a place since called Angel's Slough, near the Sacramento River, south of Chico. In 1856 they purchased a mining claim at North San Juan, Nevada County, and, joining with others, commenced opening it by tunnel. In this enterprise about $40,000 was expended and lost. The brothers had continued inseparable until 1860, when the elder, Eugene Angel, went to the eastern slope, in the Washoe excitement, and was killed at the massacre at Pyramid Lake, May 12, 1860. Myron Angel in the meantime had become editor of the Placerville *Semi-Weekly Observer*, in which situation he continued until the spring of 1860, when he returned to San Juan to take charge of his mining interests there. Upon the breaking out of the war, he offered his services to the Governor of California, and received the appointment of Captain of Infantry. Upon this being announced, the San Juan *Press*, of October 5, 1861, said:

"We are pleased to learn that our friend and fellow-townsman, Mr. Myron Angel, is raising a company of infantry in obedience to the call of the General Government, having received official authority from Governor Downey so to do. This furnishes an additional opportunity to all who are willing to serve their country in the hour of her need, to enroll their names.

"Mr. Angel received a thorough military education as a student at West Point, and knows well the duties belonging to an officer. He is a gentleman, too, in whom recruits can repose implicit confidence. Their necessities, under his care, will be promptly attended to and their rights strictly guarded."

No fund had been supplied for maintaining and forwarding recruits, and this Mr. Angel did until his own funds were exhausted. Then came the pressing demand for his time to attend to the business of a failing mining enterprise, in which his all was invested, and although appealed to by Colonel Judah, a West Point friend, who then had command of the Fourth California Volunteers, he was compelled to withdraw from the service, hoping for another apportunity when his business would be better arranged. That time, however, did not offer.

After writing for various papers, in 1863 he became editor of the Reese River *Réveille*, at Austin, Nevada. While in that position he wrote several reports on the mines of Eastern Nevada, assisting Mr. J. Ross Brown in his "Report on the Mineral Resources west of the Rocky Mountains." A little book he wrote about this time on his favorite theme of the resources of Eastern Nevada, had the distinction of being published in French, in Paris, and in German, in Leipsic, the translators into French being Emil de Girardin, who paid the author the compliment of saying that it was the best English he had ever translated. Mr. Angel was editor-in-chief of the *Réveille* until 1868, when he left and became editor of the Oakland *Daily News*, in California; then of the *State Capital Reporter*, of Sacramento; then of the White Pine *News*, of which paper he continued as San Francisco correspondent and agent until 1875, when he again became editor of the Oakland *News*. While acting as newspaper correspondent in San Francisco he also wrote for other publications, the principal being a "Pacific Coast Business Directory and Gazetteer," of which two editions were published, one in 1871, and the other in 1876, a very important and valuable work; also the historical and miscellaneous matter for the San Francisco Annual Directory. The Pacific Coast Directory comprised all the region west of Dakota and Wyoming, and contained the most complete account of the history, geography and resources yet published.

While performing these labors he was engaged in a mammoth mining enterprise, in company with Mr. M. D. Fairchild and Hon. John Daggett, in making a canal and opening a large hydraulic mine in El Dorado County. After an expenditure of over $100,000 the enterprise came to a halt for want of funds, fortune again slipping away, and the faithful pen or pencil found to be the only safe reliance.

September 22, 1879, he was married to Charlotte Paddock Livingston, daughter of Rev. Joseph Paddock, an accomplished lady, whose acquaintance extended from the days of their youth. In 1880 he was engaged to write a history of mining in California, for the State Mining Bureau, and after making considerable progress on the work operations were suspended because of lack of funds. In 1881 he was engaged to write and supervise the publication of a history of the State of Nevada, which made a grand volume of 1,000 quarto pages. In 1882 he wrote a history of Placer County, California, a book of 400 quarto pages. In this is given the best political history of California yet written; also a complete history of the construction of the Central Pacific Railroad. In 1883 he wrote and published a "History of San Luis Obispo County." In the same year he became editor of the San Luis Obispo *Weekly Tribune*, a Republican paper of much influence. At the time of taking charge of the *Tribune* the assessed valuation of all property in the county was under $5,000,000. The editor, confident of the resources of the county, and believing in the power of the press, vigorously handled, promised that $2,000,000 should be added per annum, and in five years thereafter the assessed valuation exceeded $15,000,000. The promise had been made good.

In March, 1886, Mr. Angel had the sad misfortune of the death of his wife. This lady was very highly esteemed, and her death was mourned by a large circle of friends and relatives. A handsome monument was erected to her memory in the cemetery at San Luis Obispo. In October, 1886, Mr. Angel disposed of his interest in the *Tribune* and purchased the *Daily Republic*, which paper he still owns and publishes. November 13, 1889, he was married to Miss Carrie G. Flagler, of Fallsburg, Sullivan County, New York, an accomplished lady, of a prominent Quaker family of New York, Mrs. Angel, however, belonging to the Presbyterian Church. Mrs. Angel has a valuable property at Fallsburg, but they call San Luis Obispo their home. During the spring and summer of 1890 Mr. Angel was engaged in the State Mining Bureau to examine and report upon the resources of several of the counties of the State. Having been engaged in literary or newspaper work for more than thirty years, he has necessarily accomplished much, and in recognition of his historical works had the distinction of being made Honorary Member of the Oneida Historical Society of New York.

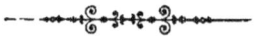

C. E. SOULE is one of the prominent citizens of Ventura County, California, and a pioneer of the Ojai Valley. He was born in Canada, December 31, 1838, and is the son of Charles and Louis (Hurd) Soule, the former a native of Canada, of English and German descent. He was the younger son and the second child of a family of four children, two sons and two daughters, and received his education in his native country. Before he had quite reached his majority he came to California, in 1859, and worked on a farm for two years, after which he spent two years as a machinist on mill-work, in the mines in Nevada. He then returned to Sonoma County, California, and purchased a ranch on the Russian River, near Healdsburg. On this he built a house and barn, and otherwise improved, and in 1874 sold the property and came to Ventura County. The journey was made in sixteen days, with two wagons, a four-horse wagon and a covered wagon for his family, which consisted at that time of his wife and four children. Mr. Soule had previously been to the Ojai Valley, and had bought land and erected a house which was ready for their occupancy when the family arrived. The valley at that time was a sheep ranch, with 10,000 sheep, owned by Messrs. Olds & Daily, and the only two houses there were those of Mr. Waite and Mr. Ayres. At first Mr. Soule obtained his mail at Ventura, and after getting a route established, the few settlers had to pay for the carrying themselves for a long time. Mr. Soule engaged in wheat-raising, but now devotes his time to general farming and fruit culture. He still retains 195 acres of his original purchase, upon which he raises fruit, hay, and horses, both draft and roadsters. His principal fruit crop consists of nectarines, apricots and prunes. He has ten acres in olives not yet in bearing. They have a dryer and dry their own fruit.

Mr. Soule was united in marriage, in October, 1862, to Miss Addie Koger, daughter of William and Matilda (Anglen) Koger, the former of German descent and the latter of French. Her father was a Virginian by birth, and was one of the pioneers of California. He was a deacon in the Baptist Church, and a prominent rancher of this State. His death occurred when Mrs. Soule was quite young. Mr. and Mrs. Soule are the parents of five children, viz.: William E., a resident of Reading; Lillian E., Nina E. and Earl E., natives of Sonoma County, and Zadie E., born at their home in Nordhoff. Mrs. Soule is a warm lover of California, and rightly thinks there is no place like the Golden West. She is a member of the Presbyterian Church, and is a lady of culture and refinement. Her family are talented, being gifted in both music and drawing. Mr. Soule and his wife were charter members of the Grange. He was the first Master of the lodge, and she has also held important offices in the same. In politics Mr. Soule is a Republican, and has been a member of that party since its organization. For four years he has held the office of Justice of the Peace; and has been clerk of the School Board for fourteen years out of the sixteen years he has resided in the town. During the building of the Presbyterian Church, a fine structure, Mr. Soule was a member of the board of trustees. He has been a member of the Republican Committee of the county for the past ten years.

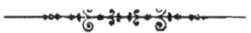

E. S. HALL, a prominent business man of San Buenaventura, was born near Fairmont, Marion County, Virginia, February 27, 1854; and his father, Robert Hall, was also born near the same town. His grandfather, Rynear Hall, also a native of Virginia, a son of Jordan Hall, who was born in Delaware, went at an early age to Virginia. His father was Thomas Hall, of Dover, Delaware, born in 1724, died in 1772. Mr. Hall's mother, whose maiden name was Sarah Hayhurst, also a native of Virginia, was a descendant of old residents of that State. E. S., the subject of this sketch, had no brother, but has one sister, who is now the wife of Henry Roberts, of Virginia. The mother died when E. S. was but two years old, and the father now resides in Iowa. The subject of this sketch was brought up by his uncle, E. B. Hall, now of Santa Barbara. His early education was received from private tuition before the day of public schools in Virginia. Later he was an attendant at public schools, and also at Lincoln Academy and the normal school. He read law in the office of his uncle, Judge E. B. Hall, who was a member of the firm of Hall & Hatch. He was with them three years, 1876–'79, and October 7 of the latter year he came to San Buenaventura, where he has since been in the practice of his profession, and also engaged in real estate and insurance. For two years he was District Attorney, his services being satisfactory to the public. He is a

Republican, but has not sought office. He owns considerable real estate. He built a good house on Santa Clara street, but, receiving a good offer for it, he sold it and is now preparing to build a better house,—one that will be an ornament to the town.

Mr. Hall is an active and pleasing business man, with a very large acquaintance in the county. His office is on the first floor, on Main street, in the center of the business, and is well equipped in every particular for the comfort and convenience of his patrons, as well as for his own health and comfort. He is a gentleman of "all-round" business tact and a well read lawyer.

Mrs. Robertine Hall, his wife, is a daughter of Judge Hines, the first Superior Judge of the county, who was a Grand Master Mason and High Priest of the order in California. She was born in Vincennes, Indiana, is a graduate of the San José State Normal School, and has a host of friends throughout the State. Mr. and Mrs. Hall have two children: Edwin, who was born in Ventura, January 4, 1884, and Alice, born in the same place, December 28, 1886. Mrs. Hall is a member of the Presbyterian Church. Mr. Hall had Presbyterian parents, but is not a member of the church. He is a member of Blue Lodge, Royal Arch and Knight-Templar divisions of Free Masonry, and both himself and wife are members of the O. E. S.

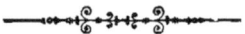

D. C. DIMOCK, whose home is so pleasantly located in the San Miguelito Cañon, was born in the town of Newport, Hants County, Nova Scotia, November 9, 1842. He attended a private school for several years, and then attended the Wolfville Academy at the beautiful village of the same name, situate in Kings County, Nova Scotia. At an early age he studied medicine with J. H. Dennison, M. D., of Brooklyn, same province, when he became proficient in Materia Medica by attending the doctor's drug store, and in a short time compounded all prescriptions, and manufactured nearly all articles there dispensed. Leaving the doctor's home he next found employment with the nursery firm of Chase Brothers, then of Sidney, Maine, now of Rochester, New York. The Doctor stayed with this company until he had earned enough money to complete his medical education, and matriculated in Bowdoin College, Brunswick, Maine, medical term of 1864, and graduated at Berkshire Medical College, at Pittsfield, Massachusetts, in 1866.

He began the practice of medicine at Renfrew Gold Mines, Nova Scotia, but the mines failing he gave it up and came to Boston, where he studied dentistry with J. R. Dillingham. Soon becoming skilled at this business he started for California, and on arriving in the Golden State he settled at Gilroy, and soon had a flourishing dental practice; was there when the railroad was built to the town; and, seeing how easy money could be made in a booming town, went to San Diego and invested the earnings of a year in town lots, which he was glad to relinquish at a small percentage of cost, and returned to Gilroy and resumed the practice of dentistry, at which he continued until the Bacon Hard Rubber Company of Boston compelled him to quit. He then reviewed medicine for one term at the Toland Medical College, San Francisco. Soon afterward he settled in Oakland, Douglas County, Oregon, where he enjoyed a large and very lucrative practice, and made money rapidly, but by an unfortunate land speculation he lost his hard-earned money and became quite discouraged, gave up his practice and returned to California, and after visiting old friends at Gilroy settled in Bakersfield, Kern County, and commenced anew, and enjoyed a successful practice of over two years.

He was elected Coroner and Public Administrator while there, but owing to illness was compelled to leave and seek a different climate. He visited Lompoc, in Santa Barbara County, in October, 1875, where he had a brother residing. He then went East and passed the winter at his old home in Nova Scotia. Early in the spring of 1876 he went to New York, and visited many of the noted places East and South; was at Philadelphia at the opening of the Centennial Exposition, and spent two months viewing the wonderful things to be seen at the greatest of shows. Returned to the Golden State in the summer of 1876, settled at Lompoc and commenced the practice of medicine, doing all the work of the valley, also establishing and managing a drug store. In 1882 Dr. Dimock sold a one-half interest in his business to Dr. Saunders, who attended the practice of medicine while Dr. Dimock managed the drug store. After one year he bought the interest of Dr. Saunders in the drug store, and soon after sold out to J. B. Dean, who has since continued the business. In 1879 Dr. Dimock bought his present ranch in San Miguelito Cañon, which he improved by building a residence and planting an orchard. In 1886 he began shipping horses from Lompoc to Los Angeles, which proved very profitable. He then invested in Santa Barbara, and engaged in the real-estate business, with Judge E. H. Heacock, which interest he continued until 1889, when he returned to his ranch, still holding considerable property in Santa Barbara, part of which he improved. He now owns 640 acres of white-pine lumber in Oregon, from which he anticipates great returns, and also a four-acre walnut grove at Carpenteria.

Dr. Dimrock was married at Lompoc, November 9, 1880, to Miss Anna L. Ruffner, a daughter of Joseph Ruffner. Dr. Dimock rents his ranch; and after a varied and eventful life, is now enjoying the fruits of his labors.

R. B. HAYDOCK is the Principal of the Hueneme school in Ventura County. He was born in Paducah, Kentucky, March 20, 1867. His father, R. M. Haydock, was also a native of Kentucky, born in 1831, and now resides in Monrovia, Los Angeles County. His grandfather, John Haydock, was born in North Carolina. Mr. Haydock's mother, nee Elizabeth Watts, was a native of Kentucky, and her father, David Watts, was born in North Carolina and removed to Kentucky, being one of the pioneers of that State. The subject of this sketch is the fifth of a family of seven children, all of whom are living. When a child he was brought to California by his parents, in 1873, and received his education in the public schools of this State. He graduated at the State Normal School of Los Angeles, December 17, 1885, taught one year in the Arnaz district, Ventura County, and since that time has been connected with the school at Hueneme, as Principal. In 1888 he was appointed by the Supervisors of Ventura County, a member of the Board of Education, which position he now occupies. In 1890, for County Clerk on the Democrat ticket, he ran 125 votes ahead of his fellow candidates, while the average Republican majority for that year was about 300. Mr. Haydock has chosen teaching as his profession, and thus far has met with excellent success, gaining the confidence and respect of his pupils, as well as of the patrons of the school. His qualifications as a teacher, combined with his love for the work, make him a fitting instructor for the young.

Mr. Haydock was reared a Methodist, but is not a member of the church. Politically he is independent in his views, trying always to select the best man.

J. H. HERBST is one of the self-made, successful business men of Hueneme. He was born in Germany, February 16, 1861, the son of Jacob Abraham Herbst and his wife, Ester (Hines) Herbst, the former a native of Russia and the latter of Germany. It was the intention of J. A. Herbst, who was a Hebrew, to educate his son for a rabbi, and his education was conducted with that object in view until he was twelve years of age. By the death of his father, at this time, their plans were thwarted, and young Herbst was obliged to work to help support the family. When eighteen years of age he started for the United States to find, in the land of the free, better facilities for improving his financial condition, with $1.75. He worked his way to New York city, and for twelve years he labored and struggled in that densely populated city, trying to lay up something, and meeting with poor success. In the mean time he married Miss Dora Cohn, a native of Germany. Three children were born to them in New York city, but the densely crowded tenement houses, with but little fresh and much foul air, caused sickness. Two of the children died and the expenses attendant upon sickness and death took all he could earn and constantly kept him poor. In 1879 he started with his little family for California, with scarcely means enough to reach the Golden West. He located in Saticoy, Ventura County, where he worked for wages for a year, and during that time saved $100, with which he started a little grocery business, on a very small scale, going in debt to a considerable extent, which he did not find difficult to do as he was well recommended. He continued at Saticoy nearly two years. In 1881 he came to Hueneme and purchased his present store and the building in which it is located. The building was then new, and they used the upper story for a dwelling. He keeps a fine stock of general merchandise, and is doing a good business. His wife often assists him in the store. Mr. Herbst has been remarkably successful since he came to Callifornia. He now has $5,000 at interest, and does a $30,000 business. He has been blessed with a family of bright children: Hattie, born in New York city, and Jacob, Herman, Ester and Moses, born in Ventura County, California. Mr. and Mrs. Herbst are both Hebrews. In political views he is Democratic. He is a well informed and progressive business man; and is another illustration of what a poor, honest man, with a strong determination to succeed, can accomplish in this State. He is also one of the many sons of Germany who have come to the United States and by their successful life are a credit not only to their native land but also to the land of their adoption.

REUBEN W. HILL, M. D., San Buenaventura, was born November 27, 1845, in Arlington, Vermont. His father, Abner Hill, was also a native of Vermont and of English descent. Their ancestors had been in that State on the original grant since the founding of the colony. The Doctor's mother, *nee* Miriam Webb, was born in Sunderland, Vermont, of Holland descent, but resident for a time equally long in America. Dr. Hill, the youngest of eight children, was brought up in the State of New York and graduated at Washington Academy, one of the oldest institutions of learning in that State. In medicine he graduated at the Bellevue Hospital Medical College at New York city. He began practice in Monterey, Mexico, and one year afterward he removed to Salto, Argentine Republic. Was surgeon on the Pacific steamship line for two years. In 1874 he came to Santa Barbara, and since that time he has practiced in Santa Barbara and Ventura. His residence has been in the latter town since 1877. Here he has purchased a home, and has been connected with all the interests of the place to the present time.

The Doctor is a veteran of the civil war, having enlisted when seventeen years of age, in Company E, First New York Mounted Rifles, and served in the department of Virginia and North Carolina, three and a half years, or until after the close of the war. He participated in all the battles of his department. After the close of the battles of the Peninsula they were in North Carolina in a raid, and did not learn of General Lee's surrender until six days afterward; and they had a sharp battle six days after the surrender of Lee. The Doctor consistently belongs to the G. A. R., being a member of Cushing Post, No. 44, at San Buenaventura, for which post he holds the office of surgeon. He has also been coroner of Ventura County, and County Physician of Santa Barbara County. In 1878 he was made a Master Mason. He is a talented physician, having a good practice and the confidence of a wide and respectable patronage.

Dr. Hill was married 1875, to Miss Mary C. Gutierrez, daughter of Benigno Gutierrez, a native of Chili and a pioneer of California. They have eight children, whose names are Emmet, Ruby, Benigno, Edwin, Jessie, Annette and James. Mrs. Hill is a member of the Catholic Church.

C. D. BONESTEL is a pioneer business man of the State, having landed on the golden shore in 1849. He was born May 30, 1826, in New York, a son of John Bonestel, who was a native of the same State. His ancestors on his father's side were German. His mother was a native of Connecticut. In their family were four sons and two daughters. Mr. Bonestel, our subject, and one of his sisters, are all that are now living. He was brought up on a farm and when grown he came to California by way of Panama, and during a part of the succeeding winter he followed gold-mining in El Dorado County, on Hangtown Creek, in partnership with three others. Intending to build a saw-mill, they obtained the material and machinery—the freight charges on which were excessively large—and the rains set in, compelling them to abandon the enterprise for the season. They continued mining until they obtained gold enough to pay these charges and other debts on the mill material, when Mr. Bonestel found he had about $700 left. Then, with a partner, he bought a log hotel in Placerville, at $3,000, with the aid of borrowed money. They ran this hotel for two years, and in 1854 erected a brick building at Placerville, a place then of 4,000 or 5,000 inhabitants. The lower story was rented for stores, and above was a concert hall. Mr. Bonestel speculated in cattle and horses, and during the winters of 1860-'63 he was clerk of the California State Legislature. In 1862 he started on a visit to the East, taking passage on board the Golden Gate, which had about 350 passengers. She was burned on the sea, only 150 passengers making their escape. The boat in which Mr. Bonestel was taking refuge was waterlogged as night was approaching. The other two boats came along, one on each side, and took the passengers out, bailed the boat and the load was evenly distributed between the three boats. During the night the boats became separated. In Mr. Bonestel's boat were four sailors, and they supposed when morning came that, as the sea was against them, they would still be found above Mancinillo. They rowed hard, and took turns at the oars all day. As night approached and no signs of the town appearing, they decided to land through the surf on a sand beach. They were upset in the surf, but got ashore. One man had $6,000 in a buckskin vest, and lest it should sink him he took it off. The sailors advised him to make it fast to the boat, and it would be wafted ashore; but he endeavored to bring it in his hands and was obliged to let go of it and it was all forever lost. Another man, who had a gold-brick of about $2,000 value, tied up in a handkerchief, fastened it to the boat and it came ashore all right.

After landing the party traveled several miles before finding potable water, arriving at a river. Soon afterward they reached a small Mexican hamlet and learned they were 100 miles below Mancinillo and could not go back on the coast, but would be obliged to make a detour back in the country to find a road on which they could travel. They were but partially clothed, as those who had clothes divided with those who had nearly nothing. They supposed that the country was infested with Mexican robbers, and were trying to engage the Mexicans to take them on horseback to the coast, when one little Frenchman, who had no garments, was particularly afraid of the Mexicans. While they were talking they heard the clatter of horses' feet and the clanking of spurs and swords. The Frenchman started into the brush as fast as he could run, to escape for his life, when the party came up and proved to be men from another village who heard of the disaster and came up to see what assistance they could render. Mr. Bonestel says he always laughs when he remembers the figure that little Frenchman made as he ran, in his red shirt and drawers, as fast as if he had been shot out of a cannon.

They finally reached the town, and twenty days elapsed after the disaster to their boat before they obtained another, on which they proceeded to New York. After remaining in New York three months visiting his family, he took passage on the steamer Ariel for California, which carried 800 men, women and children. Some apprehensions were entertained that the rebel vessel Alabama might fall in with them and capture them; and much sport was indulged in concerning the matter. Several times it was stated that the Alabama was sighted, which however proved each time to be a hoax; but when off the east end of the island of Cuba Mr. Bonestel and others were below, eating their dinner. The butler put down his head and cried out, "The Alabama is after us!" Mr. Bonestel replied, "Oh, that's chesnuts;" but in a very short time they heard the report of a gun, and he and his friends made an effort to get upon deck. They were met by a crowd of people trying to get below. The shot which they heard was indeed the Alabama firing a blank cartridge at them to make them slack their speed and surrender. The Captain of the Ariel did not stop, and soon they saw two puffs of smoke from two of the guns of the Alabama, and they saw, or supposed they saw, two large balls coming directly toward them. They seemed as plain as a base ball. One of them struck the main mast and tore a large piece out of it and caused the splinters of the mast to fly all over her deck. The Ariel was stopped and a boat was sent by the Alabama to take their captain. All the passengers were filled with surprise and terror; some of the ladies fainted, and others went into hysterics. When the officer, Lieutenant Lowe, came on deck, many implored him to spare them and asked him to save them. He replied, "Ladies and gentlemen, not one of you will be harmed or injured;" and then they began to ask him all kinds of questions what he was going to do with them. Their questions were all answered in a polite manner; and such was the gallant bearing of the officer that they actually began to admire him. It was finally decided that the passengers would be landed at Kingston; but when they arrived at that point a vessel came out, which was spoken by Captain Semmes of the Alabama. He then sent word for the Captain of the Ariel to come on board the Alabama, informing him that the yellow fever was raging in Kingston and he did not wish to disembark. He said that if the captain of the Ariel would give bonds for the value of the boat—$300,000—he would let them go. The arrangement was made and they were permitted to resume their voyage, and they arrived at San Francisco January 2, 1863.

Mr. Bonestel resumed his place in the Senate that winter as clerk, and after its adjournment went to Austin, Nevada, and speculated in mining property and also opened an office or bank, with a partner, and conducted it for two years. He then bought out his partner and the First National Bank was started there. He closed his business and was elected vice-president of the First National Bank of Nevada. At the end of a year he found his health failing, and he came to San Francisco, bought an interest in a book and stationery store, and remained there until 1871. Then selling out, he made another trip to the East, and returned in the winter of 1872. He then was a resident of San Francisco until January, 1875, speculating in stocks; and finally he came to Ventura County and four years held the position of under sheriff. The next two years he speculated in grain and cattle. In 1882, forming a partnership with Messrs. Chaffee and Gilbert, under the firm name of Chaffee, Gilbert & Bonestel, they afterward added the lumber trade to their business of general merchandising, and since then they have been carrying on these trades until February, 1890. They then sold out their lumber business. In October the farmers organized and incorporated a lumber company under the name of the People's Lumber Company, and elected Mr. Bonestel their president and general manager of the company.

Mr. Bonestel was brought up a Democrat, but during the war became a Republican, and so has since remained.

He was married in 1868, to Miss Nannie Smith, a native of Louisiana, but brought when an infant by her parents to California. Their three children, all born in San Francisco, are: Cora, Alonzo and Edith. Cora is now the wife of F. J. Sifford, of Ventura.

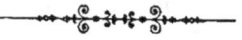

HON. B. T. WILLIAMS, Judge of the Superior Court of the county of Ventura, was born at Mt. Vernon, Missouri, December 25, 1850. His father, Dr. J. S. Williams, a native of Kentucky, was an eminent physician. His grandfather, Thomas Williams, was president of what is now the University of Kentucky. The ancestors of the family settled in North Carolina at a period so early that all accounts of it are lost. One of them, a relative of Daniel Boone, came to Kentucky with him. The judge's mother, whose maiden name was Amanda Downing, was of the well-known Downing family of Fauquier County, Virginia, whose ancestors settled in that State at the time of the first settlement at Jamestown in 1607. Her father, Henry H. Downing, emigrated to Missouri in the early history of that State, and was a planter there upon land of his own. The Judge's parents had nine children, of whom six are still living. His father came with the family to California in 1853, when the subject of this sketch was three years old, settling in Santa Rosa, Sonoma County, and there the subject of this sketch grew up to years of maturity, and commenced the study of law in the office of the late Judge William Ross. In 1869 his father moved to San Diego, where he died in 1879. In 1869 Judge Williams resumed the study of law with his brother, William T., now a member of the Los Angeles bar. He was admitted to the bar in 1871, and located at San Buenaventura, where he has since resided, engaged in the practice of his profession. Upon the organization of the county he was elected District Attorney, and served in that capacity acceptably for four years. Entering then into partnership with his brother, W. T. Williams, he continued in that relation with him until 1884, when he was elected to his present position, already stated. He is now serving his first term of six years, and has been unanimously renominated by the Republican party, the Democrats having declined to make any nomination against him, which assures his re-election. In his social relations he is present Master of the Masonic lodge in San Buenaventura, and is a member of the K. of P., A. O. U. W. and the A. L. of H. He was married Febauary 28, 1878, to Miss Irene Parsons. Their four children, all born in San Buenaventura, are: John T., Irene, Paul and Kate.

Judge Benjamin Tully Williams is a representative American gentleman, good-tempered, affable, easily approached, and destitute of pride or ostentation. He has a fine legal mind, is a ready, easy speaker, gives his rulings promptly, and usually gives entire satisfaction. By showing his honest desire strictly to administer exact justice, both when district attorney and later as judge, his conduct has been such as to command the respect of the bar as well as the best citizens of both parties. And it is worthy of remark, also, that such is his physical development that were a sculptor looking for a model he could scarcely expect to find a better specimen of the human race. He measures six feet four and a half inches high and weighs 275 pounds; and his proportions are so well balanced that his movements are easy and not in the least retarded by his size. Being but forty years of age, a long and honorable life seems to lie before him.

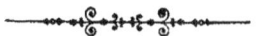

ORION C. WALBRIDGE is the second brother of the Walbridge Brothers. He was born in Texas, March 5, 1856. His father, Henry Walbridge, was a native of the State of New York, born in 1822. He was a farmer by occupation, and a consistent member of the Christian Church. His death occurred in 1883. Grandfather William Walbridge was born in Vermont, and was in the war of 1812. His wife was a niece of Commodore Perry, and great-grandfather Walbridge came from Scotland, and was a participant in the Revolutionary war. Mr. Walbridge's mother, *nee* Mary Crocker, was born in Indiana in 1829, a daughter of Orion L. Crocker, who was wounded in the war of 1812, was a cousin of the late Charles Crocker, and was a farmer and a devoted Christian man. Mr. and Mrs. Walbridge had six children, four sons and two daughters. The eldest son, William, has a family and lives in Washington. Harney M., a partner in the firm, has a wife and one child. Whatever he undertakes he aims to be the best, and will not be content with any second place. Mattie, the second sister, is a stenographer and typewriter operator, having a good position in Santa Barbara. With O. C. Walbridge reside his mother, his sister Myra and his brother George. They are an interesting and intelligent family. The whole family are Good Templars. The sister is a member of the Woman's Christian Temperance Union, and a prominent temperance worker. They are members of the Christian Church at Ventura.

Mr. Walbridge came to this county in 1873, and has been engaged in farming and in the business of pressing hay. There is not a neighborhood in Ventura County in which the Walbridge brothers have not for years run their hay press, and they are the pioneer hay-balers of the county. Their business in that direction has so increased that they now own and operate two presses. This year, 1890, they have planted 110 acres of Lima beans, of which the average crop is 1,500 to 2,000 pounds per acre. Great honor is due to the honest toiler, whose steady blows and persistent work develop the country.

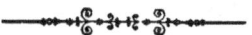

JAMES McKEE is the Nordhoff Justice of the Peace, and he also holds the office of Notary Public for the town and Ventura County by appointment of his excellency, Governor Waterman. Mr. McKee dates his birth near Napoleon, Ripley County, Indiana, September 15, 1837. His father, Samuel McKee, was a native of Indiana, and his grandfather, David McKee, was born in Vermont. They are of Scotch ancestry. His mother, Emily (Langston) McKee, was born in Indiana, the daughter of Mr. Bennet Langston, a native of North Carolina. His parents had four children, of whom he is the oldest. Three are now living. He was reared and educated in Indiana, and began life as a teacher, but the great civil war broke in on his plans, after he had taught two years in the Ripley County schools. In the year 1862, it will be remembered, the great war had become a serious matter. The brave armies of the Union had met in mortal combat the ardent and heroic armies of the South, and the former had met with many severe reverses, and many of the brave men on both sides had been slain and many had been returned to their homes mutilated for life. The outlook was dark, indeed. And at such a time as this, Mr. McKee felt it to be his duty to give up teaching and enlist in the service of his country. He enlisted in Company F, Sixty-eighth Indiana Volunteer Infantry, and was First Duty Sergeant of his company. He participated in the battles of Munfordville, and on September 12, 1862, was taken prisoner, and was paroled and sent back to his State; soon after he was exchanged. He was sent to the front on detached duty at Nashville, where he was prostrated with disease and sent to the hospital, remaining there two months. The medical directors ordered him home to see if he could regain his health. He partially recovered, reported for duty and was detached as indorsement clerk at Indianapolis. He remained there until after the close of the war, and on June 30, 1865, was mustered out of the service.

Mr. McKee then returned to his home and

again took up his old profession and taught as Principal of Napoleon Schools until 1875, when his health gave out. As a last resort to save his life, he was sent to this coast. When recovery was almost effected he returned and removed to Iowa, where he remained five years, in agricultural pursuits. He then disposed of his property in Iowa and permanently settled in Nordhoff, California, in 1887. He purchased a small ranch and has a nice place planted to fruits, vines and flowers.

In 1857 Mr. McKee was married to Miss Nancy C. Eaton, a native of Indiana, daughter of Mr. Edmund Eaton, who was born in Vermont. They have had four children, two of whom are living, both born in Napoleon, Indiana: Sarah Ellen is the wife of Mr. John Linder and resides at Nordhoff, and Clarence lives with his parents. Mr. McKee became a Republican when the party was organized and has seen no good reason to leave its ranks. He is a member of the Baptist Church and his wife is a member of the Christian Church.

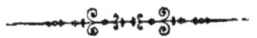

EDWARD F. ARNOLD was born in Martinez, Contra Costa County, California, November 4, 1853. His father, Cutler Arnold, came to California in 1849. (See sketch of the family in the history of Mr. Mathew Arnold, a brother of Edward F.) Mr. Arnold was reared and educated in the county of Lassen and in Sacramento, and came to Ventura County before he was twenty-one years old. When he reached his majority he owned 120 acres of land near Hueneme. In 1886, being in poor health, he sold this property to his brother and came to Nordhoff. He purchased 100 acres of land, improved it in part, and sold it in 1887.

He then engaged in the mercantile business, the firm being Arnold & Van Curen. A year later he sold out and built his present drug store. The firm of Arnold & Sager have the only drug house in Nordhoff. It is well fitted and stocked with everything in the drug line. These gentlemen, being courteous and obliging, have established a fine trade and enjoy the good-will of the entire community.

Mr. Arnold has built for himself and family a comfortable residence, has regained his health, and is now in a fair situation to enjoy life. He was married in 1878 to Miss Lou Trotter, a native of Illinois, and a resident of California since 1877. They have three children, two born at Hueneme and one at Nordhoff, viz.: Albert Walter, Lora L. and Frank. Mr. Arnold is a Republican; was elected Justice of the Peace, but, not desiring office, resigned.

GEORGE ROBERTS, a pioneer, and a prominent developer of the interests of Lompoc, was born at New York Mills, New York, May 22, 1832. His father was a machinist, and had charge of the machinery of the New York Mills large manufactory. Our subject's education was very limited, except as he acquired knowledge by observation. At the early age of ten years he began life upon the "tow path" of the Erie Canal, as driver in towing boats, which occupation he followed for three summers. He then went to Lewis County and was employed as a farm hand until 1849, when he went to New York city, and for four years was employed as driver on the East Broadway Stage Line. He then returned to Lewis County and engaged in farming until 1860, when he came to California, first settling at Omega, Nevada County. He there established a general merchandise house, and did an extensive business with the surrounding mining camps, within a radius of twenty miles, packing his supplies on pack animals and by mule teams. This he continued very successfully until 1870, when he sold out and came to San José. There he invested extensively in real estate, and also conducted a wholesale and retail merchandise store, and for a short period conducted a hotel. The store and hotel he sold in 1874, and took stock in the Lompoc Valley Land Company; he was elected secretary of the company, and November 9, 1874, attended the first sale of land in the valley, and purchased quite extensively. Mr. Roberts then returned to San José for the winter, and in the spring of 1875 established himself at Lompoc, where he was the agent of the Lompoc Valley Land Company. He started the first drug store, on the corner of H and Ocean avenues, and soon added general merchandise to his stock, which he continued until 1879, when he sold out, and since that time has given his attention more particularly to the sale of lands. He formerly owned a stock ranch of 800 acres, where he was extensively engaged in breeding horses. He now owns 775 acres of valley land, which he rents, twenty-seven town blocks, partially improved with residences, and much improved business and residence property at San José. Mr. Roberts is president of the Bank of Lompoc, which was organized May 20, 1890; he is now erecting a brick building, 50 x 80 feet, corner of H and Ocean avenues, for bank purposes. He has demonstrated by his career that the enjoyment of college privileges or the inheritance of wealth are not essential ingredients to the successful business life.

Mr. Roberts was married at Osceola, Lewis County, New York, in 1851, to Miss Nancy Green. They have no children.

J. C. BREWSTER, a well known and highly esteemed citizen of San Buenaventura, who has been connected with the growth of the place and interested in its moral and business welfare, and now the proprietor of the art gallery, was born in Wayne County, Ohio, December 31, 1841. His father, Calvin Brewster, was born in Canterbury, Windham County, Connecticut, in 1787, a descendant of Sir William Brewster who came to the New World on the Mayflower in 1620. He (Sir William) was the father of Love Brewster, and the generations in succession were Wrestling, Jonathan, who came to Windham, Connecticut, in 1729, Peleg, born in 1717, who must have removed to Canterbury when quite young, for his oldest son, John—who made the sixth generation—was born in that town in 1739. Peleg was Mr. Brewster's great-grandfather. Jedediah, a younger son of his, was Mr. Brewster's grandfather. The record of Jedediah's birth was lost; but the town records show that he was married to Prudence Robinson May 19, 1773. According to the good-fashion in those good old times, they had a good large family, and about every two years there was a record of a birth in the family. The names on the record are as follows: Elizabeth, Silas, Anson, Florina, Sarah, Calvin and Jedediah, Jr. Elizabeth, Sarah and Jedediah died in childhood, and January, 1789, the good wife Prudence died, and the next autumn Jedediah married for his second wife Miss Asenath Hapgood, to aid in the care of the family. He removed a few years later to Berne, Albany County, New York. In 1808 he sold some of his land to Silas

Brewster and the deed descends to him as living at Berne. The same year he sold his homestead to Deacon Barnabas Allen, whose son still owns it. It is about four miles from the village of Canterbury. A descendant of the Brewsters was recently there and was shown around by the proprietor. She drank from the old well that had been in uninterrupted use for more than a century. The farm is considered one of the best in that section, although a Western farmer would consider it very poor land. The old burying-ground was about a mile from the house. It was given to that part of the town by one of the Brewsters, and has been used by four or five generations and about a dozen families. Here are the names of Prudence Brewster and the children alluded to. In the lot are some stones so old that the inscriptions have become completely defaced, and some have sunk so deeply in the ground that only their tops are visible. The graveyard, however, is kept in excellent condition by a Miss Winchester, whose ancestors have been buried there for several generations. She is a spinster of eighty-five years—the last of her family. She has made provisions in her will to have the graveyard kept in condition after she has gone. She remembered old 'Diah Brewster, as she called him, and said her mother used to go over there on certain occasions.

Mr. Brewster's mother, whose maiden name was Harriet Cramer, was a native of Strausburg, Lancaster County, Pennsylvania, and was born in 1813, of Dutch ancestry. The parents were married in 1837 and had a family of six children, of whom the subject of this sketch was the second. He was eight years old when the family moved to Iowa. Before he was of age he taught two terms of school, holding a first grade certificate both in Iowa and Missouri. He began to learn the art of photography in 1860, in Warsaw, Illinois, and since then has devoted his entire attention to it. In 1862 he came to California and for a short time taught a select school in Sacramento city. Soon afterward he engaged in partnership with Frank M. Stamper, and subsequently he sold to his partner and took charge of a photograph gallery on J street, that city, and continued in its charge until the proprietor sold it. Then he went to Virginia City, Nevada, and took charge of the gallery of R. H. Vance, of New York, who was a pioneer photographer of the coast. Next he had charge of a gallery at Carson City, for the same party.

In the spring of 1865 he went to Idaho with a Concord wagon and four bronchos, for Sutterly Brothers, and opened business at Ruby City. They had good success there, and his salary was $50 a week, and board without room $16 a week. In the fall they went to Placerville and also to Centerville; thence to Salt Lake City. There Mr. Sutterly built a gallery and Mr. Brewster continued to run the tent at Douglas, three miles east. In the spring of 1866 they moved into the new gallery and did a large business, the receipts sometimes reaching $200 a day. Soon after this Mr. Brewster went to Helena, Montana, and opened a gallery for himself. In the fall of 1868 he sold it and returned to Salt Lake City, and continued in business there and at several other towns in the vicinity, with fine success, until the next spring. He then went to Nevada, and was there until 1871, with his brother-in-law as partner. They had a large gallery and fine building. Thence he went to Visalia and to San Francisco, where his mother then resided. His health had failed, but soon after returning home he recovered, and began work for William Shew, on Kearny street; but at length he was discharged because he would not work on Sunday. He then worked for Bradley & Rulofson until he decided to begin on his own account. He had a nice trade at San Luis Obispo until 1874, when he came to San Buenaventura and opened a gallery near the mission church. A year afterward he moved between Oak and California streets and built a gallery, with the privilege of moving it. In the spring of 1877 he bought his present location on Oak street and moved the gallery there, building additions to it, and has since then conducted his business with brilliant success. His gallery is splendidly equipped, and is filled with samples of his work which reflect great credit upon his skill. He was among the very first to adopt the dry-plate method, so superior to the old method.

He has recently built a nice two-story residence on Santa Clara street, surrounding it with choice flowers and young trees and shrubs. In 1875 he married Mrs. Mary O. Sinclair, widow of J. S. Sinclair; her maiden name was Mary Oberia Hadley. They have had two children, but lost the little son. Their daughter, Pansy Augusta, was born in Ventura, August 15, 1880. Mr. Brewster has been elected one of the School Trustees of the city; he is a Prohibition Republican, a business man of talent and a citizen without reproach. He is an Elder in the Presbyterian Church, of which denomination his family are also members. He is Treasurer of the Young Men's Christian Asssociation, and has been made an honorary member of the Women's Christian Temperance Union. He is also Treasurer and Depositary of the American Bible Society at Ventura.

D. A. SMITH is one of the great family of Smiths and is a worthy citizen of the Ojai Valley, Ventura County. He was born in Bedford County, Pennsylvania, September 18, 1845, the son of Morgan and Elizabeth (Martin) Smith, both natives of Pennsylvania, the former of Scotch descent, and the latter of Scotch-German descent, her father's ancestors having been Scotch and her mother's German. They were the parents of six children, five of whom are living. The subject of this sketch was their second child. He was reared in Ohio, and was attending school when the war of the Rebellion burst upon the country. The call to arms resounded through every city and village throughout the entire North and East, and the sound of the fife and drum could be heard in every town. Young Smith, filled with patriotic ardor, enlisted in Company E, Eighteenth Ohio Volunteer Infantry, as a high private, and served through the whole bloody struggle, re-enlisting when his first term of service expired. He participated in all the battles of the Army of the Cumberland. Sometimes his clothes were torn by shot and shell, but, strange to say, his flesh never received as much as a scratch. The most sanguinary battles in which he was engaged were Stone River, Chickamauga, Mission Ridge and Nashville. In these battles vast numbers of brave men were slain on both sides, besides the thousands who were mutilated for life. Mr. Smith's re-enlistment occurred at Chattanooga. He was mustered out at Nashville, Tennessee, in October, 1865.

At the close of the war Mr. Smith returned home and engaged in farming, which he continued on a farm of his own until 1872, when he sold out and emigrated to Nebraska. He there took up a Government claim of 160 acres, and improved the land by erecting buildings, etc., and resided there eleven years. His health failed at that time, his disease being asthma, and his physician advised a change of climate. In 1883 he disposed of his property and came to California, first to Los Angeles, and a few months later to Ventura County. Finding the climate of the Ojai Valley conducive to his health, he purchased forty acres of land, upon which he has erected a neat and commodious home. He has planted trees, which have grown rapidly, and his place has become an attractive one. His property joins the town of Nordhoff on the east, and he enjoys the advantages of schools, churches, postoffice and stores. Mr. Smith is engaged in raising poultry, horses and cattle, and he also produces large quantities of hay. The balmy air of this delightful climate has restored him to health, and life that had become a burden is now a pleasure.

In 1867 the subject of this sketch was united in marriage with Miss Ann G. Eddy, a native of Athens County, Ohio, and a daughter of Thomas Eddy, a farmer of that county. They have five children, all living, two born in Ohio, two in Nebraska, and one in Ventura County, California, viz.: Clara H., Fanny A., Winnie V., Ira Blaine, and Ellsworth, named for Colonel Ellsworth, who pulled down the rebel flag and was shot.

Mr. Smith was a delegate to the Republican National Convention, from Nebraska, in 1884; was sent as a Grant man, but, under the unit rule, voted for Mr. Blaine. Mr. Smith, like James K. Polk, enjoys the distinction of being Roadmaster of his district, and the district enjoys the convenience of first-class roads. He is a temperance man, a Republican, a member of the I. O. O. F., and a member of the Temple of Honor.

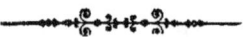

M. A. SIMPSON came to California in 1860 and to Ventura in 1861 when there were only three or four other Americans in the place, namely, William Hobson, James Beebee and Alex. Cameron. He was born in York Township, Jefferson County, New York, August 27, 1825. His father, Sylvanus Simpson, was a native of the State of New York, of Scotch descent; and his mother, *nee* Susan Harrington, was a native of Vermont. They had four sons and two daughters, and moved from New York to Ohio when the subject of this sketch, the fourth child, was eleven years old, and settled on a farm in Sandusky County. Mr. Simpson was therefore reared upon a farm, and began agriculture on his own account on a quarter section of land in Indiana, upon which he moved directly after his marriage. His wife died five years afterward, and then, in 1852, he came to California, spent two years in Los Angeles County, stopping a short time in San Francisco and then returned East, married again, and in 1859 sold his place and came again to California. This time he settled first in Santa Barbara County, in that portion which is now Ventura County. He brought with him across the plains forty head of American cows, three yoke of cattle, three mares and two wagons. In Ventura he opened the first hotel, in an adobe building on West Main street, on the south side, and west of Ventura avenue. He was also the first Postmaster of Ventura, holding the office four years. His hotel, called the American House, he sold, and also his cattle and other live-stock, and in 1865 bought his present homestead property of 150 acres, of which he has since sold fifty acres: forty acres are on the other side of the avenue. Previously he speculated to some extent until 1872, when he built his present nice residence, which he occupies with his children, whom he has given a good education at San Francisco and Oakland. Of the homestead there are twenty-five acres of fifteen-year-old bearing walnut trees, which now yield from fifty to 200 pounds to each tree. He has also twenty acres of apricots, apples and other fruit. The apples are of the varieties Pearmain, Bellflower, Rhode Island Greening, etc., and they all do well. The fruit sells at from one to two cents a pound. The remainder of the farm is devoted to general agriculture,—corn, barley, alfalfa hay and potatoes. Mr. Simpson is a member of the three principal branches of Freemasonry, in good standing; and as a citizen he has seen the country grow from its pioneer condition to its present paradisical proportions.

Mr. Simpson was first married in 1847, to Miss Eliza Smith, a native of Ohio, and they have one child, Helen L. Mrs. Simpson died, as before stated, and he afterward married Miss Sarah Bisby, a native of Canandaigua, New York, and they had two sons and one daughter: George B., Charlie C. and Sarah B. This Mrs. Simpson died in 1864, and since then Mr. Simpson has not again married. Mr. Simpson's daughter Helen is married to J. H. Walker and resides in Tacoma, Washington; George is married and lives in San Francisco; Charles is at home with his father; Sarah B. is married to G. W. Huston, a son of Dr. George Huston of San Francisco, ex-Mayor of that city.

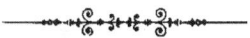

NATHAN W. BLANCHARD, a prominent pioneer of Ventura County and founder of the town of Santa Paula, was born in Madison, Maine, July 24, 1831. His father, Merrill Blanchard, was born in Abington, Massachusetts, July 18, 1806. His grandfather, Dean Blanchard, and his great-grandfather, Captain Thomas Blanchard, and his ancestors two generations farther back were natives of the same State. His ancestor was of French Huguenot stock, who settled near London, having been driven from his own country by persecution. His ancestor, Thomas Blanchard, the ancestor of a large part of the New England families of that name, came from London in 1639. In the manufacturing interest of that Commonwealth they have been active as machinists and inventors, doing a large share in the production of labor-saving machinery. Mr. Blanchard's mother, *nee* Eunice Weston, was born in Madison, Maine, on the Kennebec River, in 1804, the daughter of Deacon Benjamin Weston. At that point two generations of the family had resided. Mr. Blanchard's parents had six children, three daughters and three sons, and they are all living. Mr. Blanchard was educated at Houlton Academy and Waterville College—now Colby University—where he received his degrees.

In 1854 he came to California and engaged in mining for a season near Columbia, Tuolumne County, and in the fall went to Iowa Hill, Placer County, and conducted a meat market there for four years; then he went to Dutch Flat, continuing in part in the same business several years longer. From 1864 to 1872 he was engaged in lumbering with excellent success. Selling out he came to Ventura County and in partnership with E. B. Higgins purchased the site of the town of Santa Paula—2,700 acres. In the fall of 1872 he bought Mr. Higgins' interest and sold it to E. L. Bradley. The firm at once began to make valuable improvements on the property, in fencing and conducting water to it from the bed of the creek two miles above the town. From it they also obtained water for the lands and power for their flouring-mill, which they built. This mill and all the property were managed by Mr. Blanchard, Mr. Bradley being a non-resident. In 1885 the property was partitioned, and Mr. Blanchard now gives his whole attention to the production of citrus fruits. In 1874 he had an orange grove of 100 acres, planted by Mr. Clark, who did the work for an interest on the same; and they afterward bought Mr. Clark's interest. In 1876 they budded 1,000 trees to lemons and as many more to different varieties of oranges. The orchard remained so long in an unbearing condition that most people had decided that it would never bear; and not until 1888 did the orchard return a profit. In 1889 Mr. Blanchard shipped 8,386 boxes of oranges and 2,540 boxes of lemons. The prospects now are that it will continue to increase in productiveness for many years. No fertilizer has been used; the soil being a very deep, rich loam.

The family are delightfully situated in their California home, surrounded with the trees and flowers of their own planting, and overlooking the town which Mr. Blanchard platted and with which he has had so much to do in its improvement and growth. He has also aided materially in the construction of the academy, and is now president of its board of trustees; has also taken a lively interest in the public schools, serving as trustee of the same several years. He is a member of the Independent Order of Odd Fellows and the three principal branches of Freemasonry, having passed the chairs in both the blue lodge and the commandery and also the lodge of Odd Fellows. In his religious views he is a Congregationalist, and in his political a Republican. He is a good, straight-forward business man and unassumin his manner. While in Placer County, he was elected District Collector and served two years, then was elected to the State Legislature, and subsequently declined a nomination tendered him, when the nomination insured an election. In the Legislature he served efficiently on the Committee on Education, and was author of a bill enacted into a law which suppressed an immorality prevalent in the mining towns of the State, namely, bands of dancing girls, who periodically visited the mining communities, played the tambourine and made the drinking saloons their headquarters.

In the fall of 1864 he went East on a visit, and December 21, married Miss Ann Elizabeth Hobbs, a native of North Berwick, Maine, and daughter of Wilson Hobbs, an old resident of that State. They have two daughters and one son, all born in California, namely: Sarah E., Eunice W. and Nathan W. The elder daughter is now in San Francisco studying art.

M. L. WOLFF, the senior partner of the firm of Wolff & Lehmann, general merchants of Hueneme, is a native of France, born March 2, 1855. After the German and French war, in 1871, he came to California, and was one year in San Francisco, attending a business college and learning the English language. He then went to San Luis Obispo, and clerked for A. Blochman & Co., three years. In 1875 he came to Hueneme and formed the firm of Wolff & Levy, in the general merchandise business, doing a successful business for ten years, until 1885, when Mr. Wolff bought out his partner, Mr. Levy, and gave an interest to Mr. Lehmann, who had formerly been one of the clerks of the firm. Since then the business has continued to prosper. They have a large double store, and include in their stock everything in the general merchandise line; the stock is so complete that scarcely anything in any department of trade or business is left out. The store is well equipped with the conveniences necessary to handle so large a stock, and the arrangements of the different departments is first-class in every respect. They buy wool, grain and beans in large quantities, and have excellent storage and shipping facilities; the trade of the house extends from twenty five to thirty-five miles. The store is 90 x 100 feet, and two stories high.

Mr. Wolff was married in 1887, to Miss B. Levy, a native of San Francisco, and of French ancestry. They have one daughter, Jeannette, born in Hueneme, May 10, 1889. While he has been very assiduous in business, he has not neglected the social side of life, and has built himself and family a beautiful home, surrounded with flowers and rare plants. He spends his evenings with his wife and little daughter. Mr. Wolff is a very evenly developed business man, not an extremist in any respect, and his eminent success shows his financial ability. In his political views he is a Democrat.

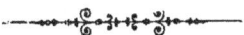

M. JONES, proprietor of the Santa Clara Hotel and an old resident of San Buenaventura, came to this State in 1852. He was born in Manchester, England, February 14, 1839. His parents, Edward and Elizabeth (Markland) Jones, were English, but his father's ancestors were Welsh. They came to America in 1847, settling in New Hampshire, where Mr. Jones received his education. He also attended school in Baltimore. His first business was in 1856, when he drove a six-horse stage-coach from old San Pedro to old Los Angeles, which business he continued until 1868, when the railroad was built. While driving stage he carried the United States Mail and the Wells-Fargo packages. His next business was buying, selling and raising sheep, which he followed until 1871, when he came to San Buenaventura and bought the hotel. He has since built additions to it, and is conducting it in a very obliging and satisfactory manner. The building was first erected in 1869, then in the center of the town, by Pearson Hornbeck and Pedro Cunstanza, and for many years was the principal hotel of the place. It was leased from 1873 to 1877, but Mr. Jones has been its landlord since 1871. It contains thirty-five well furnished rooms, is located on Main street nearly opposite the old Mission church, and a free bus is run to all trains.

Since locating here Mr. Jones has made an extended journey to the Sandwich Islands, New Zealand, Feejee Islands, etc., being gone nearly a year. He stands high as a man of good business capacity and excellent judgment. For many years he has been City Trustee, being greatly interested in the business interests of the place and efficient in aiding in its development. He was married in May, 1873, to Miss Flora Preble, a native of Maine, of which State her father, Charles Preble, was an old settler. Mr. and Mrs. Jones have three children, all born in San Buenaventura, namely, Minnie P., Charles E. and Walter M.

AYETTE BENNETT, a rancher near Lompoc, was born in Seneca County, Ohio, in 1830, and lived with his parents, who carried on farming and stock-raising, until 1852, when he started for California, going first to New York, and from there by steamer to the Isthmus of Panama. He landed in San Francisco, May 1, 1852, and went to the mines at Hangtown, now Placerville, and was engaged in mining for thirteen years, being engaged all through the mining district and in every kind of mining. He passed through the usual vicissitudes of this life with the usual success, often gaining a pound of gold per day; but the heavy expenses and losses were often very great. In 1867 he gave up mining and began lumbering in the redwoods in Santa Clara County, and also carried on general farming until 1873, when he secured a contract from a paper manufactory at Saratoga, Santa Clara County, and for four years he had charge of their bleaching apartment. In 1877 he went to Fresno County, where he took up a Government claim and engaged in the sheep industry, keeping about 500 head, and which he continued very successfully until 1880, when he came to Lompoc. He then bought eighty acres northwest of town, covered with brush and timber; he has since cleared forty acres, where he has established a comfortable home, and carries on general farming, making beans and mustard the principal crop, with barley sufficient for feeding purposes. He keeps twenty head of cattle and ten head of horses, breeding from a fine grade of mares, and securing some rare colts.

Mr. Bennett was married in Santa Clara in 1868, to Miss Malinda Orr, a native of Ohio, and they have three children.

JAMES WALKER, one of the business men of San Buenaventura who in a quiet way is doing a large grocery business, both wholesale and retail, was born in Wilmington, Illinois, March 13, 1843, a son of Elijah and Eliza (Craig) Walker, the former a native of New York and the latter of Indiana. Of their ten children four are living. James, the second child, was educated principally in the public schools of his State, removed to Monona County, Iowa, in 1860, opened a general merchandise store and conducted it successfully for several years. From 1874 to 1886 he was Sheriff of that county, giving complete satisfaction. He then came to San Buenaventura, bought property, built a house, and purchased the stock and good will of T. H. Morrison, and has since then been carrying on the grocery trade with fine success. His establishment is located in the best part of the town, but he also sends many articles to order out of town. He was married in 1867 to Miss Sarah Myers, a native of Iowa and a daughter of J. K. Myers, who was a native of West Virginia. They have three children living: Harley M., Mary E. and James H., all born in Iowa. Mr. Walker is a member of San Buenaventura Lodge, No. 214, F. & A. M., and he is also a member of the chapter.

HARRISON BISH, a rancher of Lompoc, was born in Giles County, Virginia, October 10, 1828. His father emigrated to Shelby County, Ohio, in 1830, and from there to Grant County, Indiana, in 1834, and there purchased a farm of 240 acres, where he carried on general farming, and also raised a great many hogs, which was a very profitable industry. Our subject lived at home until he was nineteen years of age. He was educated in what was known as the subscription schools. At the age of nineteen years he began teaching school at Logansport, where he remained until 1852, when he started for California, in a prairie schooner, across the plains. They had a quiet trip but were six months in crossing; they came by the way of the Truckee route and the Beckwith pass. He then came to Sacramento and engaged in cutting cord wood until the spring of 1853, and then located a ranch of 160 acres, which he fenced and worked for two and a half years. He was then obliged to surrender it, through the pernicious influence of a Spanish grant, which was a curse to so many of the early settlers of California. He then went to San José and engaged in artesian well boring until 1857, then opened a fruit store and ran it for four years, and then began again the business of well-boring, which he continued very successfully for fourteen years, and also engaged in mining more or less during the same time. In 1871 Mr. Bish went East to visit his father, and was married in Grant County, Indiana, February 22, 1872, to Miss Rachel Ann Wiles, a native of Indiana. In the spring of 1872 they went to Greene County, Missouri, where our subject bought 160 acres of land, and continued farming, remaining until 1875, when he again started for California, settling at San José, where he was engaged in farming until 1880. He then came to Lompoc and bought 111 acres, sixty-five of which he has since cleared, and raises beans and mustard. He has also planted ten acres to a variety of fruits, mainly winter apples, all of which are in bearing.

Mr. and Mrs. Bish have six children. They are the happy possessors of their own home, with no danger of creditors or Spanish grants robbing them of their possessions.

JOHN G. HILL, one of the most prominent men of Ventura, who by his intelligence and ability stepped to the front in the ranch and stock-producing interests of this county, is a fine illustration of what can be done in a country so wonderfully fertile. His birth occurred in Paris, Monroe County, Missouri, March 14, 1845. His father, James Hill, was a native of Kentucky, as were also his ancestry, as far back as it can be traced. His mother, *nee* Nancy Gray, was also born in Kentucky, of parents whose ancestors were also Kentuckians.

Mr. Hill, the subject of this sketch, was the fourth child of ten children. The family crossed the plains to California in 1852, settling in Napa County, where the senior Hill bought a ranch of 160 acres, and afterward added to it by purchase 1,400 acres. On this ranch Mr. Hill acquired his knowledge and experience in farming, which has proved to be of so much value to him and his brothers in the production of the finest horses in the State, if not in the world. Mr. Ben Hill, the noted horse man in California residing at El Cajon, is one of the brothers. In 1866 he began farming upon his own account, on his father's ranch, and after two years' work he removed to Ventura, in 1868, and bought part of the Colonia grant, 630 acres. On this property Mr. Hill has built one of the finest houses in Ventura County, planted orchards of fruit trees and groves of ornamental trees, and has made a delightful home. He is also raising fine thoroughbred Berkshire hogs, Durham cattle, etc., and he now has 150 head of blooded colts, of the Richmond, Wild Idler, Joe Daniels and Reveille strains. His young horses are not only of the best blood now in the county, but by his management they are the best developed specimens of their kind. Every lover of the horse is filled with admiration at the sight of his stock. In connection with Mr. Chrisman as partner, Mr. Hill is owner of several other fine places. At Montalvo they have a town site of 350 acres, fifty acres of land near Santa Paula, 108 acres sown to alfalfa on the Colonia grant, four-fifths of 260 acres planted in walnuts, one-third interest in 842 acres rented and sown to barley, and four-tenths of the Ventura waterworks. Mr. Hill stands high as a business man and gentleman in his county. He has witnessed and aided in the development of his locality; is an enthusiast as regards the fertility of the soil, and he really has good reasons to expect most lavish returns for his investments.

He was married, in 1866, to Miss Aranetta Rice, of Contra Costa County, and they have two sons, Ernest R. and Ralph N., both born in Ventura County. Mrs. Hill is a member of the Presbyterian Church.

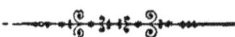

GEORGE R. WALDEN is a native son of the Golden West, and a business man of Saticoy. He was born in the city of Sacramento, December 18, 1857. His father, Jerome B. Walden, was a native of Canandaigna, New York, born March 20, 1829, and was a pioneer of the far West, having arrived in California before it became a State. For many years he was a Sheriff and detective, and is now a Justice of the Peace at his home in Sisson, this State. Twenty-two years of his life, as Sheriff and detective, were spent in Napa County, where in early days he rendered efficient service in breaking up the gangs of desperados that infested the country at that time. He was united in wedlock to Miss Mira A. Harrington, daughter of a pioneer Methodist minister of Wisconsin, a member of the first Legislature and also of the first Constitutional Convention of that State. The subject of this sketch was the first son and the second of a family of five children. He finished his education in the Napa Methodist College, and also studied two years at the State University at Berkeley. His parents were desirous of having him become a physician, and at fourteen years of age he began to learn the drug business. From that time until 1880 his time was divided between working and going to school. He was then elected apothecary of the Napa Insane Asylum, and held the position five years, during which time he compounded 47,560 prescriptions. On account of ill health he resigned the position, and from the officials of the institution received testimonials for faithful and competent discharge of his duties. In 1886 he removed to San Buenaventura, and engaged in the real-estate business with Mr. B. E. Hunt. They organized the Montalvo Land and Water Company. Eight hundred acres of land in the Santa Clara valley were purchased, and at a meeting of the directors of the company Mr. Walden presented the name of Montalvo for the town, in honor of Ordenez de Montalvo, who had the credit of first writing and publishing the name "California." The name proposed was unanimously adopted. The rush for new towns soon after collapsed, and the company allowed the land to go back, losing their first payment. Mr. Walden happily consoled himself for the loss of several thousand dollars with the fact that he had the honor of having suggested the name of the town that in the growth of the country is destined some time in the future to become a place of importance and fame.

In the summer of 1887 Mr. Walden circulated a list for signatures, and secured twenty names of native sons to organize a parlor of that order at San Buenaventura; and at the meeting at which the name to be given the parlor was discussed, Mr. Walden proposed the name of Cabrillo, the pioneer of pioneers. After giving a brief sketch of Cabrillo's life the name was readily adopted, the parlor was organized, and is still growing. It was decided at that meeting to take initiatory steps to build some day a monument to Cabrillo. In 1888 Mr. Walden came to Saticoy and opened a drug store. In 1889 he was appointed Postmaster of Saticoy by Postmaster-General Wanamaker, which position he now fills.

He was married April 22, 1884, to Miss Adela L. Frisbie, a native of Napa County, California. She is a daughter of Edward Frisbie, a native of Albany, New York, and now a banker of Redding, Shasta County, California. Mr. and Mrs. Walden have two children, a son and daughter: Arthur F., born at Redding; and Jean, in San Buenaventura. In politics Mr. Walden is Republican. He is a very pleasant and courteous business man, and is full of enthusiasm in regard to the history and great future of his native State.

JACOB K. GRIES is one of the best known and highly respected citizens of Ventura County. He came to California in 1852, and has had large experience in the early history of the State, as well as the early settlement of Ventura County. He has been a leading man—a man of nerve and of great natural ability. His early experience in the Golden State would make a book of interest; but he declines to recount the privations, dangers and exciting times that tried men's souls in the settlement of the great State in which he has had a share, and in which he has borne an honorable part, and for which he is now rewarded by having his home in the most civilized, enlightened and delightful portion of the world. All new countries have their ruffians and renegades, and California was no exception to the rule, but she has proudly and grandly outlived the stormy days, and the pioneer looks with just gratification and pride upon the great country he has helped to develop.

Mr. Gries was born in Berks County, Pennsylvania, July 16, 1830. His father, Jacob Gries, was a native of the same county, and was a soldier in the war of 1812. In early life he had been a hat-maker, but after his removal to Ohio he became a farmer. He died on his own farm, in Ohio, in 1870. The subject of this sketch was reared in Ohio. At the age of twenty years he removed to Indiana, and a year later took his course westward to the Pacific Coast. He arrived in June, 1852, and July 16, following, he was twenty-two years old. He went to Foster's Bar, on the Yuba River, and mined until late in the fall, then, in company with others, he engaged in the hotel and staging business, two very important occupations at that time. The hotel in which he was interested was the Oregon House, in Yuba County, and he was thus engaged for three years. From 1857 to 1860 he was in the butchering and meat business. In the latter year he removed to Nevada, remaining there until 1869, ranching and mining. He owned a ranch in the Washoe Valley, which he sold in the fall of 1868, and removed to White Pine County, where, for several months, he was interested in the toll-road business.

November 1, 1869, Mr. Gries came to Ventura County and engaged in farming, raising barley, corn and wheat, on eighty acres of land which he purchased of the Briggs grant, near Santa Paula. This property he still owns. He also bought 360 acres of Thomas R. Bard, on the Colonia Ranch, which he afterward sold at a great profit, and bought 412 acres in the ex-Mission ranch, still retaining it. He has a one-half interest in 426 acres on the Colonia ranch. Mr. Gries came to Nordhoff in December, 1887, and has here built a fine residence, where he resides with his family. For a number of years he has been interested in the production of thorough-bred horses, mostly trotting stock.

In 1860, Mr. Gries was married to Mrs. Elizabeth Foulks, daughter of John Turbett. By her he had one child, Belle, born in Yuba County, California. She married Norris Claybury, and they reside near Santa Paula. After twenty-two years of wedded life, Mrs. Gries died. Four years later Mr. Gries married Mrs. Mary Simpson, a native of Texas, and widow of Frank J. Simpson. Mrs. Gries is a member of the Presbyterian Church. Mr. Gries is a Republican; he was a Democrat before the war, but at that time took a strong stand in favor of the Union, and has since affiliated with the Republican party. He is a man of strong convictions, a natural leader among men, and has been prominent in Ventura County ever since its organization. He has been active in helping to maintain law and order in his county, for which he has the respect and good will of every worthy citizen in the county. Mr. Gries has enjoyed pleasant business relations with others, and has had in his employ men who have remained with him for years, all of them speaking highly of Mr. Gries, and some of them having risen to wealth and influence. It is scarcely necessary to add that he is a warm admirer of California and considers Ventura County the cream of the great State.

DR. O. V. SESSIONS is a native of Union County, Illinois, born February 27, 1852. His father, Richard Sessions, was born in North Carolina, March 20, 1820. He removed to Illinois in an early day, was reared there and became a merchant, spending the whole of his life in that State, with the exception of the first eight years. He was a prominent Methodist and a devoted Christian. His death occurred in Illinois, in 1876. The Doctor's grandfather Sessions, also named Richard, came from England to America in the latter part of the seventeenth century. His mother, nee Mary House, was born in Tennessee, September 14, 1826, the daughter of Robert House, who was of German descent. The subject of this sketch was the oldest child of a family of four sons and one daughter. He was reared in Illinois, and at the age of fifteen years began to assist his father, who was conducting a general merchandise business in Hamburg, and was engaged in the store for ten years. He then began the study of medicine, first reading with Dr. J. I. Hale, of Anna, Illinois, and afterward attended the Chicago Medical College three years, graduating in 1882. He then went to Springfield, Missouri, where he practiced two years, after which he returned to Illinois, and continued the practice of his profession at Hamburg and at Anna. He next came to California, opened an office in Hueneme, and has here met with marked success. When he came here he was the only physician in the place, and by his skill and close attention to his patients, he has established a fine practice. His ride extends out twenty-five miles, and he now has the principal part of the practice on the ocean side of the Santa Clara River. He is the owner of a nice home and office in the center of town, the grounds extending through from Broad to Market streets. The house fronts on one street and the office on the other, with an attractive flower garden between, in which the Doctor takes much pleasure and needed rest from his labors.

Dr. Sessions was married in 1875 to Miss Lucy Martin, a native of Missouri. They have one son, Kenneth V., born in Springfield, Missouri, November 20, 1877. The Doctor is a Republican, but does not give politics much attention. He is strictly a temperate man, using neither strong drink nor tobacco believing both to be injurious. He is not only a successful practitioner, but is also a good business man and a worthy and respected citizen.

PATRICK McHENRY was born in Ireland, March, 1848, and at the age of nineteen years came to America, coming direct to California. Patrick was preceded by two brothers, and upon his arrival the three went to ranching in Marin County, and engaged in that business jointly for a year and a half. At the expiration of that time, in 1869, Patrick invested in some cattle and came to San Luis Obispo County, locating in the Los Osos Valley, where he has since remained, engaged in the cattle and dairy business. His present ranch, 500 acres in extent, is located in a very pretty part of the valley, the view from which is extensive. Very many changes have taken place in this district since he first settled here. Immense ranches have been cut up and sold, and where there were only a half dozen settlements then there are thirty or more now.

Mr. McHenry was married in November, 1873, and is the father of seven children, five of whom are now living.

WILLIAM M. ZELLER was born in Hagerstown, Maryland, December 22, 1853. His father, David Zeller, was also a native of the same State, born in 1802. He had large real estate interests there, and was the senior member of the firm of D. Zeller & Co., in the wholesale commission business, Hon. Thomas R. Bard being the junior partner. His death occurred in 1884. Mr. Zeller's grandfather, Jacob Zeller, was a Maryland planter, and the ancestors of the family came from Switzerland. Mr. Zeller's mother was Mary Parker (Little) Zeller. The maternal ancestry is the same as Mr. Bard's, which appears on another page of this book. The subject of this sketch is the youngest of a family of three children. His early education was obtained at Hagerstown, where his boyhood days were spent, and in 1869 he attended the Mercersburg College. He finished his education at the Massachusetts Agricultural College at Amherst, after which he was engaged in farming in Maryland for four years. He then came to California and engaged in farming on the Colonia and Las Posas ranches. Mr. Zeller is still conducting his farming operations on a large scale, having 1,800 acres of land devoted to the cultivation of barley, alfalfa and beans.

In 1885 he was married to a San Francisco lady. Mr. Zeller is a member of the A. O. U. W. He is a strictly temperate man, and politically is a Republican.

In speaking of Mr. Zeller's father, it is just to his memory to say that while he was a Southern gentleman and at one time had numerous slaves, he never sold one, and often arranged with them, giving them wages whereby they were permitted to buy their liberty. He was a man very correct and methodical in his business habits, as well as at his home and on his premises. Seldom do we find a man in these days possessing such admirable traits of character.

F. CLARK is one of the young business men of Saticoy. He was born in Horton, Bremer County, Iowa, July 14, 1863. His father, Otis Clark, is a native of Ohio; and for the past twenty years has been a resident of California, and is now engaged in the lumber business at Yuba City, Sutter County. His mother, *nee* Laura A. Patridge, was born in New York, in 1845, and her death occurred September 30, 1888. She was a devoted wife, a faithful and loving mother, and her loss is deeply lamented by the family. She was the mother of three children, all of whom are living, the subject of this sketch being the oldest. He is a graduate of the State Normal School at San José, class of 1885. Mr. Clark spent some years in teaching, being for two years Principal of the schools of Brentwood, California, and in 1888 came to Saticoy where he engaged in farming. He has 100 acres of very choice land on which he has recently erected a handsome residence. He has selected a beautiful location for building, and when the arrangements of the grounds are completed it will be one of the attractive places of the community. Mr. Clark is the manager of 900 acres of farm land adjoining his own, the property of his father-in-law, John Nicholl. The entire tract is rented in lots of from forty to eighty acres to tenants who are mainly men of families and in comfortable circumstances, the principal crop raised being Lima beans.

Mr. Clark was married, July 27, 1887, to Miss Agnes Nicholl, a native of San Pablo, California, and also a graduate of the State Normal School. They have one daughter, born August 30, 1888. Since taking up his residence in this county, Mr. Clark has been identified with its best interests; and is justly proud of the great State of his adoption.

J. E. McCOY was born in Placerville, California, June 7, 1864. His father, J. D. D. McCoy, was born in Canada in 1835, was the pioneer hotel proprietor of Hueneme, and now resides at Portland, Oregon. His ancestors were Scotch, but residents of America for many generations. Mr. McCoy's mother, Margaret (Lynch) McCoy, died when the subject of this sketch was quite young, leaving a family of ten children. Mr. McCoy was reared and educated in Ventura and Hueneme, and began his business career in a hotel. He has owned the Seaside Hotel for the past five years. This house was built by Mr. Judkins twenty-two years ago, and Mr. McCoy's father bought it, made some additions to the building, and opened it to the public, conducting the business for fifteen years. Since it has been in the possession of Mr. McCoy, Jr., he has remodeled and enlarged the building. It is as old as the town itself, is well managed, and is provided with a good table.

Mr. McCoy was married April 17, 1884, to Miss Ina Woodruff, a native of Pennsylvania, and daughter of William and E. A. Woodruff, who reside in Hueneme. Mr. and Mrs. McCoy have one child, Maggie, born in Hueneme, March 17, 1885.

The subject of this sketch votes the Republican ticket, but is not an active politician. He is a well-known business man in the county, and has been identified with the best interests of Hueneme since its beginning.

HENRY M. STILES, one of the pioneers of California, came to Ventura in the winter of 1867. He was born in Medina County, Ohio, December 15, 1837. His father, Milton Stiles, was born in the State of Massachusetts, in 1808. A large part of Mr. Stiles' life has been spent, both in Ohio and California, in the mercantile business. He is now spending the remainder of his days with his son Henry M. in Ventura; he is eighty-two years of age. Mr. Stiles' grandfather, Dorus Stiles, was also a native of Massachusetts; his mother, Catherine (Nelson) Stiles, was a native of Massachusetts. Mr. Stiles was the fifth child in a family of seven children. He received his early education in the public schools in Ohio, and at fourteen years of age began to earn his own living by working on a farm. In 1852 he went to Kalamazoo, Michigan, and worked there for a while, and then to Minnesota, then a Territory, and, like President Lincoln, ran a flatboat on the Minnesota River to St. Paul, and was soon made captain of the boat. He had three men under him; the business was freighting lime. After being engaged in this business for two seasons, he returned to Ohio, and from there came to California, in 1856, and settled in Amador County, and with his father engaged in mining for five years. In 1864 Mr. Stiles went to Oregon, and remained there one winter, then he went to the mines in Placerville, Idaho Territory, being very successful. The next year he lost all he had made, and went to Montana and prospected for a while, and then to Salt Lake and next to Prescott, Arizona, where he drove a four-horse team for a time; thence he came to Los Angeles, and from there, in 1867, in November, to Ventura. Here he purchased a lot, erected a livery stable,—the second in the town,— which he ran for four years; and since that time he has been back and forth in the Territories several times, but has always considered Ventura his home. In 1866 he made a prospecting trip into Idaho, with sixty men and 100 horses. Getting far into the snow, the party became disgusted with their leader and separated. While two or three were out hunting the Indians shot one of them; the others made their escape back to their comrades. They started twenty-five men on horseback after the Indians, but they failed to reach them.

In Arizona Mr. Stiles made another prospecting tour, with fifty men, to the head of Black River, but found neither gold nor silver; and they were not troubled by the Indians. Since coming to California he has made three trips to the East. He is now proprietor of the Ventura Soda Works, furnishing the whole of the county with temperance drinks. In company with his brother, he also owns 266 acres of land in Pleasant Valley, which they are improving, by planting trees, sinking wells and erecting buildings. In 1874 Mr. Stiles built a brick building in Ventura, the best in the town at that time. He also built the house where he resides and owns a building on Main street above the Ventura Bank. Mr. Stiles has seen much of frontier life and has had many interesting experiences; he is now one of Ventura's reliable and prosperous citizens.

He was married in 1874, and had one son, Freddie, who now resides in Idaho. In 1885 he was again married, this time to Miss Theresia Frank, who was born in San Francisco. Her father, Philip Frank, M. D., was from Vienna, Austria, and her mother was a native of New Orleans. By this marriage there are two children: Wilbur H., born in Lead City, Dakota Territory, and Milton P., born in Ventura.

ACHILLE LEVY, one of the prominent business men of Hueneme, came to California in 1871. He was born in Alsace, France, now Germany, October 23, 1853; his parents were both natives of France. After he arrived in San Francisco he went to a business college for two years, to take a business course and to learn the English language. He then engaged in clerking and as book-keeper in a general merchandise store in Dixon, Solano County, and was there two years. In 1875 he came to Hueneme and engaged in business, the firm being Wolff & Levy, in which they continued for ten years, meeting with excellent success. In 1885 he sold his half interest, and opened a wholesale grain, commission and banking business. He handles large quantities of grain, honey, beans and wool, and ships his produce all over the United States and Mexico; he is also a director, stockholder and vice-president of the Hueneme Bank. He is extensively interested in real estate throughout Ventura, Santa Barbara and Los Angeles counties.

In 1881 Mr. Levy took a tour to Europe and was there married to Miss Lucy Levy, a "forty-second cousin" of his, and a native of Paris, where her parents reside. They have four children, born in Hueneme: Anna E., Palmyre, Joseph Paul and Julia E. Mr. Levy has built a nice home; he has bought recently a ten-acre lot on one of the best streets, about a half-mile from town, which he designs to fit for a residence, and lay out in handsome grounds in the near future. In his political views he is a Republican, and prominently identified with that party; he is a very active business man, and a member of the San Francisco Produce Exchange.

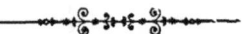

JOHN H. KUHLMAN was born in Germany, in 1827, received his education in his native country, and at the age of fifteen entered upon a three-years' apprenticeship to the blacksmith trade. His term having expired, in 1845, he came to the United States, landing at Galveston, Texas, and worked at his trade for three months in that State. He then gave it up and was employed as a cabin-boy on a steamboat, continuing that business five years, and being promoted from cabin-boy to steward of the boat. While sailing on the steamer Palmetto, he was shipwrecked on Matagorda Bar, January 9, 1851. Fifty passengers were on board, and all were saved in a remarkable manner, which is worth relating here. Among other freight they had a bull on board—a fine large animal. One end of a rope they attached to him and the other end to the vessel. He was sent overboard and swam ashore, and they were thus landed before the ship was dashed to pieces. Mr. Kuhlman sailed on the schooner European, for Chagres, and was again shipwrecked at Algrat Keys. They were rescued this time by the Apalachicola and landed at San Juan del Norte, and taken to Chagres on the steamer Avon. He remained a month at Chagres and crossed the Isthmus in April, 1851, working his passage on the steamer New Orleans. He returned to Panama May 5th. The steamer was sold. For three months he acted as steward on the steamer Unicorn. After that he went into the mines, where he was engaged until 1859. At that time he came back to San Francisco, and went on a steamboat to Olympia. From there he went to Anaheim, and from there, in 1865, to Santa Barbara. In the latter place he opened a variety store, ran it three years, and, in 1869, started a branch store of the same kind in Ventura. He afterward sold his business at Santa Barbara and moved to Ventura, where he built a store, in 1870, on leased ground. This he traded to Mr. Hobson for his present store, and has since continued business in the same place.

In 1870 he was married to Miss Maria Botilla, of Santa Barbara. They have six children: Christina, Charles, Rosa and Henry, born in Santa Barbara; and John and Flora, born in Ventura. Mr. and Mrs. Kuhlman and the children are all members of the Catholic Church. Mr. Kuhlman was brought up in the Lutheran Church.

In addition to the business interests already mentioned in this sketch, it may be stated that Mr. Kuhlman has stock in the Anacapa Hotel, and is treasurer of the company which owns it He is the owner of considerable valuable business property on Main street, Ventura, and has fifty acres in another place. He still retains a lot and brick store in Santa Barbara. Mr. Kuhlman has an extensive acquaintance throughout the county, and is regarded by all as a reliable man and a worthy citizen.

JAMES RAYMOND VANCE was born in Schuyler County, Illinois in 1824. His father was a farmer and owned the land where Nauvoo, once a Mormon settlement, is now located. His father having died, his mother moved with the family to Wisconsin in 1838. At the age of eighteen the subject of this sketch began lead-mining, which he followed for six years; then in 1849 he started for California, with older brothers, traveling across the plains with a horse-team. They were ninety days en route, coming by old Fort Kearney, North Platte river and Sublette's Cut-off. They began placer-mining and found their first gold at Steep Hollow on the Bear River. After two years of mining, with varying success, Mr. Vance went back to his home in Wisconsin for a visit, but again returned to California in 1853, and engaged in mercantile life at Forbestown and Camptonville, and what was then Uder County. In 1858 he was appointed Deputy Sheriff of Uder County, under Mat Wood, and was an officer about four years. He then went to Nevada and engaged in silver-mining, until the latter part of 1864, when he began farming again in Sonoma County, continuing until 1868, when he came to Santa Barbara. He took up 400 acres on Casitas Pass and began the stock business, having about 500 head of cattle, and continuing for ten years. He lost nearly all his stock in the drouth of 1877. The next year he moved to Santa Barbara to educate his children, and there engaged in farming. In 1886 he was elected Supervisor and Councilman, serving two years as Supervisor and four as Councilman.

Mr. Vance was married in Santa Barbara in 1869, to Miss Mary C. Nidever, a daughter of John Nidever. They have seven children, all at home. Mr. Vance has passed through the experience of all miners, having frequently "struck it rich" and then losing heavily through some disastrous speculation. He now owns twenty-seven acres in East Santa Barbara, where he resides.

HON. THOMAS R. BARD, a prominent business man of Hueneme, is the best known and most distinguished factor in the growth and development of the county of Ventura. He is a man with whom the history of Ventura County is more intimately connected than with any other. He was born in Chambersburg, Franklin County, Pennsylvania, December 8, 1841, the son of Robert M. Bard, a lawyer, born in the same county in 1810, and died in 1851. His grandfather, Thomas Bard, was also born in the same county, and his great-grandfather, Richard Bard, was of Scotch-Irish descent. He came to America in 1745, and was one of the earliest pioneers of that part of Pennsylvania; both himself and wife were captured by the Indians, April 19; 1758. Five days after being captured he made his escape, and made unceasing efforts for the release of his wife. She was in captivity for more than a year, but was finally given up at Fort du Quesne, Pittsburg, her ransom being forty pounds sterling. Mr. Bard's mother was Elizabeth S. Little, a native of Mercersburg, Franklin County, Pennsylvania, born in 1812, and died in 1880. She was the daughter of Dr. P. W. Little, and a grand-daughter of Colonel Robert Parker of the Revolutionary army.

Mr. Bard's parents had two sons and two daughters, all of whom are still living. He was reared and educated at the Chambersburg Academy, and began, at the age of seventeen, the study of law with Hon. George Chambers, then a retired Supreme Justice of the State of Pennsylvania; but, finding an active life more suitable to his tastes, he abandoned his studies of law for the profession of railroad and mining engineering, in which he received a practical training in the Alleghany Mountains. When he returned he was offered a position in a forwarding and commission house at Hagerstown, Pennsylvania, which he accepted. While at that place the war broke out, and the firm, differing in politics, dissolved, the town being a border town and excitement running high. Mr. Zellar, one of the company, took Mr. Bard as a partner, and then he commenced his business life, before he was twenty-one years of age. While in business at Hagerstown the firm there were agents for the Pennsylvania Railroad Company, and were in constant danger of rebel raids, and had to be constantly on the alert to know of the proximity of Confederates. For this purpose Mr. Bard found it necessary to do some scouting, and was on the battle-field of Antietam when the battle began, and afterward voluntarily took up arms on the Union side in that fight. He then became acquainted with Colonel Thomas A. Scott, then Assistant Secretary of War, and did valuable service for him, which was much appreciated by the Colonel. The rebels, under General McCausland, in one of their raids, burned Mr. Bard's mother's house, after which Colonel Scott induced him to come to California to take charge of the business interests here.

Mr. Bard sold out his interest in the business at Hagerstown, and January 5, 1865, came to Ventura County. His first work here was the superintendency of the California Petroleum Company, in which Colonel Scott was interested. They attempted to develop the oil resources of Ojai Rancho, and everything they required in the way of machinery came from New York, via Cape Horn to San Francisco, and from San Francisco by boat and landed by means of rafts, through the surf at San Buenaventura. This was the first attempt to develop the oil fields of California. Their work was practically unsuccessful. When they had gained experience enough to know where to locate the wells, the company became discouraged and closed the work. After this he took charge of the property in which Colonel Scott was interested, consisting of the ranchos:—the Simí, 113,000 acres; the Las Rosas, 26,600 acres; the San Francisco, 48,000 acres; the Calleguas, 10,000 acres; the El Rio de Santa Clara, 45,000 acres; the Cañada Larga, 6,600 acres, and the Ojai, 16,000 acres. In addition to this he took charge of a large part of the town of San Buenaventura, and Colonel Scott's lands in Los Angeles and Humboldt counties, about 12,000 acres, making a grand total of about 277,000 acres. This vast acreage was devoted to sheep and cattle-raising, and Mr. Bard had charge of it until sold. The business was attended with much inconvenience and trouble through people stealing on the lands, supposing it to be Government land; almost all of the vast property was involved in dispute concerning title, and much ill-feeling was the result; some of the parties were desperadoes. Generally Mr. Bard succeeded in a just way to pay the people for their losses, and all of the lands he has disposed of have been found to have perfect titles. The land was rented to the people, and many of them afterward became purchasers.

In the meantime his own affairs had grown upon his hands, during the time he laid out the town of Hueneme, and built the wharf, in 1871, and from that time the town took its start. He continued to manage Colonel Scott's affairs until the time of his death, which occurred in 1882, after which he became his administrator in California, and closed out the property.

The liberal course taken by Mr. Bard with the tenants and squatters on the lands resulted beneficially in the settlement of the county. He eventually bought the wharf and warehouses and invested in real estate, which, with the growth of the county, has become valuable. He was one of the incorporators of the first Bank of Ventura, and was its President for fifteen years; he is now President of Hueneme Bank, and of the Hueneme Wharf Company. He organized the Simí Land and Water Company, and the Las Rosas Land & Water Company. Mr. Bard is President of the Mission Transfer Company, which owns the large system of pipe lines and refineries, at Santa Paula, and which handles the whole of the oil production of Ventura County; he is also the President of the Sespe Oil Company, which control 22,000 acres of oil territory. He is also President of the Torrey Cañon Oil Company. The output of these companies aggregate 600 barrels of oil per day.

Mr. Bard has 320 acres of land adjoining his home, of which all is being farmed; he has fifty acres of ground surrounding his home, on which is a beautiful and commodious cottage, and very excellent grounds, in which he takes much enjoyment in the collection of flowers and other plants. As one enters the grounds he is confronted by a large triangular bed of scarlet geraniums, making a brilliant show of blossoms. Back of this is a large fountain, and the winding drives branch off in two directions, making curves in divers directions amid groves of trees and flowers and amid the border of evergreen hedges, until the avenues meet in front of the house.

Mr. Bard held for several successive terms the office of Supervisor in the first district of Santa Barbara, before the county of Ventura was formed; he was first elected Supervisor on the Republican ticket, against a Spaniard on the Democratic ticket, when there were not over a dozen Americans in the district. He was the Republican candidate for State Senator in 1877, in the Senatorial district composed of the three counties of Ventura, Santa Barbara and San Luis Obispo. He was defeated, but Ventura and Santa Barbara counties gave him a handsome majority, which was barely overcome by his opponent in San Luis Obispo County. He was also on the Garfield ticket for Elector, in 1880. He was a delegate at large for the State to the memorable convention at Chicago that nominated Mr. Blaine, in 1884.

He married, in 1876, Miss Mary B. Gerberding, daughter of Mr. E. O. Gerberding of San Francisco, who was one of the founders of the San Francisco *Bulletin*. Mrs. Bard was born in California, in 1858. They have five children, all born in Hueneme, viz.:

Beryl B., Mary Louisa, Anna Greenwell, Thomas G. and Elizabeth Parker. Mrs. Bard is an Episcopalian, and Mr. Bard is an elder in the Presbyterian Church. He is a man of liberal views, broad business capacities, and a quiet and unobtrusive gentleman.

WILLIAM H. RYAN, one of the pioneers of Arroyo Grande, or, as one of the citizens remarked, the "father of the town," was born in Amesbury, Massachusetts, April 28, 1833. His father, Jeremiah Ryan, was a native of Ireland, and his mother, formerly Miss Betsy Glidden, was a native of New Hampshire. He was educated in one of the excellent schools of Amesbury, and at the age of seventeen years started out in the world to seek his fortune. In 1849 he decided to come to California; took passage on the brig Ark and came to San Francisco by way of Cape Horn, arriving April, 1850, the trip consuming seven months' time. Mr. Ryan did not remain long in San Francisco, but while there was actively engaged in the dray business, and was the owner of one of the first drays brought to that place. One year and a half was spent in the city and one year in Santa Clara. In 1853, during the gold excitement in Australia, he set out for that far-away country. For one year he was foreman of an American company there. He next went to South America, trying his luck in Peru, then Chili, and in a year returned to San Francisco. He visited Washoe during the Washoe silver excitement, and finally settled in Silver Mountain, Alpine County, and built the hotel known as Ryan's Exchange, where he remained for several years. Arizona was the next scene of his sojourn. In 1872 he came to San Luis Obispo County, and here he has made his home up to the present day. Thirteen months he was engaged in business in the city, and then he came to Arroyo Grande. With the latter place he has become thoroughly identified, and has been engaged in the hotel and livery business. The hotel which bears his name and which he successfully conducted so many years, is the pioneer hotel of the place, and is known to everyone in this locality, as is also its owner. Mr. Ryan is the oldest representative in business in the place and has done much toward building up the town and making it what it is. Arroyo Grande is a thriving little town, situated in the heart of some of the richest land on the globe, and no one person residing in the place has appreciated or marked these changes more than the subject of this sketch. Mr. Ryan has retired from the active management of his hotel, having leased it to other parties, and is now living a retired life.

CHARLES H. CLARK, an early pioneer, and a prominent developer of the Point Sal shipping industry, was born in Johnson, Vermont, in 1838, and is a lineal descendant of William Clark, the chief mate of the old ship the Mayflower. Our subject's education was only in English branches, acquired in attendance at the common schools and academy. At thirteen years of age his business career began, as clerk in the postoffice of his native town, where he did all the writing of the office, and attended school during the school hours. In 1857 he came to California, by the Panama route. At San Francisco his first occupation was in the postoffice, but the opportunities being too narrow for one of his enterprise, he soon found more congenial employment in the broader fields of mercantile life. As clerk he entered the office of C. J. Hawley, an extensive wholesale and retail grocer of San Francisco. After one year, as a financial advancement, he worked on the steamboat running between San Francisco and Stockton for one year, and then returned to the former place, where he opened a retail grocery store. Here he felt the kindly influence of his old employer, C. J. Hawley, who in many ways advanced the young man's interests. Mr. Clark continued his store until 1868, when on account of failing health he sold out, and in 1869 came to the southern country for the open-air exercise, settling near Santa Maria Valley, and taking charge of the "Todos Santos" cattle ranch, where he remained about eighteen months. When the Guadaloupe Rancho was divided, about 1874, Mr. Clark bought 1,000 acres near Point Sal, and in 1884 bought 1,157 acres adjoining, upon which he has 750 head of cattle and fifty head of horses. The ranch is particularly adapted to grazing; being near the coast it has an abundance of nutritious food and Mr. Clark is farming only a small acreage to hay. His horses are well bred for general utility purposes.

In 1864 Mr. Clark was married to Miss Eliza Clayton, a niece of Hon. Charles Clayton, and they have had eight children, two sons and six daughters. The elder daughter is a descriptive writer of great merit, and all the children have musical talents. The second daughter, Minnie, has studied music under the best instructors in the State, and is a finished pianist and vocalist.

The history of Point Sal has been chiefly made by Mr. Clark, he being the promoter and founder of its extensive shipping industries. In 1872, before any wharf was established, in partnership with W. D. Harriman, he commenced unloading vessels by means of lighters, and that year ten cargoes of lumber were loaded through the surf, and over 1,000,000 feet were sold to the new settlers. In 1873 Messrs. Clark & Harriman built a wharf at Point Sal, of which a third interest was sold to Hayward & Harmon, of San Francisco. In 1876 the wharf was carried away by a storm. It was rebuilt the following spring, but the winter again destroyed it, and Mr. Clark soon after sold his interest, and is now agent for the Pacific Coast Steamship Company, whose steamers largely do the carrying trade of the coast. The present Chute Landing was built in 1880 by St. Ores, a Canadian Frenchman, a syndicate of ranchers furnishing the necessary capital, which amounted to $21,000. This is an elevated frame work, projecting from the cliff, firmly anchored to the rocks and elevated eighty feet above the water. The vessel is then safely anchored outside, over which extends, from the landing to a buoy beyond, a wire cable; this is securely attached, a traveler is safely suspended to it, which works easily back and forth upon it, by means of nicely adjusted shievis. To the traveler are then suspended cages, which by means of steam power are worked back and forth, thus discharging or loading the vessel, an engine on the wharf furnishing the necessary power. In 1881, 8,000 tons of grain were shipped by this landing.

Mr. Clark has been manager of the landing since 1883. The gypsum mines of Point Sal were developed by him in 1883, on the Casmalia Rancho, owned by Merritt & Phoenix. Mr. Clark secured a twenty years' lease of Messrs. Lucas & Co. of the Golden Gate Plaster Mill of San Francisco, which is the only plaster mill on the coast for manufacturing plaster of Paris and land plaster. The mining is all under ground and Mr. Clark is the manager of the works, and he is said to be the "Father of gypsum on the Coast," and he mines about 3,000 tons per year. Mr. Clark possesses the confidence and esteem of the community, and in early life devoted much time to the interests of the Republican party; but in later life his manifold duties have occupied all his time.

BERNARDINO LUGO was born in San Fernando, May 10, 1810. Early in life he was taken by his family to Santa Barbara and his childhood was spent at that place. It was not until 1850 that Mr. Lugo came to San Luis Obispo County. Then hardly a settlement was to be seen anywhere. He engaged in ranching extensively, and for many years was foreman of a large ranch known as the Paso Robles ranch. In 1870 he came to San Luis Obispo and has been engaged in the cattle business ever since, residing at present in the city and living a very quiet life. He is a very familiar figure on the streets of the city. When out of doors he is always on horseback, sitting as erect as a soldier. He is eighty years of age. Mr. Lugo was married in 1850, and has one son living.

JOHN M. PRICE, one of the best known veterans of San Luis Obispo County, and we can say of the State, is the subject of this brief sketch. "Old John Price" was born in Bristol, England, September 29, 1810. As a boy he was fond of the sea and at a very early age became a sailor. When fifteen years old he shipped for a three-years cruise to the Southern Ocean on a whaler named Cadmus, of London, England. At the age of eighteen he started on that eventful voyage which unexpectedly landed him for all time on the coast of California in the New World, on the bark Kent, a whaling ship commanded by Captain Lawton. The Captain was a hard master, Mr. Price rebelled, and in company with another boy quit the ship at Manzanillo, now a prominent Mexican port, but then a wild, uninhabited region, where this whaling vessel put in for supplies. The two young men escaped undiscovered, and this, in the year 1829, was the beginning of their career on the American continent. Making their way into the interior, with the aid of friendly Indians, they finally reached Colima, where Mr. Price almost succumbed to an attack of cholera. After a year's sojourn there he improved the opportunity to come to Monterey, California, on a sailing vessel. At that place he was for six years a vaquero about the ancient capital, and then, in 1836, he came to San Luis Obispo, where he has ever since been a resident. Here he first hired out to Captain W. G. Dana, receiving as wages $15 a month on the Nipomo. Two years later he was engaged on the Huasna Ranch for Isaac J. Sparks, for which he was paid $20 a month for several years. During the Graham insurrection he became one of the many prisoners who were sentenced to confinement at Santa Barbara and San Blas by order of Alvarado. In 1846 he was residing at the old ranch house a short distance above the site of the present village of Arroyo Grande. The Mexican war was in progress and Mr. Price was surprised one day by the appearance of General Fremont and his troops, who wanted him and his men (Indians working for him) to surrender. Mr. Price was willing to surrender, but suddenly the Indians were missing. It was afterward ascertained that they had hid themselves in the almost impenetrable mass of willows then growing in the Arroyo Grande Valley, where they could not at that time be found. Mr. Price states as an eye witness that the stories rife concerning the reckless depredations by Fremont's troops are great exaggerations.

On the breaking out of the gold fever of 1848, Mr. Price and Mr. F. Z. Branch started off to try their luck. They found some "big nuggets," and after a fair degree of success returned to their ranches. These nuggets Mr. Price desired to retain as splendid specimens, but subsequent hard times compelled him to cash them.

For a time he worked on the Pizmo ranch on shares with Mr. Sparks, and subsequently he purchased it undivided—7,000 acres, near the ocean shore. This place is a favorite resort. For fifty years Mr. Price has been engaged in cattle-raising, dairying, etc., and now, at the age of eighty years, he is as active and energetic as any man on his place, thinking nothing of a long ride in the saddle or of frequent trips with horse and wagon to San Luis Obispo city, fifteen miles distant. Since his settlement here he has had many offices of prominence, both under Mexican and American control. Under the Mexican Government he was Alcalde and Juez de Paz, and as an American official he was Alcalde, Justice of the Peace, County Judge and Supervisor. Many are the curious documents which Mr. Price has in his possession and which he courteously shows to his visitors, in relation to the offices he held in those times. As Alcalde he gave great satisfaction, and, taking into account the greatly disturbed condition of the country at that time, without law and without precedent, his position was fraught with great responsibilities. Many are the observations of historical interest that Mr. Price can make to a visitor, taking him back to 1840, and even earlier. Probably he is the oldest white settler of this county, and his life has been full of adventure and excitement. Cast upon the world to take care of himself when a boy, amongst a strange people and in a strange country, he has through his indomitable will-power and pluck reached a position of wealth and honor in his old age.

He was married in 1844 to Doña Andrea Carlon, a native of California, and they have had thirteen children, of whom twelve are now living. A splendid specimen of adobe work is seen in a portion of the family home at Pizmo. The walls are there two and a half feet in thickness, and as the family increased in number, rooms were added to the house. Mr. John M. Price is distinguished for his hospitality and devotion to the welfare of his family.

JAMES A. BLOOD, one of the successful ranchers of the Carpenteria Valley, resides in a handsome residence situated on a high elevation among the foot-hills, commanding a superb view of the valley, ocean and the islands in the distance. Mr. Blood was born in Boston, Massachusetts, in 1818. His father was a mechanic by trade, and a native of Salem. He moved to Rochester, New York, when the streets of that present beautiful city were filled with stumps and the town supported but one insignificant hotel. James A. remained at home until nineteen years of age, when he went to Illinois, and became engaged in the manufacture of plows. He was one of the first to make a scouring plow, and people would come a hundred miles to see it work. He did a large business for that country, and also carried on farming, owning a quarter section of land. He remained twelve years, and then sold out in 1850 and came to California.

He fitted up three wagons with plenty of supplies, and started on his long march, taking seven men who paid him for transportation. He was eighty-seven days en route, and men and animals all arrived in first-class condition, while others suffered severely from lack of supplies. He then went to the mines in Placer County, and after a short but successful experience he returned to the East, having made $3,000. He then engaged in the hardware business in Farmington, Illinois, and one year later sold out and returned to California. He again crossed the plains. This trip took six months, as he drove eighty head of cattle and suffered very little loss. He then settled at Marysville, Yuba County, where he began trading by running a pack train to the mines, and later engaged in the merchandise business with a Mr. Shannon, for two years. He then sold out, continuing his trading until 1858. In that year he went East with his brother, by water and the Eads ship canal route. They then purchased cattle on the border of Texas, and drove 1,250 head across the plains, up the Arkansas River to Pueblo, then to Denver, leaving the cattle to graze on the Humboldt River through the winter. In crossing they lost about 200 head, and later the Indians stampeded 500, thus making the transaction a losing investment. The subject of this sketch then went to the mines in the Indian Valley, where his first year's business amounted to $33,000. He was then "frozen out" by his partners, receiving only $25,000 for his one-third interest. He was in the valley about five years, as he also owned 1,000 acres of land in partnership with his brother. Mr. Blood also had mining interests in Summit City, Nevada County, where he invested $25,000 and lost every cent. In December, 1866, he made a pleasure trip to the East with his wife, going by the Isthmus of Panama, and returning to California in 1867. After returning to San Francisco, he began looking about for a place to settle, and came down the coast by steamer, landing at Santa Barbara. He purchased 117 acres in the Carpenteria Valley, all wild, rough land. After clearing the land he began the cultivation of nuts, corn and beans, and he has since added to his place, increasing it to 350 acres. In 1875 he rented the ranch and moved to Santa Barbara, where he carried on the grocery business under the firm name of Blood & Orr, for about six years, after which he returned to his ranch. In August, 1887, he sold his entire tract to a syndicate. He then re-purchased eight acres, where he has since built his large and beautiful residence.

Mr. Blood was married at Avon, Fulton County, Illinois, March 29, 1840, to Miss Cornelia L. Woods, and they have just celebrated the fiftieth anniversary of their wedding, a pleasure granted to but few in this world. Although they have not been blessed with children, their present happy relation is significant of the peace and harmony which have always existed.

ANUEL P. FREIRE was born in California in 1864, and is a son of Portuguese parents, his father and mother, now deceased, both being natives of the Azores Islands. Mr. Freire spent his early life in Watsonville, on a farm, and in 1874 moved to San Luis Obispo County, where he has since made his home. At first he leased a ranch in Los Osos Valley and engaged in the cattle business. A year later he leased for a term of years the ranch he now occupies, located on the Corral de Piedra. This property consists of 1,130 acres. Mr. Freire devotes his time solely to the dairy business, marketing the products in San Francisco with very excellent results. Mr. Freire is married, but has no children.

THOMAS B. HIGUERA was born in San Fernando, California, March 7, 1818, and died March 10, 1886. He came to the county of San Luis Obispo in 1855, and invested in property located in what is now the center of San Luis Obispo. A prominent street known as Higuera Street, named after him, adjoins this property. Most of this land has since been disposed of, and Mr. Higuera's widow and family who survive him now reside in a dwelling of their own on Marsh street. Mr. Higuera fought in the Mexican war and took an important part therein. For some years before his death he suffered greatly from rheumatism and was quite an invalid; and prior to this he was actively engaged in ranching and was very successful. In 1844 he was married to Bacilia Hernandez, by whom he had fifteen children, ten of whom are now living, one having died October 12, 1890.

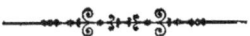

JOHN HENRY BARON von SCHRODER, proprietor of the magnificent Eagle ranch described at length at the close of this sketch, is a native of Germany, the eldest son and heir to the estates and titles of the Von Schröder family. At the age of eighteen years, namely in 1870, he entered the Prussian army and served through the Franco-Prussian war of 1870-'71, in a regiment of Hussars. In 1880 he retired from the army, and in 1882 received the decoration of the iron cross for twelve years of distinguished service. From the Hussars he was transferred to the Cuirassiers of the Guard, on which he served four years in Berlin and then changed to the Thirteenth Dragoons, of which regiment he is at present Premier Lieutenant d. R.

After leaving the army he traveled during the greater part of two years in the South Sea Islands. It was in January, 1881, that he arrived in San Francisco, and directly afterward, while on a hunting tour in San Luis Obispo County, he "fell in love" with the Eagle ranch. The original settlers on this property were the family of Francisco Siquero. In 1876 A. F. Benton came into possession of it, and in 1882 the entire property of 2,400 acres was surveyed and was purchased by Baron von Schröder. Large game are still plentiful on this ranch, many bear and deer having been killed in recent years.

The Baron married Miss Donahue, of San Francisco, and has two children.

THE EAGLE RANCHO,

eighteen miles from San Luis Obispo city, and six miles from Santa Margarita, is a work of large significance and even of great notoriety. A first thought on visiting the place is that it was a hearty lover of nature in her rugged fastnesses and her sweet solitudes who discovered and afterward appropriated this secluded domain, which has to a great extent been already redeemed from the wilderness. Making Santa Margarita station our starting point, and driving westward toward the Santa Lucia Mountains, we begin the easy ascent on a fine graded road up a little valley, crossing here and there a small brook of pure rattling water, and then winding in and out along the cañons under great live-oaks, at every turn catching views and gleams of scenery long to be remembered. In less than six miles the outer rim of hills has been surmounted and a gradual descent of half a mile brings to view the beautiful basin of sixty or eighty acres, where appear the buildings, orchard, vineyard and garden of the home part of the Eagle Rancho. On the east side of the basin are the great wooded hills we have just crossed on our way in, and on the west two dark, chapparal-covered mountains. Near the southern side of the base of the mountain are the ground and residence; and west of these, between the mountains, are the orchard, garden and vineyard. The residence of the Baron is on the crest of a handsome knoll containing about two acres and rising above the plain forty to fifty feet. The grounds are inclosed by a well-grown cypress hedge at the base of the knoll. Within this circle of cypress about eight or ten feet is a low stone-wall, above which on the bank is another hedge of cypress; while between the wall and the outer hedge is a fine graveled walk,—a charming promenade quite concealed by the cypress. The sloping grounds around the residence are laid out in unique style. On the southeastern and northeastern sides are miniature forests of thickly set cypress, forming an impenetrable mass of interlacing branches, impressing the mind with a sense of seclusion and distance as if in the heart of a forest. The residence faces the northwest. The foregrounds are laid out in rose-gardens, greensward, graveled walks and beds of flowers, at once graceful, simple and harmonious. In brief, the principal characteristic of the residence is its suggestiveness of tranquillity in retirement.

A wide veranda enveloped in clematis and climbing roses, finished with an ornamental roof, furnishes shade and shelter on the front and two sides of the house. Rooms, all on the ground floor, are numerous and ample. Rich and quiet furnishing renders the whole interior homelike and smilingly inviting, with the aid of piano, organ and harp.

In the rear of the residence and about a hundred yards distant, in the point of a rocky spur from the mountain base, is the grotto, cut into the solid rocks about twenty-four feet wide, twelve feet high and forty-eight feet deep, and opening toward the valley and the residence. It is smoothly floored and wainscotted a yard high, with wide shelving to receive vases of antique pottery and of flowers, with bright matting, lounging and easy chairs of cool rattan and other means of luxurious delectation. A grove of choice forest trees from two hemispheres occupies the little space between the grotto and the residence, while a fountain plays in front of the grotto at the entrance to the grove.

The water supply at the altitude of this ranch—some 1,500 feet above sea-level—was by no means sufficient for its many uses on the property; and it therefore became necessary to increase it largely and at the same have it pure. This was accomplished by piercing the mountain side near at hand by a tunnel at sufficient elevation to secure the desired pressure, only about 160 feet in depth being required to reach the water. The mouth of the tunnel was then walled up and the tunnel itself became an underground reservoir shut in from dust and sun.

The largest prune orchard in the world is on this ranch, in another basin three miles distant from the residence. It contains 200 acres of thrifty trees five years old, being one year old when planted there. The soil is a fine, rich slate loam, mellow as a garden bed newly made, and is kept in a high state of cultivation under the care and superintendence of Mr. Benton, the competent, courteous and faithful manager of all the business and work of the Eagle Rancho. Ten tons of dried prunes were grown on these young trees three years after planting, which took the first premium over all competitors at the Mechanics' Institute Fair for 1889, as the "best French prunes raised in the State of California." Substantial buildings, with accommodations for the ranch men, are located in this part of the premises, and are for the exclusive use of the men who are employed in the great prune orchard and on work adjacent.

Two and a half miles from the residence, on the headwaters of the Atascadero Creek, in a deep mountain gorge, are the picturesque and beautiful waterfalls which, with the great overhanging cliffs and gigantic leaning trees almost canopying the chasm, constitute one of the charms of the Eagle Rancho, and are made entirely acceptable by a delightful drive to the cañon and a romantic walk through a great thicket of wild lilac. This spot is particularly refreshing during the hot weather of summer. A fish-pond between the residence and prune orchard is an attractive feature of the place, and reveals ingenuity in its construction, location and general arrangement. The Baron proposes to stock this farm with choice fish.

One of the most expensive and delightful improvements on this property is the system of beautiful drives, lined with trees of different varieties, the noble redwood being conspicuous among them. They wind through romantic cañons, over ridges and through the valleys, revealing new views and scenery at every turn. One of these climbs the mountain in the rear of the residence quite to the summit, an elevation of 2,500 feet above the ocean level, with a wide, easy grade, over which the team trots much of the way. It is the intention of the Baron to plant the pine and redwood trees all over the great chapparal hills or small mountains, which constitute a large part of the estate; and in time he will thus transform these wastes of chapparal into noble forests, making them an admirable range for game and adding a new element of beauty to the landscape. The chief purpose of this grand drive to the mountain top, as well as most of the other work now visible at different points throughout this grand retreat, is utilitarian mainly in a spirital sense.

HENRY STORROW CARNES, of Santa Barbara, was born in Boston, Massachusetts, June 10, 1822, eldest son of Nathaniel Greene Carnes, who was a grandnephew of General Nathaniel Greene of Revolutionary fame. Captain Carnes' father, also a native of Boston, was a Captain in a Massachusetts regiment in the war of 1812, and passed the last twenty years of his life in France. At one time he was wealthy, but lost his fortune by the failure of the Bank of the United States in 1836. He made and lost two or three fortunes, and eventually lost all his property. Both the parents are now dead, and three of their sons and two daughters are living: George resides in San Francisco, Lewis is in London, England, and the two daughters in France. His grandfather was a Captain in Lee's Light Horse, and his great-grandfather was an Episcopalian minister and a chaplain in the American army during the Revolutionary War, and was in intimate correspondence with General Washington during the early period of the Revolution. His mother's family were Wainwrights, one of the early families of Boston, who came from England to this country about 1630 or 1650, and sympathized with the American cause. The progenitor of the Carnes family in America was Commodore John Cairnes, of North Britain, Scotland, who commanded the English fleet cruising on the American coast during the early years of the seventeenth century. He was one of the originators of "The Ancient and Honorable Artillery Company" of Boston, and its commander in 1649 and '52, as was also his great-grandson, Lieutenant-Colonel John Carnes, father of the chaplain before mentioned, in 1750. Mr. Carnes was but six months old when he was taken by his parents in their change of residence to New York city. At the age of eighteen he went to Paris, which city his father had previously visited, and studied languages and anatomy, under the instructions of Professors Bernard and Guy, and resided there six years. He learned to speak the French language very fluently, and is now a good Spanish scholar. Volunteering in the Mexican war, he saw much service, and came to California in the famous Stevenson's regiment. During the last war he was in the Provost Marshal's department, under Colonel Jackson; and was afterward several years in the Internal Revenue Department. He was Postmaster of Santa Barbara six years, most of the time under President Grant; after that he was not in business until recently, he became book-keeper and reporter for the Santa Barbara *Independent*. In 1851-'52 he was a member of the State Assembly; and District Judge for Santa Barbara, Ventura and San Luis Obispo counties, in the earlier years of the State, serving a part of the time by appointment; was also a member of the city council several years.

In 1850 Captain Carnes married Maria Domitila Rodriguez, a Spanish lady, whose father was José Jesus Rodriguez, and whose family came to California in the military train of one of the first Spanish Governors. Her parents are dead, but she has brothers and sisters living in this State. Mr. Carnes has nine children, all living in Santa Barbara and Ventura: John is a farmer; Lewis, the only married son, is in business; Frederick is Deputy Recorder of Ventura County, and Nathaniel is employed in clerical work. The daughters are Mary, who married Mr. Tico, a farmer; Mélanie, now the wife of Thomas Chrisman; Adelia, unmarried; Martha, now Mrs. Charles Bell, and Rosalie, the youngest of the family.

BORONDA, son of José Canuto and Francisca (Castro) de Boronda, was born in Santa Barbara in 1834. While he was yet an infant the family moved to Monterey County, where he remained twenty-eight years. His father owned a fine ranch at that place on which he was engaged in ranching. Mr. Boronda is one of a large family—thirteen children—of whom nine are still living. In 1871 he came to San Luis Obispo, and lived with his sister two years. Next he went to the mines, and seven months later came to the Santa Margarita Valley, where he lives to-day. His ranch comprises 160 acres, and is beautifully situated seven miles from the city of San Luis Obispo. As Mr. Boronda is a cordial, hearty, and in every way a popular man, his pleasant country home is always full of visitors. He was married in 1874 to Beatriz R. de Boronda. One child, Epifanio, is the result of this union. Mr. Boronda is a direct descendant of an old Castilian family in Spain, and he is justly proud of his ancestry.

HENRY W. OLD (deceased) was one of the most respected pioneers of the Santa Clara Valley, Ventura County, California. He was born in Corwin Parish,

Cornwall, England, October 5, 1834. May 4, 1845, his parents, both English people, set sail for America, bringing their family, and locating in Wisconsin. The subject of this sketch was reared and educated in that State. He spent six years of his life working in the Cliff copper mines in Wisconsin. He was after that variously employed in different places: in Illinois, then in Dodgeville, Wisconsin; in 1857 removed to Eagle River, Michigan; in 1862 went to Vermont to look after the development of a copper mine for a company, and was five months opening a mine.

While at Dodgeville, Wisconsin, on the 23d of November, 1850, Mr. Old was united in marriage to Miss Ketura Cox, a native of Plymouth, England. Before coming to this coast three children were born to them: Elizabeth A., Eliza J. and James J. With his wife and his little family he started for California, coming via the Isthmus route. He worked in the mines at Grass Valley, Nevada City, for seven years, being in the employ of a company. In 1869, with his family and his brother-in-law, Richard Cox, he came to Ventura County. Mr. Old purchased 320 acres of land in what was then a wilderness of wild mustard, where their present fine home is now located. There were no trees and no land marks, and here the family struggled along with adversity and worked with unremitting zeal, both Mr. and Mrs. Old being united in their efforts to make a comfortable home. In the course of years they succeeded admirably, their ranch being now one of the finest in the valley. They built a large and commodious house, large barns, and planted rows of Eucalyptus trees, a large orchard, plenty of small fruit, and an abundance of flowers and shrubs; and the skill and good taste combined in the planning and execution of this work have rendered it an attractive place. The ranch is supplied with plenty of artesian water. Mr. Old raised both grain and stock, while Mrs. Old took a just pride in her turkeys, ducks and chickens, which afforded both pleasure and profit. George W. and Edith were added to their family in California.

Late in the month of May, 1889, Mr. Old was taken ill. The disease in a few days terminated in heart trouble, which caused his death June 2. To his wife and children it was very unexpected, and they deeply mourn his loss. He was an industrious man, a faithful and loving husband and father, and he died with his trust in the Saviour. He is missed by a large circle of friends and acquaintances. Their loss is his infinite gain, and he has gone to forever enjoy the reward of a well-spent life. The home he made by toil and self-denial and left to his family, is his most fitting monument.

The oldest son, James, is married and resides on the place with his mother. He is an industrious young man of good health and character, and is a support and comfort to his widowed mother in this her time of bereavement.

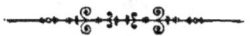

ALBERT F. BENTON, foreman and former owner of the Eagle ranch, now owned by Baron von Schröder, was born in Germany, in 1848. When he was six years old his parents moved to America, the family then consisting of four children. As soon as he was old enough he engaged in business with his brother who kept a wholesale grocery house in New York city. In 1866 he came to California, and for three years was employed in a wholesale liquor house in San Francisco. He then came to Paso Robles and bought a tract of 1,000 acres of land, five miles west of the town, and engaged in sheep-raising. He still owns and leases 640 acres of this property. It was in 1876 that he acquired possession of the Eagle ranch, and for six years was principally engaged in cattle-raising. At the end of that time he sold the property to its present owner, and is now the foreman.

Mr. Benton was married in 1869 to Miss Hannah Menton, of English ancestry, although born and brought up in the Santa Clara Valley, California. Mr. and Mrs. Benton are the parents of four children.

During Mr. Benton's ownership of the Eagle ranch, everything was in its wild state. Bears were very plenty and also extremely troublesome to the cattle-raiser. Mr. Benton describes very graphically the loss of much of his stock, and "bruin" is responsible in each case. So uncivilized was this part of the country at that time that Mrs. Benton's father strongly objected to his daughter making it her home, insisting that it was no place for women. She did not, however, seem at all distressed at the outlook, and the Eagle ranch has been her home since 1876. In early times this property must have been a favorite resort for Indians, as many relics of their curious implements have been found and preserved, among them a splendid and perfect specimen of a mortar and pestle, used by them for pounding acorns for bread, etc.

WALTER SCOTT CHAFFEE, a pioneer and one of the most prosperous business men of San Buenaventura, was born in Madison County, New York, February 2, 1834. His ancestors were from Massachusetts, but his father, E. H. Chaffee, was a native of Madison County, and was a farmer in the "town" (township) of Petersburg, where the celebrated Gerrit Smith was brought up; they were playmates together. During the great slavery excitement Messrs. Smith and Chaffee were "under-ground railroad" men, and many a one of God's poor they helped along the road to liberty. Mr. Chaffee's mother, whose maiden name was Celinda M. Stranahan, was a native of Cooperstown, New York. He was the third child in a family of seven children, and at the early age of fourteen years he began his mercantile career, being ten years a clerk in the city of Syracuse, New York. In 1858 he went to Portage City, Wisconsin, and opened a general merchandise store; but a year afterward he sold out and returned to his home in New York, where he remained a year. Then, in company with Jerome B. Chaffee, he went to Pike's Peak and bought two claims at Leadville, where he was a miner for one season. The following year, 1861, he came to San Buenaventura, when there were but three American settlers in what is now Ventura County. Two of them still reside here,—V. A. Simpson and W. D. Hobson. Mr. Chaffee started a ranch on T. Moore's grant and engaged in raising hogs. Six months afterward he sold his interest and opened a general merchandise store, and has ever since been in mercantile life excepting two years. When he began here there was but one other store in the place. He purchased his goods in San Francisco, and had them brought here by schooner. He has also been engaged meanwhile in general farming and stock-raising. He was one of the original incorporators of the Bank of Ventura, and is at present one of its directors. When the town was incorporated he was appointed by the Legislature a member of the first Board of Trustees. During the late war he kept the United States flag flying night and day upon a liberty pole in front of his store.

After several of the flags had been stolen, he guarded the next one with a shot-gun for several nights. It was the only flag south of San José that was placed at half-mast when the news of President Lincoln's assassination reached the coast. Although interested in the political welfare of the country, he has never accepted office.

He built his present brick store, 30 x 100 feet, on East Main and Palm streets, with a store-house in the rear, another 100 feet in depth. He has also built an elegant residence on a 100-acre ranch near town, and he has a 3,000-acre farm and stock ranch on the Santa Clara River, thirty four miles from Ventura, where he has several hundred head each of sheep, cattle and horses, and is constantly improving the stock. Parties are now sinking the fifth oil well on this land, the four already in operation yielding an average of twenty-five barrels per day each. Mr. Chaffee, notwithstanding the fact that he has seen forty years of active business life, appears like a man in the prime of life about forty-five years of age. He has truly seen a "wilderness blossom as the rose." From a little Spanish settlement the city of San Buenaventura has sprung up to a place of 3,000 inhabitants living in homes of beauty and refinement, with their numerous business blocks, metropolitan hotels, fine churches, model school buildings, etc. San Buenaventura has indeed been to him what the name implies,—"Good Luck."

For his wife, Mr. Chaffee married Miss Rebecca Nidever, a native of Texas, born in 1846, and of their nine children all are living save one. Walter Scott, Jr., was born in Santa Barbara, in his grandfather's house, and now has charge of his father's ranch. The following children were born in San Buenaventura: John Hyde, now teller of the Ventura Bank; Arthur Leslie, his father's bookkeeper; and Helen L., Ethel, Lawrence, Chester and Margareta, all of whom are at home with their parents. Mrs. Chaffee is a member of the Presbyterian Church, and Mr. Chaffee, although brought up a Presbyterian, has never joined any church. He is a Master Mason and a Knight Templar.

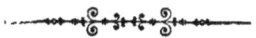

HENRY CHAPMAN FORD was born in 1828 at Livonia, New York. At an early age he chose the profession of an artist, and to perfect himself spent two or three years in Europe, studying at Paris and Florence.

Returning from there at about the beginning of our civil war, he in December, 1861, enlisted and served about a year in the army in the West and South, when he was discharged for physical disability caused by a series of forced marches in Tennessee, Alabama and Kentucky.

When in the army he furnished many sketches for the illustrated papers. While recuperating at Chicago he was induced to open a studio there and was the first landscape artist in that city who attempted to gain a livelihood by the brush.

Afterwards, when more attention was given to art and the Chicago Academy of Design was incorporated, Mr. Ford took an active part in its inauguration; was one of its charter members, and for several years its president. At that date he was best known as a painter of forest interiors, nearly his whole time being devoted to this class of landscapes. To obtain studies for these, his summer sketching excursions were extended to all the picturesque mountains of the Northern and Middle states, and to the savannas and cypress swamps of the South.

In 1866, before a railway had crossed the

plains, in company with his wife and two other artists, he visited the Rocky Mountains and spent some five months in camping and sketching in the parks of Colorado, much of the time beyond the reach of any mail. A few years later he visited the same region with a class of pupils. His studio was in the Academy, and when it was burned in the great fire of 1871, his accumulated studies of many years were destroyed.

His health failing in 1874, he was advised to seek a change of climate, and in accordance with this advice, he went, in 1875, to California, and soon after settled at Santa Barbara, finding the genial climate, picturesque surroundings, and agreeable society of that place, very attractive to himself and wife. California is the paradise of the landscape artist. Its long rainless seasons and mild climate enable him to ramble far and wide, undeterred by any apprehension of bad weather. These favorable conditions Mr. Ford did not fail to make use of; for almost every year since he came to Santa Barbara, camping excursions have been made by him until every valley and noted locality in Southern and Middle California has been visited.

In 1878 he organized a party composed of artists and of persons of scientific and literary tastes and made a long camping trip to the Yo Semite, where during the six weeks they spent in the valley he made many sketches of its remarkable scenery. But probably the most important work of Mr. Ford as an artist in California has been his labors to preserve, in a pictorial form, the remnants of the old Franciscan missions that are scattered along the coast from San Diego to San Francisco. The site of each of these was visited, and careful studies made of all that remained of them. A series of handsome etchings were made by him from these and printed; the imperial edition of which, being in attractive folios with brief historical and descriptive letter press, has found a place in many university and college libraries and art museums in America.

It is not as an artist only that Mr. Ford is known in Santa Barbara, but as an intelligent, well-informed gentleman of unusual scientific acquirements outside of his profession, as is evidenced by his having been for many years president of its Natural History Society, as well as one of the most active and efficient members of its Horticultural Society. As a botanist he has interested himself in the introduction and cultivation of foreign trees and shrubs; and as a citizen, has made himself generally useful in promoting all good works in Santa Barbara.

JOSEPH FANDREY, Santa Barbara. Among the progressive institutions of Santa Barbara will be found the art rooms of Mr. Joseph Fandrey, who was born at Berlin, Germany, in 1847. He was especially educated in decorative art work, and to perfect himself he studied drawing and painting in designs at the Vienna Academy and at Berlin. He has served as foreman in the leading furniture manufactories. He emigrated to the United States in 1882, and went to Chicago, where for two years he worked in manufactories. He then came to San Rafael, and was employed by Mr. Sayle in the furniture business. He came to Santa Barbara in 1885, and engaged with Mr. F. H. Knight as foreman of his decorating and upholstering establishment. Mr. Fandrey receives the latest designs from the leading decorators in Dresden, Vienna and Berlin. He is also an inventor in artistic furniture, the "Sultan Ottoman and Fandrey Chaise Lounge" being among the number, and are most convenient and comfortable. He received a medal in Vienna for artistic work, and in the Santa Barbara exhibition of home products in 1887 and 1889 he received silver medals for each year for his display of furniture. His show-rooms are at No. 8 East Ortega street, where he carries a fine line of easy chairs, sofas, etc., and upholstering materials.

DR. CEPHAS L. BARD, a pioneer of San Buenaventura, of 1868, deserves special mention in this work. Previous to the Revolution the progenitors of the family to which he belongs came to America and settled in Franklin County, Pennsylvania, when the colony was in its infancy. The men were men of character and ability, active in the affairs of the time. The Doctor's father, Robert M. Bard, was a native of Chambersburg, Pennsylvania, born in 1810, and for many years practiced law in that county, being at the head of the bar; was a man of talent, a prominent leader, and a candidate for Congress at time of his death. He married Elizabeth Little, a native of Mercersburg, same State, who was born in 1816, the daughter of Doctor P. W. Little. Their family consisted of two sons and two daughters, the Doctor being the third child. He completed his education in a classical course at Chambersburg Academy, and his medical education at the Jefferson Medical College of Philadelphia. His ancestors on the maternal side were nearly all physicians, and on the paternal side Drs. John and Samuel Bard were founders of the College of Physicians and Surgeons of New York. It is but natural therefore that the subject of this sketch should inherit a taste for this profession. He began his medical studies by entering the office of Dr. A. H. Senseny, a talented physician of Pennsylvania; and while he was pursuing his studies there, he enlisted as private in Company A, One Hundred and Twenty-sixth Pennsylvania Volunteer Infantry, participated in the battles of the Second Bull Run, Antietam, Fredericksburg and Chancellorsville. After his term of service had expired he attended lectures at the Jefferson Medical College; and later he passed a satisfactory examination before an army medical board, and was appointed assistant surgeon in the army. Going to the front with his regiment, the Two Hundred and Tenth Regiment, Pennsylvania Volunteers, he participated in all its successes and reverses, in the Army of the Potomac, until the close of the war. This regiment was a crack one, composed of remnants of several veteran regiments, and was commanded by Colonel William Sergeant, brother-in-law of General Meade, Commander of the Army of the Potomac, and its history shows that it ever was in the front when the battle raged most fiercely, and its casualties were enormous. Its greatest losses occurred at Hatcher's Run, Dabney's Mills, the fights before Petersburg, Gravelly Run and Five Forks. One flag of truce sent in by Lee at Appomattox passed through a portion of this regiment deployed as skirmishers. By an official order one assistant surgeon was always with his regiment in order to give instant aid, and Bard was ever with his command, and on several occasions, when meeting with reverses, he remained behind exposed to the volleys of his friends as well as those of his foes

Returning home he continued his practice until 1868, when he came to Ventura County, California, where for twenty-two years, with exception of two years devoted to study in Eastern cities, he has been identified with all the interests of the place of his adoption. He was the first American physician with a diploma to locate in this county. By devotion to his calling and ambition for excellence he has justly attained an enviable reputation.

His professional character has been shaped by his army experience and residence in a frontier country. Debarred association with the professional brethren and remote from surgical supplies, he is bold, self-reliant and full of expedients. An accomplished rider and well versed in the language and ways of the native Californians, he seems to be " to the manner born." A description of his long rides; his varied adventures in mountains and swollen streams; his contact with characters not met with now, and his reminiscences of men and things, would make a most interesting book. He has not allowed himself to become an old fogy, but by close study, and by attendance at the Eastern medical schools, he has kept fully abreast of the times. He is at present a member of the Board of Pension Examiners, President of the County Medical Society and Surgeon to the County Hospital.

He is a member of the Military Order of the Loyal Legion, Grand Army of the Republic, and Knights Templar, and is a Republican in his political sympathies and a Presbyterian in his religious opinions. His residence is one that in all its features and appointments exhibits refinement and taste.

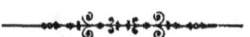

P. E. KELLOGG, deceased.—The community of Goleta parted with one of its best and most substantial citizens in the death of P. E. Kellogg, which occurred June 28, 1884. He was a native of Jo Daviess County, Illinois, born November 23, 1841. He was reared an agriculturist, and came West with his father, F. E. Kellogg, and located in Napa County, in 1846. He was twice married. After the death of his first wife, Hester Spires, he married Miss Sarah Montgomery, in 1868. He was the father of eleven children, and six are now living. He came to Goleta, Santa Barbara County, in 1875. Mr. Kellogg was a prominent and influential man in his locality, a devout member of the Methodist Episcopal Church, and a strong temperance advocate. Mrs. Kellogg lives on the homestead, a beautiful farm of seventy acres.

LEON LEVY, liquor dealer, Santa Barbara, was born at Metz, France, January 7, 1860. He came to the United States in 1870 with his parents, who landed in New York, but immediately started westward and established themselves in Santa Barbara, which was then a small settlement of Mexicans, native Californians and a few Americans. Being unable to speak English, Leon attended Santa Barbara College to learn the language, and then attended the public schools. He went to the northern part of the State and passed five years as clerk; then, returning to Santa Barbara in 1885, he opened a wholesale and retail liquor store on State street, where he keeps both imported and domestic wines, liquors and cigars, making a specialty of California wines and controlling the agencies of very fine liquors.

Being unmarried he resides with his mother.

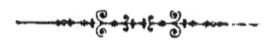

DAVID F. NEWSOM is a native of Petersburg, Virginia, born September 5, 1832. He attended school at his home, pursuing his studies at Wake Forest College for one year. At this time, his father failing in business, David went to New York and learned the brass furnishers' trade. While there he attended a free school at night, being anxious to perfect himself in his studies. So desirous was he to accomplish this that he worked ten hours for his employer during the day, and was ready to study when night came. After being in the city two years he returned to Petersburg, where he clerked in a store for two years and a half. At the age of twenty-one he came to California and to San Luis Obispo County, taking his first meal in San Luis Obispo October 28, 1853. This meal Mr. Newsom remembers well. The restaurant, so called, was adjacent to the old Mission, and was patronized on that occasion by a curious mixture of races, no less than seventeen nationalities being represented. This illustrates very forcibly the cosmopolitan character of the settlement in the city then. Mr. Newsom was County Clerk two terms, 1853 to 1857, the first term by appointment and the second by election. In 1854 he was instrumental in organizing the first public school of the county. School sessions were then held in the Mission building. He was superintendent of the school and conducted it for three years, having entire charge of arrangements. Mr. Newsom resigned his position as County Clerk before his term of office expired, and went to Oregon and Washington Territory on a prospecting tour, seeking for good business opportunities. In April, 1858, he opened a store in Bellingham Bay, Washington Territory, the first store in the history of the town. Here he met with great success, clearing $30,000 in eight weeks, which included the profits of real-estate transactions in connection with his regular business. In December, 1858, Mr. Newsom went to the town of Fort Hope, on the Fraser River in British Columbia, and there remained until June, 1859. About this time he was injured and was advised to return to California, but owing to subsequent events he did not follow this advice. He arrived at San Juan just at the time of Captain Pickett's arrival with his troops to prevent the arrest of certain individuals by the English. In the meantime three large English men of war were anchored in the bay, and, hearing that Captain Pickett had trespassed on Her Majesty's domains, the officers in charge issued orders for his immediate arrest. Captain Pickett received the officer bearing the order for arrest, with civility, and told him to tell his superiors that he would fight as long as he had a man left, and that he was waiting for them. A detachment of 500 soldiers was ordered to assist Captain Pickett, and when General Scott arrived he was allowed to depart in peace. Mr. Newsom had, in the meantime, organized a company of sharpshooters, which formed a part of the command under Captain Pickett. Arrangements were subsequently made for the joint occupation of the island, and two magistrates were chosen to represent the different factions. Mr. Newsom had the honor of being chosen the American magistrate, and Major DeCoursey the English. This excitement quickly subsided, and Mr. Newsom looked with longing toward his old home and first love—San Luis Obispo. He returned here in 1862, and that same year he was elected Justice of the Peace. Since then he has held several offices of responsibility and trust. Always taking an active interest in educational matters, Mr. Newsom has done much toward improving the system of study in the schools of the county and in the district where he has resided. He opened the district school in Arroyo Grande in 1864; and was District Clerk of that district for eight years,—1864–'72. The Newsom School District was organized in 1885.

In 1863 Mr. Newsom was married to Miss Anna Branch, daughter of F. Z. Branch, the well-known pioneer, and has a family of twelve children. In 1864 he came with his wife to their present ranch, near Arroyo Grande,—a fine estate of 1,200 acres, formerly in the Branch tract. Since their occupancy Mr. Newsom has been engaged in stock-raising, and during the past few years has established a very desirable health resort on the property. The place is naturally well adapted for such an institution, being well located and conveniently situated within two miles of Arroyo Grande. Valuable hot springs have been located on the premises, and adjacent to these Mr. Newsom has built his sanitarium. The bath houses are well equipped, and the institution throughout indicates a painstaking care on the part of its proprietor, which is worthy of great praise.

ELI RUNDELL, one of the early pioneers to California, was born in Cayuga County, New York, December 14, 1828. He was reared on the farm and received only the common-school education of that period. At the age of eighteen he was thrilled with the western fever, and though then living in Illinois he wished to push farther West, and a party then being formed for California he joined them to go across the plains. The company numbered about seventy-five, with thirteen wagons, crossed the Missouri at St. Joe, May 8, 1846. After a pleasant trip of about five months, they entered California, and arrived at Johnson's ranch, forty miles north of the present site of Sacramento, where they went into camp. Then they went to Santa Clara, with the families of those who enlisted with Colonel Fremont. After three months' service in a local company at Santa Clara, under Colonel Fremont, Mr. Rundell went to Stockton with Dr. Q. C. Isbel, and was there engaged in house building. In 1848 he joined the Stockton Mining Company and went to the mines. He was there engaged in placer mining and in clerking about one year. In 1850 he returned to San José and began making saddle trees, and in 1853 went to Gilroy, Santa Clara County, where he opened a harness shop, learned the trade and remained ten years. In 1863 he went to Silver Mountain, on Carson River, prospecting, but the result was disastrous. In 1866 he came to Santa Barbara in the employ of the Coast Line Stage Company, as agent and harness-maker: remained in their employ about twenty years. In 1883 he opened a harness shop on State street, and in 1888 built his present shop at 21 East Haley and moved his establishment. He keeps a fine stock of light and heavy harness, saddles, bridles and all effects pertaining to the stable.

Mr. Rundell was married in Santa Barbara, in 1871, to Miss Kate Magee, a native of Boston, Massachusetts. They have four children, three of whom survive and live at home.

Mr. Rundell was elected to the Town Council in 1870, and was five times re-elected. He was served five and one-half terms in the City Council. He is a member of the Odd Fellows lodge, No. 256; of the Masonic, Santa Barbara, No. 192; Order of the Eastern Star, No. 78; and Royal Arch Masons, Chapter No. 51.

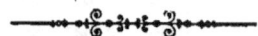

CHARLES SEDGWICK, one of the California pioneers, was born in Columbia County, New York, in 1829. At the age of fourteen years he began his business life, by accepting a position in a grocery store as clerk, and assisting in buying grain, at Hudson, New York, and continued there until he started for California. Accompanied by his father, on February 6, 1849, he started for this State, on board the ship Robert Bowne, commanded by Captain F. G. Cameron, going around the Horn. The ship carried 207 passengers, and stopped at Rio Janeiro and Callao, and after a slow but safe trip of seven months they landed at San Francisco. They then went to the mines on the Stanislaus River, and worked in placer mining, but on account of the illness of his father they returned to Stockton, where they opened a market and began butchering, which they continued very successfully until 1880. Mr. Sedgwick then ran a river express to San Francisco, and in 1882 came to Santa Maria and opened a market, which he has since followed. Mr. Sedgwick, with two children, have each located 160 acres adjoining, in Chimney Flat Cañon, north of Suey Rancho, which they are stocking with horses and cattle.

He was married at Stockton, San Joaquin County, on June 10, 1858, to Miss Mary A. Clements, a daughter of J. E. Clements, who was born in Hampden County, Massachusetts, in 1811. He emigrated to California across the plains in 1849, coming through Mexico. They had a very hard trip and lost nearly all their stock and wagons, and several of the party died from cholera. He followed mining about three years, and then ranching in San Joaquin Valley. In 1854 he returned East, overland, and brought out some very fine mares, and for thirty-five years he was engaged in stock-raising and farming. He raised the William H. Seward, the celebrated ten-mile trotting horse. In 1880, after eighteen years of litigation, he lost his ranch through the location of boundary lines, and has since lived with his daughter at Santa Maria. Though seventy-nine years of age Mr. Clements is still active and vigorous.

Mr. and Mrs. Sedgwick have three children living: the two eldest are married and one lives at home, and they have three buried in Stockton. He is a member of Centennial Lodge, No. 38, K. of P., and of the A. O. U. W., at Stockton, San Joaquin County, California.

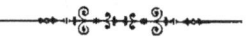

R. J. BROUGHTON, Sheriff of Santa Barbara County, was born in County Galway, Ireland, September 19, 1847. He came to Santa Barbara in the month of May, 1867. He had followed a seafaring life from the time he was a boy of thirteen years. His father, Coleman R. Broughton, was a sea captain, as were all of his father's brothers. After young Broughton landed in Santa Barbara he went upon a ranch in the Santa Ynez Valley, and later engaged in merchandising in Las Cruces. He was elected Sheriff of Santa Barbara County, in the fall of 1882, and still holds that important office. He has proven one of the most efficient and popular officers this county has ever had.

W. C. SHOW, one of the most enterprising men of Santa Barbara, was born and brought up in California, and has been in Santa Barbara twenty-two years, and in business there five years, carrying a general line of groceries, crockery, glassware, hay, grain and feed. His parents, Major Daniel and Eliza J. (Harvey) Show, were natives of Virginia, and had only two children, namely, the subject of this sketch and Ella, who married W. L. Hunt; the latter is in business with Mr. Show. Daniel Show was a farmer by occupation, a grain-raiser principally; came to the Pacific coast in 1850, locating in Washington Territory, and shortly afterward he went to Petaluma, Sonoma County, California. He died at Santa Barbara in October, 1874. Mr. Show's mother is still living, in Santa Barbara, on Gutierrez or Railroad street. Mr. Show is a strict business man, taking no part in politics, and is an exemplary citizen.

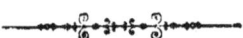

J. S. COLLINS.—In passing along the Main street of San Buenaventura, in the centre of the business portion, the eye of the observer is attracted by one of the most substantial and imposing blocks in the city. That is the banking house of William Collins & Sons. A little further up the street another fine building starts up promptly among the rest: that is the Masonic Block, built by the same firm. Mr. J. S Collins is the manager and cashier of the bank, and is a reserved, considerate but pleasing business man, of excellent business habits and large executive ability. He was born in Perthshire, Scotland, May 21, 1847, of Scotch parentage, who came to the United States, settling in Illinois upon land which they owned and cultivated until 1864, when they came overland to California and settled in Oakland. In 1869 they purchased a tract in Ventura County and were here four years In 1874 Mr. J. S. Collins graduated at the State University near Oakland and came to San Buenaventura, engaging in the lumber business as a member of the firm of Saxby & Collins. In 1885 Mr. Saxby died and Mr. Collins went into the Bank of Ventura, where he was a stockholder, to learn the business of banking, and for a year and a half occupied the position of teller and director. Having the capital, and seeing an opening for another bank, the Bank of William Collins & Sons was established, with a paid-up capital of $100,000 all owned by themselves: William Collins, President; D. E. Collins, Vice-President and J. S. Collins, Cashier. From the very start the business was large, and now they do the largest banking business in the county. Their farm they sold for $100,000. The subject of this sketch is highly spoken of by his fellow-citizens as a liberal gentleman. When asked for money, for town or church improvements, he shows his interest to the city by the way in which he " puts his hands into his pocket." Scotland has furnished many a scion to be grafted upon the United States tree, and it is a vigorous growth in the California climate; nor is it a bad tree for the country. Mr. Collins is also a Master Mason, belonging to both the chapter and commandery. He is President of the Board of Trustees of the city, is a deacon and the treasurer of the Presbyterian Church of San Buneaventura, being a faithful and efficient worker for the upbuilding of Christianity.

He was married in 1877 to Miss Belle Gerry, daughter of Waite Gerry, and a native of the State of New York. They have one daughter, named Bella Walker, and born in Oakland, this State. Mrs. Collins is also a member of the Presbyterian Church.

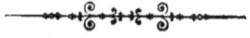

GEORGE PARRISH TEBBETTS was born in Gilmanton, New Hampshire, October 26, 1827. His father, Dr. Nathan C. Tebbetts, was a well-known physician of the same place, and also a native of New Hampshire. His mother was the niece of Hon. William Badger, a former Governor of the State.

The subject of this sketch was educated at Gilmanton Academy, and afterward studied medicine with Dr. Nahum Wight, a noted physician of Gilmanton, intending to adopt his father's profession. But in 1849 the California gold fever was at its height. Mr. Tebbetts, with many other young and adventurous spirits of staid New England, caught the infection. Breaking off his medical studies at the end of the second year's course, he set sail from Boston harbor on March 1, 1849, on board the schooner Edwin. After a stormy voyage of eight days and a half they reached Chagres, and found the Isthmus alive with pilgrims on their way to El Dorado. Means of transportation were limited—the accommodations for those in transit notoriously insufficient. The Edwin's passengers were forced to remain in Panama until May 18, when the steamer Panama, which had rounded the Horn, put into port for coal and passengers. Mr. Tebbetts, with one of his *compagnons de voyage*, managed to secure a passage. The Panama made the Golden Gate on June 4, 1849.

From San Francisco Mr. Tebbetts first went to the mining regions on the middle fork of the American River. He delved for gold with varying success, but in a few months returned to San Francisco, and on November 10 sailed for San Diego, on the brig Fremont. In San Diego he opened a store of general merchandise. In 1851 he was elected a member of the City Council and President of the Board. For several months he acted as Mayor of San Diego. In October, 1851, he was elected delegate to the convention called at Santa Barbara to arrange for the division of the State of California. This convention took the first steps toward the division of the State. Its work has not yet been completed. In this same year, 1851, there was an Indian outbreak which caused much alarm. San Diego was declared under martial law. The tribes in revolt were the Yumas, Agua Calientes and Tulares. Mr. Tebbetts was chosen as a lietenant of a company of cavalry, and was one of the thirty-one who volunteered to go to the mountains in search of the Indians, who were reported to be well armed and 1,500 strong. Major Fitzgerald, the commandante, had called for volunteers. These thirty-one responded. They marched away to the mountains, eighty or ninety miles distant, met and routed the enemy, capturing a renegade American called Bill Marshall, and a Mexican adherent. Antonio, the chief of the revolted tribes, was taken by the United States troops, who followed closely after the volunteer corps. Antonio was treated to a court martial, and shot in San Diego. The other prisoners were hung, when the troops returned, after two months of actual service.

Mr. Tebbetts was married in 1854. Of that marriage but two daughters now survive. The eldest, Frances Stella, is the wife of J. Ben Burton, only son of the late Don Luis Burton. The youngest, Mary Virginia Del Reyes, is the wife of Frank C. Prescott, of Los Angeles.

Mr. Tebbetts was married for the second time to Miss Mary Jones, of Herefordshire, England, in February, 1887, by whom he has two children, Nathan Anthony and Marjorie Elizabeth. He removed to Santa Barbara in 1865.

While in San Diego, Lieutenant Derby, the celebrated "John Phœnix," was often a guest at Mr. Tebbetts' residence, and wrote there some of his most amusing articles. These papers have been carefully preserved, as well as many others relating to the early history of California. Indeed, he had, perhaps, the most valuable collection of papers and documents to be found in

Southern California. He has always taken a deep interest in politics, but has never sought office from any party. In 1853 President Pierce offered him the consulship at Acapulco, which he respectfully declined. In 1883, having had previously some experience in journalism as business manager of the *Press*, Mr. Tebbetts concluded to start a daily newspaper, the present *Daily Independent*, of Santa Barbara, on a wholly independent and non-partisan basis. It has been successful in the highest degree. He is one of the executive committee of the Southern California Editorial Association, a member of the Society of California Pioneers, secretary of the Association of Pioneers of Santa Barbara County, and has recently been elected a Director of the World's Fair at Chicago, in 1893.

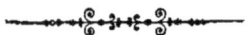

WILLIAM A. STREETER, one of the oldest and most honored citizens of Santa Barbara, was born in Great Sodus, New York, July 30, 1811. When he was three months old his father, Nathaniel Streeter, died, and some two months afterward his mother and family moved to Auburn, in that State, where he lived until he reached the age of twenty-eight years. Being naturally a mechanic, he at one time contrived to build a steam engine. He became skilled in general mechanics in Auburn. On account of failing health he went to Peru, South America, in the spring of 1842, and a year afterward he came to California, landing in Monterey, May 10, 1843, spending about a year in the vicinity of San Francisco. Finding that the climate there did not agree with him he came down to Santa Barbara with the expectation of returning to Peru, but as the only opportunity of passage was on a whaling ship, and as he liked the climate here, he concluded to remain. He practiced medicine for four years here and never lost a patient, although he had an extensive patronage among the ranchers in the surrounding country. During that time El Capitan de la Guerra was his best friend. The kindness of the old man was beyond expression. If Mr. Streeter did not reach his house every morning by nine o'clock the Captain would send one of his sons to inquire whether he was sick or what the occasion was of his absence, and on his arrival the first question every morning was: "Who is sick; does he need anything?" On being informed of his necessities he would hand Mr. Streeter the key to the store-room, authorizing him to take to the needy person whatever he thought necessary, and many times he would hand him one, two or three dollars, and in some cases as much as twenty dollars for the needy and on being asked who Mr. Streeter should say had sent it, his reply always was, "A friend." He always refused to send his name along with the donation.

As other physicians came in Mr. Streeter returned to his favorite mechanical pursuits. In 1849 he was in Stockton engaged in merchandising, in partnership; next he was in Ventura, in various pursuits, for a year; for nine years he was agent for steamers before a wharf was built and when all the passengers were landed in surf boats. In 1873–'74 he began to make inside decorations his principal business, including graining, painting, upholstering, etc. Since 1844 he has been a constant resident of Santa Barbara, although business called him away most of the time between 1849 and 1855. Since 1874 he has made general repairing a specialty.

Under Lincoln's administration he was Inspector of Customs three years; was also Justice of the Peace of the town (before it was a city) about three years; Under Sheriff in 1861–'62, and he has held other local offices. His office of Under-Sheriff he resigned in favor of his wife's brother-in-law, George Stone, who had just arrived.

Mr. Streeter was first married in 1832, in Auburn, New York, to Miss Hannah Day, who afterward died in Saratoga, leaving two children, two of her children having died. For his present wife Mr. Streeter married Josefa Petra Valdez, daughter of Ramon Valdez, and a native of Santa Barbara. Her mother is of the Ortega family. In this family are now five sons and three daughters. One son, who is married, is now employed in Hunt & Hosmer's grocery in Santa Barbara; another son, unmarried, is engaged in Maguire's dry-goods house; the eldest daughter is married to Charles Freeman, the son of Dr. Freeman; the second daughter is now Mrs. William B. Hosmer, who is in the grocery business here; the youngest daughter is attending business college in that city; the youngest son is now on the Island of Santa Catalina with his brother-in-law. The eldest son, a bricklayer by trade and an excellent workman, has for the last seven or eight years been in Mexico or Arizona. The second son is married, lives in Oakland, a printer by trade, and works in the office of the San Francisco *Chronicle*.

W. H. REILLY, a native son of the Golden West, and the youngest Sheriff in the State, was born in Yuba County, California, June 15, 1861. His father, M. J. Reilly, a native of New York, came to California in 1849. His mother, whose maiden name was E. J. Linn, is a native of Illinois. M. J. Reilly, after a residence here of only two years, died, in 1876, in San Buenaventura. W. H. Reilly, the subject of this notice, was the eldest of the children, was educated in the public schools of San Francisco and Ventura, completing a course in a business college. April 10, 1889, he married Miss Mae Beck, a daughter of Hon. Thomas Beck, who was Secretary of State of California. In November, 1888, Mr. Reilly was elected Sheriff of Ventura County, on the Republican ticket, by a majority of 352, which was far ahead of his ticket. Not long after he assumed the office to which he had been elected a circumstance occurred which demonstrated that the county did not make a mistake in his election. At noon, on April 23, 1889, the desperado James McCarthy entered the bank of William Collins & Sons, and, leveling his pistol at the clerk, ordered him to hand out the money. The clerk instantly dropped below the counter and ran out the back way. The robber seized what money he could get quickly, amounting to $4,000, and was making his escape when he had a horse to mount. Mr. Reilly heard the alarm, thought it was a fight, rushed into the street and saw the robber, who turned when the sheriff was within ten feet of him and snapped a forty-four caliber Colt's revolver at him. Unfortunately, the sheriff was unarmed, but had the presence of mind to rush into a hardware store, seize a shot-gun and load it, and succeeded in overhauling McCarthy, made him surrender, took his money from him and safely landed him in jail, where he was safely kept until he was tried and sentenced to State's prison for eight years. That was indeed an act of courage and promptness worthy of any officer, no matter how skillful. The sheriff of a California county is also tax collector. The total taxes collected by Mr. Reilly in 1889 were about $159,000. He is a man of character and marked ability, and is destined to be successful in his undertakings.

Mr. Reilly belongs to the I. O. O. F., K. of P., A. L. of H., and N. S. G. W., of the last of which he was one of the organizers and a charter member.

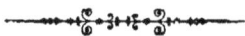

FERDINANDO CHIESA was born in Parma, Italy, June 16, 1855. He received a good education, attending an excellent school for six years. At the age of twenty he enlisted in the military service and for four years stood ready for the call to arms. In 1879 he came to America and at once located in the city of San Luis Obispo, a resident of which he has been ever since. Mr. Chiesa at once identified himself with the business interests of San Luis Obispo. He first entered the store of G. R. Maggi, one of his countrymen, and clerked in that establishment for two years. He next worked on a ranch six months. Returning to the city, he went into the store of J. Dughi, as clerk; shortly afterward, in 1885, a co-partnership was formed with Mr. Dughi, and up to the present time Mr. Chiesa has controlled a half interest in the business.

Mr. Chiesa was married April 5, 1885, to Maggie Angellini. To them have been born four children, two of whom are now living. He is a member of the A. O. U. W. and also of the Italian Society, being second vice-president in the latter organization.

DAVID SMITH MILLER was born in Indiana, September 19, 1832. When eighteen years of age he came to the Western States to make his home. His first venture was in Oregon in the fall of 1850. In this locality he engaged in ranching and remained there until 1852, when he went to Santa Cruz, remaining there for six years. In 1858 he came to San Luis Obispo and has been variously occupied during his life in this county. He ran the coast line stage between San Luis Obispo and Cambria from 1868 to 1874; was Deputy Sheriff of the county for six years and a Deputy Assessor for one term. Of late years Mr. Miller has been engaged in the wood business, cutting and supplying large quantities of it for the market. His ranch adjoins the famous Santa Margarita ranch, and is excellent woodland property. Mr. Miller has been twice married and has a family of three children.

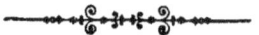

CAPTAIN WILLIAM S. MARIS, one of the early pioneers to California in 1850 (the subject of this sketch), was born at New Hope, Pennsylvania, in 1822. His father was a large manufacturer of cotton and woolen yarns. In 1830 they moved to the island of Madeira, and for nine years carried on the wine business in buying and shipping to foreign ports. They then returned to the United States and settled in Philadelphia, and in 1844 William S. Maris began his sea life by going to Madeira as supercargo, on board the bark Pauns of Philadelphia, Captain John Graham, to attend to the sale of the cargo of corn, lumber, and flour, then with the bark in ballast they sailed to Gibralter on the Mediterranean Sea, returning with a cargo of corn to Madeira. The vessel then went to Rio Janeiro, South America, with 130 emigrants, and our subject then returned to Philadelphia. He went to New York and purchased for Captain Graham the United States Government brig Lawrence, which was carefully refitted for merchant service and name changed to Don Juan. He then sailed out with the brig to South America, and after two years of service and study he became master, and took charge of the vessel. He then took a cargo of general merchandise to the river Congo on the west coast of Africa, and returned in ballast to Rio Janeiro. He also made a trip to the east coast around the Cape of Good Hope. In 1850 the brig Olindo, from Bangor, Maine, was condemned at Rio Janeiro, and the cargo of general merchandise, house frames and lumber was reshipped in the schooner Mary Pheby, W. S. Maris master, and he came to California. Selling his vessel at San Francisco he bought a one-third interest in the brig John Andrews, and started on a trading expedition down the coast, but stopping at Santa Barbara sold his interest and there remained. He has since resided in the county, mainly in this city. He was a clerk for Wells, Fargo & Co. many years, and has also been interested in the grocery business. He was first elected city tax collector, in April, 1882, and was re-elected in 1884–'86, 1888 and 1890.

Captain Maris was married in Santa Barbara, in June, 1855, to Miss Dolores Chapman, a native of California. They have five children: Isabelle, Anita, Sarah, William and Josephine, all living in Santa Barbara.

W. F. JOHNSTON, a prominent rancher and stock-raiser of Santa Maria, was born near Jefferson City, Missouri, April 4, 1836. His father, George K. Johnston, was a native of Virginia, and emigrated in boyhood to Kentucky. At the age of twenty-one years he was married at Monticello to Miss Nancy Jane Upton, and soon after their marriage they removed to Missouri. The subject of this sketch lived at home until manhood, acquiring meantime a common-school and academic education, and four years thereafter he spent in teaching district schools. In the winter of 1859, becoming imbued with the spirit of gold-mining, the excitement then existing in the Pike's Peak region, about the 30th of March he started for the mines, and arrived at the mouth of Cherry Creek, near where the city of Denver now stands. After prospecting unsuccessfully for three weeks, he decided to go on to California, and with a friend he struck out over the Cheyenne trail for Salt Lake City, thence on to the head of the Humboldt River, across the Humboldt desert to Carson River, and across the Sierras to Hangtown and Sacramento, arriving September 13. After spending a few months in Yolo County, he taught school one term in Sonoma County, near Mark West Creek. He then went to the Washoe mines in Nevada, where, with many hardships and privations in its mountain mining towns, he lived for about twelve years, but, never forgetting the beautiful Santa Rosa Valley, and one of its more beautiful inhabitants, in October, 1865, he returned there and was married to Miss Mary M. McCorkle, then a teacher in one of its schools. In the fall of 1872 he left Nevada and came to Guadaloupe, and since that time has been extensively engaged in grain-farming and stock-raising in the Santa Maria and Santa Ynez valleys, with varied success. Mr. Johnston has worked long and hard to make improvements in the valley, and his beautiful ranch of 900 acres near Lake View depot, with its thirty-acre orchard and other substantial improvements, is an ornament to the locality. He has also an eighty-acre tract near town, and some town property. He owns the Aliso Rancho of 9,000 acres on the Santa Maria River, where he has 300 head of cattle and 225 horses, and where he breeds both trotting and work horses. He owns the stallions Ben Wade and Sultan, the latter a Norman horse weighing 1,600 pounds. Mr. Johnston has for many years farmed from 1,000 to 2,000 acres. He has never been an aspirant to office. They have five children living, four sons and one daughter.

M. D. BARNARD, one of the best known pioneers of Ventura, was born in Calais, Maine, December 12, 1830. His father, W. K. Barnard, was a native of Massachusetts, and their ancestors were from England. His mother, whose name before marriage was Nancy Denny, was born in Worcester, Massachusetts. Her ancestors came to that State during its early settlement. Her father, Daniel Denny, was one of the posterity of John Denny, of Suffolk, England, who lived there in 1439. A picture of the old English home of 450 years ago is still preserved in the family, and there is also in their possession a complete genealogy of the family from 1439 to the present time. Branches of this family have established themselves in all the States of the Union. In Mr. Barnard's father's family were six children, all sons, he being the eldest. He was brought up and educated in Maine, Vermont and Massachusetts, completing his education in New Hampshire. He began business for himself as a merchant. In 1852 he came to Oregon and was engaged in general merchandising in Corvallis until 1859; he traveled for two or three years, and in 1868 came to Ventura, when that town was just starting, the American residents there being Messrs. Chaffee, Leach, Ayers, Grimes, Simpson and the Hobsons. Mr. Barnard engaged in the lumber business, and soon purchased a home place of thirty acres about a mile up the avenue; and he has also been engaged in real estate. His home place now comprises 125 acres, beautifully cultivated, and artistically arranged with ornamental trees, hedges, etc. He has 3,000 walnut trees just commencing to bear fruit; has twenty three kinds of fruit altogether. He has also two or three other farms in the valley. He has been a very busy man, accomplishing much in the improvement of his ranches and of the locality generally. Such industry and such faith in the country has had its ample return. Mr. Barnard has never joined any society, is not a politician, but is a Republican. His parents are Unitarians.

In 1861 he married Miss Sarah E. Lehman, a native of Wayne County, Ohio, and of Pennsylvania Dutch ancestry. They have six sons and one daughter, all natives of the Golden West: Frank E., Edwin L., Austin D., Charles V., John C. and Mary E., all at home with their parents.

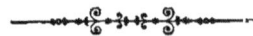

MARVIN STEWARD, a prominent citizen of Ventura, was born near Pittsburg, Pennsylvania, December 29, 1828. His father, Marion Steward, was a native of the State of Connecticut, and was of Scotch ancestry. Mr. Steward's mother, Sarah A. (Dart) Steward, was of English parentage. They had a family of twelve children, and most of them are now living. His father removed to New York, and from there to Ohio, where he received his education in the public schools. He engaged in the business of milling and distilling until 1850, when he removed to Quincy, Illinois, and engaged in business there for six years. In 1856 he removed to Hannibal, Missouri, and engaged in the flouring-mill business; he then went opposite Hannibal, and built a mill and distillery, and during the year 1863 his revenue tax was $18,000, the tax being twenty cents per gallon. He came to Marysville, California, and engaged in farming and stock-raising, and also bought the Oregon House and ranch, and continued in business there until 1868, when he sold out and went back to the Atlantic States, and also to Texas. After remaining away five months he returned and bought the Oregon House and ranch back, and after two years sold it, and went to Bangor, Butte County and engaged in mercantile business and stock-raising. He also bought a ranch on the Honcut, Yuba County, and in 1875 came to Ventura. He first settled near Santa Paula, buying 150 acres of land and improving it, and also building a nice house. He bought the property for $36 per acre; and sold it for $100 per acre; it has since been sold for $200 an acre. After selling his land Mr. Steward came to Sonoma County and engaged in the mercantile business, and in a year and a half sold out and returned to Ventura, engaging in farming and fruit-raising near Santa Paula. This property he traded for land in Ventura, and now resides in a two-story residence of his own building on Ventura avenue; he retains the town property in Ventura, which he rents. He spent one year in Grass Valley for his health, and while there built a nice house. He has been only two years in his home on Ventura avenue, but the place is a fine one, with a nice hedge, beautiful flowers and ornamental trees and shrubs in profusion,—howing what can be done in a short time in this delightful country and climate.

When Mr. Steward was nineteen years of age the Mexican war began, and he enlisted in Company C, Fifteenth United States Infantry, and served through the struggle. He was sent to re-enforce General Scott at Vera Cruz, and was in all the fights until the city of Mexico was taken. In taking the city he received a musket shot in his right foot, for which he receives a pension. He has been Postmaster twice. In his political views he is a Democrat, but always voted for the best man. Mr. Steward is not an old, worn-out looking man, notwithstanding he is a veteran of the Mexican war, and has been active so long.

Mr. Steward was married in 1852 in Quincy, Illinois, to Miss Sarah A. Abner, a native of Illinois. They have six children living: Alice D., the wife of Mr. J. Brown, of Yuba County; Rosanna C., at home with her parents; Charles Richard, a book-keeper in a wholesale house in San Francisco; Minnie D., wife of Mr. Faulkenstein, and residing in Ventura; Lora May and Mattie M., both at home with their parents. In 1883 Mrs. Steward died, and Mr. Steward has since married Mrs. Eliza McNett, of Quincy, Illinois. He was made a Master Mason in 1850 in Springfield.

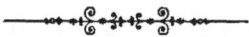

M. HOIT, present Postmaster of Santa Barbara, apppointed under President Harrison, was born in New York city, and after passing his boyhood days he removed with his parents to Virginia, where his father followed general farming. Our subject enlisted at Parkersburg, West Virginia, July, 1862, in the Fourteenth West Virginia Infantry, Colonel D. D. Johnson in command; Captain, George W. Taggart. The subject of this sketch was commissioned as Orderly Sergeant, and served in the departmena of West Virginia, and in General Crook's command, attached to the Eighth Army Corps. He served from July, 1862, to May, 1864, when he was wounded at Floyd Mountain, Greenbrier County, Virginia.. He was then ranked as Second Lieutenant, having been promoted for merit and bravery on the field. His service was largely on the line of the Baltimore & Ohio Railroad, in skirmishing with guerrillas and keeping open communication over lines of the road. He was also in General Crook's raid toward Lynchburg, in destroying Confederate stores and supplies. They were met in force at Floyd Mountain by Breckinridge, and won the fight, but there Mr. Hoit was wounded and taken from the field. He was fifteen days en route to Gallipolis, Ohio, the nearest hospital, and arrived more dead than alive with lung fever. He was there six months, and was honorably discharged in January, 1865, being about one year in recovering his health, and is still lame from the effects of the wound.

Mr. Hoit was elected Recorder of Wood County, West Virginia, in the fall of 1866 and re-elected in 1868.

He was married at Parkersburg, West Virginia, to Miss Ella W. Saunders; they have three children living. Mr. Hoit, with his family, came to Santa Barbara in the fall of 1872, and his first impressions were anything but agreeable, taken as they were from the deck of the steamer, which was anchored three-fourths of a mile out, with a prospect of being well drenched from the surf in being landed from the ship's boats. The eye rested on the San Francisco Mission, and an occasional adobe, with here and there an unpretentious structure reared by a white settler. No trees except an occasional pepper, and no verdure anywhere. He now has great faith in the town. Its growth has been slow but steady, and its future is assured.

He is a member and Past Post Commander of Starr King Post, No. 52, Department of California. He was appointed Postmaster for Santa Barbara in October, 1889, and confirmed on December 20, 1889, for the term of four years.

FRANK E. KELLOGG, of Goleta, is a native of Napa County, California, born at St. Helena, September 22, 1851. His father, F. E. Kellogg, was a farmer by occupation and a mechanic by trade, and located in Napa County, in 1846. Our subject received his rudimentary education in the public schools of his native town, and subsequently graduated at the Illinois College, Jacksonville, in the class of 1872. After a year's sojourn at Hannibal, Missouri, he again came West, locating on his present place in 1877, where he engaged quite extensively in bean culture. In 1882 he engaged in the dairy business. His years of experience has taught him that it pays best to keep graded Jersey stock, as they make the most profitable and satisfactory milch cows. The thoroughbred Jersey is best for quality but not for quantity of milk. The cross or compromise between Jersey and other good milch cows of common stock produce the best grades for both quality and quantity. This is the principle, put into practice, upon which Mr. Kellogg has built up his excellent reputation as a successful dairyman. Of his fifty to sixty milch cows, nearly all are from one-half to seven-eighths Jersey blood. The Goleta Dairy covers 150 acres of land, all under a high state of cultivation. Twenty-five acres of this tract is covered with soft-shell English walnut trees in bearing, and several acres are devoted to Pampas plumes for market.

Mr. Kellogg's business enterprise is manifest in the recent erection of a first-class steam-power creamery on his place, which has become one of the most important institutions of its kind in Southern California. It was the first creamery erected in Santa Barbara County, using the milk from farms in the vicinity. He has thus far confined himself to the manufacture of creamery butter, in which he now consumes the milk from about 150 cows, or about 2,000 pounds of milk, producing 150 pounds of butter daily, or one pound to each cow. It is put up in two-pound rolls (full weight). While, as Mr. Kellogg says, the business is in its infancy, he regards the result produced thus far as settling the question as to the practicability of operating creameries in this county. All the milk from the surrounding farms is carefully tested as to its butter value, and every farmer is paid for his milk a price determined by this test and the selling price of butter. The creamery, producing a larger percentage of butter of a superior quality, which brings an advanced price, gives the farmer more for his milk product than he could realize for it in any other way, and also saves him the trouble of manufacture and marketing. The Goleta Creamery is fully equipped with a De Laval centrifugal cream separator. This is propelled at a speed of 7,500 revolutions per minute, extracting the cream from the milk immediately after having been taken from the cow. The machine separates the cream from 100 gallons of milk per hour. The cream then goes into a tempering vat for a given period, thence into a churn, with a capacity of 300 pounds of butter at one churning. This fine new machinery is operated with an upright steam engine. The product of the creamery finds a ready market in Santa Barbara and other cities. Credit is due Mr. Kellogg for developing so important an enterprise in a county where it was regarded as experimental.

As a citizen and a business man Mr. Kellogg holds an exalted position in the community. He was Principal of Goleta public schools ten successive years, which fact is a strong evidence of his high standing as an educator. He takes an active interest in public affairs, but is in no sense a politician. Although yet a comparatively young man he has acquired a handsome property, a good business, a fine home, and is surrounded by hosts of friends, and, the greatest of all blessings, a happy family.

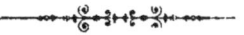

DR. W. T. LUCAS, a prominent physician and surgeon of Santa Maria, was born in Buchanan County, Missouri, March 18, 1850. His father was a farmer by occupation, and emigrated to Montana in 1864, across the plains in prairie schooners, and our subject rode a mule. The company brought out about 1,000 head of cattle and several loads of freight. They stopped at Deer Lodge Valley, took up land and ran a butter and cheese dairy until 1868, when they sold out and came to California. They settled near Woodland, Yolo County, where they farmed for several years, but he has now retired, at the age of sixty-seven years. The subject of this sketch gained his education by hard work, making expenses as opportunity offered. He attended the public schools, and then the Hesperian College at Woodland, and also taught in the public schools of Yolo and Solano counties. In 1874 he entered the Medical College of the Pacific at San Francisco, at which he graduated in November, 1876. He began practicing at Woodland, Yolo County, and also gave lectures at the college on physiology and hygiene. He had charge of the County Hospital until 1879, when he came to Guadaloupe, Santa Barbara County, and practiced until June, 1884, when he came to Santa Maria. He bought town property and also 160 acres of ranch property. He rents eighty acres, and is improving the remainder. He has already set out twenty-two acres in orchard and deciduous fruits; his present residence property he bought in 1887. The Doctor has had an extensive and successful practice throughout the Santa Maria Valley; he is a great reader, and has a large library.

He was married in Sacramento County, September 9, 1879, to Miss Lula Maupin, of French descent. They have two children: Lee Forman and Orion Lulu. The Doctor is an enthusiastic Mason, and has served the lodge at Guadaloupe as Master for four years, and is still officiating. He has been a member of the Grand Lodge for several years, and belongs to San Luis Obispo Chapter, No. 62, R. A. M., and to San Luis Obispo Commandery No. 27, and has the most extensive Masonic library in Southern California. He is an enthusiastic and consistent Democrat, and takes an active part in every campaign.

GEORGE W. M'CABE, son of Anthony McCabe and Elizabeth E. (Waller) McCabe, was born in Nova Scotia, March 13, 1857. In 1869 the entire family, consisting of parents and four children, moved to San Francisco. In 1872 Mr. McCabe and his son George took charge of the Borax Lake property, in Lake County,— property which has since developed for its owners very valuable and important mines. Young McCabe decided to learn some trade, and selected that of blacksmithing, at which he worked in Napa, Napa County, for some time. In 1879 he moved to San Luis Obispo, where he continued work at his trade. In 1882 he engaged in business for himself and is now established in one of the most important shops of the city.

In 1882 Mr. McCabe was married to Miss Steele. To them have been born three children. Mr. McCabe is a worthy and respected citizen. April 1, 1890, he was elected one of the City Trustees. He is a member of the order of Odd Fellows, in which organization he has filled many high positions. He also belongs to the A. O. U. W., in which society he is an ardent worker. Mr. McCabe is active in politics, and is at present Chairman of the Republican County Convention.

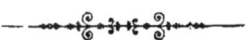

JAMES R. WILLOUGHBY is another illustration of what energy and integrity will do for a man in California. He arrived in San Francisco in April, 1853, in pioneer times, even without a hat! The cause of this was: The steamship Independence, on which he was a passenger, caught fire and burned until she sank; 200 of her passengers were lost, but Mr. Willoughby, with others, were cast upon an island, whence they were subsequently rescued by a whaleship. He lost everything. He was at that time twenty two years of age, vigorous and ambitious, and he obtained work by the day and odd jobs until he was soon able to carry on a systematic business for himself, buying and selling hogs, sheep and cattle. His business increased apace upon his hands, while he also added the wholesale butchering trade, and for twenty-nine years supplied the meat markets of San Francisco. Thirty years ago, in traveling over the State to buy stock, he saw Ventura County, "fell in love" with it, and soon afterward bought a ranch of 10,000 acres near Saticoy, and he still owns 7,500 acres of that tract, on which he is rearing improved breeds of horses, cattle, sheep and hogs. He keeps about 100 head of horses,—French Canadian, Clydesdale, Cleveland Bay and Richmond,—some of which are as fast trotters as any in the world. He has 5,000 sheep, 1,000 hogs and 600 head of cattle,—Durham, Hereford, Devon and Holstein. He has fifteen hands in his constant employ; has several barns 100 feet long, and many other ranch buildings. He has a ranch of 180 acres of fine land near Saticoy, planted in walnut and other fruit trees, and furnished with a good house and barns. Although in business in Ventura for many years, he did not reside here until 1881, when he bought his present home, on the corner of Santa Clara and Ash streets.

Mr. Willoughby was born in Canterbury, Connecticut, October 22, 1831. His father, William F. Willoughby, was a native of Connecticut and died in 1849. His grandfather, Russell Willoughby, emigrated from England to Connecticut in early life. His mother, whose maiden name was Phebe Carey, was also a native of Connecticut. Their family consisted of twelve children, and the mother is still living, now aged eighty-four years. James R., the eldest son, had charge of the business, and the cares of the farm devolved upon him.

He was married in 1862, to Miss Mary E. Holloway, a native of Tennessee, who died in 1881. The children by this marriage were: W. F., George D., Abby, Charles R. and James. The three first named are married and the others are with their father. Charles R. has recently received an appointment to attend the West Point Military Academy. August 10, 1886, Mr. Willoughby was united in matrimony with Miss Rena Roberts, a daughter of William and Mary (Fowler) Roberts, from England, and she was born in Minnesota. They have one interesting little girl, Irene Sessions, born in San Buenaventura. The family attend the Presbyterian Church and contribute to all the churches of the town. Mr. Willoughby is a member of the A. L. of H.; a Trustee of the city, and for four years has been chairman of the Republican County Committee. The county has been Democratic, but it is now Republican; and although Mr. Willoughby has been so influential, he has refused political preferment, desiring rather to attend to his private business.

JAMES FRANKLIN WILLIAMS, deceased, was one of the leading members of the bar of Santa Barbara County. He was born in the town of Manlius, Onondaga County, New York, May 14, 1818, the son of Nathan Williams, a dry-goods merchant. After attending the public schools of his native town, he attended Union College, Schenectady, New York, at which institution he graduated at eighteen years of age. He later took a thorough course in the study of law, paying for his own education. He married Miss Susan Sweet, July 28, 1845, and for three years traveled in the Southern States. He then came to California, in 1849, and spent some time in the mining regions, with headquarters at Sacramento city. In this he had average success, but he subsequently took up the practice of his profession at Martinez, Contra Costa County. He was promptly recognized as a lawyer of ability, and was elected to the District Attorneyship of his county. He served one term as Superior Judge of Contra Costa County by appointment. Mr. Williams remained there until the year 1867, when he took up his residence at Santa Barbara, and opened a law office. He was a popular Democrat, and several times chosen by his party for County

Judge, which party was in the minority. He practiced law up to within two years of his death, which occurred August 2, 1876. He was the father of three children, one daughter, now deceased, and two sons, one son dying in infancy; the other, Nathan Wallace, is a well-known and substantial merchant of Santa Barbara and a "native son." He was born at Martinez, California, November 18, 1854, and graduated at Heald's Business College of San Francisco, in 1873. He learned the carpenter and joiner's trade, which he successfully followed for about ten years. He is now junior member of the popular grocery house of Hunt, Hosmer & Co., State street, Santa Barbara.

He was married September 8, 1878, to Miss Jennie E. Orr. They have three children, two daughters and a son: Gasper Franklin, Eva B. and Gracie E.

JUDGE S. A. SHEPPARD was born May 22, 1824, in the District of Columbia. His ancestry on the paternal side were English and Scotch, and on his mother's side Irish and Scotch. His ancestors were Colonial settlers of Virginia and Maryland. His father, a native of Annapolis, Maryland, in early days was a farmer, and afterward resided in Baltimore city and the District of Columbia, and owned both city and country property. Judge Sheppard completed his school life in a classical academy in Georgetown, District of Columbia; commenced to study law in 1844, in Cincinnati, in the law office of William T. Forrest, and removed to Baltimore in December of the same year, where he continued his law studies and was admitted to the bar in the city of Baltimore, in January, 1847. He practiced his profession there and in the United States courts in Washington city until February 3, 1849, when he started for California. He came around by way of Cape Horn, and landed in San Francisco September 9, and went to the mines with a party of seven friends who had come to the coast with him. They went to the Shasta Diggings, Redding's Bar, and after prospecting there for a while they went to the Feather River, locating at Bidwell's Bar. Soon after the rains set in, the mines become inundated, and he, with others, returned to San Francisco, where he opened a law office, December 10, 1849. He soon had a paying practice, and he continued his profession there successfully ten years. He then removed with his family to Tulare County and opened an office at Visalia, and practiced law there seventeen years, namely, until April, 1876; and since that time he, with his family, has been a resident of San Buenaventura, engaged in the practice of law. In San Francisco he was Public Administrator; in Tulare County he was District Attorney two terms; was also Mayor of Visalia; was appointed by Governor Haight Judge of the County Court to fill a vacancy, and was afterward elected to a full term. While residing in San Buenaventura he was elected County Judge of Ventura County, and since a member of the Board of Town Library and President of the Board. Politically, he sympathizes with the old Jeffersonian Democratic principles. He was initiated in Washington Lodge, No. 1, I. O. O. F., it being the first lodge organized in the United States.

In 1848 Judge Sheppard married Miss Margaret L. Armstrong, a native of Baltimore and a daughter of James Armstrong, a wholesale leather merchant and manufacturer of that city, and they have now living two sons and three daughters, viz.: Isabella, now the wife of George E. Stewart, of Nordhoff; Margaret, now Mrs. Horace Stevens, residing in Batavia, this State; Summerfield D., residing at Hueneme, Ventura County; Thomas A., who is also there, in the drug business, and Annie R., the youngest, is at home. Mrs. Sheppard is a member of the Presbyterian Church, and the Judge's father was an Episcopalian. Judge Sheppard has built a nice home in the beautiful and healthful village of Nordhoff, where, with his children near him, and also his many friends whom he has known so long, he will spend the evening of his long and eventful life in peace.

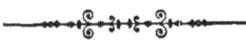

J. R. BENNETT, a rancher near Nordhoff, was born in Ireland, December 1, 1845, the son of respectable Irish parents. In 1864, at the age of nineteen years, he set sail for American, landing at Quebec, June 15 of that year. He had relatives there engaged in business, and for a time he was employed by his cousin as supercargo. They bought provisions and clothing and took them to the coast of Labrador, bringing back a load of fish and oil. After three years thus engaged he went to Thurso on the Ottawa River, where for two years he clerked in a general merchandise store. In July, 1869, he came to California and worked in a saw-mill a year in Mendocino County. In 1870 he sent for his brother George and gave him a position in the mill. Starting out in search of easier and more profitable employment, he next went to Vallejo, where he was engaged in laying water pipes until he could accumulate a little money to go still further in search of better employment. Going to San Francisco he worked for a while on the wharf, unloading vessels, and then obtained a situation in a wholesale dairy produce store, conducted by T. H. Hatch & Co. Soon he secured a position there also for his brother George. Two years later he and his brother engaged in the dairy produce business for themselves in the California market, which they continue to the present time, supplying the elite of San Francisco with "Bennett's Celebrated Butter."

While in the market, Mr. Bennett contracted catarrh, which extended to his bronchial tubes, and he was compelled to seek a milder climate than San Francisco. Leaving the business there in charge of his brother, he started in search of health, traveling the whole length of California, from Sisson's to San Diego, and found the most desirable place for pulmonary complaints to be the Ojai Valley. Here he purchased sixty-one acres of land, on which he is now building a handsome residence. He is entering largely into fruit culture, having planted French prunes, almonds, olives and raisin grapes. The property is now in a flourishing condition, and is destined to become one of the most delightful homes on the coast.

Mr. Bennett was married in 1878, to Miss Hatty Greeleese, a native of Thurso, Canada, and a daughter of William Greeleese. Mr. Bennett became acquainted with her while in Thurso ten years previous, and succeeded in persuading her to meet him in California. Upon her arrival, Mr. Bennett went to meet her, taking a minister with him, and they were married in Sacramento. They are the parents of four interesting children, the three eldest having been born in San Francisco, and the youngest in the Ojai Valley. Their names are: Lillian, Stewart R., David S. and Anita. Both Mr. and Mrs. Bennett are members of the Baptist Church. Mr. Bennett is independent in politics, but shares the views of the Republican party. He is a member of the I. O. O. F., and also of the F. & A. M.

H. MEHLMANN, one of the enterprising men of San Luis Obispo, was born in Berlin, Germany, June 28, 1846; studied agriculture and surveying; served one year in the Prussian army, in the war of 1866; and in 1869 came to America. After stopping a short time in Nevada, he came the same year to San Luis Obispo and engaged in diversified farming upon 320 acres of good land near town. This, however, he sold, and after working for several years at the carpenter's trade, and some time in a surveyor's office as draughtsman, he engaged in the sale of wines and liquors and in the bottling of lager beer, which he now prosecutes with success.

He was married March 1, 1883, to Miss Löwenstein, who was born in Prussia in 1853, and they have five children.

J. KELLER, deceased, formerly a resident of San Luis Obispo, was born in Bavaria, Germany, May 26, 1826, and at the age of seventeen left home and learned his trade, as brewer, following the business six years in a large establishment. In 1849 he came to America and resided in Cincinnati and Columbus, Ohio, for a time. In 1852 he came overland with a large band of horses and cattle to California, being six months on his way, but losing the most of his stock by death on the route. He arrived at Sacramento, and then spent considerable time at the gold mines. In 1856 he returned to Germany, intending to stay; but, not liking the prospects there, he came to America again the next year and located permanently in Newtown, El Dorado County, where he established a large brewery and was quite successful with that institution.

In 1860 he returned to Cincinnati, Ohio, and married Miss Minnie Wiegand. In 1870 his brewery was destroyed by fire, and the next year he moved to Oakland and established himself there in the same business for a period of three or four years; then he resided about four years in Temescal, a northwestern suburb of Oakland, where his residence and grounds formed one of the chief attractions of the town. In 1879 he moved to San Luis Obispo, where he resided until his death, which occurred in 1882. He had eight children, all of whom are still living.

R. W. NUTTALL.—The leading real-estate broker, formerly interested largely in our northern coast, is R. W. Nuttall, Esq. There is no better informed gentleman as to land values and the industry of our country in general, in California. He has a large extent of fruit, farm and grazing land to sell in small lots to suit purchasers.

THOMAS NORTON, M. D., a leading citizen of San Luis Obispo County, was born in Roscommon County, Ireland, December 24, 1846, the son of Dr. Thomas Norton, who was an eminent physician in Ireland, and a graduate of Trinity College, Dublin, also of the Royal University of Edinburg. He died about 1860 in his antive country, after having spent about seven years in America. He had six sons and one daughter, of whom the subject of this sketch is the third child.

C.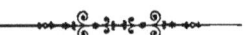 P. HALL is one of the successful ranchers of Ventura County. His father, William Hall, was a native of Berkshire, Massachusetts, and his grandfather, Parker Hall, was born in Rhode Island, and was a soldier in the Revolutionary war. They were of English descent. Mr. Hall's mother, Sarah (Dyer) Hall, was born in West Troy, New York. Her father, William Dyer, was an early settler on the Hudson River, and used to run the first ferry across the river there. William Hall was twice married, and had eight children by the first wife and four by the second. The subject of this sketch was the youngest child by the first marriage, and was born August 14, 1833. His mother dying when he was a year and a half old, he was thus early in life bereft of her love and care, and when he was four years old he went to live with his aunt. Six years later she died, and he was then put on a farm to live until he was twenty-one years old, when he was to have a suit of clothes and $100. During that period he attended school a part of the time in the winter, and at other times he was engaged in work on the farm. As he terms it himself, he was educated with the hoe and between the plow handles. He may be said to have educated himself. He then taught school in the winter and worked on the farm, by the month, in the summer. The usual price for farm work was $10 per month, but a part of the time he received $13, because he was considered a reliable hand. He received $15 per month for his first school, and taught ten terms. In the fall of 1856 he went to Iowa, and taught and worked until he was able to buy 115 acres of land. This he improved by building, etc., the whole costing him $3,300. After living there ten years, he sold the place for $6,200. He then removed to Red Oak, Montgomery County, Iowa, and bought 160 acres of land, unimproved, on which he erected buildings, residing there eight years. At that time it was considered one of the best improved farms in the township.

Mr. Hall spent the year 1882 in California, for the benefit of his wife's health. The change of climate saved her life, and in 1884 they sold out and came to Ventura and bought their present comfortable home and thirty acres of land. The house and grounds are pleasant and attractive and the locality is delightful. Mr. Hall has acquired such a habit of industry that he could not be happy unless engaged in some active employment. Since coming to this sunny land he has devoted his time to the cultivation of fruit and vegetables, has been more especially interested in the production of beans, having raised from 1,600 to 2,200 pounds to the acre. The price for Lima beans, in 1890, is $4 per hundred pounds.

October 19, 1859, the subject of this sketch was united in marriage with Miss Lucy Ann Ballou, a native of Essex County, New York. The Ballou family were Rhode Island people, their ancestors having settled there with Roger Williams, in 1645. Mr. and Mrs. Hall have two living children, Edward and Elmer E., both born in Farmersburg, Iowa. The older son resides in this valley, and the younger is now taking a scientific course of study in the university at Los Angeles. In Clayton, Iowa, Mr. Hall was elected Justice of the Peace, and served four years. He has been a Republican ever since the organization of that party. Both he and his wife and sons are members of the Methodist Church.

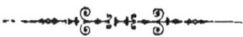

JOHN AND ALPHONSO A. WIGMORE, in 1875, purchased the Rancho del Puente, of 4,800 acres, situated near Los Alamos. The rancho was a part of the original Rancho de la Laguna de San Francisco, originally granted to Antonio Guitierrez. The ranch has been fenced and partitioned by the present owners, who have also developed the water, the source of which is obtained from a small laguna, and several large springs, which are now distributed by pipes about the ranch. The place was rented until 1889, but is now under the management of Alphonso A. Wigmore, and is being more highly improved and stocked with high grade Durham cattle, and a class of carefully selected mares, in view of breeding horses for draft purposes, from Percheron stock. They now have a large number of cattle and horses, but as the ranch affords fine grazing they propose keeping about 1,000 head. They are also experimenting with deciduous fruits, in view of setting out a large acreage, favoring also the English walnut, olive, grapes and figs. About 1,300 acres of the ranch is tillable, affording ample opportunity for the growing of all grain, hay and supplies.

W. M. ARMSTRONG, the able Superintendent of the Public Schools of San Luis Obispo County, was born in Lebanon, Warren County, Ohio, February 10, 1844, the son of John L. Armstrong, who was born in the same county in 1804. He was a miller and merchant by occupation, and a leading spirit in business, social and political circles where he lived. He was a Democrat in politics, but whenever before the people as a candidate for office his excellent reputation drew to him a large Republican support. He came West to Chariton, Lucas County, Iowa, in 1855, and engaged extensively in real-estate business, investing his money in large tracts of land. Later he took up his residence at Nebraska City, Nebraska, where he spent eight years. Subsequently he moved to San Luis Obispo, where he and his estimable wife are spending their declining years in retirement.

The subject of this sketch opened his business career as a contractor and freighter on the great plains, engaging successively with the United States Government and the Western Union Telegraph Company, who were then building the Western Union line through the Western States and Territories. He had acquired a fair education, and being amply qualified he accepted the principalship of the public schools of Astoria, Oregon, in 1864, continuing in that position two years. Mr. Armstrong then spent two years in the employ of the Government as head Quartermaster's clerk, at the headquarters of the Department of the Columbia, at Portland, Oregon. In 1868 he came to California and taught school in Monterey and San Luis Obispo counties, and for four years was principal of the public schools of San Luis Obispo city. He resigned this position, and in 1886 was elected to the superintendency of the county schools, where he served a four years' term. Mr. Armstrong attended the biennial session of the State convention of county superintendents of schools, and there took a prominent part in the amending and formulating the present excellent school code of laws, many of which were subsequently adopted by the State Legislature. During his term of office the schools of his county have risen to a rank *par excellence* with any county schools in this State. Mr. Armstrong is a man of fine executive ability, a favorite with the educational class, and is justly proud of the excellent high standing his schools have obtained and the good reputation they have abroad.

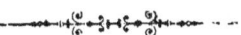

J. ROBISON, one of the prominent ranchers of the beautiful Ojai Valley, was born in Bloomington, Indiana, July 22, 1838. His father, Andrew Robison, was born in Kentucky, July 4, 1800, removed to Indiana in 1826, bought a farm and there reared his family. He was a consistent member of the Church of Christ. His death occurred in 1872. Mr. Robison's mother, Nancy (Smoot) Robison, was a native of Kentucky, and the mother of four children, of whom the subject of this sketch is the youngest. Mr. Robison received his education in the public schools of his native State, and also in the Indiana State University. He learned the blacksmith trade, removed to Ellis County, Texas, in 1859, and there opened a shop which he successfully conducted for twenty-six years. In 1882 he sought a milder climate, arrived in Los Angeles, purchased ninety-five acres of land at Azusa, which he improved by planting fruit trees and a vineyard, and also erecting buildings, and resided there three years. At the end of that time he sold out and returned to Texas. A year later, however, he came back to California, and in May, 1886, came to his present locality in the Ojai Valley, and moved his family here in November of the same year. Mr. Robison is a very successful horticulturist, and is the owner of a fine fruit ranch of 115 acres; three acres are devoted to peach trees, six to apricots, sixteen to French prunes, two to pears and a variety of other fruit. Twelve acres are in almonds, two in olives, six in raisin grapes, and one in figs. All these Mr. Robison planted, and he has also erected a comfortable residence. He intends to prepare his fruit for market by drying it. The rest of his ranch is devoted to the cultivation of oats, wheat and barley.

Mr. Robison was united in marriage, in 1867, with Miss Laura Douglas, a native of Tennessee, and a daughter of N. L. Douglas, who was born in Charleston, South Carolina. Her grandfather, Jesse Douglas, came from Scotland. Her father was born in 1801, and was a soldier in the Seminole war, enlisting when he was seventeen years of age. During his residence in Texas he was elected to the office of Assessor and Collector. He died in 1873. Mr. and Mrs. Robison have a family of six children, all natives of Texas, viz.: James M., Cynthia E. and Julia E. (twins), Annie, Marion, Ethel and Clara O. Both Mr. Robison and his wife are members of the Church of Christ. He is a Republican. Was a Southern man, but was for the Union. Through the force of circumstances he served in the Confederate army during the war. People who differ from him in political views give him credit for the honesty of his convictions.

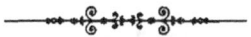

JAMES EVANS, one of the early settlers and prominent pioneers and ranchers of Ventura, was born in Clarke County, Indiana, July 5, 1839. His father, Thomas Jefferson Evans, was a native of Kentucky. The ancestors of the family were Virginians of Scotch and English origin. Mr. Evans' mother, whose name before marriage was Catharine King, was a native of Pennsylvania, and her parents were Pennsylvania

Dutch. Thus our subject has inherited an unusual degree of good quality. He was the third in order of birth of a family of five children. He received his first schooling in Missouri; afterward, in 1844, his parents removed to Missouri, in 1852 to Oregon, and in 1859 to California, settling in Sonoma County, and he attended school in each of these States. In starting out in the world for himself, he first followed farming two years in Sonoma County, and then followed mining most of the time for four years in Idaho, made some money, but lost it; then he came to Salinas Valley in Monterey County and engaged in farming for two years; and finally, in 1869, his father came with his family to Ventura County, purchased 111 acres of land, and he (our subject) bought eighty acres, which he still owns. He has therefore been cultivating his present ranch for twenty years. He has raised corn, beans, barley and flax; but his principal crop at present is beans, on which he realizes $35 to $40 per acre.

Mr. Evans has never joined any society or held office, but he has ever been a Union man and a Republican. He was married in October, 1884, to Miss Osmosen, a native of Germany, and they have two children, Plasent and Hallie, both born in Ventura.

JOSEPH HARRIS, of Lompoc, was born in the town of Suffolk, England, in December, 1843. His father, Rev. George Harris, was a minister in the Baptist Church at Rishingles; he also carried on farming, and he has been a continuous renter of the same farm for forty-five years. He is still living and preaching, at the age of seventy-four years. Joseph lived at home until 1866, and carried on his father's farm of 300 acres, engaged in general farming. In 1866 he went to Flixton, and from the estate of Lord Waveney he rented 282 acres, where he carried on general farming and stock-raising. In 1871 he was married at Drinkstone, to Miss Kate Cooper, whose father was a renter of a farm which had been in the family continuously for over 150 years. Joseph Harris, our subject, farmed at Flixton until 1877, when, on account of illness of his mother, he returned home and resided there until he brought his family to California, in 1884. He came direct to Lompoc, and rented eighteen acres in the San Miguelito Cañon, where he built his home, planted two acres in fruit trees and started a market garden. They have one son, George, who was born February 20, 1872. Mr. Harris is a strong admirer of the freedom of the American people, and regrets that he did not earlier seek a home beneath our flag.

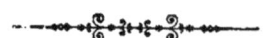

DR. B. GUTIERREZ, Santa Barbara. The California pioneers were not all natives of our glorious Republic, as among the number whom we now find prominent among the residents of Santa Barbara, is the subject of this sketch, who was born at Santiago, Chili, in 1830. He was educated in private institutions of that place and also attended a course of lectures in pharmacy, as, his father being a druggist, he very naturally inclined to the same profession. During the gold excitement of 1849 he came north to California, landing at San Francisco, and for five years thereafter he followed mining very successfully in Placer, El Dorado and Calaveras counties. He came to Santa Barbara in 1855, and in connection with Dr. M. H. Biggs, started the first pioneer drug store in the town. Santa Barbara was then a small

Spanish settlement, and the natives were engaged in the raising of cattle and sheep, marketing in San Francisco. Land was then worth almost nothing, city blocks then selling as low as $5 per block, and acre at 10 cents per acre, a radical difference from the boom of 1887, when the land on State street sold at $250 per foot. About 1872 Dr. Gutierrez was appointed School Trustee for the term of three years, and later served one term of two years as Coroner. He formerly owned much real estate, but sold too early to receive much benefit from the boom. He still owns 1,000 acres at Carpenteria, which is farming and grazing land. He also has an interest in blocks corner of State and Ortega streets, where his drug store is situated, which he carries on in partnership with Dr. C. B. Bates. They carry a full line of drugs and chemicals.

The Doctor was married in Santa Barbara, in 1857, to Miss Soledad Gonzales, a native of Santa Barbara. They have had twelve children, only six of whom survive. The Doctor is a member of the Society of California Pioneers, composed only of men who came to the State in 1849, and though sixty years of age is still robust and well preserved.

J. S. HARKEY.—Among the well known pioneers of California we find the name of J. S. Harkey. He was born in Cabarrus County, North Carolina, October 27, 1829. He was the son of Isaac Harkey, a resident of North Carolina for many years and afterward of Arkansas, from 1839 to 1872, when his death occurred in that State. His mother, Cottin P. M. (Shinn) Harkey, was born and reared in North Carolina. The progenitors of the family on both sides were German, but long residents of America. The subject of this sketch was the fourth of a family of fifteen children, and was reared and educated in Arkansas. When he became of age he rented land from his father and engaged in farming for a time. He afterward went to school and studied law. A siege of typhoid fever at this time resulted in his abandoning the idea of engaging in the legal profession. After two or three years' farming, he became a clerk in Norristown, on the Arkansas River, and eighteen months later bought out his brother's partner and engaged in business. Having met with losses in various ways, in 1858 he closed out his interests there, and, with his wife and son Thomas, then two years old, came to California. He left $1,500 due him, from which he never realized a cent. He arrived in San Francisco December 15, 1858, and the same evening left for Russian River, Sonoma County. He there lived on a rented farm eleven years, and was not out of the county during that time. In 1869 he located in what was then Santa Barbara County, now Ventura, and bought a squatter's claim in Pleasant Valley, supposing it to be Government land. When he arrived here he had, all told, property and money, about $1,500. He bought the grant to get title to his land and gained his suit, but afterward lost everything. In 1872 his wife was taken sick with typhoid fever and died February 26, that year, and he was left with a family of helpless children, without means. He manfully overcame his troubles, and cared for his family without remarrying. In the fall of 1873 he was elected Justice of the Peace of Hueneme Township, serving two years. In the fall of 1875 he was elected County Assessor, and served four years. He is a Democrat, but was nominated by both parties. In the spring of 1877 he bought twenty acres of land where he now resides, at a cost of $70 per acre. He has planted fruit trees of different kinds on his place, but his principal crop is corn and beans. The land produces from 1,800 to 2,400 pounds of beans to the acre, and they bring $2 and more per 100 pounds. Mr. Harkey has raised 4,600 pounds of shelled corn to the acre. He is farming adjoining lands.

Mrs. Harkey's maiden name was Mary Ann Petray. She was a native of Arkansas. They were married in Arkansas and had a family of six children, three sons and three daughters, viz.: Thomas N., George W., William D., Ida May, Fanny and Laura Ann.

Mr. Harkey is a man of his word, a strictly temperate man; and has been a Master Mason for thirty-seven years.

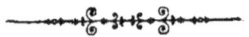

JOSEPH H. SEATON, M.D., one of the most eminent physicians and estimable gentlemen in Southern California, was born in Centerville, Wayne County, Indiana, July 29, 1836, the son of Myers and Elizabeth (Dill) Seaton. The father was a native of Pennsylvania, and also a pioneer merchant of Centerville, where he located in 1834; the mother was also a native of Pennsylvania. They raised a family of six sons and two daughters. Joseph H. Seaton, the third child, left home at about eighteen years of age, going to Louisville, Kentucky, where he took up the study of medicine, and graduated in the winter of 1856-'57. He was soon tendered and accepted the position of resident physician of the City Hospital at Louisville, which position he resigned in 1858 to go to Keokuk, Iowa, where his parents were then residing. He remained there until the breaking out of the Rebellion, when he enlisted as Surgeon of the Twenty-first Missouri Infantry, taking the rank of Major. Mr. Seaton served in the war from March, 1862, until its close in 1865. His regiment opened the battle of Shiloh, where they lost 180 men, and their division commander, General Prentice, was taken prisoner. Anything like a detailed account of the Doctor's experience during his years of active service in the war would form a thrilling narrative, and his services as an army surgeon cannot be overestimated in value to his regiment and comrades.

At the close of the war Dr. Seaton returned to Keokuk, Iowa, and resumed the practice of his profession, continuing there until 1875, when he came to California. His residence in San Luis Obispo dates from 1877, and since his residence here he has enjoyed the full confidence of the best people of the entire community, as a citizen and physician. He makes a specialty of diseases of women and children. He is affable in his manner, domestic in his social tastes, and charitable where charity is desired. He is a charter member of Fred Steel Post, G. A. R., No. 70.

Dr. Seaton was married in 1879, at Colusa, to Miss Josephine Blount, a native of California, and they have one son, Joseph, Jr. Besides other property Dr. Seaton owns one of the finest homes in the city of San Luis Obispo.

GEORGE W. COFFIN, who is one of Santa Barbara's representative citizens and descends from Quaker stock, and whose ancestors formerly lived on the Island of Nantucket. His grandfather left the Island in 1778 on account of the oppression of the English, and settled in Washington, Dutchess County, New York, where George W. was born in June, 1817. His father was a farmer, and as it is said, "As a twig is bent so the tree inclines," so it was that the early life of George W. was spent in tilling the soil, and in the conducting of a farm on scientific principles. He lived at home until the age of twenty-two years, when he was married at Patterson, Putnam County, New York, to Miss Helen M. Howland, whose ancestors were from New Bedford, Massachusetts. He then settled at Amenia, New York, where for nineteen years he carried on farming on a farm of 108 acres. Devoting himself to the high cultivation of the soil, and the improving of stock, only keeping Ayrshire cattle, and South Down sheep, but gaining notoriety as a practical farmer. About 1856 he sold out his farm interests and went to Poughkeepsie, New York, where he followed a mercantile life. He then went to St. Paul in 1864, where he became interested in manufacturing, and then to St. Louis, where for four years he was connected with the Atlantic & Pacific Railroad Company. In 1872 he came to Santa Barbara in the interests of that road. Returning to St. Louis in 1873 he severed his connection with the Atlantic & Pacific Railroad, and in 1874 brought his family to Santa Barbara to take up permanent residence. For eight years thereafter he was connected with Colonel Hollister as private secretary. In 1882 he began the real-estate business, which he has since continued. In 1884 he was elected Mayor and was re-elected in 1886. The first three years he drew no salary, but it went to a fund, called the Mayor and Common Council Fund, and was used in improving the city. Mr. Coffin was much interested in the sewering and paving of State street, which is one of the finest paved streets in California.

Mr. Coffin, having lost his first wife, was re-married in Santa Barbara in 1886, to Miss Susan Robinson, a native of Thomaston, Maine. Mr. Coffin has been quite a traveler, having crossed the continent fourteen times and by every route. He owns a large amount of property, and is now devoting himself to his own interests and in the settlement of certain prominent estates.

SAMUEL T. MOORE was born in Yorkshire, England, in 1828. His father was a stone dealer, owning extensive quarries. Samuel T. learned the trade of stone-cutting and carving in his native place, serving an apprenticeship of seven years, and becoming proficient in every kind of masonry He immigrated to the United States in 1867 and settled in Minnesota. The weather, however, being too severe, he soon afterward located in Pittsburgh, Pennsylvania, where he worked six years. In 1873 he came to California. After spending about one year in Los Angeles, he came to Santa Barbara and arranged for permanent settlement. He soon set up his business on State street, and in 1881 established his present yard in East Santa Barbara near the cemetery, purchasing the corner lot and erecting his residence in 1889. He keeps in stock Italian and Vermont marbles, and also all the popular granites of America and Scotland, and native stones. He has done much contract work in the city and was superintendent of the stone work for the residence of Mr. Dibble, also the J. F. Myer & Garland Block, and many others. For the past nine years he has been superintendent of the cemetery. Mr. Moore has thoroughly identified himself with the best interests of Santa Barbara, has been quite successful in business and owns much paying property.

Mr. Moore's first wife, a native of Cornwall, England, but a resident of Pennsylvania for a number of years, died in 1877, leaving two children. In 1878 he married Miss

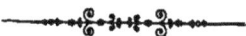

PHILEMON GARCIA is a native of California, born February 10, 1849. His father, Francisco Garcia, was a native of San Francisco, and his grandfather Garcia, also named Francisco, was born in Mexico, and came to California in an early day. His mother, Maria Antonia (Paraulta) Garcia, was born in San José, this State. They had nine children, seven sons and two daughters, of whom six are now living. Philemon Garcia was educated in the English schools, and at the early age of eleven years began to work for himself. He was first employed to ride race horses, riding Langford, Miami and Norfolk at the most noted races. They were then considered the best horses. He then worked on a ranch for H. Williams, and afterward on threshers for different parties, until he had a thresher of his own. Mr. Garcia, in company with A. B. Smith, was the first to start a cook house, in connection with threshing-machines, to board the hands. He came to Ventura County in 1873, and bought of Edward Borchard his present home place of twenty-six acres, paying $1 down, the purchase price of the property being $500. He paid it all the same year, and since then has built a house and barn and made other improvements, making his money by raising grain and threshing. He cleared a piece of land for Thomas R. Bard, and raised a crop on the same, for which he received $2,000. He is also clearing up other lands for Mr. Bard. Mr. Garcia runs a steam corn-sheller, with which he is doing a large business.

In 1884 he was married to Miss Filetica Vasques, a native of California, and daughter of Francisco Vasques, also born in this State. They have three children, Filetica, Anneta and Philemon. Mrs. Garcia is a member of the Catholic Church. For serveral terms Mr. Garcia has served the public as School Trustee. Politically, he affiliates with the Republican party.

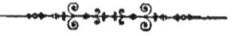

R. D. COOK, one of the founders of Santa Maria, was born in Clermont County, Ohio, in 1832. His father was a carpenter and farmer. Our subject lived at home and learned the trade of carpenter with his father. In 1850 he went to Quincy, Illinois, where he clerked for a short time. In the spring of 1851 he started for California, with an ox team; he drove the team and cooked for his passage. They came by the old Carson route, and landed in Sonoma County, in September, where he immediately began working at his trade, at $4 per day, and in two weeks became "boss" of the job, at $10 per day. He followed his trade two years, when he began farming, and on October 12, 1854, he was married to Miss Genette Nelson. He continued farming until 1855, when he went East, by the Panama route, and passed the winter in St. Louis, where, in partnership with C. C. Money, they purchased 350 head of cattle and twenty horses. They drove them across the plains in three months, with very slight loss. They landed in Sonoma County, and there continued in the cattle business until 1861, when on account of dry weather they lost heavily. The following five years Mr. Cook was variously employed at farming, carpentering, etc. In May, 1869, they started south, landing in Santa Maria Valley, which was then settled by only five American families, without a shrub or brush in sight. The location proved desirable, and he bought a claim of 160 acres, and built a two-story house, hauling his lumber from Port Harford. In October, having his house inclosed, he gave a dance, with which to raise funds to erect a school-house. He sent invitations far and near, and received for his commendable enterprise $305, and so was established the first school-house in Santa Maria, there now being twenty-eight school-houses in the same district. Farming in this valley was a failure for the first three years, the crops being eaten by grasshoppers, and Mr. Cook made his living by killing deer and gathering wild honey, which he shipped to market. He worked at his trade when opportunity offered, and at farming until 1874, when he started a blacksmith shop, which he continued until 1876. He then sold out and built his present livery stable, which business he has since continued. His land, covering the center of the town he had platted and laid out, in 1874, when it was located; and of his original purchase he still owns 125 acres adjoining the town, and 40 acres south of the town. He still continues his livery business, keeping horses and carriages suitable for the trade.

Mr. and Mrs. Cook have five children living, four daughters and one son. Mr. Cook was elected School Trustee for twelve years.

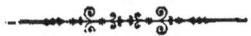

W. S. CANON, Postmaster of San Luis Obispo, was born in Crawford County, Ohio, September 24, 1837. After a thorough schooling in the public institutions of his native place, he commenced a course of study in Wittenberg College, Springfield, Ohio, with a view of graduating, but the Rebellion having broke out he turned his attention to the preservation of the Union. In 1861 (August 15) he enlisted in the Union army, under Colonel W. H. Gibson, in Company C., Forty-ninth Ohio Infantry, as a private, but was soon promoted to the rank of First Sergeant. In October, 1862, he was transferred to the veteran reserve corps (having been disabled while under fire at Battle Creek, Tennessee), and was appointed Sergeant Major of the Seventh Regiment, which was on detached duty at Nashville, Tennessee, and Louisville, Kentucky. During the latter part of his term of service his regiment was transferred to the defenses of Washington, where they remained until August 15, 1864. Having served three years his term of service expired, and he received an honorable discharge. Mr. Canon proceeded to Auburn, Indiana, to which place his parents had removed, and soon found employment at Ft. Wayne, in the office of the Pittsburg, Ft. Wayne & Chicago Railway as check clerk, which position he held one year. He afterward did train service one year, and was advanced to a conductorship, in which capacity he served about five years. He continued in the railway service, in the East, until 1876, when he came to the coast, and was with the Southern Pacific Railway Company until August, 1881, thus devoting seventeen years of his life to railroad service. Owing to exposure his health became impaired, and he located at San Luis Obispo, purchasing the Central Hotel, which he operated until his appointment as Postmaster of his city, February 19, 1890.

Mr. Canon was married to Miss Irene Snyder at Ft. Wayne, Indiana, in 1866; she was a native of Ohio, and a most estimable lady. They have three daughters and two sons. Mr. Canon is held in high esteem by the cititzens of San Luis Obispo. He has been a member of the Board of Trustees, and was two years its chairman; and is also a member of Fred Steele Post, G. A. R., No. 70, and is Past Commander of the same. In his present Federal position he is proving a most competent and satisfactory official. He is fully abreast of the demands of the times, and has located the postoffice in a handsome new building erected and equipped for the purpose. He is such a citizen as no city can do without.

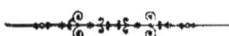

J. SIMMLER, of San Luis Obispo, was born in the city of Mulhaus, in the Province of Alsace (now a portion of Germany), July 18, 1826. At that time Charles X was king of France, and this province was an important department of that kingdom. His father, George Simmler, a pupil of the celebrated Pestalozzi, the great educator, was a professor of thirty-one years' standing in the college of Mulhaus. He was born and reared in humble circumstances and educated himself. He died at the age of seventy-eight years, in France. He had three sons and two daughters. The sons emigrated to America, the second one coming in 1835 and settling as a pioneer in Texas. He was a professional pianist and piano manufacturer in the old country. Being an intimate friend of General Sam Houston, he entered public life and lived until 1881, having three sons and three daughters.

Mr. Simmler, the subject of this sketch, received a first-class education in the old country, and learned the trade of painting, traveling two years in the completion of his apprenticeship. He came to this country in 1847, then a young man of 21 years, just after the close of the Mexican war, and resided at Houston, Texas, until 1852, following his trade. During that year his love for travel induced him to come to California. He was several months on the way, some of the time in the Republic of Mexico, and two months he was on the ocean, where his sufferings were so great as to cause him to land when the vessel struck shore near Port Harford. The story of his coming is somewhat thrilling. He shipped from Mazatlan, on the bark Holloway, and the vessel being for sixty days lost on the ocean the sailors and passengers fell short of rations. At length they saw land, which proved to be Point San Simeon, at which they landed. About seventy passengers debarked, all of whom except Mr. Simmler hastened off to the mines. He became employed as cook for an American physician named Clements, who was afterward killed by a California lion while out hunting about five miles from the town of San Luis Obispo. Afterward Mr. Simmler engaged in painting for Captain John Wilson, an Englishman then at the Los Osos Ranch, now the property of L. M. Warden. Captain Wilson was a diamond in the rough, a good man; was step-father of ex-Governor Pacheco. After working for Captain Wilson a year Mr. Simmler began farming on John Brice's ranch, and in this enterprise lost all his accumulations. Next he kept a hotel, the first in San Luis Obispo, near the old Mission where Weaver's undertaking establishment now is, on the corner of Choro and Monterey streets. Subsequently he removed with his partner to the St. Charles, on Monterey street near the Blackman Block, in Mrs. Sauer's building, now a tin-shop.

From the time he entered the hotel business near the old Mission, in 1856, he held the office of Justice of the Peace until 1858, when he resigned in order to join the Vigilance Committee. This body was disorganized six months afterward, and Mr. Simmler began work again for Captain Wilson, and was in his employ several months, pursuing meanwhile his trade as painter until April, 1859. At this time he married for his present wife Mrs. Rosa Butron de Canet, a native Californian whose husband was a Spaniard. Mr. Simmler was Justice of the Peace at intervals for ten years; also Deputy Sheriff and Deputy Assessor four years; one of the first Town Trustees; School Trustee for a number of years; first Police Judge under the first corporation and Postmaster about twenty years. Of course, during a portion of this period he held two or three of these offices at the same time. He was an efficient and popular officer, and although he was the choice of 700 citizens for re-appointment as Postmaster, he was not re-commissioned under the administration of Benjamin Harrison. At present he is book-keeper and manager for Louis Marré.

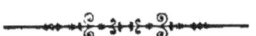

JENKINS & McGUIRE, the present proprietors of the Santa Maria *Times*. G. W. Jenkins, the practical newspaper man, was born in La Grange, Missouri, in 1854, and after a preliminary education he completed his studies at the Normal College at Kirksville, Missouri. He then began teaching in private classes, and after a course at Canton Business College, he taught day and evening classes until later on, when he engaged in the newspaper business. He came to California in 1879, settling at San Luis Obispo, where he became connected with the staff of the San Luis Obispo *Tribune*, a daily publication with a weekly edition. After three years this connection was severed, and in partnership with F. O. O'Neal they started the San Luis Obispo *Republic*, but after three months he sold out and came to Santa Maria, in 1883, in the capicity of business manager of the Santa Maria *Times*, the paper having been started by S. Clevenger & Laughlin, in 1882. In 1884 Mr. Clevenger and Mr. Jenkins bought the Laughlin interest, and continued until May, 1887, when Mr. Clevenger sold his interest to I. N. McGuire, and Jenkins & McGuire have since managed the paper. The circulation is 600 copies, and it is considered one of the leading papers of northern Santa Barbara County.

Mr. Jenkins was married at San Luis Obispo, in September, 1882, to Miss Allie McGuire, a daughter of I. N. McGuire. They have two children: Percie May and George Ray.

I. N. McGuire was born in Jackson County, Missouri, in 1832. His father, with his family, moved to Buchanan County, in 1838, and there our subject received his education. He then moved, with his family, in 1849, to California, coming across the plains, and driving an ox team all the way. They then settled at Vacaville, Solano County, and started the town by building the first house therein. Mr. McGuire then began raising cattle and horses, continuing until 1853, when he moved his stock to Sonoma County, buying 480 acres of land, and there followed the stock business for twenty years, keeping about 300 head, and farming in grain. In 1873 he came to San Luis Obispo County, and was engaged in sheep-raising until his herd numbered 3,500 sheep; he lost heavily by the dry season of 1877, and closed out the business. In 1880 he moved to San Luis Obispo, and for three years was engaged in mercantile life, and in 1883 came to Santa Maria. He was engaged in the drug business until 1887, when he bought the interest of Mr. Clevenger in the Santa Maria *Times*.

Mr. McGuire was first married in Sacramento, in 1854, to Miss Sarah Condit, who died in 1887, leaving six children. In May, 1888, he was again married, at Bloomfield, California, to Miss May Horsley. Mr. McGuire is a member of Hesperian Lodge, No. 264, F. & A. M.

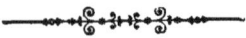

MICHAEL BOLL is counted among the early American settlers of San Luis Obispo. He is of German birth, was born September 29, 1829, on St. Michael's day; hence he received his Christian name. He emigrated to this country when a mere youth. He is a first-class shoemaker, which trade he learned in the cities of New Orleans and Mobile. In 1853 he made a trip to Europe, but immediately returned to New York city. Mr. Boll has been a very successful business man, and was also one of the pioneer merchants of Chicago, where he kept a boot and shoe store at 613 State street, in an early day. Owing to the severe climate he embarked for San Francisco, where he remained but a short time, when he started for his adopted town, San Luis Obispo, where he has since resided. He has diligently pursued his chosen calling and by judicious investments he has accumulated a competency.

July 16, 1854, he married Eliza Scheffner, a merchant tailoress. They have five children.

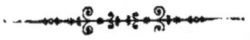

J. D. SNYDER, an early pioneer and a prominent developer of the Los Alamos Valley, was born in Wales Center, Erie County, New York, in 1853. His father was a farmer with extensive lumber and saw-mill interests. Our subject left home at seventeen years of age and went to the lumber regions at East Saginaw, Michigan, where, owing to his experience in his father's mills, he readily found employment and was put in full charge of a large saw-mill, remaining about three years, when an epidemic of fever and ague broke out, and Mr. Snyder, being quite ill, returned to his home in the East. After recovering he again started forth, and settled at Green Bay, Wisconsin, where he was engaged with a Mr. Lamont in the lumber business for two years. He then disposed of his interests and visited Portland, Oregon, Puget Sound and Seattle, and then went south to Guadaloupe, where he located in 1876, and began ranching. In 1877 he went to Los Alamos, which was then the old stage station, and foreseeing the founding of a town bought land and made the primal move toward its establishment by erecting the first business building of the place, which is now occupied by Arata Bros. Mr. Snyder also rented extensive tracts of land and engaged in farming, and in 1881, from 400 acres of land, he raised 10,000 centals of barley and wheat. During the harvest he employed sixty men, sixty horses, two threshers, a header and bailer and at the same time managed his extensive hotel business; was also agent for the Wells-Fargo Express and Coast Line Stage Company, and, as one might imagine, he was reasonably busy. In 1880 he built the Alamo Hotel, which he managed for a number of years. In 1887 he received the Government contract to carry the mail between Lompoc and Los Alamos, and the same year established a livery business.

He was married in Los Alamos, in 1881, to Miss Linine F. Keenan, a native of Illinois. They have no children. Mr. Snyder has now closed his business, rented his hotel and intends taking a much needed rest by an extended trip East.

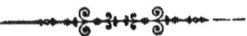HOMAS BARROWS is a native of Massachusetts, born on Martha's Vineyard, April 14, 1843. His father, James Lloyd Barrows, was also a native of that State, and was a merchant and manufacturer. Their ancestry came from England. His mother, Hannah Cottle, was born in Massachusetts, the daughter of Captain Edward Cottle, a sea captain of merchant ships. Mr. Barrows finished his education at Gorham, Maine. He began his business career at Indianapolis, as clerk in a wholesale dry-goods house. After this he accepted the position of general traveling agent for the Grover & Baker Sewing Machine Company, and acted in that capacity for several years. He next took the general agency for the Victor Sewing Machine Company, for the Northwest, with headquarters at Chicago, the firm being Thomas Barrows & Co. During this time he was a partner in the Elgin Iron Works, manufacturers of small engines and castings. Their sewing-machine business in Chicago became quite extensive, sales reached 8,000 machines in the best year, and altogether they disposed of 25,000. They were caught in the great Chicago fire and lost quite heavily, but were again receiving orders the week following the fire.

In 1875 impaired health caused Mr. Barrows to leave Chicago and come to California. He was first in Oakland and San Francisco. His disease was hemorrhage of the lungs and attending troubles, and his physician advised the mildest climate possible. The Ojai Valley was decided upon, and he arrived at this place in 1878. He purchased 160 acres of unimproved land, which, under his judicious care and management, now presents a very different appearance. He has erected a comfortable home, planted a large variety of trees and vines, and his property has become a lovely tree-embowered retreat. Mr. Barrows has long since regained his health, and is now in a situation to enjoy life, under the shade of the vine and fig tree of his own planting. His ranch is provided with ample barns. He is now engaged in raising Holstein and Jersey cattle and fine blooded horses of the A. W. Richmond stock, and is also raising work-horses; has had as high as 300 head of horses and cattle at one time. He has dealt some in real estate, and owns about 250 acres of choice land in the valley. He is engaged in orange culture both at his home and also at Pomona.

Mr. Barrows was married, in 1869, to Miss Sarah W. Coffin, a native of Edgartown, Massachusetts, daughter of Jared W. Coffin, who traces his ancestry back to Nantucket. This union was blessed with a daughter, and a few days later the young mother and beloved wife was called away, and thus a most sad bereavement came to him. The daughter, Charlotte C., is now attending the Pomona College. Several years after his wife's decease, Mr. Barrows was again married, in 1872, to Miss Ella A. Cole, of Medway, Massachusetts, daughter of Captain John Cole, a sea captain of whaling and merchant vessels. They have one child, David P. Barrows, who is also attending Pomona College, in the freshmen class. All the family are members of the Congregational Church. While in Chicago Mr. Barrows was superintendent of the Tabernacle Sunday-school and deacon in the Tabernacle Church; is now a deacon in the Nordhoff Congregational Church, and also an active worker in the Sunday-school. He is a gentleman of pleasing and genial manners, and

LYMAN L. PATTER was born in Bennington County, Vermont, November 4, 1847, son of S. J. and Flanella Patter, both now deceased. He is one of a family of eleven children, five of whom are living. February 24, 1868, Mr. Patter landed in California, having made the trip by water, via Panama. He came directly to San Luis Obispo County, and went to work for Steele Bros., and was in their employ for four years. For some time he was engaged in ranching for various parties, and in 1882 came to Santa Margarita Valley, settling on a small ranch where he now resides. This property is located in the heart of this lovely valley and there is no prettier site in the county. Mr. Patter also owns a ranch of 160 acres in Kern County.

He was married February 16, 1871, to Miss Jane Sumner, and they have had ten children, only two of whom are now living.

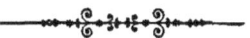

JOSE COLL, son of Daniel and Bruine (*nee* Garcia) Coll, was born in Santa Barbara, in 1834, and is one of a family of three children. The family moved to San Luis Obispo in 1841, soon after the death of Daniel Coll, and, with the exception of Jose, have since continued to make that city their home. Mrs. Coll is still living, aged seventy-eight.

The subject of this sketch came to San José Valley in 1850, and was the first settler in the place. He built the first corral, the location of which is yet easily recognizable. Mr. Coll has seen, as no one else has, the remarkable changes that have taken place in this productive valley, and having an excellent memory relates in a very interesting way his early adventures. When he arrived here the place was one thicket of brush and cottonwood; the creek, now quite a formidable stream, was then hard to find and very shallow. At one time, in company with four men, one of whom was Antonio Garcia, he went on an expedition off from the valley and caught a number of wild horses. In those days it was no novel sight to see horses roaming around that belonged to no one, and though wild were soon put to a good use.

Mr. Coll has been twice married, the second time, in 1877, to Mrs. Sweet, the widow of J. W. Sweet, by whom he has three children. Ever since living in the San José Valley he has been actively engaged in farming and stock-raising, and is now settled with his wife on the Sweet ranch.

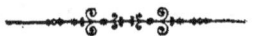

J. M. SHARP is one of the prominent ranchers of Saticoy. He was born in Cadiz, Ohio, March 3, 1844. His father, John Sharp, was born in Pennsylvania, March 27, 1797, and his mother, C. A. (Hesser) Sharp, was born in Virginia in 1808. They had seven children, all of whom are now living. The subject of this sketch was reared and educated in Oregon, and was a school teacher there. He has also been engaged in the profession of teaching since coming to Ventura County, having graduated from the State Normal School in 1871. He came to California in 1867, spent two years in Placer County, working for wages; then, for six years, was a book-keeper in San Francisco; worked one year on a farm in Sonoma County. In 1876 he came to Southern California, resided six years on a farm in Santa Ana, and, in November, 1882, moved to his present ranch where he has since resided. This property consists of 140 acres, and is most beautifully located. Mr. Sharp has built and made many improvements, and is now engaged in the construction of a fine residence which, when completed, will contain all the modern improvements of a first-class home, including gas, hot and cold water. It is being built some distance from the highway in order to afford ample room for ornamental grounds. This farm cost $40 an acre, and is not for sale, but is valued at $200 per acre. Mr. Sharp is engaged in the production of Lima beans, for which the land is wonderfully well adapted. He has twenty acres in walnut trees, which will soon yield $100 per acre. Mr. Sharp was married in 1874 to Miss S. R. Plank, a native of Pennsylvania, born in 1851, and daughter of Joseph Plank, who was born in Chester County, Pennsylvania, September 13, 1813. Mr. and Mrs. Sharp have an interesting family of seven children. She is a member of the Baptist Church, and was graduated at the State Normal School of California, in the class of 1871. Mr. Sharp is a strictly temperance man, and adheres to the Prohibition party.

JOHN RANSOM, M. D., San Luis Obispo, was born in Olean, Allegany County, New York, in 1825, the youngest of the five children of Rodolphus Ransom, who was a farmer and a leading citizen of that place, a native of Vermont, and is now deceased. He moved with his family from Allegany County to Madison County, same State, and here Dr. Ransom began the study of medicine, under the supervision of a relative, Dr. David Ransom. He graduated at Geneva College, in the class of 1849, and commenced the practice of his profession at the age of twenty-four, in the city of Rochester, remaining there about six years. While there he married Miss C. S. Brennan, daughter of Dennis Brennan, a dry-goods merchant. He next went to San Antonio, Texas, where he engaged in stock-raising with good success. Upon the breaking out of the War of the Rebellion he was shadowed as a Union man. Indeed, he did not hesitate to avow his political preference. This caused him at length to rent his plantation and remove with his family to New York. He entered the Union army in 1862, as Surgeon of the Fourteenth New York Cavalry and the Nineteenth United States Colored Infantry, and he served in this capacity until 1867, since which time he has been a citizen of San Luis Obispo, quietly practicing his profession. He is a gentleman of retired manner, and highly respected as a physician.

He has three children living: Cornelia N., wife of Mr. Hugh K. McJunkin, a lawyer of San Francisco; Florence, now Mrs. R. Manderscheid, of San Luis Obispo, and Rudolphus, of San Francisco.

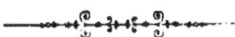

ALBERT J. BOESEKE was born at Schwedt, on the Oder River in the State of Prussia, January 6, 1828; was educated in the common schools and learned the trade of tinsmith. In 1848 he was mustered into the Prussian army, and after three years of active service he was discharged. He then worked two years, and emigrated to America in 1853, landing at New York. In 1855 he went to Muscatine, Iowa, as a pioneer, and started in business, remaining until 1865, when he crossed the plains to California, by way of Salt Lake City, bringing with him his wife and three children, and was nineteen weeks on the journey. He first began work at San Francisco, but, not liking the climate, and hearing through friends of the more salubrious climate of Santa Barbara, he came to that city, where he established himself and has since (1890) remained. He first opened a tinshop and gradually ran into hardware, and then, by taking in a partner, trouble began, as the partner defaulted and Mr. Boeseke lost heavily. He then sold out to Smith & Edwards, and, after settling up the old business, continued a one-third interest, which he held until 1889, when he felt that his health was failing, and to close up his affairs sold out his interest. He has been a hard-working man, and through thrift and economy and the natural increase in values, has attained a comfortable competence.

He was married at Comanche, Iowa, in 1858, to Miss Eliza Fluehe, a native of Hamburg, on the the Elbe River. They have six children living. He is a member of the F. & A. M. and of the Odd Fellows. He says with great pride that he is a strong temperance man and does not use tobacco, and neither of his four sons either smoke or drink. Mr. Boeseke has many interests in town, as the accumulation of his years of prosperity; and who is more worthy to enjoy than the hard-working pioneer?

CAPTAIN A. L. ANDERSON.—After a busy, bustling life in the East, Captain Anderson first came to Santa Barbara in 1878, and being attracted by the even temperature and restful quiet of the Montecito Valley, he there established himself in 1884, and his handsome residence now commands a beautiful view of the fruitful valley and the peaceful ocean in the distance. Captain Anderson was born at Croton, Westchester County, New York, and is a son of Nathan Anderson, who was an extensive trafficker on the Hudson River. Captain Anderson built that famous river boat, the Mary Powell, which is celebrated the world over for her speed and magnificence. She is 300 feet long, with thirty-four feet beam, with main, promenade and hurricane decks, and can carry 2,000 passengers. Her record is twenty-six and one-fourth miles per hour, being the fastest time of any river boat in the world. The captain ran her from 1862 to 1878, and has had for passengers all the eminent people of the East and many foreigners visiting this land, as the trip up the Hudson is one of the most beautiful excursions in the East. The boat ran between New York and Kingston, leaving New York each afternoon, Sundays excepted, at 3:30 P. M., and had the record of being so punctual and always on time that even watches were regulated by her arrival, and more confidence was placed in her running time and punctuality than in the steam cars. The Captain speaks of her with great tenderness, and she has been the pride of his life; but, owing to increasing years, his son, Captain A. E. Anderson, now runs the boat. It has been twice rebuilt. Captain Anderson still owns a beautiful home at Kingston, on the Hudson, which has been in his wife's family over 100 years. He prefers, however, to spend the closing years of his life in the more peaceful temperature of Southern California.

M. C. DENNIS, of San Luis Obispo, was born in St. Louis, Missouri, November 26, 1833. His father, a native of Lexington, Kentucky, was a real-estate operator, and in early days removed to St.

Louis, where he did an extensive business until his death, which occurred while he was yet in the prime of life. He left a widow and eight children. Mr. Dennis, of this sketch, left St. Louis in 1851 for the gold-fields of El Dorado County, California, and there spent the most of his time in the mines until 1865. Then he traveled over the Western Territories, spending some time at Salt Lake City, where he was so kindly treated that his opinions concerning the people there were considerably modified. In 1882 he finally settled in San Luis Obispo, although his property interests are mainly in San Francisco and Oakland. In 1885 he married Miss Fredrika Bombardie, an Alsacian lady, who has been a resident of this country for fifteen years. They have one step-daughter, named Mary, who is twenty-two years of age.

CHEDISTON HOUSE, a boarding and day school for young ladies. The object of the founders of this excellent institution of learning was to afford young ladies tuition in those branches of study not taught in the public schools; for example, the Latin, French and German languages, instrumental music and advanced drawing. The subjects taught in public schools are also taught if desired. The school was formed in the fall of 1888, by two highly educated and accomplished young ladies, the Misses Lilian and Beatrice, daughters of the Rev. J. Cheal. They were educated in high-class schools of England, their native country, and took special courses of study in German. In music and the languages they are especially brilliant and efficient. Their love for books and study, and their ambition and enterprise as tutors, seem to have come to them as an inheritance from their parents. Their father, the clergyman in charge of the Episcopal Church at San Luis Obispo, was, during a long and busy residence in England, thirty-four and a half years, a tutor in the public schools of that country. He is a man of broad culture and a profound scholar. For several years he kept his own private boarding school in Otley, County Suffolk, England, and for three years prior to his coming to America he held the head-mastership of an endowed institution, which was founded in 1632. He came to America with his family in 1885, and since his arrival he has thoroughly acquainted himself with the American system of education. Although he has not thought of teaching in this country, he has, as a matter of personal gratification, passed all the examinations in the State of California, entitling him to the highest-grade certificate; and his experience as a tutor in English schools of learning was promptly recognized by the State Board of Education, which board cheerfully issued a certificate to teach in any schools in the State. Mrs. Cheal, his amiable and cultured wife, was also educated for a tutorship in English schools. It is thus made clear how the children of such parents should aspire to the exalted positions they have taken in the field of higher education.

Mr. and Mrs. Cheal have a family of four daughters and three sons. All, with one exception, are residents of Southern California. Mr. Harry A. Cheal, the eldest, is a thoroughly educated man, a professional chemist and a drug merchant of Tacoma, Washington. Fred J., the second son, is a prosperous rancher and stockman of Lompoc. A daughter, Alice, is conducting classes in music, French and drawing at Lompoc.

The Miss Cheals, Lilian, Beatrice and Gertrude, have now opened a similar school to the above at Seattle, Washington, and Mr.

and Mrs. Cheal, with their youngest son, Maurice, expect to join them at Christmas. A large number of pupils have been secured, and more are likely to attend next term, which commences early in January, 1891.

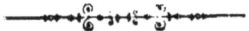

HON. McD. R. VENEBLE, a leading lawyer and banker of San Luis Obispo, was born in Prince Edward County, Virginia, September 8, 1836, the son of Richard and Magdelene (McCampbell) Veneble; the former was a planter of his native county, and the latter was of Scotch-Irish parentage, and a native of Lexington, Rockbridge County, Virginia. His grandfather, Richard N. Veneble, was a prominent lawyer of Prince Edward County, and his great-uncle, A. H. Veneble, was a United States Senator from the old Dominion State. His father died in the prime of manhood, leaving a family of five children. Judge Veneble, the fourth child, was educated at Hampden Sidney College, Virginia, and read law at the University of Virginia in the class of 1859. In 1861 he joined the Confederate Army, and fought under General Robert E. Lee in the Richmond Howitzers. His battery fired the first volley at the battle of Bethel, the opening engagement of the memorable conflict. He remained in the Army of Northern Virginia until after the battle of Chancellorsville, and was then appointed First Lieutenant in the Engineers Corps, and was stationed at Shreveport, Louisiana, where he remained until the close of the war. Mr. Veneble received a painful wound at the battle of Antietam in his left leg, from a cannon ball, which tore away the flesh, and also a slight scalp wound at the same battle. In this engagement he was acting as Lieutenant of Branch's Battery, and was in command of the center section of the battery, there being right and left sections, and it was at this time that he received his wounds.

After the close of the war, having served four years and one month, Judge Veneble settled at Farmville, Virginia, where he commenced the practice of law, remaining until 1868. On account of failing health he removed to California, locating at San José, where he remained only one year, and then removed to San Luis Obispo. His knowledge of law and his excellent social and business qualities made him many friends in this county. He was chosen County Judge of his county in 1872, serving to and including the year 1880. He was also elected on the Democratic ticket to the Legislature of California in 1887, and has also served one term in the city council of San Luis Obispo. In 1872 Judge Veneble represented California at the National Democratic Convention at Baltimore, Maryland.

He was married in 1872 in Montgomery County, Maryland, to Miss Alice Watkins, a daughter of G. M. Watkins, of that State. The Judge is an absolute conservative business man and financier; is a heavy stockholder and the president of the Commercial Bank of San Luis Obispo.

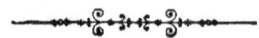

COLONEL W. A. HAYNE, one of the pioneer settlers and developers of the "Montecito Valley," whose pleasing residence commands a beautiful view of valley and ocean, was born at Charleston, South Carolina, in 1821. He is a son of Hon. Robert Y. Hayne, an eminent statesman of South Carolina, who also served as Speaker of the South Carolina Legislature, was elected a member of Congress and, later, United States Senator (which office he resigned, in favor of

Mr. Calhoun), and was then elected Governor of South Carolina. In 1832 when President Jackson issued his proclamation against nullification, Governor Hayne issued a counter-proclamation, in favor of "State Rights." Robert Y. Hayne was in the United States Senate, opposed to Daniel Webster, in that great debate on "Foote's resolution," regarding public lands, which drifted into "States' Rights" and eventually resulted in the civil war.

Colonel W. A. Hayne is a graduate of the South Carolina College. He studied law and was admitted to practice; was afterward elected to the South Carolina Legislature, and voted for the convention which passed the "ordinance of secession." He served through the war of the Confederate States; was assigned special duty at Charleston, where he was stationed much of the time; and at the close of the war, having lost a large estate, he emigrated, with a family of small children, to California, arriving at San Francisco in July, 1867. Having there a brother, Dr. A. P. Hayne, and cousin, E. J. Pringle, a prominent attorney, under their advice, he visited different localities, and, finding Santa Barbara possessing the most desirable qualities, bought a tract of 200 acres of land, in the Montecito Valley, at the rate of $20 per acre. The valley then was wild and unsettled, the ground being covered with sage brush and chapparal. There were no improvements in the neighborhood, and not a fruit tree had been planted. The Colonel began clearing and developing, bringing 1,000 orange trees from Los Angeles, and thus begun the industry, which has since proved so successful, making the valley one of the most beautiful of Southern California, and increasing the price of land from $20 to $250 per acre. His son, William Alston Hayne, Jr., is deeply interested in the development of the olive, having extensive nurseries at Montecito, and planting extensive groves in the Santa Ynes Valley. Arthur P. Hayne, another son, is in the "Montpelier Institute," in the south of France, studying viticulture and perfecting himself in wine manufacture, that he may be better able to develop the great wine interest of California. His eldest son, Robert Y. Hayne, is an eminent lawyer of San Francisco, and has been elected Superior Judge, and is now a member of the "Supreme Court Commission," appointed by the Legislature to aid in Supreme Court decisions. Colonel Hayne has two other sons who are lawyers, and one who is also interested in the Santa Ynez olive ranch.

Colonel Hayne was married in Philadelphia, Pennsylvania, in 1847, to a daughter of Edward Stiles, a gentleman of English descent, who early settled in Pennsylvania. The Colonel is a modest, retiring gentleman, justly proud of his ancestors, and of the success of his own family.

W. STEELE, a prominent dairyman and stock-raiser in San Luis Obispo, was born in Delhi, Delaware County, New York, March 4, 1830, the son of Nathaniel Steele, who was a farmer by vocation and also in pioneer times the owner of a stage line. He moved to Lorain County, Ohio, about 1836, and finally came with his wife to California, whither his children had preceded him. He died in 1861, at Point Reyes, where his son, I. C., had located; and his wife died the preceding year, at Petaluma.

The eldest daughter living, Mrs. E. Moore, now eighty-five years of age, lives in Delhi, Delaware County, New York. The eldest son, Osman N., was killed in his performance of duty as under Sheriff of that county, August 5, 1845, by men disguised as Indians for the purpose of resisting the collection of land rents. The eldest daughter died in Boston, Massachusetts, in 1886. The second son, J. B. Steele, a member of Congress from Ulster County, New York, was thrown from his carriage and killed in 1867. The third son, Major General F. Steele, United States Army, died January 12, 1868, in San Mateo County, this State. The fourth son, I. C., has resided at Pescadero, San Mateo County, since 1862. The fifth son, Judge George Steele, is a resident of San Luis Obispo. The seventh son died in 1854, of cholera, at the Straits of Sault Ste. Marie, between the great lakes.

E. W., the subject of this brief outline, is the sixth son and eighth child in a family of nine. Except those mentioned the family lived and died in the State of New York. He came to California in 1856, first locating in San Mateo County, but since 1866 he has been a resident of San Luis Obispo County, engaged in dairying and stock-raising. He also has heavy interests in San Luis Obispo; is a stockholder in the Central Milling Company, and has extensive stock and agricultural lands in the Santa Ynes Valley. He has been Supervisor two terms, being President of the Board one term; was a member of the firm of Steele Bros., first at Point Reyes until 1863, when, their leases expiring, they moved their cattle and dairy business to San Luis Obispo County. Most of their stock is Holstein and Jersey. At one time, just before and during the war period, they had 3,000 milch cows. It was they who presented to the National Sanitary Commission during the war the mammoth cheese, weighing 3,856 pounds. Half of this was sold by the commission at San Francisco for $3,000, and the remainder was sent to the soldiers of the Army of the Potomac. For its manufacture special machinery was of course devised, the bands and hoop alone costing $500. It was all of good quality.

In this county Mr. Steele has now about 5,500 acres of land, in Arroyo Grande Valley, mostly grazing and agricultural. He has adopted the modern improved methods in all the departments of the business; has a silo for alfalfa.

Mr. Steele was first married at Chattanooga, Tennessee, to Miss Julia Stanley, who died about eighteen months afterward; and in 1876, at Los Angeles, Mr. Steele was again married, this time to Miss Emily E. Smith, and by this marriage there is one son, named Edgar J., and born August 26, 1879.

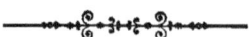

ANTONIO G. GUTIERREZ, druggist at Santa Barbara, was born in that city March 18, 1860. The biography of his father, Dr. B. Gutierrez, appears elsewhere in this book. In educational pursuits Antonio first attended the Santa Barbara Mission, then the Santa Ynez College, at Los Alamos (now Los Olivos), and the Pacific schools of Santa Barbara. In 1878 he went to work with his father in the drug business, and remained with him until February 1, 1881. He then went to work in San Francisco, and took two courses of lectures in the California College of Pharmacy during 1881 and 1882, and also was employed in the chemical laboratory of Messrs. Redington & Co., manufacturing chemists and wholesale druggists, in San Francisco. On March 15, 1883, he sailed for Chili, South America, on steamer City of Rio de Janeiro, arriving at Panama April 3, and the 11th of the same month at 5:30 P. M.

he sailed for Callao, Peru, on steamer Bolivia, arriving at Callao April 19, at 4:30 P. M., and on the 21st of the same month he sailed again for his final destination, Valparaiso, Chili, on steamer Mendoza, at 6 P. M., arriving at Valparaiso April 30, 1883, at 6:15 A. M. He was gone six years, spending the time mainly at Valparaiso and Santiago, the capital of Chili, in the wholesale and retail drug business.

Mr. A. G. Gutierrez was married at Valparaiso, Chili, November 29, 1883, to Miss Carmela Ibañez. They have five children, four of whom survive.

On December, 15, 1888, he sailed for Santa Barbara, California, with all his family, on the steamer "Corona," and arrived at San Francisco January 4, 1889, and Santa Barbara January 12, and immediately entered the drug business with his father.

Mr. Gutierrez is a member of the California Pharmaceutical Society of San Francisco, and of the American Pharmaceutical Association, of Philadelphia, Pennsylvania.

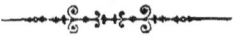

A KRILL, M. D., San Luis Obispo, has been a resident of this place since 1887, one of the leading physicians. He was born in Weston, Wood County, Ohio, May 7, 1855; completed his literary education at Oberlin College, and his medical at the Homeopathic Medical College at Cleveland, graduating in the class of 1882. He first practiced his profession for a brief period at Burton, Ohio, and then came directly West to California, locating at San Luis Obispo, where his success as a practitioner is a well-known fact. When he came here he was the only homeopathic physician in the county. He is a genial gentleman and an enterprising and popular citizen. He was married in 1884, at Burton, Ohio, to Miss Hattie A., daughter of Edward C. Rice, a capitalist of that place.

CHARLES L. HALL, the present manager of the "Miramar" ranch, which contains 550 acres and is located in the foothills overlooking the Carpenteria Valley, was born and educated in France, completing his education at the agricultural college in the south of France. This college is very thorough in its instructions and rigid in examinations. He there passed two years and a half, and in 1885 came direct to California, to take charge of the ranch which was purchased by his father in 1878. His father, C. O. Hall, is a native of New England and went to France in 1860. Being a dentist of great prominence, he now operates in Paris during the summer and in Nice during the winter months. Mr. Hall purchased his ranch through his brother, H. H. Hall, of Santa Barbara, with a view of cultivating flowers for the oil they contain. This business was conceived after a long experience in the south of France, where the industry is extensively carried on. The climate of the Carpenteria Valley being similar to that of southern France, Mr. Hall thought the flowers could be produced to advantage here. It, however, proved unprofitable, owing to expensive labor and the great destructiveness of gophers and ground squirrels; so, on the arrival of his son, Charles L., the entire plan was changed and the ranch is now being devoted to fruit. They have 3,000 olive trees planted, and anticipate increasing the number to 40,000. Three hundred of the Nostral olives were imported from the South of France. They are also largely interested in the production of loquats, which mature in the early spring, and which are considered very profitable. In addition to the fruits already mentioned, they have 1,500 Sicily lemons, 150 Mandarin oranges, and a large number of apple trees. Altogether this is a ranch scientifically conducted and must necessarily bring profitable results. Mr. Hall also cultivates many rare and novel plants here, for ornamentation rather than profit.

An important feature of this ranch is the dairy. They have a cross of Jersey, Durham and Holstein cattle, and manufacture an Italian cheese, having an expert to manage the dairy. They also have a high grade of horses for farm purposes.

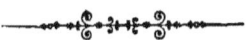

WILLIAM BENN was born at Maryport, Cumberland County, England, in August, 1812. He learned the trade of carpenter and joiner, and in 1836 came to America, first settling at Mobile, Alabama, where he worked at his trade. In 1837 he was on the river steamboat Ophelia, on the Black Warrior River, when she sunk. Only one life was lost. Mr. Benn followed his trade at Mobile and New Orleans until 1839, when he returned to England and France, making one trip as ship's carpenter. On his return he was overseer and carpenter of a sugar plantation, near New Orleans, for one year. He again returned to England, and was engaged by the Cunard Steamship Company, as ship's carpenter on board the Britannia, making four trips to Boston. He then worked for the Liverpool Dock Trustees for five years.

On the 17th of March, 1842, Mr. Benn was married at Cumberland, England, to Miss Ann Fischer. In 1847 he brought his family to New Orleans, and soon afterward started for Council Bluffs. They were wrecked on the Missouri River, on the steamboat Dacota, about seventy miles from Council Bluffs, and that distance was traveled by wagons. After remaining in Council Bluffs about three years, they traveled by ox teams to Salt Lake City, and three years later, in 1855, they moved still farther west, coming by ox teams and arriving in San Bernardino December 5 of that year. In the following February they came to Montecito. Here Mr. Benn purchased 100 acres of land at $1 per acre, carried on some farming and also worked at his trade. In 1873 he sold out and came to Carpenteria, buying four acres of land in the foot-hills and establishing for himself and family a comfortable home, overlooking the valley and getting full benefit of the breezes from the Pacific. Mrs. Benn died in September, 1885, at the advanced age of seventy-three years. Since then Mr. Benn has lived alone, his five living children having gathered to themselves individual responsibilities. Though seventy-eight years of age, Mr. Benn is in the full enjoyment of every faculty, and, surrounded by his books, animals, dogs and flowers, seems to be closing a peaceful contented life.

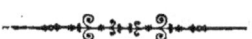

HON. MILTON WASON, a '49er, and one of the best known citizens of Saticoy, was born in Hudson, New Hampshire, January 17, 1817. Three generations of the family were born, reared and died in that State. Judge Wason, father of Hon. Milton Wason, was born November 2, 1785. He was a prominent man in his native State, having served several terms in the State Legislature, and having held the office of Justice nearly all his life. Judge Wason's great-grandfather, James Wason, with his wife, Hannah, emigrated from the county of Antrim, Ireland, about the year 1740, and settled on a tract of land on which generation after generation of the family were raised. Judge Wason's mother, Mary Colburn, was a native of the same place, she and her husband having been born within a mile of each other; she was of English ancestry.

Judge Wason, our subject, was the third child in a family of twelve; two children died in infancy, three sons and seven daughters grew to maturity, and five of the family are now living. He was educated at Dartmouth College, and took a law course at Harvard College, and also read law with Philips & Robbins, a prominent Boston law firm, and with Bradford Sumner. He was admitted to the bar in 1847, and practiced there two years. In 1849 he came around the Horn to California, where he mined for four years, with fair success. In Solano County he settled on what he supposed was Government land, where he lived and made improvements for six years, but finding it was not Government land he left it. He bought another place and lived upon it for eight years, when he sold it and came to Ventura County, April 10, 1868, and bought 275 acres of valuable land, which he has since sold at a large advance, with the exception of 100 acres, which he has saved for a home place, and on which he has built a large and commodious residence. On this property he has a complete variety of fruit, mostly for home use, and the ranch is devoted to corn, barley and beans.

Judge Wason was married October 26, 1852, to Miss Maria A. Borgnis, a native of the city of London, England. She was born February 1, 1820. They have two sons and two daughters, viz.: Maria A., now the wife of Mr. Riall G. Sparks, and residing at Santa Paula; Mary Eliza, residing with her parents; Charles Thomas, who married Ella B. Wason, of San Francisco, their fathers being cousins; they reside at Ventura; and George M., who married Agnes Jones, of Elizabeth, Pennsylvania, and resides with his father. All the children were born in Solano County, California. Judge Wason has been a Republican since 1861, and has three times been elected to the California State Assembly. When the county was organized he was appointed County Judge, and afterward elected to the office. He held the office of Deputy Revenue Collector for four years, and has often been elected a member of the Board of School Trustees. He has taken a deep interest in California and the county of Ventura. In his official capacity he has exhibited both ability and strict adherance to what he believed to be right.

DR. GEORGE BURRITT NICHOLS, of San Luis Obispo city, was born in Augusta, Georgia, November 28, 1840. His parents were both from Bridgeport, Connecticut, and at the time of the civil war his father was a very wealthy man, having been in the saddlery business in Newark, New Jersey, a member of the firm of Smith & Wright, the firm later becoming Nichols, Sherman & Co. At the time of the Rebellion, however, he lost most of his fortune. At the age of twelve years George was taken to Burlington, New Jersey, and placed in the Burlington College at that place, one of the best educational institutions in the country, then conducted by the Right Rev. Bishop Doane. After pursuing his studies there for a time, he went to sea, and was before the mast for several years. In 1858 he was in Europe, and traveled much with Robert Ballentine, a gentleman of intelligence and versed in the sciences. After his travel the Doctor commenced the study of medicine, entering the far-famed Bellevue College, New York city, then in charge of Prof. James R. Wood, where he remained three years, graduating June 22, 1871. During his study at the college, Dr. Nichols was for a time ambulance surgeon at the Bellevue Hospital, and from that office was transferred to the Park Hospital, the first sun-stroke hospital in New York, where he also received the appointment of house surgeon, a position of honor and requiring much knowledge and skill. In 1872 he came to California, and was engaged in the practice of his profession in Santa Barbara County for four years, and at the end of that time came to San Luis Obispo city, where he has since continued to reside. The Doctor makes a specialty of surgery in his practice, in which department he is eminently successful. His patronage throughout the county is large, and he is frequently called in consultation from distant points, in complicated and obscure cases. He is a man of many gifts, versatile in speech, universally popular throughout the county and wherever he has lived, and is at the present time a conspicuous figure in San Luis Obispo.

Dr. Nichols, with Alf. Walker, was the original discoverer of gas in the county at the oil wells, and at the same time owned that property; he has since disposed of it to other parties. He is now largely interested in the bituminous rock enterprise, the mines of which, located near the Corral de Piedra, he discovered in company with Alfred Walker. The Doctor is one of the largest stockholders in the company, and takes an active part in the management of its affairs. He has held various offices of importance since he came to California, politically and otherwise. He has been a member of the City Council of San Luis Obispo, and was the last Mayor the city really had. Through his efforts in that office many of the city departments have been divided and re-arranged, greatly assisting the method of the city's business. The Doctor was the County Coroner during 1888–'90, and while in Santa Barbara County was County Physician of the Third Township for a term of three years. In fraternal orders he is Warder in the Knight Templars, and King of San Luis Obispo Chapter of Royal Arch Masons; also Vice-Grand in the Odd Fellows lodge.

Dr. Nichols was married in 1873 to Miss Emma Leland, and they have two sons. His residence, located near the Mission, is a handsome structure, surrounded by an attractive lawn and flowers.

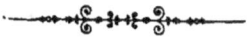

A. S. REED, the efficient Postmaster of Carpenteria, was born in Ontario County, New York, in June, 1839. He was reared on his father's farm, and remained there until twenty-one years of age, when in 1865 he went to Kent County, Michigan, where he again engaged in farming. Two years later he sold out and returned to Ontario County, where for a time he sold stump-pullers; but, not meeting with success, he returned to Hastings, Michigan, and bought an interest in a general merchandise store, carrying on the business under the name of Fuller & Reed. One year later he sold out and went into the livery business. Soon after this he left for Grand Rapids, Michigan, where he was engaged as book-keeper for nine months. He next returned to his old home and was employed in a warehouse, and also bought grain. In addition to this he purchased ties for the New York, Lake Erie & Western Railroad.

In December, 1884, Mr. Reed came to

Santa Barbara, and in the January following he located in Carpenteria, bought a small house and lot, and rented and worked land. In September, 1888, he rented H. J. Laughlin's hotel, but after a nine-months trial he found the patronage was insufficient to make the business profitable. He then bought a half block and erected his present residence, and also engaged in cultivating prunes, nectarines and peaches, in a small way. Mr. Reed was appointed Postmaster in the spring of 1889; was also appointed Deputy Sheriff about the same time, by R. J. Broughton, of Santa Barbara, then acting as Sheriff.

Mr. Reed was married in Livonia, New York, in 1860, to Miss Frances E. Risden, a native of New York State.

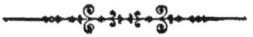

SOLON SMITH, whose fine ranch lies at the northwest end of the Carpenteria Valley, was born in Hanover, New Hampshire, in 1842. In infancy his parents moved to Kendall County, Illinois, being then pioneers to that wild, unsettled West. Solon was there reared and followed farming. At the age of twenty-one years he came to California by the Isthmus route, landing in San Francisco in 1863. The following four years he passed in Nevada and California, during the summer working at logging, and in the winter at farming in the Sacramento Valley. In 1868 he returned to Illinois, and was married at Joliet, Illinois, to Miss Amelia Bronk, who was born in Kendall County, same State, in 1846. Mr. Smith then followed farming in Illinois until 1883, when he brought his family to California and settled on his present property in the Carpenteria Valley. He owns sixty-five acres of fine land, forty acres of which he plants yearly in Lima beans, and the rest is in barley and fruit. Mr. and Mrs. Smith have three children: Allen David, Lennis Leonard and Roy Solon. Mr. Smith is a worthy and respected citizen.

L. D. GATES, proprietor of the Santa Barbara Foundry, situated on Bath street, was born in Valparaiso, Porter County, Indiana, January 18, 1864. His father was a farmer and native of Ohio. His parents moved to Chico, California, in 1875, and to Los Alamos, Santa Barbara County, in 1877. In 1878 Mr. L. D. left home, feeling that the occupation of a farmer was too narrow for his enterprising and inventive mind. He first went to San Francisco, and was there employed by the Pacific Rolling Mills. In 1879 he went to Sacramento with the Pioneer Flour Mill, and then with W. M. Guttenberger of the Sacramento Foundry, where L. D. learned the trade of machinist. He was there three years, then one year with the Mint Brass Works, in making tools. In April, 1884, he returned to Los Alamos on account of illness of his father, and there established a foundry, remaining until 1886, when he came to Santa Barbara and purchased 100 feet front on Bath street, between Ortega and De la Guerra, and erected a machine shop. He also built a foundry, where he makes all kinds of iron castings, as heavy as 1,500 pounds, and, should business require, as heavy as three tons. He is proficient in boiler-making, moulding, and with his naturally inventive mind is proficient in all mechanical work. He has invented an attachment for burning oil, and a three-cylinder engine, making his own designs and castings. His first job in Santa Barbara was setting an engine of an electric light plant in Santa Barbara city. He owns a fifty-acre ranch of valley land, and with his undoubted inventive mind is sure to succeed.

September 1, 1890, Mr. Gates married Miss Emma Brooks, "a fair maiden of nineteen summers past," and a resident of Santa Barbara.

DR. L. NORTON DIMMICK was born September 29, 1823, in Bethany, Wayne County, Pennsylvania. His father, judge in one of the courts of that State, moved with his family to Vermillionville, Illinois, in 1833, and became one of the commissioners of La Salle County. Here the boy Norton received his early education, and commenced with Dr. Bullock the study of medicine, which he afterward pursued in Philadelphia, and later graduated from the Medical University of New York. He commenced practice in Vermillionville, but soon removed to Freedom, Illinois, where he was married in November, 1853, to Elsie J. Nilson, a native of Norway, who came to this country with her parents in early childhood. They had two children who died in infancy. Here overwork and exposure compelled his removal to Ottawa, about 1857, where he opened a drug store, and there, with his brother, Philo J. Dimmick, continued in business until 1872. His health, however, not improving, and having entirely lost his voice, he sought the genial climate of Southern California and settled in Santa Barbara. Here he obtained a new lease of life, and after two years regained his voice and a measure of health that enabled him to live a quiet but useful life for twelve years. He built a home, surrounded by a beautiful garden of rare, curious and interesting plants from many lands. There with his fine cabinets of conchological and geological specimens, and his many albums of sea algæ, on which he was considered authority, made his home one of the most interesting places in Santa Barbara. The Doctor was a man of happy temperament, of clear judgment, and of a liberal public spirit, as our city library (of which he was a trustee) and other public interests will attest. He was also a member and Trustee of the Baptist Church. His death at the age of sixty years was as great a loss to to the city as to his many personal friends. Of a man so well beloved and so highly respected little need be said; for while he lived, not to know Dr. Dimmick was not to know Santa Barbara.

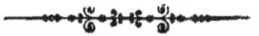

CHAUNCEY HATCH PHILLIPS, of San Luis Obispo, was born in Wadsworth, Medina County, Ohio, July 5, 1837, of English ancestry. He came, in 1864, to California, being a passenger on the celebrated ship Constitution, and first located in Napa, and soon obtained employment in the banking house of Goodman & Co., where he remained five years, his services being satisfactory in a high degree to his employers. He held the position of Chief Deputy Collector of Internal Revenue, for the Napa district, but soon removed to San José, where he received a re-appointment, and after the consolidation of the First and Second districts he made his residence in San Francisco, where he lived until November 30, 1871. His management of the Internal Revenue office at Napa, San José and San Francisco was distinguished by the most satisfactory settlements made with the Government, and also a correct and accurate system of detail work in his offices. In the fall of 1871 Mr. Phillips removed with his family to the town of San Luis Obispo, where he engaged in the banking business with Horatio M. Warden, under the firm name of Warden & Phillips, which partnership continued for two years, when the firm dissolved. The Bank of San Luis Obispo was then organized, under the direction of Mr. Phillips, with a paid-up capital of $200,000. He filled the office of Cashier and also of president of this bank until 1878, when he resigned. During the great panic of 1875 the Bank of San Luis Obispo never closed its doors, as nearly all the banks in the interior had done. Since 1878 he has devoted his energy entirely to real-estate interests, and his sale of Spanish grants and large private ranches, placed under his management, has been one conspicuous success. At various times he has purchased large estates and divided them into small lots, effecting a sale in a remarkably short space of time, and creating lively little settlements or towns in what was a vast tract of grazing country. Prominent among the transactions of this nature is the division of the Morro, Cayucos, Steele Brothers and Huer-Huero ranchos. In March, 1886, Mr. Phillips was one of the incorporators of the West Coast Land Company, an organization of which he is really the projector, and which company is doing on a larger scale only what business he did by himself a few years previous. He is the manager of the company, but with the combined capital of many prominent men in San Francisco and also in San Luis Obispo, the company is able to negotiate larger tracts of land than can be successfully accomplished by a private individual.

He was married January 18, 1862, to Miss Jane Woods, of Fond du Lac, Wisconsin, and they have the following children: Mary, now Mrs. Henry A. Sperry; Jane; Eliza, now Mrs. H. A. Vachell; Chauncey Hatch, Jr.; Josephine, Chester Delaney, and Nelson Burnham. Mr. Phillips is a man of fine physique and fine appearance. He takes great interest in matters affecting the public welfare of the city and county, and enjoys the highest confidence and respect of the community at large. Mr. Phillips has a residence at Templeton, but his permanent home is in San Luis Obispo.

ENRY J. DALLY, one of the earliest pioneers to Santa Barbara County, who, after a varied life upon the sea and land, visiting the ports of the world, came to this coast in 1843, and here he has since resided. He was born in New York city, March 22, 1815. His father, John Dally, was a sail-maker at the Brooklyn Navy Yard, where Henry J. was early put to work. Inheriting the desire for a seafaring life, at the age of eighteen years, in 1833, he went to New Bedford, and there shipped on the bark Winslow, a whaling vessel bound for the Pacific. On account of hardships, he, with eight companions, deserted at Cocas Island, near the equator; the island being barren, they lived for fifteen days on fish and sea-gulls. They were taken off by the ship Almira, of Oldtown, Massachusetts, and they remained with her for two years, leaving her at Peru. He then returned by ship to Nantucket Island, and then back to New York in 1837, after an absence of four years. Finding home life very tame and quiet, he soon longed for the excitement of the sea, and after a visit of fifteen days he went to New Bedford and shipped on the Pacific and New Brunswick, and until 1843 he followed a sea-faring life, visiting nearly all foreign ports and passing through many exciting adventures. On the east coast of Africa, because of trouble with a fellow sailor, he was put on shore, in a land of supposed cannibals, with a supply of three biscuit and a bottle of water. But he found the people friendly, and though suffering great privations, he finally shipped on a slave trader, a Moorish brig bound for Mozambique. After repeated changes of vessels and several trips to the east and west coast of Africa he started for Okotsk Sea in the North Pacific, on a whaling expedition, and being successful, returned and landed at Monterey, in 1843. Here he spent one year, then joined an otter company hunting down the coast; but, failing in that, he went to San Luis Obispo, where he took up the business of carpentering.

In 1846 he was married to Miss Felicita Rodriguez, at San Luis Obispo, where he continued the trade of carpentering until 1848, when he was elected County Sheriff, and re-elected in 1850. He resigned, owing to the dangers of the business. In 1852 he went to Carpenteria and bought land and also kept a wayside inn until 1867, when he sold out and came to Santa Barbara, where he has since resided, following the trade of carpenter, cooper and boat builder.

He has five children, all living. Though seventy-five years of age, he is hale and hearty, and having passed through the spectacle period his eyesight is now as strong as ever, having regained what is sometimes termed " second sight."

I. K. FISHER, who is a member of the City Council from the Fifth Ward, and a man largely interested in the progress and development of Santa Barbara, was born at Fisher's Summit, Bedford County, Pennsylvania, in 1836. His father moved to that locality in 1832, and established and named the town. The subject of this sketch left home in 1854, and as a butcher received a contract from the Huntington & Broad Top Railway to supply constructing parties with meats. In 1854 he went to Nebraska, and for two years speculated in lands in and around Omaha. Then for three years he was wagon master for Major Rossells & Waddell, and took charge of freight trains across the plains from Kansas City to Salt Lake City, carrying supplies and merchandise. In 1859 he went to Colorado, and was engaged until 1863 in mines, and speculating at Central City, Black Hawk, Delaware Flats and Denver. He was one of the pioneers to Boise City, Idaho, and helped lay out the town. Until 1867 he was engaged in mining and speculating in Montana, Arizona and at Salt Lake City. In 1867 he came to Los Angeles, and in 1868 to San Diego, where he ran hacks and did teaming about the city. He also had mining interests at Julian. In 1871 he came to Santa Barbara in the employ of the Atlantic & Pacific Railroad, and in 1873 he bought out the California Market on State street, where he has since been connected in business, having many outside interests. Mr. Fisher sold an interest in August, 1889, to Mr. More and Mr. Hollister, under the firm name of I. K. Fisher & Co. He also owns a half interest in a 670-acre ranch at the mouth of the Santa Ynez River, and one-half interest in a 226-acre ranch at Ortega. He also owns 270 acres near town, where he does some farming, and also keeps a fine stock of horses, about fifty head. He breeds the Richmond blood for speed and carriage driving. He owns 419 acres on the Hondo Creek, which is fine grazing land.

Mr. Fisher was elected to the City Council from the Fifth ward in 1884, and was re-elected in 1886 and 1888.

Mr. Fisher was married in Santa Barbara in 1874, to Miss Lizzie Holmes, and of three children only one survives. Mr. Fisher has been a member of the I. O. O. F. for twenty years. He is also a member of the Knights of Pythias and A. O. U. W. He is an owner and director of the Santa Barbara Water Company, and has many other interests in and about the city.

CHARLES H. McKEVETT, prominent as a business man of Santa Paula, was born in Cortland County, New York, October 3, 1848. His parents were born in the same State. His grandfather, Alexander McKevett, was born in Scotland and came to New York when a boy. Mr. McKevett commenced work on his own account in the oil business in Pennsylvania, first for wages and afterward under contracts to drill wells, and still later in operating for himself. He followed the oil business in Pennsylvania and adjoining States successfully for twenty years, and by his enterprise secured a comfortable fortune; and then, desiring to secure a home in a more genial climate, he came to California, in January, 1886. He visited different parts of the State and selected Santa Paula for a location, although at that time there was no railroad to that place. He purchased 425 acres of the Bradley and Blanchard rancho, extending from near the center of town out into the country. Part of this he subdivided and sold. The remainder he has improved. Has now over sixty acres of both citrus and deciduous fruit trees; also thirty acres of eucalyptus. Mr. McKevett was one of the organizers of the Bank of Santa Paula, January 17, 1888, of which he was vice president; George H. Bonebrake, President, and J. R. Haugh, Cashier. On September 23, 1889, the bank was converted into the First National Bank of Santa Paula. Mr. McKevett was elected president, which position he now holds. This bank has a paid up capital of $75,000, is the only national bank in the county, and is doing a good business. He was one of the organizers and president of the Santa Paula Lumber Company: this is now part of the Ventura County, Lumber Company of which he is a director. He is treasurer of the Santa Paula Fruit Packing Company, and is secretary of the Santa Paula Academy.

Mr. McKevett is a member of the Universalist Church, is a Knight Templar and an Odd Fellow, and in politics is a Republican In 1873 he was married to Miss Alice Stowell, a native of Pennsylvania. They have three children, two of whom were born in Pennsylvania, and the third, a daughter, in Santa Paula.

THOMAS McNULTA, the present City Attorney of Santa Barbara, was born at New Rochelle, New York, October 8, 1845. He enlisted November 21, 1861, and served during the war of 1861–'65 in the Fifty-third New York, Company D, Epineuil Zouaves, and the Sixty-second New York, Anderson Zouaves, and as Lieutenant and finally as Captain of a Tennessee militia company, formed from employés of the Quartermaster's Department at Nashville in the fall of 1864; and with the exception of a few months when he was disabled, was continuously in the service until the close of the war in May, 1865. He is now a member of Farragut Post, G. A. R., at Vallejo, California.

After the war he became Deputy Circuit Clerk of McLean County, Illinois, and served in that capacity about eighteen months, devoting his spare hours to the study of the law, and literary and general educational subjects, and then entered the office of Weldon & McNulta, at Bloomington, Illinois, and regularly pursued his legal studies with that firm for two years, and was admitted to practice in the Supreme Court of Illinois.

Shortly after his admission to the bar he formed a partnership with his brother, General John McNulta, and was associated with him as counsel for the Indianapolis, Bloomington & Western Railway Company, and also the Gilman, Clinton & Springfield Railway Company.

Mr. McNulta was married in Bloomington, Illinois, in May, 1873, to Miss Georgia Robinson, a native of Atlanta, Georgia, and removed to Santa Barbara in that year, where he has since resided.

He was elected District Attorney in 1877; has held the office of City Attorney by appointment for four terms, and is now holding that position and engaged in the practice of his profession.

HENRY W. BAKER, one of the prominent ranchers of Saticoy, came to California in 1859, and to his present ranch in the fall of 1875. He was born in New Hampshire, December 28, 1828. His father, Davis Baker, was a native of that State, born about the year 1790. He was a faithful member of the Congregational Church, passed his life on a farm, and died in 1842. The ancestors of the family were English people. Mr. Baker's mother, nee Hannah Church, was a daughter of Mr. Elihu Church. Henry W. Baker was one of a family of nine children, seven of whom are now living. He received his education in the public schools of his native State, and his life has been principally devoted to agricultural pursuits. He purchased a farm in Lake County, California, in 1866, which he improved and on which he was engaged in general farming for nine years, raising both stock and grain. At the end of that time he sold out and went East on a visit. Upon his return to California, he bought his present farm of forty acres, and has since added forty acres more to it. This property he has improved by building, tree-planting, etc. In his orchard he has apples, pears, peaches, apricots, prunes, figs, oranges and lemons. He is doing a grain and bean farming.

Mr. Baker is a Republican and is one of the reliable and substantial men of Ventura County. His widowed sister, Mrs. Leavitt, keeps house for him. She is a member of the Congregational Church.

A. PICO.—It is quite safe to say that there is not a family in California who has withal borne a more conspicuous part in the early settlement and history of the State than the Pico family. The name is familiar to the student of Southern California history. It has been the writer's privilege to meet several members of this honored and historic family, and he can not fail to give expression here to a sentiment which is not only founded upon pleasant personal acquaintance, but is also expressed by those who have known the Pico family in times of war, times of peace, and under various trying vicissitudes incident to the settlement and growth of the Commonwealth.

Don José Jesus Pico, of San Luis Obispo, is one of the aged surviving members of this family, born at Monterey, this State, March 19, 1807. There he lived until 1840, when he moved with his family to San Luis Obispo and assumed the administration of the affairs of the mission at that place, which duty he discharged until the change of government took place. In 1847 he held the office of

Alcalde of San Luis Obispo, and in all matters civil, business and social, his expressed wish and opinions were accepted without dissent or question. He possessed a stout heart and a clear, keen judgment in matters of private or public policy. He later devoted several years to the care of his ranch and stock interests, and now lives in retirement in San Luis Obispo city. He has five surviving children. Mrs. P. A. Forrester, a widow lady, and Mrs. William J. Graves, of San Luis Obispo, are daughters. Benigno and Fredrico, of San Fernando, and Zenobia A., of San Luis Obispo, are the surviving sons.

Benigno Pico was born in Monterey, March 17, 1837, the third of the family. For some time he pursued the hotel business at Port Harford, and in 1877 went to San Fernando and opened the present well-known and popular Pico Hotel, which he still conducts. He is a popular landlord and a highly respected citizen.

Zenobia A. Pico is a native of San Luis Obispo County, born in 1843, on the family homestead near the city, where the family lived from 1849 to 1868. He was first Assessor of San Luis Obispo County for one term of two years, and then City Assessor, in which office he is now serving his third term. He married, March 8, 1868, Miss Mary Baxter, and they have three children.

HON. C. A. STORKE, a prominent citizen of Santa Barbara County, was born in 1847, in Yates County, New York, whence in early life he removed with his parents to Oshkosh, Wisconsin, where he lived until the age of sixteen years, when, on February 28, 1864, he enlisted in Company G, Thirty-sixth Wisconsin Regiment, under Colonel Frank Haskell, who was killed at Cold Harbor. This regiment joined the Second Corps during the Wilderness campaign, under General Hancock, participating in the battles at Spottsville, North Anna, and at the terrible slaughter at Cold Harbor, where, out of four companies, sixty-nine per cent. were killed, and the rest captured. The prisoners were sent to Libby, Andersonville, Savannah and other prisons, suffering frightfully from privations and exposure. Of the twelve men of his company, Mr. Storke helped to bury eight out of eleven, one having been paroled. He himself was reduced from 165 to 95 pounds weight during the seven months of his imprisonment, before he was paroled. He went home and was discharged May 26, 1865. He now prepared for college, passing three years at the college at Kalamazoo, Michigan, then going to Cornell, where he was graduated in 1870, taking the Goldwin Smith and the President White honors for the senior year.

Among his classmates were Governor Foraker, of Ohio; J. Julius Chambers, of the New York *World*; Hon. T. W. Spence, of Wisconsin; Hon. S. D. Halliday, of the New York Legislature and others of note. From Cornell Mr. Storke went to Brooklyn, where he taught for two years in the Adelphi Academy; thence he came to Santa Barbara to teach in the Santa Barbara College. After one year he went to Los Angeles, where he founded the *Herald*, but soon returned to Santa Barbara, and began the practice of law. In 1882 he was elected to the Assembly, and served in the sessions of 1883 and 1884, and he was again elected in 1888, when he made himself a record by his work for the investigation of prison management.

Since 1877 he has been connected with the Sespe Rancho, Ventura County, then owned by his father-in-law, T. Wallace More, who was murdered there on March 24, 1877, the prosecution of his murderers engaging Mr. Storke's best efforts for some four years thereafter. Of this rancho, 600 acres are still owned by Mr. Storke, as well as 300 acres of the Dos Pueblos Rancho, and considerable city property.

Mr. Storke is a Knight Templar Mason and Vice-Post Commander, G. A. R.

Mr. Storke was married in 1873, to Miss Mattie More, of Santa Barbara, by whom he had four children; and on September 10, 1890, to Miss Yda Addis.

CAPTAIN FRED HILLARD was born in Norwich, Connecticut, July 24, 1822. His mother was a Brewster, a direct descendant of the Elder William Brewster who came over in the famous Mayflower. Fred Hillard spent his boyhood and received his education in his native town. At the age of nineteen he joined a whaling ship and for five years was before the mast, traveling extensively around the coast of Europe. At the end of this period he shipped to Chili and Peru and on the coast of South America. On this vessel he filled the position of fourth mate. He was on this coast until 1848, when he came to San Francisco, right in the heat of the gold excitement. Captain Hillard proceeded at once to the mines near Sacramento, but was unsuccessful, and soon abandoned the search for gold. After disposing of his land claim at Sacramento, he was engaged on a freight vessel, sailing between San Francisco and San Diego, and continued in this business until 1850. The steamship Ohio was then being operated on this coast, and Captain Hillard was engaged as fourth mate. In 1852 he was its captain. It was on this boat and during this year that Captain Hillard first made the acquaintance of Captain John Wilson and family, who were on their way from San Luis Obispo to San Francisco. Captain Wilson had with him at this time his entire family, consisting of Mrs. Wilson, one son and three daughters, one of whom, Miss Ramona Wilson, named after her mother, was subsequently married to Captain Hillard. This marriage took place April 24, 1853, at the Osos ranch, near San Luis Obispo, the old family home of the Wilsons. To this worthy couple five children were born, viz.: Adelaida, Charles, Mary, John and Frederick.

Captain Hillard's successful career as captain of the coast steamers may now be said to have fairly begun. As captain of the Ohio and subsequently of the Seabird, Goliath, Southerland and Fremont he acquired a reputation as a navigator which any officer then and of the present day might well be proud. In those days there were no light-houses of any description, no buoys of any kind, no pilot charts nor guides, all of which helps make navigation of the California coast a comparatively simple matter to the steamship commanders of the present day. During this period Captain Hillard brought his boats safely through many a perilous voyage, and it is not surprising when his intimate knowledge of the coast and also his splendid qualifications as an officer are taken into account, that he was known as the " best captain on the coast."

Captain Hillard moved his family from the Osos ranch to San Francisco in 1882, where he resided until his death, which occurred May 5, 1890.

When Captain Hillard married Ramona Wilson, he married into a family whom residents of San Luis Obispo County love to think and speak of. Mrs. Hillard's mother was born in San Diego, July 29, 1812, and died December 16, 1888. She first married a Pacheco, by whom she had two sons, one of whom is ex-Governor Pacheco, of San Francisco. Her second marriage was with Captain John Wilson, by whom, as was previously stated, there were three daughters and one son. Mrs. Ramona Wilson had hosts of friends wherever she lived and visited. Especially in San Luis Obispo, where she lived so long, did the sick and poor often receive a helping hand from her. To quote from the eulogy of the distinguished Father Dugan, who officiated at the funeral services of the deceased, "throughout her life Mrs. Wilson always manifested that strong faith which is a distinguishing characteristic of her race, and it had consequently been her hope in life and consolation in death."

Mrs. Hillard, the surviving widow of Captain Hillard, inherits the many noble characteristics of her mother, to a very marked degree, and her frequent visits to San Luis Obispo from the family home in San Francisco are always hailed with great satisfaction by the many who are so fortunate as to know her.

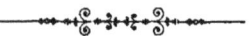

CHARLES H. SHELDON was born in Kalamazoo County, Michigan, June 9, 1839, and is a descendant of an English family. His grandfather, Timothy Sheldon, was long a resident of Gouverneur, St. Lawrence County, New York, and his father, Henry Sheldon, was a native of that place, born July 2, 1814. Mr. Sheldon's mother, *nee* Betsey Botsford, was born in Darien, New York, September 14, 1817, her ancestors being English and Welsh. The subject of this sketch was the oldest of three children. He finished his education in the Gouverneur Wesleyan Seminary. His uncle, Robert Botsford, being a blacksmith, Mr. Sheldon, early in life, conceived a liking for that trade, learned it with his uncle, and has made it his life work.

At President Lincoln's first call for troops, Mr. Sheldon enlisted; but, the quota of his State, Michigan, being full before he was mustered in, and being determined to engage in the great struggle, he went to Chicago and joined Battery C, Chicago Light Artillery. He went to Washington, where the Captain, Richard Busteed, Jr., was taken with inflammatory rheumatism. General Berry, then Chief of Artillery, went over to their camp on East Capitol Hill, and informed them that they were at liberty to join any branch of the service or go home, as they liked, the battery not having been mustered into the United States service. Mr. Sheldon then enlisted in the First New York Light Artillery, Battery G, and served three years without receiving a wound or being a day from duty. He participated in the following battles: Yorktown, Fair Oaks, Malvern Hill Antietam, Fredericksburg, Gettysburg, Auburn Hill, Wilderness, Spottsylvania Court House, Cold Habor, and several others; and during all this time he was blacksmith for his battery, shoeing all the horses and keeping every thing in repair.

In 1875 Mr. Sheldon came to Ventura County, California, and, in partnership with Mr. Vickers built their present shop. They are also engaged in the manufacture of wagons and carriages, and are doing a thorough and reliable business. Mr. Sheldon owns a ranch of eighty acres, sixteen miles from town, which he is devoting, principally, to the cultivation of orange trees, Washington Navels. Water is flumed to this place,

He is also interested in bees, having 200 stands on his ranch.

In 1861, Mr. Sheldon was married to Miss Elizabeth Young, a native of England, by whom he had six children, four born in Michigan, viz.: Frederick Henry, Emma C., Sarah S., Charles Leroy, and two born in Ventura County, Harriet E. and Maudie. Mrs. Sheldon having died in 1881, Mr. Sheldon was married, in 1883, to Mrs. Nellie Bradley, a native of Indiana, and daughter of Gabriel Newby, a Quaker of that State. Mrs. Bradley had two daughters, Edith R., born in Santa Barbara, California, in 1869, and Effie N., born in Ventura, in 1873. Mrs. Sheldon is the owner of a good home in Ventura, in which they reside. The subject of this sketch is a member of the Masonic fraternity; and was a charter member of the Grand Army of the Republic, in Ventura. Mr. Sheldon is a respected and worthy citizen, and no man is more entitled to respect than he, who by honest industry makes a livelihood and a competency.

GIOVANNI ROCCO MAGGI was born in the State of Parma, Italy, January 16, 1852, and came to Santa Barbara, California, in 1872. After remaining in that place three or four months and hearing of better business opportunities in San Luis Obispo, he came to this city, associating himself with G. Divoto in the grocery and general merchandise business. This connection lasted seven years, at the expiration of which time he engaged in business for himself and has so continued up to the present. In 1871 Mr. Maggi made a visit to his old home in Italy, remaining there six months and then returning to New York and six months later to San Luis Obispo. Four years afterward he made another journey to Italy, this time bringing back with him to this country the remainder of his family. Mr. Maggi's parents, Pietro and Katrine Maggi, are both dead. Mr. Maggi is married and has six children, all living. He is a member and Vice President of Societa Unione Italiana of San Luis Obispo.

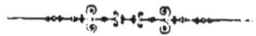

MURPHY GRAVES, son of William J. and Soldat (Peco) Graves, was born in San Luis Obispo, August 5, 1865. At his baptism in the Catholic Church (the mission) there were present as sponsors P. W. Murphy and Mrs. C. W. Dana. Mr. Graves is one of a family of seven children, four sons and three daughters, all living and all prominent men and women. He attended school in San Luis Obispo and later on in San Francisco. In the latter place he subsequently entered his father's law office, remaining there for three years. Mr. Graves is at present deputy County Clerk, a position he has held for five years. He is a charter member of the society of Native Sons of the Golden West; is also a member of the Ancient Order of United Workmen.

Mr. Graves was married January 16, 1889, to Harriet Leland, of Watsonville, Santa Cruz County, daughter of Captain Richard Leland.

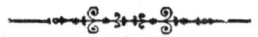

D. H. REED, one of the popular photographers of Santa Barbara, was born at Buffalo Grove, Illinois, in 1848. His father came to that locality among the first pioneers in 1829, and devoted himself to farming. The subject of this sketch was educated at the State Normal School, Illinois, taking the regular teachers' course. He then took up photography, gaining his knowledge from actual experience through photographical acquaintances and in attendance at photographic conventions. He came to Santa Barbara in 1887 and established rooms at 928½ State street, where he has since conducted business in all kinds of interior photography, and his artistic tastes in scenic views is especially recommended.

He was married at Pontiac, Illinois, in 1874. They have three children.

EDWIN TAGGART was born in Sullivan County, Pennsylvania, in the town of Montoursville, August 6, 1852. He is the son of John P. Taggart, a native of Pennsylvania, who was an assistant surgeon on the first staff of General Grant, and for some years held the position of Internal Revenue Collector of Utah Territory. His death occurred November 22, 1889. Mr. Taggart's mother was *nee* Phebe Ann Willets. She was married to Mr. Taggart in Bloomsburg, Pennsylvania, and is the mother of two children, the subject of this sketch and a daughter, Emma, who is now the wife of Lieutenant Mumford, of the United States army. Mr. Taggart finished his education at Manuel Hall, Chicago. When he was sixteen years old, he was engaged for eleven months with a surveying party, in southern Illinois, making a railroad survey. At the age of seventeen, with a partner, he started in the drug business, in Salt Lake City. In 1877 he sold his interest in that enterprise, and engaged in mining at Silver Reef, working there a year and a half. He then went to Wood River, Idaho, and mined with fair success. In 1881 he came to California, located in Ukiah, Mendocino County, bought out the drug business of Dr. Barton Dozier, and remained there ten months. At that time he sold out and came to Ventura. He here bought the pioneer drug store of the city, which is located on Main street, between Oak and Palm streets, in the center of town, and which is the largest and best equipped drug house in the city. He employs two assistants, and has established a good trade.

Mr. Taggart was married, September 11, 1876, to Miss Virginia K. Pitt, of Salt Lake City. They have one child, John K., born in Salt Lake City, December 24, 1877. Mr. Taggart is a member of the Masonic fraternity, is a Republican in politics, and is president of the board of trustees of the Episcopal Church of Ventura. As a business man he is prompt and capable, and as a citizen he is worthy and respected by all who know him.

A. DUVAL is an early settler an ad prominent business man and rancher of Saticoy, Ventura County, California. He was born in one of the Windward Islands of France, September 14, 1834. His parents and all his ancestors were French people. Mr. Duval came to America when sixteen years of age, and has become thoroughly identified with American principles and government. A part of his life was spent in the State of Maine. He came to California in 1861, went to the mines in Nevada for three years, and was afterward in the grocery business. From Virginia City he came to Saticoy, in 1868. This country was then a vast field of mustard. Mr. Duval purchased seventy-five acres of land, built a house, and at once commenced the work of planting trees. Some of the trees first planted have attained a wonderful growth. His land is now mostly devoted to fruit—apricots, peaches, plums, prunes, nectarines, apples, pears, figs, oranges, lemons, blackberries, almonds and walnuts. At the time he bought this property, land was sold at from $12 to $20 per acre. It is now worth from $150 to $500 per acre, according to the improvements made. Mr. Duval has disposed of a part of his land, but retains a fine home, where he resides; and in addition to his ranch interests he is also engaged in mercantile business.

He was married, April 15, 1855, to Miss Artemisa G. Hopkins, who was born in Frankfort, Maine, daughter of Captain Smith Hopkins and Susanna Hopkins. Their union has been blessed with ten children, nine living, viz.: Charles S., Carrie, Winton, Gertrude, Anna, Willie, Walter, Earnest and Edwin. The first three were born in Maine, and the others in Saticoy, California. They are members of the Union Church of Saticoy. In his religious views Mr. Duval is a Conditional Immortalist. Politically, he is a Prohibitionist. He is a public-spirited citizen, and is much interested in the upbuilding of his town.

J. C. ORTEGA, son of Stevan and Dogracia (Ruiz) Ortega, was born in Santa Barbara, March 19, 1850. At the age of fifteen years he left home and came to San Luis Obispo to attend school and prepare himself for a business life. In 1870 he took charge of the express business of Wells, Fargo & Co., and also the Pacific Coast Stage Company's business, remaining in that capacity until 1876. Mr. Ortega then engaged in the stationery business on his own account, continuing until 1885. Since that date he has been in the insurance and real-estate business. He was City Treasurer from 1870 to 1880, the only public office he has ever held, although requested at various times to accept nominations.

Mr. Ortega was married May 8, 1888, to Miss Mary Murphy, of San Francisco. They have one child.

J. L. CRANE.—Much credit is due to the pioneers who came to this country when it gave so little promise of being what it is to-day, who, with astonishing fortitude, spent years of labor and experiment, and who overcame the difficulties and discouragements that beset their way. J. L. Crane is one of these worthy pioneers, and is deserving of more than a passing mention in these pages.

He was born in Sharon Township, Medina County, Ohio, June 17, 1839. His father, George W. Crane, was a native of Massachusetts, and a pioneer of Ohio. He went to that State in an early day, took a Government claim of heavy timber land, cleared it up, reared a family of seven sons and one daughter, and lived there until he died, in 1885. Mr. Crane's grandfather, Barnabas Crane, was a sea captain in summer and a school teacher in winter, and lived to be eighty-four years old. They trace their ancestry back to England. Some members of the family settled in Massachusetts before the Revolutionary war, and most of the Cranes of this country are descendants from that stock. The mother of the subject of this sketch, nee Louisa Briggs, was a native of New York, born in 1815. She is now a resident of California. Mr. Crane received his education in the public schools of Ohio, and has been engaged in agricultural pursuits all his life. Before coming to California he sold his farm in Ohio to his brother, started in October, 1861, and arrived here in November. He came to his present location on the Saticoy ranch in December of the same year. His uncle, G. G. Briggs, came with him from Marysville, and bought 16,000 acres of the Moore Brothers, the price being $45,000. Mr. Crane had been married a short time before leaving Ohio, and to this ranch, in March, 1862, he brought his young wife. At that time it was a vast mustard-plant country. Their nearest neighbor on the west was ten miles away, and on the east, twelve miles. The only inhabitants of Saticoy were a few Indians. The country was full of game, and it was not unusual to see bands of fifteen or twenty deer on the hills. One could scarcely go out without seeing tracks of the grizzly bear. At that time it was thought that nothing could be raised without irrigation. Mr. Briggs brought nursery stock for his own use, and the next year 200 acres were plowed and planted. An orchard, containing a variety of fruits, was set out, the first attempt of that kind in the country. They planted the first ten acres of corn grown without irrigation. Up to that time, Mr. Crane had been in the employ of his uncle. In the fall of 1862 he went to work for himself. That winter proved to be a short one, and the drouth of 1864 caused Mr. Briggs to abandon the idea of colonizing the valley. Every one was discouraged and gave up the thought of staying or the possibility of living in such a country. Mr. Briggs sold his ranch in 1867 to E. B. Higgins. In 1864 Mr. Crane removed to Santa Barbara, and engaged in teaching school. The people of Santa Barbara at that time were so discouraged that they offered land in what is now the heart of the city for $5 per acre. After remaining in that town ten months, he returned to the ranch and planted a quantity of potatoes. They were planted too late, however, and were killed by the frost. After six years of discouragements here they were heartily sick of California, and decided to go back to Ohio, which they did. They remained only ten months, and, after all, found that California had its attractions, and they were sufficient to induce them to return to this coast. They came with a firm determination to stay, and have never wanted to leave again. He resided in Carpenteria seven years, was there at the time the county was divided, and has seen a wonderful change come over the Santa Clara Valley. Mr. Crane now has a farm of 100 acres at Santa Paula. Twenty acres of this are in fruit trees of different kinds, 700 pear, 300 apple, 100 plum trees, and all other kinds of fruit.

Mr. Crane's marriage occurred in 1861, when he wedded Miss Jenette Briggs, a foster daughter of his uncle. She is a native of Massachusetts. They have five children, all born in Ventura County: Emmit C., April 6, 1863; Lincoln P., September 28, 1865; Cora L., April 21, 1873; Charles, April 21, 1875; and Chancy, November 4, 1877. The two oldest sons are merchants at Saticoy, and the other children reside with their parents. Politically, Mr. Crane is a Free-trade Democrat.

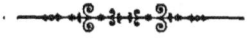

GEORGE G. SEWELL, residing near Santa Paula, is a pioneer of California, having come to the State in March, 1851. and is also a pioneer of Santa Paula, as he arrived here in 1872. He has to the present been one of the most prominent ranchers, and occupies a most delightful suburban home, graced with vine-embowered retreats, and ornamental trees and shrubbery. He was born in Glens Falls, New York, February 24, 1819. His father, Jonathan Sewell, was a native of Dutchess County, New York, born in 1770, and was an early settler of Glens Falls. His ancestors, from England, first settled in the East, in the early history of the country. His mother, Wealthy Skinner, was born in 1780, in Connecticut. In their family were nine children, of whom George was the seventh. Five of this family are still living, their ages now aggregating 376 years. Mr. Sewell went to Wisconsin in 1844, bought a farm and cultivated it for six years; he then sold out and came to California, where he engaged in mining for a few months in Placer and El Dorado counties; but exposure to cold water induced rheumatism, which compelled him to abandon a miner's life, and he located upon a section of State school land, on Auburn Ravine, near Lincoln, Placer County, on which he spent twenty years of his life as an industrious farmer. In 1868 he was elected County Clerk of Placer County, and subsequently re-elected. He is a Republican, casting his first Presidential vote for William Henry Harrison, and his last for his grandson, Benjamin Harrison. Mr. Sewell sold his fine farm at the close of his term of office, resided at Sacramento for a few months, and then came to Santa Paula and purchased about 1,000 acres of valley and grazing land. Barley and corn being the principal productions of the valley at that time, his experience in Placer satisfied him that to grow small grain for the San Francisco market, entailing the expense of labor and machinery for harvesting and threshing, would not pay. He, therefore, at once stocked his ranch with sheep and hogs, principally, and by raising hogs enough to do the harvesting and save the threshing, and conveying to market the corn and barley grown on 200 to 300 acres yearly, made his investment remunerative. The dry season of 1877 forced him to dispose of his sheep, but by growing two crops of barley and corn on land that could be irrigated, other stock did not suffer. He after that engaged in dairying for five years, milking from fifty to seventy-five cows, making butter and cheese, which he found to be profitable.

Recently he has subdivided his land and sold portions of it. His home place, one mile west of Santa Paula, contains sixty acres. Mr. Sewell has lived in four or five different States, and as many localities in California, and is best suited with his present place.

He was married in 1849 to Miss Harriet Benedict, of Glens Falls. She lived only a year, and in 1858 Mr. Sewell married Eliza Rich, of Shoreham, Vermont, who was born in 1825, the daughter of Hiram Rich, of Richville, Vermont, which place was settled by and took its name from her grandfather. His brothers came from Massachusetts and settled there. Mr. and Mrs. Sewell are original members of the Universalist Church of Santa Paula. While at Lincoln, Mr. Sewell was a member of the Union League.

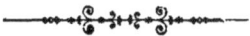

J. D. GOODYEAR was born in Tiffin, Seneca County, Ohio, October 23, 1825. His father, Merritt Goodyear, and his grandfather, Joseph Goodyear, were both natives of Connecticut. His great-grandfather, Stephen Goodyear, came from England in an early day and settled in Connecticut, and was the ancestor of the Goodyear family in America. Charles Goodyear, the man of such noteriety as a rubber inventor, and whose name is stamped on nearly all the genuine rubber boots and shoes in the civilized world, was a cousin of Mr. Goodyear's father. The mother of the subject of this sketch, *nee* Fanny Smith, was born in the State of New York. She was the daughter of Zenas Smith, who married a Marvin, niece of Marvin the great safe manufacturer of New York. Mr. Goodyear spent his early childhood in Ohio, and, at the age of seven years, went to New York State, where he remained until he reached his majority. He has been an industrious man all his life, began work when he was quite small, and has been engaged in many different kinds of employment, and among other things, has worked in the redwoods of California. He has been the owner of several pieces of property that have become very valuable since he parted with them. He thinks the mistake of his life has been that he did not hold on long enough. Mr. Goodyear has learned wisdom through the years that are past, and it is his intention to keep the beautiful ranch which he now owns. In 1887 he bought 120 acres of land. This property had been improved to some extent, and Mr. Goodyear has continued the work of tree-planting and improving and remodeling until the place is now a delightful and attractive home. There is a fine artesian well on the ranch. Mr. Goodyear's principal crop is corn. He also has a fine variety of fruit, and has given some attention to the raising of horses.

The subject of this sketch was married in 1851, to Miss Sophina Wright, a native of Illinois, and daughter of Peter Wright, who was a Kentuckian by birth. They have had ten children, six of whom are now living, viz.: Harriet, wife of Henry Root, resides in Oregon; Eugene, who married Miss Lizzie Paulson; Willie, who is at home with his father; Everett, now attending college at Berkeley; and Edward and Fanny, at home. Emma married Albert Coyle, and died in 1883, leaving one child, Emma.

Mr. Goodyear was a Democrat until the organization of the Republican party, and has been a Republican since that time. The Goodyear family is one that has seen much of pioneer life, and can fully appreciate their comfortable home, which is situated in the beautiful Santa Clara Valley, only three miles from Hueneme. Mr. Goodyear was a pioneer in the Territories of Wisconsin and Minnesota, and voted for the admission of both into the Union. Himself, wife and children represent five States, by birth.

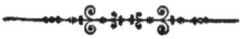

MATTHEW H. ARNOLD is a prominent rancher of Ventura County, and a pioneer of California. A brief sketch of his life is as follows: He was born in DeKalb County, Illinois, February 16, 1844. His father, Cullar Arnold, is a native of Ohio, born in 1818; has been a pioneer of California since 1849, and is now a resident of Orange, Orange County. The ancestors of the Arnold family came from Connecticut and Vermont. The grandfather's name was Nathan Arnold, and grandmother's name on father's side was Cutler. His mother's name was Hough. She was born in New York State, of ancestors who were from Connecticut and Massachusetts. Burage Hough was her father's name and Alexander her mother's name. Cullar Arnold had nine children, of whom eight are living in California. Mr. Arnold, whose name heads this sketch, received his education in the public schools and at Oakland College, California, and, since leaving school, his time has been principally devoted to agricultural pursuits. He came to California in 1852, and to Ventura County in November, 1868, and his present location December, 1878. In November, 1869, they settled on what they supposed was Government land; but, on finding their mistake, his father and two of the sons bought 480 acres, and afterward 160 acres more. Matthew H. purchased 320 acres, and to it has since added eighty acres. The first purchase was at $10.50 per acre and the last at $8.50. This land is now worth from $100 to $125 per acre. Mr. Arnold's principal crop has been barley, but the land is well adapted to the cultivation of other grains, and without irrigation. He derives a good income from the hogs, Poland-China and Berkshire, kept on this place.

In 1877 Mr. Arnold wedded Miss Eliza Perkins, a native of Maine, daughter of T. E. Perkins, now of Los Angeles County. They have four children, all born at their present home: Ralph, Chester, Jo and Alice. In politics Mr. Arnold is a Republican. He was elected School Trustee when the district was formed, and held the office twelve years. He is a member of the A. O. U. W.

When Mr. Arnold came to this ranch it was a wilderness of mustard, and there were only three or four board houses between there and the river, a distance of six miles. Since that time the settlement has been rapid and the improvement wonderful. The people who had faith in the future of the county and the courage to settle in it then, are now amply repaid.

THOMAS R. MORE, of Santa Barbara, was born in the village of Santa Barbara in 1856; attended college two years at Cornell University and two years at the Michigan State University at Ann Arbor, in the scientific course. March 24, 1880, he married Miss Mary Den, and they have five children. Mr. More is a member of the Young Men's Institute and of the Native Sons of the Golden West. His father, T. Wallace More, was born at Copley, Summit County, Ohio, in 1826, and in 1849 came to California with his brother. He and his brother, Alexander P. More, owned the famous Santa Rosa Island, which contains nearly 70,000 acres, and over which graze 60,000 sheep. T. Wallace More was married in Santa Barbara, in 1852, to a daughter of Mr. Hill, who was one of the earliest American settlers in Santa Barbara. He married a daughter of the famous Ortega family. T. R. More lived on the Dos Pueblos ranch from 1884 to 1889, looking after his fine-bred cattle and horses. While at Ann Arbor he was under the especial instructions of Professor Moses Coit Tyler, whose only son is married to Susie E. Den, a sister of Mrs. T. R. More.

Mr. More is a poet, having just completed a long poem, which will shortly be published.

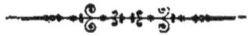

PROF. JOSEPH E. GREEN, the leading musician of Santa Barbara, was born at Hamilton, Ontario, Canada, in 1846, of English descent, his grandfather being one of the first settlers of Ontario. Mr. Green was educated at Hamilton, and in early life developed a decided talent for music, the cornet being his favorite instrument. At the age of ten years he was dressed in full uniform and a member of the Artillery Battery Band, and later, at the age of fifteen years, he traveled through the United States as soloist on the cornet. In 1867 he was leader of the Hamilton City Band, from which was formed the Thirteenth Battalion Band, which is recognized as the best band in Canada. Having a fancy for travel he left Canada in 1863 as leader of the band connected with the Great Overland Circus, and for seven years, with different organizations, he traveled through the United States, Mexico and the Sandwich Islands. In 1875 he organized the San Francisco City Band, which was chosen to escort President Hayes across the bay on his visit to San Francisco in 1879. Mr. Green holds a musical diploma from the San Francisco Musical Fund Society. In 1881 he returned to Ontario and became leader of the Dominion Organ and Piano Factory Band, remaining two years, making the band the second best in Canada. He returned to San Francisco in 1884, and to Santa Barbara in 1885, where he has since resided. He has organized an orchestra and Military Band, at present one of the best in Southern California, and for four years has catered to the guests of the Arlington in all dances and concert music, and has been the recipient of many presents and letters of commendation.

Mr. Green was married at Santa Barbara, May 26, 1888, to Miss Orisa Clifton, a very superior pianist with great natural talent. They have one child, Charlotte, born February 9, 1889.

T. CODY was born in Onondaga County, New York, September 12, 1826. His parents were both natives of Edinburgh, Scotland, and came to America as early as 1820, settled in Cicero and built the first frame house in that town. Their name, Mr. Cody thinks, originated in the north of Ireland; if so, he is of Scotch-Irish descent. He has only one son.

Mr. Cody was educated in Cleveland, Ohio, and graduated at the Willoughby College of Medicine, after which he engaged in the drug business in Zanesville, Ohio. From there he went to Cleveland and from there to Europe. He afterward made a second trip to Europe. He spent a portion of his time in Toledo, Ohio, and was also engaged in the drug business in Waukegan, Illinois, three years. In 1850 he came to California, first worked in the mines and had a trading station near Hangtown; next went to Mariposa County, and also had a trading station on the Merced River, being at that place during the severe winter of 1852–'53. From there he went to Big Oak Flat, Tuolumne County, and opened a drug store, and was in business there until 1864, when he went to Washington Territory. He remained at the latter place a year and a half, and was in the drug business nearly all the time from 1856 to 1890. He came to Ventura May 18, 1881, and bought his present store of Mrs. Simms, a sister of Judge Williams. Mr. Cody has erected the building in which his store is located, and is doing a nice business. He is also agent for Wells-Fargo & Company, having received his appointment as express agent on St. Patrick's day in the morning, and his wife took the telegraph office in July, 1882.

Mr. Cody's first wife, who was the mother of his son, was *nee* Susan Adams, of Providence, Rhode Island. Her father was a merchant in that city. The son, N. T. Cody, was born in Waukegan, Illinois, and three weeks later his mother died. Young Cody is now traveling in Europe, and writes home that the more he sees of Europe the more he loves America. In 1872 the subject of this sketch was united in marriage to his present wife.

In many respects Mr. Cody is a remarkable man. Has never run for any office, nor has he ever joined any society. He does strictly a cash business; owes no man anything, either in his business or out of it. He is averse to lawsuits, and would rather lose a sum of money than bring suit in order to get payment. He is, withal, a jovial man, and none loves fun better than he. He both gives and takes a joke freely, and if there is any fun going he is sure to know of it and have a share in the same.

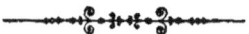DWARD M. CLEVELAND was born in Fluvanna County, Virginia, July 19, 1845. Both his father and grandfather, Jeremiah Cleveland, Sr. and Jr., were natives of Virginia. His mother, *nee* Sally Wills, was born in the same county, and his grandfather, Miles G. Wills, was also a native of the "Old Dominion." The subject of this sketch was the second of a family of nine children, eight of whom are now living, and he was reared and educated in Virginia. When the great civil war commenced Mr. Cleveland was only sixteen years old. In 1863, when the need of the South for soldiers became great, at the age of eighteen, he enlisted in the Fluvanna Artillery, under Captain Massey, in Colonel Nelson's battalion. He was in many skirmishes and in the battles of Kelley's Ford and Winchester. In the latter a twelve-pound cannon ball wounded him in the back part of the leg, near the knee, carrying away a portion of the flesh and injuring the cords. He was crippled and in Harrisonburg prison hospital twelve days; was considered unfit for service and was permitted to return home.

After his recovery he worked on his father's farm, and later rented 400 acres of grandfather Willis, which he farmed for five years. He was next employed as a clerk in a general merchandise store with his uncle, A. S. Burgess, of Central Plains, and the following year he came to California. He purchased seventy-five acres of choice land at Santa Paula, which he has improved and where he has made a very pleasant home.

In 1879 Mr. Cleveland was married to Miss M. J. Fowler. She was born in Indiana in 1855, and is the daughter of Mr. Welcome Fowler, of Indiana. Mrs. Cleveland is a member of the Christian Church. Mr. Cleveland is a member of the I. O. O. F., and in politics affiliates with the Democratic party.

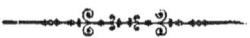D. F. RICHARDS, founder of the town of Saticoy, was born in Fairfield, Herkimer County, New York, March 8, 1838. His father, Benjamin Richards, was a native of the same State, born June 30, 1800. Mr. Richard's grandfather, Joseph Richards, was born in Connecticut, and was a soldier all through the Revolution. His mother, Hepsey (De Forest) Richards, is a native of the State of Connecticut, was born June 20, 1800, and is still living in Oneida County, New York. She was the granddaughter of Joseph De-Forest, a Huguenot, who fled to America to escape persecution in France, his native land. He bequeathed the DeForest fund to Yale College for the education of any of the De-Forest name. Mr. Richards, our subject, was the sixth in a family of nine children, only four of whom are living, and was educated at Fairfield Academy, one of the oldest institutions of the kind in New York. He came to California in 1868, and bought 650 acres of land, where he now resides. He was one of the first to raise flax-seed, of which he raised over 100 tons on 200 acres of his land; he was also a pioneer in the raising of canary seed, raising 3,000 bushels in one year, and selling it at from three to five cents per pound. He is now farming a portion of his land to Lima beans and 100 acres has been set the present year to English walnuts. Mr. Richards had the town plat of Saticoy recorded March 25, 1887. He has since sold many lots, and

there are many pleasant homes in the town. The station is within half a mile of the town, and they have an abundance of good water and a handsome Presbyterian Church edifice, of which Rev. J. M. Crawford was the first pastor, and the Rev. Dr. Bowman present pastor. Mr. George R. Walden is the obliging postmaster and druggist, and they have two hotels and a blacksmith shop, three general stores, one dentist and two physicians. The town is in the center of the Santa Clara Valley, surrounded by a wide stretch of rich level land, as choice as any in the State; it is located about half-way between Ventura and Santa Paula. The name Saticoy in the Indian language is equivalent to Eureka (Greek for "I have found it") in the English language, and is a very appropriate name for the town.

Mr. Richards was married October 4, 1877, to Miss Carrie Leavens, a native of Trenton Falls, Oneida County, New York, and a daughter of Hamilton Leavens, of that State. Mr. Richards is a Republican and a prominent citizen of Ventura County.

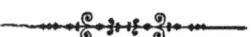

K. P. GRANT, a Ventura rancher. When the Americans began to settle at Ventura the whole face of the country was covered with mustard plants so tall and thick that one could scarcely ride a horse through it—indicating that the soil was of the best quality. The town was then a Spanish village. The American seeking a productive soil was allured by the rich alluvium and delightful climate of this region. Dr. Voorman had come to Ventura, and, being acquainted with Mr. Grant, informed him of the fine opening at Ventura, and September, 29, 1869, Mr. Grant arrived in the town, where he has since made his home and met with success so satisfactory as to render him content.

Mr. Grant is a Master Mason and belongs also to the Chapter and Commandery, having passed all the chairs. He is Past Master and Past High Priest, and is now filling the second office in the commandery. He has also held the office of District Deputy in the Odd Fellows order for seven years, and is a charter member of the A. O. U. W. and K. of P., and is a member of the A. L. of H. Politically he has been a steady Republican. Recently he was appointed by Governor Waterman a member of the commission to locate the new insane asylum. In his manner he is genial and unassuming, and in his general character a very practical man.

JARRETT T. RICHARDS, one of the leading members of the Santa Barbara bar, who came to Santa Barbara in 1868 has materially assisted, by counsel and action, in its development and in securing for it a sound city government. He was born at Chambersburg, Pennsylvania, in 1842. His father, John Custis Richards, was born in Baltimore, Maryland, June 1, 1812. His ancestry were of Welsh origin. His grandfather was the Rev. Lewis Richards of Glamorganshire, Wales, who was sent to this country as a missionary about the latter part of the last century by Lady Huntingdon, and who married Miss Custis of Virginia. The early education of Jarrett T. Richards was in Chambersburg; at the age of seventeen years he went to Europe, spending two or three years of student life in Switzerland and Germany. He began the study of law in 1864, at Chambersburg, under a preceptor. In the summer of that year the town was destroyed by a detachment of the Rebel army, and in the ensuing fall Mr. Richards went to New York, and entered the Columbia Law School, graduating in 1866, taking the second prize in municipal law. After graduating he entered the office of Brown, Hall & Vanderpool, remaining about one year. He then went to Erie, Pennsylvania, where he began the practice of his profession, and was also the political editor of the *Daily Republican*, during the impeachment of President Johnson. After one year at Erie, being in delicate health, his friends persuaded him to come to California. He settled at Santa Barbara in the autumn of 1868, immediately opening a law office, and has been continuously in practice of his profession ever since, devoting himself principally to the civil branch of the science.

In 1872 an attempt was made by the California Atlantic & Pacific Railroad to obtain a subsidy from San Francisco and the Southern counties of California, and particular efforts were made to obtain a donation from the county and the town of Santa Barbara. Mr. Richards was of the opinion that it would be disastrous to saddle an indebtedness upon the community when there was no positive assurance afforded that the road would ever be built, and the results have sustained the conviction. Even after San Francisco had declined to give any aid, it was attempted, nevertheless, to obtain a subsidy from Santa Barbara, many prominent citizens who acted in good faith in favoring it, believing that the prosperity of the community depended upon securing railroad facilities. Mr. Richards opposed it with all possible ardor and energy, and became interested in the Santa Barbara *Times*, which he edited for that purpose, and the proposition was defeated. The Board of Supervisors—Thomas R. Bard, of Ventura; Thomas W. More, of Santa Barbara; John Edwards, of Santa Barbara—refused to place the question before the people. The feeling was very bitter and colored the complexion of politics for a long time. In 1875 Mr. Richards was elected Mayor of Santa Barbara. While in office he conceived the system of having city warrants bear a reasonable rate of interest, pending the existence of a large floating indebtedness, which put city scrip at par and established its credit until the indebtedness was finally liquidated. In 1879, at the first State convention held after the adoption of the new constitution, Mr. Richards received the nomination of the Republican party as one of the Justices of the Supreme Court. There were four parties in the field, two of which, the Democratic and Workingmen's party, combined upon the judiciary ticket, and thus secured the defeat of the Republican judiciary ticket, with the exception of Judge Myrick.

Mr. Richards is opposed to monopolies, the combination of capital and centralization of governmental power, but he is no longer in active politics, attending simply to the duties of his profession.

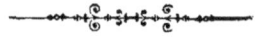

C. N. KIMBALL is one of the prominent ranchers of Saticoy, Ventura County, California. He was born at West Boxford, Essex County, Massachusetts, September 17, 1843. His father, C. F. Kimball, was born in Newburyport, Massachusetts, in 1818. He was a shoemaker and a farmer. Mrs. Kimball, the mother of the subject of this sketch, was *nee* Hannah Tyler, born in Boxford, Massachusetts, in 1817. She was a daughter of Flint Tyler, a native of the State of Vermont. C. N. Kimball was the second of a family of seven children, all of whom are living at this writing. He was reared and educated in his native place, and his first work was as a machinist. His country's claim in its time of need caused him to enlist, and he was placed in unattached service on the coast of his native State, doing duty in the fortifications. He was mustered out on the 4th of July, 1865. Then for two years he worked in the factories of Lynn and Haverhill, engaged in the manufacture of shoes.

December 31, 1867, Mr. Kimball sailed from New York for California, at which place he arrived January 22, 1868. He accepted a position on the Central Pacific Railroad, remaining in railroad employ nine months. On Christmas of that year he came to Southern California, and bought a band of sheep which he took to Eastern Nevada and traded for a ranch in Lamoille Valley. He there engaged in farming, raising potatoes and barley; and from that place he went to Eureka, same State, where he burned charcoal for the smelting furnaces. After he had been there a year and a half he was taken sick with pneumonia. At that time he returned to California, and worked near Gilroy two years. In 1876 he came to his present locality and purchased seventy-five acres of land. Here he has built a tasteful home and planted trees and flowers, making a very attractive place. In farm products his specialty is Lima beans, which proves to be a bonanza for many of the farmers of Saticoy. Mr. Kimball's crop last year averaged 1,600 pounds to the acre, the price being from three to four and a half cents.

Mr. Kimball was married in February, 1884, to Miss Carry Duval, a native of the State of Maine, and a daughter of E. A. Duval, a prominent citizen of Saticoy, whose history appears in this book. One child, a daughter, born October 4, 1888, died November 4, 1889. Mrs. Kimball is a member of the Union Church. In political views Mr. Kimball is a Republican. He is a member of the I. O. O. F., is a good citizen and a man of worth and integrity.

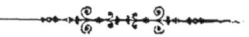

C. REMICK, son of Samuel Remick, a native of New Hampshire, and nee Olive Norton, of Massachusetts, was born in Anson, Sunset County, Maine, July 7, 1848. He remained at home, receiving a careful education, until the year 1868, when he came to San Luis Obispo County, California. March 16 of that year he was engaged on the Huer-Huero ranch as a ranchman, and June 1 of the same year assumed the entire charge of the work on this place. This vast property of 44,000 acres was owned by Flint Bixby & Co., and was devoted entirely to the raising of sheep. Young Remick did not, however, remain long on this place, and was soon after engaged to take charge of the Nacimiento ranch, at the same time also being engaged in the livery business and mail contracts in the city of San Luis Obispo. In 1875 he purchased a sheep ranch and leased it. Later on he stocked it with cattle, and met with the same misfortune that every one did in the dry year that followed. He then sold out all of his cattle interests and in the spring of 1878 established himself in the business of buying and selling meat, produce, cattle, wool, etc., and shipping to San Francisco, with headquarters at San Luis Obispo. This business has assumed large proportions and, in Mr. Remick's hands, is at present very successful.

Mr. Remick was married April 15, 1874, to Elizabeth J. Orr, of Detroit, Michigan. They have four children, two sons and two daughters. The family have been living in the city in their present residence since 1877.

Three times Mr. Remick has been elected City Councilman, and for six years he has served as School Trustee. Socially he is affiliated with the Masonic lodge, the Odd Fellows and the Workingmen's Society Mr. Remick has taken an important part in the operations of the San Luis Obispo Paving & Improvement Company; has been interested in the bituminous rock business for some time, and has been instrumental in the opening and extension of the city streets, at various times.

A remarkable fact in connection with this Remick family is its longevity. Mr. Remick had ten brothers and sisters, and such was the splendid constitution of each member that there was not a death for a period of forty-two years. The father of this family is now living, aged seventy-seven. The mother is deceased.

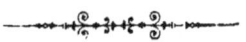

WAITE GERRY came to Ventura in September, 1873. He was born in New York in 1824, the son of Euroclydon and Pauline (Avery) Gerry, the former a native of Hatfield, Massachusetts, and the latter of New York. His grandfather's name was Nathan Gerry. His maternal ancestors were English and Welsh, and one of them, Benjamin Waite, was the hero of Hatfield, Massachusetts. Mr. Gerry's parents had two children, a daughter and son, the former being now the wife of Mr. Burr, of New York. Mr. Gerry received a common-school education and completed his studies in Williston Seminary, Massachusetts. The principal part of his life has been devoted to agricultural pursuits, but for a time he resided in Pennsylvania, where he ran a sawmill and conducted a store. He also spent some time in Indiana. In 1864 he crossed the plains with Major Bridge, and after returning he emigrated to Cass County, Missouri. Having a love for pioneer life, he continued his way westward, and engaged in mining in Utah, and after returning from this trip he came to California in 1872. For a time he was employed in Oakland, after which he came to Southern California and worked at Los Angeles for the telegraph company. From Los Angeles he went to San Bernardino, and from there he made an overland trip to Reno, Nevada, to see the country.

In 1873 Mr. Gerry sent for his family to come to Ventura County, where he had rented a farm from Mr. William Collins. On this ranch of 550 acres they lived a year and were very successful. The next year he removed to Saticoy, leaving his family in Ventura, where they had built a home on a lot he purchased. Mr. Gerry engaged in farming, in company with J. L. Starr, in Aliso Cañon, and also kept a small apiary. In 1880 he purchased seventy-five acres of choice land at $22 per acre. On this property he has built a good house, planted trees, and the place has become valuable, being rated at $200 per acre. The principal crop raised on this ranch is beans, but it also produces corn and fruits. The land yields 3,500 pounds of shelled corn to the acre, and as high as 2,500 pounds of beans per acre.

Mr. Gerry was married in 1850 to Miss Ester Craig, who was born in Pennsylvania, May 12, 1827. Her father, John Craig, was a native of Russia; came to America in 1817, and settled near Scranton, Pennsylvania. Mr. Gerry's family consists of six children, four daughters and two sons, namely: Mary E., born in New York, September 2, 1851, and is now the wife of J. L. Stone, of Los Angeles; Eva P., born in Pennsylvania, April 5, 1854, wedded Mr. A. Everett, of

Saticoy; Isabell G., born in New York, February 17, 1857, now the wife of J. S. Collins, of Ventura; Lacetta H., born in Indiana, April 24, 1861, now the wife of George E. Preble, of Tustin City, Orange County, California; Ellsworth E., born February 4, 1863, in Indiana, is now renting the home ranch; Edmund W., born April 2, 1868, in Missouri. Mrs. Gerry and the family, save one, are all members of the Presbyterian Church. Ellsworth and Edmund are members of the Y. M. C. A. Mr. Gerry has been a Republican, but he and his sons are now Prohibitionists.

P. J. BARBER.—A brief biographical sketch of the life and career of the Hon. P. J. Barber, and incidents in connection therewith, from the pen of an old friend, by whom it is dedicated.

The early home of his parents discloses the fact that he sprang from staunch New England stock, their ancestors having emigrated from old England. Those on his mother's side arrived in 1634, and were among the first settlers of Newbury, Massachusetts.

His father, Thomas Barber, was born in Canton, Connecticut, in 1773. His mother was born in Simsbury, Connecticut, in 1781: her maiden name was Percy Merrill; they were married in 1797 and reared a large family, the youngest of whom—the subject of this sketch—was born in Nelson, Portage County, Ohio, in 1830, to which place his parents emigrated in 1820, the journey being made with ox teams in forty five days, that being a remarkably quick trip. The Western Reserve, or New Connecticut, as it was then called, was but sparsely settled, there being less than two families to the square mile in the township, and in some instances three miles distant from each other, the whole face of the country being a dense forest except little clearings around the rude log houses which protected the pioneers and their families from the winter storms, as also from the wild beasts; for in those days wolves and bears were numerous and dangerous. Deer, turkey and other game were in abundance, and were brought down by the rifleman when desired for food. At this time the war-whoop of the savages had scarcely died away, and civil government was in a chaotic condition.

Mr. Barber's father, when in his prime, was a powerful man, and with his oldest sons battled with the world against adverse circumstances: forests were cut away, crops planted, and, with a devoted wife and mother, every effort was made to establish a comfortable and happy home in the then far West.

It was indeed discouraging to them when, after many months of toil in securing their first crops, and, just as a severe winter had set in, to have it entirely destroyed by fire, together with a large barn: some of their animals and all their farming utensils, and their year's subsistence and the wherewith to save the family from suffering was not at their command. During the burning of the barn an older brother came near perishing in the flames.

In 1828 sickness entered the family circle, and within fifteen months five brothers and sisters were laid in their graves. These were crushing blows to their devoted mother, and few if any at this period have the fortitude to bear up under such trials and afflictions.

Mr. Barber's father died in 1848, his mother in 1849, and before the close of 1869 nine more brothers and sisters had gone to their long homes, Mr. Barber being the only survivor of that once large and happy family!

He can speak in the most glowing terms of the honesty, integrity and patriotism of his father; of his struggles with the Tories during the war of 1812, when the devoted amongst them prayed for the prosperity of their dear Mother England, that she might come off conqueror in the war, many of the populace at that time proposing to volunteer and go to Washington and massacre the heads of the Government! He raised a company of volunteers to go to the frontier, but was thrown from his horse on the morning he was to start and his shoulder was broken in the fall, thus disabling him for service,— from which injury he never fully recovered. May it not be said that the love of liberty and country has in a measure been handed down to the posterity of that old patriot, Thomas Barber?

Mr. Barber, the subject of this sketch received his education in the common schools (that were poorly organized and equipped at that time), except an academic term in Windham, Ohio, where he served an apprenticeship as cabinet-maker, commencing at the age of seventeen; previous to that he had worked on his father's farm, where malaria was prevalent, which was the prime cause of his leaving home. After acquiring such information of the business as was possible in a country shop, he engaged himself to a firm in Cleveland, Ohio, to perfect himself in his occupation, returning to his home late in 1851, after finishing his apprenticeship. Previous to this he resolved to strike for something more exalted and had devoted much of his spare time in the rudimentary studies of architecture and building.

At this time the California gold excitement was running high, and being of an enterprising disposition assisted in making up a party from the neighborhood to go there, among whom were Colonel E. C. Smith, Ebin Earl, L. V. Hopkins, Prof. J. W. Pike, Mr. Ives and some six or eight others

The party started for New York on the 11th of February, 1852, having through tickets from there to San Francisco, on what was claimed an independent line of steamers. They had passage on the steamer United States to Chagres, thence by small boat up the river to the head of navigation, and thence on mules to Panama. Much to their disappointment there was no steamer to take them to their destination, and after many days' delay they finally secured passage on the ship Clarissa Andrews, afterward known as the "floating coffin," which made the voyage in sixty-five days, arriving in San Francisco May 22, 1852. One of their party, Barnus Ives, became delirious from sickness contracted in Panama, and on the seventh day out threw himself into the ocean and was drowned, all efforts to rescue him proving fruitless. During the voyage sixteen of the passengers died, chiefly in consequence of bad water (imperfect evaporations from the salt sea water) and from the insufficiency and poor quality of food, from which innumerable insects, etc., would endeavor to escape when it was broken open to be eaten! Nearly all the passengers were put on short allowance after the first day out from Panama. Those were times that tried men's souls; for many days death stared in the face the ill-fated passengers of that unseaworthy old vessel, it having been their choice to accept a passage on her rather than longer hazard their lives in that malarious region around Panama, where there were over nine thousand detained emigrants, many of them not knowing how they could escape. It was a touching sight as day after day they saw their shipmates dropped into the ocean to become food for the sharks that were seldom out of sight from the ship.

Fearing the loss of his health, Mr. Barber decided to remain in San Francisco for a time, but the majority of his comrades proceeded at once to the mines. From the time of his arrival until August, the same year, he worked at his trade,—for which he still harbored a dislike,—when he proceeded to Marysville, and soon after invested in the Mammoth Joint-stock Quartz-mining Company, on Jamison Creek, some 100 miles into the mountains, where, during the terrible winter of 1852-'53, the snow lay from three to ten feet deep, in which the company's pack-train of sixty-six animals all perished, and the machinery and provisions for the mill, with which they were loaded, were scattered through the mountains and lost. This, with the fraudulent transactions of those left in charge of the mine and mill during the months that the property was inaccessible, caused a failure of the company, and with this a total loss of the most of Mr. Barber's earnings up to this time.

While in Marysville he was taken sick with a fever, and for many days his life was despaired of. When convalescing, the hotel where he was stopping was burned and he came near losing his life, having his clothing and hair burned as he escaped through the flames. He finally recovered so that in December he was able to return to San Francisco, where he took up and followed the carpenter and joiner business and the study of architecture, except a portion of two seasons when he farmed near Oakland.

Returning early in 1856 to San Francisco, he worked for wages a short time, when he commenced contracting for buildings of all classes, which he followed quite successfully until late in 1868, being his own architect on many buildings which he erected, and also for others on which he was architect and superintendent. In 1868 he suffered a loss in having a large brick building, upon which he had a contract, thrown down by an earthquake. In 1856 he made the acquaintance and gained the confidence of Reuben Clark, an eminent architect,—especially in the constructive branch,—from whose plans the beautiful State Capitol, at Sacramento, was erected. The wise counsels of Mr. Clark and his lessons in architecture have been a source of great profit to Mr. Barber from that time to the present, he having followed the profession constantly since 1868.

Besides the buildings in San Francisco which he planned, he was also architect on nearly all the principal buildings in Santa Barbara, such as the county court-house, the Santa Barbara college (now the San Marcos Hotel), the Arlington Hotel, the Presbyterian church, the old Methodist and Congregational churches, Clock building, First National and Commercial Bank buildings, Crane's Hall, theatre, Third and Fourth Ward school-houses; also those at Lompoc, Carpenteria, Santa Ynes and other places; many stores and fine dwellings, as that of Gaspar Oveña, Thomas P. Dibblee, Captain Moore, John Edwards, Captain Greenwell, Mrs. Lucy Brinkerhoff and many others; and later on, with his partner, the annex to the Arlington, the Hawley block, Cottage Hospital annex to the Clock building and the three-story stone-front building adjoining the latter. Mr. Barber is now alone in business, and is engaged on a good dwelling for Judge Canfield, the Public Library, a stone church for the Unitarian Society, and the Methodist South.

While in San Francisco, in 1855-'56, he was a member and treasurer of the Elysian Club, a social organization of 160 or more young ladies and gentlemen; and every participant will carry through life the most pleasant recollections of those happy reunions. They were all that the name of the club implies. Mr. Barber was a member for several years of a cavalry company,—the First Light Dragoons,—under Captain C. L. Taylor and Lieutenant Flanders. Soon after the breaking out of the Rebellion, when the California hundred was being mustered into service, he seriously contemplated going to the front with them, and would have done so but for his young wife and child who were dependent upon him; but he regularly paid his full proportion into the sanitary fund.

He, like many others, invested in stocks during the quartz-mining excitement, and his dearly bought experience then may have proved beneficial later in life.

Mr. Barber was married in San Francisco, in 1859, to Miss Mary J. Wheaton, of New Orleans, Louisiana, and they have a family of five children: Sylvia S., now Mrs. H. A. Rogers; Ella F., Alice F., Samuel M. and Arthur B. They buried their little daughter Mary Ann in 1864, when but twenty months old, and their youngest child, Mary Beatrice, in 1888, aged eleven years.

In 1869, for the better health of his family, Mr. Barber sought a more genial climate and settled in Santa Barbara, then but an old Spanish-built town with less than half a dozen respectable American-built dwellings, and no public buildings except the old adobes. It now has a population of some 6,000 people, among whom are as refined, cultured, benevolent and patriotic a class as any city in the world can boast of.

Some thirty years ago Mr. Barber joined the Odd Fellows, and has never ceased to be a member,—first the Yerba Buena in San Francisco, then by card Santa Barbara Lodge, and was one of the charter members of Channel City Lodge, No. 232 (the name "Channel City" being proposed by Mr. Barber and afterward adopted). He was for some time a member of the Santa Barbara Encampment and holds his card. In the subordinate lodges he passed through all the chairs and has been elected three times a representative to the Grand Lodge, and served one term as Deputy Grand Master of District No. 54, and for some ten years has been a trustee of Channel City Lodge. He has been a member of the Veteran Odd Fellows Association for many years, and greatly enjoys their meetings and banquets in San Francisco, where he is privileged to meet his old-time California friends. He is also a member of long standing in the orders of United Workmen and American Legion of Honor.

He served on the Board of Health in 1878-'79, and in 1880 was elected Mayor of Santa Barbara, by a surprising majority, and served a full term, giving universal satisfaction, during which he was ex-officio Chairman of the Board of Health.

During this time the small-pox was brought into the city, spreading through one family. The work of the board was laborious and dangerous. For a long time they felt that the destiny of the place—from a sanitary standpoint—was in their hands; if the disease had been allowed to spread, and the plague had swept off a portion of the population, the reputation of the city—which now stands pre-eminent as a health resort—would have received a blow from which it would have taken years to recover.

In 1882, under the administration of Presidents Garfield and Arthur, he received the appointment of Postmaster at Santa Barbara, and served his full term of four years. The satisfaction he gave the public in this capacity has been manifested in many ways.

In 1890, after having been solicited in writing by some two hundred voters, he with much hesitancy allowed his name to be used as a candidate for Mayor, and is now serving his second term as such, and again as chairman of the newly organized and efficient Board of Health.

Mr. Barber's habits of life have always been those of sobriety, industry and frugality; his gratitude is warm and enduring for every kindness; he tenaciously adheres to his friends, come what may; is always ready to forgive any injustice or injury inflicted; is generous—some say to a fault—but never boasts of it, and the Golden Rule always seems uppermost in his mind. He has been an almost constant worker through life,—always at his post. Though fond of enjoyment and recreation, he never has had what he thinks he has earned.

In 1863 he paid a visit to his old home and boyhood friends in Ohio and other States. Though but eleven years had elapsed since leaving, many old neighbors and friends had gone to their long home. In 1887 he again sought rest and recreation, and, with his daughters Ella and Alice, took a trip to the old country. In going to New York they took a middle route through Kansas City, St. Louis, Cincinnati, Chattanooga, Washington, Philadelphia, etc. They took passage on the Anchor Line steamer "Fernessia" to Glasgow, visiting Scotland, England, Ireland, Belgium, Holland, Germany, Switzerland and France, returning by the same line, on the Devonia, to New York. When four days out from New York they encountered a terrible hurricane, which came near foundering the ship. From New York they took the more northern route for home, visiting Niagara Falls, Cleveland, Chicago, Denver, Salt Lake, etc., stopping off and visiting the old homestead in Ohio and the scenes of his childhood and such of his old associates as had not emigrated to other localities or had been numbered with the dead. The ravages of time during thirty-five years, together with those of the war of the Rebellion, were too apparent, and a feeling of sadness crept over him when, at a little banquet at the same hospitable farm-house where forty-five years before he had stepped to merry music, there could be counted upon the ends of his fingers all that remained of the scores who had been wont to gather there for youthful amusements. At parting he said good-bye to them, perhaps for the last time, and once more turned his face toward his home on the shores of the Pacific.

Since he has lived in Santa Barbara he has fostered and encouraged every legitimate enterprise to the extent of his ability; has expended some money in prospecting for minerals, oils, etc., and at this time is interested in two companies that are putting down wells in oil regions. He was for a term of years a partner in a firm that dealt heavily in lumber and other building materials. For many years he owned a small farm near town which he had properly cultivated, and planted out with the choicest variety of fruits, vines, etc., and on which he had carried on for him an apiary, and was treasurer of the Apiarists' Association of the county during its existence. He has done much work gratuitously on different churches, as he is doing at the present time; but his race is well nigh run, and when his career is ended he can say with satisfaction to himself that he has made the best use of the time allotted to him under the circumstances, and goes hence with a clear conscience and good will toward all mankind.

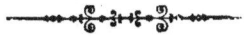

OLIVER C. CARLE was born in Trumbull County, Ohio, August 29, 1838. His father, Joshua Carle, was born in Jefferson County, Ohio, in 1800; passed his life as a farmer, and died in Illinois, in 1884. His ancestors were Germans. Mr. Carle's mother, Margaret (Oliver) Carle, was born in Jefferson County, Ohio, and was of Scotch descent. Of the thirteen children born to them, Oliver C. was the seventh. He attended school at Hopedale and finished his education at the State Normal School.

His young manhood was reached at a time when his country was in great danger and engaged in the most sanguinary struggle of its history. In August, 1862, he enlisted in the One Hundred and Twenty-sixth Ohio Volunteers, and did his duty with bravery all through the conflict. He was in the battle at Winchester, Frederick, and other places, and his division was sent to New York to quell the riots at that place. He participated in the battles of the Army of the Potomac, and at the battle of the Wilderness was captured and taken to Andersonville, where he remained from May until September. At that time they were being moved by train to Florence, when Mr. Carle and three others escaped. They spent days and weeks in the woods, traveling by night and hiding by day. They were at times defended by Union men and made many escapes, and only one of their men was recaptured. In the dark one night they were halted by seven men, with guns, and they themselves were only armed with clubs. They represented that they were Confederates going to the command, and produced a pass which Mr. Carle had written. When they were trying to light a match two or three of them were knocked down at once, and the escaped prisoners broke away in the dark, followed by shots, and made good their escape. They reached the Union lines at Knoxville, Tennessee, January 12, 1865. In the charge on Petersburg, Mr. Carle was wounded in the foot, and was at the hospital in Washington when President Lincoln was killed. Mr. Carle saw his full share of the horrors and sufferings of the war.

When peace was declared, the subject of this sketch was mustered out of the service, and engaged in agricultural pursuits, happy in knowing that the old flag waved over a united country. He bought a large farm in the vicinity of Kansas City, on which he remained about seven years, a greater part of the time engaged in farming, and for a while conducted a dairy. A portion of that ranch is now included in the limits of Kansas City, and his son, Edwin T. Carle, resides on the portion which they still retain.

When Mr. Carle came to Ventura, California, he purchased 120 acres of land, where he has a most delightful home and where he now resides. The rare taste displayed in the arrangement of the grounds and the perfect neatness which pervade the whole premises, make it one of those attractive homes for which California is noted far and wide. Its cost was $26,000. Mr. Carle has also invested in other real estate in different parts of Southern California. On his home ranch he has many fruit trees of different kinds: among them are 500 walnut and 500 apricot trees.

April 14, 1860, he was married to Miss Jennie Taylor, who was born in Louisville, Kentucky, in 1840. This union was blessed with two children: Edwin T., born March 20, 1861, in McLean County, Illinois; and Ethbert D., born May 20, 1866, now at home on the farm. Mrs. Carle was stricken with consumption and after a protracted illness, in which all efforts to save her life proved futile, died January 26, 1867. After living single four years, Mr. Carle was again married, January 12, 1871, to Miss Adelaide M. Maitland, a native of Lawrence County, Pennsylvania. She is the daughter of William Maitland, of Lawrence County. They have had one child, which they lost. Mrs. Carle is a member of the Methodist Church. Mr. Carle's parents were members of the Disciples'. While at New Castle, Pennsylvania, he united with the I. O. O. F. His political views are in harmony with Republican principles.

GEORGE W. FAULKNER is the son of George Faulkner, who was born in England in 1806, came to Ohio in 1838, and settled on a farm in Richland County, where he still lives and where, August 16, 1846, his son, George W., was born. Mr. Faulkner's mother was nee Julia A. Green, a native of Franklin County, Ohio. Her father, William Green, was a pioneer of Ohio, and built the third house in the township in which he lived. The subject of this sketch was the fourth of a family of six children, was reared and educated in Ohio, and was engaged in agricultural pursuits on the farm on which he was born until coming to Ventura County, California, in 1879. He purchased seventy-three acres of land near New Jerusalem, and three years later came to his present location, near Santa Paula. Here he bought a farm of 150 acres, on which he has made many improvements, planting trees and building a large barn. He has not yet built his new house, but has selected a beautiful building site and already has the grounds planted with shrubbery and trees. Mr. Faulkner has eighteen acres of apricots and a general assortment of prunes, apples, pears and citrus fruits, and has twenty-eight acres of bearing walnut trees. This place presents a fine appearance with its flowers, fruit-trees, ponderous barn, and well kept stock grazing in the green pastures. Mr. Faulkner is carrying on general farming, but the crop of which he makes a specialty is Lima beans, raising as high as a ton to the acre, the price being now four and a half cents per pound. He employs two farm hands all the time and often more.

Mr. Faulkner was united in marriage to Miss Roda S. Seymour, a graduate of Baldwin University, class of '72. She is a native of Ohio, and a daughter of Rev. S. D. Seymour, of the North Ohio Conference, Methodist Episcopal Church, now a resident of Texas. Mr. and Mrs. Faulkner are the parents of two daughters and one son: Alpha and Stella, born in New Jerusalem, and George Seymour, in Santa Paula. Mr. Faulkner is forty years older than his little son, and his father is forty years his senior. He showed the writer something unique in the way of a picture, the three portraits, father, son and grandson, being arranged on one card.

Mr. and Mrs. Faulkner are members of the Methodist Church. Politically he is a Prohibitionist.

JACOB MAULHARDT. In a work of this character it is fitting that the name of Jacob Maulhardt should find a place, and that mention should be made of his life and successful career as a rancher of Ventura County. He was born in Prussia, of German parents, June 30, 1841, and came to California July 7, 1867. He had received his education and had learned the carpenter's trade in his native land; and after coming to this State he engaged in sheep-raising in Contra Costa County, on the shares. In 1869 he went to Tulare County, and there devoted his time to farming. In June, 1870, he located in Santa Clara Valley, Ventura County, and here purchased 410 acres of choice farming land at $10 per acre. This property he still retains, and has since added to it seventy-five acres, at a cost of $50 per acre, and later bought 312 acres of choice farming land at a cost of $7,100. He has erected a large barn and fine residence, which can be seen for miles around in every direction—a place of beauty and a credit to the country. He is conducting his farming operations on a large scale, his principal crop being grain. He also raises fruit for family use, and for his friends. The total value of his property now is about $100,000.

Mr. Maulhardt was married in 1865, to Miss Dorothy Kohlar, who is also a native of Germany, and whose parents were German farmers. They have five children: Henry, the oldest, born in Europe; Emma, a native of Contra Costa County, California; Louisa, born in Tulare County; and Adolph and Mary, born at their present home in Ventura County.

Mr. Maulhardt is a Democrat and takes an active part in political matters, having attended the county conventions of his party, as a delegate, since 1876. He and his family are members of the Catholic Church.

J. D. AXTELL, Superintendent of the County Hospital, was born in Pike, Wyoming County, New York, in 1835. His father was one of the pioneers of that county in 1828. The subject of this sketch was educated and lived in his native county, engaged in farming, hotel-keeping, and other enterprises, up to the opening of the war. He enlisted at Pike, August 25, 1861, in Company F, Fifth New York Cavalry, under Colonel O. De Forest, there being 1,100 men in the regiment. They were first sent to Staten Island to drill in sword exercise. Leaving there in November, 1861, they went to Baltimore, and there being mounted they went forward to Annapolis and joined General Hutch's corps of cavalry. Mr. Axtell sustained an injury at Annapolis, was sent to the hospital and was discharged December 18, 1861. He spent the winter at home and in the following spring joined the Quartermaster's Department at Washington, and in 1863 was sent to Johnsville, Tennessee, to take charge of a saw-mill, sawing timber for railroad ties and bridges, and there remained until the close of the war. The following ten years he engaged in railroad work and hotel-keeping, and in February, 1878, came to California. He first settled at Lompoc, but the year being dry he did no business. In November, 1878, he was appointed Superintendent of the County Hospital. In 1880 he took up a Government claim on the Santa Ynez River, and there farmed for three years; then sold out and went to Lompoc, where he kept a hotel. In 1886 he was reappointed Superintendent of the County Hospital, and has since held the position. This hospital is the home for the sick, feeble and infirm residents of the county, and averages about twenty inmates.

Mr. Axtell was married at Castile, Wyoming County, New York, in April, 1873, to Miss Nellie M. Anderson. They have but one child living—Miss Nellie. Mr. Axtell is a member of Magnolia Lodge, No. 242, F. & A. M., and of the order of the Eastern Star, Marguerite Lodge, No. 78, of which his wife is Worthy Matron.

JOHN BORCHARD is a native of Hanover, Germany, born October 8, 1838. Both his father and mother were Germans and both are still living, at the ages of eighty and seventy-seven years, respectively. Mr. Borchard contemplates returning to his native land to visit them during the present summer, 1890. The subject of this sketch is another illustration of the way the thrifty sons of Germany succeed when they come to the United States. He came to his present location in 1871, and purchased 400 acres of land, on which he is now raising barley, beans and corn. He owns 4,000 acres on the Conejo, where he is raising cattle and hogs, keeping an average of 400 head of grade Durham cattle, and from 400 to 500 head of hogs. He also owns property in Texas, 6,000 acres of land, which he rents to four men. On his Conejo ranch, Mr. Borchard is building a brick house. This ranch is divided into six or seven pastures, and each is supplied with plenty of spring water and fenced with wire fencing.

Mr. Borchard was married in Germany in 1865, to Miss Elizabeth Chothelm, a native of that country. They have three daughters, all born at their present home in Ventura County, California: Mary, Ann, and Theresa. The family are consistent members of the Catholic Church.

Notwithstanding that Mr. Borchard is a rich gentleman, he calls himself an old Dutchman, and works as hard as ever he did, the thrift and economy acquired in the fatherland still staying by him in California. During the nineteen years he has lived on this coast, he has seen many remarkable changes, and has given a helping hand to many a German friend.

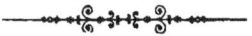

F. HAWLEY is a California pioneer. He was born in Canada, December 28, 1830, the son of Charles Hawley and Cynthia (Laboree) Hawley, both natives of Canada. His grandfather, Amos Hawley, was a native of New Hampshire, and his grandfather on the maternal side, Rufus Laboree, was a native of Connecticut, and the ancestors of both families had long been residents of America. He was the fourth of a family of thirteen children, and the first twenty years of his life were spent in Canada. In 1852 he came to California, and worked in the mines in Mariposa County, with ordinary success. After being there a year he went to San Francisco, and February 16 1853, sailed in the Monumental City for Australia, where he arrived after a voyage of eighty days. He went directly to the mines, where he worked for a year and a half, having fine success. He washed as high as $200 in gold in a single day, with an old-fashioned rocker. Upon his return to California he went to the mines in Nevada County, and worked at river mining in the South Yuba, with indifferent returns. In 1862 he went across the country to Idaho and prospected where the city of Auburn is now located. The next year he went to Boise Basin, being more successful and remaining there two years and a half. He was one of a company of five who worked four or five claims at one time and took out as high as $10,000 in a single week. Mr. Hawley took out $4,900 in one week, with five hired men, each receiving $6 per day. They employed four men to work at night, to save the water and also the gold. The water cost 50 cents per inch for twelve hours' use. When he left the gravel mining he sold his claim, and, with his brothers, went to Nevada and prospected in quartz-mining. They had hard luck and met with heavy losses. After this Mr. Hawley bought a ranch in Placer County, where he farmed four years. Then his wife died, and he sold his farm and went back to the mines in Nevada County, where he obtained a situation as a water agent and remained there ten years. At the expiration of that time he came to Southern California and at

Carpenteria rented land for five or six years, which he devoted to the production of Lima beans. When he came to his present location he purchased eighty acres of choice land, a part of which he has since sold, retaining forty-three acres. This contains a nursery of walnut trees and a variety of fruit trees.

Mr. Hawley was married, in 1865, to Miss Matty Wheelock, a native of New York. They had two children: Ida B., born at Columbia Hill, Nevada County, is now the wife of John Dickerson, and lives near her father; Frank A., born in Placer County, resides with his father. After five years of married life, Mrs. Hawley died December 18, 1870. Mr. Hawley afterward married Miss Anna Carrol, a native of New York. They have had two children, born in Nevada County, Clarence and Lee. aged eight and twelve respectively. Mr. Hawley is a Royal Arch Mason, and has been a life-long Democrat.

JUDGE H. G. CRANE.—One of the old and honored residents of Santa Barbara is the subject of this sketch, who was born at Varick, Seneca County, New York, in 1828, being the youngest of six children. His self-support began at the age of twelve years, when he was bound out to a farmer for a term of four years, getting the little education that was afforded in those early days at the winter schools. His next step forward was to Ypsilanti, Michigan, where he served two years with a harness-maker. He learned the trade and then bought a one-half interest in the business, in 1852, which was very prosperous, making many harnesses for shipment to St. Paul and New Orleans. Owing to failing health he sold his interest in 1856, coming to California by the Isthmus of Panama and settling in Tuolumne County, where he had mining interests which proved very profitable. In 1861 he was elected Justice of the Peace, holding the office four years. In 1862 he bought out a hardware and merchandise store at Shaw's Flats, which he continued until 1868, when he sold out, and in 1869 came to Santa Barbara. He bought two blocks in De La Vina street and built the pleasant cottage which he now occupies, corner of Sola and De La Vina streets. In 1871 he was elected Justice of the Peace, holding the office until January, 1883. He also became engaged in real-estate business. In 1882 he was elected Public Administrator, commencing from January, 1883, and continuing in office until January, 1887, when he was elected Supervisor of the Second District, and was made chairman of the board, continuing in that office up to the present date. Judge Crane was examined and admitted to practice law in the Superior Court of the county of Santa Barbara in May, 1890. He lost his first wife in 1883, whom he married in Saline, Michigan. He was again married in Santa Barbara, in 1886, to the very estimable lady Miss Frances Porter. Mr. Crane has one son, Alphonse, who has been a successful stationer in Santa Barbara, and with whom he is now connected in real-estate interests. Mr. Crane built Crane's Hall in 1876, and he is recognized as a man of deep knowledge and research, a man strict in the discharge of his duties.

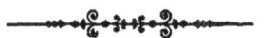

W. E. READY was born in Hamilton County, Ohio, October 25, 1849. His father, W. G. Ready, was born in the same county, and was a farmer all his life. His grandfather, Lain Ready, was a native of Delaware, was reared in Georgia, and removed to Cincinnati, Ohio, becoming a pioneer of that part of the country. Mr. Ready's mother, Margaret (Houston) Ready, was born in Cincinnati, and was the daughter of Robert Houston, a merchant of that place. His grandfather Houston was of Scotch-Irish extraction, and came from the north of Ireland. The subject of this sketch was the fourth of a family of twelve children. In 1861 he left Cincinnati and went to Keokuk, Iowa, and engaged in farming there until 1866. At that time he removed to Northern Missouri, then to Colorado, in 1877, being engaged in farming the most of the time. After a year spent in Colorado, in the spring of 1878, he came to California, and in September settled in Ventura. He worked by the month for four years, and then bought forty acres of rich farming land located two miles and a half east of Ventura. He has built upon it and improved it, and is now engaged in the production of Lima beans. This crop has proved quite remunerative, the average production being from 1,600 to 2,000 pounds per acre, and the present price four cents per pound. The average price is about three cents.

Mr. Ready was united in marriage with Miss Martha Seward, daughter of A. D. Seward, a civil engineer. She was born in Indiana. They have four children: Charles E., born October 2, 1883; Virgil E., November 16, 1885; Gracie M., January 20, 1887, and Lester, December 8, 1888. Mr. Ready is a Republican. Both he and his wife are members of the Presbyterian Church.

HON. CHARLES H. JOHNSON'S biography would form an interesting chapter in the history of San Luis Obispo, were all the material at hand, as his life has been one of stirring activity in travel, adventure and public affairs. His early years were passed in Maryland, his native State, and after graduating at college he left his home for the sake of travel to distant countries. He first visited the Pacific Ocean and China, and returned home. In a few months he again set out, this time for England and the East Indies, and China again, in company with an uncle who went as agent for a Baltimore East India house. He made the tour and safely returned home again. Meeting John Finley, an acquaintance of the family, and forming with him a partnership, he loaded the ship Rhone for a voyage to the west coast of South America, Sandwich Islands and California, while the Mexican war was in progress. He had assurance from the authorities at Washington that the Government intended to possess California. The Rhone sailed from Baltimore December 22, 1847, visited the various ports on the west coast of South America, and arrived at Honolulu July 18, 1848. There the news of the discovery of gold was received; and, instead of disposing of his goods shipped for that port, he and his partner purchased a large addition to their cargo, and on the thirty-first sailed for San Francisco, arriving August 11. His vessel was the first merchantman to enter the harbor of San Francisco after the publication in California of the treaty of Guadaloupe Hidalgo. The gold discovery and the rush of business in San Francisco caused a change in all the plans of these young merchants. Their design had been, after disposing of the cargo for Mr. Finley, to take the ship to Canton and purchase a cargo of tea for the New York market, while Mr. Johnson would purchase land in San Francisco, take an overland trip to Baltimore, and return and settle in California in the mercantile business; but the times did not permit the execution of these plans. The cargo of the Rhone brought over $100,000 in San Francisco, and the opportunity for establishing a great mercantile house offered itself and required prompt attention. Accordingly, the house of Finley, Johnson & Co. was soon established, and in a short period it became the leading house in California, importing heavily from Peru, Chili, Sandwich Islands and Mexico. Their prosperity was all that could be expected or even desired. Great warehouses were built and stored with hundreds of thousands of dollars' worth of goods; but the great fire of May 4, 1850, swept away $4,000,000 of the property of the merchants of San Francisco, the firm of Finley, Johnson & Co. being among the unfortunate. No insurance could be obtained, and their loss was total. However, they, with the pioneer merchants generally, proceeded forthwith to resume business and build up as if nothing had happened. Ships poured in their cargoes, business prospered and all seemed in a fair way of regaining the fortunes lost. The merchants of that period were generally quite free from debt, and when they lost a few hundred thousand they generally had cargoes of their own on the way, or at least a credit that secured them consignments.

But scarcely had they rebuilt their stores and filled them with goods when, June 14, 1850, a still more extensive fire swept them away, involving a loss of $5,000,000. Again the work of rebuilding was begun and business resumed. The buildings erected this time were more expensive, many being deemed fire-proof; but on the night of May 3, 1851, the cry of fire was again raised, and during the next day—which was the anniversary of the first fire mentioned—eighteen blocks of the business portion of the city went down before the flames, involving a loss of between $10,000,000 and $12,000,000! Finley, Johnson & Co. then had in store over a quarter of a million dollars' worth of merchandise, all of which was destroyed by the fire. This so greatly reduced their resources that they settled with their creditors and retired from business.

Mr. Johnson removed to Monterey, and soon thereafter was appointed Deputy Collector of Customs of the district, and afterward Inspector of Customs for the port of San Luis Obispo, coming to this county in 1852 and settling here permanently in 1856. The position of Inspector he held until 1860, when he resigned to take the seat in the Legislature, he having been elected to the Assembly of 1860–'61. During his long residence in San Luis Obispo he has always been known as a public-spirited citizen and a close student of the affairs of the world. He has written and spoken much on the early history of this county, and many extracts from his writings have been given in other works, some of which have drifted into this volume. His eloquent and instructive oration delivered before the San Luis Obispo Grange, in 1874, was published in pamphlet form and most superbly printed. On account of its rich historical allusions, we wish we had space to reprint the oration entire.

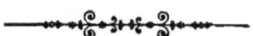

C. ROGERS, President of the Rogers Brothers Produce Company, and also of the Rogers Land Company, was born in Vermont in 1855, and is a lineal descendant of Daniel Webster. Mr. Rogers prepared himself for college at the academy at Montpelier, but commenced business for himself at the age of fifteen years. In 1875 he came to Santa Barbara and established himself in business with his brother. By dint of economy and perseverance they were successful, and when the Southern Pacific Railroad was being opened through Arizona they established a general merchandise store there. This proved a successful business venture. They afterward disposed of the store and engaged in stock-raising and Government contracting.

In 1888 Mr. Rogers was married to Miss J. A. Norcross, and has since made his home in Santa Barbara. In 1890 the Produce Company was incorporated, and the subject of this sketch was elected president. The firm is doing a large produce business, shipping for the season of 1890 over $1,000,000 worth of beans. They have established branch houses at Los Angeles and San Francisco, and expect soon to open one at Chicago. Mr. Rogers is a self-made man, one who has earned his prosperity through hard work and close application to economic business principles.

D. McGRATH is one of the old settlers and respected citizens of the Santa Clara Valley, Ventura County, California. He was born in Longford County, Ireland, in the year 1832, and his parents, Peter and Mary (Davis) McGrath, were also natives of the "Emerald Isle." He was the youngest, except one, of a family of six children, received his education in the country schools of his native place, and, at the age of twenty years, came to America. For six years he lived in the State of New York, after which he came to Alameda County, California, about the year 1861, and worked for wages on a ranch for nearly four years. He became interested in the sheep business and followed that occupation six or seven years. In 1876 he removed to Ventura County, and purchased his present tract of land, known as the Rice tract, which contains 1,300 acres. He has improved the property, planted trees, and, in 1879, built a large and comfortable house, in which ot spend the evening of his days. When he first moved to the ranch he lived in a little clapboard house, but, under his managemen, the premises now have the appearance of comfort and affluence. Mr. McGrath has made farming his life business, his principal crops being barley and corn.

He was united in marriage, since coming to California, to Miss Bridget Donlon, daughter of James Donlon, of Ireland, and an aunt of James Donlon, the Ventura County Assessor. They have had thirteen children, ten of whom are living, four sons and six daughters. They were all born in California, and their names are as follows: Mary T., Maggie, Lizzie, Nellie, Josephine, Annie, James H., Joseph, Frank and Robert. Mary T. is the wife of Bernard Hanly, a resident of Oakland, California. The other children reside with their father. After many years of happy wedded life, and after rearing a large family of children, Mrs. McGrath died of heart disease, in 1888. She was a devoted wife, a loving and faithful mother, and a true and earnest Christian, and is greatly missed by her family and many friends. The whole family are members of the Catholic Church.

In his political views, Mr. McGrath is independent, always selecting what he believes to be the best man. Mr. McGrath has seen and can appreciate the many changes that have taken place in Ventura County in the last few years. He came here at a time when people thought grain could not be raised in this section of the country; but all these fertile valleys needed was the hand of toil rightly directed. Enterprising and progressive men from different parts of the world have settled here, and the work of development has gone on until Ventura County is now one of the most attractive and productive counties of the great State of California.

JOHN F. CUMMINGS is a prominent and successful rancher living four miles west of Santa Paula on a farm of rich land and on one of the finest roads. He was born in Richland County, Ohio, September 19, 1835. His father, James Cummings, was born in Pennsylvania, in 1795, was a farmer, and lived to the age of eighty-five years. His wife, whose maiden name was Christine McMillan, was born in Pennsylvania, in 1801, of early American ancestry. Mr. Cummings, our subject, the fourth in their family of seven children, was brought up in Ohio, and began life as a farmer on one of his father's farms. In 1860 he came to California and for several years worked by the month in the northern part of the State. Taking 160 acres of land, he improved it as he gradually obtained the means. In 1872 he sold it and came to Santa Paula, bought 150 acres of unimproved land, and year by year he has been making it one of the finest ranches in the county. He has erected the buildings and fences and planted the trees and witnessed their wonderful development. He has added other land to his original purchase. On this place he has raised heavy crops of corn, and also raised and sold many hogs; but his principal business now is the raising of Lima beans. Last year (1889) he raised on seventy-five acres sixty-five tons of beans, for which he has, at date of writing, refused four and a half cents per pound. On ten acres he raised 3,300 pounds of beans to the acre; this quantity, at five cents per pound, would be for the ten acres $1,650. His crop for 1889, at the same price, would amount to $6,500. He has harvested three large crops of potatoes from one planting; has raised corn sixteen feet high and ten feet to the ears; so that the productions of his farm are truly marvelous; and yet not all of his land is in cultivation. Politically, although he first voted for James Buchanan for President, he has long been a Republican. He is a man of industrious habits, executive ability and hospitable disposition.

In 1880 Mr. Cummings married Miss Georgia Sweeny, a native of Long Island, New York, and a daughter of Charles Sweeny, a native of the same State. Their five children are: Ada B., Madge, Christine, Walter W. and an infant daughter named Esther.

HARALD L. KAMP was born in Sweden, May 22, 1824. His parents were both Danish by birth. His father, L. Kamp, arrived in Sweden (before his birth) as a commercial agent. Harald received a private education; was engaged as clerk in a book and stationery business; and emigrated to the United States, landing at New York, in 1845. In 1846 he enlisted with Colonel Stevenson's New York Volunteers, Company C., Captain Brackett; left New York for California in September, 1846, arriving March, 1847; was stationed at Sonoma. In May, 1847, he was with others sent to Sacramento under Lieutenant Anderson for the protection of the settlers from Indians; remained there until September, same year, when he was sent back to Sonoma; and remained in Sonoma to the close of the war.

After the war he left for the mines and remained there until December, 1848, when he returned to Sonoma and engaged in store business to 1856. Selling out his mercantile business he engaged in farming and stock-raising, in Sonoma County, until 1868, when he moved to Martinez, Contra Costa County. He engaged there in the wholesale and retail liquor business until 1880, then moved to San Buenaventura, continuing in the same business.

Mr. Kamp was maried in Sonoma, in 1851, to Doña Josefina Higuerra, a native of Napa County, and they have had five children, three of whom are now living, whose names are Luis Ignacio, Adriano Francisco and John.

DR. JOSHUA MARKS, one of the prominent citizens of Ventura County, was born in Richmond, Virginia, July 12, 1816. His father, Mordecai Marks, was a native of Prussia, came to the United States when a youth, was reared in Virginia, and was a merchant there for many years. The Doctor's mother, *nee* Esther Raphael, was a daughter of Solomon Raphael, a tobacconist, and a descendant of the great painter Raphael. Her maternal ancestors were settlers of Pennsylvania, her great-grandfather, Solomon Jacobs, and her grandmother, Marion Jacobs, having come to this country with William Penn and settled in Philadelphia. Solomon Raphael, one member of the family, was appointed by the Masonic Grand Lodge of Virginia as one of the gentlemen to receive General La Fayette on his visit to this country.

At the age of eight years the subject of this sketch left Virginia, and was educated in New York city, at the college of Baldwin & Forest, on Warren Street, and at the Medical College of New Orleans, graduating at the latter place in 1847. He was appointed by Major Chepin of the Commissary Department of the United States army, as Assistant Surgeon under Doctor McFale, and was in Mexico during its occupation by the American army. He began the practice of his profession in Matamoras. During his stay in Mexico, the Asiatic cholera made its appearance there, in 1849, and was most malignant and deadly. The Governor of the country advised him to follow the disease, and gave him letters of introduction to the most prominent people and also to the Governor of Durango, stating how successfully he had treated the cholera, first at Saltillo and various other places, after which he went to the city of Mexico, and was given a part of the city to attend during the prevalence of cholera. He was examined by a medical faculty of Zacatecas, and received a license, in accordance with the law. His reputation in the treatment of the disease became such that he was paid $800 for twenty days' service, and $4,000 for 4,000 doses of his medicine with directions for use. A gentleman, acting as his agent, sold $1,000 worth of the medicine at one time. He had six assistants giving the medicine under his direction, and so astonishing was its success that, by actual count, of 600 who received it only five deaths occurred. Some of this number took the medicine in the first stages of the disease. After this Doctor Marks was appointed surgeon on the steamship Independence on the Nicaragua route from San Francisco, and after making several trips both he and the Captain left the ship because they did not consider her seaworthy.

The Doctor remained in California, and was elected County Physician of Mariposa County, and also held the same position in Placer County. He built the County Hospital and sold it to the city, and was County Physician and had full charge of the indigent sick in Stanislaus County. After leaving that place he went to San Francisco, where he practiced his profession for a number of years, and was a member of the Medical Society there. In 1861 he was appointed by Governor Downey, State Vaccine Agent. He is now a practicing physician of Ventura County and has charge of the County Hospital of Ventura. His long experience and special qualifications fit him to perform the duties of this office with both credit to himself and the county.

The Doctor was married, in 1853, to Miss Catharine Curtis, in Sacramento. They have two sons: Joseph Edward, born in El Dorado County, May 20, 1855, now a lawyer of Santa Cruz; and Ide, also born in El Dorado County, February 18, 1857, is assisting his father in the hospital. Mrs. Marks arrived in California in 1847, and was elected an honorary member of the Pioneers' Society of California.

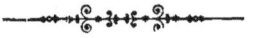

JOSE DE LA ROSA was born in the city of Los Angeles, Mexico, January 5, 1790, at one o'clock in the morning, and was baptized in the cathedral the same day at seven o'clock in the evening. He is the son of Señor Don José Florencio de la Rosa and Doña Maria Antonia Narzisa Rosa. His baptismal name is José Maria Telisforo de la Solida de los Santos Angeles de la Rosa. He has the distinction of being the first printer in this State, having arrived from Mexico in 1834. He was sent by the Mexican government, as government printer in California. In the year 1845 he was appointed by the government as Alcalde of Sonoma (which is the same in the English language as district judge). He remained in Sonoma until 1867, when he removed to Martinez, Contra Costa County. Here he resided until 1879, and in that year he came to Ventura, where he still lives, in the enjoyment of good health, at the advanced age of one hundred years. He is a devout Catholic.

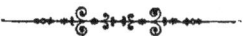

GRAHAM.—Among the rising citizens of the Santa Clara Valley, mention should be made of the gentleman whose name heads this sketch. He arrived in California, April 28, 1876, and at first worked for wages. By his intelligent industry and perseverance he now owns 160 acres of land, which he has improved. He came to his present locality December 28, 1882. Here he is engaged in farming, raising barley, Lima beans and potatoes. Last year his beans averaged twenty-six centals to the acre. Two years ago twenty-eight acres of corn averaged forty-six centals of shelled corn to the acre, which he sold for ninety cents per hundred pounds. Mr. Graham also raises horses, hogs and poultry. He keeps a hired man and a Chinaman cook.

Mr. Graham was born in Richland County, Ohio, December 1, 1848. He is the son of Samuel Graham, a native of Lancaster County, Pennsylvania, born in 1815. His grandfather, James Graham, was also a native of Pennsylvania. His mother was Rachel Clingan. She was a native of Virginia and was brought by her parents to Ohio when three years old. Her father, James Clingan, was a native of Ireland, and emigrated to America in an early day. The subject of this sketch is one of a family of six children, five of whom are living, three daughters and two sons. He was reared at Mansfield, Richland County, Ohio, and received his education in the public schools of that place. Mr. Graham has made one visit to the East since coming to California, and contemplates returning again for a visit this summer. Politically, he is a Democrat.

Mr. Graham is unmarried and consequently one chapter of his history remains unwritten!

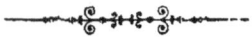

ILLAM GOODWIN DANA, deceased, was better known as Captain Dana. He was born on Friday, May 5, 1797, the first child of William and Eliza (Davis) Dana, of Boston, Massachusetts. His father, William Dana, was born in that city in 1767, and married Miss Davis, the daughter of a prominent artillery officer in the Revolutionary army. William Dana died at St. Thomas, June 3, 1799, aged thirty-two years.

Among the commercial people of the United States there has been accorded to New England the credit of largely developing commerce, and making explorations among the South Sea Islands and along the western shores of North America. Boston, Salem, New Bedford and Nantucket were localities well known to all classes of people, and their residents were regarded as the best representatives of active thought and energy. From such an ancestry came William G. Dana. His youth was spent in Boston, where he acquired a good education, and at the age of eighteen years his uncle, a Boston merchant, sent him to Canton, China, where he remained nearly two years; thence he journeyed to Calcutta, India, where he remained one year. From India he cruised to the Sandwich Islands, where he remained for a time, and in 1820 established a large commercial business on the island of Oahu, where he erected a large warehouse. Later Mr. Dana made several voyages as ship captain from Honolulu to California and to the South American coast. In 1825 he located at Santa Barbara, and three years afterward built a schooner, which is said to be the first seagoing vessel ever launched by an American on the Pacific coast. In 1835 Captain Dana having become a naturalized citizen of the Mexican Republic, applied for and obtained a grant of the Nipomo Rancho, comprising 37,887.71 acres. This grant was one of the earliest on record, and as he had his choice in a very large area of country he made a selection which, as has been shown, was for many purposes a wise one. In the autumn of 1839 they removed their residence from Santa Barbara to Nipomo, and upon his property he erected a large adobe house, which still continues to be the home of some of the family. The splendid old house stands a conspicuous object on an elevation overlooking a large area of the grant, a monument to the history of the county, second only to the old missions, and naturally around it cluster many interesting reminiscences. The Captain was distinguished for his hospitality and generosity, and the Nipomo Rancho was a favorite stopping place for Americans journeying through the country, and many are the guests who have been entertained at this place. Nipomo was the only place then on the road between Lan Luis Obispo and Santa Barbara, and it was twenty-five miles from San Luis Obispo and eighty-five from Santa Barbara. In political life Captain Dana was for a time quite active, and under Mexican rule he was Prefecto, the highest office in the gift of the government. At the first election for officers under the constitution of the State of California in 1849, he received the largest vote for the Senate, but owing to imformalities in the election the office was accorded to Don Pablo de la Guerra, a native of California, and connected with one of the leading

Spanish families of that country. He subsequently became President of the Senate. Captain Dana died at Nipomo, February 12, 1858, and his remains were interred in the cemetery at San Luis Obispo. His widow died at the same place, September 25, 1883.

He was married August 10, 1828, at Santa Barbara, to Maria Josefa Carillo, the eldest daughter of Don Carlos Antonio Carillo, the Governor of Alta California. By this union there were twenty-one children, twelve of whom are now living: William C., born May 6, 1836; Charles W., born June 27, 1837; John F., June 22, 1838; Henry Carillo, July 14, 1839; Ramon H., January 11, 1841; Francis, May 14, 1843; Edward Goodwin, December 24, 1846; Adeline Eliza, March 30, 1848; Frederick A., June 12, 1849; David A., August 27, 1851; Elisha C., October 23, 1852; Samuel A., April 3, 1855.

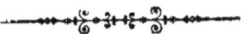

CHARLES DAVIS is a native son of California, and with his brothers Joseph and Buchanan, is the owner of 1,200 acres of land, adjoining San Miguel on the north. He was born in Monterey County, eight miles north of the town of San Miguel, February 21, 1864. He is the son of Mr. George Davis, a pioneer of the State, who came to California in 1843, and is now one of the oldest living pioneers. He is a native of the city of New York, born May 6, 1816; was a soldier in the Black Hawk war; went to the Rocky Mountains and trapped and traded on the north and south forks of the Flat River, following that business seven years. The company he was in had many fights with the Indians, whose weapons, at that time, were mostly bows, arrows, hatchets, spears and knives, while the whites were armed with muzzle-loading, flint-lock rifles. They got many bear skins, which they sold at good prices, and everything they had to buy was high. Mr. Davis followed it more for the wild, exciting life than anything else. Kit Carson was one of his companions at that time, also Doctor Newell and Bill Doty. In 1840 they went to Oregon and farmed for a year, raising wheat. They came to California overland, and had to fight their way through, arriving at Sutter's Fort in July, 1843. Captain Sutter had a blacksmith shop, and all the farmers in the county were near there, and the Captain also had a small store. At that time there was not to exceed fifteen Americans at the Fort.

In company with them was a family by the name of Sumner; and on this overland journey, fraught with so many excitements and dangers, Mr. Davis became acquainted with Miss Elecay Sumner, and soon after their arrival at the Fort, in July, 1843, they were married, Captain Sutter officiating. The newly married couple moved to Cost Creek, built a house, and Mr. Davis continued hunting. They had flour, acorn coffee and an abundance of deer and bear meat. From there he moved to the American Fork, just above where Sacramento now stands. General Fremont with his mountain men came there in 1846, and Mr. Davis piloted him and his men up to Bear River, twenty-five miles above Sutter's Fort.

Mr. Davis was one of the thirteen men taken prisoner by Castro Alvarado. He says they were well treated and paroled on their honor. The Mexican soldiers were sent back to Mexico.

With his brother-in-law, Jefferson Shadden, Mr. Davis engaged in furnishing cattle to the miners. It paid well, beef being four bits per pound. They raised melons, and received a half ounce of gold for each melon. In the fall of 1849 they engaged in mining, made money and spent it freely. In 1860 he came to San Luis Obispo County and took a pre-emption and homestead claim, and engaged in raising sheep and cattle, having as high as 9,000 sheep at one time.

Of their thirteen children, eight are now living,—four girls and four boys. His sons, Charles, Joseph and Buchanan, are farming the ranch, one-half mile from San Miguel, which comprises 1,200 acres, to hay and wheat, and are also raising valuable horses and cattle. These gentlemen have been reared in the county and are interested in its growth and prosperity.

IRA VAN GORDEN is a pioneer of California, who came to this State in 1846. He is a native of Lawrence, Tioga County, Pennsylvania, born February 12, 1820. His father, Gilbert Van Gorden, was a native of Pennsylvania, born in 1779, and a farmer by occupation; he served in the war of 1812. He married Lucinda Ives, a native of the same State, and daughter of Benajah Ives, also of Pennsylvania. They were the parents of eleven children. His death occurred when he was ninety-seven years of age. Mr. Van Gorden's grandfather was a native of New York, and was a soldier in the Revolution; he was wounded and is pensioned by the Government. The Van Gordens originally came from Holland.

Ira Van Gorden was the oldest of the family, only three of whom are now living. He was reared on a farm in his native State, and attended the public schools in winter and worked on the farm in the summer. When seventeen years of age he moved to Berrien County, Michigan, which was at that time a new county, and the State had just been admitted into the Union. For two years he worked by the month, for $15 a month. He then removed to Bond County, Illinois, where he farmed on rented land. In 1846 he removed with his family to California, and settled at the Santa Clara mission. He served as a soldier under General J. C. Fremont, for three months, as long as his services were needed. He then went to the San José mission, and from there to the redwoods, near Oakland, and sawed lumber with a whip-saw and made shingles. In 1848 his wife died, and Mr. Van Gorden took his children and went to the mines, where he mined for three months; the children staid with their aunt. Winter set in and he returned to the mission; while mining his largest pan of gold was $776, coarse grains like wheat and some pieces of $3 and $4 each. At one time he struck a pocket, which lay in a crevice between slab rock, and he picked the gold out with a pick and knife, the amount being thirty-four ounces. At the San José mission he raised three acres of onions, and sold them on the ground for $4,000. From there Mr. Van Gorden went to Los Angeles County, and engaged in raising and shipping grapes, and at this business he also did well. He then went to San Diego County and engaged in stock-raising from 1854 to 1855. From there he drove 260 head of cattle and forty horses to Tulare County, where he took up Government land, and continued there in the cattle business for eleven years.

He was married in 1841, in Illinois, to Miss Rebecca Harlan, a native of Indiana, and daughter of George Harlan, a farmer of that State. They have had three children, two of whom survive: Jerome, now residing in Cambria, and George, residing in San Simeon. In 1848 Mrs. Van Gorden died. Mr. Van Gorden was again married in Tulare County, to Miss Agnes Mary Balaam, a native of Arkansas, of English ancestry. They have six children, viz.: Gilbert, Ira, Sarah, Ann Vine, Sherman and Earl. In 1868 he came to his present ranch in San Luis Obispo County. He purchased 4,468 acres of the San Simeon Ranch, and continued his stock-raising and farming. On part of the farm is a large dairy of 200 cows. When he first moved upon the property he lived in the old adobe ranch house. In 1870 he selected a secluded nook from the coast winds, and erected a beautiful home, where he is spending the evening of his successful life with his family. On the ranch he raises hay, grain, patatoes, cabbage and fruit. In 1886 Mrs. Van Gorden died, and he has since remained unmarried. Mr. Van Gorden was a charter member of the Grange. In his political views he is a Republican, and is one of the best known and most influential citizens in this part of the county.

REV. SAMUEL T. WELLS, a former pastor of the Presbyterian Church at Ventura, was born in Greenfield, Massachusetts, August 6, 1809. His father, Calvin Wells, was born in Greenfield, Massachusetts, and for most of his life was engaged in the lumber business. He removed to Western New York in 1815, settling in Byron, Genesee County. Mr. Well's grandfather, Colonel Daniel Wells, was a soldier in the war of 1812, was a man of wealth, but lost his property by the embargo. Early in the history of this country the sovereign of England sent a man named Welles over to Long Island to act as sheriff, who settled at the east end of that island, and this was the inception of the family in America. The name Wells is derived from the original Welsh from Welles. Secretary Gideon Welles, of President Lincoln's cabinet, was one of the family, one branch of which went to Hartford, Connecticut, and the other to the South; since then they have scattered over all New York and Michigan and into other States. Mr. Wells' mother, Elizabeth Taggart, was a daughter of Domine Taggart, of Colerain, Massachusetts, a Presbyterian minister from Londonderry, Ireland. He had a Congregational Church, but had elders to govern it Presbyterian fashion. He was fourteen years a member of Congress. All of Mr. Wells' brothers and sisters are now deceased except the youngest.

The subject of this sketch received his academical education in Wyoming, New York, his collegiate at Union College, Schenectady, same State, and his theological training at Princeton, New Jersey, under Dr. Alexander. In 1842 the American Tract Society appointed him their agent in the West to establish the colporteur system, and he acted in that capacity twelve years. It was the commencement of that system of book distribution, and in the reports it was stated that his field was the best work in the United States. The forty men under his management sold and gave away a great many thousand dollars' worth of religious books. In 1855 he received the appointment of Synodical Missionary for Iowa, with headquarters at Dubuque, and he organized sixteen churches in that State. In 1860 the Presbyterian Board appointed him agent of colporteurage for California, and in that year he came to the coast. The first year here he preached for the Calvary Presbyterian Church at San Francisco, and also superintended his colporteurs, who at the end of four years had placed $22,000 worth of religious books in this State. While in Oakland, there was no cemetery there that was not in some way encumbered; and Mr. Wells became instrumental in starting the Mountain View Cemetery on the plan that all the money received for lots after paying for the ground should be expended in improvements on the property. The result is that this property of 200 acres is now the most beautiful cemetery in California.

In 1870 Mr. Wells came to Ventura and took charge of the Presbyterian Church. There was then only one active man in it and a few women. Their edifice had been sold for taxes, and they were in debt $1,600; they had about given up all hope. Mr. Wells took the field and with less than half the salary he had had at Oakland, in three years had the debt paid and the society in flourishing condition; it is now self-supporting. Since his arrival here he has served on a committee for raising the salary of pastors, and has been very efficient in that work for six years. He purchased 300 acres of land, when land was cheap, at $15 to $20 an acre. The railroad was afterward run through it and the company paid him $150 an acre for it, and this has made Mr. Wells financially independent for the rest of his life. Across the street and near the church in which he has taken so much interest, he bought a fine lot and erected upon it a substantial, comfortable and tasteful residence, moving into it November 10, 1888, where he can quietly pass the evening of a well spent life. His brother, Calvin, is proprietor of the *Press* of Philadelphia; and his youngest son, Samuel Calvin, is one of the editors of that paper.

May 25, 1842, is the date of Mr. Wells' marriage to Miss Catharine McPherson, of Schenectady, New York, and they have four children: Moses T., born in Allegheny City in 1843; Rosina M., born in Schenectady in 1845; Elizabeth Jane, in Allegheny City, in 1847; and Samuel Calvin, in Pittsburg, in 1849; and seven grandchildren. Mrs. Wells died April 12, 1853, in her forty-fifth year; and in 1857 Mr. Wells was again married, this time to Miss Eliza Swan, of Burlington, Iowa; and by this marriage there are no children.

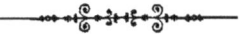

THOMAS SHARON, a prominent rancher and capitalist of Paso Robles, and an early settler in California, was born in Peterboro, Ontario, June 24, 1823. His father, Henry Sharon, was a native of Scotland, and a captain in the British army. He enlisted in 1803, and fought under the flag eleven years, when, in 1814, he returned and became a valiant soldier of the cross. He came to America as a Methodist minister, and preached as a missionary among the Indians and early settlers of Canada. He married Miss Elizabeth Moles, a descendant of the Harveys. They were the parents of twelve children, five of whom still survive. He was a minister for forty years, and died at the age of eighty-seven.

Thomas Sharon, our subject, is the second of the children now living. He never went to school in his life, and is, in one sense, a self-educated man, having been a student all his life. His father and mother were educated and gave him much help in getting his education. He left Canada for New York, and from there emigrated to Wisconsin, when about twenty-one years of age. He engaged in surveying, and after acquiring money enough he purchased eighty acres of land, and became a farmer. He has added to his property from time to time until he has become the owner of from five to six hundred acres. In 1846 he started for California, but was obliged to return on account of the Indians. In 1852 he again started for California, and arrived in Stockton, in 1853. He engaged in surveying, and opened the first land-office in Stockton, which he continued until he became a farmer. In 1855 Mr. Sharon returned East, and lost all he had made, except $275, by the failure of Page & Bacon. Returning to California in 1877, he was engaged in fruit-raising, money-lending, etc., in San José, until 1887, when he came to Paso Robles. Two miles east of the city he bought a section of beautiful ranch land, with a large spring in the center. From this ranch he has since sold 100 acres. He built his residence near the spring in a romantic spot, and planted an orchard of French prunes and other fruit. The trees have made a remarkable growth, some of them only two years old measuring nine inches in circumference. On this property he is raising wheat in large quantities.

Mr. Sharon spent a portion of his life among the Indians, studying their habits, and is the author of a book entitled "Life Among the Sioux," and also a work entitled "Viola, or Life in the Northwest." Both books met with ready sale. Another portion of his life was spent traveling in the South, before the war, a correspondent for the New York *Tribune*. While there he got a view of the institution of slavery, which caused him to become a warm friend of the downtrodden and oppressed. The treatment given by a slave-holder to one of his slaves caused him to write a little book on slavery, entitled the "Dawn of New Orleans." It was warmly received and had a wide circulation in the North. He also traveled and lectured on slavery, and did what he could to help slaves to liberty. When the Republican party was organized, and Fremont nominated for President, he delivered many political addresses in that exciting time, before many thousand people. Many times his life was threatened, and at times danger seemed imminent, but he passed through all the excitement without receiving a scratch. Those times are passed, the country is now united, and the great stain that marred the escutcheon of States has been removed, and Mr. Sharon rejoices in the humble part he was permitted to take in making this country the finest under the canopy of heaven.

Mr. Sharon was united in marriage with Miss Sophronia Burch, a native of the State of New York, in 1847. They had four children, born in Wisconsin, viz.: Cyrus K., Alice, Willis and Edward. After eight years of wedded life Mrs. Sharon died. Mr. Sharon was again married, in 1858, to his present wife, Miss Celia Ralph, a native of New York, and daughter of Mr. John Ralph They have two children, a son and a daughter, born in Wisconsin: Ellsworth G. and Jessie Maud. Cyrus resides in Texas, Alice in Iowa, Willis in Tennessee, and Edward in Dakota. Ellsworth is in Santa Margarita, and Jessie Maud, a beautiful and accomplished young lady, is with her parents. They have a fine ranch and pleasant home. They are members of the Methodist Church, and aided materially in the construction of the Mission Church at Paso Robles. Mr. Sharon has risen by his own exertions to be a man of affluence. This busy, active man cannot expect much longer to remain on earth, but he can truly say, "Lord, now lettest thou thy servant depart in peace, for mine eyes have seen thy salvation."

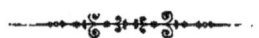

C. TWITCHELL, a farmer of Santa Maria, was born in Waldo County, Maine, in 1856. His father, M. C. Twitchell, was a school-teacher and farmer, and moved to Dallas County, Iowa, in 1857, Our subject was educated in the common schools, and at the age of sixteen years began working out, preferring that to study. He first came to California in 1876 and passed four months about San Francisco; then returned home, and in the fall of 1877 again returned to the coast, to make California his permanent home. His first business was at Oakland, where he bought an interest in a freight boat, which he ran about the bay, but after a few months sold out, and in 1878 came to Santa Maria. He first purchased 160 acres, south of town, but he has since added to the amount of 265 acres. Being somewhat of a trader in lands and also interested in real-estate business with O. W. Maulsby, his acreage property is quite variable. His farming is for stock purposes, and he sows about 200 acres for hay and feed. He keeps about forty head of horses and cattle, and has also been extensively engaged in raising hogs, which he purposes to make his chief business.

Mr. Twitchell was married in Santa Maria, in September, 1881, to Miss Mattie Stubberfield, a native of California, and they have had two children,—Eva May and Fred Martin. Mrs. Twitchell died in May, 1887, of pneumonia. In 1882 Mr. Twitchell served one year as Deputy Sheriff, under R. J. Broughton, and in 1887 was Road Master, but both positions were resigned, as his private business took all his time. He is a member of Santa Maria Lodge, No. 302, I. O. O. F.

RUFUS FISK, a prominent rancher of San Luis Obispo County, was born at Wilton, Ontario, Canada, January 19, 1854. He is the only child of Lovina Lapum Fisk and George F. Fisk, now deceased. Both his parents are Canadians by birth. When he was twelve years of age, in 1866, the family removed to the Pacific Coast and settled in Santa Clara County, California, on a farm which his father had bought and improved. When Mr. Fisk was nineteen years old his father's death caused him to leave school and take charge of the farm, where he remained for three years. He then returned to school, completing the Latin scientific course in the University of the Pacific, where he was graduated in 1878. He designed studying for the legal profession, but, his farm demanding his attention, he returned and continued in that occupation until 1882, when he sold out.

When on a trip from San José to San Luis Obispo he passed over a fine tract of land located on the Nacimiento River, eight miles west of San Miguel. He was favorably impressed with the situation, the prices, and the future prospect of the country, and on his return purchased 985 acres of the land that had previously attracted his attention. He has since added to it until he now has about 2,000 acres. It is a magnificent ranch, a large portion being plow land; and he is raising hay, grain, horses and cattle. He has built a large barn and a comfortable house for present use. Mr. Fisk and family took up their permanent abode on the ranch in the winter of 1886–'87. In November, 1890, they moved into San Miguel, where Mr. Fisk's business interests demanded his attention.

In 1879 Mr. Fisk was married to Miss Emmogene A. Barnes, a native of the Golden West, and the eldest daughter of Captain T. F. Barnes, a prominent farmer of Santa Clara County. Mrs. Fisk is a graduate of the State Normal School of San José, and a teacher by profession. They have one daughter, Stella, born to them July 2, 1884, in Santa Clara County.

Mr. Fisk is a Master Mason, a member of

the Odd Fellow's Lodge, the Farmers' Alliance, a Master of the Grange and one of its charter members. He is also a member of the A. O. U. W.; his wife is a member of the Grange, Farmers' Alliance and Order of the Eastern Star.

They take an active part in all social and progressive movements in their community; are people of refinement, and highly esteemed by their friends and acquaintances.

F. G. BENNISON, one of the business men of Santa Paula, was born in Memphis, Missouri, September 1, 1858. His father, Henry Bennison, was born in England, in 1826, and came to America in 1846. He entered the regular army of the United States, fought through the Mexican war; was then sent to Florida to fight the Indians; and also served all through the late war. Mr. Bennison's mother was *nee* Miss Agnes Perry, a native of Michigan. They had two children, the subject of this sketch being the first born. At twenty years of age he went to learn the blacksmith's trade in Galesburg, Illinois, in 1878. He opened a shop in Galesburg, which he conducted for several years. He sold out and came to Santa Paula, California, in 1884, and bought his present shop on Main street, where he is doing an extensive business for the size of the town. Three men are employed in the shop besides himself, and they do blacksmithing and carriage work. Since coming to California, Mr. Bennison has purchased forty acres of land, located about two miles east of Santa Paula, which he has improved and on which he has built a neat residence. With the exception of a fine orchard of a variety of fruits, the whole place is devoted to French prunes and English walnuts. The neat way in which the property is kept shows the thrift and enterprise of the owner.

Mr. Bennison was united in marriage, in 1885, to Miss Eda Olmstead, a native of California, born in 1867. They have one daughter, Eda B., born in Santa Paula, December 22, 1887. Mr. Bennison is a Republican, and a worthy member of the I. O. O. F.

J. B. PALIN.—Among the many active business men with which Ventura County abounds, we find the subject of this sketch the peer of any of them. He is a native of Canada, of French parents, born within twenty miles of the State line of New York, east of the St. Lawrence River, January 6, 1847. He came to California in 1869, and to his present locality in 1873. At that time there was but little farming done in this part of the county, the land being used for stock purposes. Mr. Gries and Mr. Bell had engaged in agricultural pursuits to some extent, but the whole Pleasant Valley, now so beautiful with its well-tilled fields, was then a wild-looking place, indeed. Mr. Palin first worked for Mr. Savers about three years, and then engaged in raising sheep. Three years later he sold out his sheep interests, and began farming and raising horses and cattle, continuing at that business four years. He then purchased a large tract of land, which he is having farmed. He is also farming 1,700 acres of land in Pleasant Valley, having six men in his employ and using thirty work horses. Last year he harvested 11,000 sacks of barley. This year, 1890, he is planting 170 acres to beans, 120 to corn, and the rest to barley and wheat.

Mr. Palin is a lover of fine horses, and devotes considerable attention to breeding the

Hambletonian stock. He is the owner of the valuable horse Dew Drop, which is eight years old, and is the most valuable horse of the kind now in the county. At a horse show in Santa Barbara he received a diploma for this horse, which is framed and hanging in his best room. He is also the owner of John Thompson, a very valuable and fine three-year-old colt, of this breed. He owns the thoroughbred mare, Eva P. She is the mother of some fine grade colts.

Mr. Palin is a Republican, and takes an active part in political matters. For some time he was a member of the County Central Republican Committee from Pleasant Valley precinct. In 1889 he was a Republican delegate to the State Senatorial Convention, and aided in the nomination of Judge Hickcock for Senator.

E. KALTMEYER is one of the thrifty and enterprising self-made men of Ventura County. He was born in Germany, of well-to-do German parents in 1842, and received his education in his native country. A spirit of independence and a desire to do for himself prompted him to start for the United States, here to earn a living and ultimately to establish a home for himself. He came in 1856, and settled at St. Louis, Missouri, where he learned the trade of a confectioner and cook, and was engaged in that business there for ten years; he then went to Tennessee, where he opened a restaurant. From there he went to the Paris World's Fair, and also visited his parents, returning to America three months later. At this time he engaged in the cotton and wool business, and met with reverses, losing all he had made. On his way to New York his ship was caught in a severe storm, and he came so near losing his life that the other things did not seem of much importance.

In 1861 Mr. Kaltmeyer enlisted in a Missouri volunteer regiment, and served three months, during that time participating in the battle of Springfield, Missouri. Some time after being mustered out of service, he again located in St. Louis, Missouri, and was engaged in business there until 1866. While in that city, in 1863, he married Miss Josephine Young, a native of Germany. To them were born two lovely children. During the fearful cholera epidemic in St. Louis, they were all taken with the disease, and both wife and children died, he alone of the little family being left. At this time he was broken in spirit and also met with financial reverses. With what money he had left he came to California in 1868, via Panama. In San Francisco he worked at his trade, and in the fall he went to Napa County, where he heard there was choice government land in Southern California, and that it was a fine country. He came to Ventura County in December, 1869, and settled on 160 acres of land, which, after a while, he learned was not Government land. He bought eighty acres of it at $16.50 per acre; four years later he bought the other eighty; and still two years later he purchased sixty-seven acres more that adjoined it. Nearly all this time he was unmarried and did his own cooking. After remaining single nearly ten years, he wedded Miss Pauline Ruoff, a native of Germany. This union has been blessed with five children: the first, a son, died; the other children are Matilda, Emelia, Bertha and Hulda, all born in Ventura County.

Mr. Kaltmeyer has greatly improved and beautified his ranch; the house, a very comfortable and attractive one, he built in 1883; and the whole property speaks in unmistakable terms of the taste, refinement and enterprise of the owner. After being broken up twice, he has, by the power of his will and close application to business, become independent and affluent. Notwithstanding his various experiences, he still looks young, and, no doubt, has before him a long and successful career. He was inexperienced in ranch life when he came to his present location, and many were the difficulties he encountered, but he overcame them all, and now ranks among the leading ranchers of his district. Politically, he is a Republican.

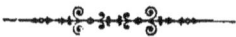

LEROY ARNOLD is a pioneer of California, having come to this coast in 1852, when a boy ten years of age. He was born in De Kalb County, Illinois, January 22, 1842. His father, Cullar Arnold, is a native of Ohio, born in 1818, and now resides in Orange, Orange County, California. The Arnolds were among the early settlers of America. Mr. Arnold's mother, Emily (Hough) Arnold, was born in the State of Illinois. For a number of generations her ancestors were residents of the United States. Leroy Arnold is one of a family of nine children, six sons and two daughters now being residents of California, and one child having died in infancy. His father, on coming to California with his family, settled in Marysville, and opened two stores of miners' supplies, one at Nelson Creek and the other at Goodyear's Bar. He was there for three years, and then moved to Martinez, Contra Costa County, where he farmed two years. After this he kept hotel in Sierra County. In 1857 they went to Lassen County, engaged in farming and stock-raising, and remained there until 1868, when they came to Ventura County and located on 320 acres of land, where the Arnold brothers now reside. After finding that it was not Government land they bought the property, and later added 900 acres more. It is a splendid tract of land, three miles east of Hueneme. The brothers have bought and sold among themselves, and Leroy Arnold now owns 160 acres of it. He has improved this by building, tree-planting, etc. He has an artesian well, with seven and a half inch pipe, in which the water rises sixteen feet above the level of the ground. He has remodeled the house, built the barns, and, under his judicious management, the place presents an attractive appearance.

Mr. Arnold was married September 19, 1876, to Miss Carrie F. Hill, a native of Indiana, and daughter of William Hill. They have had seven children, all natives of the Golden State, and all living, viz.: Effie F. is the wife of A. D. Smith, and resides in San Buenaventura; Mary L. married S. G. Sheppard, and resides at Hueneme, and the following are at home with their parents,—Martha E., Oliver B., Royston C., Alton E. and Ida L. Mr. Arnold is a Master Mason and a member of the A. O. U. W. In politics, he is a Republican, having cast his first vote for Abraham Lincoln.

M. CONNELLY is another one of the prominent ranchers of the Santa Clara Valley, who has risen by his own frugality and industry to an enviable position as a citizen and land-owner. He is one of a number of gentlemen of Irish birth who left their native land to enjoy the liberty of citizenship in the United States. Several of them have settled in the same neighborhood, and when they came here they found the country a waste; by their industry they have made it a paradise, dotted all over with the fine homes of a thrifty people. The well tilled fields of this valley, the neat farm houses with their fruit and shade trees and flowers, all go to make up a picture beautiful to behold.

Mr. Connelly was born in County Monaghan, Ireland, March 10, 1844, and came to America in 1866, at the age of twenty-two years. He first worked for wages in New York and New Jersey. In 1869 he came to California. After working some time in Contra Costa County and also in Sonoma County, and not liking the country, he came to Ventura County and was pleased with the prospect here. He was employed by Mr. Leonard and Mr. Hill, and later he rented 200 acres of land and bought a small house. After working along in this way until 1876, he purchased his present ranch of 264 acres of Thomas R. Bard. By building and other improvements he has made a valuable property of this.

Mr. Connelly was married in 1878, to Miss Eliza Cline, a native of County Longford, Ireland. They have had nine children, six of whom are living, all born at their present home, viz.: John L., Ann C., Mary, Joseph A., Frances and James N. The whole family are members of the Catholic Church. In his politics Mr. Connelly is a Democrat. He has been Roadmaster of his district for the last five years.

POLLEY is a pioneer of the State of California, and hailed from Waltham, Massachusetts, where he was born December 22, 1822. His father, Elnathan Polley, was a native of the same place. Their ancestors were Welsh people, and were among the earliest settlers of New England. His mother, Marian (Brigham) Polley, was a native of Massachusetts, of English descent. They have the genealogy of the family back to the old barony of Bludgehouse, England. Mr. Polley had eight brothers and sisters. Five of them are still living, three older than himself. He was reared and educated in Massachusetts, and learned the machinist's trade, which he followed in the East. In 1851 he came to California. He engaged in milling in Sacramento in 1852, and has the honor of grinding and putting up the first sack of merchantable flour put up in that shape in the State. After four years in the mill, he engaged in contracting and building, and also did some farming. In 1876 he came to Ventura County, and became a rancher and thresher. In 1884 he purchased his present home property, erected buildings, planted trees and otherwise improved it, and is now engaged in raising barley and fine horses.

Mr. Polley was married in 1843 to Miss Charlotte Ann Kellom, a native of New Hampshire, born at Hillsborough, September 6, 1824. To them were born nine children, four of whom are now living: Martha K., married J. Y. Saviers, and resides in Texas; Charles H., born in 1859, married Miss Ren Cunningham, and has two children. He is his father's business partner, the firm being Polley & Son. George F. was born in 1861, and is now a resident of Ventura County. Porter L. was born in 1865; is married and resides in Colorado. Their sons were all born in California.

Mr. Polley resided in Sacramento during the exciting times of the Vigilant Committee, and aided in the organization of the Republican party there; ran on the ticket for a member of the State Assembly, and stumped his district for John C. Fremont, the "Pathfinder." They were both stoned and clubbed. He lived in Mendocino during the war, and it was about as much as a man's life was worth to announce himself a Republican. At a meeting held in Sacramento city, the Republican speaker, Henry Bates, was rotten-egged. Mr. Polley saw a chief justice throwing eggs, and a county judge paraded in front of the stand with gun in hand, swearing that he would shoot the first Republican that would open his mouth. There were at one time three tickets in the field, and nine candidates met at one place. They agreed to hold a discussion, each one to have fifteen minutes' time. Among other things they were to express their opinions on the action of the Vigilant Committee. Mr. Polley said: "I will say one thing, and no man can gainsay it. Every man that the committee hung was a Democrat, and every man they banished from the State was one, and I hope none of them will ever return." Those were exciting times in California, and people of the present can scarcely think it possible that such a state of affairs could have existed. Mr. Polley is a Master Mason. Notwithstanding the fact that he has seen and been through the early turbulent times of the State, having lived here thirty-nine years, he is still quite a young-looking man.

DONLON BROTHERS are prominent ranchers of Hueneme, and natives of California. Their father, Peter Donlon, came to Ventura County in 1870, with his wife and their two little sons. He purchased 400 acres of land, which has since become valuable property. It was at that time a wilderness, and the little board house, still standing not far from their more modern home, speaks plainly of pioneer times and days of small things. Peter Donlon was born in County Longford, Ireland, in 1846, both his parents being natives of Ireland. He was an industrious and respected citizen, and by his honest toil he had provided himself and his family with a comfortable home, surrounded by fruit trees and fields of waving grain, in one of the most fertile valleys of the State. Here, when he was so favorably situated to enjoy life, a fatal accident occurred, in 1888, that terminated his useful life. He was engaged in cutting trees, and a ladder was thrown against his head by a falling tree, which resulted in his death a few hours afterward. This sad accident was a severe trial to his family, and a shock to the community in which he had resided so long. He left a family of five children, three sons and two daughters, as follows: James T., born in Alameda County, July 29, 1868; Charles, also born in Alameda County, August 30, 1869; Joseph, born at the home ranch in 1871; and both the sisters, Mary and Ida, also born at the home place.

Since their father's death the farm is being conducted by the sons, under the firm name of Donlon Brothers, and the sisters manage the housekeeping. The crop raised on this ranch is principally barley, but they also do general farming and raise horses, cattle and hogs. They are agents for 600 acres of land besides their own ranch, and 350 acres of it they are farming.

The family are all members of the Catholic Church. The two oldest sons belong to the Young Men's Institute, and the youngest is a member of the order of Native Sons of the Golden West.

D. BLACKBURN, a pioneer who arrived in this State August 12, 1849, is the founder, in partnership with his brother-in-law, Hon. D. W. James, of the beautiful young city of El Paso de Robles (the pass of oaks), now one of the most attractive and beautiful young cities of San Luis Obispo County. This firm are also the projectors and builders of the great sulphur hot springs bath-house, for which the town is now so justly celebrated as a famous health resort. They also gave to the city the nice park which adds so much to the beauty of the place, and are now engaged in the completion of their brick hotel, comprising two stories and a basement, 285 x 300 feet, and 130 rooms, furnished with all the latest improvements. This institution is a magnificent ornament to the beautiful city, and is a grand monument of credit to their enterprise and success as builders. With such men at the helm, the future of the town is assured.

Where are these men from? Mr. Blackburn was born at Harper's Ferry, Jefferson County, Virginia, April 8, 1816, a section of the Union noted for the birth and rearing of many of the sturdiest men of the nation. In 1822 Mr. Blackburn removed with his parents to Springfield, Ohio, where he grew up and learned the carpenter's trade, which has since been of much value to him. After following it six years, he became a clerk in a store and warehouse for Phelps & Summers, in Oquawka, Henderson County, Illinois. He afterward formed a partnership, the firm being Swezey, Seymour & Blackburn, porkpackers in that place, and they carried on the business successfully until the spring of 1849, packing from 65,000 to 75,000 head of hogs annually and shipping them down the Mississippi River to market.

Now a new era arrived in the life of Mr. Blackburn. His brother, William, who had come to California in 1844, was writing glowing accounts of his new home in this delightful country; and the gold excitement of 1849 gave an irresistible impetus which carried our subject, with his brothers James and Jacob, his brother-in-law, Findley, and his partner Henry Seymour and James Westerfield, forth to the Golden West. Electing Mr. Findley Captain, and Mr. Blackburn Lieutenant, and taking three wagons and three yoke of oxen to each wagon and two years' supply of provisions, they joined a company of 120 men, crossed the Missouri River at Iowa Point, May 5, 1849, and crossed the plains and mountains to the "promised land" without accident or loss, arriving at Deer Creek August 12. They were the first to do mining in what is now Nevada City. Mr. Blackburn followed mining nine days on the South Yuba, and then went to Santa Cruz and engaged in farming on his brother's land, on shares. He put in twenty-eight acres of potatoes and cleared for the crop about $16,000. The yield was abundant and they sold at six to twelve cents a pound. Mr. Blackman has paid $1 a pound in California for the seed. He also had about eighty acres of barley, oats and wheat, and he continued in grain farming until 1857. In June of that year he came to Paso Robles, in company with his brother James, and purchased 22,000 acres of land known as the Paso Robles Rancho of Petronillo Rios,— which included the hot sulphur springs—at a cost of $8,000. They engaged in stock-raising on this ranch, having as many as 10,000 head of live-stock at one time. The dry season of 1864 caught them with about 3,000 head of cattle, nearly all of which were lost. Had it not been for the hogs they had on the ranch, they would have been broken.

In 1860 the firm divided their interests in the ranch, Mr. Blackburn taking the league of land which included the springs. He sold a half interest to Mr. McGreel, who in 1865 sold his interest to D. W. James, for $11,000; and in 1873 James H. Blackburn bought a fourth interest in the property. Mr. Blackburn and his friend James kept "bach" until 1866, when two bright young ladies, the Misses Dunn, natives of Australia, became aware of their "hopeless" condition, and after the usual amount of urgent persuasion consented to share their lot with them on the beautiful Paso Robles Rancho. The couples were married at San Luis Obispo by Father Francis Mora, now Bishop at Los Angeles, and a warm friend of all the parties in the affair. Mr. Blackburn, our subject, chose Celia Dunn, a daughter of Patrick Dunn, a California "49er," and of their ten children, nine are living, viz.: James W., Francis J., Henry H., Margaret, Daniel, Nellie, Annie, Harriet and Frederick. Jennie was killed by the accidental upsetting of the wagon.

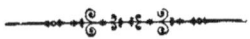

C. P. FAULKNER is a prominent landowner and horticulturist of San Luis Obispo County. His ranch is in the Ranchita Valley, three and a half miles east of San Miguel. He is a native of Guilford, Connecticut, born May 4, 1853. He was born in the house where his father, William Faulkner, and his grandfather, Charles Faulkner, were born. Faulkner Island took its name from this family. His mother, Mary Griswold (Stowe) Faulkner, was a native of New Haven, Connecticut; her father, Pittman Stowe, was born in Guilford, Connecticut, and their ancestors had been among the very earliest of America. Mr. Faulkner, our subject, was the only child by his father's second marriage, and was educated at Yale College, and completed his studies in pharmacy and chemistry at Philadelphia. His father was a pioneer of California, and in the year 1849 was one of the publishers of the *Pacific News*. He was an accomplished writer and business man. His editorials, at that early date, show a perfect estimate of what San Francisco was to be. His death occurred in 1882. Mr. C. P. Faulkner began the drug business in San Francisco, in 1873, on the corner of Mission and Fifth streets, where he has conducted a successful business continuously for fifteen years, with the exception that in the year 1876, being much impressed with the accounts given by Wells and Squiers in their works, of the richness of Honduras, Central America, in the precious metals and opals, he left his business and traveled for about a year in that country as a miner. Finding that, though the country was very rich, it was impossible to mine at a profit, he returned to his business in San Francisco.

In 1884 he recovered from a severe attack of pneumonia, and to regain his health made a trip to San Luis Obispo County. He regained his health so rapidly, and was so delighted with the country that he called it God's footstool, and believed in the great future of the county. He selected 160 acres of beautiful land, commanding a fine view of the county, and filed a claim on it for a homestead, in 1885. It is located four and a half miles east of San Miguel, and they have built upon it a pleasant and cosy residence. Mr. Faulkner, his wife and two sons reside on it, and take great pleasure in raising fruit, of which they have a large variety. The leading kinds are walnuts, chestnuts, pears, apples, peaches, apricots, prunes, nectarines, figs and cherries. They have a nice vineyard of many kinds of grapes.

Mr. Faulkner was married in San Francisco, in 1872, to Miss Nellie McMorris, a native of Toronto, Canada, daughter of Robert McMorris, also of Canada. They have two sons, born in San Francisco; the oldest is now seventeen and measures six feet in height, and the youngest is nearly as tall.

Mr. Faulkner is a Past Master of Excelsior Lodge, No. 166. Mrs. Faulkner is a member of Violet Chapter of the Eastern Star Lodge at San Miguel. They are refined and intelligent people, and their success in raising fruit without irrigation show the fruit-producing value of the county.

MICHAEL HARROLD, a dairyman near Cayucos, was born in Ireland, in October, 1828. July 4, 1849, he alighted upon American soil, the land of opportunity. For the first twelve years he lived in New York city and vicinity. In 1861 he arrived in Marin County, California, where he worked for wages for a period of five years. Then he took a homestead in Sonoma County. Later he followed dairying on rented property. After residing in that county two years he came to Cayucos and vicinity, where he entered extensively into the dairying business. In 1883 he located upon his present ranch of 320 acres, on Old Creek five miles from Cayucos, where he was engaged chiefly in dairying with fair profit.

He was married in 1866, to Miss Margaret Phillips, and has seven children: Elizabeth Dorcas, John, Mary, Victoria Lee, Margaret, Michael Dennis and Susan Fidelia.

CAPTAIN RICHARD ROBINSON is one of Ventura County's prominent horticulturists and stock-raisers, having 2,440 acres of land devoted to the above mentioned pursuits. He was for forty years, the best of his life, a seafaring man, most of that time master of a vessel, and has therefore honorably earned the title of Captain. The past eighteen years he has been identified with Ventura County and its interests. It is not a little surprising that a man who had followed the sea for forty years, should at once be transformed into a successful horticulturist, and that, too, in a county where the raising of fruit, when he began, was but an experiment. Mr. Hobart and himself were the pioneers in the business in the Upper Ojai Valley. In 1872 the Captain purchased 440 acres of land, on which he built and planted and improved. He now has forty-five acres in fruit, apricots, nectarines, prunes, peaches, apples, olives, walnuts and oranges, all yielding large returns. He has his own dryer on the ranch. In addition to his fruit interests, he is also raising horses, cattle and hay on this ranch. This property is being managed by his son, Richard O. Captain Robinson has bought 2,000 acres of land on the Santa Ana ranch, ten miles north of Ventura, where he is raising Hambletonian horses and grade Holstein and Durham cattle. He has imported a fine Hambletonian horse and several thoroughbred brood mares, and now has about 150 head of cattle and sixty horses. He also raises hay on this place.

Captain Robinson was born in Thomaston, Knox County, Maine, August 13, 1817. His father, Richard Robinson, was born in North Wales, in 1787, came to Maine when a boy fourteen years old, and was a sea captain, most of his life a master of merchant ships, principally in the cotton trade between New Orleans and different ports in Europe. The last twenty years of his life he was President of the Thomaston Bank. He married Miss Jane Wyllie, a native of Bristol, Maine, daughter of Captain John Wyllie, also a ship owner. They had a family of ten children, four of whom are living, two in California, one in Brooklyn, New York, and one at the old home in Maine. Captain Robinson received his early education in his native State, and at the age of seventeen years began to sail with his father; was two years before the mast, six months second officer, three years chief mate, and after that was master of the ship Catharine, of which both he and his father owned a part. She sailed between the South ports and New York, Boston and Europe. The Captain has seen much rough weather, but never lost a ship or had a serious accident. He was married, in 1840, to Miss Mary Wentworth, of Lincolnville, Maine, and daughter of Captain John Wentworth, also a native of that State, and a seaman. Mrs. Robinson sailed with her husband during the greater part of his seafaring life, so he was not deprived of the company of his family. Their union has been blessed with two sons, Richard O. and Charles W., both born at Thomaston, Maine. Charles is now devoting his time to the study of music in Boston at the New England Conservatory of Music. Both the sons are married. The Captain and his family retired from the sea in 1872, after a most successful career, and settled in Ventura County, where they have since resided. In politics Captain Robinson is Republican. He is a quiet, unobtrusive man, never seeking notoriety. He has purchased a neat home on Oak street, Ventura, where he and the partner of his life are quietly spending the evening of their voyage on life's tempestuous sea.

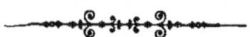

ADOLPHO CAMARILLO was born in San Buenaventura, October 29, 1864. His father, Juan Camarillo, was a native of the city of Mexico, born in 1812. He came to California with a colony, in 1834, they having for their destination Monterey, and, becoming tired of the sea, landing at San Diego and continuing their journey by land. Juan Camarillo left the party at Santa Barbara, and became a traveler and trader with the Indians from San Francisco to San Diego, selling them trinkets and receiving gold in return. The Mission Fathers were very obliging to travelers, and gave him a room in which to lodge, and there, when all was quiet at the mission, the Indians came to trade. In this trade with the Indians he accumulated $3,000, and with this money he opened a store in Santa Barbara, and there made his money.

Mr. Pedro Ruiz had a large goverment grant of land, and upon his death the heirs sold the property, 10,000 acres of beautiful land, to Mr. Camarillo. He also owned town property in Ventura. Mr. Camarillo's family consisted of four daughters and three sons. One of the latter is deceased. The father died December 4, 1880. The Ventura property was left to the daughters, who are now married and reside in Ventura, and the ranch was left to the widow and two sons. Mr. Adolpho Camarillo is the manager of, and resides upon, the ranch, while his mother and brother, Juan Camarillo, live in Ventura, the latter being engaged in the general merchandise business.

Adolpho Camarillo was educated in the public schools of Ventura, and graduated at the International Business College at Los Angeles. He has been on the ranch since his father's death, and is extensively engaged in the raising of sheep, keeping an average of 4,000 head. He also raises the horses and cattle required on the ranch. Mr. Camarillo rents 2,500 acres of land to be cultivated in corn and Lima beans, 800 acres being devoted to the latter. The renters furnish every thing and pay one-fourth of the crop for the use of the land.

The subject of this sketch was married, in 1888, to Miss Isabella Mancheca, daughter of Francisco Mancheca, a native of Spain. They have one child, a daughter, Minerva. Both Mr. Camarillo and his wife are members of the Catholic Church. Politically he affiliates with the Democratic party.

FRANK P. BARROWS, the leading general merchant in the town of Nordhoff, was born in Martha's Vineyard, Massachusetts, June 23, 1850. His father, J. L. Barrows, was a descendant of the Puritan Fathers. (See the ancestory of the family in the history of his brother, Thomas Barrows, in this book.) The subject of this sketch is the youngest son, and was educated in the public schools of his native town. He began business for himself, in Chicago, in 1867. In 1871, he, in partnership with his brother, took a general agency for the Victor Sewing Machine, and they did a thriving business, selling 25,000 machines in the short time they were there. They were in the great Chicago fire, but a week afterward were at business again and receiving orders. Mr. Barrows, on account of failing health, his disease being throat and lung trouble, was obliged to give up business, and, by the advice of his physician, came to California in 1875, and to Ventura County in 1879. He has here fully recovered his health. His first venture was to buy the Ojai Valley House, which he improved and conducted for five years. He bought 100 acres of land, and later purchased a stock of general merchandise in Nordhoff, and is doing a thriving business, employing five clerks. He has the largest store and stock of goods in the town, and enjoys the confidence and patronage of the people in the two valleys. He is liberal in his views on all topics, and has good natural as well as acquired ability for the mercantile business. He takes orders and delivers goods all over the territory which naturally belongs to Nordhoff. His customers have found they can buy no better goods elsewhere. Mr. Barrows gives only a few hours each day to his business, just enough to keep himself thoroughly informed as to how it is being conducted. He has a handsome residence near the center of town; the grounds, comprising ten acres, are dotted over with beautiful live-oaks and other trees, with flowers in profusion. A delightfully shaded brook runs through the grounds, and the whole place speaks of taste and refinement.

Mr. Barrows was married in 1882, to Miss Julia Smith of San Francisco, daughter of Stephen Smith, a merchant there. This union has been blessed with three children, all born in Nordhoff: Albert L., Stephen S. and Edward S. Mr. and Mrs. Barrows are both members of the Congregational Church. In politics Mr. Barrows is a Republican. He spends most of his time with his family, in his beautiful home, surrounded with balmy air, fine scenery, cooling shade, and enjoys a paying business. Why should he not be healthy and happy in his lovely California home?

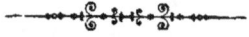

M. C. RYNERSON was born near Stockton, California, January 4, 1858. His father, C. C. Rynerson, is a native of the State of Kentucky, and crossed the plains to the Golden State in 1849. He took up a Government claim near Stockton, was, for a time, Sheriff of the county, and for a number of years was one of the most prominent men of San Joaquin County. His ancestry came from Germany. One member of the family is a leading medical authority of New York city. His father died in 1887. His mother, Mary A. (Wesley) Rynerson, was born in England, and in infancy came with her parents to America. She was the mother of nine children, five daughters and four sons, only two of whom are now living, the subject of this sketch and his sister, Mrs. Eva J. Leach, a widow, residing at Santa Barbara.

Mr. Rynerson received his education at Santa Barbara, and when prepared to enter the university his eyes became diseased. He afterward took a business course at the Heald Business College, San Francisco, and engaged in the milling business with his father at Santa Barbara. Five or six years later they sold the mill and moved to Arizona, remaining there a year, having, at this time, failing health. In 1884 gypsum had been discovered, and his father returned to California to see it, and purchased 660 acres of land. They have recently sold a mining claim to the Ventura Plaster Company, and the gypsum bed will now be worked. The subject of this sketch has improved the property which his father bought, by erecting a pleasant home and planting fruit trees; he has four acres in French prunes, three acres in apricots, and an assortment of nearly every kind of fruit, including blackberries, raspberries, and strawberries. He also has twelve acres in young olive trees. Many of his fruit trees are now in bearing. Mr. Rynerson sank a well 196 feet deep, in which the water rises to within forty feet of the surface, and he has an engine of his own to pump the water. For sixteen hours in succession the water has run without exhausting the supply. Since coming here, Mr. Rynerson has regained his health, and is now a strong man in a fair situation to enjoy life in his pleasant California home, which is a typical one, surrounded with trees and vines and with the foot-hills making a delightful back-ground to the picture.

Mr. Rynerson was united in marriage with Miss Ida C. Holmes, a native of Wisconsin, and daughter of J. T. Holmes, a farmer of that state. This union has been blessed with three children, two born at Santa Barbara and one at their present home, viz.: Ruth, Edna L., and Margery. Mrs. Rynerson is a member of the Presbyterian Church. Mr. Rynerson is a Trustee of his school district, and takes an interest in educational matters. Politically, he is a Republican. Earlier in life he took an active part in the conventions of the party, but more recently devotes his time to his ranch.

B. W. GALLY, one of the prominent business men of the Ojai Valley, was born in Wheeling, Virginia, July 9, 1852. His father, Hon. Thomas M. Gally, was a native of Virginia, a leading Whig politician, and was a member of the Constitutional Convention of Virginia in 1852 and 1854. His mother, who, before her marriage, was Miss Mary List, was a native of Wheeling and a daughter of H. List, Esq., a leading banker of Wheeling. Mr. and Mrs. Gally had but two children, a son, the subject of this sketch, and a daughter.

B. W. Gally, after receiving a liberal education, was engaged in the banking business until his health became impaired. He was advised by his physician to give up a sedentary business and seek a milder climate; and with that object in view he came to California in 1883. He purchased seventy acres of land, on which was located a pleasure and health resort, one mile east of the town of Nordhoff. This was formerly the property of W. S. McKee. Mr. Gally has improved the place very much by erecting four new buildings. The hotel is on the cottage plan, with main buildings in the middle containing parlor and dining-room, and the cottages affording home conveniences. It is situated on a beautiful lawn, shaded and made delightful by scattering live oak trees. It is both a winter and a summer resort; is patronized in summer by Californians, and in winter by Eastern people. All are delighted by the grand and picturesque scenery, which meets the eye in every direction. A fine new Presbyterian Church edifice stands near the hotel, and the beautiful tree-embowered town of Nordhoff is only a mile distant. The whole valley is noted for its equitable climate and balmy and health-producing air. In the valley are found mineral springs, and at the hotel an abundance of good water, choice fruits of all kinds, and the best of Jersey milk and butter.

Mr. Gally was united in marriage in 1885 with Miss Mary Davidson, a native of Jefferson City, Missouri, and a daughter of Dr. William Davidson of that place. Howard and Killborne, their two children, were born at their present beautiful home. Mr. Gally is possessed of those courteous and agreeable manners so characteristic of the Southern gentleman. In his political views, he is Republican. Mrs. Gally is a member of the Episcopal Church.

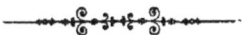

THOMAS A. SHEPPARD is a native of the Golden West and a business man of Hueneme. He was born in Tulare County, November 5, 1862, and is a son of Judge S. A. Sheppard, a native of Maryland. (His history will be found on another page in this book.) The subject of this sketch was educated in the public schools and also took a course in the Heald Business College, San Francisco. After completing his education, he went to Los Angeles, where he engaged in the real-estate business, under the firm name of T. A. Sheppard & Co., Peter Ward and William Wright being the other members of the firm. They did a thriving commission business, and continued it until 1887. They were the exclusive agents for an East Los Angeles tract belonging to Dr. J. H. Griffin, and were also agents for a Sister of Charity tract, both of which they closed out in a satisfactory manner to all parties concerned. Mr. Sheppard then removed to the Ojai Valley and engaged in the real-estate business with Mr. Stewart. He remained there until business became dull. He next moved to Hueneme, and here bought out the drug business of his brother, S. D. Sheppard, which he still continues. He has the only drug store in the town and is doing a fine business.

Mr. Sheppard was married, in 1884, to Miss Bell Hutchings, of Los Angeles. She was born on the plains, while her parents were en route to California. They have three daughters: Madge, born in Los Angeles, Florence, in Ventura, and the youngest (not named) born in Hueneme.

Politically, Mr. Sheppard is a Democrat.

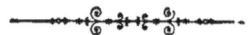

C. T. GILGER, the junior member of the firm of Livingston & Gilger, of Hueneme, Ventura County, was born in Ohio, April 13, 1865. His father, Daniel Gilger, is also a native of that State, and his grandfather, Jacob Gilger, was born in Germany and settled in Ohio in the early pioneer days of that State. He was a weaver by trade, and the family still have in their possession cloth made by him at a time when everything they wore was woven from their own wool and flax. Mr. Gilger's mother, Cynthia (Turbett) Gilger, was born in Ohio, of Pennsylvania Dutch parentage. They had three children, of whom the subject of this sketch is the eldest. He first came to California and to Ventura, with his father and family, in 1871. They returned to the East, settled up their business, and came back to this State the following year, remaining a year in Sutter County. In 1873 the family came to Ventura County, where the father purchased forty-five acres of land, near New Jerusalem, on which he erected buildings and otherwise improved, and engaged in the real-estate business, in which he met with fair success. In 1877 he purchased 120 acres of land.

The subject of this sketch had two farms near New Jerusalem, which he sold and afterward bought ninety-five acres of his father. They are both pleasantly situated and have erected comfortable homes. In February, 1890, Mr. Gilger bought a half interest in their present grocery, hardware and produce business. They have a good stock of goods and have established a fine trade.

Mr. Gilger was united in marriage with Miss Annie Middleswarth, a native of Ohio. They have one child, Fred, born in Ventura County. Politically, Mr. Gilger is a Republican.

JOHN DONLON is one of the prominent ranchers of Ventura County, California. He was born in County Longford, Ireland, in the year 1847, the son of Irish parents. He came to California, in the fall of 1870, and since that time has been variously employed. He first worked for wages at San José and in Alameda County for three years. Next he went to San Francisco, where he was employed for two years. In 1875 he came to Ventura County, and worked out for a year, after which he engaged in sheep-raising, following that business seven years, and keeping from 500 to 3,000 sheep. He sold his sheep and purchased 403 acres of land, and on this property he has since lived, engaged in farming. His principal crop has been barley, of which he has raised 3,400 sacks in a single year, which sold for ninety cents per hundred pounds. He also raises horses, cattle and hogs.

Nearly all this time Mr. Donlon lived the life of a single man. June 24, 1886, he was united in marriage with Miss Mary Forrer, a beautiful young lady, native of Utah, and daughter of Fred and Caroline Forrer, natives of Germany. Now things are changed at the once dreary bachelor's hall, for here are two interesting children: Peter A., born April 28, 1887, and William C., born December 2, 1888. The patter of children's feet can be heard and the prattle of childish voices greet the tired father as he returns from his daily routine of ranch life; and he whispers to himself, "How much I missed by remaining single so long!"

Mr. Donlon is, religiously, a Catholic, and, politically, a Democrat. He has served the public as School Trustee, and is much interested in the development of his section of the country. Living, as he does, so near the village of New Jerusalem, he enjoys the advantages of stores, school and church.

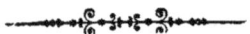

JOHN SCARLETT, one of the old settlers and prominent ranchers of the Santa Clara Valley, is a native of the "Emerald Isle," born in County Fermanagh, June 18, 1825. His parents, Richard and

Elizabeth Scarlett, were natives of Ireland, lived on a farm, and were members of the Episcopal Church. John was educated in his native country, and came to the United States in 1852. He engaged in the wool and cotton dyeing business five years. He came to California in 1857, and had charge of an engine in a San Francisco sugar refinery. Mr. Scarlett remembers Mr. Spreckles when he started a little business there at that time. After three years spent in San Francisco, he moved to Alameda County, built a hotel and conducted it from 1861 to 1870, after which he rented it. There was a deal of travel on the roads at that time and the hotel business was a very profitable one. Mr. Scarlett next engaged in sheep-raising, keeping from 4,000 to 5,000 sheep. This also proved a profitable business and he continued it four years before coming to his present locality. While in this business he lived in a tent both winter and summer. When he came to this county he brought 2,700 sheep, three men and a cook. The journey was made by land, and their diet was principally biscuits and bacon, though they sometimes got an antelope, and they slept on the ground at night. Mr. Scarlett bought an interest in a grant and when it was divided his share was 700 acres, which he has farmed since that time. When he made the purchase, his neighbors, Mr. McGrath and Mr. Leonard, were both here. The land was bought of Mr William Rice. Mr. Scarlett does general farming and raises horses, cattle and hogs, his principal crop being barley and corn. He has several splendid fields, perfectly level and in a high state of cultivation. From the highway, which passes through Mr. Scarlett's ranch, the traveler is at once impressed with the pleasing appearance of this attractive home. The house, an elegant one, is shaded and surrounded by ornamental trees and flowers, and the whole premises indicate that the inmates are people of taste and refinement. Mr. Scarlett says that the improvements of the grounds may be attributed to his wife, as he gives his time and attention to his stock and ranch.

Mr. Scarlett wedded Miss Annie Lester, a native of Australia, and daughter of Lawrence Lester. Their union has been blessed with five children, four of whom are living and all at home with their parents. Their names are Lizy, John, Sally and Annie.

In his political views Mr. Scarlett is a Republican.

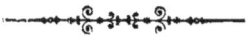

SIMON COHN is one of Ventura County's business men and the pioneer general merchant of New Jerusalem. He was born in Germany, of German parents, April 4, 1852, and was educated in his native land, and learned the mercantile business in his father's store. He came to California, in 1873, to launch out in business for himself, and has met with that success which is the reward of faithful, honest toil. He was first employed by his brother, at Saticoy, and remained there sixteen months, after which he came to his present locality, in 1875. Mr. Cohn is entitled to the honor of being the founder of the town of New Jerusalem and of naming it. The first settlers of the town were three Hebrews, the fields were loaded with golden grain, plenty of fine cattle were in the valley, there was an abundance of choice fruit, and also milk and honey; so, the name of New Jerusalem seemed quite appropriate. Mr. Cohn erected the first building in the town, and in it opened his store and continued to do business in the same until the increasing demands of his trade necessitated a larger store room. He accordingly erected the brick block in which he is now doing business. This is a double building, filled with all kinds of merchandise, and Mr. Cohn is doing the principal business of the town. He now owns several buildings, and is also interested in real estate out of the town, having sixty acres of well improved land.

Mr. Cohn was married, in 1885, to Miss Minnie Cohn, also a native of Germany and of the same name, but of no relation to him. Their family consists of three children, all born at New Jerusalem, viz.: Dora, Helen and Jacob.

The subject of this sketch has been Postmaster of the town for the past ten years. In political views he is Democratic.

EPHRAIM B. HALL, of Scotch descent, was born in Harrison County, Virginia, (now Marion County, West Virginia), in 1822. He completed his academical course, studied law, and practiced that profession in said Marion and adjoining counties from 1850 until after the commencement of the civil war in 1861.

Mr. Hall was a member of the Virginia Convention that met in Richmond in February, 1861, and was one of the fifty-eight members of that body who voted against the adoption of the Ordinance of Secession. On the adjournment of that convention in May, 1861, he returned home, and canvassed his own and the adjoining counties, against the ratification of said ordinance by the people, at an election ordered for that purpose; and not returning to the adjourned session of said convention in June, 1861, from his absence therefrom, and his active opposition to the aggressions and operations of the Confederate government and forces, and of the State government co-operating therewith, he was, by ordinance, expelled from said convention; and subsequently, under the provisions of an ordinance of said convention declaring certain acts resisting the authority of the Confederate government as constituting treason against the State, and providing for trial, in the absence of the accused, by process of outlawry, he and three others were tried upon a charge of treason against said Confederate State government, and condemned to be executed whenever the civil or military authorities of said State or of the Confederate government might be able to arrest them.

He was a member of the convention that met at Wheeling in 1861, for the re-organization of the State government on a loyal basis and in co-operation with the Federal Government.

Was a member of the convention that formed and adopted the first constitution of the State of West Virginia, and was one of the committee of five, appointed by said convention to have charge of the election, and to make returns of the resuts of the vote upon the ratification or rejection of said constitution by the people; and, if ratified, to present the same to Congress and the Federal authorities at Washington, and to secure its acceptance and the formation and admission of the State of West Virginia.

Mr. Hall was elected Attorney General of the State of West Virginia, for the term commencing January 1, 1865. He was elected Judge of the Circuit Court (ten circuits, composed of the counties of Jefferson, Berkeley, Morgan, Hampshire, Hardy and Pendleton), in October, 1865, and in December, 1865, resigned the office of Attorney General and entered upon his judicial duties. Was re-elected for a succeeding term, and after seven years' service upon the bench, he, in October, 1872, on account of the ill health of his wife, resigned his office of judge and removed to the State of California. That prior thereto, in March, 1870, he was by the Governor appointed one of the three commissioners on the part of the State of West Virginia to confer with the State of Virginia to adjust and settle the matter of the debt of Virginia as between the two States, which position he also resigned.

In November, 1873, he qualified as attorney in the Supreme Court of California and settled, and made himself a quiet and cozy home in the El Montecito Valley, some four miles from the city of Santa Barbara, where he still resides; but did not resume the practice of his profession until 1875, since when he has been engaged in the practice. He is vice-president of one, and counsel for two of the banks of said city, and in a quiet way pursues his profession, and enjoys his home, which for beauty and comfort, and in such a locality, and with such a climate, should make any one content and happy.

Thus have many done, who have passed through the exciting scenes of a border home during the war.

L. LAW & CO.—The representatives of the above firm are S. L. and P. E. Law, who were born in Chicago, Illinois. Their parents are natives of New York city, but moved to Chicago in 1837, being numbered among the pioneers. Their father dealt largely in real estate, and was at one time owner of Hyde Park. These enterprising young men came to Santa Barbara in 1888, bringing with them a $12,000-stock of well-selected gents' furnishing goods, hats, etc. By marked activity and close attention to business their store ranks with the first of the city. They make specialties of Knox's hats, of New York, and Stetson's, of Philadelphia.

S. L. Law was married in Santa Barbara in May, 1889, to Miss Martha M. More, a daughter of T. Wallace More.

JOSEPH SEXTON, nurseryman at Goleta, was born in Hamilton County, Ohio, nine miles from Cincinnati, March 14, 1864. His father was a farmer and afterward a merchant at Dent, same county; then, in 1852, he came to San Francisco on the steamer Star of the West, on the Atlantic side, and the S. S. Lewis on the Pacific side, crossing the Isthmus by the Nicaragua route. The S. S. Lewis was unseaworthy, leaking badly, and on her next trip she came near sinking off San Francisco. After arriving in San Francisco, Mr. Sexton first became a dealer in wood for eleven months. Then he went to Ione Valley, Amador County, and bought a tract of land, on which he started a nursery of all kinds of fruit trees. In 1864 he returned to San Francisco, then moved to Petaluma, Sonoma County, and bought a nursery, in company with his father, which he conducted two years; then managed the grain farm in Marin County two years, and finally, in December, 1867, he came to Santa Barbara and bought ten acres within the city limits. In the spring following he went to the Goleta (signifying schooner) ranch and purchased forty-five acres. He has since added to that tract twenty acres. Here he started the nursery business first in town and then moved to Goleta. He started with fruit trees only, and afterward added ornamental. In 1882 he bought 208 acres, and later 105 acres at Ventura; and next, in company with his father, he purchased a ranch of 8,000 acres. He has about twenty-five acres in a nursery of fruit-trees; is now setting out 105 acres of blue gum (*Eucalyptus globulus*) at Ventura. In 1872 the industry of raising pampas grass was originated at the Santa Barbara Nursery, by planting the seed—a discovery having been made with reference to selection and the mode of planting. In 1889 he shipped between 200 and 400 plumes, and since 1874 he has shipped altogether 1,388,000. At first plumes were valued at twenty cents apiece. The soft-shelled walnut also originated with Mr. Sexton, from seed purchased in San Francisco. In the nursery he has a full line of fruit and ornamental trees, the specialty being the soft-shelled walnut and ornamental palms in great variety. For these purposes he has under cultivation sixty-five acres. He has 300 varieties of evergreen roses.

Mr. Sexton was married at Goleta, in 1868, to Miss Lucy Foster, a native of Illinois, whose father, Isaac B. Foster, was a money-lender. Mr. and Mrs. Sexton have seven sons and five daughters, and all living at home.

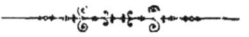

C. TALLANT, one of the leading grocers of Santa Barbara, is the subject of this sketch, who was born at Wheeling, West Virginia, in 1858. His father was a wholesale dry-goods merchant at Wheeling, and later moved to Baltimore, where he carried on business for many years. Our subject was educated at private schools, in Baltimore, and finished at the Roanoke College, Salem, Virginia. He moved to Santa Barbara with his parents in the fall of 1874. He began the grocers' business in 1877, in the store of P. M. Newall, for whom he worked five years. In 1883 he bought an interest in the business, but after eighteen months sold again, and bought in with Mr. Sweetser, continuing under the firm of Tallant & Sweetser until March 1, 1890, when Mr. Tallant bought the entire business, and will continue alone. He carries a full line of domestic and imported groceries, smoked, dried and packed meats, and dried and canned fruits.

He was married at San Francisco, in 1884, to Miss Mattie Dillan, a native of New Orleans. Her father, Edward Dillan, was an extensive manufacturer of chronometers at San Francisco. Mr. and Mrs Tallant have two children. Mr. Tallant is a member of Odd Fellows, Santa Barbara Lodge, No. 156, and of the A. O. U. W.

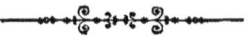

FRED A. MOORE, at present the City Assessor of Santa Barbara, and a gentleman who has been largely interested in the local press, was born at Pittsburg, Pennsylvania, in 1856. His father was a prominent merchant of Pittsburg, and later at Baltimore, Maryland. They moved to Minnesota when our subject was an infant, and in 1863, after his father's decease, his mother, with himself and sister, came to San Francisco, where he began his education at the public schools, and then at Santa Clara College. In 1867 they moved to Santa Barbara, and he attended the mission for two years, and then took a scientific course at the Oberlin College, Oberlin, Ohio, returning to Santa Barbara in 1872, and attended the Santa Barbara College for three years. He spent 1876 in San Francisco, returning in 1877 and connected himself with the *Weekly Index*, which he continued about one year. In 1878 he started *The Independent*, as a semi-weekly, and in 1879 bought out *The*

Advertiser and consolidated the two papers. In 1884 he sold out his paper and engaged in fire insurance, which he has since continued, representing all the leading American and English companies, and carrying the principal insurance business of the city. He was first elected City Assessor in 1884, and re-elected in 1886 and 1888. Being unmarried, he resides with his mother and sister. Mr. Moore is a member of the society of Odd Fellows.

ALONZO CRABB, Constable of the city of Santa Barbara, and a native son, was born January 23, 1859. He was educated at the public schools, and for five years was connected with Sherman & Eland, corner State and Ortega streets. He was elected Constable in the fall of 1888, qualifying the first Monday in January, 1889: term of office, two years. He has also served as Deputy Sheriff, under R. J. Broughton.

Mr. Crabb was married at Santa Barbara, July 2, 1883, to Miss Isabelle Maris, daughter of Captain W. S. Maris, whose biography elsewhere appears. They have qeen blessed with one child. Mr. Crabb is a member of the "Native Sons of the Golden West."

J. F. MEYER was born in the northern part of Germany, in 1850. His father was a seafaring man, and for fourteen years he was on one vessel as mate and ship's carpenter. Our subject was in the general merchandise business in Bremen for five years, and in the fall of 1869 came to New York, where he was engaged in business until 1873, when he returned to Germany for a visit.

On returning to the United States, in 1874, he went to San Francisco, where he was variously employed until 1883, when he came to Santa Barbara and permanently established himself. In 1887 he erected a fine two-story brick building at 822 State street, where he resides and conducts a billiard-room, bowling-alley and saloon, keeping a fine variety of wines and liquors.

He was married in San Francisco, in 1887, to Miss Louise Meyer, and they have four children. Mr. Meyer is a charter member of the lodge of A. O. U. W. at San Francisco.

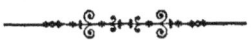

A. F. McPHAIL, a gentleman largely interested in various enterprises in and about Santa Barbara, was born on Prince Edward's Island, at Charlottetown, in 1858, his parents being natives of the island, and his father a farmer and cabinet-maker. In 1866 his parents moved to Lake City, Minnesota, where our subject attended school until fourteen years of age, when he was employed as money-order clerk at the post-office, remaining two years, and in 1874 coming to Santa Barbara to join his father, who came out in 1872. They then started a furniture business under the firm name of McPhail & Son. In 1880 our subject bought out the Champion livery stable, which he has since continued, keeping about twenty horses and suitable carriages. He was one of the incorporators of the Santa Barbara Transfer Company, which was incorporated December 14, 1886, and is now (1890) its president and manager. He was one of the incorporators of the Santa Barbara Hack and Carriage Company, July, 1888, and is still president of the company. For ten years he was manager and had charge of the street-car line, and has been connected with many of the city improvements. He was elected a member of the City Council from the second ward in 1884, and re elected in 1886.

Mr. McPhail was married at Santa Barbara, in 1880, to Miss Helen Stevens, a native of California. They have two children, Eula and George. He is a member of the Knights of Pythias.

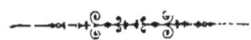

ALONZO L. GORDON was born in Caspar, Mendocino County, California, June 22, 1865, and was reared and educated there. His parents are of Scotch ancestry. His father, Alexander Gordon, was born in Montreal, Canada, and his mother, neé Christine Martin, is also a native of Canada. They have five children, of whom Alonzo is the third. Mr. and Mrs. Gordon came to California and settled in Mendocino County, in 1863, and there Mr. Gordon bought a ranch of 1,000 acres and engaged in cattle-raising and butchering. They still own and reside on that ranch. In 1885 they purchased a fine ranch of 1,000 acres of level land, located eight miles east of Hueneme, in Ventura County.

Alonzo Gordon has been reared on a ranch, and is thoroughly informed in all matters pertaining to ranch life. He gives strict attention to business, and is an enterprising young man; is manager of this ranch, and has five men in his employ. Since its purchase, many improvements have been made on this property, a house and suitable out-buildings having been erected. Mr. Gordon is extensively engaged in stock-raising, and also raises some barley, corn and hay. They have some fine Holstein cattle; and their horses, of which they keep about fifty, are mostly the Black Lewis stock crossed with the Clydesdale. They have a Black Lewis horse that is considered a very fine animal.

The subject of this sketch is a member of the I. O. G. T. Politically he is a Republican.

W. M. EDDY, one of the progressive young men of the Santa Ynez, was born in Luzerne County, Pennsylvania, in 1862. They lived at Beach Haven, and his father was engaged in running a canal boat on the Pennsylvania Canal. The family came to California, arriving at Lompoc, Santa Barbara County, January 6, 1877, where the father carried on general farming. In 1886, in connection with his son, the subject of this sketch, he purchased a ranch of 320 acres at Santa Rita, the son owning a one-half interest. In 1888 W. M. Eddy came to Santa Ynez and leased the spacious livery stable of John F. Miller and bought his stock of horses and light and heavy wagons. Thus equipped he was ready to meet the requirements of a critical public, and since that time has been successful in his business undertaking. The ranch is also in a prosperous condition, and is being carried on in the interest of stock-raising, both horses and cattle.

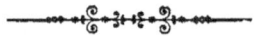

JOHN CAWELTI is the son of German parents, and was born in Wurtemberg, Germany, January 3, 1829. He received his early education in his native country, and at the age of nineteen years, in 1848, came to America. His first work in this country was in a brick yard in New York, where he was employed for three months. He then went to Milwaukee and learned the butcher business, working for $5 per month. He was taken sick there, and from that place went to Cincinnati, Ohio, where he was engaged in butchering from 1849 to 1856. In the latter year he went to Iowa, purchased 160 acres of land and engaged in farming, continuing to reside there for three years and a half. In 1864 he came to California, rented lands in Sonoma County and farmed there until 1863, then he came to Santa Barbara County (now Ventura County). Like many others, he thought he was on Government land and for a time he fought title, but when he found he could not hold the land, he rented the property, and in 1875 made about $5,000 on about 1,000 acres of rented land, raising wheat, barley and hogs. In 1877 there came a dry season and he lost nearly all he had before made. The property on which Mr. Cawelti is now located was owned by the Catholic Church. They sold to the ex-mission, and when the land was put on the market he bought 1,000 acres, at $16.25 per acre; or $16,250 for the property, paying one-third down, and going in debt $11,000. Since purchasing he has made many improvements on the place, has cleared part of the land, built two barns, at a cost of $1,000, and a nice dwelling, at a cost of $3,000; also two other smaller houses, and has built nine miles of fence. He has bought 640 acres of hill land for pasture, at a cost of $2,000; and now owns 150 head of cattle and eighty head of horses, and is out of debt, having paid up in six years. His horses are part Belgium stock, and he is now introducing Seavern blood into the cattle.

Mr. Cawelti was married, in Cincinnati, Ohio, in 1852, to Mrs. Sipp, widow of Mr. Jud Sipp, by whom she had one child, Frederica Louisa. Mrs. Cawelti was born in Bavaria, Germany, and when a little child was brought to America by her parents. Their union has been blessed with nine children, three born in Ohio, four in Iowa, and two in California, viz.: David, John Henry, Catharine, Jacob, John George, Mary E., Dora and Andrew E., all living near him except David, who is in San Bernardino County.

The subject of this sketch is one of the many illustrations how the hardy and industrious sons of Germany succeed when they come to this country. By his own intelligent industry and judicious management, he has risen from a day laborer in a brick-yard to one of the reliable and wealthy citizens of Ventura County, California. Mr. Cawelti was reared a Presbyterian and still holds to that creed. Politically, he is a Democrat; has been elected to the office of school trustee, but is not, in any sense, a politician or office-seeker. He is a quiet and unobtrusive man, and deserved the success which has attended his labors. Long may be live to enjoy the home so nobly and honestly earned!

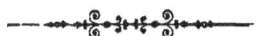

CAPTAIN W. E. GREENWELL, a distinguished member of the United States Coast and Geodetic Survey, was born in 1824, in St. Mary's County, Maryland, of English ancestry. His father, William Greenwell, served in the war of 1812, commanding a regiment which he himself had organized against the British; was severely wounded and was a sufferer on that account until his death.

Captain Greenwell, the subject of this sketch, graduated at Georgetown (District of Columbia) College; studied law in the office of the distinguished jurist Brent, of Washington, District of Columbia, and when about twenty-two years of age entered the coast survey, receiving his appointment from Professor Dallas Bache, Superintendent, who had been his intimate friend and from whom he received the recognition and appreciation his talents and fidelity merited. He first served with Captain F. U. Gerdes, United States Coast Survey, in Mobile Bay, on the coast of the Gulf of Mexico, until 1854. The next year he was transferred to the coast of California to take charge of a coast survey party, under General Ord, and kept this position until 1861. The war of the Rebellion then breaking out, he went East and was stationed at Washington during the exciting period of the Secession Congress, and was a witness of the momentous struggle. It was thought that he, being a Southerner, would cast his lot with the Southern cause, but he remained true to the Union, saying that he owed nothing to the territory of the South, but much to the Government.

In 1863 he returned to California and continued in the coast survey until he resigned, a few years before his death.

The records of the Coast Survey, which alone chronicle the arduous, faithful and skillful work of this admirable corps, show the talented handiwork of Captain Greenwell in all branches of field-work along the Atlantic coast from Maine to Florida, and particularly along the coast of California and the islands outlying the southern portion.

He made his permanent home in Santa Barbara, where he died August 27, 1886, leaving to mourn his loss a wife and three sons. He was a distinguished man and efficient officer; was well known and highly respected throughout the State of California, and was claimed by the people of the State as one of her sons. He believed in the great future of California and invested there his little patrimony, and was enabled to leave his family in independant circumstances. His life was devoted to the service of the Government, and doubtless he sacrificed a portion of his life, which should have been a long one, to regard his fine physique and iron constitution, in such service. Working in the miasmatic bayous of Louisiana, and landing where there were no wharves, through the surf on the coast, told in after life, and he was some fifteen years ago prostrated by a severe and almost fatal illness which left him a sufferer until his death. One who was the intimate friend of Mr. Greenwell for years, and who understood his true character and appreciated his superior traits, writes of him as follows:

"Mr. Greenwell was not of the ordinary class of humanity. His strong, pronounced individuality separated him from it and marked him a figure independent of his associates. There was not a tame thing about his nature, and, of course, the term was applied to him which the world fits upon those who wander from or soar above the beaten road of life—eccentric. This eccentricity caused him indeed to differ in many ways from a number of his fellows. He loved honor, truth, virtue, justice, and above all gentility, which he considered the aggregate of the noble graces. He hated and denounced charlatanism, and especially when displayed in serious matters affecting the honor, credit and standing before the world of the Government and its branches of service, he abhorred and openly expressed his contempt for petty acts of selfishness and his disgust for vulgarity and grossness. Nothing could induce him to intrigue for his own preferment or advantage, but with a child-like pleasure he would use his high standing and personal influence to promote others, especially the young men in the service whom he believed to be worthy, competent and energetic; and it is safe to say, his unselfish acts on this behalf were not always rewarded with gratitude, and the latter part of his life had in it some bitterness, instilled from repudiated kindness, unrecognized generosity and misplaced friendliness.

"The contributor of these few lines in tribute to the memory of a dear friend can say of this officer and gentleman, that there never was a more unselfishly loyal man, true to his God, true to his country, true to his family and true to his friends, and with such self-sacrifice. He hated blasphemy. While a student of the problems of science and history, and one of the best readers of nature, he was in perfect accord with its spirit. The animals loved him. He could train and control them with ease. He treated them with gentleness and tenderness, having been known to leave his bed at night to nurse a sick horse or dog. He could not tolerate the shallow sophists of the day who would make of nature the weapon of a feeble intellect to annihilate God and prostitute man; but saw in all the footprints of an omnipotent and all-glorious Creator.

"Though a Southerner by birth, his allegiance to the Union was firm and fixed. He loved the flag, and at one time rebuked and discharged an aid who spoke of it disrespectfully. He was a warm partisan of his country, and eulogizer and defender of its institutions, in comparison with those of other nations.

"The same loyalty leavened his friendship. The mentor, counselor and corrector in private, he was in public the stanch advocate, supporter and defender of his friend. His friendship was well worth having, being of the valuable sort. Rich in counsel and in practical aids, his judgment seemed to the writer almost infallible in the ordinary affairs of life; and when he submitted to it he never erred. He acted in life as he played chess, never ambuscading for a piece, laying his plans far ahead and depending upon the skillful use of his pawns. He never skirmished for temporary advantage, but looked far into and planned for the future. He cared nothing for the antagonism and opposition of the powerful and influential, and made all his battles with his equals in power and influence, whilst he displayed to his employés and the poor a careful consideration and dignified and kind *bonhomie*. It was a privilege coveted by the laborer to be of his party in the field. Hesitating, and in ordinary conversation laboring to give proper expression to his thoughts, though forcible and eloquent when aroused in a serious cause, it was difficult for passing acquaintances to gain any conception of the depth of his character and strength of his intellect. Indeed, none but his most intimate friends know how noble and great he was. The worldling and time-server could not approach him. An unfortunate barrier of pride and sensitiveness and diffidence lay between him and the hero-forging public.

"Captain Greenwell was happiest and appeared best at the post of duty in moments of action and danger, when coolness, judgment and courage were demanded. He was a perfect executive officer, and peril seemed to expand his force and quicken his wits. Some will remember his taking command of the steamer Senator some twenty-five years ago when it had been driven near the rocks of Point Concepcion, on a dark, foggy and stormy night, when the Captain was ill and exhausted and the crew were tired and rebellious; and by his command of men, skill, coolness, judgment and courage got her afloat and saved her from shipwreck, rescuing the ship and passengers at the expense of the freight, which he caused to be thrown overboard. At the beginning of his career in the coast survey, a young man, he at the risk of his own life rescued from shipwreck some sailors, with gallantry and brilliancy. Many of the old commanders of the navy thought and said that the United States had lost a brilliant and efficient officer; and yet his shore duties were performed with equal genius. He was the best surfer in the service; was an excellent mountaineer, and never forgot a landmark; and he was peculiarly fitted for reconnoissance work to map out and complete a practicable scheme of triangulation. He was thorough in everything, and was incapable of slipshod or slovenly work. The monuments he set in the fields were permanently fixed and so described that those officers who followed his footsteps had little difficulty in connecting with his work; and the work itself was faithful, exact and complete.

"As a host Mr. Greenwell was elegant, liberal and bountiful of sympathy, warmth and geniality. His house was the reunion of the young who were happy in the atmosphere of refinement. But his male friends loved most to be with him in the mountains, or on the ocean, in camp or on deck; he seemed then so free from restraint, so natural in his goodness, so noble in thought, ways and bearing, so kindly, gentle and sympathetic. It is there that they love to call him back and look upon his face unclouded with sorrow, unfurrowed with care, unmarked with bitterness against a selfish, ungrateful world, and listen to his lofty, refined sentiments and thoughtful words. The writer recalls at this moment some of his earnest utterances as he with others sat together in his tent looking at the 'everlasting hills.'

There is "everything in blood. An honorable and worthy sire begets a brave and honest son; and pure blood is the best legacy we can give to our offspring. The fact that it flows within our veins and that we are the medium of transmission, makes us guard the stream from pollution and send it onward as clean and clear as it came from the fountain head. It is the charm which preserves the scion of genteel stock in the midst of waywardness, folly and pursuit of pleasure, as well as from worldliness, from dishonor and crime; we can err in precept, discipline and training in the rearing of children, and all men do; for God alone can indisputably shape the youthful character; but we bequeath to them in our blood, jealously preserved from disease and poison, the antidote for all our errors; and we can fall asleep with the consciousness that the offspring of our body and bearers of our name can not without unnatural perversion cast upon it disgrace or stain."

W. P. SPROUT, an early pioneer of California, was born in Guernsey County, Ohio, in 1835. He remained at home on his father's farm until seventeen years of age, when he started for California. He shipped at New York on the Brother Jonathan, crossed the Isthmus of Panama and there took the ill-fated McKim, which was over crowded, shortly provisioned and very unseaworthy. They ran into San Diego harbor, and from that place Mr. Sprout walked to Los Angeles. He worked his passage from San Pedro to San Francisco on the brig Fremont. After a short engagement at Sacramento, he went to the mines at Nevada City and engaged in placer mining in Placer and Nevada counties, until 1869, as laborer, superintendent and owner, as the circumstances allowed. During the latter part of that time he was superintendent of hydraulic mining. In 1869 he came to Santa Barbara to take charge of the Belmont ranch for Fernald, Blancher & Co., an extensive fruit ranch. For four years he was in their employ. He then settled in East Santa Barbara and engaged in dairy farming on a ranch of 150 acres, keeping fifteen Jersey cows.

Mr. Sprout was married, at Santa Barbara, in 1871, to Miss Augusta Mandell, a lady of German descent. They have six children living. Mr. Sprout is a member of Santa Barbara Lodge, No. 56, and was a charter member of the encampment, I. O. O. F.

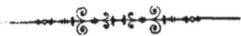

HENRY STODDARD, one of the early settlers of the Montecito valley, was born in Dayton, Ohio, January 2, 1835. His father, Henry Stoddard, Sr., was a prominent lawyer of Dayton, and practiced in that city for upwards of fifty years. The subject of this sketch graduated at the Miami University of Ohio, and afterward studied engineering at the Yale Scientific. He then studied law at Dayton, and later at St. Louis with Judge Bates, who was Attorney General under President Lincoln. In 1863 he went out on the John Morgan raid, companies being especially formed to resist the raid, but not regularly connected with the army. In the spring of 1864, when special call was made for troops, he enlisted in the One Hundred and Thirty-first Ohio National Guards, under Colonel John G. Lowe, Mr. Stoddard being a member of the regimental staff. They were sent to Harper's Ferry and Baltimore, and were mustered out in the fall at Camp Chase, Columbus, Ohio.

Returning to Dayton, he engaged in the manufacture of linseed oil and varnishes, under the firm name of Stoddard & Co. Ten years later, owing to failing health, he sold out all interests and came to Santa Barbara, California, in August, 1873. He purchased twenty acres of land in the Montecito Valley, and in the out-of-door life which he led, recovered his health. In 1876 he engaged in the real estate business in Santa Barbara, and the next year was appointed Postmaster, under President Hayes. For four years and a half he filled that office very acceptably to the people. In 1882 he was elected County Recorder, and upon the expiration of his term of office he again entered the business of real estate and insurance. He negotiates many loans for Eastern capitalists.

Mr. Stoddard was married in Memphis, Tennessee, in 1850, and has four children living. He is a member of the Starr King Post, Department of California, G. A R.

LARSEN, who is a professional dairyman, was born in Denmark, in 1844. His father being a farmer, the subject naturally inclined to the products of the soil. In 1868 he graduated from the college at Copenhagen. He had previously devoted himself to the acquirement of the science of the dairy farm. He was engaged on an extensive dairy farm at Skeyward, and there received full instructions in the making of butter and cheese. In 1868 he was married at Grano, and then became manager of several large dairies, up to 1876, when he came to America. He first settled at Easton, Pennsylvania, where as veternary surgeon he passed one year. He then went to DeKalb County, Illinois, where he built a large manufactory, bought up milk and made butter and cheese, continuing for two years. He then went to Milwaukee, and started a commission store for farm produce; but failing in this venture, in 1880 he came to California, first starting at San Francisco as veterinary surgeon, which he continued very successfully for three years. He then came to Santa Ynez, among the first settlers, and bought 160 acres near the old mission, but the purchase proved a losing investment; and in 1884 he came to Lompoc, as foreman of dairy for R. T. Buell. He then leased land and rented or purchased stock, and is now (1890) carrying on a very satisfactory business. He has 200 head of Holstein and Jersey cows, and makes butter in rolls for market. He bought the old Heacock ranch of 500 acres, in 1889, and also owns town property.

He has two children: one son at home and a daughter who is married and lives in San Francisco.

D. M. GREENLEE, one of the pioneer stage drivers of California, was born in Stark County, Illinois, in 1841. His father was a farmer, and also owned extensive milling interests, having built the first mills in Stark County, the old red Snatchwine mills on Walnut Creek, which were the only mills at that time west of Chicago. The subject worked in mills and on farm until 1855, having moved to Henry County in 1852, from which point in 1855 he started for California, with his father, taking out a number of blooded horses and fine cattle. His father was one of the largest importers of horses and cattle of that period, driving to Marysville, from which point he sold through the country. Between 1855 and 1862 the subject made nine trips across the plains in driving horses and cattle. In 1863 he went to Nevada, teaming and driving for Wells, Fargo & Co., remaining until 1868, when he returned to Marysville, driving on the old Colusa road for about two years, and in 1871 came to Los Angeles, and later on to Santa Barbara, teaming, staging and driving for Wells, Fargo & Co., until 1880, when he entered into partnership with A. F. McPhail, in the Champion Stable and in the Santa Barbara Transfer and Bus Line; also having individual land interests in the city and owning about fifty acres in the Montecito Valley. He came to Los Alamos in the spring of 1890, and keeps the Los Alamos stables, and also owns the stock of the old Patterson stable, in all about forty head of horses and wagons, both light and heavy for country driving. He also runs the stage line between Los Alamos and Lompoc, a distance of twenty miles.

Mr. Greenlee was married in Santa Barbara in 1889, to Miss Emma Bisbee. Mr. Greenlee first visited Los Alamos in September, 1876, and built the first house in town for the old stage line.

A. J. NICHOLS, the leading jeweler of Lompoc, was born in Central New York, in 1848. His father, J. A. Nichols, was a lawyer of Tioga County. The subject was educated in Tioga County, and in 1865 began his trade of jeweler and watchmaker near home and completed it in New York city. He then worked at his trade through several of the Central States, and in 1874 came to Santa Barbara, where he remained two years. He then went East and worked at his trade until 1880, when he again returned to Santa Barbara, and remained until 1883, when he came to Lompoc and opened his present business. He carries a fine stock of watches, clocks and jewelry; also musical instruments and sewing-machines.

He was married at Cleveland, Ohio, in 1874, to Miss A. J Martin, a native of Ohio, and they have two children. Mr. Nichols built his present store and residence, building 25 x 40, on Ocean avenue, in 1889, and his stock is neatly and tastefully arranged.

He is a member of Lompoc Lodge, No. 57, Knights of Pythias.

C. O. GARDNER.—One of the active and progressive farmers of Santa Ynez Valley is C. O. Gardner, who was born in the Province of Quebec, Canada, in 1848. His father was an extensive farmer in that locality, owned and cultivated 400 acres of land, also kept a dairy and dealt largely in cattle and horses. The subject of this sketch was reared at home, being engaged at work on his father's farm until twenty-six years of age. In 1874 he came to California, coming direct to Guadaloupe. He worked on a farm in the Santa Maria Valley until 1862,' when the town of Santa Ynez was laid out. Mr. Gardner at once purchased town lots and erected his present residence. He then leased about 500 acres from Bishop Mora, and later from the Santa Ynez Development Company, who bought the valley. Since that time he has been a large producer of barley, hay and wheat. In plowing he uses two gangs of five ten-inch plows each; and uses the improved large machinery for harvesting his crops. To a certain extent he is a breeder of fine work horses, keeping about twenty head.

Mr. Gardner was married at Santa Maria in 1882 to Miss Eva J. Preston. They have had three children, all now deceased.

DR. J. WILL GRAHAM was born in Hancock County, Illinois, in 1850, and came to California in 1852, with his parents, making the journey across the plains with an ox team. They settled in Colusa County, at the little town called Grand Island, on the Sacramento River. His father settled on what was supposed to be Government land, but in 1860, through the recognition of the Government of certain boundaries, a claim for a Spanish grant was established, and the tenants were obliged to buy, hire or clear out; and Mr. Graham then moved to Sutter County, where he bought a ranch of 160 acres and carried on general farming and stock-raising.

The subject was educated in the public schools of Colusa and Sutter counties, and in 1880 entered the medical department of the Willamette University, at Portland, Oregon, where he graduated in medicine and surgery in 1883. He practiced medicine in East Portland for one year, and in 1884 came to Los Alamos, where he has since carried on his profession. In 1888 he built a two-story brick house, the only brick house in town.

Dr. Graham was married at San Francisco, in 1882, to Miss Maria Gennette Drum, a native of Pennsylvania. The Doctor covers in his practice a radius of about twenty miles, necessitating long drives to see his patients.

B. P. WHITNEY was born in Corinth, Maine, on October 7, 1834. His father was a farmer, also kept a small shoe store. From thirteen years of age subject lived with his brother, who had large milling interests, and he worked in the shingle mills in summer and in the blacksmith shop in winter. In 1852 they went to Canada, and then to Minneapolis, Minnesota, always in milling interests and continuing blacksmithing. In 1856 they moved to what is now Kingston, Minnesota. His brother took up Government land, built a saw and grist mill, and thus started and named the town, and remained until March, 1859, when they started for California, driving ox team to Omaha, where they remained until May, then via Salt Lake City drove on to Red Bluffs, Tehama County. In January, 1860, they went to Table Rock, Sierra County, remaining until October, 1862, working in the mines. They then went to Petaluma, and except one year at Virginia City remained until 1868, carrying on blacksmith shop. He then went to Eel River, Mendocino County, and acted as superintendent of his brother's stock ranch, and also interested in blacksmith shop, remaining until 1882, when he went to Point Reyes, Mendocino County, and there worked at his trade for five years. Mr. Whitney's interests were identified with his brother until the death of the latter, in January, 1883. In 1887 he came to Los Alamos, first renting shop and later buying 100 x 100 feet, and establishing his present situation.

He was first married in Petaluma, on April 13, 1865; and formed his second matrimonial relation, at Potter Valley, Mendocino County, in October, 1877, by marrying Mrs. Martha Long. He has four children living, but all by his first wife.

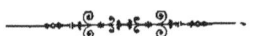

MRS. E. A. GREER, one of the early and successful settlers of the town of Santa Ynez, was born at Harper's Ferry, and was a daughter of John Cochrane, a contractor and builder of that locality. Miss Cochrane was first married in 1851; being left a widow, she remarried in 1866, at Dayton, Nevada, to Henry Greer, a native of Belfast, Maine, and together they came to California in 1868, stopping at Santa Barbara until purchasing a ranch of 160 acres in the west end of Montecito Valley. They cultivated some fruit and were among the first to plant orange trees. Mrs. Greer came to Santa Ynez in 1884, during the infancy of the town, and has since been one of its prominent residents. She purchased one-quarter of a block, 150 x 200 feet, upon which she first built her store and residence, and later a large livery stable. In 1888 she erected the town hall, called the Greer Hall, upon which she has placed a large brass bell, the first bell of the town. Adjoining her store she also established a restaurant, which she has continued with success to the present time. Her store is general merchandise, and she keeps a full line of dry goods, groceries, hardware and household supplies. She also has a ranch of 160 acres in Pinie Cañon, which is well-stocked with horses and cattle. Mrs. Greer has four children, three daughters and one son. She is a woman of great executive ability and should feel proud of her well deserved success.

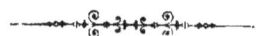

J. ANTHONY was born in Whitley County, Indiana, in 1849. In 1854 he came across the plains to California with his parents, suffering great delays and hardships from the Indians, who were especially troublesome that year. His early life was passed at his home in Santa Cruz, a part of the time being employed as clerk in the lumber business of his father, G. T. Anthony. In 1872 he went to Monterey County and engaged in the stock business on Government land, keeping about 200 head, and continuing there for three years. At the end of that time he returned to Santa Cruz, where he was occupied one year in a saw-mill. In 1876 he came to Lompoc and engaged in farming, The next year he located at Los Alamos, where he was interested in sheep-raising, and, although the year was dry, he was very successful, selling at a profit in the fall of 1877, and then returning to Lompoc. At that time he entered his father's blacksmith shop and learned the trade, at which he has since continued to work. He came to Santa Ynez in November, 1887, and after purchasing town property and building his house, he went into partnership with his father, under the firm name of G. T. Anthony & Son. They have erected a fine brick building and are doing a prosperous business, being also agents for light and heavy wagons and farm machinery.

Mr. Anthony lost his first wife at Lompoc. He was there again married in 1884, this time to Miss Louisa Manda Reed, a native of California. He has one child by his first marriage and two by the second.

G. T. ANTHONY, one of the early pioneers of California, much of whose life has been passed in pioneer work, was born in Saratoga County, New York, in 1820, and at the age of fourteen years went with his father to a lumber camp in Allegany, New York, remaining about three years, when he went to Fort Wayne, Indiana, and there learned the trade of foundryman and machinist. In 1840 he was married at Fort Wayne to Miss Hannah Hurd, after which they went to Whitley County, where Mr. Anthony bought a farm of 160 acres, being obliged to leave the shop on account of failing health. He engaged in raising sheep and general farming, continuing until 1854, when he sold out and came across the plains to California, starting with forty-eight head of cattle, six yoke of oxen, ten horses and four mules. They had a very hard trip, as the Indians were very hostile that year, and Mr. Anthony lost nearly everything except his mules, one cow and one horse. He then went to Santa Cruz and opened a foundry, with his brother, and later went into the lumber business; but, owing to depression in California in 1874, he lost about $75,000, and was financially ruined, after twenty-one years of close attention to business at Santa Cruz. In 1875 he located at Lompoc and opened a blacksmith shop, as his trade only was left to him, and by economy and energy he has reasonably prospered. He remained until November, 1877, when he came to Santa Ynez and bought town property, erected a residence and, in partnership with his son, G. J. Anthony, built a fine brick blacksmith shop. They have carried on a successful business; are also agents for wagons, carriages and all kinds of farming implements.

Mr. and Mrs. Anthony have had twelve children, five only surviving. Mrs. Anthony is living, at the age of seventy years, and on January 18, 1890, the children gathered at the homestead and joyfully celebrated the golden wedding of their happy parents, a celebration few people are spared to enjoy.

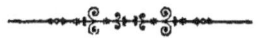

DORMER & CHALLENOR, whose beautiful ranch of 160 acres lies south of Ballard's, in the Alamo Pintado Valley, are of English birth, and were educated at Jesus College, at Cambridge, England.

Max. C. Dormer studied engineering with Professor Stuart, at Cambridge, and later with the Crewe Locomotive Works at Crewe, England. In 1887 he came to the United States, and direct to California, to visit his old friend D'Urban, who then owned the ranch, which was later purchased by Mr. Dormer, and where he now resides.

John Challenor studied for the army,

entering in 1885 the Fourth Battalion of the South Staffordshire Regiment, serving three years, until he acquired the Captaincy, and then, not caring to go into active service, he resigned and turned over his commission. He then came to the United States, and to California to visit his friend, Mr. Dormer, and soon after the above partnership was formed. In 1889 they set out 2,000 peach trees, and in the spring of 1890, 4,000 more peach and 4,000 prunes, covering about 100 acres. The land was wild bottom land when they took it, but has since been converted into a veritable garden, by their system of thorough cultivation. The old adobe ranch house is one of the landmarks of the valley, nestling as it does beneath the shade of the majestic live-oaks, and the conveniences of windmill and out-buildings which have since been added, making of the ranch an ideal home.

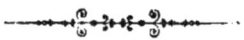

JEFFERSON B. TOWNSEND, a rancher in the upper Arroyo Grande, was born August 11, 1843, in Missouri, of Southern parents who are not now living, and was brought up on a farm. In 1856, when he was thirteen years of age, the entire family crossed the plains to California with ox teams, being five months on the road. It was the plan of Mr. Townsend's father to take a herd of cattle from the plains, where he could get them cheap, and bring them on and dispose of them as the best occasions offered, beef being very high at that time in this State. The party did bring 2,000 head of cattle. Sonoma County was reached, a place of 200 acres purchased, and the family settled there; and it was here that Jefferson continued his studies, attending for a time the Sonoma College, conducted by the Cumberland Presbyterians. From 1856 to 1867 he was at his parental home, and then he came to San Luis Obispo County, taking up 160 acres of land two and a half miles south of San Luis Obispo city, where he was engaged for eight years in farming. He then spent a year in San Francisco. Returning to this county he bought a place on the Corra de Piedra and worked that for eight years. He came upon his present property in December, 1882, which occasion was celebrated by a Christmas dinner. This ranch lies in the upper Arroyo Grande, between ranches Santa Manuelo and Arroyo Grande, and comprises 640 acres. Here Mr. Townsend is engaged in dairying and stock-raising, and also to some extent in fruit culture, the soil being well adapted to grapes. He has 6,000 vines in bearing, producing both raisin and wine grapes of excellent quality. His dwelling is situated on the Arroyo Grande Creek, which runs through his property. The view through and around the splendid trees near by is especially fine.

Mr. Townsend has been married twice— first in San Francisco, April 29, 1868, and the second time August 9, 1888. He has four sons and two daughters.

Z. W. SAUNDERS, M. D., the popular and successful physician of Lompoc, was born in Birmingham, Iowa, April 25, 1843. His father was by trade a cabinet-maker, who moved to Uniontown, Missouri, in 1858, and there bought 700 acres of timber land, and there erected a large saw and grist mill and carried on a very successful business. In 1876 he visited Lompoc, then returned East and closed his business, and in 1880 brought his family to Lompoc, where he settled and died in November,

1889, at the age of seventy-three years. His widow is still living, at the age of sixty-nine years. The subject of this sketch worked on the farm until the erection of the mill, and then became under-engineer, which he continued until the breaking out of the war, when he enlisted, on the 28th of August, 1861, at Birmingham, Iowa, in Company H of the Third Iowa Cavalry, under Colonel John W. Noble, the present Secretary of the Interior. Subject enlisted for three years, or the war, and they were engaged west of the Mississippi River, and were veteraned at Little Rock, Arkansas, in January, 1863. Prior to 1863 they were engaged in the capture of Little Rock and many small engagements. After re-enlistment they were connected with the Sixteenth Corps, and operated east of the Mississippi. They were on Wilson's raid through Tennessee, Alabama, and Mississippi, and were at the taking of the Confederate arsenal at Selma, Alabama, thence on to Montgomery and to Macon, Georgia, where they heard of the armistice between Generals Grant and Lee, which closed the war They were then sent to Augusta, Georgia, where they took the surrender of General Johnston's army, then to Atlanta, where they were mustered out in 1865, and the subject returned home. He was never wounded, though in every battle of the regiment. He then attended the Memphis High School, and in 1868 was elected County Assessor of Scotland County for four years, and at the same time began reading medicine. In the winter of 1872 and 1873, he attended the Missouri Medical College at St. Louis, and in 1874 graduated from the College of Physicians and Surgeons at Keokuk, Iowa. He then returned to Uniontown, Missouri, and followed the practice of his profession up to 1882, when he came to Lompoc. He then bought one-half interest in the drug business and practice of Dr. H. C. Dimock, and after one year resold to Dr. Dimock, and Dr. Saunders gave his entire attention to his profession, in which he has been eminently successful, having a very extensive practice and covering a radius of twenty-five miles—necessitating very long drives. In 1883 he bought half a block on H street and established his present comfortable home. In July, 1889, in partnership with Mr. F. W. Ellis, he started a very complete and attractive drug store on Ocean avenue. At the incorporation of the town in 1888, the Doctor was elected Town Treasurer, and was re-elected in April, 1890, without a dissenting vote, which was the highest acknowledgment of his popularity as a public officer. He was married at Uniontown, Missouri, in 1866, to Miss Lydia E. Hall, and three sons and two daughters now grace and enliven the household.

The Doctor is a member and present Master of Heperian Lodge, No. 264, F. & A. M.; a member of Lompoc Lodge, No. 248, I. O. O. F.; Knights of Pythias, and of Robert Anderson Post, No. 66, G. A. R., of which he was the first Commander.

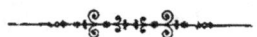

JOSE FRED BRANCH, son of the prominent pioneer, F. Z. Branch, a native of New York, and Manuela (Corlona) Branch, a native of California, was born March 15, 1853, on his father's splendid rancho near Arroyo Grande. During his youth he attended the public schools, finishing an excellent course of study in a college at San Francisco. Since that time he has devoted all his energies to farming, stock-raising and the dairy business, his ranch now consisting of 1,300 acres. Mr. Branch has erected a fine residence on his place, directly below the magnificent old adobe house of his father, not now occupied, but nevertheless in an excellent state of preservation. Jose Fred is the youngest of a family of ten children, five of whom are now living. He was married March 5, 1861, to Miss Herlinda Borilla, a native of California.

DR. FRANK P. BURGESS was born in Pennsylvania in 1840. He received a medical education at the Jefferson College, Philadelphia, and when quite a young man was prepared for the practice of his profession. He did not, however, for various reasons, carry out his original intentions, and a year later, the year 1860, found him engaged in journalism. This he abandoned shortly after the civil war broke out, and enlisted for service, taking part in a number of important engagements in that conflict. It was in the year 1866 and the year following, when Dr. Burgess was living in Nebraska and Indian Territory, among the Indians, that he discovered the powerful, salutary and beneficial effects of roots and herbs as a medicine for the human system. Doctor Burgess is a firm believer in this kind of medicine. For the past three years he has been engaged, with his brother, in this State, in circulating these medicines, known as Pawnee Indian remedies. They consist of five distinct varieties of medicines, all calculated to relieve various troubles. The Burgess Company, whose main office is in San Francisco, have a unique way of advertising their medicine. It consists of a thorough canvass of each town by the Doctor and his assistants, the assistants providing a variety of entertainments at their headquarters in the evening, while the Doctor presents the business proposition before and after each entertainment. The Pawnee Indian remedies are surely growing popular. Sales to the amount of $1,000 a day have been recorded; and, as Dr. Burgess is an enthusiastic worker and also very popular, his enterprise is bound to succeed. Doctor Burgess has been a resident of California since 1881, residing in San Diego up to the year 1887, engaged in real-estate business. At that time he organized the company alluded to.

FRANCIS EDGAR COOK was born in Napa County, California, May 17, 1860, son of Samuel and Phœbe Cook, the former a native of Michigan and the latter of New York. His early life was spent at his home in Napa County and at Monticello, twenty-fives miles east of Napa city. In 1872 he came with his father to San Luis Obispo County, his father renting a ranch two miles north of the city. Here the subject of this sketch employed the most of his time when not attending school. The family next moved to a ranch of 640 acres, eight miles south of San Luis Obispo, which was subsequently sold to and now owned by the Steele Brothers. Mr. Cook now has a fine ranch of 320 acres in the San José Valley, on which he is now engaged in farming and stock-raising. He is an energetic and industrious farmer, and is bound to succeed in the fertile valley where he has made his home.

He was married February 2, 1889, to Miss Martha A. Ballard.

D. J. BURDICK, a leading architect of Lompoc, was born in Oswego, New York, in 1842. His father was a contractor and builder, and moved to Racine,

Wisconsin, in 1855, where he carried on his trade. Subject learned his trade from his father, with whom he worked for twenty-eight years. He was married at Racine, in 1863, to Miss Fanny Hodeck, a native of Bohemia. They lived at Racine until January, 1882, when they came to Santa Barbara, and he continued at his trade. He built the Pavilion at the race track, and many of the prominent residences of the city, and in all, some 200 houses, great and small. In June, 1889, he came to Lompoc and bought a lot 100 x 140 on H street, where he is now building; and he has more contract work than he can well attend to, being architect and building the houses for Sudden and William Cantley, the Town Hall and Roberts' Block; also architect for the Athletic Club and Engine House, which will soon be erected, and has put up many smaller buildings. Mr. and Mrs. Burdick have four children—three sons and one daughter.

W. H. AUSTIN was born in Windham County, Connecticut, in 1830. His father was a farmer and a native of Rhode Island. His parents both died in the boyhood of our subject, and he then went to Putnam, where he learned the trade of house, carriage and sign painter, and for some years followed his trade in Providence, New London and Norwich. He married Miss Francis Reynolds, at Brooklyn, Connecticut, and then settled in Putnam, where he carried on his business in all its branches. He then moved to Killingly, Connecticut, where he secured some large contracts from manufacturing houses. In 1861 he enlisted at Killingly in Company B, Eighteenth Connecticut Regiment, Colonel Ely, and was stationed at Fort McHenry, near Baltimore; and there, subject received a severe injury in his foot, which permanently incapacitated him from marching, and he was honorably discharged in 1862, and returned to Killingly, where he carried on his trade until 1865, when, with his family he moved to California, coming by water and the Isthmus of Panama, with Judge Peckham and family of San José. Mr. Austin settled at Watsonville, Santa Cruz County, where he carried on his trade until 1873, when he moved to San Luis Obispo, and after five years of business he tried the hotel life as proprietor of the old Eagle Hotel; but in one year he lost $3,000. He thent went to Guadalupe and again started a hotel, and in one year he made up his last loss, and then sold out and returned to his trade. In 1880 he came to Lompoc, and bought a house and lot on K street, where he still resides. He also opened a shop and he returned to his trade, buying out the shop of John Henry, and has had a very lucrative business. Mr. and Mrs. Austin have but one child, William, who was born in November, 1876.

DURRELL STOKES GREGORY was born in Virginia, June 14, 1825. About the year 1838 he removed to Cobb County, Georgia, and was educated in Marietta. He read law under ex-Governor McDonald, and was admitted to practice under special enactment of the Legislature, on account of being under the lawful age. Afterward he was in partnership with Governor McDonald until starting for California, in 1850. He first located in Santa Cruz, in the practice of law; thence he went to Monterey, from which place he was sent as a delegate to the Peace Convention, which met at Charleston, in 1860. About the year 1862 he formed a law partnership with P. K.

Woodside, which continued many years. In 1872 he removed to the new town of Salinas, where he remained until 1882, when he came to San Luis Obispo, although for several years previous he had maintained an office here. His law practice here grew rapidly, and in the course of time he was selected by Governor Stoneman to fill the position of Superior Judge, made vacant by the death of Judge McMurtrie, which occurred February 11, 1883. At the expiration of the term of this appointment, Judge Gregory was a candidate before the people and was elected to the Superior Judgeship, which position he held until his death, which occurred at 3:30 P. M., June 12, 1889. Judge Gregory's political services to the State of California were varied and invariably in the interests of good government and order. He was twice a member of the Senate, from the district composed of Monterey and Santa Cruz counties, and of the Assembly from Monterey County.

Early in the year 1888 the Judge began rapidly to fail, being troubled with a disease which rendered him practically helpless; and so he had been on his back most of the time for a year, and utterly unable to assist himself during the four months prior to his demise. He was a most patient sufferer, always gentle in spite of the great pain which racked his every bone. For a long time the Judge had realized his helpless physical condition and looked forward to the end with calmness. A man of most loving and affectionate disposition, ever true to his family and friends, he was universally popular. As a lawyer he was bright, alert and accurate, always going into court thoroughly conversant with every detail of the case in hand. Although not a flowery orator, he was clear, concise and convincing in argument, and was generally favorably regarded by jurists. As a judge he was strict, but invariably courteous and impartial. A man of the strictest integrity, no man nor combination of circumstances could induce him to swerve from a position he knew to be right.

Judge Gregory was married August 20, 1876, to Miss Amelia Hartnell, whose family were early pioneers of California.

JULIAN GARCIA, one of the pioneers of San José Valley, was born in New Mexico, in June, 1831. When young Garcia was twelve years of age the family moved to San Bernardino, California, coming via Salt Lake City. Mr. and Mrs. Garcia spent the remainder of their lives in that place. After remaining with his parents in their California home for eight years, Julian started out for himself, first going to the mines in Sonoma County and remaining there one year. He then came to San Luis Obispo County, where he was a vaquero for Mr. Pacheco and Captain Wilson for four years. In 1856 he located in the San José Valley where he has since remained. It was while attending a lot of sheep on the shares with Captain Wilson that he first came to the valley, and he was so favorably impressed with the possibilities of the place that he decided to make it his home. Mr. Garcia is engaged in cattle raising and has a very attractive place, about one mile from Pozo.

He was married in 1851, to Rosa Herrera, by whom he has had fifteen children, ten of whom are now living. Mr. Garcia has been particular in giving all of his children a good education. Montone and Bedell, the two oldest sons, have attended college at Santa Ynez, and the others are receiving every advantage possible. Mr. Garcia was the County Treasurer one term, and for the past four years has served as mail contractor.

An unfortunate accident occurred to Mr. Garcia during his early life which deprived him of his right arm. Being one of a party near a shooting affray, a shot intended for one of the principals, struck him in the arm. The injury was a bad one and in consequence the entire arm had to be amputated. Mr. Garcia is living a quiet and retired life in his old age, surrounded by the many comforts which a refined and generous nature like his own can appreciate. Many of his sons, now all grown, reside at the old home.

JOHN BALL, whose fine ranch borders the Santa Ynez River, was born in Northamptonshire, England, in 1831. His father, Daniel Ball, was a farmer, and subject lived at home until 1850, when he came to the United States and first settled at Lockport, New York, where for three years he was servant in a hotel. Then, in 1853, he went to Oswego County and farmed up to 1856, when he came to California, by way of Panama. He then went to the mines in Nevada County and mined three years with good success, but on account of failing health he was obliged to leave; so went to Monterey County, where he rented from 200 to 400 acres and raised grain for sixteen years. In 1876 he came to Lompoc, and bought eighty acres of land, paying $35 per acre. That land was covered with brush and timber, but is now cleared and highly improved. He carried on general farming up to 1885, but since then has been an extensive breeder of hogs, of the Poland-China, Essex and Berkshire breeds, keeping about 150 head and fattening for market. He is about reducing his stock, to return to the cultivation of beans and mustard, and thus change his farming. Mr. Ball was married at Castorville, Monterey County, in 1863, to Miss Elizabeth Staley, a native of Missouri. They have but one child living, Charles Ball, who was born July 6, 1869, and he still lives at home. They lost their two daughters in 1879, with diphtheria, dying within four days of each other.

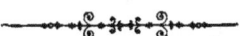

CHARLES BRADLEY.—Among the successful ranchers and sheep raisers of the Santa Maria Valley, we find the subject of this sketch. He was born at South Wingfield, England, in the county of Derby, in 1839. He had little opportunity to cultivate his mind, but his hands were kept constantly busy, and at the early age of twelve years he began work in the coal mines at Oakerthorpe, and at the age of eighteen years he began contract work, in mining and breaking suitable for market, which he continued until 1868, when, through the influence of his uncle, Paul Bradley, he came to California, first stopping at Salinas, where his uncle then resided; but in the fall of 1868 all stock was driven to the Santa Maria Valley, where his uncle had purchased land, and subject continued to work for him about four years. In 1872 Charles Bradley purchased his present home ranch of 160 acres, and added thereto by pre-emption and purchase to the amount of 2,560 acres, 1000 of which is tillable and balance grazing land. He farms about 700 acres and leases 300 acres for general farming purposes. He keeps 1,500 sheep, in which industry he has been very successful. He also has 100 hogs, and about forty head of horses and cattle. He set a small orchard, experimentally, in 1880, in a variety of fruits, all of which have done well, and his present orchard covers eight acres, apples, peaches and apricots being principal fruits, although he also includes all small fruits. Mr. Bradley was married at South Wingfield, England, on April 5, 1857, to Miss Elizabeth Booth. By the marriage eleven children have been born, two sons and nine daughters, all living. Mr. Bradley built his present spacious residence in 1873, at an expense of $5,000, including all modern improvements. He is a member of Hisperian Lodge, No. 264, F. A. & M. Mr. Bradley takes no interest in political or public life, except education, and he has served as School Trustee and Clerk for over six years. His eldest son, Charles W., was educated at San Martha's Hall at San Mateo, and at Heald's Business College at San Francisco. Mr. Bradley gives his children the higher education, of which he was deprived.

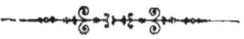

FOSTER POMEROY, the proprietor of the Grand Central Hotel, of Lompoc, was born in Indiana, on January 26 1856. His father was a merchant and later traveled for a New York house, and then on account of failing health came to California, in 1860, by the Isthmus of Panama. He then settled in Santa Clara, where he bought a ranch, and remained until 1868, when he moved to Hollister, and in 1883 again moved and settled at San Jacinto. Foster Pomeroy lived with parents to mature life; then, after a period of travel through Arizona, Colorado and New Mexico, he came to Lompoc in 1885 and was again connected with his father in ranch life until 1887, when subject bought the Lompoc Hotel, in partnership with J. C. McReynolds, continuing until the fall of 1888, when he bought out Reynolds and has since continued alone. In December, 1889, he leased the Grand Central Hotel, which was just completed, and where he is now located, running the two hotels jointly. He was married at Hollister, November 1, 1877, to Miss Mary Diana Triplett, and they have two children, one son and one daughter. Mr. Pomeroy is a member of Lompoc Lodge, No. 57, Knights of Pythias.

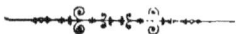

W. SWEET was born in the city of San Luis Obispo, February 24, 1864. At this time the family were residing at Paso Robles. Very soon after the birth of young Sweet, his parents moved to the San José Valley, settling on a ranch. When seven years of age Mr. Sweet's father died, and, except when he attended school for a time, he has been thrown entirely upon his own resources, working on ranches from time to time. At present he has under his management the home place, and also conducts a ranch of his own near by. Mr. Sweet is one of the few young men in the San José Valley who speaks English and Spanish both fluently. A greater part of the settlers adjacent to Pozo are Spaniards and have few opportunities for improving their English, if, indeed, they speak English at all. Consequently Mr. Sweet is called upon frequently to settle disputes and takes part in interviews where the English tongue is heard.

JESSE CASTEEL, a rancher of Arroyo Grande Valley, was born in Knox County, Ohio, November 11, 1834, of parents who were also natives of the same State. In 1848 the family moved to Missouri, and on his father's farm Jesse learned about all that was to be learned of farming. After residing there fourteen years he engaged himself in the live-stock business in

Texas, but not to a very great extent. Then he was in Missouri ten years. Colorado was his next home, for three years, and in 1868 he reached California. Arroyo Grande Valley has since been his home. The first two years he resided two and a half miles above Arroyo Grande on the creek; later he had his farm at the foot of the valley, where he lived until 1888, when he came to his present property in the town, consisting of two acres of very choice land. He owns 73 acres a mile from town and 640 acres near the Huasna Valley. On the latter he is raising stock, and on his other land in the valley he is raising fruit and vegetables, with splendid success. He points with pride to a pumpkin which weighs 207 pounds, and beets and carrots of incredible size, which have been raised upon his ground. He is a zealous believer in the great wealth and resources of that famous valley, and he is "there to stay."

He was married in February, 1856, to Miss Hingley, and they have eleven children.

WARD, the leading harness-maker of Santa Maria, was born in Santa Rosa, California, in 1850. His father, Abraham Ward, moved to Petaluma in 1853 and bought a ranch of 2,000 acres, 300 being tillable. He there carried on general farming and the dairy business, keeping 150 cows and also about fifty horses. Subject was educated in Oakland at the Breighton University, from which he graduated in 1872. He then began book-keeping at Petaluma for one year; then went to the harness shop of W. Davis, where he learned the trade of saddler and harness-maker, remaining about two years. He then worked at his trade, and other occupations, until 1877, when he went to Washington Territory, where he opened a harnesss hop and continued ten years in the business. In 1887 he sold out and returned home for a few months; then opened a shop at Nipomo, but in 1889 moved his stock to Santa Maria and bought out the harness shop of Cumis & Smith, which he has since continued. He keeps a fine stock of saddles and harness, all his own manufacture, and a full stock of robes, horse clothing and stable supplies, with sufficient hands to perform all orders with neatness and dispatch. Mr. Ward was married in Petaluma, in 1875, to Miss Lucina Lusk, and five children have been added to the union. He was a charter member and has served two terms as President of Nipomo Parlor, No. 123, of the Native Sons of the Golden West.

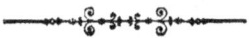

VALENTINE MANCILLA was born in Mexico in 1829. At the age of twenty years he went to San Francisco, California; remained there, however, but a short time, as he also did at Monterey, where he next journeyed. The gold mines then attracted his attention and he searched for nuggets for three years and more. Sacramento was his next stopping place, and in 1855 he moved to San Luis Obispo. Mr. Mancilla has been engaged in mercantile life ever since he came to this county. In the city of San Luis Opispo he was one of the pioneer merchants. For thirty years, barring a period of six years when he was in Bakersfield, he has kept a general merchandise store in that city, and has watched with great interest the growth of the place. When first he settled there he relates that, besides the mission building, there were only ten or twelve houses in the whole settlement. In 1884 Mr. Mancilla moved to the town of Pozo, in the San José Valley, where he now resides and conducts a general merchandise store.

He was married in 1869 to Mary A. Ortega. A gentleman of fine bearing, Mr. Mancilla has been universally popular wherever he has made his home.

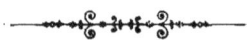

EDWARD LEEDHAM, of the Arroyo Grande Valley, was born in Birmingham, England, in 1828, and for many years before coming to America he practiced mechanical engineering. After arriving in this country he operated quartz-mills at Halifax four years, and then was for some time the engineer of a large flouring-mill at Boston. In 1875 he came to California, and for three years was the principal lighthouse-keeper at Pigeon Point,—a novel experience for him. In 1878 he bought a ranch in Santa Cruz County, and began farming, but he says with disastrous results. He came to the Arroyo Grande in November, 1879, with just $500, and soon lost it in the sand hills. He fell back upon his old profession as engineer, and operated as such in a mill at San Luis Obispo; and in 1881 was able to buy his present property. His first purchase was only sixteen acres, but he now has 116 acres. He makes a specialty of fruit, flowers and bulbs. He is an excellent authority in all horticultural and agricultural matters. He was commissioner for the Mechanics' Institute Fair in 1877 and 1878 for San Luis Obispo County, held in San Francisco. He is also president of the Arroyo Grande Valley Agricultural Society. He has been successful in a marked degree with his exhibits at the fairs, carrying off many of the valuable premiums at each competition. He and J. V. N. Young secured most of the premiums at the county fair of 1889. Mr. Leedham is married and has six children.

JOHN V. N. YOUNG, a farmer of the Arroyo Grande Valley, was born in Otsego County, New York, in 1826, of which State both his parents, who are not now living, were also natives. They had a large farm, which was the family home until the spring of 1836, when they all moved to Michigan, at a period when there was a grand rush of emigration from the Empire to the Wolverine State. Until 1859 Mr. Young remained at his father's home upon a farm. He then started West again and settled for a few years on the east side of the Sierra Nevada mountains, upon a farm. In 1867 he came to San Luis Obispo County, and kept a hotel at the the county-seat, where now the French Hotel is. Originally he intended to purchase a ranch, and had no idea of keeping a hotel; but the land bargain which he thought he had made fell through; and so he tried the hotel business. A year of this was enough for him, and he bought a ranch of 1,220 acres twelve miles west of Paso Robles, where he raised live-stock for twelve years. Disposing of this property in 1883, he moved upon his present place, which he had purchased in the fall of 1878. It comprises twenty-five acres, is near the town of Arroyo Grande, and here he raises fruit and vegetables. He still has a place of 160 acres rented out near Paso Robles. His present garden spot on the Arroyo Grande Creek is prettily situated. His orchard of fifteen acres there is one of the finest in the whole valley.

Mr. Young was married in 1852, to Miss Babbitt, of Elmira, New York, and of a family well known throughout that section of the State. They have two sons and three daughters.

CALEB SHERMAN, the leading lawyer of Santa Maria, was born in Madison County, Vermont, in 1830. His parents moved to Illinois in 1833, and to Iowa in 1839, but both died before subject became of age. His education was conducted at the common schools of Iowa, with a brief normal course. He worked at farming up to eighteen years of age, and then began reading law with Judge Darling, of Jackson County. In the spring of 1850 he started for California, across the plains, but owing to an attack of mountain fever he stopped and wintered at Salt Lake City, continuing his trip in the spring of 1851; and on the Truckee River he was stung by a scorpion, which again brought on a severe illness. With the delays the trip consumed one year; he was at death's door twice, and he lost $1,200 in horses and cattle. He landed at Marysville, and then went to the Eureka mines, remaining in that vicinity until 1855, with very fair success. In 1855 he returned to the States, by Panama, to settle the estate of his uncle. He was married in Jackson County, Iowa, in 1856, to Miss Laura Butterworth, and in the fall of the same year he returned to California, by Panama, accompanied by his wife, uncle's family and relatives. He then settled at Petaluma, and for seven years engaged in the hotel and restaurant business. In 1863 he went to the silver mines in Nevada and remained about three years, then took his family to Iowa, and he went to New York to sell mining securities. While going up the Hudson River by boat, he was asked what business he had followed in California, and in reply said, "Everything, from selling peanuts to pleading law,"—such was the diversity of occupations by the early pioneers. On account of illness Mr. Sherman returned to Bellevue, Iowa, and engaged in the livery business, and later was appointed Under Sheriff, which office he held four years; then in 1874 he returned to California, and settled at Santa Barbara, when he engaged in an auction and commission business. In 1877 and 1878 he represented Santa Barbara and Ventura counties in the Legislature, and in 1879 entered the office of Judge Heacock and completed his profession, and was admitted to practice in 1880. In the fall he went to Oakland, and practiced about fifteen months, then in the spring of 1882 he came to Santa Maria, bought property, established his home and continued his profession. In January, 1883, he was appointed Assistant District Attorney under J. J. Boyce, and in January, 1886, was re-appointed under Oglesby, and in January, 1889, under W. B. Cope. He has served as Notary Public since 1884.

His first wife having died he was remarried in Oakland to Miss Amy Wilson. Mr. Sherman has 640 acres of valley and grazing land, which he rents, but his pretty place, surrounded by fruit, flowers and shrubbery, bear evidence of his love for nature had he time to gratify his desires. He is a member of Santa Barbara Lodge, No. 156, and Encampment No. 52, I. O. O. F.

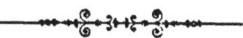

JOHN LONG was born in Norfolk County, England, in 1856. He lived at home during his early life, assisting his father on the farm excepting about two years when he worked at blacksmithing. He came to the United States in 1875, direct to California and landed at Guadalupe July 2, 1875

He immediately found employment with Hart Bros., but after three months he came to Santa Maria to work in the shops established by Reuben Hart, where our subject continued to work until 1887, when Mr. Hart closed out that branch of the business. Mr. Long then purchased one half of Mr. Hart's building and moved it to his lot on Main street, where he is now established with a fully equipped shop 40 x 60 feet. He there carries on iron and wood work in all branches of carriage building and repairing, employing three blacksmiths and one wood-workman. He was married in Santa Maria in 1883 to Miss Annie Bradley, a native of England, and the union has been blessed by two children, Charles and Sadie. Mr. Long is a member of Hesperian Lodge, No. 64, F. & A. M.

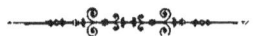

J. B. DRAPER was born in Sonoma County, California, in 1866. In 1870 his father's family moved to Cayucos, San Luis Obispo County, and there young Draper spent his boyhood. At the age of ten he went to San Luis Obispo and ran a milk wagon, attending school when opportunity offered. In 1881 he came with his father to the ranch where they now live. This property consists of 320 acres of choice land, located between the Huasna and Arroyo Grande valleys. Mr. Draper raises considerable stock on this place, but also spends much of his time in outside work. He is at present foreman and manager of the Tar Spring ranch, 4,900 acres in extent, and adjoining Huasna Valley on the west. This property was formerly in the Branch tract and has been recently purchased by Mr. R. W. Sanford, a wealthy Englishman. Many cattle and fine horses are raised on this ranch.

Mr. Draper was married in 1887 to Miss See. They have one child.

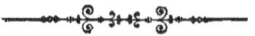

REUBEN HART.—One of the pioneers and prominent developers of Santa Maria, is the subject of this sketch, who was born in Derbyshire, England, in 1843. He was educated in England and learned the trade of carriage builder at the Stubbs Manufacturing Company at Derby city, where he remained five years. He then went to Swansea, Wales, and worked in a large manufactory, after which he came to the United States and began his American life at the Cummings Railway Contract shop in New Jersey, remaining about four years. While there he sent for his brother, also a machinist, and together they came to California in 1866. Our subject first worked for D. S. Mills at San José, as manager of his large manufactory of wagons and agricultural implements, and then went to Castorville, and with his brother established a general blacksmith and machine shop under the firm of Hart Bros., which they continued up to 1872, and then moved their stock and machinery to the new town of Guadalupe, where they started the town by establishing a large blacksmith and machine shop and also built a block of business houses; also acting as sub-agents of the Guadalupe ranch. After three years, in 1875, Reuben Hart came to Santa Maria; bought property at corner of Maine and Broadway and started the town by building extensive shops for blacksmith, repair and machine purposes, also a feed mill—with steam power—and later a store and several residences, and carried on a large business in feed and barley and in general trade with the farmers. In 1879 the firm dissolved and our subject retained the Santa

Maria property, his brother continuing at Guadalupe. In 1879 our subject started a lumber yard, and in 1880 established the water-works, piping the town and pumping the water by steam power from a well eighty-five feet deep to an elevated tank. In 1882 and 1883 he was in partnership with M. P. Nicholson in farming 4,000 acres in wheat and running a steam thresher. In 1884 he built a one-story brick building 50 x 88 feet, corner of Main and Broadway, for store purposes. He continued his shop interests up to 1888, then sold business and building, which were removed, and he began erecting his present spacious and comfortable hotel, being a two-story brick 100 x 120 feet, containing forty-three sleeping rooms with spacious parlor, smoking, reception and billiard rooms and a dining room, 30 x 60 feet, with hot and cold baths; in fact, a hotel complete in every appointment and managed by a genial host makes a pleasant place to reside.

Mr. Hart was married at Santa Maria in 1879 to Mrs. Harriet Sharp, a native of Pennsylvania, and with her two daughters and one by the last union the home circle seems complete and happy.

VICTOR JESSEE, surveyor and civil engineer of Santa Maria, was born in Woodland, Yolo County, California, in 1855. His father, Archer C. Jessee, was an early pioneer to California and was born in Russell County, Virginia, in 1821. He lived at home until 1842, when he was married, in Atchison County, Missouri, to Miss Mary Harbin, a native of Tennessee. After marriage he farmed until 1846, when he came across the plains to California with oxen, horses and mules, and was five months in crossing. He settled on the present site of Sacramento, and soon after arrival, in the fall of 1846, he enlisted under General Fremont in Fremont's Battalion, and was appointed First Lieutenant of Company E, under Captain John Grigsby. They were at the battle of Salinas Plains when Captain Byrns Foster and others were killed, and at the skirmish at San Fernando. He served through the war and was discharged in April, 1847. He then returned to Sacramento and later moved to Napa Valley, where he resided fourteen years, trading and dealing extensively in land and stock. He was the first Sheriff of Napa County and served two terms. In 1864 they moved to Lake County in same business and in 1869 came to San Luis Obispo; then to San Bernardino in 1873, and in 1876 to Arizona, where he died August 12, 1876. The family then returned to Santa Maria in 1878. There are ten children living, seven sons and three daughters.

J. Victor Jessee was educated in the common schools and the private college of San Bernardino, and there studied civil engineering, finishing in 1875. In Arizona he followed his profession in general land survey and in running irrigating canals. He returned to Santa Maria in 1878, and in 1880 joined the United States Land Survey, working with them one year, and since then has been chiefly occupied by his profession. He subdivided the Bradley ranch for the Santa Barbara Land and Water Company, and is frequently employed by the courts in cases of complicated boundary lines throughout Santa Barbara County. He has been a witness in thirty-eight land cases and has never lost a case. He does all the county work in the northern part of the county, and has done the necessary subdividing of the Suey Rancho. He has all the field notes and data of the section of country about the Santa

Maria Valley—made out by personal experience.

He was married at Santa Maria on February 16, 1888, to Miss Mary McHenry, a native of California, and they are very happy in their little one, born January 23, 1890.

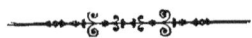

GEORGE MANDERSCHEID, superintendent of the wharf at Port Harford, was born in Germany, in 1853. At the age of ten years he was thrown as an orphan upon his own resources, and in 1872 he came to California. After spending a few months at Santa Cruz, he came to San Luis Obispo, and was for the first two years engaged in the photographing business. Afterward he worked in the quicksilver mines in Canada, and for two years had charge of a wharf at San Simeon, and also conducted a store there. He first came to Port Harford in 1877, and clerked in the wharf office; and since 1881 he has been superintendent of this wharf, where a much larger amount of business is transacted than one would imagine without investigation. Mr. Manderscheid is also Postmaster at that point, and agent of the Wells-Fargo Express Company.

He was married in 1884, to Louisa Avila, a niece of John Avila, and has three children.

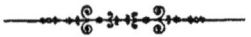

DAVID LEWTY was born in England, in 1842, and at the age of thirteen years was apprenticed to John Bond, in the town of Preston, who kept a contract and general machine shop. There David learned the trade and remained seven years. He then went to Liverpool and worked in a marine shop, and then to Crewe, where in railroad shops and mills he remained until 1869; then emigrated to the United States and direct to California. He soon found employment in San Francisco with the Ben Holliday Steamship Company. In 1872 he went to Salinas, and for J. E. Preston ran his engine for his steam threshing-machine, continuing the work to Santa Maria, in 1873, when they threshed all through the valley; and out of threshing season he worked at his trade in the machine shop of Hart Bros. at Guadalupe, continuing up to 1877, when he spent one year in San Francisco, and in the fall of 1878 started his saloon at Guadalupe, selling out in 1881 to take a trip to England, and was away fourteen months. On returning to California in 1882 he opened business at Quincy, and in 1883 at San Luis Obispo, returning to Santa Maria in September, 1885. He owns town property and fifty-seven and one-half acres on Santa Maria mesa. He is a member of Guadalupe Lodge, No. 237, F. & A. M.

ORVILLE ROOT, station agent, Postmaster, etc., at Miles Station, on the railroad between San Luis Obispo and Port Harford, has had his present situation ever since the railroad was built to that point, and he also owns a ranch of forty-seven acres. The postoffice is named Root in his honor. He was born born in Allegany County, New York, in 1821, and when of age he settled upon a piece of land in Indiana which his father had bought for him, and lived there sixteen years, and while a resident there he married Miss Elizabeth Hurd, in 1843. In 1857 he moved to Kansas and was engaged there in mercantile life for a time, and in 1863 he came to Santa Cruz County, California. Here he first engaged extensively in the lumber trade, as he did also at Port Harford for a year. In Santa Cruz County he was Under Sheriff six years. In 1870 he came to his present place, already mentioned. His ranch near by is well located and is very productive.

His children are five in number, viz.; Ruth, now Mrs. George T. Gragg; Hazard; Eliza, now Mrs. J. A. Mercer; Mary, now the wife of J. D. Armstrong; and Orville, Jr.

GEORGE C. SMITH was born in Butler County, Ohio, in 1849. His father was an extensive farmer and stock-raiser, who moved to Douglas County, Illinois, in 1863, and on 700 acres of land carried on general farming and stock-raising, keeping 1,800 sheep, besides cattle and mules. In 1869 they moved to Mississippi and raised 140 acres of cotton, but labor being high and weeds abundant they grew but one crop, and in 1870 returned to Ohio, where our subject bought ninety-five acres of land and grew wheat. After two years he went to Cincinnati, and in December, 1874, started for California, settling at Gracioso, where his father had preceded him and taken up 320 acres of land. Our subject farmed two years, then during the following five years made two trips to Ohio, returning to California in 1881 and settling permanently in the Santa Maria Valley. In June, 1882, he was engaged by Schwartz & Beebee as manager of their lumber yard, and he continued in that position until February, 1890. He has also been interested in land speculations and fine horses. In 1886 he bought land near town, and still owns 160 fine buiding lots. He formerly owned the noted stallion Ben Wade, and has raised some fine trotting horses. Mr. Smith was married at Dix Creek, in Butler County, Ohio, on March 24, 1869, to Miss Mary C. Curryer, of Scotch-English descent. They have had two children, and been deeply afflicted with the loss of both.

CHARLES W. MERRITT was born in Brooklyn, New York, in 1842. His father was an extensive dry-goods and clothing merchant of New York city, after living in Galveston, Texas, where he was interested in real estate. Coming to California in 1856 he settled at San Francisco and was connected with the grain and commission business. In 1856 and 1857 he was editor of the *Daily Post*, which later was merged with the *Pathfinder*.

Our subject came to California with his father and was educated in the public schools. He began business in 1866 as superintendent of the Huasna Rancho owned by Isaac J. Sparks, who came to California before 1840, and to whom the ranch of 25,000 acres was granted. After four years as superintendent, in 1870 he began the stock business in San Luis Obispo County, renting land up to 1882, when, in partnership with George Phœnix, they bought the Casamalia Rancho of 5,600 acres. He keeps 500 dairy cows and about 300 stock cattle. He has three dairies, all leased with stock. In 1887, with John Murray, Jr., they bought 160 acres near town and began breeding fast horses, keeping about twenty mares—graded and standard bred. They own the stallion "Electro," standard bred, by "Electioneer" from the "Palo Alto" ranch of ex-Governor Stanford; also "Saxton," standard bred, raised in New York. They have a mile track on the ranch for training purposes and Mr. Merritt also owns improved town property.

He was married in San Luis Obispo County

in 1869, to Miss Dorothy Phœnix, and they have six children. Mr. Merritt has served two terms as Supervisor and declined renomination. He is a member of the A. O. U. W.

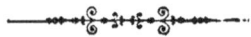

ALFRED WALKER, a prominent citizen of San Luis Obispo, was born in Somerset County, Maine, June 22, 1835, of sturdy New England parents. His father is still living, at the age of eighty-nine years; he is a descendant of a Plymouth Rock pioneer. His mother, also living, is a relative of ex-President Cleveland, her maiden name also having been Cleveland. Mr. Walker, our subject, graduated with honor at the Anson Academy. Soon afterward he went to Boston and learned the trades of engineering and carpentering. In 1859 he came to the Golden State and entered the sheep rearing business in Monterey County, in company with F. A. Goodrich. Together they owned the San Joaquin Ranch, comprising two leagues of land. In 1864, the disastrous dry year, the firm lost 10,000 head of sheep! Soon afterward they sold their ranch, at a good profit. In 1865 Mr. Walker went to Santa Cruz and operated a saw-mill until 1871. For many years after and before this date he was engaged as a contractor and builder in the construction of large buildings in the counties of San Luis Obispo, Santa Barbara and Los Angeles; also in laying street pavements, etc. He built the Blochman store, the county jail and court-house in the city of San Luis Obispo, and laid the pavement of many prominent streets in Los Angeles with bituminous rock, the latter contract involving an expenditure of $360,000. In 1886, in company with Dr. Nichols, he purchased the property known as the Oil Wells, Judge Frederick Adams soon afterward taking an interest. During the past two years this property passed into his own hands, and he now owns it, together with a ranch of 300 acres adjoining. On this place, now called Sycamore Springs, Mr. Walker conducts a popular hotel, and, being on the direct road to the ocean from San Luis Obispo city, it is well patronized. On the grounds are also valuable sulphur springs, connected with a sanitarium. January 9, 1889, the bituminous rock mine was discovered, and for a time Mr. Walker was interested in that; but shortly afterward he sold out his interest to other stockholders.

He was married in 1885, to Mrs. Clackmer, a sister of Frederick Adams, and has one child,—Blaine Walker,—named after the distinguished statesman, James G. Blaine, an old and intimate friend of Mr. Walker's father.

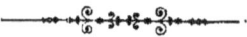

P. MORENO, a resident of San Luis Obispo city ever since 1856, was born in Monterey, this State, June 25, 1845, and has been engaged in agriculture most of the later years of his life. At one time he was foreman of the ranch of S. Blochman for a period of seven years. He now keeps a restaurant on the main road between San Luis Obispo and Port Harford, having a good run of patronage. He was married June 17, 1880, and has a family of three children.

GEORGE O. TAYLOR, a gardener and orchardist in the Arroyo Grande, was born in New Hampshire, in 1846. The family of which he was a member moved to California in 1853, settling in Yuba County for three years. The father was engaged in mining and lumbering in Nevada City, Nevada County, and that place was the family home for a time. In 1862 George was sent to school in Santa Clara County, and for eighteen months he attended the University of the Pacific in that county. In 1864 he went to sea, being gone four years and visiting South America, Europe, the Mediterranean Sea, and other parts of the world,—mainly for experience and information. Returning, he went into the stone business with his father; shortly he began farming in Kern County, and in 1876 he settled in the Arroyo Grande, where he now lives. He has twenty acres on the Monte, where he is engaged in raising beans and fruit. His orchard is successful beyond all anticipation, some of his trees being revelations in their way.

He was married in 1872, to Miss Nettie B. Jones, and has three children.

W. S. JONES has been a resident of San Luis Obispo County for twenty-five years, coming to the Arroyo Grande as a rancher with the Steele Bros. He had previously made the acquaintance of George Steele, who had been studying law with his father. He was married in 1868 to Ednarda M. Branch, a daughter of Francis Z. Branch, and has nine children. They are residing on a part of the large Branch tract, which was deeded to Mrs. Jones by her father, May 26, 1871; it is located just below the old Branch residence. She was born in 1850, in the old adobe house, than which there is no finer specimen of adobe architecture now to be found. Many are the people who have been entertained in this Branch home. Having an excellent memory, Mrs. Jones relates many interesting items in connection with her father's estate, which are printed elsewhere in our sketch of that distinguished pioneer.

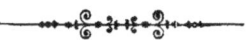

F. F. FIELD was born in Madison, Connecticut, in 1829, and in 1843 moved with parents to New Haven, where subject was educated. At the age of twenty-one years he went to Newton and learned the carpenter trade under A. W. Gory. He then followed his trade about Connecticut up to 1858, when he emigrated to Glencoe, Minnesota, then a new town, just being established. In 1862 he went to Fort Snelling to enlist, but was rejected on account of rheumatic troubles; but, thrilled with patriotism, he then returned to Connecticut and enlisted at Meriden, in Company A, Fifteenth Connecticut Regiment, under Colonel Dexter R. Wright, who later resigned and was succeeded by Colonel Charles L. Upham. The regiment was then sent to the department of the Potomac, and their first engagement was at Fredericksburg. They were then stationed at Newbern, North Carolina, for about one year, doing provost duty. They then started to meet Sherman in his march through Georgia, but in an engagement at Kingston, North Carolina, the entire regiment were taken prisoners. They were then marched to Richmond, a fifteen-days march, with little to eat, being allowed only one pint of meal each day, and that ground with the cob. They were then placed in Libby prison, but paroled after three days and the war being so nearly closed, they did no more active service, but were mustered out at Newbern, in 1865, and sent back to New York on an old disabled schooner. Mr. Field then returned home. His father had died during his absence, and the family removed to Wallingford, Connecticut, and there he remained and worked at his trade until he came to California, in 1871. He then settled at Anaheim and farmed one year, then came to San Luis Obispo County, and became manager of the Suey Rancho. He built the present ranch house and out-buildings, and remained eleven years. In 1878, following the dry year, the valley was first farmed, thus affording the settlers an opportunity to work, and also to get a supply of seed, for future purposes, as they were nearly starved out. This was the commencement of grain-raising in the valley. After the death of Mr. Newhall, subject came to Santa Maria and purchased town property and built his present residence, and, through improving his place, set out experimentally a few orange-trees, which have done well. He also worked at his trade as opportunity offered.

Mr. Field was married at Wallingford, Connecticut, in 1868, to Miss Bessie Crampton. They have no children. He is a member of Hesperian Lodge, No. 264, F. & A. M., and is Commander of Foote Post, No. 84, G. A. R.

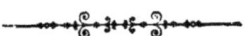

WALLACE L. HARDISON, of Santa Paula, is one of the most prominent business men of Ventura County or Southern California. Joseph Hardison, the originator of the family in America, came to that part of Massachusetts now embraced in the State of Maine before the Revolution, and it is believed from Sweden. His son, Joseph Hardison, and his grandson, Ivory Hardison, and his great grandson, Wallace L. Hardison (the subject of this sketch), were all born in Caribou, Aroostook County, Maine. Mr. Hardison's father was born in 1802, and he dates his own birth in August 26, 1850. His mother, Dorcas (Abbott) Hardison, was born in China, Kennebec County, Maine, in 1804, and was a descendant of the old Abbott family, statesmen and authors of the early history of the country. There were eleven children in his family, of whom he was the youngest. His education was received in the public schools and a short course in the Holton Academy; before reaching maturity his business had been that of farming. In 1869, when nineteen years of age he came to Humboldt County, California, where for a short time he worked for wages; soon, however, he began work for himself, as a contractor, in a small way. In the fall of 1870 he went East to Pennsylvania, and engaged in work for his brother, who was controlling the drilling of oil wells. In the course of a year he was taken into partnership, and in another year he began to operate for oil on his own account. While in Pennsylvania he was connected with the drilling of 300 oil wells. The first well he owned was the Eaton and Grant, the time occupied on it before it began to produce oil was about three months, and its production was 100 barrels per day. While engaged in the oil business in Pennsylvania, he purchased the Eaton farm in Saline and Ellsworth counties, Kansas, and afterward purchased other lands adjoining, to the amount of 10,000 acres, which he stocked with horses, cattle and hogs, introducing some fine blooded horses to improve the stock. After running this property eight years, a stock company was formed, and half of the stock was sold to F. G. Babcock, of New York, and the other half was sold the following April. July 1, 1888, Mr. Hardison took stock and started the National Bank of Saline, Kansas, and for four years owned the controlling interest and was its president until March, 1885, when he sold his interest; but he is still a stockholder. In 1882, with other gentlemen, he organized the Eldred Bank of McKean County, Pennsylvania, and was its president until 1884, and still retains stock. Through the influence of Mr. Lyman Stewart Mr. Hardison, in April, 1883, visited the oil regions in Ventura and Los Angeles counties, and was so impressed with the country—the prospect for oil, the fertility of the soil and the excellent climate—that he decided to move here, which he did in July 17, 1883. In connection with Lyman Stewart, Milton Stewart and others, they drilled seven wells, six at Pico Cañon and one at Santa Paula Cañon. Only one of these wells was a producing well, which yielded a large amount, and is still producing splendidly. They have organized the Hardison-Stewart Company, and have drilled forty wells. They also organized the Sespe Oil Company, composed of Thomas R. Bard, Daniel McFarland and others, and have drilled twenty-seven wells. In connection with Thomas Bond, W. Chaffee, Messrs. Stewart, Dolbeer and others they have built pipe lines from the wells to Hueneme, Ventura and Santa Paula, and a refinery at Santa Paula. This crude oil is shipped all over the country, and the refined oil finds the principal market at San Francisco and Los Angeles. They also manufacture lubricating oils, gas oils and asphaltum. Their crude petroleum is largely used for fuel, for the generation of steam. They built a steamboat, at a cost of about $65,000 to carry oil in bulk to San Francisco: her capacity was 160,000 gallons. It caught fire and burned at the dock, and has not yet been replaced.

Mr. Hardison has assisted in the organization of the First National Bank of Santa Paula, and is one of the directors and a stockholder. He has been a factor in the organization of the Universalist Church of Santa Paula, and also in the starting of the Santa Paula Academy. He is president of the Horse and Cattle Company. In 1883 he bought 6,400 acres of the ex-Mission Rancho, and a company was formed to which he sold the ranch. Before organizing the company he had sold interests in the ranch to his brother, Harvey, and to his nephew, C. P. Collins, and also to John R. D. Say. At the time of organization the company had about 500 head of cattle. Mr. Hardison still retains stock in this enterprise. In 1885 he imported twenty thoroughbred registered Holstein cows and a bull from Holland, through a cattle firm of Hornellsville, New York. They are doing finely. Mr. Hardison is president of and a stockholder in the Santa Paula Hardware and Stove Company, who have just completed a very large and expensive store building, an ornament to the place and a credit to their reputation. It is fully stocked to demand all the modern requirements in the line of hardware. The building is 62 x 80 feet, with a rear addition 40 x 60 feet, for stoves, making the total depth 140 feet. Mr. Hardison is also a director of the Los Posos Land & Water Company, conducting an extensive enterprise. His home place, of eighty acres, is situated in a beautiful locality in the Santa Paula Cañon, a mile and a quarter from town, where they enjoy a beautiful view of the surrounding country. Mr. Hardison has here built an elegant house, on a beautiful site, surrounded with grounds, to his taste, where he enjoys the comforts of home life. When in Pennsylvania, he represented his district in the Legislature during the exciting sessions of 1880–'81. In his political views he is a Republican; in his religious, a Universalist, and he is a total-abstinence man with reference to string drink and tobacco. He has a fine physical development and is a splendid representation of the self-made American business man.

In 1875 Mr. Hardison was united in matrimony with Miss Clara McConnell, of Venango County, Pennsylvania. Her father, William Benjamin Harrison McDonald, now resides in Santa Paula. Mr. and Mrs. Hardison have five children, three of whom are living, namely: Guy Lyman, born in Clarion County, Pennsylvania, April 3, 1876; Gussie, born in McKean County, Pennsylvania, May 30, 1880, and Hope, born in Santa Paula, April 2, 1889.

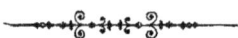

HERMANN HOLT, a cattle-raiser near Guadalupe, was born in Hanover, Germany, and came to America in 1867,—directly to California. For the first two years he followed farming in Monterey County, and since then he has been in San Luis Obispo and Santa Barbara counties. For some time he lived with his brother Henry, who owns a ranch of 475 acres on the Oso Flaco, and since 1884 he has been residing upon his own ranch of 211 acres a mile from Guadalupe, where he is engaged in raising cattle. He is a bachelor.

JAMES ALLEN DAY, one of the pioneers of the orchard business in Ventura County, came to Ventura in 1874, and engaged in horticulture, planting 100 acres to apricots. He also let 150 acres, which was planted to fruit, under his directions, and he built the first fruit dryer in the county; so that he is entitled to the credit of having faith that the soil of this county would raise fine fruit, and he backed his faith with his works. He is a native of Franklin County, New York, and dates his birth July 3, 1828. His father, Orrada Day, was a native of Springfield, Massachusetts. Mr. Day's grandfather, Robert E. Day, was one of the first settlers of Hartford, Connecticut, having gone to that State before the Revolution. They were Welsh people. His parents had twelve children, three of whom are now living, Mr. Day being the sixth of the family, and the oldest survivor. He was reared and educated in the State of New York, and his first business was the manufacture of lime and brick. He made a success of it in Oshkosh, Wisconsin, for twenty years. Before going to Wisconsin he had spent five years in Massachusetts. When he came to Ventura he invested in land. He is still largely interested in real-estate, having 807 acres in one locality, and seventy-five acres adjoining Ventura. He has more recently interested himself in the construction of some fine blocks in Ventura. With three others he built the Masonic Block, one of the grandest buildings in the city, if not the finest. It is a credit to the city and also to its builders. Mr. Day had the superintendence of its construction. It contains two fine stores on the first floor, and above are several office rooms and a splendid Masonic hall, all the rooms being occupied. Mr. Collins and Mr. Day built the Collins Block, in which the Collins Bank is located, and this building is another ornament to the town. Mr. Day has done his part in the public enterprises of the place, and has been ever ready to help in what he believed was for its success. He was made a Mason in 1860, and is Commander of the commandery at the present time.

He was united in marriage to Miss Sarah Jane Warren, of Connecticut. She is the daughter of Mr. Alonzo Warren, of that State. Their union has been blessed with four children: the oldest, Alice, was born in Oshkosh, Wisconsin, and is married to Mr. Charles G. Bartlett, of Ventura; Bera C. is now attending a university at Los Angeles; Mark E. and Lillie V.

Mr. Day has now, in a measure, retired from business. He spends his time in the lovely home he has built, on a sightly spot, overlooking the town and the ocean. He has also a nice club room, in which he may often be found, enjoying especially the company of his friends.

R. ORTON, another one of California's pioneers, came to this State in 1853. He was born in New York, March 23, 1834. His father, R. Orton, was also a native of New York, and was of Scotch descent. Mr. Orton's mother, Clara (Bicknell) Orton, was born in Utica, New York. Her people were of French and English extraction. Mr. Orton was educated in Mount Pleasant, Iowa, and, after completing his studies, he engaged in the milling business, which he learned in Iowa with his father, who owned a mill.

Mr. Orton came to California during the gold excitement, and, like others, he became a miner in Volcano. He mined for a year and made as high as $50 per day; then sold out and went East. When he returned to California he engaged in milling in Santa Cruz County, and was in the business there from 1855 to 1871. He was elected Sheriff of the county, and held the office for eight years. During that time he arrested many desperate characters, guilty of high crimes. One man he followed 1,180 miles, and single-handed arrested him in a saloon, shackled him, lodged him in jail at Salt Lake City, and took the train to Ogden and thence to California. Mr. Orton again engaged in mining for two years, after which he located in San Luis Obispo County, and went into the milling business. He built a mill and remained there four years, and from there went to Watsonville, Santa Cruz County, and milled six months. He came to Ventura in 1881, and helped build the Ventura mill. He returned to Ventura February 1, 1887, and since then has improved the mill from a stone to a full roller-process mill, and he is now doing the milling for Ventura and surrounding country, and ships some flour to Santa Barbara. They make the best of flour, and also grind meal and feed of every description.

Mr. Orton was united in marriage to Miss Elizabeth Hunt, a native of Illinois, and daughter of Mr. John Hunt, of Watsonville, California. Their union is blessed with five children, four sons and a daughter. Emma was born in Santa Cruz County, and is now the wife of William Orr, of Santa Barbara County. F. A., Edgar and John were born n Santa Cruz County, and Lucius was born in Ventura. Mr. Orton is a Master Mason, and also a member of the Ancient Order of United Workmen. In politics he is a Republican.

TYLER BITHER is another of the worthy pioneers of California. He was born in Houlton, Aroostook County, Maine, June 15, 1828. His father, Benjamin Bither, was also a native of Maine, and his grandfather came from England to that State in an early day. Mr. Bither's mother, Anna (Tyler) Bither, was a native of Maine and of Dutch descent. The subject of this sketch remained in his native State until twenty-three years of age, when, in 1854, he came to California, and for twelve years was engaged in mining in Tuolumne County. He dug from $2.50 to $100 per day, and in one pan got six ounces of gold, which he sold for $102. When he quit mining he went to San Joaquin, took up Government land, which he improved, and ten years later sold it and located in San Luis Obispo County, remaining in that place one year. In 1877 he came to Ventura and, after renting land three years, purchased the farm of 100 acres on which he now resides. This he has improved, and his home is a comfortable and attractive one. Mr. Bither is devoting 400 acres to the cultivation of Lima beans and also small white beans, and is realizing from $30 to $80 per acre from his crops.

The subject of this sketch was married in 1852, to Miss Sarah J. Ward, who was born in Massachusetts in 1836. For thirty-eight years she has shared his joys and sorrows, and knows much of pioneer life. They have reared a family of seven children, all now living, viz.: Arthur A., born in Maine in 1853, resides in the San Joaquin Valley; Marion J., born in Tuolumne County, California, in 1861, is now the wife of J. M. Coffman, of Santa Barbara; Annie S., also born in Tuolumne County, now the wife of W. S. Newell, of Ventura; W. W. W., one of triplets, now a resident of Ventura, the other two having died a few hours after birth; B. F. and Minnie M., both born in San Joaquin; and S. J. Eva, born in Ventura in 1880.

Politically Mr. Bither was formerly a Douglas Democrat, but since the war has been a firm Republican. He is a member of the I. O. O. F. lodge. His mother was a Freewill Baptist and his father a Universalist. Mrs. Bither was reared a Congregationalist.

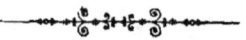

J. B. KELSEY, a rancher near Ventura, is one of the pioneers and extensive farmers of Ventura County. He was born in Morris County, New Jersey, November 8, 1838; his father, J. B. Kelsey, Sr., was a native of the same State; his ancestry were from Scotland. Mr. Kelsey's mother was Delia (Conyer) Kelsey; her ancestors were of French extraction. J. B. Kelsey was the eleventh of a family of fifteen children. After his early schooling, at the age of fourteen years, he went to work in a grocery store in Rockaway, and continued there five years, when he came to California in 1858. He remained one year in San Francisco, and then removed to Alameda County, where he rented lands and engaged in farming market produce. He continued that business until 1868, when he came to Ventura and rented land two years, and then bought and improved 182 acres of land near Ventura. He still owns the property, and has planted trees and built a fruit-dryer. He moved upon the place in 1876, and is now raising corn and beans on a very large scale, — 1,500 pounds of Lima beans, and about the same quantity of small white beans to the acre. His average crop of shelled corn is from 3,000 to 4,000 pounds per acre.

Mr. Kelsey was married, in 1861, to Miss Mary Fichter, a native of New York city, but was raised in New Jersey; her parents were of German extraction. They have had eight children, three of them born in Alameda County, and the others in Ventura, viz.: Sarah, who is now attending the Normal School in Los Angeles; Agnes, Victor, Mary (who is also at the Normal School), Della, Helen, Fred and Olive. They have a large stock ranch, of which Victor has charge, and Agnes is keeping house for him. On this ranch he is breeding horses, both Norman and Clydesdale stock. Mrs. Kelsey died September 24, 1884; they had been married twenty-three years, and the loss was most deeply felt by them all. Mr. Kelsey is a member of the I. O. O. F.. and also of the Masonic fraternity; in his political views he is a Republican. He was again married, to Mrs. Redwin, widow of the late Mr. Lewis Redwin, of Ventura. She is a native of Missouri. Mr. and Mrs. Kelsey and several of the family are members of the Presbyterian Church.

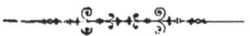

HON. L. M. WARDEN, a prominent resident of San Luis Obispo County, has been a resident of California since July 6, 1850. He was born in 1825 in Licking County, Ohio, at the town of Granville, and was the son of Gabriel Warden, a farmer who had ten sons and three daughters. The subject of this sketch, the eighth son, went with his brothers and sisters to a point near Redfield, Dallas County, Iowa, in 1844, as an Indian trader. Two brothers and one sister still live in Ohio. He came to California during the early gold-mining period, being only sixty-two days in crossing the plains, coming by way of Fort Laramie and Salt Lake to Hangtown. After mining for three months he engaged in the livery business and staging from Auburn, Placer County, to Yankee Jim's and Michigan Bluffs, same county. Three years afterward he went to Napa County, engaging in the live-stock trade; then he removed to Mendocino County, where he was Sheriff from 1860 to 1868; and then he came to San Luis Obispo County, entering the sheep business on the Atascadero ranch, and leased eight leagues of land from General Murphy for four years. Then he purchased 3,100 acres on Los Osos ranch and stocked it with 12,000 head of sheep in the fall of 1871. The season of 1876 was so dry that he quit the business, with only 600 sheep. Since that time he has sold 1,400 acres. This ranch is known as Captain Wilson's, where ex-Governor Pacheco was brought up. Mr. Warden, a Democrat, was a member of the Board of Supervisors from 1874 to 1878, and of the State Legislature for 1878–'79.

He has a wife, two sons and three daughters: one son and both the daughters are married. Frankie E. is the wife of Dr. H. M. Fisk of Chicago; May is the wife of W. H. Fisk, of Portland, Oregon; William H. is on the ranch; and Oscar L. is a resident of Portland, Oregon.

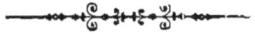

P. W. MURPHY, of San Luis Obispo, was born in Missouri, September 11, 1840, the son of Martin and Mary (Bulger) Murphy, who were both natives of County Wexford, Ireland. When Patrick was a mere child, the family removed to California, settling in the beautiful Santa Clara Valley. Here he grew to manhood, attending school and graduating at Santa Clara College. He then moved to San Luis Obispo to look after the large estates of his father, which amounted to 70,000 acres, and including the beautiful and far famed Santa Margarita Rancho. Later Mr. Murphy came into possession of this vast property, and on the ranch mentioned, twelve miles distant from San Luis Obispo, he makes his residence. Politically he is a Democrat, and is prominent in both political and business enterprises of any magnitude. He has three times been State Senator, and once an Assemblyman. Mr. Murphy was one of the originators of the San Luis Obispo Water Company, and also one of the incorporators of the San Luis Obispo Bank. He bears the title of General, having been appointed by Governor Irwin Brigadier General of the Second Brigade of the National Guard of California. The home of General Murphy, Santa Margarita Rancho, is pretty enough to be one huge park; no tourist to San Luis Obispo ever fails to visit this lovely spot. Its owner devotes most of the land to cattle-grazing, in which business he has been eminently successful.

He was married February 23, 1870, to Miss Mary Kate O'Brien, daughter of Dr. P. M. O'Brien, of San Francisco, who died in Santa Clara Valley in 1875.

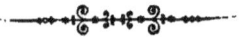

E. WHITNEY, one of the old Vermont stage-drivers at Santa Barbara, has been a resident there about six years. At one time he had charge of the Truck Company of that city, whose business he sold to George Walker. Mr. Whitney was born in Chautauqua County, New York, in 1836, a son of Ira Whitney. His father, a native of Vermont, now resides at Carpenteria, and is eighty-one years old. His mother, a native of Cattaraugus County, New York, died when twenty-four years of age, at Silver Creek, Chautauqua County, New York. Mr. Whitney married Hattie Ferry, a native of Ohio, and they are living at the corner of Ortega and Canal streets. Politically, he is a Democrat. He has a brother living at Battle Creek, Michigan.

WILLIAM E. BORLAND, a contractor and builder at San Luis Obispo, is one of the old pioneers of this county who rounded Cape Horn in 1849. He was born in the city of Washington, in July, 1828, and when fourteen years of age he commenced to learn the carpenter's trade, which he has ever since followed. In 1849, through the efforts of a prominent steamship officer, he shipped aboard the four-masted steamship Chesapeake, and August 8 of that year steamed out of New York harbor for California, and arrived at San Luis Obispo June 14 following. In those days men were paid double wages for their work; and Mr. Borland, working at his trade, made money. For eighteen months he lived in San Luis Obispo, and then worked in San Francisco six months: but in the latter place he was unsuccessful and was glad to get back again to San Luis Obispo, where he has ever since prospered.

He was married in 1857, to Josefa Avila, a daughter of Don Miguel Avila, and they reside on a part of the Avila estate between San Luis Obispo and Port Harford. Mr. Borland has held prominent public offices and taken part in all the interesting, and at times exciting, proceedings that form a conspicuous part of the history of this county. He was under Sheriff for seven years under Francisco Castro; was also County Judge for a year and a half, under appointment from Governor John G. Downey.

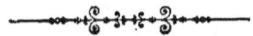

JOHN C. KAYS, a dry-goods merchant at Santa Barbara, first came to California as early as 1842, which was two years before Fremont's first visit to this country. He was born in Ireland, at the same place where ex-Governor Downy was born, and came to America in 1833, landing at New York. In the fall of 1842 he came on to California and entered the dry-goods trade in Los Angeles, which he followed until 1848, being the only merchant of the kind there with the exception of two others at the beginning of his career at that place. But during the Mexican war he served in the army, in Texas and Mexico. In company with about 500 other volunteers, he was taken prisoner at Santa Fé; and afterward he was sent out from that point to obtain provisions. Finally he was one of the number who marched victoriously into the city of Mexico. In 1849 he moved to Santa Barbara, since which time he has been engaged mostly in the dry-goods trade, his business amounting at times to several thousand dollars a day. Thus he amassed a considerable fortune, owning at one time three nice ranches; but he lost them in real-estate speculations. For a time he was agent for the Wells-Fargo Express Company. He has never been willing to accept office.

In 1847 he married Josefa, a daughter of Captain Burke, an American, while her mother was from one of the old Spanish families of Monterey. Mr. Kays has a number of relatives in the Eastern States, and now has six sons and two daughters living. Two of his sons are in business in Los Angeles—James and Michael—the latter in Coulter's dry-goods house.

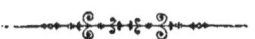

ROBERT J. HAZARD, a rancher near Cayucos, was born in Rhode Island, in 1826, of English ancestry and one of three sons. He was reared on a farm in Greenwich, Rhode Island, which was his home at intervals for twenty-two years. At the age of sixteen years he went to Naragansett Pier, one of the now famous watering places of America, and engaged in the shipping business with his uncle; and he was also in business for a year in New York city. In 1850 he came to California, and for the first four months he was in San Francisco; then two years in Tuolumne County, farming, and then engaged in gold-hunting away off in Australia, for eight months, with moderate success. He next visited Peru and crossed the Andes Mountains to the Amazon River, for more wealth, but did not find it. Returning to Tuolumne County, he remained there until 1867, when he came to San Luis Obispo County. The first two years here he resided in Cambria, where he had a ranch of 400 acres. In 1870 he came to Cayucos. For the past ten years he has occupied his present property of 430 acres, six miles from Cayucos and on Old Creek. On it are splendid fruit orchards, to the care of which he devotes much of his time, as well as to dairying. He has 18,000 grape-vines and 250 fruit trees now in bearing.

He was married in 1857, to Elizabeth Fry, of Strasburg, Germany, and they have five children, namely: Mary L., now Mrs. R. Swain; Thomas T., Robert Douglass, John and Elizabeth M.

GEORGE STONE, deceased, in his lifetime a resident of San Luis Obispo County, came to California from Mexico, having served in the United States army during the Mexican war. He arrived in San Buenaventura in 1849, having lived some time previously in Los Angeles. He was employed by Isaac Calahan, who was at that time lessee of the Mission at San Buenaventura. For a time he was in charge of a store there which Mr. Calahan owned. They were two fast friends, whose friendship grew in strength and happiness with years. Mr. Calahan died in 1851, and soon afterward Mr. Stone moved to Santa Barbara, where he took from Captain Sparks, on shares, the Arroyo Grande Rancho, with 500 head of cattle. He then returned to San Buenaventura, where he married the widow of Isaac Calahan, whose maiden name was Valdez and who still survives. In 1852 Sparks sold the ranch to Captain Mallagh and gave Mr. Stone a lease of the Huasna ranch for five years, and $1,000 in coin if he would cancel his lease of the Arroyo Grande. Mr. Stone remained on the Huasna ranch until 1858, when he delivered it and the live-stock thereon to Captain Sparks, who was so highly pleased with his management and close attention to his business that he offered him every assistance he might require in any business he desired to engage in. In October, 1858, he went to Mexico; but in 1860 returned to California, broken in health and in purse. Soon he was appointed under Sheriff by Sheriff Dennis, and his execution of duty was such as to gain for him the full confidence and esteem of the entire community. In 1862 he again took charge of the ranch on favorable terms, receiving 4,000 head of cattle, large and small; but two years afterward the dry season put an end to his stock enterprise. He was shortly afterward appointed Internal Revenue Assessor of the county of San Luis Obispo, which office he held until the county was joined to the Santa Barbara district. Then until his death, which occurred April 7, 1882, he lived in San Luis Obispo County, in or near Cayucos. He had a wide circle of acquaintances, all of whom held him in high esteem. Of quick but generous impulses, ready to take up the gauntlet when thrown down to him, he was ever ready to lend a helping hand to a vanquished foe. He left six children.

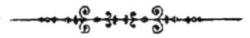

JUAN V. AVILA, proprietor of the Avila Hotel at Avila Beach, is a son of Don Miguel Avila, and was born April 28, 1845. That point has always been his home. The splendid Avila Rancho, consisting of 16,000 acres, has been subdivided and sold,—the most of it,—the subject of this sketch being the administrator of the estate. His hotel is a very popular resort, nine miles from the city of San Luis Obispo and directly upon the beach of the broad blue ocean. He was married in September, 1889, to Miss Nuthall.

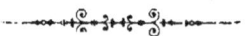

MOSES T. WELLS came to Ventura County in 1869, and in 1870 located at Saticoy, thus becoming one of the early settlers. He was born in Pittsburg, Pennsylvania, April 19, 1845. His father, Rev. Samuel T. Wells, a retired Presbyterian minister, is now residing at San Buenaventura. The history of his life will be found in another place in this work. In 1860 Mr. Wells and his family removed to Oakland, California, where the subject of this sketch finished his education at the old Braton College, now the State University, at Berkeley. Before coming to Southern California he was variously employed: was freight clerk at Oakland, four years; was pilot on the Oakland ferry for five years, during which time he became widely acquainted with the people of Oakland and California in general; held the position of engineer in the mines at Virginia City for a time; then went to Leadville, prospected all over the country, acted as engineer a portion of the time, did general mining, and, having made a study of assaying, when a Boston syndicate was formed to locate mines, he and his friend, Mr. Fink, were employed by them to prospect, and were the first explorers of the old Ute reservation, where they discovered large fields of coal.

As before stated, Mr. Wells located in Saticoy in 1870. He and his father purchased land at $15 per acre, and twenty acres, containing the Saticoy mineral springs, they bought for $100 per acre. His father bought 600 acres at above price, 300 of which he sold to the railroad company for $150 per acre, receiving a check for $45,000. Of the remaining 300 acres Mr. Wells is the owner of 180. They first engaged in raising barley, corn and hogs, and are now making a specialty of Lima beans. He also raises Jersey cattle and valuable horses, and devotes considerable time to poultry, ducks, geese, turkeys and chickens. They gave the ramie plant a test, but were unsuccessful. With like results they tried the castor-oil bean. Flax can be raised without irrigation, as is the other products of this ranch. Mr. Wells built a house, planted trees, and now has a nice home. His land extends to within one mile of the station.

May 2, 1889, he was married to Miss Annie Nicholl, a native of San Pablo, Contra Costa County, California, daughter of John Nicholl, a prominent land-owner and farmer of the Santa Clara Valley. Mr. and Mrs. Wells have an infant daughter.

Mr. Wells is a life-long Republican, takes an interest in the affairs of the county, is intelligent and public-spirited, and is well spoken of by his fellow citizens. His wife is a member of the Presbyterian Church.

JAMES PERCY, a gentleman who was thrown upon his own resources at an early age, who has participated in the exciting adventures of the hunter, who has experienced the changing fortunes of the miner, and who is now a well-to-do citizen of Saticoy, Ventura County, is deserving of mention in a work of this character. A sketch of his life will be found of interest, and it is as follows:

Mr. Percy was born in Scotland, August 16, 1850. He is one of a family of four sons, and his parents, John and Rebecca Percy, both English people, came to America and settled in New York the year following his birth. The father was a brick-layer and a contractor and builder. When the subject of this sketch was five years old, his father started to California, via Cape Horn, and died while en route. Young Percy was also deprived of a mother's care at an early age, her death occuring when he was twelve years old. He then made his home with Mr. Sells, in Iowa, for three years, after which he started out in life for himself, and worked on a farm in Iowa until he was twenty-one. At that time he went to Wyoming and was employed on a stock ranch one year. He then turned his attention to the exciting business of trapping beaver and hunting buffaloes. This he followed two years, being in partnership with Mr. Stephen Stone. They found a market for their game in Denver, and when the meat was not worth shipping, they hunted for the hides, selling them for from $1.50 to $3.00 each. During the two years they spent in hunting, they killed 1,300 buffaloes; and it was estimated that there were between 2,000 and 3,000 men engaged in the business at that time, 1872 and 1873. Beavers were quite plenty on the South Platte from Greeley, Colorado, to Julesburg, same State; and they caught 150 during one season, and sold the hides for $1.50 to $5.00 each.

Mr. Percy next turned his attention to mining, in both Utah and Arizona, and was engaged in that business six years, sometimes making and sometimes losing money. He has been in all the mining excitements of the coast, his principal interests being in quartz mines. In the fall of 1874 he was working on the McCracken mine, having had the first contract on that celebrated mine; and, while working, a ladder broke and he fell fifty feet, which resulted in a broken ankle and his being laid up at San Francisco a year for repairs. Upon his recovery, he prospected in the Tombstone district, Arizona, and there located some good mines, among the rest the Burleigh mine, for which he was paid $30,000, being in partnership with his brother Hugh at this time. The parties to whom they sold the mine were afterward offered $100,000 for the same, and refused it.

After selling the mine, Mr. Percy went East and, in 1881, was married to Miss Cora DeNice, a native of Iowa. He returned to Arizona with his bride, and engaged in the cattle business, in company with his brother Hugh. After continuing in that business six years, he sold out and came to Ventura County, California. He purchased seventy-five acres of land adjoining the town site of Saticoy, and is here engaged in agricultural pursuits. He has twenty-five acres devoted to apricots, five to prunes, and ten to oranges, lemons, apples, and a variety of other fruits.

Mr. Percy has three sons, and his brother, referred to in this sketch, also has three sons. Mr. Percy is a Republican, and cast his first presidential vote for Mr. Harrison. Previous to this time he had lived in the Territories, and consequently had no opportunity to vote for President before.

P. WEBB is one of the promising young citizens and ranchers of Saticoy, Ventura County. He came to California in 1879 from Memphis, Tennessee, where he was born March 25, 1856. His father, J. L. Webb, is a native of North Carolina, and was one of the first residents of Memphis. He was in the wholesale mercantile business, and was a dealer in cotton; was a man of liberal views, and a Democrat. The ancestors as far as known were residents of North Carolina. Mr. Webb's mother, Arina (Sheppard) Webb, was also born in the "Tar State." He is the youngest of a family of eleven children, and was reared and educated in Memphis, completing his education at the East Tennessee University. He clerked for several prominent firms of his native town and at the time he started for the far West he had the position of agent and salesman of the Alabama Lime Association.

Mr. Webb, after his arrival in California, spent eight years as a farmer at Carpenteria, and from there came to his present location, one of the most productive valleys in Southern California. He is the owner of fifty acres of choice land, ten acres of which are in English walnuts and three acres are devoted to apricots and prunes and a variety of other fruit. Mr. Webb has a nice home, surrounded with majestic shade and ornamental trees and attractive grounds. One of his principal crops is Lima beans, the land being especially adapted for their production.

Mr. Webb was married, in 1888, to Mrs. Franklin, widow of the late M. E. Franklin, who was a native of Mississippi. Mrs. Webb was born in Virginia. She has five children, Grace, Earnest, Bernard, Nellie and Bessie. Mrs. Webb is a member of the Presbyterian Church. Mr. Webb possesses those courteous and affable manners so characteristic of the Southern gentleman, and guests are welcomed at their delightful home in a charming manner by both himself and Mrs. Webb.

M. WHITE is a pioneer Californian and an early settler of Santa Paula, Ventura County. He was born in Kentucky, February 6, 1842. His father, Obadiah White, was a native of Virginia, his remote ancestors being Irish. His mother, *nee* Eliza Jane Jet, was a daughter of William Jet, of Virginia. Mr. White's parents had eight children, only three of whom are living. He was the second child, and was reared in Kentucky until fifteen years of age, when the family removed to Missouri. From that State they came to California, in 1862. Since coming to the far West, Mr. White has been engaged in various occupations; was a farmer on the Ojai; a miner at Virginia City, two years, for wages; mined for himself one season in Idaho, where he made $1,000; worked for wages in Placer County, California, at $3 per day; farmed in Sonoma County; and in 1874 came to Ventura County. Eight years he was foreman on the Blanchard & Bradley ranch. Since then he has been buying and selling lots; is now the owner of five lots, three dwelling-houses and a blacksmith shop, all of which are rented.

He was married, in 1888, to Sarah Ellen Shessler, a native of Ohio. They are the parents of twin sons, Otto and Bert, born in Santa Paula, May 4, 1889. Mr. and Mrs. White are members of the Presbyterian Church. For over twenty-three years he has been affiliated with the I. O. O. F. fraternity. Politically, he is a Democrat.

WOOLEVER is a pioneer of California, having resided in the State continuously for the last thirty years. He was born in New York, February 24, 1820, the son of Samuel Woolever, a native of Pennsylvania, one of that hardy race of well-to-do people, the Pennsylvania Dutch. His mother's maiden name was Effie Glaspie, a native of New Jersey, daughter of William Glaspie, a valiant soldier in the Continental army. They were of Scotch ancestry.

At the age of nine years Mr. Woolever was cast upon his own resources; so that hard work interfered with his getting a liberal education, and his opportunities in that direction were limited. In 1845 he removed to Illinois, and, after years of hard work he purchased eighty acres of unimproved land, on which he built a home and lived until 1860, when he sold out and came to California. He first lived in El Dorado two years, then removed to Yolo County, where he bought 160 acres of improved land. This he sold in 1864 and went to Gilroy, Santa Clara County, bought a house and lot and lived there seven years, doing some speculating and other business. He sold that and purchased a ranch of fifty acres, three miles west of Santa Paula, on which he made many improvements. Mrs. Woolever is entitled to the honor of planting with her own hands the large grove of eucalyptus trees, now about 100 feet high, and many of the other fruit trees on the property. She says that her greatest regret in parting with the place was having to leave that fine grove. Mr. Woolever has bought property in Santa Paula, a very pleasant home with large yard and garden, where he has retired from active business, and is living upon what he has saved in a life of frugal industry. His time is occupied in his garden and in the cultivation of the flowers and shrubs which beautify his home.

In 1844 Mr. Woolever was united in marriage to Miss Maria Sovereign, a native of New York, and daughter of Richard Sovereign, of New Jersey. Of the nine children born to them, five are living. Those born in Illinois are: Samuel, in 1850; Izettus, 1852; and Mary J., 1858. Louisa was born in California, and is now at home with her parents. Politically, Mr. Woolever is a Republican. He has never sought or held office, but has often served as a member of school boards. Mrs. Woolever is a member of the Presbyterian Church. She has the old family Bible which she brought with her and read on their long and tedious journey across the plains. She says when it was not in her lap it was under her feet, in the wagon, where she could easily get it.

ABNER HAINES, a prominent rancher near Santa Paula, is one of California's pioneers, who came to the State in 1853. He was born in York County, Maine, October 10, 1823. His father, Samuel Haines, was also a native of that State, born in April, 1800. His grandfather, Samuel Haines, Sr., was also born there, before that portion of the Union became a State. The ancestors of the family came originally from England to Massachusetts. Abner's mother, whose name before marriage was Silvia Woodsum, was also born in Maine, the daughter of Abner Woodsum, a native of that State and a participant in the early wars with the Indians. Mr. Haines, the eldest of six children, all living, began teaching school when a young man, but soon bought an interest in a saw-mill and worked in the lumber business and also at farming. On his arrival in California, in 1853, he engaged in mining in Indian Creek, the Middle Yuba, Forest City and Moore's Flat, with many ups and downs, finally leaving the mines with $900. As a sample of his luck it may be mentioned that one time he bought $300 worth of potatoes, at ten cents a pound, and planted them; and when digging time arrived they were so cheap that he gave them away rather than to leave his work, where he was getting $100 a month. After leaving the mines he followed teaming for a time and then obtained a section of State land, on which he raised hay and live-stock. He sold his hay at Marysville, cut about 200 tons, receiving about $10 a ton. Four and a half years afterward he sold out and took a Government claim in Sutter County, which was at that time in appearance a poverty-stricken cow pasture. Commencing in 1861 he improved it and raised grain there until 1867. Then he came to Santa Paula and purchased 150 acres of land, to which he has since added fifty acres more. On this property he was also a pioneer, and has made it a beautiful home, characteristic of Southern California. When he arrived here there were probably not more than two houses between Ventura and Camulos in the whole Marine Valley. He paid $10 per acre for his land, and it is now worth $200 per acre. The second year he was on the place he planted his orange and lemon trees, which are now in bearing. The first year he raised wheat, but he is now raising Lima beans; last year (1889) on 100 acres he raised 100 tons, which are worth five cents, but that is very high. Mr. Haines first voted for Stephen A. Douglas for President, but since that time has been a Republican. He is a member of the Baptist Church.

In 1864 he married Charlotte Goodwin, a native of Maine, born in 1833, and daughter of Governor Goodwin, of that State. They have had three children, of whom two are now living—Maud, born in Sutter County and married to Samuel Henderson, and lives near her father; Edith, born in Santa Paula, is living at home.

R. G. SURDAM, the founder of the towns of Nordhoff and Bardsdale, was born in Dutchess County, New York, August 11, 1835. His father, Lewis L. Sur-

dam, was a native of Connecticut. His ancestors came from Germany and had been residents of America for many years. Mr. Surdam's mother, Julia (Lockwood) Surdam, was born in Dutchess County, New York, the daughter of Hanson Lockwood, a native of Connecticut. His great-grandmother, Julia Williams, attained notoriety and fame during the Revolution by the daring deed of swimming her horse across the Hudson River to escape the Red Coats, with her little son, Mr. Surdam's grandfather, on her lap. The subject of this sketch is one of a family of four children, two sons and two daughters, all now living. He received his education in Illinois, and was there until 1854, when he came to California, and has remained in this State ever since. For ten years he was engaged in mining, in all the mining regions of the State, and made and lost fortunes and experienced all the vicissitudes and hardships of mining and pioneer life. In 1864 he came from San Francisco to Los Angeles, sick with bilious fever. Old Dr. Griffin sent him to the care of the Sisters of Charity, who nursed him, and to them and Dr. Griffin he owes his life. In 1865 he had charge of the mines on the Santa Catalina Islands, and had much to do in entertaining visitors to the islands and showing them points of interest.

In 1866 Mr. Surdam came to San Buenaventura, built a warehouse and handled grain and oil for ten years. He sent the oil to San Francisco, which was used to preserve the timbers of the Palace Hotel. He purchased 1,700 acres of land and the town of Nordhoff was started. He built the hotel and gave twenty acres of land for public purposes, and it soon became a noted sanitarium. He sold the whole tract in two years; and when he named the town after Mr. Nordhoff, the author, Mr. Nordhoff wrote him a letter thanking him for the honor and speaking in the highest terms of the climate and picturesque location of the beautiful new town.

Bardsdale is located about one mile north of the railroad station at Fillmore. A number of nice houses have already been built, surrounded with thrifty trees and shrubs, all supplied with a fine system of water works. In this beautiful valley Mr. Surdam now resides, and is the manager of the whole property, which is, as he terms it, his pet tract. The subject of this sketch has never married. He is a man of very generous impulses,—not so much after making and hoarding money as to help his fellow men. It may truthfully be said of him that he has done much to build up Ventura County. He has long been identified with its interests, has seen its day of small things, and has great faith in its future.

Mr. Surdam is a Royal Arch Mason, and has been a stanch Republican all his life. He is a man well known and much respected throughout the county.

DR. J. B. SHAW.—Perhaps none of the pioneers have attained a higher place in the affections of the citizens of Santa Barbara city and county than Dr. Shaw; and therefore a brief outline of his career becomes an essential part of this volume.

James Barron Shaw was born in London, England, November 4, 1813, of a Scotch father, who was born in Invernesshire, and English mother, of London. He had unusual advantages of education and culture, both in England and Scotland, up to his sixteenth year, when it was deemed necessary for him to choose a profession, as was the custom in those days, the navy being his choice, but strongly opposed by his mother; the medical profession was selected. Instead of beginning his studies in London as wished, he preferred Inverness, where he had become acquainted with a Dr. Nicol, who consented to receive him as a pupil, and never has the Doctor regretted his choice. After nearly three years' study with Dr. Nicol he went home and entered University College, London, where he spent four years, attending the required lectures, demonstrations and hospital practice. Having completed the six years' study required by the Royal College of Surgeons of London, he found several months must transpire before he could present himself for examination, the college requiring the candidate to be fully twenty-two years of age. Ascertaining that with his credentials of study and a year's residence, with lectures, at the Glasgow University, he could on examination obtain the degree of Doctor of Medicine, he went to Glasgow and in April, 1836, was successful. Returning to London, he became a Member of the Royal College of Surgeons in August, 1836.

After receiving his diplomas, the Doctor went to Paris for the winter, to perfect himself in performing surgical operations, where subjects were so much cheaper than in London, attending lectures and the various hospitals in Paris.

On returning home, and having sufficient means, he determined to take a voyage round the world, not yet being inclined to commence practice. He took other voyages, in one of which, in 1842, - being in Calcutta and finding surgeons were required for the two wars then being carried on by England, one in Afghanistan, the other in China,—he applied for China, and obtained an assistant surgeoncy in an Indian regiment preparing to leave for China. He served with the regiment until the treaty of Nankin was signed. He returned to Calcutta in 1843 and embarked with another regiment to England. In 1844 he returned to Hong Kong (via Madras and Calcutta), where he remained practicing his profession until 1849, when the world was electrified by the discovery of gold in California. As soon as practicable he embarked upon a Swedish vessel and arrived in San Francisco July 3, 1849. In August he went to Sacramento in company with a number of his fellow passengers, where they organized, and proceeded to a point on the Mokelumne River. There they worked as gold-seekers in the usual manner, until it became apparent that not one of the party was adapted to such an occupation. The Doctor then proceeded to Dry Creek, Tuolomne County, where he bought a log shanty—the best sort of building that locality afforded—and recommenced the practice of his profession. The place was chosen on account of the variety of miners, there being a considerable number of Americans as well as several companies of the Spanish-speaking race,—Sonorians, Chilians, Mexicans and Californians,—with whose language the Doctor was quite familiar, he having resided in many Spanish countries. The Americans became jealous of the Spaniards, who were more successful than themselves in taking out gold, and they determined to drive the foreigners away from their mines, giving only ten days' notice to clear out. This was literally carried into effect, not one of the Spanish race, except Californians, being left. The Americans soon repented of their injustice and came to the Doctor, asking him to use his influence to get them to return; which they positively refused to do.

The winter of 1849–'50 is remembered as the most severe in the history of California since American occupation; and when it opened in all its severity Dr. Shaw determined to carry out an intention which he had formed in the early days after his arrival in this State, namely, to go to Mexico where he had friends and relatives residing. Securing passage on a vessel bound for Mazatlan, the agent of the line introduced him, before embarking, to Don Pedro Carrillo, of Santa Barbara, who was a cultivated man, educated at Boston. Said he to the Doctor: "Surely, you will not go to Mexico without seeing Santa Barbara, where the most aristocratic families of California live!" and added that he could then easily go to Mexico if not satisfied with Santa Barbara. Thus persuaded, the Doctor withdrew his passage money from the Mexican-bound vessel, and took passage on the fast-sailing schooner Honolulu, commanded by Captain Mallagh, who had come with him on the same sailing vessel from China, and whom he had often attended professionally on his frequent trips from Bombay to Hong Kong, where the Doctor was stationed. The captain was about to sail his schooner from San Francisco to San Diego on a trading expedition, and the Doctor thought this a good time to carry out the advice of his Spanish friends in Mexico.

Starting December 18 and stopping at various points, he arrived at Santa Barbara January 6, 1850. He found only a small Spanish village, not at all prepossessing; nor did he find the imposing "aristocracy" he was led to expect; and, what was worse, he learned that he must return to San Francisco if he wished to proceed to Mexico. Not finding any vessels leaving for Mexico, he remained in Santa Barbara in the practice of his profession.

In May, 1852, he left Santa Barbara for San Francisco overland, and at last, July 5, started for Mazatlan, whence he went by way of San Blas to Tepic, and there met his friends Barron, Forbes & Co., bankers and merchants. After a visit of about four months he went to the city of Mexico in November, and six weeks later left again overland for Acapulco, his determination being to return by Pacific mail steamer to San Francisco. As the Pacific mail steamer was overcrowded and would not take passengers, he was obliged to wait in Acapulco for the Vanderbilt steamer, Independent, which though crowded gave him accommodations. This vessel met with terrible misfortune. After having been wrecked on Margarita Island, she was burned and 135 lives were lost, about 400 being saved. Magdalena Bay lies between the island and the mainland. After going three days practically without food and water, some of the men crossed the island to the bay side, in search of relief, and there saw four ships at anchor, supposed to be whalers. Returning to camp, they reported their discovery, and the Captain organized a party to carry over to the opposite side of the island one of the boats which had been saved from the wreck, with the intention of going to the ships for assistance. About half way across they met a boat from one of the ships carrying a party going to the island to cut wood. On learning of the starving condition of the people wrecked, the officer of the whaling-boat proceeded to the camp, taking for the relief of the famished ladies of the shipwrecked party the two kegs of water and some crackers, which a whaling-boat always has on board. The second officer, who was in charge of the boat, proved to be an acquaintance of the Doctor, having been under his professional care at Hong Kong, and he asked the officer for a sip of the water. "Not a drop, Doctor," replied the officer, "until the ladies are served."

The officer, on returning to the ship, took the Doctor with him, where he found a berth. As soon as the news spread among the whalers, they manned all their boats and went to the island to rescue the party. Before night all the ladies were taken off and divided among the ships, and then came the men's turn. The captain of the wrecked steamer consulted the commanders of the whaling vessels as to the manner in which the people could be supported, and tried to charter one of their vessels, but found the respective captains all unwilling to break up their whaling voyages.

Dr. Shaw then volunteered to go to La Paz to secure a vessel, and proceed on to Mazatlan to procure assistance from the American or English consul. He went two or three miles away, secured horses and a guide, and made arrangements to start the next morning. About 8 P. M., however, he heard a voice calling out, "Doctor, where are you?" and answering learned that it was the purser who had come to tell him that the captain had been successful in chartering one of the whalers, on which he requested the Doctor to return and take passage. After everything was arranged on the ship, the Doctor went aboard, where he found that the vessel would be terribly crowded and provisions scarce. Knowing that it would take twenty-five days to reach San Francisco, he determined not to go, but made arrangements with the captain of his friend's vessel to take him to the Sandwich Islands. After a pleasant voyage he arrived at Honolulu, and waited there for a vessel to take him to San Francisco. In Honolulu the Doctor was most hospitably received by General Miller, the Consul General of Her Britannic Majesty.

He arrived again at Santa Barbara, in May of 1853, and took charge of Santa Cruz Island, belonging to his friends in Mexico, which he managed for sixteen years. This island, by the way, with an area of 54,000 acres, was formerly a penal settlement of the Mexican government, who transported thither some desperate characters. The government placed a certain number of inferior cattle for their support. The prisoners made a raft, covered it with hides, pitched it with brea, and made their escape from the island, and landed abreast of Summerland. They settled at Santa Barbara and some of them became good citizens.

On commencing operations on the island, Dr. Shaw purchased from Alphonso Thompson 200 ewes. The first shearing yielded 400 pounds of very inferior wool. In 1854, having heard of a band of sheep containing 1,000 head just from the East overland, he went to Los Angeles and purchased them, and drove them to Santa Barbara, whence they were transported to the island by schooner. One of the chief difficulties which the Doctor found in working the island, was the dread the natives had of going there, supposing that it would be impossible ever to get away. Fortunately, however, he found three shipwrecked sailors of the celebrated schooner on which Dana took his remarkable trip, a description of which he published in his "Two Years Before the Mast." The sailors soon became useful "hands."

Dr. Shaw purchased a piece of land 300 feet square on the Santa Barbara beach as a corral, where he could keep the sheep when brought over until there were enough to drive or ship to San Francisco. These sheep were herded on land now covered by houses and gardens. To supply himself with a pure breed of rams, he bought 1,000 acres of land on Ortega ranch, now Summerland. He took this precaution to prevent the introduction of scab on the island, which had always been free from this disease.

The Doctor was signally successful in the management of this great sheep industry, and, as before stated, conducted it for sixteen successive years. It was then found necessary by the other owners to sell, and he turned over to the purchasers 54,000 head of sheep, and a large number of cattle and horses, the investors being a company of French and Germans. During the last year he managed the island, the gross proceeds were over $50,000. He was the first to send mutton sheep to the San Francisco market by steamer, and some choice ones brought there as high as $30 each, some dressing over 100 pounds, selling at thirty cents a pound. Some time before the island was sold Dr. Shaw bought over 22,000 acres of land on the ranchos of La Laguna de San Francisco and Los Alamos, which he stocked with sheep from Santa Cruz Island. He, however, soon found out it was much more difficult to carry on a sheep-ranch on the mainland than on an island. In the first place, supplies of all kinds, more particularly lumber for buildings and corrals, were tremendously costly; and the wretched roads on which goods had to be hauled for seventy-two miles from Santa Barbara, which were excessively tedious. A load of never more than 2,000 pounds took from the time of leaving Santa Barbara on Monday until Saturday afternoon for the round trip, costing $30 for freight and provisions for the men and horses! and then if an accident occurred to the wagons no blacksmith was nearer than Santa Barbara!

The country was full of wild animals, bears, pumas, wild-cats and coyotes, which destroyed the sheep in large numbers. At the end of nearly three years he found he had fewer than he put in. Shepherds were most difficult to procure, and were most independent and unreliable, coming perhaps in the evening saying, "I am going to quit and want my wages," and there was nothing to do but yield. He had no neighbors with sheep for some considerable time. At last scab made its appearance in some way or other, which horrified the Doctor, who never had anything of the kind to manage previously or on the island. This determined him, even after his enormous outlay in building corrals, shearing sheds, etc., to gradually sell off his flocks and put the proceeds into graded short-horn or Durham cattle, selecting imported bulls famous for beef and dairy purposes. The Doctor has sold about 15,000 acres at various times of his large rancho, retaining, however, nearly 6,000 acres, which he intends still to reduce, being convinced a smaller quantity can be better attended to and will result in larger profits upon the same capital invested.

The Doctor was married in San Francisco, in 1861, to Miss Helen A. Green, a Londoner like himself, and has had four children, all sons, three of whom have died. His first and only son now relieves him almost entirely of the supervision of the ranch, where he principally resides with his wife and children.

Of late years the Doctor has been a resident of Santa Barbara city, though he gives considerable personal attention to his large ranch interests. He has entirely withdrawn from medical practice. He is a man of rare benevolence and nobleness of character, and in the community, of which he has long been an honored member, he commands a measure of esteem well earned by a life of integrity.

P. J. HOBSON is a young business man of Santa Paula, who makes no pretensions to having a history worth writing; but, as he has, by his business tact, made himself a factor in the growth and development of his town, he is deserving of mention in the history of the county; for history is a record of the present as well as the past.

Mr. Hobson was born one mile west of the business center of San Buenaventura, on Ventura avenue, January 10, 1863. His father, W. D. Hobson, was a business man of that town,—first as a farmer, and afterward extensively engaged in pork and lard packing, with his sons; is now in business in San Francisco. Mr. Hobson's grandfather, William D. Hobson, was born in America, of English ancestors. His mother, *nee* I. J. Winemiller, was born in Ohio. He is the seventh of a family of ten children, and had a twin sister who died. Young Hobson attended school in Ventura, and finished his education at a business college in San Francisco. For a time he was engaged in farming, and for seven years worked in the packing business. He came to Santa Paula in January, 1887, and bought lard in quantities, which he subdivided and sold at a gain, and also did some business for others in the same direction. He has built twelve dwelling-houses, and owns a half interest in a fine brick block, two stories high, containing three stores, on the best street in Santa Paula.

January 10, 1888, Mr. Hobson was united in marriage with Miss Olive Hink a native of Mendocino County, California, born April 18, 1870. She is a daughter of Samuel Hink, a resident of that part of the State. Mr. Hobson has been a Republican all his life.

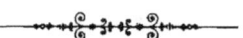

W. F. JOHNSON, Proprietor of the Petrolia Hotel, Santa Paula, California, was born in Terre Haute, Indiana, April 22, 1853. His father, George W. Johnson, was born and reared in Indianapolis. While attending school, he spent three years of his life in the family of Henry Ward Beecher. For a long time he was employed on the *Daily Sentinel*, now a leading paper of Indianapolis. Mr. Johnson's grandfather, Collin P. Johnson, was a pioneer of Indianapolis. He was a native of Winchester, West Virginia. Mr. Johnson's mother, *nee* Mary E. Kittlemen, was born in Indianapolis, and her father, James Kittlemen, was a pioneer there. Her grandfather was a soldier in the Revolutionary war, and lived to be 104 years old.

The subject of this sketch was the oldest of a family of three children. He received his early education in Iowa, Kentucky and Oregon, completing his studies at Plymouth College, Oregon. The first work he did was to help Mr. Ben Hodely construct a telegraph line. After that he was engaged for ten years in the hotel business. In 1883 he purchased the Calistoga Hot Springs, together with 148 acres of land known as the old Sam Brannan property, and conducted it a year a half, after which he sold it to Governor Stanford, who now owns it. In Sonoma County, he bought 500 acres of land and for two years carried on general farming and stock-raising. On account of his wife's failing health, her physician ordered them South, and they traveled for nearly two years, seeking health for Mrs. Johnson, but without success; and finally located at Phœnix, Arizona, on a farm of 640 rcres. There Mr. Johnson established the Calistoga breeding farm, importing and breeding fine stock of all kinds. After conducting this two years, he sold out and engaged in business in Phœnix, forming the firm of Hiller & Johnson, dealers in investments, bonds, warrants, etc. While in that business they purchased 150 acres of land, joining the city of Phœnix, which city is now the capital of Arizona, and laid out the Hiller and Johnson addition. During the last year he spent in Phœnix, Mr. Johnson conducted the Lemon Hotel— then the leading hotel of the Territory.

March, 1, 1888, Mr. Johnson sold his interest to his partner, Mr. E. Hiller (now the cashier and manager of the Hartford Banking Company of Phœnix), and came to Santa Paula. He purchased the lease of the old Union Hotel, and conducted the house successfully for ten months, when it caught fire and burned down. Three months later he bought the ground and commenced the erection of the Petrolia Hotel, which he completed and furnished in a very satisfactory manner. It is 50 x 110 feet, with two stories and a half and a basement, containing forty rooms, and having a central location on Main street. The house is lit with gas, does a good business, and is well managed. It is the regular eating-house for passengers on South Pacific trains, and it is the leading hotel of the place.

Mr. Johnson was united in marriage to Miss Sarah M. Booth, a daughter of Mr. James R. Booth. She was born in Oregon in 1857. Their union was blessed with two sons and one daughter, namely: Chester, born in Napa County, September 1, 1877; Carl, in the same place, February 2, 1879; and Pearl E., in Adin, Modoc County. Notwithstanding the efforts put forth to save the life of Mrs. Johnson, she died, of consumption, in 1884. In August, 1885, Mr. Johnson married Miss Mary F. Fornia, a native of Nebraska City, born in 1869. She is the daughter of Mr. Milton Fornia, a merchant of Leadville, Colorado. They have two interesting children: George N., born in Phœnix, May 30, 1887, and Eleanora Cecelia, born September 13, 1889, in Santa Paula.

For the last five years Mr. Johnson has been a contractor for the Government posts in Southern California and Arizona. While in Arizona, Governor F. A. Tritle appointed him Secretary of the Territorial Fair Association, at a salary of $1,200 per year. He was a stockholder in the Valley Bank, and in the Hartford Bank. Mr. Johnson has obtained every degree in the I. O. O. F., and has passed all its chairs. He is a K. of P., and a member of the military order of the Loyal League of the United States. In politics he is a Republican, but is not radical. He is a prominent business man and a very obliging hotel-keeper.

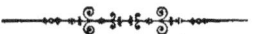

R. C. DAVIS, one of the prominent business men of Santa Paula, was born in the town of Derby, Orange County, Vermont, May 12, 1857, the son of Dudley M. Davis, a native of Canada, who came to the United States in 1838, settling upon a farm in Vermont, where he brought up his family and still resides. He has been selectman of his town for many years. His grandfather, Enoch Davis, was a Canadian, and lived to be ninety-four years of age. Mr. Davis's mother (name before marriage Lydia Blake) was born in Canada, a daughter of Rev. Isaac Blake, a Methodist minister, who was also a native of the Dominion. His grandfather was Daniel Blake, and the Blake family trace their ancestry back to the Normans of England, and their forefathers have been of more or less historical note. Mr. Davis has an uncle, Isaac Elder Blake, now living in Denver, Colorado, who made a vast fortune in the oil regions in Pennsylvania, but lost it all in speculation; yet he has regained another fortune and is immensely rich. He is a fine musician and organist; has donated to the Methodist Church a magnificent pipe organ, equal to six common organs combined, at a cost of $30,000, and he himself is the performer upon this instrument. He is still Superintendent of the Continental Oil Company. His youthful resolution never to drink tea or coffee or any strong drink, he has faithfully kept.

Mr. Davis, our subject, next to the youngest of four children, completed his school education at Derby Academy, Orleans County, Vermont, at the age of sixteen years. He obtained his certificate and taught school in the winter seasons for seven terms. In 1879 he visited the oil fields of Pennsylvania, where his father and uncle had made money, but decided to come to California, where his uncle had come two years previously, to introduce the shipping of oil on a car he had invented. On arriving in San Francisco his uncle met him at the station and offered him $100 per month to run the Sacramento station of the oil business, which position he declined because he did not feel competent. He finally went to the warehouse without his uncle's knowledge and told the keepers that he was a young man from the East wishing to learn the oil business. They permitted him to commence work, at $7.50 per week, and in two years he became one of the salesmen. During the first year in his new situation he and four others were each to receive $100 per month if they sold 300 gallons each a day; but if less than that, $75 per month. At the end of the year it was found that his sales nearly equalled all four of the others, and he was given the position of superintendent and general manager of the business in San Francisco.

In 1873 he came with his uncle to Santa Paula on a prospecting tour, and while here organized the Mission Transfer Company, for the purpose of transferring oil by pipe-lines and marketing it. Leasing the territory they obtained a royalty on the oil produced. He and his uncle held fifty-one shares of the stock, and two years ago sold out their entire interest; but Mr. Davis has revived his interest in the company, and has also stock in the Oil Company of California. He also has a large stock ranch and considerable real estate in Santa Paula. He is one of the owners of the Champion Livery Stable, is interested in the driving park, being secretary of the association, which has eighteen or twenty fine blooded horses in training. He has a neat home in the town. He is a Master Mason, being now Senior Deacon of his lodge; is also an Odd Fellow; at San Francisco he was Vice-Grand of the lodge. In his political views he is a Republican, and as a business man he is one of Santa Paula's best citizens.

He was married in 1884, to Miss Miriam Garrison, a native of San Francisco and daughter of Lewis B. Garrison, of New York; she was born April 27, 1864, of Scotch ancestry. Mr. and Mrs. Davis have had two children; the first born, a daughter, died; and their son, Walter Elmer, was born April 1, 1888.

J. HUDSON, a rancher near Templeton, is one of the early pioneers of California, having come to this State in 1845, while it was Mexican Territory. His train, consisting of 100 men, was the first emigrant train that crossed the Sierra Nevada Mountains to California, and they had considerable trouble with the Indians. When they started their destination was Oregon, but learning that California had a better and more healthful climate they decided to locate here. In the spring of 1846 a Spanish officer went to them and in a polite way gave them notice to leave the country. Finally General Vallejo came to them, and after staying with them over night and being treated kindly, he told them he would like them to leave the country. They replied that they would not go yet, as they would have to make some preparations for the journey, and would need provisions. In the morning the immigrants got together and concluded they would stay and take the country. Twenty-one immigrants and six of Fremont's men took the town of Sonoma and General Vallejo, and sent him to Sutter's Fort for safe keeping. They hoisted the Bear Flag over the town; it was made of a red flannel skirt, belonging to Miss Elliott of the party, and white cotton cloth, on which a bear was painted. Mr. Hudson's family remained in Sonoma six months, until peace was declared, and the Bear Flag party accepted the situation with joy.

In 1849 Mr. Hudson's people moved to Guilicos Ranch, and his father bought 2,500 acres, where they were engaged in raising wheat and stock. In 1854 they moved to Napa County, joining the town of Saint Helena, and bought 200 acres of land, which he fenced. He planted an orchard and vineyard, and built and ran a stock ranch until 1866, when his father died and the estate was divided. In 1868 Mr. Henderson came to San Luis Obispo, and settled near the town. In 1879 he purchased 1,000 acres of land near Cayucos, and continued stock-raising. In 1875 he sold his stock and ranch, and removed to Lake County, but returned to San Luis Obispo and purchased 539 acres on the Paso Robles Ranch. Here he is engaged in stock-raising, and has built a fine house, where he intends to spend the evening of life. Mr. Hudson is interested in mines in Mexico, and in the State of Sonora is engaged in real-estate business.

Mr. Hudson was born in Missouri, March 3, 1837. His father, William Hudson, is a native of Virginia, born in 1810. His grandfather, William P. Hudson, came from England. His mother, whose maiden name was Smith, was a native of Missouri, and of Scotch-Irish descent. They have eight children, of whom five are living, all born in California. He was married in 1863, to Miss Sarah Burtnett, a native of Illinois, and daughter of Mr. Peter Burtnett, a native of the same State. They have had nine children, viz.: Willie, John, Harry, Tina, Emma, Bertha and Carrie. In his political views Mr. Hudson is a Democrat, but is liberal and independent. He is well preserved for a pioneer of 1845, weighing 285 pounds. He is genial and cordial, and has plenty of business vim for years to come.

T. HOGG was born in the eastern part of Kentucky, May 20, 1849. His father, Herman Hogg, was a native of Virginia; was a Republican, and served as County Judge for ten years. Their ancestors were residents of the Old Dominion as far back as anything is known of them. Mr. Hogg's mother was *nee* Polly Roark, born in Kentucky, daughter of James Roark, a native of Tennessee. His parents had seven children; and by his father's subsequent marriage seven other children were born. The subject of this sketch received his education in the public schools of his native State. When he became of age, he went to Nebraska, bought eighty acres of land, built a house and improved the land, and was there engaged in farming for eight years. He then sold out to come to California, and arrived at Paso Robles in February, 1886. He purchased sixty-five acres of land, located a mile and a half south of the town. On this property he has built a home and made other improvement, and has planted prunes, apricots, pears, peaches and cherries. He keeps a dairy of twenty-two cows, and furnishes the milk supply for Paso Robles.

Mr. Hogg was married, in 1876, to Miss Fanny Grant, a native of Kentucky, and a daughter of W. S. Grant, also a native of that State, and now a resident of Paso Robles. They are of Scotch ancestry. Two children have been the result of this union: Opal, born in Nebraska; and Bernice, at their present home. Mr. and Mrs. Hogg are members of the Christian Church. His political views are in harmony with the Republican party.

D. FROST, one of the reliable young business men of El Paso de Robles, is a native of Ohio, born September 21, 1867, and is the son of William B. Frost, a native of the same State. Both he and his father were born in the same town. His grandfather, E. S. Frost, was a native of the State of New York. The ancestry of the family came to America from England before the Revolutionary war. Mr. Frost's father is still living and has the honor of having been a Union soldier in the great civil war, a volunteer from the State of Ohio. He is now traveling agent for a San Francisco firm and resides at El Paso de Robles. Mr. Frost's mother's maiden name was Miss Flora J. McKenney. She was a native of Ohio and daughter of Almoren McKenney, a native of the State of New York. Grandfather McKenney came from Scotland and settled in New York in an early day. Mr. Frost's parents had five children, of whom he was the second son. He received his education, in part, in South Toledo, and in 1876 the family removed to Milwaukee, Wisconsin, where he finished his education. In 1885 he came to the Pacific coast. In San Francisco he was appointed a station baggage master by the Southern Pacific Railroad Company; spent eighteen months at Pajaro and was then transferred to San Miguel, in the same capacity, and completed his knowledge of telegraphy. March 4, 1889, he was sent to relieve the freight and passenger agent at El Paso de Robles, for three weeks. The agent's health not recovering, he resigned, and Mr. Frost was appointed to that position, which he now fills to the satisfaction of both the company and the business men of the town. Mr. Frost is a Protestant and a Republican. He is a Master Mason; and is a young man who enjoys the confidence and good will of all who know him.

EDWIN M. BENNETT, a prominent business man of El Paso de Robles, was born in Oakland, California, July 18, 1860. His father, Nathaniel Bennett, is a native of Boston, Massachusetts. The Bennetts have lived in New Bedford, that State, for four generations. Mr. Bennett's mother, nee Miss Teresa Feleury, was a native of Ireland, of Irish ancestry, and came to America in 1845. In their family were four children, of whom our subject was the third child and the first son. He was reared in Santa Cruz County, and was educated partly in the public schools and partly by his father. When fourteen years of age he began to earn his own livelihood as a messenger boy, and then as a clerk in a store. In 1883 he came to clerk for P. H. Dunn for six years; and then, with his present partner he formed the firm of Bennett, Shackelford & LeBlanc, hardware merchants and plumbers, who have a fine stock and are doing a large business. All the members of the firm are young men of enterprise and business ability. Previously Mr. Bennett had been appointed agent for Wells, Fargo & Co.; and he is now also Postmaster; and he is, besides, a partner in the firm of Earll & Bennett, insurance agents, who represent several of the leading insurance companies; and he is agent of the Western Union Telegraph Company. Two and a half miles out of town he has a ranch of 160 acres, and he also has some lots in the city. In political matters he is a Republican, and in his social relations he is a member of the Masonic fraternity and of the order of the Eastern Star.

July 10, 1889, he was united in marriage with Miss Nellie James, a native of El Paso de Robles, and a daughter of Hon. D. W. James, one of the owners and founders of the city. On June 6, 1890, Mr. and Mrs. Bennett became the proud parents of a beautiful baby boy; so that Mr. Bennett " is one of the fortunate ones who has nearly all the good things of this life!"

COLONEL JAMES LIDDLE, a Paso Robles business man and rancher, was born in Geneseo, Genesee County, New York, May 20, 1854. His father, George Liddle, was a native of England, and married Miss Martha Jane Webb, a native of Scotland. They came to the United States in 1840, settling in Genesee County, New York, where they reared thirteen children, of whom the Colonel was the youngest. He grew up to years of maturity in his native county, learning the mechanics' and engineers' trade. In 1865 he went to Montana and engaged with his brothers in raising live-stock for several years, and while there the last of a series of Indian raids was committed on the frontier in that Territory, in 1875–'76. The Renshaw Brothers, half-breed Indians, who were ferrying on the Big Horn River, became the leaders of a most atrocious massacre of the white settlers. Men, women and children were surprised and murdered, and their dwellings burned, and their bodies most fiendishly mutilated and left unburied. The Governor of Montana called for volunteers to protect the settlers and subdue the Indians. The citizens formed a company at once, comprising ninety-nine men, who furnished their own horses and were armed by the Government. Mr. Liddle was elected Colonel of the company and had command of it during several skirmishes and two battles with the Indians.

Organizing at Sterling, near Virginia City, they went in the direction of Yellowstone River, and at Black Mountain the Indians made a stand; twenty of them were left on the battle field, while the rest retreated through the hills by the river for twenty miles, with the whites in full pursuit. The next season they were found 200 strong or more at Clark's Fort, on the Yellowstone. They opened the fight, which lasted a whole day, the Americans losing ten men; and the Indians after sacrificing many of their number withdrew and got away. Thus ended the Indian raids, as the savages were successfully subdued. They soon afterward assembled at Fort Benton, where a treaty was formed, which has never been broken. An appropriation was made by the State to pay the volunteers for this service, which was thankfully received.

Colonel Liddle, after doing for his State a valuable service, returned to his stock ranch and continued there a number of years, in Montana and Nevada. Selling out, he came to Paso Robles, arriving June 19, 1886. He purchased 800 acres of land three and a half miles west of town, on which he started the business of stock raising, and he still continues in that occupation. The town of Paso Robles starting about the same time, he spent a year in the real-estate business; then, with a partner—Mr. Short—he engaged in a wholesale and retail meat market. Soon afterward he met with a serious accident by falling down a trap-door way and breaking his leg. The firm then leased their shop and retired from business. Colonel Riddle is a Republican in his political views, and is yet unmarried.

J. B. LeBLANC, a leading young business man of El Paso de Robles, was born in San Joaquin County, California, April 13, 1869. His father, Perry LeBlanc, was a native of Louisiana, and the whole family on the paternal side had lived in that State since before the Revolution. His mother, nee Sally Hough, was born in Mississippi, the daughter R. N. Hough. Their family consisted of five children, four of whom are living. Mr. LeBlanc, the second child, was reared and educated in Fresno. His first business enterprise—the management of a bakery—was in that town; but he was burned out and he arrived at his present place August 16, 1889, connecting himself with the firm of Bennett, Shackelford & LeBlanc, in the hardware business. He had learned the art of plumbing before coming here and had become pretty well acquainted with hardware. The company now has a fine trade. Mr. LeBlanc is a young man of strict business habits and deserves the good reputation he enjoys. In his political views he is a Democrat.

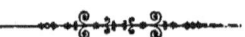

DR. SOMERSET ROBINSON.—In a very pleasant brick house on the hillside overlooking the beautiful city of El Paso de Robles, dwells the subject of this sketch. He had the house built for himself, and the block on which it is built is beautiful, with a variety of trees, including vines and orange trees. In this way the Doctor is amusing himself and prolonging his life in this health-restoring resort. The well-spread table of the El Paso Robles Hotel is only a few hundred feet from his door, and there the Doctor three times a day supplies the wants of the "inner man." Dr. Robinson is a native of Maryland, born March 6, 1836. His grandfather, Fendle Robinson, and his father, Thomas Robinson, were both natives of Maryland. His great-grandfather, Ford Robinson, came to America from England to possess a grant given him by the King; the part of the country in which he settled is called Ford's Venture, a plantation near Fort Washington, Maryland. His mother was Harriet (Gray) Robinson, a native of Maryland, and of pure English ancestry. The Doctor had six brothers and sisters. His education was obtained at the Rugby Academy and at the University of Georgetown; he is a graduate of the Medical Department, of 1858. He then entered the navy, and was a medical officer in the navy with Commodore Farragut in the Gulf Squadron, and served in that capacity all through the great war. Since then he has been continuously in the service of the Government, traveling around the world attending to his duties as a Medical Examiner of the United States Navy. After having seen all parts of the world, where American ships sail, and learning of El Paso de Robles as a health resort, he came to this place. He was pleased with the locality and climate; to him it has been the true El Dorado; he now enjoys better health than he has for twenty-five years. He still holds his official capacity in the United States Navy, and makes trips of inspection whenever he receives orders to that effect. The Doctor has a beautiful home, and is a quiet retiring gentleman, not seeking anything that would appear like notoriety. He does not object to be classed with the citizens of Southern California, and enjoys the wider relation of being a citizen of the United States.

Politically, he is independent, and seldom votes. He says he has faith in the intelligence of the people, and gives politics but little attention. The Doctor is thoroughly and widely informed on all scientific subjects, and is a very cordial and entertaining gentleman.

DR. S. J. CALL, a leading practicing physician of Paso Robles, was born in Missouri, February 18, 1858. His father, G. W. Call, is a native of Kentucky, his parents having come from Maryland and Virginia. His remote ancestors were Scotch-Irish. The Doctor's mother, Elizabeth (Johnson) Call, is a native of Kentucky, and a daughter of Colonel Tom Johnson, who was one of the active participants in the late war.

The subject of this sketch is the youngest of a family of five sons and four daughters, who, with their parents, crossed the plains to Idaho in 1864, where they lived until 1869. At that time they came to California and settled in Santa Clara County, where the Doctor received his common-school education. He then took a thorough course in the State Normal School, after which he went to San Luis Obispo and spent three years in the drug business. Next he read medicine with Dr. Hayes, and then went to the Cooper Medical College, San Francisco, where he graduated in 1884. In the spring of 1885 he began practice on the coast of San Luis Obispo County. Soon afterward he was appointed physician for the Alaska Commercial Company, and repaired to Alaska to treat and look after the health of the employés of the company; was at sea nearly all the time, visiting the stations of the company. When he returned from this trip, he brought back many curios of the country, with which he has ornamented his office in El Paso de Robles. Soon after engaging in practice at this place, he received the appointment of physician to the Hot Springs, which he now fills. The Doctor is much pleased with the effects of the water on gout and skin diseases. A careful analysis of the water shows as valuable medical properties as any in the world, and many instances of wonderful cures are noted.

The Doctor's political views are Democratic. He is a Master Mason, a member of the encampment of the I. O. O. F., and is on the way to the Knight-Templar degree.

JOHN SCOTT, a prominent citizen of El Paso de Robles, was born in White County, Indiana, January 29, 1850, a son of Greenup and Elizabeth Scott. His father and his grandfather, John Scott, were both born in Kentucky. His mother was a native of Indiana. He was the youngest of three children, and when he was twelve years of age the family came to San Mateo County, California, and after three years came to San Luis Obispo County, settling at Cambria. They purchased 200 acres of land, engaged in stock-farming, improving the place and continued there seventeen years. In 1882 Mr. Scott, of this sketch, was elected Sheriff of the county of San Luis Obispo on the Republican ticket, and served two years, retiring from it with a clean record. He then removed to El Paso de Robles and engaged in a meat market for more than a year, with good success, when he sold out and rented his shop. His attention is now turned in the direction of raising fine horses, in which he takes great delight and in which he is thoroughly posted. His favorite breeds are the Hambletonian and Almonts, standard trotters. He keeps them on his ranch, which he still retains. Mr. Scott is a member of both the Odd Fellows and the Masonic orders; in politics he is an unhesitating Republican, and in his disposition he is social, kind-hearted and liberal.

He was united in marriage to Miss Cate Lane, a native of Tennessee, and they have a son and a daughter—Edwin G. and Maud—both born in this county. Mrs. Scott is a member of the Presbyterian Church.

UGENE A. STOWELL, one of the prominent business men of El Paso de Robles, was born in Charlestown, Massachusetts, July 12, 1848. His father, Alexander Stowell, his grandfather, Abel Stowell, and his great-grandfather, Abel Stowell, Sr., were all natives of Massachusetts. His great-great-grandfather, Cornelius Stowell, settled in Watertown, Massachusetts, in 1727, a clock manufacturer, a pioneer in that business. His work was of the honest kind, made for durability, and many of his clocks are still in existence. Four successive generations, including Alexander Stowell, were clock-makers. The Stowells also took a lively interest in the Revolution. See any standard history of the United States. Mr. Stowell's mother's maiden name was Esther M. Adams, and her ancestors were the first settlers of Caroline, Massachusetts. Of the ancestry on her mother's side, David Dodge was the first city clerk of Charlestown, that State.

Mr. Stowell, one of two children—the other a sister who has since died—was educated at the Charlestown High School and at the Norwich University. His desire for adventure and seeing the world induced him to go to sea, and for four years he sailed a part of the time before the mast and the rest as second mate. Then he spent eight years with the firm of Stowell & Co., his father being the senior member of the firm. He then removed to Nebraska and purchased a large farm and engaged in stock-raising for eight years, when he sold out, and in 1889 came to Paso Robles. Becoming interested in the growth of the new and promising city, he purchased business lots and built a brick block, which is all occupied, and he has also built one of the finest residences in the county where he resides with his family. He is engaged in the real-estate business with A. R. Booth, Stowell & Booth as sole agents for Paso Robles property.

Mr. Stowell is a member of St. Andrews Chapter of Royal Arch Masons, of the K. T. and of the I. O. O. F. For his wife he married Miss Helen L. Stephens, a daughter of Major C. W. Stephens, and they have a daughter named Alice Esther. Mrs. Stowell is a member of the Protestant Episcopal Church.

It is interesting to state that Mr. Stowell still has in his possession the surveyor's instruments used by his grandfather in surveying the border between the United States and Canada.

L. F. EASTIN, the county clerk of the county of Ventura, is one of the best known and well-informed men in the affairs of the county, having acted as a clerk from its organization to the present time. He was born November 8, 1845, in Lexington, LaFayette County, Missouri. His father, James W. Eastin, was a Kentuckian, born

February 7, 1821. The ancestors of the family came from Ireland early in the history of the country. He came to California August 20, 1847, settling at Sutter's Fort. From there he went to Sonoma and engaged in the mercantile business, and in the time of the gold excitement became a miner. In 1850 he settled on a farm in Santa Clara County, where he is still resident. Mr. Eastin's mother, *nee* Rebecca A. Pine, was born in Tennessee, August 19, 1811, and died March 15, 1883. Of their five children three are living. A brother, John W. Eastin, was born in San Francisco October 9, 1848, the first child both of whose parents were "Americans" born in that city.

The subject of this sketch graduated at the University of the Pacific, in Santa Clara County, in 1866, and followed farming with his father until 1868, when he was appointed Deputy County Clerk of that county under John B. Huston, serving two years under him, and a second term of two years under J. M. Littlefield. In May, 1873, when the county of Ventura was organized, he was requested by telegraph to come and take charge of the office of this county, and everything in connection with the records of the county fell under his supervision, and the manner of keeping and preserving the records has devolved upon him. During the years 1875-'76 he served the county as Under-Sheriff, appointed by John R. Stone. In 1883-'85 he practiced law and dealt in real-estate and lent money; and in 1886 he was again elected County Clerk, and in 1888 re-elected, and he now holds the office. He is a Democrat, and generally runs ahead of his ticket in the elections. He has aided in the establishment of the fine library of Ventura and has been one of its trustees; and he has also held the office of Court Commissioner two years. He is a member of the blue lodge, chapter and commandery; has been Secretary of the blue lodge and Master several years, and since 1876 has been Secretary of the Chapter. He is also a member of the A. O. U. W., and of the Catholic Church; his parents were members of the Christian Church.

Mr. Eastin was married July 19, 1874, to Miss Fanny Sutton, who was born in Canada April 12, 1850, and they have three daughters and two sons, all born in San Buenaventura, namely: Mary A., Fanny R., Ruth, Charles P. and George Russell. Charles is attending school at Los Angeles.

PAUL CHARLEBOIS, one of the leading business men of San Buenaventura, was born near Montreal, Canada, December 8, 1848. His father, of the same name, was also born in Canada. His grandparents were brought when children by their parents from France, who settled as pioneers in the dense woods of the Dominion. Mr. Charlebois, one of five children—three sons and two daughters—was educated in the French language in the public schools of Canada and in the English language by himself. When twelve years of age he went to Ogdensburg, New York, entering a store as package boy, and remained there seven years in the employ of the house. In 1868 he took a trip to St. Louis, Missouri, and remained there a year and a half; then he was at his native place until 1870, when he came to California, settling in Napa Valley. Next he went to San Francisco, where he was a clerk for a year in a dry-goods house. In the autumn of 1871 he came to San Buenaventura and clerked for the firm of Einstein & Bernham for fourteen years. For them he had charge of their hardware and grocery department, and they had an extensive trade. In 1885 he took charge of the business of

Leach & Hunt in San Buenaventura for nine months, and he then bought them out and has since remained in business, dealing in hardware, tinware, stoves and farm implements, on the corner of Main and California streets, in the business center; of course he enjoys an enviable trade. In 1886 he was elected a trustee of the city, and by the trustees elected chairman of the board, a position equivalent to that of mayor in a city. He was re-elected to the same position in 1888. In the fall of 1889 he was elected County Treasurer on the Democratic ticket, being only one of the two Democrats elected that season; he ran ahead of his ticket about 300 votes. He has passed all the chairs in the I. O. O. F., and has been District Deputy for the order four years. Religiously, he was brought up a Catholic; his wife and children are Presbyterians. The life of Mr. Charlebois strikingly illustrates the rise of a chore boy to a position of affluence and honor, and it seems that he has many years yet to live to enjoy the fruits of early industry, enterprise and good judgment.

He was united in marriage in 1874 with Miss Agnes Ayres, a daughter of Robert Ayres, who is a pioneer of Ventura County. She is a native of the State of Illinois, and was only one year old when she was brought across the plains to California in 1858, and was brought up in Petaluma, Sonoma County; and she came with her parents to Ventura County in 1869. Mr. and Mrs. Charlebois have an interesting family of girls, all natives of San Buenaventura, namely: Blanche, Celima, Emma and Florence.

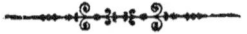

HEPBURN & TERRY, managers of the fine hotel built by L. J. Rose, of Los Angeles, in San Buenaventura. Mr. Terry was born in Massachusetts in 1850, and came to California in 1875, since which time he has been engaged in hotel-keeping. He first had the Langham House, one of the most aristocratic hotels on the Pacific coast. With his partner he afterward had charge of the Garvanza Park Hotel in Los Angeles County. G. M. Hepburn was born in New York city in 1849, and has been in California about fifteen years, and all this time in the present partnership. The Rose Hotel is a very imposing and beautiful four-story structure, and an ornament to the town as well as a credit to its owner. It has seventy-five rooms for guests, elegantly finished and furnished, with costly mirrors, silverware and rich furniture. For its size it is indeed the most expensively furnished house in Southern California, and second to none in America. Messrs. Hepburn & Terry are men of experience and ability, who understand well their business, and the Rose Hotel is destined to have a still wider reputation.

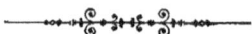

STEPHEN D. BALLOU, a well-known citizen of San Luis Obispo and at present the light-house keeper at Port Harford, came to California in 1865. He was born at Middleport, Niagara County, New York, in 1845, and at the age of sixteen years he volunteered to defend the flag of our Union, joining Company D of the Forty-ninth New York Infantry, which was attached to the Army of the Potomac, and he served four years in that department, participating in the battles of Centerville, Virginia, Lee's Mills, Yorktown, Williamsburg, Savage Station, Malvern Hill, Second Bull Run, Sharpsburg, Antietam, South Mountain, Fredericksburg Chancellorsville, Gettysburg, the first battle of the Wilderness under General Grant at Spottsylvania, later at Bowling

Green, Cold Harbor and then went into camp in the front of Petersburg. In July, 1863, his brigade was summoned to Washington, where they fought General Early in the streets of the National Capitol, and later in the Shenandoah Valley, and on the 19th of October at Cedar Creek; it was here that General Sheridan made his famous ride. Succeeding in this expedition his regiment, with others, took their position in the front of Petersburg, where they fortified themselves and remained until the following winter, and in April, 1865, a general advance was made on the city, and Lee evacuated. Mr. Ballou witnessed the fall of Richmond and the surrender of Lee, and was mustered out of the service in July, 1865.

During his service in the army, Mr. Ballou was wounded in the left leg, at the battle of Lee's Mills, in 1862, and also was struck in the face with a piece of shell at Malvern Hill, from the result of which wound he has never recovered.

Mr. Ballou then made his way to California, by way of the Isthmus of Panama, and spent some time in mining in the mountains of Nevada, and later spent one year on the United States Geological Survey. In 1868 he returned to California, stopping in San Luis Obispo County a short time, and then located in Monterey County, where he engaged in farming until 1874. He then opened one of the first stores in Lompoc, in San Luis Obispo County. After a two years' visit to Arizona he entered into merchandising and farming on an extensive scale in Fresno County, but since 1874 he has been a resident of San Luis Obispo County. He is a popular citizen and a genial companion. He is a Sir Knight of Commandery No. 27, and an influential member of Fred Steele Post, G. A. R., at San Luis Obispo.

He has recently received the appointment of light-house keeper at Port Harford, and the position certainly could not have been bestowed upon a more worthy citizen and ex-soldier. Mr. Ballou came from a well-known family in America, noted for their sterling qualities, and is only a generation or two from the immediate family of General Garfield, whose mother was a Ballou. Stephen Ballou was married at Santa Cruz, California, in 1871, to Miss Mary, daughter of J. D. Marshall, and they have one daughter.

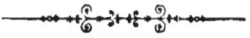

COLONEL WILLIAM WELLS HOLLISTER, deceased.—Among the American settlers of Southern California, from the early pioneer days to the time of his death, perhaps there was none other so well known and prominent, and so universally respected, as was W. W. Hollister. He possessed in a high degree the qualities of the true pioneer and civilizer, with the ability to grasp the situation in a new country, and the strength of mind and character to turn his abilities to account. So interwoven is his name with the history of this region that something more than the mention of him in a historical capacity becomes essential, and a brief outline sketch of some of the salient points in his career is given in this connection.

He was the second son of John and Philena (Hubbard) Hollister, and was born in Licking County, Ohio, January 12, 1818. His father had settled in that county in 1802, when it was a wild, unsettled region, and took an active part in its early development. Being a man of unusual intellectual power, splendid physique and commanding presence, he was an important figure in that portion of Ohio. There the Hollisters intermarried with the Welles family, which embraced among its members Gideon Welles, the well-known member of Lincoln's cabinet, a near relative of the subject of this sketch, and the one in whose honor he was given his middle name.

W. W. Hollister, with whose name this sketch commences, spent his early boyhood days amid the scenes and surroundings which usually attended the clearing up of a new district in Ohio, and after having received such educational advantages as the vicinity afforded at that time, he was sent to Kenyon College to complete his schooling. There he applied himself so diligently to his studies that he was attacked with inflammation of the eyes, which caused his retirement from college without having completed the course. The death of his father had left the farm without a head, and to this position the subject succeeded. The place consisted of a tract of 1,000 acres, but so successful was his management that the area was soon doubled, this being an example in early life of the splendid business qualifications of W. W. Hollister, afterward so well displayed in California. He also engaged in merchandising, and, in connection with farming, carried it on with varying success

The prominence which California had obtained by reason of the discovery of gold naturally attracted his attention to that faraway land, and from the information gleaned from the many reports received, he felt that there was a favorable opportunity there for well-directed effort, and in 1852 set out overland for the Golden State, reaching San José on the 3d of October. A glance over the country satisfied him that there was a good opening in the sheep business.

In pursuance of the plan formed, he went back to Ohio, and in the spring of 1853 started again for California with a company of fifty men and driving 6,000 graded sheep. Such an enterprise, driving a body of such sheep across sandy plains, often destitute of water and grass, and often met by tribes of hostile Indians, seemed desperate, but the promise of the future, in case of success, seemed to justify the attempt. He was accompanied by his brother, J. H. Hollister, of San Luis Obispo, and his sister, Mrs. S. A. Brown. There were numerous obstacles to contend with, but the knowledge of the country obtained on his previous trip enabled him to overcome them successfully, despite of many predictions of disaster by others. The route lay from St Joseph to Salt Lake, thence to San Bernardino, by the old Mormon trail. When he begun the descent into California, at San Bernardino, less than a fourth of the sheep had survived the hardships of the trip, and the remnant, wending their weary way along the cactus hills and plains, gave little promise of the future. The grass, which was growing fresh and green at Los Angeles soon restored strength to the animals, which reached San Juan, Monterey County, not only without further loss, but with the addition of 1,000 lambs born on the way. It will be seen that the enterprise required nearly a year, and that the long drive involved the necessity of arriving at the time that grass should be growing: hence the choice of the southern route, which would admit of crossing the Sierra Nevada in the winter season.

At San Juan he became associated with Flint, Bixby & Co. The first land purchased was that of the famous San Justo ranch. Other purchases soon followed, until the firm became perhaps the largest land-holders on the Pacific coast, holding at one time so much land as to admit of their offering the right of way to a railroad for eighty miles!

Although a large land-holder, Colonel

Hollister was the pioneer in breaking up the large holdings to facilitate settlement. The San Justo ranch was subdivided and sold to a colony of settlers for some $25,000 less than was offered by a speculator. The colony of Lompoc was also formed through his influence and liberality. When a hard season reduced the colonists to a condition of embarrassment, the Colonel came forward and relieved them, by throwing off principal and interest to the extent of some $25,000, thus enabling them to tide over the hard times.

Colonel Hollister was married in San Francisco, June 18, 1862, to Miss Annie, daughter of Samuel L. and Jane L. James, the ceremony being performed by Thomas Starr King. To them were born five children.

Soon after the sale of the San Justo ranch, Colonel Hollister made his home in Santa Barbara, to which place, until the time of his death, he gave most of his time and attention, having expended nearly $500,000 in and around the city. Every commendable enterprise had the benefit of his purse and judgment. The Arlington House was raised principally through his enterprise. The Santa Barbara College was also greatly indebted to him, as was also the Odd Fellows' Building and Odd Fellows' Free Library, now merged into the public libary. On the occasion of dedicating the library to public use, the Rev. Dr. Hough, perhaps the most eloquent speaker that ever made Santa Barbara his home, made some very felicitous remarks which deserve to be preserved in a form more substantial than that of a newspaper.

(Santa Barbara *Press*, September 17, 1875.)

"LADIES AND GENTLEMEN: I have the honor of presenting to your acquaintance this portrait of Colonel Hollister (here the veil was removed). If ever I was called upon to perform what our Catholic friends call a work of supererogation, it is in being asked to introduce Colonel Hollister to the people of Santa Barbara. There is not a Spanish *muchacho* in our streets; there is not a sheep-herder between this place and Point Concepcion who would not instantly recognize in that picture the representative man of California, the man who holds the plow or the pen with equal facility, the man who is equally at home in planting an almond orchard at Dos Pueblos, managing a rancho at San Julian, assisting to found a colony at Lompoc, or aiding to rear an Odd Fellows Hall and public library at Santa Barbara * * * I have entertained the idea that in the early days of the order there occurred, somehow, a mistake in the name, and that it was intended they should be known to the world not as the Independent Order of *Odd* Fellows, but as the Independent Order of *Good* Fellows. I do not know whether Colonel Hollister is an Odd Fellow or not. I know that he has sometimes been named, quite against his own taste, a "Pastoral Prince," but I am sure that neither he nor you will quarrel with me, if I combine the two, after the fashion that suits me best, and call him the Prince of Good Fellows.

"Colonel Hollister's home place is called Glen Anne, in honor of his wife, and contains 2,750 acres of land composed of plain, rolling hills, long sunny slopes, and secluded, sheltered valleys. In one of these, which, though named a glen, is elevated enough to overlook the sea for a great distance, he has built an extensive cottage some 60 x 100 feet, with wide verandas overlooking a plantation of 2,000 or more orange and lemon trees in bearing. On this farm he has 30,000 almond trees, 1,200 oranges, 1,000 lemons, 500 limes, 350 plums, 200 peaches, besides other fruits, foreign and domestic variety. Roads winding under great oaks, around rolling hills, across rustic bridges, over deep glens, now coming in view of a farm-house for his workmen, or a fanciful barn for his stock, showing here a glimpse of the sparkling sea, now a field of grain, and now portions of his orchard, are among the attractions of the place.

"In company with T. B. Dibblee he is the owner of the San Julian Rancho, situated in the western part of Santa Barbara County, which is as fine a piece of property as a prince might wish to own. It is composed of the ranches San Julian, Salsipuedes, Espada, Santa Anita, Gaviota, and Las Cruces, containing in all about 100,000 acres of land classed as follows: valley, 17,000; rolling hills, 50,000, most of which can be cultivated; strictly pasturage, 35,000. It carries from 50,000 to 75,000 head of sheep and 500 cattle. The sheep are pure merino, and the cattle thorouhbred. The annual sales are from $125,000 to $150,000, the expenses being from $25,000 to $30,000. The Gaviota Wharf is part of the property, though much produce is shipped from the Santa Ynez Valley by this wharf. It will be seen that the property pays an interest on at least $1,000,000. It is the intention of the proprietors to subdivide and sell it when it shall become worth more for agricultural purposes than for grazing.

"Colonel Hollister has inaugurated some very extensive reforms. What is called the trespass law was enacted mainly through his exertions. In early days cattle were allowed to run at large, compelling every person to fence who wished to cultivate the ground. Though a stock-raiser himself, he insisted on not only the justice, but the policy of compelling every man to herd his stock under pains and penalties of trespass if they did damage. Public opinion was much divided on the matter, but one county after another came into the arrangement, until the justice and expediency of the 'Trespass Law' is now generally conceded.

"The subject of Chinese labor is still under consideration. Whether the public will come to his way of thinking is doubtful. He wields a vigorous pen, and is evidently sincere and earnest. He is a great believer in the value of labor, and enforces his belief by being about the hardest worker in the State. As a public speaker he is to the point and lucid, never attempting to be ornate or poetical, but is often humorous and sometimes sarcastic, though it requires great provocation to bring out the latter quality. In politics he is a Republican, earnest, but not rabid. A few extracts from his writings will give a better idea of his style than any description.

"PRODUCTION BEFORE COMMERCE.

"*Antecedent to all trade is labor.* England grows rich, not because she is smarter than other nations, but more industrious. France lives and thrives, and pays the frightful war indemnity because her citizens work. Did she care for the millions of coin paid out, and fear that thereafter she would have no measures of values left inside her dominion? Not at all. She went to work, and so brought them back from all nations with whom she had commercial relations.

"LABOR, MORALITY, AND CIVILIZATION MARCH ABREAST.

"Labor is the sum total. Go to work and grow rich. If the nation continues idle, nothing can save it. If idle, it will be immoral. Poverty and crime go together. If you would have a moral community, make it prosperous. You can only do that by unflagging industry.

"*Labor is the penalty we pay for civilization.* If there is an American who does not wish to work, let him don the scant apparel suited to the climate, go to the tropics, be a savage, and nature will feed him from a tree. If he wants the comforts and luxuries of a better life, let him take off his coat and go to work.

"Without work there is no wealth. There is not a dollar added to the wealth of the nation without labor. Congress may make a promise, but it cannot create a dollar. The labor of the people alone can do that. When the Government issued its greenbacks, it simply promised to the world that the American people would create by labor a dollar's worth of property for every dollar of paper issued. That promise we must fulfill. When we have done that, greenbacks will be as good as gold, and not an hour before."

P. A. FORRESTER, deceased, was an influential member of the San Luis Obispo County bar, a progressive citizen of broad intelligence and an aggressive advocate of the cause of right. He was born in Philadelphia, Pennsylvania, in 1836, became as he grew up a bright scholar, active in educational affairs, an eloquent speaker and an influential politician. In San Luis Obispo County he was County Superintendent of the Schools from 1870 to 1872, and a brilliant correspondent of leading San Francisco papers. He was a member of San Simeon Lodge, No. 196, F. & A. M., of San Luis Obispo. He was married in that city, January 21, 1861, to Doña Maria Josefa Pico, daughter of José de Jesus Pico, a highly respected Californian of that place. Mr. Forrester died September 18, 1885, at the age of forty-nine years, leaving a wife and six children. Touching eulogies were written and officially engrossed upon the records of the bar. We copy:

"Upon the receipt of the sad intelligence of the death of P. A. Forrester, Esq., the members of the Bar of San Luis Obispo County assembled in the court room of the Superior Court on Monday, September 21, 1885, and after eulogistic remarks passed the following resolutions:

"*Resolved*, That the members of the Bar of San Luis Obispo County have received with profound sorrow the announcement of the death of P. A. Forrester, late esteemed member of the Bar of this county.

"*Resolved*, That in his decease his family have lost a kind and affectionate father, the Bar an honorable member and learned attorney, and the community a good citizen.

"*Resolved*, That as a mark of respect to the deceased these resolutions be spread upon the minutes of the Superior Court of this county; that a copy be transmitted to the family of the deceased, and that a copy be furnished the newspapers of the county for publication.

"W. H. Spence, *Chairman*."

D. H. JOHNSTON, of San Luis Obispo, is a pioneer of California, as he first landed at San Francisco as early as March 14, 1850. He was born in Green County, Alabama, a son of Chesley Johnston, who also was born in that State, in 1809, was a farmer by occupation and was twice married. By his first wife, whose name before marriage was Mary Ryan, he had one son, who is the subject of this sketch. By his second marriage he raised a large family.

Mr. Johnston left home in the fall of 1843, going to Hinds County, Mississippi, where he was overseer of a large cotton plantation until he came to California. Starting from New Orleans by sailing vessel to Panama, he came thence by the steamship Edward Everett to San Francisco. After spending eighteen months in the mines of California and passing through various business vicissitudes, he located in 1867 in the extreme southern end of San Luis Obispo County, on Los Barons Creek, where he entered the dairy business, being the second to engage in that occupation in this county. He has since sold his stock and leased his ranch of 1,700 acres, and practically retired from business, making his home in San Luis Obispo.

He was married in 1855, to Mrs. MacKinnes, a daughter of Charles Hamilton, of Scotland.

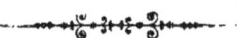

EDWARD B. DE LA GUERRA, a son of William and Francisca (Foxen) de la Guerra, was born on the Los Alamos Rancho, December 12, 1864. His father, who died in 1874, was the oldest son of José Antonio de la Guerra. His mother, now Mrs. Goodchild, was the daughter of William Domingo Foxen, one of the distinguished pioneers of Santa Barbara County. Edward spent his boyhood in Guadalupe, Santa Barbara County, to which place the family had moved; and it was there that he attended school and also entered mercantile life. At the age of fifteen years he was in the employ of L. M. Kaiser & Co., and later of M. J. Fontana & Co.,—both firms being of Guadalupe. For four years afterward he was engaged by Weilheimer & Coblentz of Santa Maria. In 1888 he came to San Luis Obispo city, where he and his brother are now engaged in the trade of gents' furnishing goods, under the name of De la Guerra Brothers, although the establishment is somewhat better known as the "City of Paris."

In September, 1888, Mr. De la Guerra was the Democratic candidate for County Recorder of Santa Barbara County, but was defeated. The nomination for this office was not of his own choosing, and was accepted only after the earnest solicitation of his friends. He is a member of the N. S. G. W., Santa Maria Parlor, No. 128. He is unmarried.

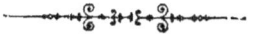

MANUEL DE LA GUERRA, of the city of San Luis Obispo, is the son of William and Francisca (Foxen) de la Guerra, and was born in Los Alamos, April 13, 1856. He received his education mainly in Guadalupe, and later, in 1879–'81, he completed his studies at Santa Barbara. In 1884 he left Guadalupe and made his home in San Luis Obispo city, where he has since resided. For three years he was in the employ of Blochman & Co., and later opened the gents' furnishing store now known as the "City of Paris." He was then associated with Meyr & Greenberg. In February, 1889, he formed a partnership with his brother Edward, and they are now conducting the business jointly. Mr. De la Guerra is a man very popular both in business and social circles. He is a member of the N. S. G. W., San Luis Obispo Parlor. He was married April 25, 1890, to Mrs. Lizzie Price.

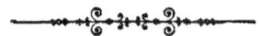

S. B. CALL, of San Luis Obispo, now deceased, was born in Newport, New Hampshire, in 1838, the youngest in a family of six sons and two daughters. He learned the harness-making trade in Boston and came to Santa Cruz, California, November 2, 1859, and to San Luis Obispo in March, 1862, where he died at the age of forty-three years. He was a pioneer in the saddle and harness business at this point. He was highly respected as a man of influence in the community, was a successful business man, and on his death he left a handsome estate.

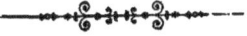

WILLIAM GRAVES, of San Luis Obispo, is the second son of Judge William J. Graves, deceased, whose sketch is given elsewhere. Born August 15, 1854, he received a liberal education, attending the public school in San Luis Obispo, a private school at Chorro Ranch taught by Mary K. Biddle, the Lincoln school in 1868 in San Francisco, in 1872 the Sunnyside High School in New Bedford County, Virginia, and afterward the University of Virginia, at which he graduated. He was admitted to the practice of law in Virginia by the Court of Appeals in 1877, and in December that year he was admitted by the Supreme Court of California and also by the United States Circuit Court. In 1879 he was busy at the practice of law in San Francisco, and was well established in his profession in connection with his distinguished father, under the firm name of W. J. & W. Graves.

In 1881 he went to Arizona and was associated with Oscar M. Brown, an intimate friend of his father, in the practice of his profession. In 1884 his father died and he returned to San Luis Obispo. Since that time he has made his home in this city, devoting all his time and energy to the practice of law, being now a member of the firm of Graves, Turner & Graves, who transact an enormous amount of business; their clients are scattered all over the State. They have participated in the litigation of about all the important suits that have been instituted in this county, as the will cases of Biddle, Logan, Herrera, Blackman, etc. When in Arizona Mr. Graves was a member of the Territorial Legislature. In San Luis Obispo he was City Attorney in 1878-'79, a member of the city board of trustees 1877-80, and is now a school trustee.

He was married in October, 1881, to Miss Lily H. Branch, a native of California, and has three children. Mr. Graves is a man of dignified presence and stately form, and is a distinguished lawyer.

ROBERT E. LEE was born in Watsonville, Santa Cruz County, California, September 21, 1866. His parents, Robert F. and Mary F. Lee, were both of Irish descent, and came from Ireland to America in the year 1850, remaining in the Eastern States some years before making California their home. Young Lee journeyed to San Luis Obispo in the year 1874, and has made that city his home ever since. He is a printer by trade, having established himself in that business in 1882. Is a prominent member of the Native Sons of the Golden West.

CHARLES L. ST. CLAIR was born in San José, California, July 12, 1854. He is the son of Arthur and Alida St. Clair, who came West from Michigan in the fall of 1853 and settled in San José. Young St. Clair came to the city of San Luis Obispo in 1860, and has since made this city his home with the exception of a short period when at school in San Francisco, where he attended the St. Mary's College, graduating in 1874. In 1878 he was married to Albertina B. Boll, of Mobile, Alabama. They have two children. Mr. St. Clair is a prominent member of the Native Sons of the Golden West, and has, during the five years of his membership, taken an active part in the management of the affairs of this powerful organization. A blacksmith by trade, he has been engaged in that occupation for fourteen years. Mr. St. Clair is a prominent member of the San Luis Obispo Band, and possesses considerable talent as a musician, a gift which has been inherited to a surprising degree by his little son, who, at the age of nine years, took part in the performances of the band.

JOHN THOMPSON is one of the prominent early settlers of San Luis Obispo County. In 1867 he located in Monterey County, and after three years spent there he came to his present locality in San Luis Obispo County. He is a native of north England, born in February, 1842, of English parents, John and Esther Thompson, and was reared and educated there. When he came to San Luis Obispo County it was a grand sheep country, with but few settlers, principally stock-raisers. At first he took sheep to raise on shares, and soon worked up a fine business, becoming a breeder of stock. This he continued successfully until 1884, when the county began to be settled more thickly, and he closed out the business. When he came to the county there was only one American at the mission, Lewis Colgate, and only a few Spaniards were there. The following year Mr. Walter M. Jeffreys landed there, and they became warm friends, the intimacy lasting until 1890, when Mr. Jeffreys' death occurred. Mr. Thompson was with him in his last illness and at his death-bed. He is administrator of his friend's estate, and the manager of the Jeffreys Hotel, the pioneer hotel of the place. Mr. Thompson has large land interests of his own, having 800 acres, located three miles east of San Miguel, where he is carrying on farming and raising horses and cattle. He is also interested, with two of his sisters who reside in England, in 1,600 acres of land in Kern County. They have stock on this ranch, and they also have property in the city of San Luis Obispo.

Mr. Thompson was married in 1863, in England, to Miss Craiton, an English lady. Two of their children, Walter and William, were born in England, and in infancy came with their parents to California. Esther A. was born in San Luis Obispo, and is the wife of Mr. Higgin McFadden. After seventeen years of wedded life Mr. Thompson had the misfortune to lose his wife by death, and since that time, 1880, he has remained single.

As a hotel manager Mr. Thompson is courteous and obliging. He is a member of the Masonic fraternity. He prefers the Democracy, but is independent in local politics, and is well informed in the affairs of his country. He is a hospitable gentleman, of pleasing address and kind impulses.

JUDGE AYLETT RAINS COTTON, of San Francisco, owning a beautiful ranch in San Luis Obispo County, was born at Austintown, Ohio, November 29, 1826. His father, John Cotton, was a pioneer of Ohio, and also of Iowa, having moved there when it was a Territory. Judge Cotton, our subject, accompanied his father to Iowa in 1844, crossed the plains to California in 1849, and after working in the mines returned to Iowa in 1851, and resumed the practice of law; was elected County Judge of Clinton County, Iowa, in 1851, resigned the office in 1853 to return to the law practice; was a member of the Convention in 1857 to revise the Constitution of Iowa; was a member of the Iowa Legislature in 1868 and in 1870, and occupied the position of Speaker of the House at the last session. He was a member of Congress from the Second Iowa District from 1871 to 1875. In 1883 he removed with his family to California and engaged in the practice of law in San Francisco. He has also taken an interest in fruit-tree culture, having planted some 160 acres in San Luis Obispo County, where he made purchase of several tracts of land, with French prunes, apricots, peaches, and other varieties.

Judge Cotton has also attained a high position in the Masonic order, having been Grand Master of Masons in Iowa in 1855-'56, and been honored with the thirty-third degree in Scottish Rite Masonry.

In 1873 he was united in marriage with Miss Hattie E. Walker, a native of Williamsport, Pennsylvania, and a daughter of J. T. Walker, also a native of that State. They have two sons, Aylett R. and Stewart W., and a native California daughter, Claudine.

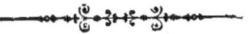

WALTER M. JEFFREYS, deceased, a prominent citizen and early settler of San Miguel, was born of English parents, in the great seaport town of Liverpool, England, January 15, 1848. He received his education in his native land, and in 1868, when twenty years of age, was married to Miss Margaret Wilson, a native of England. They sailed for the United States and arrived at San Luis Obispo in the latter part of the same year.

Sheep-raising was very profitable, and the prevailing business of Southern California at that time; he embarked in it and was very successful. He purchased a valuable tract of land, 500 acres in extent, adjoining the town, near the old mission building. In 1874 he built the Jeffreys Hotel, the pioneer hotel of the town, and for sixteen years, up to the time of his death, was its owner and manager. He was a very popular landlord, and enjoyed the patronage and confidence of the oldest and most prominent residents and settlers in the county, and was considered by all as a man of the strictest business integrity. In politics he was an active and enthusiastic Democrat, was a leader of his party in the county, and did much toward its success in many a campaign He took a great interest in the affairs of San Miguel and especially in educational matters, serving as School Trustee several terms. For twelve successive years he was elected Justice of the Peace by his party.

In the midst of his business career, and in the prime of life, January 11, 1890, he was taken suddenly ill and in a few hours the spirit of Walter M. Jeffreys had fled—the warm hearted friend, the public-spirited citizen was no more, and the whole community had met with an irreparable loss. He was a prominent chapter Mason and a charter member of San Miguel Lodge, No. 265, F. & A. M. His Masonic friends gathered around his bier and, with their beautiful and impressive ceremony, performed the last sad rites, and dropped into the grave of their departed brother the emblem of eternal life. The day of his burial was just forty-two years after the day of his birth; and he was the first Mason buried by the lodge of which he was a worthy member. His funeral was attended by a very large circle of acquaintances and friends, and by all was his loss deeply felt.

Mr. John Thompson, his life-long acquaintance and intimate friend and brother Mason, was with him in his illness and at the hour of death; and was very appropriately appointed has administrator. Mr. Thompson has charge of and is conducting his business and the hotel.

Mr. Jeffreys left no son to continue the name, and this brief and imperfect history is intended to perpetuate the memory of Walter M. Jeffreys, an esteemed citizen and one of the founders of San Miguel.

JOAQUIN QUINTANA was born on the Quintana ranch, San Luis Obispo County, December 19, 1862, and is a son of Pedro and Luz, nee Herrera, Quintana. The subject of this sketch passed his childhood on the ranch, after which he attended school at Santa Barbara and Los Angeles, receiving a good education in these cities. In August, 1889, in company with his brother and Mr. Masterson, he engaged in the general merchandise business, under the firm name of Quintana Brothers & Masterson, their establishment being located at the corner of Chorro and Monterey streets. Mr. Quintana is the senior member of this firm, a firm which merits the respect and confidence of all who have dealings with them.

Mr. Quintana was married in 1884, and has three children.

J. C. CASTRO, son of José T. Castro, was born in Monterey, California, December 18, 1845. He received a good common-school education in his native town, and after engaging in business at various times in that city, moved to San Luis Obispo in 1866, and has continued his residence there since that time. Mr. Castro is a gentleman prominent in business matters and a general favorite throughout the county and wherever he is known.

He was married in 1872 to F. Maria Jaxoli. They are the parents of five children.

PEDRO QUINTANA was born in New Mexico, January 29, 1833, and is one of the pioneers of this county. He came to San Luis Obispo County in 1843, there being at that time only three or four families residing in this vicinity. Mr. Quintana owns a fine ranch twelve miles from the city, where he has spent an active and useful life engaged in ranching, and where he is now living, quiet and retired, a gentleman universally popular wherever he is known.

He was married in 1856, to Luz Herrera, and has seven children. Three of the sons, one of whom forms the subject of a preceding sketch, are actively engaged in mercantile life in the city.

GEORGE VAN GORDEN is a pioneer, of California, who came to the State in 1846, lacking only one year of being a native son of the Golden West. He was born September 8, 1845, near Buchanan, Berrien County, Michigan. His mother died in 1848, and he was raised by his aunt, Mrs. H. C. Smith, of Alameda County. Mr. Smith, his uncle, was a Representative of Alameda County to the first State Legislature. Mr. Van Gorden attended school in Alameda County, and Visalia, Tulare County. He was raised on a farm, and, with his father, has been twenty years in the cattle business, and nine years in the same business on the ranch of Senator Hearst, the Piedro Blanco Ranhco of 46,000 acres. Mr. Van Gorden has had the care and management of it for nine years. They are doing a large dairy business, and have 1,000 cows. They are also engaged in raising horses and mules; they have 300 head of trotters, runners and draft horses. Their stock horses are of the very best breeds, and several of them are very valuable. The ranch contains a race course, and everything connected with the business. They also have the Santa Rosa ranch, of 1,500 acres, one of the best ranches in the county, on which they are breeding and raising their running horses. In the forty-four years that Mr. Van Gorden has been in this county, is comprised nearly all the American history of the State, from the formation of the government to the present time. At one time his uncle, H. E. Smith, kept a prisoner, Thomas Bell, in his house for three weeks. Bell was a noted horse-thief and a desperado, had stolen two of their horses, was pursued and captured, and when they brought him to their house the high water prevented their taking him to San José. After he was taken to San José he made his escape, and after many depredations he was finally killed. Mr. Van Gordon's people were at the San José mission when the cholera broke out, and hundreds of Indians died with it.

He was married in 1868, to Miss Annie Stiner, a native of California, born at Mariposa. She is a daughter of Mr. Calvin M. Stiner, a native of Mississippi, and a veteran of the Mexican war. Thay have three children, born in California, viz.: Annie R., George M. and Laura Emma. Mr. Van Gorden is a member of the Odd Fellows fraternity, and in politics is a Republican. While he may be called an "old-timer" and a pioneer, still he is a young man, and in the business in which he is engaged he is the right man in the right place. He is a great lover of horses, and is producing some very fine ones. He has lived in San Luis Obispo County twenty-two years, and considers it the best stock county in the State.

JAMES TAYLOR, one of the influential and well-to-do ranchers of Cambria, having one of the finest ranches in that section. He came to California in 1869, and is a native of Scotland, born October 1, 1842. His father, John Taylor, was born in the city of Cork, Ireland, January 26, 1810, while his father, Peter Taylor, a Scotchman and a British soldier, was stationed in Ireland. The grandfather, Peter Taylor, was promoted as Sergeant, which was as high as could be attained in the British army, without buying a commission. At the time of the battle of Waterloo, he was a recruiting officer for the army. He was born in Scotland, March 28, 1779, and died October 1, 1856. Mr. Taylor's father was a Presbyterian elder in the Westminster Church of Los Angeles for several years, and held the same office in the church at Cambria, where he died, December 7, 1881. Mr. Taylor's mother was Jenette (Crerer) Taylor, a native of Perthshire, Scotland. Her father was James Crerer, also a native of Scotland.

James Taylor, our subject, is the third in a family of six children, viz.: Peter, Lillis, James, Ellen, John and Jannet; the last mentioned died May 20, 1860; their mother died in Scotland July 6, 1850, and the family came to America in 1851, and engaged in farming in Delaware County, New York. It was a timbered farm, but they cleared the land and lived there until 1869, when they came to California; the family are settled within a few miles of each other. They located Government land in the mountains, and engaged in stock-raising; one of the brothers remained at the ranch and looked after the stock while others worked out. Mr. Taylor was an excellent sheep-shearer and followed that occupation in the season for four years after coming to Cambria; in that time he sheared 24,000 sheep, and the last year sheared 7,000. Mr. Taylor took 120 cows to their ranch in Los Angeles County, and with Robert McFadden engaged in making butter and cheese, which they sold in Los Angeles and San Diego. In two years he sold out, and, considering San Luis Obispo the best stock county, came back and bought 160 acres of land, where he raised stock, potatoes and vegetables, which he sold to the quicksilver miners. From time to time he has added to his ranch until he now has 640 acres of land, on which he has a dairy, and is raising grain, cattle and horses. His specialty in horses is the Norman Percheron, of which he has several splendid teams, and is also breeding roadsters. He has among many other fine horses a large gray team, which weighs 1,560 pounds each. He has property in many other places, and is one of the men who are a credit to any county in which they reside. By industry and honesty, for which his country men are noted, he has steadily risen from hard and steady work, of which he is not ashamed, to be one of the foremost ranchers in this part of the country.

James Taylor was a volunteer soldier in the civil war; was drafted September 2, 1863, at the age of twenty. On finding drafted men could not join the company of their choice, he borrowed the money and furnished a substitute; and three months later he, with eight of his neighbors' boys, volunteered and joined the Eighth New York Independent Battery, stationed then at Yorktown, Virginia, and was in active service in all the raids and engagements of the Eighth Battery till the close of the war; was discharged June 30, 1865, at Norfolk, Virginia.

Mr. Taylor was married November 18, 1875, to Miss Jennett McDougal, a native of Delaware County, New York, and daughter of Archibald and Agnes McDougal, natives of Scotland. They have had six children, only three of whom are living, and born in San Luis Obispo County, viz.: Jannie, Katie and Archibald. Mr. and Mrs. Taylor are members of the first Presbyterian Church at Cambria; Mr. Taylor is an elder, and aided in the erection of the church edifice. In his political relations Mr. Taylor is a Republican.

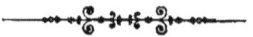

AUGUST LOOSE, one of the promising ranchers of his district, has 120 acres of land on the banks of the San Marcos Creek, three miles southeast of San Miguel. The nice young trees, the growing crops, and the appearance of thrift all bear testimony to the enterprise and industry of Mr. and Mrs. Loose, who are united in their efforts to make a comfortable and attractive home. Mr. Loose is a native of Germany, born July 7, 1848, of German parents. He was reared on a farm and attended school until seventeen years of age, when, in 1866, he came to California, to escape the oppressive military laws of Germany, and also to make a home and a fortune in a land of free institutions. He first settled in Mendocino County and was in the timber business for some years. While there he took up 350 acres of land, built a house and planted an orchard. He afterward sold out, made some money, and came to San Luis Obispo County, October 6, 1887, and purchased 120 acres of new land. On this he has built a house, planted trees and vines, and is engaged in raising wheat, corn and vegetables, being very successful.

In July, 1881, Mr. Loose was married to Mrs. Bleehan, a native of Germany. She had three children by her first husband, born in Mendocino County: Charles, Louisa and George. By her present husband she has two sons, also born in Mendocino County: August and Henry. Mr. Loose was reared a Lutheran and Mrs. Loose an Episcopalian. They speak the English language in their family, and are completed Americanized. He is a Republican and an excellent citizen.

COLONEL RUSSELL GARRETT, a resident of Ventura, had seen this portion of the State in 1849–'50, and was so impressed with the desirability of Ventura that he never lost sight of it, and in 1880 bought the property on Ventura avenue, which is his home. He has also bought a ranch of 600 acres, where he raises wheat and barley. He has built on the ranch and planted fruit trees for home consumption.

Mr. Garrett was born in Ohio, September 29, 1829. His father, Charles B. Garrett, was born in Virginia, in 1794, and was in the war of 1812, under General Scott. His grandfather, William Garrett, born also in the Old Dimiuion, was a soldier in the Revolution under Washington, in Lee's army. The family in early day had its origin in Ireland, whence they emigrated to France and became Huguenots. Mr. Garrett's mother, Maria Walker, was born in Detroit, Michigan, August 9, 1807. Her father, William Walker, was born in Virginia, captured by the Indians when a boy and taken to Michigan. Governor William Walker, of Kansas, was her brother, and R. J. Walker, Secretary of the Virginia State Treasury, was another brother. Mr. Garrett, our subject, is the third child in a family of six sons and three daughters, of whom two are now living. After finishing his education at Chapel Hill College, Missouri, he came in 1849 to California overland, and spent two years in the mines, he and his associate being the first white miners on the north fork of Feather River. They obtained on an average about $4 worth of gold to the pan of dirt, and they took out sometimes as much as $500 a day. The deep snow and mountain fever drove them from those rich mines. Returning to Missouri, Mr. Garrett engaged in farming, and when the war commenced he had a number of negroes, and in order to preserve his property he enlisted under General Rosser, of Virginia, and they were drilled all winter before the war. During the war they formed a portion of the army of General Price and participated in the battles of Lexington, Oak Grove, Pea Ridge and in the retreat from Springfield, Missouri, and at the engagement at Boston Mountain, —— Hill, Helena, and on the Red River and at Campden,—at all of which the Confederates were victorious except at Helena, where they were badly whipped by General Grant's lively regiment. Mr. Garrett was of course in many minor engagements besides the above named. He enlisted as a private; at the battle of Lexington he was promoted to the Colonelcy, when he was permitted to raise a regiment, General Jackson appointing him to that position. After the war closed, according to the advice of General Price, he went to Springfield, Missouri, with 300 of his men, intending to enlist under Colonel Grovely to go out and subdue Indians; but he was the only one of the 300 who enlisted. He was in that service from March 13, 1865, to October 26 following. Being discharged, he went to Kansas

City and engaged in agriculture upon a farm of his own; in 1880 he sold this and came to Ventura, where he has since resided. He was appointed by President Cleveland Deputy Revenue Collector of this district. In his fraternal relations he is a Master Mason.

The Colonel was married in 1860, to Miss E. J. Lane, a daughter of Isaac W. Lane, of Utica, New York, of English descent; she was born in Ohio in 1839. Mr. and Mrs. Garrett have had no children of their own, but have brought up three. The girl is now Mrs. Honeywell, and the boys are Charles M. Garrett and John McMullen, all grown up. Mrs. Garrett is a member of the Christian Church. During the war she gave her services one year to the hospital at St. Louis, and afterward had the care of the sick and wounded at Gajoso Hospital in Tennessee.

WASHINGTON WOODBERRY, deceased, formerly a lumber merchant at Ventura, was born in Hamilton, Massachusetts, in 1838, of Massachusetts ancestry. At the age of nineteen years he went to Council Bluffs, Iowa, and thence to Leadville, Colorado, and prospected for a time. Then he engaged in freighting and also dealt in produce; next he was in the cattle business in Idaho, driving stock to Nevada; and in Nevada he controlled the business. While in that State he was elected Assessor of White Pine County, which position he filled for three successive terms. In 1884 he came to Ventura for a better climate, and bought out the lumber firm of Saxby & Collins, and carried on the business successfully until the time of his death, January 13, 1890, of rheumatism of the heart, which was only of five days' duration. As he was a man of high character, his sudden death cast a heavy gloom over the community. He had just completed a fine residence in Ventura. He was married December 13, 1881, to Miss Ida Kilburn, in Eureka, Nevada. She was born in Nevada City, a daughter of Governor O. Kilburn, a native of St. Albans, Vermont. Mrs. Woodberry is a member of the Protestant Episcopal Church, and has made many warm friends during her residence here.

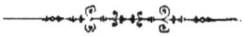

JOSEPH P. MOODY is one of the prominent and influential ranchers of Estrella. He was born in Cincinnati, Ohio, November 20, 1849. His father, Henry Moody, was born in Kentucky, December 15, 1818, and his grandfather, John Moody, a native of Virginia, was reared in Kentucky. His grandmother's maiden name was Catherine Porter. She was a native of Kentucky. Henry Moody spent fifteen years of his life as a farmer, in Ohio, and then came to the northern part of California, where he spent several years. He married Nancy L. Buxton, a native of Ohio, by whom he had four children. In 1852 he brought his family to California, and settled in Grass Valley, Nevada County. In 1858 they went to the Feather River, five miles south of Marysville, and remained there until 1869, when they came to San Luis Obispo County.

When the subject of this sketch was three and a half years old, his mother died, and he was thus in early life deprived of a mother's loving care. Having come to California when quite small, and having passed his life in pioneer districts, his educational opportunities were limited; but, while he was deprived of many early advantages, he was evidently drawn largely from the book of common sense, without which the college graduate is of little account; and through many hardships and discouragements Mr. Moody has risen to a position of prominence and influence, and is regarded by his fellow citizens as a man of integrity.

In 1873 he took up a piece of land in San Luis Obispo County, and afterward found it belonged to a railroad company; then selected another claim, and also had to give that up. In 1882 he came to his present locality, six and a half miles east of San Miguel, took up 160 acres of land, and purchased 440 acres more; has since sold 180 acres, and now (1890) owns 440 acres, on which he has built a house and barn and planted a large variety of fruit trees and a fine vineyard. He is raising large quantities of wheat, and is cultivating a section of land in addition to his own. Last year he raised nearly 7,000 bushels of wheat. In 1872 Mr. Moody married Miss Martha M. McClary, a native of New York. The following children have been born to them, and all are now living, viz.: Charles E., born in Marysville, and the others in San Luis Obispo County: William H., Lottie E., Mary E., Ellen, Arthur, Elmer, Joseph E., Grace I., Earl J., Hattie N. and Clara L. Mr. and Mrs. Moody are members of the Methodist Episcopal Church, and he holds the office of trustee in the church, and is also School Trustee. His political views are in harmony with the Republican party.

J. L. ARGABRITE, formerly of the firm of Argabrite & Cannon, grocers of San Buenaventura, was born in West Virginia, April 8, 1856. His father, Pharis Argabrite, was of German descent, and his mother, nee Rosana Jerrett, was a native of West Virginia. The subject of this brief notice, the youngest of their twelve children, was educated at Roanoke College, Virginia. When he became of age he was appointed conductor on the Ashland Coal and Iron Railway, and had that position five years. He is a member of the Masonic Order, a young business man of energy and integrity, and a good citizen.

He was married in 1879 to Miss Dora, daughter of Captain J. P. Mail, born in Augusta County, Virginia. They have three children: Newton M., Joseph M., and William Wade. Mrs. Argabrite was in poor health, and he came to California with her for a change of climate; but she did not recover, her death occurring February 20, 1887; and in April, 1889, he married Miss Clara Cannon, who was born in Nevada City, this State, and came to Ventura in 1875 with her parents. By this marriage there is one son, named Clarence C.

GEORGE W. ROBBINS, son of Thomas Robbins, of Boston, and Encarnacion (Carillo) Robbins, daughter of Governor Carillo, of Santa Barbara, was born in Santa Barbara, in February, 1847. In 1861 the family moved to Nipomo ranch, San Luis Obispo County, and in 1864, after being burned out of their home there, moved to Arroyo Grande, where they erected the first house ever built in that locality. Young Robbins opened a general merchandise store, in 1870. Three years later he built a hotel and remained in the place until 1878, when he sold out and came to San Luis Obispo. With Mr. H. W. Little he engaged in the saloon business, and in 1879 was elected City Marshal. In 1880 he was re-elected to that office, and later was Deputy County Assessor for three years. Mr. Robbins next took a fancy to the railroad business, and was employed at various points and at various times by the company then operating the railroad in San Luis Obispo County. In 1885 he was engaged in the Cosmopolital Hotel, and three and a half years later he entered into business for himself, and now conducts an establishment known as the Castle Saloon.

Thomas Robbins, the father of George W., was very intimately associated with old Captain Dana in his early life. He came to California as first mate on Captain Dana's vessel. Before the vessel's next trip, Captain Dana got married and Captain Robbins took control, running the boat up and down the coast on its regular trips.

George W. Robbins was married in December, 1876, to Miss Hottel a native of Pennsylvania.

JOHN JACOB SCHIEFFERLY was born in Zurich, Switzerland, January 1, 1831. Of his life prior to the year 1849, when he came to San Luis Obispo, very little is known, save the fact that for a short time he was before the mast on a sailing vessel, and after this he went into the mines and engaged in some light work, such as bookkeeping, etc. After arriving in San Luis Obispo in 1849 he was employed by Captain Wilson in his warehouse at Port Harford, then known as Avila Port. After being thus occupied for two or three years he established a restaurant and lodging house (all the buildings then being adobes), which he operated for a period of three or four years. Young Schiefferly clerked for Samuel Pollard for awhile, and afterward engaged in the general merchandise business for himself, and still later formed a copartnership with a brother of Pedro Quintana, now deceased. Their business was conducted on the site of the present store of Quintana Brothers & Masterson.

May 3, 1855, Mr. Schiefferly was married to Juana Feliz. To them were born nine children, five daughters and four sons, all of whom are now living. Shortly after his marriage Mr. Schiefferly purchased the Buena Vista ranch and resided there four years. He then bought the Quavitas ranch of 1,400 acres, a distance of seven miles from the city of San Luis Obispo, and lived there with his family for a period of ten years. This property is now in possession of the estate, although unoccupied by the family, who are now living in the city. This ranch is supposed to contain some deposits of bituminous rock, and if this is so the property is of great value.

Mr. Schiefferly died July 14, 1889, leaving the nine children already alluded to, and twenty-five grand children. In 1879 the subject of this sketch sent to Germany for his aged mother, met her at San Francisco, and brought her to his home in San Luis Obispo. She was a strong and vigorous woman, almost up to the time of her death, which occurred six years after her arrival in America.

Mr. Schiefferly was one of the prominent men of his time in this city. He was exceedingly active in politics, and a very important factor in all matters of a political nature. He held at different times the offices of Constable and Sheriff, and was county assessor twice. While sheriff he had a number of important duties to perform, which in those days were somewhat perilous. Being called upon one day to arrest a band of thieves in Ventura County, he left San Luis Obispo with a posse of men, and, overtaking the thieves, he called on them to halt. They declined to do so and at the same time fired on the Sheriff. The fire was returned the Sheriff picking out his man and killing him instantly. This occurred during the term of 1854–'56. Mr. Shiefferly suffered a severe fracture of the leg about the year 1870, which nearly resulted in his death at that time. On his return from San Francisco, where he had taken his son John to college, the stage in which he was traveling upset, and he was found aferward with his leg broken in three places. He was confined to his bed for three months, during which time his life was despaired of from time to time. He fully recovered, however, and was able to use his wounded limb. Prior to his death, Mr. Schiefferly was engaged in the real-estate business.

P. B. PREFUMO, son of Antonio and Anna Prefumo, was born February 20, 1844, in Genoa, Italy. He was one of a family of seven sons and five daughters. At the age of thirteen years he went before the mast, and for five years was on the high seas, making frequent trips to the coast of Italy and the different countries bordering on the Mediterranean Sea. Young Prefumo had a strong inclination for sea life, but his parents greatly desired that he should spend his boyhood days at home and pursue his studies at school. The trip just alluded to, therefore, was taken against their wishes. He came to San Francisco when eighteen years of age, as third mate of a sailing vessel. This was in 1862. He determined to leave his ship at this port, although he had shipped for a much longer period of years, but he was not satisfied with his future prospects on this vessel. He therefore secreted himself in the city, and when the time came for the boat to sail, third mate Prefumo was not to be found. He started soon after for Nevada City, Nevada County, California, and was in business there for three years, returning then to San Francisco. He clerked for a short time in West Point and next went to Monterey, where he remained for three years as a clerk in a general merchandise store. In 1868 Mr. Prefumo first settled in San Luis Obispo. At that time he established himself in the general merchandise business with W. H. Henderson. This arrangement lasted one year. Then after doing business alone for eight years, he formed a copartnership with Mr. Vallmer, and up to the present time the business is conducted under the firm name of Prefumo & Vallmer.

Mr. Prefumo was married in 1876 to Miss Ada Selby, daughter of Captain Selby, one of the early pioneers of this coast. The subject of this sketch is a member of the Odd Fellows, having joined in 1868. He is also a member of the Masonic fraternity.

CAPTAIN DAVID P. MALLAGH was a native of Ireland, and came to California in the year 1849, settling down in Santa Rosa, Sonoma County. He was soon afterward married to Juanita Carillo. To them eleven children were born, five of whom are now living, viz.: Mrs. Ellen Morriss, Mary, William and John Mallagh and Mrs. Jansen. Soon after his marriage the Captain and his wife moved to San Luis Obispo County, settling on what was then known as the Arroyo Grande ranch. Shortly afterward he disposed of this property and took the Huer-Huero ranch. Captain Mallagh was a sea captain for a period of ten or twelve years, in charge of coast steamers and sailing vessels, and at that time was very prominent in all maritime matters. He built and operated a number of wharves at various landing places in this county. The wharf at Cane Landing is being used as the regular steamboat landing. The stage and freight business between this landing and San Luis Obispo was successfully operated by Captain Mallagh, in whose charge it was at that time. The ranch of 1,600 acres, adjoining the Pizmo ranch, constituted the home of the Mallagh family until the Captain's death. He was a worthy and respected citizen. At various times he served the public as deputy sheriff and also as Sheriff. At one time he was elected Sheriff on the independent ticket.

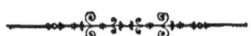

LOUIS LAMY, son of Louis Lamy, a native of France, and Maria Antonia (Ortega) Lamy, of California, was born in San Luis Obispo July 31, 1862. After receiving a common-school education in that city, he was sent to San Francisco, where he attended lectures at Hastings Law School. He subsequently entered the law office of W. J. Graves, in that city, and remained there between the years 1881 and 1884. He returned to San Luis Obispo and has been engaged in the practice of law in that place since April, 1885.

Mr. Lamy was married in March, 1886, to Miss May Finn, of San Francisco, by whom he has two children. He is a Senior Past President of Los Osos Parlor, No. 61, Native Sons of the Golden West; is also Senior Past Chief Ranger of Court Star of San Luis Obispo, No. 7697, Ancient Order of Foresters of America.

P. H. DALLIDET, Jr., a real-estate dealer of San Luis Obispo, was born on what was then known as Gabriel Salazar's place, three miles from this city, April 6, 1857, a son of P. H. and Maria (Ascencion) Dallidet. He attended school in this city, and later, in 1873, at St. Mary's College, San Francisco. He then entered into business, but owing to ill health was soon obliged to withdraw for a time. Shortly afterward he went to Guadaloupe, and was there engaged as an assistant in the mercantile establishment of Mr. Hartman, and a few months later returned to his home on the Salazar place in San Luis Obispo County. In 1876 Mr. Dallidet entered the county clerk's office, then in charge of Mr. Nathan King, and was his chief deputy for three years. Under Mr. Simmler he was also in the post-office for six months, in 1881. He then became interested in real-estate operations and has since been more or less engaged in this occupation. June 1, 1882, he associated himself with Mr. Phillips in this business, which engagement proved to be an eminently successful one. The sale of immense tracts of land and prominent ranches known to every old settler of this locality was successfully negotiated by this firm. In 1886 Mr. Dallidet established himself alone in the real-estate business, and about this time he also bought an interest in some improved gold mines, which he still retains.

October 6, 1886, he was married to Miss Dora Oldfield of Brooklyn, New York, and they now reside at Fixlini Terrace, a pretty place owned by Mr. Dallidet in the suburbs of San Luis Obispo city.

EMIL FLUEGLER was born in Germany, September 3, 1851. He received a good common-school education in his native country, and in 1866 started for America, locating at once in Pittsburg, Pennsylvania, where he engaged in the confectioner's trade, which trade he had learned while in Germany.

At this time young Fluegler was not robust and, becoming ill at different times, his family advised his return to Germany, which advice he acted upon in 1867. Again interested in the new world, he started once more for America, in 1868, and worked at his trade this time in Philadelphia. In 1873 he went to Australia and worked in the mines near Sydney. This expedition was far from successful, many lives and a great deal of money being lost by those who took part in the undertaking. Mr. Fluegler, after his unfortunate adventure in the mines, worked awhile at his trade there and then sailed for California, arriving in San Francisco in 1875. The following year he came to San Luis Obispo, remaining, however, only a short time. In 1877 he was engaged for four months in the bakery and confectioner's business in Bakersfield. From San Francisco, soon afterward, with two companions he started for the Black Hills. Soon becoming disgusted with the country there, he took a trip into various parts of the United States, visiting Leavenworth, Kansas, and Philadelphia, then back to San Francisco, Bakersfield, north to Washington Territory, and finally back to San Luis Obispo, in 1878. In the latter place he has continued to reside up to the present date, engaged at his trade. Since 1882 he has been in business for himself.

Mr. Fluegler was married, March 24, 1882, to Carrie Moltz, a native of Indiana, by whom he has one child.

WILLIAM MALLAGH, son of Captain David P. Mallagh, was born at the Huer-Huero ranch, San Luis Obispo County, August 15, 1864. He attended school in San Luis Obispo and finished his education at Santa Ynez, Santa Barbara County, taking the full business course. After leaving school he went into the railroad business, in which he was engaged for a time, and later connected himself with the Cosmopolitan Hotel, one of the leading hotels in San Luis Obispo, where he is still interested. For three years he has been a member of the Native Sons of the Golden West. Mr. Mallagh was married, May 21, 1890, to Miss Nellie Dana.

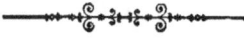

WILLIAM DOMINGO FOXEN, deceased, also known as Benjamin Foxen, of San Luis Obispo County, was born in Norwich, England, in 1798, and commenced a seafaring life when a lad, entering the merchant service. He was gradually promoted until he became first officer, in which capacity he visited many parts of the old world and finally the islands of the Pacific Ocean. Meeting Captain Thompson, afterward a resident of Santa Barbara, he was entreated by him to enter his large shipping business. Santa Barbara was reached in 1820, but it was in 1818 that Mr. Foxen first anchored his vessel in San Francisco Bay, the first vessel ever anchored in that harbor. Entering the employ of Captain Noriega at Santa Barbara, he built a schooner in the little bay, since called from that event the Goleta. By this time Mr. Foxen had given up all idea of returning to his home in England; accordingly, following the usual custom, he sought a wife among the graceful señoritas. In 1830 he married Eduarda Ozuna, of the town of Santa Barbara; but, according to the laws of the Catholic Church, he was prohibited from marrying one of the believers of that faith unless he also became a Catholic. He therefore changed his faith, and his name from Benjamin to William Domingo, and all was thenceforward "plain sailing." He had eleven children, of whom nine are now living, namely: Ramona, now Mrs. Wickenden, and living at Tinaquaic Rancho; Francisca, now Mrs. Goodchild, of San Luis Obispo city; Juana Maria, now the wife of Mr. Roth, at Ventura; Marie Antonio, now Mrs. Stone, at Los Alamos; Mathilda, now Mrs. Cartere of Santa Barbara; William José, at Los Alamos; Fred, at the same place; Thomas, at Tinaquaic Rancho and John Charles, at San Luis Obispo.

Mr. Foxen was granted by the Mexican government two leagues (8,888 acres) of fine land, called the Tinaquaic Rancho, situated about fifty miles from Santa Barbara and near Los Alamos. He died February 19, 1877. During the Mexican war he did much to assist General Fremont in his campaign, furnishing him with provisions, horses, etc., for which he received no return whatever—an experience similar to that of other old settlers. He personally made the capture of Santa Barbara city a very easy matter for Fremont, guiding him from his ranch over the mountains by the old San Marcos trail instead of the beaten road, to the outskirts of the city, undiscovered, and while the Mexican troops were all at mass in the old mission early on Christmas morning. The American flag was floated in the center of the city and the place was captured then and there. Mr. Foxen was successful as a physician, although of course without special training. He was especially available in the relief of much suffering at points remote from the towns. At his death his property was divided equally among the children, some of whom are still residing at the old homestead.

Charles Foxen, son of the preceding, was born in Santa Barbara, December 15, 1853, and was a resident of the old homestead until a few years ago, when, owing to the ill health of his wife, he moved to the city of San Luis Obispo. He was married in 1878 to Lenora Villa, and has six children. He is a gentleman of modest and unassuming manner and is universally esteemed

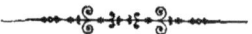

GEORGE FREDERICK SAUER was born in Bavaria, Germany, in 1836. He spent his boyhood and was educated at his home. In 1856 he came to New York city, remaining there for two years. In 1858 he journeyed to California, coming to San Luis Obispo. It was here that he met his future wife, and was married April 23, 1862. Four children were the result of this union, two of whom are now living, a son and daughter. Mr. Sauer was engaged in the bakery and grocery business, and made San Luis Obispo his home until his death, which occurred July 31, 1873. He served as City Treasurer during the years 1865 and 1866 The subject of this sketch was a man of the strictest integrity, and, as the proprietor of one of the earliest places of business in the city, occupies an important position in its history.

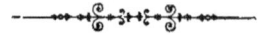

J. P. LIMA was born in the Azores Islands September 12, 1835. In 1857 he came to America, and after remaining in Boston, Massachusetts, a few weeks, he went before the mast, shipping to Charleston, South Carolina. A few months later, hearing of a good opportunity to ship to the Arctic ocean, Mr. Lima determined to go there, and for the period of three years and more was an inhabitant of the Arctic regions.

Returning to Massachusetts in 1860, he made a short stay in New Bedford, and shipped to Rio Janeiro, South America, returning to Massachusetts three months later. Apparently not satisfied with these expeditions, he determined to come to California, and in the latter part of 1860 arrived in San Francisco; proceeded at once to the mines and remained there for fifteen years. Meeting with indifferent success as a miner, Mr. Lima returned to his native country, the Azores, for a brief stay. Four months later he came back to California, settling in San Luis Obispo in 1875, where he has remained up to the present date. He is proprietor of the Luzitania Hotel.

Mr. Lima was married September 23, 1877, and has four children.

TIMOTHY CAVANAUGH was born in Ireland in 1823, and went to Canada at the age of eight years. In 1845 he came to the United States and settled in Illinois. It was there he cast his first vote for President, and General Taylor was the man who received it. Mr. Cavanaugh remained in Illinois only three years. At the expiration of that time, like many others, he caught the gold fever. In 1850 he set out for California and at once sought the mines, where he remained, however, only six months. He then traveled around prospecting, and finally settled down in Santa Clara County, in July, 1852, where for three years he was extensively engaged in ranching. During this period Mr. Cavanaugh was married, and eleven children is the result of this union, ten of whom are now living. In 1883 Mr. Cavanaugh came to San Luis Obispo County, and, with the assistance of his sons, is operating a fine ranch of 1,000 acres, near the Santa Margarita station on the Southern Pacific Railroad. Mr. and Mrs. Cavanaugh are living in a very pleasant cottage near the railroad,—the eleventh house he has constructed during his life-time.

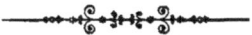

JOHN McDONNELL was born in Tipperary, Ireland, in 1846, and at the age of sixteen years came to America, coming direct to San Francisco. He was first employed in the commission business in the city, but very soon afterward went to the Santa Clara Valley and engaged in farming. For thirteen years he was engaged in that occupation, a part of the time on his own account and a part of the time for P. W. Murphy. In 1879 Mr. McDonnell was employed on the famous Santa Margarita ranch, in San Luis Obispo County, the property of Mr. Murphy, and from that time has been the foreman. Under his charge this vast property, twelve miles square, is being successfully and judiciously managed. As far as the eye can reach this beautiful piece of land extends, and every visitor to San Luis Obispo who has a day at his disposal, would miss much by not making the journey of only eleven miles to this ranch. Mr. McDonnell is unmarried.

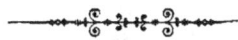

EDWIN P. BEAN was born in Corinth, Maine, May 1, 1844. He is the son of Reuben and Mary (Smith) Bean, both natives of New Hampshire and descended from early New England settlers and soldiers of the Revolution. Both are now deceased. They reared a family of twelve children, all of whom continue to make their home in the East with the exception of the two brothers, Edwin P. and Reuben, who, together, came to California in 1862. These brothers have traveled and lived together ever since, in California and elsewhere, and their interests, business, social and otherwise, have always been identical. Before settling down in this State the brothers went to Virginia City, Nevada, and opened a lumbering business, owning saw-mills and operating them for a period of nine years. In 1871 they came to Hill's Ferry, California, and for three years were engaged in farming, and later on turned their attention to raising sheep extensively. It was in 1878 when the brothers purchased a ranch in the Santa Margarita Valley, eight miles from the city of San Luis Obispo. From that time until 1889, they were extensively engaged in cattle-raising. In the latter year, the Southern Pacific Railway Company, having established a station at Santa Margarita, the brothers leased their ranch and opened a hotel at the railroad station, which they continue to operate. The hotel is a commodious building, and as the town promises to be a thriving one in the future, this property of the Bean Brothers, which consists of seven acres, is a valuable one.

Edwin was married in 1878 to Miss Rebecca Maud Sumner, a native of California. They are the parents of three children. This interesting family is so situated as to enjoy life, and their many friends always receive a hearty welcome in their pleasant home.

P. F. READY was born in Ireland in 1844, and two years later was brought by his parents to America. In 1852 he set out to work for himself and went to Virginia, where he learned the trade of blacksmithing. In this he was successful, and during the civil war he worked at his trade on the battle-field, shoeing horses for the Army of the Potomac. In 1865 Mr. Ready went to Omaha and worked on the Union Pacific Railroad until that road was completed. He then, in 1867, came to California and at once located in San Luis Obispo. Mr. Ready was employed in a blacksmith shop for five years after he settled in the city. After that time, and since the year 1872, he has been in charge of a shop himself. For some time he has been closely identified with the management of the city's affairs. In 1882 he was elected to the City Council for a term of two years; in 1888 he was again elected, and was subsequently chosen as the President of the Board—the chief executive officer of the city. He has also served as Supervisor for a term of years. Mr. Ready is a member of the Odd Fellows, the Masons, Knights Templar and Knights of Pythias. He was married July 14, 1872, to Miss Mary Somers, of Canada. Three children have been born to them.

ISAAC L. WILSON, son of James and Nancy (Barlow) Wilson, was born October 6, 1844, in Madison County, Indiana. When young Wilson was four years old the family moved to Atchison County, Missouri, where the father engaged in farming. It was in that sparsely settled country that Isaac received a good common-school education and laid the foundation for a very valuable and useful life. In 1863 he started on a prospecting tour, traveling through many of the Western States, looking for a desirable spot to settle. In 1867 he engaged in the lumber business in Montana, was there four years, and then went to Washington Territory and Oregon, remaining in those places, however, but a short time. Los Angeles was the next objective point, and a year was spent in that city. During that time Mr. Wilson worked at the carpenter's trade. Los Angelos then was not the Los Angeles of to-day, and the attractions there were not sufficient to keep him longer than a year. It was in 1873 that he first went to Santa Barbara, and it was then that he met his wife, Miss Frances Martines, to whom he was married October 5, of the same year. By this marriage three children have been born, all now living. Two years were spent in Santa Barbara, and in April, 1875, Mr. and Mrs. Wilson moved to San Luis Obispo, where they have since resided. In his business relations Mr. Wilson has always held a prominent position in this community. As a contractor and carpenter he is unexcelled. There are few structures of any note in regard to which he has not been consulted. Mr. Wilson had in charge the alteration of the old mission tower in San Luis Obispo. In 1878 the tower was cracked and became dangerous. This necessitated the erection of a frame one. This work, and also the encasing of the entire structure of adobe with wood, Mr. Wilson successfully completed—a task not difficult of execution, but of a nature always of historical importance. Mr. Wilson is a member of the Odd Fellows, and also of the A. O. U. W. At various times he has held promient offices in these organizations.

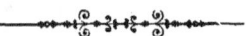

GEORGE T. GRAGG, son of Moses and Rebecca (Alden) Gragg, was born in Roxbury, Massachusetts, April 29, 1829. Mr. and Mrs. Gragg, both now dead, were New England people and reared a family of nine children. George T. received a good common-school education at his home and also learned the carpenter's trade. At the age of twenty, March 1, 1849, he resolved to strike out West for himself, and on this date sailed for California, via Cape Horn, on the ship Sweden. He arrived at San Francisco August 3, and soon went into the mines, remaining there, however, only three months. Spending the winter in San Francisco, working at the carpenter's trade, he tried the mines again in the spring, this time at Coloma on the south fork of the American River. Leaving this locality in the fall of the same year, he went prospecting, remaining at Bear River, near Illinois Town, for a short time and then going on the north fork of the American River, where deer and game of all kinds at this time were very abundant and could be shot almost without moving from the camp. In the fall of 1851 Mr. Gragg went into Mariposa County, remaining there until July, 1852. In all these places mentioned he was engaged, as was almost every one else, in mining, and with fair success. He now decided to settle down in Santa Cruz. and did make that his home until 1880. For two years he was engaged in loading vessels, then worked at his trade for ten years, and later on was in the tanning business for a period. From 1867 to 1880 he was engaged in the planing and lumber business with S. J. Lynch. During his life in this place Mr. Gragg naturally witnessed many changes in its growth and development. From a village of 300 inhabitants it grew to be a city of 5,000 population in 1880. At one time he held the office of City Trustee in Santa Cruz, the board consisting of three members during his term of service.

In 1880 Mr. Gragg moved to San Luis Obispo County, and since that has made his home here. He is the owner of a fine ranch of 700 acres, near Port Harford, which he is devoting to stock-raising and farming. He also owns a pretty home in the city of San

Luis Obispo, at which place his family reside most of the year, the children receiving the benefit of the city schools.

Mr. Gragg was married in 1868, at Santa Cruz, to Miss Ruth Root, and as a result of this union there are six children. Since his removal to this county, Mr. Gragg has thoroughly identified himself with its best interests. He has served as a member of the Board of Supervisors for the Fourth district for four years. During this term many needed reforms and improvements have been accomplished. It is a period that is, perhaps, conspicuous in that respect, in the history of that body.

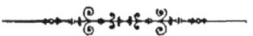

JOAQUIN ESTRADA was born in Monterey, in 1819, and moved to San Luis Obispo in 1845. He first settled on the Santa Margarita ranch, a property which consisted of 15,000 acres, and which is now considered one of the very best ranches in the State. Mr. P. W. Murphy bought it in 1860 for a trifling amount compared to its present valuation. After disposing of this property, Mr. Estrada purchased a ranch about two miles from the city of San Luis Obispo, and has continued to live there since that time. The property, a very pretty place of about 160 acres, is now known as "Estrada Garden."

Mr. Estrada has a distinct recollection of General Fremont's campaign in this part of the State during the Mexican war. It was during his ownership of the Santa Margarita ranch. General Fremont's troops were then stationed in various parts of this county, and at one time, being short of beef, they decided to help themselves to the fine cattle on the Santa Margarita ranch, which they did to the extent of thirty cows and 100 horses. The cattle were killed and for a time the Americans were well fed. Mr. Estrada states that to the best of his recollection he was never paid for the stock, neither did General Fremont offer any explanation in the matter. Mr. Estrada also remembers that this occurred while he was absent, and it was on his return that he missed his cattle. He was subsequently captured by the troops at various times, but was in each case released without serious injury.

He was the first County Treasurer in this county, W. J. Graves being his deputy. He held this office two years. Was also Justice of the Peace, and for many years served as Supervisor. Of late he has been living quietly at his ranch, the "Estrada Garden," a popular place for picnics, barbecues, etc. Many are the interesting stories this old pioneer tells of his life on the Santa Margarita ranch. At one time a barbecue there lasted thirty days. He had a band and other attractions, and people came from all over the country.

Mr. Estrada was married in early life.

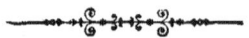

ERNEST GRAVES, a member of the firm of Graves, Turner & Graves, attorneys at law, at San Luis Obispo, is a son of William J. and Soledad Pico, and was born in the old mission building adjoining the Catholic Church in the city of San Luis Obispo, December 5, 1852. At the age of eight years he was taken to San Francisco, as the family changed residence to that city, where his father was practicing law. He attended St. Ignatius College in that city, between the years 1862 and 1864, and later the Santa Clara College; in 1871 he was in attendance at the State University at Berkeley, and then at an Oakland school. He studied law under the instructions of his father in San Francisco, afterward practiced with him there, and after his father's death he located in San Luis Obispo city, his old home, where he has since resided. The law firm of which he is a member is well known in all parts of the State, as they have been parties in all important litigation in this county for a number of years, and generally with marked success. Among the most important cases were those of the wills of Biddle, Logan, Herrera, Blackman, etc.; also the case of Schultz against McLean. Mr. Graves was City Attorney for three years, 1875–'77, the first three years of the corportate life of the city; and he was District Attorney 1880–'85.

He was married March 27, 1878, to Miss Holloway, a native of California, and he has three children.

CAPTAIN HENRY A. SPERRY, a leading citizen, agriculturist and stockman of San Luis Obispo County, is a native of Boston, Massachusetts. He was born December 22, 1842, is a son of Henry Sperry, a successful real-estate dealer of that city, and a native of Vermont. The subject of this sketch spent his boyhood and youth in his native city, and received the advantages of a fair public schooling. He entered the war of the Rebellion in 1861, a member of the Thirtieth Massachusetts Infantry, Company D, as a sergeant. He was advanced through the various official grades with the rank of Captain of his original company. He served nearly five years in the army, and was then sent South at the close of the war, to do Provost-Marshal duty.

His experience as a soldier was rather an unusual one, having engaged in so many battles at times under the hottest fire, yet never received a wound. After serving under General Butler in the army division of the South, he came north under General Phil. Sheridan in the Shenandoah Valley, when Early invaded the city of Washington. He was in the battles of Winchester, Fisher's Hill, and Cedar Creek, when Sheridan made his famous ride. After having been mustered out of the Government service, he, desiring to see California, came to Stockton, where he remained about one year and then went to San Francisco, from 1868 to 1872, where he engaged in mercandising. In 1872 he came to San Luis Obispo County, leased a sheep ranch of Ziba Branch, Esq., one of the wealthiest and most successful old settlers of the county. This business venture proved a success, and in 1875 he wedded Miss Louise, one of the accomplished daughters of Mr. Branch. The wife died in 1879, and her two children, Henry Scott and Elsie, died later. Mr. Sperry married for a second wife Mary Woods, daughter of Mr. C. H. Phillips, a prominent and influential citizen of San Luis Obispo, and the results of this union is three sons and one daughter. Mr. Sperry is a stanch Republican, a member of the Ancient Order of United Workmen, and a leader in the Harper Post, G. A. R., of Arroyo Grande.

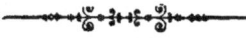

C. FERNANDEZ was born in San Luis Obispo County, February 12, 1855, and is one of a family of ten children, seven sons and three daughters. The family ranch is located on the line of the city limits, and there Mr. Fernandez has spent the whole of his life. At present he holds an important position as agent for a San Francisco meat and produce establishment, and has in charge the buying and selling of cattle for them. He is also engaged on the ranch and in various other enterprises. Mr. Fernandez is personally a very popular man in the city and well known throughout the county. He was married in 1881, and has five children.

HON. CHARLES FERNALD.

Conspicuous among the homes of the Channel City is that of the Hon. Charles Fernald, perhaps the most widely known as well as the oldest New England resident of Santa Barbara. An entire city block is dedevoted to the culture of fruit and forest trees, upon a slight elevation in the midst of which stands the dwelling. The exterior is a true indication of the hospitable home within, for the Judge and his family unite to the simplicity and character of social life in New England, the genial hospitality and grace of the sunny South.

Judge Fernald traces his lineage to one of the oldest stocks of American progenitors, being a direct descendent from Dr. Renald Fernald, who came from England to New Hampshire with Captain John Mason's company, in 1631, and settled in Piscataqua in that year. The Doctor had the distinguished honor of being the first surgeon who settled in New Hampshire, where the family has continued for more than two centuries.

In 1640 appears the name of Renald Fernald as one of the grantors of fifty acres of glebe lands settled by the government and inhabitants of the Piscataqua Rivers to the church wardens for the advancement of the cause of religion. The city of Portsmouth has since been built upon the site of this grant. With this city the name of Fernald has been deservedly connected to the present day.

Dr. Renald Fernald and is brother Thomas Fernald, who came from England with him, became proprietors of the island, or the northeast shore of the Piscataqua River, and their descendants held the same for a century and a half, until John Fernald, Jr., of Middleton, New Hampshire, conveyed away the middle one, known as the "Lay Claim Island," and also as Fernald's Island, which afterwards on June 15, 1806, passed into the ownership of the United States and is now the site of Fort Sullivan in the Portsmouth or Kittery navy yard.

The Fernalds have ever been a brave and loyal race. In 1776 Mark and Gilbert Fernald appended their signatures to the solemn engagement, to oppose the hostile proceedings of the British fleets and armies against the United American Colonies, and Hercules, or Archelaus Fernald, as he was sometimes called, the grandfather of our present subject, then only twenty-seven years of age, and a resident of Kittery, York County, Maine, enlisted in the Continental army in the regiment of Colonel Francis, when he marched to the Heights of Dorchester near Boston and engaged in the defense of his country. He afterward did much other patriotic service.

The subject of our present sketch, Judge Charles Fernald, was born at North Berwick, County of York, State of Maine, on May 27, 1830. After completing the preparatory studies for college under the tuition of Professor Harrison Carroll Hobart, at the age of eighteen he joined that band of hardy and brave youth sent forth by New England to California, arriving at San Francisco June 14, 1849, being one of the Argonauts to pass through the Golden Gate in that memorable year,—which honor the Judge still preserves by a life membership in the California Pioneers' Society. After a few months spent in the mines he returned to San Francisco in November 1849, and was engaged in editorial work and law reporting until May 1852, being upon the staff of the *Morning Post* and *Alta*, the two leading journals of that day. During the time of his residence in San Francisco, he pursued his law studies with steadfast ardor, although interrupted greatly by the fire of May 4, 1851, which blotted out the city and for a brief period checked business pursuits. On May 4, 1852, a conflagration again destroyed the growing city and swept away his entire library, which he had accumulated in the meantime. This second disaster seemed to have changed his determination to remain longer on this coast, and he resolved to return to Boston. Having many friends and acquaintances in Southern California, the Judge resolved to visit them on his way home, stopping at Santa Barbara and at Los Angeles, intending to take the Panama steamer at San Diego where it then touched. On June 30, 1852, he arrived at Santa Barbara, where he met his friends, Edward Sherman Hoar and Augustus F. Hinchman, who were among the leading lawyers and citizens of what was then an old and respectable Spanish settlement.

At this period the law-abiding citizens of Santa Barbara were carrying on a vigorous campaign against an organized set of bandits who, disregarding all laws, had so terrorized the peaceful residents that their lives were a daily burden. They had compelled the officers of the law in the county to resign their trusts, and anarchy and terrorism ruled supreme. At a public meeting of the leading citizens of the town it was resolved to make a firm and determined effort to re-establish order, and they invited Judge Fernald, then a young man of twenty-two, to remain and assist in the good work, desiring him to accept the office of County Judge. He was not a man to decline a public duty thus imposed upon him, and finally consented to remain. Upon the application of the leading citizens of Santa Barbara, Governor John Bigler, on March 14, 1853, appointed him Judge of Santa Barbara County. To this place he was elected September 5, 1853, and re-elected in 1857. At these elections the Judge was the unanimous choice of the citizens of the county, only a few votes being cast against him. Among his first official acts was the appointment of Russel Heath to the office of district attorney, with a strong and efficient corps of county officers throughout to take the places of those who had resigned. To these the people gave loyal support and the county government was successfully reorganized, and so strictly and impartially were the laws enforced under the new *regime* that no public disorder or resistance to the laws was attempted for many years, notwithstanding many "bravos," outlaws and desperados were at large in some of the adjoining counties.

On January 7, 1860, by a joint resolution of the Senate and Assembly, Judge Fernald was granted five months' leave of absence from the state, in order to transact some very important business and visit his old home in the East.

The Judge spent six months in Massachusetts and in the East. On his return he was again elected County Judge, in 1861. In 1862 he again visited his old home in New England, and returned in October of that year accompanied with his bride, who was Miss H. H. Hobbs, of North Berwick, Maine, ever since and now the universally esteemed and honored wife who has so well aided in making an ideal home in Santa Barbara.

In 1862 the Judge resigned his office on account of the inadequacy of the salary, and entered upon the active practice of his profession in Santa Barbara and throughout

Southern California, where he has continued his practice with signal success up to the present time. He was admitted to the bar by the Supreme Court of this State on September 2, 1854, and the Circuit Court of the United States for the District of California, September 2, 1857, and to the Supreme Court of the United States at the October term, 1874. He was appointed Judge Advocate of the Fourth Division of the California Militia, April 26, 1854, by Governor John Bigler.

Judge Fernald was almost unanimously elected Mayor of the city of Santa Barbara in May, 1882, and held the office for two years, to the great satisfaction of the citizens and honor to himself, declining to accept any salary, provided by city charter, for his services as such.

For more than thirty years Judge Fernald has been identified with all the important litigation of this and adjoining counties, and throughout Southern California, and has numbered among his clients the most distinguished citizens as well as the largest non-resident land-owners; and during that long period has maintained his great reputation in his profession for fidelity and signal ability. He is said never to have lost a land case.

Nearly all the great land-owners, including John C. Jones, late of Boston, Massachusetts; Colonel Thomas A. Scott, T Wallace More, Henry M. Newhall, Dr. Nicholas A. Den, Thomas B. Dibblee, Dr. J. B. Shaw, Ellwood Cooper, Lazard Freres, the Pacific Coast Steamship Company, and the Southern Pacific Railway Company were numbered among his clients. He has never been identified in any way with any doubtful or questionable litigation, refusing retainers in inequitable cases as well as declining criminal practice.

He is strong physically and morally, alert, an acute observer, and possesses the great and natural advantage of a good memory of facts and occurrences at a trial, as well as tireless industry.

His services to this city in finally settling the title to and fixing the boundaries of its municipal lands, as successor to the ancient Pueblo of Santa Barbara, by obtaining a patent therefor (four square leagues) from the United States Land Department, the first patent ever issued to a pueblo in this State, were of great value to this city and its inhabitants.

Fortune has smiled on the Judge's professional career, and bestowed upon his exertions ample pecuniary rewards. He is now an extensive land-owner in Santa Barbara and its vicinity, and a stockholder in many of its leading corporations. The Fernald Block, in which his elegant offices are located, is a striking ornament on State Street, situated in the heart of its business center. He has ever been one of the foremost in all local enterprises for the improvement of the city, and he has contributed in no small degree to its business prosperity.

There is perhaps no citizen of Santa Barbara more widely known and respected than Judge Fernald. He is deeply read in ancient and modern history, in English, French and Italian literature, and familiar with the principles of the civil as well as the common law; also a close student of international law and the science of government.

He has ever taken a deep interest in fruit culture and in forestry, being a life member of the American Forestry Association. The first experiment in planting, and in the cultivation of the olive tree in Southern California, outside of the old missions, was made by him. As early as 1865–'66, and long prior to the greater and more successful experiment of Mr. Ellwood Cooper, he purchased the "Belmont property," about seventy-five acres of land, near the city of Santa Barbara, and planted it out in olives of the mission variety, for the purpose of establishing the fact that the soil and climate of Southern California was alike favorable for the production of olives for preserving and for making oil of the best quality.

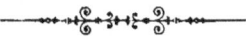

J. A. BARKER.—In traveling east of Santa Paula a mile and turning to the south a quarter of a mile, one comes upon the lovely sequestered spot, under the spreading oaks, and numerous shade and fruit trees of the owner's own planting—the cosy home of the pioneer, J. A. Barker. The house is nearly hidden from view by the endless variety of fruit and other trees that surround it. The first intimation of life on the ranch is the friendly greeting of the harmless old house dogs, which by their wag and twist seem to say, "We are glad you have come." Next, the visitor is met and taken by the hand by the pioneer himself, who, in his frank and hospitable manner, invites his guest in and makes him feel at home.

Mr. Barker was born in Louisville, Kentucky, December 3, 1833. He is a son of John Barker, a native of Kentucky, born in 1802, and a grandson of Stephen Barker, also a native of the "Blue Grass State." Both Mr. Barker's mother, nee Mary Asheroff, and her father, James Asherhoff, are Kentuckians by birth. The subject of this sketch is the youngest of a family of ten children, only four of whom are now living. He was educated in Missouri and lived on a farm there until twenty years of age. In 1853 he came to the Golden State, in search of its rich treasures. For six years he mined in Nevada County, with good success, his average per day being from $7 to $14. He came out of the mines with what to him seemed satisfactory results. He makes the statement that he has seen a piece of quartz rock seventy-six pounds in weight, that contained $8,250 in gold. After leaving the mines he engaged in freighting, and received $35 per thousand for drawing lumber seventeen miles. There were very few settlers in this part of the county when Mr. Barker came here in 1869. Mr. J. Crane, Judge Wason and Mr. George M. Richardson were here, and soon other settlers came and the work of development was pushed forward. Mr. Barker took up a Government claim of 160 acres, which he has improved, and where he has been engaged in general farming, raising corn, barley, beans, horses, cattle and hogs. Mr. Barker is only one of the many who have come here and have made for themselves and families beautiful homes in this sunny clime.

He was united in marriage to Miss Sarah Lee, a native of Ohio, and daughter of Joseph Lee, who was born in Massachusetts. They have had a family of eight children, six of whom are living: James, Benton, Mary Ella, Sarah Isabel, John Wesley and Hattie. Several of the children are married and live near him. Mr. Barker's political views are Democratic. He and his wife are members of the Baptist Church.

www.ingramcontent.com/pod-product-compliance
Lightning Source LLC
Chambersburg PA
CBHW081140290426
44108CB00018B/2397